ALSO BY SHERWIN GLUCK
Private Good Luck
T.R.'s Summer White House, Oyster Bay

pappus

The Saga *of* A Jewish Family

Gluck, Sherwin
Pappus
The Saga of A Jewish Family
A companion to *Private Good Luck* and *As I Remember…* / Sherwin Gluck / Maria Gluck
p. cm.
ISBN 978-0-9672543-6-4 (Perfect Binding)
ISBN 978-0-9672543-5-7 (Hard Cover Binding)
ISBN 978-0-9672543-7-1 (Electronic)

Gluck, Irving, 1921-2016.
United States. Army. Armored Infantry Regiment, 6th.
United States. Army. Military Police Division, 67th.
World War, 1939-1945--Regimental Histories--United States.
World War, 1939-1945--Campaigns--North Africa.
World War, 1939-1945--Campaigns--Italy
World War, 1939-1945--Campaigns--France
World War, 1939-1945--Campaigns--Germany
World War, 1939-1945--Personal letters--American.
Soldiers--United States--Biography.
Jews--Czechoslovakia--History--1921-1938
Jews--Czechoslovakia--Personal letters
Jews--Hungary--History--1938-1944
Holocaust, Jewish (1939-1945)--Hungary--Personal letters
Holocaust, Jewish (1939-1945)--Romania--Personal letters
Jews--United States--History--1938-2016
Jews--Israel--History--1948-1994

Printed and bound in the United States of America
First Edition
Book Design by Sherwin Gluck

Introduction

Seventy individual letter writers, all interconnected. 1,823 letters that tell one story. *Pappus, The Saga of a Jewish Family*, is a remarkably comprehensive collection of letters written just before, during, and after World War II that documents the experiences of an observant Jewish family from Polyán, Czechoslovakia — a small agricultural village. The main letter writers were members of my close knit Hungarian speaking, religious Jewish family (Glück) and our extended family (Schwartz - Mayer - Klein) living in Czechoslovakia, Hungary, Romania, and America. Written predominantly in Hungarian, English, or both, these letters memorialize and illuminate the lives of ordinary people enduring extraordinary events. Through them, experience history as it unfolds. Read letters from children learning to write, grandparents living out their golden years, family, friends, and neighbors — Jew and Gentile alike. Some will become martyrs, others survivors. A few will be enablers, collaborators, and perpetrators. Painstakingly written on thin airmail paper, v-mail, or plain stationary, they bear postmarks from Czechoslovakia, Hungary, Romania, New York, Ohio, Texas, Pennsylvania, California, Missouri, Algeria, Italy, France, Germany, Iceland, Sweden, the Philippines, Florida, and Israel. This volume contains the complete personal correspondence in the family's special collection now housed in the United States Holocaust Museum in Washington, D.C.

There were six siblings in the Gluck family of Polyán. The second oldest sibling, David (Dezső), emigrated to the United States in January 1938. He had just turned 28 years old. David's entry to the US was sponsored by his father's elderly brother, Julius (Jonás) Gluck, who lived in Columbus, Ohio. As soon as David had arrived safely, his four younger siblings — sisters Hermine (23) and Marie (Mariska) (21), and brothers Herman (Hershmendel) (19) and Irving (Ignác) (16) — started the process to leave for America, too. They soon secured affidavits of support from Julius' son, their first cousin Arthur Gluck, a well-known Ohio industrialist and owner of Bonded Scale and Manufacturing.

However, in October 1938, just as their voyage to America was being finalized, Germany took over the Sudetenland, Czechoslovakia no longer existed, and the village of Polyán was returned to Hungary. The Gluck siblings, now considered Hungarians, were able to keep their Czechoslovakian quota numbers, but had to transfer their paperwork from the American Consul in Prague to the American Consul in Budapest. Their emigration was ultimately delayed for another year and a half and they were only able to leave Europe in February 1940. By that time, their planned voyage on a British owned Cunard Lines ship was no longer possible. Cunard was no longer sailing passenger ships across the Atlantic and the four siblings were switched to the SS *Vulcania* of the Italia Lines. Their intended port of departure was Trieste, Italy. However, their departure by train from Budapest was delayed and the Vulcania had set sail from Trieste to Naples before they could arrive. They rushed by train through Trieste and continued to Naples in order to embark there. They sailed on February 11, 1940 and arrived at Pier 92 in New York on February 21, 1940. Their first cousin Bertha (neé Gluck) Weingarten (45), who had emigrated to the US in 1915, met them at the dock. The four siblings subsequently travelled by train to Columbus where their brother David, Uncle Julius, and their cousin Arthur lived. David had been employed as a nightwatchman, a cab driver, and a drapery installer in Columbus. Irving initially worked at a paint factory, Herman at a machine shop, Marie as a seamstress, and Hermine as a nanny.

David registered for the draft in 1940, but was classified as IV-F, physically unfit for duty due to varicose veins. He moved to California in the fall of 1943 to work in the Navy's shipbuilding industry. Herman registered for the draft and was inducted in January 1941, but was honorably discharged in February 1941 due to stomach issues. Irving registered for the draft in 1942 and reported for his military service in March 1943. He was sent to Camp Wolters in Texas and trained as an infantryman. In August 1943, he was sent to Oran, Algeria but wasn't permitted to fight in combat until he became a naturalized U.S. citizen on November 18, 1943. Irving left for Naples on a ship that sailed on December 28, 1943 and was then assigned to the 1st Armored Division, 6th Armored Infantry Regiment/Battalion, Company B. He fought in the battle of Monte Porchia just south of Cassino during January 6-14, 1944, for which his unit earned the Presidential Unit Citation, in the battle of Anzio from January 24 to May 28, 1944, in the capture of Rome on June 5, and continued in pursuit of the Germans as far north as Leghorn (Livorno), until his unit was reorganized at the end of July 1944. Irving subsequently worked in an army PX in Naples until December 1944, then served as an MP in France, then Germany with the 67th MP Company, for which his unit earned the Meritorious Unit Citation. He returned home to Ohio in November 1945 and, by January 1946, was taking classes at Ohio State University under the GI Bill.

Irving earned a BA in Economics at Ohio State University in 1949, and after a lengthy job search worked for the United States Atomic Energy Commission as a buyer assisting in the construction of the gaseous diffusion plant in Portsmouth, OH. Irving and his other siblings all ended up relocating from Ohio to New York. Hermine was the first to move in June 1946, eventually getting a job at the Paramount Movie office and encouraged Marie to join her soon after, which she did in October that same year, ultimately working as a cashier in Ratner's restaurant in Manhattan. Irving joined them in 1954, and David joined them in 1963 after several business ventures in the Long Beach area — a lighting store, a drapery store, a restaurant, and a bar— went out of business. The impetus for his move to New York was a misdiagnosis of cancer.

The first letter in the collection is from 1937. At first glance, it appears to be irrelevant to the story of my family. However, it's importance won't be realized until years later. In this letter, a Christian neighbor (Juliska Szabo) who had been employed by the Gluck family to care for their dying mother back in 1932, writes to ask if they would now be willing to sell some land to her for her grown son. The letter is significant because this same Christian family, Szabo, would be appointed the Christian partner to the Gluck family's farm under the Hungarian government's anti-Jewish decrees. They would claim that the produce of the farm belonged entirely to them. As we will read in his letters, Jeremias Gluck, the siblings' father, takes them to court, using a Jewish lawyer who is also forced to have a Christian partner. Jeremias Gluck wins.

The letters of 1938 begin with two notes just before David leaves Europe, and then they continue in earnest after David arrives to the U.S. There are letters from his father and his five siblings in Polyán and they go into great detail about all of the complications related to his siblings' efforts to emigrate, as well as life on their farm, their village, and its environs; letters from his brother Lajos' young children; his maternal grandparents [Schwartz] who lived in the neighboring village of Lelesz; his uncle Marton Schwartz (his mother's youngest brother) who lived in the neighboring town of Kiralyhelmec; his second cousins in Romania [Mayer]; various friends and business associates from Europe; and from his first cousin Bertha Weingarten in New York. Bertha's letters to David document her attempt to advise him on how to handle himself with their Uncle Julius and cousin Arthur in Columbus, so they would agree to sponsor his siblings' journey. They also discuss letters that both David and Bertha receive from David's cousin — and Bertha's half-sister's daughter — Jolan Mayer in Romania. Her letters, and the discussion between David and Bertha about her situation, document her repeated attempts to find a way to emigrate to America, her effort to convince David and Bertha to help her, and her anguish at failing to do so. There are even a few letters that were received by the family while still in Europe. An especially important one is from David written in 1938. He writes to his father describing issues related to the logistics of his siblings coming to the U.S., what they should bring with them on the ship, what they can do to make the voyage bearable, life as a young Jew in America, his job, and his strained relationship with his Uncle Julius. One postcard from Hermine's friend Helen Perl from Szürte, Hungary documents her advice to Hermine regarding ticket prices for ships to the US and their availability. These two letters were brought by the siblings to the U.S. in 1940 when they immigrated.

Once the siblings were reunited in Columbus, Ohio, there are letters to them from their father, brother Lajos, sister-in-law Etelka —with whom Hermine and Marie were especially close— their grandparents, uncles, aunts, cousins, nephews, nieces, friends, and non-Jewish neighbors, all of whom write to America detailing the deteriorating situation back in Czechoslovakia: restrictions on Jewish owned businesses, the flooding of the Latorica River, the planting, the harvests, the debts, the lawsuits, the synagogue's roof collapse, and the compulsory military service in the Hungarian army that their brother Lajos and their uncles (Marton and Lajos Schwartz, brothers of their mother) had to endure. By November 1941, letters sent by the siblings to their father and relatives in Europe were returned as undeliverable. They didn't receive any more mail from Europe until after the war's end. Hermine continues to correspond with her friend Helen Perl, who had arrived to Cleveland, OH a few months before the siblings. Helen makes two attempts to be a matchmaker for Hermine by introducing her to Gilbert Rosewater, and Louis Goldblatt. Helen's letters help provide a window into Hermine's suitors, the difficulties of being single, and the joy of getting married.

In 1943 with Irving's induction to the army and David's move to California, a second period of "triangular" correspondence between the siblings begins which would continue throughout the war. It doesn't taper off until 1954, when telephone calls begin to supplant the written word. The letters, often via special delivery travel back and forth from Ohio to California, and from Irving's army post to either Ohio or California. In these letters the siblings discuss their jobs, their whereabouts, and their work, and they weigh the various social and economic aspects of life in California, Ohio, and eventually New York. The letters document the hardships of their day to day lives, their work hours and pay, their ration tickets, their romantic relationships, Irving's basic training, their worry over Irving's life in the army, and their many care packages to him. Irving's wartime experience in North Africa, Italy, France, and Germany is documented through his postcards, letters, and v-mail. The letters also include a lengthy correspondence between Hermine and Marie with Lajos Schwartz, a distant cousin who arrived in the US just before the siblings. He lived in Youngstown, OH until he too was inducted into the Army and sent to Iceland.

Most of the letter writers who remained in Europe, including the young children of the siblings' oldest brother Lajos, were murdered by the Nazis in 1944. Letters from survivors ultimately document the fate of the family who had remained behind. Letters from Emil Schwartz, a first cousin who survived Auschwitz, Mauthausen, and Gunskirchen arrive soon after the war ends. Emil is the son of the siblings' mother's brother, Uncle Marton Schwartz. Emil's parents and all his siblings perished. The letters from Emil, and later from his wife Lili, document his eyewitness account of the family during the Holocaust, the help he received from Hermine and her siblings in America, his difficulties getting to and living in Israel, and his small, but steady successes rebuilding his life in Israel. His letters continue through 1994, documenting some of the major milestones in his life and in the history of Israel, culminating with a memorial service and yizkor book commemorating the 50th anniversary of the murder of our family and the Jews of the Zemplén district.

Ignác Klein and his sisters Manci and Rozsi. They were Etelka (neé Klein) Gluck's brother and sisters. Etelka was the siblings' brother Lajos' wife. Manci and Rozsi document their eyewitness account of the family during the Holocaust. Ignác was appointed the caretaker of the Gluck's property in Polyán after the war, later claiming the property should belong to him because of Etelka's dowry which the Klein family had given upon her marriage to Lajos. Etelka perished in Auschwitz. Lajos perished in Mauthausen Gusen. The letters from Etelka's brother and sisters document the view the survivors had of the non-Jewish residents and the conflict that arose when the survivors returned. Other post-war letters come from the Kleins (Lipot, Margit, and their daughter Lulu) who also survived and lived in Budapest. Lipot was the siblings' 1st cousin, the son of the siblings' Aunt Zseni (their father Jeremias Gluck's sister) and Uncle Izidor Klein.

There are several post-war letters from the family's Jewish neighbor in Polyán, Malvin Lefkovic. Her younger brothers studied with Irving and Herman with the melamed (the tutor) that the two families hired to teach the boys Jewish studies. She survived and was brought to Sweden to recover. Two letters from Rozsi Hausman, Etelka's cousin, who was also brought to Sweden to recover, are included as well.

The collection includes pre- and postwar letters from non-Jewish neighbors of the Glucks in Polyán (Török, Gereny, Szmolyák, Deak, Toth, Ragány) which document the roundup of the district's Jews by the Nazis. They testify about the arrival of the Nazis, how the Jews were taken, what efforts they allegedly made to help bring food for the imprisoned Jews, and the ultimate disposition of our family's personal property. They also describe their own family's struggles during the war years. There are letters from the postmaster of Lelesz, Jana Fabianova, who helped finance David's trip to America. Her letters document her close connection to the family, despite being a Gentile. In pre-war letters, she is mentioned several times by the siblings, their father, and their Uncle Marton as being a very special person. Her postwar letters document the siblings' efforts to repay her loan by sending care packages to her after the war. Also are postwar letters from Pál Lengyel, a public notary and lawyer from Polány, an old personal friend of the siblings' father, Jeremias. These document his wartime situation and discuss the Glucks' personal property and real estate; these letters provide a contrast to the letters from Ignác Klein and his sisters.

The letters are all encompassing and their historic value is immeasurable. As primary sources, they give a contemporaneous account of the events the writers lived through, undistorted by the passage of time. They touch upon peacetime immigration —both to the US and Israel—, the quota system, the Sudetan crisis, the dissolution of Czechoslovakia and its ramifications, restrictions on Jewish businesses, economic hardships in Hungary, religious observance of the Jewish community, the legal standing of Jews in Hungarian courts, the difficulties involved in getting travel documents, the perilous journey to escape Europe, the joy of arrival in America, assimilation in America, the war years, life on the home front and as a Jewish combat infantryman on the front lines, the Holocaust and its aftermath. The collection includes the heartbreakingly poignant first letters from Holocaust survivors after being liberated from the death camps, their accounts of what they found upon returning home, their testimony about who lived and who died, the contradicting claims about real and personal property from non-Jewish neighbors, everyone's pleas for financial assistance, and finally the rebuilding of new lives — all in their own words.

This volume includes correspondence from dozens of letter writers, ranging from mere children learning to write, to grandparents living out their golden years, Jew and Gentile. It is the definitive companion text to *Private Good Luck* and *As I remember…*

This is my family's story.

1943/11/8 Irving to Family, North Africa (Book 3, 134)

November 8 - 1943 North Africa

...Do you know that yesterday my dearest, I had a little time, *so I made all those letters that you wrote to me into a book and I read it*. Those that you have written to me from day to day. Up till now I received 23 letters from you. I'm sure that you must have been writing to me more, but they did not arrive yet. I left my old job and I'm waiting what the future will bring. Don't worry, the Almighty will help. I remain with hope until we meet again. Kisses from your little brother, Irving.

*italics added by the editor

Prologue

For a long time, it was just a cardboard box sitting on top of a six foot tall filing cabinet in my father's basement office. We shared the office, his desk and papers and my Lionel train layout, so I passed this box throughout my childhood, not knowing its secrets. I didn't even know what it contained when I started interviewing my Dad, and recording his history for posterity. At some point, after I had married and started raising children, my Dad must have started cleaning, sorting, and organizing his office. There were years of accumulated business records, and family papers. Little did I know that the cardboard box contained the motherlode of family papers!

In an attempt to ameliorate my Aunt Marie's loneliness and boredom, my Dad brought the cardboard box to her apartment in Flushing, Queens, and she began to sort through it. She took letters that had been read and stored away seventy years earlier out of their envelopes and placed them into "magnetic" photo albums, cutting an envelope or refolding a letter to make it fit the album's page. Her effort to organize them, although haphazard and a bit destructive, led directly to this volume. Had she not taken this first step, these letters may have languished in their cardboard tomb, only to have remained undiscovered and unknown, perhaps to be thrown out. Yet she did, and she shared the most poignant letters with my Dad, who in turn, shared them with me, translating them silently from Hungarian into English in real time as he read them out loud to me, usually with tears streaming down his face, often interrupted to regain his composure.

This led him to want to share his history, and what he was rediscovering with others. He answered an advertisement in the local paper placed by the Syosset High School Librarian, Lynn Ortleib. She was looking for area residents who were veterans willing to be interviewed by students for the Library of Congress' Veterans History Project. They spoke by phone, and then agreed to meet before the students conducted interview. To this first meeting he brought just one of the albums that my Aunt had assembled. Ms. Ortleib was astounded, and quipped that she felt like she was holding history in her hands, which she was, and that it should be in a museum. Unfortunately, at that time none of the letters were translated, and my Dad could only share those written in English with her, or like he did with me, translate one or two of them on the fly.

After this meeting, and the subsequent interview for the Veteran's History Project in 2007, I convinced my Dad that these letters should be translated, and that who better than he to translate them! I bought him an Apple laptop and taught him how to use ViaVoice, a new program for the Mac that transcribed the spoken word into typed text. After an hour training session to "teach" the computer to understand his voice, he was using a computer for the first time in his life at the age of 86. He translated (in his head), spoke the translation aloud into the microphone on the headset, and let the computer transcribe his translation of the most important letters that he came across.

At the same time, I realized how fragile the paper could often be, and that the adhesive in the albums my Aunt had put together risked destroying many of the letters entirely. My wife Hanit and I set out to remove the letters from the magnetic albums, and put them into archival grade plastic sheet protectors. There were so many letters, that we couldn't spare any time to actually read them while we reorganized them. For several Shabbat afternoons in a row, we left our young children to entertain themselves while we disassembled my Aunt's work, and reassembled the letters as best we could, hoping to revisit them one day.

This actually made my father's work at the computer easier, since he could hold each letter in the plastic sheet without damaging the paper or smudging the lettering upon it. Slowly, but surely, he translated and transcribed many of the most interesting letters, following a file naming methodology that I recommended he use so we could locate and sort the files as he translated them - year, month, day, letter writer, letter recipient, any special note. Perhaps two years passed in this way. When my Aunt Marie, then 93, fell, we decided that it would be better for her to move into my Dad's house rather than stay in the rehabilitation / nursing home. After a week or two, she began to recover and thrive. Cleaning, gardening, cooking, baking…it was as though the move to my father's home had renewed her lease on life. She wanted to learn how to use the computer as my Dad had done, and help translate the mountain of letters that remained. After several hours training the computer to understand her heavy Hungarian accent, she too learned to use ViaVoice. Now, at the age of 95, she began to create transcriptions of letters in English that she herself had written 70 years earlier in Hungarian.

Despite their diligence, my Dad and Aunt only translated less than half of the letters in this collection. I'm sure that they felt they had translated the most meaningful ones, and that many of the others were not worthy of translation. Additionally, my Aunt especially, used her newfound voice to write her own memoir, *As I remember...*, dozens of notes and letters to her nieces and nephews, and her own short story. Those two years, between age 95 and 97, were an amazingly productive period for her! Before their deaths, they both read, and approved, an unfinished version of my father's memoir, *Private Good Luck*, which I wrote in his voice, using my interview with him, the most meaningful letters that they had translated, the many documents and mementos that my Dad had saved, and the documentation which we had acquired from the US Holocaust Museum, the Holocaust Archives in Bad Arolsen, and the Red Cross.

Yet, it bothered me that so many of the letters from that old cardboard box remained untranslated. What secrets did they hold? What else could I learn about my family? What advice might lay hidden in the lines of writing left locked away? Fortunately, a tenant of ours, Monika Markacs, a young woman from Hungary, had majored in English in university. I inquired hesitatingly if she would be willing to translate "some" letters into English. To my surprise, she was thrilled at the opportunity, and I uploaded at first one, then fifty, then fifty more, and so on, to my Dropbox, and she painstakingly translated the letters written in cursive one by one. Many of the newly translated letters gave me details that added to the richness of my father's memoir. When she had translated everything through 1947, and I felt there was nothing left to add to the memoir without ruining its pacing. Although some discrepancies existed between my Dad's memories and the newly translated letters, I decided to end my work on *Private Good Luck* and switched hats from writer and editor to publisher. It really felt good to finish it.

However, I soon realized that there was more to be done to truly finish what I had started. While it was being printed, the US Holocaust Museum replied to my inquiry from the previous year regarding my offer to donate the entirety of my father's letters, documents, and artifacts to them. We met with the curator, and he was astounded by what we had accomplished. After meeting him several more times, the donation was complete, and I again thought I had finished this journey. However, there remained many letters after 1947 that I wanted to read, so after more uploads to my Dropbox, Monika translated almost every letter left. I learned to read Hungarian well enough to input anything that wasn't clear into Google translate. With great effort, these letters, along with all the earlier letters, appear in this volume.

As proud as I am of his memoir, I think these letters represent something so much more than I could have ever created. Had I been able to interview my Aunt Hermine, Uncle David, or even reinterview my Dad after having read these letters, I would not have been able to get a more complete, a more accurate, a more faithful account of their lives from 1938 to 1954 than what these letters contain. Each letter on its own is fascinating, but when taken together as an opus, the effect is intoxicating. Each letter writer is connected in some way with another, a mention of a name here ties in with a description there. Fact and feeling unfold in real time, as they lived it, as they experienced it. You feel their hopes, their dreams, their fears and frustrations, and their love; the anguish of lives extinguished and the joy of life renewed. Everything is available to those patient enough to peel back each layer of this proverbial onion.

A note about the title, *Pappus*. A pappus is the tuft of hairs on each seed of a dandelion, which assists the seed's dispersal by the wind. Two of my favorite stories growing up were *The Winds of War*, by Herman Wouk, and *Roots*, by Alex Haley. How apt I thought to incorporate them both in this title. The *winds of war* have blown the pappus which carried the seed of our family across the ocean to establish its *roots* in the new world. It is my hope that these three books - my father's memoir, *Private Good Luck,* this collection, *Pappus,* and my Aunt Marie's memoir, *As I remember...*, will be the fertilizer which nourishes our family so that wherever they may go, they will always know from where they have come.

Summaries by Year

1938 Summary

David (Dezső), the second oldest of 6 siblings arrives to Columbus, OH from a small village in Czechoslovakia called Polány (Bodrogmező). He travelled on a Czechoslovakian passport and quota number, with a guarantee from his Uncle Julius (Jónász) and Julius' son Arthur, both of whom live in Columbus, OH, and with financial help from a lady friend, the postmaster of the neighboring village of Lelesz - Jana Fabianova. David's 4 younger siblings - sisters Hermine and Mariska (Maria) and brothers Herman and Ignác (Irving) begin their preparations to come to America as Czechoslovakian citizens. David, with his first cousin Bertha, who lives in New York, discuss how to make this happen, as well as what his sibling's living arrangements will be upon arrival. Bertha has a half-sister, Sarolta Mayer, who lives in Szatmar, Romania. Her daughter, Jolan Mayer, begins writing to David and Bertha, pleading for their assistance to get out of Europe. Uncle Julius gets the wrong impression of David. He thinks that David is being disobedient when in fact he's just trying to work, learn a new language, make and go out with friends his age, and attend synagogue -albeit not his Uncle Julius', all while sending money home to help his family. Uncle Julius is now reluctant to sponsor any of David's siblings. At the same time, David's father Jeremias proceeds with plans to send the 4 siblings to America, while fighting several lawsuits and trying to sell off land and property to pay for the imminent travel. Herman is called up to serve in the Czechoslovakian army and is taken to a labor camp, but he soon returns home. After the Sudeten crisis and the First Vienna Award, the siblings' plans to come to America quickly change. The region they live in has been returned to Hungary and they have become Hungarian citizens. All the previously filed paperwork to emigrate to America must be transferred from Prague, the capitol of Czechoslovakia to Budapest , the capitol of Hungary. Most importantly, they can still use the Czechoslovakian quota numbers they already have. Other friends and relatives (Helen Perl and Louis Schwartz) are in the same situation. However, those like the siblings' Uncle Martón Schwartz (David's mother's brother), who have only just begun thinking about emigration, will need to emigrate using the Hungarian quota, which by the end of 1938 would put them on a two year waiting list.

1939 Summary

The siblings are uncertain if they will be able to leave Europe at all. Their first hope is to travel through Prague without having to make new passports. Friends and relatives besiege Bertha in New York and David in Columbus to help them get guarantees. Bertha's sister, Mariska Schőn, wants her children Tibi and Clara to emigrate. Jolan Mayer continues to ask Bertha and David to help her find a way from Romania to America either as a tourist or as the fiancé of an American. Uncle Martón asks David to intervene on his behalf to get a guarantee from Uncle Julius. David's actions are all interpreted by Uncle Julius and his son Arthur as being disobedient. Bertha begs David to comply with their Uncle Julius' wishes for the sake of bringing David's siblings to America. Meanwhile, the siblings' hopes to be in America by Passover are dashed when they find out that they need to use Hungarian passports and get releases from the Hungarian military for Irving (Ignác) and Herman. Their father Jeremias has sold property, but used the proceeds to settle a court case. He wants to sell their new house, but the sale is postponed until the local notary approves it, and the notary was fired because he was Jewish. Money from the sibling's paternal grandfather's estate is available to use for travel. However, it is in 3 orphanage accounts: one in the name of Herman, one in the name of Irving, and one jointly held in the names of their eldest brother Lajos' oldest children Emil & Lenke. The money may be used only for bona fide travel and only after the children turn 18. Herman immediately files a petition for the money. Irving must wait until his birthday in November to do so. Economic conditions in the village and its surroundings worsen. Stores close, including one owned by Samuel Schwartz, the siblings' maternal grandfather. Food is scarce, but David's father Jeremias was able to purchase a cow and calf for milk, and waits desperately for a good harvest later in the summer. The Levente, a Hungarian paramilitary group, begins training young men. Irving must participate. Herman is inducted into the Hungarian army, but expects to be released since he's a Jew. The siblings had hoped to bring Hungarian money to America to repay their Uncle Julius for the ship tickets. Instead, Julius insists that they must buy them in Europe. In order to do that, they must pay for them in dollars. Jana Fabianova, the lady friend of David and postmaster in Lelesz, offers to loan the siblings money to travel to America. The 4 siblings travel to the American Consulate in Budapest for their visa hearing, and their visas are approved even though Herman is missing various documents. They won't be able to travel until Herman is released from the army. As soon as Irving turns 18 in November, he too will require a military release, but by then the monies held by the orphanage in his name will also be released so they can buy tickets. Clerical errors in the paperwork lead to Herman's passport being denied, forcing the siblings to submit corrected paperwork. Hungarians begin confiscating Jewish owned land, so selling more land to pay for the ship tickets appears impossible. The longer they wait, the less money they will have to buy tickets because they are spending what they have just to survive. Their friend, Helen Perl, bought tickets on Italia Line, and advises them to do the same since the Cunard line is no longer sailing passengers. Helen is going to Cleveland, OH. The American consul finally approves everyone's travel visas, but other documents have now expired and need to be updated.

1940 Summary

Hermine and Herman rush to Budapest to finalize the paperwork. This includes bringing Irving and Herman's military releases from the Hungarian army and the moral and district certificates, and correcting the error in Herman's birthdate on them. They had planned to sail on a ship owned by the Cunard Line, but it's no longer sailing ships across the Atlantic. They make arrangements to sail on a ship from the Italia Lines. Marie and Irving travel from Polány to Budapest and together the four siblings go by train to Naples, Italy. They sail on the SS *Vulcania* on February 10th from Naples and arrive to New York on February 21st. Bertha, their cousin, meets them in New York and advises them to immediately apply for US citizenship. They travel by train to Columbus, OH where David meets them. David telegrams his father Jeremias that all four siblings have arrived. Meanwhile, back in Polyán, the siblings' eldest brother Lajos' wife, Etelka, gives birth to Zoltan, their fifth child. There is heavy flooding in Polyán forcing the extended family to come by boat to the bris, and delaying mail delivery. It remains muddy for a long time. Etelka reports that Mityu and Gyuszi, her 3rd and 4th children, are inseparable and that Gyuszi still has shoes that fit him. Jeremias, the siblings' father, settles his lawsuit with his neighbor, Mihancki, but his problems continue. A local lawyer accuses Jeremias of getting false passports for his sons Herman and Irving. Additionally, the bank that loaned money to him calls in its loan. He is going to try to get the money from his father's inheritance held in Lajos' oldest children's names (Emil and Lenke) , but it won't be released unless the children plan to travel to America. Although Jeremias would consider coming to America, and discusses selling the barn to the village, he is not in a rush. Instead he tries to sell some land to a neighbor, Gyula Szabo. The land commission doesn't approve the sale. The winter wheat crop freezes, but Jeremias plans to have his son Lajos plant potatoes, sunflowers, oats, millet, and poppies. Lajos will have to hoe and plant by hand because the horse and carriage were requisitioned by the Hungarian army. Eventually, Jeremias is able to bring the horse and carriage home, and the horse gives birth to a colt. Soon after, Lajos and his mother's brothers - Uncle Martón Schwartz and Uncle Lajos Schwartz - are drafted into the Hungarian army. Many other Jews volunteered but were not needed. Some, like Irving's friend Sanyi Klein, who used Irving's wooden gun for training after Irving went to America, were taken to do forced labor in the Fenyves Valley. Uncle Martón is a corporal in the Hungarian army - a rank he earned in World War I. He is stationed in Patak along with Uncle Lajos. Uncle Marton's wife, Aunt Etel, visits him in Patak with some of their children. Uncle Martón and Uncle Lajos remain there for four months. Mariska, Bertha's sister, also lives in Polyán with their father Lazar (Jeremias' oldest brother), her husband Miksa Schön, and their two children Tibi and Clara. Her husband Miksa is also drafted. Without Lajos at home, his father Jeremias has nobody to help on the farm and no money to pay for help. Yet, the crops that Lajos had planted earlier grew very well, except the wheat that had been damaged by frost. The local school shuts down because the teacher left. Emil Gluck (Lajos' oldest child) goes for only one month. Etelka reports that Emil's younger sister Lenke reads and writes beautifully. Restrictions against Jewish businesses are enacted. Shopkeepers must keep their stores open on shabbat (and only 4 of the many shopkeepers in Lelesz, the village next to Polyán, were Christian!) and animal traders are prevented from selling. Jews can't buy land, even if they have already paid for it. Gyula Szabo, who had been appointed Jeremias' Christian partner mistakenly believes that he will get all the produce from the land. He thinks that Jews have no rights. Jeremias brings him to court. Another Christian neighbor, Julis Simon , sues Jeremias claiming that he hasn't been paid, but Jeremias wins both lawsuits. A friend of David's, Rella Veizer, writes that her father had surgery and closed his shop, they have no money, and they need help. Everything becomes expensive, forcing the synagogue in Lelesz, whose wall had collapsed, to shut down. It remains in disrepair, and is eventually demolished. This includes the mikve, the ritual bath. Since building materials were so expensive, Jeremias disassembles his barn and gives the wood to his brother-in-law, Uncle Lajos Schwartz, so that he can complete building his house. Jana Fabianova, the postmaster in Lelesz who loaned David money to go to America, is transferred to the city of Miskolc. The siblings' brother Lajos is discharged from the Hungarian army to return home in time for the harvest, and a harsh winter. Louis Schwartz, a cousin who also travelled to America and settled with his extended family in Youngstown, OH, works in Leonard's Clothing shop. He has a high draft number so he doesn't worry yet about being drafted. He communicates with his family back home. They too have Christian co-owners , but are able to have their farm mechanically threshed. Bertha recommends to the siblings to send money home through Israel Zsupnik. He lives in New York, but has family near Polyán. When he receives the money in New York, he directs his family to give an equal amount to the siblings' family in Europe. Uncle Julius had asked his brother Jeremias to send a Torah with the siblings, however, they couldn't travel with it. Jeremias decides that he is no longer in favor of sending it to America.

1941 Summary

The situation in Polyán is precarious. Jeremias has no money. He uses sunflower stems and corn stalks to heat the house during the brutal winter. Prices are rising everyday, and even if they had money, most items are scarce including lumber, which his brother in law Lajos Schwartz needs to finish building his new house. Jeremias removed the roof from the tobacco building in order to repair his own house. Meanwhile Lajos Gluck, Jeremias' eldest son, is concerned that he may be inducted into the Hungarian army again. The concern is realized when both he and Miksa Schőn, his cousin Mariska's husband (who also lives in Polyán), are inducted again and are sent to Bacska. Lajos' wife Etelka's sister dies, as does Lazar Gluck - Bertha and Mariska's father and Jeremias' oldest brother. Jeremias' Christian partner, Gyulia Szabo calls the police to prevent Jeremias from using his own land. Nonetheless, Jeremias borrows money to plant corn, barley, oats, beets, and potatoes. Bread is scarce until the wheat can be harvested. Jeremias' other neighbors, the Török family, wait patiently for Jeremias to repay a loan and they also ask David to contact family of theirs in America. The colt that was born in 1940 to Jeremias' mare Sari now belongs to the Simon family. The siblings in Columbus continue to send money to Europe through Bertha's contact, Israel Zsupnik in New York, but this becomes more and more difficult. Uncle Julius (Jónász), Jeremias' brother, dies in Ohio. The siblings stay in touch with Louis Schwartz, who visits them in Columbus. He tells them that he heard from his family and that they were able to harvest. Unfortunately, 90% of the profit went to their Christian partners. The siblings' letters to Europe are returned in November as undeliverable. Hermine also stays in touch with her friend Helen Perl from Szürte who still lives Cleveland. She had been staying with her uncle, but now that he also died, she is living with strangers.

1942 Summary

Herman Gluck receives his induction notice for the US army, while Louis Schwartz passes his army medical exam but is sent home because he's a foreign national. He gets drafted anyway in June. The siblings' cousin Jenny Frye, who lives in New York, plans to marry Harry Weinberg in August. After their Uncle Julius died, the siblings move to a new apartment. Their cousin Arthur, Julius' son, refuses to let them take the furniture. Bertha receives a long delayed letter from Miksa Schőn, her sister Mariska's husband, telling her that her father Lazar has died. Louis Schwartz meets with the siblings on Labor Day. Irving Gluck, the youngest sibling is called in for his US army medical exam in September. Helen Perl, Hermine's friend from Szürte, marries Sam Goldstein.

1943 Summary

Irving is inducted into the US army and travels by train from Columbus to Camp Wolters, a base near Mineral Wells, Texas for 13 weeks of basic training. He is first assigned to the 57th Infantry Training Battalion , and then to the 55th for heavy weapons training. Infantry training includes learning to assemble/disassemble his hand gun and machine gun, learning about grenades, and experiencing live fire exercises. Irving enjoys life in basic training. He excels on a sharpshooter exam, enjoys the hot dry desert air, and describes hiking through mosquito infested cacti while wearing sunglasses with full equipment weighing 60 lbs -and using a gas mask. He receives letters and packages from his sisters in Columbus. Although he shares the chocolate and candy from the packages with other soldiers, he keeps Hermine's baked goods (kifle) to himself. He tries to keep kosher, even during Passover when he attends a seder in Fort Worth, Texas and at the USO. Irving is given the choice to be a medic, an infantryman, or go to officer training school. Irving speaks to his siblings by phone occasionally. His siblings even surprise him with an early morning phone call. Irving makes a wire recording in Fort Worth and sends it home, and he also corresponds with Flo Meizlish. He will correspond with her occasionally throughout the war. After 13 weeks of basic training, Irving has a one week vacation in Columbus. Hermine first, and then Marie begin news jobs at the Lazarus Department Store, Hermine as a salesgirl and Marie in the men's suit department. David receives his American citizenship, while Herman applies for his. Herman gets paid 60 cents an hour. Louis Schwartz gets inducted into the US army and does his basic training in Fort Belvoir, VA,. After his furlough, Irving returns to Texas only to be transferred to Camp Shenango in Pennsylvania. Here he learns the skills to be a military policeman: escorting prisoners and doing guard duty. Although he has sent much of his salary home for safekeeping, Irving is robbed while he is asleep and his siblings send him some money. He is unable to attend synagogue in Camp Shenango. They practice packing and unpacking constantly, until mid August, when Irving is shipped to North Africa , where he works with a typewriter in an office processing replacement soldiers. Weeks go by before he receives any mail from home. The Jewish New Year arrives and Irving breaks the Yom Kippur fast with a French family. He likes the family's daughter and visits with her again. His sisters send him many letters and packages. Irving must request items (like candy) in order for his sisters to send it to him. Finally, a Federal judge arrives to North Africa and administers the oath of citizenship to Irving. Once a citizen, Irving is shipped out to the combat zone and ends the year at sea, en route to Naples, Italy. Meanwhile, David leaves Columbus in the Fall and drives himself to California. He applies for, and receives, a Californian driver's license. He takes a job hanging drapery with dreams of working in a movie studio, even taking a professional head shot. Instead, he gets work as an electrician's helper building a repair ship in Los Angeles. He studies to be an electrician. David lives in a small, one room apartment with a shared bathroom in a large building for shipyard workers in Wilmington, CA. He begins working 7 days a week, but finds time to join the Wilmington Counsel. David stays in touch with his siblings in Columbus, and has someone keep tabs on Herman to be sure he is eating properly and paying his fair share of the rent in the apartment he shares with his sisters.

1944 Summary

Irving arrives in Italy and is assigned to the 1st Armored Division, 6th Armored Infantry Battalion, Company B. He is sent into front line combat for the first time at Monte Porchia. After just over a week of combat, he is pulled back -only to be shipped out again days later with the same unit to Anzio. He will remain on the front lines at the Anzio beachhead until breakout at the end of May. Irving loses many friends including Buddy Hunecke, who was killed in January according to his wife's letter. Irving wrote a letter home on behalf of Buddy before combat. His wife commented in her letter how Irving's handwriting was so similar to Buddy's. Irving describes the situation of the local Italian population as the 6th Armored Infantry moves north. It took Irving's siblings 3 weeks to receive a letter from him after breakout. During that time they had no idea whether he was dead or alive. David thinks he recognizes Irving's photo in a newspaper. David sends old photos of his mother overseas to Irving in time for their mother's yahrzeit. Irving would like a photo from the French girl he met in Africa. The 6th Armored division is reorganized, and Irving is sent to a replacement depot to await reassignment. He is transferred to a non-combat role and works in a PX in Naples. He works there until the end of the year when he is sent to another replacement depot to await a new assignment. Irving sends money home to his sisters. They buy war bonds for him with it.

Back home, Hermine is hospitalized. David sends a matching snail shell necklace and earrings for Hermine and Marie to share, but one of the earrings was damaged. He also sends medicine for Herman's nervous stomach - this was the reason for Herman's honorable discharge. David learns that they can send small packages overseas to Irving in the same way that they send letters. They send large 5 lb packages to Irving, too. These packages include cookies, fruit cakes, and even salami. David also sends Irving liquor in small bottles of mouthwash or suntan lotion. He also advises his sisters in their dispute with the landlady over the rent payment for the garage. He asks for their help in getting tax papers from his former employer, Spitler, the owner of the taxi cab company in Columbus for whom David drove a taxi. Hermine's friend, Helen Perl Goldstein suggests that Hermine come to Cleveland. She has two men that she wants to introduce to Hermine: Louis Goldblatt and Gilbert Rosewater. Louis is sent overseas, first to Hawaii, as a dentist and a Jewish chaplain. He is much younger than Hermine, but his mother, whom Hermine meets, likes her very much and encourages him to exchange pictures with Hermine. Gilbert is much older than Hermine, and David discourages her from becoming serious with him, however they do correspond and go out. Irving meets David Kornfield from Eperjes, Czechoslovakia, and he knows Gilbert Rosewater. Louis Schwartz writes to Hermine and Marie from a US base in Iceland. Marie takes various jobs including one at a barrage balloon factory and another at American Education Press, Inc. David gets training as a marine electrician. His sisters are worried that he can get hurt working with live electricity. He reassures them that he doesn't. He has an easier job at the shipyard coordinating part orders and deliveries onboard the ships being constructed. He encourages his sisters to come to California. As the Russian army nears Ungvar, a large city near Polyán , Marie suggests bringing the family out as soon as possible. David predicts that jobs will be better in Europe after the war. David follows the news from the Eastern front very closely. Once Ungvar falls to the Russians, David hopes that the family back home is well. David reads that the Red Cross is helping Hungarian Jews. Polyán and the surrounding area are captured by the Russians , and so is Szatmar, Romania. David asks Herman to send him Canadian Club whiskey and asks his sisters to send him their ration coupons. David moves from Wilmington to Long Beach. He now lives in an apartment with a private bathroom and a kitchen, and he learns to cook for himself with advice from Hermine and Marie. David works 70 hours per week. He wants to learn interior design. Once again he encourages Marie to come to California - at least to learn the new style of drapery so she can bring it back to Ohio. Instead, Marie works as a cashier at Neill House, a hotel in Columbus. David encourages Irving to register to vote and to come to California to open a kosher butcher. Flo Meizlish, a girl who went out with Irving before the war, and who is corresponding with him, recognizes Hermine at synagogue on Yom Kippur.

1945 Summary

Hermine has an appendectomy but doesn't write anything to Irving about it immediately. She doesn't know that their cousin Arthur already did. When she finally does write to Irving, he feels hurt because she didn't tell him. Again, David advises Hermine against Gilbert Rosewater. If he was in the army, and then subsequently sent home, something is wrong. He advises not to rush into anything. Hermine eventually breaks up with Gilbert Rosewater. David still works at the shipyard, and he writes about going on the sea trial of a ship he worked on, and about the radar system he helped install on it. Irving is waiting in Naples in a replacement depot for new orders. He has been reclassified as I-B - limited military service, non combat. He receives a package and letters from Flo Meizlish and another package from the US Army Mothers of St. Louis - an organization that includes his friend Buddy Hunecke's wife. He sends Flo a small table cloth from Naples. He also buys a cameo for his sisters, a cigarette case for Bertha, and other gifts for Arthur, his wife Flora, and their children Samuel and Jennie. Shortly thereafter, Irving is reassigned and sails to Marseille, France, and is assigned to be a military policeman (MP) with the 67th MP company. He patrols by motorcycle and foot in Dijon, Toul, and Nancy in France before being stationed in Germany where he serves as a guard for, and speaks to, General Arthur R. Wilson. The General writes to Irving's sisters. Irving is in Mannheim, Germany when VE day is declared. With the war's end, his letters go out uncensored and he writes a letter to his family in Czechoslovakia. He also asks for permission to visit them. He hopes he can before he has enough points to be sent home. Irving is transferred again to transport German prisoners of war from Germany to a prisoner of war camp in France. He hopes to be transferred home soon after, but is reassigned to a replacement depot outside Paris. He would like to visit the city, but must wait his turn. Since there is poor communication with Eastern Europe, he does not get the approval to visit his family in Polyán. He saves money for when he does get permission to visit them. Finally, he's sent to Chamarande, France to wait for a Victory ship to take him home. Irving still has no news about his family in Czechoslovakia and no permission to go there. Irving reaches out to the Red Cross and they advise him to file a Missing Persons report with the International Red Cross. He's transferred to Camp Lucky Strike, and from there sails to the USA on the Victory ship Frederick. He hopes to return to Europe as a civilian to help his family. A buddy of Irving calls Bertha to say Irving is ok, he's just been delayed by the lack of available shipping. Irving arrives to New York and calls his sisters in Columbus before going on to Pennsylvania to be discharged. When Irving arrives home to Columbus, he thinks about going to school under the GI Bill and quickly applies to the Ohio State University.

There was a water shortage in Columbus because of the heavy snow with no thaw. The world premiere of a film about Eddie Rickenbacker was held in Columbus, his hometown. Everything was decorated in his honor. Hermine, Marie, and Flora apply for citizenship at the same time, but Hermine and Flora get their interviews and citizenship first. Marie had to correct her citizenship application because it mistakenly listed Hungary as her origin, not Czechoslovakia. Louis Goldblatt's mother says he isn't interested in marriage yet, but Hermine meets him anyway. He gets stationed in Oklahoma as a dentist and is then sent overseas. Marie loses her cashier job at Neil House since she wasn't feeling well. She starts a new job at the A&P as a cashier. Herman is unemployed. Louis Schwartz is still in the US army in Iceland. David works 77 hours a week at a new shipyard repairing ships. He complains that there is barely a minyan in Long Beach. David visits Hollywood and goes to the Palladium. He sends a letter to his family in Czechoslovakia via Irving. David goes fishing and gets seasick. David goes to a Russian restaurant, but the musicians were Hungarian so he spoke with them and danced the csardas. Although there are job cuts, David plans to stay in CA and he encourages his sisters to come there, too. Marie and Hermine write their 1st letters home to Czechoslovakia, but they are returned as being undeliverable.

Bertha hears from Jack Eigner that the family may have been murdered in Europe.

Uncle Martón's son, Emil Schwartz, the sibling's cousin from Kiralyhelmec, writes the first letter to Hermine and her siblings after returning home from Auschwitz, Mauthausen, and Gunskirchen. He describes in detail what happened to the family.

Ignácz, Manci, and Rozsi Klein, the brother and sisters of Lajos Gluck's wife Etelka, reply to Hermine after they took Hermine's letter that was addressed to the sibling's brother Lajos and father Jeremias in Polyán. The Kleins detail those who survived and those who perished in Polyán and Lelesz.

The siblings' Christian neighbor, Ilonka Török, writes to the siblings about those who survived after being taken in April 1944: Malvin Lefkovits is in Sweden. Ignácz Klein is in Lelesz. Miksa and Tibi Schőn are dead. She wants to buy land from Bertha.

Another Christian neighbor, Margit Gerenyi, writes that Etelka, Lajos' wife, had another daughter, Kornelia. She writes that the Jews were rounded up in May and taken to Sátoraljaújhely. Her husband drove the carriage that brought them to Sátoraljaújhely. She writes that Ignácz Klein returned and he has asked her to give him the sibling's father Jeremias' watch.

Another Christian neighbor, Mrs. Deàk, writes describing the roundup of the Jews. She claims to have brought food to the family held in Sátoraljaújhely. She buried 5 of her family in 3 years, including both of her daughters who were friends with Marie and Hermine. She describes what happened to the siblings' house and furniture.

Hermine inquires about the family through the Jewish Agency

1946 Summary

As Hermine and Marie receive letters from Europe, it becomes clear that the family the siblings left behind are victims. Although they have their cousin Emil Schwartz's letter detailing the fate of the family, the siblings hold out hope that perhaps their brother Lajos survived, and since Emil Schwartz survived, then perhaps Lajos' son, Emil Gluck may have survived, too. Hermine and Marie try to maintain correspondence with, and send packages to, the few relatives who did survive: Emil Schwartz - their Uncle Marton's son who returned to Kiralyhelmec and is staying with his cousin Zoli Pollak until he can make his way to Palestine; their cousin Lipot Klein, his wife Margit, and their daughters in Budapest; Malvin Lefkovits, their neighbor's daughter, who was taken to Sweden to recover after being liberated; and their brother Lajos' wife's siblings - the Kleins (Manci, Rozsi, and Ignácz) who have returned to Lelesz. These Kleins detail the fate of the Jewish community of Lelesz and Polyán, as well as the disposition of the sibling's property in Polyán. They also describe the gentile neighbors in Polyán, and their interactions with them. Over time, the sibling's relationship with the Kleins in Lelesz deteriorates because of the way they seem to be deceiving the siblings about the state of the land, their interactions with the neighbors, and their use, or misuse, of the packages that the sisters are sending them. Rather than using them, they seem to be selling them at inflated prices, at least according to the non-Jewish neighbors. Hermine and Marie also write to these gentile neighbors and get several replies from them detailing the roundup of the Jews and the occupation of the village by the Germans. Margit Gerenyi informs the sisters about Ignácz Klein and how he is demanding that she return the earrings that were given her as a "gifts" as well as the siblings' father's watch, chain, and pipe. She describes their own economic difficulties and how Ignácz Klein is selling everything (furniture, clothing, shoes) that he repossessed from the neighbors at prices they can't afford. Istvan Toth recounts life during the war, and describes the sibling's family being taken. She tells that their father, Jeremias, took his children's photos with him, and that German soldiers were quartered in the Gluck's house. She claims that those soldiers wanted to use the furniture for firewood, but her family, and other neighbors, offered to do laundry for them in order to salvage the furniture. She admits to taking the beds and mirror. Ignácz Klein wants to take it back from her in order to sell it and buy a calf, but she argues that she, and her newly married daughter Margit, deserve it for all the help they gave to the Gluck family. She complains that she had funeral expenses for her husband and that her daughter is expecting and needs baby clothing. She also claims that Ignácz took the photos that she had of the Gluck family. Ignácz exacerbates the distrust that the siblings now feel towards him by claiming that they owe him the dowry his sister Etelka brought into the marriage with their brother Lajos.

Jolán Ragàny, another gentile neighbor, writes that she took furniture from the Glucks to protect it from the Germans. She also claims to have done laundry for the German soldiers in order to protect the furniture. Malvin continues to write from Sweden. She writes that she gave jewelry to Gyula Szabo for safekeeping, but that Gyula denies ever having been given the jewelry. Malvin gets an affidavit of support to come to America. Rozsi Hausman, a cousin of the sibling's sister-in-law Etelka, and an acquaintance of Malvin's, writes the sisters from Sweden, not asking for anything, but just to correspond with someone since she believes she has nobody left in the world. She details her survival in Auschwitz, Dachau, and Bergen Belsen. Despite her belief that she is alone, two uncles in America recognize her name in the lists of survivors and submit an affidavit of support to bring her to the US. Until then, she, using her meager salary from her work in Sweden, is sending packages to other survivors in her home town of Agárd. Finally, Bertha receives word that Irén Mayer from Romania (Bertha's half sister Sarolta's daughter) survived. Bertha tries to think how she can bring her to America. Irving finds out that his friend from Polyán, Sanyi Klein, survived as well. Sanyi writes that he was in a labor camp for 2 years and then spent 2 years in Russia.

Meanwhile, back in the US, Irving starts studying at the Ohio State University. He takes classes in economics, English, speech, and psychology. While there, he receives an invitation to Flo Meizlish's wedding. She had been corresponding with others as well as with Irving while he was overseas. He sends a card to her parents, but does not attend. Louis Goldblatt, the young soldier interested in Hermine, gets stationed in the Pacific as a dentist and chaplain/rabbi. Hermine has given him her picture, a big deal at the time, but he has not yet given his picture to her. He details how he helps refugees in Manila, the Philippines and how he helps to conduct services for the orthodox soldiers there. He also finally sends her his photo, and even though he isn't ready to get married, he plans to visit her when he is on leave. Hermine makes the monumental decision to visit Bertha in New York in June. If she finds better opportunities in New York, she intends to stay. Bertha, and her husband Mannie, allow Hermine to stay with them in their apartment, and Hermine goes to learn how to use a comptometer, and eventually gets a job working for the Paramount Movie theater. She meets and dates several guys: an optometrist at a Hungarian picnic, a Polish guy who is rich, but too short, and a 43 year old Hungarian who is too old for her. She encourages her siblings to come to New York because the job situation is good and it is much better for them socially. Although David still tries to convince his siblings to come to California, he advises Marie to join Hermine in New York, which she does in the Fall, and discourages Irving from coming to visit him in California until Irving finishes school. Hermine feels guilty for staying so long with Bertha and Mannie, so she and Marie stay in one room of an apartment that they share with an older woman named Mrs. Kugler. It was very difficult to find an apartment/room that was affordable. Both sisters worry about Irving and Herman being alone in the apartment in Columbus. Who will maintain it? And who will look after Herman? He doesn't feel well, he's very anxious, and is not eating properly. It's getting worse, not better, and he needs help. Marie hesitated going to New York because of this. However, once Marie is in New York, she goes on one date that turns into a serious relationship. His name is also Irving. Meanwhile, David encourages Hermine to write to the US Consulate to try and protect the siblings' property rights back in Czechoslovakia. This is especially urgent because a neighbor (Sandor Koszyto) offers 1000 dollars to buy Bertha's property there. Hermine and the siblings send a letter of inquiry to Pál Lengyel, their father's friend and the village's notary, as well as to their brother Lajos' in-law Ignácz Klein to find out what's happening with their property. She also reaches out to Kalman's son to help get their property back. (Kalman was a resident of Lelesz. His father's home was used for services after the synagogue there was condemned back in 1941.) At her job, Hermine waits patiently for a promised salary increase, but it is always being postponed. Although she wants to send money and packages to those in Europe she can't afford to send to everyone. She stops sending to the Kleins in Lelesz because of her feeling that Ignácz Klein is dealing deceptively with her regarding the sibling's property. After an additional package or two, Hermine also stops sending to the Kleins in Budapest because Lipot has written to Arthur for help, and Arthur graciously agrees to send them aid. Lipot continues to receive medical treatment because he has had ongoing health issues after being liberated. Hermine arranges for their neighbor, Mrs. Ivany, to receive help from a Catholic charity and sends a package to their neighbor Mrs. Deak, but not to Mrs. Gerenyi who has asked if the siblings' house in Polyán is for sale. The non-Jews Puskár and Horvyak live in the siblings' house in Polyán. Hermine makes the decision that the only person that can, and should, be helped is their mother's brother Marton's son, their cousin Emil Schwartz. Arthur will consider sending a guarantee for Emil to come to the USA. However, while in New York, Hermine meets Emil's uncle, Louis Lefkovits (Emil's mother Etelka's brother). It is through Hermine that he learns that Emil survived. Lefkovits does nothing for several months because he is waiting for Emil to write him. Hermine continues to send packages to Emil since he asked her to send him clothing. He still plans to go to Palestine, but he also wants to study dentistry. His cousin, Zoltan Pollak, with whom he has been staying, will marry the Rabbi's daughter. Hermine's friend in Cleveland, OH, Helen Perl Goldstein finds out that her parents and sister were killed. Hermine is still hopeful, especially when she receives word that an Emil Gluck has been found alive. However, it was a case of mistaken identity.

1947 Summary

Marie's boyfriend Irving wants to propose, but Marie isn't sure what she will say if he does. Soon after, she breaks up with him. She starts working at Ratner's - a well known, kosher restaurant in Manhattan. Hermine quits her job at Paramount because they never gave the raise they had promised. She finds a job as a comptometer operator at a department store, and then a different job at Warner Brothers, working in their foreign service accounting department. Louis Goldblatt comes to visit her in New York and wants her emigrate with him to Palestine where he will work as a dentist at Hadassah Hospital or study in a yeshiva. After lots of consideration, Hermine decides to say 'yes' to Louis even though she would be leaving her family and country. Marie supports her decision. David is against it. In the end, Louis doesn't have as much money as he needs to go to Palestine with Hermine. He proposes to marry anyway. He would go to Palestine alone at first, and Hermine would come later, but she refuses. Hermine is determined to set a date to say kaddish for her father, her brother, and his family. She asks Irving to ask a Rabbi. She later finds a Rabbi who recommends saying kaddish for the family, and advises her to just pick a day that fits best. Hermine starts taking classes in English and history twice a week at Roosevelt High School and votes for the very first time in her life in the November election. Hermine continues to coordinate among the siblings to send money to Emil, but she stops writing to the other survivors because she can't afford to do anything more to help them. Everything is expensive for Hermine and Marie, but Mrs. Kugler, the kindly old woman with whom they share an apartment, helps them get wholesale clothing. Marie and Hermine buy winter coats.

The siblings fill out paperwork regarding the property in Europe. They want to remove Ignácz Klein as the caretaker. Manci Klein, Ignácz's sister questions why the siblings want to take control of the property away from Ignácz. The siblings hire Belo Fenicky, a lawyer in Helmec and a former notary, but he sits on their paperwork and does nothing to help. Instead, he sells his own property and advises the siblings to sell theirs. Irving writes to Pál Lengyel, his father's friend and notary to help preserve their property rights by the Oct 31 deadline. The siblings agree that Bela Fenicky should no longer be authorized to act on the family's behalf. Pál Lengyel reports back regarding the property - the house needs repair or it will collapse. Regarding the tax assessment, he writes that the property hasn't been confiscated and that Ignácz Klein has merely been appointed as the administrator of it. Furthermore, the siblings can change who administers the property at any time. Ignácz now wants Emil and Lenke's share of the property because of Etelka's dowry.

Jana Fabianova, the postmaster from Lelesz, writes to David and the siblings to their Uncle Julius' address. She was in Italy during the war. Hermine and Marie send dresses to her. She hopes David is well after his recent illness, and that he will write to her. When he doesn't answer, Jana writes directly to David, hoping he will reply. She asks for various small items hoping that David will send them, along with his photo. David writes to her and she sends him her photograph from 1944. She asks for stockings, nightgowns, camisoles, and a raincoat.

Irving is still studying at OSU, trying to decide his major. He writes a term paper, *"Planet of Oneness"* which envisions humanity living peacefully. After his exams, he visits his sisters in New York and meets Hilda Goldberger, with whom he corresponds with upon his return to Columbus. He receives a letter from Ruth Balbach, a woman he met while on patrol in Germany. She addresses the letter to "Irving Berlin", the pseudonym he gave her while in Germany - to "conceal" his Jewish identity. She describes the conditions in Germany for her family.

Bertha goes to Florida, alone, for about 2 months. When she returns, she proposes a scheme to use Irving to help her niece Irén Mayer get a visa to come to America from Romania. She wants him to bring her as his war bride. Maria advises Irving in the strongest possible way not to listen to Bertha.

Herman returns to work for Arthur again at Arthur's company, Bonded Scale and Manufacturing. He remains there until the factory burns down in one of the largest fires in the country that year. He and Irving still live together. Hermine recommends that they rent out the girls' room in Columbus to help them with the expenses there.

David considers coming to New York, but Hermine discourages him. It's hard to find a room, never mind an apartment, and whatever he would find would be very expensive. David tries to convince Irving to be a homesteader with him in Alaska because ex GIs can get 160 acres of land there.

Malvin Lefkovits will leave Sweden and return to the Czech Republic. She can't come to America for at least another year.

Lipot Klein is hospitalized in Budapest with pleurisy.

1948 Summary

Ignácz Klein goes to court and claims Emil and Lenke's share of the property in Polyán. Hermine writes that they may still be alive, and if they are not, it will be more difficult to sell the property. Ignácz's claim is denied by the court. The siblings organize documents to submit to Czechoslovakia regarding their property. Hermine asserts that if they haven't heard from anyone by now, then they didn't survive. She asks that they pick a yahrzeit date and the boys should say kaddish. She also insists that they must help Emil because his father, Uncle Marton, took out a loan in order to loan the siblings money to come to USA. Hermine dates a wealthy Hungarian guy named Irving (ironically because Marie had dated an 'Irving', too!). He breaks up with Hermine because she had a lingering cold and he thinks she is sickly. Hermine is planning to meet the Lefkovits girls in New York. They lived in Kiralyhelmec and came to New York in 1946.

David surprises his siblings by suddenly marrying Dorothy in CA with one week's notice. David, short of money, asks Irving for a loan in order to marry. David and Dorothy get an apartment together in Long Beach, and Dorothy admits that David is the far better cook. Hermine suggests buying a silver dinner set as gift, but worries that perhaps it's too expensive for Irving to afford. Both Hermine and Marie are angry that David hardly writes to them after the wedding. Dorothy goes home to visit her family in Chicago by train. It's a 39+ hour trip. Although she wants to meet Irving and Herman, she experiences hemorrhaging on the train just before arriving to Chicago and is hospitalized. Meanwhile, Jana Fabianova, the postmaster from Lelesz, gets another package from David. Everything in it was perfect. She writes him again asking for cookies and canned goods, coffee and tea. She also sends a drawing of her shoe size.

After appearing in a German play ('A Man Must Marry') at OSU, Irving goes to Chicago to visit Dorothy and her family, as well as his friend and former classmate Herb Baum. Herb is studying for his PhD at the University of Chicago. Irving then goes by train to New York and visits his sisters, and Hilda Goldberger - with whom he still corresponds. Irving is not the only one to visit the sisters in New York. The siblings' and Bertha's mutual cousin - Fred Gluck, the son of their late uncle Martin Gluck of Mt. Pleasant, PA, visits with his wife and daughter. Louis Schwartz and his brother Joe visit New York to welcome their nephew who just arrived from Europe - at Ellis Island. Hermine also describes the Jewish protests on behalf of Palestine in New York. After Irving returns to Columbus, his friend Herb Baum visits with his girlfriend Renee. Irving hopes that his sisters will come to his graduation in 1949. Hermine and Marie promise that they will.

When Dorothy returns to California, David goes alone to Bakersfield to help open a store. Dorothy joins him on subsequent trips there. David freelances in the drapery business. On Dorothy's birthday, she wins a laundry machine at the grand opening of a furniture store. Hermine suggests that after Irving finishes at

OSU they would all move to California since the weather is better and Marie wouldn't get sick so often. Dorothy recommends Los Angeles because there are more single Jews living there than in Long Beach.

In Budapest, Lipot Klein is very ill. He has a cancerous tumor in his forehead. Bertha wants to hire someone named Zsiga to take care of her property in Polány. Zsiga wants to take care of the other Gluck Property, too.

Marie doesn't get a bonus on Christmas like her co-workers because her employer says Jews don't believe in Christmas.

1949 Summary

Hermine continues the discussion about saying kaddish for the family. Many Jews discuss saying kaddish for the victims on Jan 11 (Note: International Holocaust Remembrance Day is eventually established on January 27th). Hermine is against it because that date coincides with David's anniversary, but she insists they must set a date and say kaddish. A Rabbi advises her to set the yahrzeit date for the 2nd day of Passover, the day the Jews of Polyán and the surrounding district were taken to Sátoraljaújhely. He suggests that they can always change the date if new information becomes known. Hermine writes about her latest suitors and about her once a week English class. She strongly feels that Herman should come to New York, get a good job, and meet a nice girl. Herman is unemployed because he was let go by Arthur's company after the fire, and Hermine insists that he must collect unemployment. In order to do so, he must say that he is willing to work and he must keep searching for a job. Marie agrees that he should come to New York because the way he lives is not living. Life is passing him by. Herman begins thinking seriously about coming to New York. Hermine advises him to leave his job after Christmas. She also meets Eugene Solomon, a Hungarian immigrant from Romania, and starts dating him seriously. Nonetheless, she visits Herman and Irving in Columbus. Marie goes on vacation to the Catskills where she enjoys playing tennis. She hopes to visit Irving in Columbus and David in California within the next year, but she must save up for it.

Irving's graduation from OSU is quickly approaching. He and his siblings discuss what he will do after graduation. He will either visit David in California, move to New York, or go to graduate school at OSU. Since these all cost money, Marie suggests that he becomes a Rabbi, which he can do for free. The siblings discuss what to do with the apartment in Columbus, and if the boys leave, what should be done with the furniture there. Irving graduates OSU with a degree in economics. None of his siblings attend the graduation. Hermine broke her ankle and is on crutches and didn't tell Irving because she didn't want Irving to miss his graduation or to worry. Irving's friend, Herb Baum, asks his girlfriend Renee to marry. She'll work while he finishes his PhD at the University of Chicago.

In California, David and Dorothy set up their new apartment. Despite the noisy neighbors, Dorothy's mother visits them for 6 weeks. Dorothy is pregnant again and is expecting in October. She confirms that she had a miscarriage last year. Dorothy suggests they all go into business together, but Hermine discourages the idea. Irving doesn't want to go into business with David, and is unable to loan him money to start one. He has decided to go to graduate school with the dream of studying the economic conditions that lead to war, and hoping to help prevent another one. As for the loan to David, any extra money Irving has is invested in the stock market, and taking it out would be a huge loss for him. David takes a loan from Dorothy's father instead and opens his own store in July. Dorothy gives birth to Frederick Jerome.

Arthur rebuilds his factory after the fire. Irén Mayer, Bertha's niece is arrested in Romania. She receives permission to emigrate to Israel, but Bertha is trying to get her to Canada. Helen Lefkovits' sister will marry in New York and invites Marie and Hermine.

1950 Summary

Irving visits Elsie, Arthur's sister, in Cleveland. Hermine initially plans to marry Eugene in February, but then sets the date for March 5. Hermine pleads with Herman to attend her wedding. Herman is unwilling to spend money on himself and live properly. Hermine and Marie both try to convince him, and Irving, to come to New York. Herman doesn't attend the wedding, but Irving does and while in New York he looks for a job. He eventually gets one, but works there only briefly. He returns to Ohio and takes a civil service exam, which he passes, and waits to find out which government job he will get. Hermine and her husband Eugene find an apartment on Long Island. It's located at 36-19 167th Street and they will move into it in August. Hermine is busy buying furnishings for the apartment. She also asks Irving to send her the dunná that they had brought with them from Europe. Hermine wants to try to bring their cousin Emil Schwartz to America, but she is also afraid that he would be drafted to serve in Korea. She makes sure that the Lefkovits girls will talk to their, and Emil's, Uncle Louis Lefkovits. Hermine again encourages Irving and Herman to come to New York.

Dorothy flies home to Chicago with Frederick Jerome. Irving and Herman go there to visit with Dorothy and her family. Irving also meets with his friend from OSU, Herb Baum. David and Dorothy move to a house at 3242 Maine Ave. in Long Beach, CA. Long Beach is being built up and they hope that their business will go well. Dorothy works in the store with David. Marie reserves tickets on a train to Columbus, Chicago, and California, leaving September 30. She buys a round trip ticket, but is open to staying in California. David meets her at the station, but doesn't recognize her at first. Marie suggests that Irving could come to California and help David. She may start working in California and David tries to convince Irving to come to California, too since there are plenty of jobs, just not enough men. Marie decides that there is nothing for young people in Long Beach, and thinks that Los Angeles would be better, but she doesn't know anybody there, and the jobs don't pay well. She concludes that she doesn't want to work with David, and returns to New York. She asserts that it is better for everybody to be in New York, even though she lives about 1 hour 45 minutes commute from Hermine. Additionally, she recommends that Irving should not go work for David either. David and Marie are both worried that Irving will be called up to fight in Korea since he was in the infantry.

Jana receives a large package sent by David that includes the shoes she asked for, and women's clothing.

1951 Summary

Irving is working hard in his new job, although it is night work. He eventually leaves this job and returns to work for Arthur. Hermine has stopped working and plans to take a 1 week vacation. She loves how her apartment turned out, and she loves her husband. Both Hermine and Marie again encourage Irving and Herman to come to New York and marry. It is hard for Marie to find someone to marry, but she is hopeful that G-d will help. Hermine and Marie frequently talk by telephone, but it's too far for Marie to visit often. Marie suggests to Irving that when he writes to Hermine, he should also include *Eugene* in his salutation, so that he doesn't get insulted.

Emil receives a package that Hermine and Eugene sent and is overjoyed to eat from it. Hermine strongly suggests to her siblings that they all care for Emil like he was their brother. She reasons that their Uncle Marton took a loan and gave them money from it so they could come to America, therefore they should repay the loan to his son, Emil. Emil receives a check sent by Hermine. It takes at least 2 weeks to get it converted into cash, and he writes that it is better if she sends packages, since he especially needs clothing. He explains what happened to the money his father had hidden, and how he became impoverished. His cousin, and guardian, Zoltan Pollack used it for his own wedding, and other expenses, without Emil's knowledge. Hermine and Marie send $15 to Emil through an organization. Emil is studying dentistry.

Dorothy writes that business is slow in California. Freddy is growing nicely. Hermine would like to see Freddy, and would travel to Chicago if Dorothy goes home to visit her family in the summer. Irén, Bertha's niece, finally arrives to Israel.

Arthur Gluck's sister Elsie Schallheim's daughter Jane goes to Columbia University to be a teacher. Hencsu Lefkovits from Helmec marries in June, and Lester Gluck, Aunt Jenny's son, gets engaged and marries in August. Eugene's brother Milton Solomon, a trained tailor, manages a store that rents out men's suits.

1952 Summary

Hermine recommends that Herman should pay attention to what he eats. She thinks that his nervous stomach disorder might be from ulcers. She has a court case for an injury, perhaps from when she broke her ankle. Hermine is pregnant, and once again encourages Irving to relocate to New York. She wants to set Irving up with someone nice. Hermine now uses the telephone to stay in touch with their relatives, but Bertha and Jenny Frey need to be invited separately since they don't get along. Hermine would like to get a television. She invites Marie for Passover, but since Marie lives very far and works very hard, she isn't sure that she'll be able to go.

Irving contributes to packages for Emil, as Hermine requested. Although Irving tried to start a business, it failed, and he and Herman finally move to New York. Irving works for Atlas Construction. Their cousin Sam Gluck, Arthur's son, applies to graduate school at Columbia University to study philosophy. He wants to leave his father's business (Bonded Scale) completely. He asks for Irving's advice, and gets it.

Emil Schwartz lives in Jaffa, Israel. He goes for 5 weeks reserve duty in the Israeli army , and consequently loses his job as a taxi driver. He receives another package from Hermine and every item in it is perfect. He describes the current economic conditions in Israel. Emil wants to marry Lili Feuereisen, but he doesn't have money to rent his own place so can't ask her to marry yet. He asks Hermine for a dowry gift to give to Lili.

Sam Fried also details life and economic conditions in Israel. He asks Irving to help get parts for machines from Arthur.

David doesn't write anymore, only Dorothy. David was upset that Irving was too busy to write to him. David and Dorothy move their store to a larger location that has parking in front.

Irén Mayer, Bertha's niece, will go from Israel to Canada in May.

Tonti and Bill Zuhl, neighbors/friends/landlord of Irving in Columbus, help him to sell his car because Irving left Bonded Scale and moved to a new apartment/job.
Roberta Gluck, Fred Gluck's daughter from Mt. Pleasant, PA, having met Irving only once, corresponds with him.

1953 Summary

Marie goes on summer vacation in the Catskills

Irving gets a new job in Portsmouth, OH at the Portsmouth Gaseous Diffusion Plant. He plans to work there to get experience, but doesn't intend to remain there for years. Marie hopes Irving has luck meeting young women. Hilda (maybe Goldberger), Irving's former girlfriend, calls Marie, however Irving is in a serious relationship with a woman named Lee. She lives in New York, but she visits Irving in Portsmouth. Hermine invites her to come over to visit Linda, Hermine and Eugene's baby daughter. Michael Conley, a friend of Irving's from Ohio State, writes to him from Germany and describes the conditions there. He documents both the destruction wrought by the war and the rebuilding effort. Irving shares his thoughts with Michael on war and peaceful coexistence.

Herman stays in New York, and is upset that Irving left to go to Ohio again without telling him that he wasn't coming back. Herman visits Marie every night, but he stops visiting her entirely when Marie moves to a new apartment, refusing to even call her. Marie wanted a change, and decided to no longer live with Mrs. Kugler. Instead, she shares a 4 bedroom apartment with another elderly woman. Although she doesn't really like it, she will stay there for now. Hermine thinks it's good to leave Herman on his own, since he'll be forced to change his behavior. Herman doesn't like his job, but his sisters feel it's his own fault since he waited until the last minute to find it.

Dorothy visits her ailing father in Chicago with Freddie. Hermine is unhappy that Dorothy and David haven't written in a long time, but the reason is that business is slow in California, and they are struggling. David and Dorothy must close their store and liquidate everything. They consider going into the restaurant business. Flora and Arthur visit New York and call Hermine. Thanksgiving is spent at Eugene's brother Milton.

Emil's wife Lili gives birth to their first son, Misha.

Irving gets engaged to Lee. She continues to live in New York, and she often goes out with Marie. Sam Gluck, Arthur's son, also meets with Lee. Marie thinks Sam likes Lee, too. Sam admits that had he seen Lee first, he would have dated her. Lee and Irving begin planning their wedding, and she wants him to come to New York during Passover to do so. Marie agrees that he should. Marie also meets Lee's mother over lunch. Herman and Marie come to Hermine's for the seder, but Irving doesn't come to New York until after Passover. Afterwards, Lee and Irving meet midway between New York and Ohio for a weekend, and again in Washington. Irving worries about not having a steady job because the work at the gas diffusion plant is coming to an end. He may return to look for work in New York. Hermine suggests that they have a small wedding, but leaves it up to Lee. However, Lee's mother wants them to have a big wedding, so Lee might pay for it. The wedding date is set for September 19th, but Irving is let go from his job at Portsmouth Diffusion, and the wedding is put on hold.

In a work accident, a shelf falls and breaks Herman's leg. He spends 7 weeks in the hospital, upset the entire time that he has to continue to pay rent for his apartment when he's not even living in it. He hires a lawyer to get injury compensation. Although Herman often yells at Marie, he still wants her to live with him, however, she wants to live her own life. Marie advises Herman to get a suit in preparation for Irving's wedding. He doesn't want to and she asks Irving to talk to him. Marie is busy trying to organize the tax papers for Irving, Herman, and herself. Nonetheless, she is able to take a vacation at the Pine's Hotel in upstate New York. Irving buys her a watch, but she insists on paying for it

Hermine is also expecting a second child, and gives birth to Diana in July. Irén Mayer, Bertha's niece, comes to New York from Canada. She is remarried (her first husband didn't survive the Holocaust). David and Dorothy go into the restaurant business.

1955-1994 Summary

1955
Rosalind Rowsey, a 19 year old co-worker of Irving's from Portsmouth, is engaged.

1956
Irving flies to visit Dave and Dorothy in California. David is trying to sell his restaurant, "The Main Stop". Irving takes the train home and visit's Dorothy's family in Chicago. He gets fired from his job for arriving later than expected because he took the train. He goes into the vending business.

1957
Hermine and Eugene move to a house. Eugene loves gardening.

1958
Dorothy has surgery. Her stepmother dies. David opens Freddy's Place, a bar/pizzeria serving mostly foreign beers.

1960
Irving loans David money. Pál Lengyel writes about the siblings' property in Europe. Jews who left renounced their ownership, and property owned by Americans was confiscated and made communal. The siblings' house was confiscated and sold to Sandor Puskar. Ignácz Klein moved to Nágymihaly to live with his sister Rezsi. Samuel Schwartz's property was sold to D'Oczy. All movable property was auctioned or stored. Pál Lengyel obtains land registry statements for the siblings' property and sends it to Irving. According to Pál, the siblings' father, Jeremias Gluck, paid his debt to the credit union. However, Pál requests that the siblings repay a loan that he personally gave to their father.

Bertha asks Irving to help regarding her property in Europe, too

Selma Jaeger introduces Barbara Nagel to Irving. After dating 1.5 months, they get engaged in May, and marry in September.

David undergoes a spinal tap. He looks and feels fine.

1963
Jerritt is born to Irving and Barbara. Arthur's wife Flora undergoes major surgery.

1967
Arthur and Flora are aging. He is nearly crippled, she is losing her eyesight.

1968
Emil Schwartz considers coming to the US as a cantor. He sends Irving an audition tape.

1972
Emil receives a taxi permit, buys a car, and works during the *daytime* as a self employed taxi driver. He had been waiting for the permit for 20 years. Their oldest son Misha is serving in the IDF.

1973
David's son Freddy visits Israel, but fails to spot Emil and Lili who were waiting for him at the airport
Misha finishes his service in the IDF. Dudi works to earn pocket money.
When Israel is attacked on Yom Kippur, Misha is taken from synagogue straight to the front in Sinai as a medic.

1974
Lili describes the economic situation in the aftermath of the Yom Kippur War and the Arab boycott.
Barbara begins to feel ill. Lili hopes Misha will study medicine.

1975
Misha is studying at Hebrew University in Jerusalem. Dudi is a Lieutenant in the IDF.

1976
Lili works in the sales department of a shoe factory
Misha is progressing very well with his studies
Dudi is still in the IDF (perhaps studying, or wants to study Eastern Studies)

1978
Misha, and his wife Adina, both continue their studies at Hebrew University

1980
Dudi marries Chana and starts studying.
Misha will get his doctorate soon.
Barbara's illness continues to worsen.

1981
Linda travels to Israel and visits Emil and his family
Emil and Lili become grandparents when Chana gives birth to Limor. Dudi is studying to be an attorney
Misha and Adina finish medical school

1982
Emil and Lili receive an invitation to Irving's 2nd son Sherwin's bar mitzvah
Michal Schwartz is born to Misha and Adina

1987
Barbara's illness progresses.

1990
No cure for Barbara's illness - MS
Emil stops driving the taxi.
Misha is a dental surgeon with a private clinic in Jerusalem and at Hadassah Hospital. He and Adina have 3 children.
Dudi is a lawyer, studying for his doctorate at Bar Ilan University. He and Chana have 2 children with one more on the way.
Irving reads Torah in the synagogue

1992
Sherwin, Irving's son, corresponds with Limor and Michal, Emil's oldest grandchildren

1994
Jerritt has a steady girlfriend and plans to marry.
Barbara struggles to write a few lines to Emil and Lili
Emil and Lili prepare Yizkor Book for 50th anniversary of being rounded up in 1944

The Letter Writers

Their ages in January 1938 and their relationship to Irving

Letter Writers in 1938

    Juliska Szabo, Christian neighbor, 40s?
    Aunt Helen Gluck, Uncle Jónász (Julius) Gluck's wife, Columbus, OH
Dezső (David) Gluck, brother, 27, Columbus, OH
Bertha (Bertuska) Gluck Weingarten, first cousin, 42, New York City

Herman (Hersmendel) Gluck, brother, 19
Hermine Gluck, sister, 23
Mariska / Marcsa (Maria) Gluck, sister, 21

Emil Gluck, nephew, 7, brother Lajos' son

Ignác (Irving) Gluck, 16
Jeremias Gluck, father, 62

    Jónász (Julius) Gluck, uncle, 69, Columbus, OH
    Ilona Gerenyi, Christian neighbor's child

Jana Fabianova, postmaster, early 30's
    Blanka, a friend of Dezső's
Jolan Mayer, 2nd cousin, 24, Romania
    Arthur Gluck, 1st cousin, 41, Jónász Gluck's son, Columbus, OH
Irén Mayer, 2nd cousin, about 20, Romania, Jolan's sister

    Mariska Deák, Christian neighbor, about 21
    Lajos Schwarz (Schwarz's), Dezső Gluck's wholesale supplier/manufacturer of blinds
    Dezső Grunberger, Dezső Gluck's friend/acquaintance

    Sarolta Mayer, 1st cousin, 47, Romania, Jolan and Irén's mother
    Samuel Schwartz, maternal grandfather, 86
    Lajos Schwartz, uncle, 49, mother's brother

Marton Schwartz, uncle, 42, mother's brother, shoe salesman / Yeshiva tester
    Lazar (Lajzer, Leizer) Gluck, uncle, 74, Bertha's father, Jeremias' brother

New Letter Writers in 1939

    Berta Veizer (mother) and Rella Veizer (daughter), a friend of Hermine's and Mariska's
    Lenke Gluck, niece, 6, brother Lajos' daughter
    Mityu Gluck, nephew, 4, brother Lajos' son

New Letter Writers in 1940

    Jozsef Lefkovits, neighbor in Polyán, Irving's godfather, Malvin's father.

Etelka Klein Gluck, sister-in-law, 32, brother Lajos' wife
    Lajos Gluck, brother, 33
    Magda Schwartz, 1st cousin, ~16, Marton Schwartz's daughter, polio
    Aunt Etelka Schwartz, ~40, Marton Schwartz's wife
    Hersu Schwartz, ~14, Marton Schwartz's son
Louis Schwartz, distant cousin from Europe, from Szürte or Nagyrapos [maybe Veľké Kapušany, Hungary], ~16, Youngstown, OH
    Mrs. Ivany, a neighbor
    Sanyi Klein, Irving's friend and classmate from Polyán, ~18
Helen Perl Goldstein, Hermine's friend from Europe, Szürte, ~23, Cleveland, OH

New Letter Writers in 1943

Irene and Howell Walters, neighbors in Columbus, OH

New Letter Writers in 1944

Flo Meizlish, Irving's friend, USA
Frey-Yenkin Paint Company, Irving's employer
Flora Gluck, Arthur Gluck's wife
Jane Schallheim, 2nd cousin, Arthur Gluck's niece
Louis Goldblatt, Hermine's suitor, ~20, soldier in Pacific
Gilbert Rosewater, Hermine's older suitor
Margaret Hunecke, wife of Irving's soldier friend 'Buddy'
Aunt Helen Gluck, Uncle Julius Gluck's wife
Leo Seide, Irving's army acquaintance

New Letter Writers in 1945

Earl Wetzel, fellow soldier from 6th Armored Infantry Battalion, Company B
Paul Imhoff fellow soldier, MP
Elsie Schallheim, 1st cousin, Arthur's sister
Emil Schwartz, 1st cousin, 16, Marton Schwartz's son

New Letter Writers in 1946

Klein (Ignácz, Manci, Rozsi), brother and sisters of sister-in-law Etelka, brother Lajos' wife, Polyán
Neighbors: Török, Gereny, Szmolyák, Toth, Ragány
Malvin Lefkovits, Jewish neighbor's daughter
Rozsi Hausman, cousin of sister-in-law Etelka, brother Lajos' wife
Klein (Margit, Lipot, Lulu), 1st cousins, children of Jeremias Gluck's sister Zseni, Budapest
Pál Lengyel, Czechoslovak lawyer, friend of father Jeremias Gluck
Belo Fenicky, Czechoslovak lawyer
Hilda Goldberger, Irving's friend

New Letter Writers in 1947

Ruth Balbach, German woman Irving met on patrol

New Letter Writers in 1948

Dorothy Gluck, sister-in-law, 26, brother David's wife, Chicago
Herbert Baum, Classmate at Ohio State University

New Letter Writers in 1960

Selma Jaeger, Irving's ex-girlfriend who introduced Irving to Barbara

New Letter Writers in 1972

Lili Feuereisen Schwartz, Emil's wife

In Hungarian, the following are often added after a given name:
bácsi = [title of esteem/respect, Uncle]
néni = [title of esteem/respect, Aunt]
-ka/-ke (-kam/-kem) is attached as a suffix to add an affectionate touch to the name.
For example, Etelka = Etel -ka.

The Letters

1937/11/2 Juliska Szabo to Hermine and Marie (Book 2, 248-249)

Dear Herminka and Mariska!

I'm sure my writing to you is unacceptable. I have been waiting for you to remember me with a letter, but I can't wait any more. I decided that I will write. Maybe you will not misunderstand me if I get in touch with you with good intentions. We spent so many happy days together. We talked about many good and bad things and argued about one thing or another. Now, I would only like to have a discussion about many things, because I can hardly write down what happened here. It would be hard to even tell you in person. I am very happy when I think about you, but my heart aches when I think back about the family and the past. I kept vigil with [your] poor [father] Mr. Gluck and Lajos's family the last week. We sometimes cried, and sometimes consoled each other. We said good bye to each other, with a broken heart, since our family and the Gluck family were such good people. I could write a lot of things. But, if you get this letter and, if you think it's worth responding to it, then I will write more another time. I have a family picture. [Your father] Mr. Gluck and Lajos' family are on it. Besides, Lajos and my little Neli, are very precious to me, but I know that for you they are even more precious. If you think that you don't have that picture, I will send it to you. I could write many things, but I don't want to bring up the past because it hurts me too. I know it is even more so for you. Another time I will write more. All of us, thank God are alive. I already have a big son. I have lots of troubles. My father and family are alive, but they are weak. This situation would kill even a buffalo. I am Juliska, Mrs. Szabo, so you can make sense of this letter. I thought that I will just write a few lines, but I'm not crying from the writing yet. I'm only afraid [that I will] get started. I would just like to write everything shortly, some other time. I'm asking you a very important thing. Please, do me a favor and respond. I'm asking you very much to write an answer. If the "Kelkej" [perhaps the name of a section of land] would be for sale, we would be interested, because Tibi is 20 years old. Time flies. I would not like it if three families would live together, because Mama is so old, but you know our entire life. I also know yours entirely. Write to me. I'm counting on it because I know you will not come home to live. Let me know about everything. If you will respond, I will write more also. I hope you will not despise me, that you will not write. I remain faraway, with loving greetings to the three boys and to you always with love, kissing you many times, one faithful friend. Juliska

[It seems that she may have been a family helper when our mother was sick. Her family, Christians, will be appointed by the State in 1941 to be "administrators" of our family's farm.]

1938 Undated Aunt Helen to Dezső (Book 6, 150)

Dear Dezső!

It's very nice of you to finally remember the promises you made a long time ago and you have to change. I am very happy with the confirmation of something, but it will be even better to see you again here in the very strange world. Until I will see you again as soon as possible. Best, Helen

1938/1/10 Dezső to Ignác (Aunt Marie's album)

Remember!

If with the time passing we will ever be far from each other and will only hear rarely about life's destinies, think about this thought, who wrote these lines a long time ago...

Dezső Gluck, Polyán 1938.I.10
Gluck Ignác
Polyán

1938/2/28 Bertha to David (Book 5, 37-38)

1938 February 28
New York

Dear David!

Only a few lines to let you know that regarding myself I am well and hope to hear the same from you. We received a letter from Jolan asking that I should help her in reference to the situation. But Brother! I received a letter from a young man and he writes that if Jolan leaves home, he won't be able to carry on. Dezső dear, I thought that she doesn't have any man, and that is the problem, a potential young man. I wrote to Jolan that it will be better if she gives up the visit to come out here, because she wouldn't be able to stay longer than two years or so. Because of that, everything is finished unless she wants to wait for the quota system. That will be different. That would be the best decision. I can't put down hundreds of dollars because I don't have it, and I can't take it from my husband. What can I do? Workers get only pennies in income a week. If a person lives well one can't give it up from oneself. That is the whole story and you understand me. The people there fail to realize that here in America, if one lives nicely, it does not mean that that they have any [spare] money. I will not write more at this time, I'm waiting for Mannie to come home for supper. Now it's 9:30 PM, he doesn't have time, and no one would believe it. With loads of love, Bertha.

1938/3/1 Undated Ignác to Dezső (Book 4, 297-298)

[Dated by Dezső being in America for 4 weeks]

My dear brother Dezső,
We got your awaited letter and I read it with happiness. We were waiting for it so hard. I could not imagine what could be the reason why you did not write, because you have been there for 4 weeks already. And when you wrote, you did not write about everything. I'm asking you, please, in your next letter write everything about your traveling. What did they ask you in Prague when they gave out the visa? I am letting you know about the latest news. The post lady is already in Helmec since March 1st. and [a replacement] came to replace her from Kassa, and she is also very nice. When the new lady came, I was just there. And she [Jane] introduced me to her, and she said, if I will go to the post office, then please give out the mail. And she [the replacement] promised that she will. Although I was there the day before, and I mentioned to the K [kedves = dear one], if the new lady comes, she should tell her to give out the mail. And we went to the post office every day on bicycle. Dezső, wouldn't it be good if I would be there with you, by your side. If it would be, I would help you to feed the boards [the dogs in the kennel], but God will help with that. Soon I will write an English letter to you. And thank God I'm healthy, I will close my letter with this. I kiss everybody, you separately. Your faithful brother, Ignác
[On the side of page 1] Here I'm sending a few stamps. Write how much they cost, and what's going on with the rest of them. Kiss you,
Ignác Gluck

1938/3/1 Hermine, Marie, and Herman to Dezső (Book 5, 117-119)

Dear Dezső, "Borech Ha Shem"
We have received your letter dated the 14th of this month and thank God that you have a job now. You write that you are working very hard. As soon as you are able to speak a little bit more English, it will be much easier for you. This is the worst part, at this time, in the beginning. About ourselves our father will advise you of any news. With regards to the Eszenkei lawsuit, the village district won the lawsuit [and the] money, and from here on he may have to pay up. The little girl from the post office has been transferred to Helmec. This came also to my mind to tell you that the elder Fridman brother died about three weeks ago. In your next letter let me know how much they pay you per day, and about everything. On March 2, Lajzer Bácsi went to Szatmar. My situation is the same as it was before, there's no outlook here. Wishing you good health and lots of luck in your job. Kisses to all and separately to you, your brother Herman.

[from Mariska]
Give our heartfelt regards and kisses to Jónász Bácsi and to dear Aunt Helen and to the rest of the relations. Also wishing good health to all of you, Mariska

[from Hermine]
Dear Dezső,
We have received the long-awaited letter that you mailed us, and in it you are replying to our letter. No other letters came, except the card from the port or perhaps it was from Prague? How are you? How are the relations and dear Jónász bacsi? We are very happy that we have such wonderful relations there. I can understand and imagine that you're busy, but despite that, you should still write about everything and frequently, since you know how much we're waiting for your letters! This week we received a letter from Iren, in Szatmar and her future husband. In this letter they say that they had their engagement and they would like to have their wedding shortly. She has written because of their account that is due them from Miksa [Shon]. The question now is, is there any money for Jolan for the journey to America? It would be a shame that she would depend on that. Nothing else that I could write about. Our grandfather wanted to write to you, however our father is taking the letter to the post office in Helmec. We have had guests for an hour: the

Ujloki Imil bacsi. He was in Bolyba [the next village from us] to make an arrangement for his son, with the Panet girl. Emil, Lenke, and Mityu would have liked to see you and Emil wanted to write to you also, but he's not at home. Lenke and Mityu are waiting for a baby and a motorcycle. All of us and the children are sending their kisses to you with love, Hermina

Give my love to all the relations and also to dear Jónász bacsi, with lots of love.

[from Mariska]
Dear Dezső!
I hope that my lines will find you in good health and I thank God that you are well. The sewing situation is still continuing and it has improved somewhat. How are you otherwise? You have written that it is difficult for you because you do not speak English. To study here at home by oneself is very difficult. The men from Csap paid only 30 kronen on February 4. I'm not writing any more this time, since our father and family have written about everything. Please write to us more frequently about everything. You know how bad it is if one does not write and does not receive letters. We wish you good health and good luck. Many kisses to you, Mariska.

1938/3/1 Undated Emil to Dezső (Book 5, 150-151)

Dear Uncle Dezső,
The letter that you have written to me made me very happy. I would like to see you. How are you? Write to me always because it is difficult to wait for your letter. When I receive your letter, I'm happy and I'm diligent to reply. I never ever thought that you would be in America. So I too, may be there one day. Love, and kisses, Emil, Lenke, and Mityu.
Regards and kisses to Jónász Bácsi.

1938/3/2 Father to Uncle Jónász (Book 5, 82-83)

1938/3/2
Polány

My dear loving brother Jónász and dear sister-in-law Helen. To 120
I do not understand how it has been two months since we have received any letters from you. I ask you my dearest brother please write more often. How are you? Write about yourself. We are, thank God, in good health and that's what I hope to hear from you. I've received the $10 that you sent me and it amounts to 283 kronen. I thank you for it and God will repay you for what you do to help us. How are your children? And how are you my dear brother? How do you feel? Please let us know about yourself. How does my son Dezső behave? I hope that he will behave. Our dear brother Lazar left yesterday to Romania to visit his daughter Sarolta for about two weeks. Yesterday we had Yahrzeit and on the 31st next month there will be another one again. I hope you are not upset that I'm reminding you of this, however, I'm writing this just in case you forgot. My best regards to your children, individually many times. My brother Jónász and dear sister-in law, wishing you love and kisses, many times. I remain your faithful [youngest] brother, who will never forget you to 120 years. Amen [written in Yiddish]. Jeremias Gluck

P.S. My father-in-law and family send their regards to all of you, and you especially, and to my dear son Dezső. And Patyu [Marton] said to tell you that he is also sending you his best regards to you all. I remain with love, as above.

1938/3/2 Undated Uncle Lazar to Uncle Jónász (Book 4, 343-344)

[Dated only because Jeremias complains also that Jónász hasn't written in a long time, otherwise this could be placed anywhere before 1940]

My dear little brother Jónász!
You don't deserve that I write to you, since you, like my younger brother, never give any sign of life about yourself. You could ask if I am in good health or how am I, because I am an old man. I am, thank God in good health, and I hope you don't miss that as well! Dear little brother, you know how the Hungarians say it, life is long, so don't feel bad about writing, so write slowly with your brotherly love. I close my lines. I kiss and respect my sister-in-law and children. I will stay your faithful brother, Gluck Lazar

Unfortunately, that the good God visited with the fall harvest. Indeed, not much showed. The good old ones are gone "_ _ _ _? [meaning unclear]

As above

My child [sends] regards to all of you Especially write a lot.

1938/3/3 Jane the Postmaster to Dezső (Book 1, 186-187)

Dear Dezső,

I received your card today, and for a long time I was gazing at that ship floating at sea, whose occupant you still are, and prayers ascend to God that He may protect you and help you in the future too. Dezső, a great work regarding your life has reached its completion! Right now you, an honestly struggling young man, are flying across the faraway seas toward a country with a better future. And I am so happy that this is now a fact; apparently my encouragement was not in vain. But I cannot take credit for it, neither can you. Here it was the good God helping the young man who waded through innumerable difficulties, and who loved his parents and his siblings. Dezső, please, never forget that!!! Always keep in mind that you are a Jew, and that everything you begin and finish needs God's blessing. Never forget our true heavenly Father, who never abandons us. He will always help you, and help you in everything. Besides, do not forget your earthly father who was left behind. For a father's love is so deep and touching. He visits me frequently and talks about you so lovingly; he tells me about his sleepless nights. Tears are running down his honest and kind face, and he is not embarrassed about them in front of me. With tears in his eyes he talks about his dear child whom he let go far, far away from under his paternal wings! Dezső!! Your kind father needs to be loved with happiness!!! Let his respectable head shine with radiant joy from his son's grateful love, because he deserves it. Also, be an obedient nephew to your Uncle, who also raised you with a fatherly love and he gave a helping hand to access a happier future. If you keep all this in mind, then God's blessing will follow in your life!!! If you are still on the ship, I urge that God will have you under his protection. If your letter will arrive from America, I will continue [to write] more and will send it immediately, so you can get it. On March 1st, I got your letter and, on my way I gave it over to Gluck bacsinok right away. He was very happy. He had many sleepless nights. Also, III [March] 1st, I gave the office over. Currently I'm on vacation and I'm going home. I will live in little Helmec. I have a nice apartment and I'm very happy about my new place. Believe me, I feel so good that I will leave Lelesz. And you Dezső!! I can understand you a lot and as always I will give the truth. I know you suffer a lot, but this is the price of earning bread!!! Everybody is the same with this. I encourage you to be patient and endure. God is good, and helps you through the new hardship and tests your patience. Think about me. I'm fighting too and I could solve the everyday situation easily when I go. Be brave with your life and everything good will come this way. Trust in God. He will help and with the language barrier [overcome], everything will be good. Dear Dezső, I would be very satisfied if you will send $20 once a month. I didn't put it up to torment you, rather to help this way. I am going to Kiraly Helmec as the postmaster, instead of the postal bureau. I will be very happy to [receive] your lines anytime you write me and I will always answer willingly. I will send the picture here also, and with a couple of stamps. Yours is being put away, in another letter. On the envelopes I'm also sending nice stamps, right? I'm very happy about the swallows fabric, and I'm asking for 3 meters. I am almost clapping in my happiness. The other pictures were burned and can't work, but it will be done for Easter. I will wait for your letter very much again and I would like it, [that] if you want to talk to me, then talk to me. It took a long time for the letters to come, from February to March. I don't really know any news now. I need to enjoy the beautiful freedom of carefree days. My Aunt sends her greetings and she wishes you well and much luck to you. I also wish the best and am waiting for your letter, After sending the money, [I] will give the signed family document over either to you or to your family. Don't be worried, I also hope, but also sending greetings with much love. Jane

Leles 3. III.1938

[The woman who wrote, Jane Fabianova was the post lady and this is the one who gave the money that we borrowed]

1938/3/15 Undated Hermine and Marie to Dezső (Book 4, 269-270)

[Dated by mention of Purim, which was on March 10, 1938, Marie mentioning she'll write more on Friday, and the other letters sent on the 20th]

[from Marie]

Dear Dezső!

I'm sorry that I don't write. Friday night I will write more details. I'm in a hurry with the sewing. I sent 240 korona for the details. God will help and I'll have a job all the time, so I will send in some now also. Other than that, I'm fine. I hope that my lines will find you in the best of health. Write about everything. I kiss you countless times and I stay with respect. Your sister, Mariska

Your Uncle Lajos sends his respects to you and Lenke is mentioning you.

[From Hermine]
Dear Dezső!

We got your lines. Although, you wrote about you situation there, I still think, at least partially, it's better there than here. You can hope better in America. You wrote, that I should go first. I can only say, that I don't care about anything, I can take more work, only it is hard. But now the question is, if Uncle Jónász will agree to give the guarantees. Even though, like they say, it does not cost anything, it is possible that he will find that it is too much. About the cost, like you wrote, we don't even think about having you send it. Dad agrees also. Furthermore he also said that it is painful for Marcsa that he isn't going. If it's possible he should go also. But that would be very hard. You arrange it the way you think it's best. My birthdate is 1914 April 5.

Do you think it would be successful for me to get out? And how much time would it take? I think it would go a little bit faster now. Everybody is recommending to us to go. Although we are substituting your situation a little, from every point of view. And imagine, that Malvin [Lefkovics] is getting ready to go to America also. She already wrote to her uncle. She is showing his letter to everyone there and yours as well. I'm writing discretely, that her mother doesn't have too much hope for her being a bride. But they say, at least they will divorce. Or he will travel after her. How are the documents going for Jolan from Szatmar? Is she getting ready already?? If the traveling would be successful, that would be very good. But somehow, I don't believe it. Don't be surprised, that my writing is so sloppy. I work in the garden all day long and only write at night. Weinberger was at our home. He stayed for a night. He came for the fair. Very happy that you are there already. Did you write anything already to the relatives?

Uncle Marton is always wondering about you and he can hardly wait to hear something from you already. Many people envy you. The entire Török family is wishing you good luck and the Gerenyi family sends their regards. Our grandfather and family wish you everything good and Grandmother asked for a little picture. There are a lot of people still going to America from Lelesz. The Kovacs with his wife and kids from Helmec came back from Prague, although he sold everything. Write about everything. I kiss you and send greetings. Your sister, Hermin

Etel [Lajos' wife] made peace with Schőn. Szeré nenni called him in at Purim to Mindu. How was your Purim?

1938/3/20 Father to Dezső (Book 4, 205-206)

My dear son Dezső.

Your letter, which I was waiting with difficulty for, finally arrived on the 7th. First, it makes me very happy to know that you're spending time with my brother and especially today. But you don't mention how my brother and his family are feeling. Are they okay? It makes me very happy, that thank goodness, you are well and that you are working. Thank goodness we are well also. I hope you will be able to stay well. You're asking what's new about the building, they want to decide what is paid with the money and I just paid them interest this month on the 1st. The letter arrived to Shon in the store, and in it he asked if I would sell 3 pieces of farmland which he would accept in payment for the debt. I told Shon to tell him that yes, I will do it. And he talked to his mother. She told him she wants only money. After that they went to Helmec to the police and were asking questions about what he can do to get his money. They advised him to take it to court. Rider also reopened the case and took me back to court. The hearing was on February 14th. I went to see Rider and asked him what he wants from me. He's doing it because I didn't give it to him. He found an excuse, he wants to do whatever he wants to get [money] from the tobacco when [it's] sold. Uncle Isidore [Klein] was there too, and he also spoke with the lawyer. He didn't even talk to us. You should pay the money he owes them. Then he will miss the case if I don't pay the attorney's expenses of 200 Kronen. He will pay half. About the building, there wasn't any meeting yet. Slovakia is suing us for 800. And the price for sharing a border and the tax included is still due on the 8th. That would be also 63 korona. The Rider case is 460 korona. I didn't know what to do, therefore I was forced to sell another piece of land. My son Lajos was very angry with me because he didn't want me to sell. And I had to open the Gambos case for a lawsuit again. Then he told me and therefore I sold to Beninek Szabo that one piece of land which is near the cemetery for 8250 korona. They gave me up front 3000 koronat and the rest of it they will pay on Sunday. He's going to take it out from the bank in Lelesz. That's the money I plan to give to Rider in 2 parts. The fee for the lawsuit is set by the price of the auction on the 8th and I'm going to the lawyer tomorrow to see how much I owe them and Rider, also. I sold a piece of land to Geza Simon for handling the case in which he was involved so to settle he will give me credit on that and yesterday I paid Gambos 1500 K[orona]. Now there is a new bill. I owe 268K. He will not charge now that the case is closed. I asked for the receipt. He promised he will give it to me tomorrow. He was asking for the stamps that I owe him. [That,] and the other bills I will pay him tomorrow. And also with the Slovakian [case] I don't know what will be. Last week on Saturday he came out to see what he can take. He was looking at my clothing and at Hersmendel's [Herman's]. He wanted to take all the American clothes that weren't Dezső's. Also the daily newspapers because we were reading it. He left it all on the table. He left very angry. Someone is in jail like a criminal. Did anyone meet you at the ship when you arrived to America? Did you see Zseni or Nacit? Do you know what will be? We could not pay. Here Motner Odon was paid 61 korona. He told me that you sent the money to him. I want to thank you for everything that you are doing helping us even more than you can. Now I will close with my best wishes for good health and happiness to you, your loving father, who will never forget you not even a moment. Your loving father, Gluck Jeremias.

P.S. Ferenc Kün from Eseny writes that you have been charged 30 Korona. You should write to him about it.

[I typed this letter in the computer in October 8–012. The letter is more complicated to read because nothing but heartaches. Maria.]

1938/3/21 Blanka to Dezső and Dezső to Hermine (Book 5, 230-231)

21-III / 1938
[from Blanka]
Dear Dezso!
I got your card and I was very surprised, that I came to your mind from a far away.
Dear Dezso, you wrote that you did not get any response from me until this day with the pictures you took. I got everything, but processed this thing differently, that we will talk in person one more time. That is why I did not have the courage to respond to your letter. But surely it had to be that way. But now I will be in a hurry to respond [since] hearts feel for each other. Dear Dezso, write everything in detail. What do you do over there? What is your profession? Do you plan on staying there? If you would know how many times I mentioned you to my acquaintances, but nobody could give me a sign about you. At Purim I went to a theater and I met with someone named Galocsi Klein who was with us the last time and he said that you went through the water to tell news. I asked for his card and I laughed at myself. Just in case I did not let him read it, only sign it and stamp it. Dear Dezso, I feel very good. Sometimes I go to party, but I don't forget about you. Otherwise how are you? How are your days going? I'm sure it is going very well in a big city like this. Write a lot because it takes a month to receive a letter.
I believe I wrote everything. Send a picture of yourself. I'm sure you got mine, unless you lost it. I will stay faithful respectfully. Blanka

[from Dezső]
Dear Herminka!
I'm attaching this letter, so you can see how the girls are. Do you know whose delicate wedding that's in Ungvár. While I was at home, this is what I was dealing with. You didn't write a response to my letter and what kind of a response will you give to my simple card? You would think that maybe the one who writes it there, that they are for each other, but unfortunately you are clinging to the wrong place. My heart is like a stone, it does not feel stupid things like that. I wrote to more places anyway, so they can see what happened. I am writing to this stupid girl with a good heart, and I will write today, tomorrow I will be almost stingy. I'm just an assistant right now. I know with her that for me to say goodbye I must have a little...

...revenge to this annoyance, that's why hasn't she written to me. And I will be pleased to let her know that I am pleased to respond to anybody's letter, until she can't even write. The fashionable ladies are like that. Herminka! Don't forget what I am writing here! Do not listen to anyone's promise and word, because we can't believe anybody these days, because everything is business! Everybody is trying to see how they can deceive the other. There is a lesson in this letter as well. I read this too to Uncle Jonás because it came to his address. I knew he will be interested in it. He might think, who knows who it is...It is enough for today. It is 2 o'clock at night and I have to get up at 6 am. At 8 A.M. I will take the letter to mail it to you. Hope to see you soon. Will talk more then. You will understand everything in person. Thanks for the kisses from Gerenyi and others. I'm sure it was really like the content of the letter. Do not be sad since the summer is coming now.

[Upside down, then in the middle, then on top, then down the right side]

Hersmendu wrote a lot of money is in the pocket...
Write immediately upon receiving it!!
Lajos shouldn't write that he's coming. It is possible that Arthur may agree that he would come now, but I'm not sure if it's good for him to come later. -everything is going to be arranged- Next week I will write to Patyu [Uncle Marton] and the little postal girl. We have to write to our grandfather's relatives in German, if he is able to do that. It is enough for today. Dezső

1938/3/24 Ignác to Dezső (Book 4, 203-204)

1938 March 24
Polány, Cheskoslovensko

My dear brother Dezső, live to a hundred years.
We have received your letter, and as I read, you are going to send me a dollar. You have plenty of time, just use it yourself for your own needs, because you have to work for it yet and you've plenty of places to pay. I hope that God will help so that everything will be alright. I wish that we will succeed with the American travel, since you know that I would like to be there as soon as possible, near you. Here at home there is not much of an outlook. I'm asking you to think of me. Do not wait for the induction date, that will be for some time. Otherwise I'm healthy and well. There is no special news. Now I understand a little English. Kisses to everyone, and to you separately, goodbye. Your brother, Ignác
Sany [Klein] is sending his regards.
Kisses, Ignác
1938/3/24 Polány

1938/3/25 Father and Herman to Dezső (Book 4, 233-234)

March 25th/1938
My dearest son Dezső. I'm very happy to hear that thank goodness you're okay. We are okay here too. I'm surprised about my brother Jónász that he mentioned to you he would like to have a Torah. If I could send him the one that I once promised, I would send it to him. When you're going to see him you could mention that my son Lajos would also like to go to America and then I would send him one Torah with my son. I would do anything for him. Just ask. Your grandfather asked me to write to you if you would please write to his family in America. They did not hear from them for years now so they could mail them or have [mail from] them they would be happy and appreciative. He will send you the address. So your uncle Patyunak [Uncle Marton] thinks you are angry at him because he is waiting for your letter and can't see why he doesn't hear from you. Please write to him with a few lines for all of them. He wanted a small picture of you. Your grandfather asked me to give them a small picture of you. They were very happy to see you. They kept that picture. Also, they asked me to remind you to pray everyday and not to forget. You see some samples from some companies and the Schwartz [company] will have new prices. I am sending you that my son Lajos' birthday is September 13/1904 and Hermine's, you know she told you. Mariska is crying that she would like to go also. Ignác he would like to go also.– Hersmendel also. With me, do not worry. Now give my best regards and my love to my brother and his family. I still didn't get the money that you mailed me. Mihancki reported me to the authorities that I owe him money. I told Mihancki to wait after I get the weeds and the other crops ready and I will pay him back what I owe him. My best wishes to you my dearest son. Gluck Jermias

[I paid] Rider this week [from] the land that I sold to Beni Szabo's son. I wrote to you about that last week. [From] 4700. K I paid out 500 K. I asked to allow me to have that money so I would be able to pay to Simon Geza what I owed him. Therefore, they allowed me to have that money so this way Gombos dismissed the case and I did not have to pay for him. I still have the straw and the Gombos boy was convicted and arrested for one year and Svarc for 8 months digging, but I think he is still free.

P.S. You never mentioned your cousin Naci and Jenny. Did you have a chance to see them or talk to them? You never mentioned it before [so] please let me know. With all my love. Your father Gluck Jeremias.

My brother Làzàr came home from Szatmar. He's sending you his best wishes.

P.S. Anna Gerenyi neni hasn't heard from you as of now. When she received the picture from you she kissed that and all of the children. Please write about everything. This month I received 30k from this 2nd 50 K. For my brother I will write next week. Many kisses, your father Jeremias.
Also if you met my brother Marton's children at all please let me know.

[This letter is from our brother Herman]
Dear Dezső,
We received your letter today and are happy to hear you're well. At this time thank goodness we are well also, [but] not as good as it should be. Here it could be better. At least you'll have a better chance to be happy. At this time we have nice weather. Next week I have to report to exercise to learn to be a soldier. Now we are still working with the straw and getting ready to bring it in. It's a very difficult job. Thank goodness we will not have to do it for too long. You asked me who will take care of the tobacco. The previous people, Kantor and Fustos Jani or maybe Bolint, one of those 2 people. I wish I could be there with you. It would make more sense to work there, no matter how hard, it would be much better. Here you can see how hard it is and you can have nothing for it. I can imagine our God helps everyone. I hope he will help us one day. I say it's slow, but we'll get there sometime. I want to wish you the best of all happiness and a good job and lots of money to go around in your pocket. Your brother with kisses and love, Herman

1938/3/28 Jolan Mayer [Szatmar] to Dezső (Book 5, 181-182)

Szatmar 1938 March 28
Dear Dezső!
I got both of your letters and I knew that you wondered why I did not respond to them yet. When I got your second letter, you probably got my letter at the same time. You also wrote to me from Prague that I should write to you. I wrote to Bertuska too, but since then I didn't get any response from you. So my Dezső, let's get down to business. I'm asking you very much to please listen carefully to what I am about to say. You asked me to send my Birth Certificate to you immediately. I did not send it yet because it's really pointless to send it until I know something for certain, since do not think that it is so easy to come out from here in Romania. From you all I already did some research and they said if somebody would put down a downpayment [caution money or deposit] for me, then maybe. But who is going to do that? I know, if you would have it, you would do it for me, but unfortunately, you aren't there yet. They also said that, if somebody would adopt me there, it would be easy to get out. They don't say that it's impossible to get out, but that it could take a long time. And I would have to live in the uncertain for at least two years. It would be very hard. Now dear Dezső, it's up to you. Please give me advice on what to do or what can we do. I can send my birth-certificate any minute because this week I have to get it anyway since I need it for the citizenship certificate. And I'll get two copies. Until then I didn't write because I was waiting for your response to my letter where I have all the details. Your first letter was very depressing, but don't think that you scared me away with that. Not at all! If anything, I would love to be there even sooner [America]. I know and I'm prepared for it, that one has to work and I don't think about it otherwise, that I would just go to America and be done and everything would be perfect. For that, I would need a year and only after that can I get a work permit. I'm working, but in the watch repair business. It is not too much and it is a terribly hard profession. If I would know for certain that I could get out, since it takes at least a month until one gets all the documents, etc., then I would start in a foreign country because I understand how to do it, I just don't have the competence. So, that is the situation. Dezső, now you be the smart one and make a decision for me. You can see I even write a letter to you because it's not so important that everybody has to see it. However, if you want to show it to anyone, you can. But I will note it one more time to you that I'm not scared from

doing any kind of jobs. And I would rather work than live the way I do...I can study English here, which relatively doesn't cost that much. I already talked to two teachers and possibly I will start with the first. But I'm asking you very much dear Dezső, to write me immediately and write everything exactly to me. And then I will send the birth-certificate. And please take actions like it would be your case. Other than that I'm fine. My little sister didn't make a decision about the wedding because a lot of things are missing for the wedding. Give my best to Uncle Jónász and also kisses to you countless times. Kisses from my mom and everyone in the family. Your Cousin, Jolan

1938/4/20 The State Industrial Bank Re Arthur (Book 7, 11)

The State Industrial Bank
21 West Gay Street
Columbus, Ohio

April 20, 1938
To whom it may concern:
The undersigned has been personally acquainted with Mr. Arthur Gluck, President of The Bonded Scale Company, Columbus, Ohio, for more than fifteen years and takes pleasure in recommending him and his Company to anyone contemplating dealing with him. During the many years that Mr. Gluck has been known to the writer, I have had occasion to represent banking institutions and transactions involving extensions of credit to him. Mr. Gluck possesses a high personal sense of honor and has always taken care of his business and financial commitments in a prompt and conscientious manner. As a business man, we believe Mr. Gluck has demonstrated an unusual ability and success in his chosen line. Based upon our observations, he should have no difficulty in fulfilling any contracts or obligations which he sees fit to incur. Very truly yours, Clyde C. Shively, President - Treasurer

1938/4/21 Bertha to Dezso (Book 1, 170-171) pages 1-4

New York
Apr 21/38
My dear Dezső!
I don't even know how to start my letter, because from what I got out of your letter, you are still not familiar with the situation here. You want to have your little brother and your two sisters come out here. I don't doubt this, but what are you going to do with your little brother, because you don't have the type of situation that you can supply all of them. With some things, yes, if dear Uncle Jónász and his dear son could help you. Dear Dezső, you have no idea, what a big responsibility it would be to me to figure out their existence here. You know very well that the girls at home are very sensitive, just like you were, too. If I were to say something that they don't like, they will write home. And then, if we would place them at a house, they would not be impressed and they would feel unhappy. This way, everything might be blamed on me. You know, my Dezső, I only want to do the right thing. After I asked her, Aunt [Jennie] said that she will try [to take in] one of your sisters, and that she would be with her until she gets placed and trained how to work in a house. Dezső, my dear, we can promise this much, that Mannie and I will try to place your sisters somewhere here at a good Jewish house, but only if your sisters would be willing to do the kind of work at a house. You know that from home, what a shame it would be to have your father brought here. It would be a deadly mistake, because remember when Uncle Albert [Frye] came here, he was very unhappy. He could not get used to the kind of life here. If your father would see that his children are "mehale sabeszok" [violating the Sabbath] in that way his heart would be broken. Do not forget, that your sweet father lived the best of his years and he lived his entire life in that abandoned town of Polyán, like my home. Now, I would like you to explain everything to me in details about your dear sisters, so they will not reproach us or you. I would never forgive myself, if they would bring me to that. So don't rush anything, because this is a very serious thing and I am afraid. I hope you will understand it like I do.

1938/4/21 Undated Bertha to Dezso (Book 3, 362-363) pages 5 and 6

If the girls would feel disappointed, they can't maintain themselves, and if they will travel back to Polyán because their traveling takes long and it costs a lot. My dear Dezső, think about what you say or write to home. Dear Dezső, somehow you give me many complements. I am just scared that I will be conceited if you repeat them to me many times. And that will not be good for me, but forget about this. Dear Dezső, I don't understand why a letter from my dear father did not come. I hope for the best or maybe they put something into his head in Romania. I don't know what to think. Please, if you know something, don't hold it back from me and notify me immediately. Now I will not write more, because I think it was enough about this. Kiss you with love, Bertha and Mannie

Greetings to those who ask about me.

1938/5/1 Undated Hermine to Dezső (Book 1, 162-163)

[Dated by mention of Helen Perl on May 18, and harvest by Feri Szabo]

Dear Dezső!

I was very happy to [receive] your letter, and I understand, that writing could make you a little tired. But the knowledge that you make me happy, should overcome the tiredness. Regardless, we know how busy you are, and it takes time until you write to everyone, but even then, the first thing that we see, is if you write to everyone. I am at home, but still I have very little time to write, because you know better, that there is always something to do here. Although, I wrote to you that I'm out of patience, yet I have to finish my work every day. I think that you can understand my impatience, because you tried it as well, and you know what is like to wait.

With God's help, if all four of us can go, that gives a lot of work to do, because besides that, there is the ordinary daily work we are used to and the furnishing, because I want to do that as well. While they do not buy the house, in other words, until they pay all [that's due], I will not start. What else can I do, what am I waiting for...I write it like, Helenke Perl wrote from Szurti. She wrote to the agent and they responded, that she could wait for the notification every day. She is traveling to Cleveland. Maybe it will work out that we can travel together, because she gives her documents to the consulate on May 18th, and ours is on May 19th. I was in Garany [Slovak: Hraň ; Hungarian: Garany is a village and municipality in the Trebišov District in the Košice Region of south-eastern Slovakia.] accidentally with Uncle Laizer with a car. We left in the morning and we were home by night. They were very happy to see us and did not want to let us go. They were wondering about you a lot. They heard from a local man that you traveled away.

You can imagine the surprise, when I told them, that we are getting ready to leave also and shortly. Whoever we spoke to would want to leave, too. I wondered about Pataki. He does not have a job yet, and regrets it so much that he travelled there. There is no mail from Csehi until this day. The man from Csap promised that after the harvest he will give it, but they said that they already auctioned it. Don't be surprised about my writing, but it is already late, and I'm doing my best, this is my second letter already. The majority did not write yet, so my writing is different. They started to harvest the grain today. Feri Szabo is the one who is capable [kepès].

Grandmother had guests. The Munkacs siblings and his brother in law. Grandpa (and others) send their greetings. I always forget to write what is most important, that I'm learning English, and you wouldn't be able to sell me. What do you say to that? I have a very good book, a dictionary combined with grammar. I'm learning how to read now. It's just that I have very little time to do that. I wanted to write to dear Uncle Jónász, but it's too late now. If I will have time tomorrow, I will write. I learned that he had his birthday, so even if it passed already, give my lucky wishes to him and I wish him to live in happiness and health for 120 more years. From my heart with love, kissing you many times, Hermin.

I will not write more now.

I kiss you with love. Also, [kisses to] dear aunt Helen in the hope of seeing each other soon and [to] dear Arthur and his family.

[On the side:] Write about your well being!

1938/5/1 Undated Maria to Dezső (Book 4, 227-228)

[Dated to after Pesah and before Shavuot, and Marie mentioned sewing only in 1938]

Dear Dezső,

Don't be surprised because in the previous letter I wrote to you only a few words, but I thought you gave me advice about what I should do and I am answering it the way you asked me to. The reason is I did not have too much time to write more. I thought it is better to write a few words than nothing because they were waiting here for that letter. Believe me I wrote so fast I don't even remember what I told you. First of all I was behind for 3 months. I received a notice that I should pay now because I am late in payment. Otherwise I will lose the [right to make a] monthly payment and I would have to pay the balance that I owe them. I really did not know what to do. I had just enough money to pay for it, but I did not have the money in my hand. And you know dear Dezső, they [the customers] are always promising that they will pay me, but I only get promises and am waiting. It seems weeks and months go by, but I still did not get what they owe me. The girls owe me 200 ck [Czech korona] and others owe me 200 korona, but they are good for the money, therefore I just have to wait. And do you know how else it is? This is just ironic because you get it. [You know very well the situation we are having?] I wrote to the factory to give me more time and I will try to make up as soon as I can because at this time I'm not able to pay. I hope in the near future I will be able to pay the total amount. I am asking them if I would pay the total amount how much of a discount would they allow me. I received an answer from them that they will allow me to take off 2% from the back payment and 4% from the rest of the bill before Punköz. I mailed them 100 ck. And then I did not mail them any. As of now I did not send them or write to them. According to me if it would come down to that I hope they will come down with the price by 10% more as you mentioned. Now I'm waiting for that. Dear Dezső, believe me, whatever I can I will do everything in my power. I hope you understood me that when the time comes to pay the balance I am very careful to try to save every penny, but it does not help. I hope in a couple of days I will be able to send them more. I will repay a total of 350 ck and it is now up to 4 months. I mailed the money to Alisz the next day. I would have paid her before Passover. I also owed to our grandfather and I made up for him at the same time at Hol HaMoed. The good God helped me and I was able to mail them the money. Now I think it's worth it. Now I can't get anyone to come and learn how to sew because the work season has begun and will be busy. It is more important for them than to come and help me sew. [In the springtime usually they start on the farm and get ready to start planting the seeds.] Now I think I wrote enough. I hope you will understand me. What happened to that man who was asking about you. If you find out anything more please write to me about everything. I am interested to hear from you. I know as busy you are you don't have much time left to take to write me separately. Otherwise I am okay thank goodness, but I hope you will be well also. Now I'm wishing you all the best, good health, and happiness. And many many kisses to you until we meet again in America. Your loving sister, Mariska

Lipot [Klein] from Perbenyk and his family are sending you and to Uncle Jónász and his family the best regards and many kisses to all of you. They are very surprised that you never sent them not even a postcard after you arrived to America. They are always asking about you. Lipot tells me that you forgot about them. I told them you already sent your best wishes and regards to them. They were very happy to hear. Also, Margit Gerènye and her family and Anna send kisses to you.

Dear Dezső, as of now we still haven't heard from the American Consulate. We do not know what will come out. I am very concerned about that. It seems like it's taking too long to notify us. We have nothing except waiting and hoping for the best. Your sister Maria.

1938/5/1 Undated Herman to Dezső (Book 4, 263-264)

[Dated by planting the tobacco after clearing out Lesna]

Dear Dezső,

We got your registered letter on the 11th of this month.

Thank God, we had enough to read. Write a long letter like this always. You wrote that we should write at least 1 letter a month. I promise you, that it will be this way if our travel to America would work out, and the dear God will keep us alive. Furthermore, you wrote, that I should be a good boy. You know the way one will be is [because of] the way the situation is. We got a response to the request that we sent up to the police. The cop was out here on the 7th. I requested that we get a definite response this week. With the tobacco planting already alright the "nanuek a lesna" that we cleaned out. That was also planted with tobacco. Now the weather is very good for everything, especially for the tobacco. There is plenty of rain. Thank God it will be time for the harvest soon. At least another 4-5 weeks. The fruit crop will not be good, because of the cold and the caterpillars barely left anything. Poor old Veisz died. You know, Dezső, we got a letter from you that was not sent registered. We got it regardless, but you send them the way you think. I hope my letter will find you in the best of health. Also, dear Uncle Jónász and his family. Until I will see you! I kiss you, your faithful little brother, Herman.

Separately kiss dear Uncle Jónász and his family.

1938/5/1 Undated Ignác to Dezső (Book 1, 204-205)

[Dated by after Pesah, gift came just in time, nothing happening]

My dear brother Dezső!

We got your letter, that we could hardly wait for. I was very happy to hear that, thank God, you are healthy. I hope my lines will find you in the best of health, also. We got the package you sent this year for Pesah. The part that came for me, came just in time. Thank you. The hat is very good for me and thank you very much. I'm sorry that I'm writing everything so briefly, but one can lose patience. Also, I don't go anywhere and because of that, I don't know what to write. And it's not like only one of us would write from the family, because [in that case] that one only would have something to write about, but if all of them want to write, then eventually the final result is the same. That is why I write less and I know that no one wrote this before. We don't know anything about the traveling yet. I can tell from your letter that you are busy because you don't write [to each of us] separately. But, I'm only asking you to take care of your health. There is no special news. Everything is the same old. I kiss you many times. Your little brother, Ignác.

Reply immediately.
Greetings to all the relatives.

1938/5/2 Undated Bertha to Dezso (Book 1, 109)

[Dated to here because Jolan will receive a discouraging letter from Bertha see 1938/6/9 Jolan Mayer to Dezső (Book 4, 295-296)]

Dear Dezső,
If you think that I wrote the letter nicely or intelligently to Jolan, and if you want, mail it in the post office, but if you don't, then tear it apart.
I will leave that up to you. Bertha

1938/5/4 Iren Mayer to Dezső (Book 7, 214-215)

Dear Dezső!
First of all, I'm sorry that I only write one card, and that I would dare to bother [you] unknown, but I think I'm a niece to you, like Jolan my sister is to you, right? Dear Dezső, your sisters encouraged me, so don't be surprised, that I simply dare to speak up. We would like to go to America, my fiancé and I. I wrote a 4 page letter today to Aunt Berta, where I gave broad details about the finances and everything else. I'm asking you nicely to ask for it and read it with patience, because I'm hoping so much for your involvement/intercession, only because of the narrow space here. Just one thing, that my fiancé is a painter, like you know, I have a little bit of a dowry, that is plenty enough for the cost. Dear Dezsőke, will you read this, my letter written to Berta? Don't think I'm ill-mannered, that I'm only asking now, how are you? We all are, being filled with hopes, doing well enough. We have faith in the love of relatives and in your patronage. I'm waiting for your response as soon as possible. I kiss you, your unknown niece, Irên!
Do not worry. I sent both of our birth certificates. Next time there will be a letter as a response, I promise. Please write!
My address is below:
Mayer Iren
Str. Aureliana 27. ["tompat"]
Satu-Mare Romania

1938/5/12 Jane the Postmaster to Dezső (Book 2, 291-292)

Dear Dezső!
I was endlessly glad for the telegram, that you already got used to the new environment.
I get your lines accurately, and even if not, [I] always welcome your lines willingly and I'm very happy about it. Your uncle here got the money, slowly mine is running in soon. I'm not angry that you are sending it in installments, and I'm willingly waiting, since my intention wasn't to torment you with demanding, nor to get profit, but to make a goal possible for a honest, diligent man, to overcome a hard obstacle at the beginning of life. And that was managed successfully, thank God. I was reading your unsatisfied lines with smiling, and I know that this is only hard at the beginning. But, if you will learn the language, I predict a nice future for you, and you know, that my sayings always come true. Endure and be diligent, and good results will come. Do not mind the work that you do. It is the way it is, so you will be able to appreciate your better future that way. Don't forget that every beginning is very hard!!! The situation with the fire is astonishing, but it is also a life test, and everything you lost, can still be replaced. I know you are sad, but look, these are only things that one can get bored from. The most important thing is that you are healthy.

The rest will be restored. It is a noble thought that you take care of your good father and siblings. How beautiful life will be, when you are all together!!! My new situation is good, but it did not change a thing about me. I'm quiet and peaceful, like I was, and modest too, I don't care about entertainment nor parties. I know many people, but I don't go anywhere. Imagine, I haven't even been to the movies, even though I like to do that. I'm an obscurantist, small town girl, and at night at 11 o'clock I don't know anything about myself or anyone else. Life like this is not my world. My apartment is a nice, small villa, the place, if you know it, is at the bottom of the acacia forest, at the base. It's a little expensive 150 K[orona] per month, the furniture is mine, but there is a bathroom and what's important for me, nobody can come in to me that I don't know. That's what I invest in and for that I have to pay. I'm gentle natured and this way nothing can come to me even if I can't figure it out. So, I don't have a boyfriend even here. I will not, rather I will stay an old-maid. My aunt is still ill. Every 2-3 weeks I go to her, but the road is exhausting and long on foot. Thank you very much for your kind offer, that will help Loci or me to go to America. It's truly kind of you, and one can never know, when I will be in need of that. If yes, I will take it with confidence. If possible, your father will pay that amount to me giving the document, and if you would ask in front of the uncle here, I will destroy it. Mother and family bought a house in Gyomo. The building is not so modern, but it's nice, and it is full of fruit there. I'm so happy about it. About my health I'm not bragging, no trouble, but I do have iron deficiency. I'm tired and chilly. Although, the new environment is where the memory is. I can't send the picture, unless [your] father has one, because yours are burned and all my plates/negatives have been destroyed. I'm so sorry for the lens. Too bad that your machine has burned, because this way I will not get landscape pictures anymore. But this can be done later, can't it. Yes the fabric with the swallows on it, is very important-you know why!!! You could smile about this, of course. Write whenever you can, I will be happy about it. Much diligence and endurance for studying and work. Sending greetings many times
Jane
12.V.38

1938/5/12 Undated Deak Mariska to Mr. Gluck (Book 5, 105-106) mentions fire

[Dated by mention of the fire]
[Unfortunately the whole family with the exception of the mother passed away due to an unknown illness at that time - Irv. typed in 5/5/010]

Dear Mr. Gluck!
With great happiness I'm acknowledging that I thought you have forgotten about my being. You're asking regarding my journey? I'm still at the same stage as I was when you left. It has been said that "one succeeds and the other does not." I believe I'm also with the latter because it doesn't want to succeed. I would like very much to travel, but I believe that it will not happen. My uncle would not take me because he's an old man. At this time, I believe in God that he will help in some way, sometime. My mother was born there and she too would like to go back, but she can't because there's no one to help in this matter. We would pay all the expenses and even then we can't succeed. From M. Szwurty, 3058 W. Boulevard, Cleveland, Ohio U.S.A. This is the address and Ihel. Agardi is there and he promised that he will look to help and as of now there is nothing, no news from him. The girls were telling me that due to a fire you lost everything. Here I am including Gellèrt LORRIN, 300 Su St. Duquesne, Pa. He lives nearby my uncle. I do not have any hope that I should succeed. I will write to you in the future about everything in detail, exactly and readable. Now I'm only writing from a chair as you can see from my writing because also they are waiting for my letter to take it to the post office. How are you otherwise? Thank God we are healthy. If someone asks how I am, my answer would be I don't know. I wish you good health from our whole family. Be courageous in the big strange place! With my acquaintances would help, likely the relations are behind our back, but it is your benefit that your brothers and sisters could go so fast. Next time much more, regards with my few lines and wishing you the very best.
Deak Mariska, Polan

1938/5/13 US Consulate Prague Emigration Number (Book 1, 67-68)

Gluck Hermine, Maria, Herman & Ignác

Regarding the questionnaire you have filled in and submitted to Prague in which you asked to be put on the US Emigration waiting list, we are notifying you that on May 13, 1938, in the Czech Republic. we listed it. Pre-registration number: T-825-8. In time, we will tell you when it will be on the list. Keep this notice clean. The waiting list number is not the quota number.

Send a change of address to the Consulate General. Any kind of urgency will be completely disregarded, and the content of such may be ignored.

1938/5/22 (a) Father and Hermine to Dezső (Book 4, 169-170)

Polány May 22. 1938

My dear son Dezső.
I just want you to know that I received your letters dated 2/24, 3/2 (the letter to the little woman), 3/6, 4/10, 4/18, 4/24, 5/5, and the check you mailed. I'm very happy that thank God you are well. I hope my brother Jónász and his children are also well. About us, thank God, we are well. Regarding our budget know on the 11th I received the papers from Prague for all of the 4 children and I have seen my lawyer to fill them out. We mailed them back right away. About Hersmendu, I went to see the doctor who is in charge to give the health report to legally be able to get out from this country. Also we need the citizen papers. 1 week has passed since the lawyer mailed in the papers legally for all of the family. I was there Friday to make sure they mailed them in. I asked if it was once or as soon possible. They just received the papers. On Friday it was 40, I gave already 500. On the envelope I wrote that he received that and the money left over, 25, I gave to Uncle Marton. Beside that I gave to the lawyer for stamps that I still owe. Their lawyer promised the legal papers. He will help when I will sell the house. They offered 38 thousand korona. But some people are trying to break off their deal. Therefore I changed my mind since they did not give the money yet. I asked someone to check how large the property is. As of now I don't know. I'm waiting for the result. He has to make a drawing...

1938/5/22 (b) Undated Father to Dezső (Book 4, 215-216) page 2

...and submit it to the district office before the Bibor council for approval. Just when it will end [with the approval] I do not know, but nobody else does. The engineering salary can be 150 korona required for the district office. If they need another legal permit that would also cost 150 korona. You know I've always had enemies, but even now the way they talked about Jozsi bacsi's home today also. When I asked him about it, he denied it. If the opportunity is right then it might be worked out. Until then, I cannot and will not sell any land until it's necessary because I do not want to get burned with it. That way, I'm not going to be the first one. In the previous letter you mentioned you will write again next week and I was waiting for that letter. That is the reason I didn't write to you before. I received that letter on the 19th and the 2nd one I wanted to take care of it on Friday. 220 remained. At this time I can't write anymore. I would like to mail this letter from Helmec. Your grandmother and your grandfather sent their best wishes to you, also. Your Uncle Marton also wants to write to you. If the lawyer will do the job, [and] they will allow him to leave the country, then I will go to Ungvár. Until then I'm wishing you good health and many kisses, your loving father who will never forget you, not even for a moment. I want to thank you very much for your gift. I hope my brother Jónász knows about this. Again wishing you all the best and all my love, your father. Gluck Jeremias.

1938/5/22 (a) Father and Hermine to Dezső (Book 4, 169-170) (as in previous letter)

[On the same letter my sister Hermine wrote to my brother David]

Dear Dezső!
We were very happy to hear you found a very fine family that you are staying with. As you tell me, the cooking is very good and you will learn. Here the relations are thinking. They will not have the chance as you know their situation. As you know, I hardly could wait to be there and do whatever I need to do. It doesn't matter how hard I have to work to leave home and leave our family, but we must have a better future. We have none here. xxxx!
We trust our God that he helps everyone who has a problem. I know you know it very well that there isn't any thing that I would not take. Anything I can I will do. The only thing I hope is that God will help to be able to get to America. That's all my dream. I would be grateful to the relations. I received a card from Helene Perl from Szürte. She heard that I'm going to America. I should write and tell them what ship I'm going to go on. She would be very happy to go with us. Maybe I will tell her, but how I don't know if we will ever get out from here. You know the reason. Everyone is asking about you. They send you all their best wishes. I do not have any patience to name them individually. You must be very happy that you're there. At this time, I do not even know what to write to you, you know everything. The only thing I am

asking you is to please write to us. I'm waiting every moment to hear from you. I would have written to you before, but I was waiting to have something positive to tell you about the papers, but I am sorry as of now I do not know. Next time I will try to write to you more, but forgive me at this time I cannot. I have no patience. Many kisses to you and the relations with all my best wishes to you and the relations. With my love, your sister, Hermina.

Dear Dezső,
I will not write much at this time. I'm wishing you a better life than we have here. I send kisses to Bertha, for you, and our relations. From Miksa Soen [Last name is unclear]

1938/5/22 Herman to Dezső (Book 4, 277-278)

Dear Dezső! 1938 I 22
I got your letter and I'm glad that, thank God, we got good news from you. About me, I can write that probably this week we will go to Uzhorod, with the request in person. I will write about the decision in our next letter. Although I think the request will not mean much. You know or think why...it's possible, that if it's not it, then it could succeed. Only if one way, then we will know shortly already, what it's going to be, "hay or straw" [it's a common idiom/expression].
You wrote, that I didn't write. First of all, it's because I was not at home when they sent your letter, and that is why you didn't get any writing from me. Yes, if we take one thing, then you deserved that. Why? I will write it. You know, to that letter that I responded, you know that you still didn't even mention my name in it.

See, how bad it felt, that I did not write to you, right?! It felt as bad to me, as it felt to you. Although, I did not follow your example, only I was not at home, when you sent the letter. And at the end, you did not get anything else from me. The weather is beautiful. Since January 12 Lajos Török, the neighbor, is here. They took away from him for one repair 6,700 korona. This guy has luck like that. I hope my letter will find you in the best of health and I wish you a happy Shavuot holiday. Kisses to you, your little faithful brother. Herman
I kiss separately, Uncle Jonàsz and his family. Next time in [spoken] words!

1938/5/22 Undated Marie to Dezső (Book 4, 301-302)

[Dated by Little Olga is going to America. She will leave 6/8]

Dear Dezső!
We got your letter, that we could hardly wait for. And you cannot imagine the day, how hard we waited for your letter! And it feels good to hear that you ended up being at a very nice family, and that you are healthy. Dear Dezső, give thanks to God, that you are already there and you are over with everything! I wish we would be there already. Dear Dezső, no matter what kind of a situation you are in, you still have to be happy that you are there and you don't need to be impatient! I wish we could be there already too. But now who knows when can we go. Bozske Braun will go to America just today from Helmec. She got the visa already and also, Little Olga from Lelesz, but who knows how!...! Dear Dezső, if we will be able to go to America. Would [this] be a problem at the visa delivery? My throat is the way it was at the time you were at home, and my legs are the same way also, only when it hurts it goes blue, about the size of an egg. There are little dots one by one sometimes, somewhere, and I think the vein shrank. And I think that all this is from my tonsils. Since the last time it has been a gap of at least for 2 months, and now it started [again], and I'm afraid that there will be an error with the visa, and who knows, if they will let me go. God will help us from that, I am only saying this, so I can see what you say, and what can I do, so it will be good. I think that you know everything better than we do! Dear Dezső, if God will help us and we will be there, I will take any kind of job. I'm sorry that I only write this much, but I will make up for it next time. Yes, we got the application from the agent at least two weeks ago. And now we should get some kind of notice. We should get the citizenship in these days. I think that dad wrote everything, but I'm in a hurry, because we want the letter to go now. Dear Dezső, write a lot about everything. Do not follow our example. I kiss you countless times, and I will stay with love and I wish you everything good.
Your little sister, Mariska

Give my best to dear Uncle Jónász and dear Aunt Helen and also to the entire family/relatives.

May 31, 1938
New York,
Dear Dezső,
You will forgive me for not replying to you [and] your precious lines promptly, but I am lazy of the pen since I don't know what to do with my niece's interest. I would have liked to help both Iren and her future husband with the paperwork, but my husband is only a worker and you know that his income does not cover the papers as they desire to bring out three people, and I do not know to whom to turn. I was thinking that perhaps if you ask our dear Jónász bacsi to send the papers, that is, the affidavit, to Jolan only. I don't want to disturb him by asking our dear Uncle that, however there is no other way and they likely would only mail to Jolan the required papers. As Irene is writing that her fiancé is an accomplished individual and it would be a shame that he should live his life there for years and he has a future here with a little luck. I believe that in my next letter I will return to you Jolan's birth certificate and if it succeeds it would save time, and if not please return it. Believe me, I have a deep problem. Dear Dave, you are writing that Jolan is impatient because she would like to be here. Rome wasn't built in one day. She should have thought of that two years ago. Her father was always asking for money and we couldn't help, so if the girls would have come out, it would have been a very good future. Here I think we could have paid to rush the immigration. That couldn't have taken place from Romania and then probably she could secure the tickets for the ship. Don't write that to them because this time since we do not have anything, and we are not sure of anything, let's wait for their thoughts. Do you know my dear Dezső we have a lot of problems, and you know it. Our Menyuson has a family at home and yet they want to bring out his niece from Czechoslovakia. Shall I come to you with more problems, I don't like to do that. That much you know. My dear Dezső, as I see it from that letter, Iren has courage. She has been blessed and she would be able to live and survive upon the ice. You're asking me then reply to your sisters that they should purchase things here in America even though it may cost more, but they would be up to date. Therefore, it would be better if they would bring money with them and they would purchase what they needed. If you don't think like that then it's up to them. I hope you feel well. We do not have that money. I have been suffering in sickness, asthma, and it's difficult to get rid of it. The climate is not the most desirable and because of that it's more difficult. Now I will not write more. Regards to our uncle, and with kisses, Bertha and regards from Mannie and the relations.

1938/VI/2
We received your letter and we're happy to hear good things from you. Thank God I am alive. There's nothing new to write about since the other members of the family must have written about everything. The only thing I know I can write to you is that the wheels are turning very slowly. It would be wonderful if a person could fly. [We've] been waiting for a very long time and there's no end to it. We hope for the best and with that we reassure ourselves. I wish you the very best of everything and good health. With love and kisses to you, your brother Herman

[from Hermine]
Dear Dezső,
Don't feel badly that I'm writing to you a small note, but I have been very busy. It is before the holiday Pünköst [Pentecost = Shavuot] and there is a lot of work to be done. It's true that I don't care about anything since I don't have any patience. You have already experienced that, if someone is getting ready to go somewhere, especially at this time, it is difficult to wait. I'm not writing about anything because you know almost everything better there than we do here. It's just very difficult until we can go. We must have hope that God will help all of us. Little Olga, from Lelesz, will travel on June 8th. Our father wrote to you that we have gotten a letter from cousin Arthur, and in this letter, he tells us that in America we must work. I should try to explain it to them, but I don't have time for that. I had to do the wash late at night and this is the only time I can write to you. I hope they can understand from my letter that they should not worry about it. We are not going there to rest. Please write about everything and I will write more next time, too. I do not know whether the picture is no good or if you lost weight! We mailed Csehinek a package without silk, but you did not write anything about it. Please write exactly what you want us to buy. I would like very much to take bedding with us. I feel sorry to sell the beautiful pen, who would buy it!? There aren't any buyers for that, I don't know why. I'm still questioning our journey. I think that slowly the time will come and we too can go. With all the difficulties it would be better to know. You could comfort Uncle Julius [by

saying] that we are accustomed to work and he will not have any aggravation with us. It seems like he is hesitant. Where does Jolan from Szatmar stand regarding her travel? Maybe we will be traveling together? We are well. Kisses and love to you, Hermin

P.S. Mityu always mentions you and is waiting for the motor bicycle. Emil is in Lelesz. Lenke is getting ready to go to America.
[These are our oldest brother Lajos' children. note by Irv.]

1938/6/2 Undated Hermine and Ilona to Dezső (Book 5, 78-79)

[This note was written by my sister Hermine and our neighbor's daughter, Ilonka Gereny to Dezső, sometime in 1938. Dated by the type of paper Hermine was writing on and the color ink of the pen Herman used in the previous letter.]

This little girl ran home to write a letter to you. Please reply to her because she always asks about you and talks about you. Our brother Lajos' son Mityuka is getting ready to go to America. Lenke and Emil also send their kisses and are waiting impatiently for your letter. Mityuka is very cute and he is a very good boy. He's always waiting for you to come back home. Hermine

Dear Dezső, how are you?
I'm very well. What's new in America? Here there is nothing. Is it good for you in America? When are you going to come home to visit us? I would like to see you! Wishing you the very best, you're older political neighbor. With respect G, Ilona

1938/6/5 Ignác to Dezső (Book 5, 111-112)

B"H
Dear brother Dezső, until 120
I was very happy to [receive] your letter and I thank God that you are well. Don't be angry that I wrote little in my last letter, I wasn't at home. I was in the field in the area called Leszna, for tobacco and when I arrived home our father was writing you a letter and I had to return the wagon to this area again to pick up more tobacco. We have plenty of tobacco, but not enough space for it. It is difficult to find a suitable place to store it. One of the large buildings is full and we have another area called Dioszog. There aren't any rentable places in the village, therefore we may have to build to enlarge the carriage building into a smaller building to make space for the additional tobacco. We cannot have it dispersed in different places. We must be able to watch it, so we can look out for it. Our father will write you more about it. I wrote last time that I may have to have a military permit to get out of this country, but later we were told that no, it's not necessary, because I'm only 17 years old and not 18. They claimed that it was an error on their part. We will be ready shortly to make our journey. I do not know when yet. I understood everything from your letter!!! Our grandfather and grandmother were very happy and he too has written to you. Here the weather is very undesirable it's raining constantly, cloudy and we would like to have some nice, sunny days. We also have corn and it is very beautiful out in the field. Don't be angry that I do not write any more this time, but next time I will write more. Loads of kisses to you, your brother, Ignác Gluck

PS Regards to the Arthur and his family. Ignác
Please reply as soon as possible and a lot! And Kisses, Ignác.
1938/VI/5

1938/6/5 Undated Mariska and Hermine to Dezső (Book 5, 50-51, 54-55) Marie's missing first page and Hermine's maybe wrong spot

[from Marie]
The boys are occupied because at this time they are accumulating the tobacco from the field. Kantor and Fustos Jani are doing it. Our tobacco is very beautiful at this time and we have more than we have space for it. Now we must build another warehouse because there is no place to rent in the village. The main thing is that we should succeed that they'll pay well. I'm writing this to you because I know that you're interested. The other produce is being brought home and we hope that they'll pay well for it. Now you see, I've written about many things. Mariska

Emil is not at home he's going to school in Lelesz. He said he would like to write to you when he comes home. He sends kisses to you from him separately. He takes your picture with him wherever he goes and was very happy and he thinks of you a lot.

Lenke is waiting for the baby and Mityu is mentioning you a lot.

[from Hermine]

Dear Dezső,

It's better to address the letter to your address, because this way you'll be able to find out Jónász bacsi's opinion. The consulate did not advise us whether they received a letter from America. I'm asking you to do something, you can see how the situation is. I've just written to the agent and they too are neglectful. I've written to the consulate that if the boys do not get the passports then only two of us would travel. He wrote saying that we have to agree to that. I mailed you the papers and I'm sure you understand that better. Only God knows if anything will take place with our traveling. Helen Perl will leave on November 24 with a different shipping firm. I'm going to ask for the address and I'm going to write to them. Ask Uncle Jónász if he can assist us then he should. Kisses, Hermine

1938/6/7 Father, Hermine, Marie to Dezső (Book 4, 293-294)

My dear son, Dezső!

I was glad to read in your letter that, thank God, you are in good health. And we are also in very good health and I hope that this letter will find you in good health. Last week I sent a letter to your address. I hope you got the response to my nephew Arthur's letter and gave it over. It is still high/tall 38. A little bigger 40, and also sometimes higher and, if Uncle Jonas could do [it], if he would be ok with that, he should only do [it] that way. The weather was good for the tobacco planting and hope it will be good from now on. I wrote about the house and Hersmendol in Uncle Jonas' letter. Since we sent the completed sheets the agent didn't write back, if it's good or not. Today, I plan on writing a letter to him. Greetings from your grandfather and grandmother too, and the crop, thank God, stayed sustained. May the good God keep it preserved. Kissing you with respect, Your father, who will never forget you, Gluck Jeremias

[from Hermine]

Dear Dezső!

We were happy to read your letter, but I'm sorry, that we didn't write so much to you. If God will help us, shortly we will be able to tell you everything in person. When we will know everything exactly, then I will notify you. How are you? I am great, thank God, but I'm very busy all the time. I am in a hurry to write to you right now, also, because they will take the letter to the post office. Many people wonder about you, and from this town many are leaving to America. Little Olga from Lelesz got her visa, and she came home and only last week went away. Leczo Erzsi travels on Monday. Juhasz Ilon doesn't know yet. Her documents have been ready for a long time and her passport is ready too, but she doesn't know the date that the boat she will go on [sails]. I will write more some another time. Kissing you with Love, Hermin

[from Mariska]

Dear Dezső,

We got your letter and I'm glad to hear that, thank God, you are healthy. We understood everything In the letter. I would love to be finished with everything, but I hope that time will come soon.

Dear Dezső, before Pentecost [Shavuot] I had a job. I've replaced sewing at night [instead of or in addition to] during the day so I can finish because there was only one week and I was alone, so it was definitely [a lot of] work. 100ck [Czechoslovakian Korona] was my clear earning. But that's not a lot for that much work. I should have gotten more. This week I sent 100ck for the payment, although I'm behind with the money. But I'm hoping when I get my receivable amount, then I will be compensated. I wrote to the factory on May 23rd, but I didn't a get reply yet. If I want to sell the machine, I'm willing to accept 1500 ck and I will not buy a coat because, if we are going in the summer, I will not need it. Based on the sample you sent, the style/fashion is the same as here at home. I'm sending countless kisses and I will stay with much love until we see each other. I'm sorry, that I write that way, but our father is taking the letter to the post office and I don't have time. Your sister, Mariska

1938/6/7 Ignác and Lajos to Dezső (Book 5, 43)

1938 JUNE 7

Bodrogmező,
My dear brother David LEBEN TO 100
We have received your letter and I'm very happy, thank God that you are well and in good health. We are very impatient with regards to the traveling. In your last letter you wrote about the traveling. I understood everything. We have not received anything yet from Prague. I don't know what could be the reason. The news is that Veizer from Imreg died. There's nothing else to write, next time I will write to you more. I would ask that please dear Dezső, that you write to me a lot not like I do, but immediately. Kisses to everyone and to you separately, your little brother Ignác----- good by.

[In the same letter you will find a letter from our brother Lajos.]

Boruch Hashem

Dear Dezső, LEBEN TO 120
Don't be angry that I am somewhat late replying to your letter, you probably know that I don't have patience. How are you otherwise? We are so, hope that it will not be any worse.
How is Uncle Jónász bacsi? Give my regards. I don't have anything else to write about. Lots of kisses, your brother Lajos
PS. Can you pray? Do you have Tefillin? Don't abandon it because that [way] is not for a Jew.

1938/6/7 Undated Herman to Dezső (Book 4, 1-2)

[Dated by Veizer from Imreg dying]

Dear Dezső,
I read your letter with lots of love and understanding. Surely, you are right about my siblings who have written, but nothing more on this, to the others you wrote to all of them separately. I'm not angry at you, but you wrote in your letter that I did not write, and I'm only responding to that. [The letters] that you didn't send by registered [mail], we did not get. [We would each give a] house for a letter already. Please! The next time you send it, send it registered with the post office, because this thing bothers me. My traveling is not certain. The answers should come in two weeks, and then we will know everything. As long as my travel isn't definite, I won't study the tailoring [terms] in English. I won't spend time with it, until I know something for sure. This year I mowed the clovers. I learned that it is a very hard job, but it is bearable. If one is healthy, then slowly one can proceed nicely. The tobacco on the Leszna land is developing nicely. In the other land it is growing nicely, too. I will be very happy if they will release me from the military, and I can go to my new home, because [here] at home, there is only work. As you mentioned about the cents, I will look into it, and if there is, and they will give it to me, we will buy it for sure. I met with Yoshàvol Kopasz. Every time I meet her she asks what you are doing. She would have gone also, if she would have had someone who would have taken her. I got the [razor] blades and I thank you. From the three you left home, I shaved with one of them at least twice, but I only used the used one. One blade is enough for me to use for 5-6 weeks. You asked if Joska Fekete doesn't live with his wife, now he's not a fool, because the good goes to his reputation, and the bad even further. I think I wrote about Vajner from Imreg, his wife died a week ago. Also, the collections with the letter were sent back together to Czech[oslovakia]. We received a letter from him asking dad, that if he has bins and is an honest man, then give it to the tax office, and let the persons know the exact address. And if we don't send it back, he sent the settlement invoice. I think it's around 800 on you, so he would need to get at least 60 K[orona], but he isn't demanding anything. I hope I wrote enough so that you will not have any complaint about me, [and that you'll] only have enough patience to read it. I don't have patience to write nicely and the ink isn't so good either. I wish you good health and everything good. Kiss you, your faithful brother, Hermann.

This letter paper should be proud that it goes on a ship a second time until you receive it.
[Dezső must have sent them the paper to write on]

1938/6/9 Bertha to Dezső (Book 4, 401-402)

New York
June 9, 1938
Dear Dezső,

I will try to answer your letter. I'm glad to hear that your hand is better. Don't be afraid of a little emergency. It's not that easy to die. Dear Dave, I'm sorry, but I am not clear about your letter. After I read it, first of all, I sent you Jolanka's birth documents. I hope you got them. I could say, that our cousin Arthur must be a nice guy. I'll wait for a little while, and if I don't hear from him, then I'll have time to bother him. Dear Dave, you can't bother a business man. Give him some time to get the documents. Now I will ask you something, do not answer Uncle Albert's question, because if you will write one word, they will make it into five. Grow up already, dear Dave. Everybody should mind their own business. We also have all kinds. I don't know then you will get into trouble, I don't remember why I would not have responded to your last letter, but sometimes I don't know what's the meaning of the word. Somehow I still can't read your handwriting right. Dear Dave, get everything the right way. Don't worry yourself about every little thing. Don't be afraid, your sisters will come, just give them a little time. My Mannie is also trying to get the documents. You know, to a business man [things] don't go that fast. We will do whatever we can. Now in turn, after a 1000 letter, visiting the relatives, they always ask about you and send their greetings. I got a letter from my father also. Thank God, he is well and is asking about you also. Now, I won't write anymore. Give my personal greetings to dear Arthur and our dear Uncle and his wife, and to you separately, and to all of you, Bertha and Mannie.

1938/6/9 Jolan Mayer to Dezső (Book 4, 295-296)

Szatmar
1938 VI 9
Dear Dezső!
I got your letter yesterday, and I'm already responding today. I'm very surprised that you didn't write for such a long time. I already started to think that my letter was lost along with my birth certificate. Dear Dezső, it's not necessary to send my birth certificate back. I will get it again because I have to put the stamps on them anyway. I got our certificate of citizenship also, because now our citizenship is revised and everybody had to get it, so maybe I will have to go in person, I hope. If not, unfortunately the bigger trouble is, that I did not get encouragement or a favorable letter from Bertuska. She also says that it could take 2 years until I can get a visa. Bertuska should send all of the documents that I need. My sister's preparation to leave is only half done now, because they did not take an oath and they are still young, and they have time, even for two years. They will still have the money then too, because they live in a house and it could be sold in a moment. In a way, I'm strongly asking you to write to Bertuska, [and say] that right now she should deal with my case. After all, we shouldn't leave our home at the same time because we can't cause our parents such pain. If God will help us, and I will be out of there, we will deal with that then. I would like you to arrange this already from there and ask from the consul, because I will go up alone to Bucharest. If not, then the one who will do my passport because he has close ties and he arranges a lot, will. We already talked to him about this, but until they notify us, he can't do anything. Write to me [telling me] exactly what I need to say, to whom I need to go and why, etc. In one word everything exactly, because, if Bertuska does not deal with that, then we are going to try something else, but until then, there is nothing we can do in the world. There is a Veisz girl who is going from here now to New York. It took them 5 months to deal with everything. They are already making her passport. Dear Dezső, you can't even imagine how much I want to go already, and I still have to wait for two years.... I can't even imagine anything more terrible than that. Mother has already entered fully into the spirit of it. Everything is fine, I could just go already. I'm already learning English, too. It's a hard enough language, but the teacher (female) says I have a good sense of the language, she hopes that I will be able to do that. I took the "orásagat" out also, in other words, I took it very seriously.
Therefore, my Dezső, I'm asking you very much to arrange everything you can and as soon as possible. The "Eùhresztikùs" [Eucharistic] Congress was in Budapest just now and I wrote to my girlfriend, that if she sees something interesting, like stamps, she should send it to me and this was one of them that I'm sending here. I'm not sure if you still collect them, but I will send it to you just in case you do. I'll be glad if it would be good for you. I'm sending here an amateur picture of me, my sister, and my brother in law. It could have been better. If there is a picture of you, send one to me too. I think I wrote enough, I'm asking you very much to write, because if you don't write, I'm so impatient. I kiss you with love, Jolán

1938/6/9 Lajos Schwarz (Schwarz's) to Dezső (Book 5, 369)

Dear Mr. Glück!
I have the honor to take note of your precious letter dated above. I really didn't expect to get a letter from you from America. I will pass the sent card to your dear father at the same time. When your letter arrived to

me I almost envied you, that you left to a more peaceful, calmer place and that you turned your back on this restless Europe. I believe that for you the price of the blinds is much lower in America. But don't forget the fact that they have the advantage of having two or three kids of different sized windows. Until we can produce for the orders, only then can they produce for inventory. Then as I am informed they don't work with that big of a selection like we do. And then don't ignore that big bulk that can be produced and can be placed there. That will also make the selling price cheaper. In any case, I would be very interested in what qualities go in the market there. And if it would be possible please to get a collection in and send it to me. I would be glad to cover the costs. Besides the samples I would be interested in the prices also, what the traders are asking for. Regarding your account, I would like to inform you that the balance is in favor of me as I showed you on November 11th last year, Kc. 69.60 [Czech korona] makes it up. Although, in case I would not be able to get the Ferencz Varga's shipment's value, then the amount will rise to this : Kc. 103.60 Like you know, this buyer above was being sued. I hope my letter will find you in the best of health and if you will write the next time, I hope you will forget about this. By then you will be half American, and you will speak the language already also. And that you will have a more favorable situation. I still wish you everything good. With full respect, Lajos Schwartz

1938/6/15 Dezső Grunberger to Dezső (Book 19, 34)

Grünberger Dezső
Král. Chlumec

Dear Mr. Glück!
You must be surprised, that although it is about my own interest I am so negligent. It sounds ridiculous, but I did so that no book has remained to me. I was ashamed to go and get one back from anybody. So I took it back from somebody who did not pay. It took me a little search. But finally now I got the book and I will be in a hurry to send it to you. I hope that since then you made some acquaintances because this way you could be helpful to me in a more effective way. I am terribly envious of you, that you are there and believe me I am thinking about how can I get out there night and day. You know every trouble starts when people have no money. Do something so you could have a lot and then you will put down the guarantee instead of me. I could get the travel expenses for myself, but I am afraid that you are very far away from [being able to do] that. I would like you to write an exhausting letter about what you do, how much money you make and what are your plans…etc. It is better if I write less about myself. I am still suffering with these three occupations. And I am terribly bored about things. The man's nerves could terminate the service in this. One more time I am asking you to be hurry, to squeeze a little something out of this book. I am waiting for your response impatiently. We are all sending greetings to you from our heart and wish you lots and lots of luck to you. Until I will see you again. D. Grünberg and his wife
Král. Chlumec 1938. June 15.

1938/6/23 Hermine to Dezső (Book 5, 1-2)

June 23, 1938 Polány

Dear Dezső,
We have received with happiness your lines to [our] letter that we have been waiting for so long. We read it and [since] last week we have been waiting every day for the letter that you have been writing, [but] we have not received it. Truthfully I regret [to say], but do not mail any letters except registered. I understand everything from your letter, I only ask of you, in the future please write about everything. Thank goodness we are well, however we are waiting to travel which is very difficult to wait for since I have a lot of work to be done by then. However this is something that we have [no choice but] to wait! We have written to the agent [asking] what is the matter with our papers. They replied that they mailed it to the consulate in May. Presently Pista Juhasz's daughter left without time to say goodbye. Poor Ilonna Juhasz [the daughter] did not have enough time to get ready because she received the notification in the evening that she had to be in Prague by 8 AM the next morning. It was a holiday and there was no post. She has called them and they postponed it for the following day so that she would arrive. I wouldn't like it if we would be in the same situation. It's true, we are not in that particular situation. First we are waiting for the notification to make passports. Our father went to Helmec because of Hershmendu's situation since today. They're going to reply to the questionnaire and give a reply to attain a passport that we could make for him.

You can't complain that I'm writing a short letter this time, however Ignác will report to you punctually about everything. This too has a reason. He works in between, but it comes to his mind and he makes notes to himself and by the time you write he has the answers. By me it is somewhat different. I have it in my mind, however when the time to write it comes, I forget. I have put the bread away and I prepare dinner and in between I hurry to write, so that the letter could be mailed. Anyone that sees how much you're writing, [thinks] that he has a good time and that he doesn't work, because he wouldn't have time to write. There are no words of that, we are satisfied, that you write, I know it gives work for you. If God will help, we'll have to write from there, because if more of us are there, it will give you less work regarding to writing. Our grandparents are very weak. They always want to write, but it always remains [for me] to send their best regards to you, as well as to dear Uncle Jónász. They always send their love and they cried a lot because they have never thought that their grandchild Dezső would write from America. It's sad to go to their place because they constantly cry. I would have a lot that I could write to you, but I must put it aside so if and when we are there, with God's help, something should remain...... I've written to the Perl girl, however she didn't reply. I just mailed a card to Gizi from Szürte, that she should talk to her and then advise me. Bela Stark, the youngest, is also getting ready to go to America. She is from Leles. Probably her passport is ready. When she'll go or leave I don't know. It wasn't long ago that she was preparing to go, but now she is ready. I don't believe it. There isn't any other news except the Lefkovics girl is not yet engaged, but will be getting married to the Beregszaszi fellow who is a psychiatrist. His mother died and now he is a good catch and this is what was mentioned in secret and not open to the public. It doesn't pay to talk to them, and I do it like you wrote about it. Anyone that throws rocks at me I should give them bread, as it's being said. What she has done at our house and she has the nerve to send us 'csolent' every Friday to cook in our oven. This was enough from all of this. Lots of kisses and love, your sister Hermina

The ship I believe will be the same as Jolan from Szatmar.

1938/6/24 Father and Hermine to Uncle Julius (Book 4, 193-194)

Polány June 24. 1938
Received your letter of recommendation

My dear brother Jónász and dear sister-in-law Helen.
I just want you to know that thank God we are well. I hope you have the best of health. My dear brother, I hear you are not feeling well. Please take care of yourself. My son wrote to me you are still working very hard. Please take care of yourself. I received the 12 dollars that you sent me. I received 38 korona [he meant to write 48] from the bank, four for each according to the exchange rate today. [In Yiddish קראנען 38 האבע

דאפיר בעקאממען פיער דען שטיק - I got 38 korona for it[,] four a piece]. I thank you very much for sending me the money my dearest brother Jónász. I went to shop this same day for whatever we needed. Last week our brother-in-law from Szürte was in Helmec. I met him. He asked me to tell you to please write to him also. He and his family are well and send you all their best wishes to you and to your wife. And especially for you I'm wishing the best of health, your loving brother, with many kisses. Gluck Jeremias.

[Next page continues my sister Hermine]
Polány 1938 June 23
My dear Uncle Jónász.
When we received your letter it made us very happy to hear you're well. I cannot even tell you [how] I hope I could tell you in person. It would make me very happy to be able to speak to you in person. I hope our God will help us. Just like in our home as a young girl I remember it was very nice even to think about it. I remember when I put flowers every day in your coat lapel. From my heart, I'm very happy if I would be able to see you in America. It is true our happiness does not come without some heartaches. And we feel at the same [time] some sadness. I hope after the sadness will follow the happiness because if our dearest father will see and know we are happy he will also be very happy to hear that his children do not suffer and are happy. He will be very happy too. I think it does not matter how hard it will be to do and be able to have a job. It is better to hear good news. It does not matter how far we are, than to be close by and to watch their suffering. I am sorry I do not mean to bore you with my long letter my dear Uncle Jónász. I will never forget what you are doing by helping us. I am wishing you all the best of health and happiness to Aunt Helen and you especially, dearest Uncle Jónász and the family. I hope I could say I'll see you soon. With all my love, your niece– Hermin.

Dear Uncle Jónász,

We were really happy to receive your dear letter Uncle Jónász. You especially made our father very happy with it. We hope that you will write more often than before. Uncle Jónász, I would like to talk to you in person already. But God is good, and the time will come and we will be able to talk in person together. I hope my letter will find you Uncle Jónász, and your family, and also Aunt Helen in the best of health. I wish you everything good! I kiss everybody.

Your faithful little nephew, Herman

My dear son Dezső,

I got the registered letter and I was very happy to read that thank God, you are in good health. We are in good health also, and I hope that we will only hear good things back from you.

I got the 16 D[ollars], [In Yiddish] I sent a sum of 28.60 korona in the year 38, after which there was an increase in the value of the coin, and then I sent a sum of 29 korona. [In Hungarian] I sent the collection with a letter to Czechoslovakia, but I didn't get a response. I put the letter in the package. I asked the Pollack boy yesterday if Czechoslovakia sent the 35 korona to him? He hasn't written back yet. It's still his allowance and he asked if there would be a good traveler to whom I can give the collection to? Doci Odon and Kullik, who are always in the post office, also talked to me. I told him to write to Schwarc and then I will give him over the collections. Herman's request to the registrar came yesterday already, and he wants to be an American resident, and the gendarmerie [police] will consider him as an American resident, so this way he will get the discharge sooner and I read in it that the related documents need to be sent in. The Jaras doctor said that based on this, he will get discharged, and it is necessary to wait for the notary because of the house. He made the contract and we will sign it next week. After 14 days it will be administrated in the district office.

Until this case is settled with the orphanage they will not give any money from the bank. I hope our God will help us. I gave to the Post Master lady 500 korona and I asked her not to be angry because my son Dezső can't pay at one time. She was very happy. She said that my son Dezső is a very good person and please ask him to write to me more often because I'm waiting impatiently for his letter. She will write to you very soon, too. At this time I don't have anything more to tell you. My best wishes and many kisses, your loving father who never forgets you forever, your father Jeremias Gluck.

Your grandfather and grandmother send their love to you. As of now I did not receive the citizen papers. Monday I will go in to see what goes on there and why was it delayed. I will try to ask if it is possible to work on it faster. You mentioned before that you mailed us a letter which we did not receive yet. No one mentioned it last week.

My dear brother Dezső,

I was a happy to receive your letter and I'm glad that thank God you're in good health. I could not imagine why your letter was so late, but I see you have written, but we did not receive it. In the future, don't spend 20 cents more because that means you overpaid 38 Czechoslovakian kronin. Dear Dezső, don't be angry that I'm writing it so, but it bothers me that the letter was lost and the things that were in it. Please let us know what was in the letter that was lost. Imagine that Veizer from Imreg was fine in the morning and in seven days she died. She was getting everybody ready to get to the market and it seems like a vein popped in her head, and that was it. Don't be angry that I'm the writer for the news about personal tragedies. No one wanted to write about this, but I know that you are interested to know what goes on here. It's true, it's a very sad situation. Otherwise I believe that everyone wrote to you about everything else. I spoke to Joskaval Fekete. He wanted to write to you, but he's too busy. He is well with his wife as it was before. I didn't even write about Jóska Kopasz. On May 1st, Jani Haraszty and Pista Kusnyir jabbed Gyorkit and Kopaszt with a knife. It wasn't serious, but it was enough for them. As you see, you can hear nice things from this village. I did not give your regards to him yet because I didn't speak to him. Jóska Csorosz did not receive any mail from you. You do not write about the old Csorosz bacsi's death. Kosztojék sends their regards. It would be good to tell you all this in person and would be interesting to write pleasant things in a letter. Otherwise, I'm okay. Kisses to Uncle Jónász bacsi and Aunt Helen, also dear Arthur and the rest of the relatives, and to you especially, your little brother, Ignác.

1938, VI/24

1938/6/27 Bertha to Dezső (Book 4, 403-404)

New York
June 27 / 38
Dear Dezső!

I already believed that you became unfaithful to me and you love other relatives, not me, but finally the waiting brought news from you. The thought that you met the two [university] students makes me happy. You will see that here it isn't what one does [that's important], but rather who is a man. A scavenger hasn't been looked down here, and I already told you about this. That's why I'm asking you to be natural and don't humiliate yourself, because here if you have a little luck you could proceed one way as well as the other. Truthfully, it takes a little opportunity also. My Dezső, an intelligent man who thinks normally, knows that money doesn't matter. Truthfully, without money one can be paralyzed, but that will come too. [I wish you] only luck with your radio and with learning English. My Dezsőke, mourn and then everything is going to be good. But forget about this one too. My Dezsőke, it would be very nice to get Jolanka's documents from Arthur, but I wouldn't like to bother him because I know from Mannie that if he comes home from work, he is so busy and especially in this heatwave, it wears him out. But this week I will ask. My Mannie will write the letter in my name. Arthur can be sure, that Jolanka's being here will not be a ten [tizhelne]. God save me if I have to wash the floors, even then it's not sure that I can hope that we will have the opportunity, in some way, to repay it to the unknown dear cousin Arthur. Like they say, a mountain with a mountain doesn't match, but a man with a man does. In the letter, I can't show my appreciation and give my thanks, but you never know how the wheel will turn. Dezső in the past we were, picnicking [In Hungarian - "zosárnak" = in the basket] I will call it, at a very nice forest. Jenni Frey finally got there and my Mannie made a good lunch there. I thought about you, if you could be with us. There are a lot of things we could do with you. They made baked corn and snitzlit [schnitzel]. There was enough and it would have been enough for you too, but never mind, it will be this way again. I think it was enough about this too. I wish you good luck with everything, with love, Bertha

"adàt üdv hitünket" [Faithfully]

To the dear relatives [there], the dear relatives from here send their greetings

1938/7/1 Bertha to Dezső (Book 5, 223-224)

New York
July 1 / 38
Dear David!

I received a letter from Jolan in which they sent a picture from home with her sister. Will send some information. The problem exists there too. Dear Dezső, I sent you a letter to our cousin and I was thinking if he would send the visa to Jolan it would be better if he sends it now [because] it would take even longer from here. If he sent it to me here, I would like to get a chuppah and a future husband. You know, we didn't want to do things until we are sure because Jolan is the firstborn. Therefore it would be better if she comes first. I still didn't hear from my cousin. I hope the answer will come soon so we would be able to mail the papers, that's what's important. Otherwise, how are you? I hope your pay got better and that your English has improved, too. Also, I'm hoping that you have heard from your sisters. Are they coming? Somehow I didn't hear from my sisters. Maybe they're angry maybe it should be that way. If they ask questions they will see that I want only the best for them. I will close my letter now. Give my best wishes to our uncle and his dear wife and also our cousins and family unknown. You wrote that it would be important for Jolan to know how big Arthur's family is and how old they are. You let me know because you know better about their lifestyle and their ages. If not write to me, and I will send it to them. Many kisses and best wishes many times. Bertha

1938/7/8 Father to Dezső (Book 4, 217-220)

Polány July 8, 1938.

My dear son Dezső.
I am delayed writing a reply. I was waiting until I would have any positive news to tell you about Hersmendel. As of now, I still don't have any information because I didn't go to the office in Prague. Last week when I was there, I was told we have to get the permit to release him because he is at the age that he must go to the army to serve as a soldier. I wanted to know why he needs the permit. They wanted to know if he is an American citizen. Then I would have to bring in those papers to prove it. I'm waiting now for those papers. I still did not hear from Prague [and I'm] still waiting. The lawyer submitted the papers to those legal offices. As of now I still did not hear from them. I still don't know when the sale of the building will come through. At least he was asking about the price in advance. I am not even sure if we can get the citizen papers now. I have to get the passport 1st. As soon as possible I'm going to get the papers.

You are asking me about the Torah. I promised my brother Jónász. I must ask if I need a permit to take it out from here to America. It has to be a Temple to be able to take it out from here. And [since] men and women are together therefore my brother Jónász does not have a Temple. This year the wheat is good. We had a little ice damage to the tobacco. Yesterday they started to get ready to go on the farm. Feri Szabo and his family are working on it. I paid 10 K. And the squash I sold it for 18, The squash crop came in well, the hay also. Because we did the work for ourselves from the group of 27 therefore they will auction it off in our home. I don't know where I will get that money 585K to transport it at another 500k. I mailed in early spring, but the balance remaining is 300 and the fall also. They will harvest the tobacco and the hay and I will see how much I will get. They wanted to take it all for nothing. They find all [kinds of] excuses. Therefore there will be a hearing scheduled. They wanted to lie and cheat, but somehow it did not work out. The letter you are asking about I received. Thank you very much for sending it. I received [the ones you sent on] 5/21, 6/8, 6/13, 6/20. I sent a request to the agent who is in charge about the advance of 825 korona on the tobacco. They denied it. I wrote to them because I know I do not owe them at this time. I didn't get the reply from them. I paid them before what I owed them. Otherwise I don't have any more news to tell you at this time. There is nothing special. Therefore I wish you all the best and many many kisses to you and all my love, your father who never forgets you. Gluck Jeremias.
PS
Your brother Lajos sends you his best wishes and Miksa [Schon] too.

[Note from Maria. I typed this letter in the computer 10/9/012. This letter like all of them very difficult to type nothing but heart aches.]

1938/7/8 Herman to Dezső (Book 4, 305-306)

B'H
1938, until 120, VII/8
Dear Dezső,
I received your letter gladly, even if it's in one piece or separated. It doesn't matter. I'm sorry that I don't write about everything in detail now, but I don't have time. Otherwise, I'm sure that our father has already written about everything that was interesting. Believe me Dezső, one can work through the entire long day. So when it comes to writing, I'm completely exhausted. About traveling to America, I still can't write anything yet to you. The answer should come in these days. I hope that God is good and will help, and this is how my days are passing, day after day. I know that writing is difficult for you too, when a man is tired all day long and overworked himself. But God created man for work. And as long as you are alive, you have to go through a lot. In my next letter, I will write about my occupation. I hope my letter will find you in the best of health, and I wish you health and everything good. If God is good and will help and I will be in America, then we will talk about everything. It's Friday afternoon at 4 o'clock and I'm in a hurry so I can send it today, as you can see from my writing. I kiss you, your little brother, Herman

Separately kiss Uncle Jónász and his family.

The Stor type straw which was sold, he gave 100 Korona. He made us wait and encouraged us and at the end he didn't take the straw. So we ended up taking a loss because of him, about 400 Korona because we received about 170 Korona from the straw. And then he wanted his 100 Korona back because he is a poor man. This only came to my mind since you asked in your letter, and I saw that none of them wrote this yet to you. That's why I wrote it.

1938/7/9 Bertha to Dezső (Book 4, 405-406)

New York
July 9, 1938
Dear Dezső

[Here are] a couple of lines so I can let you know about everything. The documents have arrived from our cousin. But I was advised here that it would have been better if he would have sent them with the rest of the documents at the same time. However, we sent them to Jolanka with the letter that Arthur wrote to me, so they can see that the rest of them were already sent to Bucharest directly. My Dezsőke, if you can possibly see our cousin and ask him if he sent his birth certificate. If it's with him, [he should] send it to Jolan. We can save some time like that. They have not offered to do Iren's documents. I'm sorry I don't know how to do it. It's possible that they can come here in two years from the time the documents are done and they send it. They will get it from them from that date if they start this way. Now I don't write more, because I don't have patience. I have to write to many places still and I don't feel the best now. I'm very nervous. It's too hot to sleep. I can't eat. I hope our God will help, so that my sickness will end. Also, I think Mannie's sibling is getting married on the 14th of this month. I will not write anymore because I'm tired, but I don't know why. Give my kisses to our dear Uncle and our dear unknown cousin and to his dear family. If I could write in English to him I would correspond more often. No reason why, only because he seems to be a very fine man. Kisses, Bertha

1938/7/12 Iren and Sarolta Mayer to Dezső (Book 5, 271-272)

July 12, 1938
Dear Dezső!
I don't know how to begin this letter because Iren and Jolany address your letter. I wrote an eight page letter. Dear Jolany my sister didn't mail it out to you. Why not? And what was in it I do not know? I know that you made her very angry. You made her feel terribly because now you think that to a beautiful letter you were answered on a card and I didn't answer. Therefore you can see I'm not the cause. And you will forgive me, yes? Dear David, if I would be you and someone wrote a card I would be satisfied. With Bertha's letters, you will read it. Thank you for the card, but in this beautiful letter which we didn't mail I was writing and I will repeat it again here. Only you can do something in our interest. If my Jolan cannot write anything god forbid that I do not want to. She is the oldest. You write that we will also be able to get out in less than two years. I do not know where you heard that. We received a letter from my sister Bertha telling Jolan that we will not be able to go before two years. We thank you for letting us know. From Szatmar, her fiancé will forgive her. I'm a watchmaker? You didn't understand. It's no wonder, I'm sorry I write so badly and I can't change that, I was born that way. I write again that I'm a homemaker, nothing else. If I would go to teach with my fiancé in Satmar, he is a painter. Here I'm sending you a picture. And I'm wishing you all the best. I hope your wish will come true as soon as possible. Kisses to all of you and to you 1 million times. Iren Forgive me, okay?

Dear Dezső,
I am mailing you a few lines in which I send you kisses and simply to Uncle Julius and his family with love, Sarolta

1938/7/12 Jolan Mayer to Dezső, Romania (Book 5, 56-57)

1938 July 12
Szatmar, Romania
Jolan to Dezső

Dear Dezső,
I received your letter and I'm in a hurry to reply to you. I cannot write anything in this letter regarding Bertha. My teacher had an operation and from the 20th for about 15 days I couldn't go to study and I can't go to another because of a few days. Today I received a letter from Bertha she writes very dearly! Uncle Mannie also wrote a few lines in English. I'm going to write to them after I go back to study watchmaking

and I must reply to them, regretfully I can't yet. You can't imagine how much I would like to learn and know, but it is very difficult as you write "just study" and everything will be fine. These words lift me up.........

Bertha tells me in her letter that you're going to write to me punctually about everything because she has difficulty because she does not know the language well enough. To me it doesn't matter who writes it as long as it comes here. Until now I did not receive anything from Bucharest. I'm sure I will get something. Dear Dezső, give to Arthur my sincere thanks until I will be able to thank him in person. Also, tell dear Jónász bacsi that I wish him the very best and many, many happy birthdays and he should see his children and grandchildren, and the same to our Aunt, with hand kisses. I did not know his address so I could have written directly. I believe this is just as good or will be good. I'm very happy that you have it good socially and they like you. I am not surprised since such a good boy as you is difficult to find. Now you might think that I'm writing this because I'm trying to butter you up, but you ought to know me by now that I can't do that.

My dear Dezsőkem, please write to me punctually what I should do and I will follow you and we'll do that. Don't be angry that I'm writing here and there but I'm nervous because all things came together at this time, I would like very much to talk to you a little bit about myself to you in person. How is the trip with regards to your sisters' traveling? I've written to them and two weeks ago [sent] a card, but I did not receive any reply yet. I don't know if they received it? Then it should have been returned if they did not receive it. My dear Dezső, I will close these lines now and I hope that you will write to me soon. If I receive anything from Bucharest, I will advise you immediately. The one that is best to you and the best of friend, my best wishes to them. How is the radio activity? Probably well..... This was your old desire to work in the radio, hope that God will help you with that, that you will succeed, and all the very best. Kisses, your niece Jolan
[In English] So Long

1938/7/13 Grandfather Samuel and Uncle Lajos Schwartz (Book 5, 44-45)

1938 July 13
Lelesz
[From Uncle Lajos Schwartz, my mother's brother]

Dear Dezső, Leb to 120
I read your treasured letter with happiness, and I'm rushing to reply; about ourselves, I can only write to you that we are going backwards, the business thank God is going, but slowly. Did you learn the local habits already? Living there in the beginning is very difficult, but I think that you are not in a strange place because you have a very good uncle bacsi that thinks of you and that helps a lot. How are they otherwise? Lots of love and kisses from Aunt Etel [my wife] and Lajos bacsi. Give our regards to dear Jónász bacsi and his family, without knowing them

[From Grandfather Samuel Schwartz, my mother's father]

Lelesz 1938 July 13
My dearest grandson Dezső, I love you from my heart. Leb.to 120
I'm replying to your question. It seems that you're interested in my hand writing, the only thing I can write to you is that thank God we are in good health. Your grandmother and I wish you good health from God and I ask you that you behave well, be careful and don't forget that you are a Jew, uphold it as a religion because we don't live forever: I will bring to your attention that you have a good Bácsid [uncle] that is, Jónász bacsi, I'm asking you to listen to him because he is like a father there and he means well for you.--- I do not have patience to write because my hand is shaking. The store is as it was before and we are! Please give my greatest regards to dear Jonasz bacsi and the whole family with my pure heart. I remain your grandfather and your grandmother with love and kisses, I and your dear grandmother many many times. Schwartz Samuel, Lelesz and grandma Hàné [Haje]
If you are going to be interested in my handwriting, if we live then I will write you again.
[Note by Irv: As far as I know my grandmother's last name was Moskovics]

1938/7/13 Uncle Marton [Helmec] to Dezső (Book 3, 402-405)

Dear Dezső

I received your letter with the money. I am lazy to write, as you know. It is already too much, as I begin to write, but your father came in and showed me your letter, therefore, I will write to you. The postmaster lady spoke about you with me. She's working in the post office in Helmec. She helps me with the mail. She's a very fine lady and said that she's going to write you and will tell you to pray every day and observe the Sabbath. I really like that a Christian girl would say that.

I also beg you to take care of your Jewishness, that is the only hope, even though this world is bitter, and we live daily in constant fear and the thought of this is sickening. Otherwise we are well, thank God. Just now I've returned from Lelesz, there was a salesman,... but they are well also thank god. And I cannot write any good news. And after eight days, Menyhert Broun, that is on Thursday, will be two weeks to everything, all the good things, happiness were taken away.

The business has died here. Feno's son inherited it. Hazai Mano died the same day, he was an insurance agent at Lipot Klein. After a long sickness, he died in Ungvár, in the community house. He was 36 years old. Broun would have been 58 years old in August. Gedaljovics also died. In Lelesz the old Mrs. Hermel died last week. We live somehow. Keller Kalman also had lunch in Kenderes. He did not have any problem, but after 5 minutes he died. So one can't be certain in one's own life. In the 3 sad weeks [before Tisha b'Av] I plan on going to Szobrancz for at least 2-3 weeks because the itchiness did not go away completely. Two weeks ago I had grandfather and family over as guests from Lelesz. The aunts and one uncle. They went to Palocz from here. Whenever possible get work amongst nicer and better people because [otherwise] you will stay where you are. You will not learn the language. And because of that you will not get ahead. Knowing the language is important. Be educated so you can become a traveler, not a peasant [someone who is uneducated] because mowing-scything needs strength and that is not common in the Jews. The girls wish to go out already [to America]. Before Shavuot I was in Pest with Magda. It's possible that they have to do surgery on her. After the big holidays I will go with her again. I'm just hearing that Szekely is getting ready for the after life also. What a shame. Rather his wife should substitute him. Hevra Kaddisha Keren Kayemet will send out 25000 I don't have anything else to write about. We kiss you all countless times. Also, the kids and my wife send their greetings. Separately I'm sending greetings to Uncle Jónász and his son, without knowing him. I will ask the good God to give him a long life in good health and strength for the good deeds that he does for your father. He saved their life and from the edge of the cliff brought them back to humanity. There was no way to buy bread. It was out of the question to buy a dress for the big girls. They would have become the shame of the whole world. They would have been thrown out of the house and the land as a result of the auction. They would be hungry and thirsty if your Uncle Jónász did not pay them. The good God will pay him 1000 times more for that. [Örök ólam habüst szerzett maganak] And furthermore one can no longer be in business. Lajos is working very hard, but is unable to buy even a piece of rag for his family. I am hopeful that your mother, my sister, will help us from the other world. Wishing you the best of everything and kisses to you all, Marton
Helmec, 13/VII/1938

1938/7/18 Undated Marie to Dezső (Book 4, 255-256)

[Dated by Uncle Marton going to Szobranc spa]

Dear Dezső!
I was in Helmec today and Uncle Marton was not at home. He went away to the bath/spa in Szobranc. And it's possible that I wrote to you since then, because it's been at least two weeks since he said that he will write to you. But you know how it goes. Miksa Sőn [Shon] doesn't write because he is angry that you addressed him informally by his first name! But now you know how it goes! [It was] the harvest and they were at the house so they have no time. Dear Dezső! The situation is exactly where it was in May. I'm sure you know everything, but I will write it again anyway. When they mobilized us, approximately 100 soldiers from Helmec [went] to the Perbenyik border. [The mobilization] is very big from the other towns as well, but from Polány only Beni Simon. In Helmec they brought down [men] from Ungvár and they were here for 4 weeks and in Lelesz, also! And now, the same ones who got the call up, [were told] that they should get ready, When exactly? I don't know. Although there is no bigger change, it's possible that the dear God will help and nothing is going to happen, because they don't want that! But who knows what the future will bring! I'm only writing this because I know you are interested in everything. The news here is that at least 40 thousand Jews are in Prague, who are appealing to the American Consul for permission to immigrate and the consulate only gave it to 2400. Although, there are refugees from Vienna and the rest would get it, if Vienna would give their wealth back, but it does not want to. And only our approval could come sooner. I have written enough! Kisses, Mariska

New York
July 18/38
Dear David!
I'm in a hurry to respond, so it will be on time. Good luck to you on your new position. Knowing this makes me happy. I have a feeling that you will be a lucky man one day. Like at the same time I said, whoever can't bear their own destiny, doesn't deserve the good.
My Dezső, we must work everywhere! My Mannie worked from early morning in the day Monday until 6 at night because he did not get the working uniform to the next day. This is America! But we have to thank this one too to the dear God, that it is still not like at home. There is no need to ask [anything] from the Emperor for the Jews-that is, us- otherwise maybe we would be cast out. My Dezső, listen to your older cousin. As I took it from his letter written earlier, he is a very nice man and he sacrifices a lot for his relatives, and that's hard to find, and that is why [you must] try to work from your heart! When it is warm it is hard to work, but do what you have to do and how, because he bears a lot on his shoulder, if he would take you there. And you have to try to be with open eyes and don't talk too much with the workers! They should not even know that you are a relative. Talk to them only what you must, good morning and good night. Don't worry about it if maybe somebody gives you a compliment. Let it fly over your ears! But it is enough about this because I don't feel good, my lips are overwhelmed. Thank God it is also over. You know this little angina wore me out so much.

I had to lie down in bed for three days. I am not too strong today and plus there is no help, but why do I even complain to you as though you could help. Don't worry about your sisters coming here. It was certainly not done in a day. Every demand in time [illegible], but I will ask you not to save money on your stomach because you will have to give it to the doctor. Eat well so you can bear your work before it's too late. Do not forget this! Now greetings! Are they bringing the Torah to you? I kiss you separately, Bertha
Manny sends his greetings and good luck from the both of us.

Dear Dezső!
I got your letter, that I could hardly wait for, and I read it happily that thank God you are in good health. I am, thank God in good health, which I hope I will hear back from you also! And dear Dezső, we got your registered letter written on the 6th day and 4th month, where you mentioned that you also wrote to Jòska Csorosz and in it to Gerenyi also, and we gave it over, but our father and the others together, forgot to write about it, and I did not have time to write this in detail to you yet. But now I looked after it and I realized, that you were right. These neighbors are always wondering about you, and sending their kind greetings. You have know idea, how happy you made Ica Gerenyi. She has been coming all week long and asking if you wrote yet, and when she got it, she danced in her happiness, and it felt very good for her parents that you remembered about it. They will write everything in detail. And you asked how the Ajgner girls are doing? We didn't get letters from them since then, but I heard, Lipòt Klájn [Klein] said, that they came home when the messy confusion was there, and ever since then, I don't know anything about them! Simon from Szürte and the others are the way they were! Dear Dezső, we don't know anything about the documents [even] until this day. We wrote on the 12th of this month to the consul and to the Agent, to find out what is with the documents. The response came from Agent on the 14th, that since the documents were processed on the 13th of May, for that reason, we are waiting for the notice this month. And we did not get an answer from the consul, but we are waiting for the notice every day. We don't know what would be the reason why it is late, but in case we don't get it this month, then maybe it would be good if you would write [them], because here, there is no one who can arrange it. Who knows how much longer they can delay it? Like, for example, in Lelesz, the Rez girl started before you, and she is where we are until this day. And now she hired the lawyer Barnat Klein from Bacs, to act in this case, and she can't even imagine what is the reason for the delay. Little Olga would still be at home, if she would have not hired that lawyer, because there was a little error with the documents, and he set it in right, and in a few days, she got the visa. She already wrote from America. It didn't take two months for Erzsi Lecò and Ilon Juhasz, and they could travel out. I talked to Rezeda the last time, and he said, that he recommends to practice being a tailor, because if I were to travel to America, I might be able to take advantage of it. Although, I can sew any kind of design alone, it wouldn't hurt to know exactly. And whoever I tailored for was a success and everybody likes it. So what do you have to say about that? It's completely different in America than at home. Dear Dezső, I'm thinking about

everything, and I don't know what to do. In Ungvár at the Lada storehouse, the machine edged handwork would be good to learn, at least to go for 1-2 weeks and learn it, since it doesn't cost anything, and it's an opportunity, and maybe there I could take advantage of it. What do you say? Don't mind that I write about all these, but I write whatever is on my mind because I can write anything, but you don't have to do anything about it, if you don't think it's good! Bőske Gecse goes to sew. I don't have a lot of work these days, but I have enough, so I can cope with it easily. I did not send the payment yet, because I would like to send at least 2-3 payments at the same time, but it takes time and it's hard to put it together. Every time Mrs. Szeré Lefkovics meets with all of us one by one, she always asks about what you write. And, she knew here at home what kind of a boy you were, and [she asks] if we are going to America for real, but she is sure [we will] in a short time. But she asks this pretty much everyday. And she can't take it that we are going, but she has to stay. Because, it's useless for her to write, since their Uncle Vilmos doesn't respond, and since you wrote, they didn't get anything from him. I don't have any special news. I think the others wrote everything. We got Uncle Jónász's letter with yours at the same time. We got a letter in English also from Arthur last week, and he was wondering why we can't travel yet. We did not write to him separately, but give him, and the entire family, our cordial greetings. I think that I wrote everything to you and from this he will know everything also. As soon as we get the notice, we will let you know immediately. I kiss you countless times and I will stay with much love. Your little sister, Mariska

I am sending my greetings and kisses to Uncle Jónász and to dear Aunt Helenke, and dear Erzsikének [Elsie], and especially to Bertha.

Emil is not at home, and that is why he did not write.

Mitya and Lenku send kisses to you

[On top of the page] Ica Gereny travelled away with her grandmother to the bath/spa [Hungary is famous for these baths. They cure a lot of health problems. Americans call it spa, but it's nothing like an American spa], because her leg and heart hurts a lot. She is sending her greetings and next time she will write to you. She wants to write now, but she didn't know when we are writing and she had to go away.

1938/7/25 Hermine to Dezső (Book 4, 239-240)

Dear Dezső,

We received your letter and we are very happy to hear that thank God you're okay. We did not answer the previous letter you sent us because we were waiting for something we could tell you in more detail. Also we were waiting for this letter that we just received. Our cousin Arthur is very sweet. He also wrote beautifully to us about you. He complimented you that you are very good person. He asks us that as soon we have any information we should let him know about the papers. We should let him know as soon as possible if we know the date when we can leave. He wrote in English and it was a difficult to translate it to Hungarian so we can understand. I tried to and have finally succeeded with a dictionary. Some words were difficult to translate. As of now we did not receive any notice yet about our trip. I wrote to the agent and also to the consul what is the reason it took so long and we still haven't heard from them. I received a letter from the agent. They answered that we should receive a notice from the consulate this month. For you it must feel very good to know that in a strange country there is someone close to you like family. You couldn't find someone here like the person who gave you the radio. No one cares. It seems in America it is a different world. I understood you very well. Little Olga from Lelesz wrote that she still wasn't able to get a job. Hopefully, maybe next year. Even though she is in a very good place with an aunt who lives alone and who is quite well to do. She also wrote that she was on one week vacation. If it's true or not, I do not know. As she writes it, she misses her home. I saw the picture that you took on the ship of both of you. It stands out from the other group as I see you have all kinds of people there. There are many different countries [represented]. It seems they are very hard workers, you can tell. It was very nice to see. It felt very good to see [them] with the hope that we will be there soon. For the four of us it would be different. I hope it will be soon. That would make me happy. Also, I hope that maybe we could go at the same time as my friend [Helen] Perl from Sürty. I think our friend in America could not find a job because she would not do just anything she could get. The only thing is that she's not telling the truth. I am hoping we will have better luck and will find a job. I don't care what kind. About the building it's still the same. We did not get paid yet. Maybe it will take another 2 months. Maybe it's a possibility that we would be able to leave before we get the money. That's what happens when it comes to dealing with Village leaders.

Now we are shopping at Rieder's. He is still here in Adolf bacsi's building.

Marcsa Deàk is still alive. She would like to write to you but she thinks it's not very nice for her to write to you. She is very ill. She thinks she will not be able to go to America. Here the weather was raining constantly. We were not able to work on the farm. We have losses from the damage. The 168 cross weight of wheat, 61 k.gos [kilograms?] We will most likely harvest it with the tractor so we can use it. Our father signed on the 3rd line. He will be next. Pastor Joska got married. P. Kusnyir got engaged. P.S. Jolan broke off the engagement and if you would see her she looks beautiful like an actress. Lajos Fekete is also planning to go to America. I was laughing because I was visiting Lefkovic and Miklos Leczo was speaking English. He wanted to know if I understood what he's saying. They were very surprised that I understood what he was saying.

They thought I'm just saying it, but now they were surprised that I really was able to talk to him. I told them I would like to practice with someone who knows English. That way, I could learn faster from someone who could help me. Schvarcz didn't write about the bag. I did not hear from Csehie either. Lajos from Szürty he is in Perbenik. They just bought a machine. [He's working on that machine to clean out from the tenant usually that's what they have to do before they are ready to make the planted flowers.] And Gizi writes that the documents are still as they were. They did not have time to sort it all out. At this time I think I wrote to you enough. You were asking me to write about whatever is happening here. At least you have something to read. Our neighbor Borcsa neni is not getting along with Yoska. She left and moved to Boly. She had lots of problem with him. Since then she came to visit. She wants to know how you all are. She is very happy that we are going to go to America. I got to know America maybe like you do, but not really as good. But I will try to learn all about it by the time I arrive there, at least some knowledge. Until we meet in America, I remain with all hopes and many kisses, your sister. With love Hermine.

[Side of first page] Our Uncle Marton is in Szobránci resort on vacation.
[Side of second page] We will take pillows with us and some linens, maybe one blanket.

1938/7/25 Undated Herman to Dezső (Book 4, 261-262)

[Dated by father signing on line 2 or 3 for threshing machine, transporting the harvest]

Dear Dezső,
We got your letter, that we could hardly wait for, and I read your lines happily. Now, I want to be careful with my lines, so they will not give you a hard time reading. Next time write if it was easy to read my letter. Since, if we can leave out the bad writing and substitute it with good writing, then why not. I can't write anything certain about my traveling, but very likely, that it will be good in every aspect. We will start the transporting this week. Wheat and grain all together 2.30 Kezeszt. From this we will give out 30 kezeszt. For the Kepes will stay 200 kezeszt. For our part from this, I think, since the wheat and the grain was rich, therefore I think, that at least it has to be 60 q [1 quintal = 100 kg]. But I will write for certain after the threshing. Because like dad says, Don't be too wise in advance. This is the blessing that comes. [Yiddish - "szetazein komen dsz bruche"] The threshing is the way that at least for a year they did not do anything. The manorial from Lelesz is counting on bringing a machine to our town. They were here to write things out to see about how many signatures they can get. Our father was the second signatory. So, as soon as we will transport it [the grain] in, we can thresh it immediately.
I note, that it will thresh for 9 percent, but they will need workers for the machine, at least 18 people, as I heard from our father. If we will be alright with all this, then again, we will start the second cloverleaf mowing. The last week we had a big rain, it helped everything, except the kezeszt. Because they got rained out and because of that it held back the transporting. But, thank God, that we have nice weather now. We don't have any fruit, only a few apples, but even that is nothing, because of the worms. That is the only reason why I was waiting for the summer, so we will have a lot of fruits. And now it really messed me up. But it's ok. It will be in America. The tobacco from the Lesna had a little frost, but it is bearable. It only caused harm to the bigger beans. This week we have remaining a sea [of tobacco]. We rented out the business place to the commune, until it will be bought by the town. It could bring some profit. It will come in handy. It is better than nothing. From July 15th the starting rent is 100 korona per month. There is no response from the Czechs since they went back "the collection" "Szvarc" did not ask for the bag. They replaced the lady at the post office again in Lelesz. Her replacement is a smiling woman, but she is a very fine lady. Since she is there, I was only once at the post office. I hope you will not have any to take issue with me since I responded to everything. I wish you and dear uncle Jónász and his family good health. Kisses. Your faithful little brother,
Hermann

[Dated by mention of Kusnyir getting engaged]

My dear brother Dezső. Until 120 B'H

I was happy for your letter, that thank God you are healthy. At least you wrote me a good, long letter. Sometimes I write a long letter and sometimes a short letter, because there hasn't been gathered much to write about. There would be things to write about, but I will only tell you those in person. Now, first I will start to write about the good news, that I think you are also going to be happy about. Thank God, we got rid of the goats. We sold them at the fair in Helmec. Two of them for 240 K. A goat trader came from Kapos, and he bought all of them. There were 4 old ones and 1 little one, for 380 K. We sold them cheaply, but it doesn't matter. [I would] rather give them cheaply than they would die. And they won't yell after me, we aren't "Jews with goats." I just ask the dear God to help us, that we could buy a cow as soon as possible, and that our traveling would work out. Now the harvest has ended [and] already this week we will transport it thanks to the threshing extract. The others already wrote everything, I'm sure. Starting from the time the mail comes to Lelesz, I count from that day until the day we get mail again. I will go on [counting], until the letter comes. When I go to see our Grandparents, which is every 2-3 days, they are always thinking about you. Grandma asks "When will we see David" [Yiddish - "Ven elehdeh zén mán Zájde Duvedi"] I say [to her] don't be sad grandma soon he will be home to visit. Yes, but that my eyes see him in life [Yiddish - "Yaya ich viekleh zán, sajn óch indőrhájm"]. And they asked if I go away, would I write to them? And we should not forget that we have an old grandfather and a grandmother. And, if Passover comes, since Hencse will not be home, will we think about them? And I am encouraging them that [we will], no matter what!!! News, Husnyir is engaged to a strange girl. Yes, I forgot to write about this in my previous letter, that Braun Nagy from Helmec died and Tarkany who was in the home magazine, he died too. I gave your greetings to Uncle Lajos and he sends his best also. Joska Kopasz, also sends his greetings, and he will also write next time, but he has no time now and he thanks you for your greetings. Kocsis sends his greetings also, and he thanks you for thinking about him from the big world. He still lives where he lived. Nothing has come from the consul yet. Since June 15 there is a different post lady in Lelesz. She also gives out the letters. Now that the two registered letters came, I asked her to give out both letters and she gave them out with out a word. She gave it easily, she just said that if I bring it down, then she will give it out at other times as well. The postmen in Lelesz and Polány send their greetings to you! As for me, thank God, I'm healthy. I kiss all the relatives. Ignác

1938/7/25 Jane Fabianova Postmaster to Dezső (Book 7, 52-53)

Dear Dezső!

Your dear father brought your letter and the money immediately after it arrived. I will write to you as soon as I receive your new address. I am well. Our situation hasn't changed. I'm happy when you write and tell me about everything. The material is white and it will be very beautiful if the leaves are 6 cm large. The other blue material is also beautiful, I trust that. I can write more about this in a letter. My best regards, Jane Be diligent and persevere!

1938/7/27 Father to Dezső (Book 4, 257-258)

My Dear son, Dezső!

I have read your letter, one that I could hardly wait for, with happiness. Thank God you are okay. I was very impatient because your letter was late. I understood the reason why. The item you sent luckily arrived. Until today 32 is the promise, I'm still waiting on it. I got the advance for the tobacco 3000k. [korona], and from that, 825 k [korona] was forbidden for the Slovakian debt. With the deficit I sent 585k as a contingency [konitigental]. And for the costs, I wrote a letter and I asked to let it go for me, but I didn't get a response to that yet, and I asked to stop the auction. It was scheduled for today and the notary asked me to give 2000 korona because he promised 1000 k [korona] to the commissar. I took it to him and he didn't take it. I told him it's not enough and I didn't get anything until I don't get money, then he was like, he won't take responsibility for it. I put the money away. There is no place to get a loan from. It is what it is. I asked him to send the documents over, because time is going by quickly, and he, once again stipulated with the judge to post it publicly for 15 days. It's going to be next week on Tuesday. The one in charge of the proceeding is on leave. And they sent the invitation 8 days before the meeting. I talked to Kobori, he promised that he will be on my side.

and I told the notary, that I'm in his hand. He responded that he can't ask that from me, because it's not allowed, one can be sent to prison for that. He wants it because he promised it to the komiszar [administrative officer], but I would say that he just wants an assurance for himself.

I still didn't deal with the passport, because the consulate did not let us know if the papers are good. The agent wrote that they are making the passport and it will be done this month. Hersmendal's papers are not ready yet. I will go to the district office tomorrow. They asked for the authorized communal certificate, that he is unmarried, and the birth certificate. I asked from the person if he will get discharged. He answered, 'yes', it just needs to be sent to the military commander. But you know how it goes, we need to wait patiently. The money is not even in the child's hand, but he wants to fly. Impatience. It's already been two weeks since I got the letter from my nephew Arthur, but I didn't respond to him because I still can't write anything about the papers to him. I still didn't get anything from Czechoslovakia yet. He didn't send the money to Polak. I was at the man in Csap. I got 20 k [korona] in April. He promised that after the harvest he will give me money. He will leave next week. The neighbors said that they will put his house up for auction in May. Little hope. We had to cover the barn, because it got damaged by the wind.

I will talk to the lady to give my greetings to my nephew Arthur. My brother Lazar sends greetings. I can't write about the Torah until Hersmendel's trip is certain, because it's a big deal to take it, because it can only be carried. Uncle Izidor [Klein] sends greetings from Szürte. The Grünberger's son said that he wrote to you at least a month ago. He doesn't know if you got the letter. I kiss you respectfully, many times, your faithful father, who will never forget you, Gluck Jeremias

[On the bottom of the 2nd page:]
...and I will ask a relative how much it is worth

[On the top of the 1st page:]
...at your departure you told me to bring home the name-board/sign-board [company's], and when I asked for it, the sister-in-law said Ptak took it. I asked him 'Who did you send it to?' He answered that to my son Dezső. If it's true or not [maybe he means, he doesn't know, if it's true or not]

1938/7/27 Undated Marie to Dezső (Book 5, 62-63)

[Dated by New position on 7/17/38 (Bertha), Emil not home 7/24/38 (Marie), sewing machine. Might be a little later because of the pictures and Ignác mentions on 8/16 taking pictures]

Dear Dezső,
We have received your letter which we have been waiting for with difficulty. We were very happy to read and to know that you are well, thank God. Otherwise we are also well and hope that these few lines will find you likewise. Don't be angry that I'm not writing in detail, but our father has written about everything regarding our travel. We are waiting for the notification. If God will help us then in a short time we also will be there. With regards to the [sewing] machine I will try the best. I'm not writing more this time because I can't think of anything to write. When we meet in person I will tell you more. Kisses to you many times and I remain with love until we meet again. Wish you good health and good luck in your new position and I believe also that your reply is on the way and we'll be on our way also. I remain with kisses to you, your sister, Mariska.
I'm also sending my heartfelt regards and kisses to dear Uncle Jónász bacsi and dear Aunt Helen, to dear Arthur and his family and Elsie and her family. Emil was not at home, but will write an answer to your letter in the near future. Here I'm mailing you a few pictures. It's true they're not very good, especially Ignác's, but it is better than nothing. He made 10 pictures.

1938/7/31 Undated Hermine to Dezső - VISA (Book 5, 65-66)

[Undated, but before 7/31 as indicated in the letter]

Dear Dezső,
I do not know how to begin this letter. And do not be angry that I did not reply to your letter immediately but I wanted to write you the exact information. In your letter you wrote that you have sent a telegram to Prague, we would be very happy to go there on July 31, We have been requested to come in at 9:30 for the visa to be able to receive it and they have to have an affidavit and any other papers that are needed to be

bring with us. At the present I will go to buy some cheap custom dress for Marie. However, I'm leaving that and I return to the more important things. That is, poor Herman was inducted into the army and because of that I did not write to you immediately because we thought we can apply for a permission, however there is no possible way. We tried without success. Because of that, you can imagine our situation! Up to now, we have been worrying about the transportation and for all that perhaps this is better as it is. We hope that God will help us more so that it will be otherwise. They may also discharge him from the military and then he'll be able to travel to America. Since we have a file at the consulate that states if we cannot get the documents now, they will sign that I can assume that later that we have the right. I hope that it will not have to be that way. The passport was not mailed, but it's getting ready and if we are going to expedite it so by then we should receive it. Father mailed the important papers that we need by registered mail. We hope that Arthur will help us and will do that [fill them out] since it came to our attention that Arthur is not happy because he thought that [filling them out] meant asking him for money for the transportation and that we are not happy with the guarantee, while others would be happy just to receive the guarantee. The situation is such that, Uncle Jónász wanted to look good in front of his son and therefore he is making himself look good by saying that we have been asking for it [money], but it is not true, we did not ask. As I wrote to you, Arthur emphasized that if we want money he will take the affidavit back from the consulate. Thank God this will not come to this point, if he does not send the documents, then we cannot go. We are hoping that by then they will pay for the building and it will be somehow. From whom I have learned this information what Arthur has done I'll write it in such a way that it will not be a misunderstanding. They became friendly with Bertha and she has written a letter to her father, Lajzer bacsi, calling it to our attention to tell it to us that we should not ask money from them. I'm glad that we didn't ask, but I will thank him for his offer to us. I will write to you if I have anything important and if we can travel. I will definitely advise you, and also Uncle Jónász.

Hermin

P.S. Helen Perl and Lajos [Schwartz] have not received an invitation to go and they have sent a telegram that they called us in!!!

1938/8/1 Undated Maria to Dezső (Book 4, 241-242)

[Dated by Juhász Ilonka permission to travel.]

Dear Dezső,

We received your letter and were very happy to hear from you. I'm happy to hear thank goodness you are well. We will continue to be well also. Ilonka Juhász received her visa. Her father just came home from Prague and he informed us about everything and she will be on the ship on the 28th of this month. I hope we will get it very soon also. I hope it will be sooner than later. How are you dear Dezső? Otherwise I'm okay. I hope my lines find you in better health too. The sewing shop is still open for sewing, but now I'm convincing myself. Saturday I went to visit our grandparents. They are thinking about you all the time, day and night. She asked me to tell you that you should take good care of your self. And Margit Gerenyi was dreaming that you came home to visit them. You had a big conversation and told her about your trip and she was very happy. At least she was able to speak to you in a dream just like when you were at home. Every time I see her she speaks warmly about you. She felt badly because she did not give you anything before you left. At the time she wasn't feeling well, because she was planning to give you something when you leave. She also sent you best wishes from her heart. All her family sends their kisses and their love, each one of them separately. At this time I think I wrote to you about everything. Many kisses to you, I remain with hope that we will see you soon in America. Until then, all my love, your loving sister. Mariska.

Dear Uncle Jónász, we received your letter and we were very happy to hear from you. We were waiting impatiently to hear from you. Also, we were happy to hear that thank goodness you and your family are well. I hope in the future we will continue to hear the best from you and your family. Wishing you all the best, many kisses to follow you individually or otherwise. With love and I hope that we shall see each other soon. Mariska.

1938/8/1 Bertha to Dezső (Book 4, 407-408)

New York
August 1, 1938
Dear Dezső!

I'm glad to hear that you are in Columbus already. Although it's so hard to work very hard, at least you are among people and besides, you are lucky that you have a job. There are many natives who would happily welcome any kind of job, if only they could create an existence. Dezső, America will make you a man. Just don't take it away from your stomach, because you know the man will then keep the doctor. Eat right, [be sure] that you dine well, this way you will get energy. Do you exercise? Dezső, my Mannie did not write in English to Jolanka. That was me, because Jolanka wrote to me in English that they spend all their time on what I have been saying, so I replied a few lines about that to her. What Mannie wrote was in Hungarian. My Dezső, I don't expect you to write me every week, if it's once a month, it is enough. I know very well that you have to respond to many letters. I only want to hear that you are proceeding well for your own good. Kiss you with love, Bertha and Mannie

Give my greetings to Arthur and his dear family also.

You say that we don't visit you? Even if by a picture, it's better than nothing.

1938/8/1 Undated Secretary to Arthur re Dezső's family coming from Europe

[dated by Aunt Helen writing to father, mentioned in 1938/8/15 Father, Uncle Lazar, and Marie to Dezső (Book 4, 195-196)]

Sent you yesterday about the Gluck's coming over from Europa. Father Gluck says he wants nothing at all to [do] with these children. That they are all probably as bad as Desider [Dezső] and he wants nothing to [do] with them. If they come they cannot even stay at his house or anything. You should take care of everything. He also said that they had the money to buy their own tickets and that they could be bought at that end, that is, in Europa. Dunn and Bradstreet called and said that they finally received word from the American Consul at Bucharest that they received the report from Dunn on you [for] Yolan Majer.

1938/8/7 Jolan to Dezső, Romania (Book 5, 26-27)

August 7, 1938 Szatmar

Dear Dezső,

In the first place, this is where I shall begin. I can't imagine what may be the reason that you did not write to me for so long, perhaps I offended you with something, but I don't know of it. My dear Dezső, I have received the immigration papers to travel to America from Bertha. I mailed them immediately to Bucharest. On Friday, I received a reply from them. They have written to me with a lot of questions, like how old is Arthur? I replied to them that he is 38 years old, his wife's age I don't know, how old are the children, or how many? I wrote that he has one son. Also, do I have relatives? So I wrote down Jónász Bácsit and Bertuksat. Also, they're asking when did Arthur write to me? I did not reply to that. They also asked me when did I receive money from him? I did not reply to that either. They asked why do I want to travel? Why do I want to go to America? I replied that my uncle is very wealthy, and I'm going to go to him to help in the house. [They] wanted to know what is his occupation, and I wrote that he is a watchmaker and I would maintain the home. They are finished with it, however they still had some more questions. Be so kind dear Dezső, ask Arthur that he should write to me [a letter]. It should say that he cannot comprehend why I am not coming to America, that they are so busy and they need me. I have to send it to them, that is, to the consulate and with all this it won't be any problem. Only I have [a problem] since I do not know anything to show them. This is a mistake. He should write what he thinks about this so it will be good together. I am sorry that I always have to turn to you with everything, since you started it please complete it. What do you think...do you think that he will write to me? Please ask him. In my observation they may ask him also and I don't want a delay with all this. The agent that is making the papers said it's important to have it. Right now nothing has to be done. He has written to the consulate. He is an upright individual and the correct travel papers is the only thing they do here for everyone with an American passport. A friend of mine went to America three months ago to New York. They make corsets. She has written to her sister that this is what she is learning since that is a very good occupation and she earns $18 a week. What do you think if I would learn that also? This would be a very good occupation. Here too they are paying quite well. In 2-3 months I could learn all that. I will tell you my dear Dezső, that the watch repair business is very difficult and it takes a long time to learn it. If one is not an expert in this field, then it's worthless. Dear Dezső, write to me immediately because I would like to do this corset [job]. I could learn this. Please write to me what shall I do. Since I cannot go there to fix watches, first I could learn from both of these trades, both of them are very good. I'm waiting for you to see what you're going to write to me. I did not write to Bertha yet about this subject until I hear from her first. My dear Dezső, if Bertha will surprise me with a ticket ship ticket, I have no knowledge of it. Please write to me immediately and Arthur, too. It is very important. Give my regards. I'm asking you to please write. With loads of a kisses to you all, Jolan

1938/8/15 Bertha to Dezső (Book 3, 360-361)

August 15 /38
New York

Dear Desider!
First of all, we want to thank you for the calendar. It was very dear of you to surprise us with it.
Now I'm diligent to reply to you that my dear Jolan's papers were mailed registered and already I received a reply. In fact, there is a letter which dear cousin Arthur mailed to me, and that I mailed it with my letter and I wrote that I will wait for her and she will remain in New York by us. Everything was explained as I've written and Mannie wrote also because perhaps he could explain it much better than I. We received a reply to this letter. I'm glad that I didn't have to disturb Arthur. You wrote that it's possible Eigner would like to come to America. Brother, not only he, but everybody. The only thing I feel sorry for is that my niece Rezsi twice had an opportunity, [once] before she got married and the second time after she was married. Her husband was to go to Canada and he had the money to pay for it. He had the opportunity, well that has been, after the rain you do not need a raincoat [we hope for the best].
Inform me about your dear sisters arrival. Give my kisses to our relatives. Bertha

Mannie is sending his regards.
As above.

1938/8/15 Father, Uncle Lazar, and Marie to Dezső (Book 4, 195-196)

Polány 1938 August 15
My dear son Dezső.
I received your letter and am very happy to read that thank God you're well. Tomorrow on Friday they'll have the hearing about the building. And the end of this month they will decide to buy it and then they will decide if they will pay me or they will buy the home. I wrote a letter to my brother Jónás. I received one from my sister-in-law in which she wrote to me that my brother Jónász is upset about us. She's telling me he doesn't want my children to come to America anymore. I never mentioned anything to him about the outcome or that I heard about.
The barn is being made now by Pista Szabo. It is 8m long and wide at the end of the eaves. The shell is like the wood of the fence. I purchased the wood that we need from Keszler and the tile from Kajzler from Csap. Now we will deliver the tobacco. They are supposed to pay. Now I'm going to go to Helmec to the lawyers to see them. They are in charge with this legal part. My dear son, [In Yiddish] I am wishing you a very happy new year. To hundred 20. [In Hungarian] From your father, my best wishes and many kisses your father who never forgets you not for a moment. Many times over, forever. Gluck Jeremias
[At the top of the first page] My respects to Arthur and his family

My dear child Dezső,
I can't even tell you how happy I was to hear from you. Thank goodness you're well. Here thank goodness I'm well. I can't tell you anything special. I am wishing you all the best for the holiday. Also, please give my best wishes to the relations. And many kisses to all, especially to our Uncle and his family. Your mourning uncle, [N. B sirig = nagy bàtjat sirág]
[In Hebrew letters] Uncle Lazar Glück

Dear Dezső.
Don't be angry at this time I will be very brief. It is very important to mail this letter today. Thank goodness, I am well, which I hope you will be well too. About our travel I still cannot write. Our papers have been ready for 6 weeks. The only problem is about our brother Hersmendel. His permit is missing. We did not receive it. Until we do, we can't get our papers because all 4 of us are connected for the passport. This week our father was in Ungvár to the military office to see what they did with the documents. There he was told they mailed it to Kasa and from there they will mail it to Prague. As of now we are waiting every day, but only God knows when we will get it or how long it will take!! Our father is going to Helmec to see what is going on with those papers and why there is such a delay. If we cannot get the permit for Hersmendu, then

Page 36

they may issue the passport to only 3 of us. We are waiting in an uncertain situation. As you know, in today's climate the uncertainty is not very good. Also, with our brother Ignac it must be ready to go. We cannot delay any longer. We must leave before we will have more problems. The money, I hope, is supposed to be received this month. Jolan from Szatmar received a letter from the agent. He told them she might have to wait 2 years. Maybe then they will be able to let her know when she can go. They are very disappointed and very upset. Ignác Grosz would write, but sends you his best wishes, good luck and many kisses to you. Mariska Deak was here. She was very happy to hear from you and sends her best wishes to you. Until next time, with my love, your sister Maria.

[On the side of the 2nd page] Our grandmother and grandfather send many many kisses to you. They would write to you but at this time he's busy.

[This letter, and letter above to David. I dictated in the computer October 4/012. Maria.]

1938/8/15 Undated Hermine to Dezső (Book 5, 161-162)

[Dated by mention of the Torah and train ticket purchase in Prague to which Dezso will respond to in the next letter home]

Dear Dezső,
It came to my mind to write you a few lines in reference to the Torah. Relax, it will not be left here at home. I have mentioned it to our father from the beginning, it would be impossible to leave it here. However, the religious life there is different and you cannot keep religion as we do here. How can you think of not maintaining religious practice and being withdrawn and not even thinking of being Jewish? It is a little bit difficult for father, he would like to give it to a proper temple. I cannot find the address for Lovasz, I looked for it. I don't know if you knew it, but Uncle Jónász wrote a letter and suggested that we should buy the train ticket in Prague to go from New York to Columbus. Uncle Laizer received a letter from Bertha. He asked her why she couldn't be helpful to help us as relations! I know it's true and sad that we have to do whatever Uncle Jónász dictates. With regards to our travel, I will advise you as soon as we know. We hope that it won't be long with God's help.

[There must be a continuation of this note.]

1938/8/16 Cunard White Star to Hermine (Book 1, 92)

1938. August 16th.

We are responding to B. letter and attaching the Public National Welfare Ministry's permission to issue a passport.
With the document please apply to the district office there, at the passport department. The license for issuing the passport is in Hermina, Herman, Maria and Ignác names. Although it's a consulate decision, if there is Herman two times, it was a mistake, do not be worried. The emigration passport will be issued to all of you, please let us know about it. We will remember/note until then, With full respect, Cunard White Star

1938/8/16 Herman to Dezső (Book 5, 93-94)

1938, VIII/16.
Dear Dezső,
We have been waiting for your letter patiently. It took 25 days to receive it. You mailed it on July 25. On the same day we received the registered letter also. I can't write down how happy you have made all of us. In one day two letters came. We have been waiting for it for two weeks, 'double or nothing'. It is true that you are in the same position as we were, in reference to the letters. We mailed a letter on July 26 and we have not written anything since then up until today because we were waiting for your letter. Enclosed you will find one picture, similar to that which will be on the passport. With regards to the Torah, I can tell you that we will take it, but whether it will be belonging to the community or ours, at this time, I cannot tell you for sure. Do not be angry that I write only briefly, however, God will help, and we will be there shortly, then I will double what I missed this time. I wish you everything the best in good health. With loads of love, your little brother, Herman.

PS. Individually to Uncle Jónász and the family.

1938/8/16 Ignác to Dezső (Book 5, 95-96)

[This letter was with the one before, but has a separate file]

Don't feel sad that I write to you so briefly at this time. I hope that you will understand me. Next time I will write to you more in detail. The police were out here taking pictures. If they come back, and if I can, I will buy a picture from them. I will mail it to you. When you write next time use a different envelope because this can be opened from three different sides. In Budapest's they have censored the letter. I hope that you do not feel badly that I write so badly today. If you cannot read it, please let me know!! The rest of the family must have written to you about everything. Grandfather sends his regards to you. Uncle Lajos from Lelesz asks about you and sends his regards. A lot of people were called in for military service. You probably know more news than we do here. In Lelesz, business permits have been taken away from Lefkovics and Herskovics. Not everyone is in such a situation. Kisses to you from your little brother Ignác.
In the near future I will try to write better and more. Now we are going to go to the field to cut grass for the horses.

[On the side of the first page] For the home guard training they gave us to wear on holidays black pants and white shoes.

1938/8/16 Uncle Lazar Gluck to Dezső (Book 5, 64)

Bodrogmező, 1938 August 16

Dear precious nephew Dezső?
I am very sorry that I have written such a short letter that there wasn't much to read----? but that is not a serious thing. I thank God, I'm well and in good health and I hope that you are not missing that either. Please give my brother Jónász and his wife my regards. Also, not knowing Arthur and his wife, give my respect and kisses and all the good wishes to all of you. I just received a letter from my daughter Bertha. I have just written to her also. My respects to them and I wish them good health. Be happy, your mourning uncle until the end. Lazar Gluck.
I would like to be there for an hour with you to drink a glass of wine. Wishing happiness to all our relations, by the above.

1938/8/16 Undated Uncle Lazar to Uncle Jónász (Book 1, 108)

[Dated by his request for a long letter from Aunt Helen. She sends one, and Hermine mentions it in her letter of 1938/9/5]

My dear little brother Jónász and sister-in-law Helen,
Do not think that I wish you to write me so often, but the love of siblings bring it to itself, so one can talk things out through the letters. Otherwise…my sister-in-law Helen, I expect that you will write me a long letter. The kids don't hold you back, so they would not be your excuse that there is nothing to write about. I am, thank God in good health, and I hope you don't miss that as well. I will close my lines. I kiss you and hug you, your faithful brother and brother in law, Lazar Gluck

1938/8/17 Ignác to Dezső (Book 5, 76-77)

My dear brother Dezső, Live to 120!
I have received your letter and it was very difficult to wait for it. It took 25 days. I don't no why it took so long. It arrived at the same time as the express letter, but [despite] all of that I was happy to know that thank God, you are in good health and that is the most important. I am, thank God, in good health, too. Don't be angry that I am just writing now that we received from Prague! on the 30th! the approval. The only reason we have been delayed, we were waiting to hear from you. We began to make passports for all four of us. Imagine! A few days later, a little annoyance. Our father went to the passport office and they said that I need to have a permit. Our father came home and went to the Lelesz office, and [they] said that I don't need any because it begins at age 17, and I am not 17 yet. He said if they demand it, then he will write an official letter and he will take care of it. I just remembered that you went to the doctor. Did you receive any money from the doctor, due to the fire that you had? Please write and let me know about it. Don't be angry that I

do not write more because I only think to write to you what I think is interesting to you. I hope everything will be fine! I will write to you more next time, loads of kisses to you, Forever, Your little brother, Ignác 1938/VIII/17

P.S. Reply at once! I am learning the English language, slowly- and a lot!

Szinykoné her book is very good, she does not want to sell it.

[In English] Good By!

1938/8/22 Jolan Mayer to Dezső (Book 4, 251-252)

Szatmar
1938 VIII 22
Dear Dezső!

I can't imagine why you haven't written to me in such a long time. I ask many times, why not? Did I say anything to hurt your feelings? I don't know if I did, and don't recall any reason. Dear Dezső, I heard some bad news that I have to tell you. I wrote to Bertha about it, too. I was notified it would take 2 years from here to be able to get the visa. Can you imagine, how sick I am now after waiting so long. My hope is all gone. And the disappointment that goes along with it. I can't imagine what I will do now? I can't even dream about it. I wrote to Bertha that maybe she can try something in America. Maybe from there she could do more to help me to get out faster. From here there's nothing I can do. It's a dead end. Maybe if I had some money, I could go in person to the consulate in Bucharest and do something. As it is, it's hopeless and I don't know what else to do. It is a terrible situation and it makes no sense. I never even thought that this would happen. Today I received a letter from Bertha. She advised me to write to you and maybe you can help. She sent some papers. I'm trying to take care of it. I just mailed a letter from the consulate to Bertha. She can translate it and she will see what they write. Dear Dezső, try to speak to cousin Arthur. Maybe he can help in some way. Maybe he has more authority as an American businessman and he could help me. Maybe he can do something. Bertha wrote that Arthur sent a letter to her. He is willing to help with anything, but Bertha does not want to bother him at this time. She asked me to write to you Dezső because maybe you will be able to help me. Therefore you speak to him. I would appreciate whatever help you can give me. If I could write in English I would write to him, but as you know, I can't. I'm too far from that. You are very capable, please would you try to speak to him on my behalf. If I cannot get any help from anywhere I'll have no choice but to mail back the papers. There isn't any reason I should keep it here any longer for after two years it will expire and I will need new papers. Dezső, I was thinking of something, but hope you're not going to be angry at me. Let's say that there is a young man who is an American citizen, and he is willing to come and get married. Maybe this way, as his wife, I would have a chance to come to America sooner and with less complications. Afterwards he could do whatever he wants, with no obligation to me, and we could separate. I'm trying to think of everything that could be possible. I think so much that I'm making myself sick because of it. From here I can't do too much. I know you are very smart and will find a way to help me. I want you to use your judgment in whatever way you can help me. I will follow your instruction, whatever you want me to do. I appreciate whatever you do to try to help me. I haven't heard from you for a long time. And in the last letter you did not answer me, even though I asked you a very important question. I've wondered why? I am still waiting for that reply from you. I will have to mail back the paper to the American Consulate explaining why I do not have any answer for them at this time. I am going to wait for your answer before I mail back the paper. I hope you will answer as soon as possible and before you do, that you will talk to Arthur. I received the picture from Bertha it seems you didn't receive any picture from what she sent. It came out very nicely. My mother cried when she saw it, but what can she do. She felt helpless. My parents tried to accept the thought that I will go to America, but now I don't know what will be. I'm so obsessed with the idea, but I should not worry so much. I was so sick because of that. I lost a lot of weight. I was hoping that I will go somewhere and here is one disappointment after another. Now the time is come, my parents have accepted it, and they definitely want me to go, but I can't because if I leave I have to report the 2,000 lira, and until my little sister gets married I can't go anywhere. Therefore I just keep on complaining to you and mentioning to you. If you would write to Bertha on my behalf maybe she wouldn't be so angry at me. She always thinks I want something from her. I try to be very careful when I write to them, but I'm so full with that feeling. I can't even write anyone about how I feel. It's impossible to imagine what I'm going through. Therefore, I'm writing to you hoping you will understand. I think dear Dezső that I've written enough. I hope I did not disturb you too much with my headache. The one thing I'm asking you is to try and speak with cousin Arthur. He is the only hope I have. Please write me at once. My dearest mother thinks the reason you aren't answering my letter is because I did not write to your sisters. I haven't written to them at all. It seems they've forgotten all about me. Give my kisses to our dear Uncle Jónás bacsi and his wife and his son Arthur, and to you especially, your cousin, Jolan

My dearest mother and my father send their best wishes and love to you all. Please answer me right away. I'm waiting very restlessly for your answer.

1938/8/26 Father and Hermine to Uncle Jónász (Book 4, 191-192)

Polány August 26 1938

My dearest brother Jónász and my dearest sister-in-law Helen. I received your letter, thank God you are well. I received your gift of 476 Korona. That is what I received here for it about 2 weeks ago. They notified me that there is a package in my name with a note and I have to sign it to give them the right to examine what is in [the package.] I did. As of now, I did not hear from them or [know] what happened to the package. I didn't hear from Dezső. About the papers I submitted to the office about my son Hersmendel, now the question is, will they allow him to leave this country. Also my son Ignác because he is 17 years of age. If it will be okay then we have to mail the passport to Prague. There is another question, if I could sell the house by then, the city will have to agree. The man who is in charge was on vacation and he has to okay it. I'm in agreement with their lawyer. He understood that there were only 20,000 korona earmarked for housing. The offer was that. And now for 1939, the expenses are not allowed to go more than 18,000 korona. If I agree to that price they would pay me by January.

In case I still want 20,000 korona, they have to pay now, before the supervisor dismisses the case because he requested a new agreement, too. If that happens now, they have to have another okay from those city leaders who are in charge. And now the 20,000 koronat will be earmarked for housing next year. Next week the notary will do it again on Tuesday because he was anxious. He didn't want to do anything until I gave him 2,000 korona. He may have taken two more years, and I lost more than I should have, just because I wanted to give them the money to be sure the deal will go through as soon as possible.

Our brother-in-law Izidor told me not to speculate [take a chance] because [better] to give him the work to do one month earlier while the city leaders were not here at home, even if I had to. But now I don't know what will be, how long it will be delayed and when will we hear when they will be able to leave. The lawyer told me he will try to help me whatever he can. When the notification is okay for my children to leave, they will have to go to Prague to pick up the visa so they could leave at once. I am sorry I am bothering you so much my dear brother Jónász, With all my best wishes and my love, many kisses from my heart to you, my sister-in-law, and your children. Your brother, Gluck Jeremias

I also wanted to wish you all the best and many kisses you my Uncle Jónász bacsinak and your family, with my love, your niece, Hermina.

1938/9/3 Grandfather Samuel Schwartz to Dezső (Book 5, 48-49)

Lelesz 1938 September 3

[It was still Czechoslovakia until October 28,1938 - Irv]

My dear, precious grandson Dezső, I wish you as much good as the many teardrops I shed while reading your letter and which [fell] on the one I am writing on to you. You have journeyed from me so that I will not see you again and you're taking the other members of our family from us. It pains me a lot. I have never expected it. God has given them that. I would like to ask you while we are alive, don't forget about us, because every day passes by as if we would have strength--------. I really understand a lot about you from your writings and your well-being and if you can, don't forget the religion that is sweet, our dear religion, you have always to keep it in mind a lot and it will help you.------ I am happy that you are keeping the Sabbath.----- and that is a big deed and [as for] the rest, think to yourself that I wish you could do that. I will not write more except that thank God I and your grandmother are healthy. I gave your letter to my son Lajos. With our love and kisses to all our relations individually with respect. And give your uncle and his son our best regards, from our heart forever, with respect from your grandfather and your grandmother. The business has been going thus far for us, the only thing we should have is health. I'm asking for a reply. I wrote with a pencil because I do not have a pen. I wish health to all of you. Samuel Schwartz Lelesz to 120.

Polány September 5, 1938.

Dear Dezső my son,
I got your letter that I waited so hard for, and I'm very happy that, thank God you are in good health. I'm very surprised that you already know about Uncle Jónász's nature, that you need to obey him and leave everything to him based on his mood and do everything the way he wants, so there will be no trouble. It's been already a week since I got a letter from Helen in German. She wrote that Uncle Jónász can't take the annoyance that you did to him. You told him that you will write to your siblings not to come to America. Well, he wrote the same, that he will have more annoyance, so it's better if they stay home. He is a sick man. He won't be able to stand it. I did not respond to him yet. I will write to him tomorrow too, just don't forget anything also and be good. Now, I will go to Helmec to the office about Hersmendel's document, if it came already. The gendarmes were there, but while there is no dismissal, we can't proceed with it. As soon as it arrives, I will let you know. The notary will arrange everything today also. The tobacco, thank God can remain, so we must have a finished barn that is at least 8 meter long. And we have to tear down the eaves. I expect to have something done to its place, but I don't have a korona/dime yet. I'm going to the wood trader to see if he will give me any of the main material.

It's approximately 3000 kronen to replace the roof with tile. I couldn't secure a place for the tobacco, therefore we had to fix this one. I took the envelope with the handkerchief to the post office Lady. It had a stamp on it also. She will write to you soon. The fellow that used to give out your letters to me asked me to ask you for some stamps. There's not much more that I can write. I remain with best wishes with love and kisses, your true father, that will never forget you. Gluck Jeremias

Dear Dezső,
We received your letter which we were very happy [that] thank goodness you're all right.
Also we received one a day before from our aunt Helen. I can't even imagine what happened there that she would write that letter to us. And also we haven't heard from you for such a long time we thought that maybe it got lost, but now I can understand the reason. I hope my letter will find you well. We thank goodness are well. I hope we will hear better news in the future. I hope this will pass and it will be better for all of us. After the bad news will come the good. Otherwise nothing special. I spoke to Lipot Klein the other day. He mentioned that he did not hear from you yet. I hope next time you will make up for not writing to him. He expects that in the future you will remember him. We will write more often. He sends you his best wishes and many kisses from his family also. Dear Dezső, we received the hairstyling machine you sent me. You're very observant and I thank you very much. I will use it after every time I wash my hair. It costs too much if I want to have it done here. And with this maybe I can save all that money. We already tried it, and it is very beautiful. Can you imagine, who ever saw it they can't get over how beautiful it looks. They ask us to do it for them also. We told them you have to have long hair to do that. Malvin Lefkovics could not believe that you are so attentive to mail us this machine. This week Szeré nénni is going to write to you because you deserve the best. She read the letter you wrote to them over and over. They should not ignore it without answering that letter soon. You know very well she is a very smart lady. You can imagine what goes on in her mind. She mentioned to Malvin that you could help her to come to America. You should ask our Uncle Jónász for a guarantee and she will pay back all the expenses. We told them you can't even think about because he will not do it. He has enough family who needs to get out. As you see there are types of people who don't care how, but expect to have everything they want. The best thing is to ignore it. We will talk about that in person when we are there. At this time, I think I wrote enough. I hope it will not be boring. Now many kisses to you and I remain with love. Also, give my best wishes to our family. Your sister, with love. Mariska.

[From Hermine]
Dave Dezső.
We received the letter. At first, it wasn't very pleasant to hear [what was written], but it's besides the point [because] it already happened. Our father wanted to write to you immediately, but since today is Friday we

would like to write to you right away. It is unbelievable what Uncle Jónász wants to do. Maybe it's best just to ignore it. I hope with our God's help we will be able to get out sooner, and he will help us. We received a letter from Aunt Helen. She mentioned that our uncle asked her to write to us because he doesn't have the strength. He was deeply hurt when you told him you will write to us that we should stay at home. He does not want us to come there. You didn't appreciate what he's trying to do to help us. In this case, when people get older, they become very nervous. You have to forget about it and ignore it. I was thinking we can stand anything if we have to. The situation here is getting very complicated. I had a similar experience with Schőn. I was trying to prepare chicken in her place. She wanted us to have it for the trip because she promised us, but it seems she was looking for an excuse to be angry. The whole thing came out and she was asking for the 500 korona that we owe. Somehow she found out that Lajos was delivering some wheat. For this our father gave them 200 korona and at this time he cannot give anymore. She should understand that we haven't received anything from the house yet and we've had so many expenses for the papers. If she had any feeling for us
she would understand and try to help us, instead of demanding. She called me on Friday. I went over the next day on Saturday and she wasn't very nice. I told her off also. Now I'm saying goodbye to her. The dog doesn't deserve it. I just walked out. Our Uncle Leizer was visiting us since he's not angry even though none of us are visiting them, not even the children.

1938/9/5 (b) Undated Hermine to Dezső (Book 1, 115-116) page 3-4

We got the card from Jolanka from Szatmar and we only waited with the response because our father wanted to write about everything accurately. Jolanka wrote that she sent the birth certificate already and asked to arrange the documents so we can travel together. I hope it will work out and God will help us soon enough, because we are all very impatient and it's hard to wait the time out. It would be great if the sale of the house would work out also. We are hoping.

Other than that we are well. Everybody is wondering about you. And, if our traveling will be successful, I will whistle to everything. [I will not care about anything]. I would have written to Uncle Jónász, but I sent the letter already, which would not be necessary anyway and maybe he would have felt badly that I bother him. I would have written him only because you wrote that our father should write, but I wrote. I kiss you, Hermin

1938/9/5 (c) Undated Hermine to Dezso (Book 5, 18-19) page 5-6

Here I am noting an address from Weizer, the hat makers. These are their relations. They're very wealthy. They would be very happy if you would talk to them and to help them to get a guarantee to go to America. They would pay all expenses. Both of them know how to make hats. If you can do it for them. They wrote to you before, but it wasn't important. I'm only mentioning it to you because they are waiting for a reply. Her mother translated the letter. This person has translated Arthur's English letter perfectly. As a child she was in America. The present situation is such that a person must ask favors. Our father traveled to Ungvár to clarify an Insurance claim that he paid already. Love, from Hermina.
The address is as follows:
Mr.. M. L. Bayer
922 South 22nd Street.
Columbus, Ohio, America.
The new address is;
M.L. Bayer, Atlas building.
8 East Long Street
Columbus, Ohio, America.

1938/9/5 Undated Jane Fabianova to Dezső (about shipping packages) (Book 5, 273)

[Dated by finance department settlement, so I think they're still living in Czechoslovakia, not Hungary and reference to mailing with a fabric package that Hermine referenced before sending it without silk. Therefore, the letter should be around here.]

Dear Dezső!
Thank God that we are alive and well, but I have too much work so I will write only briefly. Your Dear father settled with the finance department completely, and I'm very happy that it came out ok. It is better to send things in a fabric package, but wait until you receive the gift shipped to you and then you can ask how they mailed it out. Best wishes, Jane

New York
Sept 7 / 38
Dear Dezső!
I got your letter also. The telegram does not help much because the ship ticket was bought in Czechoslovakia. This way they can't give any information here in the Cunard Lines office until the ship arrives. I am calling the offices every day until then. This is what they recommended. They did not want to take my visa because they said that if they would write it for everybody who calls them, then there would not be an end nor length to it. I should not bother them with this. But you should not worry because I am paying attention to the ship arrivals. Everything is going to be fine my dear Dezső. And we can't keep the boys here because they don't have a place to sleep. You know our apartment well. You wrote that I should send Jolanka's letter. Yes, I'm sending it here. I will forward to Jolan the letter from Arthur that was sent to me also. Maybe he sent that to the Consul, too. I don't understand why it was being denied?

If dear Arthur would be so kind and write to the Consul, and find out what could be the reason that Jolan had to wait for so long, I'm sure that he will get an answer to that. You know it well that I am also very busy. I don't even know who to turn to in this case. But do you know what I was thinking? If maybe Manny and I would have sent documents to her, maybe that would have been better, because we are an Aunt and Uncle to her. Find out somehow and then we will send it to her, too. The fact that we did not send it to her sister [Iren] was her fault because we were going to send the documents to her, but then we changed our minds. And also they were waiting for Jolan to come and I thought that Arthur's affidavit is going to be enough.

Maybe by the time he writes his request the quota will get filled up for me. They said at the office that in one year you can't come in for sure, but it will take two more years for Jolan to come here. I was surprised about your letter because I thought in the office here that maybe they did not know what they were talking about. Dezső you also bring up the letter that Arthur got from the Consul in Bucharest. You will see that they will not say that they will be in a hurry to get Jolan's passport, but they will say that they are "saluting the law" [saluting/following the law] I can't pronounce this in Hungarian - to take action that she got the documents back. I think she will be under the [quota] numbers so she will have to wait until she gets her turn. They told me that here, too. Dezső, I can't do anything about her case. And I don't even think that anything can be done with money.

I wish we could do something to rush her coming out. But my Dezső it is childish to be so worried like Jolan is. It is not helping, rather it will give health problems. And will that be better? My Dezső, I believe that it is your fault because until you came here, none of them wanted to come here to America. I am not surprised that Jolan has no money to go for a change of air and does not take much from her grandfather's dowry. Dezső, I can't help anyone. You know that well. We have enough [people] in the family that need help. Now I'm asking you not to send telegrams because they scare me. I almost jumped out of my skin when it came. There is more for Jolan you write whatever you want. You see I'm exhausted, God forbid…Kisses, Bertha

Dear Father,
I got the letter today, the one that you sent to Uncle Jónász's address. He brought it from the factory, but he didn't talk to me. I didn't go in, but it's better that way. I don't want to get along with him, because it would end the same way again. I don't know the reason why, but I wrote a letter and sent it by air mail on August 17th and on the 26th our father wrote, but it didn't arrive. I don't know the exact dates about my letters, but I sent it twice by airplane because it's simple. The last one went registered and by air. The one from today, will also go that way. Therefore, I will send the exact facts shortly. As from the attached letter from Bertuska, you can see that she already found a place for one in New York, but by the time they get here, both girls will have places. I would say they should thank God that they will stay there, because if they want to keep their religion, they can be the type of Jew they want to be. There are opportunities for everything, but here it's not the case. There are many Jews, but they live spread out from each other in too many different places. There is a Hungarian Jewish synagogue, where the family goes, and there is one for Russian Jews where I say kaddish, and there is one for German Jews, Eskenez, I will go to that. Unfortunately, you can't do it any

other way, but still, I want to go to the temple. Here it is not like at home, you need to take the tramway anyway, because if I don't go to the temple, I still will want to go [to that area], because I won't sit in the factory and the heart of the city is 7km, therefore I can't help it. Tomorrow I will go to the temple. I was in the Jewish store this week. I bought some canned food to eat, but it is truly Jewish, because it's tasteless, because it was made with coconut. It says on it that [it contains] no meat nor milk. It goes like this for a few years now, for the families. It's easier because they can buy kosher goose, chicken…etc. Therefore, the boys will come here straight after they arrive, and it's possible that the longest they can stay in New York is one day. There is no place for them there and a guest room costs a lot. So don't feel badly [that it will be] this way, that the girls will stay there. It has to be that way. They can have their budget until Columbus, if they stay there. So they will buy whatever they will need. They can't be without their needs. But none of them should buy the train tickets at home, there is time [to do that here] and the money should be saved, because if they won't let them go, they will be like I was. Therefore, they have to have money to show it. I got a card from Arthur. He is letting me know that they will arrive home next week. Poor Jolanka from Szatmar got denied by the consul. She can only get a visa after two years. But if Arthur comes home, he is going to recommend it. Maybe it's worth it to try. Why don't the girls write to him? Poor thing, he got sick. He lost 48 kg. The doctor recommended a change of environment, but there is no money for that. So I will announce that they have to follow orders and do the way I recommend it. They already know that the girls will not come here. But there will be time to come here, if it's not going to be good there. There it will be better. I wish I could have stayed there too. It would be so much better for me. Don't forget! That is the world's first city. There is an opportunity for everything there. But here it's almost like in Polány. The Father recommended, because the lady told him, not to look for company. It is stupid, but please don't tell him that…since I'm not a hermit. I'm a young man and I only have two days [off]. Should I spend it locked up, like him? I'm not saying that I have to party, but the boys I hang out with are not the party type. They are good boys and if you plan to learn the language it's better. It's a must to get together with people. That is what Arthur recommended. Now, I point it out that when Father, you will say: [In Yiddish] Erhat Kein zitzfleis nicht [He doesn't have the will to sit still], but still, I'm thinking how I can go to some place else, because as I can see here, time goes very slowly such that during the day, it won't be a lot of work and at night guard duty will start. From October 1st, I'll need to stay up every night and sleep during the daytime, which would not be a problem, but the factory is outside of town, in a desolate, scary place. Arthur said that there is no need for a revolver. I would not even get a permission for it. I only have a "billy club". But, if anything were to happen, if I couldn't get to a telephone because someone was breaking in, it wouldn't be acceptable for me to hit them with a club, or I would call for the police. However, I don't like this place and I won't let the 2 boys [come] to this hotel. Why? Because if there is something better, an apartment for $60 a month, approximately, I would need $10-$15 for the 2 boys. This way the monthly cost is $30 for each of them. So, that's not a good deal. Besides, it's still summer, so no need for the coal and nobody is stealing it. But here everyone has fuel for fire. I saw homes in poverty a few days ago. They don't have anything to eat and their clothing is ripped. Although they are vagabonds, they don't want to work for cheap. They would rather live on city welfare. They will go to steal, I'm sure, because where we are, it's still summer. They will not steal coal, rather they steal the wheels from the wheelbarrow. It was in another building, since here we can walk on the roof, because it's flat. Therefore, it was not so high up. They could climb in through the chimney and they stole it that way. They called the police to come the next day because of the theft and they are there today again. I'm not going out at night because I can't sleep. I can't sleep many nights because after 9- they bring the coal and then after midnight they bring it again 2 or 3 times, so I can't sleep. I think I know when the theft happened. It was on Monday night when I heard that something flew/glided under my window. I went out through the window, but where I saw them, the grass was as tall as a man. So I didn't go there. Later I heard a hammering noise. At 12 o'clock at night the coal truck came and they got scared from it and they ran away. Three weeks ago, during the daytime, they climbed into the factory through the window. When I'm in the city and my fruit was outside, they eat it. It's possible that they were kids because they are very bad. Therefore, I thought it will be necessary for me to stay because there is no better place, but I will not leave the 2 boys in a nice, friendly place, like this. But I will work on getting a revolver because even the two phones are worth nothing. But forget it. So, it's very important to write to Bertuska about when will they leave so she can wait for my siblings by the ship. Write to her immediately because she said that for days we don't know anything. She calls the ship company everyday and inquires about the Gluck family's arrival. She is very impatient and she deserves to know. We have to let her know. This is the situation, but don't say a word. About what I wrote to the postlady, what I saw here on a girl, but when I was in the store, I looked at it, but it's like cardboard and I need silk. I walked through the stores here, but I couldn't get any or it's not something she needs. She wants it with blue swallows on white fabric. And here they have the opposite. But it can't be gotten from America because it's from Paris. The most delicate silk

1 yard 80 centi[meters wide] is almost $2. But I asked the company how much it costs and if they can get it for me. [If they can] I can send it home by October 10th. So I'm waiting on the information these days because he let the main New York express purchaser know to check out every similar sample and [place the] order for the required fabric. So they must have it without fail. If that won't work, then I will arrange for the company from Paris to ship it [directly] to the lady. But she is obsessed by this and she has to have that fabric. She deserves it, even if it would cost double. She has to see that I did not want it for free, but I'm afraid that the fabric will not be enough. But don't put me to shame because I wrote. I don't want her to think that I gave back the guarantee paper, she doesn't care about me, I know. That's why I want it with interest, so I can replace it. I will write next week to Cechi with registered mail. I will demand the abstract [statement] from him. And I will warn him, if he doesn't settle up, I will [file a] report to Dunn and Bradstreet that his company does not settle up with his traveler. They will put it on the black list. Unfortunately, there is no proof left. Everything has burned [in the fire], but I hope he will deal with this. I believe, I wrote enough. I was clear about everything, because everything is going so hard. But we can't help it. If we would have to wait for two years, it would be even sadder. I'm sorry that I don't send money now. But when my siblings come, I have to send money to Bertuska so she can buy anything they need. I don't know how much, approximately I will send $10-15. I hope everything is going to work out well. Many kisses Father. Until I will see you again. Your faithful son, Dezső

My Dear siblings, Herminka, Mariska, Herman and Ignacka.
I'm sorry that I write everything together, but I wrote everything to Father already. So, I'm only doing this so we don't get anyone angry. Although, only Ignác and Mariska wrote to me with the letter for Uncle Jónász's, it's ok. Although, I waited for a meaningful letter, but as I can see, my airplane letters did not arrive before the regular letters, but I will send this the same way, anyway. Maybe this will get there sooner. Without fail, I wish it will be that way. Will you boys come here? Don't be sad! You will not have to eat dry bread, even if you will not work. I will make sure that I will cook well for you, even if it's not like from a restaurant. Even if the great Uncle will not give any, so don't worry. Although, don't forget, I will have the most trouble with you, because I will have to keep you safe and take good care of you all. You shouldn't be in a situation like I was. Additionally, if you want to see something, only with me in a way that I will be on every picture, because with our uncle you will only get to the middle of the room. I better tell you before, so it will not be like in Polány. It depends on you, if you will be ok. I will give you my last cent, even if I won't have any left. But, if you will be the way you want to be, then you will be like I was with our dear uncle. That's why, I try to spare you from that, because I know what that is like. So the girls should stay with cousin Bertuska and they will be happy with her. Although, the boys could stay there too, but what would the uncle say, only that that's an impossible thing. For the boys, there are two suits here, not new, but in good condition. They are good for Ignácz and Herman and there is one winter coat too that's good for Herman. I will not buy anything, until they come here, so it will be proper for them. But, you girls, without any fail, I will wait every week for you to write about everything. But, if I don't see that I can get for you a nice place there, then I will work on keeping the family together, like I wrote many times.
Columbus is not really modern and nice, but it wouldn't matter at all, if I could study English. I would love to leave this place because there is no hope for a good ending, because a lot of stores are closed and there is no traffic at all, you can only earn about $20-$50 because Ohio is more like an agricultural country. Everyday I look at the ads in the newspaper, but they are only looking for farmers or otherwise, agents with weekly traveling cost. They cover $10-$20, besides that proviso, it is the way it is. I don't know what to do with Grunberger's book. Next week I will write to more Hungarian newspapers. I will ask for advice. If there would be a Jewish newspaper in English, it would be possible to get it translated, which is faster, but it would cost a fortune. The hourly payment costs at least $1, but it could be more...I hope that from my many letters, you understand everything. You know, I will never forget it if you don't do as I say, because I was up many nights until I wrote everything exactly the way it is to you. Everything I wrote is based on my experience and is for your own good, therefore, if you won't do the way it is, it's not my fault. And, if you will do exactly like I said, then God help me with his power, to hold my back for everything. I don't know anything special. Write to Jolanka without fail, because she is very sad. I wrote to you, to Bertuska, and Jolanka today. I really get tired from writing, since I have to write to everybody. So, do it in a way so I don't have to write everything to each one of you separately. Come here and see that I only told the truth and verify the truth. Next week, I will send out the New Year's greetings. I will send the list of names to whom I sent them to. I hope you will be here for the holidays already. Although, I recommended it to our father, if he wants to go in a strange/foreign land to synagogue, I will cover the cost. But wherever Father will be, even if in Lelesz, the entire family will cover everything during the holidays. In the beginning of next week, I will send my old debt. No matter how much it will cost, just please buy it [a holiday seat?]. If it's possible,

please buy the Maftir for grandfather, either day of Rosh HaShana. But, no need to tell him that I wrote this, but you can tell him that it was my wish, that it will be that way.

Boys, it will not feel good to be in a big strange place, but anyway, it will be better here, because you won't be alone. I know, on the boat you will suffer, but you know, I saw a movie this week, where a family goes to see Paris from America. It demonstrates that when they are on the ship they get really sick. They throw up whatever they eat. I got a big laugh about it, because when others get sick I laugh, but when I was coming, I wailed/suffered. But, it's ok. It will go away after the first two days. Everything is going to be ok. Do not take the advice of anyone in Polány, when they say it's better not to eat. It's not true. You need to ask a doctor, he will tell you also, that it's easier to throw up from a full belly, than from an empty one because [on an empty stomach] you only start [to throw up] and that is even worse. It's ok if it will come out. Eat again, because it only happens from the dizziness. If you will come with a small ship, it won't be that bad. Since it [sails] slower, you will not get dizzy. The best medicine is to be outside on the deck. Second, walk around and around quickly, in a way that's in synch with the ship's movement, [you won't] get so dizzy that way. Eat and drink as much they give you. If it's not enough, then ask for more. Don't worry about anything. When the girls or boys are sick, and they want to eat, they will bring the food up to them, because there are many who are weak and can't go down because of their sickness. When I was coming, the young people were dying, especially the women were throwing up every second, but there was a 76 year old lady, who did not have any problem. She was okay because she drank palinka [Hungarian liquor]. It really is a good medication, but if it gets you drunk, you don't know what's happening to you. A little isn't worth anything. There has to be a big bottle of sosborszesz [salty wine, another type of liquor, used for medication]. And something with a strong smell, like patarck dust [a smelling salt] that you will also need. Besides that, you can bring anything you want. They don't declare what you need. Now I'm thinking, if maybe there won't be space available for blankets [Dunná a large puffy blanket], then the 2 boys can bring them here, but don't bring too much because there is not too much space to put them and it will only cause trouble. You know, there are beautiful camisoles, silk, you can buy here, from 25 cents. Underwear from 25¢. So there is a lot of stuff that is cheap, but stockings are very expensive. In part because they come from there to here, so it is worth it to bring them from there. So you don't have to buy them here, but only good ones in nude colors. You know for 78¢ and $1 there are beautiful purses. They are fashionable. Many are very expensive, but many are cheap, but you will be in New York, where you will buy everything for less money, because the sellers on the streets are very cheap. They are cheaper because they sell things from the stores that are wrinkled or dirty, because laundry is expensive. A little sleeping ware is 10¢, a shirt is 12-15¢, underwear 10¢, and for that much you can buy 2 pieces for 25¢. It's not worth it to have them washed too much. I have countless stuff like this in my bag already. They are waiting for some good luck. If I can get the [post] lady's material, then I will send more packages. But, if not, then I will only send working clothes to Lajos, by the end of the year, that is iron strong. Although it's for the summer, he can dress under it warm in the winter. Also, for Emil it's a little too long, but it won't get ripped easily. Ties, like the Uncle sent home 10¢ per piece. It costs more by us. Also, I will send bubble gum, that everybody eats. Not tobacco. I believe, everyone better quit smoking, because one can chew one piece of gum for a half a day. So, if I will send a package, I will only send what is important and pays off, because it isn't worth it to send heavy stuff. But first of all, I will find out about that newspaper where it was written that we can send new things without declaring anything. If not, then I won't send anything, because it's not worth it. However, if it would be without declaring, then they wouldn't have opened father's package. I wonder, who sent it. I want to know, if I can get the lady's fabric, ho's address should I send it to, so it could go with out a declaration. I have to ask her, because we can only send 'used' stuff even in gift packages, as I understand it. Give me some poor person's address, so we can get the poverty certificate, then we don't need to declare anything. If I can get it, I will send it and will cover the cost for the [customs] declaration also. Here we can't pay it [the customs fee] afterwards, but he could find out about this in Prague. After $1 how much do we have to declare, because here we have to write out the price also. They declare it based on the price. It's enough for today. I am sending kisses to everyone, happy holidays, and good health. Good Bye, Dezső

1938/9/12 Bertha to Dezső (Book 5, 20-21)

New York
Sept 12 / 38
Dear Dezső,
Once again I'm rushing to reply to your precious letter. In my letter to Jolan, I wrote dear Arthur's address, all the family's names and their ages, too. I have copied it from the affidavit. I see Jolan did not sit down calmly, to read the content of the affidavit. Also my husband Mannie has written a letter explaining

everything for her exactly. I wrote in May to Arthur because of her letter, so he can see that she is not crazy, but I see that she is not a thoughtful girl and she does not use her head as her dear mother Sarolta used to do. What Sarolta wanted to do was to have her daughter get married. Dezső, you don't have to run your health down because of a girl so that her daughter Jolan can come out. She would help her so that she would be able to get married. All this had been arranged, after the Coresz [the problems], and to be sure after the children become adults legally, that shouldn't be painful for the girl that her sister gets married first. I'm glad I do not have any family because I only have heartaches from their children's parents because they cannot give the things that are necessary for the children. I do not know anything, I only know nothing [this phrase was written in Yiddish]. Dezső, do you think that your sisters will arrive for the Jewish new year? If not, then we would go, my husband and I, for a few days away because my nerves are wrecked. Perhaps this travel would help me now. Do you know what I was thinking, if Jolan cannot get her passport then she should come out as a visitor and extend her passport to make enough money that she could go to Canada and then could return to this country. Dezső, I cannot grab a man to marry my niece when she comes out here and after the wedding they could divorce. That would also cost a lot of money and I do not have it. And after that we will have the responsibilities, we have enough problems.

[On the top of the first page] Bertha and Mannie. I miss you.

1938/9/15 Uncle Marton to Dezső (Book 5, 101)

Dear Dezső to 120

Inasmuch as I have a headache, I applied a cold towel on my head, however your father was here and he had a letter opened and asked me to write a few lines to you. The situation has been very difficult and that is why I have a headache. I would like to switch with you. Don't upset Uncle Jónász, don't forget what he has done for you, accept everything in good faith, because he deserves it and one should not take it so seriously. Accordingly, you may ask for forgiveness and be polite. You will get further with good words than with words that are undesirable and in the front of others.....My hands are shaking, I will close these few lines because my headache is very painful. I'm wishing you..... Pleasant holidays. Pray in a religious temple and ask for the best of everything from God. Kisses, Marton.
Regards to the relatives and I wish them also good holidays.
M.
1938/IX/15

1938/9/17 Bertha to Dezső (Book 3, 358-359)

New York
Sept 17 / 38
Dear Dezső,
You have said that I should ask Jennie Fry to go to meet your family. My dear Dezső, in this country everyone is occupied and you know that, Jennie is in business and she is working to make a living. I would have liked, only if it is necessary, that one would stay and sleep in her place, but she doesn't have any place. Dezső, here everybody is for himself. You can't judge them because they don't have time for anything besides business. It will happen some way. Dezső, do you think that it's just my illness and nervousness in itself, you're mistaken. I don't advertise everything, brother, everybody has a problem. A person does not advertise everything telling everyone in the world so they must know everything as everyone says. Dear Dezső, if I would be you, I would not say a word to Uncle Jónász because he is still an old man, and with his personality it's always best if you're fine and be smart. Regarding his son, speak to him and Uncle Jónász, and you can accomplish much more than by being against them and spiteful. The son is like his father, if he would be mad he would not have written to Polyán. You must not know about this, as if you would not have known anything about it. It is a small situation and you must deal with the bigger problems. I will not write more at this time. I must go because they are waiting for me. Have a Happy New Year with love from Mannie and Bertha.
PS. Please think it over when you speak, it's easy to spit the words out, but it's difficult to take them back!

1938/9/28 Herman to Dezso (Book 5, 207-208) pages 1-2

1938/IX/28
Dear Dezső,

We received your letter. We were very happy to hear thank God it is better there for you than it was at home, and that you are well. My health is the same as when you were here. Sometimes it's better other times worse. Unfortunately, I can't go out for a few years. We have to keep quiet about going somewhere. We asked for some information from a lawyer. He told us that at this time it is impossible. They will not let you out. After I read your letter, he will look into it. In maybe four years maybe we will be able to go. Today people are not sure if even by then you can. They closed down the border or the exit. No one can leave. Believe that God willing it will be as it is. We cannot change it or do anything about it. You can write over for the name then I will be able to leave with the others. If I could save a little money here a penny. You know from yourself when you're here, you understand how it is out here for a person. It too late to talk about it. I would not write you about it. You know all about how the situation was when you were here. You always made a couple of pennies sometimes more, other times maybe less, but you had a chance. I wrote you before what happened. I believe in God. The weather is very bad, raining all the time for the whole month of April. I went for the army exam. There were 13 Jewish boys and they didn't take me this time. From the 2 Stark boys in Lelesz they took Mendu, the youngest Stark. The oldest is not well therefore they didn't take him. Also from Polány they took four. From this they took three of them and two they didn't. Therefore from Polány three soldiers.[illegible] I would not mind if they would take me, at least it would be over within two years. I wrote you about this. Maybe you are not interested to hear. From Lelesz they took 15 older Foroknak IV/ 23 [illegible] Svart Miki told me that because you didn't answer all the questions only a few words therefore he doesn't write. Wishing you good luck

1938/9/28 Undated Herman to Dezső (Book 4, 213-214) pages 3-4

He whistles to it, but we trust it and we hope that the black soup is still behind us. The good God will help us come in 4 or 5 years. And if God will keep us alive, only then the situation will turn out well. It would be good to live in Polyan, if there would be a well with money and we could always dip it out like water. It would be necessary. You know, Dezső, the iron needed to be hit while it was hot because now it's already too cold to hit. Now only patience helps. Kisses, your brother, Herman

I got a very bad pen and that is why it was not written so well and in a hurry, and it will be difficult to read.

It came to my mind too to write it to you. The post office in Lelesz will be taken away and replaced by a new one in Helmec. In Lelesz and Boly it happened because it comes out better for the state/government. It is like this everywhere not only here, but in general.

1938/10/4 Jolan Mayer (Romania) to Bertha re; Dezső (Book 5, 80-81)

Szatmar 938 X/4
[On top to Dezső] You do not have to mail it back to me, Bertha.

Dear Bertha and Uncle Mannie!
I can feel that you are unhappy with me that I am replying to your letter so late. I'm not at fault because I've written to the consulate again, that is, I translated that letter that Dezső sent to me. Arthur received a letter from the consulate about two weeks ago and I haven't received a reply. I do not understand it, since I was holding back with my reply to you since I thought that I could write you something worthwhile, something good, since that could have been helpful for us. I want to inform you that Friday my sister received her approved government application for their marriage on November 6. I can hardly wait that it should be over, since you know my dear Bertha, what it means in today's world, a poor man's daughter. I don't mind, since we hope that God will help us. Here enclosed you will find a picture that I just made for the passport. Accept it from me with great love, 'is being said', mailing it to you. Are Dezső's sisters there already? What are they doing? Please write about them also. Yesterday, we received a letter from our dear grandfather and he said in his letter that he would like to come to see us for the holiday [Szukasz]. I replied to him that he should definitely come and could stay for the wedding and thereafter. We are very happy that our grandfather is going to come. My mother is crying constantly. If you could come also and be with us at this time so that the family could get together, I know it's a difficult, long journey. Dear Bertha, please forgive me for not writing to you more at this time, but it is the evening of Yom Kippur and I have a lot of work to do and I also want to write to Dezső. Dear Bertha and Uncle Mannie, I am wishing you the very best of everything and a delightful holiday and everything should turn out as you want. With true love, your niece, Jolan

PS. Our parents are wishing you a happy New Year. They are not writing to you at this time, since I'm writing this letter from the store. Kisses, as above.

1938/10/4 Jolan Mayer (Romania) to Dezső (Book 5, 67-68)

Szatmar, 938/X/4

Dear Dezső!

I received your letter last week, but I didn't answer you until I received information from the consulate. I will note that I've written two weeks ago to them, but as of now I've not received a reply. I made a copy of that letter that you sent me and I mailed it to them, but I've not received a reply. Why? I do not know even though I mailed it registered. I don't have any news and I'm sure you don't have, or do you? I believe that now I can resign from going to America. As I digest this is it all true? I already have been aggravated a lot. I did not reply to Bertha because I was waiting [to hear] from the consulate, but I'm not going to wait [any longer]. I'm going to write. Hermin and the rest are they there? They must be very happy that they were so lucky. I only am waiting as it will be, it will be. Here I am enclosing my picture which I made recently for the passport. It turned out very well, accept it from me gladly. One of your nieces will be civilized. The wedding will be on Friday, November 6th, with God's help. I can hardly wait that it should be over, because I have a lot of things to do yet. Please Dezső, send the address of Uncle Jónász and Arthur, too, because we plan to send them an invitation. How are you otherwise? What are your brothers doing and the girls? Please write everything about them to me exactly, because you know I'm interested. Dear Dezső, at the present time I can't write a lot. I have to write to Bertha and it is the night before Yom Kippur and I have a lot of work yet. Give my best to dear Jónász bacsi, and best wishes for the New Year, also to Arthur and his family. At present I do not write to them individually, because you will give them our regards. It's true! I'm asking you to please write and let us know what the consulate has written and so forth...

Dear Dezső, I wish you all the best in the new year, lots of luck in everything and it should be the way that you wish, with love, your niece, Jolan

1938/10/7 Bertha to Dezső (Book 1, 178-179)

New York
Oct 7 / 38
Dear Dave!

I'm glad to find out that you will start to go to school. Just be diligent, because that is very important, particularly for a man. For you, the future looks good. If you will be diligent and you will listen to your cousin [Arthur], since like I understood from his letters, he is a very intelligent man and one could learn a lot from him. Listen to him, because he only wants the best for you, even if you have to work hard, but you will have an advantage because of it, with time. The knowledge that you get from being around a man like that, with his fine manners and wisdom, will make you happy. Dave, I hope you will understand, you [think] that you are very unlucky, but I don't believe it. It only takes time and you will see. [You'll begin] to understand this when you have more experience. Although, from the situation here, man is chased by his destiny. But sometimes it's good, because it gives a little enlightenment to the people. But enough about this, too. Dave, I wouldn't mind, if only we would know when your siblings will come here. They will be so tired from that big trip, that we would like them to stay in New York and they could see something about the city. God knows when they will be able to come back.

Dave, you just do everything like dear Arthur says. If he says that the girls should go there, yes they should try it. If not, then they will have to accept that. You just send them back to New York. My dear Dezső we can't annoy the uncle, because he won't tolerate it, and if they wouldn't allow it I wouldn't for myself, because the entire world would blame it on us. So you just look at this: whatever is assigned to whoever, we will find it anywhere. Look at this! We can't look at ourselves. We have to look at others as well. As I can see, our dear uncle wants the best. He doesn't understand better. He thinks that he is everything and we have to respect that and his years/age and we have to try to do what the heart wants to do for him because don't forget he has a big responsibility, if he will undertake himself for everybody. Now I'm asking you not to talk to your siblings. Not even a word about how sweet your American life has been here. Let them get familiar about it by themselves. This way things won't hurt them as much. Just ask them to have a lot of patience. It is your duty to bring them to visit with our dear uncle and be gentle with them. And do things the way our Uncle likes it. You cannot catch flies with vinegar.

Be thankful for your late mother's picture that he sent to you. You should think that you are dealing with a small child and this way you will feel better. The "lamb will stay in shape and the wolf will be well fed too" [a saying]. Now, I am kissing everybody with love. Bertha

1938/10/11 Herman to Dezső (Book 4, 187-188)

Dear Dezső,

I was very happy to read your letter, but I don't even know how to begin to write this letter to you. I can see how they say it's your luck. If you are meant to be lucky sometimes it just happens to be and if not you can't do too much about it. If you have money, you can do anything you want. You could go or do anything you wish. I'm sorry we are not that lucky. We can't do what we would like. I am hoping our God will save us and help us. We will have a better day with his help. Please take care of yourself. Our health is more important than anything else. We must have patience I understand. You must have strength because it is very difficult to wait. Thank goodness we are alive. About the trip, I think the girls wrote to you what is going on. Therefore I can't tell you more. About the tobacco, it's not ready yet. I wasn't notified yet when we are supposed to deliver it to them. I'm sure it will be sometime in January. I estimate about 3, 3.50 Czech korona. We are worried because we do not know in advance what it will be. I wish we would be there already. I hope it would be better for you also. Please write as soon as possible. Every day we are waiting for your letter to hear from you and because of that, we delay our writing, too. We stopped going to shul ever since we have the problem here. By the rule change, you can go with your family to temple. Today's weather is heavy snow, and very cold. The cold winter started too soon. The situation now changed a couple days ago. They took Lajos to serve in the army. I hope God will help him there. I hope for the best it will get better. The situation is serious. Now I want to wish you all the best, good health, happiness, and many kisses. Your brother. With all my love, Herman.

[The letter was written by our brother Herman to Dave from the time the Hungarians in control of part. I typed this letter in the computer 10/2/012 - by Maria.]

1938/10/11 Undated Emil Gluck to Dezső (Book 4, 231-232)

[dated by Rosh HaShana, Lajos to the army, to Dezso only]
[this letter is written by my 9 year old nephew, our brother Lajos' son.]

Dear Uncle Dezső,

I hope you're not going to be angry because you did not hear from me for such a long time. I hope you will write to me [and] you do not forget me. When my grandfather wrote to you I wasn't here. I was away in school at that time. I was in Lelesz. From now on I promise I will write to you all the time. From now on I will go to school here at home. Tibi [Miksa Schon's son] came home from Helmec because we do not have any more Slovakia. Dear Uncle Dezső, ever since I did not write to you or you didn't hear from me, many things happened to us. My dearest father had to go to the Army to the town of Homokra to serve as a soldier. He also had to take the horses with him and the wagon before the holiday, Erev Rosh HaShana. You could imagine how we felt, the heartache, crying you cannot imagine the holiday. It was nothing without our father. At the Temple we had only the older people and those children. You could imagine how badly we all felt that everyone was gone. My Uncle Hermus still did not come back. He was also a soldier. At this time the only thing I could write is that we are going to go to Aunt Regus soon. Thank goodness we are okay. I hope you're well also. Many kisses to you and my best wishes to Uncle Jónász and his children and family. Your little nephew, Emil.

[from Etelka]
Emil just came home and he's trying to write to you before we mail this letter out.

1938/10/26 Father and Marie to Dezső (Book 4, 199-200)

Polány, 1938 October 26

From my heart loving my dear son, Dezső.
I received the letter that I was waiting so impatiently for. I was very happy to read it and to hear thank goodness you're okay. Thank goodness we're okay, too. The last letter we received was one on the 24th and the 2nd one on the 25th. All the envelopes were open and it was censored. The 2nd one was open, but closed.

I received them and I gave them to your grandfather to read. He was very happy to hear from you and was also crying. He told me he will keep the gift that you sent him as a memento to remember that you Dezső, his grandchild sent it to him. About the building it is still the same in today's situation. I went to see the lawyer and tomorrow I will see him again. We can't do too much if there isn't any money soon. Even if they call me in about the visa I don't know what will happen if our territory will change.. If everything stays the same way then they might ask for more papers. The government wants their own regulation. You have no idea how bad the situation is. Your gift came just in time. My dear son, I don't have one penny left. My dear son Dezső, you are asking me how much was the price of the wood for the building. At Keszler 3380 K for tile, to break apart 680 K. to build 500 K and some of the parts from the old building. The other items, nails plus anything else, they need to be charged 5000 K. So I'm guessing it will be 35m which I needed for the tobacco. The only thing I don't know is who will cash it and what will be…

[continued below Mariska's letter on the next written page]

Tomorrow I am going to Helmec. I am not sure if your post office friend will be there. I'm going to find out if it is possible to speak with her. I cannot explain what I should do or will do. They can't find the letter because the letter may have been destroyed. In the letter I wrote to you about a lawyer. I wrote about the situation that is happening here. I don't know at this time what will come about. I hope it is for the best. Today the banks do not give out money. I hope by the time we need it, we will get it. Now I want to wish you all the best with health and happiness. Many kisses to my dear son Dezső, from your loving father who never forgets you. Gluck Jeremias

You ask what happened to the crop what was the outcome. There were 4 wagons on one of the meadows. For the millet for porridge the machine was 5m and it will have it done right away.
Now give my best wishes to my dear brother Jónász and his children, and dear Arthur and his family. Last month I received $10 from him. Love as above, your father.

[From Mariska]
My dearest Dezső,
We did not mail this letter yet. We just received another letter and thank you so much for your gift. It was very nice. The other handkerchief we gave to Mariska Deak. Therefore we will mail the letter out tomorrow. Please give my best wishes to the relations. I am asking you please, you must have patience for a little longer. Don't worry so much. You can see it doesn't do any good because we cannot do much about it. We must trust our Almighty. He's the only one who could help. And as you know nothing lasts forever. We must just have patience. Now I want to wish you good health and happiness and a happy new year, better than ever and [enough] money to make a living wage. Now I think I wrote to you enough. I kiss you with understanding and it's good that you wrote because we saved it. Mariska
Jancsi Smolyák was here and sends his best wishes to you. We received a letter from Iren from Szatmár. She invited us to the wedding. It will be on November 6. Today I heard that the Hártumbaum girl from Perbenik was called in to Prague to pick up the visa. She started the same time as we did. One of her uncles already went to America at the same time that you did.
M. [Mariska]

1938/10/26 Undated Emil and Lenke Gluck (Lajos' children) to Uncle Dezső (Book 5, 46-47)
[Dated by mention of handkerchief and Smolyák]

[from Emil]
Dear Uncle Dezső,
I was very happy to get your letter. I thought by now I would not receive a reply, it took a long time to get here. Ignác was going to the post office every day last week and returned without a letter. Finally the postman Szmolyák bácsi brought it on Saturday. You can imagine how happy Lenke and I were for the handkerchief and we thank you very much. Other special news for my part is that regretfully, I am not going to be Hebrew school and Tibi [Schon] is not going either.
I already know the Hungarian national anthem, Lenke and Mityu, too. I was not in Agardon, my father, my mother, Lenke and Gyuszi were. I will be going during the summer because now I do not have a coat to wear and it is very cold here. How are you? We are healthy. Kisses to dear Jónász bacsi and his family and dear Arthur bacsi and his family and to you Uncle Dezső, kisses many times, your nephew Emil.

[from Lenke]]
Thank you for the handkerchief. I'm writing with my father. He is holding my hand. Lenke and Mityuka.

1938/10/26 Herman to Dezső (Book 5, 156)

1938 X/26

Dear Dezső,
We received your letter. We knew the reason. Don't be angry that in reply to your long letter I will write very briefly. I know the family wrote to you. Just to keep you busy isn't important. They told you about everything. Therefore, you will understand me why I'm not writing to you more. Kisses to you, your brother, Herman

1938/10/27 Grandfather Samuel Schwartz to Dezső (Book 4, 201-202)

Lelesz 1938 October 27

My dear, precious grandson Dezső,
I was very happy to take into my hand your precious letter and read good things. Thank God, you have acknowledged my teaching regarding the religion. I have shed many tears while reading your letter, grandmother too, because we were worried if we would ever hear from you, because I am an anxious person, grandmother is able to handle it better. Thank God that otherwise we are healthy. I cannot write anything else except to thank you for the one dollar gift that you sent us. I know that you are working very hard for it. I wish you health and wealth and respect and kisses to you many times, and to your uncle and his family, as well. I would like to write more, but at this time I'm praying. Behave the same in front of God as in front of man, because God will help you everywhere and I'm wishing you all the good things. Once again I'm thanking you for the gift of one dollar that you sent me. I will keep it as if I would see you. Thank God that you are now in the great country, America. Here in our place the atmosphere is very confused. Only God knows what will be with us. We remain, your grandfather and grandmother forever with respect to the whole family, and please write something. You will give me happiness. My writing came out very well, I'm weak in my physical being. With respect and love, from your grandfather and grandmother.... Schwartz Samuel

[In Hebrew] B"H Yosef Shemaya Schwartz

1938/11/7 Bertha to Dezso (Book 1, 180-181)

New York
Nov 7 / 38
Dear Dave!
I hope that you are in good health! I started to worry since you did not show any life sign about yourself for so long. What do you hear from home? Or maybe your sisters are already there with you? It makes me think why don't they write. Well, let's hope for the best. Please write even if it's only a card because I am worried. I would like to ask one thing from you, that please ask your dear cousin [Arthur] to write to the consul in Bucharest for Jolanka's sake. Once every month Jolan's case can be pressed for her to come out because that young man came out of Szatmar and his relatives did this here and this way he only had to wait for a year for his documents. I believe that even the woman accountant could write to Bucharest. This way we would not need to bother to ask dear Arthur. I will write to Jolan [so she can] show our letter also. Maybe it will help with something. This week I got an invitation to Jolanka's sister's [Iren] wedding. It was held this month on the 6th. About something else, the late uncle Henry's wife travelled away for a week with her daughter. I think they might visit you too, if her time will allow it. But let's leave this too. I would have written to you sooner already, but I was very busy with painting the apartment and then the struggle wore me out so much that I had to lay down. Finally I could start [doing] things again. I do not know what else to write anymore. Give my best to the dear relatives. I kiss you with love. Bertha
Mannie sends his best.

1938/11/15 Undated Dezso Grunberger to Dezső (Book 5, 364-365)

Dear Mr. Glück!

Page 52

Maybe I should be ashamed of myself that with so much time that has passed only now I write to you. But you know there are so many things that have happened here since then that even things that seem most important are also dwarfed. We got back to Hungary, to express it in Hungarian, we got ourselves back to Hungary. There was a little mobilization beforehand, and we already thought we wouldn't get away without a world war. So, the fact that I did not write to you does not mean that I forgot about it, I have been thinking only about you, and [other] people who were born under the same lucky stars like you, who are already out there like yourself and who have no burning problems like this. The mental state from worrying and many such extraordinary events, the entire book [of samples] and the past somehow lost its topicality and I did not want to bother with this.

Since then the conditions are changed so much that surely it would be for the best if every Jew would get the hell out and would go wherever the road takes them. Nobody knows where the road takes us. Although, it serves with little consolation, that there are good friends out there for us in the big world. And when it's truly needed then everyone's conscience speaks out and runs for help.

Thank God you have decent relatives there. My relatives are terribly closed minded people. Despite that, I have two uncles there and two aunts, neither one of them are moving their tail to do something in our case. My sister Helen wants to go out there too and my relatives already promised that they will send documents for her, then these noisy happenings got in the way and somehow they stopped.

As I heard you became a traveler. I don't know if you get into other towns as well, but if yes, then in that case I will send my relatives' address here and it would serve me greatly, for me as well as for my sister, if you would talk to their conscience and enlighten them about what great people we are, that they will not be ashamed of themselves, if they will help regarding our traveling out.

Based on this letter I am seriously asking you to do everything possible that you can to give the most important information below:

Please let me know, when will the New York world exhibition take place. Maybe it's possible to go to that exhibition from here, that is, from Hungary and from the areas that were reattached to it.

Please be so kind as to find out if there is a technology trade school in the United States. And what kind of documents are needed there from foreigners to sign up. Is it possible to stay there for a longer time based on the sign up? And how many years does a course like that last? My boss is a skilled miller and he would like to sign up for a school like that.

If you would also be able to please find out if there is a school like that in Canada? And under what kind of conditions foreigners [can] sign up to it. These are all unnecessary efforts, but now it is a gift for you a real business too where it could be searched:
There would be two mills for sale. Both of them work great, but the owners would like to sell them. If you know anybody who would want to move back here and would like to be a mill owner, then please let them know about that.

With my knowledge many will come back, those who want to spend the rest of their lives here. We should advertise the same in some Hungarian newspaper also. I will write the text for the article separately here. Unfortunately we don't know the cost, but I assume that it could be very little and give credit to a mill's owner. As soon as they will write the cost of it we will send it to you immediately. We would like for you to work on that intensively, because a lot depends on this. I gave a lot of mandates to you that you will surely have to hire three people to have this case be successful.
I repeat, I'm asking you to make this possible for me, that I could wish you a Happy Passover to you there. Do not use me as an example, and write as soon as possible because I have every faith in you. I'm waiting for your response. Your most honest supporter, D. Grunberger

In the meantime, my sister Helen's documents arrived from the consulate in Budapest.

[In English] How are you getting on with your English. I learn again and hope, that during 3 month I shall be perfect in the English language. God save you!

Dear Dezső,

On XI /2 we received letters and again on XI /18. I'm not surprised that you didn't get any mail from us in so long. This is because there wasn't regular postal service by the Hungarian Mail service yet. It wasn't very nice that that service was late. Therefore everything in person was done differently. It is much longer to write about it in a letter. Otherwise we cannot write to you as we want to. In the last letter I forgot to mention when it was the holiday where we prayed [where we held the minyan]. I want to mention it today. It was in Lelesz with our grandfather and our uncle Lajos. I read how good hearted a man Arthur is, to give you a hard time. They say the rule is that after the bad comes better days. The good God will not fail to act. I wish that all of us would be there out from here. I am not afraid of that. I would choose it at this time, but there are so many problems I don't know if I will be able to go. This is a question. So you see Dezső, in a short time everything is ready for the girls. The only thing that is missing 3250 korona, [???] For the time being, the autumn revenue is 20 q [1 quintal = 100 kg] of wheat. 3 q of mushrooms. I hope that we should be able to get back 8-10 q and the expense we have if it is for the ship. The money is still there. Maybe we would have been able to sell, but the man who was in charge wasn't at home and because of that we couldn't make any deal to settle the problem, and therefore the deal is off. About the tobacco we're still missing [money] because of that. When the building will be all ready it will be 8 by 8 m. It will cost 5000 Czech Korona. Andras Simon is the judge as of now, but only until there is an election. The immortal Tomacs did not beat him. I hope my letter will find you in good health. I wish you all the best health and happiness. I do not have patience to write better. I know it will be hard to read my writing. With kisses, your brother Herman

1938/11/20 Father and Ignác to Dezső (Book 4, 197-198)

Polyán [Bodrogmező] November 20, 1938
My dear son Dezső,

I received you letter which I was waiting so hard for, and I was very happy to hear that thank God, you're okay. We are also well. We received your letter and your gift. I hope that you have received my reply. Your friend from the post office wrote but it was opened. That was the rule. I'm sure you will understand. You know more about it. Thank God we became Hungarian again.. I hope everything will be better. The lawyer left. About the sale of the Building it's still the same. The reason that they didn't accomplish it yet is because the office still isn't set up. I have to wait. When they are ready then they can get together and then they will work on this case. The only thing is now we will have to use Hungarian money [pengő]. As of now I do not know what will be. They will notify me. I do not have the money for the children. Tomorrow I'm going to go to Helmec and I will try to find out how they can travel. I will go to the agent to find out about Hersmendel's records to see if he can go or not. I was supposed to get a letter from my brother Jónász, as of now I did not receive it. I got one of your letters that arrived on the 17th on the 18th in the evening, but just the Express page because there was no regular post office. I hope that you will get them sooner than we did. I want to thank you for your gift. Please give my love and best wishes to my dear brother Jónász, his wife, and son. Last week I wrote to them in your letter. I am wondering by now you should have received my letter-- both of you. Give my best wishes to Arthur and his family and especially to you, many kisses and my love many times over, your loving father who never forgets you, not even a moment. Jeremias Gluck

Your grandfather and grandmother and your Uncle Lajos bácsi all send you their best wishes, love, and many kisses to you.

[This letter was written by Ignác]
Dear brother Dezső,

We received your letter and we were very happy to hear that thank goodness you're well. Please Dezső I just want you to take care of yourself and your health. About our trip you heard we do not have any definite answer. I could tell you one I hope our fortune will come our way. I hope maybe that there is some possibility we might be able to go sooner. Therefore we live in an uncertain condition from all around us. I'm sure you must have heard what goes on here. We changed our country because the Hungarian's just took over. I would be happy to tell you all about it in person. Sometimes it can change in a hurry someone else told you about the same thing. Sometimes that is what's happening. And sometimes when asking a question no one answers. Therefore don't be surprised if it is not the same as you think. As you write in your letter, it would be okay. I would like to do that if it would happen. I wish it would be sooner, but we don't know. Please

Dezső write more. Thank goodness I'm okay. I am sending you many many kisses with my love, your loving youngest brother. Ignác Gluck [In English] Good by!

[In Hungarian] <u>Please write to me at once!</u> Also, please give my best wishes and love to the relations.

[Here is an additional note from our father.]

Today I went the State office to see maybe I can find a way to get the papers sooner. I was told that Herman's papers are still in Ujhel. Legally they moved the office there. They are waiting to hear from them. And if he will be able to go they will okay it there. They are asking me how much will I pay for it 5 to 60 Koronat. It would be better. I will try to work with them. I will see their lawyer there.

1938/11/20 Undated Jane to Dezső (Book 1, 166)

[Dated by Jane mentioning she's writing in the letter from our father and the letter above in which he writes that she wrote]

Dear Dezső,

I'm endlessly happy that you wrote a long letter. I would love it if you would always write. I am unfortunately in a situation where I don't have time to write. I believe, that you know about everything, and I was also away for 3 weeks. Your dear father was kind enough to leave me space, so I can write. Dezső, it's possible that I have to leave this place shortly, but I still don't know the address, and I can notify you. Otherwise, your father will know where I am!!! I am very happy, that you are there!! I'm in a hurry, I have a lot of work. I will continuously trust to God's goodness and care for us, Greetings with much love, Jane

Write, do not wait from me to write more, because I can't, but if I will be calm I will write a lot.

Wait with the material yet, until I write. So much tiredness and spending, I did not think I would get it so soon, even sooner in a little old business. It is truly kind, but it's a lot from you. Therefore, wait until I will know where I will be because after 2-3 weeks I would start again.

[Dezső received the letter and writes a note on it. I'm not sure who he is writing it to, maybe]

Pardon, I only write blurry, but right now I don't have ink in hand. I wish you all the best for everyone with love, I kiss you, Dezső

Also, your dear husband.

Kisses,

I will let you know my new address. Now you can write.

D Gluck

110 W Park Ave. Colombus Ohio.

I'm sorry, but first I started to write with pencil, and then I looked for a pen. So one more time I wrote it over so you can read it.

[I can't read everything in the right corner its very blurry.]

1938/11/21 Hermine to Dezső (Book 4, 237-238)

Dear Dezső,

I received your hard to wait for letter. Unfortunately, I am sorry you had some problem. I'm very glad you did not get hurt. You're lucky, it could have been worse. How is your arm? You mentioned before that we should write to Uncle Jónász about our trip. I think it is not worth it to bother him. If he doesn't like it, he just won't give us the guarantee. There isn't too much loss. This way our father will not aggravate himself. Our Uncle will not feel that we are always bothering him with something. At this time I'm really very happy. It would be so easy to give that guarantee and our father would like to have it that our brother Ignác also would come with us to America. So many people are jealous of us that we are able to go all 4 of us together. It is better this way. I wish I would be able to go sooner. I wish I would be there already. Here we can see nothing. They make-believe that they're your friend when they are not. Ever since you left I couldn't tell you, we didn't have any place to go, no friends. This week we are planning to bring our grandmother here for a couple of days. She would like to see us here. She works very hard at home. Every year before Passover she does all her cleaning. Uncle Marton is not happy because you did not answer his letter and he's waiting so hard for it. He was here. Mariska Deák says the same that you are writing to everyone and not to her. In May, Ilon Juhász and will have their 20th grandchild. Malvin [Lefkovics] would be very happy to go. She is waiting for an answer from her uncle. I think they broke off the engagement. I'm sure she's not going to get married with this man. She wanted to thank you for your best. I believe this was a fake engagement. She thought this way, maybe someone will come forward and [she'll] find someone else. They do not have any money to give for the dowry, so therefore no wedding. If you write to Lajos, he won't write much because he is naughty. Marcsa wrote about I am sure of it. It is not worth it to waste so much time, that's for sure. If someone is listening for themselves then they will hear it. And if they overheard their conversation she had choices either to go home or to come in because it wasn't nice to listen in what goes on inside, namely our Aunt Etelka. Now we finished our visiting until the time comes that I am leaving to America. As of now everyone is asking about you. People are very happy for you. They can't even think that they might have a chance to leave to America. By now I hope you received our letters in which we sent you our birthdays. My birthday is April 5/1914. I hope you received that. Maybe you must learn and be careful how you talk to our Uncle and recognize his whims. I wish I could be there already. We still didn't write to Szatmar. Now I will try to write to them also. Our Uncle Leizer was visiting his daughter Sarolta. He was very happy. It was the first time he visited them. They are very poor. They have nothing there. But can you imagine, beside all this, for Purim she sent us shalahmones. It was all cream, but it was very good. There are people who can't stand that you did whatever you could for Jolan. Bertha wrote to Mindu. I am sorry my writing is not the best, it happened that my pen is not the best. I don't want to waste more time to look for another pen therefore I'm finishing with this one so I could mail out this letter today. Many kisses and love, your sister Hermine.

Hello and kisses to Uncle Jónász

1938/11/21 Maria to Dezső (Book 4, 235-236)

1938 XI/21

Dear Dezső,

I was very happy to hear from you that thank goodness you're well. I would like to ask you to take care of yourself. Make sure you are eating well. That is very important. About myself nothing special and thank goodness I'm well. The only thing is that I am very concerned about our trip, [but] we cannot do much about it. I'm sure you must have read about what happened. When they took over Kiraly Helmec it was a big celebration. It was advertised on the radio all over. Even in our home it was a big celebration. Yesterday the Hungarian government took over the Russian part of Slovakia. As of now we don't know what will happen. It's true that here we can't do more except hope for the best for us. The sooner they settle down the sooner we are able to get ready to work on our papers so we could get a faster response. Now I just wait and see. We were ready to go. I did not get any work in between this time. This changed our life and now, because of that, we have to start all over again. I am behind in my English. I should start studying again. Also I am behind in my payment for the machine. I was thinking that before I leave I would sell my sewing machine. At this time they are not asking for the payment. I trust our God. He is the only one who could help us. You know Dezső, our God especially cares and tries to help us. Until now, at the last minute, I received help and was able to manage whatever I needed. You must hope to survive. Now I think I wrote enough. I'm sure you know more than we do here. It makes me feel better if I tell you what goes on here. Otherwise nothing new here. I'm sure the rest of the family wrote to you all about it. Many, many kisses to you and our Uncle Jónász and his wife and their family. I do not want to think that we might not able to go, God forbid. I could not accept or live with it. I do not want to leave my father and my brother. It breaks my heart. The only thing I think about is that when we settle in America we will be able to bring the rest of the family out, too. Otherwise I could never leave them behind. This is our dream. I hope we will never be disappointed. This is my thought as I am writing this letter today. I am going to close at this time. With love and many kisses until next time, your sister, Mariska

1938/11/21 Uncle Marton to Dezső (Book 4, 212)

Dear Dezső, live to 100

Your father has written a letter and I am enclosing this letter with his. Thank God we are well. We have met Mayer bácsi since now thank God we are Hungarians and one does not need a passport. What is with our papers? I cannot mail it yet? I'm waiting for a guarantee and hope that you can expedite it. Loads of kisses to you. Marton

XI / 21 1938

1938/12/1 Undated Hermine to Dezső (Book 4, 245-246)

[Dated by change of government and Bela Stark's daughter sent home on Nov 17]

Dear Dezső,

We hardly could wait to hear from you and finally we received [your letter] and I was very happy to read it. I understood what you are saying. I just want to tell you you must have patience and take care of yourself. I hope our God will help us to be there soon. When we will be there it will be better for you, too. At least you will have a family together. At this time we will have more difficulties, but I hope it will work out for the best. When we will be together I hope we all will be able to take care of ourselves. Bela Stark's daughter from Lelesz is going to Prague for the 2nd time. On November 17th day they sent her back home even though she already has the visa. The agent advised her to come back on the 21st because she already has the ship, but she could not get there in time. Our father asked the agent to notify us as soon as they can, whenever the papers are ready. We became Hungarian since our country was taken over on this date. Our visa will be good because they were already notified from Czechoslovakia that it was okayed and ready, therefore we could transfer all those papers to the Hungarian government in Budapest to the American consul. We would be much happier if we could be there already, but I understand we need more time and patience. And waiting makes it very difficult I admit. There is always [the fact that] sooner or later it will come to an end. Whenever they call us in we will let you know as soon we hear from them, whenever we are ready to leave. Otherwise we are trying to manage the best we can. Thank goodness we are well. I could write to you much more, but I think I'll leave some for next time. Or until we will meet again in America I hope. About the delay with the mail, at this time they aren't organized yet. We are the same way. We didn't hear from you for a while and then all of a sudden we received 2 letters from you and then we received a card a day later. I want to thank you for your pictures past and present. Whomever sees them is very jealous that you are there. I know you know about everything that goes on here. I am hoping for the best in the future. I'm sure you've heard or read what is happening here, the celebration, it is very nice and everyone is happy. As you mentioned about Jolan from Szatmar, I am very surprised how she behaved with you. Especially in today's world to think even the way she does. You cared seriously about her life because you know the situation she is in and how good it is if someone cares and tries to help and is serious. It is also true that here those who have heard that what you and many others are going through it, and you are serious. I always think that the townspeople make sense, but I don't think it's all the same. At this time I think I wrote enough about everything. You will be tired to read it. Whatever comes to my mind I mention it to you. Last time you're asking us where we spent the holiday and where we went to temple. I forgot to mention to you that we went to Lelesz to see our grandparents and our Uncle Lajos. They led the services in the Temple. We are not visiting our uncle at this time. We visited only our grandparents. Otherwise we're not going anywhere, we have no place to go. Only Mariska Deak comes to us or we go to visit her. She received the handkerchief. I just gave it to her. I repeat myself, please take good care of yourself. When we had the celebration in Helmec it was very crowded. Therefore they had 3 mishaps. All from Perbenik one was 13 years old, one 12 years old, because of a car accident. Also by accident, on Saturday afternoon Uncle Lajos' business acquaintance's 3 grandchildren were together in a car accident. One of them died instantly, and two got hurt there. They have hope they will survive. You can imagine how much heartache their parents have to go through. I forgot to mention, do not forget to eat. It is very important. Since you mentioned how many hours you are working, and that could destroy a person. You are over doing it. Although you have to work, you need to rest also and to eat regular meals on time. You should do the best you can.

Aggravation is not a solution. It does not solve anything. You should do the best you can. It seems when you are working, they don't know you as well. Now take care, wishing you nothing but the best, many kisses to everyone, and for you many kisses, and all my love, your sister Hermine.

I sent a card to Szatmar with congratulations for the bride. What will happen to us, that I do not know.

1938/12/7 Dezső to family in Europa (Book 5, 58-61)

1938 December 27
Columbus Ohio

My dearests! L.M.E.S. 120

Forgive me that I am just writing the letter that I promised you. Unfortunately that's the way it goes. If a person does not have a proper home one doesn't want to do anything. One doesn't have the desire when a person comes home from work in an ice cold room. Gas heat takes a long time to warm up the room. Let's forget that. As noted in a letter written by Hermine, I indicated that I'm working in a traffic business, I don't know if I'll be staying here or not, however as I see it, they are satisfied with me because the previous boys were not packaging better, in fact worse, so I trust in God. Presently they are asking me to go to a paint factory. I wrote about it to you before, however, I don't have any desire to do that. I would prefer to be a businessman instead of a factory worker. I would be able to go to learn the furniture business. If I can remain in this business it will be better. Here it is a warm place and it's clean and no one dictates because it is one company owned by Hungarian Jewish people. They have stores in different towns. Here one days' income would help our father. This Christmas week they brought in $10,000. It's a lot of work, but it is better to be doing this than to work for someone that drives you crazy. What I would like now is to have my family here and to know when they're coming? I'm by myself. I cannot speak to anyone anywhere. I speak to Eigner bácsi. I go there once a week on Sunday for dinner and after that he takes me to the movies. I thank him for it............ Forgive me, today I only write to you a little bit, and tomorrow I will continue writing about myself.

Brief news, briefly, that Lajzer bacsi has written a letter to Jónász bacsi to take out the letters from Lefcovitcs and Lenke that they mailed him. He is asking to send him some used clothing because he doesn't have anything to wear and it will come in very handy. He writes to send to our father also, since he doesn't have any either. If our father should write to him, since our uncle has not received any mail for the past two months, then he would send something because Uncle is waiting to hear from home. That is a good excuse for him! You must write to him as soon as possible because he will not do anything otherwise! As far as what these people are asking about a guarantee, Uncle's guarantee is no good. He is an old man who can't do anything for anyone and can't bring anyone out-------- especially with the present conditions in this world---- also from there no one can come.--- He regrets that everywhere is dangerous. There is a man in this world saying that in Bolivia, South America, they would allow a Jewish state for farming. Lenke has written from Kassa of the situation there. They asked for papers and would like to come out and are asking for help from Arthur. If I would be more as I was, but today I couldn't even mention it to him because we seldom speak to each other. As it is, I have to wait before I can do anything. If Fisher has any money then he should ask an agent and perhaps they would let him go to England. From there he may get permission to come here. If they put down $500 there, perhaps then we'll be able to get help to get out. Everyone wants to come out from there because of the terrible stories that we hear only about the Jews. And this is also from Romania, I received two letters from Jolan. Her father Lipot [Majer] writes to me that I should help because he has debts due to the wedding. I regret that I can't do anything. I gave his letter to Jónász bacsi. They will not have results because he just can't do it. You cannot speak to Arthur because he also has some debts, however I think that if Lipot does not have any money, then he shouldn't have made a big shindig of a wedding. I will not answer this letter, but I will mail it to Bertha. I don't know what's with her. She hasn't written me for four weeks because I wrote her that I left Arthur. I also told her that I do not know him any better than she does from New York. Perhaps she got offended, but I will mail this letter to her anyway. It's true that Lipot from Romania need not know anything about this letter. I am also poor without any assets. Jolanka is asking me again for advice. She wants to know what to do so that she could come out as a visitor. I regret that I've written to her a lot and told her that she should return to the local agent. I don't know what it is with her, the poor thing, she cannot understand my directions. Bertha was telling her that if she could, she would send her the ship ticket and any papers. I mailed the letters to Bertha. Don't mention anything to Lajzer bacsi about this. Verbally, I can only write so much to anyone to have hope that there ever will be any help from here because it is a big responsibility. The only possibility is that if they would establish a state here in America for the Jewish people, but Fisher couldn't do anything for one or two years. The English language is important. I would help, but I can't. They would only understand more, [knowing] that the Uncle's wife has two members of her family one in Karlsbad that should be helped, and [another] in Grojoba because of the problems there, but no one would send any papers for them. Therefore there is not much hope for anyone to be brought out here. I've written so much that no one will have any patience to read it, especially my bad writing. I observed that some of the German Jews must be quite rich because they brought out their furniture with them to America. It may cost at least $2000. They live here like someone who has no problem. It's impossible to understand and to listen to all the news that there is. When I was offered a job [just] to live, they replied that that wasn't a future, it's better if one doesn't work. [Maybe] that is why the situation is bad in this world, they only want to live easily? They should be happy that they are here. There are some that would take anything, even to fleece the Lamb [Baranyt]. Some families came out with $9000 and therefore they do not have to work. This is enough at this time. The Rabbi went back to Palestine, and he was a rabbi at the temple where uncle was going; presently there is another person--- an attorney who wants to be a Rabbi here. This rabbi knows as much and as well as in Europe and speaks perfect English, but he cannot be a Rabbi here. I can only mail you $3, I cannot mail more at this time. I know it will come in handy. Perhaps I can help in the week of January. I will mail you again. It has been one year that I left and arrived on January 12 to America. When I receive the letter from my family, I will make a package together in January and I will mail it home [with] things that you can use. Forgive me that I combine everything! I will mail a pipe to Lajos, straight lined at the end of January. I will be getting it from the store at a discount rate it will go as no value, as well as a hair straightening thing. Please write to me, if you want dark or light or rounded or six sided small or general. I will send a very fine pipe that very few people will have. It costs about $10-$15! However, I'm going to send it [anyway], you don't have to think about it.............. Therefore please reply at once.

1938/12/8 Jolan Mayer to Dezső (Book 5, 320-321)

Szatmar 938 XII / 8
Dear Dezső!
I don't even know how to start. I have so many things I would like to write. It seems that you are not writing anymore because you have nothing special to write. I wrote so many things to Bertha. She should write to you and explain the situation. Why aren't you writing to me? Maybe I hurt your feelings? But under any circumstances write to me, even just a card if nothing else. And do me a favor, I'm sorry my aunt Mariska is also very uncertain. It is very difficult to get the visa. And especially for me, until we have some changes here or it settles down and we have peace in this world. Dear Dezső, I know we should [???] Then I would be able to go to the world fair, I would like to go. Maybe this way it will be easier to get out. Who knows how long I would have to wait to get in under the quota! That could take even 2– 3 years. This way, [????] I would be able to go. Bertha is so sweet. She wrote to me that she will send me the ticket for the ship and she was telling me I can stay with her because she does not have children. I wrote this to the consulate. As of now I didn't get any answer. Even the first one didn't get anything yet from what you mailed me. Arthur received papers from the consulate too, and I copied and mailed it. As of now I don't have any answer. Dear Dezső, I would be very happy if you would start something now. Bertha will help me and send whatever papers I need in order to start new paperwork for the visa. I am asking you Dezső, if you can please write to me and let me know about it. If you want to help me, then I will start getting ready here. Unless you start I will think you are tired of it. But now at least, think of a good deed, and if this doesn't work out then I will give up the idea. I hope you are not angry because I am bothering you again, but I have no other way out. I know very well you're working all day and you don't have time to run around. But you can write, you can do it. Either way I trust you! Or write to Bertha what she has to do. I was very surprised that before my sister's wedding we received a letter from Hermine telling me that they are in America! How is it possible Dezső that they are still here? At that time I already had a visa. Please Dezső, I would appreciate it if you will write to me about everything. You know I'm interested to hear what's happening. Otherwise how are you? Are you working where you were working before? Thank god we are over with my sister's wedding. It has been four months already, and it was a very nice wedding but I'm sorry no one was there. She felt very sad and was crying. Did you receive the invitation we sent to everyone? No one except Bertha even sent congratulations. That's the way the relations are. I think I wrote about everything. Please just have a little more patience! I hope you're not letting my letters go unanswered and will write to me soon because I will be very angry. Until then, I send my best to the relatives. Many many kisses to you, your niece Jolan

Our mother and my new brother-in-law and all the rest of the family are sending their love and kisses. If it would not be Friday, then they would all write you. At this time they're very busy. I'm writing now from the business.

1938/12/25 Father to Dezső (Book 4, 273-274)

Polány December 25 1938
From my heart, with love, to my son Dezső.
I was so glad that I could read your letter which I could hardly wait for, and I'm happy that, thank God, you are in good health. We are, thank God, also in good health. They did not discuss about the house yet because until now, only the military authority gives orders. The public administration is being taken over already. When the civil authorities and the district caucus will exist, then it will be discussed. I hope everything is going to be fine this way, because I gave in the documents to the office before the Hungarians came in. I hope it will be arranged in the month of January. About the money exchange in the bank. That is conducted by Deics Mara and Dobos. They are in charge at the bank and they asked about the sale of the house. How will it be exchanged? I will see when the sale takes place and then I will check the actual currency balance. When it will be sold the magistrate will give us the confirmation, because the town always insists on that. When will they travel to America? I don't know. But you know Csidert who was with Zombori? He is here

now. He says that the Hungarians will discharge Hersmendel. A request needs to be sent to the Dandár Commander. I gave him 3 pengo for the stamp. In the meantime, they sent the documents to Pest and the agent wrote that we have to get the passports done, and then let them know. I let them know and then he asked when we were born. We wrote back on the 21st, but we still did not get response. Prague sent over everything that was needed. It is about the land that was taken and about how many children I have. The documents that stayed here I took it to Csider and he said that he only has to send a request. I did not take the money to the Dandár Commander yet. For the farmers, the situation is hard now. Uncle Jónász sent $6 on October 28th. He wrote that he sent it and I did not get it until today. May God give us a good/calm life. They started the tobacco exchange. They took 35-40-50 average from the town on Friday. They will ship it in January. When exactly? I don't know. I wrote enough. I respect you and kiss all of you and please be good and patient to everyone. And listen to Uncle Jónász because he has experienced so much. Hugs and kisses from your faithful father, who will never forget. Gluck Jeremias

The monopoly ceased on October 15. So I don't have [the grass cutting machine]. Feri Hegedus still has the wagon and he got the pub. They took away the wagon from Lefkovic. Everything is there in the commune and they took away Uncle Lazar's tractor [?] also.

1938/12/25 Hermine to Dezső (Book 5, 3-4)

Dear Dezső,

We have a received your long-awaited letter. It was delayed, but we were happy to receive it. We were just about to write to you when your letter arrived. The situation is the same everywhere and it is important to have inner strength, that is, we cannot be downhearted. As long as we are alive we must have hope! That is all true, it's a very difficult situation that we live in. Many situations are such that we would have given up because there is no hope, but God makes a miracle and helps. I do not have to write to you about the present conditions, since you know about it. I'm very happy to know that thank God you're healthy and I'm asking you to take care of your health. As for ourselves, I don't know what to write to you, what could be, I think that God will help us as it will be decided. I wouldn't mind if I will be beyond this, who knows whether it will be better? As you're writing, everything is very cheap here, but the money is very dear. There would be a lot of news that I could not write down, it would be very lengthy. Our papers, first of all are in Budapest with the same shipping company and they asked us whether we have the Hungarian passport ready. We need a Hungarian passport, I believe that we will only need a permit to be attached to it with stamps. We are not sure yet since we are waiting for a reply from the agent. I asked them when will we get the visas. Ignacz Grosz from Lelesz received a letter from the agent requesting birth certificates and it will take years before it will be his turn. Miki Schvarcz knows nothing and their girls cannot travel. They took away the liquor license from them. You can imagine how they are! The shochet [slaughterer for kosher products] that comes out to our house and others' must move, to where, we don't know. Adolf Lefkovics lives in Kassa. He was here for a short period in Polyán. Lajos from Szürte is also getting ready to go to America. He was advised from Prague and Budapest to prepare a Hungarian passport. The Perl girl [Helen] is still at home. There are a lot of people that are planning to travel to America now. Bela Stark went by third class on the ship and she has arrived. More likely Bertha will be writing about her and that she will be settling in her neighborhood. She also took some package with her. Until she has arrived to this particular position she went through a lot of problems. She went three times to Prague. Little Olga from Lelesz regretted that she went to America. She doesn't have a beautiful situation there. Everyone wants to go to America even though they know the situation there and there must be a reason for that also. Last week Miksa [Shon] received a letter from Bertha and he was asked to submit the birth certificate also for his little son Tibi and she will send a guarantee, so that they could travel to America also. I do not know whether they plan to go or not. I do not believe anything will come from it. I did not give the letter to Mariska Diak since it is Christmas, and I'm in a hurry to send this letter as soon as possible, because of neglect the letter remains. I think that I've written enough about everything. Tomorrow the rest of the family will write and I want them to have something to write about, also. That's why many times [there are] things I'm not writing to you so that everyone can write, too. I'm asking you to write and don't worry because it doesn't help and take care of yourself. Thank you for the pictures. I have been reading the Hungarian newspaper from America that Ilonka Juhasz has sent. I understand that she has a very good situation. I cannot write to you too much about the studies of the English language since in this situation I didn't feel like studying, but now I must start. Everybody is asking about you. Jani Balint sends his regards. His father is very strict. With hearts full of regards and kisses with love, Hermine

The weather was very good, but now we have real winter. It's not too pleasant to think of the ship, but as it comes it will be.

1938/12/25 Undated Marie to Dezső (Book 4, 271-272)

[Dated by mention of Janos Balint and Uncle Marton will write]

Dear Dezső!

We got your letter that we could hardly wait for, and I gladly read that thank God you are healthy. About us I can only write, that thank God we are in good health. About the situation, I think, you know more than we do. Uncle Marton from Helmec changed the sign board to his own name. And he also mentioned that he will write to you. I was in Lelesz 2 weeks ago, at our grandparents. Thank God they are healthy and they can hardly wait for your letter. They can't write anymore the way they used to, but they send regards to you and kiss you countless times and they talk about you a lot. About our traveling, dad and the others wrote everything, where we are. The post lady in Helmec and Janos Balint were wondering about you and sending their best. I'm sorry that I write so briefly, but we could talk better in person. I hope everything is going to be okay. And Dear Dezső! I'm asking that you take care of yourself! And don't think too much, let it come that has to come. God is good and will help all of us. Believe me dear Dezső, that I know very much how hard we have to work, but believe that we are ready for anything, because now it's like this way: the whole world is in turmoil [Yiddish- "dősz gance velt iz ajn core"]! And that is the way it is. But while a person is alive, he has to try many things. And now, we are hoping that in the future we will hear good things about each other. Now I don't write anymore. I kiss you countless times. I wish you good health and luck in the future, your little sister,
Mariska
Gecse stayed here.
[Up side down:] Thank you for the pictures.

1938/12/25 Undated Ignác to Dezső (Book 5, 97-98)

My dear brother Dezső,

We have received your letters, to which I have been very happy to learn that you're well thank God. I was concerned since your letter was delayed. It is not surprising because the post office and its system was not in order. Dear Dezső, don't be offended that I do not have any news to write to you, because everyone has already written about everything, I can only tell you that I'm well. I do not have any patience for writing because when I think of it that we are still here at home. Because of that it is better if I don't think about it. Do not be upset that I only write this much however, in my next letter, I'll write more. Let's hope that God will help that the next letter I would be able to tell you in person. Loads of kisses, your little brother Ignác.

Give my kisses to all of the relations! Goodbye!

1938/12/28 Uncle Marton to Dezső (Book 4, 229-230)***

Dear Dezső,

On November 6th I received your card. It is very interesting that you're complaining you didn't hear from your father, [and] why isn't he writing to you. Your poor father is complaining, too. He was telling me that you didn't write to him for 8 weeks. On the other hand, it seems both of you are writing to each other. You'll have to mail them with insurance otherwise it seems to get lost. It's also because the situation is changing here so much from one day to the other. I'm sure you learned from the newspapers what is going on here. After 20 years the government leadership is changing all around us.. Thank goodness, we hope it's going to be better.. We became Hungarian again after so many years under Slovak government control. According to the post lady your letter got lost or delayed at this time. It takes time to change over, especially the mail. Therefore you just keep on writing. Don't wait at this time for the other mail to come from your father. You will get it. The only thing now is you have to put it down that the country where you are sending the letter is now Hungary. About the girls' passports, I wrote to Budapest. They received the documents from Prague. It is not ready or certain, but most likely they transferred the papers over, but we do have to do start from scratch again to get from Budapest all those papers. It will take again time and money to be able to transfer those papers from Czechoslovakia to Hungary. Otherwise, how are you what are you doing? How much are you making? Can you speak well in English? Did you have an opportunity to see what can you do for us? You promised you will try to find a place to be a hazzan [a cantor]. Also, I studied to be a shochet. I am able

to do whatever needs to be done. I am qualified. If I could come I would like to make enough to support my family. I qualify even to be a Rabbi. I hope you find someone to hire me if I have to under any circumstances. If it is possible I'm ready and capable to do the job. Maybe if there is chance to ask your Uncle Jónász maybe there is a possibility he could help to give me a guarantee so I would be able to go to America. I do not need any money for our expenses, I will cover it all, just the guarantee. It would not cost him any money. I would do anything to help a Jew migrate. That would be the only solution to get out if it is possible. I'm sure you know very well what goes on here. For the Jewish people it has become very difficult all-around, more so every day. I am reading in the newspaper every day all over in Europe. Now from here it will be easy to get out. The government promised it will help whoever wants to get out. Therefore it would be easier if you could help me to get a guarantee paper. It especially wants to help the Jewish population to get out as fast as they can because this government is trying to do whatever to help them. Thank goodness this government is better than the other. The leaders are the same. They do not care for anyone therefore at this time someone somewhere tries to help us. In other places they don't care what happens to you. The situation is the same here too. All over Europe there is hatred of the Jewish population. The president and the leaders know the situation and are making it easier to be able to get out before it is too late. Whoever wants to get out fast, they will do everything to let them go. If I want to go, now is the time to get out. I'm still young and able to do the job. Later on it would be more difficult. One of my uncles is here from 'Raclusnesz'. He also needs help for his family. Mr. Murer doesn't know when he will come, but he's well and he's strong and he's waiting every day. Otherwise thank goodness we are well. The store is okay at this time. I received beautiful shoes from Budapest, much cheaper than before when it was the Czech government. My wife and children send their best wishes to you with many kisses. Lenke and my brother-in-law send their best wishes to you. At this time I don't have anything special to tell you. Many kisses to you and your Uncle Jónász. I'm waiting anxiously for your reply. Please answer this as soon as you can.
Marton.
XII/28 1938

My brother Lajos from Leles was here today. Tobi from Palòcz is going back home. He was here today also. Your father was here last week. Your grandmother and your grandfather are well thank goodness.
Marton.

1939 Undated Ignác to Dezső (Book 5, 157-158)

My dear brother Dezső, live up to 100 years.
Received your letter and I've read it with pleasure, knowing thank God that you are in good health. Dear Dezső, I wrote my last letter with a pencil because I didn't have any time to write with a pen. Please let me know if you were able to read it. We are very anxious, because we would like to be there already, but I do not know if anything will happen with our traveling, since you know what's going on here!! After I received your letter and read it, I was like a new person. You made me happy. I felt like I had someone to encourage me, because here no one cares about anything. Only I had to do it. My dear brother Dezső, please write to me long letters more often, I love to read them. Don't be afraid that I may not read them, even if it were five times as long, then too, I would read it. Even now I'm reading it and rereading it many times, so it would be appear that it's an even longer letter. Please write always good things and as soon as possible! The rest of the news, with God's help, if we get out of there, we will talk all about it, when we get there. Give our kisses to dear uncle Jónász and the rest of the relations. Kisses to you individually, your faithful brother, Ignác

[In English] Good by
[On the side] miss you very much [written in English, but Hungarian spelling].

1939 Undated Ignác to Dezső [regarding Jane Fabianova] (Book 5, 84-85)

'Baruch Hashem'
My dear brother David, Leben until One Hundred Twenty!
Father was in Helmec and spoke to the postmaster lady. She said that she will write to you, too and will mail it from Lelesz with Kocsmaros. As I came to pick up the mail she did not write, but she was also there in Lelesz and I spoke to her. I asked for the letter, and she said that I should write to you that she didn't have any time because she's busy from early morning to late evening and she has a lot of work in the office. Her father passed away this week. She will be here until spring time. She's well and sends her regards. Ignác
I'm writing this in a hurry in Lelesz.

Dear Dezső!

We have been waiting for your letter, finally I was happy to read that thank God you are in good health. Also, I'm glad to know that you have a position. Dear Dezső, please take care of yourself so that the supervisor should be satisfied with you, since you know the situation and it's better that you don't notice it because they can take revenge against you when you don't even expect it. Please don't be angry that I'm writing this to you, I write what I think. Now I will turn to the travel situation, do you know Dezső that if we had gone during the fall we had the money [in the currency] that was then, we would have been there by now, because of that we are at home as of now. Mr. Klein wrote to us last week that when he met our father during the fall he asked how far we are with our travels, and he asked if we need any advice. He writes now that if father would have given him the authority then, we would have been there by now and even now he could solve the problem, but it would cost money. I thought that it would have been worth the money so that we would have already been there. By now, we would have earned his share and would have able to save the amount that would have to be given. It would have been worthwhile to pay him to prevent any disappointment. They're not talking about one person, but four people that would give anything to go. You know how it is here and I'll bet you can understand it. Our father spoke to the old Mr. Klein that his son is asking too much money and he should reduce the price for this work. We gave the case to him, since he said that he can solve the problem. We have written about two weeks ago to Prague and finally we have gotten a reply. We asked the agent to help us with this case and we will pay him any expenses that may have occurred, but we didn't get a reply. We have gotten a reply from the agent in Budapest in which he said that he can't do anything until we mail him the required information that he asked for. We thought that they mailed it to him from Prague and that's why he wrote to us. If it's all possible we will try to do anything we can to go through Prague because then we would not have to make new passports and who knows how long it would take before we would be able to get in line, and besides, it would cost quite a bit and even then we wouldn't be able to go right away. As you know we had enough of waiting, even for a good thing it is too much. One can't tolerate this situation and one can't even write it down. I hope to be able to tell you in person. I believe I've written quite a bit up to now. I didn't want to write this to you, but now I think at least you know the situation and maybe you could help. For myself, I hope that I will receive a reply from America from you. We did not give the letter to Vajzer girls, but we shall do so this week. Otherwise we are well. The news is the same as it was. We wrote to Uncle Jónász, we did not receive a reply. He wrote that he mailed us six dollars, but we did not receive it yet. I wish you good luck, many kisses, and good health. I remain until we'll see you again. Mariska

Don't follow my example, write! We have been accustomed to waiting every day, throughout the [whole] day, we are only waiting!

1939/1 Undated Father to Uncle Jónász (Book 4, 160-161)

[Dated by mention of pengo, so after November 1938, otherwise could go anywhere]

Dearest loving brother Jónász and dear sister-in-law Helen,
I do not know why I did not hear from you for 1 year. I would like to know. Here, we are thank God, well. Hope you are well also. I wish you and your children best wishes and many kisses to you all, with all my love, your brother who will never forget you.
My son Lajos also sends his best regards. Gluck Jeremias

You wrote in the first letter about 75 pengo that you mailed to us. As of today we still did not receive it. The recent letter you sent to Uncle Marton's address, as of today we did not hear about it. Please write about everything, best wishes and kisses to you all, your brother who will never forget you. Just write more about everything. Love, Gluck Jeremias.
We received a letter from Sarolta from Szatmar. She tells me that she's corresponding at this time with her father Lajzer bacsi. She sends her regards to all of you.

1939/1/9 (a) Bertha to Dezső (Book 5, 39-40) pages 1-4 missing pages 5-8

January 9 / 39
New York

Bertha

Dear Dezső!

I can't figure out the reason why I didn't hear from you for so long, that you do not give any life signs about yourself. I hope that it is only from neglect. Please advise me of your being, because I'm very impatient. I hope that you are in good health. We are also well and not missing it.

Our cousin, Jennie Frey is not very well. Last week she was in bed, she had a cold and she's not very strong. I will be going back to see her tomorrow. Last week I was preparing our supper there for all of us. Thank goodness that she is better, but she's very weak. How is our dear Uncle Jónász bacsi and dear Aunt Helen? What do you say regarding the war? I wrote to Miksa [Schőn] by registered mail [saying] that after all this situation, I would like to have his oldest son [Tibi] and my sister Marcsa to come here, but I didn't receive any reply. I don't think they have received it and I also mailed 2 packages for them. I cannot know what to think because I'm afraid that every day it will be worse and perhaps even later they will not be able to come here. It worries me that he may have gotten angry, that is my brother-in-law, because he wrote last year that he wants to come here to America. I replied that he cannot leave his family and cannot bring out the whole family and if he is not capable to help them well, then they should do as they want to. Let them see that only I have a terrible personality, that I should worry. Let's leave this. I don't know why I am disturbing you with this. I only want to inform you that we are not strangers. I did not hear from Jolan for a long time. I mentioned to her that she should proceed to get a visitor's visa to see the world fair, otherwise it would be difficult to come out here. She is a city girl, but she does not have "spunk" if you know what I mean.

1939/1/9 (b) Bertha to Dezső (Book 17, 33-34) pages 5-8

[dated by Bertha making aprons]

I'm afraid that later it is going to be too late, even if I would want [her] to come. So, I can't promise too much to her and if she would be here already, you know one can't be heartless. You know, before the New Year I was very busy. I decided to do aprons, so I can make a few dollars. And it was successful because the aprons came out so nice that I sold them. Although, I gave some to the Boleszt +others as a gift. At least six of them and I gave five dollars as a gift also.

I think I'm doing it right. What do you think? People think that I have nothing to do without siblings and things. I can't live where my kind are suffering at home. I wish I could give them at least a part of what I have. But it hurts that they don't understand me. You know since you wrote a few lines, I did not get any [letters] from my sister Rezsi. But I'm …

not angry at them because they don't understand me. I sent one of the packages to them. Although that country makes people so wild, that is why I am not being understood by them. Like I said they don't know better! That is why I know from my heart, that I am not ruined [emotionally] and, even if yes, I don't mind. I don't want to be that because we are siblings. and we have to behave advised.

I just realized that my letter got pretty long. I hope you will not get tired from reading my letter! Give my best and kisses to all the relatives. I kiss you also. Your cousin, Bertha. Greetings from Mannie. Let's hope that the New Year will bring lots of luck to you! As above

1939/1/29 (a) Bertha to Dezső (Book 5, 41-42) pages 1-4

New York
Jan 29 / 39
Dear Dezső,

I don't know how to begin writing this letter, because I would like to ball you out one minute and in the next minute I feel for you because it's difficult for someone to understand those that want to do good things, and brother I'm speaking to you from my experience and understanding. If your position presently is good at this time, it would have been greater in the future with Arthur. Since you're not a child, you have had enough time to suffer like that, cabbage without meat. After three years you would have had a future and you would not have had to suffer for a few rotten dollars. Within one thousand people one would not have such a future as you would have had. Brother, this is my wish, that you would not be sorry because you're still not familiar with living here. Do you think that when someone speaks to you nicely that they are sincere with you? You are making a mistake. Never talk about your family or about yourself to anyone! Not even about your liking or (disliking) or to give a complement! That is cheap! Please be considerate! I am also asking you to think it over, even though it is painful, as a responsibility to dear Uncle, visit him, and to dear Arthur also, and listen to him. Brother, if you're going to get hit on your face, you will accept it more so from a smart man than a kiss from a crazy person.

Dear Dezső, your family depends upon your dear Uncle [Jónász] to be able to come here. If you show them that you are helping the family with whatever amount you able to afford it. [Show] to the Uncle that you are suffering for his help because your family depends upon it. Do it to [show] your thoughtfulness and suffer again, I'm asking you to think it over and be kind and visit the relations and act as a relative. It does not cost you any money. To meet pleasant sociable people is difficult, and I'm asking you, please, for your future, put everything in your pocket and listen to our Uncle's words with understanding. He is a very very fine, intelligent individual, and you can go further if he would accidentally ask you to return to work for him. If you don't want to, then tell him you are very grateful for his asking, [but] what you would like to do is to learn the English language working with people, so that you would be able to use it and then you would be able to consider his proposition. Trust in Arthur because he's the only one who could help. That is all at this time. Now I'm going to refer to my dear Jolan.

1939/1/29 (b) Undated Bertha to Hermine (Book 4, 283-284) pages 5-8

[dated by lined paper]

Jolanka has no patience to wait, even though I wrote that we will finance the ship tickets. So I don't have to ask the family to have them come here as "szokot" [maybe szokott=escaped] people. In the meantime my sibling's situation is not more favorable. That is why I thought if Miksa's son [Tibi] would come out first, and then if Marcsa [Bertha's sister] would be able with the kids, and maybe we could have my sweet mother come here. I don't want to mention that for now because I don't like to promise. Although, dear Arthur already sent a affidavit for her and for Tibi at the same time. Now Mannie will have one written too. Yesterday he talked to a person who will probably be able to help for a lot of money. Miksa and the others will have to get here by the quota because if they close the quota, it will take at least 4 or five years until they could come out. So, let's hope that we will have luck to bring him out here. Now I am asking you, do not mention any of this at home because then it is going to be trouble. If I will find out that you mentioned any of this to our relations because you know the letters are being censored. You should just learn to be quiet as a man. It is never hurts. Too much talk brings one into trouble. You can mention about Kalman's children. When you were here maybe Aunt Jennie could have told you that she would want to see Kalman's kids. You must have mentioned something to your siblings here! Now they wrote to Jennie too. So, do you need this?! So everyone will resent you? That is why I'm asking you honestly, if you hear anything, forget it, if you are not interested in it. Everybody should mind their own business. Everybody should look after themselves! You should think about yourself also and your family as well! God forbid, you are the only one who they can turn to. You know that well. In case Miksa coming here will be successful then maybe you can rush their coming here too because of that. But I'm asking you again! God forbid, don't say anything to anybody because we could get into trouble. You hear what I'm telling you?! Don't answer these few words to me because I don't want my husband to know that I told you.

1939/1/29 (c) Undated Bertha to Dezső (Book 3, 373-374) pages 9-12

[I am continuing from page 9]

I will begin to write to you about Jolan. She met now a young man and this young man has written to me a letter that I should advise him what he should do because he is in love with Jolan and he cannot carry on if she should come to America and he should remain there. It is a very well written letter, but it's not for me to answer this question. What he should do is to get advice from his relations, since I'm not in a position that I could give him advice. My niece may not be too clever, because she thinks that since we do not have any children then we do not have any problem, but I worry more about my family than she thinks. Dear Dezső, they think that we have a tree and we shake it and the money will fall down. I'm enclosing Jolan's letter to you. She writes in her letter that she thinks that she will get into difficulties because the consulate in Bucharest will believe that she is coming here to work if she comes in a quota. If she only comes for a visit, then they will not return her. She's afraid of her own shadow. It is natural that if she's coming to the world fair they will not even think of questioning her about anything. Please speak to them because they think that you can give an affidavit to everyone. If someone works for others, I don't believe that Jolan is a shrewd girl. My dear Dezső, this is enough of my thinking. Now I'm going to ask for your advice. I began to make aprons so that I could make a few extra dollars to help them, otherwise I can't. God knows our heart, you can see it's good, but this is not bad, and God will help us. I will not write more at this time. I believe that you will be satisfied with this letter and you are not writing about bringing them. Lots of luck with whatever you have started. Kisses, love Bertha.

Also I send kisses to the relations. Thank you for the pictures. Forgive me for my natural true me. Please give our kisses to our dear relations. I ask why don't you have complete confidence in yourself, because you understand everything better than anyone else. A smart man does not talk like that to himself.

1939/1/30 Father, Emil, Ignác, Marie, Hermine to Dezső (Book 1, 207-210)

[From Marie]
Dear Dezső!
Don't be surprised that I did not write to you, but we were waiting for your letter everyday and your letter was a little late, but last week it arrived luckily. I was glad to read that thank God, you are in good health. Dear Dezső, I can't even write down the situation here. We are nowhere with our traveling. The whole thing is so terrible, but what can a man do, and where to start, because whomever we talk to, gives a different opinion and the agent is not like the one we had from Prague. He responds to our 5th letter in a way that he should have responded to the first one. We are running out of time. I don't know if it's true, but I hear that the immigration permit/visa will be only valid for 6 months, and that is until the end of March. The way everything is going, who knows if we will be able to travel because here the days go by without anything and with impatience. Dear Dezső, what you wrote in a few lines. You know, if God would help us, and everything would come true, then God would have a special care for us. But we are at the point where we don't know what to write to you. We hear that we can urge the American Consul from there, so then we could arrange it without the quota. We would be able to travel in a short time. Although, we are also being late, because we have no notary, but he should be here [soon] already. The notary has to approve the house also, and then we need to send it to a new [office] place, because of the approval. So until there is a notary in Ujhely, there is nothing that can be done. You can imagine the whole situation. The tobacco exchange was done also, but not like it's usually done. It was 29 quintals [1 quintal = 100 kg] and we got 40 Hungarian forint. But compared to what others got, ours was not bad. So we did not get anything for our money, because we had an advance. I will not write more and I think you understood everything. I wish you a lot of luck in your new job and good health. I kiss you. Did you know Fernè Brandorzs from Helmec, poor thing he died. And the old Lajos Török died also. Give my best to dear Uncle Jónász and to the other relatives. Write about everything, we will write. As soon as we will know anything we will let you know. Good health and kisses, Mariska

[On the side] Thank you for the picture. Uncle Marton is waiting for your letter.
[On the top] Aunt Lenke Lefkovics is being taken to America by her brother, if it's possible to travel.

[From Hermine]
Dear Dezső!
We got your letter, which we could hardly wait for, with happiness, and [are glad] that your present place is good and you have less time for the quarrels-arguments. I can only write that you should rather try to get along with them, especially now when you could do that. Uncle Leizer got a letter from dear Uncle Jónász, where he writes that he has a lot of annoyance with you. However, I believe that this came in handy for him at the same time, because Uncle Leizer wrote twice already about the Lebovics case. And he ignored it again. And he did not write anything again about the guarantee. Also, it's been two weeks already since Feri from Szürty wrote our father asking for our uncle's address. Lipot [asked] as well and he got the uncle's address. Maybe Uncle Jónász won't be happy that dad gave it, but we can't refuse to. And why should we be the bad ones? It's also true that they will write the same way that Feri will: [That] he heard that he could give a guarantee. Also, he needs the guarantee in the first place, he thinks the cost comes afterward. He did not write about this out in the open, but I know. And he does not even think that they would deny it. I don't even know what to write. I would have a lot to write about, but now it is Thursday night again and I'm in a hurry to write. Although, I don't know if I can send it tomorrow, so I will get back to the American trip. Everyone would be happy if they could get the necessary guarantee. And we have all these with all the documents, but still, it's so hard.

About all the documents, here and many others I could write about a lot, but what for, when with having those we [still] cannot get anywhere. Dad is going to Helmec tomorrow and he'll be able to get some things done in our case. Our Uncle Marton was just in Budapest, but he could not get anything done, because they are waiting for something to know. Everyone is the same way about that, but it's truly a hard case. I believe dad will try to ask the lawyer in Prague, Klein from Bacska. Maybe, it would go easier and a new passport would not be necessary. I got a card from Lajos from Szürty. He also plans on traveling just as H[elen]Perl. She's also planning on it and [getting] a Hungarian passport done.

The Bolyi Guttman relatives from Helmec, the Herskovits girls, are in Prague for months, but they don't have money to travel away. Therefore, it seems it isn't good either way. But I'm hoping and I could hope, too. It would be better if it would go the way we would like it to go. Write about everything and don't be surprised [or] worried if you don't get an immediate response to your letter. Our traveling is going very hard. But what can we do?

Uncle Marton wrote a detailed letter to the son of Hermel from Helmec. He is a lawyer in Prague, who indicated that he was interested in our case. Maybe, if it's possible, we would travel to Prague. I'm curious, what will he answer? If it is impossible, then we'll need a Hungarian passport, and many are asking for that. Dear Uncle Jónász doesn't even know to whom he should give it [a guarantee]. I believe we came off well, that we agreed to it back then, because now he wouldn't do it. If only God would give us help, so we can go already. I wrote everything in this letter honestly, because it will go to your own hand. It would not be good for others to see. I'm in a hurry and writing very messy, but don't pay attention to it now. I guess I wrote enough.

Kiss you with love, Hermin

[from our father]
Bodrogmező, January 30, 1939
My dear son Dezső!
I'm letting you know that thank goodness, we are in good health. I hope that this is something you are not missing! I respect you and kiss you, your faithful father. Who never forgets you. Gluck Jeremiah
Thank you for the items you sent. The kids wrote everything. I'm sending my regards to Uncle Jónász and his family. Now I don't have more time to write.

[from Emil, my brother Lajos' son]
Dear Uncle Dezső!
I'm sorry that I don't write much to you, but I'm going to school now. I kiss you many times, your little nephew Emil. Lenku and Mityu too. I kiss you.

[from Ignác]
My dear brother Dezső! We got your letters and we were very happy that thank God you are in good health. I hope that my lines will find you in the best of health! We are very impatient about the trip, otherwise, we are fine. Very blessed, waiting for our good luck. I'm asking you dear Dezső not to be angry because I'm only writing this much. I wrote everything down in the previous letters, but still it would have been nice to write more. Next time I will write, but please write to me. I kiss you many times and the rest of the relatives, too. Ignác, your brother

1939/1/30 Herman and Grandfather Samuel Schwartz to Dezső (Book 4, 265-266)

B"H
1939
I/30
Dear Dezső, until 120
We happily got your letter. We are happy that thank God, you are in a good and peaceful place. I'm sorry that I will write only a few lines, but I will make it up next time in a letter or with words [in person]. We are, thank God, alive. If the good God would help us, I would like it that we could be there as soon as possible. But we hope, that God is good, and this case will end, but it takes up a lot of time. Now I wish you the best and also good health. Countless kisses, Herman
Monday I/30 1939

Lelesz 1939 January 7th

My dear loving grandchild, Dezső,

In my great happiness, I don't know what to reply. As I heard, thank God, that you have for yourself a good and a respectful place. [However,] what's important, that on Saturday, you are going to work. I also like this job, but I can see that whatever road a man is trying to apply to, he will get an answer from the good God. However, I warn you about something, that our Saturday is the day of rest, and therefore, if it's possible, go to the synagogue, where you can learn and by this you will get better news and you will always get to better places, because the good God, will not forget about you. Instead, there is no other place to go except where they learn Hebrew on Saturday afternoon. Do not be ashamed from the others and so go back and see exactly how [zosz czimbù zaktol tsze sanuly zuszat - זוס צימבאו זאקטול צא שאנולי זוסאט] because you need to consider the soul. Therefore I can't write more to you about what kind of situation the Jews are in here. Thank God I'm in good health here, Grandmother is also. We wish you good health and youthful energy, and forgive me that I discipline you so much. I'm writing it from my heart.

I will countlessly stay faithful,

With our regards, your grandfather and grandmother also, and from my son Lajos.

Samuel Schwartz

Joseph Samuel Schwartz from Leles [In Hebrew]

I ask for a good answer.

1939/3 Berta Veiser, a friend, to Dezső (Book 5, 72-73)

1939 March
Kiraly-Helmec

Very respected Mr. Gluck L/m/ e/shuna [to 120].

I received your esteemed letter from your dear sister and my whole heart was touched by your willingness to find our dear relatives. We are very glad that your hard work was crowned with success. I imagine how amusing it must have been when you telephoned [them] in English even though you are still having a hard time.

Does this relative remember me? It's really good, I remember them and I regret and am sorry that his wife passed away, my dear niece was such a person, a real Jewish woman that if everyone would follow her belief then this world would be different. Mr. Gluck, I thank you for your kindness and continue your work further, especially in this world. It is a big 'Miczve' [a good deed] in today's European state and there is no other thing for us, but to get out of here.

My children are diligent 'Bechoved' [with honor] respectful, smart intelligent, healthy beings and I would not worry if they could get out, but this is the biggest problem that the quota system makes it very slow to get out. One cannot live nor die. Perhaps, if they were adopted, I ask Mr. Gluck speak to the dear Bayer relations because with an affidavit it would take too long to get to America, because the quota system may have been filled and if there will be any way to adopt them then perhaps through Josephine Pepi, a Bayer relative. I do not know their address, but I heard that they are rich, but don't have any children. My children would not be of any difficulty, but they would forever be grateful to them. What should I write to you Mr. Gluck! I know that you are reading the newspapers aren't you? Please give our sincere regards to the dear relations and their son and I'm asking them not to forget about us. And to you Mr. Gluck we are thankful for your diligent work, your sisters Hermina and Mariska are the best of friends to my daughters and they love them, for your sisters are kind hearted people.

If you have a little time please advise us regarding the above.

I remain with respect.

[Mrs.] Henrikne Veizer born

Berta Grunfeld.

1939/3/8 Bertha to David (Book 5, 225-227)

March 8 / 39
Moroff's Hotel

Dear David!
I'm trying to answer your letter as soon as possible. I mailed what you wrote to Jolan, but I think it would've been better off if you would not have written to her that she should write to Arthur. When I asked Arthur be kind enough to give an affidavit to Miksa [Schon], he sent me a reply. After that, I would never bother him again for the whole world even if he will give me gold. That is true, what he wrote me was enough, even if he sent me an affidavit only. From now on, I would never ask any paper or anything else from any one of the relatives. If Jolan wants to wait for when she will get the quota it will take years from there to come because she has more aggravation and worries. She will make me more aggravation. And I'm not that strong of a person that I can undertake that responsibility [and] to take care of myself. As you, I have to leave my home for a couple of days because I would destroy myself with every person's problem. At least if I would be able to help them, but I can't. The quota is so full it would take years. Dear Dezső, it will be better if I gave up from everything before it will be too late because I am so worn out. I am not able to function with all these problems from all sides. I can't bother Mannie about my family and he has his family also. Now he wants to bring his parents out. Dear Dezső, for a working man it is too much and I eat myself with aggravation and save everything to be able to help others. It's better if a person looks out for themselves. I've lost weight. Therefore I need some time to myself and I have to get away for at least 10 days. Sunday I will go home. And after, I will try to rest every afternoon. If I don't, then for a long time I will not be able to take care of my health. I know how to take care of my health, and I want to do more as my strength allows, it's worth paying for it. I think it is enough for now. Wishing you all the best with affection. Bertha

1939/3/8 Emil Gluck to Dezső (Book 4, 209-210)

[from Emil]
Dear Uncle Dezső,
I received the letter that I had been waiting for. Before I received your reply to my letter I thought that you may not want to write to me. I began to be angry, however, I'm not angry now because you answered my letter. And my dear Uncle Dezső, I want to thank you very much for wanting to send something for me. I'm really looking forward to receiving something from you. Tibi received something from his Aunt Bertha, so I'm also waiting for something. Lenku and Mityu are happily looking forward to getting a package. I don't know what to write you this week. It was Purim and I got 80 Fillert. How did you spend your Purim? My dearest Uncle Dezső, I hope that I can be in America also! I hope that God will help us, like you have been helped in doing everything to get out from here. There are a lot of people that would love to get out from here. I already know 15 words in English. I'm kissing you 1,000,000 times. Your nephew, Emil Gluck, Bodrogmező, 1939 March 8.

Dear Uncle Dezső, we are also kissing you, Lenke and Mityukam.

1939/3/8 Father and Ignác to Dezső (Book 4, 3-4)

My dear son Dezső!
I got your letter, for which I hardly could wait, and I'm so happy that you are, thank God, in good health. I did not know what to think that you didn't respond to my letter. Also, my dear brother Jónász doesn't write and I didn't get a response since October 28. Uncle Jónász wrote that he sent to me 6 dollars and until this day, I did not get it. I let my brothers know. Dear son, I don't know how to start to write, but I am speculating, but it's not worth anything. About the trip, Klein B. in Prague asked 1000 P [to find out] if the trip to Prague will happen. I told his father I will give 500 p. so he can write this to his son. Now I'm waiting for the response. The deputy sheriff put the documents from the house's sale to the orphan's court. I will arrange everything in this case with the notary. I will respond tomorrow in person. I will take the documents in person, so it will be done sooner so it will be approved. They can pay off its cost. I sold the land already because there wasn't anything [else] to do nor [money] to pay. It was necessary. Already 2 buyers signed up for the house, but I'm obligated [to sell it] to the commune. Two weeks ago I talked over everything with the deputy sheriff. I asked, if they will approve or reject the buyer. He promised me that he will approve it. On his part it will be settled. My brother Uncle Jónász will send to Lebovics and Feri, an affidavit and I read the letter briefly that Uncle Jónász wrote about you, that he is not satisfied. He suffered so much because of you. I'm asking you my son, be good. I respect you and kiss you countless times. Your faithful father, who will never forget you. Gluck Jeremias

My dear brother Dezső,

We got your letter that we were waiting so hard for. I was already thinking that you forgot about me, since your letter was late for a long time. But it's ok. The most important thing is that, thank God, you are in good health. I hope that my lines will find you in the best of health. And, if God helps us all, I hope we will be on the ship for Passover. I can't write anything new. The others wrote everything already. Yes, it's been two months since Joska Kopasz signed up to be a gendarme [police] and they accepted him. They called him in for 6 months training. He has it good out there. [IN YIDDISH:] Nor zenen ále resúem dé náje lád, ober nor cím jid (TRANSLATION: Even though he is in a good situation as a csendőr, nevertheless the " náje lád", the new csendőr trainees are evil, roshoyim / resúem, but only to the Jews.)

I'm not asking for anything, only for God to help us all. I want to tell you about the things at home in person not in letters. I kiss you many times. Your brother who thinks about you a lot. Ignác Gluck
Write often, don't wait for the response.

1939/3/8 Undated Hermine to Dezső (Book 4, 309-310)

[Dated by mention of Purim and Passover, two weeks after Lajos applied for passport he received it]

Dear Dezső!

We read your long awaited letter with happiness, that you are in good health.

We could not imagine, what was the reason why you sent a letter in Uncle Marton's letter we got. Although, now you have a part in writing letters, but we did not write until now, because we were waiting for your letter. We got used to waiting for our letters so much, so we are always waiting, only sometimes we get lucky to get our long waited letters. I can't write anything about us, because we did not do anything with the traveling. It is very difficult. We were notified to request the new passports and the shipping company from Pest sent two applications to fill out, and [one of which we would have to] send to the consulate in Prague so they could officially document which place we are in the quota and send it to the American Consul, and the other one filled out to the agent. But until today, we did not do anything because we hoped that it could work out to travel with the old passport. One letter went to Klein in Prague, and he would arrange everything for 1000 pengos, if it would work out. 200 pengos, if it doesn't work out. For now, it's up in the air. If we could agree, that way it would work out shortly. Lajos from Szürte has a Hungarian passport already. He requested it with Helen Perl at the same time and she did not get it yet. It's been two weeks already. It would be good to know when can they travel.

My special wish to God is that the moment to travel to America, the moment that we can hardly wait for, should come already. You may say that I wrote a lot about my sorrow and painful situation and we are still wishing. But you should think back, how much being patient can leave you so restless. That with so much hope we wait. It looks like we must make peace with everything. And it would be good to be over with everything, or it would be good in America already. Many people are getting ready, for example; Keszler who was Braun's aide, will travel to Prague. It's possible, that it would be very easy to arrange ours, but it's no use to write to the shipping company in Prague, they will send their response to Pest and I would get it from them. I leave it alone already. I wrote enough also, and you should write, because we can hardly wait. I can understand your situation also, you have enough on your plate also. Have you not met the Uncle or Arthur yet, since then? Well, with God's help, we will be there, however it is, he will not be happy for us, for sure. I don't remember exactly, but about a few weeks ago, our Uncle wrote to Uncle Lajzer. He was wondering why can't we travel and we should write [the reason] immediately. Allegedly, Uncle Lajzer did not answer yet, but it's possible, that he's just saying it and he will send some kind of winter clothes. Also, when our father was in Ungvár, he took off at Szürte, and there they said that Uncle Jónász gives a guarantee to Lebovits and to Feri. I don't know if they will go, but the point is, whomever is waiting for a guarantee, will hope. But we have everything and we are just milling around in one place. How was Purim? Did you go anywhere? Or maybe you didn't even have time to think about it. We truly don't know about anything. We don't go anywhere. What I wrote is enough. Kisses, Hermin

I wish you good health and take good care of yourself. Have a pleasant Passover. In person, we will pay the cost per person. From the money we got from the lands, we paid Mihanszky off. He did not take any interest.

1939/3/13 Blanka to Dezső (Book 5, 119)

1939 March 13
Radvancz,

Dear Dezső,

I just want to remind you that after you left, you finally wrote me a card and I was in a hurry to reply to you and as of today I have not received any reply from you. Dear Dezső perhaps you have not received my letter because the international letters got lost, but I'm still hoping that you will write. Please write me the reason or perhaps you did not feel it's important? With all respect, you are always in my mind and especially when I look at the albums and I see all those pictures that you have made. Don't be disappointed that I'm writing on this type of paper, however I'm taking this with all uncertainty, perhaps you will receive this letter a year later. I hope that you will receive this letter and you will not leave it without a reply. With heartfelt regards to you, Blanka.

1939/3/26 Jolan Mayer to Deszo (Book 3, 390-391) pages 1-4

[green ink lined paper]

1939 March 26
Szatmar, Romania

Dear Dezső!

I received your letter and I'm in a hurry to reply. I'm so surprised that I cannot even write it down. I did not write those things to the consulate, not a word is true. [There are three lines blurred I cannot read it]. Do you know Dezső, I see everything that you wanted to take me out to America and now I am connected with the boyfriend because he wrote to Bertha. I did not know a word about anything, and I was very surprised when Bertha wrote about it. I gave him what he deserved. Even though I'm writing this, you will not believe it. However, God should help me so that I should be out there in America real soon. Since then I'm not friendly with him. I know very well that if I'll go, I couldn't take anyone along with me and I wouldn't. I could go there as a visitor, and I wouldn't have to live here in fear. This is what's happening here. Dezső, don't think that you have scared me by what you have written to me, that you are sorry because you went out of the way. I do not get scared from anyone, even then it's better because you are not under constant prosecution...... what I have written I see it quite well. I can see that whoever has a small relationship in America is in a hurry to get help in any way, in any form, so that they could go out. I've written to Bertha, that God forbid, I do not want it to cost her any money by sending me that ship ticket. And I've said in my letter that I would send her money to repay her expenses and ticket. And when I begin to work I would not live there, I would earn enough from day to day to make a living and I would not run home.... You must know Dezső that it depends upon the goodness, if I wanted to do that [then] I would go to the World's Fair for six months. Once out there then some arrangement could be made that I could remain there. Because of that I'm asking all of you, don't find any excuse, that is, because of the boyfriend and because of that and running away from this. I would not have written about this because it would not have been a great unfortunate thing that he has written to Bertha. She could have answered him a few lines and not throw me away....... and not to find any excuses, because it would have made me feel better that very simply you would have written it [like this], 'Jolan,

1939/3/26 Jolan Mayer to Deszo (Book 5, 232-233) pages 5-6

[green ink lined paper]

We have a much closer relative and he/she is the one who we have to bring out. You can't come now only after 5 years' and I would thought it over. And believe me it would have sounded better that way. As you or Bertuska wrote. Because Bertuska also wrote that she wants to bring out Marcsa's [Mariska Gluck] two kids [Clara and Tibor]. I can understand it, that [it can be done] only for closer relatives than I am. It makes me feel so very badly, but [it's] in vain, I'm so unlucky. I'm sure that Arthur does nothing for me because if he would've done it, I would have a result. It is not really nice of him...Dezső please don't be mad at me because I got a little out of myself, but if you read my letter well and you think it through well, you will realize that I am 100% right. Although, it is true that I won't go too far with it, but at least you should know. And don't think that I was waiting for some help from you, God help from [asking] that...only that you can talk [up] in my interest. I will not bother you anymore. I kiss you, Jolán

1939/3/31 Bertha to Dezső (Book 17, 12-13)

New York
March 30 / 39
Dear Dezső!

I got your letter, but forgive me I could not understand the content, since the writing was rushed. And it comes very hard for me to recognize the flashy letters. So, please write a letter with an explanation so your mail will not go to waste. You wrote that our Uncle sent documents to somebody, but I could not understand for who? Brother, if you want to be smart, then see everything, but know nothing about anything and anyone! This way you will get along with everyone and everyone will like you. If you don't like someone, keep them by your side because you never know who is your well-wisher. The world got cold, even the priest is not faithful. Now, I'm asking you, whatever the uncle says to you, you must visit them! Also his son. Be smart! You know there is only one net, a proud smart way ahead. Dezső, you don't want my words. Blood will never turn to water! You have to look for them sometimes and be kind to them! You know that to catch a fly [with honey] is easier than with vinegar. Your sisters were looking forward to the trip! I never like to postpone something I could do now, but to no avail. After it rains, there is no need for a raincoat. I hope you don't need to wait 4-5 years, like the others at home! We wanted to bring out the two older kids as students because we thought that this way we don't need to get a quota, but no use, it did not succeed, but there is no way, they can only come by the quota also. So it is unnecessary to do paperwork and visa again because they are students and the oldest son was sent one already by Arthur and by my Mannie. Now I think it was enough about this. I wish you a happy holiday! With love, Bertha
The relatives send their kisses.

1939/4/7 Undated Hermine to Dezső (Book 3, 223-224)

[Dated by reference to hol hamoed = Pesah and Friday]

Dear Dezső!
We have received your letter which we have been waiting with difficulty, the package too. We did not write to you immediately because we were waiting for the package to also arrive and it came on the holiday evening. I thank you for the things that you sent me. Today it's Friday and it is hol haMoed. I do not want to wait with my letter writing, so I'm writing now. Our father is not at home yet. He went to Ungvár to meet with an attorney, when he comes home we will write to you about the results. About ourselves, I do not know anything except that it would be better if we would be there. In the last letter the shipping company from Budapest wrote that we should fill out the form and return it to them, then the Consulate will request the quota from Prague and according to the numbers, [the rank], if it is our turn, then they will advise us. We have mailed in the application and we are waiting and now we can begin to make our passport. What I hear is that many individuals are waiting and this comforts us. Imagine how successful Marcsa Diak is. Their mother is an American, she was born there, now she lives here in Hungary. She can travel to America without the quota system and can take with her two underaged girls. The important thing is that she has to secure the birth certificate and a witness that could prove that she is the same person that they are speaking of. She already has received the birth certificate and now in a short while will succeed. Her grandfather died in Agard, and they have an inheritance and it can be sold. As you know we are not going any place at all, to this you may not be interested. Yes another story, Manci Klein from Lelesz is very sick and as you know they took her to the hospital in Ungvár with malaria. The younger sister Rohcsi has inherited from Samu, who was a policeman, furniture and many other things, and it is made from hard wood. She took care of him and this was in his will. There are a lot of things I could write, but it cannot be done because we try to write something and so things come about that you're not interested in. You know much more and better than we. Do you have a radio? And how are you? Thank God that we are alive. Father bought a cow and it is beautiful. He bought it for 260 pengos. The calf is one week old. The cow gives about 12 liters of milk. Now you know how much happiness it has given us because at least we have that. I wrote to you in the last letter that our father sold a piece of land, but I didn't explain it to you because I thought father would have written it to you. He has sold the Helyes pasture land that was plowed to Gyula Szabo for 1250 Pengos and the Sulymoskát to Andras Toth for 1140 Pengo. We have paid off Mihancki and [our father] gave some to the lumber people and purchased the cow. We have in the Leleszi bank 700 Pengo so that if we need it we shouldn't be held back. We also sold the furniture from the store for 80 Pengo. As you know everything here is very costly. The cheapest lady's shoe is 10 Pengo and 12 Pengo. Emil's shoe is 8 Pengo. When you calculate it, it is very costly. We hope that God will help us because here there's not much hope. I understand you and your situation. Don't worry! Take care of yourself. Where did you go to celebrate Pesah? Uncle Jónász bacsi does not write to us! My handwriting is not the best because I'm in a hurry. With kisses to you, Hermina

[the following information as I remember it, see below, with regards to the exchange rate until 1938 under Czechoslovakia. Then under Hungarian rule the exchange rate was counted with the monetary system as Pengo, now it is Forint. One Hungarian Pengo =7 kronen,

30 Czechoslovakian kronen= 1 US dollar. Now Slovakia is a separate state that uses kronen. also the exchange rate varies. With One Pengo you purchased one kilogram of sugar which amounted to Seven Czechoslovakian kronen. A farm worker was getting six Kronen for one day's labor, that is, from sunrise to Sunset. - By Irv.]

1939/4/7 Undated Marie to Dezső (Book 1, 202-203)

[Dated because just after Passover]

Dear Dezső!
Do not be surprised that we were late with writing a letter for too long, but it is always waiting, so we know something accurate to write about our traveling to you. And even until today we don't know anything. The last time I mentioned to you about Klein from Bacska, that he would have taken [the case], but we found that what he asked for was too much. And now we are lucky that we did not pay for it, because I think that he would know better. The Battyanyi's daughter paid him 500p and even today he is encouraging them to be patient, because it will get done soon. Now he sent her documents from Prague to Budapest and he said it has been taken care of and the amount should be paid to him. Since there are Germans over there they would not have sent it.

But you know Dezső, that is only an excuse, because we were like that also and the application needed to be filled out, so one Consul can take it over from another, and we needed to attach 1 pengo 80 f[illert] to the document and we also sent it in 4 weeks ago to the agent in Pest. We still did not get any notice. We hope that [it is] going to be sooner, not like you wrote, what the "jok" said. Maybe the good God will help and will make our wish come true, that we will be on our way around the time of Shavuot. Although, I could never even think about that yet, that we will spend Passover at home, but it doesn't matter. We have to have peace with the many changes. You know, those who would like to be at least where we are, are innumerable. We will just start the Hungarian passport and everything from scratch. Before we would start we had to travel to Ungvár to the Prosecutor's Office, to see if they will permit the passport and they probably will tell already, if there is a request necessary for the boys and if they will allow [them]. The notary told our father that he should be calm, because they will permit it. So let's hope for the best. Our father will be home this afternoon already, so we will know everything. How are you? Otherwise, we are alive. In the letter where you mentioned what you will send in the package, we got it, but since then no letter came. The gift that you sent me, thank you. For the package, we needed [a] poverty certificate, The whole thing did not cost a lot. Imagine, we are still not right with the house. Now we had to give in the approval again to the law office and if they approve it, only then will it be sent out to the Prosecutor's Office, to see if the town will approve it. You know, Dezső, many times I have such sorrow, that it costs so much and searching for our many documents. It costs a lot and now we would have had done the passports again, but we are afraid, God help us, the air is still not clear around us! You know how I think!! We have a lot of acquaintances who are like we, only they don't have the passport. The agent from Pest wrote to us first, that we should be patient, because we are traveling through the Czech quota. I just have to encourage him, so they can show what place we stand in the quota. And only when the Consul definitely approves it will they write and call us in for the visa. New news, Joska Kopasz and Gabor Leco just arrived home for Easter in police uniform. They became such big men that you would not recognize them. There is no other news. How did you spend Passover? You were in our mind a lot. Did you meet our Uncle? He does not write to us since then, although we don't write either. He wrote to Uncle Lajzer, but he did not respond either. I think he will write after Passover. He is also well. He was home yesterday. Grandmother is also in good health, thank God. Now I think I wrote enough, just have the patience to read it. I wish you good health and good luck. I kiss you countless times. If you would meet the dear relatives give them my kisses to all of them.
Mariska

[Up side down:] We got your registered letter with today's mail.

1939/4/9 Father to Dezső (Book 4, 173-174)

Bodrogmező 1939 April 9
My dearest son Dezső,

I received your letter and was very happy to hear that thank goodness you are well. We are well. I did not hear from my brother Jónász since October. Why don't you go to visit him? He has to forget whatever happened. Start again, you must forget whatever was. I was in Szürte [to visit] my brother in law Lebovics and Feri, and Joliek. They received the guarantee from America from my brother Jónász. I did not ask in whose name was it. I have forgotten to ask about their passport or if they have all their papers that they need to get out, their permit to leave the country or if they were ever in jail. To get that paper to prove they are clean you must go to Ungvár, to the legal office located there. It will take time to get those papers since there is an application to fill it out and then you have to send it back to them and this takes time. They make sure you've paid the taxes and if they find anything, they could deny it. And only then you could start to get the passport if they give you all of those papers and it is okay. About the house, 18,000 Czech koronat will be paid to the three banks like the children's share from the orphanage. I will make payments from it and they will try to settle the case legally. I hope it should be in the near future that the American Consulate will be ready with the paper. By then I hope their money and the papers will be ready for the children to go to America. How much it will cost I have no idea yet, the passport also. Thank you for the gift you sent me. In February, my brother [Lajzer] received from his daughter $10. He exchanged it here and got 100 pengot for that. [Jónász] doesn't care that there is no future here. I know you will understand what I mean. I was forced to sell a piece of farm because we did not have anything to eat. We were very lucky that I didn't start with Klein's son because I would have lost for ever. I sent him a letter, but he never answered. Lucky it was settled that week. At least he could have answered my letter saying he will not be able to be there. At this time I can't tell you any more. All my best wishes to you and many kisses many times, your loving father, who never forgets you. Gluck Jeremias.

I'm going to go to Helmec. I will show to Uncle Marton this letter. I ask you again, please go and visit Uncle Jónász and his family. You should be nice to them. I'll write to them also. your father.

1939/4/9 Undated Ignác to Dezső (Book 4, 299-300)

[Dated by: goes nowhere = no school, everyone writes the same = no news, hate everywhere]

My dear brother Dezső,
We got your letter, that we could hardly wait for. I was very happy that thank God, you are healthy. I'm only asking you dear Dezső, that you take care of your health. I just want to be there already, so you will not be alone. Since you spend your free time with thinking. First of all, you are not doing that right, because nothing is worse than when one is lonely and has an opportunity to think. Believe me, dear Dezső, I criticize the situation there too, I can't tell where is better. The whole world is full of hate. {Yiddish - "sziz ájn core indez gancer vekol"]. Many times I think that you are a lucky man because you are there. Everybody thinks that. I think that too many times. Although, things are not always the way we think. The situation is equal in the entire world, even in letter writing, too. We sit down to write to you at the same time and everybody writes to themselves, and when it's all written, then we wrote the same [thing].
We don't go anywhere, we are only at home, so everyone knows one thing, therefore don't be surprised about all this. In your letter they asked, if I wrote everything. I am doing fine. I kiss you, your little brother, Ignác
Write.

1939/4/14 Bertha to Dezső (Book 4, 410-413)

Dear Dezső!
I will try to respond to your letter. Again I will give you a lesson: please visit your relatives, even if they throw knives at you, but they won't. "Blood doesn't turn into water" [A saying that means: They are finer than that, they would not do that] and you do not want to see the visa [lost], you should do that because of your father, but God help us do not tell anyone that I wrote this, because then you will not hear from me ever again by mail. I did not hear from this girl, who you mentioned came to New York. Dear Dezső, I wrote to Jolan, that Mannie was inquiring on her behalf and the answer was that it doesn't make sense to bring out ["kihozatni"] individuals on a visit, because seven years ago the law became so tough [1932 Immigration law drastically restricted immigration] that … it is hard ["Nehez] after six months to renew the stay, but if she will do it there, because it can be done only there ["smirelni"?] and it will cost a minimum of $500 so this way we can urge her coming-out. Dear Dezső, for Marcsa's children, maybe there is no way to come out, only with the quota and we thought, that way, that Arthur and Mannie already sent documents. Miksa and his oldest son. [We] can't do anymore for anyone. If a child has no one at home, then some way the

child could be brought out sooner. You can write this to Jolan. My Mannie has a sister at home and there is nothing he can do to bring her out. I'm sorry, but Jolan does not want to believe that we would like her to be here with us. Tell her that she will not be in trouble because she said to the consul that she is coming to America to work. It was not the reason why, because [you know] yourself it is obvious/self evident, if someone comes here, they are not coming to visit. That person comes to make a living, and if she wouldn't write this, then the consul would think that she will rely on the state. Dave, that took away from my health a lot, because you know better, that I only want the best for my people, even for strangers. They always think that because I wasn't close with the relatives, you know that I'm not corresponding with my sibling, only with our father, that I don't want to listen to their "czoresz" [problems]. They also had relatives come here, especially for Rezsi and [she] did not come. Once we sent to my brother enough money, that they should go to Canada, but [he did] not......, but I can't do anything for anyone, because the man lives nicely and then believe that ....I'm sorry, but I can't do anything. Jolan always consoles me. Jolan always wants to know what to do and we can't get out of it. You know better, that I am like a grandmother, what I have on my tongue / lip I have on my lung ["grader mihel [vogyak] vász ich kòb on mein cùng labick on my ùn lùng" [Yiddish - needs translation - maybe, "I say what's in my heart"] I'm not afraid to tell the truth. Although, I wrote to her to come to the exhibition, because the late uncle Henry's wife suggested this, but later we found out about a Romanian girl. She came here like a medical student and she had go back to Romania. Although she found herself a young man, she still had to travel back. If she was afraid it would be better herself, then still good, but, if no, then the heartache is bigger. So that's why I wrote to dear Jolan, to try to come permanently, but it's useless. And I will get a nervous breakdown from the whole thing. You know, that a poor man has a good heart, but yes there are relatives here from her mother [Sarolta and Bertha were step sisters, and Bertha is referring to Sarolta's mother's family] and she tries them. They are smarter and they can take care of things better than I. Although, I don't know their addresses, but once that person brought me a letter from Lipot Majer - from his brother-in-law, so they need to know their addresses. Dear David, I wish you good luck for your big brother [Lajos] coming here. But he should have enough money with him, because when someone comes to visit, he must have enough money to travel back. Although, to America, yes maybe he will be the lucky one, who will successfully stay here. I wish him much luck, because he needs it. Let's stop with this whole thing, enough about this. Dave, don't worry, the package will arrive to Europe. I sent two packages also. On January 9th and last month on the 27th once again. 39 pounds and on Monday I will send [one] again. In this package everything is for the children and I will "honit" and something to send. See, if you would be smart and you could seek out [visit] your relatives, they would give you something also, that you can send home. Listen Dezső, only a fool is proud, but a smart [person] uses their brain. I will close my lines. I have done more than you [unclear].

with love-
Bertha
Greetings to everyone
I'm very tired.

1939/4/15 Rella Veiser to Dezső (Book 5, 74-75)

Dear Mr. Gluck! L.M.SHONA
We are very grateful for your lines and we thank you very much for all your effort. Until now I could not write because I was waiting for my dear Bayer bacsi's letter, that did not come as of yet. I'm asking you my dear Mr. Gluck to continue your effort, we would forever be grateful to you. I would like very much that my niece Lilly and I [could] enter America. Would you be kind enough to ask our relations to give us Aunt Jozepfine's address and perhaps she would be able to do something on our behalf, my dear mother met her and knew her in person. The situation here is not rosy, what should I write? I believe that in America you know much more. For example, everyone here is worried about getting their permits to be in business. Lilly has an established business and she is a very successful person. She has been in business for five years. I too know how to make ladies' hats, sewing, baking, cooking and so forth. What is the most important thing is that I'm willing to do any type of work, we're not afraid of work. Therefore, once again I'm asking you to be kind enough do something on our behalf. Besides all this, how are you? Did you get accustomed to America? Do you speak English well? Please give my kisses to Bayer bacsi and his dear daughter and the whole family. I'm awaiting a reply with regards
Veizer Rella
Kiraly-helmec 1939 IV 15th

New York
April 26, 1939
Dear David,
By this letter I'm also asking that you put your ugly, stubborn nature aside and visit the Uncle. Even if he doesn't send help home. Consider it in honor of your dear father. First of all, he does not owe anyone to send anything home. If he does not want to, you can not blame it on the Uncle. Also, it comes out looking badly that you don't go there, Dave. You don't think properly a little. I'm afraid that you are still angry with me because I saw the whole thing in a different way. My dear Dezső, Americans don't mess with each other. If the Uncle sent home a package to someone, he did not do it to take a revenge on your father. I ask you, that God help you, don't dare repeat this to anyone in the world, because they will think that you are not a respectable man. A grown up man does not understand it like that. Moreover, you can see that he wants to help whomever he can with the documents. It is good that there is someone to turn to for immigration documents because many people would not even do this. The conscious makes me happy, that you don't forget about your loved ones and you will help them as much as you can. God will help. I'm glad to hear that there is hope for your sisters' emigration. Dezső, I'm only asking you, be more considerate and don't be afraid that others would want to defy you [and] don't be envious of anybody for something good. Do not talk too much about your relatives [referring to Arthur and Jónász]. God help them if it comes back to them. It would not be nice and it would be very unpleasant to you. If you think something about someone, you just keep it to yourself. I'm telling you this, because I wouldn't like you to have a problem with anyone. I hope you will understand me and you will do like I write it to you. I know how hard it is for someone who is starting a new life, a new language, and [is trying] to make it better, starting everything from the bottom. But time will bring everything by itself. I don't remember if I mentioned to you, I sent a package home again, but only clothing. I washed everything so that they will not declare anything. I hope everything will arrive without any trouble. Now, I hope you are satisfied with this long letter. I ask you again, don't be angry about my bugging you, but I only want the best. I hope that you will forgive me that I wrote so openly. Now, accept my kisses, and Mannie also send his greetings, to the relatives too. Bertha

Bodrogmező, May 7,1939.

From my loving heart to my son Dezső.
I was very happy to read your letter. Thank God that you are healthy and hope that my lines will find you in good health. On May 2, I traveled to Budapest. There was a national fair. The traveling was half of the usual price. I went because of the passports. No one was allowed to go the consulate office, only by an invitation through the mail. As soon as they will receive the documents from Prague, they will notify us. They are very slow in Prague. They are overloaded with paperwork, however, when they receive our papers they will notify us immediately. I spoke with the agent and they too are promising me. He said that it was regretful that I had to travel to Budapest, because if they receive [the papers] they would immediately notify us. The Czech passport is not valid, so we will need a new passport. The Agent said not to make the passport, even though we already began to make it, until he notifies us. Thus, we have to wait. Someone was asking the travel agent, when will their time to travel come, [he said] maybe two or three years. I asked the travel agent if my children's journey will take place this year and he answered positively. I received a questionnaire from the consulate to fill out and mail it to them in order to find out what happened to the documents if they had arrived yet from Prague. It has to include a self addressed stamped envelope, then the consulate will reply. I have difficulty with the building also. The 18,000 Czechoslovakian Korona are in three different banks. The underage children and the children's money has to be deposited in the bank. The only part that can be taken out for travel to America, is namely, Herman's and Ignac's. I have to petition the office of the orphans to secure all the traveling monies that needed. This office decides the amounts for each. They are demanding Emil's and Lenke's share of 627, Herman's and Ignác's share of 627 pengos, that is 1871 pengos [total should be 1881] to be paid to the orphanage office. I will try to determine some way what to do. I was in the orphanage office and spoke with the president there because we are not going to have enough money for the travel expense. God will help us. I wish we would be at that point. I received a letter from my brother last month on the 23rd and he enclosed $10. Don't be an antagonistic to my brother. My brother Jónász asked me if the affidavit is good. I replied that I don't know, and I asked him to ask you. I showed the letter to the

travel agent in Budapest and he said it's fine. About that you will also let me know. Best wishes and kisses, your true father that will never forget you. Gluck Jeremias

I received the gift that you sent me and I thank you. Your grandfather asked Ignác if we have written to you that he closed his store. Best wishes from him also. Your father, Gluck Jeremias.

My dear brother Dezső,
I received your letter and I was very happy that thank God you're well. Hope that my lines will find you healthy. Thank God, with problems excluded, I am well. We are waiting for a better future! Forgive me, but I'm writing to you so badly, I have no patience and I'm in a hurry but I know that it doesn't go to the stranger. I hope that you're going to be able to read it. Yes, are you wearing your eyeglasses all the time or just in business, let me know about it. You know, if you would write to me separately then I could write you much more. I was over to our grandfather. They mention you all the time and are complaining that they are living from savings. They are reminding you that perhaps you will think of them. Otherwise they are well. The military exercise began and [it takes place] every Sunday morning for ages 12 years of age to 21. Filip Miklos, the elementary teacher, is teaching us. The Polish person returned and now we have a minyan [a quorum], so as of now we had services in our temple. Loads of love and kisses your brother, Ignác Gluck 1939 V/7
Please write to me separately and a lot and so will I. Write a lot. [In English] Goodby!
I don't feel like studying English because we will forget it anyway, sometimes I study a little bit.

1939/5/8 Undated Hermine and Marie to Dezső (Book 4, 281-282)

[Dated from father going to Budapest]

[from Hermine]
Dear Dezső!
We got your letter, that we could hardly wait for and we try to write. Although, if Friday did not get in our way, we would have written a response immediately. I'm glad, that you are, thank God in good health, we are also doing fine somehow. Dad bought a pair of eyeglasses for himself in Pest. The doctor and the glasses costed 30 p[engos]. Dad tells how beautiful everything was at the Exhibition. You can imagine that even from Polyán people travelled to the fair. But forget this one, too. Imagine our happiness, we got a letter from Uncle Jónász, and truly he writes [in a way] that nobody would believe it. Although he wrote that we should not write about this to you, I will write it anyway, but please never mention this to anybody. He is wondering about our traveling, and he said he will do anything, [we should] just write [what we need] to him, as though it would be for his own children. And he said that if money will be a problem, he would send it too for all four of us. He wrote that we should not think that he is doing this out of obligation, no! He does it gladly and willingly, because our father does not even know, how much he loves him. And he will do anything, we only have to write it to him. Although, Bertuska and our father are writing that you ought to visit him, but if you do visit him now, he would think that we wrote to you [about what he has written]. He noted, if you wouldn't have caused any trouble to him, he would have already sent the tickets for the ship last year. But I repeat myself, never mention any of this to anybody, because I would not want this to get to them or that he will worry about us. We are doing everything so he will not have any annoyance because of us. However, about [what he has written], we were thinking we will refuse it, unless it does not work out in any other way. I know that it will cost a lot, but it is better that way, than not at all. I was thinking with this hope, what if the time to travel will come and we will not have the money? In this, the worst case scenario, we will not stay at home because of that reason, [that Uncle Jónász has offered to pay]. They called Mrs. Deak to Budapest on July 6. The way it appears, she will travel to America. I have hope that by the summer we get our turn, too. Although it would be nice to get the entire thing over with, we can't help that. Did you write to Terebes? I wrote, but they did not respond. They must not be ok. Write about everything and may God give us that your response will not find us still at home. I'm so sick of the whole thing already, that I can hardly write it down and I can hardly wait for the moment when we can go. Emil does not go to heider, he is at home, in Lelesz. They can't support a child and here they hire a direct teacher, but it will be somehow. I kiss you all with love,
Hermin

P.S. Emil, Lenke, Mityu kiss you. I'm asking you to destroy this letter and do not mention it to anybody. I'm only writing this, so you can know also.

[from Marie]

Dear Dezső!

We got your letter, that we could hardly wait for. I'm glad to hear, that thank God, you are in good health, just take good care of your eyes. We are also well, besides being so impatient, and I'm sorry that I'm so brief with my writing, but I think they wrote everything already and they want to send the letter. Imagine that they already called in Mrs. Deak on July 6th to Budapest. She doesn't yet know why. I kiss you with love, Mariska

1939/5/8 Herman to Dezső (Book 5, 86-87)

1939 V/8

Dear Dezső, 120 yr.

We've received your letter. Do not be angry because I did not write an answer to your previous letter. That was because I wrote to you before and this time I just overlooked it for some reason. Thank goodness we're okay. It would be better if we could be there also. How are you? Write more. Our father went Budapest regarding our trip. I believe that he wrote to you about it. I don't want to repeat it. To be precise, the situation is difficult especially now with today's conditions. We hope that everything will turn out to be all right. I don't know any special news,. The weather, thank God, is good, only we could use some rain. We have a received the permit, but it is less than it was before. Miksa Shon did not receive it. It would be better to speak to you in person. I do not have patience to write in letters. Thank you for the package that you sent me. I hope that my lines will find you in good health. I wish you good health, your brother, Herman.

1939/6/2 Father, Ignác, Hermine, Marie to Dezső (Book 4, 285-290)

My dear son Dezső,

I got your letter which we waited so hard for and we gladly read in it that, thank God, you are in good health. I hope that my letter will you find you in good health as well. I am letting you know that we are also in good health. I hope you don't miss that either. In your last letter you wrote that I will get a registered letter from you. That's why I didn't write yet. You were late with the response so the writing got delayed day by day. I went to Helmec yesterday and your Uncle Marton and his entire family got a guarantee, from his brother-in-law Lefkovics, for the American travel, and he already sent it up to the consulate. He wrote that the Magyarkata will be enlarged, so the view is that it will be taken into place sooner. I believe that I wrote it in the previous letter to the agent to urge it, but I did not get a response yet. One came from the consul in Budapest that said there is no registration yet. They did not send the documents over from Prague yet. I believe that the children wrote Uncle Jónász. Regarding the letter you wrote, you can send 10 d[ollars], I just only ask that you look, if you add to it. Her wish somewhat needs to be fulfilled, if it's possible. Regarding Lenke Lefkovics who stayed in Karleszbad, she is in America with her family already. Now Marton spoke to her mother about the 12 d[ollars] she sent. She exchanged it in America for 720 pengo. And there it was sent to the post office as 720 pengo, not based on the actual currency. And others got it that way also. You'll have to inquire, if it's possible. The case with the house is still not settled. I hope that in this month it will be over. In Mülhetek the weather was rainy and it's still cold even today. Barnai is suing again. Now the Vatos and Klein from Prague are sleeping. I don't know what will develop from this, if there will be anything, I will write about it. I know, Judge Andras Simon, T. Csoros mainly, Peter Gerenyi, Feri Maroi, Hotos Kasznoci, Mr. Elnok, and Lajos Török, now 6 of them will a have hearing because they contradicted [themselves]. If I will get the answer from my brother to what I wrote at the beginning of last month. I'm curious what he will send to the children because he offered a ship ticket. I wrote back that I don't know when the money from the sale of the house will be available. If he is kind, he will send it and [I] will have the children take the money back with them. But my brother wrote that we can't let you know about that. I respect you and kiss you, your faithful father, who will never forget. And thank you for the gift. Gluck Jeremias,

[from Ignác]

Dear Brother Dezső,

I'm sorry that I write so briefly, but unfortunately, I can only write a lot, if they write me a lot. Like you are writing in your letter, that I signed the card, yes I wrote it because our father was not at home. He was in Budapest at the time and I did not want to wait for two days. We were curious and I believe you would have been, too. Thank God I'm fine. Please next time write me more. If you write me more, I will write you more. Grandfather is sending their greetings to you. They were wondering about you. Thank God they are healthy.

About the traveling we are where we were. The Puskas from Polyán and the Lekeszi are sending their greetings. I kiss you many times, Your brother, Ignác

[from Marie]
Dear Dezső!
I got your letter that we were waiting so hard for and I'm glad that you are in good health and your eye got better a little. You just take care of yourself. And like you wrote it, we don't write too often. I believe that you can understand our situation, that is, what terrible days we live through here. And we wait everyday and the days are passing by, but there is nothing about nothing. Think about the way [it was] when you were here. It was better for you then, but now our traveling process is 100% harder. And they only encourage [us] day by day. We are trying to write something encouraging, but we don't know what to write. We are used to it, that we are only waiting. We got a reply from the consul, and he wrote that they don't have these names in the registration. We can now have more grief about that. What can we do? Although the agent said, until they get the documents officially from the American Consul in Prague, they don't know anything either. They can't do anything about it for us. Now we can hardly wait for Uncle Jónász's response because we wrote everything to him so maybe he can help us. We can urge it by the American Consul and they would send our documents down from Prague. It's been three weeks since they called in a girl for a visa, from Csicser. But others are still waiting like we are. I heard it was faster for her because they urged it from America. I didn't hear anything else about her. See, Jónász was not right. But, God is good and will help all of us. I don't know if we told you yet, but we sold the advantage/rights for 40 pengo. Imagine, dear Dezső, what a miracle God did, in the past few days, adding to this, in a small town like this. First you have to recall Gyula Juhasz. He was born here and also lived in Ujhely. And Gyula was learning to be a pilot for 7 years. He came to visit the relatives on Saturday. But at night he already left to Ungvár because they just relocated him there. And just the next day, on Tuesday he went aboard and was sent out to somewhere and on his way back, what God is giving, near to Gabor Szabo's garden, where Pastor Gyuri's garden is, to be exact, he crashed. It happened in a few minutes the entire thing and two of them were sitting in it. Gyula got killed instantly. The other one survived, but he got a concussion of the brain and his stomach. I'm not sure if he will stay alive. He was Archduke Jozef's son. A very fine man. The funeral was great and gorgeous. He was buried as a second lieutenant in rank. The reason why they had the funeral here because, God is good, he died in the town where he was born. He had to crash right into that garden. It was terrible to see it, but the funeral was beautiful. There were a lot of people. It is enough for today. I kiss you and wish everything good, with love, Mariska.
Magda [Uncle Marton's daughter] wanted to write to you also, but I am just going to Lelesz now.

[from Hermine]
Dear Dezső!
I guess you won't be so mad at me that I only write this much. We got your letter today. It's Friday and we want to send this today. How are you? I'm alive and hoping! Otherwise, thank goodness, I'm healthy. I wrote everything in detail in my last letter. Now I'm in a hurry and don't have time to write. I have to cook. You just write, because we can hardly wait! I kiss you and wish you every good, with love Hermine.

1939/6/2 Herman to Dezső (Book 5, 70-71)

1939 VI / 2
Dear Dezső,
We received your letter and it was difficult to wait for it. We are happy that you are well. Thank God, I'm living! But it would have been better to be there with you. I've been waiting for your letter with great difficulty. They just began the exercises that will be every Saturday afternoon from 2-5 pm. This is the levente [Home guard]. Tomorrow we will begin to cut the wheat and assemble it. Last year we thought that we will not be at home at this time. Time goes by, even while you're sleeping the days are progressing. How are you? I hope you're well. There is not much I can write about anything special. I wish you good health and everything the best. Love from your brother, Herman
PS. Please write more frequently because then we will write too.
Emil, Lenke, Mityu send their kisses to you.

1939/6/9 The State Industrial Bank Re Arthur (Book 1,6)

The State Industrial Bank

21 West Gay Street
Columbus, Ohio

June 9, 1939
To whom it may concern:
This will serve to introduce Mr. Arthur Gluck, president of The Bonded Scale Company of this city. Mr. Gluck is prominent in business circles in this community and has for many years, engaged in real estate and manufacturing activities. The writer has known Mr. Gluck personally for more than fifteen years, and during that time has had numerous banking transactions with him involving extension of credit. During these years of business association, I have had occasion to observe at close range, the many sterling qualities he possesses. His character and integrity are of the highest order and the success which he has attained in his various business endeavors is the logical result of his intelligence and industry. The writer can truthfully say that he has never heard of an instance where Mr. Gluck has failed to keep an agreement or meet an engagement in a satisfactory manner. While he is not financially wealthy, he does possess reasonable means necessary to consummate any ordinary commitment or undertaking. Very truly yours, Clyde C. Shively, President

1939/6/14 Father, Maria, Hermine, and Ignác to Dezső (Book 4, 221-226)

Bodrogmező, 1939 June 14
My dearest son Dezső
I was very happy to hear from you and thank goodness you're well. I am very concerned about you. I know you are very upset because of the situation you are in. It is very difficult sometimes. People cannot understand you and they can cause you more problem, especially in America. They do not understand whatever is. I just want you to know, do not worry about us. Thank goodness at this time we are all right. I also just received from Uncle Jónász a letter in reply to the letter I wrote to him [in which I was] asking him, as he mentioned before, to give the tickets for the ship like he promised, and if I get the money from selling the house, the children will take the money back to him that he is giving me. The answer was that we should get the tickets here because the children can't take money with them to America. His son wrote to Prague to the American consulate and also to the one in Budapest asking them to try to get our visa sooner if it is possible. Last week I received a letter from the American Consulate with some papers to fill it out and we must mail it back to them. I mailed it back. I am not sure that it was according to his request. I let him know that the agent already submitted it on March 23rd to the consulate. He let me know about this. About the home sale it is still the same. We don't have any money–and there isn't any place we can turn to get money. To eat we must. If I need the money from the house if we sell it then I have to ask my brother Jónász if I have to.
Last week Uncle Lajzer received a letter from Bertha. She wrote that Uncle Jónász is there visiting her. I did not read the letter. He will bring it to read it, but he didn't bring it yet. He only told me to be full of thanks that my son Dezsö is in America. My daughter wrote that Uncle Jónász said no need to know anything about this. Kisses countless times from your father who will never forget you. Glück Jerémiàs

[from Hermine]
Dear Dezső,
We were very happy for your letter. We are grateful that God has improved your situation and that you are healthy. I don't even know what I'm writing about for you, I would have written a lot, just my patience is little. I know you understand our situation with the great unrest we have a part in. You can also write in detail about the situation there, but it would have been better to be there. It's against my will and I am impatient. We are not going anywhere and even though we have enough to do, it would still be better to make money in America on such long days. Leave your comments, because we can't help it anyway, and I hope the good God sees us too... because it can't end soon enough. As I wrote about your offer in the letter, we did not ask because we want to spare ourselves the requirements. He also has a little joy. I think there is a time when we can no longer be without your help. I just got a card from Gizi from Szürte and Lajos writes that he is being asked for the affidavit so they can request the visa. So he hopes to travel soon. I'm done with the passport. And imagine one day they request to do this with Helen Perl and Helen will only receive it now, Lajos' was all ready in 3 months. We are of the opinion that it has not even been sent because the shipping company has informed us that we will catch up anyway, because the consul will notify us in advance. Yes, it would be better if we were okay with that, but we already had one!! Therefore we prefer to wait for the boys because of the petition and the clerk said the waiver would be for "jud". Lenke and Jolanka

from Košice can go within three months because her husband is Polish and so she is booked in this quota - so I heard, how much is true I don't know... I wish you good health and kiss you with love, Hermine

[from Marie]
Dear Dezső!
We were very happy and thankful to get your letter. I hope our God will help us that we should be able to leave sooner than later, because as you know, for the boys sooner is better, but yes, you know it is all up to our God the way it will be. That makes us think it will happen because he will help us. I don't think I understood everything that you are saying in your letter. I understand the relations in America, but I really want to work. The only thing I am sad about is that we are wasting time here at home doing nothing when I could work and make a living. Here we have nothing, our mind becomes dead, there is no meaning, everything stopped, there is no future. Blank. You know what I mean here. Our grandparents, Uncle Lajos, Uncle Marton send their best regards. Emil is in Agard. He went for this summer to be able to learn Hebrew because here we did not have any Hebrew school. Lenka, Mityu and Gyuszi– are sending many kisses to you. If you would see them you would not recognize them. Emil has become a big boy and the little Gyuszi, he's such a sweet and beautiful child. He started to speak. I must say he's a beautiful child. They always ask about you. They want to know when are you coming home. When we are ready to leave here we will take their pictures so you could see what beautiful children they are. But now I wrote enough about everything. Now I want to wish you all the best, besides good health, and happiness and many kisses. With all my love, your sister, Mariska

[from Ignác]
My dear brother Dezső,
I want to thank you for your pictures and I think you should write more often, too. I was very happy to receive your letters and thank goodness you are well and thank you very much for your letter. Thank goodness we are alive. My English is coming along very slowly. I hope by the time I will be there I will be able to understand something. Here I try to study. Every Saturday afternoon from 4:30 I have to go to [the military] drill. We have become soldiers. On Sunday it was a big holiday for the flag. Gyorki Menhert [lived across from us] was with me. Officials were there and lectured to us. Kisses, Ignác
[on the side] Here the weather is very hot today.

1939/6/15 Herman to Dezső (Book 5, 109-110)

1939/VI/15
Dear Dezső to 120 [Borach Hashem]
I hope that you have received the letters we mailed to you on May 8 and June 2. We have received a letter mailed on the 30th of last month. Thank God that you are well. As you see, I am alive. I'm writing this letter, but I don't have patience to do so. We just came back from the field cutting hay.[szenat]. And I want this letter to go out and I wanted to write something, and all of a sudden something came to my mind and I don't want you to think that I am angry. This type of work is really not for us, but someone has to do it, because it would take seven days, and it takes money to hire people and we don't have it. We hope from God that this will be different. We would like to succeed that on the seventh or eighth month we could be there. I do like money, here the only thing you can say is that it is in the other person's hand, and my hand is empty. I believe that everything has an end and also for the ministers too. It can't be this way forever. I can't write in detail how we are, because our father and the girls have written already. I do not want to repeat it. Homeguard exercises are every Saturday afternoon from 2 to 5 PM. July and August will be "rest". From the ages of 12-23 it is required to attend. "They should live so long as I like them".[Written in Yiddish]. In Lelesz, Lacsni, the official's sister, became the post master. There is also now a district Dr., but it doesn't belong to the Helmec district. In the next village Fulop, the teacher, is also in charge. Hencse [Hermine] has rebuffed him. I believe that you will not be able to read my writing, but I'm writing it as it comes. I will save you some time with this. It's brief, but it can be more. It is as it is, this is what I'm going to write. I hope that God will help us that we shall be there soon. I will not have to break my head to write things like this. I hope that this letter will find you in good health. Try to reply as soon as you can. Waiting is the most difficult thing. Kisses, from your brother Herman.
On June 19 there will be an induction to the Army for people born in 1918. I also have to go. 4 of us from this village will be going. Three days ago it was declared by the "public drummer" to the public that this induction will take place.

New York
June 20
Dear Dezső!

I hope that you are in good health. I will disturb you with my lines because I received a letter from Arthur and he wants to take back, through telegraph, the affidavits from the girls. You know that you will lose the future for them. You must not forget that you washed your hands of everything, because everything is going well for you. I'm here 25 years and I do not know half of the questions from my relations and you began so fast and you're responsible for whatever he does. Even if they kick you out of the house, you must return and ask forgiveness from them. You know no one owes that has to help one. It is very nice from such a relation who wanted to help----- consider the luck you are destroying for your family because of your [false pride]. Dezső, you should show Uncle Jónász and Arthur how much you are sending home to your dear father, take it with you, so they can see it that you are thinking of your family back home, your father and your brothers and sisters. Dezső, this is my last letter in which I'm going to disturb you. I don't want to take the responsibility. The truth is that the girls may remain back home and be lost and it depends upon you, show it to them that you have feelings. I'm asking you with God's help, don't take anything lightly, because Arthur does not want your sisters and brothers to come here and he asked me to write to you if you're sending any money home to help the family because if you're not helping the family, they want only to create problems for you and they can do that and you will not have any position in Columbus. This is the last time that I'm asking you. You spoke a lot, therefore I beg you to listen to everyone and tell the truth and you just listen. You know very well that a stranger would destroy a person in a spoonful of water if they could. Dezső everything depends upon you. Do it for all of us, go to Uncle Jónász and Arthur, be calm in front of them and be like a fine gentleman and tell them your errors in front of them, as they wanted you to do. That you did not understand how you have behaved, and about the living situation, as you would like to. If I would be strong enough, I tell you, I would go to see you all and I would iron it out. Please, I'm asking you not to bring any shame to our relatives, and don't aggravate them because there must be something, that you're not behaving as a gentleman, Brother.... I'm not after you with any interest, but for our family. I wish that you shouldn't throw away that opportunity, and your father really gets from you everything [here she is referring to money that my brother was sending home. He didn't tell the relatives what he is doing with his money, that's why they were angry at him. This is my observation from the letter].

This week he wants at least 5 dollar. Write it to your Dad to be honest with Bácsi [our Uncle] and write it to him, because it will show your dignity. Dear Dezső, understand me well, what I want and you must send an answer to Arthur shortly. He wrote what will happen to your family. He does not know why I am the victim. You also know how hard it is to take the girls to me because, if they are trusting, with your nature, and me a weak "veztelathattal" [not clear] when you were here and me especially the way our family agrees at home and, if I would want anything, they would think that I want it for me [not clear] My thinking is within this letter and, if you won't behave like a considerate man, then let's forget about corresponding, because I don't exchange letters with someone who does not look after his family's future. Moreover, even your situation cannot be pleasant, where everyone says all the nice and good things to Arthur's family and to Uncle [Jónász]. The nephew had come out a year ago and..... there are irregularities [Yiddish - mirefhedjen]? Do I know what it is. Dezső it will be hard to get a new affidavit for the girls. If this will be asked, you know what to say: I got a letter from my relative, and tell them what I wrote. Like that, they will see that I want to make everything better. Whatever I can, whatever you can, do what Arthur wants. You will be a man, your words, the way you state it, that you are sending money, proves it that it's true, so they will know the truth. Dezső, it's hard to get back what one had once it's wasted. Just listen and don't answer foolishly to Arthur. If you only knew how sick I was and [yet] I got out of bed to write this letter to you, but the trouble is today to listen. In theory, you could also tell [them], that you rarely write to me, because I don't even know what they think about me, [or] about what is going on between me and you. If you don't mind I'm writing like this, but I'm desperate, [to know] why something like that would happen between people. Dezső, I will not send Arthur's letter to you, but think about it like a man, not a child, and act and answer, because I have to give an answer about the girls coming here. And write to your dad, [tell him] to do anything he can, even if he has to pledge his property, he has to buy the ship tickets or, if you could send it to the girls [and they will] repay you. It could be done maybe "kányzlisal" [not clear] will send something. Now I think it is enough about this, because I asked, if they let you know give me the truth.

Tell me what you want, but you can't do anything about it and from now on it's a test of what it's like to let a kiss kiss you and be a gentleman. It's not as hard as making a life at home. Dezso, not everyone can get documents and if the girls already could get it [behave] so it won't be rejected. Maybe they will never get a chance to get here because of your behavior, it could happen. I will respond to Arthur and I will tell him that you are senile and can't find the letter since May, but I will try to find it.

I will write a letter for you and explain the entire thing. I can't do anything more. Then your dear father should write to the uncle too, but he should not write always crying in a letter. He should be happy if his two daughters would come out with what he had, and then they could be a help. He shouldn't wait for the uncle to send him [a letter]. I think the uncle has been the best to you all and don't forget that! I'm waiting for the response. I kiss you, Bertha

1939/6/26 Bertha to Dezső (Book 5, 33-34)

1939 June 26
New York

Dear Dezső!
If I could I would visit the relations [in such a way] that I would [behave] as [though] nothing has happened. You should show your father's letter so that they could see that you're helping them. If they are apprehensive, tell dear Uncle that I didn't tell you because I was afraid that you would get sick and I wouldn't have liked it that because of me you, or my dearest Arthur and family should suffer. If they say something just bite it and think of your family back home. If you see any flaws, just utter the truth with brotherly fineness that you only make $15 and you have a problem with your eyes. Go like a storyteller as you rub the hair of the dog. I will write you news. A few weeks ago our Uncle was here with his wife in a relaxing atmosphere and said that if your sisters will come out as they want to, I should take the responsibility. And this is what they want.
My dear Dezső, as you see I'm not a very strong woman and your sisters are very sensitive and if I would say something that they should make it so they would be hurt and I wouldn't take it for the whole wide world with all the money. And secondly, if Jolan will come out at the same time and my husband's father is coming and we are waiting for him every day and you know we do not have a separate room. I am happy to help them for one or two weeks if the rest will not arrive by then. What will I do if they also arrive at the same time as Jolan and the rest. You know very well the food does not matter. You know I'm a weak person. Last week my uncle's wife and his beautiful daughter [Helen and Elsie] came. I just got out from bed so that I can mail this letter because you are curious to know its continuation. My husband doesn't want to give any advice because he's afraid that God forbid that things may not turn out to be, if they say something. I know it's all the same and just listen and say that he is right for the Uncle and I will listen and follow as much as I can and then you do what you think is best. I wish my strength would allow me so that I would go to Columbus, but unfortunately I'm not so strong that I could make a long trip. It is very difficult to understand the "Barai" letter that was mailed to you. If the letter would be shorter and understood better it would not affect me. Now my heart has gotten a little calmer because I was afraid that if I did not undertake it, then they will also ask to return the papers to Arthur. As I see it, the Uncle is not an angel and because of that destroy the letter. If it comes from me because you don't know who's going to read it and who's going to interpret it [and] how will they understand that. After reading it I will not write more. It is a serious illness. I can hardly stay on my feet and I lost weight, good luck to everything. With love, Bertha
Regards to everyone

1939/6/30 Herman to Dezső (Book 4, 291-292)

Dear Dezső

[Upside down:] I wrote this letter last week, but I want this letter to go, so I'm in a hurry.

Your letter [that] was sent on the VI/18th, we got it, and we are so happy that thank God you are well. I hope you got our letter which we sent on the 15th. Have you? I can only write about myself, that I'm alive, but I can't even think about [the possibility] that I will travel with the others. What do you say? They drafted me to the military. We went to the conscription. Me, Pandi, Fekete and little Janos. Only Pandi's son got in. They classified me to the hussars. I would make out well if I would get in there, right? The day of the joining is October 1st and again in the month of February. The call will be two times. They did not reject me for sickness because they did not examine me. They only asked if I have a medical certificate, but of course, I didn't have it. They took 4-5 Jewish boys from Helmec also. Only [those born in] the year 1918 went and from what I heard, whoever has been drafted did not have to go anymore. The Balint boy was good in the Czech [military] and they sent him home from there. The Hosztyo boy came home last week as well as the others before who were good. I think that 85% stayed. Dad asked the notary, if we need to get the request done. He always said that he is Jewish and they fired him because of that. That is why the request is being delayed. It was already three days late before that. It said on the conscription that he [meaning Herman] is planning to travel to America, and of course I did not hear it, and because of that, I asked him if he mentioned this. He answered 'yes' but he doesn't know anything. If there is a request, if all my documents are ready with the passport, then I could have hope that they will release me, since I'm a Jew. I talked to Ignacz Grosz, and he said that Polek is counting on traveling, and since I met him again he said that he can't even go there. Thank God the harvest/crop is beautiful, the only question is if they will still pay for it. The harvest will start next week, we don't know exactly who the "kepés" [don't know the meaning] will be. The weather this month was very rainy. I was in a hurry with writing because there will be covering [agricultural term] in the afternoon. It's possible that you will have a hard time reading [this letter], but it's hard to be patient. I wish I would have gone with you when you left, because here at home the suffering is worth nothing. Kisses, your little brother, Herman

1939/6/30 Ignác to Dezső (Book 6, 115-116)

Polyán, 1939, VI / 30
B"H
My dear brother Dezső, live up to 100 years.
I was very happy to receive your letter that thank God you are well and in good health. Now I can see that you have not forgotten about me and about our people at home and you remember the past when you were at home you understood them. Now the problem is that you don't write enough, but now at least this is a Gluck, if you have the will to write something, it can help at home. People can be helped more with knowledge than with energy, so it is said. This week we have mailed papers to Budapest to the consulate. More likely there'll be some result because of you. I was in Helmec and I asked about the postmaster lady and I was told she is at Rozsnyő. this is her address; F.. Janka, Hungary. Miki Schwartz is in Helmec. After he finishes his work on Saturday he goes on a bicycle. It's America here for him from this point of view. The Leleszi Urban girl is not going because his father became a judge. The other members of the family will write about everything. Thank God I am well. I remain with kisses, your little brother Ignác.

Thank God I'm in good health. Please write as soon as you can! I thank you for the letter directed to me. Good by, Ignác

1939/6/30 Jeremias to Uncle Jónász (Book 22, 1-2)

Bodrogmező 1939 June 30
My dear beloved faithful brother, Jónász and dear sister-in-law, Helen.
Please forgive me that I only respond just now. You wrote that your dear son is pressed for travel [documents]. The notification has arrived from the consulate with yesterday's mail about the July 31st appearance in Budapest. If we can get all the documents for that time, here my brother-in-law Marton made a copy of the notice and here I have attached it. And I'm asking you please to send those down. I'm sending it by airmail. And my dear beloved brother, I'm letting you know that we are thank God in good health and I hope that my lines will find you in the best of health.
I'm letting all of you know that unfortunately my son Herman was drafted to the army [to be a soldier] and there is no way of seeing how [they'll] let him go. So this way, poor him, will stay behind, because I can't help him. I hope that I will manage the cost for the traveling. I respect you, your dear son, your family and my dear sister-in-law. Once again, I'm asking you, dear brother Jónász, please send the necessary documents. I remain your faithful brother, who will never forget you. Gluck Jeremias

And I'm asking you for the affidavit that the consul sent here. It's in two copies. Gluck Herman and Gluck Hermina. I wrote this to the agent and he responded immediately that it is only a mistake. Because my birthday is hers, since she was born in 1914 April and if it's possible for you to check so that it's not going to be a mistake. It must have a copy there, because I don't have time to write more. Your brother, Jeremias If at that time my son can't travel, there is a notification that has to be made so he can get the quota number for later [and] can keep the advance booking.

1939/7/1 Lajos Schwarz (Schwarz's Blinds) to Dezső (Book 7, 88)

July 1, 1939
Dear Mr. Glück!

Back then when you wrote to me, I replied to you how much I envy you for getting to such a nice and good place. Also, because of that you are so far away from the troubled situation here. Although, back then I did not think that after barely a year I would have to think about my own plan to travel away from here.

Under the treaties, I remained Czech Slovak citizen for as long as the Republic was standing. Although, I did not employ workers, but worked alone. This however has changed so much. It has been a month already since they closed down my places. They were only open in these days so I can do inventory, since there is interest in the business.

I turned to your father for the address, who was so kind to send this to me by mail. So this way I am able to ask you to inform me about the situation there. Specifically, I would be interested [in knowing] how I can bring myself for now and my family after me later. What would be necessary for this and if you could be of help to me. Also, I would like to ask you, what could I do there? I think that I can't count on making blinds. I am a skilled textile technician. I graduated as a technician. This way I would like to work in this field.

Your dear father is asking me at the same time to tell you the address for the Czech Company - Zbecnik. This company exists in the protection zone. Today add to the address that it is next to the "Náchod" so the company will get your letter for sure.
I'm waiting for your precious response and I remain with full respect. Lajos Schwarz

1 International reply voucher

1939/7/3 Maria to Dezső (Book 5, 137-138)

1939 VII / 3
Dear Dezső!
Don't be upset that I did not reply to your letter immediately, but in between we were waiting so that I can write something definite to you regarding Hersmendu [Herman] our brother. It's very regretful that it is without a result as of now. Do you know dear David, I am glad that I have written to you and also to Arthur to urge the consulates, without which it would have taken several months. I believe I have written to you that Arthur has written and urged them in Prague and in Budapest, and due to that we have received documents from the consulate that we had to fill out and return it to them with money. Here the agent has been asking for the quota number that he needs and now the consul has written that he needs the documents. The consulate has written that we could have gone in May according to the Czech quota system, however [we couldn't] because they did not have any acknowledgment from Prague. Now they have called us for the visa discussion for July 31. You know that I have another problem. I worry since the consulate has written that we ask again from America to guarantee in a sworn statement that he [Arthur] will take care of us and that we will not be dependent upon the government. Also they need a bank statement to show that he has money and where he works to show it officially and how much he earns because without that information we cannot go in for the visa hearing. The consulate sent us additional documents to fill out since we do not want to lose the visa. We are asking the consulate to maintain our number so that we can go, God forbid that we should lose our number in the present quota. It is true that our father has written to Uncle Jónász via airmail and Uncle Martin has also asked that he should send the documents to us immediately by July 25. I believe that he [Jónász bacsi] would be afraid of God since everything is ready from our part. If he has a heart he would not neglect it and he would send us the document. God forbid. It is terrible even to think of it. I believe that you can understand me? [Regarding] our passports, we hope that by then all will be

completed. With regards to Herman. We will try to inquire perhaps we could get permission to let him go also. I would like him to come, this is in my mind. At the present I will not write more. I hope that in the future we can talk about everything in person in America. There isn't anything that does not have an end. I trust God. If they do not let Herman out at this time, then maybe he will be discharged at the military exam and then perhaps he can succeed with the present quota system and will be able to go to America at a later date. We are going to go to Helmec to mail the letter. Otherwise we are living. At the present we started to harvest wheat on the farm. The weather is not good. There's not much news. There are many people waiting for numbers to succeed but without hope. Until we meet again, my best regards and kisses many times from my heart in America. Grandmother and grandfather send their love and kisses. Mariska [Maria]

P.S. A woman from Lelesz went to America and is engaged to marry.

1939/7/12 Arthur to US Consul in Budapest (Book 1, 63)

Bonded Scale Company
Columbus, Ohio

July 12, 1939.

United States Consul
Budapest, Hungary.

Dear Sir:

I am writing you relative to Maria Gluck, female, Hermin Gluck, female, Herman Gluck, male, and Ignacz Gluck, male, all residing at Polany, Post Office, Leles, Bodrogmezo, Zemplen, Megze, Hungary, formerly of Czechoslovakia. These are cousins of mine and I've taken care of filling out the necessary affidavit of support and the verification of my ability to back up the affidavit by submitting a report to Dun and Bradstreet and a letter from my banker. I am under the impression that all details are satisfactory to the Consul at Prague, and also to your office as you have these details in connection with an other case, in which you acknowledge that everything seems to be in order. This other case is Dr. Pista, (Stephen) Roth, who is a physician. (File No. 811.11 EVP / McD). I received word that the above people are to appear before you for examination on July 31st, and that you would like additional affidavits, letters from my banker. These are enclosed. I further definitely state herewith that I am prepared to support these people for all the necessities of life, if necessary, and guarantee they will not become a public charge. I have also asked the Dun & Bradstreet. Inc. to send you by air mail, another statement of my financial conditions. Very truly yours, Arthur Gluck

1939/7/17 Zemplen County Orphanage - Herman (Book 7, 7)

Zemplen County Orphanage
Page 10559/1939

Subject: Minor Glück Hermann
Adult Resident of Bodrogmező

Attached

DECIDED

The application is granted, and for Glück Hermann Bodrogmező who was born in Bodrogmező on the 16th of November, 1918. As a full-fledged man, he is privileged to lead his affairs and to manage his property independently.

Glück Jeremias, a resident of Bodrogmező, the father, is summoned to give his guardian's grandfather's wealth to his guardian as his own.

JUSTIFICATION

He applied for his seniority.

The child is dated to the age of 20 according to the birth certificate of the presented child.

Page 86

By the testimony of the village of Bodrogmező on May 31, 1939, it was verified that the minor's own affairs were sufficiently mature and moral objection could not be raised.

The applicant demonstrated that it is necessary and useful for him.

The parent and closest relatives are in agreement.

Taking these into consideration, we have found it appropriate to reach a decision in accordance with the provisions of the relevant section

Against this final verdict there is an appeal to the administrative committee of Zemplén County.

The appeal can be filed or filed with us within 15 days from the day after the receipt of our final decision.

We will notify the following:

1. Glück Jeremiás, Bodrogmező
2. Glück Hermann, Bodrogmező
3. Municipality, Bodrogmező
4. The county council of Sátoraljaújhely

Sátoraljaújhely, July 17, 1939

In the name of the Zemplen County Orphanage

1939/7/26 Lajos Schwarz (Svarcova Blinds) to Dezső (Book 5, 368)

26.7.1939
Dear Mr. Gluck!
I acknowledge receipt of your precious letter. Receive our thanks that you sent that letter with airmail, so it could be in our possession sooner. Regarding the sale of the plant, I can't write anything further yet. I don't even know how much money can be taken out of here. These are the kind of issues that only arise for clarification when I already know where I will go. In any case, all I would say is that if our assets can be sold at normal values, it will take about 250,000 Korona -which at 30 korona exchange equivalent for one $ (dollar) is about $7,500. We used to live in a part of former Czechoslovakia, which was attached to Germany with the name called, Szudeten-Gau. So in my view, we would fall into the German quota. In that case, we would emigrate to North America. I will obtain the required information and I will send it to you the next time. However, I do not know that information company you mentioned. I know about the operation of two American companies. One of them is, Wys Muller & Co, and the other one is, R.G. DUN. I believe, that you are thinking of this latter company. Please let me know what your acquaintance asks for the intervention, which of course, would only be due if I use their efforts and that's only if it will be effective. In the event that I did not take the steps, no fee would be due. My birth details are as follows:

Schwarz Lajos, was born in Rakospalota in 1895 January 19th Hungary Czech Protecturatus Citizenship
Schwarz Margarete, was born in Trient, in 1893 December 21st.
Schwarz Greta, was born in Braunau 1919 July 28th.
Schwarz Evi, was born in Braunau in 1920 June 20th.
Schwarz Susanna was born in Tandorf in 1925 December 25th.

I believe for now this data will be enough for you.

Regarding the Czech company, Zbečník. With my knowledge the company is first rate and your claim can be recovered. The company probably will not settle with you because the claims are not settled yet or because the reward is being held against the losses. Regarding that, I can tell you as much that under the formal Czech-Slovak law, the company is not entitled to do so. That after a transaction for which the consideration has not been received, they will not pay a commission. I don't just consider it natural, but it is also legal. However, it is against the law that he would hold your commission back when the buyers have settled the invoice and that they use this amount to cover their losses. With my knowledge, you did not undertake it on credit. I advise you to ask from the company for an exact statement, then discuss the conditions with them, which you agreed [with] the representative about. And then I will tell you about the next steps you need to take. I'm waiting for your response as soon as possible. With full respect, Schwarz Lajos

1939/8/3 Father, Marie, and Hermine to Dezső (Book 4, 181-186)

August 3, 1939

Bodrogmező, 1939 August 3

My dearest son Dezső I love you from my heart,

I have received your letter on the fifth of August. I did not answer you immediately because I wanted to write to you regarding Budapest. I believe that Maria has written about everything. Now I only hope that God will help with the cost for the trip. The money from the house is being paid off already. Ignác's, Emil's, and Lenke's share, over 1254 pengos, were put into the orphanage bank and, if and when it is needed for Ignác, then [they will release it] but only if the passports are ready and available. They need you to be present for the orphan court , then they will negotiate and they will allocate it, the president of the bank said. I believe that my daughters, Mariska and Herminka have written about everything to you. God will help us so that every thing should succeed. My dear brother Jónász sent all the necessary papers. The consulate said why so many papers? So he [the official] gave it back to us and said that we must rush the passports. Last week, the postmaster lady [Jane] was in Helmec I have taken her with our coach to Lelesz. She was very happy because I said to her that you are fine and well. She will be in Miskolc beginning August 1 at the main post office. She will be working there. With my respect and love and kisses, your father that will never forget you. Gluck Jeremias

[from Marie]

Dear Dezső!

Don't be surprised that we did not reply to your letter right away, but we wanted you to hear everything accurately about us. First of all, as we have written to you on the 31st we were called in for the visa hearing. We received the documents that we requested from Uncle Jónász. Everything is good. The consulate personnel interviewed us about everything: our birthplace, our occupation, and also for pictures. Then, with the 4 pictures, we signed everything individually. The official made us take an oath that everything was true that we submitted. They also asked if we are healthy, since we had to take our doctor's report from home. When it was done, the consulate official signed the visa. That means it was approved. We did not get it though, because by law they could not give it to us, however it is already as if he would have given it to us. Our passports were done, but on Saturday we were instructed by a person here that they still could not give them out. So we left without the passports. The official wrote that we can appear at the visa hearing without them [the passports]. But when we arrived, the agent spoke quite differently, [and told us] that we can't appear without the passports. We appeared before the consul anyway, and you can imagine how terrible it was, until we were finished with it. I will go back to the passports. They did not give out the passport to Ignác, since he has already turned 17. Consequently, it needs to be sent over to the Ministry for approval, but it does not need a request. For Hersmendel we have made a request. But the notary is [illegible] and did not attach the passport to it. So we will be getting his passport done just now, when we will get the request out. And you can imagine, that Herman had no documents at all, because the notary did not want to give them out. Only the 4 pictures and the American guarantee documents. But despite that fact, he got the visa also, anyway. The lady who arranged everything said that we will have to send everything in the mail. We did not even have the doctor's certificate.

We will try to get the passport as soon as possible and we will send it in so we will be able to travel faster. As soon as we get our papers, either today or tomorrow, we will send it to the consulate. I can't tell you when we will be able to travel exactly because they only got the registration number from Prague. We will still need the quota statement and, if we will have everything, then they will notify us, But at the consulate they said that we can travel in September or October. But now the question is if anything else, some other obstacle, will happen again later. You know what I think!! They recommended a lawyer, who [works] in an emigration office and who would arrange everything for free of charge. We went to them because of the boys because perhaps he could give us some advice. This lawyer advised us to go to the military ministry in person, because it does not require a lawyer, and ask if the documents have arrived and what is going on with them. But you know, we did not have the [case] number, under which they sent them in. We did not take it with us. So, first we went to the castle, to the registry and there they looked for the number and from there, down to the ministry. So there, we showed that the request had already been sent on the 16th. Hersmendel's and Ignác's passport did not arrive yet, but they promised that as soon as they do arrive, they will arrange everything immediately. So they can send it as soon as possible. We asked, if they will dismiss them. They said that they are pretty sure they will let them go. I think I wrote enough. Maybe I also wrote things that you are not interested in. I only wrote them so you can see that we arranged everything alone, in person, and free of charge. Here at home everything costs and nothing is the right way. Now our father wrote to a lawyer from Ujhely, who would come with us and arrange everything for Hersmendu. And it's ok, if he has no documents at all. He will arrange it. However, finally, today we went. He [the lawyer] stayed [behind] and because of that we did not have anything. But now we are happy, that without him, we arranged everything. It's only for the 4 of us. But our advantage from this, is that this way, Herman came [with us] and he got it also. I arranged for somebody else too. Pest is a beautiful city. We are now writing to Uncle Jónász also, because imagine, we can't get dollars for the visa anywhere, and we can't pay with anything else. Therefore, the agent said, that we must ask [for it] from the American relatives. [We need to write] that they [the consulate officials] have requested it and to explain why we are asking for it, and that we will pay it back to them. Now, we are writing to them that we had no intention to ask anything from them at all, but we are asking only because we can't get any kind of money here. We will pay it back to them. Although, we need the 40 dollars [for each of the] 4 parts, don't send just that exact [amount], [because] when they sent so much for the guarantee we didn't need it all, and they gave some back from that. Now I will not write anymore. I kiss you and wish you good health and I will stay with the hope that I will see you again. Mariska

Now it seems as though we are still in Pest. We were there for 3 days. We stayed in a hotel. We got back last night and today I'm already writing so you can know something. Now we are asking the good God to help us with the traveling. Answer about everything, immediately. Kisses, M.

[from Hermine]

Dear Dezső!

I hope you are not angry that we didn't write right away, but now we are trying to write and send it as soon as possible. Mariska already wrote everything. That is why I'm writing everything briefly. What is important, is that, thank God everything worked out!! That is the only thing that matters and it should be that way evermore! We did not get the visa yet, but it's being promised, or it's already there, but they will only give it out for the traveling. And Hersmendel showed up without all the documents and he took the oath also, just like we did. Now we have more hope! True, the atmosphere is not really pleasant! But there are some people who don't get acknowledged about the traveling, also. Everybody is following the example of the uncle with the hat [a proverb/saying]. I hope you understood everything. Now I will also write to Uncle Jónász. Iren Schvarcz, Uncle Hermus's daughter, was called in August 14th to the consul for the visa hearing. Helen Perl [was on] August 7th. I kiss you, Hermine

I'm exhausted from traveling, that's why I'm only writing this much.

1939/8/3 Undated Ignác to Dezső (Book 5, 52-53)

My dear brother Dezső,

I was very happy to [read in] your letter that you're healthy and well. We went to Budapest. Everything was a success. Chief consulate was a very fine man. Swore us in and he began to say, good good, and he signed the visa. The others have written everything and because of that, I don't want to disturb you repeating that. If we have to wait long, then it would be a good idea to rush from your side and then maybe they would act faster. As we were traveling to Budapest and people discovered that we are coming from the north, they came together, they were very interested, but I must note that they did not know that we were Jewish. Some of them were crying with happiness because we know more of what was going on!!!. It would be good to get out as soon as possible and talk to you in person.

We hope that my few lines will find you in good health. Thank God, I'm well.

Kisses from your little brother Ignác.

1939/8/4 Undated Father's letter to Dezső (Book 5, 11-12) has passports

[This letter might come later]

My dear son Dezső,

My hope is that you have received our letter in which I replied to your letter. We are healthy thank God, which I hope that it's not missing from you. I've written to my brother Jónász and I told him everything and he will tell you all about it. I wrote to the agent because there was a mistake in the affidavit, it was twice written to Herman and should have been written to Hermina. The passport is written Hermina, Maria, Herman, and Ignác. The Agent told us it will be no problem, I remain with love and kisses, your father Gluck Jeremias.

1939/8/4 Herman to David (Book 5, 15-16)

1939 VIII 4

Dear Dezső,

I just want to write to you a few lines, don't be angry. In the future I will write to you in detail. I believe that my sister has written the latest news to you. I also went for the hearing without the necessary papers, but they promised [it to] me as well as for the others.
Your brother Herman.

1939/9/1 Herman to Dezső (Book 5, 115-116)

1939 IX / 1.

Dear Dezső,

We were happy to receive your letter and to know that you are thank God well. Your aggravation, as I read your letter, it's regretful, but that is life. We hope that it will be better. I am alive! However, we are still at home, I'm not going any place. I only know what happens here at home and I'm sure the other members of the family have written to you about it. I do not want to write anything that isn't interesting to you. Tomorrow again, we will start the military home guard exercises. I do not know anything about the permission, however, they have asked twice for papers from us and in the past two weeks, we mailed to them. Now it depends on what will happen, that's all I have. Always, the hope and wish to be there, so I could work, that is the outlook for me. Wish you a pleasant and healthy holiday. We are going to the temple in Lelesz for the holiday. Hope that God will help us and we will be there soon, then we will tell you about everything. Kisses, your brother, Herman.

1939/9/1 Undated Father to Nephew Arthur (Book 5, 104)

Dear nephew Arthur, to 120
I'm wishing you and your family a happy new year and good luck in the new year. Regards, and many kisses, always your uncle. Gluck Jeremias

1939/9/1 Undated Father to Uncle Jónász (Book 5, 134-135)

My dear brother Jónász and dear sister-in-law Helen.
I want to inform you that we are well and we hope to hear from you the same. I want to wish you all happy new year and good luck in the coming year. My regards and kisses to all of you with love and especially you my dear brother Jónász. Your brother forever, Gluck Jeremias.
It will also make me happy with a few lines so I can see your handwriting......your brother, Jeremias.

1939/9/7 Father and Hermine to Dezső (Book 4, 175, 179-180)

9/7/1939
[from Hermine]
Dear Dezső,

I received your letter in which I was very happy to hear that thank goodness you're okay. I understand the situation that you are going through, but don't get angry that I will write at this time very briefly since today is Friday. I want to be sure I will write to you a short note. I know you're waiting very hard to hear from us. I'm waiting for the money. I am very concerned about what our uncle will say if he hears that. We never expected to get it from him. Unexpectedly the shipping company told me we can't get the tickets here. They asked anyone who was there from America who had a ticket they can go. They purchased it before with American dollars. Even those who have been there and had dollars they will not accept them from everyone. Just 2 weeks before we leave we'll ask for it. Irene Schvarcz from Leles was also called in to report for the visa. But she does not know when they will call her in since there is no date yet. Maybe in September she might be able to leave. Lajos and Helen from Szürte are on the scene. [have become an important part of the situation]. I think you had a lot of trouble from our Uncle, but the good God will help us even though it seems like there is no way out. I hope our almighty will help us somehow. About us I'm sure you know more than we do. We will take with us only what is very important –1 pillow–and one quilt. From that we can make 2 pieces from it. I think I am taking it just to remember our home and where we come from. About my English, I can understand a little, but to speak is much more difficult. Now I must start working harder to make sure that at I will be able to understand what they are saying. Now I want to clean up the home before we leave. Next week we will try to organize to get ready for whenever we leave to America. At this time I don't have any special news to tell you. I don't have the time. Next time I will write more. Until then I want to wish you all the best good health. Kisses with love, Hermine

4 weeks ago a son was born to Uncle Marton in Helmec. Malvin Floringer from Ladmoc was also called in for the visa. He got married before. He was asking about us.

[From our father]
Bodrogmező 1939 September 7

My dear son Dezső,
I received your letter and I'm trying to answer you at once. Thank goodness we are okay here. I hope you will be okay to. At this time I did not receive a passport for Hersmendu and Ignác. I'm hoping we will be able to get it and there will not be any more problem. I hope that God will help us. The Svarc girl was in Budapest to receive her visa. According to the agent, we must have the payment in dollars otherwise we will not be able to get the tickets. As of now, we do not have dollars. As of now I do not know the reason. Now it is getting late. It is Friday and I'm trying to finish so I will be able to mail the letter today. I want to wish you all the best, good health and happiness and many kisses, your father who never forgets you not even for a minute
All my love your father, Gluck Jeremias.

1939/9/7 Undated Marie and Ignác to Dezső (Book 4, 307-308)

[Dated by late on Friday, waiting for Herman's passport]

[from Marie]
Dear Dezső!
I'm sorry that we did not write separately now, but it is Friday and our father wants the letter to be sent today. There is no special news. I hope that everything is going to be good with our traveling. The passport is already done and we only have to wait about Hersmendu. I will not write more now, I will make up for this next time. I kiss Uncle Jónász and dear Aunt Helen and dear Arthur and you separately. Kissing you many times. Your little sister, Mariska

[from Ignác]
I kiss you, your little brother, Ignác

Emil wanted to write, but we are in a hurry, only next time.
I kiss you, Emil, Lenku and Mityu

1939/9/12 Undated Hermine to Dezső (Book 5, 88-89)

Regarding Manci [Lajos' wife's sister] She is not in Ungvár. She was not taken in there because she had to go to Budapest or Debrecen to be in the sanitarium due to nerves. Our father went to Ungvár regarding our journey. When we get any information regarding calling us in for our journey, I will let you know. Lajos from Szürte and Helen Perl received their new passport. We hope that we will get ours soon. Since our boys must have an application, questionnaire, to let them go freely from the Army, this takes time. I will also add at this time write to the Ship company if they know anything. If you would like to write to them here is the address.

Cunard White Star
Budapest. 8,.
Rakoci St, Number 56
Even though I was in a hurry to write this letter on Friday, it was not nailed, so it will be going on Sunday from Helmec. To rewrite this letter, I don't have any patience. Kisses, Hermin
[On the side] Lajos is sitting here, but does not feel like writing.

1939/9/12 Undated Hermine and Ignác to Dezső (Book 5, 5-8)

[from Hermine]
Dear Dezső,
Don't be angry that I'm just answering your letter. I'm very surprised that it's been such a long time that you have not received letters from us. We have replied to every letter that you sent us and we always write long letters because I know that you are waiting for it. I have a lot to write to you, but now I'll make it very brief and next time I will write more. About ourselves, so I think I can write to you regarding the travel, that our passports are ready, but Herman's permit to travel didn't come in yet. On September 10, we received [a letter] from the agent and they wrote the same thing as you have, that from America they're not paying for the traveling. I don't know how they can think of that. They think that if we are unable to purchase the tickets then we would give up our journey. When we can travel we do not know yet. I'm going to write to the agent because they asked us what is the reason we are late. I'm writing to them that if it's possible they should send from the consulate and from themselves requests, regarding to Herman's permit, to the people in the Ministry that we are waiting for the papers from them and then we would be ready to go or we would pick up the visa and then I would wait. If Ignác does not travel by November 16, then he too needs a permit. On September 12, our father went to Ungvár because the permit was mailed to Prague, and who knows whether they will let him go due to the present conditions and it's not desirable to remain here....... You know everything. I want to write about it, but I think that I may have written to you about it before and it sounds like I did. This is the reason that I want to get over with the travel. I know God will help us and the time will come. The papers for the Perl girl are ready and she will be traveling on October 3. She was called in for the visa. We are waiting for the reply from the agent and then we will mail them the numbers for the passport. We hope by then the money will be released from the [sale of the] house because they promised it to us. If not that we have to wait for Herman [Hersmendu] we would have been able to travel soon. The Stark girl from Lelesz went to pick up her visa. If we have to wait for a long time for Herman's permit it's more likely we will be traveling in October also. I wrote to Szatmar, but we did not get any reply. Otherwise we are [existing] somehow! Our father wrote to Uncle Jónász Bácsi and Aunt Helen. I did not write. I have only a little patience and we trust that it will come. I hope that you received our last letter and only if you can, please write home. I do not know what may be the reason that you have not received our letter. The only news I can tell you is that the Cimerman girl from Csernyi got married. The Barkaszoi girl that had her picture married Alli Berner from Helmec. If we succeed then we'll talk about everything in person and until then, I hope to see you soon, with love and kisses, Hermin

[from Ignác]
Dear brother Dezső,
The letter did not go out on Wednesday so I will write a few lines so that you could see what I'm doing. Many times between work I make a few notes so that I would have something to write to you everyday. Sometimes I write a short letter, [even though] I would have things to write about, but I would like to tell you in person. I'm making notes to myself so I could tell you everything when we get out from here. I'm leaving this behind for the next letter so that the other letter could be as big as this one. I am asking you that you too should write a lot. As of now, I'm satisfied with your writing and I thank you for that, you write so much and I know, I believe you understand me in every letter. Many kisses and with lots of love, your little brother,
Ignác Gluck, goodby! [was written in English]
Give my kisses to dear Uncle Jónász bacsi and to cousin Arthur and his family and the rest of the relations. Reply immediately!! [In English] Goodby!

1939/9/29 Undated Marie and Ignác to Dezső (Book 4, 176-178)

[Dated from Miksa's appendix surgery that Hermine writes about on 10/1 and written on Friday (Ignác mentions this in the next letter on 10/1. Could be earlier because Marie mentions Sukkot and that will be in just a few days after the letter is written]

[from Marie]
Dear Dezső!
I know that you are surprised that we did not write to you for a while, but I think you can understand me. We got your letter and I gladly read that thank God you are healthy. And I also saw that you are slacking off from your writing a little. That is why you don't get a letter from us so often, because we are expecting it from you and days go by with nothing happening. Please don't follow our example. You just write and as soon as we find out something accurate, we will let you know immediately. Just have a little patience also. We all hope that God will help all of us because only he can help. Believe me, dear Dezső, that I would love to leave all this behind already so much, but who knows when that will happen. Our situation not very bright, but God will help us to get there again where we were once! Our passport is in Budapest at the Consul. As of today, Herman's and Ignác's have not yet come. We are waiting for them everyday. Like you said, our Uncle may be able to urge it, so he can help somehow. Dad wrote once to our Uncle that if the conditions are changing about the Torah, we should take it out. So he wrote what you wrote, that now it is not necessary, but it is very possible that we will take it because it will have a better place there. I knew what our relatives are, but that they will be that dirty [Yiddish - "smiceg"], that is terrible, but forget about the whole thing. It has been two weeks tonight since Miksa suddenly got sick and they did appendix surgery on him in Ujhely. Thank God it was successful. He is at home already. Uncle Izsidor was sick also, but he is better. Our Grandparents, thank God are well. They send their greetings. Uncle Marton is wondering about you, how you are doing, but despite that, he doesn't write. Imagine, I don't know if I wrote this already, but our father met with Janka [the postmaster lady] in Helmec. She came to Lelesz and our father was very happy to see her. Our father was with a carriage, so he gave her a ride. He took her all the way to Lelesz and meanwhile they were talking. She said it herself, that if Mr. Gluck's children run out of money, she would give them and help them out. And, if it's necessary she would give half of her inheritance/property, because she trusts us so much. Our family is very dear and she said that anytime we need money, we should send her a card and she will send the money right away. But our father did not ask money from her. I'm only writing this to you so you will know what this woman is capable of. It is very rare. Today, not one relative would give, but she offered it herself. Other than that, we are well, and the cost until we need it, we'll have it. We are hoping for the best. I don't write anymore, because I'm in a hurry. I kiss you and I wish you pleasant holidays. Maybe we will meet by Succoth. Mariska

Sari Simon and Beni Szabo got married last week.
Bozsi Simon and Miklos Szabo will get married next week.
Jici Török and Janos Pali's daughter also. In the motherland, a boy is very rich.
I'm sorry if I wrote something that you don't care about.
Emil, Lenku, Mityu, Gyuszi kiss you

[from Ignác]
Dear brother Dezső!
I'm sorry, that I don't write [to you] now, but I don't have time, because it's Friday night.
Thank God, I'm well.
I kiss you, your little brother, Ignác

1939/9/27 Undated Marie and Hermine to Dezső missing page 2 (Book 2, 272-273)

[Dated from can't buy ship tickets in pengos and the next letter that they did research and can buy dollars from the national bank]

[from Marie]
Dear Dezső!
I can not imagine what could be the reason you did not write yet for so long. We wrote 2 letters to you already and we did not get any response to those either. Although, I thought by the time the reply would come, we would already be in America, but unfortunately not everything is the way we would like it or want it. The others already wrote about everything to you, that we truly can't count on it, because as you can see, we are doing everything we can, but it looks like it's all useless. It is useless to have the money, if we can't buy the ship tickets with it, because they don't sell them for pengo. And now there is nothing to do. We will leave it to the destiny. We are like those who are being chased by their destiny. Unfortunately we can't help it. Now, it all depends on Uncle Jónász. Although, this week we got Erzsie's guarantee, and I can see that they are trying to do anything they can.

[On the left:] Greetings from my heart and kiss you with love, Mariska.
[On the right:] and I wish you good health and everything good.

[from Hermine]
Dear Dezső!
Uncle Leizer was just here and he also wrote to dear Uncle Jónász. He knows that we don't want to take advantage of his kindness/goodness. But there is no other excuse and please don't mind anything. I know what's coming next, but there is nothing I can do and I must make peace with it. Now you can see what the situation here is like. The whole thing depends on this. Now I can see myself in the destiny, what it will bring to me. It is going to be the way it is. Please notify the authorities immediately. You know what it could mean to us, but especially for the boys, if it won't be successful for them to get out. You know, whoever is registered in the Czech quota, their turn is next. I can hardly wait for the response that will decide my destiny. I kiss you and send greetings with love. Hermin

1939/10/1 Hermine to Dezso (Book 4, 6) missing page after first

Dear Dezső!
We did not get a response from you to our latest letter, and we can hardly wait for it. We would have written already, but we were waiting for your letter. I don't even know what to write about us...since you know everything very well. Thank God we are healthy, and we are hoping that you are, too! Otherwise, there would be things to write about, but I'm keeping them until I can tell you in person!!! But it's very hard to wait it out, but I can't write it in a letter. About our traveling I only know that we got a letter two weeks ago from the shipping company, and they wrote us to wait patiently for the notification from the Consul and then we have to notify them too, so they can pay the fee for the visa. Right now, we can travel to Italy, but we have to pay for the ticket for the ship in dollars. We did some research already and it's possible that we can get dollars from the national bank. The way it comes it will be...It would be nice to be over with this! Ignác did not get his passport yet and they rejected Herman's. Now they aren't giving them out, if they will, he will get it. They say that on the first day of this month we have to go there where Hersmendu officially needs to go and because of that, he can't travel. We hope that everything is going to be ok. We are waiting for the invitation also, but I would not mind if it would be cancelled. How are you with the uncle? In a letter that he wrote he did not mention a word about not giving the money. I guess you missed that, but it happened already, we can't do anything about it. We should get a reply from him too. I wished happy new year to him. I don't even know if I wished that to you. If I did not, then it is still good now. So, I wish you good health and a happy new year, like it's been always. We went to the temple in Lelesz. Uncle Lajos led the prayers. He [leads] on Saturday when he is at home. I don't know, if we wrote to you that they did surgery on Miksa Shőn for his appendix.

1939/10/1 Ignác to Dezső (Book 4, 5)

Dear brother Dezső!
I'm sorry that I didn't write much in my letter the last time. I didn't write so much because I only found out on Friday around late afternoon, that we are going to write, so we were in a hurry to catch the next post delivery time. Ever since then we didn't have any delivery, as I would think, you know that as well, but why we hope for the best. For a Jew it's not a good [answer] to the Jewish question, because now he can't have land, I don't know exactly how much land it's possible to have or how much land is allowed to have. The public was informed that whoever needs any could request it. At our place both times there were 60 requests, and 40 [of them] were requested from the Dioszog [the town's lands in Polány]. However, they sent out a printed sheet, that was bigger than the tobacco permit. We had to fill it out to say who works on it, how much did we get it for and many more things. When you remember you talked to Jozska Csorosz that here if it would be like in Deutsch country [Germany] you would also "bake it or beat it" [it's probably an expression] but then he said, no, don't be afraid! There wouldn't have been anyone who would buy it, but now he is the first one on the line and he thinks he will have the land for free. I will be ok, if God will help us all. [Leventeség] is very strict. They took the Stark boys from Lelesz to a camp beyond Budapest, because they had an incident. The instructor said Jew, and they fought each other. The man said, "he said" [someone got kicked, but couldn't make it out] and then somebody sued them. The post officer lady is in Miskolc. Someone was visiting there and [she] was wondering about you and is sending greetings to you. How are you? I am, thank Goodness, very healthy. I'm sorry that I'm bothering you with all kinds of things, but the

last time I wrote very little. Now I'm making up for it. You also, write a lot. I hope my letter will find you also in good health. I wish you a very happy new year! Kisses, your brother Ignác.

1939/10/4 Father to Dezső (Book 4, 207-208)

Bodrogmező, 1939 October 4

My dear son Dezső, live to 100,
In your letter you have advised me that you have given the money to my brother Jónász. He also wrote to me that he received it. Regarding to traveling, when it will be really, I do not know, only God knows. We are in good health and hope that you too are well and you're not missing it. Rozmán initiated a lawsuit, however before the hearing I gave him 150 Pengos. [I will pay him] 43P. on January 1, 1940 and on September 7, 225 P. What will be I'm sure you know more there, than here. They want take the Jewish [owned] lands. This month they will be making decisions. The boys' passports are still at a standstill. The orphanage office is holding the money. I will not receive it until Ignác's passport is available. It will be very difficult to take out Emil and Lenke's share. I have not received any letter from you. We are writing and are hopeful that you receive it from us. Write frequently, don't forget about us, with respect and kisses your father, with love. Gluck Jeremias

I wish you a happy new year and if you meet my brother Jónász, give my regards to him. If he has received my letter, by now I would have gotten a reply. Your father.

1939/10/4 Herman to Dezső (Book 5, 154-155)

1939 X / 4

Dear Dezső,
The last letter I received from you was a long time ago. I know we have delays in the mail. We wrote a long time ago and we should have received an answer. We were waiting to hear from you. We hope everything is okay with you. Please write us as soon as you can about everything. I can't write anything good, therefore I didn't write before. If you listen to the news then you know what I mean. I'm sure the girls wrote everything to you, about how we are living. It is not the best. On the fifth we would have been going into the army, but because of the holiday we didn't receive the letter. I will have to go in February. If I will have to go sooner, I will write to you. At home, we are soldiers by their rules. I was in Lelesz to the temple for the holiday. It was in a small room. How are you doing with your English? I don't have any passion to learn because I don't know if I ever will be there. We didn't hear from Uncle Jónász either for a long time. We can't travel until we have the money in dollars to buy the ticket to go to America. We moved out from our new house. 4 weeks ago. I don't really like it, that is, we live like animals. We can't even go out. Where can we go? We're waiting for a better future. In person we could talk much more about it. Hope you are not angry that I don't write often. Hope you are well. Loving kisses, your brother Herman

1939/10/5 Father, Hermine, and Marie to Dezső (Book 4, 267-268)

[from Hermine]
Dear Dezső!
It is true, that last week we sent one letter to you, but this letter from the consulate in Budapest came in. Since Arthur gave sponsor statements to more relatives, it's necessary for Arthur to give a statement, under oath, and signed in front of a notary, regarding how many relatives and acquaintances he has given [sponsorships] in the past two years. What kind of affidavit and for what nationality. Until he does this our visa is suspended. I hope that our dear Uncle Jónász [K[edves] J[onas]] will do this for us at least. Now, it's important that he has enough wealth/possessions so he can give a guarantee to more of us. I also thought that, so we don't waste time with corresponding, if in case it won't be done like the consulate wishes, then he can withdraw [the sponsorship] from the others, so it won't prevent us from traveling. We are the first ones and [it's] already cost us a lot so far. Our traveling will depend on this. Most importantly, it [Arthur's statement] must be here as soon as possible. You can see the tremendous impact it's had on our traveling already. I wrote to dear [kedves] Uncle Jónász also. How are you? Write! We have been waiting for your letter, but did not get one yet. Thank God, we are in good health and we wish that for you too. Kissing you with love, Hermine

[from Marie]
Dear Dezső!
I think you will be satisfied with us because we are sending our second letter, meanwhile we did not get one letter from you. Although, I thought I can write something good to you now, but unfortunately, it is the opposite. The others already wrote to you and now I don't even know how to write it to you. I don't intend to cause more worry, but our trip is being cursed and I do not believe we will be able to travel. Like now, for example, it's only a tiny thing, but still what an obstacle. Time is passing and I'm afraid the most about the traveling. Who knows where our money will be for that because when one lives from what we have, we will spend more or less until we will be able to save some. We can't even sell additional land anymore, and who knows what more will come!!! I want to go there so badly, already, but only if it's the 4 of us, the way we started. It is not worth it to go if it will be less than that. I hardly can think about it. I can only leave it to destiny. Don't worry yourself either about this. Although, I can't help it anyway. I'm sorry that I write like this. You can understand. Kissing you with love, Mariska

[from our father]
Bodrogmező, 1939 October 5
My dear son Dezső!
I'm letting you know, that, thank God, I'm healthy and I hope you aren't lacking that also. We are waiting for your letter every day, but it is not coming. I wrote a letter also last week, but it was only sent by regular service, if you got it. Now on the 3rd, we got a letter from Pest, that Arthur Gluck gave more guarantees during the past two years, [and they are asking] to whom and what relatives and what kind of nationalities he gave, and that he confirm [his answer] in front of a notary under oath. If he will send this in to the consulate, then they will be willing to negotiate our case. Until then, the visa is being suspended. This document needs to be sent by Uncle Jónász by airmail. I hope he will arrange that. I kiss you respectfully, your faithful father who has you in his mind in every step of the way, forever. Gluck Jeremias

1939/10/6 Bertha to Dezső (Book 5, 204-205)

New York
October 6, 1939
Dear Dezső!
Please accept our thanks for the New Year's cards. Hoping the new year will bring to our family and all of us and to you the best of health also. Your bad temper should behave, your happiness [depends on] just that, [and] your health. Sometimes I worry because in a strange, new country you didn't learn the language. It would help if you could speak better with understanding. You will be able to socialize. Do you have any friends? I hope you have! Because then it will be easier to learn and get used to it. If you are here in America there's life, thank goodness. Do you get any mail from home? Ever since the trouble started I didn't get any mail. From Miksa I received one on the first of September. The latest report was he wrote this letter from the hospital. I can see from his writing that he was very weak. Hoping that you will hear the best for your family, if you will hear from them anything. What do you think about everything? What will be about your family coming to America? At this time I've written enough for now. The relations are asking about you. They are sending their best wishes. Mannie and I are sending kisses and best wishes to you. Please let me hear from you about yourself. Bertha

1939/10/15 Bertha and Mannie to Dave (Book 3, 366-367)

New York
1939 October 15
Dear Dave! Accept my thanks for the information from home, you have made me relax. Yesterday I received a letter from Miksa. Finally they received the package which I mailed them at the end of March. I had a lot of aggravation to ship it. Finally I decided to write to the American consulate. Then the shipment by airplane cost a lot of money and it took so long to get to them. I really don't mind it now at least I know that they have received it. Again I'm going to send them whatever I can get together because I know is that there it costs a lot of money to secure it, especially clothing. My niece's papers are not ready that they can get out from there shortly. There is no information about my father. Dear Dave, I mentioned to Mannie that you have expressed that you would like to go to a larger city to reside. He recommends that one doesn't know what will develop from this war. Be conscientious. Forget it at this time to secure a new home. Learn to

speak English, that's the most important thing. Spend your free time on that because if you neglect that now, later you won't have as much time as now. There are schools where they teach you for free and you can learn a profession and you would get much more than in Polyán. Believe me, it will take about four years before you really become an American person. If you are going among people don't feel backwards. You will see it in the future, especially for a man. Allow me once again to predict that if you can get to know that I mean well, not only for you but for all of the relations. It's enough about this. I seize the opportunity now to reply to your letter since my Mannie went to a ball game, so I am alone at home. I wish you to be happy, with love Bertha and Mannie.

1939/10/15 Undated Hermine and Marie to Bertha (Book 1, 167)

[Dated by Bertha wrote to Dezső that she hasn't heard from his sisters. Hermine writes that they may arrive in November or December, so this letter must be around here]

[from Hermine]
Dear Bertuska! Until 120
I guess my lines that I write to you will surprise you a little, but I heard so many good things about you. The way Dezső is writing, he thought we got on the ship already. The restlessness, which you are a part of, I understand, and for that reason, so you can be calm I bother you with my lines. When we will know something certain about traveling, in other words, when we get our visa, we will let you know immediately, just like Dezső, as to which ship and when, so you can wait for us. Also true, that if weren't for the conditions, we would be already in America. Right now, I only know what the shipping line has written, that [it will be in] November or December, but it's possible that we will get a chance even sooner, [and in that case] I will write to you. It only depends on the conditions. The waiting and the restlessness will come to an end finally when everything is going to be fine. That is why it is necessary for us to be calm, it's a little hard, but it is what it is. I send heartfelt greetings and kisses to all the unknown relatives, to you, and your dear husband. Your [cousin], Hermin

[from Marie]
Dear Bertuska!
I am sending my heartfelt greetings also, to you and to your dear husband, and also to the rest of the unknown relatives. I will remain until the hopeful reunion. Your [cousin], Mariska

1939/10/15 Grandfather Samuel Schvartz to Dezső (Book 5, 17)

Lelesz, October 15 1939
My dear grandson, Gluck Dezső,
I write to you a few lines about my son Lajos. I only can tell you that we are well thank God, I hope to hear from you the same. I can only write to you that I have closed my store and I'm not in business anymore. I would like it if you could look up my relations.

Luisz Berger lives in Brooklyn. The other (girl) relation, Eszter Deits, is in New York. I haven't received a letter from them in a long time. I don't know if they already have a son. Deits is the wife of Luisz Berger. If you have an opportunity to look up Lajos Lefkovits, he is my son Marton's brother-in-law. I'm not going to write anything else. We are hoping, waiting that God will help us, your grandfather and grandmother respectfully, Schvartz Samuel, Lelesz.

I'm waiting for a reply, only good things.
[Grandmothers maiden name was HAJE MOSKOVICS]

1939/10/18 Uncle Lajos Schwartz (Lelesz) to Dezső (Book 4, 253-254)

Schwartz Lajos
Haberdasher, Spices and Mixed Trade
Leles 1939 X / 18

Dear Dezső.
I think you will be surprised to hear from me. I just remembered to write to you a few lines. I was visiting your family yesterday. They are well. I just hope they will be able to get out soon. At this time I have nothing

else special. Thank goodness we are okay and so is your grandfather. I think you have more information about everything that goes on than we do here. I cannot tell you anything at this time. Your family must have written to you whatever was happening there. If our God could help us. Please write to me something good I hope otherwise you are well. How is your Uncle Jónász? What are you doing at this time? Can you speak well in English. Please write to me about yourself, what you doing, how you managing and please write some good news. I'm happy to hear from you. Dear Dezső, at this time I'm trying to turn to you with a question. I mentioned it to you before you left to America. Now the time has come to get help for any tragedy can happen here. If we can get away or if he can get some protection for all my family before it is too late. If you have time, but if you could get some information from all your friends to help our Temple.. We need a new roof. It is in a very bad stage and we need help for that and the walls need help. We cannot afford to rebuild what we desperately need. The mikva was closed down. It has to be rebuilt. It is in a very bad condition. Now you could imagine now in this bad situation that we are in we are not able to repair it. Therefore I am turning to you, maybe there is the chance you might be able to help us. I'm sure you know how to get around and what to do. I hope you can help us whatever you can. I hope maybe you can write or ask your Uncle Lajzer's child maybe they can help a little. Also your Uncle Jónász and his son. Please believe me that I would not bother you if it would be possible to do it otherwise. It doesn't have to be at this moment. We could wait even if it takes a little longer. The only thing I am asking is to not forget about us, to think of some solution. After all, we are Jewish people and you will understand I was thinking maybe you could advertise in the newspaper. Maybe that would help. It would be the best, maybe better. Over there it would be less expensive. Here it would cost much more, 5 times more. The work can be done much cheaper here. I would like to ask you a favor. I know if you want to really help us I understand you will be able to do whatever you want to. I'm not asking for myself. We need to have a mikve. Here we do not have enough people to ask for help. Now I want to wish you the best with many kisses to your Uncle Lajos. Please give my love and best wishes to Uncle Jónász and his family.

[On the side] I'm waiting anxiously for your answer. I hope I don't have to wait too long. Please write about everything. I hope you will succeed. I do not ask you to give. I do not expect that you will pay for all of that.

[I know about the Temple and also about the leak. We used to go to that Temple all of us.
Our grandfather and our Uncle used to be very active there. That was before the Holocaust. - Maria]

1939/10/25 Bertha to Dezső (Book 3, 364-365)

New York
October 25 / 39
Dear David!
Arthur has interesting questions, forget it, I don't want to hurt him or make it difficult for him, he means well. He will be helpful and was interested in my family back home. I would have been very grateful, but I don't want to disturb him, because he has enough problems with my family. We are lucky that we can get the necessary papers to our Miksa, therefore the numbers will remain when it will become there turn. Dear Dezső, Arthur is very nervous. I would not like it that because of me he will have a heart attack. Let me think that I do not have anybody, so I have to manage as I can to help my sister, I'm not going to bend my knee for anyone. If it is so ordered, and in another way we can succeed. And it is up to Arthur, in his last letter he wrote to me that he may have to ask to return the papers. And I have written to him about it that for mine he could send them and he should be kind enough and if he can't afford it, then he should arrange it the best way as he sees it. My brother in law, and son and Jolan can take care of the up keep with her relations and if he needs stamps and the insured mail. Perhaps the best thing is to forget that I will disturb him as he has enough problems with his business. Last Friday, I received a letter from Miksa. They have received a package that was sent in March. At the time when he wrote the letter he thanked me in the name of Marcsa and the children. He does not mention anything about my father. I hope that I sent good things, clothing to Zoli. However I forgot the number and that is what I wrote on the package. And I addressed it to Boj Street, Kiraly Helmecz. Do you think that he will receive it? Also I have written on it Miksa's address, if they do not find Zoli. I will not write more, except my thanks for the registered letter.
Kisses, Bertha, and regards from the relatives and Mannie

1939/11/16 Helen Perl to Hermine and Marie (Book 13, 317-318)

Dear Herminka and Mariska!

I received your card and as you can see I am responding immediately, since I can already write it exactly that with God's help on Sunday, in other words on the 19th, I will travel by overnight train to Pest. Ready to go. I too would have been happy if we could have travelled together from Szürte and we didn't go together. As far as the Italian company is concerned, write to the company exactly when you had the visa interview and when they promised the visa to you at the consul. And request that they will write to the American embassy in that case. Don't mention the Cunard company for now, that's later. The price of my ship ticket is $225, in other words, two hundred and twenty five dollars, but I am traveling with a cheaper boat because that ship will leave only next month and it is not advisable to wait today. The cheapest ticket price is $165. I advise you to write as soon as possible to this ship company. They will arrange this in a short matter of time. The exact address for the Italia shipping company is: Budapest district 5 (V) Vaci street number 4. My next address will be American if God will help me to get there with luck Sam Freedman Shoe, Buckeye Road 11618 Cleveland, Ohio. I will close my lines with wishes for lots of good things. I am sending greetings from my heart to both of you. Helen

1939/11/21 Zemplen County Orphanage - Ignác (Book 7, 5-6)

Page 15637 193/91

> Subject: Minor Gluck Ignác of Bodrogmező
> Application for a Resident's Seniority
> The report on the basis of the response, request for decree, etc. number
> > Attached
> > Deadline

DECISION

The application is granted, and for Glück Ignác Bodrogmező who was born in Bodrogmező on the 14th of November, 1921. As a full-fledged man, he is privileged to lead his affairs and to manage his property independently.

Glück Jeremias, a resident of Bodrogmező, the father, is summoned to give his guardian's grandfather's wealth to his guardian as his own.

At the same time, we searched the district of Kiralyhelmec that all the registered properties are now controlled by the above legally. This incorporates the Bodrogmező fields 415, 147, 285, 522 and 521, of the official registrar.

We know that you have become self-righteous to see the accounts at the guardianship authority, in the view of the guardian, t. t. proclaiming a guardian; otherwise he has the right to make copies of his calculations and documents; and if they have objections to the counting, they shall report their observations to the Guardianship Authority during the course of the six months of the present invocation. However, if during this period the guardianship authority does not declare it, the guardianship authority shall issue a guardianship for the guardian, who is the lawyer of the acquittal.

We are released from our bankruptcy-managed cash, so therefore we call the county council of Sátoraljaújhely to take the necessary measures on the basis of the voucher attached to this final decision, to the benefit of the inhabitant of Bodrogmező Glück Ignác, common orphans XVII, page 131 of 623 Pengő 80 fillér i.e. six hundred twenty-three Pengo 80 fillér cash and the interest on the last day of the month before the day of payment of the sum Glück Ignác of Bodrogmező the increase in the legal rank of this final decision and after it is communicated to the resident m. kir. send a savings bank.

The Lelesz notary public, I informed by means of a guardian that Glück Ignác of Bodrogmező had reached the privilege of resident.

DECLARATION

He applied for his seniority.

The child is under the age of 18 according to the birth certificate of the presented child.

By the official document #4331/1939 issued by the village of Bodrogmező on November 14, 1939, it was verified that the minor is capable of decisions and is mentally well balanced without reservations.

The applicant demonstrated that it is necessary and useful for him to become an adult.

The parent and closest relatives are in agreement.

Taking these into consideration, we have found it appropriate to reach a decision of approval in accordance with the provisions of the relevant section.

Against this final verdict there is an appeal to the administrative committee of Zemplén County.

The appeal can be filed or filed with us within 15 days from the day after the receipt of our final decision.

We will notify the following:

1. Glück Ignácot, Bodrogmező
2. Glück Jeremiást, Bodrogmező
3. Chief Attorney, Local
4. The Land Registry Authority Kiralyhelmec
5. Notary Public Bodrogmező, minor was raised to a legal level
6. The county council of Sátoraljaújhely is informed with a voucher, sátoraljaujhelyi

Sátoraljaújhely, 1939, November 21

1939/11/24 David to President FDR (Book 7, 3)

Dear Mr. President:
We are thankful celebrating with you our second Thanksgiving. May the Lord let you carry on your blessed work.
David Gluck
Otto Neubauer
420 S. Monroe

1939/11/24 FDR's Secretary to David (Book 7, 4)

The White House
Washington
November 24, 1939
My dear Mr. Gluck:
Permit me, please, to acknowledge the receipt of the telegram from you and Mr. Neubauer, which I shall be glad to bring to the President's attention when he returns to the city. You may be sure that he will be most grateful for this evidence of your goodwill. Very sincerely yours,
M. A. LeHand
PRIVATE SECRETARY

1939/12/15 Undated Helen Perl to Hermine and Maria (Book 4, 243-244)

Dear Herminka and Mariska.
I am a little delayed in my writing. Usually I do answer soon. I was very happy to hear from you. I was wondering why you still haven't received your information that you need and are waiting for. Sometimes it gets lost or delayed. I'm very happy to hear Dezső promised that he will bring you to visit me in Cleveland. Please when you decide to visit me let me know beforehand so I would have a chance to prepare something. As an old friend I would be very happy to see you again. I hope you will not be upset I would like to celebrate. I'm very happy to hear the best about all of you. I would be happier if my brother would be here with me.
But sometimes it is not the way you would like it to be. We wish that it could be this simple. About myself I could also write I'm working all time. Dear Maria you are asking me what I am doing in my spare time. I

do not have too much time. I can't brag about or say that I have. I do not have too much free time, maybe it is my fault. In the daytime I am working in a factory on dresses. Also at home I am sewing privately for myself. It helps [to have] a little extra money. I would like to establish my own business. My family would like to have it also because you can make a nice living here being able to sew. I would like to know maybe first if I had one customer then the 2nd one will follow. This way they will get to know me and I will be able to lift myself up. It is hard work, but nothing comes easily even in America. It always comes in handy. They always needs someone, especially if you are a good worker and are able to sew. I don't go out. My relations are not the outgoing type [so] they're not interested. At home I suffer a lot. If I mention I would like to go out they are not happy. As I look back, my sister and I used to go out everywhere [and] we had a good time, but now what we go through. My family worked at hard labor–they are suffering. In my heart it is very difficult to accept. The people who are here much longer than I am cannot understand me. I hope you're not going to laugh about it and

you will understand me. I know in your heart you feel the same way. The pain I feel I'm sure you feel the same. Some people cannot accept or think about anything except themselves. How are the Reich girls? They were here at Christmas time visiting me in Cleveland. I never visited them. They were very hurt because I haven't visited them. They like to talk about themselves. I think maybe you know about them better. I am not anxious to keep up our friendship. Here I have enough relations. I think I wrote to you enough [and] hope that I am not boring you. Please write about everything. With all my best wishes and many kisses to both of you. Also best wishes to your brother. Your friend, Helen

1939/12/19 Lenke, Father, Ignác, Hermine, and Marie to Dezső (Book 2, 287-290)

[from Lenke]

Dear Uncle Dezső,
I'm happy that I can also write to you already. Write to me, too. I kiss you many times.
Lenke

[from Hermine]
Dear Dezső!
We were very happy to read your letter, we could hardly wait for it. We did not know what to think, but your lines were a little consolation for us. I will also write to the consulate now, because we did not get any notice yet. You may know more than we. If you sent a telegram to the consul, then you know the answer already. Otherwise, we are in good health. [If only] the good God would allow us to travel already. As you can see, Lenke is trying to write to you and if you would hear how good she is at reading. She's a very good student. Now I can't write more. I kiss you with love, Hermina

[from Ignác]
I'm looking forward to a better future!
With kisses, your brother Gluck Ignác

[from our father]
Give my respects to my dear brother. I will write a letter to him when they will get the notice from the consul. Gluck Jeremias.

[from Hermine again]
Dear Dezső,
As you could see, I'm continuing to write the letter because our father has no time to write, and we already wrote everything anyway.
Please write more often. If we will know something definite, we will notify you. Hersmendel is still here at home, and if the call-in [to the consulate] would come in a short time, then maybe everything would work out. He says that he doesn't know what to write to you and that is why he does not write. Give my greetings to the relatives and thank them very much for all the arrangements. Now, the only thing that matters, is if everything arrives to Budapest. Kiss you, Hermina

[from our father]
My dear son Dezső,

I got the letter you sent and thank goodness, you are in good health. I hope that we will have a result from all the effort. I did not do anything about the boys' cases. The consul did not decide it yet. Time is short and money [is being] wasted. I kiss you respectfully, your father who will never forget, Gluck Jeremias 1939 XII/19

[from Marie]
Dear Dezső!
We got your letter, that we could hardly wait for. We didn't know what to think, that your letter was so late. Until then, we did not know what to write, either. As you can see, as of today, we don't know anything about our traveling. I'm very happy to hear that you are in good health. As you wrote that they sent the documents last week, it is incomprehensible what happened. Maybe we wrote it to you, Helen Perl and 5 others travelled at the same time from Szürte. Lajos Shvarc and 1 more boy were in Budapest last week and at the consulate they promised them that they can definitely travel in the first half of January. Now, it is out turn. It's about time and, if the good God will help us all, we will be able to travel with luck.
Ever since Iren Schvarc travelled, they did not get any [news] except that the agent's list said that the ship has arrived. Now we are writing to Budapest. Uncle Marton traveled to Budapest also. His business still exists, as of right now, but other than that, they are well. I was at Uncle Lajos and he is waiting for you to write to him. He is also well. Also, grandfather's family is well. They are both sending their heartfelt greetings and kisses to you. You know, nobody here even believes us that we are going to America. Although, I cannot believe it myself, but I hope the good God will help everybody and it won't be long that it will end. I see that you and our uncle are doing everything in order to help us. The only problem is that there is no normal postal traffic. It is holding us back, and that's also the reason why you rarely get a letter from us. Dear Dezső, please write more often. If we get something definite, we will write immediately. There is no other news. We are sending greetings also and kiss you. Give my best to the relatives.
Mariska

[On the top of the page] Accept my thank you, until I will return it in America to you.

1939/12/22 American Consulate General Re Visas (Book 1, 16)

American Consulate General
Budapest, 1939, December 22

Misses: Gluck Hermina and Maria
Mr's: Gluck Herman and Ignác
Bodrogmező, u.p Lelesz

With reference to the "vizum" permits to go to America, the chief consulate advise you that the visas have been approved.

We wish to advise you that the following documents have expired: moral character, addresses (where you live), doctor's reports. Please mail the new documents so that the visas can be issued.

Sincerely,
Acting Consul General,
Milton C. Rewinkel,
American Consul1940/1/14 (a) Undated Hermine to Dezső (Book 2, 293-294)
[Dated by mention of January 8th and father's letter on the same day in which he writes that Hermine wrote already]

[on top] I kiss you countless time, your little brother Ignác [illegible] Good by.

Dear Dezső,
I know you will be angry at me if I tell you what request I had for dear Uncle Jónász. Like I wrote, the consulate notified us that if I renew the documents, then we should send them in so the visa can be issued. We arranged the boys' passports also and they are good. I took them on January 8th in person, and they said at the consulate that the Cunard White Star line does not sail to America. Now everybody is traveling from our town with a ship from the Italia shipping company. I inquired from the manager of Cunard, if it's true.

He said the consul has no information about that. I went to the Italia Lines, it's an Italian company. They only sell tickets for dollars. So, now we are under the necessity of asking dear Uncle Jónász for the ship tickets. I am truly sorry that there is always some kind of request, but I never thought that we would have to come to this, since we have the money. You know this well, also. The town took over the house and our dear father has sold land also, but that doesn't matter, because the Cunard Line gave [the tickets] for pengos. Now they are holding their passengers until the last moment, and in the worst case scenario, they can transfer [the money] to the Italians and then they will also take a percentage from it. The consul also promised that in the first days of February they will send out the visa, and then with God's help, we can travel, as long as we have the ship tickets. I guess, you can understand our situation today. We did whatever was possible. But, you know better, that everybody has ship tickets from America, and things like this don't occur with others. Dear Uncle Jónász will do this if he can, and if he can't, then everything is over. Don't mind me, that I'm only writing so briefly, but my entire patience is gone. Only a person who has lived this, knows what it is. Now, Mrs. Eizner from Lelesz had a visa interview, and in February she will get the visa also. The lady admitted that if it was not for the documents, then we would be in America already. It wouldn't be inconvenient. She can't help with anything, unless we get our turn. The Visa division is on February 15. But it would be so great, if Uncle Jónász would send the ship tickets as soon as possible, because we will get the visa in the first days.

[in the corner] Kisses, Hermine

1940/1/14 (c) Undated Hermine to Dezső pages 3 and 4 (Book 4, 303-304)

[dated by context, and matching paper and page numbers]

Everybody is very surprised that all four of us can go. Ignác's picture is not good, but at least you will see [him]. Emil is not at home, that is why he doesn't write, but he can hardly wait for your letter. He is already counting how many dollars he will get from America per month. Mariska Deak suggested that if you can't read her letter, have her taken to America, so she can read it to you. Molvin [Lefkovics] is always joking also, but I will give the correct answer. I will write to Jolan shortly. Although, I should have written to her already, but it always remains [to do]. I would love to get the response to the letter in America already. This letter came after 25 days. Kiss you with love. Hermine

Our father does not know what to write to dear Uncle Jónász, because if we all go away, what can he write. It doesn't work that way. He needs to be supported with everything, there should be no excuse and I know how much he deserves it. And our father says it too, that he would like everything to be as it used to be. He doesn't write because of that. In turn, if he will find out that we will go, he would not come.

1940/1/14 (c) Father to Dezső (Book 2, 277-278)

Bodrogmező 1940 I/14

My dear son Dezső,

Herminka wrote everything already. I am letting you know also, thank God we are in good health, and I hope you don't miss that also. To that question for my dear brother, I had a hard time to decide myself, but we did not want to leave it to the last minute because we don't know the situation, and what develops from it. Last month on the 24th, I sent the previous letter to you with AirMail. I did not get a response. I can hardly wait for Uncle Jónász to act. You be patient with whatever my dear brother says! Write about everything and how you are doing. Your grandfather and grandmother send their regards to you. I don't even know what to write to you. My dear son Dezső, when God will help, your siblings will tell you everything in person. I respect you, kiss you, your faithful father, who will never forget. Gluck Jeremias

1940/1/15 Herman to Dezső (Book 19, 28-29)

1940 I / 15

Dear Dezső,

Forgive me for not writing to you so sooner, however I don't know what to write you now because the girls have written to you in detail. I'm writing to you about myself that I'm alive and I hope if God will help something will change. How are you? Write a little bit more frequently because we are waiting for your letters. If God will help us it will be that we will be there then we will talk about a lot of things. The big news in our village is that Joska Juhasz is engaged to Anna Deak. Time goes very slowly because we are waiting and it's very cold here so we stay indoors without being able to do anything. We are thinking of the necessities to stay warm hoping that things would change so that life won't be so boring. Otherwise there's not much to write, and I believe when you finish reading our letters then you'll know about everything. I hope that my letter will find you in the best of health. With kisses, Herman.

1940/1/16 Uncle Marton to Hermine [in Budapest] (Book 5, 274-275)

Now on Thursday afternoon I received a letter. Today in the morning I already mailed a letter and I'm responding to the 2nd one also. Nothing new here. I didn't get any mail. That person must be a very bad person. Don't trust yourself with this kind of person and don't talk about anyone to them or anyone else you know, because they can cause lots of problems for you. Be very careful and take care of yourself. If the two boys can go on the 7th then let them. If you get the tickets for the ship, even if it's on Saturday, it would be wonderful, whatever you believe. But, it would be ok if Herman can go near the ship with Ignác and there they could wait for another, a 2nd ship, on the 20th. Please ask the shipping company if they think it is possible. Kisses, Marton

[Postcard postmarked January 16, 1940]

1940/1/18 American Consulate General Visa Issued (Book 1, 17)

American Consulate General
Budapest, 1940. 1. 18.

Gluck Hermina Ms.
Bodrogmező, p. Lelesz

We are advising you that the money for the visas for you and your sister and brothers that we requested has been paid to the Cunard

organization. Consequently, the chief consul has permitted the visa numbers to be issued. You can obtain the visas after the 25th.

In the meantime, we have attached the new affidavits to the existing documents. It was approved after Mr. Arthur Gluck sent the documents.

Sincerely,
Acting Consul General
M.C. Rewinkel
American Consul

1940/1/25 American Consulate General (Book 1, 18)

American Consulate General
Budapest, 1940. Jan. 25.

Mr's: Herman and Ignác Gluck
Bodrogmező u.p. Lelesz

We are informing you that you both need to submit your military certificates in duplicate immediately so that your visas can be issued.

Sincerely,
Acting Consul
Milton C. Rewinkel
American Consul

1940/1/25 Cunard White Star Lines to Hermine (Book 1, 19)

Cunard White Star
Budapest, 1940. January 25.

Attention:
Miss Hermina Gluck
Bodrogmezo

Referring to our last letter.

We are aware that the American Consul General of Budapest has written to you today regarding the military certificates of Mr's Herman and Ignác Gluck.

We are asking you to acknowledge that these military certificates will secure it. We will submit it to the American consulate tomorrow. Our expense in this matter is 3.20 pengo [$21.60]. We are asking you to reimburse us.

Please send in the return mail, the certificate of moral character and a district certificate for Mr. Ignác Gluck. These documents must be authentic. The moral and district certificates were returned by the American consulate and instead we need duplicate copies of the certificates to be mailed to us.

Also we are returning Mr. Herman Gluck's official moral character certificate and district certificate and are requesting you to obtain duplicate copies and return it to us.

We call to your attention that the birthdate for Mr. Herman Glück is different on the moral character certificate and the district certificate. We are returning Mr. Herman Gluck's birth certificate and we are asking for duplicate copies of the district certificate and the moral character certificate. The birthday must match November 16, 1918.

Most sincerely,
Cunard White Star Limited

Please return the birth certificate also.
Enclosed
Registered mail

1940/2/1 Undated Jozsef Lefkovits (Jozsef, Szerenke, Malvin) to Dezső (Book 4, 339-340)

[Given to Hermine or Marie before they left to send the accompanying letter to Mr. Vilmus Sofier. See 1940/2/1 Undated Jozsef Lefkovits (Jozsef, Szerenke, Malvin) to Victor Sofier (Book 5, 90-91)]

My dear Dezső!
I would like to be there when they will take our letters out and to see their arrival when your tears of joy will fall from your eyes into your lips and you will enjoy a thought from home when you will first meet. Although, if we could enjoy our destiny, it is a hard thing. My dear Dezső, I will ask you again a favor, we all will thank you in advance. You should write to my brother-in-law, that is, to Vilmus Sofier, so he will not forget about us completely. He wrote to us when he got your letter. In case it will wake him up [tell him] that he has a sick sibling and an unfortunate older brother at home and they have nothing to live from! They were ruined, they took everything from them. I'm writing this with a big heartache. Please look them up, maybe he could help them right away separately. Your dear siblings will tell you everything. I don't mean to share in reading the letter, only what I am asking you. I hope you will do it! I'm thanking your big favor in advance. I will remain your well wisher. Szerenke, and Joseph and Malvin!
Wictor W Sofier
c/o Hotel Webster Hall
2
Pittsburg, PA
America

[note from Dave] I just talked to dear Uncle Jónász on the phone and he is also sending his greetings to you. Also the housewife sends her greetings. And if the dear God will help all of us then they will have the entire family come here. I hope you will get my lines in your hands and I'm waiting for your answer. We are sending our greetings. Dave Gluck

1940/2/1 Undated Jozsef Lefkovits (Jozsef, Szerenke, Malvin) to Victor Sofier (Book 5, 90-91)

Beloved dear brother-in-law Wilmus!

I'm writing with shaky hands. I take the pen to my hand so I write a few lines to you. I wrote a few letters. I did not get a response to any one [of them]. [Perhaps] I do not know the exact address. Or I don't even know what to think. Maybe you don't even want to hear about us. Now the two Glück girls and the two boys are going to America. I will send my letter with them so you can receive it. I hope you will not leave my letter without an answer! It is enough that the destiny left us. At least you could help us. With just one letter they took the "Kurcsma" from us. They don't give us any kind of industry, so what do we have to live from? I don't mind working in anything. I am 62 years old, but I would do anything just for my family. I could give bread to my dear Szerenke. She has diabetes. She was put on a hospital's diet. She would live if we could do it. And she grieves more grief. Herman is getting old and I can't give him enough food. I am not able to buy clothes for him. Dear brother-in-law Wilmos, I am asking you and I'm letting you know that on Tuesday, March 5th is the blessed day of mother's yahrzeit. On Monday night should be kaddish. To say it in [the] Jewish [date] 25th day of Adar I [Adar rishon]. I hope that you will get the letter by then. Write how you have been. I hope that you are healthy! And God forbid that you are sick and that is why you don't write.

Dear Wilmos! At least a letter. Make your sibling feel better, [and] as I think, our entire family. I'm asking you to write again. [Otherwise] I think there will be a complaint! We kiss you countless times, your siblings too. Your brother-in-law, Szerenke and Jozsi

1940/2/6 Hermine (in Budapest) to Dezső in America (Book 5, 128)

Budapest 1940 II/6

Dear Dezső,

It's February 7th. We are in Budapest and we're leaving by train to Napoly [Naples, Italy]. From there we are going on the steam ship Vulcania. We are leaving from here on the 10th and will arrive on the 21st in New York. We hope that God will help us so that we will arrive safely. We are traveling all four (4) of us together. I will write to Bertha, also. Our travel has been with a lot of difficulties. Thank God, everything is alright up until now. I would have written to Uncle Jónász if I could, however, I will try from the port. Tonight, I want to organize our papers so that we can travel. Kisses to all, as well as Uncle Jónász and the other relations.

With lots of love, kisses, Hermine

And to you, also. Until we meet soon in America. Until now I could not write only that it's a miracle that we can travel. As soon as I finished, I am writing to you immediately.

1940/2/19 Etelka, Lajos, children to Us (Book 4, 365-366)

[from Etelka]

Dear Herminka and Dear Mariska,

We got your letter very late, which we could hardly wait for, from Naples. We were happy about it. We already started to get impatient, although it had a reason to be late, because since you left, there is a huge winter. The snow is so deep on the ground, it's on the same level with the houses, so this caused the bad delivery. What can I write first to you, maybe about our happiness, that you got to your goal. This happiness was interrupted with Lajos getting drafted. We don't know how much longer he will be at home. The traveling caused a big sensation in the town, as it would in a small town. I'm very happy that you had a nice trip, and am hoping that you felt well on the ship,. We mentioned you many times. Only that beloved [golden] Gyuszi does not want to believe that you went to America. He said that Hencsu is in Szürte. This is the way it is, as you can see,. he who dares to lie once, will not get credit anymore. There is no news in the town since you left, only that the winter is terribly strong. The kids don't even go to school because of the cold. Thank god, we are all in good health. The cold has a bad effect on me a little. Olga is here and she spares me a little [by helping]. We can hardly wait for your letter from America. Who could have been the first one who gave you a hug when you arrived? For dear Uncle Jónász and the dear Aunt give my kisses to their hand and kind greetings. Also to Arthur and to his dear family and to all the relatives, whoever you meet, give my greetings. I kiss you and Mariska with love and I'm thinking of you many, many times.

Etelka 1940 II/20
[from Lajos]
My loved siblings,
You know very well that I have no patience to write, that is why I'm only writing a couple of lines. I just got your cards and I'm surprised that Herman and Ignác did not write one word, but after this they will. From Dezső, we haven't received any letter until this day. I kiss everyone, Lajos

[from Lenke]
Dear Hencsu and Marcsa!
I kiss all of you also, Ignác, Hersmendel, Dezső, Uncle Jónász and his family.
Gluck Lenke, Mityu, and Gyuszi

[from Emil]
Bodrogmező. 1940 II/19
Dear Aunts and Uncles!
I don't know what to write now, because my mom (and others) already wrote everything. I would have loved to be behind you when you were kissing Dezső and Uncle Jónász. Send pictures about the first encounter with the relatives. Ignác, you left the gun. here and my dad became a new recruit. I also would like to be there among you. I'm sleeping with Grandpa [Zajdi] in your beds. I kiss all of you. Dear Uncle Jónász and dear Aunt Helen, Uncle Arthur, his family, and Uncle Dezső. Gluck Emil

1940/2/19 Father to us (Book 4, 325-326)

[The writing on the top]
When I go to the house, I'm alone and [with just] the four walls, but [complaining is] in vain, if it should be so - your father.

Bodrogmező, II 19, 1940
My dear children,
I got your letters, that I could hardly wait for. I happily read it, that you arrived luckily to the port in Napoli. Also, that you are well there and I hope that God will help all of you even more, now that you have arrived [with] luck to my dear brother, Jónász and to my dear son, Dezső.
[Hopefully] you arrived across that large sea, in good health. I only hope the best for you. I got your letter last night. They sent it from Lelesz. The winter is very bad here now, since Mariska travelled away with the others. Only that week the weather was milder. The next day we dried the tobacco. It was 1156 Ki [I'm not sure what measurement "Ki" is, maybe he meant kg? It seems to be a lot then] it would have been, 300 pengo, but they did not give anything, because [they] did not have the amount. I'm sure they will come to search. Since then, there is a big winter. Howling winds and strong weather. The trains are stopped. We did not even have postal service this week. So, I'm wondering how everything is with Lajos. Poor thing, he was conscripted into the military service. They are waiting for the call up each day. Dear children, I'm asking all of you to take good care of yourselves. How is my dear brother Jónász and his dear family and Arthur and Elzsike? I send my respects to all of them. My dear son Dezső, I'm asking you to look after your siblings. I can't imagine why I still did not get any answer to my letters. I'm only asking you to write about everything. How was the traveling and who waited for you at the train or rather, the ship? Dear children, the school master/grade teacher asked for the levente [the members of the paramilitary youth organization]. The lieutenant has been told that the 2 Glucks went to America. He answered, that it's not a big deal, it will only be 2 less of them. He did not even consider it as being important.

1940/2/19 Undated Father's letter to us #2 (Book 5, 13-14) missing first page

Everyone knows now about the travel. My dear son Dezső, once again I'm asking you please take care of your brothers and sisters. Please don't forget to write punctually also to your Grandfather, Grandmother, and Uncle Lajos bacsi. Patyu [Uncle Marton] was happy that he was there at the farewell. He would not do it for any money once again. He was very satisfied with you all. I mailed the papers that you sent me to the attorney in Budapest, the ones that I made in the central professional that I did not mail yet. He did not write the reply. I asked him what I needed for the National Bank regarding your communication. With lots of love, kisses to all of you individually, your father who will never forget you, Gluck Jeremias.

1940/2/22 Etelka, Lajos, and children after we arrived in America (Book 3, 199-205)

[from Emil]

Dear aunts and uncles.

This week I've written a long letter, so today I don't know what to write. We were very happy to get your dear letters and the dollar. I ran to grandpa's to tell him that we have gotten a letter from you. You can imagine how happy he was. Sanyi Klein is working at Fenyves Valley. The instructor entered the Army. Kisses to all of you, kisses to Dezső and dear Jónász bacsiekat and dear Arthur bacsiekat. Your nephew Emil.

[from Etelka]

Dear Herminka and Dear Mariska.

Did you rest up after such a difficult trip? It is very difficult to wait for your letters. How was the trip? Who shared with you the reception? We would be, but anytime, any day, now we are waiting for Lajos induction into the Army. What will be with us by ourselves? By me, there's no news. Mrs. Kocsis died in December. Marcsa Deak may also follow her. Kisses to you and to dear Jónász bacsi and family.

With love, Etelka.

[from Lenke]

Dear Aunt Hencsu and Dear Aunt Marcsa,

Kisses to you all, Dezsőt, Ignacot, Hersmendut. Gluck Lenke.

Mityuka and Gyuszika also send kisses to all of you.

[from Lajos]

Dearest brothers and sisters,

Thank God we are healthy and hope to hear the same from you. I am asking you to take care of yourselves. Why doesn't Dezső write? Father and Etel my wife are always waiting to hear from him. Father has written the news already. Believe me, I don't know what to write because I have a headache and my mind is somewhere else. The weather is very bad. The wheat has to be plowed over because the frost killed the seeds. If you would see Zolit, kanahare [without the evil eye], the way he salutes, you would eat him up. If I will have some money I will mail you a picture of him. Gyuszi kanahare, is big, rough, and is not afraid of Mityu. How long I'll be home I don't know. The horse gave birth to a colt. Presently, if we want to sell the cow, we would be able to get approximately 500 Pengot. With regards to our relations and kisses to all of you, many times, Lajos.

[from Emil]

We are also sending our kisses to all of you, Lenke, Mityu, Gyuszi, and Zoli. Mother has written everything. Alte Zajde [great-grandfather] sends his regards. Emil

[from Lenke]

Dear Herminka and Mariska, Ignác and Herman and Uncle Dezső,

I kiss you, Lenke

[from Etelka]

In the near future I will send you a recipe, at this time I didn't have time. I had to be with the Lefkovics family. Malvin is in Agard. I gave to Borsinek and Manyunak your letter. They said that they're going to write you. Presently they are occupied with the harvest. Leizer bacsi received your letters. We will write to you soon. Again kisses with love, Etelka

1940/2/26 Bertha to us (Book 5, 166)

New York

Feb. 26 / 40

My dearests!

Only a few lines to let you know that I'm mailing an airmail letter home telling my dear father about your arrival. I ask him to tell your father because I was afraid that your letters may not be mailed out in time, so I want to be sure that if your letters will be somewhat delayed, at least it will be mailed by me in time. Good luck, with love Bertha

[The note on the top:]
....and Hersmendel's back does not hurt. Write about everything.
Bodrogmező 1940 II/28

My dear son Dezső,
I gladly read your letter, that I could hardly wait for. I'm so glad, thank God, that you are in good health, and I hope that your siblings who have [just] arrived have it too. Lajos and his family, and I, thank God, we are all in good health. I hope that my lines will find all of you in good health as well. My dear son Dezső, the telegram arrived on the 22:12.0 55p [the 22nd at 12:55] to Helmec. The post office notified Uncle Marton that a telegram came from America and [asked] what to do with it. He answered that he will take it. The postmaster said that he knows we are related, so he [Uncle Marton] took it and he had Imre Hegedus, the shoemaker, bring it out. He gladly searched, who is in from Bodrogmező, who he can have the telegram sent with, to me. He searched at the end of the town, because on those days the winter was terribly big. We also were very happy that, thank God, they are all arrived luckily to you. May God give you happiness, with your dear siblings, in good health. Your dear siblings informed you about everything from here. In the letter I sent on the 20th, I already let you know that Lajos got drafted. They are waiting for the call-up everyday. Also this week, the old Gyula Simon was qualified as a hussar at the inspection [(originally) one of a body of Hungarian light cavalry formed during the 15th century, so a member of a class of similar troops, usually with striking or flamboyant uniforms]
In a row, I respect you and kiss you with love. Your faithful father, who will never forget.
Gluck Jeremias

My dear children Herminka, Mariska, Herman and Ignác,
I'm letting you know, that thank God, we are in good health. I hope you don't miss that also.
The telegram that my son Dezső sent, made us all very happy. Whoever heard it, was surprised how fast the trip over to America happened. May God gladly help all of you forevermore with everything, so you can be lucky. You are in your grandfather's and grandmother's mind, always. They [send their] regards to you. It's been two weeks since I was there with them. [he changed it to singular from here. I guess he talks about the grandmother] She was crying so badly and asked God to give you much luck to travel through....and your grandfather was just bringing in the wood from the tree, the one that Hersmendel cut for him, and he was showing it crying. Write to them, my dear children about your traveling. I don't want to bother you. I'm sure you wrote about everything already. And write about everything in detail and what is your occupation/profession. Write about everything, how is Uncle Jónász's health and his dear wife. How did they welcome you and write about everything one by one. Do not forget about praying and what you have been accustomed to do. I send my regards to you one by one, all of you. I kiss you countless times, your father, who will never forget. Gluck Jeremias
...and how did Bertuska welcome you? Was Zsenike [Aunt Jennie] also there? My brother Lajzer got a letter from Berta also, that she is already waiting for you.

1940/2/29 Emil Gluck to David (Book 5, 159-160)

Bodrogmező [Magyar Orszag] 1940 II / 29
[from Emil]
Dear Uncle Dezső
I received your dear letter and I'm happy that you have encouraged me that I could also be with you in America. Dear Ignác and dear Hersmendu you would not switch with me.
Dear Hencsu-kam and dear Marcsa, we mention you every minute. Did you rest up from your long journey? Kisses to all of you, Your nephew Emil.

[from Etelka, Lajos's wife] Lajos sends kisses to you and also to Uncle Jónász.

1940/3/1 Bertha to Hermine (Book 5, 179-180)

New York
March 1 / 40
Dear Herminkam!

I hope you will forgive me that I did not reply to the first letter up until now. I was in bed for a few days. At this moment, the postman rang the bell and I had to go down to sign the air mail letter. Now that you're here with 'mazzle' [mazel - luck] I hope that [it will] continue. I was in bed, maybe you believe that I was just being a little bit lazy. I'm happy to know that you are satisfied with everything. I was talking to a lady and was happy to hear that everything turned out to be okay with you and hope that from here on it will continue to progress. Be sure that you go to school and I'm sure that in a short while you will be accustomed to the life here, even though it may be a little bit difficult. Your life is just beginning and as of now you have been able to handle good and bad things. I wish Columbus would not be so far. I would look you up for a few days and would be able to be with you, if my health would permit. No one knows what can happen, but during the summer, I don't promise, but I'll say it that I'm missing you and our relations also. This will be enough of this. I'm afraid that you will be spoiled. I'm not afraid, but it's not so easy to flirt with a smart man. At this time accept my kisses from the rest of the relations and from us once again with love, and loads of luck. Bertha.
Also kisses to Dezső from me.
When you write to Patyu bacsi [Uncle Marton] give my regards to him!
As above.

1940/3/5 Hermine and Dezső to Mr. Sofier (Book 4, 335-336)

Dear Mr. Sofier!
Here I have attached dear Aunt Szerenke's letter, which I think will explain the situation.
My siblings and I arrived to America at the end of last month. We did not have a chance until now to write a few lines and that is why I did not send the letter immediately after we arrived.
Dear Aunt Szerenke [and others] asked me to send their letter to Mr. Sofier, since they wrote many times, but they did not get a response yet. Although, Dezső wanted to write all this, he is very busy and he mentioned that he would have written a year ago, but couldn't find the address.
I only ask you Mr. Sofier, to please respond to your dear sibling, because she is a very sick woman and she needs to be under a doctor's care. She would have peace with the inevitable, but wishes there would be enough for the cost. The state took away their last permit already for their pub/bar and Jews are not allowed to have any other business. And in addition to this, Hermann is with us also and there is no money to satisfy him. Also, Malvinka, needless to say, would be happy if somehow she could get out of there to America. Especially in today's situation, there is no purpose for a girl in Hungary. Now, I'm only asking dear Mr. Sofier, do not mind that I'm bothering with my letter, but I promised dear aunt Szerenke. In the present situation, even complete strangers are helping too, if they have a chance. I believe this letter won't stay without an answer to your dear siblings. With the end of this letter I'm sending my kind greetings,
Gluck Hermina.
P.S. Polyán is currently Hungary

u.i. [utóirat = PS] Dezső, and also my other siblings, send their greetings too.

Dear Mr. Sofier!
I just came home and my sister wrote, so I will write a few lines also. I'm asking you to please write to Polony, because, poor things, they went bankrupt. As you can see, my Uncle Jónász Gluck, has brought my siblings out. I am here for two years and he sent emigration permits to at least 25 people, therefore I will not talk you into it, but if you can do this please, do whatever you can. I really hope that you will respond to my letter to say that you received our letters. As for me, thank God I'm getting used to the situation. I'm currently working in a grocery store.
I'm sending my greetings and I wish all the best, with respect. Dave Gluck

1940/3/11 Bertha to Hermine (Book 5, 213-214)

New York
March 11, 1940
Dear Hermine!
I'm trying to write to you right away before you're going to work. You will get used to it. I want to wish you lots of luck. Dear this is your first job. The only thing I'm asking you, don't try to be perfect, and to overdo things so you get hurt. The window cleaning or washing don't try to overdo it. Take care of yourself, you come first. Tell them that at home you were doing the cooking. Now it is up to you how you will start

[otherwise] you would have to do more all the time. It will be as you want to plan for. In a home there is always something. She might not understand you at first. At least there you will be able to get a couple of dollars to save. The only thing, you must try to learn English. That is or should be the first [thing]. Don't get bitter or upset. You must trust or believe in God. I'm sure you will not be disappointed. The only thing I'm asking you is that Maria will be able to work too. And the boys, you must teach them to help you at home. Did you see Aunt Jennie's boys? They're even washing the floors and the windows too. Even for Dezső, it will not hurt him there at home. Maybe he can open his own business. He can make coffee, that is good and it is also easier. Tell Dezső that it wasn't easier for my husband because I wasn't feeling well and he didn't complain. He just did whatever he had to. My husband was working very hard. Only people knew us. Tell Dezső with love [what you] hope to accomplish, especially with the sisters 'you have to help' and give his time to help you to ease your life because it is not as easy as it looks. I will never forget [how difficult] it was when I came here even though it was 26 years ago. Dear Hermine, it is not important for you to mention every detail to me, all the children's details. For those I do not answer right. The problem is sometimes [there are] misunderstandings between some people. Do you understand me? Therefore I have to go because I have more important things to do. I have to tell my dear father what is going on here. Please just don't worry about it, take it easy. Wishing you all the best when you start, all of you, with all my love, Bertha

Give our best wishes to the relatives. Also sending you some stamps. You should have some. It takes time until you go to get it. At least you don't have to spend that time. Kisses again and love to all of you, Bertha

1940/3/12 Jeannie and Nathan (Frye?) to Hermine and Marie (Book 5, 167-168)

March 12, 1940
Dear Hermina and Mariska, just now I was able to get to reply to your letter! I was happy to hear and hope that you have gotten accustomed a little to America! I know it's difficult for a while, it takes a little time for a person to get accustomed to the situation. I'm positive that Uncle Jonas will do everything to make you happy if you listen to him! Here, there is nothing new. There's not much business around here. We hope that the season will begin. I was to Bertha on Sunday for supper. She doesn't feel too well. We are OK, thank God. Hope to hear the same from you. I hope that you are not going to wait too long with your reply! Write about everything. Wish all of you with love, Regards. Jeannie and Nathan
P.S. Give my regards to Jónás bacsi and his wife.

1940/3/15 Undated Gluck family to father (Book 3, 177-179) - draft

[dated to 1940 or 1941 before Passover. Most likely 1940 since they just arrived and might be learning and practicing their English]

[In English]
Dear father,
It makes us happy that we shall hear from home. We are healthy and working. How is dear father, grandfather, Lajos and relatives? Are the uncles at home? Kiss to Etelka, children and love to all. Many kiss to you dear father and wish you happy Easter - Holidays. Your children. Gluck family
Answer at once

1940/3/17 Helen Gluck to Hermine and Marie (Book 5, 255)

Dear Hermine and Marie!
By accident, I learned that you finally arrived to this fairy tale country. I want to wish you all a lot of good luck and a happy future. I hope we'll have the opportunity to meet each other in person. I would not have thought that lucky arrivals would not know me. I'm closing now, with best wishes and luck to all of you, all the best, Helen

Cleveland 17 March [1940]

1940/3/19 Bertha to us (Book 5, 177-178)

New York
March 19 / 40

My dearest!

I hope you'll forgive me that I will not disturb you with this letter. First of all, I would like to know if you have begun to learn or are you getting used to the new country and living here? I hope you're getting used to it and are busy and have a good job? I wish you all the best in life, whatever you want, with God's help it will succeed. I wish everything to you all. Hoping to hear from you soon. Otherwise I hope you found a job. A little while ago I received a letter from Miksatol [Miksa Schon] and he writes that they called him in to the army. I think if you have time it would be kind to ask cousin Arthur if you would be so kind to start some papers for Jolan and Tibi on their behalf. I don't want to bother them all the time with my letter, but because he was very nice before and wrote to me that I should give more information about them, therefore if he asks you for information, then you will be able to answer him. I am sure that he will ask and you will be able to help me with this important situation. I am asking you to do that. If unexpectedly you cannot see Arthur then speak to the Uncle. Just ask him if Arthur talked about them and if he started the papers on their behalf. First I want to thank you in advance, wishing good luck to all of you dear ones and give all my kisses and best wishes to uncle and all of you, and kisses, Bertha and Mannie

And to all the relations

1940/3/20 (1) Undated Father to Bertha and Dezső (Book 3, 219)

[We arrived to America February 22. Bertha wrote on 2/26 to her father]

My dear Bertuska,

Thank you very much for your attention and prompt advice regarding my dear children. I read your precious lines and I was very glad to read that the whole family was at your home together with my children upon their arrival. I'm very happy and thank you all for the reception of my children. I wish you good health, good luck and happiness and respect to your dear husband and to all the relations and especially to you. I remain with kisses to you many times, your sincere Uncle, Gluck Jeremias.

My dear son Dezső,

I received your telegram sent on the 21st at 11 hours and 41 minutes from Columbus and it was posted on the 22nd at 12 hours and 55 minutes and it arrived in Helmec. It brought and caused a lot of happiness. With my respect to them and the whole family. As above

1940/3/20 (3) Uncle Marton to us [after arriving to USA] (Book 5, 120-121) page 1-2

[Uncle Marton, Emil's father (Schwartz-Israel) to all of us.]

My Dearest Children - May you live to 120 with G-d's blessings!

We have received your telegram, and the two letters (the one mailed by regular mail, and the one mailed by air). As soon as I received the telegram, I brought it to your father. I also received a card and a letter from the shipping company in Napoly in reply to the letter I wrote them. Your telegram from Columbus came in first. Imagine that after you left, Goldstein [Sandor Goldstein, owner of the place where Hermine stayed in Budapest] paid to himself individually, because of that the trip would cost more. Of course, I did not discuss it, but I paid. In a small way he was 'schmucig' [dirty], but I will not live at his place because of what he did. Please write to him a letter, but don't mention anything about this.

My Dearest Children,

I cannot write down the heartfelt feeling I felt as I remained by myself at the train station. I looked dazedly as the train was leaving. I was there for a longtime and my heart was crying...Will I ever see you again someday? These were my thoughts, and I couldn't walk with them in my mind. I was in such a daze that I didn't even know what people were saying to me. I am sitting alone in your empty house and I miss you as much now as I did the day you left. I am reminded that my dear sister, your mother, is no longer alive. As I write to you, my heart feels the same as it did when she died. It felt the same way when we said goodbye at the station. Last week, and today your father and I cried together feeling very lonely, but at least today we also cried happy tears because thank G-d you are safe and sound and in a good place. You are not alone because your family is there with you and they have been very good to you! I hope that G-d will give you the very best in everything.

Now I'm going to go to the temple for evening prayers...

I've now returned to my own home and I'm continuing this letter there. All day I've been reliving the moment at the station as you were leaving. Dear Dezső, more likely than not, it is difficult for you to think of me since I'm not writing to you. Please don't take it from me, but you know very well that I'm the lazy writer that I am. Furthermore, you wouldn't be any better than I if you were here. Ask your own brothers and sisters, especially how of all [people] my son, Leibuka [Uncle Marton's youngest son] , that you do not know, for the past two weeks has been sick. Although he feels better now, he is grumpy, but that goes along with it. I'm writing this letter sitting by him. I closed my business at seven o'clock in the evening. I live here now where Davidovics lived, the fellow that used to live here doing sewing. This apartment is larger than the previous one. Dear Dezső, you must have been so happy to see your brothers and sisters! I wish I would have been there to see it! Who knows if that will ever happen in this life? If G-d would make peace in this world then perhaps it can. Herminka wrote a letter from Budapest to be mailed to you and to Bertha, did you receive it? I have written also to Bertha and I asked her to be kind enough to wait for them at their arrival at the shipping port. Children, I thank G-d that you have arrived safely. I was waiting impatiently for your telegram. Please be good to each other and respect one another. Learn English so that you can be a gentleman everywhere. Keep a kosher home, observe Shabbos, and pray as you did at home, because that's all we have. G-d will help us if we just follow our philosophy. Maintain the greatest respect for your Uncle Jónász. Forgive and ignore any misunderstanding that might arise which happens once in a while because he has done a lot regarding you and your family. The whole district cannot imagine how 4 children were able to get out at once. Maintain the Sabbath as you did at home. Ignác and Herman pray every day. Get up earlier in the morning and think smartly, study diligently, because this is the first thing, the basis of survival. Please write me often and I promise to reply. I wish you from my heart the very best to all of you, to your Uncle Jónász, and to his family. Happy Purim to our Jewish friends.

1940/3/20 (3) Uncle Marton and Magda to us (Book 1, 113-114) page 3-4

The Eszter dance [for Purim] is just tomorrow. The Lord of the sky would give every heart a cure and we could put the past behind us with happiness. The past that Haman did with the world.
Who did you meet from the relations? Write about everything, because I'm very interested about everything. I kiss all of you countless times. I send my greetings to Uncle Jónász countless times and to his entire family. Arthur too.

Marton
Kiralyhelmecz, 20/III 1940
P.S.
I finished the letter yesterday, but I waited until today, Friday morning after the Purim holiday, and I just got a letter from you and also one for Zeidi [Grandfather] and Uncle Lajos in it. I sent it home to Lelesz, also. They already inquired from your father about what kind of passport the boys used to leave with, but I hope there will be nothing about it, because I will talk about it. Anyway, the important thing is, that they are there. Etus Schwartz from Lelesz is already gone also. Thank God, Libuka is well. I trimmed her [hair] today because it was overgrown. Leibuka was sick for 2 weeks, but he is better now. We are all doing well. We kiss you and wish you a good Purim.

[from Magda]

Dear Herminka and Mariska,
I'm very happy that you are well, and have luckily arrived. I wish I could be there where you are now. How do you spend your day now? How are you? Me, thank God, I'm doing well. The doctor said in Pest, that I should have an operation on my leg after Passover. We did not decide yet. Write about everything exactly. What kind of nice things did you see? I'm sorry that I'm writing so little, next time I will write you more. I wish a happy holiday to all of you. Write often and about everything. I kiss you many times,
Magda
Smulku and Libuka kiss all of you. Libuka is going to you in America.

1940/3/20 Undated Emil Schwartz to Hermine (Book 4, 321-322)

[dated by arrived to America and his father and sister write in the above letter]

"Ávrumeli"

Dear Hencsuka, I got your letter. You must be pleased that you went to America [since] you are feeling good there. In your next card, write about it. When we got your letter, we were very glad. Next time write back to us. I wish you a good Purim and Passover. I kiss all of you. Next time write to me for sure! Emil Schvartz

1940/3/22 Aunt Etelka and Hersu (Book 5, 269-270)

March 22, 1940
[from Aunt Etelka, Uncle Marton's wife]
Dear Hermine and Marie,
I cannot even write our happiness that thank God everything went well with each of you and you finally arrived safely to America. Now you can see it is our God who wishes this and I hope he will continue to help you all and that you will continue to be lucky in everything in the future. Please write about everything. What are you doing and how is your health? What did your uncle think about you? How is Dezső? Has he forgotten about us? I hope you girls will always write about everything. Lili is always talking about you. She also will go to America to Hencsu [Hermine]. I hope it will not be bad there for all of you. We hope the situation here will get better. Kisses to all of you, Etelka

[from Hersu, Uncle Marton's son]
Dear Hermine and Marie!
I was very happy to get your letters and happy to hear you are well. Hope you will continue to write in the future. God should continue helping you. How is Dezső? We received a letter from him also. When you have time please write about your trip to America on the ship. We hope one day we will be able to go and our God will help us. When you will have a job, write us about all of you individually. What kind of work do you do? For Dezső also, tell him to send some stamps. Kisses many times your nieces and nephews. How are Yitzhak [Ignác] and Hersmendu [Herman]? Please write more often, we want to know.

Hersu
Kiraly Helmec
1940 March 22
I'm wishing you all the best for Purim and Passover

Hersu

Magda also kisses all of you and will write next time

1940/4/2 (a) Father to Uncle Jónász (Book 4, 353)

Bodrogmező April 2, 1940

My dear loved, faithful brother Jónász and dear sister-in-law!
I got your respects in a letter that I received from my dear children. I'm glad that you are, thank God, feeling well, and that my dear sister-in-law is as well. We also, thank God, are fine. I hope that my lines will find you again in the best of health. I respect you and kiss you. With dear love, my faithful brother Jónász and dear sister-in-law, I wish you a Happy Passover, forever. Your faithful brother, who will never forget. Gluck Jeremias
My son Lajos is sending his highest regards.

1940/4/2 (b) Undated Father to Arthur (Book 4, 354)

My dear nephew Arthur,
My dear children wrote, that thank God you are well, and you have two beautiful children. May God give you everything good and I wish lots of luck and happiness to you. We are also, in very good health, thank God. I hope my lines will find all of you, in the best of health. Thank you very much for the heroism you did for my children. I respect and kiss your dear wife, your children and especially you. Your faithful Uncle, who will never forget. Gluck Jeremias

And, I send regards separately to Erzsike and her dear husband and family members. Your faithful uncle, Gluck Jeremias

1940/4/2 Father to us in USA with birthdates (Book 3, 208-209)

My dear son Dezső.
I was awaiting with difficulty for you a letter that I received today and thank God that you are all together and I'm glad to hear that you are in good health and I'm not missing that either. You're writing about the torah. I inquired in the post office regarding it. First of all, I have to get permission from the National Bank [and] an official statement, and to submit it with the permission. Additionally the insurance would cost 2 pengo/kg. After 2000 Pengo, it would cost 21 Pengos. I would have to send it to the National Bank in Ujhely. I could not go anywhere at this time because of the flood, however I will proceed as soon as possible.

You are asking the birth dates; [Their age they were at the time they were taken away.]
Jeremis Gluck 1875/November/5 [68 years plus 6 months]
Lajos 1904/September/13 [39 years plus 4.5 months]
Etel 1905/July/ 16 [38 years plus 8.5 months]
Emil 1931/ January/15 [13 years plus 3.5 months]
Lenke 1933/ July/ 19 [10 years plus 9.5 months]
Miklos 1935/ October/ 3 [8 years plus 6 months]
Gyula 1937/ October/ 8 [6 years plus 5 months]
Zoltan 1940/ March/ 10 [4 years old]

With respect and kisses with love, sincerely, your father, Gluck Jeremias Lajzer bacsi sends his regards to all of you.

Bodrogmező 1940 April 2
My dearest children whom I love from my heart sincerely,
I have been waiting with difficulty for your letters, however I was reading them with great happiness. As of today I received four letters from you. Today's letter came after 14 days. I'm happy to know thank God that you are all well and in good health. I also thank God that I am in good health. I hope again to hear from you the best and my letter will find you that way. I was delayed with the letter writings because of the flood until today. The water came up to where the potatoes in the backyard were and the straw was under water at the end of the property. The water came up in our village to Mihaly Török. Today it was [your brother] Lajos's child's circumcision. Uncle Lajos bacsi from Lelesz came and the mecco [the mohel] came in a boat, but in the afternoon they went home in our carriage. Shon Miksa was the godfather [kvater].

Dear Herminkam and Mariskam, Hersmendel, Ignác, my children.
Please write to me so that I know about you all. [In the] same way as you started to, write us every week, so that at least I can read your letters. Many individuals in town are jealous that my dear brother Jónász has supplied everything for you. Now I am sending you the fourth letter and hope that you will receive it also. It does not pay to send it through airmail because it does not come any faster. Yesterday the police came regarding to Mihancki's case. The lawyers found the papers and they have had a hearing of Mihancki and he declared that he had no demand or any claim against me because I have paid all the expenses of the court and that he has forgiven the remainder of the interests. They tried to twist me and said that I have transferred the property to the children so that I do not have to pay my debt. I said to them I did not. The fact is that I paid all the debt with my children's [property] and it's in the official report. I do not know yet if there'll be another hearing. I did not mail the statement to the National Bank of my income from the rent of your share. Lajzer bacsi has written a letter that he doesn't have a cent. I was angered because he told me after I have mailed the letter to you and now you know the reason. Grandfather and grandmother send their respects to all of you and I also respect you and kiss all of you many times. Your sincere father who will never forget you. Gluck Jeremias
Bela Stark's daughter did not take it with her and returned it to us and did not mail it.

1940/4/3 Etelka, Emil, Lenke, Lajos to us (Book 3, 195-198)

Bodrogmező, 1940 IV / 3
[from Emil]

My dear Aunts and Uncles,

We read all your letters and I am very happy to know that dear Arthur bacsi did not forget us. The news from home is that there is a great flood all around us, the Kazna is full and you can use a boat. I wish you all a pleasant Passover holiday and think of me also. I'm in a hurry to complete this letter since I have to go to school. I kiss your hands, Arthur bacsinak and Jónász bacsinak and Dezső, and to all of you. Your nephew, Emil.

[from Lenke]
Kisses to all of you and Arthur bacsi and his daughter. Let me know in your letter her name.
Gluck Lenke

[from Etelka]
Dear Herminka and dear Mariska,
Don't be angry at me that I'm writing to you with a pencil, however I'm very exhausted and I can't write in the evening, and now father is writing with the pen. As you know grandpa was with us and I am by myself. We had the [bris] for the child after 3 weeks and 2 days. I was helping the guests because the girls from Lelesz were not able to come here. Szeré neni cooked because I had enough beside the regular work. We made paprikas from three chickens and noodles. It was a nice festive evening. Marcsa excelled as godmother. We had a very nice celebration. Only Olga was missing, but the transportation could have been only by boat so the ladies remained at home. During Purim Regus was our guest. She sends her regards to you. Mrs. Pataki was here to visit with me and I gave her your regards. Marcsa Diak was walking this way and I told her that you have mentioned her in your letter. She replied that she has been sick for the past six months and who knows what will be, that it's almost certain that during the springtime she will be taken. I'm very busy and I hardly know what to do. Please write frequently because the only happiness father has is when he receives a letter from you. We are also very happy when you write. At this time I will not write more because the child does not allow me to write. I wish you all a pleasant, kosher Passover holiday. Also to dear Jónász bacsi and dear Arthur and his family. Give Arthur our regards and thanks for his good deed that he thinks of us. Kisses to you all with love, Etelka, Gyuszi, and Mityu also. Kisses to all.

[from Lajos]
My dear brothers and sisters,
I want to advise you that thank God I am well and I hope to hear from you the same. Father and Etelka have written to you about everything and about the flood. There is plenty of work, perhaps in May we will be able to work. The horses are here at home and we are waiting for the flood to recede. Szmojak, the mailman, sends his regards to you. I'm in a hurry because the post man will walk away. Kisses to all of you, many times, your brother, Lajos.

Our father made a note that he's sending the stamps back with the date on it to show that the letter was returned from Columbus.

1940/4/6 Undated Mariska Deak [neighbor/friend] to Hermine and Marie (Book 4, 144-147)

[Dated by Etelka mentioning in 1940/4/5 letter above that she saw Mariska. Mariska also complains that they didn't say bye when they left. It could be a little earlier, maybe in March/April, but not later than June because Etelka writes that then that she already wrote that Mariska's sister Ica *died*.]

My dear friends Hermine and Maria,
I received your letters and I'm going to answer your letters at once. I don't want you to think that I'm angry. First, I would like to wish you the best of health and all the best. I asked our almighty [for this]. I am sorry I cannot brag about [myself] or say I'm well. My health is not so good. Only God knows what will be. I have a problem. I am having this illness for a long time and my nerves are affected by it. I do not like to talk about myself. It is true that I would like to live. I do not want to die so soon, even though we are living in such a terrible world. I'm sorry. It seems some in my family in the past would rather part from this world. They thought it will be better in the other world. Since they left us so early in life they all chose the other world. Now we are just the 2 of us here with my mother. [Ica her sister just died]. For how long I don't know. I have become very bitter. A sick person cannot be happy. You are asking to write about myself. About myself I cannot say anything good from one day to the next. Only our almighty maybe [can help], but that is not much hope. Why don't I write that I'm thinking a lot about you? Such a sincere girl as I cannot believe everything. At this time you must think I'm lying - Oh no. I will prove it to you that I'm not angry

because the day after you left I went to visit you, and here you can see. I knew very well that I went to you for no reason, but only because you were "Jews" and because I wanted to rid myself from my Jewish girlfriends. True, not from all of them, because I'm even better friends with the Klein girls from Agard than I was. They don't even know that I'm not always honest. There was a time when you were also arguing about which woman is my better friend and to whom I was a better friend. Here I was right because you proved that both of you were the same. You wrote that I shouldn't be angry that you didn't say goodbye before you left, but I don't even think I was angry [from that]. When I was really sick between life and death you didn't come to see me or miss me then, but I expected you to come since I had no problem with you, thanks for this little attention. I think I'm a little bitter, but I can't be any other way except honest. I wish that you have an honest girlfriend like me in the far away strange country that you can talk to her and trust her like me, and are able to share with her the good and bad. My dear mother is very busy. She has too much trouble. At least she is well and we are together. We talk about many things. I'm closing at this time. I am wishing you all the best. Whatever I'm wishing for you, [I wish] for the boys, too. Your father is well. I see him every day. Your brother Lajos is okay. I think I've written enough for two to six weeks. Once again, we, my mother and Anus wish you very well and send kisses. At this time I'm closing my letter with all the best, many kisses to both of you. Your not really honest girlfriend, Deak Mariska. Bodrogmező

1940/4/14 Father and Etelka to us (Book 4, 351-352)

Bodrogmező 1940 IIII / 14
[from father]
My dear beloved children,
I got your letter, that I could hardly wait for and I was very happy. Thank God, you are in good health. I hope that my lines will find you in the best of health again. You asked what is going on with the tobacco. I think I already wrote about it. They sent 141 pengo in the tax. Fostos' share did not come yet, because there was missing a couple of kg from the tobacco. And the others didn't get it either because it was missing. The flood is ebbing. It's going back nicely. In Szürnyeg [the land] washed out and 17 houses collapsed. Last week from Lelesz, Mici Kovendi brought a letter. The old Mrs. Kalman Bodnar sent it with her. The post lady sent it in an open envelope. She gave it to the Biro girls, so they can give it over and here in an attachment I'm sending the letter for you, my son Dezső. Because of the bad weather and from the flood, we still could not walk and I did not send the request to the National Bank [about the torah]. My dear Herminka, take care of yourself. Do not put too much stress on yourself. Mariska also. Ignác my son, you did not write about what kind of job you do. And Herman my son, based on what you wrote, are you working since then? In the last month, Uncle Marton sent a letter to all of you. Also, Uncle Lajos' family, and grandfather's family. You must have received them. I have been at grandfather's a week ago. They are well. It was Yahrzeit and we went on a wagon. The road was still under water. It was almost up to our knees. Uncle Lajos got a letter today too from Bertha. He got one last week as well. She writes that you are corresponding with her, and she is satisfied with you very much. You are very nice children. You don't even look like someone who was raised in a small town. Now I don't know what to write. We are, thank God, in good health, and it's what I wish to hear back from you. I gave your regards to Lefkovics. My son Dezső will look for the brother in law's address. Write to me about everything, about what you do. Also, maybe we'll be able to plow, if the weather is going to be nice. Then Passover will come. Poppy seeds and carrot and walnut, is the third to sow, but the water is still deep. I did not sell the pasture yet. I already wrote about it, that we can't sell it to strangers. I send my regards to all of you with love, and kiss you one by one, all of you. Your faithful dad, who will never forget. Gluck Jeremias

[from Etelka]
Dear Herminka and dear Mariska,
I'm only writing briefly to you now also, because the work before Passover keeps me very busy and exhausts me. Not even the weather is like it used to be, but it's kind of Hungarian. May God save us from a spring like this. It is so uncommonly cold. The children are coughing and they wish to go out, but the weather is harsh. Dear Herminka, you wrote that I should take care of [your] father. He takes care of himself too, because he has nothing to do. If he is in a good mood, he plays with the kids. He's only in a bad mood if he hasn't gotten a letter from you in a long time. For example, it's been two weeks that a letter didn't come from you. [Your] father was very upset and finally a letter came.

1940/4/14 Undated Etelka, Emil, and Lenke to Us (Book 4, 363-364) page 3-4

[dated because before Passover, mentions geese, eggs, beet soup. The paper is thicker than the other undated pages so the children can write on it]

[Etelka continues]
Mityuka and Gyuszika kiss all of you and they are waiting for a little radio.

[from Lenke]
Dear Herminka and Mariska, we are happy in advance for the package because we did not get any clothes for Passover. I kiss Dezső, Uncle Jónász and Ignác, Herman, Marcsa and Herminka
Gluck Lenke

[from Emil]
Dear Aunts and Uncles,
I will try to write to you so you can have something to read. I was very happy for your letter. I brought it home from the post office. I can write to you boys that if they whistle to the Leventes, then we always mention you. Sanyi was so happy for your letter, but he will not write now, because he is not at home. Dear Ignác, even the teacher [male] mentioned you this week. The Hegedus's son spoke up [made a sound] at the singing lesson that we did not sing Ignác's "what do you see" [mitláte] and then the teacher said 'that he should go to America and ask Ignác what he can see.' Yani Balint sends his greetings also and Kocsis too. Gerenyi and their family send their greetings and Anna Pataki too. It is almost Passover. My mom will stuff a goose also. We have eggs, thank God. We will give some to our Grandfather too for Passover and beet soup [ciberèt]. We just don't have milk, because the calf drinks it. We must eat the cow for Passover.
I kiss you dear Uncle Jónász and Uncle Arthur. Kisses for Dezső, Hencsu, Marcsa, Hersmendel and Ignác. Your little nephew, Emil.
I will write one more [piece of] news, that they give sugar and blocks of fat.

1940/4/20 Bertha to us (Book 5, 221-222)

New York
April 20 / 40
My Dearest's!
Only a few lines to you about our lives. I'm mailing a letter from your dearest father which was mailed to me. I was very happy to hear that Dezső made his father very happy [with] the short telegram that he received from him [telling] what was going on.

About me, I felt a little better. It's about time! All winter I wasn't feeling well. I wrote to you about it. I'm under a doctor's care and taking x-rays trying to find out what's wrong. The doctor told me that I have to watch what I'm eating. Also I must slow down and not worry so much. What do you think about that? I hope that this problem will not last forever. Even though this is already a problem, it is enough. Ever since I started to watch what I am eating it should help. I waited long enough. I told you about this because I don't want you to think that I forgot you! But, I'm happy that I'm alive! I hope that my letter will find you in the best of health, all of you, and the boys too. What is the news there? Are you continuing to go to school? It is very important and it will [help to] be able to work in a better job. My dearests, I understand that it is very difficult to change. It will take at least two years and you will think differently. Dear Hermine and Mariska, here if you have a wealthy person you have to twist his head so that you don't have to be so long in that type of work. If Dezső would have a good opportunity I believe that this would be practical, don't you think so? Don't be angry that I'm involved with this type of thinking, but I think this would not be the worst, if this would come forth sooner.

Wishing you lots of luck in every step and a happy Passover. I wish that we could spend the Seder together. Naci [maybe Lucille] and Zseni are here by us, we will think of you.

How is dear Herman? I forgot to ask in all my previous letters. I wish all of you the very best.
Kisses to all of you individually, Bertha
Mannie is sending also his regards and my father-in-law and the relatives, too. Also give my best to the relatives there.
Signed by the above.

Bodrogmező, 1940 IIII / 25
My dear children whom I love from my heart. Live to 120.
I cannot tell you how hard I was waiting for your letters, every minute I was hoping to hear from you, finally I was very happy to hear, thank goodness, you are all okay. Thank goodness we are okay too. Those important letters we will mail out tomorrow to the Consulate to Budapest. I just received the money for the tobacco from the Leleszi office. 142 pengo. Half of it and 48 pengo was due from Fustos. They also counted for the taxes they claim I owe them. I read your letters to your Grandfather. They were crying. They are sending their love to you all. The Leleszi lawyer's office asked where are the boys? I told him you are in America. He also asks where are they working? I told him at my nephew's factory. He wanted to have the address where you are working. He asked, 'How did they leave?' He said probably false passports! I replied to him 'How can you imagine such a thing today, it's unthinkable. You could inquire from the consulate and I even have the papers with me that they were released from the army and that they could leave.' As of now, they did not receive any information in their office and he did not believe it and did not accept it and wasn't happy with my answer. My dear son Dezső, you stated that I should sell everything now. Today it is very difficult - we must have patience. I will try to get to America if maybe they need someone as a worker. Here they offer 47 acres for sale from the left side as we are going from our village to the next. They are selling off these properties and thereby reducing the price of the land since they are interested in selling 200 acres. [They were breaking up the feudal system, this property was owned by the priests]. With regards to my immigration to America at this time it isn't important, it's not an emergency. First of all, only when your situation gets better, then you can think of me since we still have to know what would be with Lajos' children's share of the 630 Pengos being held at the orphanage office. They are still asking for proof why the money is needed. They want to know about the debt. I mailed them the bank statement and it still wasn't enough. If the orphanage office approves it, I wondered whether it could be transferred to the American orphan office or they might keep it in the 2 children's names. I'm not sure, but probably they would give out the cost of the transportation. I will try to find out what could be done. As of now I did not pay Uncle Marton what you gave me because I didn't sell land from the farm and I don't know when it will be possible to succeed. I did not have a chance to go to the National Bank and talk to them. I wrote to you in a previous letter that I told them you are not here, you live in a different country, and maybe they can help. I do not know what to write to you at this time, but I heard that Uncle Izidor bacsi was very sick and was in the hospital in Kassa. I did not hear from him for quite some time. I have not been anywhere except to buy some wine in Helmec. I went to see the Veizer girls and I gave your note to them. They were very happy to hear from you and they said they will write to you. I did not give your address to them yet. This Saturday I received the letter you wrote before Purim. My dear children take care of each other so that everything should be alright and don't worry about me, God is good and will help all of us. I wrote to you in the last letter regarding to Mihancki. This week I received [notice] that I was released and they closed the case. With respect to all of you, individually and many kisses from your loving father who will never forget you, not even for a moment. Whenever I see your clothing, I always think that you are still here, but I can't speak to you. With all my love, again, forever, your father, Gluck Jeremias

1940/4/25 Undated Lajos to us (Book 3, 206-207)

[Dated by flood, reseeding, frost damaged wheat, not yet in army]

My dearest brothers and sisters,
I was very happy to read your letters. Please don't worry about us. Thank God we are well and hope to hear from you the same. You're asking what happened to me. As of now I did not have to report to the Army, but I don't know when I'll have to go. Hersmendu, are you still working at the flower gardener? How much are they paying you? Here the seeding is very difficult and it cannot be done yet. The wheat is not worth much because of the frost. The Dioszog was partially underwater and that has to be plowed. As of now we still have the horses. I'm afraid to sell them because then I won't have anything to work with. On Passover, we were in Lelesz at the temple. When we arrived home Etel was wearing Hencsu's dress. Gyusi came to me and said that Hencsu is here. When I ask him where she is, he always tells me she is in Szürte. I tell him not there, but in America. Joska Csorosz will open a bar. That is good for him because he won't have to go too far. There is no other news. Ignác you must take care of yourself when you work. Many kisses to all of you from my heart, your sincere brother, Lajos.

[This is my information as I recall it. This was not in the above letter. I want to say that there was a Hungarian gardener. His name was Katona. He paid Herman one dollar a day. He would work from early morning to late at night and he stayed there during the week and he came home on weekends. - Irv 2009/9/30]

1940/4/25 Undated Etelka Gluck and Children - Passover (Book 5, 185-186)

[dated by Passover and the synagogue wall collapse]

[from Emil]
Dear Aunts and Uncles,
We are very happy that we have received the official papers. So we hope now that I too could be in America. I will write to you only a few lines at this time because I have to hurry to school. Grandpa bought me a new suit for 14 Pengo for Passover and a pair shoes for nine 9 Pengo and 50 fillert. We are going to Lelesz to the temple. However one of the temple walls collapsed, so now we go to Kalman bácsi's home and that's where we pray. Our kisses to all of you and to dear Jónász Bácsi as well as dear Arthur. Kisses to all of you, your nephew Emil.

[from Lenke]
All of us send their kisses Lenke, Mityu and Gyuszi.
For Passover we used Mariska's clothing and had it made for us.

[from Etelka]
Dear Herminka and dear Mariska,
We have received your letter on the first evening of Passover with the documents and we hope it will turn out to be for the best for ourselves and for our future. I understand from your letters that you are very busy and every minute counts. The main thing is to be healthy and then the work is not difficult. Believe me, I'm also quite busy with the children. The children disturb me all the time, when one stops the other one begins. The little one is very beautiful. I did not go anywhere since you left, as a matter of fact I became lazy with walking, however I took little Zoli to his god mother, Szereny neninel. We were there for a few minutes and she said that she would like to write to you a few lines but does not want to put it in the same letter as ours and make the letter heavier, so I replied to her that the postman would be able to carry it. Therefore she said she's going to write, the question is when? Otherwise you know them. We have been talking about you and wanted to know how you have set up your Passover? Do you have any Passover dishes? We had a very good red cabbage soup. Most of the people in the temple got the red cabbage soup from us. I fattened a goose and also we have eggs of our own. Thanks to the Almighty we also have 16 chickens. I put the duck eggs under the hen and I would like to have some. I also planted about 20 pengos worth of corn. Our backyard is all seeded. We had snow till the end of March. Only during April did it begin to be warmer and feel like spring. It wouldn't have been good for you to be here at home at this time because it would not have been warm enough and the weather wasn't too good or to desirable. Other news that may be interesting to you, there isn't any, even this letter will be somewhat boring for you. But my dear Hermine, you're asking how we are, that's why I'm writing you a lot. I hope that Lajos does not have to report in yet to the Army. I hope that after this he shouldn't have to go. Presently he's plowing in the field, namely on the Tablan. Even though we had a long winter, thank the dear God, our dear father, Lajos the children, and myself remained in good health and hope that you too are in good health. We would like you to send us some pictures of you. Pataki received your card and was very happy and is sending her regards to you. My letter is somewhat disorganized, because Zoltan is helping with the letter writing. I wasn't to Lelesz, but father and Emil took eggs, milk and 'ciberet' [beet soup] to grandfather and grandmother. Father also took ciberet to Patyu [Marton bacsi]. In return he gave us a bottle of wine as a gift. With kisses to you and dear Jónász bacsi and dear Arthur with love, Etelka.

1940/4/25 Undated Sarolta Klein [Uncle Izidore's daughter] to Hermine and Marie (Book 3, 389)

[Aunt Marie thought this letter is from Sarolta Majer, Bertha's sister, but the handwriting doesn't match. The writer says her father was sick in Kassa, that would be Uncle Izidore, as our grandfather mentions above. The writer says her father is with Lenke, that is, Izidore's daughter, again as our father mentions above.]

Dear Herminka and Mariska!
We were happy to receive your lines. It felt good that you thought of us. Although I do not know why you didn't come to say goodbye when you left. This week Lajzer bacsi was here and he said that you were angry

at us, but why? You have to listen to both sides and then judge. Let's forget about this conversation, it was a long time ago and may not have been true. What are you doing? What does our dear Jónász bacsi do? Is he in good health? And his dear wife? Our dear father was very sick for almost 4 months. He is in Kassa. He was also in the hospital, but the doctors didn't want him to stay longer, so he is at Lenke's, and they are treating him there. It costs quite a bit, God should help that he should improve. Manyu Broun was congratulated this week. Gizi Schwartz was there and asked about you wanting to know how you are. What type of work you are doing? What does Dezső do? How is Bertha and Zseni [Aunt Jennie] ? Do you ever meet them? From ourselves there's nothing special that I could write about. Kisses to all of you. Write because you know that we are interested. Sarolta

Agi also sends regards to Mariska because she only knows her.

1940/5/5 Father to us (Book 4, 327-328)

[Date is incorrect. He must have meant May because he references where Passover services were held]

Bodrogmező 1940 4/5
My dear, loved, faithful children.
I read your longed for letter happily. Thank God you are in good health, we don't miss that as well, thank God, and I hope that when my lines arrive, they will find all of you in a best of health. You asked me, if I sold the barn. Not yet. I did not have a buyer for it yet. I already wrote in my previous letter about the pasture and that with the lands we only need patience. We must wait until we get the money from orphan court. I needed [it for] the debt payment and now I'm waiting for the response, because they already asked for those documents and I sent them in. My dear Herminka, you asked if we still have the horses. I wanted to sell them like we planned, but Uncle Marton talked me out of it. We need them for work. The water has damaged the sowing and the wheat froze out like over a sea of cloverleaf field [an expression meaning 'over a very large area'] and it died out. We seeded a sea of it. We seeded poppy seeds to the grove of walnut trees, like a sea of cloverleaf and we will seed potato and oats and we are planning on seeding millet and sunflower also. I don't remember if I wrote it to you already, but [news] came from the prosecutor's office that we are being released from the [Mihancki] case. My dear children, I'm only asking you to take care of yourselves and whenever you can, listen to my brother Jónász, because he is an experienced man. Do not make him angry, just talk to him nicely and if he tells you something, listen to him. My dear children, as I can see, if Hermine would not write, your letters would be very short. Do not be lazy to write, because I'm also curious about everything, what kind of job you have…Uncle Lazar gets a letter every week from Berta. He also [sends his] respect to all of you. Uncle Izidor is still sick. He is in Kassa at his daughter's. Grandfather and grandmother send their regards to all of you. Write to them also. Uncle Lajos and Uncle Marton are waiting for your response to their letters. You must have gotten them already. I attached a law description and what it contains. It was sent from the consul in English. He wrote [telling] me to send this document to America. He sent a document that needs to be filled out and sent in in order to get the quota number. The pre-registration number is not a quota number. I did not give anything to Uncle Marton yet. The tree sold by the village from the Varaja forest was bought by Lajos Pandi for 2 p[engo] per meter. He will mill it. The village got the money now and an advance, so, maybe they can buy our barn. I did not write in my previous letter that the back corner in the synagogue in Lelesz collapsed with the elder, and the roof has been supported/braced by posts [atugakkal = with posts/piles]. The prayers on the first day of Passover were in the small room [in Yiddish 'kol stibli' = קהל שטיבל]in the synagogue, [but] it was condemned on that day. The notary and the doctor closed it, because it's not allowed to pray there, and since then they pray in Kalman's house. My dear children, do not forget about praying and keeping the holidays, whatever you can. Try to organize in a way, so I can get one letter every week from you. Mrs. Pataki sends her greetings, [as does] Mrs. Gerenyi, and Mrs. Csorosz with the Bron boy. He gave me the address for the lawyer and he said he got a card from you, that you are well and studying. He was in a hurry, only said a few words. I respect and kiss, separately, each of you, who are in my mind night and day. I wonder what you are doing. Hersmendel wrote that he is very tired and can't write. What's with him? Gosh, he isn't sick, is he? Write everything. Your father, who will never forget. Gluck Jeremias

1940/5/5 Emil, Lenke, and Etelka to us (Book 3, 210-211)

Bodrogmező, 1940 V / 5
[from Emil]
My dear Aunts and Uncles,

We received your letters which I have been waiting with difficulty in which you write dear Aunt Hencsu, that you have only received 2 letters from us. As of now we have mailed you 9 letters. As of now we have written to you all the news. At this time we really have no news here. We thank you in advance for the package that you sent us and we are waiting for it with difficulty. Please write to us the name of Arthur bacsi's daughter and son. Please send us pictures so that at least we would know them and recognize them by their pictures. Dear Ignác and Hersmendu,

Saturday's Levente outing [exercises] began and you were missed from the group. Mityu and Gyuszi were looking for you and asking where are Ignác and Herman. Are they in the front or in the rear? Dear Ignác, Grandpa gave your [wooden] gun to Sanyi [Klein]. Give my regards to dear Jónász bacsi and dear Arthur bacsi. Kisses to Dezső, Hersmendu, Ignác, Marcsa, and Hencsu, until we meet again in America. Your nephew Emil Gluck

[from Lenke]
Dear Aunt Hencsu and Marcsa,
I will only write to you a little bit because I don't know too much yet. My kisses to Uncle Dezső, Jónász bacsi and his family, and Arthur bacsi and his family, and Ignác and Hersmendu and Aunt Hencsu and Aunt Marcsa.
Lenke, Mityu, and Gyuszi

[from Etelka]
Dear Herminka and Dear Mariska,
Forgive me. I will write to you a few lines because I'm very tired and sleepy. If you have received my previous letter, this will add to it and next time, I will write more. As of now, there is no news. Kisses to you and Mariska and the dear relations. Etelka

1940/5/15 Undated Jane to Father with letter for Dezso (Book 4, 320)

[dated by springtime, Ignác writes in Oct 1939 that she asked about Dezső and will write, that her father died, and our grandfather doesn't mention her in any letter up to this point in 1940]

[addressing our father]
Dear Mr. Gluck!
Soon it will be one and a half years that I haven't written to Dezső, and I did not get anything from him either. I am free today on a nice spring afternoon, and I'm thinking of my dear acquaintances-and so I write. Dear Mr. Gluck! I got the letter that was sent to me. Although, I could not give a likable answer. I tried everything, but I could not do it. And now, I'm also not the way I was in other times. I hope you will understand this and will not be mad at me. Please be kind enough to get these few lines to Dezső. Thank you very much and I'm sending greetings to all of you. Jane

Dear Dezső!
I believe it will be a surprise that I'm writing to you. I have definitely been quiet for one and a half years. Since then my boat is sailing all over the place on the sea of life. Presently, I ended up in Miskolc. I thought about writing many times, but I was tired. Many things happened. My dad died, my mother stayed in my care and Laci also. I am alone here. It is very hard like this. Me, who was so used to Laci. Now I would need a passport. I am very interested in your destiny. I know that you became a very great and honest man, since you were the same here.

Write a lot about everything.
My address: Miskolc Main Post Office
I'm sending my best and waiting for your letter.
Jane

I did not get married and I don't want to. I don't miss it.

1940/5/16 Bertha to Hermine (Book 18, 289-293)

New York
May 16 /40
Dear Hermina!

I'm late again answering your letter, but don't take it badly because the situation at home takes away all my passion. Also, my father-in-law wasn't feeling well. I myself wasn't feeling well either and I don't have time to rest. I'm whispering this to you. I have become lazy and I don't even care, whatever will be, will be. Hermine, you know what I would like you to do? Make sure that you apply for the citizenship papers. It is very important. You must have them, apply as soon as possible. Do not neglect it! Now I'm going to gossip about my Mannie's younger sister. If she succeeds, she is supposed to leave from Kassa the 1st of next month. On Sunday we are going to meet Jennie Frye so we can spend time. I prepared dinner and Saturday we were there for dinner. I wish you would be closer to us. At least once a week we could see each other, [but] it's not a problem. At least you are here, over that horrible life. Even if it is not easy here, at least you are safer. We don't have to live in fear and shiver about what is coming next with the country. The only thing, you must take care of yourself, your health. You [should] eat right and sleep enough. Also, you must go out for pleasure. This is very important to you all. I hope your work is tolerable. I believe it is not easy for you all to write so many letters, but you should try shorter letters to everyone, except for me because I love you all. We hope to hear the best. I'm not selfish. Now I really don't have much to write that would be interesting to you. Give our kisses to your family and the relations. Kisses to you all separately and love, Bertha

1940/5/23 Father to Us (Book 5, 122-123)

Bodrogmező, 1940 V / 23
My Dear Children, Dezső, Herminka, Mariska, Herman and Ignác, to 120!
I received your letters in yesterday's mail. I've been waiting for them with difficulty. It took 36 days and I've been going to meet the postman daily, just as when you were at home you were doing the same. My dear children you can imagine how difficult it is waiting. Szmojak, the mail carrier, is sending his regards to you. I went to Lelesz to your Grandfather. [Uncle] Marton bacsi was there and I had the letter with me and we were reading it. They were very happy to know that you are, thank God, healthy. We too are, thank God in good health. I hope that this letter will find you in the best of health also. After we read the letter we cried ourselves out. [Uncle] Marton bacsi was reading the letter that you sent to him, crying. It took 74 days for this letter to arrive due to the weather conditions. It rained almost every day [so] I did not go to Helmec or Lelesz. The roads were muddy. The letters were mailed to Lelesz and I was reading it now. It came to [Uncle] Lajos bacsi. Grandma and Grandpa are sending their respect to all of you. I received the gift from you, thank you. Please do not take it away from yourselves. It has been said that "share it and keep some for yourselves, also." I thank you my dear children, take care of yourselves, each and every one of you. We still have the horses. Many people do not have straw and the weather was very bad. We did not get the permit from the National Bank regarding the Torah. Dezső, be patient as soon as I get information or the permit I will let you know. During the winter, Miksa Shon sold his horses and purchased oxen. He made some money on it. They are very suspicious regarding business. They're watching every move now. They [the Jews] have to merge with non-Jews in order to stay in business. With today's mail, I received a note from the bank in Helmec that I should pay the monies due them since they gave an extension, until I receive the money from orphan's office to pay them. However, as of now I have not received it, so tomorrow I have to go in. If I don't receive it by next week, I have to do something because I don't want to pay interest. My brother Lajzer bacsi, sends his regards to all of you, so does the old Gerenyi and his family [the neighbors] and all the other good people who come. I did not ask Uncle Marton if he replied to your letters. The flowers, all three Olijander, were in the kitchen and due to the cold weather they froze, but across the street at Gerenyi's, it was in the house and that one is okay, but at Shon's it froze also. On May 5, I mailed a letter, I hope that you received it. I will write separately to my brother Jónász next week. My regards to them and to Arthur and his family, too. My love to you, individually, and kisses from your father. Day and night I always have you in my mind. You are in my thoughts in every step of mine. Once again my kisses to you all, forever, your father.
Gluck Jeremias

If I do not receive it [the money from the orphanage], then tomorrow I have to go in, or if I don't receive it by next week, I will have to do something because I don't want to pay interest. Write to me more often, so I'll know about your well-being.
As above.

1940/5/23 Lajos and Emil to Us (Book 5, 132-133) pages 1-2

1940 V/23 Until 120
[from Lajos]
My dearest brothers and sisters,

I am informing you that thank God we are well and I hope to hear from you likewise. This week an automobile transportation [service] began here from us [Bodrogmező] to Lelesz and Helmec. It comes in the morning and afternoon. In my last letter I have written that. Now I want to tell you that the weather is terrible and it rains almost every day. I had to plow under the area in the "Dioszog" , the area where the water was, also at the "Leszna." We planted wheat there, but it had to be plowed under. I replanted some corn and sunflower seeds [there] and at the "Tablara" with poppy seeds. This Saturday, everyone from the age of 2 years to 60 had to be vaccinated and we were very sick from it. About the conditions here, I'm sure you know more about it. I will not write about it. Did you plant the "Becsi Tök" [squash/pumpkin] seed? We planted plenty. I'm asking all of you to take care of yourselves and each other and do not take any dangerous jobs.

Give my regards to uncle Julius and his son. Geza Pandy and his friends were inducted. In the morning, I will go to the granary [and] will take wheat and rye to mill it into flour. When it's milled the price is 24 Pengos and it is costly [along] with everything [else]. Kisses to all of you, your brother, Lajos

[from Emil]
Dear Aunts and Uncles,

We are still waiting for your letters, it becomes very difficult. Your letters come less frequently. The registered letter came after five weeks. This letter came after a longtime. I believe that by now the package should have arrived too and it would come in handy. We hope it comes in by the holiday Punkos [Shavuot]. What would you say to that? Our teacher is at the Shon's. We are learning and it is going quite well. I hope that it will be better in the future and I will progress.

The big news is that Kocsis is going to marry Ilonkat Leco. [Unsigned, maybe missing a page]

1940/5/23 Undated (a) Etelka to Hermine (Book 4, 313) page 3 - finish Emil's letter

[dated by vaccination]

[written by Etelka]
Dear Aunt Hencsú!

I will finish Emil's letter because he was sleepy at night, and in the morning he was in a hurry to go to school. Lenku. also does not write now, because last night I washed her head. She lay down and in the morning, I didn't have time to stand beside her while she is writing. I can only write about her, that she is writing and reading beautifully and she has two nice braided ponytails. They stared at Gyuszi's head at the vaccination. If I could only get nice clothing for them, but Gyuszi is still in his shoes today.

Emil, Lenku, Gyuszi, Mityu kiss all of you and dear Uncle Jónász. Send me pictures. Kiss you,
Etelka

1940/5/23 Undated (b) Etelka to Hermine and Marie (Book 4, 318-319)

[dated by Kocsis getting married]

Dear Herminka and dear Mariska,
Since your letters about your work, you can see about mine also. Particularly now, I'm writing this letter on Thursday night and it is late. It is almost going to be morning and we have to milk and to bake. What can I write to you? I can only write about home, because I can never go anywhere. This week I was at home for an hour. Since you are gone, I'm mostly busy with the children and the little chickens. I have 47 chickens under 3 broody [a hen inclined to incubate eggs] and 11 little ducks. The planting, if God helps me, I will start for the harvest. We still have 19 hens. They lay very nicely, but the eggs are very cheap. It's 8 filler for now and 10 filler per a pair. The ducks will also lay. Now I will write about the children. Thank God, they are all nicer everyday. That Gyuszi, kanehare [against the evil eye] has no match, not to his beauty nor to his smartness. Now he is home with me, because the others go to the "heider" [school], but he is so eatable. The rest of them are also diligent in the "heider". They can hardly wait for the packages for school, because their clothing is very inadequate, for sure. Little Zoltan is like Gyuszi, only he has blue eyes. He is cute. He is already laughing. Zajdika [Grandfather - Jeremias]] chose his name. That is why his name is Zoltan. It's no problem, he should just have good luck. Emil will write the news and next time when we will write, we

Page 124

will not be in a hurry to send it, then we will write a better letter to you. I kiss the relatives and all of you with love, Etelka

Aunt Iren always wants to write.
What do you say about Kocsis? He is marrying Ilont Leca. [Mit szoltok "Kocsis-hoz ? Leca Ilont veszi"]

[On the side:] In the morning I will bake cheese Danish. Don't you want to eat some?

1940/5/27 Jeanie Frye? to Hermine (Book 5, 209-210)

May 27 - 40
Dear Hermine,
First forgive me that I'm answering your letter a little late, but believe me I wasn't able to. I wasn't feeling well and every night I was working 11-12 AM and that was enough to get sick. Life is not easy in America. Thank God for that too. If we don't have a job, that is not good. And if we have good job, that is no good either. Therefore, there is always something that we can complain about. In a sense, I'm worn out. I can hardly wait for my vacation. I'm happy to hear that you are all okay and that you all are working. Every beginning is difficult. You must have patience, then you'll manage more easily. And you are well, and that makes it better. I didn't get any mail from home. I can imagine what they are going through, therefore we must appreciate what we have. Thank God for being here in America. How is Uncle Jonas and the Aunt. Maybe I will visit our Uncle this summer? I hope you will write, with love and kisses to all of you, Jeanie

Give my best wishes to Uncle Jónász and Aunt Helen in person

1940/5/29 Father to Uncle Jónász (Book 4, 347-348)

Bodrogmező 1940 V/29
My dear, beloved brother Jónász and dear sister-in-law, Helen.
My dear brother, I don't know what is the reason that you haven't written a couple of lines since February to let me see how you are doing. We are, thank God, in good health. I hope my lines will again find you in the best of health. Please, I'm asking you my dear brother, to write about my dear children, and let me know if you are satisfied with them. I hope, the dear God will help us all, so everything will turn out to be good. Although my children let me know in every one of their letters that their dear Uncle Jónász sends his regards, it still feels better when I read your writing. I can see it and read it. At least, I can cry myself out next to it. I hope you will do it, won't you, my dear, faithful brother, Jónász. Separately I'm asking you to please do me a favor. Give my regards to my dear nephew and his dear family and to your dear daughter and to her family. Please, I'm asking you, my brother Jónász, to give my regards to my children. I send my regards to you separately and I kiss you, and my dear sister-in-law with love.
Your faithful brother, Gluck Jeremias

1940/5/29 Father to us (Book 4, 345-346)

Bodrogmező 1940 V/29
My dear, loved, faithful children.
I got your May 8th letter. It came on the 16th and I sent a response to your registered letter on the 23rd. I am letting you know that, thanks to the good God, I'm in good health and I hope that my lines will find you in the best of health. My dear children, just take good care of yourselves and each other, so everything will be good. The Simon's horse and wagon, one bridle tool and the belongings are gone. Sari [it's a common horse's name] is tall and strong, she is being released. There is sowing to do still, where the water was, but it's still wet. I don't know what to write. You can write more than we can. We had to go to Gàlòcs to take and give Waszszi Kasznai's horse. They attached 13 horses from the commune. We don't know anything about what will happen yet. There is water in the channels and the pasture. At this time the weather is nice. 2 letters came from Bertha at the same time. I don't know what she wrote. I did not talk to Uncle Lajzar. He is sending his regards to all of you. Grandfather and grandmother are sending their regards and they wish good health and lots of luck to all of you. You should write a couple of lines to them, also. Now he/she isn't traveling K. sz. helmec, he is a soldier. Now that's [In Yiddish] it! [In Hungarian] I don't know what else to write. [In Yiddish] There is much to do. [In Hungarian] I'm sending Uncle Hermus' [Schwartz] daughter Iren's address now. She doesn't work. She did not get a job yet. She wrote that she is at her father's uncle.

My dear children, regards to you and kisses to all of you, one by one. Your loving, faithful father, who will never forget. Gluck Jeremias

Uncle Izidor, thank god, already feels better. He is still is Kassa at his daughter's. Otherwise Gyula Szabo still didn't approve the contract with Simon. There still did not come any answer.
I remain your faithful father, who always has all of you in his mind. Jeremias

[Side note:] The approval just arrived. They still have a right to appeal for 75 days at the ministry.

1940/5/29 Undated (a) Lajos to us (Book 3, 217-218)

[Dated by seeding and land still muddy from flooding. Went to Galocs and father mentioned this in the letter above]

Dear loving brothers and sisters,
We received your letter [and] I was glad to know that Herman has such a position. I believe it is a very difficult one. Herminka if you can, I would like you to get an easier job because in my opinion, this is too much for you. As I've written to you before that I'm working in the field, whether there will be anything from it, only God knows. I have turned the ground with the hoe in the cornfield for planting. I still have another field for corn and sunflower that has to be turned over by hand. It is located in the Leszna area. The Dioszog was partially underwater, but now it is muddy. We do not have the horse and carriage at this time, and I do not know yet what could be used to plant there either. Ignác, you are not writing about your work. Do you like it? Please write to us more. When Dezső left to America he wrote a lot, but now he doesn't feel like it. However, because he is not working he should have plenty of time to write. Marcsa, how are you feeling? What does Uncle Jónász say to Dezső's behavior since he's not dependent upon him? Is he still uptight? About two weeks ago I was in the town of Galocs with Klein bácsi. His son mentioned that he met you both, Dezső and Hermine, somewhere at a wedding and he spoke to you. I believe that his daughter knows you. She went to England and a couple of weeks later he was advised that she died. It came to my mind that Iren Schwartz got married. I believe that I have covered the odds and ends. I have a headache. The time is now 11 o'clock at night everybody is sleeping. Kisses to you all, your brother, Lajos, Mityu, Gyuszi. Give my regards to Jónász bacsi and his family.
Tomorrow I am going to hoe [to turn the ground] by hand to make it ready for seeding.

1940/5/29 Undated (b) Etelka to Hermine and Marie (Book 3, 215-216) pages 1-2

[dated by Lajos to Galocs and Kocsis is going to marry Ilonkat Leco.]

Dear Herminka and Dear Mariska,
I am representing in this writing Lajos and the children. Lajos is tired. He came home late at night from Galocs. He handed over the horse and the other equipment and carriage. The children are in school and father will be taking this letter to the post office. Thank God that we healthy. No news here, only the wind blows a lot.....Dear Herminka we are very happy to learn from your letter that you are sending us a package. I wish it would be here already. Let's hope that it will arrive. Many thanks for your good heartedness. You are writing so warmly to us and think of us from far away and believe me that it means a lot and we think of you also. Marcsa, I cannot imagine her to be serious in America as I do you. The children always mention you and I would like, if you can, send us a picture so that the children would get to know you. Mariska, how are you? How is the cooking going along for you? I can imagine that you have a beautiful home, nice and clean. I too try to maintain everything in order. Believe me, from early morning to late at night I haven't stopped. It wouldn't be too bad, if only the wind would stop blowing already... Little Zoli has a cold. Kisses to Jónász bacsi, Arthur and his family. My regards to Erzsike if she'll be there. Kisses from all of us with love to you and Mariska. Gyuszi and Mityu went to Hebrew school and took with them some food. Love from them also.
[On the top of 1st page, upside down] Lajos stayed in Galocs at Erno. Also, Ilona Leco became Mrs. Kocsisne.
[On the bottom of 1st page, upside down] Manci [her sister] was here to give me a welcome kiss. Etelka
[On the top of 2nd page, upside down] Emil and Lenke are well and are in Hebrew school.

1940/5/29 Undated (c) Etelka and Lenke to Hermine (Book 4, 323-324) pages 3-4

[dared by package sent in April still not arrived, so after April. Irene Schwartz got married which Lajos mentions above in his letter. Water damage from flood]

Mityuka and Gyuszika kiss you and they are waiting for your package.

Even if the war could avoid us, we have a bad year because of the tremendous water damage and frost damage. [There] will not leave any progress. In our town there are a lot of lands that remained fallow because it is not capable to dry out from the continuous rain. Since this spring there was no nice weather, only rain and wind. My dear Herminka, I'm very sorry that you did not send the package yet, because whoever sent it in the beginning of April received it here on time. For example, last week Uncle Leizer got very nice things and Veres and others, but only God knows how it will be later…Only patience is the main thing for today. There is nothing going on in our town at all. No news presently. Malvin took over the letter, but when will she write, that's the question. She always promises that she will write. As I hear it, Iren Schwartz got engaged in America!

[from Lenke]
Dear Aunt Hencsu and dear Aunt Marcsa. Thank God we are well. Today we got a break and now I will learn Hebrew. I kiss Uncle Dezső, Hersmendu, Ignác, Uncle Jónász, Uncle Arthur and you Hencsu and Aunt Marcsa, Gluck Lenke

1940/6/1 Louis Schwartz to Hermine and Marie (Book 18, 152-155)

Youngstown 940 V / 30
Dear Herminka and Mariska!
I'm sorry that I am just responding to your precious letter. I truly did not do it out of laziness. I am very busy during the day time. I'm usually in the store, and at night I'm at a language course, and I only come home late at night when I don't have patience to write already. I don't even remember what you wrote. I hope you will not follow my current example and you will write immediately. I promise, that from now on, I will respond normally. If I remember well, dear Hermine, you wrote that you don't think that I will look after you with my letter although I am counting on doing it as soon as the conditions will allow it. On Sunday, two boys from Szürte visited me from Pittsburg. One of them has been here for 4 years, the other one for 17 years. Last week I got a letter from home. Unfortunately they did not write anything good. Supposedly the stores need to be closed by the end of May, if nothing changes. What do they write from your home? Maybe I already wrote this, that I got a letter from Helen. As she wrote it, she has a good thing going on. Surely you are corresponding with her by letter. I did not even respond to her. I would like to visit her, too. Also, I got a letter from Iren Schwartz from Lelesz. She was not working at the time. I would like you to write about everything in detail and about the relatives, about what you do, and where you work. How do you live? I hope we will always stay relatives, regardless of the big distance which destiny brought us to from the people at home. Also, write about how you are doing with English. Relatively, I know a lot already, but unfortunately not enough to serve [customers] in the store, nor with the relatives where I eat and live, which is very uncomfortable for me. The kids only speak English, which is very hard for me and it gets me down many times, but I have to get through this. Here there are very few Hungarian Jews, especially young people. Surely there are more there. Write it to me, if you met with any acquaintances? Do you have company? What do you spend your free time with? If you have pictures of yourselves in America, send them to me. Now I will finish my lines with the hope that you will respond shortly. Lajos. Give my best to Jónász bacsi [a term of respect] and to his family. How are they? Give my best to Jenő Eigner.

Dear Dezső!
I am only thanking you now for your good wishes. You're definitely a total Yankee already!! I would like you to write to me again about yourself as well, what you do, etc. There is no news here. I am living a "greeners" [lacking experience] life, which is a little bitter because of the missing language skills. We should get through this. Greetings from my heart.
Lajos

1940/6/3 Margit Fischer to Hermine (Book 18, 15-16)

Sweet Herminke!
I was very happy to get your letter. Forgive me that I did not write sweet Hermine, but I am not angry at all, you did not give me a reason. I take it as you would be my sibling. I will write more. I divided my father's

store in half and I supplied it for myself with sugar, seltzer, newspapers, cigarettes. You would be glad that I am settled and I cook for myself and for my father too. You know the man is alone, but he listens to me. I go in the morning and I come at night to sleep at my aunt. Since I talk so much about you, send 1 picture to let her know you. You will send one, won't you? Forgive me, I could never do [unclear] who saved my hair like it would have been my love. Do you remember being jealous? I kiss you and dear Mariska.
Margit. I will wait (for the reply)

1940/6/8 Mrs. Ivany to Hermine and Marie (Book 4, 337-338)

Bodrogmező 1940 June 8th
[This was written by Mrs. Ivany, as I can see, she did not sign her name - Maria]

My beloved, sweet Herminka and my Mariska. Thank you so much for remembering me, that you did not forget about me. Dear Herminka and Mariska, I know that I'm not in your mind as much as you are in mine, because when you left from home, I could not find my place. I was going all over the place so I could hear something about you somewhere. I already felt ashamed about it. I went to your father all the time to wonder about you. When I heard that thank God you are all out there in America, I did not know what to do in my happiness. But believe me, my dear darlings, if you would be mine, not even then would you be in my mind the way you are now. My dear Mariska, you wrote that perhaps I don't even go to your house. Of course I do, just like when you were at home. Believe me, my darlings, you would not believe what a great housewife Etelka is. For poultry she has chicken and duck, so it's good to see. If only you would see how nice and clean your father is always. Your father's room is always nice. Etelka washes his sheets and clothes and irons them. There is never an argument between them. Your father has such patience for the children. The children are very beautiful. Your father looks great and healthy. Etelka looks very good too and she is also healthy. She is very clever for everything. Dear Herminka, if I go to Lelesz I always go to see your grandparents. The last time I was there they were crying about you a lot. They can't forget about any of you. They sent a message to your father, that they want to read your latest letter, at least. I want to let you know, that Margit was not at home yet. I don't know when she will come home. My dear Herminka and Mariska, I'm asking all of you very much, if God will help you and you could do that, do not forget about me. I'm sure that there it is not like here at home. Do not forget about me, even in a situation like this, because you know that the family that I have, cannot even get a rag for themselves. I will return it to you at home. We respect you very much and kiss all of you. We wish you only good health. [Unsigned]
[On the side] Good health and a lot of good luck. God be with you.

1940/6/9 Father to us (Book 4, 331-332)

Bodrogmező 1940 VI/9   Until 120
My faithful children, who are loved from the heart. I read your letter that I could hardly wait for with happiness. I'm glad to hear, that thank God, you are in good health. I can only write the best about us, thank God, we are in good health also, and I wish to hear that from you as well.
The letters from May [V] 15th and from the 22nd have arrived. One came on the 18th and the other came on the 16th. I sent one letter on the 24th and another to my brother Jónász on the 29th. I wrote to you also in that letter. I hope you got it. I was at grandfather's on Friday and I read the letter for them. They were very happy that thank God, you are well, and they are sending their regards. Uncle Lajos also will write a short letter. I'm writing some news. Uncle Hermus's daughter, the one who's address I sent to you, is a bride. Her father got a letter from her. Her fiancée has a business and a 6 bedroom apartment. He owns them, according to her father. My dear children, just take care of yourselves, always. I forgot to ask from you about the train trip from New York to Columbus. How are you? Hersmendel doesn't live with you anymore? [annoyed that Hersmendel doesn't write]. Write to me about everything. I hope that my son Dezső has a good place now. I think everything is going to be good, with God's help. About Uncle Marton, I can write, that "Tzom Militar" [Yiddish - "to the army"]. I will write more about it. Your grandfather and grandmother know about it. You can imagine the rest. What else can I write. You can write more than we. I send my regards to my dear brother, Uncle Jónász and his family, and to Arthur and his family, and one by one to all of you. I kiss all of you, your father, who will never forget. Not during the day nor at night. Your father, Gluck Jeremias
Uncle Lajzer is sending his regards.

[Side note] There is still no buyer for the barn.

1940/6/9 (a) Undated Etelka and Emil to Hermine and Marie (Book 4, 333-334) before Shavuot

[dated by mention of Shavuot cleaning]

[from Emil]
Dear Uncles and Aunts,
Now I will respond to two letters, because two letters came in a week. We were very happy for your pictures. I'm notifying you that I had my exam in school. Our report card is very good. Of course, there are better, but there are also worse. I got the worst grade from writing, because my writing is very piggy [sloppy]. Father is at home now, because he had to go to the drafting, and he only goes back after Shavuot. Now we can hardly wait for the package. Now I'm having sewed a pair of dark blue pants from Zajdiak's [grandfather Jeremias] pants. Dear Hersmendel, if you eat good things in that hotel, then think about me also. If you get a tip, then send [some] from it to me, too. There is no special news. I kiss all of you and dear uncle Jónász and dear Uncle Arthur, Dezső and all of you. Your little nephew, Emil

[from Etelka]
Dear Herminka and dear Mariska!
Despite the bad delivery system, your past two letters got here on time. We also try to respond to every letter of yours, but the question is, if you get them at all? We were very happy for your pictures, but as I can see, dear Marcsa, that your face looks very skinny, so please take good care of yourself. Eat whatever feels good. There, I believe you can select your food and not worry about putting some weight on. Herminka, as I can see you are in good health, although your picture is enlarged. I am asking all of you not to be worried about your father because he has no problem other than his financial problems. Thank God he has no trouble and one can get used to what we have. Especially in today's situation, even if…

1940/6/9 (b) Undated Etelka and Lajos to Us (Book 4, 355-358) before Shavuot

[dated because before Shavuot and matching paper]

it brought his mood back. You asked what does that golden Gyuszi do? Well, he is becoming cuter everyday [in Yiddish - ùm berufen = is called/becoming] [and] is doing Levente things with Zajdi and Mityuka, but you have to eat him up. Gyuszi is developing very nicely, but I can't clothe them. We only made clothing for Emil and Mityuka for Passover from the remaining clothes. Imagine there is no calf available to buy. They kill them at every house and they price it at 60 filler per kg, but we still have it. It is a very good example, and this price is still very good, so it's just fine…….
I don't know any news because I barely have time to go to the gate. I will go down today to paint the kitchen. I kiss all of you, also dear uncle Jónász and Arthur and family. Etelka.

Based on your letters, I like Arthur and his dear wife very much. Mityu and Gyuszi are always crying that they want to write to Hencsu also. Mityu remembered this week that Hencsu does not tell him not to whisper anymore.
Kisses, as above

[from Lajos]
My beloved siblings, thank God we are well! I think you are well also.
I read from your previous letter that Dezső is getting ready for a different business, although Uncle Marton said that he doesn't approve his change. I think Hersmendu is all right with the job he has taken, because it's easy work. I think that Herminka's job is very stressful, change it if it's possible. Dezső should write more. Write at least one letter every week. Uncle Jónász should write already also. Our father is waiting so hard for it from him.
I kiss you with love, Lajos

[from Etelka]
Dear Mariska, you asked if Ilon nenni [comes] to help? It definitely doesn't pay to have a housekeeper these days. I can barely believe we have whatever we need. You can't imagine how much more expensive everything here. It's more futile than it's ever been. I arrange my things the best I can. The day is very long now, but there is no stop. I can hardly get the laundry done. Little Zoli is somewhat of an obedient child. He is very nice, but Gyuszi, if you could see, he is like a child "umberufen" [knock on wood; God forbid (saying to ward off the evil eye)]. Now he is fat from the buttered bread and a rare one, a very smart, attentive, and

happy child who does not leave my little Mityu alone. They literally have grown together. It is a joy to watch those two kids together. Today I made a big clean up for Shavuot. I cleaned up my room, [and your] father's room last week. Maybe you make fun of my letter, that I write every foolish thing together to you, but I can't write about anything else, only about my fate, because I don't go anywhere ever. The last time I ran home for an hour was because my mom, unfortunately, is not healthy. Her leg is hurt by the sugar again [diabetes]. She was very happy for your greetings, though. The girls send greetings as well and she sent greetings back to all of you. She kisses all of you with love. Dear Uncle Jónász and dear Arthur, too. Hoping for the best. Etelka

1940/6/9 Sanji Klein to Ignác (Book 5, 148-149)

1940 June 9th [Bodrogmező] B"H

My dear friend Ignác!
I was very happy to receive your card. I never expected that you would honor me with a card. I can write to you only about myself that I'm working, if there is anything [to do]. Sometimes I farm with a hoe and do whatever comes along. I was in Fenyves Valley at a military installation that they were building. I was working there for two weeks, however I didn't find it worthwhile to be there so I came back home. I know that you're a happy person, I wish I could be there also. I am thinking of you when I do the home guard exercises since I'm by myself. There's nothing much new around here that would interest you. I'm sure your family writes about everything. My best regards to all of you, from me as well as from my parents. A true friend of yours, Sanji

[The reason he's thinking of me is that my family gave the wooden rifle to exercise with, since I was in America at this time - Noted by Irving.]

1940/6/27 Bertha to Hermine (Book 5, 145-147)

New York
June 27 / 40
My dearest Herminkem!
I don't know how to even begin writing to you in this letter because I feel guilty for not writing to you for so long. I have become very lazy to write but sometimes the situation makes it that way. Even with the best situation or under the circumstances it brings it on. My dearest, you always express yourself that you feel you write too much. Maybe because you have more people to write to therefore I can understand why you feel that way. For me, I don't have enough to read and I'm very happy you're writing to make me very happy. The village that you are living in in America is not like in Czechoslovakia with your sister and brothers. I know and understand you're worried about what you are all going through. I would like to ask you one question: did you get the first papers to become an American citizen? Don't let it go, you must apply at once to become a citizen. This is very important. You must do it without delay. This is a must, at once. At this time that I'm writing, I don't have much more to write. What would interest you? In the afternoon I'm going to visit Aunt Jennie. She is in the hospital. She had surgery. I think it was her appendix. Thank goodness, she's better. For a couple of days she had pain. At this time, about two weeks later, she will stay in the hospital. The weather at this time is not the best. It was raining, but we didn't need it. During the whole summer we didn't have good weather, [but] we can't change it. We have to take what we get and we have to be happy about it, but I've had enough of this. Give my kisses to your sister and brothers and also to your uncle and his wife and all the relatives, our cousins, and to you with all the best wishes and kisses, Bertha and Mannie

My father-in-law and all the rest of the family, all the relatives here, send their kisses to you.

As above

1940/6/29 (a) Undated Etelka to Hermine and Marie (Book 4, 371-372) pages 1-4

[dated from mention of summer, wheat, no food in the fall, cooking. Same paper type as next letter]

Dear Herminka and Mariska!

Your dear letters are arriving beyond our hope, [and] that makes us very happy. I gave you the truth that we should write to you every week, also. But, if your dear father does not write, then I will not force it either. We always think that you never receive them anyway, so we only write when yours arrive. Two of your letters arrived after 3 weeks of waiting. What we wrote [to you], also came back from Columbus. One of our letters went at the worst of time. I wonder, if you got it? Ilon nenni wrote in it too. You ask in your letters, my darlings, that I should write a lot. I would love to do that, but can I write what I want?...There is no small town gossip of any kind because now everybody is focusing on themselves.

[upside down:] The letter that came back I will send again, so you'll have something to read.

The worry [cara se] is definitely big. The rain is falling the whole summer, so we can't collect or harvest hay. The grassy little wheat we have will be rotten from all the rain. And all the bad news we hear about the Jews all the time makes us nervous. So, I don't know how it is going to end. You owe to the dear God, that he helped you out. Your two dear Uncles got drafted and the same [happened to the] Jews of this town like, Kalman bacsi, Hermel Zelcer, Keszner bacsi, Weisz and many many more, you can imagine...and the non-Jews ["gajak" = goyim] countless times. I'm scared, that I wrote too much. About myself, I can only write that I'm very busy with the kids. Besides that I worry a lot. Only the children give me happy moments. That golden Gyuszi with his black eyes, that light up so sweetly [Yiddish - "zisz"] under those blonde locks, there is no match for that. Little Zoltan is very cute. He listens nicely and his eyes are like the nicest violet. Dear Herminka and dear Mariska you wondered so thoughtfully about my mother and the family, I cannot write the best about them. I can only write badly about them, because my poor mom's legs hurt her so much that she can't walk. Every time I run home, she wonders about you. Manci is away now to Tiha, because she needs a change in environment also and a little peace, since you know that she was very sick, too. Olga, sometimes runs by us. Hermus joined the army. While I'm writing this letter, Pataki passed by with Amis and called me out with the kids because they are wondering about you. She can't write because her mother is very sick and she is busy with her. She says that they slander them because she was in good terms with all of you and you did not leave anything for her. Gerenye is also annoying/rubbing against me every morning and talks to me at the cow herding. You my darlings were wondering about the kindness of friends ["komanem" means friend/pal in old Hungarian]? Her heart is a little broken, but it's never going to be complete. I break a little sometimes, she will be with me sometimes and I am by her. But she announced, that she only will do things in return. She admits that I'm very nice to her. My writing is ugly, because the kids are bothering me. You were wondering if Rozsi Ragany still comes to me? Since you left, I don't have any kind of housekeepers. I can barely live my life. I get whatever I can. Besides that, nobody can get anything. Ilon nenni does the milking on Saturday. Thank God that we planted the new beans and the new potatoes. Just new bread is far away because the weather does not let us harvest. I'm very happy darlings, that you are in very good circles. I can only send a recipe if I go to Lefkovics. Malvin is away in Ligand.

1940/6/29 (b) Etelka and Emil (Book 4, 370) page 5

For my part, I only know that the scone slice will come out in the fat, roasted. I'm sure you have a good pantry and then cooking and baking is not hard. You can be trusted with those. Write what kind of gift you will send. If you will send a package, only wrap it until 8 kg. We will make it through the summer, but for the fall holidays, if we are still alive, we will have nothing. I kiss dear Uncle Jónász and dear Arthur and his family. I kiss you with love, Etelka 1940 VI/29

[from Emil]
Dear Aunt and Uncle, I'm letting you know that thank God we are in good health. I hope you are as well. The school [Hajder] unfortunately lasted only a month, because the leader [Yiddish - "Lener"] could not stay here. Although we loved him very much and we were glad for the studies. Tibi will go to high school [Polgari]. He does not mind. Now there is work [avoda] through the harvest. Gyuszi (and others) have been a few times, but every day it costs 2 filler [Hungarian cent] a child.

1940/6/29 (c) Etelka and Emil (Book 4, 361-362) pages 6-7

I wrote with difficulty a letter to "Gecse Pilot." Dear Uncle Dezső, I would love to be with you. I kiss you dear Hencsu and dear Marcsa, dear Ignác, dear Hersmendu. I kiss all of you, dear uncle Jónász and dear uncle Arthur. Your little nephew, Emil.

[from Etelka]
I'm ashamed that Emil writes so badly, but I don't have time to stand next to him. Lenke is writing so little also, because I can't stand by her. I have to go in many directions.

[from Emil]
We wrote already that Ica Diak died. Marcsa will not be alive for too long either. She is sick also. Anna lives at Juhasz (and others). The barn burned down there with the threshing machine in one quiet afternoon. I go to the field now to spin and to cover [harvesting expression]. It will be interesting if we will eat pumpkin from the homegrown seeds, [and] a little fruit from the other garden.

[Up side down: from Etelka] You can fry scone like chicken, shake the protein part foamy and at the end scramble it.

1940/6/29 (d) Undated Etelka and Lajos to Us (Book 4, 367-368) colt born, sunflowers

[dated by mention of colt being born (see letter 1941/3/10 Father to us (Book 3, 220-222, 225-226) missing last page, rain, a sea of sunflowers which ripen June/July.]

[In the next page there are recipes for linzer crust, rum punch, roast meat and meat cutlet. Also palacsinta (Hungarian pancake) and dobos-cake.]
[Etelka continues]
Kneaded linzer crust,
30 dkg flour
30 dkg sugar
25 dkg butter
25 dkg grounded walnut or peanut
2 whole eggs
1 baking soda
We work the whole crust/pasta together and we divide it in half. In one half we put 5dkg cocoa. We put one part with the cocoa to the bottom of the baking sheet. We grease it with fruit flavor [I put jam on it, any flavor] and put the other half on the top. We bake it and cover it with chocolate glaze and we slice it cold.

Rum Punch:
24 dkg sugar
20 dkg chocolate
20 dkg flour
6 whole eggs
mix and stir and bake
then 40 dkg icing sugar with 1 deciliter rum pour it on the crust/pasta and slice it warm.

Meat roll:
skinny, large, windy scapula slice stuffed with meatloaf [this is Hungarian meatloaf. It's different than the meatloaf in USA)
1 hard boiled egg placed, here and there inside. This one has to be wrapped tightly with skinny string and roast it.
The string should be removed before serving.
I hope you'll understand that you make this from raw meat..and then fry the meat. First you put it in flour and then in egg yolks then to breadcrumbs and finally in foamy eggs white. Fry it In fat under cover.

Make palacsinta [Hungarian pancake or crêpe] with meat with carbonated water and egg and like the dobos cake put them on the top of each other with jam.

In the last sentence :
I will not write anything else. Next time again. The children will not write now because the letter will be go out.
Kisses from all of us.

[from Lajos]
My loved siblings,

Page 132

We read your letters, that we could hardly wait for, with great happiness. I'm in a hurry to write now, because I'm going to go to cover from the rain. We can't proceed with any work like this. The wheat only grows with weeds. The sea of sunflowers is beautiful. We still have only one horse. The Csarga whelped [gave birth to] a stallion colt. I will not write anything else because I have no patience. Thank God we are well, and I hope to hear that back from you. I kiss the relatives one by one and you as well. Your faithful brother Lajos.

[from Lenke]
I kiss everyone, Lenke, Mityu and Gyuszika

[from Etelka]
[Upside down on the bottom of this page:]
Bozsi and Manya were very happy for your letter and they said, that they will understand you. Gerenyi (and others) send their regards also.

1940/7/2 Father, Lajos, and Etelka to us (Book 3, 189-190)

Bodrogmező 1940 VII / 2
My dearest children that I love, sincerely, from my heart.
I was waiting with difficulty, but I was very happy to read in your letters that thank God, you are in good health, and I hope that my letter will find you in the best of health. As for ourselves, I want to inform you that thank God, we are healthy and we hope to hear from you again the best. My dear son Dezső, you're not writing about your position whether you have one, and you did not write anything about my son Hersmendu and he didn't write either. I am very impatient. My dear children write if only you can, so I'll know about you and how you are. Your Uncle Marton was at home for Saturday from Patak and on Sunday was in Lelesz at your grandpa with Henry, they are together. Your grandfather and grandmother send their regards to all of you. They asked that you should write to them. It has been raining here for three weeks and the flood drove the cows off the grazing areas. We cannot seed the grazing area. Both the Dioszog and the lower part is full of weeds. I don't know yet what we are going to be able to harvest. I did not sell the big building where we used to dry the tobacco. There wasn't any serious buyer. I heard that Uncle Izidor bacsi is feeling better thank God. He is still in Kassa by his daughter. I would have a lot to write, but I am mailing this letter via airplane to get there faster since there isn't any other way through the regular post office. On May 24, I mailed a letter to you and in the first week of June I mailed one to Uncle Jónász. On May 29 [another] letter to you and hope that you have received it. My dearest children, kisses to all of you, individually, sincerely forever your father who will never forget you and you are in my mind every minute. Is it not so, my dearest children, that you are the same away, forever, with sincerity your father. Gluck Jeremias.

Separately, my respect to my dear brother Jónász and his family and dear Arthur, his son, and his family, also Elsie and her family, countless times, forever, your brother that will never forget you. Gluck Jeremias. My brother Lajzer also sends his regards to all of you. As above
Lajzer received a card from Bertha by air mail.

[from Lajos]
My dear beloved siblings,
I'm letting you know that with God's help, I am well, which I hope to hear the same [from you]. Uncle Marton is not at home, but he was. He sends his regards. I want to be well, [but] I have no patience for anything, not for oil or cabbage. Kisses to you, and Uncle Jónász and his son and his family. Lajos

[from our father again]
My dearest children, I received the gift. I thank you all. God should help you to all good things, that's my wish. Your father that will never forget you. Gluck Jeremias.

Dear Hermina and dear Maria.
My last letter was more extensive it would be a shame if it has gotten lost. Please let me know if you received it. Will you? Mrs. Ilon has written in that letter also and now Margit is at home she developed quite well. Ilon Diak was buried Saturday and it was a big affair. Her sister Marcsa
is up, but looks terrible, she may hold out perhaps until this fall. My letter this time is not well organized. I cannot write the things that I really would like to. Everything here is very costly. I'm very sorry that the

package has not arrived yet because the children are missing a lot, especially Gyuszi. He is the most beautiful child on the street. That little one is very beautiful and sweet. We received the package that was shipped in April. The people are surprised that you did not mail any at this time. I saw Uncle Marton. He has a golden rank as Corporal. His face is very clean shaven and he went by us in a bus. Please write frequently because it's very difficult to wait. Lajos is very nervous to write because every minute new reports are coming out. Our horses are not at home and they are being taken from other towns. With Kisses and Love to all of you, also to Jónász Bácsi and dear Arthur and his family and their children, congratulations even after the holiday. Etelka.

[from Lenke] Kisses to everyone. Lenke, Mityu, Gyuszi

[from Etelka]
Emil does not want to write because he's not happy to have such a small piece of paper. Please write more about yourself [and] about where you are a housekeeper. How large is the family? Do you know that everything interests me. Perhaps it would be better if you would look for a social life. I wrote to you that Irene Schwartz has made a good party in marriage, so she now lives without any problems. Please hurry up do likewise.
Kisses to all you, Etelka, Gyuszi, Mityu.

1940/7/5 Louis Schwartz to Hermine and Marie (Book 17, 157-158)

Youngstown 940 VII/5
Dear Hermina and Mariska!
I read your dear letter with happiness. I'm glad that you all are well. I thought Dezső will write a few lines as well. But he must be very busy with work and with the girls?! Or maybe he became so [good in] English, his writing doesn't work in Hungarian anymore? Last Sunday I unexpectedly visited Helen. My cousin [older and male] and his family travelled to Cleveland, so I went with them with my brother. She said that you will probably visit her soon. Is it true? And when? The last time I got a letter from home, unfortunately, there is no good news. The grace period for the industries has expired on May 1st. The butcher shop by us was also closed when the letter was dated, although I hope they will extend it. And when did you get a letter from home? What are they writing? Gizi was wondering about you in every letter and about what you are doing, but I could not give her too much information. Now I'm getting ready to write to home. Allegedly, I can only send it with airmail or maybe it has changed because of the conditions, it is doubtful too. The English language is going pretty well [although] I rarely go to school. And you?! Write everything about yourself and about what you do? How many hours, days etc…There is no change with me, everyday I'm in the store from 8 to 6 and then, if I have patience I study. I will end my lines. Many kisses, Lajos.
If you have pictures send them!

1940/7/9 Helen Perl to Hermine (Book 5, 234-237)

Cleveland VII / 9
Dear Hermine!
Don't take it in a bad way that again I delay my writing. I was waiting for you to come to your girlfriend. The Reich girls will come, but this week I was disappointed. They send their best wishes to me and set a good example, and [wrote] nice things about themselves. She told me about the situation. I'm asking you Hermine, here we must accept whatever is. We must clear our heads from whatever heartaches and worries and we must cover them with happiness and a smile. About myself there isn't much I can tell. I live with my relatives. I'm doing some sewing like before. Still, at this time I do not have too many friends. Last Sunday I had very nice friends come over. Lajos Schwartz and his brother Jozsi. They are very nice and I enjoy their company. They promised they plan to visit you very soon also. Please write more about you all. We often write very short letters, but now I'm interested to hear more about everything that happens in our lives as though you would be my closest relatives, even though we hardly know each other. Please let me know if you have the relation's address. I'm closing this time with all my best wishes, [and] kisses to all of you [and] your family, too. Helen

1940/7/12 Bertha to Hermine (Book 3, 370-374)

New York

July 12 / 40

My dear Hermine!

It makes me happy to know that thank heaven you're well, in good health, and they put you in a good location. The longer you are in America with that, your luck will increase and [you'll be in an] acceptable position. This is not a bad beginning for Herman. In fact, if he gains experience then he will have a good future. You don't realize how lighter my heart is when I can hear good things from my dearests. Dear Ignác is a smart child and his future is rosy and he will get ahead. He won't speak to the employees like Dezső, this way he will have a great future in a few years and with patience. It may not be so good in the beginning, but after that it will be worth 1,000 [pieces of] silver. My dear Hermine, I will ask you one thing, don't write to me in every letter that you're afraid that you will be bore me with your dear lines, because if it would be that way then I would make sure that I would not receive any letter from you. I'm not communicating through letters with you because I must, but I love you, really, all of you, and I like to hear good news. I will not ask you to write me frequently, but at least once a month. That isn't much, is it?

Let's leave this for a moment. I want to tell you that our dear Aunt's son Lester came home from the hospital yesterday. Thank heavens that now he can walk, but he's very weak. I'm sure that it will take him a few weeks to regain his energy. Yesterday, there was a burial for one of our relations, but you did not know him, but Uncle Jónász does. His name was Adolph Gluck. He wasn't a young man. He suffered a lot with heart pain. On July 4, Nate and Jennie [referring to Aunt Jennie] and I spent the day in Atlantic City, all three of us. We had a beautiful day. I felt that being away, I've lived one day from early morning late in the evening. I never believed that a change of air can do so much for me, and it did good for me as a person. Since I returned home my health has changed for the better I believe. I'll write about what you're interested in, the weather isn't the best thing here. We have had many rainy days. It's not very good for the stores now. Kisses especially to your siblings. Hi to our dear Uncle, dear Aunt, and to all the cousins. With love and kisses, Bertha and Mannie

Greetings from my relatives here. As above

P.S. Is Mariska alright? You will allow me not to write to you separately won't you? This letter of mine is also to you, plus I am also lazy to write too much. You allow me. I kiss you, Bertha

---

1940/7/13 Father to us (Book 4, 349-350)

Bodrogmező 1940 VII/13

My dear beloved, faithful children.

I read your letter, which I could hardly wait for, with happiness. I'm glad that, thank God you are well. Also, we are, thank God, in very good health. I hope my lines will find all of you in the best of health. I received 6 letters with simple post service and I got the airmail sent at the end of last week. Grandfather got it also at night. Will you keep the Yahrzeit my dear children?

Your Uncle Marton was at home on Saturday. The harvest isn't done yet. Lajos scythed himself, because the kepés [some old agricultural term] left it there because everybody's filled with dust. I don't know if it's going to be as much as we sowed into it. We can't even get a day laborer, and I don't know what will happen with the land that was sold. Last week the economic supervisor/overseer came out and he wanted to force us to sell the land for 600 p[engo] to Gyula Szabó. I answered that I'm not selling and he demanded that I give the money back. My children took it to America and used it for their expense. He threatened me that he will take it for 300 p[engo]. It's a disaster to take it away and for 1 year he will block the sale. I answered him that the law can do whatever it wants, and I told him that the crop is owned by the Glucks. But I did not have it yet. He reaped the best of the wheat, and I'm counting on the crop, so I can give it to him, that way we had a bargain. A letter came back from Columbus for the Weizer girl. Here I attached a little letter from her. It's been already 13 weeks that her father is lying [recovering]. He had surgery on his leg. He is asking his relatives to help him because it costs a lot here.

There is a new order that Jewish stores have to be open on Saturdays, because they are threatening them with eliminating their business. Keszler is a soldier and he was invited this week for a visa hearing, since then he did not travel from here to America. The horse and the wagon are still there. I did not sell the barn yet. They were interested in the pasture. Today there are no buyers. With the bad crop and the new law, it can only be sold cheaply. But you knew about this, I already wrote it to you. I don't know anything about Uncle Izsidor. I don't even know what to write to you, my dear children. I'm only sorry, that my son Dezső can't get a good place for himself. Write to me about everything. How are you my dear children? Just take good care of yourselves. Grandfather and grandmother are in good health. They send their regards to all of you. Uncle Albert asked me to write to you, if Zseni could send a couple of dollars to him via airmail so he can have some to live. Although he wrote a letter yesterday, he is not sure if it will arrive. In the last month,

I sent 3 letters to you. I hope you got them. I kiss each of you, one by one, and with love, forever. Your faithful dad, who will never forget. Gluck Jeremias

Uncle Marton sends his regards. He said that if he gets a chance, he will write from here. Uncle Lajos was not home yet. Give my respects to my nephew Arthur and his family and to Erzsike. Uncle Lajzer sends his regards to all of you. Again I kiss all of you, your father, Gluck Jeremias

[from Adolf Lefkovics]
Before I close the letter, here I am taking the opportunity to give you my sincere greetings and don't forget that God is with you. Adolf Lefkovics

You can not imagine my dear children, how happily I took your letter from Szmolyak's [the postman] hand. One day and the next just everybody who I met lined-up and was wondering if I got a letter. Of course, there were also letters from May between them. What is Lajos Schwarz from Szürte's occupation? He did not write about it. The horse trader and the cow trader did not get business, only Bela Stark from Lelesz. They keep their eyes on the traders and forbid trade for the Jews. What's left in K. Helmec is 10 Jews all together and 1 beaten prairie. What else should I write, you know everything better than we do.
Again, regards and kisses to all of you. Your loving father, Gluck Jeremias

1940/7/13 Undated Lajos to us (Book 4, 369) summer harvest, floods

[Dated by flood, plentiful harvest, not yet finished with the hay, wrote with father on other dates, maybe 7/1940]

My dearest sisters and brothers,
We were happy to read your letters. I do not know what to write to you since more likely you know more about everything there. We still have flooding in our village. I don't know whether it will go under our hay. We have yet to tie about 25 crosses of wheat and the rest was already tied together. The total would be about 100 cross and that has also weeds. The corn and sunflowers are beautiful. Herman you're asking if we have ponies. I wrote to you several times that we have a male pony. We also have about 30 or 40 kg of beets. Gyuszi was looking at the picture of Hermin and said she does not recognize me now. Thank God they're healthy and hope that you're also. Give our regards to the relations. Dezső, you could have written more since you're writing very short notes. Herman you too could write more. I remain with kisses, your brother, Lajos.

1940/7/27 Father to Uncle Jónász (Book 4, 373-374)

Bodrogmező 1940 VII / 27

My brother Jónász and my dear sister-in-law, who is loved from my heart.
I'm letting you know that, thank God, we are in good health, and what I hope is that you don't miss it either. It's been 2 months that I wrote a letter separately to your address. I hope that you got it. I will attach again a couple of lines about us. The crop this year is very bad. It froze out and the flood added to it, so it takes a lot of work to harvest whatever is left from the heavy rain, that is, if we will have anything left from it. I can't write anything better/different.
I send my regards and kiss you, my dear, faithful brother Jónász and dear sister-in-law Helén, with love, your faithful brother and brother in law, Gluck Jeremias

And my regards separately to your dear children, Arthur and his precious family and Elzsike and her precious family, Your faithful brother, Jeremias

1940/7/27 Father to us (Book 4, 375-376)

Bodrogmező 1940 VII 27

My faithful children from my heart with love, until 120. I got your letters, that I could hardly wait for. With the postmarks dated June 13 and 26, and I read them with happiness. The letter addressed to my son Dezső was sent back from Columbus on May 22. I will attach this also in my letter. I'm glad that thank God, you are in good health. I hope that my lines will find all of you in the best of health. You did not write, if my son

Dezső has a different job. Let me know about everything. You were wondering about the crop. They started the harvest. It's raining everyday. The small wheat that is left, is surrounded all around by weeds. Feri Szabo encouraged me [saying] that he will harvest. The Leszna meadow has already been scythed for 11 days and it cannot be covered. Uncle Lajos, Pityú [Uncle Marton], Henri, Lipot, they are still in Patak. Grandfather and grandmother, you can imagine, they are suffering a lot. Write to them separately a little letter. Andras Juhasz's children were burned as was the threshing machine, that was shared with Monár. The fire was during the daytime 2 weeks ago. Uncle Marton was at home last Saturday and he was in Lelesz on Sunday. There is a car service to Helmec, Bodrogmező and Lelesz 2 times per day. My dear children, I don't know what to write about myself. Even if I don't write, you know everything. I still think that you all left for a party and I'm waiting everyday for you to come back. I take your pictures out of my pocket and look at them, it's easier that way. I cry to myself where nobody can see me. My dear children just write to me about everything often. I send my regards to all of you and kiss you countless times. Your faithful father, who will never forget. Gluck Jeremias

I don't know anything about Uncle Izsidor.

Uncle Lazar sends his regards. The sale with Gyula Szabo is still not approved. It is under negotiation now.

1940/7/29 Etelka to Hermine and Marie (Book 5, 175-176)

1940 VII / 29

Dear Hermine and Mariska,

I leave everything happily to sit down to write and answer your letters because you saved us from a terrible agony and worry. I think you remember only that we didn't have any money to buy any food. How happy we were when we received any help at the last minute. That was happening at this time. We didn't have any food. We don't live now either. It's a smaller amount of bread than before. Our God ordered [it in the] last minute. Yesterday we sent you a letter, but one [sent] in Dezső's name came back from Columbus. We mailed it back again. This letter was mailed by express for the only reason that we want to show you how grateful we are to you. Please write. I know you worry about us a lot. Please believe it we also think about you all the time. If you would be here you would know how many times we mention your names. The only thing that is different is that you are there and you would like us to be there. We are grateful that you're there away from hunger and this terrible life and all this agony and suffering. I don't write this to complain or that I'm jealous! Or that I would like to be the one to be there. But it is very hard to eat bread here and the garments are kept only by the breath. It's not worth buying here either because it's very expensive. Gyuszi and Mityu are walking in bare feet. We are too all summer. It has been raining all summer and therefore they can see it here that we don't have it. I'm very ashamed that we don't have and we are forced to live like it. We also do this outside in the street. This summer is over therefore we are happy for the winter is coming but then it will be a big problem for us. The holiday is also coming! Hope is giving us strength. That others are worse off makes us keep going every day. Whoever doesn't have a home has to give up. Yesterday in our letters we wrote much more and about everyone and everything. I hope you will receive them because they were big letters. Yesterday I spoke with Diak and said hi [from you]. She is sending you best regards and she told me that Marcsa wrote to you. She will not be in heaven until maybe the fall. She wants me to tell you that I'm up and busy working until 3:30 at night. But the trouble never leaves even though I cannot fall asleep as the problem is always there. Small items are very difficult. The pantry of the whole village can be said to be empty. Those who have a little bit are saving it because they need seeds to plant for next year. Now they are only reaping grass, the season [for wheat] is over and there are not many sheaves of wheat because we had too much rain. From now on we will write you every week, even though yours is not arriving. We received 2 letters from you on Saturday and last night we received two more. We are very happy when we get your letter. The small children are very beautiful, all of them. You see how crazy a mother is. I'm very proud and happy they make do. I should not talk like that, but I feel they are beautiful and give me life. The youngest is a very good child and all are beautiful. I cannot tell you how happy I'm with them (kánehare, must say that). Both eyes are beautiful and shine like stars in heaven. About your dear father, don't worry so much because I take care of him. I'm not as bad hearted a person as I look like. Thank God, that we have milk and butter. I divided it so that your father has some also. At this time I don't bake too much and when I'm baking I'm giving father also. I take it in for him to have challah also. Therefore I am make sure I take care of him too. He is the first one you know, even before myself. I take care of him first. After that Gyuszi and Mityu share it. Dearest I understand that your Uncle Lajos is there with your Uncle Marton [in the army]. Countless other Jews were about to go but they did not need them. Yesterday [according to the] drummer, the law is that he [Jews] cannot buy land even where he already paid for it. You can't imagine how terrible it is for a poor man at this time. Do you forgive me that I will stop writing because I want to cook. I'm in a hurry because father is going this afternoon to Kiraly Helmec to take care of whatever he has to at the bank. I don't know if the children will be able to write because we don't have the time to stay with them. Father will take the letter so this way it will arrive faster to you. Many kisses to you all. You are all very wonderful people for your goodness. God should give you the best of health, and happiness. I'm wishing you all the best to all of you. What we have is the most important and thank goodness we have it, too. Many kisses to all of you from all of us, Etelka

1940/7/29 Father and Lajos to us (Book 4, 329-330)

Bodrogmező 1940 VII/29
My faithful children, who are loved from my heart. I read your letter happily this month on Saturday the 26th. I got 2 letters from you, on June 11th and on the 26th, and I responded to them with yesterday's mail. So it arrived with the mail yesterday. It was sent on May 28th and I got the airmail letter on July 18th, ten days ago. It was opened in Pest, but the envelope was closed legitimately and they put the $6 back and wrote on the envelope that there is $6 in it. [The original envelope] was placed into a bigger envelope. It was stamped/sealed with spanish-wax. Luckily it got here. The large envelope was addressed the same as the one inside, front and back. It's a fine wonder, right. Yesterday and today, the weather is very nice. The leszna meadow was [put into square bales], ["felrudasol" may be reinforcements or ingots? But it isn't a word in use these days. I think it means to collect the hay on the meadow in a hayrick or haystack after the grass has been cut and dried.] but it still needs to be put in a rick/stack. It has 35 square bales, because the entire thing was scythed. There was enough space where we put the bales [to keep them] from the water [getting wet]. The sea [perhaps poetically = the field / the flowers] is beautiful and so are the carrots and poppy seeds. The wind broke out a lot. The sunflowers are like a forest. The wheat is very weak. Feri Szabo started the harvest today. There are a lot of weeds in the wheat. He won't harvest [just] for weeds. He stated that wherever [the wheat] is the best it should be given to him. There are 13 sheaves of grain on the lake sands. I don't know how it will be with Gyula Szabo, because the economic commission does not want to approve him, because they think the 1000 pengo that is in the contract is too much. Sönét sold Vitéz's land. They already approved it, because it was only 700 p. written on the land and Zizgor helped him with it. In July it will be decided. They told him that he uses the entire land, because the wheat is good on it. He was already up in Helmec and talked to Zsiga about our case. He told him that I have to agree with him. I don't know how this is going to work out yet. About us, I can write, that thank God, we are in good health. I hope that my lines will find all of you in the best of health. Grandfather and grandmother said that it causes them great pain that their two boys are not at home. Sunday was already two weeks since Uncle Lajos left from home to Patak.
In the past, 5 dollars was 5 pengo, 53 fillert. I have 1 Dollar in the bank. This goes by the currency. I don't know any other news. I did not go to Leles this week yet. Grandfather and grandmother send their regards to all of you and I do as well and kiss you, my dear children. All of you, one by one. Your loved, faithful father, who will never forget. Gluck Jeremias
Regarding the Levente: The instructor has joined the proceeding/marching [vonul=marching, proceeding, be van vonulva=it has been in the proceeding, marching. It's used mostly when one joins the military]. The little boy, Sanyi, is still at home. He is working in Fenyves valley.

Separately give my regards to my dear brother Jónász and to my dear sister-in-law, to Arthur separately and to his family and to Erzsike and to her family.
His little brother, who will never forget. Jeremias

My loved siblings, live until 120
Your letter gave me happiness, since, thank God, you are well. We are doing our daily job. Tomorrow I want to help with the Kepes, because it's full of weeds, and so the ears of corn barely show. The man does not have a good mood for this life, because everything is going that way. You can not imagine, what bad weather we had. The water came out to the meadow so many times, so we thought it will never end. It may be improving by now. We were able to start the job yesterday on the meadow. The hay is all cleaned up. There are at least nine hay heaps. I would write more, but there is no more space. I kiss everyone. Lajos

1940/8/1 Bertha Weingarten to Hermine (Book 3, 187-188)

Aug 1 / 40
Dear Hermine!

I'm glad to know that you're progressing, but thank God that you our progressing with the use of the English language, it will be a little bit easier. If you could learn how to make ladies hats that would improve your income. They said back home, that you cannot sit in two chairs. However, if you could save a few dollars and you get a vacation, you could come to my place for a time it would not cost you anything. Aunt Jennie would also be able to help you. I thank you for the pictures, but I know that you're not interested. If you have any opportunity when you're free look for friendship with young people. Don't always be with your Uncle. You don't have to be afraid of him because they only want you to pay them back their money. You're young people. It will take quite some time until you pay them the full amount of money, according to my view. You'll be destroying your energy. If you have a good opportunity you have to grab it, think of yourself. You would have a better opportunity to pay him! I wish Columbus would not be so far, I would go and would speak about everything between ourselves. We could talk to each other and I would like it. Somehow I wouldn't want to do everything that the uncle wants just because he won't come [otherwise]. He doesn't know any better. You live a different life. He doesn't know and does not understand. My dearest, life is short! What we sow that's what we're going to gain. As you know about your dear mother, how difficult it was during that time. We have learned enough, experienced enough. If there is an opportunity you must grab it. Don't allow yourself to be used. It's enough of this. About Dezső, I'm sorry to hear about him, he is not a child. I always ask him in every letter that he should take any type of job, whatever, to make a living. This is only solution for him. If there would be a wealthy party [a girl] for him and then his father-in-law would put them in business and then he would have a future. I don't know, that little boy worries me. I did not reply at this time to his letter. I wrote to him before. I told him the truth what I was thinking, for his own benefit. Perhaps it's better if I don't write to him at this time. I can't agree with him [and] he may not like it much. I get letters very frequently from Europe, it's not good. This will be enough at this time. Kisses to Maria and the dear boys and all of you, lots of love, kisses, from myself and Mannie, Bertha
P.S. Regards from the relations and don't forget this letter and its content.

1940/8/5 Berta Veiszer and Rella Veiszer to Hermine and Marie (Book 7, 113-116) pages 1-4

[Unsigned, but handwriting matches next letter 1940/8/8 Berta Veiszer and Rella Veiszer (Book 5, 143-144) pages 5-6]

Kiralyhelmec VIII / 5
Dear Herminka and Mariska!
I will sit down to write, but believe me, I don't know what to write to you. Mr. Gluck gave me your letter approximately 5 weeks ago. I can just now respond to it because my father was in bed for X [the number doesn't show] weeks with an inflammation of varicose veins. They did surgery on him, and then they closed Lili's store. They took the industry/business away from her. The awareness of war took away the good mood. I meet often with Mr. Gluck. For example, he was over at our house on Friday, also. He talked a full hour about you entirely, and his eyes are tearing, that thank God, you are out there in America. I'm also, truly, very happy and I give my gratitude to the Lord, that you luckily got out here. I think about you everyday a lot, maybe more than you do about me. I kept the post-card from Napolyi [Naples], this way you are always in front of my eyes. You can see, that I can't even forget about you. If you would send a picture, I would be very happy. Do you think about me sometimes in the new world? Now we are Jewish [In Yiddish "Jidenak" = Jewish] compatriots, I don't have to write the reason, since you know better. My sweet Mariska, you asked me if I miss you. Well, I can't even write how much I miss you. But destiny is like that! My parents, thank God are well. My Dad is already recovering. They closed Lilli's store, but now she will become partners with a dear lady, if she wants to work. The Oszterci girls are doing well. Anyway, we don't get along with the entire family, because you know well how weird they are. The Keszler's still did not go to America, now B.I.D. soldier. I will answer accurately, the way you ask. Am I still not a bride? Surely I'm not yet. No way that I will be one now because the boys are in the military. I'm happy, that thank God you are all well, and you have a job. I'm happy about everything you write. I'm almost hopping in my happiness, that the good Lord saved you and gave you a better destiny. You have a good life and they let you work. But they don't let us live, nor die. We were at a wedding in Kispest. What kind of outfit did I get for myself? I had a dark blue "komonlot" [it's an old word], a summer coat and a dress. They said it's very nice and I look good in it. The fashion, like you wrote, is like in Europe. The locals are wearing a kerchief, so the whole world is a city. [maybe it means it's a small world?]. The Pesah went well here too, although, I understand already, and imagine, I got [the letter] back. I sent it on May 10th and on the 27th it was in Ohio and it came back with today's mail. You can imagine how annoyed I am. You must be thinking that I don't want to write, but I'm letting you know that I sent two letters and a postcard to you already. From Pest, but it's possible that it won't get to you either. Maybe the address is not right. Mr. Gluck gave me the address

and it is the same as I got from Svarc. Herminka write about everything, because I'm interested in everything that happens to you. In dear Mr. Gluck's letter you wrote to their address. Send it to my address. I am only asking it to my address so I can respond to it in person. I can't write "Nyogot", [maybe its nyugottan-easily/relaxed?] since you know everything about us!

1940/8/8 Berta Veiszer and Rella Veiszer (Book 5, 143-144) pages 5-6

[from Rella - cont'd]
Do you talk to our relatives? I will write to my dear aunt Eva also. There can be no word about us to go to America. Write about everything and send pictures. You know this from me that there are bus rides in Lelesz, Boly and Bodrogmezo etc., towns. Sometimes I would like to go to you, but then I remember that you are not at home. Then who would I go to? You should know my darlings that my tears are falling while I'm writing this letter, that we are so far away from each other. And who knows if we will see each other even in this life. I hope I wrote about everything. And maybe I already bore you with my lines. I send my best to your dear brothers. Herminka, Mariska I kiss you countless times. Your forever loving girlfriend. Rella Lilly is kissing you also now. She is working!

[from Berta]
Királyhelmecz 1940 Aug. 8th.

Dear Mariska, Herminka and the boys. Until 120
Rachu said I should write to you also. So I will write, but I know you barely have time to read it. So I will try to be brief. Last week your dear father was over. He brought greetings from all of you. "Kane hare" he looks so much better now than after you travelled out from here. It seemed he was very sad back then, but now that he gets good news about you, he is happy. His face just shines when he tells one thing or another about what you write, that thank God you are all well. That the uncle took you all out of here to the green and promised [land], that he will take you out more often etc. You all should just write many good things. It makes your dear father very happy. I can't write the best about us now. My husband has been lying [in bed] for 15 weeks. They operated on his varicose veins. You can imagine how much it cost. If you talk to the relatives about the girls, as I can see, they can not be taken out anyway, so help us out now with a little money. Our business went to literally nothing. While my husband lay down we sold the horses. And now there is a bad outlook for the harvest, we would not even get enough [if it were] for double the amount. That is how we went! My husband is still lying down. This week Rella's letter got returned from Columbus. Who knows if this will arrive?! I kiss you with love and I wish you everything good. Next time write about yourselves a lot. The girls should look for a good company/party [match]!

1940/8/11 Rohci ? and Berta Veiser to Hermine and Marie (Book 4, 249-250)

Dear Hermine and Marie!
At this time your dearest father is here. I just want to send you a few lines. I will mail it tomorrow because I wanted to get the address. I must tell you I'm thinking of you both many times. I'd like to hear from you nothing but the best. Please write to me about everything. I'm going to try to write to you more briefly. I don't have much time to write at this time since your dad is waiting for it. Best regards, Rohci.

940 VIII 11th

Dear Hermine and Maria and your brothers. Until 120!
Dear children I just want to send you a note. My husband Veiser bacsi had surgery. All of our pennies were spent on that and we have no money left. I am asking you please can you help us here? Please send us some money. We need your help desperately. Would you ask your aunt or family, maybe they can help us. Please remember me to them. With best wishes to you all.

Henrikne Veiser
single name was Bertha Grunfeld

[This letter speaks for itself. Every one we heard before or after the Holocaust nothing but heartache. It's very difficult to even write about this letter or note. The 1st one came from our cousin from Satmar. The other note from a friend of mine from home. It is unbelievable how desperate they are. What I can understand because I hear it every in and out all other countries but the Jewish people suffered before during and after the 2nd world war. Here if I really would like to help them which one should I do first. This goes on all the time one letter after the other. Whom should I help first, our father and my dearest brother and family 5 children 1 to 9 years of age they suffered so much. No food and not even their father is there to help them. He was picked up and taken away we don't even know where they took him for hard labor and then the family, his family, our family including our father, our grandmother–uncles, should I go any further - All perished in Holocaust unknown where, but they never survived. This is a very disturbing note. I am going to finish it right here. I wrote many articles about trying to remember our life history and many many letters I translated from Hungarian language to English. Maybe some day my nephew will publish it whoever will have the opportunity to read it maybe just then I hope they understand our freedom what it means to me and I treasure it for my own life and always. Now I'm going to come to close this note wishing you all the best - Maria]

1940/8/15 Aunt Etel to us (Book 5, 99-100)

[Aunt Etel is Uncle Lajos bacsi's wife]

Lelesz 1940 VIII / 15 [Borech Hashem]

My Dearests,
I hope that you will forgive me that I'm writing it together, but I don't think I can write as much because I've been alone for the past six weeks.... It's been four weeks [since] I went to visit, however, it would have been better if I wouldn't have because I can't sleep since then, he looked so badly that you cannot imagine it. If only I would be able to know how long this will take, that is, every sickness is different, to carry on unknowingly is difficult. You are asking where we live? You can't even imagine it, that is, nowhere. We began to move, renovations, and now everything is at a standstill...... I believe I've complained enough and that would have been unnecessary because only God can help, and I do not know what else I can write. And we are hoping that the Almighty will help us and gives us strength. It's regretful that not all sicknesses are the same. Give our regards to Dezső, Herman and Ignác, all of you and many kisses, your Aunt Etel.

I hope that you can understand me and that you are not taking this [to heart] that I do not write to you frequently, however as soon as God will help that Lajos will be better I will let you know. As above.

1940/8/27 Father to us (Book 5, 126-127)

Bodrogmező, 1940 VIII / 27

My heartfelt love to my dear children, to 120
I read your letters with great happiness and I was glad to know, thank God, that you are in good health. Thank God we are also well. The enclosed gift 6 [dollars] has arrived, also the picture, the ribbon and handkerchief, we thank you for it. When I received it I gave it to your grandmother. She kissed your picture with great happiness. Her sons have not returned there yet, [who knows] when? My dear children, I wrote in the last letter that Gyula Szabo, Simon, and I was there in their house to separate the wheat. They wanted to take all the wheat for themselves. They also offered 900 pengo [Hungarian money] for the land. We had an agreement and I kept myself to that agreement and I did not receive from the court statement that the sale was canceled and he believed that the governmental agency that overlooks things approved it. I said to him that I have nothing to say about it. He remarked that if I want to take it, I could eat it, then he will let me go. Then he said that they will not take it either until it's resolved. He thought that he will get all of it. I went Sunday to look at the land and it was empty. I called them to the judge and then he said that it was approved by the office of the overseers that they can take the whole thing. He thought that a Jew can't do anything with him because today [a Jew] doesn't have any rights. Yesterday I went to the attorney and he listened to the whole story and he will discuss it with his associate because he too has to have a Christian partner. He told me that I should return Thursday and he will let me know what can be done. I also reported to the judge that since the agreement to have the products [wheat] has to be reviewed, even though he has taken it to his property, he should return half. They also asked that I should return to him 400 pengo, so he could rob me. His father tried to negotiate it, but the son said why do you speak to Jermus bácsival and [he kept] repeating that it was approved by the overseer and also that a judge will positively decide in their favor. They want to be their own judge. My dear son Dezső, maybe it would be a good idea to call up the American Consul because a person in Bacska, Rozental, the family left to America and they wanted to take their property.

However, the American consulate told them that they have no right to take it. I'll find out more about it. I will also mention it to the attorney on Thursday. You know my dearest children this has been enough....How are all of you? I ask all of you, to love each other, I respect you and [give] kisses to you children individually, your father forever who will never forget you. Gluck Jeremias

My dear brother Jónász,
I'm still waiting to hear a reply from you to my letter and then I will write a more detailed letter. With respect to you and kisses, my dear brother Jónász and sister-in-law Helen.
Gluck Jeremias.
Separately give to Arthur and his family and the children my respect.

1940/8/28 Grandfather Samuel Schwartz to us (Book 4, 314-315)

Lelesz 1940 August 28

My dear grandchildren, who are loved from the heart.
I'm letting you know that I got that dear letter from you, which made me very happy and...today is the big fast [should be "böjt"] which you should also keep ["amit ti is tarjatok"], so I write [an answer] to you so I can put it in Father's name ["tehat irok nekted valaszt hogy az apa neveben be tudjam tenni"], but I note, that I can't write anything good to you, because my heart hurts so much. First, my two dear sons are soldiers [for the past] three months in Pátoka and Lajos works in the worker squad. It's hard to find a job. Lajos wasn't home not even once. Marton is home on Saturday and he will come to see us too. You can imagine how a business goes, if the boss is not at home. The Jews in Lelesz are almost conquered, the stores are closed. I am myself closed, because nobody comes. I am like a dog, my money is not enough. I was counting that I will receive a debt and there will be enough to live by. But I was afraid, because they ridicule people, because we are being looked down on. And from now on there is a new law announced, that we have to keep the stores open on Saturday too. And in Lelesz there are 4 Christian ["kereszteny"] shopkeepers. My son's store is also becoming weak ["megyéngul"], because these [products] are not available, and I also live on my son's shoulder. He keeps us. Grandmother was in bed for 3 weeks and Aunt Etel sent everything and even now she is sending everything we need, because I can't bear the cost. My son also helps us with whatever we need at the house. With money, with challah bread. But now they are asking from me 150 pengo. I give and nothing with nothing ["níncsrá semmi"] nothing it's all the good God could help me. What will happen to me I can't see, although my heart can take the great pain when I have you in front of my eyes, because thank God, you are in a good place. I wish I could be there with you. So I wrote everything to you. You can hope with God's help. The good God will help. Grandmother already feels better, but she is weak. I am standing, but on weak legs. Yet my heart is beating. What will happen to me in my old age, I don't know. How will I move here? I can't write any other news. I write the temple collapsed and it's closed down. At the Feiereizen's there is a temple, but the bath-house is closed down. The Jews in Lelesz have become very poor ["szegenyedve"] all without a profession ["mind par nelkul"] soon ["mahonap] they will be without their bread...
I will close my letter with this, you will feel everything from this, because it's not allowed to write about everything. I will stay faithful and loving from the heart, your grandfather and your grandmother, who have you on their mind in every minute, but I will not see you ["De latni rem fogjak benneteket"]. I kiss you countless times. I'm sending my regards, give them to Uncle Jónász and to his family, countless times.

[In Hebrew] Joseph Shemaya Schwartz from Lelesz
Schvartz Samuel, Lelesz

If you see my cousin Luisz Berger, in Brooklyn, write to me. Dr. Joszef Berge, the father-in-law of his brother, is in New York. Looking forward to reading something from you. We got your pictures and it adds to my happiness. I talk to you, but you don't answer. I wish good health to all of you,
Your grandfather

1940/9/15 Irving to Jeremias First English Letter (Book 5, 69)

175 1/2 W.2 ND Ave.
Columbus, Ohio
Sep. 15, 1940

Page 142

Dear Father,

I am glad to hear you are well. Since I have been in this country, I've been very happy. It wound be fine if you were here, also you must come over as soon as possible. One week ago, I started school at the Everet Junior High School and I am going every day. How is Louis and all of the family? You must write to me soon and give me the news. I wish you good health. Your Son, Irving

1940/9/23 Samuel and Haia Schwartz (grandparents) to us (Book 4, 152-155)

Lelesz 1940 September 23rd [Writing in Yiddish is illegible - appears to contain Lelesz, where the letter was written]

From my heart to my loving grandchildren. I just want you to know that on the 23rd of this month I received your letter which I was very happy to read. I received your gift also, which I did not expect. My dearest children I thank you very much, [both] me and your grandmother. It came in time and we appreciate it. Here everything is so expensive and we cannot even get it. This time I'm going to write to you that, thank God, my two sons just came home. Our heartaches got a little better. 4 months they were doing hard labor on the land.

Also your brother Lajos was inducted 2 weeks ago already and Miksa Shon was with him. We did not get any mail from them. We don't know where they are. This is very difficult for your father because he's now all by himself and he can't take care of the farm. Also, the most important thing is he does not have any money to get someone to help him at home to bring the wagon to bring the straw in from the farm. It is already 3 months. He cannot take care of it. What they will need for himself they won't have and he cannot buy it either. Your letter and with mine I will send to your father because all week I haven't seen him only on Saturday. I am mailing this letter with my son Lajos. I want to thank you again for your gift that you sent to me. Wishing you all the best good health. And your grandmother thank goodness is feeling better, but she's not very strong. She is 84 years old, therefore thank goodness, I'm well. I am sending my best wishes to all of you and kisses. Also give my best wishes to your Uncle Jónász and the family. I remain with the best wishes as your loving forever, grandfather and grandmother.

Uncle Lajos and family are sending you the best until next time.
Why doesn't Dezső write to us? Is he well–or does he not have the job.
Your grandfather, Schwarz Samuel, Lelesz

[On the back:]

My dear children,
Your wish is that you would like Grandma to write, but she doesn't like it because her hands are shaking when you don't sit here by me when I am writing. Kisses to all of you. Schvartz Hanika

1940/9/25 Lajos Schwartz to Us (Book 4, 275-276)

Dear children, I'm letting you know, that thank God this past week I arrived home together with Uncle Marton, everything should just be good. It has been a very long time, but I hope that it will be ok. How are you? Did you get used to being there? Dezső, how is he? I'm already getting out of the habit of the world, I'm not in the mood for anything, I just stay at the house. I can't write anything special, since you know better than we do. There is nothing else, only patience. Grandfather got a letter from you already and he was very happy. I have nothing special to write about. I kiss all of you with love, your uncle Lajos
I'll leave some space for grandfather,
Lelesz 1940 September 25
Especially your Aunt sends greetings. The previous letter didn't come. Did you get your Aunt's letter?

1940/10/4 Bertha to Hermine and us (Book 5, 217-219)

New York

Dear Hermine and all my dearests!

I'm not waiting for your answer because any minute your aunt will bring the package. Probably the address was wrong. I haven't heard of the Fürst family, but I'm finally writing these few lines about it to you. It should be off your list, so at least you will be able to write home that when the package is here you could tell them I tasted the pogácsa cookies. [It's all because] Fürst didn't bring the box down until then, but I said that it would have been good for a week. In the past it was very good like it was back there. Last night I spoke to my husband because everything was sitting with me for a week [and] I couldn't leave from home. I was worried. In the evening, since I wasn't able to leave the apartment until late I stayed in bed. This way we were visiting our relatives, Jenny Frey, for dinner. After that we visited our Uncle Gold. He especially likes to talk to my husband. Oh it was very late by the time we came home. Today is Sunday and my husband made breakfast for us and this way I was able to stay in bed longer. Don't say or tell anyone how lazy I am. Anyway this is the way it is. I know why. I'm telling it to you only. I will tell you a secret. I do not have anyone to write to and I do not have much to write. Sometimes it feels good to write silly things even for the dear relatives to read. I showed your writing to them and your wishes and kisses. Jennie will write to you. Maybe I wrote enough. All the best wishes and kisses to all of you. Bertha and Mannie

Also give our best wishes to the relations with all our love Best wishes
The above

1940/10/15 Father and Etelka to us (Book 4, 166)

Bodrogmező 1940 X / 15
From my heart. All my love my dearest children. I patiently waited so long for your letters [and] finally received it. I was very happy to read that thank goodness you all are okay. We also are well, and hope you will keep well in the future, too. You sent this letter to Leles. I was told they sent you an answer. They received it on Yom Kippur. My son Lajos was inducted 1½ months ago. He serves in the army near Patak. He came home for 2 days for Yom Kippur. It's been 3 weeks since I brought the horse and the wagon home. Today we have the hearing against Julis Simon our neighbor for hundred 135 pengo. I gave it to him legally and he denied that. I received the gift you sent me. Thank you very much. I still did not sell the tobacco building. The grain is 74 kilo bag should have been 100 ki–corn they are holding and they just took the sunflowers in. Uncle Albert bacsi did not hear from Naci [Nathan Frey]. He wrote to them that he just got married. Also our cousin Bertha mentioned that he got married. I am wishing you my dearest children a happy and healthy New Year. And good luck. I received a card from Szatmar in which they mentioned they received a letter 6 weeks ago from you. My dear Mariska, your grandmother would like to have the picture that I have here from you. We have a small one that we can enlarge. I am sending my best wishes to you all and many kisses with our love your loving father who never forgot you. Gluck Jeremias.

[On the back]
[from Etelka]
You should see my little Zoli. He is very beautiful. He always calls for Zajde. If you could see him you would eat him up. He's very sweet and very beautiful. We try to show them and tell them about you. This is our entire conversation because that is all we have. No other interesting news. I will stop here and there is no more room to write. Wishing you all the best, a happy and healthy new year and many kisses to all of you. And our dear God save us from this terrible life without hope. Remain. Many kisses to all of you. Your sister-in-law, Etelka

Lajos did not have the time to write to you at this time. He is also wishing all of you the best and a happy new year. Lajos was on his way before he was enlisted.

1940/10/15 Undated Etelka to us (Book 4, 162) 1st page only

Dear Herminka,
We previously wrote this letter to you, but on thicker paper. As you see it would cost us too much money to mail it. Therefore we have to rewrite it on a thinner paper that Uncle Marton sent to us. Now I will send it back to him to mail it out to you all. We will write only a short note to be sure we will be able to mail it out. Here we are very busy at this time. About ourselves, your father and I are not happy, we are very upset. On September 8, my dearest husband Lajos was unexpectedly taken to Patak. At the same time they [the men] were called in all at once from all the other places. No one remained at home. They sent Miksa [Schon] home because he just had surgery. I'm very bitter. Later Lajos came back, but this was only for a couple

days. I am praying to God at least he should be able to come home even for one hour [so] we could see him for even a short time. Until now he had a better arrangement. I hope from now on he will at least be in the same place so he could come home for an hour which would make me happy. I hope he will find out how long he would have to stay there. Our Uncle Lajos and Uncle Marton just came back after serving 3½ months. So we imagined that our situation would be difficult. There is no one to help our dearest father. He's working very hard. He has only Gypsies [to help]. You have to pay them at once and we do not have money even to pay them. At this time our Uncle Lajos lent us the money and before that Uncle Lajzer bacsi gave us to pay for the workers. Lajos needed money before he left because he has to get his food every day. He lives on only bread and he gets some fruit. He tries to keep kosher so it makes it very difficult. We are sending him packages. Uncle Marton sent him packages twice already. I have so much more to write to you, but I have no patience to sit down and write. For now I'm working very hard from early morning until the late hours in the evening. By the time comes I'm so tired I can hardly move [and] I can't write. I'm sending you only half of the letter I wrote previously because at this time I do not have the time to rewrite it and the children wanted to write. Thank goodness we are well. Gyusi and Mityu got permission to get shoes only and some clothes. It's very, very cold. [missing next page]

1940/10/16 Undated Uncle Marton to us (Book 4, 163-164)

[dated by the paper and Marton mentioning that he sent thin paper to Jeremias, and he's writing on Erev Sukkot]

My nieces and nephews,

I was in the army for 4 months. I just came home healthy. These letters I wrote a week ago. I could not mail it because I wrote it on a different, thicker paper. Now I bought a thinner paper for 3.60 pengos and sent it to your father to also rewrite the letter. It is much cheaper to mail it. My brother Lajos came home 3 days ago. He was serving in the region where I was. I also met relatives. My main job was like in Mitzrayim [Hebrew = Egypt]. 'Avodah kasha' [Hebrew = Hard labor]. Uncle [Bacsi, maybe referring to Uncle Lajos] was there, too. I heard Uncle Jónász and Roth bacsi become friends again. Deutsch bacsi is very ill and will not live long. I'm waiting to hear from them. For Rosh HaShana grandfather and grandmother were here. Thank God they are well. Now I would like to hear from you all. I would like to know everything. What are you doing? Working hard? And how much are you getting as wages. Did you meet anyone nice to get married? I hope you're very happy. I'm wishing it to you all. Did you go to the Temple to say Yizkor? Thank goodness we are otherwise fine. I hope you are well also. At this time I do not have much time to write because it is Erev Sukkot. I was cutting some wood in Patak. They charged 20 fillert to cut a hundred pieces. In one day here I am make 5 Pengo. I would not give it to them because I am very angry at them. I am wishing you a better and happier year to all of you and for all of us. G'mar chatima tova. [Hebrew - May you be signed and sealed in the Book of Life].

Please give Uncle Jónász our best wishes, and to Arthur and his family, and I wish them also a G'mar chatima tova. Regards to all the acquaintances. Help us as soon as possible. Many kisses to you all and love. Marton.

[On the back] Magda and all the other children and my wife Etelka are also sending you many kisses. They do not have the time to write today. Marton.

1940/10/27 Bertha to Hermine (Book 5, 211-212)

New York
Oct 27 / 40
Dear Hermine!
I will try to make this answer happy for you. I hope that Ignatz [Ignác] didn't neglect school because he will be a good and smart man, you'll see. We are waiting for my husband's niece before Yom Kippur. I just received a letter from home this week three months [after it was sent]. You can imagine my life, how worried I am living through that news. They took all the men in the military, and my dearest father has all the trouble and everything to take care of. I'm mailing you a postcard with the name of the person [Israel Zsupnik] I used to send $20 to my father the day before the holiday [yontov]. He will get there 150 dollars [note: she probably meant pengos]. It will be there sooner, his wife is at home. The man told me the money that he gets here that he will keep it here and his wife will take care of it like a business. When I write home I don't mention anything about this. Therefore his wife will be able to do it, otherwise his wife will be in big trouble.

If you want I can mail you how so you can mail your father also. I will contact this man again and will help you. Also, I do not write you so frequently [because] this takes time. My husband and I do not feel well very often. I don't even bother with anything for a couple of days. I only move around a little. Therefore my husband, like my sickness has sciatica. The doctors cannot find the problem. My poor husband walks with a cane and wears a belt or a corset. Now I live like this, don't take it to heart. 50 years later we don't get it back. Dear Maria doesn't feel well. When I will be able to do it, I will write letters to our relations. God gives us strength and helps us in every step. I hope dear Arthur is okay. I'm asking you, please write what the doctors are saying. Hope the situation will get better. I'm so hopeless and I cannot even offer my help to you. If my health would be better I would be able to help you. As you know, as the saying goes "The poor person has a good heart." You don't have to believe it. I know it's easier to say than to do it. Wishing you the fastest recovery dear Maria and the new year and all of you with God's help you will meet a nice young man to get married with and he will take care of you. Wishing you all the best to all of you. With love, Bertha and Mannie

1940/10/28 Amster Kirtz Co. Recommendation - Dave (Book 21, 276)

October 28, 1940

To whom it may concern:
This will serve to advise you that David Gluck was in the employ of this company for 18 months, resigning in April, 1940. Mr. Gluck was an energetic worker and performed his duties honestly and well.

The Amster-Kirtz Co.
M.J. Lieberman, Mgr.

1940/11/4 Louis Schwartz to Hermine and Marie (Book 17, 165-167)

Dear Herminka and Mariska!
I am just responding to your letters. I thought that we will go to visit you on Saturday night because one of our acquaintances was planning on going to a gathering in Columbus, but the plan fell through. I think I already wrote this in my last letter, that Jónász bacsi was visiting and he must have told you also. He praised you a lot. It looks like he likes you a lot. I got a letter from home last week. They still threshed for the season and my father had it done temporarily by a Christian who has the business under his name, and for which he got 40% for it. My father is running it continuously and he [my father] is like an employee for him [the Christian], but just as a formality. Otherwise there is no news by me. I am living my usual, uneventful life. I work and I study. I'm curious what kind of conscription number he got? Mine and my brother's are a very high number, 6500-. And how are you? What do you do? You Mariska, why did you not write? Do you work a lot? What do they write from home? Do you meet with acquaintances? What do the boys do? Do you correspond with Helen Perl? What does she write? I will close my lines and I'm waiting for your responses as soon as possible. Kisses for everybody. Lajos

1940/12/3 Father to us (Book 4, 380)

Bodrogmező 1940 XII/3
My dear children, who I love from the heart, I happily read your letter, the one that I could hardly wait for. Thank God, you are well. We are, thank God, well too. I wish we hear only good things about each other. My son Lajos was at home on this Sunday for one day. When is it going to be over, only God knows. You can imagine, my dear children, what a good life I have. My sorrow is that I was left alone here. And I don't know what to think, why my son Dezső has not written a few lines. Your Grandparents, Uncle Lajos and Uncle Marton are well and send their regards and Uncle Lajzer does, too. On October 15th there was a vote at the first hearing and it is an approval/confirmation order. The lawyer introduced it to the magistrate and the magistrate gave them 8 days to agree with me, and give everything out what is contributed, because he has no right to take my crop/harvest away, [just] because the lot/land is approved by him. So it was his turn. His father and Julis started that they brought it to their farm because the economic supervisor gave him the advice and Mr. Gluck knows about that also. The lawyer responded to him in front of the magistrate, that of course, you wanted to deceive and your luck was that you did not frighten Mr. Gluck, from your own shadow. Julis answered that we didn't pay them either. The lawyer responded that a deposit will go out and he will bring that.

Then he came before the hearing, like this, and I agreed with him for 175 kala [a measure] of wheat and 20 pengo for the hay. The lawyer's fee was 32 Pengo. He paid all these.

The bastard wanted to deceive me. If I wasn't careful enough, he would have already destroyed me. The economic supervisor conspired and thought that it is his time now, because the Jew has no rights. So if he frightens me he would get half of the money back. He would have laughed in a big way, I think, like I wrote in that previous letter, that we came home at 9 o'clock from Helmec. He is wrong, I realized that at night, they can't deal with a legal case like that. I was not frightened from it and everything is fine, thank God. Hersmendel my son, you ask what kind of harvest we got from the spring. The house was filled with the maritime [the abundant harvest] and [we harvested] 12 wagons of carrots. There were 15 wagons of potatoes. I sowed 14 bushels of wheat. I had to hire a day laborer, but the sunflower was not ready. The day laborer cost only 200 Pengo. I worked with Gypsies. The sunflower is 22 1/2 P[engo] tubular. The maritime [abundant harvest] would be worth 10P[engo] 1m. [Regarding] this.....I sold it for this expense, but I did not pay the tax. I wouldn't have paid compensation if the maritime [abundant harvest] would have dried up. It's reassuring to sell it already. I already wrote enough about this to you. It's been a week since I got the New Year greetings from Uncle Jónász. I thank him and I send my regards to him and his entire family, his dear son and his family, and separately to all of you. My dear children, just write to me if you can, so we can hear something good.

Your forever faithful father, Gluck Jeremias

I got your 1 dollar.

1940/12/3 Undated Etelka to Hermine and Marie (Book 4, 381-382)

[dated by Lajos being home for one day on Sunday]

Dear Herminka and Mariska!

I'm sorry that I write so rarely, but it's not my fault. After Yom Kippur we sent a letter to you and we were waiting for the response, but your letter was late for a long time, so we did not write, because we did not get a response. I can't write much about ourselves, only that it's been 3 months of tremendous troubles [nagy córesz = great tsuris]. We don't know how long will it take until Lajos will be dismissed from the military, but we will only know that when it will happen. This week on Sunday Lajos was at home for a day off. But it passed very quickly, so our happiness did not last for long. It's been already three months that he is not at home. But, if you could only see him, how good he looks. He changed to his advantage. What kind of people do you think he has been surrounded by there? There are big shots and all kinds of honorable people. He is eating Kosher. I send a package from home to him and money. What stress it gives me, but I must! Uncle Marton sent a little package to him also. His business goes the way he wants it and Uncle Lajos' also, but he did not send anything to Lajos yet. He [Uncle Lajos] is building his house. They took the barn apart and he wants to buy the other one also. I did not get welfare yet because the notary was stingy to me, but I will wait it out, because it comes in handy. I would dress the kids from that. The kids would like to write to all of you also, but I don't want them to write on this thin paper because they will mess it up. Unfortunately, they can't learn Hebrew because it is not allowed. They will take them to the military. I would say we would not complain, if Lajos would have been home, but he had to leave in the best season and what we could have spent [money] on clothing, [instead] had to spend it on the labor. If I get the welfare, then I will buy a dark blue coat for Lena [Lenke]. I am writing instead of Emil, that the Levente is here at home in the community building. They fixed up the apartment nicely and furnished it. So in other words, we have gendarme in the long hall. Our neighbor, Regina opened a pub, only we don't have a head for that. There is no other news. In our town, everybody is busy with their own situation. It got very hard for everyone. Little Janos just joined the army. About the kids, I can only write, that thank God they are developing nicely and they look good, They mention you a lot when I bake pumpkin. I have above 100 dkg in the garden, which substitutes many things for us. Do you eat pumpkin there? Dad is now beating the boredom with a little memory. If you could see my little superhero "umberufen" [Knock on wood; God forbid (saying to ward off the evil eye)] an angel, nice and an especially good kid [referring to Zoltan]. Gyuszi and Mityu are the same. They are big and they have the same overalls. They are nice together like that, only they make too much noise for Grandfather's [Yiddish - Zajdika] ears. Everything is expensive, 50 pengo a pair of boots, 8 pengo a half a sole, 7 pengo for a baby's. We did not even buy one. I have a little fat from last year. It's 5 pengo for one m. For a few weeks it's not available. After all this, you'll be the judge of everything, because I will not write, I ran out of paper.

[Vertically on the fold of the page] I would like to kiss all of you and the relatives, Etelka

1940/12/10 Undated Etelka, Lajos, Emil to Us (Book 4, 385-386)

[Dated by Lajos coming home from the army]

[from Etelka]

Dear Herminka and Mariska!

I would like to write a lot to you, but don't know what because I am very busy with the children. The wind is also very strong. Thank God, Lajos came home in good health and he looks good, but it was very hard to wait for his homecoming. I'm very embarrassed that my writing is so sloppy, but my hands are so tired from a lot of work. There is a lot of laundry to do weekly. We are struggling to be ok somehow, but I wish we would struggle for a good reason and they would leave the people in peace. But when will we be able to live in peace? The children were very happy to [get] your letters also. I don't know any interesting news, because I don't go anywhere, I can't even go home. Thank God, we are healthy. Little Zoli is a very nice and a good kid. Gyuszi has become a big stray and it looks good on him. Mityuka is the best kid. He also would like to write to you. We all kiss all of you and Arthur (and others). Etelka. Kisses to you, Mityuka.

[from Lajos]

My beloved siblings, I am letting you know, that thank God, I'm well, and I hope I will hear the same back from you, too. You are always on my mind. You can imagine, if you would be here! I wasn't the only one who had you on my mind, but many others as well. During my billeting [in the Army] the days were passing with the problems from home. But finally that day came also. I met with Lajos Hirskovits. He was wondering about you and about many other things. I am so anxious that I'm not able to write. I kiss Uncle Jónász and his son and you countless times. Lajos

[from Emil]

Dear Aunt and Uncle,

I kiss all of you also. I don't know any news. We use oil with wood to make the fire, not only us, but half of the town. The Levente practice here. Kisses to dear Uncle Jónász and dear Uncle Arthur and Dezső also and you. Your little brother Emil

1940/12/25 Father to Us (Book 4, 387-388)

Bodrogmező 1940 XII / 25

My loved, dear, faithful children. I got your awaited letter that I could hardly wait for, and I read it with great happiness. Thank God I am in good health, which you don't lack either. We are all, thank God in good health. My son Lajos, came home this month on the 10th and he got released from his job. Three weeks ago I sent an airmail letter to you and I have already written everything about me. I hope you got the letter. Everything is fine with him [Julis Simon]. The land that Schön sold had to be given back, and the money returned. The land shall return to dream, and the land shall be desolate. Jozsi Lefkovics is not allowed to sow anymore. I did not sell the barn yet. There is no serious buyer yet. Everything is very expensive, everybody who could, supplied themselves. You remember that also, whoever had the money for it they bought it. Now a pair of boots is 50 pengo, for a pair of boots that was 35 pengo. That is true for all merchandise. God should just help you all to have health and luck and for us too, that we could only write about good and happy things to each other. You my sons are there [Yiddish - zind dort], otherwise everything is the same. [Yiddish above - איז ארבייטסלאזער ???? = ???? is unemployed] Grandfather and grandmother are healthy. They send their regards to all of you. Uncle Lajos is getting ready to write to you also. The house is under construction. The walls are walled up and the roof is on the top already. They will continue the construction in the spring. He planned it well. He will build a room for grandfather also. They will live with him, if there will be someone to sell the house to. In my past letter I already wrote that you sent a present to grandfather and me and luckily I received the last one and the present one. The letter came, it was censored. My dear children, we blame each other that we don't get letters. The letters don't come, that is what cheats us. You just write more often, but everyone [should] write a few lines and you can prepare that in advance. No need for any excuse. My dear children, you would not know it, [but] at that time I would not write to the National Bank. I didn't write because I wasn't in favor of it anymore. My dear children, I wish you much luck, good health, and happiness. I respect you and kiss you one by one, all of you. Your loving, faithful father, who will never forget. Gluck Jeremias.

My dear loved brother Jónász and dear sister-in-law Helen,

I am letting you know, that thank God I'm well and that my son Lajos came home. I hope that my lines will find you in good health also. I kiss you my dear brother Jónász and dear sister-in-law and dear Arthur and his family and one by one you my dear brother.

I will stay with respect, your little brother Gluck Jeremias

1940/12/25 Undated Etelka to Hermine and Marie page 1 (Book 4, 390)

[dated by synagogue in Lelesz condemned, Lajos being nervous, Janos Pandi will marry Malvin, harsh winter]

Dear Herminka and Mariska!
I don't know what to write about to you because there is nothing special in our town that would interest you. Dear Hermine, we gladly read that you changed your place. At least you work at a sweet place now! Yesterday I was in Leles, there is no news there, either. Unfortunately the Jewish synagogue needed to be taken down by the magistrate's order because it was in a dangerous condition. There is no good news anywhere, life is very hard here. Everything is very expensive. I still did not [prepare a] stuffed goose yet. We bought two of them. It was 8 pengo a piece and three ducks for 4 pengo a piece, but now it's not available and it's like that with everything. I already wrote to you that Janos Pandi was engaged to Ilón Simon, but the party is over and now he will have a match with Malvin. The children, thank God, are in good health. Little Zoli is very precious. Young Gyuszi is a big stray/urchin. They are doing Levente activities in front of the commune now. This way they can learn it too. Now and then we have a very nice tea party.

1940/12/25 Undated Etelka and Lajos to us page 2 (Book 5, 136)

[dated by matching the paper to the previous letter]
[Etelka continues from previous letter/page]
Life is still a little bit difficult. I would have been waiting with more patience if the products would be here as in your place. It is very difficult to shop here. Here a shirt cost 3.60 pengos and you can't even buy it. You can't get it. Uncle Lajos bacsi from Lelesz was here. We gave them tea and [some type of] cake. He asked for the recipe to give it to his wife, Etel neni because it looks like they will refer to it.
I will write also a little [something] funny from Lelesz. Moricne Lefkovics and Dezsőne Veisz will be baptized. The same thing would have happened to Boriska Adler and Tuci Lefkovics if they weren't prevented. I'm writing this above with just one purpose, to fill in the paper so that it wouldn't go out blank. Kisses to all of you and the relations, Etelka

My dearest brothers and sisters,
We are well and I hope to hear from you the same. There is nothing new. I'm nervous I could hardly write these few lines. Your brother, Lajos.

One load of wood costs 60 Pengo. The winter is harsh and the sleigh can be used.

1940/12/30 Israel Zsupnik to Bertha (Book 1, 38-39)

Ms. Weingarten, very respectfully
Hereby letting you know that I got the $10, in other words a ten dollar check. And based on that I will transfer 75 pengo to Mr. Jeremias Gluck in Bodrog Mezo.
With all the respect, Israel Zsupnik

1941/1/1 Bertha to Hermine (Book 5, 215-216)

New York
January 1, 1941
Dear Hermine!
I hope you forgive me because I let you wait for my answer. Before the new year I was very busy. Besides that the money you all sent to your dear father, he received it. I will ask you one thing. Don't mention, don't talk about anything to your father how you mailed it to him because that person might be in big trouble. Just a week after sending the money, write that someone will receive ten dollars for that $15, that's all it takes, but don't mention how and from what city. Knowing will make you feel good. How is Maria? Does she feel better? Wishing her a fast recovery. Wishing all of you all the best in the new year.
How are the boys? How is Dezső coming along today? I hope so. My dearests, in my view, a woman can benefit from a better job, even if she earns less. I would suggest a woman have a laundry. It wouldn't be so hard, and you still get paid even if you aren't there, [and] there's a lot of money in that. If anyone has this

profession as a woman, I don't know. Every day would be worth it if a girl had such a profession. You only earn a little money for anything, but it would be better than no house or no sugar [Yiddish - czùkerlit rokol]. We had a guest from Pittsburgh, the granddaughter of Uncle Marton, who spent a week with us. Rai's [Regina's] daughter. She's very nice and beautiful. It is very boring without her because she just left today to go home. I am asking you not to aggravate yourselves. You think you bother me too much. It makes me very happy to hear from all of you. The only thing I would like to hear is the best news about you [and I] would be happy. Hoping dear Maria [that] you will forgive me that I didn't answer you separately. I have to write more letters tonight. Good luck in the new year. All the best, love, Bertha and Mannie

1941/1 Undated Frey-Yenken Paint letterhead Irving Biography (Book 3, 433)

[Dated by the following letter 1941/1 Undated Hermine, Marie, Herman, Ignac to Mr. Averria (Book 5, 267-268) - draft. It seems like an appropriate place to put this one. It can't be after January 1942 because he doesn't mention Herman being inducted. It also can't be in 1940 because Irving just starts school in September 1940]

Frey-Yenkin Paint Company

I would like to recount in detail my trip to Amerika [sic]. This was my greatest desire. I will tell you what caused all of our worries in making our trip to Amerika [sic]. In 1938, one of my older brothers had a great desire to make a trip to the United States of Amerika [sic]. At that time our country was Czechoslovakia. In a short time his papers were ready so he started to the land of freedom. When he came to Amerika [sic], the first thing was to ask for papers from the relatives, to send to us, so that we also might come. And so my uncle sent affidavits for my two sisters, one brother and me. As soon as the affidavits arrived in Prague, the cuncil [sic] wrote to us to complete the passports. We had everything ready to make the trip, when unfortunately the Czechoslovak, German and Poland war broke out. Hungary took over a part from Czechoslovakia, where we were living. Then we had to wait another year until we could come to the United States of Amerika. We came from Budapest through Yugoslavia into Italy and I was in Rome and from there I went to Napoli and I was there 5 days and then we sat on an Italian boat. After all the worries we arrived to Amerika. It took eleven days for our boat to cross the ocean. We could come only by way of Italia. If we could have come through France, we would have been here in five or six days. They stopped [at] more islands, so I had an opportunity to look at Palermo, Gibraltar and the Lisbon islands. In February 22, which is Washington's birthday we landed in New York. In New York our cousins were waiting for us. We had a very good time with our relatives. We were in New York three days, and then we came to Columbus, Ohio. We were happy to see our uncle and cousin and other relatives. Now, I can not thank God enough to come safely, to a land of freedom. Amerika means a land of freedom. There are no diktators [sic] nor any monarchs in this land. Of course, freedom does not mean of following any temptation, but freedom of resisting temptation. There is one very important freedom, too. This is religious liberty. Amerika grants all religion the right to practice here. After when Hungary took over that part, then I had to be in the army and to do what they told us. If we did not do, then they lock us up. And so we had to watch what we were saying. Our schools were very different. Our teachers did not explain like here in that schools. Only they came in for a half an hour to give us our work to be known the next day. There [it] was very hard to become anything, because it took 5 years longer to learn a profession. Now, I want to learn the English language and I want to be a good citizen. I also want to get my citizen papers. Irving Gluck

1941/1 Undated Hermine, Marie, Herman, Ignac to Mr. Averria (Book 5, 267-268) - draft

Columbus, Ohio

Dear Mr. Averria:-
It is almost a year since our safe arrival in America and we have never stopped talking about you and your great kindness to us on the boat coming over. I have long wanted to express my thanks in a material way and have been waiting until I could send you some money in appreciation - but I have been ill practically this whole time, my headaches continue and I have been under a doctor's care. I only hope that I will soon be well so that I can go to work. My sister is out of work also but my brothers have jobs. We all live together of course and are happy to be in this great country. I hope you and your family are well and will write to you again when we are "on our feet" which we hope will be soon. In the meantime I can send you nothing but our sincerest thanks and best wishes from all of us. May God bless you and yours with health and

happiness and everything that is good. Gratefully yours, Maria Gluck, Hermine Gluck, Herman Gluck, Ignatz Gluck

1941/1/9 Louis Schwartz to Hermine and Marie (Book 17, 139-140)

Dear Herminka and Mariska!

Forgive me that I am responding so late to your precious letter. Now, if I remember well, Mariska did not write, but as you know before Christmas and the New Year we were very busy. Usually after 9 at night we are closed, when I am tired and don't want to write. But this, like everything else, has passed. This way I'll be in a hurry to write, although I can't write anything particular. I spent the holidays at home pretty normal. We were going to go to Cleveland with a group, but we changed our mind. And how did you spend it? We got a letter from home last week. Gizi was wondering about you and is sending her greetings to all of you. Unfortunately they don't write anything good about the situation, moreover if there is anything then the Jews' situation is getting even worse there. How long only God knows. And when did you get a letter? What do they write? Do you still correspond with Helen Perl? Write about everything in detail, and everything about all of you. How are you? Also, about Dezső! Also, how are you with English? Do you study diligently? Now I will finish my lines because I don't want to wear everyone [out]. Waiting for your response as soon as possible. Lajos

1941/2 Louis Schwartz to Hermine and Marie (Book 17, 160)

[Undated - probably early 1941 since they still received mail from Europe]

Dear Herminka and Mariska!

I got your dear letter and pictures and I am trying to respond to it in a hurry, although I can't write any news to you. Maybe one thing is that on Sunday, Regine Feuereisen from Lelesz with her brother, who is a groom with his bride, were here. He told me to give his best to you. We talked a lot about you. I got a letter from home three weeks ago. They don't write any news. When did you get a letter from home? Last week I got a letter from Irene Schwartz. She wrote that she got married in June with an Austrian boy, who she speaks with in German, that is, in Yiddish, because he does not know English. I am moving slowly, but surely with English. I hope you are as well. Otherwise, how are you? Do you work hard? Write about everything and about all of you. I kiss you, Lajos.

Dear Dezső, I read your very short letter. You must be very busy. Inadvertently I did not have a lot of time to write, but I just found myself to do it.

1941/2/9 Helen Perl to Hermine (Book 5, 169-170)

Cleveland Ohio
February 9, 1941
Dear Hermine!

You can't even imagine how happy your letter made me. In a strange country in a different world at least with your letter we can hear from you. Not long ago in the past we took a breath of air here. If those people we loved could have been here it would be much easier. We would not have to worry about them. Then it would be much easier for us. Hermine, I think the way I remember that in the last letter I answered that somehow I didn't get it here. It's impossible for me to remember. It's a new year, but you seem to be reluctant to travel here. Before Christmas I was in Chicago to visit my girlfriend. I really enjoyed myself even though she is Christian. For us to go there and come back it is 24 hours round-trip. Columbus is much closer to us. You are closer but you don't come to visit us. We don't often hear from home. We received yesterday with happy tears because they are at home from the terrible ordeal the Jewish people have survived the nightmare. My dear [older] brother and [younger] brother are writing they are very weak when they came home. They brought with them heartaches and it's a scary time living it. They are very thankful for what you all have here and safe. Maybe you don't appreciate it. Even if you do, we will be here [and] we too will feel that way, but at this time we feel that it is impossible to accept. I think I have written enough for you about everything. Please you should write also more about everything. How are you all and your brothers too? Even though I don't know them, I'm interested. How are you getting along? I'm waiting for the previous letter. I'm closing at this time with love to your sister without knowing her and also to you, Helen

P.S. How is your brother David?

1941/2/19 Ilonka Török to Dezső (Book 4, 151)

Dear Dezső!
Forgive me if I bother you with my letter. Ever since you left to America we were waiting to hear from you or the girls. Ever since they left we were concerned. They left so fast I did not have the time [and] I was waiting to hear from you. Since then here we had some changes in our family. On May 18th, 1940 our father passed away. Dear Dezső, I am asking if you can write to their relations. Here it is very difficult to make a living at this time and the mother of the children is alone. You will understand what the situation is here. I am mailing you a relation to address.
Best wishes from Andras Török and Ilonka.
This is the address: Steve Rigó, Copper City, mich boy 162. This is Rigóne, my mother's brother. He doesn't have any children. The other one is Endij Geci Astabula Ohio 36, 25 They have children, a dear daughter! Dezső, if you get this letter, give them these few lines. I am waiting very much to hear from you as soon as possible. I am not angry. I do not want to keep you any longer. I remain with love, your friend, wishing you everything good, Ilonka Török
Andràs Török – Bodrog mező 1941 II/19

1941/3/10 Father to us (Book 3, 220-222, 225-226) missing last page

Bodrogmező, 1941 III / 10
My loving children from my heart. It was very difficult to wait for the letters that I've been waiting for, but it has arrived. I am very happy to read, thank God, that you're healthy and hope to hear it again. The letter from December came. It arrived to Uncle Marton in Helmec on Thursday. I received it on Saturday from Helmec [and] that evening and I have given it to Lajos bacsi. He was very happy to have his letter and sends his respect to you all. Grandfather and grandmother are healthy and send their respects. About ourselves, I can write to you that thank God we are well, and hope to hear from you the same. My dearest children, I am very surprised that my son Dezső got tired of writing so soon. It's enough that it takes three months to get a reply from each other and those few lines we should not hold from each other, because at least then one knows that he's alive! What is love to a father? If his children with a few lines would make him happy and when I finish reading it, I can cry by myself. We had a flood again for a week and it was all over. Uncle Abris [Albert] complained to me that since his son Naci [Nathan] got married, he [his son] and his daughter Zseni are not speaking to each other and went to live separately.
I did not sell the tobacco building as of now. My son, Hersmendel, you ask if we have a colt. I believe I wrote to you about it, it's yellow, he is big, and it's about 10 months old already.

[This letter may or may not belong here. It is from Özoreg Gerenyi, the neighbor, an old lady who wrote to Dezső, *after* family arrived to America. It was together with the above letter.]

My dear son Dezső.
Our good neighbor, we have been waiting for your letter to hear what you're going to write about my children. You did not write anything. We did not receive even a line from them. Please write at least one line about them. We hear that you're lucky. Let the good God be very glad in the goodness of all your work. Kisses to all of you and God be with you.

[On the back, written by our father] Özoreg Gerenyi wrote this

1941/3/10 Uncle Marton, Aunt Etelka, Magda to us (Book 4, 159)

Dearests, your father asked me to write a few lines to you with his letter. I also wanted to answer your letter. Last week we received a letter to my address to your father from you. The money you mailed them in my name we did not get it yet. I wish it would be here already. The situation here is very bad. Without money you can imagine how bad the situation is. Your father still did not sell the tobacco building. Your father owes me money that I lent him for the American trip for you all. Now I need that money, but I do not want him to sell below the price. If he sells it for the price they offer it would be just enough to cover the expenses. He would pay only the expenses, but he would not have a penny left for bread and clothing and food. The price of everything is rising day by day. Your father does not want to write and complain to you. I also feel an obligation to write to you about the situation we are all in. It is so bad. I could not wait. Someone has to tell you the truth. I will tell you a secret. All winter they did not have any heat in their home. Instead of wood they only had gorit [these are sunflower stems or corn stalks] to have some heat. It wasn't enough. That was all they had to keep their home warm. It was a very cold winter. I still lent them pengos a few times. I can't stand it either because I have to help your grandparents. They need everything. They need shoes also. As for my family, thank goodness we are well. We need help with the business. It's very bad. The government controls the shoes. I could not sell [any]. It's not allowed. 3 weeks went by as of now therefore I need money desperately also. I see how they are. I have no heart to ask for the money they owe me. I see they do not have even one penny. Therefore I do not ask them. I do not want him just to throw away the building for nothing. This is the reason I'm writing to you. I could write much more about the situation. I do not like to complain. I feel it is time to tell it as it is instead of just saying everything is okay or tell you a lie. I hope you will respond and will try to help. You must do everything to help your father and family. I understand you work hard for your money, but you must do it. It is very important. The situation is the same all over the country, prices are going up. Today money is very scarce and there is never enough because of the situation we are in. When [the fast of] Esther came, we were fasting. We did not have a choice The business is open but we were not allowed to sell it until further notice from the government. I hope it will get better soon. As of now, thank goodness, we have whatever we need. If you have money, then you can buy whatever you need–food–clothing. It's very expensive. If you do not have the money then you have nothing. Thank goodness, at least we are well. We are wishing you a kosher Passover and all the best. Kisses to all of you from all of us. Please write about everything, and what you are doing to make a living. Marton.

[Upside down first page - from Aunt Etel]
Dear Hencsu, there is no longer a good place to write.
Kisses to all of you. Etel

[On the side of the 2nd page - from Magda]
Many kisses, Magda.

1941/3/10 Undated Etelka to Hermine and Marie (Book 4, 165)

[Dated by Zoli's birthday, March 10, 1940]

Dear Hermine and Maria,
We were very happy to hear from you. [It's been] a long time. Also it was a long time since you heard from us. The reason is your father neglected the writing. His excuse was he does not know what to write. Therefore I waited for whenever my children let me sit down and write to you. My dearest son, the youngest Zoliknak [Zoltan] has his birthday. He is beautiful. He looks like an angel. If you would see him you would eat him, you could not stop loving him so much. He's an adorable child. Believe me, not because I'm his mother, he's so precious [and] such a good child I can't tell you enough about him. But now I want to write about the other children. Mityu has become a beautiful child. Lena grew a little. Gyuszi is the biggest fighter. Emil doesn't feel well. He has a cold because his shoes are very bad, torn and worn out. In cold weather we can't buy a new pair at this time. Father slept here this winter. Thank goodness now we have the spring coming. I cleaned up his room and he then went back to sleep in his room. Dear Hermine, you ask if we have any milk. It is very nice that you are thinking about us. You know, I do not wait, I asked the doctor when I was there. The children needed milk. Zoli received ½ a liter as a gift. Monthly from Török 15 liters and I bought 15 liters more. Now I can make butter or cheese. So as of January our house isn't empty. How long this situation will exist that we cannot tell. In January we received 3 kg sugar for the children and since then once a month. I am getting 1 pound from the doctor. I made him a goose liver that I made especially. I made it with fat only. I have a pound. For a goose you have to pay 10 pengo–the turkey has 18 db – eggs thank goodness we have. Today I planted the first planting. We did not have any heat. We could not get any wood to heat with. We use only gorit.. Lajos was not here therefore we were not able to get. And now God knows when we will be able to get. I wonder what the future situation will be. The situation here I could write much more but I cannot. In Agard my aunt passed away. You can imagine what is going on there. As of last week, Mr. Hoch slept here for 3 months. He married the Braun girl from Szürti [named] Molnar. Malvin got married to Janos Pandi. They had 200 guests at the wedding. It was sensational. They met at the time when Pandi was already engaged to Ilonka Simon, that was her wish. They separated by now. And now Ilonka became engaged to Jesy Benivel. I can say that despite the hatred against the Jewish people the neighbors in our area are very nice to us. We only dislike the Gerenyes, and there will never be anything with our dear Mrs. Schön because she only loves the peasants [morons]. Now she has to give over the Kosztyu lands [and] the lordship has already been taken away from her. Now they may be told to go after the rest [other lands]

as well. Let's leave it, they aren't worth filling out the paper with them. My passport is already here. Feigenbaum liked your picture very much, and sends greetings to you all. We are very glad that you can only write good things about yourself. Hermine [asks] why we didn't write about the children. They are adorable. They ask all the time about you and Mityu always asks me, mommy why hasn't Hermine written yet. I am asking you please write to Yucinak a few lines because now she's coming to milk our cows. Ilon is not coming anymore. She thought they will get everything you're sending us. She thought she will be the first one to get it. I cannot write about the situation we are in at this time. Many kisses to you all. Also give our best to Uncle Jónász. Love, Etelka.

1941/3/10 Undated Uncle Lajos Schwartz and Aunt Etelka Schwartz (Book 4, 389)

[Dated because he's indigent now, but not saying that he is in the new house yet. He moves in there by 7/1941 according to our grandfather. It could go anywhere between here and July]

[from Uncle Lajos]
Dear Hencsu and MaryamHendel,
I'm trying to write a couple of lines, so you may get it. I already wrote a letter and you did not get it. How are you? We are well, only the good God will help all of us. I'm indigent now, also with building the house, but I hope it's going to be alright. Dezső, Herman, Ignácz, How are you? I'm writing in a hurry, therefore I'm writing briefly. Dear girls and boys just write to us. Only attach 2-3 lines, I don't ask for more, because I'm lazy to write and [I'd like] to read something good...especially. Many times I can't write a response. Kisses to all of you. Uncle Lajos

[from Aunt Etel]
My darlings, accept my many, many kisses.
Your Aunt Etel

1941/4/7 Israel Zsupnik to Bertha (Book 1, 42-43)

Ms Weingarten with respect,
I am notifying you, that on March 28th I got the $10, ten dollars and I sent it over to Jeremias Gluck's address. Still, with respect
Israel Zsupnik

1941/4/15 Undated Etelka to Hermine and Marie (Book 3, 241)

[dated by Etelka's sister's death just before Passover. Shiva ending on Passover, so the letter is written sometime after. Trouble in Bacska on April 14 was the reason for the induction]

Dear Herminka and Mariska!
With great pains I'm going to write this letter to you. It is very difficult to write because of the unfortunate situation that has happened to us. Our dear sister Olga left the living on April 7. I know you'll be surprised, but unfortunately, that's the way it is. I will write [about] all of it to you in detail. The last time she was with us was after the wheat thrashing. Her brother-in-law from Agard was inducted into the Army. She went to Regus and she spent the whole winter there. She sacrificed herself with her goodness. She returned home for Passover, and after five days, death robbed her from us. She was lying in bed with tuberculosis and she suffered. Regus was with her to the last minute and she died in her hand. All this happened within five days. She never complained that she was sick. I was there twice within the five days. And on the second Sunday, before Passover, she died at noon and without a sound in Mancie's hand. It was a terrible situation and no one should experience that. You could imagine our pain and what a big problem it caused us, because we were without a penny, we couldn't even see buying one onion. With all that czoresz [Yiddish - suffering] every problem stopped. There weren't any more things that were missing. If we were fortune tellers we would have been able to foresee it. Joszi was here before Passover evening as I was sitting [shiva] and on that evening before Passover, I got up. I was heart broken and sick with all the czoresz. This week Hermùs, along with many others from Lelesz was inducted. We are afraid that Lajos may also be called in. We cannot tolerate it. We do not have any reserves from what we have cultivated during the fall. The planting that was done in the Fall has been lost and it was too late to do anything. Now Lajos seeded with barley. Thank God that the winter is over. We heated the house with corn stalks, but the problem was we didn't have enough. I could write to you a lot about the czoresz, but I'm going to leave that. We have taken in as our child Hersu Zinger's son because Marcsa did not want to undertake it. It is very difficult for us, but a child cannot grow

up without learning. I have chickens, nice chickens. We plan to plant so we can gather vegetables from Saturday to Saturday. We still don't have any small fish. We buy milk for five pengo. Kisses to you all and relatives. Etelka

1941/4/15 Undated Father to Us (Book 4, 379)

[Dated by take apart barn for wood for Uncle Lajos to finish his house, maybe pay Török when the weather is warmer so before May]

My dear children,
I will write, that I did not write to Uncle Marton what is for him. If I don't sell the barn, I will take it apart. Uncle Lajos needs 100 more boards, beams and they need it for others as well, so I can give the money to him [Uncle Marton]. It is a big miracle that Török is waiting with great confidence [encouragement]. If the weather will warm up, I will do my best. There is no material for those looking for wood. Your father, respectfully, Gluck Jeremias

1941/4/18 Louis Schwartz to Hermine and Marie (Book 17, 86-88)

Youngstown 1941 IV /17

Dear Herminka and Mariska!
For a change, I'm the one who is unreliable with responding, but believe me before Passover we were so busy in the store. We worked normally until 9 at night and then arrived home tired and I did not really have patience to write. In the meantime we heard the news about Jónász bacsi's death. Also, I was in Pittsburg on Sunday to return a visit with the Klein boy from Szürte. You, Mariska probably remember to Linou's cousin [older male]. He is here in America for about 4 years. He promised he will come soon. I will go by car and I will go to you. If you go to Cleveland, then write before, just in case we go before. I got a letter about two weeks ago from home from Feri. He sent pictures from when he did compulsive labor with many Jewish boys. Also, we got a letter from our cousin [younger and female] in Pest. They are waiting for a call in from the consulate. She wrote that the ticket for the ship costs $600 now. And how are you?
I will close my lines, which I'm writing quickly because it is too late at night and I still want to write additional letters. Write about everything. Kisses to all of you! Lajos

1941/4/20 Undated Helen Perl to Hermine (Book 17, 294)

Cleveland 4/20
Dear Hermine and dear all of you!
I read your card with great embarrassment, but unfortunately we can't help it. We have to put up with the arrangement of fate. So, accept my condolences from my heart! And I hope to hear the best about all of you from now on! I got a letter from home and they are going through terrible days. I am well. I am working. The boring days are going slowly and home sickness is lying in my heart always, [but it is] better than in the first months. Please Herminke write a lot, you would not believe how good it feels to read your lines. I was in Detroit during Passover for a standing tour. In the same trip I visited my relatives. They are in a hurry to keep their promises and come whenever the time is favorable. Now I am closing my lines because the time is getting late and the alarm is on for early morning when I need to get up! Greetings to all of you, and to you I kiss you many times. Helen

P.S. Where are your dear brothers? Dezső?

1941/4/25 Bertha to Hermine (Book 17, 31-32)

New York
April 25/41
My dear Hermine!
Unfortunately, we have to hear the news about our dear uncle [Jónász] that he is gone. This is life for all of us first and foremost. At least he lived a nice [number of] years. How is dear Aunt Helen? I think it's the hardest for her, since she was with him night and day. Flora let me know. I hear that Marton bácsi's [Martin *Gluck*] daughter went to his funeral. I hope it will not alienate their kids with you. I don't know what to do

about the money because if they still did not get it, I'm afraid to suggest what kind of way would be the best. I did not get a letter from home for a long time. I can't even remember the [last] time.

Yes, I was with my cousin Fred and his family for Pesah. I had the seder at his home and 6 days with Fred and his family, no need to mention. We should talk about the days because as soon as someone can get together with his own kind, that feels good immediately. I can say that they have nice daughters in every respect. They are well raised and that could make one happier also. I hope you will have the opportunity to get to know them in the future. I'm writing a new response, but this should be only between you and me. I'm aware that Uncle Albert [Feuereisen] wrote to his son and his son sent money for him from a foreign country. I know it will make you happy.

...you know that, but let's leave this. About me, this week I was not in the best shape and it's been an hour since I woke up again. I got a cold so I had to stay in bed for a few days. I postponed my response. I hope my letter will find all of you in the best of health. Did you get together with the relatives since our late uncle died? Please write about yourself because I would like to know how it goes with you. I hope the best about all of you my dears!

Give my kisses to you and to the relatives! To you and Marcsa with love, Bertha and Mannie

1941/5/2 Jennie Gluck [Arthur's daughter] to Marie (Book 2, 250)

May 2, 1941
Dear Marie,
How are you? I will bring my doll to see you next time I come to see you.
Much love, Jennie

1941/5/11 Etelka and Children to us (Book 5, 139-142)

[from Lenka]
Dear Aunt Hencsu and Aunt Marcsa
I received the one ribbon and one handkerchief. It is very nice and I thank you. I am waiting for the rest. When I start going to school, I will write nicer. Kisses to my Uncle Dezső [Dave], and Uncle Hersmendu [Herman], and Uncle Ignác [Irving], and Aunt Hencsu [Hermine] and my aunt Marcsa [Maria]. Lena

[from Mityu]
Dear Aunt Hencsu [Hermine], I'm out of breath and I can't wait for the red boots. Mityuka and Gyuszika.

[from Etelka]
Dear Hermine and Marie, this time I'm also writing only briefly because I don't have patience like you do. Also, because so many people died and I have lost my patience and we have to live with the trouble. They do whatever they want to do to us. Can you imagine that that dirty Gyulit Szabo will not allow us to use our own land? He called the police and told the government agent that we will sell it for 600 pengos and later they can just take it away. Julis [Simon] was arguing that the law is that we have to measure half of the harvest and that we should not bring it in to us because whatever we will bring from the other half [his half] he will make big trouble for us. After this you can imagine I don't want to see him because if I do I'll tell him something about how I feel about that problem he caused. It is better these days to just keep quiet and not say anything. Until now I would not believe in panicking, but now I believe it because ever since that day I don't feel like living here anymore. How they make you feel, even with us. This sharing [of businesses] is very bad. What other people go through I can't even write about. Also we can't work on Uncle Jòzsi's land because they took it away. I don't know what to write you because it makes me very sick. My heart aches. I'm very afraid thinking of what will be next. As of now we didn't do anything. We didn't cut the wheat and the straw is all still outside on the farm, unharvested. We are together with Lajos Török. Yesterday it was Tisha b'Av. Marcsa was here. It looks like our life is going back to the old Tisha b'Av. Marcsa is very sad and upset about our life as we see it. She's afraid, like I am, because her husband is far from home, like mine. Again they started to gather the names, it is a long list. On Saturday Father bought ready-made challah and regular bread. It was lucky he was able to get it. We gave your letter to Marcsa Diak. She told me she received one of your old letters this week. I can write you this much, I do not want you to waste your time greeting or giving your best regards to these girls because they do not deserve it. Behind your back they do not like any Jews. Even the best change, all of them have hatred and your best friend is ready to kill.

So the properties, whatever a Jew has, they are able to get it for nothing, even from their own friends. They are dogs and dogs eat each other. Since the spring Lajos Török comes to our home and garden all the time to pick up our straw and in the beginning the horse brought in the grain on a wagon. He brought it from Perbenyik. He promised that the Village leader will buy our tobacco building from us, but now it is scary because they might take the money away also. We will not have anything. Therefore I can't write anymore. I'm going to grind the poppy seeds. Lajos didn't write because his throat hurts and with the big trouble around he lost his patience. Kisses for all of you with all our love, Etelka

I hope you will not be angry because I'm not writing more and I sound so down and bitter. I wish I could write better notes. Give our love to Uncle Jónász, and cousin Arthur and family. Emil's space is empty because he is not here.

1941/5/26 Bertha to Hermine (Book 4, 148-149)

New York
May 26 / 41
Dearest Hermine,
I'm very happy to hear that Maria is feeling better and she's at home, that is good news. As I mentioned I mailed some money to my family and forget to tell that he [Israel Zsupnik] made a mistake by not writing the total to his wife. Because of that the money was delayed. That is what she is saying. She received that letter 21 days ago. Usually it should take only a couple days to give it over to my family. I told him his wife failed to give the correct amount to my father. I told him it should have been 72 pengo. He told me he will write to his wife to give the three pengo. I also told him it should have been 8 pengos for a dollar. He claims to have only one thousand pengo. He can't telegraph any more because he did not have any signed arrangement, so his wife would not be able to understand. I cannot give any advice to you. Do whatever you think and want to do, and be happy with it. You can send the total directly to him if and when you decide whatever you would like to do. You can mail the money to the address I gave to you. It was 5 months ago since I heard from them [my family]. I haven't heard anything about the money either. I have no idea if they received it or not. The person says they did. I can't understand why my dear father did not notify me about that or I did not hear from him. If you know something, please do not keep it from me. Let me know because we have to accept whatever it is. We cannot change, our life comes sooner or later. Until then I am not sending any money to my father. I'll wait until I am sure what happened to him. Other people get mail from home so I can't understand why I don't. I hope everything will work out. I remain with best wishes and love and kisses to you all. Your cousins Bertha and Mannie.

1941/6/15 Helen Perl Goldstein to Hermine (Book 17, 347-349)

Cleveland Ohio 1941 / VI 15
Dear Herminka!
Despite that I usually don't do that, I am responding late to your precious lines. I don't want to get into details about the reason, I will tell you everything when the time is right. I hope my lines will find Mariska in the best of health. The Schwartz boys were by me and at the same time I had another 4 boy visitors. Two of them were the Klein boys from Szürte, Uncle Izidor Klein's sons. The two boys spent their Sunday here very pleasantly, but if you could have been here I would have been even happier. Surprise me next month on the 4th we will have a sunny vacation again. I can't write a lot about myself. I work all the time, there is no view on vacation really, although I could accept a few days. What do they say from home? I haven't gotten letters from there for a long time, I only know what I hear from others, which is a very terrible news. Write a lot about everything, how are the conditions. I will wait for you to reply as soon as possible. Until then I kiss all of you with love. All the best wishes to the loved ones. Helen

1941/7/3 Bertha to Hermine (Book 5, 228-229)

New York
July 3, 1941
Dear Hermine!
I hope you're not holding it against me that I am a little late with my answer. God knows it is so hot here this summer. I hardly can do my housework where I can find a little cool air to cool off. My apartment is closer to God so it is even warmer, but I give thanks for that too. Dearest I'm asking you only one thing. Be

careful, take care of yourself, don't ruin your health with so much worry because that is not going to help. We can't help by worrying for our dearest family at home because you will ruin your own health. Then you will be all alone. No one will be there to help to take care of you. We have to hope for the best. When I received a letter [from home] at the same time I received a letter from your father, but it's almost impossible to read. It is so bad and it's changed so much. She [Mariska] writes that my brother-in-law Miksa is very seriously ill and her husband is a soldier in the army. Dearest, I'm very happy that just now I mailed her some money which will arrive just in time. I hope before the trouble started. $10, [and] also for my father $20. I do not believe we will be able to write or send any mail until it will settle down for a while. Dearest I will ask you only one thing, at least try to live a more relaxed life. If not, the way you are aggravating yourself you will have trouble with your stomach. I know from my experience. My husband and I are feeling better. At least now I'm taking my medication, vitamin B 15 mg, and this gives me strength and a good appetite. I'm just worried that I should be able to take my pain. My husband tells me it will be enough from this. Sorry that Maria still is not feeling better. I'm afraid that she's worried day and night. Nothing is worse than worry. It is poison. It is better in summer [because] you can get around [and] will be able to get better faster. You have to take life as it comes. We cannot worry all the time. I know we are relatives because I was doing the same thing. With that is enough. I'm trying to finish my letter because I'm waiting for Mannie to come home for dinner. Now I'm closing with kisses and love to all of you dears, with good health for our family and dear Maria also. I hope you forgive that I didn't write to you separately a short letter. Next time I will write more. I hope we will hear better news for all of us. Sending you kisses and love to all of you, Bertha and Mannie

Don't forget about the money. Don't forget we will not be able to do much.

1941/7/8 Father to us (Book 3, 212-214)

Bodrogmező, 1941 VII / 8

With love to my children.
I want to inform you that thank God we are well and I hope to hear from you the same. I want to let you know that the 236 Pengo was received from my brother and I thank you. It came in handy because I owed too many people. I bought half [ol] of firewood. From the tobacco building I took off the roof to fix the roof of the house and because of that I was delayed in writing you. My dear son Lajos is not at home. He is in Bacska. I would like to sell that whole tobacco building, but if I can't, then I'll take it apart and sell it in pieces so that I can give some to Török and I would like to give some to Mihaly Török [also]. He is very nice to me and very friendly and waits for me [to pay] with encouragement. You are asking about the farm, Istvan Török gave me 1M barley on credit. Corosz also helped me, [and] through him, I got 1M oats. I also borrowed a loan from Feri Szabo and we also had a little bit of seed so I could plant. A third each of corn, potatoes, and beets. I was lucky that my son Lajos was still at home and plowed and sowed the land before he left from home. The horses are still at home, but for how long I don't know. Simon's stallion has a small stripe [of coloration] from Sari [our mare], and it is out on the pasture with his mother. Last week Uncle Lajos bacsi moved to his new house. Grandma and grandpa are well and healthy and send their respect. My dearest children, I don't know if you have received my letter from last month in which I told you my brother Lajzer has died. Bertha wrote that poor Jónász bacsi also died. Please let me know about everything. Does his son say Kaddish? Did he leave you anything? My dear sons Dezső and Herman, why don't you write at least a few lines. How much are your earnings? [Miksa] Shon is also in Bacska, but he's not together with my son. My dearest Hermine, you ask me how I live. The same as before in the front room. The cow did not give birth yet and we miss the milk. Bread is scarce. We have one loaf of bread per week. I hope to do something about it. We did not have any wheat because we had to plow it under due to the frost. I bought myself two brown shirts for 20 Pengos. I didn't have anything to wear. I hope that my brother's wife Helen will not give his clothing to other people. How is she? Are you in good relations with her? How is Arthur? How are you with him? Give my regards to him. Mariska, you did not mention to me how you feel after the operation. Last week in my dreams you were at home. I wanted to speak to you, then I woke up. Many times I dream of all of you. With respect and kisses to all of you, individually, forever your sincere father who will never forget you, Gluck Jeremias
[On the inside crease] I received 3 letters from you. In one letter you mentioned [mine] did not arrive yet.

1941/7/8 Undated Etelka and Rella Veizer to Hermine and Marie (Book 4, 167-168)

[This letter is from Etelka my brother's wife from Europe. Rella was one of my friends. She was visiting my family from Helmec. - Marie. Dated by Lajos in Bacska, trouble getting bread.]

Dear Hermine and my dear Maria.

With my heavy heart I don't even know what I should write to you. Please don't be angry that the children don't write. They are in heder [Hebrew school] and we would like to mail the letter as soon as possible. Besides we cannot write the truth about what is happening here, otherwise you would not be able to get this letter. Very soon we will write more and will try to send you a picture of them so you could see how raggedly they are dressed and because Lajos also asked for a picture of them because he hasn't seen us in two months. We do not know when is the next time we will be able to see him or he to see us. Only God knows. At this time he is far from us near Szabadka [the administrative center of the Bacska district] with Sògor and Andor from Agard. They have more from nearby there. Don't be angry if I forget something you would like to know. I forget sometimes what I should tell you. This week I wasted a huge amount of time running around trying to get to have some food or bread for my family. There are some people who still strive to reach out and help me with one bread. Pataki does me a favor sometimes and Simonek. It will only be hard these 3 or four weeks because they aren't harvesting [the wheat]. This week Gyusi is telling me mommy give me just a little bread. Mariska with your dresses–I can imagine you're making beautiful dresses. You have the opportunity with your taste. I want to thank you very much to both of you for writing so, and caring for us, with loving feeling to us. Our children love you so much I don't know even how to write it to you.

Veiser bacsi was here with his daughter this Sunday. They were looking for a place where she [would] want to get married. Since she wrote on a heavy paper [to you] I have to rewrite it on thinner paper because otherwise it would be very expensive [to mail]. Thank goodness, we are well. The big problem in life is we don't have any clothing for the children to wear. If you have the money maybe they have a chance to make it. And those who don't have the money, the children are hungry and you can't feed them. At this time from one pengo you cannot imagine black coffee or if I am able to get 2 liters of milk, but only if they have it. I went to look in the village this summer [because] we didn't have milk. There was a lot of water [flooding] on the pastures. I received a letter from Lajos my husband. He is also asking for clothing. I really don't know how I can even get it, there's no way. Now I will have to stop because the friend of yours would like to write to you a few lines. We send kisses to you all and the relations. Etelka.

[from Rella Veizer]
Dear Hermine and Maria.

I am here today and I would not want to delay it any longer therefore I am just sending you a few lines so along with your father Gluck bacsi's letter you will receive mine. I wrote to you before. I received one of your letters and was very happy to hear that you are well. Thank goodness we are well. Our income and living is more difficult, but the most important [thing] is our health. My father was very ill last summer. He's feeling better today. Lili is okay. We are thinking of you all the time. I must say I made a good choice to be your friend. I am not disappointed. I could see from your letters how you are such a caring person. You say that if it would be possible to send us a guarantee to come to America you would try to help me. I want to thank you very much in advance for that. At this time, the news is I will soon be engaged and will get married. Next time I will write more about us. I remain with all my best wishes many kisses. With love Rella Veiser.

[from Etelka]
Also give my best wishes to your brothers. Now we have new potatoes. That is what we are eating today. We have nice chickens and a few ducks. Love, Etelka.

1941/7/11 Louis Schwartz to Hermine and Marie (Book 18, 286-287)

Dear Herminka and Mariska!

I just have a chance to respond to your dear letter. I'm happy that you are well. Also, I'm curious Mariska if you are working already? I was very happy that Dezső visited me, although I did not have a lot of opportunity to talk to him, because I met him late. It's been more than three weeks since we got a letter from home. And you? What do you do? I would like to know if you will go anywhere for vacation? And if yes, where? I believe a little village air and rest would not hurt, especially for Mariska. The relatives are renting an apartment not too far from Cleveland, for two weeks starting from Sunday. I can't go during that time because I have to be in the store. If you plan anything, write it to me immediately. I kiss all of you, Lajos

1941/8/8 Israel Zsupnik to Bertha (Book 1, 44-45)

Ms Gluck with respect,
I'm responding to your precious letter, that a small amount of money, the cost of the mail, will be deducted there, at the present price, afterwards will be 240P.
With full respect, Israel Zsupnik

1941/8/14 Israel Zsupnik to Hermine (Book 1, 40-41)

Ms Gluck with respect,
I got the $30 check. Thank you and I sent over the 240 P. I hope that like before, it will arrive with the best accuracy despite the fact that the situation there got worse. With full respect,
Israel Zsupnik

1941/8/29 Bertha to Hermine (Book 5, 249-251)

New York
August 29 / 41
Dear Hermina!
I hope you're not angry that I didn't write to you sooner. The reason is I have an infection in one of my fingers. For a couple of weeks I wasn't able to write or hold a pen in my hand. Finally, I'm better and will try to catch up with writing. I will tell you all about it. First, I want to thank you for your little brother's pictures. I can see he looks very nice. How are the rest of your family and how is dear Maria's health? I hope that she is getting better. How does she like it there? About the news I can't write that the aunt's daughter went through surgery on the ear. They are [????] But after the surgery they found that above the brain there is swelling. I can't find how they call it in Hungarian. But thank goodness, she is getting better and soon they're taking her home. Dearest, I see the relations only very rarely, especially the [aunt?]. She moved out from New York. Otherwise nothing special. I didn't have mail for a very long time from home. We are hoping they are alright. I'm also asking you don't worry so much, because you are not going to help. Instead you will destroy your own health. Then what will happen? You didn't help and you will be suffering too? How will that help you? [Yiddish - fúr zich got fúr únz álle]

I received a letter from aunt Helen. She wrote in German and it's so hard for me to understand. Do you know how to speak in German? I put it in Hungarian. I still cannot speak a lot of English. I learned only a little. This is enough for this time. Many kisses and love to all of you. Bertha and Mannie

1941/9/19 Louis Schwartz to Hermine and Marie (Book 17, 151-153)

Dear Herminka and Mariska!
Since I visited you, I just have the time to write and thank you for the nice hospitality. We had a very nice trip on the way back. We spent about two hours in Columbus when we left from you, but we were already back in Youngstown by 10 pm. My cousin [older male] asked me why I did not bring you with me? Of course I told him the truth, that you did not want to come. We got a letter yesterday and today from home. Gizike was wondering about you. Unfortunately they can't write anything good. Our machine threshed, but we had to give 90% of the profit to the Christians, based on the new law. Our Feri, and the Garanyi boys are still in town. They don't know when they will get home. Gizike also would like to come here, although she was not in the mood so far. Only God knows, if it's going to be? And how are you? And the boys? I will finish my lines now because I'm writing this in the store currently. I kiss all of you. Lajos
P.S. We wish you a happy and lucky New Year "k mng" [kedves mindeg = dear all] F. [as above]

1941/10/3 Bertha to Hermina (Book 5, 35-36)

New York
Oct 3 / 41
My love Herminkam,
Don't be angry that I neglected writing. It is probably because of my laziness, but I hope that you are, all of you, well. We ourselves are so so. How does dear Mariska progress with her health and with her work? Do

you know I would have written to our dear Aunt Helen but I lost my address book and I had everybody's address in it and because of that I can't write. Did you receive any letters from home? As soon as I received your letter I wrote home a registered letter. I wanted to be sure that they receive it. I also will know and see their handwriting, at least it will show that they're alive. Please be kind enough to write and let me know how you are. Good or bad, whatever, please let me know. I want to know. It's very important to me. Did they take the men folks into the army? Don't keep anything back from me please. How's your dear father and your brother at home? Please write about everything. If I can't see them in person, at least through the letters we speak to each other. I guess this will be enough of this. It's Friday afternoon and I have to prepare things for Shabbat. Give my regards to the dear relations, if you get together with them. With kisses, Bertha and Mannie

1941/11/25 Ignác to Father and Lajos - returned undelivered (Book 5, 163-164)

[This letter was returned to Columbus, Ohio]

11-25-41

Dear father and Lajos,
I do not know how I should begin my letter. It has been such a long time that we received a letter from home, it's been about three months. About myself I can only write to you this, thank God, I am well and in good health, which we hope to hear the same from you soon. We hear daily news and we know what is happening there. It's regretful that we can't do anything about it to help you, except trust and hope. Do not worry about us. Here everything is fine and good. Please write to us as soon as possible. We are waiting restlessly for your reply. And you Lajos, how are you? What are you doing? How is the seeding? And how is everything? I hope that you are at home. Please write about everything. I ask you all again to write about everything. I remain with lots of love, your faithful son and brother, Ignác.

Dear Emil, Lenke, Mityu and Gyuszika,
How are you all? What are you doing? Write. Lots of kisses, Irving
Regards to all our family and relations individually and to grandfather, Uncle Lajos, and Uncle Marton.

1941/11/26 Hermine, Herman, and Marie to Etelka (Book 5, 171-172)

[from Hermine]
11-26-1941
Dear Etelka, Lajos, and children,
I know you're waiting impatiently for our letters. We also get impatient waiting for your letters. Please write more about everything. I'm hoping Lajos that you are at home. And you Etelka, write about yourself and the children. Please write about our father and all the other relations. I really don't know what to write about because I'm very upset. We didn't hear from you for 3½ months. When did you get the last letter from us? Please write. Kisses with all my love to you to Lajos, Emil, Lenke, Mityu, Gyula, and little Zoltan. Please write to the cousins and Shön and all the others who are asking about us. Unto all the relations with kisses and wishing you all the best. Take care of our father. Dear Etelka, don't let him worry and get upset. We hope it will get better in the world!!!! Please don't worry. Take care of all of you. I'm wishing you all the best with all my kisses and love to every one of you. Hermine

[from Herman]
11-26-41
My dear father and my dear Lajos,
It is a long time that we did not hear from you either. Otherwise how are you all? Lajos, are you at home? Please write about everything. Was the tobacco building sold? I hope that our father and Lajos and the family are in good health. Many kisses to them. Your son and brother, Herman
To our grandfather and grandmother, Uncle Lajos and to Uncle Marton and his children and to Emil, Mityu, Gyula, and Lenke. Kisses, Herman

[from Maria]
Dear Etelka, Lajos, and children!
I can't even write how very worried I am about all of you. My dear father, we can't even think why we haven't heard from you for such a long time. Even though we can understand the reason, but still we worry.

We thought that maybe you are waiting for our letters, therefore you didn't write to us. I hope I'm wrong about that because I can't believe that was the reason. I will leave that, too. How are you? I hope dear Lajos you are at home and you are okay. Please write about everything, about yourself and you too dear Etelka. How are you? How is everything? We have newspapers and everything!!!!? They write about it all. And you Emil and Lena, Mityu, Gyula and Zoltan - how are you all? Please write. Is your room warm? Do you have heat? Did you have a big snow? Are you going to school? Please take care of yourselves. Be careful when you walk outside. When did you see our grandparents in Lelesz? How is everyone? We wanted to send them some pictures, but we weren't sure you will get it. It is too big. We will make a smaller one next time and will mail it to grandfather. When will they mail us something because we are waiting. I'm fine. I'm working in the same place where I was, at the furrier where they make coats. About myself, I don't have anything special to write because we don't go out anywhere, so we know nothing. The weather here is nice, it's a real spring day. The snow fell once for a week and it was very cold. Before that it was raining. At this time I am closing. From my heart I'm sending you many kisses, wishing you the best of health to you all, many times to all of you, loving you all forever. Just take care of yourselves and our dear father and please write at once about everything, Maria

1941/11/27 Helen Perl to Hermine (Book 5, 192-194)

Cleveland 1941-11-11

Dear Hermine and Marie,

I know you would not believe why I didn't write before. Why my silence? Believe me, it is not because of my negligence. Recently, I went through so many things I can't begin to write about it. My mother's sister's husband brought me here to this free country and he helped me with all the best in their house and all their love. Unexpectedly he passed away. He was never sick and he worked until noon. After dinner, he got very sick and called the doctor, but it was too late. He had a heart attack. He was only 42 years old. You can imagine how we all felt. What his poor wife went through. He loved her so much from the day they were married 14 years ago, and now she lost him and she lives all alone. Therefore we cannot even write our feelings about the pain. The Schwartz boys are all very good [and] very handsome. We can't change it. All of life is unpredictable. We have to take it as it is. We can't change it. It is very difficult. I will also have to change my life because I was living with relatives, but now she has moved to her sister. Now I too have to move to strangers. This time I have to move to a place where three or four kinds of nationalities live. It doesn't matter how good they are as people, it is still not the same as when you have your own family or relations with love and everything. You can imagine the comfort surrounding you. You never can replace such a life again. At this time I'm getting used to it. I'm satisfied with the way it is. I have a new home. The beginning was difficult. In my life I have never lived with strangers and here we are too far from our family and anywhere you want to go it is too far. We have to go through so much. I'm a housekeeper for 8 hours. After work I come home and then I cook for myself sometimes for two days. I know I'm not the only one. In Europe, they would be happy to cook if only they would have the food to cook. Do you get any mail from home? The last letter they mailed from Pest was without a sender or date on it. You can imagine how hard it is to get that kind of letter. It drives you crazy. You can't get away without that here, and now it is already very sad. I wrote to them also a very sad story. I hope to hear from you the best soon. I hope one of the weekends I will be able to see you and it will be a very happy reunion. Please forgive me that I'm making more mistakes in my letter and not writing clearly because I am upset and I didn't want you to wait any longer for my letter. Many times if I could fly I would stop there amongst my family. I can't even imagine how a girl lives through so much. What they're going through, how they suffer home. I asked God from the heart to save them. I'm closing now with lots of love and kisses with all the best wishes. I'm waiting to hear from you as soon as possible! Helen

1941/11/28 Marie and Hermine to Father (Book 5, 173-174)

1941 XI / 28

[from Marie]

My dear father!

I'm very restless and I don't have any patience to write my letter. Dear father, I didn't hear from you for such a long time. We didn't get mail from you for 3½ months therefore we didn't have any news from you. I worry about that very much. I'm very restless. Since then we wrote many letters, but we never received any answer from you. We don't even know what happens with the gift we mailed to you. Dear father, how are you? Are you okay? Please answer us as soon as possible. I hope and wish that our letter arrived to you safely and the previous letters too. And will find all of you in good health. Also how are you father, at this time I cannot write anything new. Even though we know everything that's happening dear father please try to write to us as soon as possible about yourself and also about the family. And our brother Lajos. Do you have enough food? Do you have wood to keep you warm? I know all this, you don't have what you need and you have to go without. How was the farm with all this? Were you able to raise the wheat or other items? Dear father I thank goodness I'm okay and we are all working. The only thing I'm asking you my dear father is that you should not worry about us. We are in the best place and all of us are well. I wish you and the family would be here also. Then we would be much better and happier also. We are thinking maybe our letter got lost or delayed. Therefore you and father worry about us too, but don't do that and just take very good care of yourselves. Are you working hard at home? And Lajos? Are you doing everything by yourself? How are our grandfather and grandmother? And Uncle Lajos and Uncle Marton and their families and also the other relatives? Here our relatives are okay, and our Aunt is alright. She lives alone. She was here visiting us. Arthur and his family are also okay. I wrote in my previous letter that they live in a new building. Flora and Arthur were here two days ago in the evening, too. We are very busy now. We are not going anywhere to socialize. At this time everything here is expensive and the prices are going up. We hope everything will be okay. We received a letter from Lajos Schwartz from Szürte. He wrote that he received a letter from home. There was traffic. We are the ones who can't get mail. It seems maybe it was delayed. Now I will stop it because others– Sister, brother want to write also. Wishing you all the best and good health. Many kisses to you our dear father all my love forever. Your daughter who never forgets about you. You are always in my heart. Never forget [that] I will never forget you. Your daughter, Mariska

Love also to all our family and relations from my heart with lots of kisses. We are waiting for your letter

[from Hermine]
Dear loving father,
I don't know how to begin my letter because I worry so much everyday about not hearing from you for such a long time. We thank goodness that all of us are okay. Hoping that you and family are also okay? Still don't know what happened to the 75 pengo and the second 240 pengo. Please write about that. We would like to know. Please write about everything. We are waiting so hard to hear from you. Is Lajos at home? Our grandfather and grandmother how are they? How are the other relations? Are they okay?

I will continue my job, too and it is still good because it is not very cold to go to work! If it had been bad, I would have repeatedly sent a letter..... Please write to us as soon as possible. We are waiting very impatiently. We are trying to write again. Maybe you will have received our letters. Lots of kisses to you dear father, lots of love, your loving daughter, Hermine

1941/12 Undated Hermina to Anna and Margit Gereny (Book 5, 92)

[to our neighbors Gyuri Gereny and family across the street in Bodrogmező. Dated by Christmas, no letters from home, and Jónász's death so 1941]

Dear Anna nénni, and Margit nénni!
I do not know how to begin my few lines since we haven't heard from each other for such a long time. I know it will surprise you to receive this letter. I believe that perhaps the previous letters were not received by you. I do not believe that I would not have received a small note from you by now. First of all, I want to wish you a pleasant Christmas holidays and a happy new year. And I hope that all of you are well and in good health... How is Gyuri bacsi? And how are you Margitka? Ilonka, Gyuszi, and Lacika? Regarding ourselves, I can only say to you that thank God we are all of us well. We have somewhat gotten accustomed to our situation. It is not as strange as it was because we almost feel like being at home. It is regretful that our dear Uncle Jónász bacsi was with us for such a short time [he died]. We have been together with him for many pleasant hours. He tried to help us with everything as if we were his own children. I'm sure that our dear father has been telling you about everything. I do not know what could be the reason that we haven't heard anything from home for the past three months. Once again I'm asking our dear all of you that you write a few lines that will make us very happy. Wishing all of you a lot of good things, regards from our hearts and kisses with love. Hermina Gluck
Please convey our love and regards, kisses to our father and to all the members of our family.

1941/12/7 Bertha to Hermine (Book 3, 149-151)

New York

Dec 7 / 41

Dearest Hermin,

A thousand apologies for the long silence, but it happened against my will. For two weeks I had to stay in bed and you know for women there is always something that comes in between. First of all is the weakness that wants everything and then I wanted to paint and that was not enough. I promised my association that I would make binders and bridge covers and sell them. I would get my share because I thought I could do it myself, but I was afraid that they will look down upon one person, so I took a person as partner, that means forty dollars for both us to do the job. If there is the willingness to do it and, if health permits it. Whoever can make it financially and if men would help it will be great, but we were living for ourselves. It has been six weeks since I received any letters from home. God only knows when we'll be able to hear from them. I mailed $25 on October 30. I hope they received it. My niece Rezsi heard that we should be patient. The men went to a work camp. It's better to forget or leave it alone. Hermine I received an address through my friend, an acquaintance, and she said that her friend is also an acquaintance in Cleveland who works for a newspaper, probably his weekly income is about $50. I would like you to send me a picture so that this person could see you, if not in person at least on a picture, and perhaps he would want to meet you and then would help your responsibility. I'm sending this information to this individual and the relation there. You could research it, perhaps you could find someone nice there. I don't know which way would be best to give the impression for this fellow. Well this will be enough since I am tired from nothing but worry and nervousness does affect a person. Please forgive me if you do not understand me in this letter as I explained it. Kisses and love to all my dear of you, Bertha and Mannie.

1941/12/16 Louis Schwartz to Hermine and Marie (Book 17, 177-180)

12 - 16

Dear Herminka and Mariska!

I read your dear letter. I am in a hurry to respond. Although, it is a little late and I'm starting to feel tired to write, since this week we will keep the store open until Christmas night and usually I close at 9pm, since my cousin [older male] goes home earlier. This way the traffic is so much more. I'm writing this letter at 10pm. I don't know a lot of news. We are all well, and that's what I hope to her from you too. Unfortunately, I have not gotten a letter from home for a long time again, which worries me, and only God knows when we can get one again. Considering that there is a war situation in Hungary, even if they don't communicate. It is possible that they will call me in for military service. I would like you to write [and tell me] when did you get a letter from home and what do they write? It is good to know about news, even if I don't hear it directly. Yesterday, that is on Sunday, I visited the Klein boy and his friend with a boy from Ujhely. We planned for the Spring that we will drive by you if nothing else comes up. Mariska, you must know him. He is Lino's grandchild. Of course, if there is an opportunity I will visit you, even if it's unexpected. I did not respond to Feri yet, which is really not nice of me, but I will make time for it at once. And how are you? What do you do? Do you work hard? And Dezső? Is he at home? And the boys? Did you get a letter from Helen Perl? I was in Cleveland not too long ago, but I did not visit her. What does she write? Now I will finish my lines. I kiss all of you and the boys. Lajos

Write to me a lot as soon as possible!!!

1941/12/26 Israel Zsupnik to Hermine (Book 1, 36-37)

Ms Gluck with respect

I am responding to your precious letter with happiness, that I am aware of the fact that it is being taken care of, because I got the last letter that was written on November 11th. Besides this, I got a telegram notifying [me] that everything is taken care of. With respect, Israel Zsupnik

1942/1 Hermine to Bertha (Book 10, 31-32)

Undated [The letter can be dated to about 1/1942 since Uncle Herman was inducted on 1942/1/9. See Book 21, 232]

My dear Berthuska!

I got your letter with happiness, but I'm sorry that you did not feel well. I thought about it a lot, that maybe you are sick, which was unsettling…I'm asking you as much as you can be calm and don't be worried because it is about yourself, about your health. Yes, there is always something that doesn't let you rest from worry. We did not get any letter from home for months. I am out of patience, but we can't do anything before the holidays. We sent 31 dollars, but no response came. Other than that we are, thank God, well. Herman got inducted to the military and he has to go in a few months. He got the notification two weeks ago. And surely considering the situation, the time will come that others will have to go as well. It is truly a lot that creates problems. My dear Berthuska! You are so kind that you are trying to help me. This is very nice of you! This is really interesting that I know that Fisher. Otherwise, there was a get together for some Hungarians and even the newspaper editor came. David introduced him to us. He already knew him for a longer time. He is an absolute gentlemen and very fine. Surely he has different needs. Although, I did not talk to him [alone] only in company. He spoke for a short time. He used to live here so everybody knows him. As a matter of fact, he is not so young. But I will send the picture to you and you do what's best for you.

1942/2/2 Bertha to Hermine (Book 17, 46-49)

New York
Feb 2 / 42
My Beloved Hermina!
A thousand pardons for my silence, but something always happens. First I was sick and then my husband was sick for a few weeks. Sciatica is getting into my buttocks and the suffering is unbearable. And I am going crazy [thinking what] if something happens to him. It makes me glad that you are, thank God well. That finally we are missing also. My darlings, I don't even know what to say, but lots of luck to dear Herman! And let's hope that his unit does not have to go to the battlefield. At the same time, the Germans will be destroyed just like the Japanese. I don't even remember the last time I got a letter from home. Let's hope for the best, but if we are worried, that is not a help to us. So we have to have patience. Although, that is not much. It is hard to give any advice. The point is that a person has to have his health, because where there is life, there is hope. I can't write anything special to you, because I don't see the relatives, only a note- Frey T. and his wife are well. They are fighting like everybody else, my husband also. The businesses are not the best, especially the evening gowns, but we give thanks that we are in this country. We are better off here than over there. Now I wish you all the best to all of you! Especially to dear Herman! Kisses with love, Bertha and Mannie.
Regards to our relations

1942/2/22 How I feel about America - Irving (Book 22, 5)

How I feel about America.

My name is Irving Gluck. I was born on Nov. 14th, 1921 in Bodrogmezo, Kiralyhelmec county, Czechoslovakia. When I was a little boy, I heard a great deal about America. One uncle paid visits to us, and in that way I got an opportunity to ask about America, the New World. In 1938, one of my oldest brothers came to America. On February 22, 1940, Washington's birthday, we arrived in New York. Today, February 22, 1942, we are celebrating that day and we cannot thank God enough that we have come safely to the land of freedom. For America means to us a land of freedom. There are no dictators nor any monarchs in this land. Of course, freedom does not mean the following of any temptation, but freedom of resisting temptation. There is another important freedom too. This is religious liberty. America grants all religions the right to practice here. Now I want to learn the English language and I want to be a good citizen and I also want to get my citizenship. Today we are at war, whenever this country calls upon me, I'm ready to serve this country. America is worth fighting for. Thank you.

1942/2/22 Louis Schwartz to Hermine and Marie (Book 17, 162-163)

Youngstown 1942 ; 2 , 22
Dear Herminka and Mariska!
I was very happy for your dear letter, especially for the pictures. Dear Hermine, I received it on Saturday on Valentine's Day, although it was dated on Friday the 13th. I could say that it's a very well done picture and if I remember right, it is very life-like. I introduced you to the relatives who were honestly of the same

opinion. I hope you will not be offended for my honesty, but I hung your picture up in a nice place. Dear Mariska, if you have a picture done then send it as well. If nothing will come up in the near future I will probably visit you, since two weeks ago I was at a military exam where they have found me qualified. Shortly I have to go to a second exam, and if they will take me, we will have to go to our city in Columbus, where they will put us in service and we will go to fight against our old country for our new country. It is possible if the conditions allow it, I will visit you 2 days before. Write to me the phone number, just in case, so I can get connected with you. I think I already wrote that I wrote home by the Red Cross. And you??? Otherwise how are you? Write me as soon as possible. I kiss all of you, Lajos

The boys, too.

1942/2/23 Bertha to Hermine (Book 5, 252-254)

New York

Feb 23 / 42

My dearest!

Reading your letter made me very happy, especially to hear you are well. Dear Hermine, I received your pictures, and many thanks for sending them to me. It came out very nice. I'm sorry that I made you spend the money. With this picture we might have a chance to meet some people. Also, I'm happy that you bought a winter coat. Wear it in good health. What color is it? I know you have good taste. I also hope that they will not take dear Herman to go somewhere else from Columbus. I'm happy also to hear from Irving that he is getting along in English. I'm jealous of that because I have a terrible head that can't learn and it makes me feel terrible. I'm trying very hard. First, I don't have the patience. It gives me a headache and it doesn't register. I can't remember. It takes too much time. If you want to, send me 26 words which I can send the Red Cross [to send a telegram]. I heard about this. This week I will go down then I will ask you about some information. I don't know anything special because I'm not seeing relations, no one, not even Frey. I see them very seldom. I hope my letter will find you all in good health. Dearest always with love and many kisses to you all, Bertha and Mannie

1942/3/13 Helen Perl to Hermine (Book 1, 188-191)

My dear Hermine!

Please don't be angry at me, because I made you wait a little for my response, but I truly didn't do it on purpose. It was a close call, that I didn't respond in person, but as you can see, there is always something that gets in our way. "Everything comes to he who waits" ["what is delayed won't pass" is a Hungarian saying]. We will just walk some other time. My Hermine! I can hardly write down how happy I was to [see] your pictures. You look exactly like in my memory. It's a nice, lifelike picture. Your blue smiling eyes, wavy blond hair. Isn't it too bad that you were not born to be a boy? But I won't worry about you, I'm sure you have a good looking boyfriend. Do you? Because that is in fashion here in America. Otherwise, it's easier for you to get to know nice people, since you are there with your brothers, who I'm sure are good company. Life for me, being alone in the big world, is very hard, but I wish everything would be the way it is, except for the chaos happening that has divided us. It separated us from our dear parents and from our siblings. Many times I hear the news and read the newspaper, and I get excited. If it would be possible, I would fly back home. What a terrible situation it is there. Perhaps they will not even survive. Thousands of people die from starvation. It's been 3 months since a telegram was sent with the Red Cross, but I did not get a response. Ugh, I will not dwell on the sad subject anymore. Anyway, how are you? I'm sure you are all working. I am also, and I'm working all the time, and I'm making good money. I live slowly and simply, just like I used to at home, not like the girls in America. Please Hermine, don't be mad and write a reply to me. Soon I will explain things in person. Until then, I kiss you with love. Mariska separately and the boys without knowing them. Helen

1942/4/21 Louis Schwartz to Hermine and Marie (Book 17, 147-149)

Dear Herminka and Mariska!

Laugh it out! As you can see I'm writing again from Youngstown, which I did not expect. They sent me back with two of my friends because of our hostile nationality.

Supposedly they will call us in soon also because based on the new law, they take aliens too. In that case, we won't have to go for another medical exam because we are done with that, and they have found us qualified. If I remember well, you wrote that Herman is being drafted. I wonder how could that happen? I would be happy if you would write me immediately, if he serves? And how? Or maybe they drafted him because Hungary is at war against America? Otherwise how are you? I am pretty well, except for the uncertainty that I don't know when they will call me in. It makes me a little uncomfortable. My break at work lasted only a day, when I went for the drafting process, the next day I was already at work again. My boss and relatives were very happy when I unexpectedly came back. Write to me, if you still correspond with Helen Perl and possibly [send] her address. I heard that she is not in Cleveland. Her uncle died and she is supposedly in Detroit. I have not heard about her for a long time. I did not get a response from home yet to the letter that I sent by the Red Cross. Now I think I wrote enough. Write immediately!!! I kiss all of you and the boys. Lajos

1942/6/8 Louis Schwartz to Hermine and Marie (Book 17, 115-117)

Dear Herminka and Mariska!
As you can see, I am still at home, but not for long since I was drafted on Friday. On Friday the 18th we have to go to Columbus where we will be for a few days roughly. We are leaving in the morning with the 11 o'clock train from here. It is possible that I will have a chance to visit you. Write your phone number so I can call to get in touch with you. The only news is that I live with our cousin [younger female]. She got married last Sunday, unexpectedly. Her husband is a naval officer and got a daily break. In this way they arranged it in a hurry, but there were many people at the wedding. The young couple went to California right away the next day, where they will live. Now I can't write more. I believe I'm not the one who owes someone with the writing. If you have a chance write. I kiss all of you. Lajos

1942/6/20 Louis Schwartz to Hermine and Marie (Book 17, 169-171)

Dear Herminka and Mariska!
I didn't notice it myself that I'm starting to follow your example when it comes to responding, if only by 50%, even that is too much when it comes to me. In your last mail you wrote that you are counting on renting a new apartment. I wonder, if you did that already? If I remember correctly, last summer I proposed that we should spend the summer vacation together, but then [it was met] without success. I will repeat my proposition now. I would be glad if we could do it this summer by the end of July or August. I believe you could use a little rest too. I would like to spend a week at a nice calm place by the water. It should not cost a lot. Make a decision because time is passing. Will you get a vacation? I hope so. Otherwise there is no news by us. I did not get any notification from the military , neither did my brother Joe. Tomorrow, that is, on Saturday, it will be our cousin's Bar Mitzvah, the one who we live with. They are expecting many guests. And how are you? What do you do? I did not get a response from home yet. If you have Helen Perl's address, write it. Write as soon as possible!!! I'm in a hurry because I don't have a lot of time. I kiss all of you. Lajos

1942/6/28 Bertha to Hermine and Marie (Book 5, 201-203)

New York
Jun 28 / 42
My dearest,
The knowledge you're here and thank God you are okay. Many times I want to wish you all the best for your new home with every step you make. I'm writing news that Jenny Frey will be married in August with mazal. Dearest don't be amazed about anyone because they are so small they didn't allow you to have the furniture. Take life as it comes, [and] people as they are. The main thing you should be well. The only thing is God help all of you with good health and happiness. You should be able to, with God's help, be strong and be able to depend on yourself and be healthy so you will be able to hope and will meet someone. Also, on Friday I received a letter from Miksa [Schőn]. For nine months he was running around and in the letter he tells me that my dearest father passed away and when was the funeral, what date he was buried. The good news is he received the money I sent, which you sent at the same time in their name too. We [are] alive somehow. I still don't feel as well as I should. I think the change that women get in my age is very unpleasant, but what can you do. This is not life. Believe me dearest if the outlook for the business would be better I would be surprising you all with a visit. A poor person they say has a good heart. How is Dezső? I hope that he will understand me in time. He doesn't know what dear sisters he has. We hope maybe by today he's changed a little. At this time I don't have any special news. I'm very busy with my sewing items for Bundles for America [The organization was a national war relief club, providing regulation garments, "service kits" and furnishings to the Armed Forces during World War II]. I have to cut short my writing because I have to

go to buy a stamp. Our neighbors' women were also chosen for that, but it is because we are in a strong country. Sending you kisses, with love to all of you. Bertha

Mannie sends his best wishes to you

1942/7/14 Louis Schwartz to Hermine and Marie (Book 17, 173-175)

Dear Herminka and Mariska!
I'm in a hurry to respond to your dear letter. First of all, I wish all of you good luck on the new apartment! I'm glad that you are satisfied with it, even if it's not fully furnished yet, but that will be done soon, too. As far as the vacation is concerned, I would like to do that in the first week of August or the second week, if you could do it at the same time. If it is better for you a week later, even then I may be able to do that. I'm not sure where. They say that there is a nice place not too far from Cleveland, called "Anis Field Camp". Supposedly it is a nice, cheap place and we can [rent] it out from about $20 for a week. But of course, if you know another place that is fine by me too. I just want you to make a decision as soon as possible. As I wrote already, a little rest would not hurt you either, [it's something] that we can't do many times. It is possible that one of my friends will be coming, too. Write immediately. I would like to spend that week with you and if there is something else write it quickly. The important thing is that it should be near you. Also write who else do you plan on coming with you? Now I will finish my lines. I kiss all of you. Lajos
PS: I would like to get something from you this week, if you could do that!!!

1942/7/23 Louis Schwartz to Hermine and Marie (Book 17, 95-97)

Dear Herminka and Mariska!
I just got your dear letter and I am already responding, because I still think that there is time to decide, if you want to spend the vacation together. I am keeping the decision on hold, until I get a response from you to my letter. I believe you are entitled to a little vacation, you work through the entire year. As far as the winter vacation is concerned, that is not even close to [being] the [same as the] summer one. Try to decide a little harder and it will be done. I don't even mind if you know a place close to Columbus. This way the boys could come out after work at night, if they will not get their vacation at the same time. I would like to be by the water, of course, and if it's possible then one or two weeks from Sunday. It should not cost more than [being] at home. We got a letter through the Red Cross from home. It was dated in February. They don't know any news. I will finish my lines. I hope that despite the fact that I am writing this in a hurry, you will be able to read it. Write to me immediately. If you have a phone or your neighbor has one, write to tell me. Maybe one day it will be useful. During the week until 6 mine is 31525-then 66379. I kiss all of you. Lou

1942/9/2 Louis Schwartz to Hermine and Marie (Book 17, 142-145)

Dear Herminka and Mariska!
I am writing a few lines in a hurry. I want this letter to go now, so I can get a response by Saturday from you. If nothing particular will come up, I will more than likely come down to you guys on Sunday by bus. If I get a response by Saturday, [and] if you are at home, since it will be Labor Day on Monday and the store will be closed, this way I could stay with you for two days. But if you are planning something write it to me, of course. I don't want you to change because of me. Also, write your possible phone number, so I can get in touch with you. I think I gave you my number. Day time from 8-6 in the store-315125-later my apartment-66379-
Now kisses and greetings for everyone. Lajos
Write to the new address:
Louis Schwartz
251 E. Fed
Youngstown, Ohio

1942/9/10 Louis Schwartz to Hermine (Book 22, 293-296)

Dear children!
I will use the first opportunity so I can write to you. Thank you very much for your hospitality! It was really nice to be together with you, even though it lasted for a short time. But still, it shows progress compared to

the previous ones. My road on the way back was very long. I just missed the 9am bus. It left right in front of me. This way I came with the 11 o'clock bus and I was in Akron until 7 in the afternoon and I arrived home at 9. You surely rested yourself out from the walking and the insomnia that I caused you since then, but which I enjoyed very much. I am curious if the pictures came out already? Or it is possible that my precious personality ruined them??? My cousin [older female] was in bed. She is not feeling very well, but my cousin [younger male] is better and next week he will join [army?] again. I believe that since we are before the holidays, you can use the opportunity and write to the relatives a few lines. Also, New Year wishes etc..if you want to the store address or "J Eigner 1835 Coronado Ave", which is my apartment's address. Now I believe I wrote enough. I wish all of you lots of good luck and to dear Dezső for the language on the threshold. [kuszobon=threshold. If something is on the threshold, it means almost there, you almost got it. It's an old saying]. I'm sorry that I did not have a chance to meet and talk in person with Dezső, but one day we will have a chance.

Now I kiss you with love. Lajos

1942/9/28 Bertha to Hermine (Book 1, 185)

New York

Sept 28 / 42

My loved Herminka!

It is about time to write a response to you, right?! B. I don't even know what to respond to your lines, that your brother, Irving got taken. I hope they will find a defect in him and they will send him home. Only good luck to both of them and to all of you as well. This is life and we have to make peace with it. If the house is very hard, it's easy for someone from afar to talk. My mother in law ["mahder un larcz"] for a while kept me very busy. A very good acquaintance got sick. It's been three weeks since he/she is in the hospital. He/she has double pneumonia and asked me to come every afternoon from 1:30-4 o'clock in the afternoon and it took away a lot of time and energy. Then we spent Rosh Hashana in Atlantic City. On our way back my husband got a cold and he is still coughing. Somehow, he can't get rid of that coughing. This is an epidemic here, and I was all worn out, so that on Saturday I went to bed and I got up today at 12:30. On Monday afternoon we don't have anything to do. It's strange, I don't have what else to write.

Kisses dear, to all of you with love, Bertha and Mannie

1942/10/9 Louis Schwartz to Hermine and Marie (Book 17, 112-113)

Dear Herminka and Mariska!

Today is Friday afternoon and I'm in the store. I'm writing this letter in a hurry, so you can get it this week. I'm glad that the boys are still home. Maybe they will be released, which I wish from the bottom of my heart. My brother had a doctor's exam two weeks ago. They will probably call him in shortly as a class 1-A [Available; fit for general military service]. At least three weeks ago my younger cousin already went back. Supposedly, they will transfer them overseas soon. As far as the pictures are concerned, if you could recognize people in them, then send me some from them or did my presence ruin them so much that they were unrecognizable?? Otherwise there is no news by me at all. I am well. I hope you are as well! I kiss all of you, Lajos

Greetings for the boys!

1942/10/21 Helen Perl Goldstein to Hermine (Book 17, 396-397)

October 1942 - 21

My dear Herminka!

I was really happy for your lines and as far as the response is concerned, I let you know that I wrote a letter to you a long time ago which you probably did not get because of the address change. You don't even know how happy I will be for your visit. We will talk a lot about everything. I will write surprising news about myself. My life's situation has changed. On the 14th of this month I swore eternal fidelity to Sam Goldstein. As you can see, it's been a week since I am a very happy woman. I did not do a wedding. There were only two witnesses with us at the oath/swearing. My husband is a nice man. I dated him for a year and I was his fiancée for 6 months publicly. Thank God I am my own woman. We have our own little home and a little garden. My husband travels and is only at home with me. I will tell everything in person. Until I will see you again, I kiss all of you with love.

Helen

I don't have a phone for now, but you can find me easily at this address.

1942/12/10 Bertha to Hermine (Book 1, 182-184)

New York
Dec 10 / 42
My loved Herminka!
I don't remember, if I owe an answer to you [about] anything? I hope my lines will find all of you in good health. About us, thank God we are well. Somehow I'm so busy that I don't even know what I'm doing right now. I would like to know if you like to sit down to sew. This is a mania, but I can't help myself because it's the best for my nerves. Otherwise, how are the boys doing? I hope, that they are still at home. Please write about everything because I'm curious, How is Mariska's health? And do you see the relatives? Aunt? Did dear Arthur go back to Columbus? Here there is nothing unusual. Whatever I would say, you already can read it in the newspapers. So let's hope the best for all of us. Give my kisses to your dear siblings. I kiss you separately with love, Bertha and Mannie

1943/2/17 Bertha to us (Book 5, 259-262)

Feb 17 / 43
Dearests!
I'm asking you to forgive me because I'm late with my letter. I was unable to write sooner because I was sick in bed. I had a bad cold, but now I'm feeling better. It took me a long time to get better especially since I was at home. Finally, I had to leave home to come here [The Columbia Hotel, Lakewood, New Jersey]. I can say that I'm well. The first week I was sleeping here day and night. I wasn't able to hold a pen in my hand. Let's forget about that. It makes me happy to know that you are all well. Dear Hermine, try not to worry so much about your family because it will not help. What will happen if you get sick? You can destroy yourself. I'm very happy to hear Elsie is very nice to you. I didn't have a chance to get to know her and Arthur. I never had the chance to meet him either. Even the relations here I don't see them, especially Nate Frey. It was because of me that he got married, but then he was happy. Maybe this is for the best. I do not have to aggravate myself. Let everyone be happy. As for the rest, it will be as it comes. Jenny Frey was visiting with me with her husband again while I was sick and in bed. And now I think it's enough about me. How are the boys? One time you mentioned they will go to the army if the American army will take them. What happened? I hope everything will work out for the best. I'm asking you to write about everything because I'm interested, if you have the time. At this time, I want to close. I wrote enough. With kisses and love to you all, Bertha

I will go home on Sunday. My husband is coming home this evening.

1943/2/24 Undated Marie to Elsie (Book 89-90) - draft

[dated by Bertha mentioned that she's glad Elsie is nice to you in the letter above]

II / 24
Dear Elsie and family!
We received your letter and we are very glad to hear from you. It was very sweet that you were thinking of us. We would like to see you, and your family! How are you and your family? I hope everybody is all right. I'm feeling fine. Now I thank you for your invitation. We hope that we can be there someday. I'm sorry that I can not write very well English, but I hope next time it will be better. My love to you all and please write to us again. Maria Gluck

1943/3/3 Louis Schwartz to Hermine and Marie (Book 17, 102-104)

3-2-940 - 10 P.M.

Dear Herminka and Mariska!
It is truly horrible that I am responding so late to your letter. Believe me, many times I started to write in the store, but I was busy with work and I always had to leave it in half. Now I will not mess around anymore and I'm writing the letter at night at home, although it is a little too late. In the room next to me my cousin [older male] is having fun with his guests. The room is a little loud, but somehow I will finish this letter, I hope...Do not follow my example and write as soon as possible. I haven't heard from you for a long time.

Although, it is partially my fault. I get a letter from my brother often, more often than I write [him]. He is well, considering the conditions. I am waiting for them to call me in also. One of my friends joined the army yesterday. He is also a foreign citizen. Also my friend from Columbus, maybe you know him? Eugene Weisz. He is Dezső's friend. He was here for a few weeks, and a week before went home to Columbus before he had to join the army. I'm curious if you met him? His sister was here also for at least two days. She knows the boys. They don't live far away from you. Below 600 Linwood. There is no news by me. I am busier than ever. The boy who is helping out in the store has been sick for about three weeks now. Also, my cousin's [older] wife, who also helps a lot, does not feel her best either. This way, most of the work is on me, although I'm not telling you this as a complaint. I really love it when I'm busy. And how are you? Do you work hard? How do you, that is, how did you spend the long nights? How are the boys? I hope they are still civilians?? Write as soon as possible! I kiss all of you many times. Lajos

Sending greetings to the boys from my heart.

1943/3/29 Irving to Family-1st Letter from Camp Wolters, TX (Book 3, 1-8)

Monday 29th 1943

My dearest brothers and sisters,

I am in a hurry to write this first letter to you so that I can give you some happiness. I will write again as soon as I have a proper address. Tonight at three o'clock, we arrived at Camp Wolters, Texas. We do not know yet if we will be stationed here. As we left Columbus, Ohio I've seen a lot and experienced a lot. If you take the map you will see that we are not too far away from Mineral Wells, a small town about 3 miles from our camp. I don't know how to start to write to you about this. I thank God I'm well. It was delightful to travel. On Saturday morning at 3:30 in the morning we woke up to organize everything in order that they could inspect us. I was traveling with young men from college, many were from Ohio State University. I really have felt very well. If you could be here with me, you would tell me that this is like heaven. The clear skies are a beautiful blue, not a single cloud in the sky. It took 48 hours by train to arrive here and from the train it took us an hour to come to the camp.

I can't even begin to describe to you how beautiful the terrain was as we traveled. Not all of us came here, but mostly volunteers came. They are very intelligent individuals. Since I left home and come here I've met a lot of Hungarians Jews. As it happened, I was told to note all of the newcomers' coat numbers and I had to match their name. I spoke to about approximately 100 individuals. I was doing that so they wouldn't be so tense because everything here is in a hurry, hurry up!! Do it! They didn't know what to do first. When my turn came to read their name on the roster I knew where they came from. When I spoke to them they were smiling. I spoke only a few words. I knew they will never forget me. I know of myself that I have already become accustomed to being a soldier, as if I would have been one always. A soldier's life is very nice, but it's a difficult assignment. There are those that are lucky have a good time. Up until now for me so far it was excellent, however I sleep very little, about two hours a night. It's true - it doesn't even bother me because there are so many things that can be seen that it doesn't pay to sleep.

As we left Columbus, Ohio, [traveling] westward, we did not know where we are going. We looked at the map and we were trying to figure it out after we left the city and arrived to the wilderness, the forests, between mountains and rivers, here and there we found villages not unlike Polány. Here and there the people were waving to us from their home. The buildings are built on posts or legs. Great sandy terrains and mountains, etc.. I have seen a lot. Here as we have been approaching Texas [and] from the beginning of the border it is filled with oil fields, petrol, and benzene pumps and wells as they suck out the oil from the ground and they burn the benzene out of the oil. There are tall chimneys and wells. It is worthwhile to take a trip like this. In the oil field the land is elevated and flat, and it's full of barrels as they pump it out. It really is a miracle. The climate is warmer and the earth is red. I know that by the time I get home, I will look differently and I will speak English. Here the people don't speak like in Columbus. Here they drag the words and speak very slowly. When we arrived, we were told to tell you not to write to us until we are settled, and we can write, but that's about it. We are going to rest for a week and perhaps after that will be going further. I'm now in the infantry. I do not know exactly, so because of that don't write to me yet until I give you the exact address. I like this place very much. The food is excellent. Back home you would have to pay a $1.50 for a dinner like this.

This morning was our first exercise. It's warm here and the wind is constantly blowing and it blows the sand. If I stay here I will get accustomed to it because the territory is very beautiful and the whole area is very green. In the morning, when the sun rises, it's impossible to describe in writing how beautiful it is. I will stop writing now because we have work to do. As soon as I have free time I will continue writing. I believe I have written quite a bit and I know that I will not get a reply, but I can give you my address now:

Private Irving Gluck
Company B. 57th Infantry Training Battalion
Camp Wolters, Texas.

Again please do not write to me until I write you first because I will not receive your letters. As soon as we arrive there [to our destination], and I'm able to tell you, [I will] but nobody knows about it yet. My dearest Hermine and Marie, how are you? What are you doing? Please don't worry. And you Dezső, how are you? How do like the apartment? I hope that you like it and you get together as normal brothers and sisters. I'm writing this because here in the Army everyone is like that. They agree! It's interesting that when they gave us their Bibles in Columbus, I said that I'm Jewish and so I received the Tanach [the bible] and T'filem (a small English prayer book). The boys asked me for it and they were reading it. They asked for one for themselves also because they liked the information inside, so we were reading it all the way through our journey. How about you Herman, how are you now? How are the wheels turning? I know it would be beautiful to ride the bicycle here because the weather is like in the old country. Only in dreams can you imagine it. It's extremely hot here, but we are dressed so that we don't even realize it. In one place the wind blows the sand and in the other place the air is nice and fresh. There isn't anything better. I know that you would love to be here, but wait until I write to you to come!! Otherwise, what are you doing? Did you get an increase in your wages? And also you my dear sister Mariska, are you working where you worked before? Just now a friend of mine and I went to send you a telegram instead of a letter since the letters will not go out and it takes a week until you know something. Oh yes, what is with the ration books? Did you send it in? Mail it! I really could write to you a lot, but there is always something that comes in between before I can complete the letter. Here in the Army it can only be done after 5PM, but then something else has to be done after that. One has to shave every day, whether you need it or not, and you must have a clean shirt and take a shower, and make the bed so that there isn't a wrinkle. Should there be one on it, you are in trouble.

I must note for you that everything is going well. I will be an infantryman for 13 weeks. I don't know yet what shall be doing, but during the 13 weeks everyone has to go through this. There are no exceptions. Only after the 13 weeks will they transfer you out from here. I do not know if I'll be in this territory. I've just returned from dinner everything was very fine. For this type of work one has to her a strong, determined person. I believe that I shall close this time at this letter since I write an English letter to our next door neighbor in Columbus. How did the picture come out that I made at the Morehouse National? Don't write an answer to that until I write to you first.

With kisses to all of you with loads of love, until we meet again, Irving

1943/4/1 Irving to Family, Camp Wolter Texas (Book 5, 317-319)

[Company B. 55th Infantry Training Battalion.]

1943 IV / 2
Camp Wolters, Texas.

My dear brothers and sisters.
I will inform you that tonight I discovered where I will be stationed. On Saturday I will be going there. I will be transferred to heavy weapons which means that I will not have to march so much. At the present time very good friends are here. There are 2 of them. One will become a doctor and the other one will be working with the intelligence services. How are you Hencsukam? What are you doing? Is your work very difficult? Please do not work hard, take care of your health and you also Mariska, how are you? Are you working in the same place as in the past? Don't worry, everything will be successful. I have exercised this afternoon. We played ball. Here they have all kinds of sports. Dezső, how are you? What kind of a car did you buy or are you going to buy? How's business? Are you earning nicely? Write about everything. And Herman how are you? What are you doing? Did you get a wage increase? I feel quite well, thank God. My writing isn't too good, but the reason is that I'm in a hurry and I'm in a very low chair. You can imagine it, this is the army. I will close this time. As soon as I get to the other place I will write you immediately in detail. Until then, kisses to you all, individually....... with love, Irving

Friday

April 5, 1943

Dear sisters and brothers!

Finally I have arrived to the new place where I will be for 13 weeks. Here I haven't done anything yet, just to relax from the other barracks. The first place I had a very good time. The guys were telling us good stories. They were happy. We knew each other. At this time we are only three of us who know each other. We can only get together in the evenings in this place and here they have heavier guns. At this time I don't know for sure [how it] compares to the previous place. How are you, Hermine? What are you doing? What's new there? Write about everything. I'm writing also and will try every day when possible. Yes, at this time I will try to write more. I'm writing on my bed. My writing is not the best. Tomorrow is Sunday and I'll have more time. I will write a whole page just for you. The question is if you have the patience to read it. Here it is very hot. My face will be black by the time I go home. You will not recognize me. Hermine dear, please ask the neighbor if they received my letter. I will write more and ask him that he should also write. Please let me know when you received the telegram.

Irving

Dear Maria!

I know you too would like to get a long letter from me, but here we don't always have time for that. At this time we don't have to pack the guns, but next week we will begin that also. At this time we are just doing what you used to do for me, that is, washing my stockings and white clothing every night. I must do that so it should be fresh. Also we have to make our bed so that not even a wrinkle should be on it. You know we have to get used to it. I think it is very good, but I think I wrote about myself enough. I ask you also you should write me more too. How are you? Do you have lots of work? Did you change jobs? Please write about everything. Dear Dezső! I know you are wondering why I did not write to you first. You know the English saying, "Ladies first." Therefore I don't have to explain anymore. About myself the only thing I can write is thank God I'm okay. Hope you are all well also and to hear the best from you. Please, I'm asking you to write more about everything, as I told Herman [to do] also. Tomorrow if it's possible I will write more. Dear Herman! How are you? Are you working hard? Don't forget, over there it doesn't matter how hard you're working. You can tell your boss, but here if you like it or not, you can't say a word. Just do it. In case he didn't give you a raise, then you should ask for it because now is the time. Whoever is at home makes money. At this time I am closing my letter, many kisses individually to Hermine, Marie, Dezső, Herman

Irving

I wrote to the neighbor one card and one letter

Say hello to Walters

Tuesday 6th 1943

My dearest brothers and sisters,

I hope that by now you received all my letters and postcards. I would love to hear from you all very much. I hope you are all right! Thank God, I'm doing fine. Yesterday afternoon I got a shot again [immunization shot]. My arm hurts a little although that doesn't mean anything. Today, on Tuesday we were doing some exercises and went to the movie theater to learn what a soldier must know during his 13 weeks. It'll be a lot of hard work. Today I'm completely armed so that tomorrow we can start to do the real work. My friends came to visit me on Sunday evening. Since I relocated to this place, I am in the 57th infantry regiment. Here we only use a hand rifle. There in the 55th regiment we used hand rifle, machine guns, and a smaller cannon. Now we only practice with rifles. Since I came over from the other barracks I couldn't imagine why there are all kinds of people mixed together here. It bothered me a little.

But on Monday evening I moved my stuff into a different barrack. Here it is not so bad, because the boys are better, and it's on the first floor. Suddenly I can't think of anything, except every day there is more work.

Today, we had a talk about freedoms, [which] you can't get for the next 13 weeks. The town is not too far, but you need a permit to go there and they aren't giving any permits unless I know all the rules. But even then, they let you go only twice in the 13 weeks. It's very strict around here. Everything would be fine, if we wouldn't have to run, but I believe I will get accustomed to it, because it's mandatory. It isn't necessary to tell anyone what I write here. The hot [weather] is terrible. When the wind blows then it blows the sand so much like it blows the snow at home at winter time. Please write a lot, because I can barely wait. I will close my lines, I stay with much love, and send kisses many times separately to each one of you. I still didn't get any letters from anyone. I will write more next time. Kisses, Irving

1943/4/7 Irene Walters to Irving (Book 4, 36-38)

Columbus, OH.
4-7-43
Dear Irving,

We want you to know how very much we appreciate hearing from you. Glad you like Army life and everything is going well with you. We have been working day and night this past week. We have one man off sick, and let our colored girl go as her work was not satisfactory. There isn't much time for a breathing spell. However, we aren't complaining. The first and foremost is getting this war over. Perhaps then, we will be able to relax and take a deep breath. I was just over to see the girls and Herman. They are fine, but miss you like we all do. However, they are enjoying your letters very much and I know any word you get from them is very helpful to you. They tell me you have taken on a lot of tan since you arrived in the west, and we won't know you when you return which we hope won't be too long. Mother is fine and asks me to send you her warm greetings. Best wishes and glad to hear from you when you have time.

Sincerely, Mrs. Hasson, Howell and Irene Walters

1943/4/7 Mrs. Hasson to Irving (Book 4, 39-40)

Columbus Ohio
April 7, 1943
Hello Irving:-

Just a note to also add my bit to what Irene has already wrote. They want you to know we think of you a lot. But as I told you before you left you do not have anything to worry about. Your attitude is right. I don't know of anyone I have talked with feels like you, and expresses a desire as freely as you. Keep it up. Well things here are going along about the same only piling it on. This is the first night we have been here for over a week. So thought we had better rest a little and start out fresh tomorrow. Oh yes! I see Herman starting out every morning on a new bicycle and so far he has not even got a scratch on it. So I think he's getting along alright. And as for the girls about all they seem to be doing is writing some fellow every night. By the way I forgot to get that lady friend's address and telephone number-so when you think of it send it along, and I'll take care of things here for you. Had a young man in today who is stationed in Kansas. He brought everything home with him even his blankets because he said if he left them he would never find them because of the sand storms. They must be terrible. Well Irving:-take care of yourself and let us hear from you (when you can). Your friends and neighbors,
Mr. and Mrs. Howell Walters and Mother Hasson

1943/4/11 Irving to Family (Book 6, 117-127)

Dear siblings,
Today is Sunday and I have more time to write a letter. Dear Hermine, I can't tell you how happy you made me with your letter. I really could hardly wait for it. You know it's hard to imagine because when I wrote my first letter, I knew I couldn't get an answer to it. And when I wrote the second one, I wasn't even sure that I will get a response. But, when I got your first letter, I felt like I talked to you in person. It makes me happy knowing, that thank god, you are healthy. I'm so happy to hear that you stick together like siblings because, you know Hermine, if anyone is being bad to you just tell them, that they should try to live in a strange land far from home, then they will realize that they have a good sibling like you. You know dear Mariska, don't be worried, like I read your card, you would like to be here with me, but I don't know if that would be possible. I hope that the time will come that we will see each other again soon. When I came here

I got a short hair cut, but yesterday we had an inspection and I had to cut it even shorter. I went in the evening and I'm almost bald. Here they call it GI [in Hungarian this is a type of cut by the government].Therefore I barely have hair. Now, if you would ask how many pieces of hair I have? I could answer it, because I don't believe I have more than 4 pieces. I will note, though, here there is no time to comb or brush hair. Everyone is like this with that, I'm not the only one. My Hermine, like you wrote it, that [when] my pictures are done, you would like to get one. You also asked me, if I got letters from the girl? Yes, 3 pages. I wrote a card for her, but today I will write a letter also. Yes, I got a letter from the neighbor. I was very happy about it. Did you know how beautiful her writing is? I can truly say that she's like an actress. You can't see writing like that, really beautiful. This one is very interesting, the neighbor is asking for the girl's address, but I won't give it to her. Also Hermine, I got your card too and while I was reading I was thinking about you. Here they don't make such good things like you! You know that Petofi [a Hungarian poet] said that the brown bread is better at home than the white one in foreign land. That is so true. Here sometimes the problem is that they give us bacon and then I can't eat, because I won't eat bacon. A peasant [a poor farmer] could be satisfied with that, but for me, I drink instead. Milk or coffee and bread with butter, also an apple or orange with it, sometimes corn flakes with milk. One can get full, but the difference is that the day is long and hard. From 5 o'clock early in the morning until 5 o'clock at night. We rest before we have to go for a run. For example, we get 10 minutes, but at the same time 4 minutes run and for the next 6 minutes we sit down to relax. Friday, we had our first marching, we walked 4 miles, with complete equipment. But really it's nothing because we need to do more. I will write more about that. Now I have been writing so many foolish things, if you will have patience to read. Otherwise I'm doing fine, today the weather was beautiful. It's very warm here, but there's no wind. Today, if you would've been here, we could've gone for a picnic. Yes, how come Herman and Dezső don't write? Maybe they're angry? I wrote enough, and if they don't write to me then they don't deserve my letters. Or maybe they are tired? But even then they could write. I know about myself, here we have enough work to do, when the night comes I could sleep for a week, but I still write a couple of lines. So they could write too. Now I kiss you all many times one by one, Hermine, Mariska, Dezső, and Herman with much love, Irving

Dear Herman, Sunday 4/11/43

While I was writing one of my letters I was thinking about you, what would be the reason why you don't write. I thought that maybe you are angry, or maybe I knocked you off from the bicycle? But as I'm reading your letter, well you aren't angry, only writing doesn't agree with you. You know why I'm saying this, because you only write a quarter of a page and you send half of the letter. Here in the army it isn't so bad, you just have to be smart and clever. There are all kinds here, smart and dumb at the same time. The town isn't too far because there are buses. The only problem is that it's not easy to get permission to go to the town. The weather isn't bad, only when the wind is blowing, then it's like at home in the winter when the wind is blowing the snow. And when it's raining, then there's lightening in the entire sky. And if starts to rain then it pours. Now I don't know what to write, because you barely write me. But maybe I should write more. Then you would realize how great it is when someone writes a lot. I know how hard it is to write, but if you would see me then you would know how you could do that. I need to think in a way that if I can walk, I must, so you can write because you must. Although, nobody is making me write. But I'm alone thinking that if you would be in my place then it would be really great to get one letter every day. I believe that I wrote enough for you and I'm hoping next time you will write me an entire page. I kiss you many times and wish you a Happy Passover. I will see you later, Irving

My dear Hermine,

I believe, that you are surprised when I write your name. But believe me, when I write it, I think so. What I wrote in my other letter I expressed myself differently. I will send that letter to you also. Now I'm responding to your letter from today, in other words, to the April 6th letter.

Now I will try to write separately to everyone. I can believe that Mariska was angry, that you wrote. But you know, that your letter felt good. You know from so far away, it doesn't hurt to get a letter every day. Now, imagine we are very busy every day so when the night comes, in our free time, I have a little time to think about you. When I got your first letter we just went for a march and I didn't have time to read it from noon to night, but I was very happy that I got a letter from all of you. It was not a problem that not everyone wrote, here one day without mail means a lot.

I note, when they yell it out that there is mail, then I have to go outside and listen if there is mail for me. And, if there is one letter or card that came for me, then you can imagine what it means for me. I would be much happier than if I would just run out and there would be nothing. Now I will finish my letter, because I really wrote a lot. Before I got your letter today, I had already written one to you. I believe you will need patience to read what I scribbled-scrabbled, but if you only have patience, please read it and write to me a lot. I wish you a very Happy Passover and much love and kisses many times. Until we will see each other again. Your little brother, Irving

Dear Dezső, How are you?
Write to me, then I will write to you also.
I wish you a Happy Passover. Kisses many times your brother, Irving

Dear Mariska,

I just got your letter. I could say that I was very happy for it. Although, I already wrote a letter, I will respond to this one too anyway. You know, I'm not angry at all, that you didn't respond to my first letter. But you know you got me very happy with that card. And now I'm really happy for your letter. Like you mentioned, Hermine wrote everything. Don't forget, it's not that easy to write everything, although, I only write one also. But still every letter of mine sounds different.

My dear Marcsa, don't worry, you know that is bad for you. Here everything is available for money. Do I have money? Yes, thank God! I do. Believe me I am the same way with the writing like you. When I have to write, I can't think of anything. But if I start, I can't stop I have so much to say. Today I went to the synagogue, but I don't know yet, if I will go to the town on Passover. I need permission to go. If it's possible I will go, but if I can't, then I will go to the synagogue here. Here in the army it's very hard to do, because I would get to leave at 5 pm and I have to come back by 12 am and the town is about 50 miles away. Although there are buses, it's still hard because I have to work all day long. I wish you a Happy Passover. I will write separately to the rest of my siblings. As you can see I'm writing with a different ink. You know I have a friend here. I asked for more ink and he gave it to me and when I started to write the letter with this ink, but now it's too late to change it. Here at this new place there are a few nice guys, but my old friends come to visit me sometimes. Please don't be sad. Everything is going to be fine. I kiss you many times, your brother Irving

Write me a lot, like you did these days.

Thank you for the laundry!! When I will do my laundry I will think about you!

1943/4/13 Irving to family (Book 2, 206-210)

Tuesday 13, 1943
Dear siblings,

Yesterday I sent a card and I wrote that it's possible I will call you on Sunday morning or in the afternoon. We are very busy here and we don't know when one can write a few lines. At night when one has some free time, there is work to do also. Yesterday, I worked in the kitchen and when I finished I went back to practice. Yesterday they called me to the commander regarding the residency papers. He asked me where I came from and why didn't I come to America earlier? I told him why. Also, I told him that I wished to come, but I couldn't. He asked me who came with me and what do they do for work? The main question was, if I would be in Slovakia, would I fight against the Germans? I answered, yes. The reason he asked me that is because, if I'm against the Germans, I will get the papers. If it works out, it's possible that they will switch me to another company. I could have a better job because the commander said that he is going to need me. Before I came out, he asked what is my religion? I said, Jewish, and he said, I don't look like it because I am blonde. Today, it is Tuesday night and I had to cut my writing in half, because they're calling me to school again...As soon as I come out of school, I will start to write again. You know they asked last week who wants to study in the officer training school, in other words to be a Lieutenant etc. I signed up for it too and they asked me why do I want to be that? I said, it would be great only if it would work out. During another [session] the commander asked, what I would have wanted to be, if I wasn't in the military? I thought it would be good to answer that I wanted to be a doctor. But when I told him that, he asked then why am I being signed up for a combat unit? I answered that here in America it is worth being signed up for anything. But they also asked, if I would like it better as a medic? And I responded yes, so this way I can't go to study at the officer training school. He says that a medic wants to help, not to kill, and an infantryman studies how to kill. So, I think it's better, if they will move me to be a medic. The best thing would be to be home. Unbelievably, I don't know what to think and I don't know what will be. One thing for sure is that it's hard and dangerous everywhere, but suddenly I thought that it would be better as a medic. I had to stop writing because it was getting dark. Today is Wednesday morning and I want to finish writing so I can send it now. Thank God I'm fine. I would have wanted to send this letter by airmail, but there is no time to go to buy a stamp. I will call you on Sunday, if it's possible. Now I'm closing my lines, kisses many times all of you separately, Irving

If you have time and patience then write. I will write to all of you as soon as I will have more time. Kisses, Irving

1943/4/14 Herman to Ignác (Book 3, 34-35)

1943 April 14

Dear Ignác

I was very happy to receive your letter. I'm going to write to you, but don't wait to get long letters from me. I'm not saying that sometimes I may. I'm well. The news is almost the same as it was. I did not get a wage increase. Their excuse was that he sent for permission to Washington to be able to give a wage increase. He did not receive any information so he cannot give it. Two weeks ago he said that he told the girl to give me an increase, but she didn't give me anything, then he left and did not say anything more. I don't even care. I was inquiring about the citizenship papers and they said that I could receive it, but I have to mail in the papers. If you try you succeed, that's what they used to say. I didn't mail it in yet. I don't know how to fill it out, but I will try to fill it out. The weather here for the past few days was very bad. The wind blows and it's snowing just like in the winter. The bicycle tire was punctured and the weather is bad, so I didn't have it fixed. And with the work, I will look for another job. If I can get a defense job then I shall not work for him for the money that he pays. I don't care how good he is, but this is the time to make money, if not now when. Perhaps it would be good to be a soldier. You see a lot and you learn a lot. I believe this was enough and I will write to you next week again.

I wish you will have a happy Passover. Kisses, Herman

1943/4/14 Hermine to Irving (Book 10, 63-64)

April 14, 1943

My dear Irving! Otherwise [In English] sweetheart OK.

[In Hungarian] We just got your air mail letter today and I know that you can imagine my happiness. You know little brother, today I stayed at home because where I work they did not give me a raise, [they] only [pay] by the piece we make and that is very hard. I talked to them, but I did not quit yet. I think that one of these days I will go in to quit and to ask my two weeks' pay. I should not write this to you because you will be upset because I will not have money now. But I just thought that I have a little money now and I got shoes and a coat and I can wait in this way a little bit until I get a good job. I just called Mrs. Hawkins and she said that she got a card from you and she already responded to you yesterday. I asked what you wrote. She explained about your picture and she read to me over the phone what you wrote. She was very happy that you wrote to her. You know little brother, yesterday and today it's snowing just like in winter. Although in the past days it was almost like summer. Don't think about my job and don't be upset by it because I would have a job where Mrs. Hawkins works, or I could go back to where I worked, but they are very big men [big shots], that is why I left them. In the past weeks a lot of people left them. Right now I did not talk to the neighbor, but they always call us and they are kind, but I think it is not to good to get along too much.

Hope we will talk on the phone shortly! I kiss you with love. Hermina

1943/4/14 Maria to Ignác (Book 3, 32-33)

Wednesday, 1943 April 14

Dear Irving!

I received your airmail letter and it made me very happy. As I see you receive mail even on Sunday. Am I mistaken? You know my dear Irving, I'm happy to hear that you are well. I know we can't help you to do anything about it, but I would like to know how you are with the dinners? As I see in the morning you eat breakfast and in the evening you eat supper then when do you eat dinner? I would like to mail you a package, but we are going to wait for a reply to the last letter. What are you eating? Do you know, when I eat I always think of you, that is, the larger portion remains for you. My dear little brother, I know it is difficult for you to eat non kosher products, but you must eat because if you don't eat you're not going to be strong and energetic and it's important that you take care of yourself as much as you can. Thank God I'm well. I hope to hear from you. Now I'm working in the same place as I did before. I work every day. I haven't seen our neighbor since then. I don't know why she was interested to get the address of the girl. I do not want you to mention it to her what I write about this. Last week, she came over one evening and our own lady from our house and the neighbor's husband came out and do you know they are garbage because they got together and then the woman threatened him. After that I don't know what happened. I am really not interested and I know, you too are not interested. I am just writing that the next day the young woman came over and said that she's sorry because on the street it's not polite to argue and she knows it and she gave the water tank, but at first she didn't want to do anything and then she said it will be somehow, someway. Do you know my dear little brother I'm in a hurry to write you every day if not much, but a little. Here the weather is like winter, snowing [and] windy and I was thinking of you about the sand how the wind blows it. Listen my dearest Irving, just now you know the news. I called our relations, the lady wrote to you a card. Arthur didn't feel well so he stayed at home, however, he said that he feels a little bit better. I don't know anything special to write to you and as for Passover do what's best for you. God knows how things are. You can't maintain the holiday so don't worry about it, as it comes, it is. Take care of yourself, that's what God commands you. I wish you a pleasant holiday. We can talk to you on the telephone and so long! Many times many kisses, your sister, Maria [In English] By. By. By.

1943/4/17 Flo Meizlish to Irving (Book 17, 224-229)

Saturday, April 17, 1943
"One Day Closer to Victory"

Dear Irving,
I mailed you my picture Tuesday so you should have it by the time you get this letter. I tried to get a leather frame for it but I couldn't find any to fit it. It would have been better for you than something with glass but I just couldn't find it. Am I forgiven? On your postcard you said you'd write me a letter some day so I waited until I'd receive your letter before I'd write again but I guess you forgot because I didn't receive any letter this week. I bought a beautiful new outfit for spring. My father was kidding me and he said he didn't see why I bought a new outfit, since there weren't any men around any more to admire it. But I told him I just had to have something to keep up my morale. When you come home on furlough, I'll wear it for you, so you can admire it. Is that alright with you? Shirley was saying the other day that "As the old saying goes, In the spring a young man's fancy lightly turns to thoughts of love. The only trouble is there aren't any young men around this spring." Last Sunday Myron and I went up to "Mirror Lake" on the Ohio State campus to take pictures. Myron has a camera that cost about a $100. But the best pictures of me were taken on my camera. And when I took them in to be developed, the man in charge misplaced them and so far they haven't been found. But if they are found and the pictures come out good I'll send you the snapshots of me. If he doesn't find them, I think I'll be tempted to sue him. Well that's about all for now, so General I think I'd better let you get back to more important matters. Write soon, and forgive this messy letter but you boys in the army aren't the only ones in a hurry. Right now, I am. As ever, Flo

1943/4/18 Irving to Dezső (Book 5, 243-245)

[Company B 55th Infantry Training Battalion, Camp Wolters, Texas]

4-18-43
Dear Dezső,
I was very happy to receive your card and letter. It was pleasure to read it. You have surprised me with your writings. As you mentioned in your letter, that in the beginning I used to write a lot, you were that way also when you came to America. I can only write when I have a chance. As you know, now I will begin the exercises with rifles and weapons. Tomorrow, Monday, will be the first day that we will be using real bullets. Up to now we're only learning how guns, weapons function. Now we're using handguns, machine guns. Thank God that I have been accustomed to the military life. You know David, for Passover I will be going to the city and will have a Seder at the Jewish United Service Organizations (USO) They have organized it. We have a permit from the commander that any of the Jewish individuals may go if they want to go. As I'm writing this letter, I'm waiting for the telephone with some difficulty. While waiting for the telephone there is a Czech fellow, who is very funny and he too is waiting for the telephone. Do you know that we are very happy that we are able to telephone home, however, it takes a long time to wait for our turn which takes between 2-3 hours of waiting. As you mentioned in your letter that I should call you frequently, that would be wonderful, however I can't do that since today is Sunday and we have things that have to be done. This week I was lucky that my rifle was clean. Sometimes it happens that some soldier's was not clean and he

can't get any free time. You asked me if I would like to have a stripe? Yes and no. As I was talking to the captain and asked him if it's better to be a captain or private? And he replied that it's okay, but on the other side [overseas] it's no good. If I get any stripes I will write to you about it. I'm sending my love and kisses and hope to meet again.

Your little brother, Irving

Write me lot it!! I also wish you happy Passover!

1943/4/18 Irving to Family (Book 5, 240-242)

[Camp Wolters, Texas]
Sunday 4-18-43
My dear sisters and brothers,
I can't even write down to explain to you how happy I was talking to you on the telephone. Probably it cost you at least $15 those few minutes, however when I heard your voices I felt like I was at home. Believe me my dear family, brothers and sisters, you cannot talk too much in a few minutes, however we spoke quite a lot. I'm sorry that Herman wasn't at home. I want to thank you Dezső and I will reimburse you. As I mentioned about the packages, if you can mail me, I would like to get the green eyeglasses that attach to the eyeglasses. I have them at home. Here I will be getting 2 new eyeglasses, the very round one won't be coming with me. Also, I will get socks. As I mentioned to Marcsa, to send me some chewing gum. I thought to send me something round like lemon drops or orange drops. Otherwise I don't need anything else. If you need any money for the expenses and for the telephone call, take it out from the bank and I will pay for it, it was worth every bit of it to speak to you. Presently we are getting ready to go to the temple. We are going to go to Fort Worth. More likely they will be giving us matzos for the week. I will write about it tomorrow. My dearest Hencse and Marcsa, I know that you two were surprised when you heard my voice. Please write to me and tell me how it sounded. I spoke to you from about 2000 miles away and it sounded like I was next door, it is amazing. I will write more in the near future. Kisses to you all individually many times and write even though just a few lines!
Irving.

1943/4/19 Undated Marie to Irving (Book 9, 253-254)

[dated by phone call on Sunday, see letter above]

Monday
My Dear Little Irving!
Your telephone call yesterday surprised me so much, since it came so unexpectedly. But, believe me, I was very happy for that. Although, we did not talk a lot because I would have wanted to talk to you already, but you know we can't talk too much on the phone. But it is enough, if we can hear each other's voice. And we can talk the rest out in the letters. How are you my little brother? Do you know if you will get vacation days? And when? And will you get relocated? I hope everything is going to be fine! You know, my little Irving, don't be surprised, if you heard loud words on the phone, because you know, everyone wants to talk more and that minute is so short so there is only so much we can talk. And you, in a big hurry, could not even talk. I'm asking you my Irving, to write to me. You know, whatever you can. And you know the weather is bad here too. It's raining all the time and the air is cold. Today is Monday morning and I only need to go to work at 12. We were very busy yesterday, we had a big cleaning. But today everything is alright. So, I hope it will be enough for awhile. Did you get used to the air there? Last week we did not get mail from you either. I thought about you a lot. And I thought you must be very busy. Or maybe tired. What did you do yesterday on Sunday? You know, my Irving, when you called yesterday it rang and I picked up the phone first, and you know the volume was so low, that I could not understand. I knew that it was you, but I was not sure so I called Hermine and she understood immediately. I was very happy. Did you pay it or did you have to pay for it in advance? Dezső said that he wants to pay for it. But you know, he was sleepy because I woke him up. I'm only asking little brother not to be sad and take care of yourself. We are hoping and trusting the dear God that he will help, so everything is going to be fine. We are all well. I'm going to find out what my job is going to be today. I kiss you countless times. I will stay with love until I see you again.
Maria

1943/4/19 Undated Hermine to Irving (Book 10, 21) - phone call home

[dated by phone call home, and David is still in Columbus[

My dear little brother!

I am truly happy that you called us, even if we could not talk for long. Mary [Mariska] picked up the phone first and did not understand who it was, but I knew that it was you immediately. I heard as though a woman would have said something like you have five minutes to talk. That is why I told Dave to tell you what is important because if you need to pay it will cost a lot. The last time when Dave called you it cost 4.50 or 5 dollars, but before that it cost a lot and they charge tax on it too. You know my little brother, I was very happy to hear your voice, but I'm sorry I told this to David because there could be a lot to talk about and it could be not important in a letter. I hope you are well and I understood that you are very busy. The weather here is very bad. It is raining most of the time. Today on Monday I have to go to work at 12 and I'm in a hurry to write to you. Although my writing is pretty bad, but [there's] not much time [I] need to finish the cleaning and then I will have time to finish. Do not think that Dave is that angry. He is still behaving well as much as he could. It is nice from him. Do not mention this to him if you write and I'm waiting for your lines. As soon as you can, I will do the same. Kisses, Hermine

1943/4/20 Irving to Family (Book 1, 146-149)

Dear siblings,

Today is the first day of Passover, unfortunately here we can't keep it like in Columbus or at home. However, on the first night I was in Fort Worth and it was very good. The rabbi read the haggadah, but he read very little, only a couple of words from everything. The Passover dinner was great, they had kneidlach also. On a note, I did not see many civilians there. I barely saw maybe thirty of them and we were 200 soldiers. On that note, in camp there are approximately 20,000 soldiers. We were leaving at night at 6 o'clock and the bus ride took 1 hour and 45 minutes long. The cost was $1.25. The city is beautiful, and it's much closer and nicer than at home in the summer. The view is spectacular, only the situation is military. Yesterday I took a sharp shooting exam. We had to shoot 20 bullets in 60 seconds and it had to be aimed exactly in the circle. Mine went well. Every shot is worth 5 points if you can get it into the circle. If you can't, then it's worth 4, 3, or 2 points. This is the circle (see drawing above in letter). I shot from approximately 200 meters and got 90 points, put in another way, out of 20 shots I missed only 2 and this is very good. It is possible that I will get a medal for it. Next week we will start the machine gun exercise. You know it's interesting, the weapons just make a crackling sound here. Do not be worried that I could have an accident. That is impossible here. For example, when we go to the shooting range everything is very strict. We can not turn the rifle tube backwards and if anyone would even try with an empty rifle they would deal with that person. I'm writing this so you won't be worried! My letter is going to be late today, because I started it three times. Today is Wednesday, yesterday evening it was a very good seder here. I'm attaching the paper I had. I'm noting that I thought about all of you a lot. I could write a lot, but will write more only Sunday. Today on Wednesday we went for a hike with the complete equipment. We have to do 4 kilometers in an hour. It was good enough, because the wind blows all the time. They say that it's cold here. True, the nights are cold, but in the day [you] are melting. I could write so much, but Sunday I will continue. Today I got a letter and a card from you, but I have no time to read them. I will just skim through them. It's 9 o'clock at night and I cleaned the rifle, but because I'm writing I won't take a shower. You know, here it has to be dark [lights out] at 10 pm and nobody is allowed to be in the shower. But it's very nice to hear that you are all doing well. And you Hencsú, don't be sad, you will have a better job. I hope you will look for an easier job, so you won't have to work too hard. I will write about this more. A note, that I'm sorry I write your name differently, in other words that I call you in different ways! Also Mariska, don't be upset about the vaccination. It's healthy in hot weather like this. It's necessary to make you stronger. Herman, don't think about joining the army because many people are homesick. And you can't believe how hard life is for a soldier. You can get used to everything, but it's better to be home. Dear Dezső, I don't know what to write to you. Thank God I'm doing well. I will write on Sunday. We get home late these days around 6-7 o'clock at night and we have a lot to work on until 10 pm. And after 10 I can't believe I can go to rest. Today I saw a beautiful movie. You know, when the Germans conquered Czechoslovakia and the other countries. Everything about how it started and since the Germans came to power. You can't see this picture as a civilian, but here there are movies everyday and we are learning from it. Also, they introduced the Skoda [it's a Slovakian car] factory and they said that it is the world's best factory. Now, I'm sorry that I don't respond to all of your letters and cards, but on Sunday I will. Now I'm sending kisses many times to all of you.

With lots of love. Irving

Federal Security Agency
Social Security Board
Interoffice Communication

Date 4/23/43
Mr. Huesel:

This will introduce Hermina Gluck who has made application with us for employment. It has been a little difficult to place Hermina due to her delay in getting citizenship papers. She is an excellent applicant in our opinion, and during a conversation with Mrs. Helen Bitterman, who you know, I uncovered the fact that there is some possibility of placing her in your organization. I believe her appearance and personality will speak for itself and also that she would be a very apt student. Any consideration you may give her will be greatly appreciated by both Mrs. Bitterman and myself.

Sincerely,
Grace Miller
Interviewer - U.S.E.S.

Mr. Huesel
Associated Public Utilities
Mills Bldg - 3rd floor
77 S. High St.
Columbus, Ohio

4-25-43
Dear Dezső, I have a little time to write today. I received your regards on my sister Mariska's card. It's true, I would like to receive a letter from you. I know that you're busy. For the holidays I went to Fort Worth. It's a very nice town however, I realized the prices are very high here. Last night I went to Mineral Wells. There everything costs much more. There are a lot of soldiers there and it doesn't pay to go there. Do you know Dezső, if everything is in order then I can go to the city at any time. For example from evening or from Saturday evening to Monday morning. But you must have a definite place to go and you must show the invitation and or reservations. How are you? How's everything going for you? Are you earning nicely? I thank God I'm advancing quite well. If I hear anything about the transfer I will let you know. I'm supposed to get a reply this week. I will explain everything to them. Otherwise I'm okay and I remain with love and kisses, your little brother Irving.

Dear Herman,
How are you? What are you doing? Are you working hard? It has been three days already that I haven't heard from you any news or letter. And do you know Herman, that Bnaj Brith is sending me a newsletter and tells me what's going on. I believe that you should also join them, it would be good for you, too. Are you working during the holiday? I do, here everything is different. Do you still want to be a soldier? This week we marched so much that as a civilian I would be never able to do so much walking. Down from the mountain and up the mountain and completely equipped with 60 pounds. That's enough.
I shall write more, kisses Irving.

Dear siblings,
I'm just at home in the service club and thinking of all of you. Today I wrote a letter already and maybe you are bored that I wrote so much. There is music here and they are partying. Although I went to the synagogue tonight, I came in to look around. If it's possible I'll make a recording and I will send it home to you. It doesn't cost anything because Pepsi Cola organizes it every week. As I can see it's late [to make one] already, since it's only allowed until 5pm. I will send it as soon as possible so you can hear my voice. I think I wrote it in my other letter, that I didn't get letters from you on Thursday. I hope you are all in good health.

How are you? How's everything going? What's the weather like? Here I'm melting. Mariska, you asked if I have any friends here? Yes, I do, mostly good guys and you know, there is a strange one. If he gets a package I have to open it for him, and he always offers from it. And, if I don't want to accept it, then I must anyway. He gets a package almost every day. Hermine, tell me when will you get pictures done with Mariska? Or Herman? I would love to see what you look like already. Since I left from home I weighed myself and I'm 165 pounds. I think I put on some weight, but I don't know how much.

Herman tell me, how are you? Does the bicycle ride well? Watch wherever you go! Do you still work at the place where you worked before? Did you get a raise? I will get my first check next Friday. You know it's hard to wait it out, but this is how it goes! Write, if you can!

Dear Dave,

I'm only writing a few lines, because I wrote a letter already once today. But since I'm in this Service Club and I got a table it's easier to write than on the bed or chair. What's new? Hermine wrote that you called the girl, I wonder what she said? I got a letter from her, but I'm not in a hurry to answer. True, she writes and it's interesting to read it. I think that I wrote enough today. Tomorrow, I will write more, if I will have time. You mentioned that you will come to visit. I don't even know what to say because here it is very expensive for a civilian. It's worth it to come only if you have a lot of money, and if you have a lot then it isn't so much. Have you gone to synagogue? I have, but there are mostly soldiers there, and it's boring to see only soldiers in town. I can get a day off every week, if I'm not on duty and everything is in order. It has been all good until now, and I hope it will stay that way. I will close my letter and sending kisses many times, Hencsu, Marcsa, David and Herman separately with much love!

Your little brother,

Irving.

I will go to synagogue.

Don't worry!

Write to me as soon as you can.

Irving.

1943/4/25 Irving to Hermine (Book 3, 11-14)

4-25-1943

Dear Hermina,

At the present time I can reply to your letters, which I was very happy [to receive]. This week I did not have much time to write. Here every day there is always something new to learn. For example on Thursday I used a rifle to shoot out at night. Before we do anything like that we get a lecture. This morning we woke up at five o'clock we ate at 7:20 AM and then moving fully equipped we went marching to the mountain, valleys, throughout. You can imagine how this goes here. We got an order as we were going up on the mountain to put on our gas masks and this made it difficult to breathe and made us tired. But don't worry, here we must learn everything as if it would be real and must know it like if we're going in combat. My dear sister Hencsu, how are you? As you know I received your two letters but I could not read them until this evening. This week I have not received many letters, more likely you are busy. How are you otherwise? Are you working hard? Did you get a good job? Don't worry about work. God will help you. You'll get a good job. I also know it's difficult to wait. Also I want to tell you not to worry about me, everything here is okay. At this time on Passover it is difficult with the eating situation, but we must eat, that is I must eat, and I'm sure it's permissible. I got a package from the USO. The package contained the following: matzos, nuts, salami, cookies, and honey. Everything was very good, but there's no special time to eat it. And the honey, I don't even know when I will be able to use it. The baked goods, salami, and nuts I shall consume slowly. I would offer you something, but we're far away from each other! I believe that I was missing at your Seder, but I'm glad that there is someone who thought about it. I hope next year for Passover we shall be together. Now I'm closing my lines, many kisses, your little brother, Irving

I'm curious how much you get for the telephone conversation course? Please let me know.

With love your little brother Irving

You know, my sister Hencsu,

As I'm writing these lines, I'm laughing and I'm imagining, what you're thinking about my beginning, I hope you're not going to be angry that I'm writing this way. Every Friday evening we are quite busy because on Saturday they inspect everything. The first thing is to clean your rifle so that not even a morsel of dust will be on it. Your hair has to be in order, and clean the barracks and all the equipment with it. My rifle last week was the best between 60 soldiers. This week also mine was good and I was happy for it. You know last evening, that is, Saturday evening, I went to the city. When I'll mail you a card, I will note where I was. It doesn't pay to go there because there are many soldiers. Do you know Hencsu! I wanted to make a picture there, but there were too many people in line. I didn't have patience to wait for hours until I would have had my turn. I also wanted to have the watch fixed. You know, they were asking $3 to fix the winder, so I didn't have it fixed. If I have an opportunity, then I'm going to send it home, more likely it is cheaper to have it fixed there. At this time I'm going to go to the temple and I shall continue this letter after I return.

As soon as I arrived home I am continuing this letter. Today I had a chance to lay t'filem and pray. Today, Sunday and tonight, I will go to the temple also. At 7:30 PM there be something to drink and then they're going to pray. Do you know this is the way it is here! You ask in the last letter what have I done at the wedding? Here's a Jewish fellow with me and he told me that he was invited to a wedding. I met the rabbi and he asked me to come to the wedding. I drank a little wine. It was interesting to observe the military wedding. Here everything is definitely not like in civilian life. Now I'm going to sign off. Loads of kisses, your little brother Irving

It's Jiskar [Yizkor]. I will be in the temple.

1943/4/25 Irving to Maria (Book 3, 9-10)

4-25-43

Dear Maria,

At the present time I have time to write and because of that I will write a few pages. Thank God I'm well and I hope to hear from you likewise. I received your card that you sent me and I was very happy to receive it. You are worried about me. Please don't worry because here everything is different, it's not like at home. Here the days are long, but it goes very fast. We are very busy, and there was little time to write this week, because of that I did not write a lot. However, I hope that you will have time to write to me a lot. I am waiting and I find it difficult to wait for your card, although I know you have a lot of work and you're tired also. You're asking me if I'm tired? Yes and no. Here I must get accustomed to it. I wrote to all our relatives, but I didn't get a reply. I hope that I will receive [something] from them in the near future. How are you Marcsa? Write to me a lot. If you're busy and you can't, just drop me a card, that will be sufficient. Probably I'm disturbing you with the writings but you can write to me about everything. How are you with your work? Are you working very hard? I believe it's quite difficult. I hope that you will find a good job. This week we have practiced with guns [and] grenades, and tomorrow we are going to use machine guns to get experience. It seems like it's going quite well for me. But at my first opportunity I shall mail the letters I have home because I want you to know and to see what they write to me regarding my English letters. Otherwise I'm okay. During the holidays I went to the temple and today I went for Jizkar. I have written a lot about everything. It's likely you'll get tired of reading it. If you have time, please write me a lot. A lot of kisses to you, your little brother, Irving

[On the side of the 1st page] The address? You don't have to write the number. If you write it, it's okay, if you don't write it, it's okay

[On the side of the 2nd page] Today I will find out if after 13 weeks I will get a vacation. I hope that I will get one.

1943/4/26 Frey-Yanken Paint to Irving (Book 3, 431-432)

Pvt. Irving Gluck
35633941
Co. B - 55th Infantry
Training Battalion
Camp Wolters, Texas

Dear Irving:

We were very glad to get your letter, and are also very happy to hear that you like it so well. All of us here feel certain that you are a fine representative of our company in the United States Army, and we are very proud of you. If everyone feels his duty as keenly as you, Irving, this country hasn't a thing to worry about. Don't let that Texas weather worry you. After all, isn't that out where "men are men" and the women just laugh at the whole idea? The entire office and factory send you the very best of wishes and luck. We're posting your letter on the bulletin board so that all can have your address. I'm afraid that this will be all for now, Irving, for there is work to be done, and as you know, it's up to us back here at home to do it. So until the next time, lots of good luck, Irving. Sincerely yours,

Management and Employees
Frey-Yankin Paint Company

P.S. Irving, I just thought I'd add a note. I was very sorry I wasn't here to see you before you left, but you know that I send you loads of luck. I'll bet you look real cute in your uniform. Lola Zuccarelli

1943/4/26 Undated Hermine to Irving (Book 2, 112-113)

[after writing to Mrs. Hawkins and sending home a photo. Selling gloves. Letter from Elsie.]

My dear Irving!
I got your letter as well as your card today and surely I am happy when there is news about you. Tell me, that is, write about it my little brother, if you think about little Hencsu [nényuza = little one] as you call me sometimes. You know my Irving, I miss you. I don't even have to write about that, but let's hope that we will see each other soon. I put the package together on Sunday to you my little brother. I hope it will work out. I can't write anything particular about me. Today was the first day I started selling and I sold 8 pairs of gloves. Although it's not the season now, it went pretty well. Although, I had help with it. You know the cases, if you take credit, you have to be put it out and the names will be hard to get used to, but I hope it will go easier tomorrow. The girls are very nice currently and I hope I will like to stand [for] work - [what] do you think? I wish you could be here my little brother, so you can come and visit me. Otherwise I'm well and we are all also. I'm sorry that I write so rarely to you, but I will truly be in a hurry to write to you. Believe me that your picture came [out] great at home. Sometimes I fool around and play with it and Marcsa kisses you with yearning, if you would see it. You know, if you would be home maybe she would not let me get close to you. I only write this because it would be good to fool around with you as I could. And I always mention you and I'm sorry if I rarely write. I'm very happy to get your cards. I'm collecting them in an album. If you could do it, just write anyway. I am truly interested what they write in the English letters because I can imagine Mrs. Hawkins said that she is proud of you. It is very nice of you. But if you are tired, it is not necessary to write too often. How often do you respond to them? Although, do the way you see that it's best. Did Elsie write to you from Cleveland? You know I did not get a letter from the relatives since then, only from Cleveland a card. Louis sent a social card that he probably scribbled together. I don't know why Bertha did not write. I am very busy also and if she doesn't write, why should I? But I will try to write to her sometimes. I kiss you with love and many times. Hermine
I wrote so much nonsense to you.

1943/4/27 Elsie Schallheim to Irving (Book 17, 284-287)

April 27

Dear Irving:
I was very glad to hear from you and to know that you like army life. How is the food? Are you putting on weight? I hope you will meet some nice boys that you will like. According to your letter you are learning a lot of things. However, try to be careful. I got a letter from my brother [Arthur]. He isn't feeling very well and Flora will need an operation in June. I'm busy everyday because I help my husband in the office. My daughter's school will be out the first of June. She studies hard. I hope that in a couple of years she can enter college. I hope the hot weather in Texas won't bother you too much. Have you heard recently from your brothers and sisters? Give them my love when you write. I hope you will keep well and let us hear from you when you can write. Best regards, your cousin, Elsie Schallheim

1943/4/27 Irving to Family (Book 6, 134-136)

Dear siblings,

Here everyday is a big day, and when I have time to write, I don't know what to write about first. Today we went to practice with the entire equipment and we made fox holes. This is how we learn how to shoot and while they are watching us from a plane, we have to hide. We had to dig out fox holes as deep as one's height. It was interesting to watch, how it was done in old times. You know, when the planes are coming they are very curious to watch, but we have to hide during that time. The real work is just getting started. This afternoon we went to learn how to shoot with machine guns. During the lessons we almost fell asleep in the warm weather. Here it is very hot, but we can sleep at night because it's cool enough. You know Hencsu, it's very kind of you that you want to send a package, but I can't ask you to do that, because here everything is available. But, if I will need anything, I will ask you. Dear Marie, I'm sorry, but I can't respond to your letter because I didn't get the package yet. I understand that you are trying to help me, but I have been having my laundry done about 2 weeks already, and it's a little easier that way. But I have enough work to do, also, my time is running. You mentioned that I should do everything slowly and don't do it in a hurry, true it would be good, if I could, but I can't. You know, here everyone has to do everything that I need to do and if it's possible I'm not in a hurry. Where I can, I won't rush for sure. But don't be upset about this, I will write about this more. Otherwise, I'm doing well and don't be upset. Dezső, how are you? Write! And Herman, what do you do? You write too. I will write more tomorrow. Now until I will see you again, kisses to all of you with much love, Irving

I don't know anything about moving out, but as soon as I get news I will write immediately. Write, if you have time because I can hardly wait for your answers.

1943/4/28 Irving to Maria and Hermina (Book 3, 17-22)

4-28-1943

Dearest Marie,

I will note that you are saying in your letter that you're not a punctual writer. But don't be surprised because you are very punctual and beside that, you believe to tell me the time when you're writing, in which minute you've been writing it. In the army that is very important. Here one minute is very important and it means a lot. I'm sorry to hear that Arthur is not feeling well. I don't know what could be the reason why they haven't written to me. When you speak to him give him, and the family, my regards. You are also surprised with my writings as I've written to Hencse that there are many situations when there is no time to write or to think. So I write as it comes into my mind. If you want me to, then next time I will send you an English letter.

I'm glad that the picture turned out to be successful. Sometimes I take your pictures also and I think of you. As you know, it's interesting to write an empty paper full. You certainly did it. But Herman does not do it. Why is it that Dezső and Herman don't write? Loads of love and kisses, your little brother, Irving

4-28-43

Dearest Hermina,

You really made me happy with your letter and I'm happy even with two lines. I also know that you are quite busy. That's no problem if you write me only a little, but please continue writing. I hope that you will like your work. Please write me about it. Please let me know how much the telephone expense was. You also mentioned that you were surprised that you're going to save my cards if I will write to you a small amount that I will manage on a card where I have been in which town. Also you're writing that they praise my English letter, however I'm writing it as it comes to me. If you want to, I will write to you an English letter also. You know it's difficult to think about it that I've to write. When I receive a reply I read it and I think about it a little and then I sit down on the edge of my bed and I write. I can tell you that I draw it out from my little finger. In my last letter I wrote a little bit, but I draw on something in each letter. Don't be angry, but I will close the lines for today. Work was similar to yesterday's. Today we are learning how to assemble the weapons, how fast it can be done. We have to assemble it within 8-10 seconds, it took us 15-20 seconds, sometimes it takes even longer, but we must learn to do it within 8 seconds. In this you must succeed, if not there's no choice but to do it. While we learn this we're on the ground so you can relax better. Sometimes I become sleepy, but cannot sleep, because then you have to run each hour for 10 minutes. One has to run a long way before we can rest. I believe that I scribbled so many things together that you will be tired to read it. With lots of love and kisses, your little brother Irving.

[In the lower corner] Here I am enclosing a news article, also a piece of paper on which you'll find the train on which I came here. This is as a remembrance for me when I get home and I'll have time to read it.

1943/4/30 Louis Schwartz to Hermine and Marie (Book 18, 282-284)

4-30-43

Dear Herminka and Mariska!

So, your letter found me at home, but purely by accident. Yet, if this letter will be as late as this was, it will definitely not find me home. Since I got the call, that is, they asked me to get ready to go in about May 13th. I will have to go to induction then, and a week later I have to join in. Although, my relatives requested three weeks delay because it's my cousin's [younger] wedding. She is a 19 year old girl with her boyfriend who volunteers for the Navy since January. He will get his commission at the beginning of May. At the same time they will have their wedding. I doubt that I will get it. I went up to the Board and they said it is impossible to do that.

I got a card from Irving, but I just had a chance to respond this week. I was very busy before Passover in the store. I hope that my letter will find you at the same place. Otherwise there is no news here. Like I said, Passover passed by unnoticed. Normally there is a big party at the seder, but now that the two boys are missing from the house, the mood was a little uneventful. What's up with Dezső? Does he know about the draft? And how are you? I am well, considering the conditions. I hope you are as well! I kiss all of you.

Louis

PS: Joe is in California. He hopes that he will stay there while the war lasts.

1943/5 Undated Hermine and Dezső to Irving (Book 10, 41-42)

[Undated - but by the content is just after Passover 1943. On 1943/5/5 Irving mentions the package they write about in this letter and that he has to share it, probably referring to the baked goods]

[from Hermine]

My dear Irving,

Today on Monday I will hurry to put a package together. It is possible that Dave will finish it. You know, my little Irving I tried to bake something good for you, but you know how it goes? When we want the best, it does not work out. Although, I can't bake just anything because some could go bad or get moldy. This way, I could only make something that will last. The kiflí [croissant] was stuffed with walnut, the other one with figs and there are a few plain in it. The rest of them are a new recipe and I don't know if you will like them! Little brother, write how they were when they arrived. Maybe start with the figs first because it could go moldy. You know one can live and learn. I bake good things, but one can forget or I don't even know why. I am only concerned that it is not good. But write it to me little brother. I will truly love you then. I am just getting ready for work at 12 o'clock. Thank God I am well. Also, all of us are well. Just write whenever you can. Now I am in a hurry, therefore I kiss you countless times with much of love. Hencsu OK

With the hope that the baking will get better by the time it will get there to you. Kiss you Hermine

[from Dezső]

Dear Ignác!

Currently I have no time to write to you at all because I have to go to work, but still I will write a few lines to you. You know I was inquiring from a soldier here [what will be] if you are in the infantry. He said, if you will stay there that every soldier gets 12 weeks of infantry training [and] after that's done, they will send them away. It is possible that [it will be] near by to Columbus, so don't be sad. You know the USO wrote a letter to Herman from M. Wells. He wrote that you are a very fine boy and you are behaving well. They were at the Seder on Passover and messaged that he will do whatever is possible in your case. The rabbi wrote also. So little brother, if he is willing to get to know a Jewish family [girl] we asked him to do that. His name is Abraham L. Feinberg. If you need more packages, I will send [them]. Write a lot. I don't know about the telephone call yet.

They will tell you there if you call the post office. If you want call me on Sunday. If you call me there is cheaper, but if you call, ask for only this : EV 6223 not a name. Kiss you, Dezső

1943/5 Undated Hermine to Irving (Book 10, 72-73)

My dear little brother Irving!

We got your letter with your picture today and I was really happy for it. You know little brother, tonight I went to help at the number 3 ration to prepare an address book to spread it out. You know they asked the workers at Lazarus, and this meant me too. We were all in the Masonic temple. We have to go on Thursday night. Today was the first one. After work we went to the Fashion. Lazarus paid for that. We work there from 7 to 10. It feels good to get fresh air, we can get so refreshed. I scribbled so much to you already that it is time to write about something else to you. So, I only read your letter late. Thank God we are well, I just miss you my little brother. And I don't really have patience because I am home so much. But don't worry about anything. Everything is going to be fine. I hope that they will move you over nearby, but if they don't, you will get a letter from us, don't worry. And believe me that I am thinking of you a lot and I hope that you will be home shortly with us! Don't worry about the [citizenship] papers, maybe it is better if they are late. You know what I mean? I can imagine how busy you must be! But besides that I know that they need a man there and you can stand up for yourself. I'm thinking of Herman, but believe me he could use some studying. Although, I wish I could do that, I would go too. Especially if you are there, too. How wonderful it would be! You can laugh at me, but I'm just imagining. Your picture is really not bad because a picture like this could not be that good. I did not hear any news about the relatives. I have very little time to call everybody either, although I get ready for it so often. It is really nice that you get a letter sometimes from others because sometimes there is something to read. Write if you need anything. We will send it to you. And don't worry, they will not bring you to places like that and I'm asking whatever will come, even if you just write your name and only greetings, still write. So, I will know that you think about me because you have nothing to worry about, since you study a lot. They will not take you over, I hope! And if you can, call us and take care of yourself. Don't be worried, think that we are waiting for you to come home and if you study that will be to your advantage. I'm sorry that sometimes I get delayed with writing. I kiss you many times. Hermin

1943/5/1 Howell Walters (neighbor) to Irving (Book 2, 211-214)

May 1st, 1943

Dear Irving:

Your letter received and we want you to know how much we enjoyed hearing from you. To know that you are getting along alright is not surprising. I said that before you left here. As long as your attitude is such nothing can stop you. Keep your chin up and your heart light. We are going along about as usual. Plenty to do and not too many to do it. We are even having further difficulties getting shoes. They tell us now how many pairs of certain type of shoes we can buy. The thing is when you have the money to buy, they say you can only buy so much. They tell me the day is coming when we will go up to a new customer, and we shall have to tell her we have nothing for her. When I started this letter I was going to tell you the folks were out eating somewhere. But now I see they are home, so we know they are in. We try to keep our eye on them. I suppose since you kissed the bride (and Mrs. Walters) you will be the next one to use the altar. Have not been able to reach your friend by phone. Suppose I'll have to stop down and see her. So when you write be sure to tell how I look - Don't make me out to be old enough to be her grand-pa. Mrs. Hasson just called to me to be sure and say "Hello Erving". She just about the same as usual. The only thing I see she eats about as much as usual. That's too much - that's why Mrs. Walters (Irene to you) and I are so thin. See Herman every morning getting the car off the back porch - He sure takes better care of it now. Saw him one nite walking it home. Had a flat tire. At first I thought he thought the bicycle was tired. Just giving it a rest. You know how thoughtful he is. Well Irving! (have spelled your name 3 or 4 different ways.) I am about out of news and nuisance, but just remember this - we think of you quite often though we may not write. Let's hear from you whenever you can. Regards from the folks next door. Mrs. Hasson, Irene and Howell

1943/5/2 (a) Irving to Family (Book 2, 225-229) pages 1-4

5-2-43

Dear brothers and sisters,

I believe that you will be surprised, when you get my [wire] recording that I did yesterday night. You know that here I can't speak other than in English and they censor what I say. I hope you will be able to understand it. I asked you to send new pictures in it for me. Although, I could only say what was allowed, but if it's possible I will send it again. If it's possible, I will do it in such a way that it will be an answer to your letters. I hope it will work out. It might be hard for you to listen to it, since you don't have a gramophone. But I'm sure you'll have a place where you can listen to it. Dear Hencsu, you won't believe how much I was laughing when I was reading your letter you wrote on the April 26th. I read it already twice. When you wrote that Mariska ran down one morning and hid the letter and gave you an old letter for you to read. I wonder, what could you have said when you read the old one and then the new one after? I think the letter was longer this way because you read more. Also, you and Mariska asked for more pictures to send, unfortunately I don't know when I will be able to. It's possible that I will go to Dallas in a week and I will be able to have it done there.

Also, in the multi-page letter, I mentioned that I will send money home. I don't need that much money here and I'm afraid that someone will steal it. Herminka, you asked if they will place me to another place. I do not know until this day, if that's going to happen. It's possible when the 13th week is up then they will place me. Friday they called me about the citizen papers. I hope I will get it soon. I don't know if I wrote, that this place is a replacement center and they send the soldiers out from here. On the second week in July will end the 13 weeks, I'm glad that one month passed by already. You know, here there are new people who come all the time and it's interesting to see them. I wouldn't want to go through again the things I went through already. Believe me, it's better to be an old soldier than a new one (rookie). I will note for you that for us "the black soup" [this is an expression] is just getting started. First, it's very hot here. Second, we have to walk night and day with complete equipment. On Saturday afternoon we went to exercise with machine guns and to crawl on the ground while we had to pull 30 and 40 pounds and add the backpacks to that on the way up and down the hill. It's very hard at the beginning, but I could get used to it.

Next Sunday I don't know if I'm going to write because we are going to a big exercise. Here they call it "the bottom of hell" and its mandatory to go through with it. Don't get worried. I can show it better to explain this way. They will shoot at us with machine guns and we have to crawl on the ground while the bullets will totally go above our heads. I would love to write a lot more, but I think it's better if you don't know about it.

The weather is getting hotter. You know, if it's really hot at home and you are thirsty, then take salt three times per day, that is really good against sweating and thirst. I take 3 tablets every day. Also, I'm glad to hear Herminka, that you got a good job. I hope you will like it. Write a lot about it. Herminka and Mariska, how are you? I asked, if you are lonely. I think I know the answer. But don't be sad because we will see each other again.

Today is Sunday, I was in synagogue in the morning. They mostly pray in English and broken Hebrew. It's almost like in the Broad St synagogue. but maybe they pray more there. Like I mentioned, that this week we will be very busy, in case I would not write, then don't be sad!

Dear Dezső and Mariska, I was very happy for the package, although there is only one problem, at this time there are many friends. The chocolate was in good condition and the candy is very good and I think I'll take it with me when we go for a long walk. We can't drink water all the time so it could come in handy. I didn't open the chewing gum yet. I truly thank you for all of it. And Herminka, you are also included because your letter was in the package. Mariska, as soon as I read your letter, and Hencsu, I see that you are very jealous of the photo.

1943/5/2 (b) Irving to Family (Book 2, 223-224) page 5 and 6

When I think about it, I just read with a smile on my face and imagine it as if I were there with you. Please don't be sad, everything is going to be fine. Dear Herman, I was so happy for the picture, and I think that you look great. I think it's warm there too, because your face got tan. Although, mine is red. It's 100 degrees here, that's good enough. However, it will be hotter than that. Otherwise I'm doing great. I think I wrote enough today. But I don't know, if I will be able to write in the future. I'm asking all of you don't be sad, everything is going to be fine. You know, Dezső, the brown sunglasses are the best, because the sun shines so brightly, it's very hard to look at the sky, even when I'm wearing them. But at least you don't need to squint. Just sometimes it's not too good having sunglasses on, because they give you an order and they need to be put away in a hurry because you need to put on a gas mask and walk in that for a while. Walking on the hill is the hardest, but one can get used to it, because it's necessary.

Dear Hermine, you asked, what kind of wedding I attended? I think you will laugh, if I'll tell you. You know, it was a small wedding. It was at least the 20 of us and we drank a thimbleful wine. And I thought it would be great to put a letter together, because I just got a letter from the neighbor. I think I wrote about this already. I note, if a man wants to write, then he needs to add something so that the letter will sound good.

Like you asked in many letters, where did I get the letters that I write in English. You know, sometimes it's necessary to add a little so it sounds good. Now I have to respond to several letters to relatives, and I don't know yet what I'm going to write about. But if I will have time then I will think of something. You know I'm getting the hang of this writing slowly, but unfortunately I have to close my lines, but I will write as soon as possible again. Now, I will stay with much love and kisses, write often! Your little brother who thinks about you a lot, Irving

1943/5/2 Kenneth Beighley to Irving (Book 17, 277-278)

2101 Huntington Drive
South Pasadena, California
May 2, 1943
Dear Irving,
It was a surprise to receive your card--and so promptly. I hardly expected my original card to get to you. Your being in Texas reminds me of what one fellow at Columbus said this last summer. When I invited him to see us whenever he got anywhere in California, he replied that he'd come even if he got to Texas. He is one of those Ohio boys who have not travelled very much. To him, Texas was next door to California. He probably knows better by now, however. I take it from your address that you are in the infantry, and have not been in for a year yet. I would expect you to be a corporal by the end of the first year. Don't disappoint me. I can easily understand how army life would be much different from Czechoslovakia. Give me the details on it, though. In just what ways is it so much different. Life here is very busy. We have several army friends stationed near, and see them quite often. We expect the same of you if you ever get stationed close to us. School keeps me pretty busy too. There are a lot of extra duties, such as tennis coach, to make life anything but boring. And I, too, will be in the army, and just as soon as school is over, June 19. Be sure to write again. Always, Kenneth C. Beighley

1943/5/4 Bertha to Irving (Book 18, 124-125)

New York
May 4/43
Dear Cousin Irving!
Please forgive me for not answering your most welcome post card and your letter sooner as my husband Mannie was ill for awhile and when he got better I got ill. At least we are feeling better. I am happy to learn that you are O.K. How is army life? It must be quite interesting even if it is [as] hard [as] I imagine. Please don't make fun of me if I am asking you which one of the brothers are you? The youngest or the blonde middle one? Well, lots of good luck to you cousin Irving and do write to us. We'll be glad to hear from us. Please let me know what [it] is that you need most. I shall be glad to send it to you. I haven't heard from your sisters for quite some time. I guess they are kept quite busy keeping house and besides, working is hard. The weather here is miserable. It is May 4th and we are wearing winter clothes. It doesn't look like it will get warmer. I shall try to answer your mail promptly. It was lovely of you to write to us. With best wishes from Mannie and myself. With love, Bertha and Mannie

And please don't [use] "magáz" [Hung. polite form of 'you'] We just say you

1943/5/5 Irving to Hermine and Marie, Camp Wolters Texas (Book 5, 342-346)

[Pvt. Irving Gluck Co.B.55th. Inf. Bn. Camp Wolters, Texas]

5-5-43
Dear Mariska,
I'm sorry to hear that the card I mailed you on April 28 wasn't up to par because I did not mention any reply to your card and letter. Probably I annoyed you with my card. I can understand that because I tried to write about myself since I don't have time to reread the letters to which I'm supposed to reply. Dear Mariska, if you only know how much free time I have then you would understand me, because of that, I don't reply and I write about myself only. Today I also received a letter dated 5-2-43. In this letter you mentioned that the rabbi has written to you. I know that he has written because he was asking about everyone's interests so that he could write home. He is a very fine man, however he is a very military man, and a major, and that's why he is that way. I believe that I have written to you on Sunday and told you what I was doing. I went to the movies. On Monday I worked in the kitchen. When a person works in the kitchen he has to get up quite

early. After that, you go to exercises as well. You mentioned in your letter that you're going to mail me a package. I was wondering why, since I didn't ask for anything. I mentioned in my last letter yesterday that if you mail me anything please don't, because I have to give it to the various people. I hope that you did not mail it, because half of the package is distributed to the fellow soldiers. It is laughable that you could not open up the basement door. I bet it would be good to go home and help you to open the door, what do you think? Directions how to open. First is to go twice around the circle and stop at the 13, then go once again around and stop it at 24, and return back to number two and pull the lock, and then it will open. I hope! Today the weather was quite dusty and the wind blows and one could hardly see for more than 3-5 feet. It would be good if there would be a good rainfall. I hope that you will forgive me, but I will close my letter and I will write to you again. This is the Army, one can't always write or even rest. I remain with love and kisses, your little brother, Irving

5/5/1943
Dear Herminka,
I received your card and a letter. I was very happy. Dezső mentioned that your work is quite difficult that I wouldn't believe it. I believe you because you're not accustomed to it. After you come you have more work. You always find work. Take care of yourself. Do not work too hard. It sure is different here in the Army. Believe me Hencse, those who are in the Army and become civilian would appreciate the civilian life. Here we stand 20 hours on our feet and one never knows what he has to do. Today is Wednesday. We were completely dressed with all the equipment and went for a long walk. It was eight o'clock. When we're ready, they told us to put everything away, and go to the movies. We listened to a lecture there. At noon we had to go get ready. Completely dressed with all the equipment. The wind was blowing the sand so you could hardly see and you can imagine the situation how it was. Here you do things that in civilian life that if they would pay us, we wouldn't do it. Dezső mentions that you are showing off, because you're working for Lazarus. Please write to me how you got the job, who recommended it? In your letter you mentioned that you're sending a package. I wish you would have written to me that you intend to send me because it's not worth it, because one has to give it away to the people around us. At that time everybody is your friend! It bothers me to give it to them, but they come for it. The problem is when the package arrives everybody's there and they come to see what is in the package. I gave them from the O'Henry chocolate, but I saved the chewing gum. I'm well otherwise. I have written a letter, but I did not have a chance to finish it. And if I have left something out just mention it in your next letter. Dear Dezső, How are you? Write to me if you can. How's business? And Herman, please you too write! How are you? I will close at this time my few lines. If I can, I will write tomorrow. You know, we're going to use machine guns all day tomorrow. I'll write more about it. Loads of kisses your little brother, Irving
Flora and the family didn't write it to me...........
[Upside down top of last page] The aunt wrote a page again. She wrote a very precise letter!

1943/5/9 (a) Irving to Hermina (Book 3, 29-31) incomplete

[this letter belongs with the one below 5-9-1943 that begins with my dear sister and brothers]

Saturday
Dear Hermine,
I received your package and I'm just replying. I wrote a card, but I couldn't write much on it. I'm thinking of you a lot. Thank you for your effort to send me all those baked goods. They were very good, excellent! After I received it, you have created a little problem with it. However, I was lucky that it is Saturday and I'm in the barracks and I'm on duty, so I had more time to look over what you have sent me. I will write you about it. It was interesting when I received the package. I did not know what to think or what to do, so that I don't have to give it away to the fellow soldiers. I was successful. When I brought in the package I put it into the bag and I began to read your letter and card that I received from you. And the rest of the fellows were also busy reading their letters, so I was lucky to make it disappear so that they won't see it. I only thought of how will I open it. That too was successful. I was alone in the barracks this Saturday on duty and I began to open the package. I almost forgot the interesting thing, I couldn't sleep Hermina because I wanted to know what kind of baked goods are in the package. With little difficulty I was able to open it. I took a razor blade and slowly I opened it and I got a few pieces and ate it. When I tasted it, it had 1000 tastes!!! Truly, I want to thank you and I think a lot of you. I would have been upset if I would have had to share with the rest. I'm happy that I didn't have to do it! Everything is fine!! It was like you just have taken it out from the oven. You know I'm going to try to eat it! During the day I do not have much time to come into the barracks to eat from it, but in the evening and Sunday I have the time and I will look into the box and

select which one should I take first. Every one of them were fine. It has been quite some time since I have received such baked goods. Perhaps because of that, it's worthwhile to be far away from home. My dear Hermina, don't worry that the baked goods will spoil! I'm here. I won't let it spoil! On Saturday morning from five o'clock to midnight I was on duty. Then the commander comes in and I have to report and continue my work.

1943/5/9 (b) Irving to Family (Book 3, 23-28)

5-9-43

My dear brothers and sisters,

As I began to write to you yesterday I didn't have a chance to finish it. Yesterday morning from 5 AM till 12 o'clock midnight I was a on guard-duty and it was a long time before I was able to go to rest. I fell asleep immediately. I slept like a beaver when the corporal came to me from the office and told me that there is a long-distance telephone call. I was so sleepy, however, I went in the office to pick up the telephone and the time was 12 o'clock. As I was asking you what time it is and you told me it was 6:15 AM. I was wondering after I hung up the telephone and I looked at the clock and the clock was standing still. Believe me I was so sleepy and I told you it was 12 o'clock midnight and it was really 6:15 AM just like at home. Here it was cloudy and dark. At that moment I couldn't think of anything else, I was just asking myself why I'm being called to the telephone. I spoke quite loud but something was with the line and it wasn't clear enough. I was afraid to speak too loud because the Commander was sleeping. Since last evening we are on reserve and one must be ready at all times because we could be called out any minute in case of a riot. This was like real training and will be mostly day and night. If we have to go somewhere and there is some activity we have to be ready to make order in the area.

Do you know my dear brother Dezső! I want to thank you that you called me. It wasn't too good because I wasn't prepared for it and I didn't know what to talk about and the commander was there sleeping in the office. I probably woke him up since I spoke quite loud. This already happened. If you're going to call me again, please write to me first. If I call you, I could talk to you better and I would be speaking from a place that I could talk loud. I was happy to hear that you are becoming a citizen. I know it's quite difficult to study the law. Perhaps they won't ask you too much about it and you will be able to answer the questions. I am writing this letter after our telephone conversation, since we don't know what happens from one minute to the next. Do not call me next week. I will call you if I can, and I will devote the time if I have to wait in line.

Tomorrow is Sunday and I have to work in the kitchen. There's not enough time even to take a breath of air. Don't be angry, my dearest Hermina, if I leave anything out, but if it comes to my mind, I will write about it. I also received a letter from Bertha. After I reply to her, then I will mail the letter home. It's interesting and she's writing that her husband didn't feel well and she too was not well and because of that she could not write. She asked me if I need anything and said that just tell her and she will send me anything. Dear Dezső, you're asking me if I need any chewing gum? No. I don't need it, since I have enough that it will last me until I return from the Army! As you mentioned that Feinberg wrote to me from the USO. I spoke to him after Passover. Since then I didn't have a chance to go anywhere. I will write again about it if I have time!

Dear Mariska, thank God I'm well. Believe me, that you're writing is beautiful, the only problem is that I don't know when I can answer your letters. Lajos wrote that he too will have to go to the Army this month. The neighbor in Columbus wrote to me, but I do not know when I can answer him. Write me a lot! With kisses and loads of love, Irving.

I did not mail this letter, therefore I'm going to continue. I don't know where I am because every minute I write a few lines and I don't have a chance to read it. Dear Herman I spoke to you today a few words and I wrote that I was very sleepy and erred on the time. Think of working 20 hours straight, and after four hours of rest, get up and that's enough. For a while it will be this way, one has to be ready night and day. I wrote a lot of things together and I hope you'll be able to understand me. Mariska mentioned something on the telephone. Please write to me about it. Also Hermina write to me about your work! Thank you for the package 1000 times! Also for your work and it made you tired! Everything is very fine! When I have time, I will write to you when I will be [able to] telephone you. Now with kisses to all of you with lots of love, Irving.

[On the side of the first page] I will write you again. Until then, kisses to all of you, loads of love your brother, Irving. My writing is not good because I'm in a hurry!

1943/5/10 Undated Hermine to Irving (Book 10, 44-45) - Blue Star Service banner

[Dated by phone call that woke Irving]

My dear Irving!
I know you are surprised [and you wondered] why you were bothered so early with the phone call, but as soon as Dave came home from work he started to call you since he thought it will take long [to get through]. I am truly sorry because I know that you were tired and sleepy. I did not know about the big time difference. I'm sorry that it worked out that way, but I hear that you talked and that is enough, just it is terrible to bother you that early. Did you get scared my Irving? I hope you are alright! As Dave mentioned in the writing, to simplify, it can't hurt, but maybe it is a small thing, and if they censored it, it could hurt too. If it's possible just write because you make me happy my little brother if I find a letter, even though I am a very lazy letter writer. Sorry, I will be in a hurry to write to you. What do you say? The news is pretty good and it is possible that they will deal with the Germans. On Monday after 12 o'clock I have to go to work and in the evening I stumble like you do, you know. But it is interesting, if I am busy I like it, but if I have to stand I don't like it. You know my Irving, it would be good if you would write about the magazine because I wrote to Springfield. Their office is in Ohio and they wrote a response that they will take action and they have their office in Ohio and they sent the case by it. They say they paid for the magazine for a half a year and so they can't stop it. In case you want, you can write to them. We did not give them money since then. I could barely get the address and if you write, write to this address:
The American Magazine
Woman's Home Companion
Springfield, Ohio
I'm sorry that my writing is so unorganized, but I left the writing for later and I am in a hurry. Did you get a letter from Bertha? I did not get any and I don't know what could be the reason. Arthur feels a little better, they say. They don't come here and you know that I don't go anywhere. I miss you my little brother and if you can, find out when you can come to visit here. I'm waiting for you little brother. You know we bought a nice star and we put it out in the window [the Blue Star Service banner]. If you come home you will see. Did you have trouble because of the package? I did not know what to bake. I was afraid that it will get moldy. Write what you would like and then I will bake for you. Ok my Irving? Don't mind my writing and take care of yourself. Next time I will continue. I kiss you my little brother with much love. Hermine

1943/5/10 Undated Marie to Irving (Book 6, 107-108)

[Dated by phone call that woke Irving and Marie responds to Irv about sharing from the packages]

My dear Irving!
I am sorry that we woke you up from your dream, but we didn't know it was night. Plus we thought that the connection will take long again. And you know my little brother, when David came home at 7 from work, immediately he called the phone company that he wants to talk to you. He thought that he can talk about noon and you know you called two minutes later. It surprised us and we are sorry that it was night time and we woke you up from your sleep. But besides all that I was very happy I could talk to you. I already woke up because you know it was morning already by us on Sunday. You know my little brother I know how it goes over there and you were tired. What did you do today on Sunday? Did you go to the movies? I saw a film yesterday about the war. You know how it goes on the other side? Besides that I mentioned to you on the phone, that I changed jobs too. You know my Irving, where I used to work, there was always something there. Once there was no work and once they were on strike about the money. Plus, it was a hard job. And this week workers left them who had worked there for 10 years. So did I. Although with the excuse that my eyes hurt and the doctor said that it is better if I don't sew and thus, I want to look for another job. This way I got the resignation immediately. My boss was very sorry for me and she said that if I can, I should come back because she was very satisfied with me. She wished good luck to me. She was asking me to visit her. I was at Lazarus and at first I did not say who I was. I asked for sewing and they wanted to pay me $20 for a week, but to sew fur and I did not know what to do. I did not know what to do because I can sew. The next day Hermine asked the man there in the employment office and he said he did not know who I was. He called me to go in and he will arrange things. I went in the next day and he asked me what kind of job would I want? You know my Irving, I did not know what to say. So I said I would like to sell. He said it would be good if I could work in the storage for a little while. This way I will learn. Then he sent me down to the third floor. There they sell women's clothings and hats. I talked to the boss and this way I don't know how it will be. Only when I went in I asked the man if I have a chance to get hired, if I'll take this? He said yes. He just

wants me to learn for a little while. I will start on Monday and now I have to work 6 days for 18. But they will give a raise later. I believe they will put me to clothing, since I said that I am a tailor. I will see what it's going to be. I wanted to surprise you too with this. I will write tomorrow how everything is. And I'm asking don't be sad, just if you could write. We did not get anything from you yesterday. You will have to have patience reading this much nonsense. Until now, nothing special. Your name was in the newspaper *Already in Parade*. I know my little brother doesn't like having to share from the package, but I am glad you ate from it, too. It was sent to the dispatcher in Texas. I kiss you countless times with a lot of love, until I see you again. Maria

1943/5/11 Irving to Family (Book 6, 137-141)

Dear siblings,
I got a letter tonight from you and since I am lucky I can respond to it immediately. Today there was a big practice, but the rain was pouring and they didn't call me to practice. I will only go tomorrow. Approximately half of the soldiers were at practice and the other half will go tomorrow and I am in that group. Like Dave mentioned, I don't want to write anything about our jobs, but don't be worried, everything is going to be fine. I'm glad to hear that dear Hermine likes the job. I hope that there is no need to work hard, even though you have to work 5 days, you won't have to ruin your eyes with sewing. It's very nice that they wrote from the United Service Organizations (USO) to you about me and you can see that there is no need to be sad about me, because everything is fine.

I responded to Bertuska [Bertha], I'm including her letter so you can see what she wrote to me. She asked me not to address her formally and I wrote in English to her so it will be easier to respond. You know how hard it is not to be formal in Hungarian. However, she wrote me in English. First I wrote a card and then a letter. I wrote the letter in Hungarian, but I see that it's better writing letters in English. Someday I will surprise you with a letter in English, too. The neighbor [Howell Walters] wrote, but I don't know what to respond to him, because he wrote about the girl again. He mentions that maybe I think she is too old and that's why I won't give the girl's address to him. So I need you to think for me what to answer. I talked to you on Sunday and I'm sure you got a letter from me where I wrote what happened to me. That's why I think it's better, if you don't call me, instead I will call you and will write to you when to expect my call. If the business will be quieter, then Sunday I will be free and will write to you about everything. I didn't send the money home yet. I will, if I will have time or I will go to the post office, and I will ask if I can put it to the post fund so I can save the money here.

[Note: In Hungarian there is a so called 'formal' address, that may need some explanation. It's a respectful way of talking to women, especially for men, or to elderly people. It's not exactly the same as addressing someone formally in English. It's not just adding Ms., Mrs., etc. before someone's name, rather using an entirely different vocabulary for those who are entitled to that "formal address". It's very important to understand this, because Hungarians don't take this lightly, especially in the days these letters were written. There is only one way to get released from using 'formal address', if, and only if, the entitled person offers it. However, even when they do, it's very hard to follow up on it, because of respect in our culture and tradition. For example, when I was young, my aunt once offered me the privilege to address her informally. I felt honored, but it took me a while to get used to it. So when he was saying that Bertha offered not to address her formally, you understand the struggle that he had had with that. So his solution to this was to write her in English. This is exactly how I deal with this matter sometimes. :) Monika Markacs]

The pastry was delicious and I am eating it slowly. You know Hermine all of them are delicious, but since you wanted to know which one was the best, I can only say that the one with figs are all gone and I'm eating the one with the walnuts. Meanwhile I'm eating the candy too. Thank you so much for your effort! Don't send me anything for now because whatever I have is enough for a while. If you want to, you can send me the article that I was in. I don't know anything about the transfer. It's possible that when I finish the three months of basic training, they will transfer me. But don't be sad about that. I wrote a card to Lajos. I will send you the letter that he wrote to me. He wrote that he had to go for (conscription) recruiting (US draft) this month.

Dear Mariska, how are you? I read your letter, but I assure you that I will write to you as soon as I can. But you write me also. I'm glad to hear that people wonder about, and are interested in me. You know, I would love to write to Miss Mason. When I'll have more time, I will write to her. I already mentioned about the package to Hermine. I hope you know what I mean. Don't bother to send other packages, because I have everything. The chewing gum is going to be enough for as long as I'll be a soldier and I will work hard to finish it so we could see each other again. The weather got cooler here because of the heavy rain, but I'm afraid that it will be hot after the rain. Dear Dezső, sorry that I'm not writing separately and to Herman also. I hope when you get the letter, you will be an American citizen already. And you Herman, you also should try to find out about the citizenship papers. Maybe you could get it also. Now, I'm closing my lines and kissing all of you with much love, hugs, Irving

Save Bertuska's letter, because that was the first letter she wrote me. It came by plane. I will save the envelope [kopertáts - Yiddish]

1943/5/13 Irving to Family, Camp Wolters, TX (Book 5, 298-302)

5-13-43
Camp Wolters, Texas

My dear brothers and sisters, 120
I was very happy receiving your card and letter. It has been two days that I haven't heard from you. Thank God I'm well. Do you know that the difficult exercises that we have done is over. It has been six weeks that I have been here. The commanders are saying that there won't be anything more difficult than what we have done thus far. We will have to march and we must get accustomed to it between 25 and 30 miles a day. We have been marched 12 miles in half a day. This week we have been on night and day to exercise. We are learning what we must know in the future.... There is not much time for writing... Otherwise I'm well. They called me in today regarding my citizenship paper. Within 6 weeks I'm told that I will get my citizenship papers. That is what the commander stated. I hope Dezső that you received also your citizenship papers.

Please let me know what questions they have asked you regarding to the citizenship. They didn't say yet when, but soon. I have written to Elsi in Cleveland. What do you say to Bertha's letter? She is really a wonderful relation as you see it in her letter. Let me know if you want to read the letter that I have written to her. I did not write to Yenkin's as of now because I didn't have any time to sit down and relax and reply to their letter. Imagine that I did not even reply to the girl's letter that I received a week ago. I do not know when I will. I do have time, but I'm not in a hurry to reply. It's good to receive your letters from home, but here in the Army it is difficult to reply since we are busy day and night. If I can, I will call you on the telephone, As for when, I do not know. If anything important comes about, then I will call you or I'll send you a telegram. Do not worry because I will be here for another 6 weeks. It would be great if I could get a permit after 6 weeks to visit you. I'm not sure that they're going to give me time off. [In English] I hope they do! [In Hungarian] Thank God, our troops are progressing according to the newspapers and I hear it also on the radio. Here every day they read all the current news of the daily events.

Do you know sometimes I sit down to write when I have time, but I don't have patience. You probably can recognize [the reason] why. As you know, I cannot write everything in the letter and even talking on the telephone it's probably monitored. It's true, I do not write anything except what the other boys are writing. They also write about the daily activities. There's nothing more to write about and you cannot say anything else anyway. Someday, I hope to be able to go to the USO. There is a Jewish group there. They write to us every week and tell us what's going on. This Sunday they told us that in the near future the Jewish people will be coming from Dallas and they will tell us, then I will go to Mineral Wells. The club of the USO is located there. I hope that I will be able to go. I could go from Saturday noon to Monday morning 6 o'clock. I would be free to go up till then. It would be wonderful if you lived not too far from here and I could go home. I couldn't even make it on an airplane to fly home and return in the amount of time that is given. I was thinking that if they would give me enough time off, I would fly home. The government pays half of that. I have time to think about it yet, if I get some time off, then I'll know what to do. I would like to conclude this letter but I don't want to mail it half empty.

Dear Herman, what are you doing? The neighbor mentions you in every letter that he sees you with a bicycle. One day he saw you pushing the bicycle. He thought that you ran out of gas because you were pushing it, then he saw the flat tire. Also he mentioned that you are taking care of the bicycle very well just like I did, and it is very clean.
Hermin, our neighbor Mr. Walters saw you through the window that you are at home and that you are well. He said that the situation is very difficult in the shoe business. He can't get the product that he wants and

the customer does not want the shoes that he has. He's complaining about the situation. He's still asking for the girl's address and he tells me that I think that she's too old. His letter is very interesting. After I reply to his letter, I'll mail it to you. If he is asking about me, tell them that I will write as soon as I can. I'm not in a hurry to reply since I'm busy [and] there is not much time. I only write this to you. They asked me the name of the paper which we receive. He wants to put something in it because the morale office is organizing it. I will write you. Kisses to all of you, and lots of love until we meet again, your brother, Irving

1943/5/16 Irving to Family (Book 2, 218-224)

Dear siblings,
I was very happy I got your cards. I'm glad to hear that you are doing well. Yesterday on Saturday, we were very busy and I didn't write, but today I'll make up for it and I will write. I thought I already wrote this week about the resident papers. You know, yesterday at noon they sent me to the city to have my pictures done for the second papers, and they said that I will get the papers shortly and I will be an American resident. I also had pictures done to send them home. Here it is very expensive and they only make it from one film, in other words, they only shoot once. It will be done this week. I could not have done less than 6.

I hope it will work. You mentioned in your cards that you will send me packages. I still have stuff from the other package. I'm asking you not to send anymore because the commander-in-chief is checking the bag and the cookies can't be older than two days. He said that we have to divide them or throw them out. I'm thanking you very much, I know you are sending it with a good heart. But, if I need anything, or I run out of something, if that happens, I will write and then you will send very little. Today I read through all the letters, because the one that is not worth keeping I throw away. Actually, this is an order. I want to send them home and you'll save them for me. When they relocate me, I can't have any letters on me. So you understand that it's not worth to keep them. I thought that I could collect them, but I can't. The ones I collect I will send home. I started to read the first letter and it lasted 3 hours until I finished them all. I felt badly to tear some of them, but it happened already and whatever is left, in the future, I will send home.

The days are going fast. Sometimes it's easy and sometimes hard. I think you had a question in one of your letters I read, I can't remember. I truly don't remember. If you know that I didn't answer any of your questions, then let me know. What's going on by you? Do you still like the house where you live? How are the neighbor's doing? I didn't write to them yet. I want to wait until they forget about the girl's address. I won't write about her anyway. You know, if I would write about her, they would go to visit her. and then the girl would think that she is truly on my mind a lot. Unfortunately, I didn't write to her for a month already, only a card. You know, it's great to get a letter, but it's hard to respond. A letter sounds serious, but I couldn't care less. That's why I don't write. The less often I write is better. Yesterday night I was in the United Service Organizations (USO) club and I met the chief of administration.

He is a fine man. Mr. Feinberg who wrote to you. I talked to him a little. Some kind of party will be next week and maybe I will go, if I can. If I will have an opportunity I will learn how to play on the piano. I tried here a little, and might be getting the hang of it slowly. Don't worry, when you need someone who knows how, you can just say that you have a little brother who plays on the instrument. As soon as I learn the first musical piece, I will let you know. I will note again, that don't send anything to me! If I need anything, I will ask, because it's very strict. In case they would check my bag and chest, and that they do often, they will see the same package that I had before. And then I will have to work the entire Sunday and I won't have a day off for the week. It happened before that they found a shoe in a bag. It wasn't mine, but I want to be careful, so I won't have to work, if it's not necessary. I will write more next time! You can write me too! Thank you for the package many times. I've been thinking about you a lot! Until I will see you again, kiss with much love, Irving

1943/5/16 Undated Marie to Irving (Book 8, 11-12)

[Dated because Irving is in basic training so it's 1943. The only month with a Sunday the 16th is May]

Sunday 16

My dear Irving!
You know, don't be surprised that I was so lazy, but I hope you'll understand it. As I mentioned, that I changed my job and because of that I did not have a chance to write to you as I usually do. Plus, today on

Sunday we have a big cleaning at our home, That is, they papered the room and cleaned it. The walls will be done by tomorrow as well. I will write when I come home from work. Somehow I was very tired because I work every day. I think about you a lot, but I hope and I promise, that I will write to you again properly. Yesterday, no mail came from you. I can't write anything particular about my job. It's a little hard because I have to take out the clothes and what we have to the third floor. However, my boss is very satisfied with me and he/she said, not to worry because he/she will take action, so everything will be OK. Only wants from me to learn a little. So, I don't know what it's going to be this way. Otherwise I don't know anything particular. How are you my Irving? How is everything? Bertha's letter is very nice the way she writes. We want to write to her as soon as we will have some time. We did not go anywhere this week. Did you get a letter from Flora? I talked to the neighbor and he said that he wrote to you. Dezső went about the citizenship papers and Uncle Roth and Flora were the witnesses. They will not give the citizenship papers yet. And you know little brother, you mentioned that we should send you a shoe [ration] ticket. You know my Irving, we thought that you don't need it, and this way we bought shoes. Dezső said that you can ask for one there because they will give it to you there if you need one. I don't know when we could get one here and we can't get the other stamp yet. And maybe you could get one there faster. I'm sorry that you didn't say that before because we could have sent it to you already. And since you wrote that you don't need it, we got one for it. Write what will be or if you can buy one or what we can do to help you with this.

My little brother, I am very happy to hear that you received the package successfully, that they did not see it. Also, that you like it. I am happy that I did not listen to you because I knew that you will like it, you just don't want us to send you. I understand why you said that, but I thought that it doesn't matter because even if you give away from it you will have leftover for yourself. It's more than you would buy there because you know we know what it is like to have something from home. And if you want something then write it and don't worry about it. We are glad to do it. Although, I would not mind if you would be at home already. I would love to see you already and talk to you. What do you look like? Did you gain any weight? How's the weather there? It is still cold here. We can still wear the winter coat. The wind is blowing and the rain is raining for three days. They say it has not been weather like that for a long time. Now I will close my lines and I kiss you countless times with love until I will see you again. Don't be upset and take care of yourself. I will write to you again. If I will not have time for a letter, I will send a card. I kiss you again and I wish you good luck! Maria

1943/5/16 Undated Hermine to Irving (Book 10, 60-61)

[Dated by mention of shoe ration ticket and wall paper]

My dear Irving!
Maybe you are angry at me because I write so rarely, but believe me we were very busy today. The man was here to do the [wall] paper and to peel the paper and he will come tomorrow too to finish. So, we were very busy. Although I wrote a lot of foolishness last time about it in my exhaustion. Bertha wrote a very nice letter to you. I am getting ready to write to her too and to Elsi and the others. Otherwise we are well. My job is pretty good. Write my little brother whenever you can and take care of yourself. I will find out about the shoe ticket and if we can, we will send it now. If you would have written about this last time, we could have sent it to you because we had the stamp. I'm sorry my little brother that I write so little to you. I kiss you with much love. Hermina

Did you give the address to the neighbor? Maybe he is just teasing you.

1943/5/23 Herman to Irving (Book 14, 298)

5-23-43
Dear Irving,
I'm sorry that I am such a rare writer, but this is the way it is. Don't you follow my example. If you have time, then write. Last week I was at the bank and the older lady asked how come you did not write to her? A young man who was a teller is now in Africa. It has been two weeks since I bought 1- $100 bond. I got a 05¢ raise, it is not yet approved, it's just that he gave me for overtime. Now I get 60¢ an hour. I don't know anything else in particular. I will write more shortly, if I will have time. I kiss you, Herman

1943/5/23 Irving to Family (Book 6, 142-146)

5-23-43

My dearest brothers and sisters;

After work it is great to relax, and yet I have time to write to you. Do you know that this week I have not received any mail from you and I think that you are probably very busy. Here I'm always busy, so that I don't even know if I could answer your letters. This week, day and night, we have been working, as I think. The weather is rainy, but it doesn't matter here, because you know what an infantryman does! It's raining, the wind is blowing, [and] we go from early morning 5 a.m. until 2 p.m. We come back and we lay down our weapons, and it is our turn to sleep about four hours. As you know you have to get accustomed to everything. I too slowly get accustomed to it. It was interesting this week, we went and the rain was pouring down. It was at night, we couldn't see anything, but we still had to go and the road was such as back home in the forest, muddy, and when you step on it you sink into it. And sometimes, some of us fell, with a neck full of mud. After we have returned all of us had to do the cleaning. It was two o'clock in the morning when we went to sleep and in the morning at five a.m. again [we] begin to work. As I've written it, just now we are getting black soup. But don't worry, everything will be all right. We have 5 more weeks, and then only God knows where we shall go. We were supposed to have 6 more weeks, but today they told us only 5 weeks. We will get a total of 12 weeks of training. In the end of these 5 weeks we will have black soup. We shall be going to a new place where everything will be real. And to write it down one cannot, however you know what I mean! And don't worry, all will be well. Tomorrow I will speak to you, that is, it will be Sunday. Otherwise there is no other news, everything is the same. Everyday we are learning something new. However, there's only one problem in the infantry, walking!! I have become accustomed to the walking. In the beginning my leg was painful and I thought many times that I will not be able to do the walking. I went to the doctor to check my leg a number of times and they told me that I will become accustomed to the walking and then the pain will disappear. We are now doing a fast walk of 16 miles and we take it. When we return [to the barracks] it's a little bit difficult, but we are hardened and we don't even feel like we were walking. I often say it's enough to go up the mountain at first, but when we go any further we can't take it. This week the rain made walking very difficult, but we had to go. The road is very bad at night because it's raining and it's dark in the forest like in Polány. "It's muddy" so you can sink into it. If the sun shines one melts, but when it rains it pours! Don't tell what I'm writing to anyone, because this week I believe that if we go home we will write something. Then we'll tell you back home what we're doing. Nothing should be written about our work. While we are in this country it may be better for you if you have gotten any mail from me in which I'm writing you what I'm doing, that is, you understand what you think you cannot keep, tear it up. Otherwise I'm okay, don't worry. Work peacefully. As you're writing my dearest Hermine and Marie, that you think of me a lot. And that is very beautiful to hear from you, but don't worry. Because if you think of me a lot that means that you're worried.

I haven't written to our next-door neighbor, I do not know when I will be able to. I do not write to Flora, I'm sure that they are also busy. It's true one cannot answer every letter, because it takes time. And I don't have much, but when I do have it, I must rest. If anyone asks about me just tell them my best regards and that should be sufficient. I've just finished the pastries, many thanks for your hard work. Until we meet again loads of love and kisses your little brother Irving

If you can, please write. How come that Dezső and Herman don't write? I made some pictures and when they're ready I will send them to you.

1943/5/23 Irving to Herman, Hermine, Marie, Dezső Camp Wolters Texas (Book 5, 322-326)

5-23-43

Dear Herman

I hardly talked to you, but I think you wanted to save someone, because I asked you how you are and you were in a hurry, you did not reply. That's okay. If you want to, you can write to me. I know that you do the same work, however you can write about anything and everything. I also asked if you had any dates because our sister Hermine said that you left home. I have heard you and spoke with you, you were at home. Here, there is nothing much. Looking forward, the weather is not too good, but very soon it will be the hot season of which I'm afraid of. Well, I have to close now, please write to me, if you want and if you have time. Your brother, Irving.

This week I'm going to mail you a picture. Write a lot!

5-23-43

Dear Dezső, Today I created an expense for you again, however don't worry, when I get home God will help me, I will reimburse you. It's about two weeks now that it has been raining and it's cloudy. Today's telephone call went quite rapidly. I called at nine o'clock and I spoke at 11 o'clock. It will cost $3.55 with tax included. I was wondering who was that person that you were skating with? Write to me about it, don't forget! And you write about yourself. How are you? How's business? There are five more weeks of basic training, then I will go to another place. How's the weather there? The only thing good about it that it's raining here, is it's not hot. Once the sun comes out, it's more difficult to march. Take care of yourself, the girls too. Don't argue! There's no benefit from it. Write a lot! A lot of kisses, your brother, Irving.

5-23-43
Camp Wolters Texas

Dear Herminka and Mariska,
I really spoke to you very little, but the minutes went by quickly. It was $3.55 which isn't a lot. I could have spoken more. When I get home I will pay you all the expenses and until then many thanks to you. I will be here for another five weeks and then thereafter will be going somewhere. I do not know if I'll get any furlough because they're not giving it so easily. It is possible that I will be close to home, then I will be able to go to visit you on Sundays. That would be good, then I could speak to you about everything. It's not worthwhile to speak on the telephone, because one can hardly speak and the time flies. And besides that you can't think of everything that you want to speak about. There's no news, nothing special. I've just received a letter from Cleveland. Elsie writes that she's very busy helping her husband in the office. She notes that "You write very good English letters." Sometimes I wonder if it's true, but according to that it must be. Flora has not written to me yet, but Elsie said that next month they will be operating on Flora. I am sorry to hear that, but I hope it will be successful. I do not know if I should write to Arthur, or I should wait until they write to me. My dear Herminka, do not work too hard. I'm sure that you're working at home also as much as at work. If you can, please write to me, and don't worry! Everything is fine and it will be! Also Mariska, you think of me a lot, but don't worry because that's no good. If you have a chance, write to me about everything. I will also write to you when I can. Forgive me this time, however I wrote so much that you will be tired of reading it. Kisses to you all individually with love, Irving

I will receive the citizenship papers. Write about everything. At the end of this week, I will send you the pictures. Kisses to all, Irving.

1943/5/26 Irving to Family (Book 2, 215-217)

Dear Mariska,
I always read your cards and letters gladly. You must have been worried a lot also, as I see and I'm reading in your letters. Please don't be sad. As for me, thank God, I'm fine. I hope your job is better than before! If you don't like it, then leave it, and look for a better one since you can't work too hard. Although, in this world, everybody works hard. Please write if you can, write about everything. How are you? Do you have headaches? Don't be sad about me! I know how much you think about me, but no need to think too much because it gives you a headache.
Like you mentioned, Dezső met that girl and she wondered about me. I got a letter from her yesterday. She writes beautifully, three pages and it came by plane. Today, I'm thinking about responding to it. If they didn't give "cipo" [meaning unclear, perhaps "cheap"] stamps from the office then forget it. It's not necessary to send it then. I will write some more for you another time. Now I'm sending kisses to all of you with much love. Write to me whenever you can. Dear Dezső and Herman, How are you? Write to me!! When I will have more time, I will write to you separately. Nothing new.
[Written on the side] I got the article. Also, the Jewish girl sent me one from another newspaper, but it was put in wrong, kissing you with much love, Irving

Dear siblings,
I'm sorry that I'm late responding, but I'm very busy here. I stood guard today for at least 24 hours. They change guards at all hours. It's a pleasure to be outside at night. It's been a couple of days that the weather is nice. Thank God, I'm fine. In your cards and letters, I was so happy to hear that you are all fine. You mentioned in every letter, that it would be great if I could have a break, but I don't know if it will be possible for awhile. How are you? How does the cleaning go? I'm sure it's like here on every Friday? The only difference is that no one checks after you. They check after us, in such a certain way that we can't leave a

piece of dust anywhere. Everything has to shine. But in a way that's good because everything is clean and healthy, which is important. Dear Hermine, you asked in one of your letters if I sent the address to the neighbor. I didn't send it and also I didn't write them yet! I will wait to reply. What do you say about that? Write about it!

1943/5/29 Undated Marie to Irving (Book 8, 14-15)

[May 1943 - Since he's in basic training and she mentions in this letter that she was mistaken about the date by a day…]

Saturday 30

My dear little brother! Today I got a letter from you again and I was very happy about it. You know I can hardly wait for your mail. When I get home from work and I can't find anything from you, then you know I am very upset. Don't be sad. I know that you are a soldier and don't have a lot of time. How are you my little brother? How do you look? I would like to see you already. Your letter today was very short, so I read it twice. And I can see through everything, how things are there. I also know that it is not a game. Just take care of yourself and don't be sad. I am well and I will work tomorrow on Saturday. I got it wrong with the title [above] because it is only Friday 8:15 at night, and I'm in a hurry to write you. There is no particular news here, since I did not see anything. You know my Irving, don't be surprised that I make mistakes so many times with the writing, but you know that the radio is on and we are talking too. My Irving, I wanted to ask you yesterday, if you are not afraid to shoot or from the noise that there is. Did you get used to it by now? We miss you a lot at home. Yes, we mention you a lot. Next time we will try to take a picture alone and we will send it to you, but I would like to see you as well, my little brother. Did you buy a pair of shoes yet? Do you have already a cap with a round top [helmet]? Do you still have money? I know that you did not have much salary yet and if you need it let me know, I will send some. Otherwise, what's new by you? Do you go anywhere at night, like to dance? What do you do for fun?

Do you have any girl friends? I did not go anywhere since then. I don't want to go. Flora was not well on Sunday and it is possible that we will go [visit]. Yes, we want to bake on Sunday and we would want to send some to you on Monday. I hope everything will be fine! I am asking you little brother, not to be sad, and take care of yourself and if you can, write about everything because I'm interested in everything that happens to you. And I hope that they will move you! That is, to a better place. I wish it would be easier for you already. It is terrible in that town and it is horrible to run or walk that much. How's the food? Do you like it? Are there any mixed fruits there? Do you work in the kitchen there? What kind of clothes do you wear there - do you have thin clothes? Or only that thick one? The weather here is very cold. Last week was warmer already. Did you get any mail since then? It has been a week since I called anybody on the phone and this way I don't know anything. Now I think I wrote everything together, maybe you will not even have patience to read it, but I don't even know what to write about. Dave is not at home. He is working. Hermine is reading a newspaper. Herman is sleeping. And me, as you can see it, I'm writing to you. And you, what could you be doing? I would be happy if I could see you at least from the side. It came to my mind just now, that you do a lot of cleaning and it is hard. Let's hope that we will have a good world coming! Even the sun will come out and shine on us a little. Now I send my best and I kiss you countless times and I stay with love. Your forever faithful sibling, Maria
Write if you can.
I will write and Hermine will as well.

1943/5/30 Irving to Family (Book 5, 288-294)

Camp Wolters, Texas
May 30, 1943
Dear sisters and brothers!
With today's mail I mailed you pictures that I mentioned previously. They didn't come out as I mentioned before. I had to have them redone and enlarged, because they couldn't do it. I'm curious what you will think. This time, I'm not telling you if I gained or lost weight. I want to hear that from you and to know what you think. Definitely write to me about it. I'm mailing three pictures, even though they're all the same. But here we haven't any other choice, they make only one film and that is what they work with. In the office, I was told that it was the best place when I went to make what I needed for my papers [citizenship].

Today I received a card from you. Thank you very much because you're very prompt in answering my letters. I'm getting slower with my writing. You know how it is. Here we have to work. I need more time to write this. I have to answer more letters, not like you. In case I don't write more, you know why. Don't worry about me, I'm okay. Yesterday there was a review of the entire regiment. It was a lot of work, but everything is okay. At least I'm over with this, too. Here time goes by because there is always something you have to know. Tomorrow we'll have payday with an increase. As you see it, that's what I am waiting for. I didn't put the money in the bank because that is not the best. When I need it, it would be difficult, and I would not be able to get it. If I get paid tomorrow, maybe then I will send home some. It is not good to have money here. In case they find out then they come and they want to borrow. I don't want to make it a habit that I should give them money. I will write tomorrow or whenever I have time. Herman, you mentioned the banker asked why I didn't write to him. If he will ask you again, then please write his address and his name or give him my address and let him write me. You know, the girl who talked to me about Dave already wrote me a very nice three page letter. When they will transfer me from here, I will have to send home all the civilian pictures, items, and letters. It is very interesting, when I have time I read someone else's letters, and what they write to me. You will laugh about this. This way I don't have to go to the movies and I have a [in English] good time at home! Yes, [in Hungarian] Did you understand what I said on the gramophone recording? Do you want to get another one? Let me know [and] I will send you [one] right away or would you prefer that I send you mail instead because [what I write] is in Hungarian. I can't make [that] into Hungarian. Today I wrote to Yenkin, the neighbors, and the girls. And now I have to write to Cleveland. I'm wondering why Flora and the family don't write. Maybe they are angry about something? Or they don't feel well. Even then they should write a few lines. I will not write to them until I will hear from them. I sent them a letter and a card and they should have written something. For the aunt I wrote more letters. She answers only with cards. Last week I didn't have a chance to write. I mailed her only a card. Maybe she's angry because of that. I'll wait in case I do not hear from her. Then I will write to her. Do the Roths ask about me? Who asks about me? If you get tired from reading my letter try to rest for a while. Kisses, Irving

1943/6/1 Arthur and Helen to Irving (Book 17, 196-198) - Megillat Esther

Columbus May 31 [1943]

Dear Irving, Enclosed you find a "Megilah" (The book of Esther) , the symbol of Jewish history and survival. May all our boys who are in the U.S. Army be included in our prayers for their safe return. Take care of yourself. Love, Helen

June 2, 1943
Dear Irving:

Please forgive me for not writing to you sooner. I have been very busy with business and personal matters. There is an acute shortage of labor available for the factory. We have plenty of materials but the customers must have a priority before we can sell them scales. Sam is taking some National Service courses at the University that should help him when he gets into the army. He, very likely will be in this fall. Flora isn't well and will go to the hospital soon for a major operation. May God grant her a speedy recovery. The girls were over last Monday and told us how well you are getting along. The army is a great experience. My advice is that you should learn your courses well, as they will come in handy when, and if, you are ever in action against the enemy. We all send our love to you and wish you the best of luck. I am, as ever, Your loving cousin, Arthur

1943/6/3 Irving to Hermine and Marie (Book 1, 157-161)

June 3rd, 43
Dear Hermine and Marie,
I got your letters that I longed for in which you sent photographs. You look very good in the pictures. I think Marie looks so much better than in the old ones that I have here. Hermine, however, you look very serious in it. I would love you to smile better at me. Marie, your hair looks great, you absolutely have to wear it that way. I wonder what you will say about my pictures. When I will get your response, then I will write everything, whether or not I put on weight. First I would like to know [what you think], and then I'll respond. Your pictures are very good, but I would love to see all of you in person. I believe you feel the same way about this, but I hope that soon I'll be able to get days off. It's very hard to get them here.

Dear Herminka, you asked, if I got a letter from Jenkin [from Frye Yankin Paint Store]. Yes, I got one from him. I already wrote an answer. As soon as I get [more] letters from them, I will send this one home. Until then, I will keep this here. I don't know if I wrote about it! You know Jenkin's letter is very interesting. It's worth reading it, not just once, but more than once. Mariska mentioned some holidays? What kind of holiday was it? I don't know about any holiday. June 9th will be the first day of Shavuot, but here it won't be celebrated. I still have three weeks at this place, but believe me the days and weeks go really fast. We are having the hardest days now. The heat is terrible, we are melting. There is only one way why someone would like to live in this part [of the country], that is, if it's easy to live and do the things that one wants. This week we did drills many times at night. Don't forget, we were doing drills in the daytime, also. The nights are short! So short! Saturday afternoon we are free, but even then there are things to do. Sunday goes very quickly. I would've loved to go to Dallas, but I'm tired and I rest, if it's possible. But I can't even do that always. Why not? I will write about it next time or maybe you'll figure it out.

I will respond to the May 30th letter, because I didn't have time to read it leisurely. You know, that if I want to write, there is no time to read. I will write about the income tax on Sunday, but I won't until then. You can also call the office, I believe, and you can say that I'm a soldier. Unless, I will have time, and then I will, but here there is no time for anything...

I don't need anything, many thanks to you that you think about me so much. You know I think about you a lot also. How are you, though? What are you guys doing? Do you have everything you need? Maybe I will send home a check, if I can, approximately $45 or $50. I can't go to the bank yet or to the post office, but I will be going on Saturday afternoon. Now I got $29.50 for one month! One dollar for each day and 20 hours a day!... The Hungarian man from Yenkin wrote to me and said that they are very busy. He works 28 hr. overtime.

Jenkin is working because they can't get another worker. Herman, what do you do? Do you like your job? Why don't you write? Dezső, where were you? What are you doing? Write to me! I saved your first letter to remember, so I can read it again sometimes. When I read it first, believe me it felt like I'm in Europe. Your words sounded like that from you. I hope you will write to me when you can! Now I don't know what to write about, because everything is the same....., But as soon as I read your letter, tomorrow or when I'll have time, I will write something then. I could write a lot, but it's not worth it, because I didn't even read through what I wrote [now]. I have to hurry with everything, even with writing. I have to be alert all the time. That is why it's like this. Kissing you many times, and with much love, Your brother, Irving

I got a letter from the Jewish girl and she asked why don't I write often.
You know I hardy think I can spare a minute to write to you! Write!

1943/6/5 Irving to Family (Book 3, 36-40)

June 5 - 43
My dear sisters and brothers,
I am free from noon so I shall began to write to you a few lines today, and tomorrow I will again write to you. I thought that I will be going to the city, however the rain is pouring down and therefore I believe I'm not going to go anyplace. I shall be in the barracks. In the evening probably I'll be going to the movie, I don't know yet what will be playing. Do you know this is the best time to sleep, but here one can't do it. If I'm not going anywhere then they tell you that you're lazy and they'll look for work for you, which I don't want, so because of that I'm going to go someplace. At this moment I am in the recreation hall, they're playing ping-pong and the radio is on. There is a table here and a person can sit down and write. However one can't think because all the noise that exists. As I look out through the window, the rain is pouring so heavily that you cannot look through the street. And it's a large heavy rain. If it stops raining, then I will be going to make a check of $50 and I will send it home. I will receive another pay check before they transfer me from here.

Dear Maria, You are asking me how I'm proceeding with the education? Until now I have studied eight different guns [and] weapons. Next week we are going to study newer weapons. If I would write their name you would not know what it is. I understand every one of them, but I do not know each individual name. I have a book from which I can learn and study, but there's no time, because there is so much work and you must learn different things that I don't know which one I should study first. So I know a little bit about every one [of them]. When they transfer me to another place then there I'll know which weapon will be mine, then I will study that the most. I believe I mentioned it in my previous letter that in about three weeks I will be transferred. It would be great if I could be close to you. I could then go home every weekend. I hope all things will be well! Otherwise I'm okay. Tomorrow I hope to hear from you also. I will write to you tomorrow about the taxes. Maria, I wrote to you about the stamps that you don't have to send [them to] me. I will wait until they transfer me.

I just reminded myself that I didn't write to you about the newspaper or magazine. I cannot find the address. I believe that there is an office there on East Broad St. If I remember I gave you the order form and the address is on it. Please write to me as soon as you can about it, since I want to know what it is. I don't have time to think about it. If they still send the magazine, then return it and then they will stop sending it. I am glad to hear that everyone is well. I received a heartfelt card from you Herminka. You wrote to me quite quickly especially before you went to work. I wrote you a card also between my work.

I worked from early morning to late at night and I went out in the evening to work, however before we went I wrote a few lines. We returned at night after 12 o'clock. I want to thank you for the few lines! Hencsu my dearest! My dearest Maria, you wanted to know if I listen to the radio. I do, but you cannot listen too much, only once or twice a week. I don't read the newspapers like at home. I know a little bit about what goes on, since they read it to us every day what is happening, but to sit down and to read the papers one can't, since we have to do other things that must be done. I did not receive a reply from the New York [relatives]. I don't know what could be the reason. I wrote a letter to the neighbor in Columbus. I'm sure they will read it to you. Sometimes I meet the fellows with whom I came here, but all of us are busy and we cannot get together frequently. The rain stopped and I returned from the post office. I mailed a $50 check to put in the bank. If you Hermina and Maria need it, please use it for anything. If and when you have, then you will return it. Please forgive me for calling you different names in each letter. Write to me. Loads of kisses to you, your brother, Irving.

1943/6/6 Irving to Family (Book 5, 295-297)

June 6 - 43
Dear sisters and brothers!
Yesterday, I mailed you a letter that included a $50 dollar check. I hope you received it. Nothing special, everything is well with me. Today I received three cards from you. I was very happy to get them. It is true that it wasn't much, but at least you all write, even a card. I hope tomorrow I will get more, maybe a letter. Today I wrote about the tax. I will pay them after the war. Today I received from Arthur a letter telling me I should not be angry because he didn't write sooner. But they're very busy. They have merchandise, but they don't have anyone to sell it to because they need permission to buy. He typed the letter. Poor Flora will have surgery this month. God help them so she should be better soon. He doesn't have enough help in the factory. Samuel goes to university and studies army classes. In case they call him in, then he would be more knowledgeable. Also Monday you were visiting them and were talking about me. He writes that I should learn everything that they teach because it is good to know. Today the weather is very nice here. Only in the afternoon, it started to rain. Dear Hermine, I'm not angry as you write in your card because you think I am a little boy. When I was reading your card I heard your voice in my ear. You wrote that you were at the movies and the other girls did not come in. What do you think, who was the other girl? Who was that? Please write if you want to. Maria, I hope you will like your job. Please write about it. What are you doing? How many hours? What are you doing on your time off? Are you going to see a show at the movies? Write about everything. I will answer you as soon as possible. Dear David! I really was very happy to get your card. It is too long that I didn't hear from you. You really don't write me. If I need something just send it to me. I still have one and a half dollars and the gum. I already wrote a letter to the neighbors. Probably they will show it to you all. I don't know if I will get a furlough. I will write about it if I do. Many kisses, your little brother, Irving

1943/6/7 Hermine and Marie to Irving (Book 9, 53-57)

Sunday 6.

[from Marie]
My dear Irving!

We were very happy to receive a card from you yesterday. And I'm very happy to hear that thank God, you are well. You know, my little brother, in the past few days I was very busy and did not write to you. But now I'm in a hurry to make it up to you. How are you, my little brother? I'm well. We just got home from Mrs. Halkens. You know, she is a neighbor from 2nd Ave. And you know, we took your picture to show them. They liked it very much and they said, it is a good picture of you. And write it to me honestly, I would love to know what you look like in real life. And they were wondering about you a lot. They are very nice, and they always call us. They bought new furniture for the rooms and they are well furnished, but I will leave this now.

Now I will go back to me. As I mentioned that I work at Lazarus and I think I wrote it to you that I was in the jacket department [takban]. And you know little brother, I don't really like it because it is pretty hard. And in the meantime I wanted something else. Besides that, it was possible that I would not be [good] enough. But there was no vacancy, so I looked for something else. And now, I'm on the second floor where they sell and fit men's clothes. If there is something wrong with it, I examine it before they send it out. If there is anything wrong, I file the number and I don't have anything else to do with it. Sometimes we are very busy, other times not so much. I think that it won't be so bad. Currently I do this alone. I think, if they will be happy with me, I can get into a better place easier. You know little brother, in a big place the opportunity is bigger. I don't know how much the salary will be because I didn't ask yet. When I was in stock, I only started with $18 even though they gave more. I hope at this place, maybe, maybe, they will give more. Now this week on Wednesday I will get a paycheck and I will see it then. There is a discount if I work there. They give me 10% from everything, although it is not a lot. I just got a dress for myself. I will take a picture and you will see. Somehow I always forget to buy film (for the camera) and can't buy it from somewhere else.

Yesterday I also got a bond in the movie theater. They gave a movie ticket with it. But I will leave this too. You know my little brother I wrote so much foolishness already, so you will not even have the patience to read it. Now, I will get back to you. What did you do today, on Sunday? And you mentioned, if you should send a record disc. You know, little brother, if you have a chance and money, you can send it. I talked to this old lady, who lives here, you know who, Walters. She mentioned that you wrote to them also and that you mentioned about the girl. And you know I only talked to her for a minute and she already said it. They will write to you. I don't know when. The weather is humid. Yesterday the heat was immense and today it is raining again. How's the weather by you? Now, I'm asking you to take care of yourself. Everything is going to be ok. Only rest as much as you can, and eat whatever you have, even if you don't like it. I hope you have a good appetite. We think about you a lot at home. I kiss you countless times. Forever your faithful sibling, Maria, who thinks about you a lot.

[From Hermine[
Dear little brother!
Today is Sunday. I will be in a hurry to write a few lines. Thank God I'm well. I hope that you are as well. This afternoon it rained and we were at Mrs. Hawkins to visit them, since she invited us many times. You know that I took your picture to show them and they said it is pretty good. We didn't show it to the neighbors here, since it seemed that they had company over. I will show it one of these nights to them. I know, you are surprised that I always write to you in a hurry. It's not like I would work too much, only I get home late and maybe I am lazy. Although you are on my mind a lot. Yesterday night after work we went to the movies. It was a pretty good piece and in the newsreel they showed how the life of a soldier goes. It was very real. I would have loved for you to see it. You were in my mind little brother. You know Irving, maybe you are upset at me because I call you like a little boy, but I truly do it from the heart. At least you can laugh at it or maybe you are angry at me?!!! I was very happy for your picture and I will buy a frame for it and maybe I will have it painted. Write to me whenever you can. Don't be sad little brother. Everything is going to be fine and soon everything will pass and everything will be fine. Thank God, they say that maybe it will not last for long, because they are doing well.

Side Note: Although, you know that. Kisses, Hermine

1943/6/7 Irving to Hermine and Marie (Book 2, 237-239)

Dear Mariska,

As soon as I got your card, I wanted to respond. You wrote that the picture is not good. I believe you. Also, you wrote that I lost weight! These are all things that can happen here, because during these 13 weeks, everybody loses weight and then gets fat later. When I took that picture, I was 150 pounds. When I left home I was 160 pounds. But don't worry! I put on 12 pounds since then. I just weighed myself today and I'm 162 pounds. You know my hair makes me look a little skinnier, too. It must be hard for you to believe me, because you don't see me, but I will send another picture if I go into town. That way you'll have proof! What I gained here is not fat, but strength and muscle! That's the way it goes in the military. Everybody loses weight at the beginning. The hot weather sucks the energy out of you. But don't worry! Thank God I'm fine! If God helps us, we will see each other soon! I am hurrying with the writing and it's not going so well. Kissing you many times, Irving

Dear Herminka,
I got your card at night and I was so happy to hear that, thank God, you are well. Interesting, you wrote that the picture isn't so bad! Mariska said otherwise. Although, Dezső writes! I look very good. So it's very difficult to answer, but I have already written to Mariska. Everyone should know that during these 13 weeks, everybody loses weight, because no one is used to it. Besides that, my hair is missing and that means something [has an effect]. Don't be angry about that! I hope I will see all of you in person soon. Today I got from the Aunt a megillah for Purim. A beautiful scroll! Attached was a little letter. It says! "Enclosed you will find a megillah. The symbol of Jewish Victory and survival. May all our boys who are in the U.S. Army be included in our prayer for their safe return" What do you say about that? I will reply on Sunday to them. Dear Dezső, I got one of the packages. Thanks for you. I will have more time on Sunday to write and I will write with more details. Herman, how are you? Write! Kissing you many times, Irving

Dezső I got a response from the girl! A very interesting and smart letter!

1943/6/8 Flora to Irving (Book 4, 27-30)

Columbus, Ohio
June 8, 1943
Dear Ervin:-
Many weeks have elapsed since I promised I would write frequently and please believe me that I had every intention of doing so–why didn't I then? The usual reasons– I admit it is inexcusable but I am counting on you to forgive me and I'll try to do better. About two weeks ago I saw (At 50 Linwood Ave.) the picture of a handsome young man and I couldn't help thinking that if only a few other people see it he would be receiving more fan mail than the movie stars. You can see what effect it had on me! That expression shows the right mixture of sweetness and determination and will help to get you places. The girls spent an afternoon and evening with us–they both look well and had a lot of interesting things to tell about their work–they are to be congratulated in their success in the business world. The family is well – I am looking forward(??) to an operation soon–it is a simple one that the surgeons insist they can perform it in their sleep or at least with their eyes closed so why should I worry? I don't-except I should prefer to be absent the day they're doing it. But since that can't be I'll just have to be present and behave myself. Well Ervin, keep well and good luck– may all your own wishes be realized and your fondest hopes fulfilled! Love from us all, your cousin, Flora

1943/6/12 Herman to Irving (Book 14, 239-240)

6-12-43
Dear Ignác
I hope you are not angry that I don't write so often, but you know everything takes patience. I was glad for your letters. Write to me about how everything is going whenever you have time. I am well, I'm doing the usual. I was happy to get your pictures and I think that they are pretty good. I put the money in the bank. I saw the woman and she told me that the man who was at the cashier is in England and he wrote that everything went well through it and he experienced a lot. He wrote to them that the food was different, but he got used to that also. How does speaking go for you? I guess that you are already perfect. I am not really progressing. I don't go to the school, and at home I am lazy to study. This way studying always remains and fails. But I hope we will learn it somehow. How's the weather there? Here it is very warm. Yes, it is about time. Write about everything as soon as you can. [In English] So long
I kiss you, Herman

Sunday 13.

[from Marie]
My dear Irving!
Today is Sunday and I am trying to write to you. How are you my little brother? I sent a card to you yesterday. Also, we got two from you and I was very happy about it. You know my Irving, as you mentioned in your writing, you write very good letters for that matter. Especially, about how busy you are. But I understand all that. I thought about you a lot today. I hope to hear the best from you. And now I would like to write you exactly about my job. I believe that I mentioned it to you. You know my little brother, I don't even know if I like it. I have to look through the men's clothing that they fix. That is, they sell new clothes and they fix it and iron it and then there is a ticket on it with numbers and I have to look them over to make sure the entire thing matches and then I have to record that I gave it out.

And I have to be careful not to mix the suits because you know, I could get in trouble for that. Although, I am not afraid of that because I take a good look at the number on it, which is important. There is only one reason why it is not good, that is because it is very warm there. They iron in a small place in the back. There is only a small fan there. I think maybe I will get used to the warmth. I was amongst the stacks before for a few days and it was very hard. I got $18 for a week. And now the boss said that they start with $20 here. I hope I will get more! What do you say my little brother, Dezső works there too, he just started now. He left the driving for some reason. And as I hear he takes the blinds out of what they sold at Lazarus and he is installing them. I'm not sure how much he makes. I think about $30-$40 a week. I just don't know if he will like it. You know how it is. And the previous boss told me to learn to speak better and then I could get another job sooner. Since as I can see they are happy with me and they told me they will not let me work at this place for long. The boss here is a very fine man. He also came here from Germany a couple of years ago. When Lazarus was in Europe he lived with him. Then their trouble started so he had him brought here. He was a very wealthy man at home as a factory owner. That's the way it is. Once it is up and then it is down. I will leave this too. Maybe I will bore you with all this foolishness, but I always wanted to write about this to you. And you asked me how I spend my free time. You know that I don't have a lot of free time because like today we were at home, and we were busy. We went to the movies one night this week, but only to the neighborhood [theater]. The film was very good. And I will go to work on Monday, and I will come home at 5:30. I work 6 days (45 hours a week) so I don't have a lot of time. And what did you do today? We gave your picture to have it painted and we had one framed already and it is so much better. It is above the stove with your big picture and everybody likes it, because in it you look just like in real life. The neighbors were wondering about you. This week one morning they took us to work. Did he write a response yet to you? The Aunt is really nice that she sent it [the megillah] to you and wrote nicely. You know that we call her sometimes on the phone, but she does not call. Flora, too. We don't know when they will operate on her yet. I will write it to you. Take care of yourself and don't be upset. Everything is going to be fine. I hope. Only you know that it makes me restless, if you go home [to Europe]. [On the crease:] I hope from there not too far from us, you know what I mean! [On the top:] And do you still work so hard? [On the edge:] I kiss you with love Maria

[from Hermine]
My dear Irving,
Since today is Sunday, I have time I write to you. I have not written a long letter for a while anyway. Although you don't have time to read it. I don't even know what to write to you that you would be interested in. Thank God we are well, and like always, there is some work on Sunday, too. We really don't go anywhere, just like when you were at home. Yes, I like to go to the movies whenever I can. And we visit those few good people of ours. Although, even the neighbors are calling us too, but I don't have a lot of patience for them. The lady neighbor would like to gossip. She is already saying hello, but she only wants to know the news and maybe to come to visit us. When you will come home little brother we will go everywhere with you. David is pretty busy and maybe Herman will never have a clue [how] to deal with this. It is true that we are busy and don't have too much time. I like my job and so it's a lot of fun. I meet with many kind women at lunch. There is an hour lunch time, just for the workers, and I eat there too, whatever is Kosher because there are a lot of things available there. You know my little brother, I bought a frame for your picture and you look pretty different. Much better. Dave had a picture made too, and I bought

the same frame. Although, you are just smiling for us there. It feels good when I come home from work and I can see you smiling. Although, I know that you work hard and surely is enough, but the good God will help that it will not take long. You know my pictures were not good, but if it the weather will be nice, I will send you a new one. Flora and the others are well, but she does not know when she will go to the hospital. Lajos wrote that he got called in. This week he will be in Columbus. I did not get any news from Bertha either. If you know anything about where they took her, write it to me. I hope everything is going to be fine because life is hard, but it is better if one knows everything. And they want to teach the boys this way. So, my little brother don't be worried. The dear God will help. They show in the cinema saying that if maybe there is a spy in the audience then he can count the legs of the soldiers. The last movie was pretty good. It was like you could have been there too. You know, they show how they teach the soldiers. Do you see good movies? I will write again shortly. Now I will kiss you with love. Hermine

1943/6/13 Irving to family Camp Wolters Texas (Book 5, 306-312)

Camp Wolters Texas
June 13 - 43
My dearest brothers and sisters,
I have received your letters and cards, I was very happy to read them. Today is Sunday, [and] at this time I read all the letters that I've gotten during the week. Believe me, after I finish reading them, I could write a book for you. There are a lot of questions and at that time I do try to answer all your questions. However, this week's letter did not have to many questions, therefore, I am going to write about myself [and] what has happened during the week. Yesterday evening I was at the movie and I have seen a very good picture. I can't remember the title. After the movie, I went to the USO club and I saw in person Bob Burns the radio commentator. They gave us a card and his name was on it. I went to him asking him to autograph it. He played his horn! The name of the horn was bazooka! We have a new weapon, a very famous one with that name. Probably you've heard about it! In other words it was quite interesting. His name is on the card that I mailed to you. I received it from headquarters. As you will see I made a notation on it. They were giving it to everyone because we are not going to be here too much longer. I think that they will be sending us to the other side. On the first week of June we will be leaving from here. If we are leaving I cannot call you, just write to the same address and they will forward it to us. In the next 2 weeks we're going to travel and will be there for a few days. I do not know whether I'll be able to write to you because it will be an exercise as if [we're] on the other side. This will be a real activity. If I do not write to you, don't worry we will be outdoors day and night quite a way from this camp. I will not receive any letters from you for a few days. At this time it's 11:30. I'm going to have lunch and continue after lunch! We eat after the whistle blows.

As I have returned from the lunch I am sitting down to write you again. I have also received today's mail. Only a card from Maria. I'm sorry that Lajos has to go through what I went through. If he's going to be there tell him to write me. It's possible that he will be placed here. In the beginning it will be very difficult for him as for everyone, however when he gets accustomed to every week of military life, then he will not even notice it. The word "man'" means a lot here. At the present time we are only students, however in 2 weeks from now the general will say from today on all of you are men. So it is, whether you're ready or not. As you know, a couple weeks ago I've made some pictures with another fellow which didn't turn out to be good. Here I'm enclosing them to you. I know you will say that it is not good. If you want to throw them away. I will be making another one once I'm in town, but I don't know when, it depends on whether or not I could go.

Dear Mariska, you mentioned and wanted to know how much money I have. Believe me, I haven't thought about it since I left home. This week there is even a letter from the Hungarian at Fry Yanken's factory and he said that he will work and he has extra time that he is to work. And I thought at that time it would be good for me to be there to earn extra money, however today I'm here, and everything is different. Money is no good if you have it, it does not interest me, since I love the things in my mind. I hope that God will help and I will be home in the near future. As you know I went to say Yiskar [yizkor]. I went to look at the guest list and on May 28, 1943, a Sidney Gluck from Akron, Ohio was there. I do not know whether he was a soldier or he was just visiting. I would have liked to meet him, but I couldn't, except if I would look for him in Akron. This town is not too far from Columbus. Do you think that he's related to us? He's Jewish! It was written that way. If you know anything about it and will find out, write to me about it. Here the weather is very hot. Don't worry about it because I've been accustomed to it already.

I will return to tell you that I didn't tell you before what was for dinner. Everyday we have potatoes, meat, coffee, bread, butter, oranges, eggs, lekvar, pancakes and so forth. You don't have to worry about it that we do not have anything to eat. However they're not making it well everyday. I don't eat much and some days nothing. Every morning they have ham and eggs mixed together! At that time I only eat bread with butter on it, or lekvar, milk or coffee, an orange or an apple. If I can, I pick out a little egg [from] where it is! and potatoes, potatoes every day. I wrote you this week that I worked in the kitchen. I worked long hours, but it was good because I didn't have to go to the exercises at night. I ate fruit as much as I wanted. By the time you finish reading this letter you're going to laugh that I have written all types of mishmash too!

As of now I have not received my citizenship papers. I do not know much about it. I believe I've written everything. You know, the girl Dezső mentioned wrote to me. I have replied to her and I received a reply from her also. She writes very nicely and I have to answer her today. I don't even know where I will pick up some of the words that are used. Did you receive my English card? Did you understand it? Please write about it. I will close my lines since I do not know what else to write. Before I leave this place I will call you. If I can't call you, then I will write you. Don't worry, everything will be fine. The next two weeks will be the most difficult and after that they'll transfer me and it should be easier. I don't know where yet. I'll only know when I'm there. I will write you about it! As soon as I will arrive, I will send a telegram to let you know where I am! Write to me! Loads of kisses with love, individually, your brother who never will forget you and thinks of you always! Irving

Until we meet again!

1943/6/14 Jane Schallheim to Irving (Book 17, 280-282)

Sunday

Dear Irving,

Perhaps I should introduce myself first. My mother is Elsie Gluck Schallheim to whom you have written previously. I don't know if we have ever met. I think we have though, because I was in Columbus about two years ago and met your sisters and some of your brothers and probably you.

I have two more years of high school, but at the present time we have vacation and I am working as a cashier in the cafeteria at Western Reserve University. I didn't expect to be a cashier but was given the job unexpectedly and I like it now. Is it very warm in Texas? Right now most of Cleveland's population are working in their victory gardens or taking a sun bath. It is very warm here today. We feel the heat quite a bit here because it is so damp. I would be interested in hearing about your camp life. What time do you have to be up and do you have to work very hard? There is a swimming pool within walking distance of my house and I and so will my friends be glad when it opens. We can go there after work as it is open all day and evenings too. Every one is working much harder now than last year. Very few students are loafing this summer. Most of them are working or attending summer school or both. For the first time we are having a senior graduating class at the end of summer school. There isn't much more space so I'll close.

Sincerely,

Jane Schallheim

1943/6/15 Frey Yenkin Paint Co to Irving (Book 3, 176)

June 15, 1943
Pvt. Irving Gluck
Co. B - 55th Infantry
Training Battalion
Camp Wolters, Texas

Hiya Cowboy!

Well, at least if you're not one by this time, you'd better get started. Can you lasso a steer yet? What's that? Oh, you've been too busy "lassoing" Army regulations and what makes a 30 caliber machine gun sound like Rosie the Riveter on her day off from Lockheed. We're really beginning to feel the heat. Summer has set down upon us with no mercy on any of us. The office force has been trying to talk the management into turning the place in[to] a swimming pool office, but the idea hasn't taken foot as yet. (I can't understand why). We receiving a card from Bill Johnson. He's stationed at Camp Roberts, California. My, it must be nice, what with Lana and Hedy and all the rest. Well, don't feel bad, Irving. They say some of the prettiest girls in the world come from Texas. I'm enclosing Bill's address so you can write to him and compare notes of what Army life has got to offer. Best of luck, and keep smiling.

Sincerely,
Management & Employees
Frey-Yenkin Paint Co.

[Attached at top]
Pvt. Wm. Johnson
Try. C 537 ng Bn.
11 F. A. Tng. Regt.
Camp Roberts, Calif.

1943/6/15 Frey-Yanken Paint to Irving (Book 3, 434)

June 15, 1943
Dear Irving:
I thought I'd drop a note myself again this time. You paid me a very nice compliment and thank you very much, kind sir. My boyfriend has been away on convoy duty for a little over a month now and is due back anytime. I missed him very much, but then, I have learned to take it. I just stop to think of all the other girls whose boyfriends are out of the country and especially those who have husbands overseas. A couple of weeks ago, I went horseback riding and did the most beautiful fall you ever laid eyes on. You know me, I couldn't take an animal that was gentle. Oh, no, I had to get one full of spirit. That was just fine. Only he had too much of the stuff. He got the bit in his teeth after about 45 minutes of riding and tore off with me, I lost my right stirrup and proceeded to slip off the side of the horse. It wasn't long before I was on the ground unable to move. A car pulled up along side the rode. The people had seen my stirrup swaying in the breeze and knew doggone well I was going off sooner or later. I wasn't going fast or anything, just over 40 miles an hour. In a car, that isn't much, but on a horse, Brother, that's not just trotting along! I was laid up for three days. I have suffered, Irving, believe me, I have suffered. I still have a black and blue hip, so you know it must have been pretty bad. The doctor said I have the most beautiful bruises he had ever seen, but how I escaped a broken hip was more than he could figure out. Well, Irving, I just had to relate this little experience to you. It was the first time I had ever gone horse back riding. I know one thing. I don't have to worry about going any faster, or having a horse run away with me. I know what to do now. Just quietly fall off the side of the horse, and if you're lucky you'll only be laid up for a week or so. Ben has been yelling at me to get back to work, so I guess that's all for this time. Everybody says hello. Sincerely, Lola Zuccarelli, Frey-Yenkin Paint Company

1943/6/15 Irving to Family (Book 5, 330-332)

Camp Wolters, Texas
June 15 - 43
Dear sisters and brothers, (until 120)
I received your cards and was very happy to read that thank God, you are all well. Do you know that one person can endure so much that we cannot believe it. Today, the heat was 100° and we were walking with all the equipment. Until now this was the most difficult march. It was so unbearably hot and we had to carry 40 kilogram packs. Here they have tall, stone mountains and thick trees like at home, but also cactuses. I think you know what I mean. It has needles sticking out. Here they have lots of that, the hills and the forest is full of them. Wherever you go, they stick you. You would like them because the flowers are very nice. In case you don't know what I am talking about, I will explain it to you. It has 2 or 3 branches and very stocky roots. Nobody likes it. I want to tell you something else. If you remember Ödön basci [a person back home] he used to say, there are bugs who eat human blood and if you scratch yourself, it becomes very bad, open sores. Some of the grasses have them. The fields are full of so many of them that some of the boys we're so full of it, they look like roasted meat. The bug [bite] is very small, and red, but in a few days they disappear. The problem is we get one every day. We have a couple of very small ones and then later, it itches so much you could scratch for a whole week. But don't worry about that. I'm just mentioning it because I remember Ödön bacsi used to talk about it. I did not have it, some of the boys had it. I knew what to do about it. If it is possible I watch where I'm sitting down. Even though you never can be sure where it is. Otherwise, I'm well. This week and next week will be the hardest days. If we can take it, then everything will be okay. I

will write when I can. Many kisses, with all my love, even if I can't write, you continue to write to me!
Irving

David and Herman, why are you not writing to me? Kisses to all

Irving

1943/6/16 Hermine to Irving (Book 3, 185-186)

My dear little brother Irving,
Since I think of you a lot, and besides, I didn't have enough time that I could listen to your recording as of now, so today, Tuesday, I was quite nervous and I decided to go over to the Roth girls if they are at home [because] I would like to listen to the recording that you sent us from Camp Wolters. I wish I would have thought of it sooner or I could have listened to it at the Lazarus store. What's important is that it turned out to be very good and you speak well and put your words together very well. I hope that you can imagine how much happiness you have given me with that today. There was no mail from you today. Dave and Herman did not hear it yet. My little brother, I understand what it means when someone is busy or was occupied. I hope that from now on, I will have more time and I can write you more frequently. I will see to it that I will mail you some pictures if I have a good one. Presently I don't have much time. In the daytime I'm in the store, working. By the time I come home the stores are closed. I do like it. However I would have liked to have you see me at my new workplace. Did you know that today you can't wear any colorful, patterned prints, dresses come only in one color, namely brown, black, dark blue, gray, or beige. Most of them are of [the kind of] colored dresses that I never liked. I did buy a very elegant light brown dress that I could wear with a yellow, green or white [blouse] with a collar. They say it looks very good on me. I will wear those old dresses that I have that I did not like. My conversation goes so-so, but you know it's interesting, if I give credit and they don't have a charge card —you know whoever has good credit has a piece of paper preceded by their names on it and we print it on the slip, that is, in the book, but if I don't know his name, address, or something like that, he'll tell me, and if all went well, they would realize here that they had to tell me more slowly. Otherwise they're very nice to me. Like everywhere, there are all types of people. However, I'm progressing quite well. You know my little brother, I used to have a lot of gossip about it, but I ignored it. So read on if you have time for all this nonsense. We're all fine. I'm looking forward for your pictures and I have a hard time waiting. The recording is very good, thank you a lot for it my little brother. It is very nice of you that you think of me. Also, I will write more in the near future. Kisses and lots of love. Hermina
June 16th
I didn't have a chance to check into the postage stamp. If you want me to, I will mail you stamps next time.

1943/6/16 Undated Marie to Irving (Book 6, 109-110)

[Dated by recording and before June, shoes]

My Dear Irving!
I was just at the Roth's to listen to your recording. And you know my Irving, that it is pretty good. They said it too, that you speak well. I think the same as you do, that I would love to see you. You know that we miss you very much and the house is very empty without you. I'm thinking of you a lot. I wish they would transfer you here somewhere close by and then we would see each other more often. I hope you will get a vacation! Otherwise, how are you? Are you tired? What did you do on Sunday? Yes my little brother, did you buy a pair of shoes? I am very sorry that we could not send the ticket for the shoes. You wrote it before, that you don't want it and this way we bought something for it. But it will be good for another in June and I will send it by then to you. Otherwise do you need anything? If yes, just write it. Right now Dezső is not at home. Hermine is getting ready to write to you. Herman just came home, he was riding the bike. As for me, as you can see just writing to you at 9:15 at night. The weather here is still strong and cold and I don't know when the weather was like that before. Besides that there is no particular news. I have not spoken to the neighbor yet. We haven't been there since you left. They always call us, but we are busy. We did not go to Arthur yet. Now I am asking you to take care of yourself and don't be sad. Let's hope for the best! I will take a picture and I will send it to you. Do you have any acquaintances or good friends there? Although that can't substitute much since it's only a stranger. But in your free time try to forget your worries and try have a good time, then the time will pass easier. Now I kiss you countless times and I remain with much love until I will see you again. Maria

June 18 - 43
Camp Wolters Texas

My dear brothers and sisters live to 120.
You know, it's Friday and I am lucky that I can write to you. I couldn't even think of [doing that] yesterday when I received your letter. Today I'm working at the warehouse where they keep food supplies therefore I have time to write to you. It's 8:00 in the morning and at 11:00 the trucks will be coming on up so that I can do as I please. Therefore I began to write to you. I'm working here for the first time today. It's only for one day, every day is different. This is when you can take time for yourself. The rest of the gang went out to exercise. It's very difficult outside! I'm glad to hear that all of you are well and that the other pictures look better than before. It's interesting isn't it? Do you know Herminka, that in the movies it was interesting to look at the end as they show and teach the soldiers. Those that are in it think differently. Last evening I saw Mickey Rooney's "Human Comedy". Last time you told me that you're seeing it also. The picture was very good, for those that are not in the Army. If you notice everything happens in Texas. We know the things that he played, he played very well, Somehow it wasn't interesting to me. And I was with a friend who said the same thing. We are in it every day and are interested in different types of movies.

My dear sister Maria, I can imagine where you work must be very hot. If it's possible it would be a good idea to change to another position. You know, try some salt in the morning and the noon. I know that from the heat you can collapse, but if you take salt it is much easier to tolerate more. This week I wrote about how we were on a very high mountain. It was very difficult, full of rocks and bushes that had sticky leaves and besides it was very hot by the time we got to the top. We believed that we could not tolerate it any longer. If we had to go any further, then everyone would have fallen out. We had to go through valleys and high hills with complete military equipment. A man's stomach feels like it's full of sugar and his face is burning. We take salt 2x a day and we take water along and salt. If not for the salt, we could not have tolerated the heat. It is not much that you're making, perhaps you could get an easier job with more money. I hope that you will able to locate a good job that you will be happy with and satisfied with it. I believe that you can get the best job now because almost everyone is in the Army and there is demand for workers! Don't worry about where they will transfer us. We will not go into it yet there. Actually we are going to exercise and will be there for a week and then we will finish our exercises. We're going to eat, sleep, and shower outside. Shower!? We will practice day and night. When we get a half an hour off, we will eat, sleep, take a nap and then we'll take a handkerchief dipped into water and wash our face, hands, and feet. This is what we call a bath. One of the exercises will take place for 2 days and then we'll get one day off and go to another place for 3 days. Most cases we walk at night. These exercises are very good, but difficult! It's still good because you can learn a lot from this. If we will need to know, then it will be much easier. Hope that everything will be fine! Once again I'm asking you not to worry about my transfer because nothing can be done about it. This week we were for a small exercise and the captain made some pictures of us, about five of us. I was in it also. If it comes out well, then he will give us a picture of us. Dear Herman, I'm not angry that you write so little, but it takes only five minutes to write. What are you doing after work? What would you do if you were like I am? I can imagine it! If you can, please write me again next time. Dear Dezső, how are you? I hear that you changed jobs. How do you like it? Please write about it. I'm waiting for a long letter from you! Days are going by very fast. I almost finished three months. Kisses!
With love to Hermine, Maria, Dave, Herman. [In English] With love, Irving

My dear little Irving!
Today is Monday before noon. I'm in a hurry to write a couple of lines before I go to work. Lajos is here in Columbus and he was here yesterday during the entire afternoon. He does not know how long he will he stay. I hope you are well, and if they will move you, then hurry [and] write to us your new address. Please don't be worried. [Cousin] Lajos has a pretty good thing going on and I hope you will have as well! After the third month it will be easier I'm sure. Marcsa left to work this morning, but I only start at noon. You know, it was interesting when we sat outside at the front of the house. The neighbors thought you are at home. They just stared at us. Other than that we are all well. Do not worry and write as soon as you can. If you need anything, write it. I have a hope that maybe they will move you in the near future. Then you can come home to visit us. You can be proud, my little brother, that soon you will be over with all this. That is

the hardest thing! I don't even know what to write, maybe you don't even have time to read it. But whatever is important, Marcsa will write it to you. I'm sorry that my writing is so messy. My little brother, write to me! Good luck with your new location!

I kiss you with love,

Hermine

1943/6/21 Irving to Family (Book 3, 44-50)

June 21 - 43

Dear sisters and brothers,

Today in Columbus is the first warm day, that is, it's summer time! Here we were so busy that I did not know what day it is. But when you think about it, the days are flying by. It's been three months since I came here from home. What do you say to that? You see, the days are going by! But do not worry, everything is well and will be. We have work every day and when a person works that's good, because when we sit down then we fall asleep. Here it's quite warm. The military helps so that we do not fall asleep because if someone falls asleep then he has to get up and run quite a bit until he wakes up. It's ridiculous, isn't it? But that's the way it is.

Dear Herminka,

You have given me a great pleasure with your letters. I believe that you're progressing quite well with English since you can fill out the ration book. You shouldn't worry. Chin up! Everything will be fine. This way you'll be able to meet friends or people within the English gatherings. How was the supper? Was it kosher? This word which I used can't be mentioned here. I do not eat a lot of meat, but before I do, as I enter into the mess hall I look at what kind it is and if I see what it is, since I know it quite well after looking at it. To me, meat doesn't count anymore. If you would prepare it, then it would not make any difference what kind it would be, I would lick my mouth after it. Don't worry, it won't be long [and] I will receive a furlough and then you will prepare fried chicken! It won't matter really what it will be, but it will be very good. Again, I hear rumors that we are going to get a new assignment and before that we will get a few days off. A friend of mine is in a different group and they are going to get 5 days, plus travel time.

Yes! I'm not laughing because you can't be a soldier, but I really would not like it if you would have to go through all this as we have. When you see a picture about a parade it looks very nice! Those that are preparing for the parade are getting plenty of heat. They had to practice so that they're not going to make any mistake. You cannot move when they stop. We had a parade a few days ago and a Captain returned from combat. He was wounded and he showed that he was in the parade and told us where he was, but I don't remember it. Sandor Petofi, the Hungarian poet said that it's better to be at home than to be far away. You have mentioned that the army would be good for Herman, God forbid! I don't know if you would like it one day. What do you say to that? I don't know what I can write to him about it, there isn't much time to write. If I did, I don't know if you'd get it while I'm here. I hope to see you again someday. Don't be angry, but I want to write to Maria also.

Dear Maria,

Forgive me for not writing you separately, but tonight I'm tired and I'm in a hurry to fix the bed, shave, shower and to finish this letter. Every Monday we receive fresh beddings. We take the beds outside and in the evening we bring everything in and it has to be made properly, [we] also [have] to clean the shoes. In your letter you are saying that it's difficult to understand what I write. If it's difficult, just write to me and tell me what you don't understand, please let me know and I will tell you! Do you know that I think a lot about our father and I'm thinking how they are. I hope that in the near future we shall see them again! I made a picture today also with a fellow soldier and if it's comes out okay then I will mail it to you. You are asking if I'm brown? Yes. If you would see me, my face is brown and my neck also. If I would stay here during the summer, I would be completely black! On my face sometimes I have a few pimples but it's nothing, since there is no time to play with it. On Sunday I am able to wash my face, but that's it. You will see me if God will help me to visit you. Thank you for mentioning the packages, however I do not need anything at this time. When they transfer me, then I will write to you if I will need anything. I still have candy. I don't eat it because it's very hot here and I eat salt. It's ridiculous, isn't it! But it's better than sugar. With lots of love and kisses, to each and every one of you, Herminkat / Hencsu, Mariskat (that is you!), Dezső, and Hermant

Irving

My writing is not good because the edge of the bed is iron, and it's not like a table.
Write!
Kisses,
Irving

1943/6/22 Marie to Irving (Book 9, 49-51)

Monday 21
My dear little Irving!
I sent you a card today that I wrote in a hurry. Now I'm trying to make up for it. How are you little brother? What did you do yesterday? Write a lot about yourself, if you can. We got a card from you today that I was very happy about. Because you know, I have a very hard time waiting [to hear] from you every day. I also mentioned [that] Lajos is here in Columbus. You know, even he started it [military service] like everybody else and you, too. Currently he is still here and I don't know for how long. He just called me on the phone, but he was very busy. Currently, I don't know any special news. Flora went to the University hospital yesterday. They will operate on her tomorrow, or on Tuesday. I hope the good God will help her and she'll be over with this with luck. I will write about her. And, if you will write to the Aunt [Helen], do not mention it to her because she [Flora] does not want her to know about this. Only after!

But don't be sad and take care of yourself and eat because you can't do anything else there. Do you go to the town often? Otherwise, where is the movie theater that you usually go to to see a good show? I did not go to the movie this week. But, if nothing comes up, I'm planning on going one night this week. You know, here it is pretty warm, although at night it gets colder and it's nice. I am very busy at work. I could use it to be less. I hope you are all well also. Here everything is as it used to be. So uneventful. Lajos told me that he wrote to you last time and you did not respond.

You know how it goes. They moved his brother already a long time ago and he likes it better that he is farther. I will hope that you will get closer to us now. This morning I went to work with the neighbors and they were wondering about you. They did not mention if they wrote to you or if you wrote to them. You know, they always call us to their house and we were not there since, though it's not nice of us. And if we can do it, we will go over to them this week. Yet, you know that I don't really have patience for anything somehow because people are so strange these days. You know, I got a letter from you on Saturday also, that I understood. And it is enough besides the heat and the walking.

But now I wrote so much foolishness, that I will bore even you. Hermine wrote a letter today to you and I did not have time to write. I have to go out at 9 in the morning and [stay] until 5:30 at night every day now. Please write whenever you can, even if it's only a few lines, and so will I. I'm only asking you not to be sad and take care of yourself, because you know you have to take care. And rest whenever you can. Is there fruit for you? We already have watermelon and when I got it I thought about you first, and how much you like it. I hope you have everything there too, since it is a warm area. Now so long, bye bye until I will see you again. I kiss you countless times, your forever faithful sibling, who thinks about you a lot.
Maria

1943/6/23 Hermine to Irving (Book 11, 5-7)

My dear Irving!
We got a letter from you and it really feels good to get a letter from you. Although, your situation is a little hard, let's hope that everything is going to be fine. Here it is warm, although this is the time for that. How are you doing with the studying? You are right, that it is good to know everything. The only news is that Flora had surgery yesterday and, thank God, she is feeling better. I called Flora's sibling and he/she told me. Later we will go to visit her when she can accept visitors. Besides this, there is no particular news. Lajos, yesterday, in other words on Monday, called us on the phone. But, it is impossible that he already left from here. I will continue at work. Although I have to go to work, it is late when I get home and I spend the entire day with it. But maybe it is easier like this and I like my job. You know, little brother, if God will help, you'll be home soon, since the war will not last for too long. So, we should open some kind of business for ourselves. Are you as interested as Herman? And you wouldn't have to work for Yenkin, either. Bertha still

didn't write! Did she write to you? Write whenever you can. I kiss you many times with lots of love, Hermine.

1943/6/24 (a) Maria to Irving (Book 3, 180-182)

VI / 24

Dear Irving

We have received a letter from you today. As you can see, I'm trying to reply as well. You know my little brother, first of all, I'm well. Hermine is not at home, she wrote to you about it. They're giving out the third ration book. She goes every Thursday evening to help out. She should be home about 10 o'clock evening. Dave went to the Sontal home because they're arranging for the citizen papers. This is the last week that he has to go. He has been questioned and it's over. Herman is in his room. The neighbors are asking about you. A neighbor across the street always talks to Dezső. Just now I called Flora's sister. She said that Flora's operation luckily is over and she's better, but will not accept visitors at this time. We can't go there this week either. If I can I will write to you more. Also we haven't heard much from Lajos. We received a picture from you. I understand your letter. I hope that I can hear the very best from you. I hope that you can get the furlough.

I ask you not to worry. I remain until we hear from you again, Maria

I just remembered in your letter you said that you're going to mail me a little shawl. As of today we have not received it. I think when you return home finally we will have something to remember. That is quite interesting and I hope that we'll see each other shortly in good health.

You know my little brother, the neighbor stopped by the window, the German family,[Lindek]. You know her name and she said to be sure to write to you that she sends her best regards with best wishes to you, and she said don't forget she will ask you if you got her regards when you come home, also from her little daughter, the tiny one.

Once again kisses and love until we meet again. As you see I'm continuing my writing, take care of yourself wherever you go [and] whatever you do and please write when you can. I think it's better this way and you know what I'm thinking. I'm thinking like you, it's good as it is. With God's help we hope for the best. Otherwise you can't do anything. If you can, write a card and about yourself. Did you get your citizenship? Are you going to school in what you have been volunteering? Arrange it the best way as you can. About my work, I'm very busy. It was very hot here today. It was the hottest day. Now I don't know what to write to you. Again take care of yourself and don't worry, kisses many times, love, Maria

1943/6/24 (b) Hermine to Irving (Book 3, 183-184)

[Dated from previous letter from Marie that accompanied this letter and giving out 3rd ration book]

My dear Irving;

We have received your Sunday's letter and I understand you quite well. I give you an approval that the machine gun is better because you are further away from the enemy. Our school teacher in Polyán, Filep Miklos, was in that type of unit when he was in the Army as I remember. Tonight I went again to help with the third ration book distribution. It goes quite well for me, I thought that I won't be able to do it.

The girls were talking that they heard that within six months the war will be over and then I thought they won't need you. If they ask you whom would you fight against, the Japanese or the Germans? Just tell them against the Germans. Because then you're protecting our father and family and there is more hope and also that the war will end with the Germans much sooner. I should not write to you about this, you could destroy this letter.

How are you? I'm well, but I am a little lazy. Perhaps a little military would be useful for me.

I haven't heard anything from Lajos from Cleveland, more likely he went away from here.

I asked about Flora and I was told she feels a little better. If you write to Aunt Helen, do not mention to her about Flora, she does not know anything about her situation. Do you write to any of your people that you used to know from the beginning? I did not stop over to our neighbor because I was busy and they are not at home when I am able to visit them. I would like to show them your picture. Tell me, or write to me, whether I am your sweetheart and am I in your mind? Do you think of me, my little brother? You know that you are always in my mind every moment as I come home from work. I will immediately write to you as I arrive home. I want to improve with my writing!!!!! Many kisses with lots of love to you, Hermin.

Good luck with your transfer. H.

1943/6/26 Herman to Irving (Book 14, 241-242)

[In English]

6-26-43

Dear Irving,

We just received a letter from you. Now I have a little time and will write you. It is raining and I can't go no place anyway. We were very hope to hear from you. How are you now? I hope you are fine. Write us from everything if you have time. How you are getting along with the English language? I hope you are perfect now, not like me. I don't know much more than I did before. I am lazy to everything. I am fine. Still I am working in the same place where I did before. I make now 60¢ an hour. I had in mind to ask for a raise. I would like to make about $35 a week. But before I ask for one I will look around because in this kind of days we make more. Do you think it is right? The other men having a vacation and this week I was just alone.

I had some trouble with the bicycle. I was out for a ride 2 weeks ago which is Sunday and I did get a flat tire, a real bad one. We started to fix it but it did not work out. After I got home I did take it off and I did fix it. In the mean time I saw the shelf was bent. I did take it apart and after I had the new part to it I started to put it together but it did not work out right. But now after a hard work finally I found the right way out. Write me how hard time do you have to read this, and write me if I had very much mistake. I hope you are able to read this. If not, then just write me so I will know it the next time. Write soon you can. Love, Herman

1943/6/26 Hermine and Marie to Irving (Book 9, 59-63)

[from Marie]
Sunday
My dear Irving!

Yesterday we got that pillow case you mentioned that you got from the unit. Even though you mentioned that it is a scarf, when we opened it, we realized what it was. It is very nice! You know, little brother, currently I put it away, we don't use it. How are you my Irving? What did you do today? I am well. We visited Flora today in the U.N. [university] Hospital. They did surgery on her on Monday. Thank God she feels that she is better, although it will take some time until she recovers. Also, we went for a movie today, but it was just in the neighborhood. The show was good, but I have seen it before. There is no particular news. Here it was very hot today and it rained for a few minutes also. We got a card from Lajos yesterday. He went somewhere on Tuesday. He only wrote from the train. Otherwise, everything is the same. At my work we are very busy. Did you hear anything about the furlough? I sent a letter on Friday, I hope you got it. I'm waiting for a letter from you tomorrow. Take care of yourself wherever you go and whatever you do. Don't be sad. We hope for the best. You know, little brother, if God will help and you will visit home, I will take vacation days. Also, Dave got the citizen[ship] paper on Thursday. How are you doing with that? Maybe you have to wait for it too for a certain amount of time. If you can, write a few lines. I will also write soon. How are you doing with the English? I think you can speak English perfectly. You understand everything. Kiss you countless times. Don't be sad. Everything is going to be good. Let's hope to see you again soon. Lots of love, Maria

[from Hermine]
My dear Irving!

Today is Sunday night. We visited Flora in the afternoon. Thank God, she is better, just weak. It will take a little time until she gets stronger. We went to the movie next door at night. It was a good show, but I have seen it already. It isn't as interesting that way. Besides that, I don't know any particular news. Thank God, we are good. We got a card from Lajos from the train. I hope you'll be nearby so you can visit. I almost forgot to write that we took flowers to Flora and she loved them. Maria and I paid 2.60 and it was pretty nice. She was one of Dave's witnesses and maybe he will send her some too. I did not call him last week, but I will call him sometime. I talked to Walters and he was wondering about you. Did you write to him? I will write a longer letter to you tomorrow. Take care of yourself, and if you can, then write.
Hermine

1943/6/29 Marie to Irving (Book 9, 65-66)

VI/29

My dear Irving!

We got a letter from you yesterday that I was very happy about. As you can see, we did not get any mail today and I think you must be very busy. I'm well, very busy as usual. And how are you? Have you heard about your vacation already? I hope you will get it. And you know, my little Irving, I would not mind, if we would be over with this war. I can say that I am tired of it. I'm not sure, if I heard it correctly in English. Somehow the English language does not want to come easily. Although it should, because I could use every word. I listen to the radio and the news. I hope, and my biggest wish also, is that we would be over with this war. You know, little brother, we would like to see you very much. I just called Flora's sister to see how Flora is doing. Thank God she is doing very well and she is starting to get better so she will come home by the end of this week, with her sister's help. I think I already wrote that on Sunday we went to visit her. She was very interested in you, and so was Arthur. We told them that you were very busy.

I hope you will have time later when you come back. You know, if you have a couple of minutes, write a few lines to them. Did you get a letter from anybody since then? We did not get any from Bertha. Besides that, write me how you are. Is it very hot there? Here the weather was very nice and cold. We did not hear anything about Lajos. He said that he will write to you. The neighbor was wondering about you again. Yesterday he took me to work again because he also leaves about the same time from home as I do. There is no particular news. Dave just got home. Don't be surprised that he doesn't write, you know how lazy they are to write. As you can see, I try to write to you every day. I hope I don't bore you, but sometimes I write a lot of things together because I think you might be interested in some silliness. We called Aunt [Helen] also, she is thank God, well too. Did you write to her? She was wondering about you also. It would be great, if you would be home already. So many weeks have gone by since you left. You know the days are so long, but the weeks are short this way, the time goes so quickly.

Now, my little Irving! Don't be worried, just do whatever you think is good. As soon as you can write to me. I will too. I kiss you countless times.

Maria

I will stay with love until I will see you again. I wish it would be already!

Bye, Bye

[side note:] What's going on with your picture that you mentioned? Just send it!

1943/7 Undated Dezső and Hermine to Irving (Book 10, 15-16)

[from Dezső]

Dear little brother! Until 120!

I don't know any particular news to write. Everything is the same. The girls write everything to you, there is nothing left to say. Currently I work at Lazarus [in the] curtain [department] and in rolls. My job is to measure the exact size and to install things the way it is needed. It is hard, but I try. It pays nicely 40.^{00} weekly, 45 dollars with overtime about 5-10 hours a week. From 8 in the morning to 5 in the afternoon. Currently there is a lot of work. Yes, the girls already wrote it to you last Friday I got my citizenship! This way I am an American citizen. I'm sorry that I'm not writing a lot, I don't have patience to write! Yes, I am attaching a coupon for you here for a pair of shoes. Don't be sad, there are plenty for me too. Do not send it back! I am not writing an explanation. A blessed Jew understands this [In Yiddish - A jid Broch zu haven farstand]. So, I hope my letter will find you in the best of health and please write where they are training [you] to work. Yes, right now like Lazarus has, [there is] an A. and P. gas coupon! It is 8.00 for a month. I kiss you, your older brother, Dezső

So, I'm sending my greetings to everyone. Let me know if you need more candy and chewing gum. If you need them, I will send them to you. Write it like this: Columbus-6-Ohio. We live in the 6th ward.

[from Hermine]

My dear little Irving!

I wrote a card from work this morning. Although, I don't even know what to write, since you don't have time to read it. The air got pretty cold here today, which I truly enjoy. I still did not get a letter from Bertha. Maybe I should write to her again? But my nature is truly changing because I am so lazy to write. I just talked on the phone with Mrs. Hawkins and she said that she did not respond to you yet because she was

very busy. Little brother, buy the shoes for yourself, if not now, then when they will transfer you. I am well. I kiss you many times. Hermine
Write whenever you can.

1943/7/2 Irving to Family (Book 6, 147-149)

Dear siblings,
There is loud music and noise tonight, but I'm still thinking of you. True, I'm thinking more about you than not. Just tonight I went to look if I should buy something for you, but unfortunately everything is very expensive here and it is not worth it to buy anything.
I'm sorry that I write so little, but we are always very busy. Tonight I'm not doing anything, but thinking of you. The boys called me to dance, but I'm not really interested. Tonight, at least three hundred of us are here and you can imagine what it is. In case I can't call you then I will send a telegram. I believe I can buy the same at home as here. I hope you will forgive me. If I go on the train, then in a station that I can get off I will buy something. I didn't write anybody else that I'm going because I don't know for sure. Here in the army they can change their minds everyday.
Tonight I will close my lines, because the boys won't leave me alone. They want me to be with them. But don't be sad, God will help and everything is going to be fine.
I will stay with love, and am always thinking of you.
Kisses many times. See you later, Irving

1943/7/3 Flora to Hermine and Marie (Book 17, 309-310)

Friday

Dear Marie and Hermine:
Thank you so much for your visit and the beautiful flowers. The colors were lovely and I have never seen a prettier arrangement. They gave me many hours of enjoyment. I expect to be home by Monday afternoon and hope soon after to be able to see you! With loads of love to you both and many thanks again, Flora

1943/7/8 Irving to Hermine Telegram - furlough (Book 1, 150)

1943 Jul 8 PM 4:00
Miss Hermine Gluck
50 Linwood Ave Columbus Ohio

Will arrive 2 AM July 9

Irving

1943/7/15 Irving to Family (Book 3, 41-43)

July 15 - 43
Dear sisters and brothers,
I arrived in Mineral Wells at 6 o'clock in the afternoon and I'm in a hurry to write to you, but I already sent a telegram from Fort Worth. Arrived here at 1 o'clock in the afternoon and it appears to me like if I would be in the camp itself. I was not late to the train. There were individuals that couldn't get on the train because there are so many people. I believe there is a difference in our timing between your time and the time here, but the important thing is that I arrived here in time. As soon as I finish this letter I will continue to go to the camp. I left Columbus and it took about half an hour before I had a chance to sit down. Everything was fine, but if I take a similar trip next time, then I would arrange it differently.

When I arrived to St. Louis, I thought that we have one hour and I will go to eat. But I couldn't because there are so many people in line, so I went back to the train. I was lucky, those that came late had to stand and I was able to get a seat. I can tell you one thing, if you take a trip like this I suggest you take some sandwiches along because you can't get [any] here because when they did bring sandwiches they charged double. And when I went to the dining room they only give dinners, nothing else and they charge a dollar for it. When we arrived to a station, I don't remember its name, I bought a pie [and] the price was twice as much as it was worth. I'm writing this because next time if I go somewhere, I'm going to take sandwiches along. Today I don't know what to write to you. Nothing new around here I traveled with a young man together for a while. We got off from the train and came to the United Service Organizations (USO) to write a few lines to you. I really want to thank you very much for your wonderful hospitality. I'm sorry I couldn't stay longer.

When I will get another vacation, I will make up for it. I'm going to ask you not to worry if I don't write punctually because I don't know whether I'll be able to write to you or not. My dear Hermina [Hencsu Nenyu] I cannot forget the cabbage. It was excellent, delicious. I can't forget it it was so good. It would have been a good idea to have it all the way along the road, although I would have to have a whole barrel full. It's ridiculous, isn't it! But I liked it because it was really very, very good. I write this because it was delicious... When I arrived here it was very hot, but the air was fresh. Quite different from there, I would have liked to have you come over here for a little fresh air to inhale it. I have combined so many things in this letter that you are tired of reading it because I was just at home. When you receive this letter, please write to me a few lines. Don't be angry that I do not punctuate my words because this makes my letter writing much faster [note: the letter is typed in Hungarian without diacritical marks]. It's possible that it may be difficult for you to understand it. I close my lines at this time, kisses to all with love, Irving.

1943/7/15 Irving to Family- Telegram (Book 7, 37)

WESTERN UNION TELEGRAM
CA403 4=WD FT WORTH TEX 15 138P
             1943 JUL 15 PM 4 25
MISS HERMINE GLUCK=
   50 LINWOOD AVE COLUMBUS OHIO=

I ARRIVED SAFELY LOVE=
     IRVING.

1943/7/18 Irving to Family (Book 3, 51-54)

Dear brothers and sisters,
I'm writing to you today. I received a letter from you also. It's important that I should reply, What would you say? Thank God, I'm well. I've written to you regarding my travel. As I arrived here, I began to work. It doesn't go as it would be at home, to rest for a week. It would be a good idea to have Herman read this letter because it would be more interesting to him. The day after I arrived, they put me to work. It's Saturday evening and I was busy all day. Before noon we marched 4 hours. In the afternoon, we went in to the movie to see a few films. It took about two hours, then again we went to exercise. That's the way it goes here. I don't know if I'll be able to write tomorrow because I'll be on guard for 24 hours. I do not know what I will be watching, more than likely prisoners. It is an interesting job, but you have to watch them so that they shouldn't escape. It was quite warm here today. Believe me this heat is not like it is in your place.

I would like to write to our neighbor that I have arrived safely, but everything takes time. I'm writing this letter in a hurry. You can see from my hand writing the only difference is that I'm writing on the table instead, as sometimes at the edge of the bed. I received a letter from my friend, a soldier, we came together from Columbus. While I was at home he left from here and was transferred to another camp in Texas and is going to school. He speaks Romanian and is still studying. It will take him 12-24 weeks before he will finish the school. They are going to place him or send him across the ocean. Tonight with kisses to you all and much love and please don't worry! Kisses, your little brother, Irving

Write!
Until we meet again!
1943/7/21 Irving to Family (Book 2, 230-232)

Dear siblings,
I will try to write a couple of lines tonight, because I don't know if it will be possible tomorrow. It's possible that I will leave this place tomorrow, but nobody knows to where. Don't be worried, as soon as I arrive to the new place, I will write, or perhaps will send a telegram, and you will get my address. Don't be sad, if

God will help, I hope everything is going to be fine. They will put me wherever they want to. The news is the same as before. Today we walked again for a few hours, but it's nothing. However, the heat is hard to take. Just imagine, it's 99 degrees out at 6 o'clock.

It's not everyday, but a man can't ignore it. Imagine, I earned $5.49 because I was at home. Here they calculate 70 cents a day, so I ate that much. You know a stuffed cabbage is worth that much. Right Herminka? Yes, I'm thinking about it a lot. Dear Mariska, don't you think that I'm hungry? This way I'm not. In case you write to this address that I have now, write me your numbers also. How are you? I'm sorry that I write everything together, but it's easier and faster this way. Thank you for your cards. Dear Dezső? How are you? I hope you are not mad at me? But if you are, forgive me. Write! Herman, be careful with the bicycle! Write! I can't write anymore now. I'm kissing you all many times, Irving

[Note: I meant to tell you before, that in English there is no difference between singular and plural, when it comes to certain words, such as, 'you', but 99 percent of the time he means plural. For example, when he asks how are you ? He really talks to all of you. Or at the end he says kissing goodbye, it's really to all of you. When he asks someone specifically he starts with their name. For example, "Herminka, how are you?" That's for the person specifically. - Monika]

1943/7/22 Irving to Dave (Book 5, 286-287)

[In Hungarian] Wednesday night
[In English]

Dear Dave, to a 100 years
Just a line to let you know, that I'm fine. Tomorrow we are going out from here. I can't tell you where, because we don't know it, but as soon as I get there, I'll let you know. I have written to the family, but later I have decided that you might be angry. So please forgive me for not writing to you. You know Dave, the army keeps us very busy and that's why I have not had time to write you. I'm hoping to hear from you soon, Love from, Irving

1943/7/28 (a) Irving to Family (Book 5, 263-266) pages 1-4

CAMP SHENANGO
PERSONNEL REPLACEMENT DEPOT
GREENWILLE [sic], PENNSYLVANIA

[Note at the top] As you read the camp name that means the address in the short writing on the envelope.

July 28, 1943
Dear brothers and sisters, (until 120 years!)
It really surprised me to receive $15 because I only asked for $5, but it's not a problem because when I get paid, then I will send it home. Here I have to watch over everything because they all go just like me. Always something in this kind of place, they will take even a watch. If they catch them, they will pay for it. I hope that you received both my card and the letter. Thank goodness I'm okay, hope you are too. As of now I did not hear anything about what will be with me. I know this much that next to my name there were more numbers than those who came with me. For a couple of days it was with the same as my number. As I heard, it means what you were doing when you were a civilian. Others say it is the Army police, and those who wear glasses are stock clerks or that type of job. They separate them and send them in separate barracks. I write only what I've heard. Here we don't know until it is really happening. This morning until 6 o'clock in the evening I took prisoners, those who escaped from the army that were here before, to send them out to the other side. You have to be very careful. Five of us were taking 16. After that someone else took them over from us. The five of us were taking the prisoners from a large jail to a smaller one. There another soldier took over. This is how it goes in the army, if they don't listen to what they tell them or if they want to escape, then he will get caught. That's how it goes. Here they have lots of prisoners, this is the type of place it is. They're very close to their home and try to go home. They think they will get only 30 to 60 days and that is nothing. And then they would not have to go to the other side. I think this is enough. Here everything is different and not like the other place. The only reason it is better here is because there are less people. The weather here is the same as it is in Columbus. This place is smoky so I can't write more. If I would remain

here in this place I would be able to go home on the weekend. A visit would take only a short time. Youngstown is one hour. As I am now, they give 12 hours furlough every four days. If I would be sure I would be here for awhile, I would tell you. We would be able to talk and would be able to see one another. After that, I think maybe it is possible that I will be able to go home if I get a weekly furlough, but I don't know if they will give it or not. Do you think I should go to Youngstown? To the relations? Maybe I will write to them. But I don't know when because I want to write to you first. Up till now the time goes very quickly. I didn't write anyone until now. Again I thank you for sending [the money]. But if it ever happens that the guy will be back, he will only live that long!

1943/7/28 (b) Irving to Family - Greenville, PA (Book 5, 283-285) pages 5-6

How are you? What do you think about what I'm writing to you? I know I'm making it difficult to read because I'm in a hurry. You can imagine how much patience I have for everything after this. There are a lot of people, and sometimes they manage to get caught, but unfortunately I have to pay for it, too. What's new over there? I'm in a hurry to write to you. As soon as I get paid I will mail home the check. It is dangerous to keep money here. Can you imagine, they steal from the money belt also. They take it out when you are sleeping. In the other camp, someone stole $60 and a watch from one boy, and they sent him away for a couple of years. It is said that this kind of person isn't needed in the army as a soldier. If they catch them on the spot they can even ship them [out]. Even that doesn't help because if they are thief they will do it again whenever they have a chance. Don't be angry that I'm bothering you with this. I know you have your problems too. The only difference is at home you can change the place, but here we have to live with them and live with the thieves. Now I'm closing, many kisses individually to each of you, with lots of love, Irving

Here they give out all new clothing. I'm anxious to know where they're going to place me. I hope everything will be okay

1943/7/29 Irving to Hermine and Marie, Camp Shenango, PA (Book 5, 313-316)

Camp Shenango, P.A.
July 29 - 43
Dear Hermina and Maria,
I have received your letters and I was very happy to [get] them. The address wasn't completely correct, but I received it. I wrote to you already that the money has arrived. Today all day, we were at the firing range. Today, I won a medal using real bullets. Here I do not know yet where they're going to transfer me to. This coming Sunday, a few hundred soldiers will be leaving this place. The space has so many people one can hardly move around. Different organizations. Here they transfer you, hopefully to a better place.

The news is the same, thank God I'm well, hopefully you are well, too. Probably I will try to call you on Sunday. It will not cost too much from here, it takes only a few minutes to call you. If you want me to, let me know, and then I will call you. As you know, I would like to talk to you since I'm not too far from Columbus. The problem is that they give only 12 hours of freedom, from 6 in the evening till 6 in the morning. If I want to go home, I would need more time. If I would be stationed here, then I would get more time or freedom.

Here they teach you how to become a policeman. If I remain here, then it would be like in Columbus. You work and get a rank, which means you do not go overseas.

On the other side, they are advancing quite well, you probably know that better than I do. I do not have time and patience to read. I read a few lines, if it's interesting then I continue, otherwise it's not worth it because there are other things do.

As of now I have not written to anyone except you. My best regards to all and to you with kisses. Tell Dezső and Herman to write to me. Probably Dezső was in this particular territory. From Youngstown to Columbus it will take only an hour. I will go there also. Kisses to all of you, Irving.

On Saturday is the prayer for the new month. On Monday we have Jarceit [yahrzeit]. I don't know how I will be able to say 'Kadish'. Here every Tuesday and Friday evening there are services in the temple. I hope that God will forgive and I hope that in a short while I'll be home and I will make up for it and do more.

Wish you all the best. Please write to me. Today it's been a week since I left Camp Wolters, Texas. It was a different world there. Kisses, Irving

1943/7/30 Irving to Hermine (Book 2, 297-301)

Dear Herminka, as I mentioned in Maria's letters, I will write to you too. So as you can see, I'm keeping my word. You know, I wrote that letter at noon, and I had nothing more to write, so I added that I will write to you. Although, it's possible that you will get them at the same time and they will also sound alike, but not all my letters [do], right? I know, that you will understand me, I write this just because of that. I think about you a lot, but now I'm close to Columbus and I still can't go because I only get 12 hour freedom [passes]. I don't know if I will go into town yet, but I might go tomorrow night. I still don't know how long I will stay here, but if I leave, I will send a telegram because it only takes a couple of minutes and it doesn't cost as much as it does to call you. Although I want to pay for it, I don't need you to pay for it. Here I can't get rich anyway, from the payment I get. I will bring up the payment?! Yes, I will get paid tomorrow, I don't know how much they will give me for being in this place yet. It's possible they won't pay me in full, that they will only give a tenth.

If somehow they will pay me like usual, then I will send some it home, because as I learned, one can't show it, or have trust even in one's best friend. Here many end up like I did at the old place. Here the trouble is that you can't be careful enough, because you always have to change clothes quickly, and the place is loaded in a way that you barely have enough space, but we must get used to it, or like they say, must get away. Tomorrow I will write again, kisses many times, your little brother, Irving,
Tomorrow there are prayers for Rosh Hodesh [the new month]
It's not allowed to go to the synagogue, but I will not forget the day we have Yahrzeit. And, if God will help me, after the war, I will keep it. God will forgive all, because on occasions like this, man is helpless. Tonight is Friday and first I will go to the chapel, if it's possible, and I will talk to the rabbi. Now I remain with love, Irving

1943/7/31 Irving to Herman (Book 2, 302-305)

July 31 - 43
Dear Herman,
Yes, I have been thinking about writing to you in [the] English language. But you know, that I have been transferred and have not had time to write or rather we couldn't write until we got into that camp. Here it isn't so bad, because we are waiting for shipping and that is why we aren't doing much. Sometimes we have physical training and a few more things. Well Herman I hope that you can read my writing. Today is Saturday and we got paid. It isn't like home. You can say home sweet home, because that's right. I received a letter from Hermine and Maria and they say that you'll become an American citizen. That will be nice. Yet I think, I will be called out for some reason, so until I write some more. Give my regards to the rest of the family.
Your brother,
Irving

Please write me soon!

1943/8/2 Irving to Family (Book 5, 278-282)

August 2, 1943
Dear sisters and brothers! (until 120 years!)
Today, we have yahrzeit [for our mother]. Here we cannot go to the synagogue because we don't have anything nearby. I can't get the Jewish boys together. In the army, we can't do what we want, therefore we have to do what we can. Here I'm mailing $30. From this, take out whatever you and the rest need. Get whatever you need, it's up to you. If at anytime I need some, then I will ask you to send it to me. This way, I'll know that when I need it, it will be there. At this time, I have enough until payday. Don't worry about me, if I need something I will let you know.
As you can see, I'm still here in this place. Today a few of them were sent out. I'm still here. I would like it if they would keep me here at least for awhile. Here whenever they need someone, they send them out. As they say, maybe we were supposed to leave today. I want you to know everyone likes it here better than the

old place because here we don't have to work. At this time, I'm closing my letter. Maybe later I will write more. The cards I wrote you came from the old camp. You should know before I got on the train I was writing it and mailed them, because we were not allowed to write after that. You should know when I write, I hope you were able to read. I know my writing was very bad, but here I'm not always able to sit down at a table to write. Whenever I have a chance, that is when I'm writing. I didn't write to anyone else. Whenever I will be placed in a camp where I will have a permanent address, only then will I write to Arthur, to the neighbors, and also the other relations. What do you think Hermine? Maybe I should send a card, but this is the way it is. I do not have any patience to write. If you would know how long I have to wait for the mailman to give out the letters you would say I should write everyone because you have to wait anyway. Maybe they're not interested that I am still here. Maybe tomorrow I will be in another place. Maybe tomorrow I'll have more patience because I will know where I will be sent. Then it'll be much better to sit down and write. As I am now, you are the only one I'm writing to. You will give them my best wishes until I will write to them. They don't have to know that I have time to write here. I'm not writing this because I'm running around and I don't want to write. I told you that when I was home what I will do. The neighbor's picture is very good. When I will have more patience or will be transferred, then I will write them also. You tell them when I will know if I will remain here, then I will write to them too. If not, as soon as I can, I will. I think it is better if I do not write so often. Please write, kisses Irving

1943/8/4 Irving to Family, Greenville, PA (Book 3, 70-74)

My dear sisters and brothers.
I am hardly able to wait for your letters. I cannot write in this place like I did in the previous place. This afternoon they transferred me to a new battalion [Co. H, 15th Battalion, 4th Regiment], the address is on the envelope. I do not know how long I'll be here, possibly for a few weeks. As you know they'll never tell us how long, the only time they tell us is when we have to pack. We woke up this morning and it was like every day. We washed everything. We finished everything. At nine o'clock in the morning they called our names to pack and that we should be ready to be on the way. By the time we got the pack ready, a few minutes later we had to unpack to check if we have everything. This took about three hours. We walked about seven blocks. We will stay here for a while. The barracks look nice and so does the area, but inside it is the same as the other barracks. I don't like it because we have too many people in it, and everyone is unknown to me, and I must watch everything, which is impossible. Mostly they play cards and if they lose their money then they steal until they get caught. Every day they steal from someone. Because of that I hate to be here. The work is nothing. We are not doing anything like we did in the old place, that is at Camp Wolters. There the place was beautiful and they would not let anyone play cards. Here they do what they want. I hate it here because there are more thieves than you can imagine. Here they play until one o'clock in the morning. When someone wins he goes out with $300 or $400. It is difficult to believe it, but that is a fact. Those that lose, go and steal. This is the best time for them because there are opportunities, people are moving and everything is in the open and one can't be everywhere. If you are there they will take it anyway. Last night they stole from six individuals and the billfold was returned empty.

Everything would be fine, I only ask that this war should be over soon and I would be able to get away from all these types of people. One does not know who will sleep in the upper or lower bunk. The bunks are arranged so that one sleeps on the top, and one sleeps on the bottom. It's impossible to watch out with this arrangement. As I see it, we hardly arrived here and they began to play. You can't speak to anyone. One wins and the other loses. Those that lose need to steal. On Sunday they can't play. I hope God will help me that everything will be okay. Now kisses to all of you, with much love, Irving.
The address is:
PVT. Irving Gluck
35633941
Co.H.15th.BN.4th.REG.
BKS.2111 S.P.R.D.
Greenville, P.A.

[On the side]
Please write, all of you!
I will write to you again tomorrow..

1943/8/8 Irving to Family, Greenville, PA (Book 3, 55-58)

Sunday morning

My dear sisters and brothers,

It's 8 o'clock in the morning, and yet I'm still in bed. I already had breakfast. I can do that today because our barracks were the cleanest. It was very interesting because from the six barracks ours was the best. This morning, as they began to check our barracks, I spoke to the corporal that we should be exceptional, that we should stand according to the height of each individual, therefore we will look much better. We had a contest to show whose barracks will be the cleanest. Later the corporal came to me and told me that I should be the barrack's leader. As the captain came in, as he began to talk and look around real fast it took only a few seconds, but he found three errors, one was that a shoe wasn't punished, the second was that there were cigarette ashes on the floor, and the third a match stick was on the window. And in the other barracks he found errors. I said the same thing as I was told at Camp Wolters, that is, when you report to the captain or the officer that does the investigation, if you report properly then they overlook any error and it's important that you stand properly as you speak! to the captain and if anything is not clean you must answer as "Yes sir!" That means a lot. Since I performed well the barracks got the freedom.

I just returned after speaking to you. You know Dezső, I mentioned to you how much thievery goes on here. When I returned one soldier in this barracks where I am said that they stole from him $70. This is terrible, now I know that it doesn't pay to keep any money here only if you use it right away. Now kisses to all of you, Irving.

Write! I will write again.

1943/8/9 Bertha to Hermine (Book 17, 5-7)

New York
Aug 9/43
My Darlings!
Forgive me for my laziness, but the heat is making me so weak that I can barely move.
How are you? About us, we are fine, which we wish to hear it back from all of you. Although, this summer is not going well, because as you can see, my back hurts. But it's OK. I'm still here and I'm krecking [?] and while there is life, there is hope. I wrote to dear Irving and I'm hoping for the best [and] that he is well. They must be very busy in the military. Last week Jenny Frey was here. She is very well since she got married. She furnished her home nicely. Thank God they live well. I am the happiest in the world because they did not want to get married at the beginning because her brother got married first. They live very happily. Thank God! That is why I don't have anything to write now. I wonder how Dezső is doing? Write something about him. I wonder, did he got married? That would be the best for him! It is enough about this. There is a big heatwave here still. I don't have patience for anything. I am just being lazy. If you believe me, I'll tell you something better. Give my kisses to Irving [and] to you like a sibling. With love,
Bertha
My husband sends his best.

1943/8/9-10 Irving to Family, Greenville, PA (Book 3, 59-69)

Aug 9 - 43
Aug 10 - 43
My dear brothers and sisters, (until 120)
I was really happy to receive your wonderful letters and I'm glad to hear all of you are well thank God. Today I haven't done anything. We woke up in the morning early [and] we had some physical exercise. As we woke up in the morning we went out to exercise, however I slept more than exercised. This was before noon. In the afternoon we went to the movies and after that went to a baseball game, however I don't play that so I went to the forest and I laid down to sleep. So I slept all afternoon. When I woke up everybody, most of the soldiers went back to camp, with a few exceptions, some were sleeping. Here and there were some sleeping soldiers. As I came into the camp I had just enough time that I could wash up and change for retreat. This happens every evening. At 5:15 PM. they take down the flag and the trumpet sounds and I just arrived in time for it. After that we went to eat. Before we went to eat, an order came that no one should leave this area until we get further notifications. I don't know what it will be. I think there is something. We'll know soon if we have to pack our barracks bag. As it seems to me we will be leaving this area shortly.

It could be days, or hours! Before we leave they will check everything to see if anything is missing. Yes, I received a letter from Flora and she writes very beautifully to me. If we are not leaving shortly then I shall reply from here, if not then I will write from the new place to her. If I cannot write for some reason before I leave, then please tell Flora that I was very happy to receive her letter and as soon as I arrive to the new place I will write to her. As of now, I am waiting with my writings. It is possible that shortly I'll know something if we're going to go. As it seems to me, as I see it, some of the soldiers are going to leave. I will continue this letter in a while when I return.

The whistle blows and I must go to listen what will be. I know that you will be excited to read this letter, but we're accustomed to this. It happened this morning also to some to get out in 10 minutes. Where they went, I don't know. I hope that that they will give us a little more time to get ready. Although we are always ready. We dump everything in the barracks bag and we are ready.

As I have returned I will continue my letter. The only news is that a few soldiers are going to leave. I don't know yet when I shall be going. We have to wash everything and if anything is in the cleaners we have to get back. It could be that we shall be going this week. I will continue tomorrow to write this letter.

I will write again today to you and have mailed your card yesterday. I hope you have received it. This morning we went to march eight miles and it was nice and cool, thus I did not get tired and I realized how easy it was to get accustomed to it. In the afternoon we went out to play, but I went to sleep. Believe me I became lazy. I sleep every afternoon. To sleep is not bad if they don't bother the person.

I received your card this evening. You mailed the card on July 20 to Camp Wolters and they mailed it to me here. I received the check and I was puzzled why you mailed it to me because I said that I don't need it. Here it doesn't pay to keep any money. If I need any, there is always someone that would give me. Tomorrow, if we are still here, then I shall go to Youngstown. I would like to receive a reply by tomorrow to this letter, but it's impossible. Why? I will write it to you. I received a card from Rose Eigner and she writes that she sent my letter to Lajos. She wants me to go there at any time and I can be in their place as long as I want to, however I do not know them. I don't know who this Rose Eigner is. I don't know whether she's still Miss or Mrs., but tomorrow evening I will be going there and I'll find out. It would be better if I would know in advance before I go there. I have her telephone number and I believe I will try to call her tomorrow evening before I get there so that she would meet me at the rail station. She writes to me very nicely. I'm sorry that I have to leave this place because it would have been good to stay here since I would able to go somewhere while I'm here. However, I hear that this week we will be leaving. If I stay until Saturday evening, I will call you. If we're going to go before that, and we'll be able to call, I will give you a call too.

Today, those who packed, started out. Their winter gear was taken from them, and they only went with summer [things]. That is, they will go, unless it will change. We will be inspected tomorrow afternoon, that is, Wednesday afternoon, [to see] if everything is there and if it is clean. I don't know what to do because I can take only 3 pairs of underpants from here, and I have 8—. And so it is with socks, I have 6 pairs that shouldn't be taken. Civilian shoes aren't allowed either, but I'm still waiting to send them home to you if I have a chance and return after the inspection. In the worst case, they will take them away and I'll send them home if I can, because it's a shame to throw them away. Here you never know what they can do.

I believe that I have written to you plenty in the past two days. It is probable that I will upset you with this letter. You're not accustomed to this. If I would be in this place then I could visit relatives even though it would cost money. It is 1.40 for a round-trip to go to Youngstown. It wouldn't be much, but the problem is they only give you 12 hours. Evening from 6 PM to the morning 6 AM. One must sleep also, because of that it would be great if they would give me a three day pass. However, then I would prefer to go home.

Until we will meet again, many kisses to all of you and take care, Irving
Don't worry, God will help and everything will be all right. I thank you for the check David. You did not have to tire yourself because of that. If I can, I will call you on Saturday.

My Dearest Family,

As you see, I am continuing this letter. As I hear rumors that more than likely we are going to move. I will be sending home the shoes and anything extra that I have. The boys are telling me that it's impossible to take it with me. I will wait until I can. More likely I'll be sending it home.

Yes, I'm going to go more likely to the other side...... I won't be able to tell you or to write to you where I am. If I'm going to Europe then I will write saying that I'm going to visit our father then you will know where I am. If I go to Africa, then I will write you about Szatmar, if I go to England then I will say that I'm close to our father, if I will go to Austria then I will say 'Yellow paper.' I hope that you will understand what I mean by these words. I'm writing this because I don't know when I will be going and then if I'm going, I will not be able to write to you only in English. I have just found that out so I'll have to remember these words. I hope that I will not have to go across, but one does not know. It's good to know in advance. Now kisses, Irving.

Don't show this letter to anyone. Write to me while I'm here because we can hear from each other more frequently at this time. Kisses, Irving.
If I'm in Alaska, then I will say to you how was the dog? You will know that it's cold outside.

1943/8/16 Irving to Hermine and Marie (Book 2, 240-241)

[In English]

Camp in USA
August 16 - 43
Dear Hermine and Maria,
I haven't received any mail from you yet. I hope you're all well. As you said in your letter that you changed your job, I'm very glad that you like it. What do you do? Or rather what do you have to do? Do you have to work very hard? If you do, you should come here, you could relax all day long. You wouldn't have to do anything like me. By the way, did you receive my letter from Camp Shenango, PA? Before I left I wrote to you. Say, how is the weather there? I'm only about 600 miles from home. Did Bertha write you? She is okay. Tell me Marie, how are you? Can you make out my writing? Would you like to have a picture from me? Well, when I go to town I'll make one and send it to you. The check came very good. I thank you all very much. I have written a card to the neighbor, Flora, Eigner, and Jenkins, I hope they received it. I wrote them in a hurry. I wonder if they got it. Please ask them if they understood me and tell them when you see them that I'll write them sometime. Now please don't worry and I'll write you as often as possible, but first I would like to hear from you. With all my love to you, Your brother, Irving

My ADD.

PVT. Irving Gluck
35633941
A.P.O. 7129 C/O postmaster
New York, NY

PS Say hello to Dave, Herman and friends

1943/8/19 Irving to Dave (Book 6, 154-156)

[In English]

Camp in USA
August 19 - 43
Dear Dave,
Yes I received your lines, you know Dave if you would write me a few more words, then I would have a letter from you. You know you would make me feel much better and give me something to do. I do hope that you will understand me and write me. Listen Dave, if you write me a few pages, I'll write you too. Wait and you'll see it. However I'll be busy for a while and I might not be able to write you but when I have time I won't forget to write a whole page for you. Well I hope you are feeling fine and don't work hard. Give my best regards to the rest of the family. Yes I hope to see you soon and waiting to hear from you, With love, Irving

PS I'll see if I can meet Emil and I think he will know me soon.

1943/8/19 Irving to Family (Book 2, 306-307)

[In English]

Camp in USA
Thursday 19 – 43
Dear sisters and brothers,
I just received a letter from you and I had a few minutes to write you. As you were saying you have received my letter I hope that you have understood me. I have written that in a hurry too, just like that. Yes Dave is always busy to write me, but I believe I'll write him only the same amount that he does.

By the way, Maria, you were saying that you have received that picture, how do I look on it? Do you think it looks okay? Please write me all about it. Also I saw that show that you were mentioning in your letter. We have the newest pictures here.

Well I really don't know what to say, but I want you to know that I'm well and I'll write, whenever I can. Give my regards to the relatives and to my friends. Please write me soon, Love and kisses, Irving

1943/8/24 Bertha to Irving (Book 1, 128)

B Weingarten
124 E.176th St.
August 24. 1943.
Tel. Tremont 2. 3427

Dear Irving. Just received your letter from August 16. Very much surprised you did not try to call, you can find the number in the book or information would give it to you. End of last week I sent you a postal card. You probably received it already. Maybe we could go to see you if you can not come to see us. We are all alright, hoping to hear or see you soon, Love, Bertha

P.S. I will give you Jenny Gluck's address
Mrs. Jenny Gluck
234 – 04 Seward Avenue
Bellerose, LI

Jenny Frey or Mrs. Weinberg
508 W. 166 street

[NOTE - Many of the V-mails were written in English. I left the incorrect grammar and spelling, without marking it as such because it would interfere with reading the letter. I also removed paragraph spacing to save space]

1943/9/3 Irving to Family, North Africa (V-Mail, slide 1)

September 3, 1943
Dear sisters and brothers,
I arrived safely and good health, in north Africa. Please don't worry I'm getting along all wright and most of my friends are with me. I had a nice trip to come here and plenty to eat. I took a few showers on the ship and I felt good. I was swimming today. The only difference is here when you go to town you have to speak Arabic or French. You all know or read about it. Remember the stories of Africa. How are you all? I'm hoping you are all well and in the best of health. Please write me as soon as you get my mail and regards to you all, and to my friends, Love, Irving

1943/9/7 Irving to Family, North Africa (V-Mail, slide 2)

September 7, 1943
N. Africa

Dear sisters and brothers,

Just an other day and I want you to know that I'm in the best of health. I hope you have received my letter. Here everything is as usual. How are you all? Please do not worry about me, I'm doing my best. When you'll write me, right about everything, because I want to know how every one of you are doing. Please give my regards to the relatives and friends. I'll write to them whenever I get time. Say, by the way, did you read any stories about Africa? Well if you didn't, I suggest that you should. It's very interesting continent. Well now don't forget to write me a lot… I'm hoping to hear from you soon. With love, Irving

1943/9/8 Irving to Family, North Africa (V-Mail, slide 3)

September 8, 1943

Dear sisters and brothers,

I hope that you have received my letters. Today just another day in the new continent in Africa. It's really an old continent, but it's new to me. The city is a few miles away and it's very interesting. Before I arrived here, I knew all the stories of Africa. I think you have heard it too. Those stories are true.

How are you all? I hope you are all in the best of health. I'm as usual, feeling fine, and learning something every day. I hardly need it to know, but someday I go home and tell you some good stories. I wonder, did you received my letter from the camp in America? You know which I mean. What did you think of it? Did you understand me? I'm hoping to hear from you soon, I remain with love and kisses, your brother, Irving

Give my regards to my friends.

1943/9/9 Irving to Family, North Africa (V-Mail, slide 4)

September 9, 1943

Dear Sisters and brothers,

I have written a few letters, but my A.P.O. Number always changed. Today I have the same as when I left the states. A.P.0. 7129 Postmaster, New York. Here in Africa the weather is like in Texas. I was used to it, when I arrived here. I knew how it will look like.

You know sisters and brothers, I would like to hear from you. Days are going by I have not received any mail. The only thing I can do, to read your letters over and over, and then it seems, if I would just received it.

As soon as I hear from you, I will send home some amount of money. Please let me know as soon as you receive this letter. I'm feeling fine and hope to hear the same. I'll tell you the adventures, when I get back home. Till then with all my regards and love, Irving

1943/9/11 Irving to Hermine and Marie (Book 1, 142-145)

North Africa, 9 – 11 – 43

Dear Hermine and Marie,

I hope you have received all my letters and found you in the best of health. I surely would like to hear from you, but I guess it takes time to get mail from each other. It's not like in the States. How are you all? I hope everything is okay back home. I hardly know what to write you about me, but I can say that don't worry! I'm in the best of health and that's the main thing around here. I don't know how long I'll be here, when ever I get a chance to write I'll! Here I'm enclosing a money order of $20 and I hope you'll receive it soon. Here I don't need any, because I can not spend it. As much as I need I have, so don't worry. Listen! Get yourself anything that you need. I want you to have this. If I get paid in full, I'll send you some more. Well, how are you Dave and Herman? I hope you are fine and well. I hope you will write me a lot this time. Here I'm as I was back home. I don't think I can say anything else. But remember to write me. As I have said everything is okay with me, and hope that everything is over soon. I hope to see you all soon and in the best of health. Please say hello to all my friends. I remain with love, Irving

Money order enclosed! $20 Irv

September 12, 1943
N. Africa

Dear sisters and brothers,
How are you all getting along? I hope fine. Today is Sunday and thinking about you all, waiting to hear from you. I do hope that you have received my letters and a money order of $20. I sure hope that I'll get home soon. There is different, but it won't be long. You have heard the news! I know that it's hard to wait until it's over, but this year will do it. I can't say it, you will have to guess. I'm getting training here and getting used to the real army life.

Till yet I haven't received any mail from you, or from anyone. I didn't get time to write to Walter's and to the relatives. Please tell them I said, hello. I'm hoping to hear from you soon and I remain with love, Irving
PS write me a lot!

September 18, 1943
Dear Herman,
How are you? I hope you're feeling fine. I'll bet you were surprised to hear for me, from North Africa. It's more than a month that I left the USA not much to say for myself except I'm in the best of health. How is everything back home? Are you working in the same place as you were? Please write me all about it. I sure hope you will write me a lot. Here it's just like in Texas, sometimes the sun shines and raining. I know you heard the stories of Africa, remember the old timers, when they used to talk about it.
Well, I guess I sign off for this time, and will write you soon. Love, Irving

PS regards to you all, and write me!

September 18, 1943
My dear sister Hermine,
I have read your letter many times over and over again. I always find something interesting. Since I came to North Africa, I haven't heard from you. Yes, it really takes a month till we hear from each other. How are you? I hope you're fine and in the best of health. Not much to say for myself except feeling fine and in best of health. Please do not worry about me I'll write you whenever I can. How is your work coming along? I hope fine. I wish you all could come to see the movies with me tonight. We have different shows every night. Well I guess it won't be long and we can go together again. Give my regards to the friends and neighbors. Don't worry! I'll see you soon! Love, Irving

PS my special regards to Mr. and Mrs. Walters and Mrs. Howell

Dear Irving!
As you can see we received only one letter since you arrived. How are you my little brother? I hope to hear the best news from you. It's very hard to wait for your letters. There is nothing new here. Only Dezső left for California for a vacation. At this point I don't know how long he is planning to stay there. He mentioned that he will write to you. From here a lot of them went together. You know my little brother, if he decides to do something nobody can hold him back. But I'm asking you Irvingkem, not to be sad. We are well and take care of yourself. We are very busy at work. I'm glad to hear that you can be with your friends. Do you need anything? Write what you need. Arthur and his family are well and they are back from vacation. And they are sending their greetings. And also the neighbor. Now I wish you a very fortunate and happy new year. And let the good G-d help you as soon as possible, and wishing you luck for your return in good health. Endless kisses and with love in hope of reunion, forever your loyal sister Maria.
Write a few lines if you can.

September 19, 1943
Dear David,
Times goes fast, doesn't it? It's more than a month that I left the U.S.A. How are you? I hope you are in the best of health. My friends moved out, but I'm still here. I hope I'll be stationed here. I'm reading your letter over and over until I receive from you again. As usually you write me a few lines only, I hope now you will write more. I sure would like to see you. I hope it won't be long and everything is over so I could go back to the U.S.A. As I haven't anything to say, so until the next time. Love, Irving

PS say hello to the rest of the family.

September 19, 1943
North Africa

Dear sisters and brothers, yes indeed, I have written the few letters today and I hope that you'll receive it soon. However it takes time until we hear from each other. I also have written to Mr. and Mrs. Walters. I hope you understand me. On one of the letters I mark to say hello to Mrs. Hason, But I guess I marked to Mrs. Howell. Anyway you know whom I mean.

I wish I could talk to you personally, I hope it won't be long. How are you all? Here is not much to say. Please write about you all, and don't forget to answer all my letters. I'm hoping to receive your answer to my letters. I remain with my best regards to all. Love, Irving

PS Write!

September 19, 1943
My dear sister Mary, since my friends left as they moved ahead. I have more time to write you. Today is Sunday and looked at your pictures and read your letters. I'm very glad that I brought some letters with me, at least I have something to read. Yet it takes a month to receive mail from each other. How are you? I hope you are feeling fine and in best of health. Not much to say for myself except I'm in the best of health. Please don't worry about me. I hope you received the $20 in money order. Are you still working at Lazarus'? How do you like your job? Please write all about it. We have movies every night. I saw last night "the golden boy" did you see that picture? Every night a new show. All right more next time, love, Irving

September 22, 1943
Pvt. Irving Gluck, A. S. A. 35633941
Co. B.10th Repl. Bn.
A.P.0. 9885 % P.M. New York, New York

Dear Irving:
Well! For goodness sakes! Why don't you let a person know when you decide to visit Africa? No, we didn't receive your letter from Pennsylvania, and it's too bad you didn't receive our last letter too. You were probably in the process of moving. See any good locations for a paint store in North Africa? We're thinking of letting Kenneth branch out the store. He and Nate Zeff could probably sell those natives anything! You've got to be our most frequent letter-writer, Irving, as you are the only one of the boys who is overseas. We wish you the very best of luck; and we feel quite certain that you'll be back here before long. We're doing all we can to see that you and all the rest do get back soon, too. Sadie tells us that she saw your sisters at the Junior Sisterhood Dance Sept. 4th, and she says that they looked very nice. She was talking to your sister and so Sadie had an inkling that you were being sent across. Al Marback has written to you already so you will have already probably received his letter. Liz has asked for your address and is going to write to you too. We're very proud of you, Irving, and we feel confident that you'll never disappoint us. Everyone here

(that is, we few who are left) are all very wall. Football season opens next Saturday with Ohio State pitted against the Iowa Sea Hawks. The betting is going hot and strong. We'll be sure and let you know how it comes out. Ray Chittum was home on a ten day furlough and he is really looking good. Boy, is Frey-Yenkin ever going to be glamorous after the war, what with all the good-looking men coming back. Nate Gatoff was here for a short visit also. We haven't heard from Larry Capitini for ages. Ervin Kohn and Uri Munro, our Navy men are both working hard. Ervin is on active sea duty, while Uri is going slightly daffy with facts and figures at Harvard University. He's really putting in a tough grind of study. There he is, a chemist at heart, working like the very devil in electronics, radio, etc. Hey, we've got an idea! How's about enclosing a picture in your next letter? Well, Irving, that's about all the news here for now, but we hope to hear from you very soon. Kenneth says he's going to deliver this personally, so here comes a red-headed something-or-other for General Eisenhower to worry about. (Kenneth probably will not appreciate that at all, but I'll look good with my head all smashed in, I guess!) Write real soon, Irving, and let us know how the native girls treat you. After all, what's Humphrey Bogart got that you haven't got? Sincerely, EMPLOYEES AND MANAGEMENT FREY-YENKIN PAINT COMPANY

Best of luck, Irving. The Yenkins

This letter was written to you for the firm by Lola whom we have placed in charge of correspondence to the boys since she is a natural born humorist. Sincerely, The Yenkins

Write as often as you can

1943/9/25 Irving to Family, North Africa (V-Mail, Slide 12)

September 25, 1943
North Africa

Dear sisters and brothers,

Just an other line to let you know, that I'm feeling fine. How are you all? You know I'm waiting to hear from you. Sometimes I wonder if you receive my letters, well I guess it takes time to hear from each other. I was to the show last night and I met a fellow named Schwartz. He came from Béske [probably Bés/Beša, in the Michalovce District of Slovakia]. He went to America in 1938. Finally he is a relative to us. Probably you know him too. I'll talk to him sometime tonight and I'll write more about. How are you all? I hope you are all fine in the best of health. Yet I'm working in an office. I can't tell you more about it. Please do not worry! I will write more often. I'm hoping to hear from you soon. Give my regards to the relatives and friends. I remain with love, Irving

PS Write soon!

1943/9/28 Irving to Family, North Africa (V-Mail, Slide 13)

September 28, 1943
Dear sisters and brothers,

It a month that I have been in Africa and haven't received any mail from you. Time goes fast doesn't it. I'm feeling fine here. How are you all getting along? I hope fine. I wish I could be home and speaking personally. How is everything please write me about everything. I hope you receive my letter in which I have said that I'm working in an office and doing clerical work. I like it fine. I'm trying to think to write something, but I can't. I sure hope that I can see you all soon. How are all my friends? Please tell them, that I said hello.

I'm hoping to hear from you all soon and wishing you a happy new year. I don't know if I can go to pray, but I know that God will forgive me. Until I hear from you, love

1943/9/30 David to Family (Book 12, 1-5)

Los Angeles, 29-9-43!
My darlings! until 120

I just got a chance to write in detail. I will report about my leaving from home. The guy who talked so much, the old man, I left him in Saint Louis since he did not like it on the first day. The home did not look like it would be new. He paid 20 dollars. I think he regretted that he left. Maybe he went back home.- This way the little Firje and me left. The traveling was beautiful. It took 5 days until I arrived. 2,460 miles. I sent original pictures to you also! So, the next thing was to get an apartment. That is extremely bad here. The rent is cheap, but they just aren't available. I finally managed to get one at a private house. but I will look into it and will go to Hollywood because I will mostly work there. So, this is Los Angeles. When we get up in the morning, it's pretty cold. The daytime is warm like summer. It is cold again at night so it is fine. The traffic is heavy. At least there are 30-50 routes [highway] with so much traffic like in front of Lazarus. There are many people. The cost is cheaper than a proper lunch or dinner 50-75 cents. It is 30% more expensive than home. The other thing is that movies we get here we saw at home 3-6 months ago, and there's a 75 cent/ day entrance fee. The streets are dark at night, [because] they are not allowed to light them up. There are no more lights on the main street than on Linwood Avenue. It's a lot and you only make as much money like at home. I wanted to go to the shipyard, but it is very far, at least 30 km. As a tailor, one could make 60-70 dollars per week. To me, whoever comes here to live, must get a state job. It is only allowed to hire someone private after 30 days, which means, you can't work for 30 days. But, if you have a state job and you left it, you have to wait for 60 days. So, this way I would rather be clever on my own.

Yesterday I recognized a decorator, who works in (install curtains) in at least 30 Hollywood studios. I will work with him from now on. They make different kinds of curtains than in Columbus - I always make a mistake and say, I'm coming from Helmec- and they install them differently. I have a plan, and if it will work out, it will work out well! We go to the wealthiest houses here. Tomorrow we will go to the actress Lillian Russell. She only matters here like any other person. When I will work for some of them, I will send their autographs. ok! So what is Hollywood, would you want to know? So, what is that beautiful Hollywood? It is just as beautiful as Los Angeles, just like other cities, so simple just like other streets and cities. There is no difference here. There are some streets that are nice or there are nice sections, spaces where the rich people live, just like in Columbus in Arlington. There is no difference. There are nice night clubs, although I was not in any of them! It looks like Broad Street, High Street. The movie studio looks just like a factory or storage [facility] from the outside. It only sounds nice on the radio. I could have worked in Hollywood already, at Max Factor nails at the factory where they make beauty products, (cosmetics) for $40 per week. They don't pay much, however they belong to the number one companies. You know, Hollywood is like Munkacs, there is more Judaism. Wherever you go they either speak Yiddish or German. Here in Los Angeles even more so. The sellers are Jewish, and the buyers are mostly Jewish too. This city is a Jewish city, to say it better. So, if you want to come also, there are enough jobs. You can make 30-40 dollars. Here the women almost make just as much as men in sewing K.B. [korulbelul = approximately] 60¢

There are a lot here. You know it's only good to come here, if there is somebody who already knows the directions [how to get around]. I'm starting to get familiar with where is E.W.S.N. directions. It is easy to get lost. There are houses available also, for the same money as in Columbus and nicer, but it is hard to find one like it there - So, I wrote enough for today. I wrote to Ignác, too. Send my greetings to him, I will write to him tomorrow also. I'm sending my best to the neighbors and acquaintances. If they are asking what I do, tell them whatever you want, that I work for a Hollywood Studio.
P.S. I will try to get into a Film Studio, but it is pretty hard. I would want to learn before about the jobs here and maybe I will get in.
How are you? Write! Even, if I don't write straight. How is Ms. Maria?
And you Hermina and Mr. Herman! How are your jobs going? Good?

What did Flora say about me being here? There are so many things [that] are here, one can't believe how much one can see. Maybe I will go to a radio show, one that you can listen to also. I have to get a ticket first. The time difference between Columbus and Los Angeles is 3 hours. When it is 5 at night here, there in Columbus it is 8 at night. So, I'm closing my lines. I don't know anything else. Oh yes! How did you like the big souvenir present I sent you? Send me the mail from Ignác. After I read it I will send it back. I wish you a happy New Year's to you and to the relatives. Yes, here there are at least 10 Glucks in the phone book. I will call some of them to see who they are. Maybe [they're] relatives.
So, good bye!
Dezső

1943/10 Undated #1 David to Family (Book 12, 32-33)

[1943/10 ? Date based on David's arrival to CA]

My darlings,
I'm asking you a favor, whoever has time should go to East Broad St and to 3rd St, on the right side the first building on the corner of 3rd and Broad St. They call it, Rovland Building and you should go there. The

elevator guy will tell you which floor, the 2nd or the 3rd. Do the following, he has my insurance for the car, if there is something wrong with it or I get stuck, they will pay for my cost. Yes, it has been 3 weeks since it happened, but if he will say anything, tell him, "Mr. Dixon is the President." I was late to send it because here in the phone book I have found an address that is theirs and I thought that it was the same and it was not. This way I was late and I don't speak English well anyway, that is why I did not send it. Give my address to him, so he can let me know about the agent's address here. The following address:

The Republic National Insurance Co. Cols. Ohio Broad + 3rd St Contract No Police. A73446. The first case $7.75 Sept. 21 943.

It happened in Santa Rosa New Mexico, 13 miles from the town. The fan belt broke and I got stuck in the mountain and it cost 6^{50} cents for a man to come out and give me service. I certify it on the other side of the letter. The second case. I got stuck and the man totaled 5^{50} for his help. The car had a problem with the carburetor. In case he mentions it, the repair is included. Not another company repaired it, but him. I hope they will pay me for that! So, I am entitled for the first case 6^{50} and for the second case 5^{50}. All together, 12^{00}.

This is what the insurance company owes me. If they will transfer it to me, I will appreciate it very much. Otherwise I could not do much. In case there is some girl who wants to deal with this, tell them that you want to see Mr. Dixon. He is the president. A very fine man. I am only writing this because these two letters are the receipt and if you lose it in a little mess, I will not be able to prove it. But if the boss will take it, then we don't have to be afraid. Thank you very much in advance! I repeat, if he will ask why I did not write before, say I am very busy. Thank you very much! I kiss you.

Dezső

1943/10 Undated #2 David to Hermine and Marie (Book 15, 15-16)

[1943/10 ? Date based on David's arrival to CA]

Thursday evening 11 o'clock

Dear Mariska!

I got your letter and I am in a hurry to respond to you today, even though I have to go to work soon. Although, I don't think you will get it before Monday, but still I will write it anyway. I don't know any news, everything is the same. You asked me about how the house where I live? This is in a public/state Defense house in a new building with at least 50 rooms. It was built in such a way like a hotel. At least 5000 live here, but they are still building more. They clean every day and they give clean cloth every day. So, it is clean and there is a center where there is a cafeteria that has 24 hour service. It is good to know because it is necessary since they are working in three shifts, night and day. So, the work goes well. I like my new job. It is better than the other one. I don't know any news. I am asking you to write a lot. Oh yes! What is going on with Herman? Since I made him blush, he does not even write to me. I am not surprised. He makes a lot of money now and he does not care about anything. So, good luck and write to me. I am waiting for your lines. Greetings for everyone, whoever you think that it's worth sending greetings to. I kiss you, Dezső

Dear Herminka!

I got your letter, and I'm glad that you are well, but as I can see you are still only working for $18. You know, that is no money today. Even if you can learn a lot, if the pocket is empty, the skill is worthless. Whatever that president woman is sending I don't care, and if it's possible it is not important to get along with her, even if she is the president. You know, she is not that famous and nobody chose her anyway to be the president. She worked as a secretary and married to the president. This way everything has fallen on her, because currently there is none - In other words - only the mob belongs to that unit. Tonight I don't know what to write. I'm in a hurry to write because I have to go to work. I will write more on Sunday. I don't know any news anyway. It is very quiet here. It is very nice and warm during the day, but at night it is cold on the boat so I have to put on a sweatshirt. But the air is good and healthy. Good luck and write to me a lot. Greetings to everyone and you better take care. I'm sending my best to Herman too. Yes, I will send the insurance next week. I will write to them. Kisses, Dezső

1943/10/2 Irving to Family, North Africa (V-Mail, Slide 14)

October 2, 1943
North Africa

My dear sisters and brothers,

I hope you received all my letters, time goes fast and I haven't heard from you. I know it's not your fault, but you know how I feel knowing nothing, just waiting every day that I might get some letters from you. How are you all getting along? I hope fine. I wish I could fly home and talk to you. October [September?] 30, 1943, I have been in Temple on a special pass. Everything was different, not like back home. However it was very nice and good. I also will get a pass on October 9, 1943. I'm thinking of you a lot. I hope that next year in the same time I'll be home. Here I'm doing OK. And do not worry. CENSORED. I go almost every night to the movies, with my old and new friends. Please do not forget to write me a lot. Give my regards to all my friends and relatives. I'm hoping to hear from you soon, love from, Irving

1943/10/3 Irving to Dave and Herman, North Africa (V-Mail, Slide 15)

October 3, 1943
Dear Dave and Herman,

Just another day and I want you to know that I'm feeling fine. How are you Dave? I hope getting along fine. I sure would like to hear from you. Maybe you'll drop me a line. I know that you're always busy, but now I cannot call you up and talk to you, like I used too. Now the only way we can talk is by writing to each other. So don't forget to write as often as you can. How are you getting along Herman? I believe you are a man now and doing fine. You also don't forget to drop me a line. How are your friends? Well I guess I'll sign off for this time and I'm hoping to hear from you all soon. Give my regards to my friends and relatives. Your brother, Irving

PS write soon!

1943/10/3 Irving to Family, North Africa (Book 3, 102)

1943 October 3
North Africa
written in Hungarian.

Dear brothers and sisters.

Today, again I'm writing to you a few lines and hope that all of you are well. Thank God, I am also well. As of today everything is as it was. I believe that I'll be receiving in a short while the papers. I hope that all will be well. I would like to speak to you. I could discuss a lot of things with you. I do not know what I could write to you. Everything is well and don't worry. Since I moved here there was no mail. More likely I'll be getting it all at once. The package should have been here by now, too. At the present time I am not a punctual writer. I did not reply Arthur's letter. As soon as I can, I will write to him. I did not receive the pictures from Dezső. He wrote in his letter that he will send me a picture. When you write to him, give him my new address. And as soon as I can I will write to him also. Kisses to all of you with much love. Irving.
A.S.N.35633941
PVT. Irving Gluck
Co. A. 33rd. Repl.Bn.
A.P.O.7129 p.m., New York

1943/10/3 Irving to Hermine and Marie, North Africa (V-Mail, Slide 19)

October 3, 1943
North Africa

Dear Hermine and Marie,

I hope this letter will find you in the best of health. How are you Hermine? I hope fine. Tell me, did you receive any mail for me? I don't know what to think about it. On Saturday, I read your letter, but I received it before I left the States. You have written on August 16, 1943. I read it over many times and I'm thinking of you a lot. How are you Marie? I hope you feel fine too. Can you read my writing? Sometime I'll try to write Hungarian, however I think it will take a few days longer before you'll receive it. Today is Sunday, I'm writing this letter in the office. That's beside my work. You know Marie, I met a friend of mine here in

Africa. We went to Camp Wolters together and he left me from there and later I moved out. Today he arrived here, I sure was surprised to see him here. I'll write more later with all my love, Irving

1943/10/4 Irving to Family (Book 2, 266-267)

Dear siblings,

I hope you got my letters. I noted in my letter yesterday, that I will write in Hungarian to you. As soon as you get my letter, write to me immediately. Since I came to Africa, I didn't hear from you. Maybe, it's not your fault. Believe me, I can hardly wait for your letters. I know, Mariska will be very happy for this letter, because I'm writing in Hungarian, and she will understand it better, right? I mentioned in my last letter that I'm working in an office now and I'm writing this letter from there. I work two days, sometimes I go to town and then I'm free. I was in synagogue on the holidays and I was thinking about you a lot. If it's possible, then send me candy and an "Oh Henry" bar. It will take a long time until it arrives, but I hope I will be still be here. I wish you happy holidays. I kiss you many times, Irving

1943/10/4 Irving to Herman, North Africa (V-Mail, Slide 16)

October 4, 1943
Somewhere in north Africa

Dear Herman,

Here is that letter that I promised you, remember, yes it's almost 3 months isn't it. Time goes fast. Anyway, I hope you receive mail, and I have written to the family. How are you getting along? I hope fine. Here I'm doing OK, and working seven days a week. I get time and [a] half for overtime. How about you? Are you on the same job as you were? Please write me all about.

Did you have a good time on the holy days? You know Herman, I have been thinking about you a lot. The best place is home. I sure would like to be there. I guess it won't be long, and I can tell you many things about Africa. Well, I guess I will sign off for this time and I wish you a happy new year. Till we meet again. PS write me soon! Irving

1943/10/5 David to Family (Book 12, 7-9)

Monday evening 4-10-43
My Darlings!
I can not understand what is the reason why I did not get any mail until tonight. Maybe, you don't want to write to me? Or what is the other reason? I don't understand! Please write to me because if you don't write, I announce that I will not write either. So, please write to me immediately! I don't know any particular news from here. Although, I work a job like in Columbus. The difference is that we do a little better work here. Write to me about a lot. What did Ignác write? Send me his mail. How are you Marcsa? How does the work go? If it's hard, leave it! There are enough other jobs out there. If you want to come here there are plenty. How about you Hermine! How are you? How does the office job go? If Marcsa has to work hard, take care of it. So, what does Mr. Herman do? You don't kill the devil here either, you "steal the day" [we say that about lazy people] like in Columbus. There is no difference whatsoever! So you don't need to be better than "Mrs. Deak's canvas" [it's an old Hungarian saying, it means no better than…it's just the same]. I bet that you would want to be here better. You know there are beautiful flowers to see here, big ones the size of an apple tree. The air is delicious. It is so warm during the day and at night it's good to sleep in the nice cool air. How's the weather there?

Do you have to wear a winter coat in daytime? Here we can totally be in summer outfits. What a difference! And we are only 2400 miles from each other-If you think that you want to come here, let me know-So, if you will write, then I will write to you also and about everything- You know, as I can see it, there are many religious Jews here, just like in Columbus. You can see people just like Herman- write to me about everything! Ok? Greetings to the neighbor! I did not write to him and I will not. I don't have the patience and why should I write anyway?! If you need the ration book, I will send it home- As I heard they only give 2 gallons of gas for two weeks, meanwhile here they give 4 gallons for a week. They will probably lower it here too in a few days to 2-3 gallons- If I want to sell it [the car] I can get $400 for it- So I'm waiting for the mail from you. I hope I will have mail from you tomorrow morning! Until then, I'm sending greetings from the heart to everyone. Have a nice Yom Kippur! I will go to the temple. So, good bye! Write! Respond immediately! Ok? Greetings! Dezső

P.S. If anyone is asking for the address, no need to give it, unless you think it's important.

1943/10/5 Irving to Family, North Africa (Book 3, 103)

COMPANY B. 10TH. REPLACEMENT BATTALION
APO 776 C/O POSTMASTER NEW YORK.
OCT 5TH. 1943
WRITTEN IN HUNGARIAN LANGUAGE.
NORTH AFRICA.

My dearest brothers and sisters,
Today again I'm writing a few lines and hope that you will receive this letter in good health. How are you? I can't imagine what is the reason that no mail is coming from you. It's high time by now that I should receive a letter. I had time yesterday so I began to write to our relations. More likely they'll be telling you that they received a letter from me. It's true that here there is nothing to write about since everything is as in the past, that is, every letter sounds the same. In my last letter I mentioned please mail me some sort of candy. More likely you were surprised about my asking, but here you cannot get any as it was back home. Today they paid us. I will mail home some amount. I will close at this time, until we meet again and much love with kisses, Irving
P.S. Write to me immediately

1943/10/6 Irving to Family, North Africa (Book 3, 104)

Company B. 10th. replacement battalion.
Written in the Hungarian language.
Oct 6 - 43
North Africa

Thank God that I am well and I hope that my letter will find you likewise, in the best of health. Forgive me that every letter sounds the same, but there's nothing much I can write about. Every day I'm waiting to hear from you. On Saturday I will be going to the temple. Every day you are in my mind. I hope that in the near future we can talk in person with each other. What is new at home? What are you doing? Every evening I'm going to the movies. They have some good shows at times. I would have liked to go with you to the Palace in Columbus. Tonight I'm going to watch Boston Blackie. I have seen that at home. What have you seen lately? Please write to me about everything. Since you know how difficult it is to wait. Much kisses to all of you, with love from me. I think of you always, Irving
P.S. Regards to the neighbor.

1943/10/6 Irving to Marie (Book 2, 242-243)

Dear Mariska,
I can hardly write how happy you made me with your letter. I already wrote a letter to you, but when I got yours, I started to respond immediately. You wrote September 19-43. I know, you were happy to get my letter also, but I don't know if you can imagine how happy you made me. Tonight I read it through at least ten times, and I will read it until I get another from you. How are you? How come that the rest of you didn't write me? I hope they wrote me and I will get those letters soon, too. Why did Dezső leave from home? Maybe, to explore the world. I'm glad that my letters arrived and that you understood me. Yes, I hope I will meet with Emil, but I would like to wait a little, until I'm in a better mood. I hope soon. My darling, don't be sad, everything is going to be fine. God will help me and I will be home soon. Now thank you for your letters again and I hope I will hear the best from you again. Now I will kiss you many times and the entire family, until I will see you again, Irving

1943/10/7 Irving to Hermina and Maria, North Africa (Book 3, 105)

1943-10-7.
Somewhere in North Africa.

Written in Hungarian

Dear Hermina and Maria,

I was very happy to read your October 4 letter. Thank God that all of you are well. I also thank God that I'm well and don't worry about me. You know Maria, I will be very happy to receive the package after it arrives, until then, many thanks to you. Please send me some v-mail [stationery]. One cannot buy it here, we get only a few a week. You know my dearest brothers and sisters that when I possibly can I will write to you. But I must wait, and ration it, until I receive the package of v-mail [stationery] from you. I did not receive any mail from our relatives. I believe that I will receive the citizenship papers shortly. How are you with that? How are you progressing in school? My dearest, I'm sorry I must close this line, but I'll write you again tomorrow. At this time many kisses to you, also to David and Herman. Until we meet again, your little brother, Irving.

1943/10/8 Irving to Family, North Africa (V-Mail, Slide 17)

Oct 8 - 1943
Somewhere in North Africa

Dear folks,

How are you all? I hope you are all in the best of health. It was very nice of you Maria, to write me every other day, however I have received one letter only. Probably I'll get it all at once. I usually write almost every day, home… don't you think that all my letters sound the same? Well if it does, I couldn't help it. Because sometimes you cannot say what you do. That will make it more interesting, when I get back home. How is everything there? Did you hear from Dave lately? I hope he is doing fine. Yes Maria, I don't know about that picture you might get it later. You know, they told me it will take time, however it's difficult to wait. If I get a chance I will make a picture here and send it to you. But I cannot promise when it could be done. Well, I guess I will sign off for this time and I'm hoping to hear from you all soon, love, Irving

PS write a lot…

1943/10/10 Irving to Family, North Africa (V-Mail, Slide 18)

October 10, 1943
Somewhere in North Africa

Dear Hermina, Marie and Herman,

I'm feeling fine, and in the best of health. I hope you are the same back home. Yesterday after the services Schwartz and I were invited to a French family and had supper there. We had a very good time. I spoke half English and half French. It seemed just like as it was three years ago. Some of the French people speak English quite well. I wish I could speak French as well as they speak English.

Guess what we had for supper, well we had fried chicken. But let me tell you, that no one can make it as fine as you Hermine. Boy, I remember, when I was on furlough and it was delicious. That was in the good old days. I hope next year in the same time I'll be home and you will make real fried chicken for me. Won't you! How is Dave? Did you hear from him anything? I hope he is fine. Please don't forget to write me, I'm hoping to hear from you soon. Love, Irving

1943/10/10 (a) Irving to Marie (Book 2, 246-247)

Somewhere in North Africa
Written in Hungarian

Dear Mariska,

I was very happy to get your letter and I'm glad to hear that, thank God, you are in good health and you got a good job as well. You wrote this letter on 9-24-43. This was your second letter. Tell me Mariska, how come that Herminka does not write to me? Maybe she's angry at me, I hope she is alright. I would like to hear about her. What's new at home? How were you at the holidays? How was your fast? I went to the town and I had a really good time. On Sunday I was invited to a family for dinner. Everything was good, but I would have loved to be at home with you all. However, this prayer [leader] was very good and everything was just like at home in old times. He sang as beautiful as Uncle Lajos. He was a French soldier, originally Polish. I already wrote about everything to Herminka's address. Now I kiss you many times and thank you for your letter and write again, Irving

1943/10/10 (b) Irving to Family (Book 2, 244-245)

Dear siblings,

I don't even know how to start with my lines, since until today, I only got a letter from Mariska. I hope all of you are in good health. How did you feel through the holidays? Did you fast all day long? Were you not hungry? You know, I felt really good. I went to the town with Bési Schvartz. I fasted all day long and at night we were invited to a family and there we had a lot to eat. I drank wine and delicious drinks and the dinner was really good. When we finished the dinner, it was ten o'clock, and we were off to go back to camp. I travelled on a truck on the way there and back. The town is approximately 12 km from the camp. The first prayer [leader] was praying just like Uncle Lajos. He had a beautiful voice. That soldier came from Poland and now he is a French soldier. Everything was really like home. I will continue this letter. Kisses Irving

1943/10/10 (c) Irving to Family, North Africa (Book 3, 106)

1943 October 10
Somewhere in North Africa
Continuation of the previous letter. Written in Hungarian.

Dear brothers and sisters.

A continuation of the previous letter hope that you will receive it both at the same time. If I would know that if I could get a permit to return to the place where we ate supper, I would take them some sort of a gift. I don't think I could get a permit because this area is off limits. Only a Rabbi would be able to give a permit. Do you know that things don't go the way we think. I go to the town every week, but we can't enter this area. We can only go where we're permitted. Mostly we eat near the Red Cross and see a movie and I try to write sometimes a letter from there. Say, Hermina why don't you to write to me? Are you angry at me?

Hope that my letter will find you all in the best of health, and we will meet again. With kisses always, your little brother, Irving

1943/10/11 Irving to Family, North Africa (Book 3, 107)

October 11 - 43
North Africa
Written in Hungarian.

My dear brothers and sisters,

I'm writing again today a few lines and hoping that my letter will find you in good health. I thank God, I'm well and I hope to hear from you also. I hope that you have received my letters as of today. I received letters from you. I'm puzzled Hermina. I would like to find out why you do not write to me? Perhaps you're angry at me or perhaps you don't feel well. Please write to me as soon as you can. I do not know what to make of it. How is Dezső? What does he write to you? Perhaps he doesn't even write. He does write to me. And you Herman, how are you ? I hope you're well. Marie you are the best writer. I thank you very much and don't worry, when I get home I shall not forget you. Unfortunately, sometimes I don't know what to write, but I cannot write what I would like to write. Please let me know how my letters sound to you. The most important thing is that I'm writing to you everyday. I remain with kisses, Irving

Until we meet again.

1943/10/12 Irving to Family, North Africa (Book 3, 108)

Oct 12 - 43
Somewhere in North Africa
Written in Hungarian

Dear Hermina, Maria, and Herman,

How are you? Thank God I'm well. Hope that my few lines will find you in the best of health. Today, up till now, I've been working here where I began as I've written to you before. I became accustomed to this place, but, as the Hungarian poet said, namely, Sandor Petofi, it's better to eat brown bread at home than white bread far away. Here I eat the type of bread that my dear Hermina you used to bake. Believe me I think of you lot. What will the future bring, only God knows. If everything is finished, I would like to visit our family back home. I hope that this will end well. I'm not too far away from the other side. When you receive this letter, let me know how many you received. What is new at home? What does Dezső write? How is he? Regards to him. Please write to him and tell him to write to me. I remain with much love, until we meet again, kisses, Irving.

1943/10/13 Irving to Hermine, North Africa (Book 3, 110)

Oct 13 - 43
Somewhere in North Africa.
Written in Hungarian.

Dear Herminka,

I cannot even write down how much happiness you have made with your letter. I couldn't imagine what would be the reason that you did not write to me. Your English letter was very good. Whatever language you are writing in, it takes the same time to receive it. At the present time, I am writing in Hungarian to you and this is what I'll be doing for a while. How are you my dearest Herminka? I hope my letter will find you in the best of health. I thank you very much for your wishes for my birthday and New Year's. Please don't worry, everything will be alright. I will also write to Dezső. Why did he leave Columbus? Please write to me about it. Your letter was written October 1, 1943. I am mentioning this because I'm sure you must have written other letters and this is your first letter that I have received. Dear Hencsukam, don't worry, everything will be well and God will help that this war will end soon and we will see each other.
And now with kisses many times, Irving

1943/10/13 Irving to Marie, North Africa (Book 3, 109)

Oct 13 - 43
Somewhere in North Africa
Written in Hungarian

Dear Marie,

I'm in a hurry to reply to your letter of today and I thank you very much. You wrote this letter September 30, 1943. and I am very happy to hear that you're well. I did not receive, my dear Mariska, the Chronicle paper. I'm sorry that they have made a mistake with the article, but if you want to, place it again and then it will be correct. I thank you very much for your wishes and hope that soon we'll be seeing each other again in the best of health. I believe that you miss me. You do know that I think of all of you a lot. Once again I'm asking you not to worry about me because all things should be well. How is Herman? Is he like he was in the past or maybe he changed for the better. Please tell him to write to me. Regards to Dave and I will write to him soon. Now many kisses to you and don't worry, everything will be well. I'll write you tomorrow again. My regards to everyone, Irving.

1943/10/14 David to Hermine and Marie (Book 12, 11-14)

Wednesday night
Dear Hermine and Mariska!

I got your lines (letter and card). And to you Mariska, thank you very much for the $25, but a few days ago I figured it out also. I don't know any news. Everything is the same. Please write a lot. Please write if you received the Bond. I bought two of them. Send me all the mail that comes to my address. You know, if there is something official coming, do not take it, if there is some kind of official letter that came to East Bond Street and, if he is wondering, I do not live there and [he can] go to hell. So, you know, particularly about me, I can only write that I am in the shipyard for 3 days and the day goes flat. You Marcsa, don't work too hard because here everybody works so slowly. Although, it's true the day goes hard. I'm working on a ship that's ready as an electrician's helper. It's not hard, but I thought it will be better so that I can learn something, yet here there is not so much to learn. You know, the man learns on his own skin. I get 95 cents, but if I would have known the job, I would have gotten 1.20 easily. But it's too late. After 30 days they will give me 1.03 and after 60 days, I'll get 1.08, after 90 days, 1.20. I will see if I will like it, and if I won't like it, I will get out of it somehow.

The trouble is that in every job, one can only get out of it with a good excuse. I believe, I will be able to do that. If I'm not going to like it, I have to only tell them that my leg hurts, [that is] my varicose veins, and they have to lay me off. But I will wait and I will see what it's going to be. On the ship what we are doing we will still be doing it for about 2 and a 1/2 year to 3 years. They are all special ships. You don't need to tell this to everyone. It's the kind of ship that does not take long to make. But this is a repair ship. For example, if a ship is sinking or is in danger, this ship is going to help and repair it. It will go out shortly, which will be the first ship [of its kind] in the world. Nobody has a ship like this. It is like an empty factory. They started to make this before the war and it was just completed. You know, you can see a lot of countries' ships when they come for repair. Do not tell this to anyone. You know, when a man wants to work here, they don't really like it. There is a closed union with a 10 dollar entrance fee that you have to pay. There is lunch at 12, but at 12:30 they don't do anything anymore. At 4:30 they can leave to go home, but at 4pm everybody goes to stand on the line already and they are hanging around all day long. But it is enough for today. Thank you for the New Year's greetings! I wish you the same back! Good luck!
Kisses, Dezső

Side note: What's going on with Mr. Herman Gluck? God improved his business! He does not even write anymore. He is so proud.

1943/10/14 Irving to Dave (Book 2, 283-284)

Dear Dezső,
Herminka wrote your address and this way, I will write to you immediately. How are you? I hope my letter will find you in a best of health. Did you get a good job? What's the news over there? Why don't you write to me? Here in North Africa the weather is very fall like, sometimes it rains. In the morning, it's quite cool in here. I got used to it here, but I would rather be home. I hope this chaos will soon pass, and we can see each other again, in the best of health. Otherwise, I'm fine. I went to visit the city of Oran. What do you think of the new city? Please write to me, because I didn't get a letter from you yet. I will write to you often, but don't forget to reply.
I will kiss you now many times and in the hope of reunion. Your faithful brother, Irving
Greetings to Herminka, Mariska, Herman: PS: Write!

1943/10/14 Irving to Family, North Africa (Book 3, 111)

Oct 14 - 43
Somewhere in North Africa.
Written in Hungarian

My dearest brothers and sisters,
I hope that my few lines will find you in good health. I wrote today to Dezső. I hope he will reply to my letter. Perhaps he is neglectful in writing. How are you my dearest? I think of all of you a lot. How's everything going? Do you like your work? What is with the house? Do you still live there? This is a childish question, but I don't know if it's difficult to keep up such a building because David is not there to help. If you need any money, you know what to do. God will help me and when I return home all things will be well. I went to visit Oran. It's an old town. One can learn a lot. Otherwise I'm well. We will be traveling like Dezső! Hold your head up! Don't worry, God will help. With kisses, Irving

1943/10/15 Irving to Family, North Africa (Book 3, 112)

Oct 15 - 43
Somewhere in North Africa
Written in Hungarian.

My dear brothers and sisters,

I will surprise you with a few lines today again and I hope that this letter will find you in good health. I'm well. Here on holidays one doesn't even realize it that one could make any difference between days. Yesterday it was the beginning of Sukkot. I was thinking how it was back home. It's regretful that it's a different world. Today it's raining here. It can rain for days. It is the winter season. How's the weather there? Tell me my dearest Herminka, are you angry at me that I write to you like this? And my dear Mariska what do you think of that? If I could speak to you in person it would sound differently. I'm laughing. In the letter, I always sound the same. The only time that you would know is if you get all letters at the same time and you would read them all at once. I'll write you again, until we meet again, kisses to you many times, your little brother, Irving

1943/10/16 Irving to Hermine and Marie, North Africa (Book 3, 113)

Oct 16 - 43
North Africa
Written in Hungarian

Dear Herminka and Maria,
I received five letters from you today. I cannot write it down, how much happiness you have given me. One letter came after 13 days and the other 18 days. After I finished the letters, I began to reread them and I took out your pictures and I was thinking as though you were here with me and I would be speaking to you in person. I regret that you weren't here. I hope that our desire will come through for us and again we will meet in the best of health. Dear Marie, I don't know if I gained any weight. I didn't have a chance here to weigh myself. The most important thing is that I should not lose weight. I can't send you any pictures of myself from here. If I can make any then I will mail you. Otherwise I'm well. My dear sisters and brothers, I would have liked to write more but on V-mail you can't write too much. We only get two V-mail a week and one cannot purchase any, so one must ration it. Now, with many kisses, and my dear Hermina and Marie, I think of you always from my heart. I am sending my kisses to Dave and Herman from far away, Irving.

1943/10/20 David to Family (Book 12, 16-20)

Tuesday evening Oct 19 - 43
Darlings!
I did not get any mail today from you. I hope I will get it tomorrow. I don't know any particular news from here. If you are interested, I will send newspapers from here to you, so you can see what is happening here. The weather here is excellent. At night and early morning before the sun rises, it is so cold that we need a coat and by about 10 am, it is so warm that we can be in short sleeves. This is California. It is a joy to live here. It is very cold at night, so it is easy to sleep. I am writing a little foolishness to you. I will send a few newspaper clippings here. No. 1. is an interesting case that must be true because it's about a worker in a suit, I can hardly tell if it's a man or a woman, No. 2. - I applied to go to school also and I want to study to be an electrician. They don't teach a lot, but it's easier to get a raise. Our company's name is Los Angeles Shipbuilding. No. 3. the Saturday night dance is announced every week. Here and in our home as well. No. 4. On Sunday there will be a famous dance Radio Show. I'm sure that the Saturday and Sunday event will be in the newspaper there (in Columbus). The time [difference] is 2 or 3 hours, it is 9 o'clock here, about 11:00 or 12 o'clock [there].

If you pay attention to the newspaper, you will see these names and they will broadcast it. It is possible, but it's not certain. If it's possible I will say something in it (but it's not for sure) Listen to the time /hour there, if it will be in the newspaper. The Sunday event that the factory Union will organize, I will be the part of it too. I have to be because it's a union shop. I can't tell you any other foolishness. If I will stay here and I will work here from this week, then every 4 weeks I have to get a 25^{00} Bond. It is good for me to be here only because [it's] a Bond per month. So, write to me. You know, I only write this foolishness because I don't know what to write. Hey Marcsa! You know you could easily work in the shipyard and you could get 95¢ an hour, without understanding about anything. You too Herman! Wouldn't it be good to make 49^{00} per week? It would be good, wouldn't it? Many girls work there, and hell, it does not kill them. Here you know we can also go to the United Service Organizations (USO) because a man is a defense worker, but I haven't been there yet. I will go on Thursday. There will be a big show. What else should I write? Yes, it's not worth it to me to kill the devil. Oh yes!! I was at a fortune teller. There are so many here like stars in the sky. He told me not to be sad, everybody is well in the family. In Polyán as well, and it is going well for Ignác especially.

Everything is fine and he will come home to Columbus in the best of health. He emphasized, not to be sad. He is in a good place. Far away from the shooting. What else? I will attach a little description to Herman to take to the draft board to let them know my address. They must know what I do. My current job is that I am like a soldier because what I do is 100% secret and is completely a job for the Navy. There are all kinds of ships coming that are on the sea and what is wrong with them and that's why it is a secret. If you want to see what kind of job I do and where we are working, you have to watch the movie called "Good Luck Mr. Yates". In this movie they will show about boat making/manufacturing. For my work, I go to the boats from the sea level to the deck. I go places you see in the movies. If you don't get it, watch it. But I believe you saw it. It was shown in Ohio at least in about [the past] 3-4 months. They just started to show it here. The ticket is 75¢ to enter. It is cheap! Right? I really don't know what to write. It is already 1/2 [before] 11 o'clock at night [10:30PM]. I need to lie down. It is 2 o'clock already at home [by you] in the morning. So, write to me if you want me to write more foolishness. Oh yes! I have a good neighbor. He snores like a pig. The walls are made out of boards and I can hear everything. If it will continue this way, I will change rooms. The address will remain the same. There are at least 50 houses and the address is one - one, one building. We live with 50-70 people. There are at least 400 people here in the entire town. So it's good.
Write and good luck! Thanks for the letter!
Kisses, Dezső

1943/10/20 Irving to Family, North Africa (Book 3, 114)

Oct 20 - 43
North Africa
Written in Hungarian

My dear sisters and brothers.
I'm sorry that I have delayed writing this letter to you, but I was occupied and I couldn't write. Thank God I'm well [and] hope to hear the same from you. Herman, I received your English letter and I was very happy. You write very well, keep on practicing, it will go much better.
Dearest Maria, your English letter has not come in yet. I'm happy to learn that you all have good jobs and that you like it. I have it in my mind that when I return to the United States, I will take a vacation for a year. I know you'll be surprised, but I still have time to think about it. How are the relations? I haven't heard from them as of now. Do you meet with people that I know? Does the Yenkin company ask about me? I've written to them also since I've been here, however I have not received a reply. What does Dezső write? How is he? Please write to me even though I may be late with my letters. I remain with much love and kisses to all of you until we meet in person. Your little brother Irving.
Don't worry, God will help!

1943/10/21 Irving to Family, North Africa (Book 3, 115)

Oct 21, 1943
North Africa
Written in Hungarian

My dear brothers and sisters,
I cannot tell you how difficult it is to wait for the packages. I hope that they will come in a few days. I hope I will be here because when I wrote to you to mail it, I was questioning if it will arrive so I can receive it, because of that I was afraid to ask for it. As soon as I get it, I will write to you. If I'll need anything, I will ask for it again. You have not written to me what you were sending. I'm sure it will be something good. I would like to have it here now. How are you my dearest! You are in my mind a lot. I wish it would be all over so we could see each other. Herman, if you recall your letter you will remember that nothing is as we imagine and that we think of. One can learn a lot, but one can live without it. Don't forget to write again because it's very difficult for me to wait for [your letters]. You write to me about everything, even if I don't write. I remain with much love and kisses. Irving
Dezső also.

Thursday evening 21.10.43

Darlings!

I got your letter, thank you so much for it! You know Marcsa, you wrote that this man was asking where I work. Who is that man? Only give the address if you know him, and you know who that is. Although, it would be a lot of trouble because you know there are 5000 letters coming this way daily. This address is like a Hotel address. Write to me about everything. How much does Herman make? I'm sure it's more than I make. I believe it because we only work 48 hours and he works 60 hours. Let it be his fortune, I did not regret that I left. So, I don't know any news. I already wrote a letter and a card this week to you. I hope you will get it. Do you need 6¢ stamps? If you do, I will send them to you. I don't need them here. Hermine, how much do you make? Still 18 dollars? You know that is not money! Give my greetings to your girlfriend. Maybe I will send something home occasionally, something made by the Indians. I can send one that you have exactly and then you could give one to the girls. It is difficult to obtain it here, though. It is not available everywhere. Marcsika, if I can get one I will send it. Last week I saw one pair of boots like yours, or they were 3x as big as yours. If you want it, I will buy it for you.

Forgive me, if I don't write a lot today. I have to go because I'm hungry and I did not eat yet, it is already 9 o'clock. I came home from work and went to bed and I fell asleep. So, I hope you are well! Write to me a lot and often, if you can send it with airmail, it is faster. If you want to, send Bertha's address to me, maybe I will write to her. So, I don't even know what to write. The air is starting to get cold. It is good for the skin rash. I will write to Ignác tomorrow. I will try it in English. You know, if you want to write a letter to the New York address. A.P.O. 7129 Army, and write it to them what Rp nos [replacement number] is written, give Ignác's number and ask whether or not you can write it in a different language. I don't think if it had this, it would have been sent back. Marcsa, be careful with your work because you can easily have trouble. Work slowly and correctly! I do my job pretty well, but if one needs to relax the day is very long and I don't like that. But this is how it goes everywhere. So, it is enough about this. Until I will see you again, Oh pardon, don't think that I want to go home, but I hope that someday I will see you again. Goodbye, kisses Dave

October 22 - 1943

North Africa

Written in Hungarian

My dear sisters and brothers,

Your letters are coming in late, but it's more likely because I've changed my address. The new one is A.P.O. 776 % P.M. New York., it's today's address [and] they'll expedite your replies. How are you? I'm well and hope to hear from you likewise. Yesterday I was in the city and I made a V- Mail picture, that is, it's long by hand. One can have this made twice a week at the Red Cross. I must tell you that it's not good, but I cannot make another one so fast. If I'll have an opportunity I'll have one made and mail it to you. Here everything is very closely. Here I bought hair oil. It cost me 60¢ and back home you could buy it for 10¢, that's what it's worth. And besides, you can't get what you want. Bertha wrote to me and as of now she doesn't know that I'm in Africa. I've written to her again and by now probably she has received it. When she wrote that letter I was already on the ocean. Poor Bertha, she was waiting for me desperately or she would come to visit me. I could not call her on the telephone and also I could not write to her while I was there. I will continue this letter, with kisses, Irving.

I also received a letter from Frey-Yankin. They are very proud of me that I'm overseas and I'm the only one from their factory. Sadie spoke with you and said that, thank God, all of you look well. I would have liked to receive a picture from all of you so I could see you. The manufacturer asked me to send them a picture also. I did not reply to them yet, but when I'll make pictures I will send you and them also. I haven't heard from the rest of the relations. What does Bertha write to you? I will write to her also and to the rest of the relations in New York. Bertha sent me Mrs. Jenny Gluck's and Jenny Frey's address. Not knowing them, I will write to them. I will be curious if they'll answer me. Otherwise I'm well, kisses to you all. Until we meet again. Regards to Dave. I did not receive any letter from him. Write to me a lot. Kisses to each and all of you, Irving.

Company B. 10th. Replacement Battalion.
Oct 23 - 1943
Somewhere in North Africa.
Written in Hungarian.

Dear Dezső,

I cannot tell you how happy you made me with your letters. This letter was dated October 11. I didn't know why you didn't write to me. Hermina gave me your address, 937 W. 18th Street, Los Angles, Calif. I hope that you have received my letter by now. How do you feel being away from your family? You are quite far, I am only 1000 miles away from Lajos. It would take four hours by air plane to get there. I wish that this disturbance would end, then we could see each other once again. It must be beautiful there. A bar there would be worth more than a castle is [worth] here. Presently I'm well. I'm working in an office seven days. Since I am going to the town every week, I work only six days, but sometimes I work at night. My friends have gone. Only a few of us are left over. My papers were not in order. A friend of mine from Texas arrived, we were together there. I received a letter from Bertuska, she did not know that I was in Africa. Poor thing, she was waiting that I would visit them. I am really happy because you're going to mail me some pictures. If I can, I will mail you some also. Loads of kisses, Irving
Please write!

October 23 - 1943
North Africa
Written in Hungarian.

My dear sisters and brothers,

I received four letters from you today and I'm glad to know, thank God, that you are in good health. All four letters were written in English and it was very interesting. I was surprised how well you write. Keep on practicing your writing and pretty soon you will be writing perfectly. I'm glad to know that you found jobs and you like them. What type of work are you doing? Why don't you write about it?! I received a letter from Dezső. He is well, working, more likely he has written to you about it. I did not receive the package. If you did not send the V- mail [stationery], then please send it to me since I cannot get any here. Presently I am getting some, but I cannot get it always. I have written to Bertha. She thinks that I'm still nearby her. When she received my letter, I was already on the ocean. Otherwise everything is all right here. I'm waiting for the package and hope that I will receive it shortly. In my last letter I have changed the A.P.O. It's better if you write the number 7129 because that seems to be faster. Write immediately! Lots of kisses, your little brother, Irving

October 23 - 1943
A.P.O. 7129 % P.M. New York
North Africa
Written in Hungarian

My dear sisters and brothers,

I strive to write you everyday, but I don't have any patience. When you receive a letter and it does not sound too well, please forgive me. What do you think of the pictures? I'm sure that you have received it by now. Please send me of yourselves whenever you can also. What does Dezső write? What is the news in town? Where did the Aunt travel? [In English] I'm feeling fine. You're always in my mind. Don't worry, all will be well. How is the situation there? As Marie you said in your letter that you could speak a lot about everything in person, but I could also. I'm going to save it so that I'll have something to talk about when I'm at home. I hope it won't be long, but it more likely will be quite some time before that happens. God only knows how long it will take. If I would be close to Emil I wouldn't mind. I would stay there for a while in that area. Now we should ask the Almighty that this war should end real soon. Till we meet again! Love, Irving.

Best regards to Dezső and the relatives.

1943/10/24 Irving to David (Book 2, 268-269)

Oct 24 - 1943
A.P.O. 7129 % P.M. New York
North Africa
Written in Hungarian

Dear Dezső, until 120
I hope you got my letter from yesterday. I can't write too much by V-mail, so I will continue today. It's possible you will get both at the same time. How are you? How do you like your job? How much do you earn weekly? There everything is more expensive than in Columbus. I got a letter from Herminka also, they are well. They also changed their jobs, although they didn't write me what they're doing, only that they like it and it pays well. You know Dezső, I got a letter from Yenkin and he is very proud of me since I'm the only one from his employees who is overseas. He thinks about me a lot. Although, it's easy for him, I wonder, if I would go back to work for him, who would be the first. I'm sure whoever gets there first. The other boys were just there to visit him. They are still at home. Some are lucky! Now it's Sunday and I'm writing this letter before I go to the office. Don't forget to write to me. Kisses many times until I will see you again. Your little brother, Irving,
Greetings to the family!

1943/10/24 Irving to Hermine, Marie, and Herman, North Africa (Book 3, 120)

Oct. 24 - 1943
North Africa
Written in Hungarian

Dear Hermina, Maria and Herman,
As soon as I finished dinner, I immediately began to write because later I'll be quite busy. Today I ate good fish and it was made like schnitzels [Yiddish written in Hungarian - snicli]. There was also cooked peaches, lemonade. Every day we get bread, potatoes, and salad. You probably see in the movies how it is here. The only difference is that here all a person does is always stand in line...
Now the Red Cross opened in this camp and every evening one can buy a piece of cake and the coffee is free. This week we had ice cream, but I was busy and I couldn't go. Tell me, did you see The African Diary? You probably can see it in the movies. I saw it and it was quite interesting. On the film everything is very nice. If you have seen that, please write to me about it and what you thought of it. Otherwise I'm well. It's raining today. It would be good to sleep, but I have to go to work in the office. I will write again tomorrow. Many kisses with love, Irving.

1943/10/25 Irving to Family, North Africa (Book 3, 121)

October 25 - 1943
North Africa
Written in Hungarian
[In English] Hello!
Dear sisters and brothers, until 120
I hope that you have received my letters, however I haven't heard from you for the past three days. Perhaps I will receive it all together. The package should have been here by now. Everything is slow. I have you in mind many, many times, but I do not have time to think. Hope you're well and we'll see each other again real soon. What does Dezső write? How is he? He must be lonely. Many times a person would want to talk [even] to a stranger, but there is no one. Fate teaches everyone! Don't worry, the Almighty will help. Please don't be angry if I do not write to you every day, if I can I will. I know you're busy also and there are times that you can't write. But if you can, please write. Now, with kisses and love until we meet again, your little brother. Irving
Regards to Dezső! Does he write to you frequently?

1943/10/26 Louis Schwartz to Hermine and Marie (Book 17, 90-93)

Service Club
Fort Belvoir, Virginia

Dear Herminka and Mariska!
Forgive me that I am just responding to your letters. I came home yesterday from the military training. Now it is late Saturday night when I am writing my lines. Tomorrow I will travel home to Youngstown for 7 days vacation, and shortly after we will transfer somewhere else. We don't know where yet, but more than likely it will be somewhere overseas. It is possible that it will be close to our home country. I would be happy if you could write to me your brother's address. I did not get any letter from him since Shenango, although he promised that he would. Also, Dezső's address and what he is doing next week. If you write, then write to the Youngstown address, you must have it. As far as our corresponding goes, it is natural that relatives from home know each other. In this big world, if it is possible, we should at least be in touch by letter, even if we don't meet. But of course, if it takes too much effort and it is not comfortable, I can't wish it from you to write. I'm always happy when I hear about you. For me, even if it's not a relative, but just a good acquaintance or a friend. I am corresponding with at least 3 people, who write more often than I do. I try also, even if many times I write when I'm tired, but I still respond because it feels good to hear from them. Believe me, I got letters many times from someone I did not even want to correspond with, but they wrote, and that felt good. Of course, I responded gladly when I had a chance. Otherwise I'm well. I spent Yom Kippur at a military exercise, and only got free time at night. I went to the temple. Now I have to finish my lines. I have to write more letters. Kisses, Lajos

1943/10/27 David to Herman and Hermine (Book 12, 26-30)

Dear Herman! I got your letter respectfully. You have become an excellent writer in English. But so we can be on the same page, I hope you'll be able to read my letter as well. I'm glad that you are making good money. This way at least you don't blame me that it's my fault that you work there. This way you are satisfied. Unfortunately, I'm not in the situation to write you in English, since I barely even speak Hungarian. But, if you want, just write in English and I will be able to read it. Don't worry, it was written well. It looks like you will win a medal. You are not as dumb as they think of you, right? But at the same time, I hope that you are a gentleman also. The house rent and the cost should be paid. I hope you pay them, at least half of it. Hermine only makes 18.00 and you can't ask her to pay 1/3. I hope you understand now. You have a private room and don't have a [reason] to complain.

You know I pay here 23.00 for a month for a little room. Your room is separated and you paid only 13.50 and I make less money than you do. I only work 48 hours. You are luckier. I don't even make as much money hourly that you do. So I hope the same way you can learn English, you can be a gentleman also. Will you be loyal and pay your part of the payment properly and without a fight? If you will write to Ignác, send my best to him. Today I won't write. I hope you are not mad at me for my remark. Ok, you know where I work, the noise is so much louder than in your factory. You know, when they build a steel boat and 1000 or 1500 people are working on it, with all kinds of things, it's very noisy. The weather is nice here. We can wear summer outfits. So, good luck on the new job, but you better take care.
Good Bye, Dezső

Wilmington, Tues 26.43
Dear Hermine!
I got your lines and thanks for the warning! You know, here at the company, they don't want us to work hard. You know, this is only my 3rd week. I work in the shipyard and I'm doing the 3rd kind of job already. I did not like the first one because it was hard and there was nothing to learn there. At the second one, I had to work with an old Jewish person and you know how smart the Jews are? They want other people to do their work. Also, he liked to complain. So, I announced that I don't want to do that job because it needed to walk a lot and I asked them to send me to school. Today was the first day in the school and for the most part they teach the basics of electricity. It will last about two weeks. This way I will have a decent job. I hope it won't be hard! So, I don't know any particular news. I hope you are well! Sometimes when the wind blows, I don't like the air because not too far from here there are tons of oil factories and oil pumping and sometimes it stinks very badly. If I will stay at this place for sure, I will be able to get an apartment in Long Beach. So, I will go to live there then. It is very nice there by the beach. Please write to me about everything in detail because, if you don't write, I won't either. So, I'm waiting for your detailed letter. I'm sorry if my writing is bad. I'm in a hurry because it is already 11 o'clock and I want to write to Marcsa and Herman also. But I

hope you'll be able to read it. So, I wish you good luck on your office job! I hope you got a raise already! How much? I hope you are not a donkey to work for 18.00? If yes, then you are a big D [donkey]…, you will be, if you are. This is not a future, even if you are an office lady, but to work for $3 a day when others already get $6, is not kosher! You better ask for a salary raise! You are entitled to it after 3 months of work. Good luck! Dezső

1943/10/27 Irving to Hermine, North Africa (Book 3, 122)

October 27 - 1943
North Africa
Written in Hungarian.

My dear Hermina.
I received your letter and I'm glad to hear that all of you are well. I was very surprised that you have written in English. I must tell you you're writing beautifully, very well. I couldn't find one error in it. When I read it, it sounded like you were here speaking to me. Hope our thoughts will be fulfilled. I'm glad that you have good jobs and you like them. There are opportunities to meet people and if your friend will write to me, if I can I will write back to her. Dear Hermina, how are you? Do you know that I did not write to that woman that worked with you at Fenton. I can't think of her name. If you think I should write to her, then please send me her address. You probably know whom I mean. Also I want to tell you that I did not write to your lady friends! You know of whom I'm thinking! I do not want to mention names. I'm not interested in them. When the Almighty will help and this war is over, then I'll have time to think of everything. We trust in fate! I will write more, although I cannot write too much on a V-mail. Much love and kisses to all of you, Irving
Write soon! A lot!

1943/10/28 (a) Irving to Marie, North Africa (Book 3, 124)

October 28 - 1943
North Africa
Written in Hungarian

[In English] Hello, [In Hungarian] Dear Maria, until 120
I received your letters tonight and I was very happy. One letter came in 14 days, the second took 16, the third took 18 days. These are the dates when you wrote it. Your lady friend writes very beautifully in English. Do you know my dearest, I believe that it's difficult to write in English, but you could write in any language you want. When you write in Hungarian or any language, it arrives in 10 or 11 days. The English letter takes the same time to arrive. The important thing is that the address has to be correct. Dear Maria, I am glad to hear that all of you are well and that you have good jobs. I'm hoping that God will help us, that this terrible war really ends soon. Don't worry about me, everything is very good where I am now. While I'm here, I'm alright. Now, thanks for your letter and also your girlfriend's. I'm glad that she helped you to write in English. I received a letter from Arthur. I'm sorry that Flora is still weak. I wish the very best to you and to them. With kisses, until I write to you again, Irving.

1943/10/28 (b) Irving to Family, North Africa (Book 3, 123)

October 28 - 1943
North Africa
Written in Hungarian.

My dear brothers and sisters,
As I finished writing to Mariska, I began to write to the whole family. Thank the Almighty, I am well. Dear Hermina, I want to thank you for your lines. I believe that you have been writing to me, but more likely the mail slows down somewhere, but it will come here. Some letters take more time to arrive. Can you imagine how badly it feels not to receive a letter one day? I am that way. I can understand it and it's not your fault. That's the time I sit down and write to you. I have no patience and because of that I'm writing. I believe that you do not write every day as I do. But it seems to me that you're writing quite frequently. Tonight I'm at the office and have a little work. At 10:30 in the evening, I shall be going home to lie down. At six o'clock

I get up and probably will go to the city. It's true there is nothing there. I only go there to look around! Kisses to you all, also to Dezső. Your little brother, Irving

1943/10/30 (a) Irving to Hermine, North Africa (Book 3, 125)

Oct 30 - 1943
North Africa
Written in Hungarian

Dear Hermina,

You have made me very happy with your letters dated the 17th and 18th and I am glad to hear that, thank the Almighty, you are well. I wrote to you in the last letter that I was going to the city. I was there yesterday, [but] there is nothing there. Many times I was thinking that I will not go, but I went. I thought that I will be able to make some pictures. It could have been done, but they're asking too much money. It doesn't pay to buy anything there. I had in my mind to send you something, but it doesn't pay to send anything from here. I recommend that you buy for yourselves whatever you need on my account. When God will help me and I will return to the old country I will take something from there to you. At the present, don't worry, everything will be all right I hope! I will write you again tomorrow. Until then, a lot of kisses, I hope to meet you again. Your little brother who thinks of you a lot. Irving

1943/10/30 (b) Irving to Hermine, Marie, and Herman, North Africa (Book 3, 126)

Oct. 30 - 1943
North Africa
Written in Hungarian

Dear Hermina, Maria, and Herman.

How are you? I hope well [and] in the best of health. At this time I will write a few lines to the family. I wrote to Hermina in Hungarian. Yesterday I was in town and ate a sandwich, coffee and ice cream at the Red Cross. Since I left America, this is the first time I ate ice cream. Here it's a novelty. In the city you can get it, but it's not clean as you know. I have you in my mind a lot and I'm glad that you are progressing at work. Here every day there is something to do. The main thing is that I am well and don't worry. I weighed myself yesterday for the first time. I am 80 kg, that is 176 pounds. I don't remember how much I weighed before. It wouldn't be bad to gain 10 pounds. I would like to send you pictures. As soon as I can I will. What does Dezső write? How is he? You should also send me some pictures. Dezső wrote that he's going to mail [some to] me too. Kisses to you each separately, your little brother, Irving

1943/10/31 Irving to Family, North Africa (Book 3, 127)

October 31 - 1943
North Africa
Written in Hungarian

My dear sisters and brothers,

You can't say that I'm not a constant writer even though my letters always sounds the same. What do you say to that? You probably think that I write 10 letters a day and every day I'm sending you a letter. Perhaps that would be a good idea since there is nothing new that I can write about. If a person wants to write, one must think it out and see whether that can be written. The only thing I can write is what's permitted. Thank God, I'm well and in good health, which I hope to hear from you also. Do you know that this sounds very well and I hope that in the near future we can meet again in the best of health. The nights are very long and the days are very nice and fresh. I wish I could talk to you in person about everything. This is just like when you're learning English and you cannot express yourself. I hope that in the near future everything will be okay. My kisses to all of you, until we see each other again, Your little brother, Irving.

1943/11/1 David to Family (Book 12, 35-37)

Sunday morning

Dear Herminka!

I got your precious lines and only now I'm replying, although I'm sleepy. I just got home from work. You know, I changed my work to night shift. From 12 to 7:30 in the morning. And it pays 15% more and you will be surprised, but what I wrote to you, it happened in that shipyard. I got in with 95¢ and I should have had to work for 3 months in order that I would have gotten 103 cents. So I managed to get out and I went to a different shipyard a small distance from where I live and I started the job with 105¢ and I will work about 30-90 days and get 120¢ for an hour. So, now I get 138 cents for an hour for the night shift. That is 63 dollars a week and at the other place I only got 49.[40] and I worked 8 hours per day and here I only work 7 hours. So, shortly we will be working on the double [shift]. Here I will have a better job and I will study also, which is a must in a shipyard because I need to know a lot. I hope I will get 100 per week in a few months. I don't know any particular news. Yes, it is not important to tell anyone about my raise or job change. I am working currently on a battleship. It is so much smaller than the one I worked on before. There it took 3 years to make one and here it takes 1/2 a year. Here in the shipyard I work as a outfitter and I can learn a lot, but I can't be an electrician, I need to study also. It will be a nice summer day here. The sun is shining. I will go to the city this afternoon. Currently, I'm free until 12 o'clock on Monday night. Write a lot. Kisses, Dezső

Dear Herman!

You know the insurance also sent me a letter, to fill it out and send it back to you, and then they will send the money back.

Kisses,

Dezső

Write me a lot.

1943/11/1 Irving to Family, North Africa (Book 3, 128)

November 1 - 1943
North Africa
Written in Hungarian

My dear sisters and brothers,

As you see, my address has been changed. This is the Army life. One day here, the next day somewhere else. The main thing is I'm well and I am in a hurry to write you diligently a few lines. I hope the package will arrive, but it may take a little longer. Presently I'm still in the same place where I was before. The only thing is that I have moved because the other soldiers left. Hope that the Almighty will help me and everything will be well. I don't know if I will be working in the office with new soldiers. I will write you more about myself in the future. Don't worry, everything will be all right. I hope you understand my letters, but I'm writing in a hurry so that as soon possible you will receive my new address. Otherwise, I'm well. Lots of kisses with lots of love until we meet again. Whenever you can, write. My regards to the relations. Irving

1943/11/2 Irving to Family, North Africa (Book 3, 130)

November 2 - 1943
North Africa
Written in Hungarian

My dear sisters and brothers and sisters,

I believe that you will receive this letter on my birthday. I really thank you for your good wishes and I hope that the Almighty will help me so that everything will turn out well and my wish will become reality. The years are going very fast and I hope that at my next birthday I will be at home and we will celebrate like a holiday. What do you say to that? Do you know my dear Hermina, you will cook for me the food that I like most. I don't want to write to tell you which one, but you do know don't you? I wish I would be at home, how wonderful it would be to have a little cabbage! This is only a reminder so that you don't think that I have forgotten how well you made it in the past. A person is always full of hope that the Almighty God will help and that everything will turn out to be as it should be. Otherwise I am well and sending a lot of kisses, from your little brother, especially today I am thinking of you. Irving

1943/11/3 Irving to Family, North Africa (Book 3, 131)

November 3 - 1943

North Africa
Written in Hungarian

My dear brothers and sisters,
I do have a little time [so] I will start to write again a few lines. How many letters did you get from me? What do you say about my writings? Do you get letters from me frequently? Do you know, when I have an opportunity I write to you immediately. It's true that many times there is not much to write because I can't write to you what I want. I hope you understand me. The news, I'm sure you know better than I. I am waiting for a better future! I hope it comes soon. Write to me a lot about yourselves if you have time. I'm sure you must be so busy that you can't even take a breath of air, but it's very good when I receive a letter from you. If you write to me the same things every day it is still very good. Perhaps I should also write about ten letters and mail you one everyday. But don't believe me because when I finish writing them I'm immediately mailing it to you even though it may be the same thing! I know that you too are waiting for my letters and it is difficult to wait isn't it?! With kisses, Irving

1943/11/4 Irving to Family, North Africa (Book 3, 132-133)

November 4 - 1943
North Africa
Written in Hungarian

My dear sisters and brothers,
Since I have an opportunity, I'm going to write on a typewriter to you. I believe it may be easier for you to read it. How are you my dearest? I do not know anything special to write to you, everything is like it was. As of today I did not hear anything regarding the papers. Since I left the other group I did not hear from you. I hope that it will come. Each time they place me in a different place, it takes time, and it's difficult to wait for letters. One cannot help that. The package should have been here by now and this is why it's a little late. I can't even write down how difficult it is to wait. Tonight, it was the first time that I got a Clark candy bar since I left the States. As you see, you can't get any candy here, that's why I was asking for it from you.

What's new there? I hope all is well. How do you like your work? All of a sudden I don't even know what to write and I have to hurry to end this letter because it's night and I have a little work in the office. Mostly I'm occupied and when I write to you I am always in a hurry. But you could tell that because I'm not a frequent writer. What do you say to that? I believe you agree with me.

At the present place I am doing well, I would like to stay here but I do not know how long I will. I hope that the Almighty will help me and everything will turn out to be okay and I hope that it will. Up to now it's been very good that it happened this way and I'm in the same place as when I arrived. My friends and fellow soldiers left a long time ago and they left me here. But don't worry, one other soldier was left here, too, and we get together frequently and we have some fun. That is why it's important that letters should come. When I do see letters from you I have something to talk about. When I don't receive letters from you then I always read the previous letters and I feel that it's as if I would have just received it. Don't forget to write to me and then everything will be fine.

Many times I can't think of something and therefore I would like to speak with you and discuss something, but unfortunately I can't because we are too far apart. At this time it's not like I could make a phone call and call you and speak to you like in the past. I hope it won't be long that we can speak to each other in person. Now I will close my few lines because I have to go to work. If I can, I will write to you again shortly. Kisses to all of you with lots of love until we meet again Irving.

1943/11/4 Irving to Family, North Africa (V-Mail, Slide 20)

November 4, 1943
North Africa

Dear folks,
I am wishing you Christmas greetings and a happy new year.
Irving

Co. A. 33rd. Repl. Bn. A.P.O.
7129 % P.M. New York, N.Y.

November 5th - 1943
North Africa
Written in Hungarian.

My dear sisters and brothers.
Don't you worry if my letters are delayed, but there's always something that comes in between. As of today, the post office is not open, all my letters were returned because we had to get permission that I could write in Hungarian. As soon as I received the permission, immediately I mailed the letters. I know it will be delayed a few days. The reason is that I moved today, once again. I received a letter from you and I was very happy. Thank the Almighty that you're all well. After I read what you are sending I was asking the Almighty that it should be here now. In today's world everything is late.

I do not know for sure, but more likely I will get my papers. It's true, after that everything can happen. I hope that the Almighty will help that everything will be well and everything will be finished and I will not have to go there.

Many times I'm thinking that if this situation is finished, then I would like to go to visit our family. I believe that from what I see it won't be long and I will be going there. Do you remember where you started out to come to the new home? I began to save a little bit. If this [war] is finished, then I would give our dear father so that he would have whatever he needs. I'm sure that they are lacking a lot of things there. I regret we can't do anything about it at this time. We must wait until everything will come to an end and I hope soon...

As you know I don't want to keep a lot of money with me. I'm going to send you $60.

I have written in many other letters to you that if you need anything, don't be afraid to use it. Money is not everything. It's good if one has it. At this place where I am, it's worthless. Here they give you for $1 = 50 francs, but you can't buy anything for it. Everything is very costly. You could imagine how it could be at home.

I believe I have written a lot. Tonight I was again in the office and because of that I'm writing with a typewriter. It goes very well, but the only thing is that I must rush because soon I must begin to work. If you find a lot of mistakes, please let me know. If I have time I can think, and I can write better.

I received a letter from Arthur but I didn't have a chance to reply to him. It's true that they only wrote a few lines and I will do the same.

I know that my letters always sound the same, but when I don't have time or patience to write, I have no choice. When I write, it must sound good and pleasant, otherwise it is very sad.

Tonight it's seven o'clock and in a few moments I have to start to work, so I will end this letter. I was lucky to have a job like this up until now and I could write to you almost every day.

If I can, I will write you again tomorrow but it may be that I'll be going to get my papers. You must know that I will write even though only a few lines and briefly.

Now I remain with lots of love and until we meet again kisses to all of you and lots of love. Your little brother who thinks of you a lot. Irving
[In English] P.S.Write soon.

1943/11/6 Irving to Family, North Africa (V-Mail, Slide 23)

Dear Siblings,

Your letters are always late, but [I'm sure] there is a reason for it, yet I am impatient. How are you? Thank G-d I am well. Yesterday and today I was busy inquiring about my papers. They were asking questions like they did when I was at home. I hope that with G-d's help everything will turn out alright. You probably received the letters I wrote to you recently. Today at noon a few of us left our jobs because they are expecting new ones, and if they will be a few people short they will call me again. Nothing else is new, I received a letter from Berthuska. She wants to send me a package, but is asking me to write to her, because otherwise they will not accept it at the post office. I am writing to her now. Many kisses from your younger brother, Irving

1943/11/8 Irving to Dave (Book 2, 285-286)

Written in Hungarian

Dear Dezső,

I didn't get your pictures yet, but I hope I'll get them soon. I hope my lines will find you in the best of health. Thank God, I'm fine. As you can see my address has changed again. That's the way it goes. A soldier's life is one day here and the next day, only God knows. For now I don't work in the office, but it's possible new troop[s] will come and I will work there again.

Otherwise, how are you? I hope everything is well. You know this week I went about the [citizenship] documents, but I don't know anything yet. They just asked me the same things, like at home. But I'm sure you remember. I think that perhaps it's good. Until then, I don't know anything else. Take care of yourself also. You are in my mind a lot. Kisses, your little brother, Irving

PS I got a letter from the relatives. I will write again.

1943/11/8 Irving to Family, North Africa (Book 3, 134)

November 8 - 1943
North Africa
Written in Hungarian

My dear sisters and brothers,

Today once again I will strive to write to you, but unfortunately I don't know what to write about because what happens here you won't be interested in it. I wrote to Arthur a reply to his letter. How can you write a brief letter to the five lines that I received. Can you imagine how to write a brief letter, but he will probably show you what I've written. Do you know that yesterday my dearest, I had a little time, so I made all those letters that you wrote to me into a book and I read it. Those that you have written to me from day to day. Up till now I received 23 letters from you. I'm sure that you must have been writing to me more, but they did not arrive yet. I left my old job and I'm waiting what the future will bring. Don't worry, the Almighty will help. I remain with hope until we meet again. Kisses from your little brother, Irving.

1943/11/9 Irving to Family, North Africa (Book 3, 135)

November 9 - 1943
North Africa
Written in Hungarian

My dearest sisters and brothers,

Again I had a few moments to write to you. I know that you're waiting for my letters. As of now I don't know what to write you, everything is as it was. You are in my mind a lot, but you cannot help that. I hope that the Almighty will help to end this war shortly. It's better that a person does not think of it, because you can't do anything about it. I hope that our wishes will come true. Dezső had a little truth, as it is being said; where there is hope there is truth. I have written to him yesterday. I have just reminded myself that if you cannot mail the package than show this letter to the post office. [In English] Please send me cookies, chocolate's, and the V- mail, that is a request. [In Hungarian] This was written in English because I must ask this way from the post office so they will accept the package. I wish I would be at home faster, so that I could forget all this that a human being goes through. You would not believe it. Don't forget to write to me. Kisses from your little brother, Irving.

Dearest Siblings,

I know that you can hardly wait to receive my letters and still I write so infrequently. But I am always very busy and I am unable to write. Last night I received your letter that I was eagerly waiting for. I didn't know what to make of it, that since I joined the new unit, I haven't received a letter from you. It took five weeks to receive your letter. I was wondering if you wrote to me and how often. Please write if you can. What photograph did you receive from me? The v-mail? What did you think about it? Recently I have been working in the kitchen, it's bearable. I can talk about it only in person. If you remember during the holidays, I was in the city and I received a few addresses. So this week I went in and I enjoyed myself a lot. I am invited for this Sunday again. I will write again shortly. The package has not arrived yet. Love and kisses from your brother, Irving

HELLO TO EVERYBODY, PLEASE WRITE

November 11 - 1943
North Africa
Written in Hungarian

My dear sisters and brothers,

I went to the city yesterday, so I did not write to you. As of now I do not work in the office. I hope that the Almighty will help me and all will be okay. My new acquaintances left already. That's the way it goes. They're always good fellows here. I only want to be with good people, but here you can't be choosy. Every one of us wishes that this war would end and we could return home. I wish I could talk to you in person. I have a lot in my mind now. I assume that when I get home I will not be able to speak to you about anything. It is nice how much a person can tolerate. My dearest, don't forget to write to me. It's already four days that I did not hear from you. I know it's not your fault. With kisses, your little brother, Irving.

Wilmington, California
1943 November 12

Dear Mariska

I received your letter and today I'm going to endeavor to reply. I can't write you anything about myself because everything is the same. Oh yes, probably I will have a little success, I'm not sure, I hope I will succeed. When I arrived at this new place to work you must belong in the Union for this type of work. I was going to pay the Union 27 dollars to belong. But, somehow they made a mistake and recorded $52. So, I discovered that instead of the company paying $1.38 an hour, now they will pay $1.57. The union said that I will get back pay at the rate of $1.57 per hour since it's the company's fault. I have high hopes that I will get it. I will find out tomorrow. If I'm not getting the $1.57, then at least I'll be getting $1.51. It was a holiday yesterday and therefore they paid time and a half. Some people work Sunday and I think I will also, but I'm not sure yet. On Sunday, they pay double and then if I could work seven days I could earn $100 a week. Please write a lot and I will do the same and will endeavor to write you. Many kisses, Dezső.

Dear Hermine,

I received your letter and I'm glad to hear that all of you are well. I don't know any news around here. It's cool at night [and] in the daytime it's very warm, but not very hot. I received a letter from Ignác and he writes that he was in Oran, that means that he is close enough to that town. I wrote to him a four-page letter. Hermine please send me that letter in which he is asking for candy so that I can send him some, because that's the only way I can send anything to him. Forgive me, but I'm quite sleepy and therefore I'm going to conclude my sleepy letter. If you need oranges please let me know, and I'll send you. The work is quite good, people steal more than work, [but] don't mention it to anyone. I'm closing these long letters and wish the very best from a very sleepy person. It's 12 o'clock noon and I will go to sleep, the sun shines and it's good weather. I could get 450 to $500 dollar for my car. Therefore, look up for success. Kisses from Dezső.

Friday night.
My Dearests,
I'm getting ready to go to the Long Beach Temple. There's no news, all is as it was. I believe that you will receive my letter Monday. I will write to you on Sunday. I don't know what to write anything more exceptional. How is Herman? Why doesn't he write to me? More likely he is angry at me. I hope that he will make peace with me. Hermine, why didn't you send me the mail that came to your address? I will mail you the cost of mailing it to me. It's enough of this. Good luck and until we meet in California, good! Would you like to be here? It is very cool like in Columbus. During the daytime it's warm and the weather is beautiful and the nights are cold and foggy because we are close to the ocean. So, good luck. Kisses, Dezső.

1943/11/13 Irving to Family, North Africa (Book 3, 137)

November 13 - 1943
North Africa
Written in Hungarian

My dearest brothers and sisters,
This week I haven't heard anything from you. It's true, the post office isn't restored here yet, that may be the reason. I hope that you are getting mail from me rapidly. Now I am not writing frequently because in the daytime I'm out in the exercise area and in the evening I don't have any patience to write. Last night it was quite cold. During the day it's nice and warm. I believe that I will put on my woolen underwear. How is everything there? What does Dezső write? Tomorrow is my birthday. I hope and wish that this would be over and in the future we could to get together to celebrate this day. What do you say to that? I can only write to you that I hope that shortly I'll be home. I'm sorry that everything goes very slowly. Many times I don't want to think of it, because I can't help. We are asking the Almighty that this war should end as soon as possible! Write. Kisses, Irving.

1943/11/14 Irving to Family, North Africa (Book 3, 138)

November 14 - 1943
North Africa
Written in Hungarian.

My dear brothers and sisters,
I did not think of this a few years ago that I will spend my 22nd birthday in Africa, but unfortunately, this is life. At this time I only ask the Almighty to help me to return to America, to the same condition that they have taken me to be a soldier. I do not have any greater wish than that. Because I remember cases, that with such an illness, life is worthless. The daily news reports do not interest me, because every day I hear the same thing. You probably know the day's events better than I do. Last night I was on guard duty and I had plenty of time to think of everything. I was thinking of you also. I cannot wait for the moment that this war would end. If, after that, I would have to stay here for awhile until everything is in order, I wouldn't mind it, my heart would beat more easily. Until we meet again, kisses to you all, your little brother, Irving
[In English] P.S. Write soon.

1943/11/15 Irving to Family, North Africa (Book 3, 139)

November 15 - 1943
North Africa
Written in Hungarian

My dearests,
I hope you're getting more frequent letters from me than I from you. It has been a week since I have heard from you. You can imagine how impatient I am. It's true that it can't be helped. Your letters are there somewhere. As far as that goes, it will come back, it takes time. Many times I don't know what to write about because I can't! Everything that I write in every letter sounds all the same. More likely it may be tiresome to read my letters. When the Almighty will help me and I will be home, I'll have patience and will answer anything that I didn't in the letters. It is quite cold here and it is raining, but this doesn't affect our

work. I can tell you I'm waiting for a better future. As soon as this war ends, we'll all feel much better. Otherwise I'm well. Don't worry! If I can, I will write you again briefly. You write to me, even though I may not write to you as frequently as I have. Ask Herman how does wet wood burn? Very slowly, doesn't it? If you remember, I was telling you, but you didn't believe me. Kisses, Irving

1943/11/16 David to Hermine and Marie (Book 12, 39-43)

Nov 16. 943
Dear Hermina!
I got your letter and it really surprised me that finally for once you did something smart. What you did to that lady, was worth the money. She should know not to be dirty when she does not give you the money. Ask for a receipt from her that proves you paid [the rent] for the house. I believe it's been more than two years that you lived there. Yes, don't pay her more than 25.$^{\underline{00}}$ per month either and she should keep her garage for it, but nobody wants it in the summer, so you don't need her garage, she can keep it for herself. So, it is enough about this. I hope you got my airmail yesterday! I don't know any news, everything is the same. I hope my plan will work out and starting today I will get at least 1.51 or 1.57 cents per hour. Currently, I get 1.38 per hour. I wrote to you that the union had written to me and I reported to the foreman that for my present job I am only required to pay a 27 dollar union fee and I will pay 52. He said we will rewrite my work class/schedule and I will make more money, 1.51 or 1.57. This is nice, isn't it? At the other place I got 95¢ an hour and I had to work with tons of people

...and take orders, but here there are only the 3 of us and nobody gives me orders. And one can only play here because there is nothing to do. Do not tell this to anyone! As I can see, you are working during your break and we get 1 1/2 [time and a half] for it. Currently I like my job. It is not hard and [there's] no need to rush. What can be done in two hours, we play with for an entire night. I eat. It is the same every place. Some people lie down and sleep. You know I work on the bottom of the boat (inside not outside) and nobody comes here and there are a lot of dark places, so they come here to lie down. Even the boss doesn't mind. He comes and wakes them up. See this is life! Poor soldiers are suffering and the men at home after a job like this get a deferment. But you can't help it. It goes like this in the whole country, even in Columbus. Oh yes! I am enclosing [an article] about a train accident from Columbus. As I can see, it happened at the K.B. or next to Arthur's factory at 5th East. It must have been in the newspaper there, too. [Note: November 14, 1943, James Rd., Columbus, OH, a Pennsylvania Railroad passenger train collided with an automobile. Four people were killed and three injured.] I want to write a little message to Mariska too. So, good luck and you better take care of yourself. When will you get a raise? Ask for it. Write! Kisses, Dezső

Dear Mariska!
I got your card and letter from yesterday. Thank you for trying to write to me. Some things I had to write to Hermine because she wrote about it, but I left some to your part so you can get some news too. So, I start! I got two letters from Ignác. One today and one on Saturday. He wrote that he is well. He does not know anything new. He is about 1000 Km away from Polyán. He got a letter from Bertha and she is well! He wrote on October 23rd. What I got from Ignác's letter is that he stayed there because he is not a citizen yet. Other than that, he is well. So Mariska! Listen to everybody. It is not a shame to work in a shipyard. A lot of Jewish people and Jewish girls also work in the shipyard. Hollywood is lousy. You know, ever since I lived here I have not even been there. It's 25-30 miles away from here, but there is nothing to see there. If one has a lot of money, it is easy to spend it because everything is so expensive there. You know, I'm used to not going to the city here anymore. The traffic is heavy and it is hard to park with my car. Long Beach on the other hand is 4-5 miles away and it is a very nice little place.

You know, here in Long Beach there are good looking Navy boys. They have a big dock for them and a big shipyard. On the beach there is a coast guard and there are a 100 guards on the ship watching against the enemy. You don't need to tell anybody that! So write to me even if I don't write to you promptly. I will make it up to you, if you'll write. Yes, I will write to the Selection Board. I will give them the address. I don't even know what to write. Oh yes! What happened between you and Hermine? You did not write together! There must be a reason! You better write it! What does Sir Herman Gluck do? Is he getting close to his millions? Here the weather was nice for awhile. Today the sky is dark. It looks like it's going to rain. I don't know how the weather is going to turn out yet. It's a secret of the future. So, I wish you good luck and everything good! You better send me Ignác's letter where he is asking for candy or a package because only then can I send it to him. You better write a reply! Kisses, Dezső

November 16 - 1943
North Africa
Written in Hungarian

The days go by and no news from you. Since I changed my address everything stopped. I hope you're well. Today I've taken some of the old letters and I began to read them again. I found an interesting article in the July letter. You have been waiting for me to come home for leave, how is it that it has been five months already. But time flies very fast, regretfully one can't help it. You mentioned it then and hoped that shortly I'll be at home, discharged. It is very difficult to wait for that moment and it appears it will take more time than I thought. We hope it will become a certainty shortly. It was interesting because last night it was very cold, so the boys decided to make a fire and in a few minutes it was quite warm and full of smoke. I was ready to get my gas mask so that I could tolerate the smoke. Finally, we put out the fire and we stayed inside with the smoke. I think that we are going to give up making fires inside. We will sleep in the fresh air and send you fresh kisses, Irving

1943/11/18 Irving to Family, North Africa (V-Mail, Slide 25) - Oath of Citizenship

Dearest Siblings,
I don't even know how to start this letter, because I write in vain and I don't receive an answer from you. As you can see my address has changed again. I don't know if the package will ever catch up with me. Maybe it's better if you don't send packages anymore because it's just causing problems. Today I took the oath for the United States and as of today I am a citizen. I never thought I would become an American citizen in Africa, but it seems that anything can happen in today's world. Don't be upset with me that I write so infrequently, but I can't do it, I can't write more often. My handwriting is not so good either, because my hands are cold and you can imagine how that is. Don't be sad, with G-d's help, we will see each other again. I will write as often as I can, but if I don't write, don't be sad. I am well, it's raining and it's windy! Many kisses your brother, Irving
GREETINGS TO DEZSŐ!

1943/11/20 Irving to Family, North Africa (V-Mail, Slide 26)

Dearest Siblings,
Today I am trying to write a few lines, that thank G-d I am well and I hope to hear the same from you. I still didn't hear from you. Now I am just waiting. It probably will take a couple of weeks until I receive a letter from you. I don't have any patience to write to anybody, because I don't get a response. Now if I want to receive a letter from you, I have to give you my new address. You can imagine how everything is. How are you my dears? I don't know what to write about myself. I always do the same thing and there is no benefit from it. Please write to me more often. If G-d helps me and I return home, then I will talk to you about everything. Now I'm kissing you with a lot of love. If you write to Dezső, give him my new address. With kisses, Irving

1943/11/24 David to Hermine and Marie (Book 12, 45-47)

Wednesday Nov 24-43
Dear Hermine and Mariska!
I'm sorry that I [write] you all at once, but I can write more this way and I will not write something twice. So, forgive me that I did not write before. You know, I'm sleepy and one will stay a "papol" for the other. I don't know any news, everything is the same. I was in Hollywood this week and I went to Radio City. I was at the Blondy program [Blondie] that will come out on Monday night. And I was at another, I don't know if you can hear about this there, the title "I was there" and the city's mayor Barimore was there. There is nothing to see, except that you must see it [performed] live once. That's all about it. I was at the post office again and I figured out one way to send a package. In case there are two different addresses, therefore I have two letters, one is 776 the other is, 7129. So, this way I will send a package to him on Saturday. Thank you very much for the picture. I will hold it for a few days and then I will send it back. I did not get anything from him this week. I hope I will get something. Currently, it is nice summer weather here. At night it's a

little cold. A sweater comes in handy. You better forgive me that I did not write before, but that's the way it goes. I did not get a raise yet. I hope I will get it in a few days. You know, the picture of Ignác is excellent. If you write next time, send me Ignác's new address. What can I write? Believe me, I just got up and I'm sleepy. There is nothing special that comes to my mind. I hope you will not mind, if I don't write a lot. This week I'll buy the weaving needle that I mentioned,

and I will send it to you. Maybe I will go to Long Beach tomorrow. I hope you will like it. You know, this is how it needs to be worked on it. This is a sample of a wood frame, where you stretch the fabric to, and it needs to be strengthened with nails, so the fabric will be strong on it. You can make different wood frames also and you can make it in all kinds of sizes. The frame depends on the size and the fabric also! So, now the needle has to go on the frame and will be done based on the color. The bottom has to be pierced up. For example, like this [hand drawing]…this is a yarn, they are all the same. I will send one that is started, so you can see how to do it. I hope you will like it, since they sell it in Columbus. If you will like it, then I will send more.

How's the weather in Columbus? Hermine, don't you dare work for 19! That is not enough money these days. You can not buy anything for it. You asked me if I have gasoline, you know it is available now, I have enough. I wrote my address to the Selective Bond! This week I did the Californian license. I needed to go to a road test to see if I can drive, and if I know the Californian rules. So, I have a license from here now. So, I don't know anything else. I will write more next time. I wish you good luck and everything good. Happy Thanksgiving! I will work. We don't rest on holidays. They will pay 1½ times more.

[In English] Good Bye until I will see you again. Kisses, Dezső

1943/11/26 Irving to Family, North Africa (V-Mail, Slide 27)

Dearest Siblings,

I hope you received my letters and you are trying to write to me. It's been almost 3 weeks since I received a letter from you or anyone else. I don't know what to think, what could be the reason. I hope you are all well [and] in the best health. There is nothing new with me, like they say, I'm waiting for a better future. But every day counts. One day can make a big difference in one's fate. So we hope that soon we will see each other again in the best health. If my letters are delayed don't worry, because often I can't write and that's the reason for the delay. As soon as I know anything about my situation, I will write again. I haven't heard any news from the Aunt. I received only one letter from Dezső. He wrote that he will send a picture of himself, but I haven't received it yet. Kissing you with a lot of love, your little brother, Irving
P.S. Write!!!!!!!

1943/11/28 Irving to Family, North Africa (V-Mail, Slide 28)

Dear Siblings,

Today is Sunday and I have a few minutes to write. Unfortunately until now I haven't received any news from you. I hope you are well. Thank G-d I'm well. Do you receive letters from me? If you haven't received my letters and they send back your letters, then please write to my new address and I will hear from you faster. I don't know what to think, what the reason is, [that] since I moved I haven't received a letter from you. The package should be here also. It would be good if I receive it by Christmas. There is nothing new with me, everything is the same. I trust in G-d! In the hopes of a reunion, kissing you, Irving
GREETINGS TO THE RELATIVES

1943/11/30 Irving to Family, North Africa (V-Mail, Slide 29)

November 30, 1943
My Dear sisters and brothers,

Today just another line to let you know, that I am feeling fine and hoping to hear the same. I hardly know what to write because months have passed since I heard last from you. As you see time goes very fast even in North Africa, however when I'm waiting for mail call from one day to the other, it seems like a year. I cannot express my feelings when I glance at the pictures, my thoughts are with you more than ever. I met a very fine young man, he is a likable chap. We chum around together. I hope someday we can meet again and introduce him and his wife, his child and his sisters. My darling sisters, please do not worry about me, I'm well, God is with us. Hope this war ends soon and we will meet again back in the good old U.S.A. With all my love, Irving

1943/11/30 Louis Schwartz to Hermine and Marie (Book 1, 139-141)

Dear Hermine and Mariska!

I will forgive you that you respond so late to the letters. Not too long after my vacation (holiday leave) I was sent here to Camp Reynolds. That is not too far from Shenango where your brother was shipped out from. This has been the third week I've been here, waiting every day that they will ship us out the way they told us, but somehow the "runday" is late. Our officers told us that most of our regiments will be shipped out of the country and only a small unit will stay in the country. So there is some hope, even if isn't much, that I will stay. Thankfully, I would not mind, if I were to leave, especially to Europe, but for now, I can't do anything other than wait for what destiny will bring. In the meantime I'm very often for two-three days in Youngstown. I spent every Saturday from noon to Monday morning in Youngstown. At least some good comes out of this. Youngstown is 23 km away from here. I can do it easily. I'm curious how you all are doing? What have you heard from your brother? I only got a mail from him from North Africa. That was a long time ago. What's with Dezső? I'm getting ready to write to him also, but somehow now I'm neglecting my correspondence since things are in the air and I'm not staying here permanently. I hope you will still respond, and if it's not late, it will still find me here.

Write about everything. Kiss all of you, L[ouis]

1943/12 Undated David to Marie (Book 16, 416-417)

Undated [It seems like it belongs to 12/1943 based on the style and content...]

Dear Mariska!

I got your precious card. I am very glad that you are well, but you just be careful when you are working and don't work too hard! Nobody works too hard. You better take care and eat normally and don't starve! A glass of milk and a piece of bread for breakfast is not enough! You know I live about 3 miles from the shipyard. There is a lot of traffic and it is hard to drive. It takes 15-25 minutes to take that road, but there is another shipyard here that is 1/4 mile from my apartment and I can hear the noise and the hammering very well from the ship. One can get used to it and does not even notice it. So, I don't even know what to write. You can write with more details too, a little good gossip. You used to tell stories at home and now you only send a card. If you write to Ignác, send him my best. Don't forget! Ok?

I will find out if I can send a Christmas package to Ignác, that is how I will send something. You know, if you want to send some kind of "hard candy", not the one that melts, then Marcsa or Herman should go to 75 E. Rich St, A. Kutzweil and tell MR. LAFIEVER the manager, that they are my dear sibling and they would like to send chewing gum and etc. to our little brother...this way he will give it you. You can give my best to him. It is possible that this name is still there, "Timi Callory." He is also a good guy and he will give you, just tell him you are Dave's brother, who worked here. They know me well, they will give it to you. So, good luck! Hey, you also will get a raise! Right? You just better be careful and not to rush anything with the work! I wish you good luck and everything good from a sibling far away, who you don't like too much, right? You don't look forward to letters from me, only from our little brother. You know he is not too much farther than I am. Kisses, Dezső

1943/12/1 David to Family (Book 12, 49-53)

Wednesday afternoon

My dearests!

I got your letters and I'm thankful. No news or mail from Ignác. No news, everything is the same. Hey! Hermine don't sue me since I didn't give you the 2.35 yet. I did not send it yet. But I will next week just because I spent too much this week. With today's mail I sent to Ignác 5 pounds of candy, 20 packages of chewing gum and mixed candies (hard) and 20 boxes of razors. He asked and I sent them to your address today. I am going to send a package now and I'm sending all that's in it to Hermine's address, 2 hand needles, Hermine and Marcsa and for a bigger heavier carpet/rug. But you can only sew it that way, when it is stretched out and when it is backwards, that is the original side of it. You should learn it and if you need information, you better ask. I will let you know that way. [With] 14 rolls of cotton, [which] if you can't get them there, I will send them, but you can use whatever you want and what you want, and [make] 4 sofa cushions out of cotton so you can have it in every color. I hope you will understand. You better ask for information, if you don't understand!

The military woman's necklace that I bought I don't know what it's worth because I bought it at auction. Write if you like it! 1 big landscape from all kinds of material, it will be good to hang in your room or wherever you want to put it. Also, different kinds of pictures of France. I think [they're] nice landscapes. I bought them at an auction. I'm curious if they sell them at Lazarus'. If yes, find out how much and write it! If you don't need it, sell it. Also, 2 boxes of candies that did not fit into Ignác's package and I kept them out. Write if they're good, if [you think] Ignác will like them! Also, a dress, lipstick, shoes, a hat, a few dishes and boots for whoever wants them. Also a tablecloth ("kovès" - stony [pattern?]). 4 great pictures that I got at an auction. Write if you like them! Good luck! Kisses, Dezső
Respond
PS: There is one crystal powder for you and a perfume bottle with 2 crystal cases. I will send them, they're about 5 pounds and from glass
Good luck!
Hermine, when you get a chance, go in, or you Marcsa, to the Insurance and give this letter to them. It's not urgent.

1943/12/2 Bertha to Hermine (Book 17, 19-22)

New York
Dec 2/43
My darlings!
Maybe you all think that I forgot about you. No way, only God ordered out something for me, so I can be busy. Or sometimes I get lazy and then I hesitate and that is the thing and, if you believe me, I will tell you something better. I hope that you all are in good health. About us, we are good now. We got a letter from Ignác. Thank God, he is well. I'm just sending a package to him. I was away in the past days. I got back this week. My cousin Fred, thank God he is well. He is with his family. He has two beautiful daughters. Believe me it feels good to see. It belongs to me. I wish you would live a little closer to New York. But it is very hard this way. Write about your days and how you spend them and what you do. I have nothing special to write about. I kiss you with love, all of you.
Bertha and Mannie also.

1943/12/4 Dezső to Family (Book 1, 151-156)

Thursday at noon

Dearests,
I got your letters and for you Mariska I'll note the following: whatever is happening in the factory does not mean anything. Here it didn't happen, but supposedly at some places they fired workers. That doesn't mean much. In your factory I don't know what you do. Today if you get through the plan and the contract is prepared, than naturally until you get a new order they won't get material. But don't worry, if the war will end, they will work anyway. They didn't fire you and they will not. I know, if they will fire you, you will still want to stay anyway. Go to the man where you were first and talk to him. You know, they will have work even after the war. But if they happen to still send you away, if you won't get a job where you can make good money, don't work because after two weeks of waiting you will probably get $20-25 unemployment. Do not worry, you will not be the only one. There will be many. But the fact of the matter is that there is a labor shortage. At most, you will come here. Don't worry there are enough jobs. If you want you can run to Hollywood too. Therefore do it to make everything good.

I don't know any news from here. Today is very warm. I hope you got my letter from yesterday. I just got a letter from our little brother today (his new address 33 RD, Co A). He asked me for a photograph. I didn't promise him. I wrote that I will send Californian pictures (landscape) and I will send it. I have a small picture of him in the letter. I will send it to you today. You will only get this letter on Monday. I will send it with special delivery, so that you'll get it on Sunday. If I will know any news I will write it. Oh! Yes! This upcoming Sunday at 11 o'clock or in the afternoon at ½ hour before 2 or 2 o'clock listen to the radio, maybe it will be or not, but our shipyard will get the army and navy "E" and there will be Ruddy Wally [Rudy Valee] with the Dance band. Supposedly there will be a big ceremony. I believe they will broadcast it. If they will, I will be there also!! I believe I already wrote this, starting next Monday I will get 1.51 an hour – as far as your factory is concerned, everything can be done to prepare them for production. But the factories will produce more than they did before the war and supposedly it's a steady job there. But if you don't want to go anywhere else, go back to work in Herman's factory or come here.

Lots of luck. Kisses, Dezső

Thursday afternoon

My Darling!

There is no news! I don't know what to write to you. I gave everything out to Marcsa already. I've run out. There is no news. I enclosed with yesterday's mail a Christmas Seal [a label placed on mail during the Christmas season to raise funds for charity]. If you didn't buy one, you can use it. I sent nothing and I'll enclose a couple today. Also, I got mail from the little brother today. He didn't write if he got my letter.

You Hermine misunderstood me. I already got the driver permit, only I didn't write the car over to my name. I drive it here with the Ohio license which will be good until next year March 1st, just like at home. And you can relax completely. I hope I can take care of myself like you all!

I don't sleep well. The reason is that it is very hot here, not like in Columbus and it's very hard to fall asleep. Also the houses are built out of boards and they are very warm!

I hope you got the package I sent. Pardon, I don't think so. I believe you'll only get it on Monday or Tuesday. I hope you'll like it! If you need anything from here that you don't have at home write it! If you need anything, I will send it. And please write what's up with money for the garage! Did he give in to the woman already? How did you get out of the situation? Did Herman pay?

Did you buy coal already? Are you starving and cold yet? I'm sure, yes! You see, if you would live here, you wouldn't need coal because it's warm here! I can't even know what to write. You can write to Ignác, if he writes only in Hungarian then his letter will be simple. But I believe, if he writes English then it goes well so you can write this to him, that he can write a normal letter. Just like we write from here. If he has one, he can write more. You better write to me! If not, even for some of you one by one. Don't be childish that the card wasn't addressed to you! Sometimes I write separately, but it doesn't make any sense. I can't write two addresses on one card. So, I believe that's the kind of thought that wasn't addressed to me, it's kind of a Polyáni talking! So I'm closing my lines for today. "The machine is empty" [ran out of thoughts]. I don't know any gossip. But I'm warning you that in the future you will hear a lot of gossip about the war and what's going to happen in the factories. But don't listen to anyone because nobody knows more than you do! And do not fall for any complaints! Be careful! Lots of luck and enjoy your food. I believe, you'll get this around lunch time. I will write for little brother also. Merry Christmas!

P.S. Why didn't I get mail from anyone from home?

1943/12/7 Irving to Family, North Africa (V-Mail, Slide 30)

Dearest Siblings,

I am sorry that for a couple of days I didn't write, I was not in a position to write. Thank G-d I am well, I hope to hear the same from you. I haven't heard anything from you up till now, I hope you are well. I received a letter from Bertha's husband and he wrote that you are well. He was very happy to receive a letter from me and he will send me a package and he will write again at the end of the week. Berthuska travelled to her cousin's wedding. As soon as she comes home she will write to me. Also, she will go and visit you next summer. My friends left again, it goes like this everyday. I hope the good G-d will help me and everything will be good. Right now I'm in the city and I'm writing this letter from there. Kissing everybody, your little brother who thinks a lot about you, Irving

1943/12/13 Irving to Family, North Africa (V-Mail, Slide 32)

Dearest Siblings,

Today I will write only a couple of lines, that thank G-d I am well. I received from you 2 letters via airmail and one v-mail. These you sent on Nov. 20-23-28. I was really happy to receive them. Unfortunately, lately I don't write very often, but dearest siblings, forgive me, you are always on my mind, only the good G-d knows it. As usual it's raining here. We often wonder, how much a human being can endure. Unfortunately, I cannot write to you about everything. It's been exactly four months since I spoke to you on the telephone. I hope with G-d's help we will see each other again. Walking doesn't bother me, even if I have to walk in knee deep water. It's ridiculous because right now I am just waiting for the summer to arrive so my feet can

dry. It's true, many times we laugh, but only inside. I'm sorry, but I'm not good at writing letters. I hope you understand. Kissing you many times from far away your younger brother, Irving
Write!

1943/12/12 Dezső to Family (Book 1, 135-138)

Sunday, Dec 12, 1943
My darlings!
I know you will be surprised that I didn't write you a letter this week, but that happened because I was waiting for mail from you and it didn't come, therefore my letter stayed too. I wrote a card yesterday. As of right now I'm getting ready to go to Los Angeles since I'm here and I wasn't on Sunday. This week it rained every day. Today the weather is nice. What do you say that 20-25 miles from here there is snow and they closed the traffic down. The weather here is like in Polyán. It rained and is raining, who knows when it will stop? Today, regardless of the rain obstacles the weather is nice and sunny. This is California. There is no news. I didn't get any mail from our little brother this week. You wrote a lot that you liked the things [holmi]. Tell me if you need anything else. How does the sewing go? I'm telling you you are very lucky to work for 35-40 cents. It's a shame when they pay so well here. This is your business, but how are you able to make out of that much…? What's up with garage's money? Did that lady give it back already? Hermine, this week I will send the money that I owe you. What do you say about Herman writing to me this week?

Herman wrote a letter to me however, he doesn't write anything. A wonderful boy, just like Lajos [Louis] Schwartz. He wrote a card here. I will attach it. I won't even respond to it. Christmas is coming. I'm sure he's waiting for a package. "Whistle to that!" (I don't give a damn!)
Write a lot! Yesterday night they moved me to another ship. The one that I've been on is ready. And I feel that we will work on Sunday too. It must be ready. So next Sunday I will work. I don't work this week because the union has to approve it beforehand. But next Sunday night I will work. They pay double the hourly wage, 3.02 cents an hour, not bad 21-22 dollars for 7 hours. Tell Herman that today I will not write to him because I'm in a hurry. It's 3 o'clock now. I have to get up and I'm hungry. And I will only be in LA. Here it's the "Cost Ronda" and if it wouldn't rain that much, I would go back to LA to live. There are too many people living here and they can't keep up with the cooking for 24 hours a day. They are all eating at the same place. At least 3-4 thousand per day. Mostly I go to the town to eat. So I don't even know what to write. I like my job, the boys are good. True, they are all older men.

You know that here women make the same money as men. Some make $150. They work 7 days a week for 10 hours daily. Oh! Yes. We got permission this week that we can go to work for 4 hours per day. The Government Air Corps "dipora" pays 85 cents for one hour. I also went. I thought I will make $20-25 per week. It would come in handy, but sure enough the work was too hard. So after the first round I did not go anymore and others didn't go as well. They said there are all kinds of jobs, but when you got there, you had to load large packages. So I will not go anymore because the 4 hours pay is 3.40 and I don't want to lose 10.50 for that. Do you see? To me 85 cents is not good and for you 35-40 cents is good. This is life! I don't know what to write! What's going on at home? Is anyone interested about me? You Marcsa! You were foolish, you changed your job. You could've gotten welfare and you shouldn't have to work like you do now! There are a few people from Ohio, but there isn't anybody from Columbus. There is one person from Columbus, but he lives here in Los Angeles. He is a sibling of that Jónász who is on Broad Street.

He has a Funeral Home. They work together- some know that I am a Jew and some don't. There are many here too, but luckily I don't work with any of them. They don't really like the Jews because they know how to complain. Oh yes! I have a good position! I don't know if I wrote this already, here on the Wilmington Counsel, and I'm a member too. I represent the building that I live in. At least 50. Our job is to vote for certain things. Now there will be a big Christmas show and we're asking for advice about the tenants' request. Do you know how much they pay for a good group here? H. Ruddy Wally [Rudy Valee] or O. Kugart [maybe Xavier Cugat] and for things like that on a Saturday night from 9-1, 1000-1500 dollar and for the new year, 2-2500 dollar. Nice money right?! Our job is to vote on what to do and don't think it is for salary! I wrote enough now, let's leave some for another time, too. I'm sending greetings to all of you, and the acquaintances. Flora too! And if the old Roth is interested, then him too! What's his address? 77 Latta or 63 ?
Kisses,
Dezső

Wilmington 1943.12.15

Dear Herman!

I was not in the mindset today to write to you, but I got a letter from Columbus. <u>Not from the girls.</u> When a person reports to you, do not think they don't write about everything. I'm corresponding with many, and many will report, if I'm interested. So I'm writing the letter to your address, so the girls won't see what I write. So, this thing happened. I wrote to one person and asked to report to me about what you do at home. The next letter came, but I needed to promise I won't tell anyone. It would be polite to know the name who reported the situation and if you also read it, burn the letter! This way no one will know about it.

So this is how it happened!

To your question, I can let you know about the following. The girls are doing well, although their situation isn't a good life. They aren't in the position to make money because they have a job that doesn't pay at all. And what they make isn't enough for their livelihood! Particularly to your interest about your sibling Herman, I'm notifying the following. Along with my very good people I examined very accurately the situation. And this is a true fact.

Herman works 7 days a week. But just to tell you the truth, I am ashamed. Don't get angry at me because he is your brother. But you asked the truth!

So it's here, (this was written in English) the money he makes, he puts it into the bank. Which would require a complement. But when a person who makes good money doesn't spend it on himself nor does he think of others, then that is shameful. He doesn't spend and doesn't eat like a man. He starves more than he eats. He feels badly to eat because god forbid maybe he will eat from the girls also. He is capable to last for days without a normal meal. Oh yes! He eats an apple and bread because they are cheap! And nobody takes it away from him! But what's important for breakfast! His belly hurts and his back. The doctor that is in the house can't help him. Why don't you write to him. He says there is nothing wrong with him because if he would have any problem, he would not be able to work 7 days a week. This is his medication. If he follows that, he won't need a doctor. I promise this. He should go and eat like other people 3 times a day a decent cooked meal and he shouldn't be stingy on his belly because he is going to end up giving his money to the doctor, if you don't talk to him.

Why don't you write to him that the 3 of them should stick together. The girls would prepare for him with pleasure. But I will note, if I would be his sibling, I would put him into his place for good. First of all, if they live together they are obligated to help out. Not paying for 1/3 of what they eat. He makes 5 times more than the girls and only pays 1/3, besides the girls have to clean up the house and to cook also. And he offers what? Nothing. He should be obligated to give enough money for the cost. So all three of them could eat because if he would go to a restaurant it would cost him more. But what's important, that he spends on his doctor? Write to him to take a test. Eat like a real person for 3 months. But eat! Not 30 cents worth of swill, that makes his stomach go bad. I promise that he won't have any problem. But if he'll continue this behavior 7 days of work and nothing to benefit the body just a hamburger sandwich, he'll have a lot of problems in a few years and then he will have to turn to the girls for sure with his complaints and problems. But now when it's not too late. He only lives for the bank. But it's not a human solution, it's madness. It's ok to have concerns about someone, but not the way he thinks. What he makes today he will give it to the doctor and no good will come out of that. He could live like other people today and enjoy life now. Believe me, if I would be in the girls' situation, I would not live with him. Not even for a day. I wouldn't even take care of him. Why? He only takes care of himself and doesn't think about others. I'm sorry that I talk that way about family, but you asked me the truth and this is it.

So, K[edves] (dear) Herman I'm not adding anything to this. As you can see others know this situation as well. And it's a shame! You might get angry that I wrote this to you, but I want you to know what they think about you. So I am only notifying this. I spend for rent and expenses $20 for a week and what do I get for it? You could eat until you are full for this money there and shouldn't need to visit your doctor. So, if I will hear from you shortly then I'll see how smart you are! But if I won't get a response from you, it means I have to deal with Makoch (Hung - stubborn) Herman and he doesn't deserve corresponding. So write.

Greetings Dezső

P.S. I'm very sleepy, but I want to finish the letter and I will write to the girls too. I won't even mention that I wrote this for you. So if you won't say anything, they won't know. Greetings, Dezső

1943/12/15 David to Hermine and Marie (Book 5, 195-200)

12.15-43

Dear Hermine and Marie,

I just received your cards. I'm trying to answer you right away. Thank God you're okay and I hope you all will be too. I thank you very much Maria for your acknowledgment about the package. Was the necklace in it? I hope you will like it. How did you like the sewing needle? And for you Hermine, thank you for your card in the letter that I received yesterday. I haven't received anything from Ignác for two weeks. While he does not write me more often, I wrote him many letters. It is true that for the last 10 days I did not write any. What is his address written in this letter? What I mailed, took eight days! And how much did it cost? And how much money are you getting? And Maria why are you not working? [Are you] in a better place? Are you not in the factory? You see, you are smart. I apologize, but in that place there isn't any future and the salary doesn't increase. At this time you have an opportunity to do better and get a better job. You can get now a better job, why aren't you looking for one. Even if you don't get paid more, at least you will be happy and like what you're doing instead. Even though no one knows what is instead, you are not alone in this world. Don't worry there will be more jobs again. There are a lot of people all over in many places that they don't need anything. The soldiers at this time they do not need them. In another place they have more work. If you came here you will get one. Don't worry about Hollywood. Get a job. Also, Hermine you know here it will be easier to get a job because the whole city is looking. You know, here I found the job on the radio. There's everything every day and I didn't know about it. Maybe you didn't hear it there. They call it chat radio. They are Jewish Christians. They preach like Jews, and just like the Christians they believe in Jesus, so they are interested in Jews but the Hebrews see them as Christians here. There are many scuffles in Los Angeles. I was amazed when they sang in Hebrew and preached according to the Christian religion. Here it is a very nice weather. In the evening it is very cold, no wonder, it is near the ocean! The ocean is about 500 steps from me. Would you like to live here? For you Hermine, tomorrow I will mail the money that I owe you. You wrote that you want to send something. I do not need anything here. I have what I need. Yes, I thank you for it, maybe I will ask you for a favor if I cannot get it here. The liquor, they don't have it here. It is rationed here. Therefore we cannot get it here. They're keeping it for themselves and selling it to their private customers. Therefore I would ask you to get a bottle. Get one quart of Canadian Club or 4 Roses, but not at this time yet. When you do mail it to me, you can buy it on your name. In the mail you are not allowed to mail it only by express. Will you do it if I will ask you for it? I'll mail you the money. Sometimes it is good when I cannot fall asleep. At this time I do not need it. I mention again by mail you cannot mail it, only by express delivery, maybe two or 3 pint or 1 quart. Herman can buy also, but only the best!! No need for Rum or Brandy. I've had enough! Oh yes, Herman can go for me on the phone and call the man I was driving the car for, Mr. Spitler, who lives at 777 Fairwood. You can find the telephone number in the phone book or if Herman would go there to 200 East Rich St. and ask him what I was earning under the permit in 1943 when I was there or would call him on the telephone at the last address and ask him how much I earned with the taxi when I was working for him. And how much taxes he took out and withheld from me? I want to know. It is not an emergency. I have plenty of time. Do you still have your telephone? Therefore I wrote plenty at this time. I'll leave some for next time. I'm getting sleepy. Oh! Oh! I almost forgot, soon I will have made a picture of myself. If you write to Irv you can write to him at the 23 address, that it will be an oil picture and it will look like a man in a synagogue, a movie star. I will have it colored and touched up, and send it to you. Wait until you see it. Sensational! Ha Ha! [most likely IMG_0561.JPG] But at this time it's enough with all the best wishes and a happy holiday. Best wishes for the relatives and whoever is asking about me kisses also. Dezső

Give my best to Herman and why is he not writing to me!!

1943/12/16 Irving to Family, North Africa (V-Mail, Slide 33)

Dearest Herminka,

I'm trying to answer your letter, although it's late, but I'm sorry I couldn't write sooner. Now everything has changed. I believe G-d will help me and we will see each other soon. I was very happy to read your letter, that you wrote how well I write. I'm sorry that fate changed everything. I hope you understand. I also received a letter from Dezső and he sent me five pounds of candy. Truly very nice of him. I haven't received your package yet. It looks like we will leave from here. So I don't even know when the package will catch up with me. Also Berthuska and family are sending a package. I received a letter from them and they are well. Forgive me that I write so infrequently, but as soon as I am able I will make up for it. Kissing you, your younger brother, Irving.

Mariska how are you? Why don't you write? Kissing you, Irv

1943/12/16 Irving to Family, North Africa (V-Mail, Slide 34)

Dearest Siblings,

Today I write a couple of lines to you again, that thank G-d I am well. I would like to hear the same from you. I receive letters from you very infrequently, I can't imagine what the reason could be. You are probably very busy. Nothing much to say about myself, just that I am well. As you can see my address is changing again. Right now it is the same as when I got here. It looks like we will be going somewhere. I hope the good G-d will help me and everything will be fine. You are often on my mind, but unfortunately I don't know how to express it. Don't be angry with me for not writing like I used to, but now everything has changed and I am not able to do it. I can talk about this only in person. In hopes of seeing each other again, kissing you, your younger brother, Irving

P.S. Write!

1943/12/17 Irving to David, North Africa (V-Mail, Slide 35)

Dec 17 - 1943
North Africa
Written Hungarian

Dear Dezső,

I cannot tell you how happy I was to receive your letter. I regret it, but I can't write to you as frequently as I used to. As you see on my address, I'll be going again somewhere. I hope that God will help me so that everything will be alright. In person I could talk to you about a lot. The package that you sent did not arrive yet. I thank you for it and I hope that it will be coming shortly. Hermina mailed two packages and they did not arrive yet. If I will be changing my address constantly, somehow I will not have patience to write. Please write to me even though I may not reply, because I won't be able to. As soon I can, I will write and make it up to you. Kisses, your little brother, Irving.

1943/12/19 David to Family (Book 12, 55-58)

Saturday

My darlings!

Until today I did not get any mail this week. What's going on with you? Write ok? I don't know any news here, everything is the same. Maybe I will work tomorrow. It would be good because when one gets a paycheck, there is nothing left from it after the many deductions. I will attach the 2.35 here. Hermine, if you write, send a few stamps to me because otherwise it takes a long time. There are blessed days here, the rain is raining again! Allegedly, it is raining sometimes all winter. The air is summery, but, if the rain is raining then what is it worth? I did not get a letter from Ignác for two weeks. I wrote to him this week. What's the news there? Did it snow a lot? I was in Hollywood last Sunday. I went to see a new place. You [hear it] on the radio every Sunday at night about 12 o'clock, here it is 9 o'clock.

They broadcast music and dance from the Palladium in Hollywood all over America and the entire world. Even to Ignác! You must listen to it! It is possible that it's on the radio earlier. I can't write anything else. I'm in a hurry to the post office and I still did not eat anything. I'm hungry. You should know that I go to the town to eat because the prices [here] are lousy and it is expensive. In the town (small town) there are good prices, cheaper, and there is no need to stand on line. There is no news here. So, I hope you are well! And how is Herman? And you Marcsa? And you Hermina? This week I applied for gas. I wonder if they will give it to me because I live close to the factory. Allegedly, there are a lot of jobs there without workers! Most people don't like it here and many go to Oklahoma where the weather is better. If I get a chance, I will go check it out. About 20 km from here there is a lot of snow! I have not seen snow for a long time. What does it look like?

So, good luck and Merry Christmas!

Kisses, Dezső

PS: Hermine, what's going on with your raise? Did you get any? Write it!
And you Mariska, are you still there? There is no good place? Do not be ashamed! You will find [one soon] enough.
So, I'm waiting for the mail. Write to our little brother to write.
Hey Hermine! Did the housewife give you the garage payment? If not, do not pay the house rent! She can't do anything if the O.P.A. [Office of Price Administration] said that you are entitled to get a payment from her.
Good Luck!
Kisses, Dezső

PS: Hermine today is Saturday and here they don't give [mail] vouchers on Saturday and sending mail before Christmas is very hard. I'm afraid it's going to get lost. So, I will send it on Monday.
Thanks,
Dezső

1943/12/20 Undated David to Hermine and Marie (Book 17, 2-3)

Undated [but because of the reference to people writing about Uncle Herman's behavior, it is 12/1943...see the letter from Dave to Herman on 1943/12/15 to corroborate, so sometime after, so the 20th or 27th because written on a Monday]

Monday

My darlings!
I got a letter yesterday with special delivery. Thank you so much! I don't know any news, everything is the same. Also, I got your post card too, Hermine. But you can tell Herman that he can be calm that you did not write the letter about him. What is important is that since then there is another letter that came from a couple of people. If he will be interested, I will send it to him and it will make it for certain that you are not the one who is writing the letter. If he will respond to me then I will send the letter to you. Ok Mr Gluck? I did not get a letter from Ignác for 3 weeks. He writes 5 letters a week to you and nothing for me. So, I will not be in the hurry to write to him. If I will get a letter from him, then I will write to him too! I worked last night and we were free on Saturday night. You Mariska! I bet you work for free! If you can't make good money being a tailor, then do not do it! Do you understand?? Doesn't it hurt your eyes and head? If you don't make at least a 100 an hour, then don't do it!

I guess you sew a dress for 1-2 dollars. You are silly! If you sew, you better take a good job where you can charge 5-10-15 dollars. If they don't pay you well do not sew!! There is enough work, but there is no one to do it. Don't be silly and be happy for the work if you can't make 6-8 dollars with 8 hours of work a day. Do not sew! And don't sew more than 8 hours a day! And don't be happy for the Jewish costumers because they want it for free!! They will only bring junk stuff to you to do! Why don't you specialize yourself, if you can do it. Ladies slacks, that needs to be done the same way and you can better make more money with it. And it can be done in 2-3 hours. You surely sew like before two shirts for 3 dollars. Do you understand? If they pay well, then it's ok, if they don't then they should go to hell with it! So, it is enough about this. Be smart and be careful not to become another's fool! Listen to Hermine, and ask for her approval! Do you still have the phone? So, I don't know what else to write. I will attach a picture, maybe you will like it. I did not send any to Ignác yet. I'm waiting for a letter from him. Good luck for the New Year! I sent to Arthur, to the neighbors, to you, to Mr. Roth. So, Hermina I kiss you. Dezső

1943/12/21 Undated David to Hermine and Marie (Book 12, 74-76)

[Dated by the 2.35 payment to Hermine that he promised to send on letter dated 12/19]

Wilmington, Tuesday after 8.

Dear Herminka and Mariska!
I got your letters which I was very happy about and I'm waiting for you to write more often. Hermine, I will attach 235 to you. Forgive me that I did not send it yet. Put the picture wherever you want it. I don't

understand anything about it! I don't owe Lazarus. If I do, then go in and check it. I paid everything at once. What's going on with the insurance at State St? Did you go in to see how can they transfer it to here. You, and Marcsa too, know Ignác's address and he wrote that you will send it, but no one is writing it. You better write it immediately and I will send a package to him again. And you better send it by airmail because it takes 6-7 days until the letter gets here from you. OK?! Thank you! Mariska, I don't even know what to write to you, if you left it then good for you! Why don't you arrange it so you can get unemployment, about 20 dollar for a week, and then you can work at home. Learn how to do the worn ones, it pays well and it does not cost a lot. You can make money on it and it's not really hard.

I will find out how much it sells for here. I sent the necklace to someone who will wear it. It is not important to tell that I sent it or maybe Ignác sent it then it does not really have a value. Maybe between 5 and 8 dollars- I don't even remember what kind of picture I sent to you. But I did not lose weight so then the picture is wrong. Marcsa, in the future do not forget to write Ignác's address. You wrote me a few times that he has a new address and none of you sent it to me yet. He did not write to you for awhile. Ok yes. I did not work on Sunday, only the good workers could work. So, I wrote enough for today. Greetings to all of you, Herman also, and you better write to me. I wish you lots of luck and happy holidays. And Happy New Years! Oh! Oh! Almost forgot, today the weather is nice, the sun is shining. Otherwise it's raining night and day. I don't know any particular news. Oh Mariska, I still work there. Sometimes I like it, sometimes I don't! I can't make more money anywhere else than here. So, it's not worth it to change. So, more next time and you better take care and I will, too! What's the news in Columbus? Did it snow? Is it cold? So, Good Bye and luck is [looking] up! I will go to bed. I am sleepy. They will organize a Christmas party here on Friday at the Wilmington Hall. They will give food for free and there will be dancing, too. Kisses, Dezső

1943/12/19 Irving to Family, North Africa (V-Mail, Slide 36)

My Dears,
Today I am here in the city and trying to write you a couple of lines. Thank G-d I am well. Yesterday I sent seventy dollars via telegram, so you will get it sooner. I think by the time I arrive at Emil's I will have a sum accumulated. I can hardly wait to be there. It is possible that I will go there. I asked G-d for it to end, the sooner the better. But who knows what the future will bring. Also I received two v-mails yesterday that you sent in November, it took exactly one month to get here. Forgive me that I don't write more often, but if I have the opportunity I will make up for it. You are always on my mind! I also miss you. But all this I have to keep to myself. If you need something, please take from this sum. Kissing you with love, your younger brother, Irving
Money is not everything!

1943/12/20 Hermine to Irving (V-Mail, Slide 37)

December 20, 1943
My dear brother Irving,
We received a letter a few days ago and I was very glad to hear from you. We are always thinking about you and wondering what you are doing. I know you do the same, but don't worry Irving. We are all in good health and hoping this finds you the same. My work is nice and I like it very much. My girlfriend visited me yesterday. She is very nice, but her boyfriend is coming home and they will get married. I will miss her, but maybe she will stay at the job. There are nice girls here too. Are your friends there [that] you were talking about them. Take care of yourself and we are wishing you a very happy new year and I hope to see you soon. Write me if you get a package from home. My best wishes and good luck to you with all my love, Hermine

1943/12/22 Irving to Hermine and Marie, North Africa (V-Mail, Slide 38)

December 22, 1943
North Africa

My dear sisters Hermine and Maria,
I just received 33 letters, and I'm very glad to know that you are all in the best of health. Sorry I can't answer all your letters, but as soon as I can I will. Here they keep me busy. It's not like it used to be. I hope that God will help us soon, the sooner the better. Until now I haven't received your packages, I think it won't be

long and it will follow me here. Some of these letters were written in August, September, December. I cannot tell you how much enjoyment I get when I get news from home. I think everybody is that way. You know my darlings, I think of you 1 million times a day. You must forgive me for not being so prompt with answering and writing you. But you know me, if I have only a little time, I drop you a line. Please don't worry. I hope God is with us. That French family are very fine people. Sometimes I drop in and see them. There's a very nice looking girl. I'll write you more later. With all my love, Irving

1943/12/23 Irving to Dave, North Africa (V-Mail, Slide 43)

December 23, 1943
My dear brother Dave,
I just received your long letter, which you have written sometime in August. Your letter explains everything. Sure hope that God will help me to do my best. That will be a happy moment, when I'll drop in to see the folks back home. However everything moves so slowly, it's very difficult to wait even one day. In the last few weeks, I'm doing more [military training] than I used to do when I was back home. You know, what I am talking about? I'll bet you do. It was very nice of you to send me that package you mentioned. I hope it won't be long till I'll get it. Please forgive me for not writing as often as I used to, but there is always something to do, and I really mean it. Anyway, whenever I get a chance I drop you a line. Thinking of you a lot. Sometimes I think you were right… Hope to see you soon. With all my love, Irving

P.S. Write soon!

1943/12/23 Irving to Herman, North Africa (V-Mail, Slide 42)

December 23, 1943
North Africa

Dear Herman,
How are you o' boy? That's a surprise for you. As you see I'm still writing and think of you too this afternoon. However I think of all of you, but over here is a little different even to express myself. I'm glad that you are there not over here. There one little house is worth more than over here the whole continent. Sure would like to be there to tell you all the details. Someday, I hope I can do so. Meantime here isn't anything that you would be interested in. You should write me more often. I bet with you, that you have more time to write than me. I'll be waiting for your answer soon. Take care of yourself, don't work hard. Money isn't everything. Remain with love, Irving

1943/12/23 Irving to Hermine and Marie, North Africa (V-Mail, Slide 39)

December 23, 1943
My dear sisters Hermine and Marie,
Just another line to let you know that I'm fine. Hope to hear the same. It was wonderful to know that you understand me. From here, I haven't anything to say. Please don't worry. You know my dear sisters, I'll tell you a little true story. Hear the people are not like back home, because the people back home are not like back here. If here you want to have a date with a nice and intelligent girl, you will have company. That means that you'll stop into the girl's house and from there the girl and her mother goes along with you. Tell me, isn't much easier to get a date in the good old U.S.? Yes sir, I hope to be back someday! Soon! And now I'll remain with all my love,
Your little brother, Irving

How is Mr. and Mrs. Walters? Please tell them to write me. Regards to them all

1943/12/23 Irving to Hermine and Marie, North Africa (V-Mail, Slide 40)

December 23, 1943
North Africa

My dear sisters Hermine and Maria,

Today also received 2 letters, both were written in English. Believe it or not it's perfect, you really are doing better than I thought. To learn a language it takes time and lots of practice. As I said in my last letter, that I met a French family. Whenever I go to town I stop in to see them and have some fun. One of the girls speaks a little English, and you can imagine how much I enjoy hearing it. It's just like hearing or remembering you, the way you and I used to talk. Should I say, that was in the good old days. Hope it won't be long that we will meet again. How is Herman? Please tell him to write me. How is Aunt Helen? She hasn't written to me since I left the States. I hope you all are in the best of health with all my love, your little brother

PS I have written to Dave

1943/12/23 Irving to Hermine and Marie, North Africa (V-Mail, Slide 41)

December 23, 1943
North Africa

My dear sisters Hermine and Maria,
For certain reasons I stayed in this afternoon and I have time to write you a few lines. It might sound all the same, but as you my dear sister said, it does not matter until you receive any word from me. So I decided just to write and nothing else, but write you all. How are you all getting along? I hope fine. How are you Herman? Why don't you write me. I have received one letter, but you wrote in August. Before I can answer to all your letters I'll have to read them over again. But as you know I have little time to do anything. I'll try my best. Please do not worry. I believe in God, and he will help me. Please write me whenever you have time. I hope you received $10 I cabled to you. Till we meet again! With all my love, your little brother

1943/12/24 Irving to Dave, North Africa (V-Mail, Slide 45)

December 24, 1943
My dear brother Dave, here I'm again to let you know that I'm fine and hope to hear the same. How are you there? Hope you're doing okay. I received 35 letters from home in the last few days. You can imagine how much I enjoyed reading it. However they were mostly old letters. Also received from Broad Street Temple a mezuzah and the 10 commands. As they say, they think of me. Well I believe they should. In your letter you said that you belong to both temple. How can you do it, if you are not home. Do you have any friends in California? I met a nice-looking gal here. She speak a very little English, but we get along O'K. I'll write more about later. Now please don't think of anything serious. Just studying French! With love your little brother, Irving

Why in a H* isn't this war over... Till we meet again.

1943/12/24 Irving to Hermine and Marie, North Africa (V-Mail, Slide 44)

December 24, 1943
My dear sisters Hermine and Marie,
Here I'm again dropping you another line. As you see thinking of you all the time. Your letters are just like receiving a present or package. You can understand that a package over here means a lot the same is [a] letter. Hope that you'll continue to write me as often as you can. Do you remember how many packages you sent me? Please let me know, so when I do receive them I will know how many more it's on its way. One more day to Christmas and sure would like to have from one of those packages. When I'll get it or them, I will drop you a line wright of way [sic]. That will be another happy moment. Hope to hear from you soon, and wishing that this horrible war ends soon

P.S. Write Soon

1943/12/26 Irving to Family, North Africa (V-Mail, Slide 46)

PVT. IRVING GLUCK
A.S.N. 35633941
A.P.O. 7129 % P.M. N.Y. N.Y.
December 26, 1943

Page 266

My dear sisters and brothers,

Just a line to let you know that I'm OK and hope to hear the same. Here on December 25–we have had very good turkey. Everything was fine and my thoughts were with you. My dear Maria, you are wright [sic]. I'm going to see Emil, as I said the last time. My dear Hermine, you know, when all the 4 of us were together you wrote to Emil that you and Maria are all OK. You left me out. But now everything is fine. Say by the way, do you have that address from that man? He worked in that hotel, remember? I hope that God will help me to go on and return to America. Probably I cannot write you as often as you did, but please don't worry I'll write you, whenever I get a chance. Haven't received the packages yet. From now on use this address as you see above. I'll be thinking of you a lot. I hope that this war ends soon!! Never thought of it that it will go on so long. All my love, Irving

P.S. Tell David I said hello. I'll write him too soon!

1943/12/29 Irving to David, At Sea (V-Mail, Slide 48)

December 29, 1943

My dear brother David,

Just let you know, that I am [censored] somewhere on the [censored] and thinking of you too. I would like to picture myself, but as you know it can't be done. It seems to me that the old country changed a lot. I'm not there yet, but you probably have some idea. Anyway I sure wish to be back and have some good homemade food of any kind. If you want to have some American peaches, I mean a can of peaches, you have to pay very nice for it. It's only one dollar and sixty-four cent. That's not much if you can get it. Well my dear Dave, there isn't much that I could say, only wish that everything ends soon. Don't know, how to explain the situation with me. God is on our side. Please write me whenever you get a chance. I'm hoping to hear from you in the future more often. With all my love, your brother Irving

1943/12/29 Irving to Family, At Sea (V-Mail, Slide 47)

December 29, 1943

My dear sisters and brothers, just [to] let you know, that I'm [censored] somewhere on the [censored] and thinking of you all a lot. Believe it or not, I sure wish it's over, when I get there. Many things it's in my mind but it cannot be expressed in a letter. So the best thing is to let it go and wait. Someone who believes in God and trusts him, he does not have to worry. There where I come in. Please do not worry, as I explained it above. Received a beautiful pen from Flora, before I left Africa, but haven't had time to write her, I'll later. Regards to them all. When I'll get there, will write some more, if there be a chance. Remain with all my love and hoping to hear from you all. Love, Irving

1944/1/2 David to Hermine and Marie (Book 15, 106-108)

January 1, 1944

My Darlings!

I got your letters yesterday and I'm glad to hear that you are all well. I'm well here, but I don't know any news, everything is the same. It's been 3 weeks or more that I did not get any mail from Ignác. You better tell him to write, otherwise I will not. We worked last night. Also we will tonight. It is possible that we will tomorrow too, but I don't know that yet. It's a nice sunny day here today. Oh yes! Poor Marcsa, I feel bad for the accusation, that they think that she is a Mrs., but we can easily fix that. You better put my picture away and not leave it out! This way they will not think that. It is not important to have my picture out. There is no value in it that way! It's just a picture! So, I hope it will help! Also, you better call the phone company and tell them that I don't live there anymore! Change it to your names and that way your name will be established there. And, if somebody will ask for information, they will give your names then. I'm sorry, but I totally forgot this entire case and I did not think that something unpleasant will come out of this. I hope if my picture will not be there, that incident will not happen again. How did you spend the New Year? I did not go anywhere. Currently, after writing this letter I'm going to go to Long Beach and I will have lunch there! So, I wish you a Happy New Year and everything more! Yes! It is not important to keep the picture I just sent in the room. It is not good in a paper frame, it should be a glass frame so it could keep its normal shape because it is an oil picture/painting.

How are you? Can you pay for the rent? Does Herman help? The person who wrote about Ignác was wondering from me, if I wrote to Herman. I don't know what he thinks, if he improved or what happened. as I saw it on the newspaper, he was or is in a protest strike! He was protesting too? Currently it is 6:30 by you. You must be at the cinema! I don't know what to write, nothing comes to my mind! Ever since I'm here nobody called me on the phone and they haven't sent any mail. What's the news in Columbus? How much money is Marcsa working for? Who did she buy the sewing machine from and for how much? I will close my lines. I don't know what to write. Please do me a favor and write to me and send the letter by air mail because otherwise it comes in 6 days and with airmail it takes only 2 or 3 days. So, I wish you good luck in the new year! How are the 2 paintings? They sell them at Lazarus. And how does the handwork go that I sent to you? If you don't understand, I can explain it to you again. So, good luck!
Kisses, Dezső

1944/1/4 Irving to Family, Italy (V-Mail, Slide 49)

January 4, 1944
Somewhere in Italy

My dear sisters Hermine and Maria and brothers Dave and Herman,
Just want you to know, that I arrived safely to Italy. I mailed today a money order I hope you will receive it. It's $60. From now on my trust is in God. I hope he will not fail me. Please do not worry. If I haven't time to write tonight to Dave, please tell him not to worry and I'll write to him whenever I get a chance. I also have a note in the letter with the money order. Now with all my love till we meet again. Please tell Flora that the pen is beautiful and thanks! I'll write her when or as soon as I can! Love to you all Irving

P.S. Did you receive cabled $70? P.S. Write!

1944/1/6 Irving to Dave, Mt. Porchia, Italy (V-Mail, Slide 51)

January 6, 1944
Dear Dave,
I hope you have received my letters in the best of health. Here I'm thinking of you a lot. Sure would like to be with you. I'm OK. Please do not worry, because that does not help. Yes it's a little difficult to say, but you know my thoughts. I have written to Hermine and Maria and mostly I write to them, but thinking of you too! You will have to forgive me if I'm not very understandable, but everything comes at once. How are you? Please write to me. Now Emil is almost here. So I will write you some more later. Well, I hope God will help me and will meet again. With all my love your little, Brother Irving

1944/1/6 Irving to Family, Mt. Porchia, Italy (V-Mail, Slide 50)

January 6, 1944
Somewhere in Italy

My dear sisters, arrived to another spot and thinking of you. How are you my dear Hermine and Maria? I hope you are all in the best of health. I'm OK. How is Herman and Dave? I should write to them too, but from here is a little different. I should write to Flora, but I think she will have to wait till the war is over. I hope it won't be long. But you my darling I do want to write whenever I can. However I am not very good in writing. Please do not worry about anything, God will help us and we will meet again. How is everything back home? Please write whenever you can. I am remaining with all my love, your little brother, Irving
P.S. Write!

1944/1/11 David to Family (Book 3, 161-163)

January 11, 1944
Monday evening [no date on this letter]

My Dearests!
I received your letter, forgive me for not writing to you up till now. I received it on the fifth of this month. As you know one doesn't have the desire to write after work. I don't want to forget that you called me on

the telephone. I was going with the automobile with Spitler to California and I would like to have you ask him to give you in writing how much he paid me during the trip towards California, so that I can show how much I earned because shortly I'll have to show that statement. You can then mail it to me. If not, I will write to him.

I don't know anything to write you because I am working every day, only seven hours per day and [in] this particular work at times it's very difficult and you have to work very hard. Now I switched to another class. Where I was before there were five Jewish people and there always was a problem with them. Here at this place they are Christians. I'm the only Jewish person and I work all by myself. The work is such that each individual works by himself. The manager is a nice fellow. At the present time I am getting $1.51 an hour. I feel badly, I didn't get the one dollar and 57 cents. It's only $.06 difference, but in the long run it amounts to $25. I would have to be here for 10 weeks for the extra I am looking for. So I must accept it as is.

I received a letter from Ignác written on December 17. He wrote it in Hungarian. At this time he was preparing to go to a new place and used his old address to write. He wrote on V- mail. He doesn't write any news. He did not receive the packages from me or from you. I hope by now he received them.

This is the second week that the weather is good. It does not rain and it's sunny, but sometimes during [the] night it's very cold. Maria, you're writing how much you're earning. If you're working on a dress two days for five dollars, then you put in 10 hours that would mean 20 or 25 cents an hour, so your weekly wage for 60 hours would be approximately 15 or 18 dollars, is that true?! I would think you would like to know how much you earn per week? I hope that you will write it to me or tell me. This is enough for today, but in the near future I will write you more. Good luck. Please write. There's nothing new at this time. It's 9:30 in the evening and in a few minutes I will have to go to work. Therefore, good luck to you and everything the best. Forgive me, but I don't know what to write this time because I am not going any place even though I'm very close to Hollywood. Kisses, Dezső

1944/1/14 David to Hermine and Marie (Book 2, 87-89)

January 14, 1944
My Darlings!
Forgive me that I didn't respond this week, but I will make up for it soon. This week I got three letters from our little brother. But he wrote them on the 17th and 21st, it's good. I wrote to him a long letter. He got 35 letters from home on the 20th and all of them are mostly old. I'm hurrying with the writing right now because I want to mail it myself, so it would get there this week. So, you'll get it on Saturday. And I sent a picture to him also, it's good. I'm sure you got from him this week also.

I don't know any news. I believe I will work on Sunday also. So Mariska! I'm waiting for a report from you. You know I'm in a little trouble right now. I sent New Year cards to at least 20 people and I got responses. I'm afraid to respond to them because my English is not good, but somehow I will do that. So you better write me. I'll write you as well. Maybe I will write tomorrow also. I don't know any news this week. Everything is the same. This week there is nice summer weather. Yes, I saw it in the newspaper for 200-250 dollar it's available to go where Ignacz is, a round trip ticket for a boat ride is 4-500 dollars. Would you go Mariska? But first you must [get] the approval from Washington. So that's enough about this for today. So I'm in a hurry. The post office closes at 6 and it's 1/2 6 [5:30] already. So good luck! And you better write some gossip from Columbus to me. You write nothing. Send me a Sunday [Dispatch] "Dispats" I will send one to you too. On Sunday, I'll have to send one to our little brother, too. So I'm waiting for your lines.

You better write a lot. If you need anything, then you better ask for it. If I will work on Sunday, I will buy something for a price that nobody has in Columbus, which I should not write, but I will, a necklace that's made out of little snails. How beautiful! Real little ones and with matching earrings. You will love it [have a wonder about it]! So, you know what? Next week, on Monday, if God helps me, I will mail it. I'm telling you, it's beautiful! And you'll be surprised how much it costs. I will write you. Did you know that I had my birthday on January 11th? So the present will be there next week. Kisses, Dezső

1944/1/14 Irving to Dave, Mt. Porchia, Italy (V-Mail, Slide 53)

January 14, 1944

My dear brother Dave,

Hope this letter will find you in the best of health. I was in combat. I'm OK. I haven't written to Hermine or Maria about. If you want to let them know, so go ahead and tell them. Please do not worry. God is with us. I really don't know what to write you. Only I sure would like to be with you home. I'm hoping that God will be with me again and help me. There is no one but him! Please don't worry. I will write some more again. Here above you will find my new address. That the address I'll have until I return to the Good old America. Till we meet again! With all my love your little brother, Irving

Hello to Hermine, Maria, and Herman

1944/1/14 Irving to Family, Mt. Porchia, Italy (V-Mail, Slide 52)

January 14, 1944
Italy

My dear sisters Hermine and Maria and brother Herman,
I hope this letter will find you all in the best of health. I'm OK and hope to hear the same. Since I left Africa, haven't received any mail, but I guess it will follow me up someday. Please do not worry! I hope it won't be long and will see each other again soon. How is everything back home? Here isn't anything that I could tell you, but when I get home we'll talk about something that you might want to know. Regards to the relatives! I'll write to them when the war is over. I hope it won't be long! Till we meet again! Love from Irving

In God we trust!

1944/1/14 Irving to Family, Mt. Porchia, Italy (V-Mail, Slide 54)

January 14, 1944
Italy

My dear sisters Hermine and Maria and brother Herman,
Please forgive me for not writing you sooner, but I was very busy as you know how it is. Please don't worry, I'm OK and I hope to hear the same. God was with me and I hope he is going to be with me! He is the only one! I have written to Dave. Well my dear sweethearts I do not know what to tell you, but please don't worry. I'll write to you whenever I can. Here above you'll see my address, that's the one I'm going to use till I return to America. I hope it won't be long. I'll write you some more sometime in the future. Till we meet again! Love to you, your little brother, Irving

1944/1/16 David to Hermine and Marie (Book 15, 98-100)

Saturday night
My Darlings!
This afternoon I sent to Mariska's address an insured special delivery package, which means, if it will be broken you better report it at the post office and they will pay for it. But I hope it will arrive alright. There are 2 necklaces in the package from snail shells and a couple of earrings from 2 snail shells in matching color. Make sure,

...to exchange it with each other sometimes. That is not a shame! It's your business to agree about this. So, I will note in case it happens that somebody asks you to order something like it for them, the answer is NO! Currently, based on my calculation, only you will have something like this in Columbus and another girl. So, there will be 3 necklaces in the entire town. I hope you will like it! But you don't need to know about the third necklace! But the third person knows that I sent it to you too! So, do not think that it is foolishness. It is not polite to write about the price, but only so you know

the necklace was 3.95, there it's at least 4.35, the earrings 2.80 a pair. So, I'm only writing this so you know, it was not 50 cents! Please write whether you like it or not?! And if it's possible to get these in Columbus?!

I hope you are well! I'm thank God well. I hope you got my mail from yesterday! Yes, you better watch the "North Star" movie! It is pretty good! Lots of luck and have fun for everyone! I kiss you. Dezső
This week I did not get anything from you!

1944/1/16 Irving to Dave, Italy (V-Mail, Slide 56)

January 16, 1944
My dear brother Dave,
How are you? I hope fine. I'm OK for the time being. I hope you have received and understood my letter. It's not like in the movies! Yes my brother Dave, you are the first one to whom I mentioned being up in the front. And I don't think I will write to anyone till the war is over. I have written to Hermine and Maria, but didn't mentioned anything to them. I hope you will write to me. Please don't worry! God is the only one and gives strength to everything. It can't be explained, I hope it will end soon. That cannot go on much longer. Till we meet again! Take care of yourself! Say hello to Hermine, Maria and Herman. Remain with all my love, Your little brother, Irving

1944/1/16 Irving to Hermine and Marie, Italy (V-Mail, Slide 55)

January 16, 1944
Italy
My dear sisters Hermine and Maria,

Today is Sunday and have a little time to write you. How are you feeling? I hope fine. I'm OK. Please don't worry! Everything is OK. I have written to Dave and hoping to hear from him. I hope someday God will help me to return to America and the best of health. Dear Maria, thanks for the suggestion, but I don't need anything. I hope to be home soon in the best of health. I'll write to the relatives, but yet I haven't enough time. Please tell them. They will have to forgive me. Now I'm hoping to hear from you soon. I hope that it won't be long and God will help me and we will meet again! In God I trust and there is no one else! Remain with all my love, your little brother, Irving

Hello Herman?

1944/1/17 Irving to Dave, Italy (V-Mail, Slide 57)

January 17, 1944
Dear brother Dave,
Just a few lines to let you know that I'm OK. I hope you're fine. I have written our sisters. Yesterday I received a small package with candy bar from Hermine. It was delicious. I think now I'll get them all. How are you? Please write me whenever you can. I'll write you too. But if I don't write please don't worry. God will be with me and help me. I hope it will be over soon. One minute is enough of it. Please write me, that will satisfy me and don't worry! I hope to see you soon. Till we meet again! I remain with all my love, Irving

Regards to all!

1944/1/18 Louis Schwartz to Hermine and Marie (Book 17, 129)

Somewhere in Iceland 1-18-44
Dear Hermina and Maria,
As you see your letter which I just received had to make a long trip to catch up with me. It was nice to hear from you in this corner of the world. I hoped to be nearer to Irving but we soldiers have to go where they send us. I wrote last week to Irving in his first APO number, hope he'll get it, even if late. I've not heard from him for a long time neither from Dave. I'm glad that Irving likes the place where he is. I guess I'm going to like it here after I get used to this climate. I'll have to!! I spent Christmas and New Year's eve on the boat in a rough ocean doing nothing. We were glad when we arrived. I've to write you in English. You can write either way you want to but write often. It's nice to hear here from over there. I'll write you more next time. Love and best wishes, Lou

1944/1/20 David to Hermine and Marie (Book 18, 111-114)

January 20, 44
Dearests!

I know you will be surprised that I did not write for a week to you, but it is your fault. You did not write to me either. I did not hear from Ignác since Jan 20. If you have heard from him please send it to me. Here there is nothing new. It is raining here a lot, but if it wouldn't, I would have gone to Hollywood. I saw in the newspapers that there will be a dance given by a single girls organization, but because it is raining I'm not going. Mariska, I'm thanking you for taking care of things for my tax that I should get it. If he didn't send it, please call him again and ask him to mail it and I will pay him the expense, but he must mail it at once because it is 3 weeks late as it is. If he still doesn't want to mail it, I don't know what I will do. Maybe Herman can go there. It is not too far. Maybe if you will call him once more, the woman on the telephone is his wife, and tell her would he be so kind to do it and Herman will go and pick it up, or mail it and I will pay for the shipping. I don't have anything new. How are you all? How are you doing on the job, Hermina? You still have to pay it? How much do they pay? I'm happy that Maria likes her job. If you speak to the man who hired you, I am sending him my regards. Herman, do you like your medication? I know you can't object to it because I know it's good. If it doesn't help then let me know, and he will give back the money, but I'm sure it will help you. Just write to me. I thank you for the letter, the money, and the newspaper. Therefore, for today it is enough. Good luck and wishing you all the best. Kisses, Dezső

1944/1/20 Irving to Dave, Italy (V-Mail, Slide 59)

January 20, 1944
My dear brother Dave,

Today is just another day and I want you to know that I am OK. Hope you are fine and in the best of health. I hardly know what to write you, because I haven't received any mail from you. However I received a letter from Hermine. They are all well. The letter came more than a month. From here on, I believe I'll get my mail better or faster, because they have my correct address. Hope to receive that package you sent me. I sure wish that I could be with you. I hope this war will end soon. Please write me and don't worry. God will help me and everything will be all wright [sic]. How is your work coming along? Please write me all about. You tell me your work, because I can't tell you mine. Hope to see you soon. Time goes fast! I feel like an old man. Hope to be one!! Till we meet again! With all my love, Irving

1944/1/20 Irving to Family, Italy (V-Mail, Slide 58)

January 20, 1944
Italy

My dear Hermine, Maria and Herman,

Just received a letter from you my dear Hermine and I was glad to hear that you are all in the best of health. That letter came more than a month. Yes it takes time to follow me up. Hope that it won't be long now and I'll get all your packages. How are your work coming along? Please tell me or write me all about. Please don't worry if I'm not writing as often as I used to, but you know there is always some things that keeps me from writing. I sure hope that this war will end soon and then will have time to do everything. I have written to Dave and hopefully he will write me soon. Did you receive the cabled seventy dollars and money order of fifty dollars? I hope you did. Next payday I'll send home some more. If the war would end till then I wouldn't. You know why? Well, with all my love, Irving

1944/1/22 Maria to David (Book 3, 152-155)

January 22 - 44
Dear David!

Today is Saturday and I received your special delivery letter. I'm in a hurry to write to you. This week I was very busy and I couldn't write. Last evening Mary Cay was here, Hermine's friend and her husband, who was at home on furlough. The difference is that he in this country for a while. We are well. Hermine is working and I'm in a hurry to mail you this letter. Hermine's other friend made arrangements for a party for tonight, so she can't write you today, but will write tomorrow.

I'm glad to know that you are well. We received the package and I think we wrote you about it. One earring wasn't good, so I took it to the post and mailed it back to you. They said that you will make the arrangement. I believe by now you should have it. This was the yellow necklace. There's nothing new here. I don't know yet what will be with the sewing activity, I'm not sure whether I'll continue at present. I'm going to try it, if it's worthwhile, but I don't know. I do have good customers, but I had another one with new and old clothing and it was very dirty as you can imagine. I gave everything back to her this week that I didn't want to sew. My desire for this type of work disappears. For the first two weeks I earned about $40 and everyone was happy with it, but since then it has changed. I will be waiting a few days. I have to clean the house because I'm at home and I have more work. I know you are surprised by it. Please write what you do. We received a letter from our little brother from Italy. I hope God will help him. Kisses to you, Maria.

Irving also sends his regards and kisses.

1944/1/28 Dezső to Hermine and Marie (Book 4, 12-15)

Friday evening

Dearests!
At this time, there is nothing new. I received your letters today from Maria and from Hermine, too. You know, Maria, yours was late because the weather was very bad there. Therefore the plane was delayed because of that. Next time, mail it regular mail. If I mail it tonight by special delivery, you will receive it on Sunday. Hermine, you must be very busy because you forgot to seal the envelope. I went to the post office about the earring. I have to sign some papers and they wanted $6.60 to mail it. Next week, I will send another earring and a pin. Oh yes, listen, I wrote to you before about Spitler, the company where I worked and drove the taxi. I will have to get a statement from him on the phone. Please call them up. It is in the phonebook. The name is D. Spitler, 777 Fairwood Ave. Or Herman can go there when he has time, anytime late in the afternoon about 5 o'clock at 200 East Rich St., where their station is, that's where you can find them. How much did they take in withholding in 1943? Don't forget to mail it to me. It is very important. Therefore Maria, listen to me. I wrote to you about it. You should not work so hard, especially sewing. I want you to listen to me because you started the sewing already. I would not stop. I would keep it up, but I would not do it so cheaply. I would charge more, otherwise it's not worth it. I would advertise. This way, you can work yourself up to $15 or $25 or more and I would send you from Hollywood the latest looks and styles of the best dresses. 1 or 2 dresses a week. You can announce on the telephone that the cheapest for a fine dress is $15. I'm sure we will get you more. You can have better customers. You will get more money this way. Hermine, I didn't write for you yet. I don't have any news. Everything is the same. I did not hear from Irving. How did you like my pictures that I sent you? Irving's picture is with it. Please write as soon as you can. Here the weather is nice and [it's] like summer at 7:30 PM. I'm going to Long Beach. Maybe I will go to the temple there. But by 11 o'clock I must be back because then I go to work. Therefore, I'm wishing you the best of luck, in all the best, and be careful and take care of yourselves. Is the medicine helping you Herman? I hope it helps you. Until the next time, love, kisses, Dezső

1944/2/2 David to Hermine (Book 15, 117-121)

Feb 2. 44
My darlings!
Today I got a special letter from you Marcsa. I understood the situation. I'm sorry about my letter from yesterday! As far as the medicine is concerned, I only sent it to Herman and, if it's good or bad and if it's allowed to take it, I can only note this, Herman's medicine is not made out of chemicals, but from mint leaves and similar plants, which is good for anybody. It's been already the second week I'm taking it. This is a better stomach cleaner! So, it is enough about this for today.

Mariska, from today do not send me mail by special delivery, since my address is direct to the post office and this way I will get 24 hours 7 days [a week] service. I will get the air mail as fast as a special letter. I hope you will understand. So, my new address,
David Gluck
Box 894
Wilmington California

I'm writing what is surely the most important. Last week I sent Ignác's picture back home. I was sure that it was him on the picture. It was in the Jan.14th newspaper that means, it happened on the 13th. So, I got this letter from Ignác with today's mail in English.

[In English] My Dear Brother Dave, [In Hungarian] - I hope this letter will find you in the best of health. I was in combat (in battle) and I am OK. I did not write to Hermine nor Marcsa about this. If you want to let them know about this, go ahead and write it to them.

[In English] Dezső, do not worry! [In Hungarian] The dear God is with us. I truly don't know what to write to you, only, I would love to be with you at home in America, and I hope the dear God will be with me! And he will help me. There is no other help, only him! [In English] Please don't worry! I will write some more again. Here above you will find my new address. That's the address I will have until I return to the good old America. Till we meet again with all my love your little brother, Irving

Hello to Hermine, Maria, Herman

Address

PVT Irving Gluck

A.S.N 35633941

Co B. 6TH ARM. D. INF.

A.P.O. 251 % Post Master N.Y.

[In Hungarian] I did not send the letter because I want to send a package this week. He wrote the letter on Jan. 14th. So, as you can see, I was right that it is him in the picture. For that matter, it is allowed to put it in the newspaper since the censor allowed the new address and he was in combat. I would put it in the newspaper anyway, so let them see that he is a man! If you will show the newspaper and that it was sent from California, they will even put your pictures in it. So, Hermine! Finally I see that you are thinking smartly.

I hope you are feeling well and you know, that there is "Hospitalization" for you that pays for the surgery and hospital expenses. As long as you were at Dr. Clark it does not matter, tell him and he will deal with it for you. I did not write anything to Ignác about this and I just sent an 8oz candy that he will receive as a letter. So, I wrote enough for today. Yes, I live where I used to live, only I changed post offices. Yes Mariska, if I will get anything from the tax office, about my new tax information, please send it to me. OK? So, lots of good luck and good health! Kisses to you many times, and I wish you everything good until I will see you again! Kisses, Dezső

1944/2/3 David to Marie (Book 15, 123-130)

Wilmington Tuesday Afternoon Evening

My darlings!

I can't understand what is the reason why I didn't get any mail this week from you?! Although, I sent a newspaper cutout to your address from Ignác and I can hardly wait for the response to that and there is nothing anywhere. It seems to me that I still need to beg now, like I did before, if I want to ask for something. I hope you will write, otherwise I will behave the same way with the writing. I'm doing a favor anyway for his majesty Mr. Gluck and he didn't even write - 'You dog why did you send it? I did not ask for this!'

So this is how it goes. But I am the fool because I'm writing. But I can do it differently also. It's not important for me to write, when it isn't even worth it for you to respond to me. I know you are busy, but still! You should've responded to that letter! But I hope that I am wrong and I will get a letter from you!

Mariska! I got from you an airmail on Saturday. I understood everything. But do you remember that I wrote everything to you beforehand? I knew it before that you will not earn more than 25-30¢ an hour. But this is your problem- If you sew, you better earn from it and not struggle! If you sew, you must earn at least 5 dollars per a day! That is the minimum! But you must make at least a dollar per hour! In a factory, without any responsibility, and you have to make 75 cents per hour.

It's been two weeks and I didn't get any mail from Ignác. Hermine, for your earrings and brooch you need to wait at least 2 weeks because that company will get something like the one that was broken. Currently it comes in only one color. If you need it in one color, I will send one to you immediately. But if you need a "combination" [matching one] then you need to wait!

What's going on with the housewife and the garage you talked about?! If no, you better not pay her for two months' rent! And you better let her sue you! She will not. Don't worry! She knows that you will not do that. That is why she doesn't want to pay. What's the news there? I don't know any news here. It looks like it's going to rain. Did you get mail from Ignác? I hope you are well!

How are the dear relatives? Oh yes! Did you know that you can send an 8oz package every week to Ignác? You can send a candy bar in it. And you should send one! It's the three of you there so you can send 3 little packages. You can send 3 different days or you can send more. You can note my name as well. But you need to send a simple package. But you better be careful because you can only send 1/2 pound because they will not take a heavy one. In a small package like this at least 3 candy bars fit! He will get this as fast as a letter since it will go like a letter. So, I believe I wrote enough for today! I hope I will get a proper response! Marcsa, I will send the package to you this week. Ok!? You better tell Mr. Gluck that I thank him very much for his kindness. Marcsa, I absolutely need the tax statement from "Safety Cab". If you don't ask for it, I have to from here. Please let me know. What's new in Columbus? Hermine and Marcsa, what do you think? Should I send something to Arthur's little daughter? You better write it to me! Does the German man still live there in the neighborhood? What does he do? Does he still have a big mouth?

So, I'm closing my lines for today, I wrote enough!
So, I'm waiting for a letter from you before I will write again. I will send a little picture, I think it looks like me!
So, I wish you good luck and you better write. I'm waiting for your lines and I hope it is about good information. Kisses, Dezső

1944/2/5 David to Family (Book 2, 95-97)

My Darlings!
Today I didn't get any mail from you. I hope you are well. Hermine, you as well. Nothing came from Ignác. Did you get any mail from him since then? Hermine, you know, if the house wife doesn't want to give you the garage money go to the O.P.A. and ask if you can take it out of the monthly rent. I believe yes. I did not send the package to him yet. Here, it goes a little harder than in Columbus. But next week I will send it for sure. You better write to me! Did Herman get the medication? They sent it on January 25th. I don't know any news. Maybe I will go to the dance today, the "President's Ball." Oh! Supposedly there will be something here too- actors are going to be here! For now, I don't even know what to write. I hope you have the new tax statement from the tax office showing the salary and the statement from Spitler. Please send it to me as soon as possible! Today the weather is pretty nice.

Hermine, can you eat normally now? And you, Mariska! Don't kill the devil! It's not important to work so hard. Why don't you take a job like Hermine? Hermine, let me know if the insurance company paid anything. They should pay! By the way, if the surgery and room isn't your responsibility as long as you are at home, you can go to the hospital for a few days. You pay for 21 days a year. If the clerk will send you down, then you can go to the other place.
So I wrote enough for today. You better write a lot and about everything! Can you see that I was right about Ignác's picture. He wrote at the same time when the picture was in the newspaper.
Oh, did the picture come on January 14th? I wish you good health and everything good. Today I wrote 2 letters to our little brother. I wonder if he got any of the packages yet. I kiss you and wish you good luck and you better take care of yourself! See you later! Kisses, Dezső

1944/2/6 Undated David to Marie (Book 15, 110-111) Spitler file

[Dated by Spitler file and Dave's mention of writing about Pearl Harbor the day before in the next letter on 2/7]

Sunday afternoon

Dear Mariska!
Just got your special del[ivery] letter and I'm in a hurry to write a few lines in response. Like you indicated that our little brother is in the 6th Division. That does not mean anything. They belong to another Division, as you can see in the newspaper article, the 5th Army is indicated, and in the fifth there are a lot of Divisions, but it is not allowed to write how many of them are in it. So, when they mention the 5th Division, the little brother is there too! I hope you got the Special Del[ivery] that I sent this week, where I notified about the letter to our little brother. Also, Mariska, if the medicine will work for Mr. Herman, if he wants to repay the

2^{10} for it, you better use that money for stamps! You and Hermine! I will be in Long Beach to see if I got it already, because I ordered earrings and a necklace. Oh yes! Mariska, I'm not surprised that you are in trouble when you go and sew for the Stern girl. You know, if she will not be satisfied, she will gossip about it in the entire town. Please send a Sunday paper to me!

Be smarter in the future, please! You don't depend on waiting for beggars. How would she have the money? Just let her pay for it, so she will have something to gossip about to her mother. The entire town will know what they did and how they lived etc.. So, I hope you will be smarter in the future! What did they say about it? I don't know yet, if it will work out or not, but I did do an application to go to Hawaii, to Pearl Harbor to work in a navy shipyard, if they pay well. And there I could work for overtime a lot. I will get a response to that in two weeks. They will pay for the cost back and forth and the salary starts when I will leave the address. It is warm there for 12 months a year. I believe that a contract lasts for 18 months. I have to be there for that long. This is a civil service job and constant, and is good for 6 months after the war is over. I don't know any other news. You know, they pay well here too, but there is no overtime. We will see what it's going to be. So, lots of luck and everything good. Kisses, Dezső

P.S. You better write a lot this week and absolutely send the Spitler file statement about the tax! I will send a newspaper to you!

1944/2/7 David to Hermine (Book 15, 113-115)

Monday evening

Dear Herminka!

I got your precious lines and I am in a hurry to respond. Thank you for our little brother's letter and I will send one letter from him also to you. Please send it back to me! Ok? You know, I thought of something. I have at least 3 new letters and I have older letters. I will go to different post offices and I will send 2-3 packages this week. You can also do that! He should have enough over there. I will send at least two packages tomorrow. Canned plum for compote and peaches too, figs and a package of candy, and a candy bar. Tomorrow I will get candy and gum too. So, I will send it tomorrow, this way. Poor thing, he wrote it in the past that it's 164 cents for a can of peaches. This way I will send 2-3 cans and I will send other things. But, if you will send too, that way Herman, Marcsa and Hermine should and maybe Dezső will also, so he will not be like one address. But do not forget to send this letter back! OK? There is no news. There is a nice summer weather here. I hope you are well! How is his Majesty Mr. Herman Gluck? I hope he already owns his own bank. You better write to me a lot! OK?

That means, that Mariska would come here. My answer is no. Only, if you are coming too! It is hard to find an apartment and if there would be one, the entire family could live in it for that money. As far as the town goes, here Marcsa could make good money. She could get into easily to a Hollywood Studio to sew. What do you say Marcsa?! To sew clothes for movie stars? Do not think that I'm joking, you can get in easily. It does not go the way it goes there. Here they are not that picky - I wrote it yesterday that it's possible that I will go to Pearl Harbor. I could make good money there. I don't know if they will take me because I need to know the job well. Although, I know about it a little- So Mariska, if you want to come here, only the two of you.-Herman can stay there. This will scare him, at least he will get better this way. For that matter, Ignác would not mind it. He would like it here better.

So, this is enough for today. Kisses, Dezső

P.S. Hermine, please absolutely send me the Spitler tax statement. Yes, you know you can deduct from your tax the winter coat you paid 10% tax and sales tax on the package and materials. etc

1944/2/7 David to Irving (Book 18, 74-76)

L[ong] Beach 2.7.44

My Dear Brother Irving!

I received the other day your letter and may the Lord Bless You and help you to be O.K. and help you to come back. Between us - and I am sure that God will help you to come back. - As I can figure it out you are not at the beach and you ain't at Rome, so you must be again in the front line, away from Rome in fire again! Oh Boy you have plenty, please if you can or may please let me know what you are doing, gun crew or machine gunner what I hope you ain't. As I think you are about 300 miles from Polány I hope you be there soon and safe. But be please be very careful-

Your letter was really wonderful and you now are a perfect English writer, you are doing very fine. I made my lunch today, it was very good "gulyas (meat stew)" [Hungarian - meat stew] and roast. I wish you could be here and help me to eat. Don't you think you have a chance to get a furlough? Some came home for a few weeks - you know the papers aren't oft[en] with Italy news, France is the main. You know we have plenty of Italy's prisoners of war here and they come and go free. [The] only thing they have on their American uniform [is] the country they [are] from. Oh Boy are they hungry - are they good to you boys there? I hope they are. I don't know no news, nothing is going on. Today we have a good day. I am going out to the beach and will send you newspapers and you will have in it some funnies! Did you get the packages from me? Please if you care from home to get something please let me know - Please forgive me if I don't write to you often for now. I work 10 hours a day and have to take care of everything - you know if you would come to L.B. you would like to stay here for good. You know this is a good place to stay. But you know I will try to write you more often - But if you won't hear from me often please forgive me, will you? I will do my best - Hoping to hear from you, and do hope to hear - Best of luck and wishing you everything the best. Please be very careful what ever you do. Dear Brother boy til now - hoping he be with you soon in the U.S.A. till then with all my best wishes to you, and thinking of you always with the best thought. [Illegible] with love to you to a happy safe return to us home. God Bless you!
David

1944/2/8 Dezső to Hermine and Marie (Book 4, 7-11)

Feb 8th, 1944
Dear Sisters,
To surprise you I will write to you this letter in English. I wonder if you will now [sic] to read it, I think I make plenty mistakes, but I write to different people and the[y] now have to figure it out. I have received a letter from ocskös [little brother]. He wrote this the 20th of Jan. He received a letter from Hermine what she wrote to him about Dec the 20th. He is okay. I think he is in the front line. I have sent him a package today and I hope to send him this week more in some one else name. You know I have more letters with the new A.P.O. and the old and this way I will make it. You think so, I try to write to as often as I can. The last few days I wrote to him 1 or 2 a day. I hope he will get them. Please write me. How are you Hermine? I hope okay.

How about you miss Mary. How is business, O.K. I hope that you have better customers, I won't work for jerks place. Be careful with your wonderful customers!! How is Mr. King Gluck, I hope he likes the medicine. It is okay. I know he can see that it is in good, it is perfect and it will help him for sure, but he has to eat like a man, not like a dog!
[In Hungarian]
So, I don't know, if you will be able to read the Letter in English. But I hope yes! You better write to me and to Ignác as well. Mr. Gluck [Herman] can write too. He could do that much to think that he is there also. And what would happen if you wouldn't write to him either and would not make as much money at all. So he could at least send a package to our little brother. So I'm waiting for your letters. I wish you lots of luck and kisses. Dezső

You better send me the tax paperwork! Ok? I absolutely would not want to go to jail for that. I hope you don't want to see me there!
I hope you won't get angry about my comment. So you dear Hermine, I will continue to you for now. Now the way you notified it, that Saturday you'll be working all day. Surely they will have a son for you! No?! The weather is wonderful here. There is pretty nice weather like in the summer at home, only a little cold at night. If you see Mary Kay give her my best. I wrote her greetings, but didn't know the correct address. I don't know if she got it. Her husband is home for good or only for vacation? So I really don't know what to write right now. I want to write to the Kedves Gluck [Herman] also, so I will finish. You better write so I will write more often as well. I hope you like the necklace! I repeat, no need to know that a 3rd person has the same. I repeat, the 3rd person knows that the two of you have the same chain also!
So enough about this. Good luck!
So very respected, very much worthy and deeply loved Mr/Sir Herman Gluck!
I believe with this [form of] address you can be satisfied! Yes? If no! Write it to me and I will come up with a better one! Good?! So this week in your case I did the following:

I went this week to Long Beach. I saw a doctor that is specializing in the problem you had or have. Therefore tomorrow I will mail you some medication. You will receive what I send maybe Tuesday or Saturday. I hope you will like it. You have to take it twice daily 15-20 days and a glass of water. When the first glass is finished [drink] the second glass. When you finish you will feel better. Therefore one or two weeks you will feel better and your stomach pain will stop. And your back also. After that you will feel better. If it doesn't help, he'll give me the money back. Therefore I hope it will help you. Besides this, you have to watch your diet also. You will owe me only $2.10 only if you want to give it, otherwise you don't have to, but [you should] because you're making as much as I do. I was taking similar medication. Also, just to be sure it is good, eat an orange once a week with the skin, the same way like an apple. You'll see in one week you will feel better. The 210 cents we'll be worth $210. Therefore wishing you good luck. Kisses to all, Dezső

P.S. Herman, if you think you don't want to have the medication, then don't pay for it.
[On the side] Hermine and Maria this medication is good for everyone. Especially Maria. I promise it's good.

1944/2/8 (a) Irving to Hermine and Marie, Anzio Beachhead, Italy (V-Mail, Slide 61)

February 8, 1944
Italy

My dear sisters Hermine and Maria,
Time goes fast! It's almost a month that I have written to you. I hope this letter finds you all in the best of health. In the last couple days I have received 29 letters from you. And also a package from Dave and Bertha. You know how I felt after all this time of waiting. Oh yes, I received a big package and a couple small ones from you too. I have written on January the 18th but the letter returned to me. Guess the reason. Well my darlings many thanks for your thoughts in your letters and thanks a million for the package, and I hope God will help me to return home soon in the best of health. Today I'm OK and I'll try to write some more, however I want to write to Dave and other relatives. Remember 4 years ago, and today! I cannot say anything, just hope and trust in God! That is about all! How are you Herman? I hope fine. I remain with all my love your little brother, Irving

The candy was DELICIOUS!!

1944/2/8 (b) Irving to Dave, Anzio Beachhead, Italy (V-Mail, Slide 62)

February 8, 1944
My dear brother Dave,
I hope you have received my letters, that I have written a month ago. Since than [sic] there wasn't any mail service, that's why I haven't written. How are you? I hope fine. I have received a package from you. The candy was delicious. Many thanks for it. You know in a few minutes and it was gone. You know how it is. I also received a letter from you. It's nice to know that you really think of me! Also received a package from Bertha and 29 letters from home. That's really something! I hope you'll write me again soon. That picture you sent me is not so good. If you get a chance please send me a better one in your next letter. Remember 4 years ago in this time, well today is just the opposite. I hope and trust in God! That's about all. Till we meet again with all my love your brother, Irving

1944/2/8 (c) Irving to Family, Anzio Beachhead, Italy (V-Mail, Slide 60)

February 8, 1944
Italy

My dear sisters Hermine, Maria, and brother Herman,
I hope this letter finds you all in the best of health. I have written one letter already and now I'm trying to write some more. I hardly know what to say. Your letters made me feel better. Here letters means a lot. It's not your fault at all that the letters come in late. But there wasn't any mail service for a while or since I have written to you last. This month is a famous month. Many things happened to us 4 years ago. I hope that God will be with me and help me once more. Time really goes fast. Remember the first week in February 1940?!

Today I'm almost like it. I trust in God and hope that my wish will come through. Till we meet again, remain with love your brother, Irving

1944/2/11 Irving to Dave, Anzio Beachhead, Italy (V-Mail, Slide 66)

February 11, 1944
My dear brother Dave,
Received a letter from you that you have written some time in October. Believe me I want to write you as often as I can. But a couple weeks ago I told you what goes on. I can't explain anything. I know you understand me well. Even though I don't write you, you just go ahead and write me. God will help me and when I get back I will tell you the rest. For the time being I'm OK. Please do not worry! I have received 17 letters yesterday, but I can't answer it at once. I'll try to write each day some. Hoping that it won't be long and everything will be all wright [sic]. Till we meet again! Remain with love, your brother, Irving

1944/2/11 Irving to Family, Anzio Beachhead, Italy (V-Mail, Slide 65)

February 11, 1944
Italy

My dear sisters and brothers,
As you know you cannot plan anything in the army. In the last couple of days I plan to write home and to the relatives. But something always came up and I had to do first. However I was glad to do it, because over here you know what goes on. And if you do it or able to do it, you are all wright [sic]. To all that we have to be thankful to God. Wherever you are if you think of Him you feel better. At the present time I'm OK. Hoping that, God will help me and listen to our prayers. Sooner is better! Please don't worry! You know me, if I'm able to write you I'll! Hope this letter finds you all in the best of health. Remain with all my love, your brother, Irving

P.S. Regards to the relatives!

1944/2/11 Irving to Hermine, Anzio Beachhead, Italy (V-Mail, Slide 64)

February 11, 1944
My dear sister Hermine,
Once again received 17 letters from home and I'm glad to know that you are all in good health. It was a surprise to get that picture of you Hermine with your girl friends. You know the first thing came into my mind, that I was back home with you. After looking that picture I find myself home sick. Wondering why can't I be there. That's life! Hope that it won't be long and God will help me to return home. One minute is enough of waiting and hoping. However that's all we can do. Thanks a million for your letters and please give my regards to the relatives and neighbor. Hoping to see you soon, your little brother, remains with love, Irving

P.S. WRITE ME

1944/2/11 Irving to Maria, Anzio Beachhead, Italy (V-Mail, Slide 63)

February 11, 1944
Italy

My dear sister Maria,
Hope this letter finds you in the best of health. I sure was glad to receive all those fine letters that you have written to me. Sorry I'm not able to answer all of your letters as I should, but I know you'll forgive me. I received letters from New York, Cleveland, Janny, and from Louis Schwartz and wasn't able to answer it. As I said in one of my letters, that you cannot plan anything in the army and that's why I'm forgiven. Hope they will understand me someday. Please don't worry even though I don't write as often as I used to. It will come a day that we'll all be happy and our dreams will come through. Till we meet again, with all my love, your brother Irving

Please don't worry! God is with us!

1944/2/17 Irving to Family, Anzio Beachhead, Italy (V-Mail, Slide 67)

February 17, 1944
Italy

My dear sisters and brothers,
Just a line to let you know that I'm OK and hope that this letter will find you all in the best of health. I wish I could fly home and talk to you all. Hope that someday our dreams will come through. Please don't worry! God will help us and everything will be all wright [sic]. Dear Marie, I'm glad that you like your job. Please take care of yourself. Herman, don't work too hard, however I wish I was there, and do anything but that! Your letters are wonderful dear Hermine and Maria. Please write me whenever you can. I know you think of me a lot, believe me so do I! Give my regards to Dave I'll write to him maybe later. I remain with all my love, Irving

I have not written to the relatives yet. Regards to them all!

1944/2/15 Undated Dezső to Hermine and Marie (Book 4, 18-19) missing last page

[Dated by necklace Dezső sent, the letters received on Dec 26 and 29th, lecture about sewing, mentioning Mary Kay again]

Dearests,
Two days ago I received from you 2 letters, but I just came home. I was just writing to you yesterday. I was very sleepy. Even though I'm still sleepy it is difficult to sleep during the daytime because it was very hot like summer, therefore I didn't have a chance to write before. I wrote to you as miss Maria. I hope you will see I'm right. Therefore as you wrote who your buyers are. Therefore I thought it is good to arrange it in advance if you have a better class of people as your customer. Then let's do it this way if you want to if you have lots of work at this. You take it only two or three weeks or more only if you finish whatever you started and it's already there you should not take anymore. This way you can get out of it [by saying] because at this time I'm very busy and am not able to take more. And you won't need to get someone to help you. Only take what you can do yourself otherwise it is not worth it because you have to give away more than you get. It's not worth it. Anywhere you will go, you'll see, take any kind of work, even when they do only one or two months they promise they will not make it before. This way you will see it is not worth to do it. Work less. Even the better places do this. Next week I will go to Hollywood and will get you the latest styles. I hope you're not going to work for nothing. By the way, you never told me about the five dollar dress. How long did it take you to make it? Probably three days. You know in Europe for only five hours they charge for one day. One is too much. Therefore, you do what is the best. It is up to you, not me. I hope by now you received the necklace and you like it. From Irving I received the letter that he wrote to you December 26 and what he wrote to me was the 29th. From what he wrote I can see the letter that he wrote to you was from Italy where you were in the same hotel. Therefore he mentioned if you remember. And a letter for me have to pay if he can get it. He sends his best regards to you all. Here I don't have anything new at this time. It's 7 o'clock [and] I will leave to work at 11:30. I want to mail this letter tonight so you will receive it Sunday. I hope you are not angry for the lawyer's address therefore dear Hermine I will continue at this time. As you mentioned all day Saturday you're working probably they will pay you extra. At this time the weather is beautiful here like summer at home. Only at night it sometimes gets cool. If you see Mary Kay give my best wishes to her. I sent her New Year's wishes. The post office address I did not know. I don't even know if you received it or not. Her husband was finally at home or just on furlough? At this time I'm sorry I can't write anything special. I want to write! Therefore I want you to please write. I will try to do the same. Will try to write more often. Hope you like the necklace. I mention again that you don't have to know the third person.

1944/2/22 Helen Perl Goldstein to Hermine (Book 17, 381-384)

Cleveland Ohio
Feb 22 - 1944
Dear Herminka!

I know my unexpected lines will surprise you. But, as you know, there is no mountain that long, that will not end. I did not hear from you since 1942 Nov. 2nd, therefore today I am writing. But, if I remember well, I sent a New Year greetings too that did not get a response. Besides that, I hope to hear the best about all of you. My dear husband and I are well, We live in great happiness and agreement, my man is an exceptional man. May the Lord keep him.

My Hermine, to get to the point, let me write the following, the other day I had guests and there was a noble woman. She noticed your picture and she was wondering about you. She asked me, if I can ask you, if you would be willing to get to know him for the purpose of marriage with a local, specifically handsome man? The person is looking for a European girl, and adding to it a blond, and pretty. The mentioned woman found you very beautiful and she believes that the young man's relative is well off and about 34 years old. So, if you are interested write it and decide a time when you can come over. Naturally, you will be our guest. What do you know? Maybe it is God's will? I'm sure you heard that An Reich got married and how well. I would have never believed that she'll have such good luck and that guy would marry her. So, my Herminka come on over! I hope you will not regret it! How's Mariska? And the boys? I hope to hear the best! Waiting for a quicker response, kiss your brothers and sister. Helen

P.S. In the past week I got a message from home through the Red Cross. Although, a short one with few words, that they are healthy and I should write often. What do you hear about the Shvarz boys. I haven't heard anything about them for years. I hope we will talk more about everything in person!
Helen Goldstein

1944/2/23 Irving to Dave, Anzio Beachhead, Italy (V-Mail, Slide 69)

February 23, 1944
My dear brother Dave,
Just received your letter from Feb. 5th and I'm glad to know that you are well. I'm somewhere on the ANZIO beach head. I know that you were surprised to see it, however I don't know if my sisters know it. I have not mentioned anything to them. I guess that way is better. They would worry too much. Please Dave don't worry! I know you do! But I'm saying again not to worry. God is the one that makes our heart to relax. I hope he will be with me and help me! Yet I should be home and celebrate with you and family. Yesterday was Feb. 22nd. It was a grand day four years ago. Look at me now?! Well, I guess that's the way it was written to be. Thanks a million for your package and your thoughts. Also received that long letter and cards of California. I hope to be there with you someday! Love from your little brother, Irving

1944/2/23 Irving to Family, Anzio Beachhead, Italy (V-Mail, Slide 68)

February 23, 1944
Italy

My dear sisters Hermine and Marie, and brother Herman,
Received a couple letters from you and I'm glad to hear that you are all well. I'm OK too. I should've been home yesterday on that celebration! It was February 22 I know you all remember it. That day cannot be forgotten. However look at me now! Almost there where I started from. Now I'm hoping that it won't be long and we will meet again! Back in the good old U.S.A. I trust in God that he will help me to a safe return to America, soon! I have received the box of cookies my dear Hermine, and many thanks for it! It was delicious! My thoughts are always with you. Hope to be back soon and then we will celebrate more than ever. I remain with all my love your brother, Irving

1944/2/24 Irving to Dave, Anzio Beachhead, Italy (V-Mail, Slide 72)

February 24, 1944
My dear brother Dave,
Hope that this letter will find you in the best of health. I have written a letter yesterday and I hope you will receive it. How are you Dave? Hope that you are well. How is everything in California? On that post cards everything looks so nice and quiet. I sure would like to be there with you. Any place in America. You have written in your letter that you would like to drop in and see me. I would rather say that! Stop in and stay there, oh boy! That would be wonderful. I hope that God will help and we will have many good and happy

moments together in that good old U.S.A. In closing this letter in God I trust and till we meet again with all my love. Your brother, Irving

PS WRITE SOON!
Regards to the family!
Back home!

1944/2/24 Irving to Family, Anzio Beachhead, Italy (V-Mail, Slide 71)

February 24, 1944
Italy

My dear sisters Hermine and Marie, And brother Herman,
If I would begin to write you all day even then I couldn't answer all of your letters, so you must forgive me if I just answer of the letters received yesterday. I'm glad that everyone is well. I know if I was there I could talk to you all day long and never tire. I hope that God will help me and it won't be long that we will meet again back in America. Yet at the present time I'm saving your letters. When I get a chance I'll read it over again and someday it will bring back some memories. I'm OK and thinking of you all, always. Hope this war will end soon. Till we meet again I remain with all my love, Irving

P.S. Take good care of yourselves and don't worry

1944/2/24 Irving to Herman, Anzio Beachhead, Italy (V-Mail, Slide 70)

February 24, 1944
Italy

My dear brother Herman,
Just a line to let you know that I'm thinking of you too. How are you Herman? I hope you're feeling fine. You are pretty busy I guess, you haven't written to me for a long time. Hermine and Marie told me all about you, even Dave told me some in his letter. Well Herman if you are busy and cannot write me a letter, so just drop me a note. How about it Herman?

I haven't much to say this time, but when I get home you will see we will have a lot of fun together. You will take a vacation and we will go some nice and quiet place. Please write me whenever you can. My trust in God! Till we meet again! Remain with love, Irving

P.S. Love to Hermine and Marie

1944/2/26 David to Marie (Book 2, 90-94)

Thursday night

Dear Mariska!
I got your letter today and you will see that it was your fault not mine that I didn't write. Like I noted in my previous letter, I did not get any mail from you for a week. So I was waiting for a response from you. But if you write to me, then I will write to you as well. I will attach a letter here from our little brother, in case you did not get it, you will see it then. But please be so kind to send it back to me! OK? Poor thing, the way he said it that the package was ripped apart in a few minutes. What a miracle that they stick together there, what is necessary to be that way! And it indicates that it's been 4 years since he came and today he again goes back there. I hope God will help him. He is there where they fight on the beach head at Rome. Since he wrote there was no letter. But I hope that after February 8th he went back to rest. I wish I am right. You know last week I was at a supposedly famous psychic and he said that our little brother is ok.

The good God will help him and you will see him in the same health the way he left. It will be 1½ year until he comes back because the war will take 1½ year until it ends. And luckily he will see the family in Polyán again. So, I have faith in that, thank God, the dear God, will help him and everything is going to be fine. Thanks for the news, Hermine. It comes handy to read a little gossip in the newspaper. Did you subscribe to it? So Herman, how does the medicine taste? Did you get better? I know for sure, it helps for me. Write it! (let me know) How much do you make now? How many hours do you work? How much do you make an hour? Do you regret that you left the rubber business? So you better write! And more importantly, write to Ignác! Yes, here it's important for you, you know, you made $200. You don't believe it, right? But it's here.

Listen good. You were being drafted to the army and you got honorable discharge papers. So, you will get 200 dollars, understand!! This is not a joke, it's serious! Find out where to go to sign up. I believe at the Veteran Administration. Check in the phonebook where the building is and go and you will get 200, why would you be better than others, others get too so you could as well! You better write what happened! Write for sure about it! I don't know any news here. Today there is nice warm weather! It rained yesterday! I don't know any details about Pearl Harbor. I will see what's going to happen! You know I want to make money and they pay there. I don't know the total because they will pay from the day I leave from here. But I don't know what it's going to be, maybe they won't even hire me because I don't have any experience. So I will write what it will be!

Marcsa, you asked me about my car. I still have it and it's worth more than when I bought it. If I leave, I will sell it. The weather is nice there for 12 months. This week I will get my raise. 6 cents for an hour, which is the highest here. So I will get 157 instead of 151. But I have to pay for the Union 25 dollars for more membership. But that's the way it goes. The monthly salary is 6 and 7 dollar! Have you seen the News Reel when the President gave a ship to the French? Did you see it? We make the same and I believe that it was from our factory. - You know, a shipyard looks nice on the film, but to be in it, one can get bored! I work on a ship that is ready already and it's on the ocean (in the harbor). Here you only see ships everywhere, small and big ones. This is the main place for the boats! So this is enough for today. It's not important to pass it around. Good luck and kisses. Dezső

P.S. You better write a lot. It's not important to send anything because I am here 24 hours 7 days a week. By by

1944/2/28 Ann Unknown to David (Book 14, 78-80)

Feb 28, 1944
Dear Dave:

Very glad to have heard from you again. Your letters are very enjoyable and will always try to answer them as soon as possible. Also glad to hear that all is well with you. Have been feeling much better myself and the children are all right excepting the little boy has a slight cold as yet. But I guess that goes with the climate here. One day it is nice and the next day bad.

Feeling like I would like to travel again soon so as I said before if my husband goes overseas I will try California. According to the way he writes it doesn't look so good for him, I hope not though as after all I wouldn't like to see it. However, if I do come there, hope you'll still be there as it would be wonderful to have a real friend in a strange place.

Went to a move today and saw a picture called "Sahara." It was a good show. Do you like the moving pictures and have you seen any movie stars since you've been there? My cousin, who is in the army was there and he says they're not what they're put up to be. Just have a lot of money. Wish I had some of it. I could sure do great things. But guess I'll have to be satisfied with my measly allotment, at least for a while anyway. Can't do much on that. Would like to see that Los Angeles paper you said you would send. I find things like that interesting. Well, Dave keep on writing me as it's really good to get your mail and I really look for them. Will close for now as I'm pretty tired and think I'll "hit the hay." Hoping to hear from you again soon. As ever,
Your friend, Ann

1944/2/29 Marie to David (Book 8, 34-35)

Dear David,
I got your letter yesterday and I'm happy to hear that you are healthy. We are well. We got a letter from our little brother yesterday. He is ok, only very busy. Poor thing he is on the frontline. Every minute is a lot from

that and he got from [what we sent] 32 letters at first and then another 17 also. He wrote that he got a package from you and from Bertha and a big one from us and a smaller one.

I hope God will help him and he can go home soon in the greatest health. I will change the subject to my job. Yes, I already met that man twice, but it really isn't to my taste since then. Yes, my present job is very different. They just opened up a new kind of job in a new department. They did not give it out yet. The place is clean, fresh and the job is not so hard. In other words, I have to work.

But the job is small and I work for quantity. Approximately 15 cents an hour payment for now. I'm making [barrage] balloons [ballonokat=balloons] for the war. 100% defense job. And I like it. I'm not working on a machine. I wrote enough now. There is no news. Only it is winter, as it shows, since it's been snowing all day long. You better write and take care! I'm very busy.
Greetings and kisses,
Maria

1944/3/2 Irving to Dave, Anzio Beachhead, Italy (V-Mail, Slide 76)

March 2, 1944
My dear brother Dave
I have received three letters from you, that you have written on February 7-8th. I'm glad to hear that you are well and in good health. Your letters remind me of lot's things that happened a long time ago. However after reading it, it seemed [as] if it was only yesterday. Time really goes fast. Doesn't it? I sure would like to be that young as at the time, when those things happened. Today I would not have any problem to solve, because somebody else would do it for me. That's you. Yes I was glad to see you back on the [train] station, but time went so fast that a person hardly realized it only after it's gone. We are hoping together that it won't be long till it's over and we will meet again in the best of health in the U.S.A. Please don't worry about things that happened. My trust in God, with all my love, your brother Irving

Give my love to Hermine, Maria and Herman.

1944/3/2 Irving to Dave, Anzio Beachhead, Italy (V-Mail, Slide 77)

March 2, 1944
My dear brother Dave,
This is my second letter, that I'm hoping it will find you in the best of health. I'm OK, as usual and I don't want you to worry about it. I received 21 letters from home yesterday. They were telling me about that article in the papers. I don't know anything about it. I'll see when I get the paper from you. Did you tell anything about me to them? In their letters they are guessing, but not sure of it. That way they are not worrying so much. Their letters sounds different than yours. They think it's almost like home. I don't have to tell you, because you know what it is. For example, waiting for the next minute to come and when it came to be glad of it and then hope for the next minute. A Jerry plane just came over and I have to put the candle out and sweat him out in the dark and hoping that he will drop his eggs some place else. As you know, I trust in God! Hope to see you soon, good night, with all my love

1944/3/2 Irving to Family, Anzio Beachhead, Italy (V-Mail, Slide 73)

March 2, 1944
Italy

My dear sisters Hermine and Maria,
I have received 24 letters and one package from you and Maria. I'm glad to hear that you are all well and in good health. It was very sweet of you to send me that birthday present. Your thoughts explained everything. I read it over and over again and I couldn't find any ending. That is because I think of you so much. Believe me I do. God is the one who really knows. Hope that someday I can prove it to you. Thanks a million for your thoughts and the cookies were very good. It tasted good. However it did not last very long. When I get a package, we all gather around it and in a few minutes it's gone. That is the way in the army. You know, Dave is writing to me regularly. He is OK. Well, I guess I'll close for this time with all my love, your brother, Irving

March 2, 1944

My dear sister Maria and Hermine,

I should begin and write you all day long even then I couldn't right answer on all of your letters. So I just want you to know that I'm OK I hope to hear the same. I have and will write you whenever I can. I know you understand me. There isn't anything I could write you from here. You know the every day happenings better than I do. My dear Hermine, you are right about staying in Columbus until I get back. Then we will have time to discuss all that. If God will help me to see our father and then I'll see what I can do. Do not worry I know what to do. I'm hoping it will be very soon. It's hard to wait but there isn't anyone who could do anything about it. The way God wants that's the way it's going to be. Hoping to hear from you, I'm remaining with all my love, your brother, Irving

March 2, 1944

Italy

My dear brother Herman,

How are you Herman? I know you're busy so I concern that I'm not. I am OK and thinking of you a lot. I have received about a month ago a small package and it was sent by your name. So I guess you know something about. Anyway I thank you for it. It's nice to receive a small package like that every day. Do you like your work? Please write sometime when you get a chance. That doesn't make any difference how you write you can write in English on v-mail and in airmail you can write the way you want to and whatever you want, because nobody checks it or anything like that. Till I hear from you, with all my love, your brother, Irving

P.S. Regards Hermine, [obscured by V-Mail]

Italy March 2, 44

My dear sisters Hermine and Marie,

This is just a note to let you know, that I'm enclosing seventy dollars for you. If you need it for anything please don't hesitate to take it. I'm giving it from all my heart. I can't give you or send you anything so please buy a present for yourselves and we will think that I send you from here. Hope that this war will be over someday and then I will send you myself something so then I will know that you have a present from me. I'll write some more on V-mail. Please do not worry! As I said money isn't everything. "I'm" remaining in Trust in God, that we will meet again! With love your brother, Irving

Regards to Dave and Herman!

March 3, 1944

My dear brother Dave,

Just a line to let you know that I'm OK and thinking a lot. I hope that you are well and in good health. Hope you have received my letters. You know I could talk to you all day long about things that I can't write. You are very sweet, because as Hermine is saying that you write home regularly and she also said that you have sent her a very nice gift. Talking about gifts, who is that you are saying is going to send me a package? The plane came and gone nothing to worry at the present time. They mostly come at night. I'm remaining with all my love, Your brother Irving

P.S. REG[ARDS] TO HERMINE, MARIA AND HERMAN

March 4, 1944

My dear brother Dave,

Today just another line to let you know that I'm OK and I hope you are well and in the best of health. As you see I'm writing you whenever I can. Please do not worry if my letters are a little late. Did you make any friends down there? You probably did. There everything must be beautiful. I hope that it won't be long and God will help me to go home in the best of health. Then you will take a vacation and we'll go to a nice quiet place. Boy! That will be something.

By the way, when you write me you can write me anything in any language. If you write on v-mail put on the language that you write, but by air mail you don't do it. My regards to the folks back home. Till we meet again! All my love, Your brother Irving

1944/3/4 Irving to Family, Anzio Beachhead, Italy (V-Mail, Slide 79)

March 4, 1944

Italy

My dear sister Hermine, Marie and brother Herman,

Today also a line to let you know that I'm OK. I hope this letter will find you all in the best of health. Sometimes I have more time to write, and I'm writing extra to every one of you. Yet you must forgive me as you know how it is. I have started to write to the relatives, but never able to finish it. Sometimes I figure, that I will wait till the war ends and then I'll answer all the letters. It's a shame that I haven't written to Flora and Bertha, but somehow I'm going to explain that to them. Please write me even if I'm late with answering it. No Maria, here isn't any snow, I can see it on the mountain though. Till we meet again! Your brother, Irving

1944/3/7 Marie to David (Book 8, 43-46)

3/7/44

Dear David!

We got a letter from you yesterday and I'm glad that you are ok. And we don't get letters from you that often either. It's been a week since we got mail from our little brother. I hope he is ok. Yesterday it rained a lot and today is snowing. Otherwise nothing particular. We are busy. We will work on Saturday too. You better write! What's going on with the statement? Did you get what I sent to you? I don't know anything in particular. We are doing fine. We are just very busy. You better take care where you go and what you do. And don't forget that money is not everything. Yes, money is everything, but that's not how I mean. It's a miracle that you figured it out that it's not worth to carry that much. Other than that, I will leave this alone also. You better take care and write! Greetings and kisses.

Maria

And you better write.

Send the letter that I attached here back to me.

1944/3/10 Marie and Hermine to David (Book 9, 1-2)

[from Hermine]

March 10, 1944

We have received the newspaper from you and thank you. Also received a letter from my little brother that I'm enclosing. Thank God that you're well. I am happy to hear from you that you have a wonderful job. The main thing is to take care of yourself at work. Save as much money as you can. How much did you save up till now? I'm not asking because I want you to enumerate it. However, I'm interested. I am not saving a lot because I had to pay the doctor, also I bought a beautiful dress and shoes. I knitted a handbag. They were asking $28 dollars for such a hand bag. I looked at it very closely and I made it and it came out beautifully. We are all well. You too should write whenever you can. Maria is going to write also. I'm closing now and I will continue to write to you in the future and will tell you all the gossip. Please take care of yourself. With kisses, Hermina.

[from Marie]

March 10, 1944

Dear David! Today we have received your newspaper and also a letter. I'm happy to hear that you are well. We are also well. We are busy at this time. It's a little late in the evening, so I am going to lie down. There is nothing new. Take care of yourself and don't forget to write. I received a letter today from our little brother. He is well. I will close this letter at this time. With love and regards and kisses. Maria. Please take time and rest and please write to us.

1944/3/15 David to Family (Book 12, 60-66)

Wednesday

My Darlings!
I got your letter that I unfortunately did not respond to yet. Forgive me, but I haven't gotten used to working longer yet, so it will be. I got Herman's letter also and yours too, Hermine and Mariska. Hermine, you wrote to send you a smaller necklace, so this week on Saturday or on Sunday I will go and buy it. I saw new photographs, I will choose one photo. Did you know that the smaller is cheaper? I will attach 2 letters above about our little brother. You better send them back to me. I will send your two letters back in my next letter. I hope our little brother is well!

The place where he is now is by the beach and surely a big place because I saw it in the newspaper that 10000 people who lived there had to move away from there. There is no news here. The weather is starting to get nicer. Do you see? Little brother would like to come here also. Hermine, I hope you will not let the house wife break the lease. I still had to pay 119 dollar what is over there 390 dollar. Good money, right? What is the news over there? If you want to come here to live, you can earn good money. Every person will be for the military and women make the same money as men. The only thing is, if you come here it will take two years until you can become a resident. Oh yes! Can you see Ignác was in the picture. He wrote it here that he is "surprised to see it". So, I am always almost right. If I were you, I would put it in the news paper-

[In English] - Brother in California recognizes his brother's picture in the [news]paper and his brother acknowledges that it is him landing in Italy Anzio Beach Pvt Irving Gluck 50 Linwood Ave and 4 years ago left Italy to the USA and today he is back there fighting for the U.S.A. [In Hungarian] something like that. It's not going to be trouble since the censor allowed it in our little brother's letter. Or something in the Jewish newspaper. Call him up! Allen Tarshist, you will find it in the phone book and give Ignác's new address and mention Ignác's case with the picture to him- And you can tell him if he asks where I am, that I work in the shipyard 20 miles from Hollywood. If he's interested in something, I will do it for him and thank him for the birthday note. Write to me, unfortunately I don't have a lot of time to write. I go to Los Angeles twice a week.

I treated the varicose veins on my leg at the doctor. It looks better already. I hope in two months only the mark will be there. If I have time someday, I will put together and send home the nonsense I wrote a long time ago. Herman, you go to Rich and High St, take the citizenship papers with you, and register at the East side there, at the clothing store upstairs to vote. You are a resident so you can do it. And you better do that for me at the same place to send me an absentee ballot document so I can vote also, because I have to live here for a year to do that. So, I hope you understood it and I wish you everything good!
Kisses, Dezső

P.S. It was a week ago on Sunday since I went to the Czechoslovak party, at least 40 km from here. I saw a Č.S.R. [Československá republika] movie and there are nice homes. There is a large Czech carnival like in Czechoslovakia [with] Czech music. And you know, not too far from here, there are big mountains. It was nice summer weather there too and on the mountain there was snow, just like in Ohio. So, I wish you good luck! You better write to me a lot. Marcsa! How much do you make? And do you still pay a lot? And you Herman? Lots of luck! Kisses, Dezső

1944/3/15 Irving to Dave, Anzio Beachhead, Italy (V-Mail, Slide 82)

March 15, 1944
My dear brother Dave,
How are you my dear Dave? I know you were thinking of me a lot. You probably didn't know what to do for you haven't received any mail from me. Well you know how everything goes. Even if I haven't written,

but you were and are always in my heart. I have received from you a couple long letters and a small package. Yes, and a very nice present from you. That picture! I was surprised, but the first thought I had, boy I wish I was there beside you. You know Dave, your letters are not censored! You were asking me in your letters. Please forgive me for not answering all your letters, but first I want you to know that I'm OK. I'll write some more later. I remain with trust in God, till we meet again! Love, your B[rother], Irving

1944/3/15 Irving to Family, Anzio Beachhead, Italy (V-Mail, Slide 81)

March 15, 1944

My dear sisters and brother, please forgive me for not writing to you as often as I should, but as you know I'm writing whenever I can. I have received about 30 letters and three small packages from you. Many thanks for it. It comes in just like mail. It was a very good idea. However now your letters are coming in straight. It doesn't take much time to get it, like it used to. How are you my dear Hermine, Marie and Herman? I hope you're fine. I'm OK. You don't know how much I'm thinking of you. God is the only one who knows. I'm hoping in him that he will help me to return to America in best of health. I'll have plenty to talk about the greatness of God. I'll close for now, with trust in God and all my love to you. Your brother, Irving

[Note - Irving will write 10 letters on the 16th]

1944/3/16 Irving to Dave, Anzio Beachhead, Italy (V-Mail, Slide 88)

March 16, 1944
My dear brother Dave,
You certainly know everything, however please do not worry so much. That doesn't help none of us. The only thing we can do, to ask God to help us. Be faithful! Trust in him! That is what I do! I see on every letter you mark it, write soon! You know brother Dave, I was up on the front again. Believe me I was thinking of you and the family. I took your picture out of my pocket, I can't tell you anymore. I was and I'm asking God to help me to return to America so that we can and will meet again! Over here you have no friends, you are alone and hoping that God is with you. Till we meet again! I remain with love, Your B.[brother] Irving

1944/3/16 Irving to Dave, Anzio Beachhead, Italy (V-Mail, Slide 89)

March 16, 1944
My dear brother Dave,
Just another line to let you know that I'm OK. Hoping that you are in the best of health. I read your letters over once, when I get more time I want to read it over again. Yet I have a little time so I'm just writing and not answering all your questions. By the way don't worry too much. You know I had a rifle and the number on it was 251–my A.P.O. is the same and back home the paint company address is the same. Yet I have one and the number on it 1736, well I concern that Emil's home has 36. You know it sounds nice, doesn't it. Well I hope in God that he help me soon. Till we meet again, Your brother, Irving

1944/3/16 Irving to Dave, Anzio Beachhead, Italy (V-Mail, Slide 94)

March 16, 1944
My dear brother Dave,
I have written one letter yesterday and I'm writing to you today again. There isn't anything that I can say. It's like you figure it. I just want to tell you I'm writing this letter in my house, that is a friend of mine and I have built a house under ground. So that is the safest place to be. It's pretty comfortable. Sometimes we are sweating inside, but that is the best place until we get more ground. Sometimes I figured we should have dug it so that we could go to Rome without difficulties. We hope it won't be long! My trust in God! Love, Irving

1944/3/16 Irving to Family, Anzio Beachhead, Italy (V-Mail, Slide 84)

March 16, 1944
Italy

Page 288

My dear sister Hermine and Marie, and brother Herman,

I have written one letter yesterday in a hurry. I didn't have time to read it over. Even today I'm just writing to tell you that I'm OK. There in your letter my dear sister Hermine, you are asking if I'm praying or if I have time to pray. Well I can say this to you, that here, who someone never prayed, will pray. Because here you have no one, only God. God is the only one who helps! You have to ask him to be with you wherever you are. Believe me if you say a prayer, wherever you are, you feel better, you know and hope in God, that he is with you! With love, Irving

1944/3/16 Irving to Family, Anzio Beachhead, Italy (V-Mail, Slide 92)

March 16, 1944
My Dear Sister Hermine and Marie and brother Herman,

Here I'm again as you see thinking of you all. I'm OK. I have received some letters from you today again. I'm glad to know that you are all well. Received also 2 letters from Flora and Samuel. Yes and one from Louis Shvarc. I'm sorry that I can't take enough time to write to every one and answer all letters. As I said before you are the first one to whom I'm writing. I sure wish if you would see me. I hope that God will help me and this mess will end, so I can be home with you and talk about things that today I'm not in the mood. Love, Your B. [brother] Irving

1944/3/16 Irving to Family, Anzio Beachhead, Italy (V-Mail, Slide 93)

March 16, 1944
Italy

My dear sister Hermine and Marie,

Hope this letter will find you in the best of health. I'm OK. Hope to stay that way. Today a year ago I was inducted in the army. Yes time goes fast. Now I'm hoping that next year at this time I'll be home in the good old U.S.A. and in the best of health. I'm hoping in God all of you will be in the best of health. Received some letters from relatives and so I'll have to close for this time and write to them too. Remain with all my love, your brother, Irving

1944/3/16 Irving to Hermine, Anzio Beachhead, Italy (V-Mail, Slide 86)

March 16, 1944
Italy

My dear sister Hermine,

Whenever I have time I'm thinking of you with writing. However you are always in my heart. So don't get me wrong. Sometimes there isn't time to write you, but I'm thinking of you and I know how you feel if I don't write, you will not receive any mail from me. My dear, you know, that's not my fault. I do write you. You are the first one and then the others. That is a good idea sending me small packages. That way it comes more often and lasts longer. Many thanks, for your thoughts. Regards to my friends from your b[rother] Irving

1944/3/16 Irving to Hermine, Anzio Beachhead, Italy (V-Mail, Slide 87)

March 16, 1944
Italy

My dear sister Hermine,

Here I am again I want you to know that I'm OK. I have received letters from you and relatives. I sure will try to answer some of them. You know I have received a letter from Aunt Helen and the v-mail was damaged, so it came five months. Yes here is something interesting, I have a letter from you that you have written August the 19 - 43. That was the day when I left that good old U.S.A. Since then many things happened. I hope it won't be long till we meet again! With all my love your brother, Irving

1944/3/16 Irving to Marie, Anzio Beachhead, Italy (V-Mail, Slide 83)

March 16, 1944
Italy

My dear sister Marie,

How are you Marie? I hope you're feeling fine. I'm OK. You'll forgive me for answering your letters in English. But as I mentioned in Hermine's letter that from here that's the only language I can write. Anyway I understand you and hope that you understand me too. Yes, Marie I have received your package with v-mail in it. For the time being I don't want anything, but those small packages are coming handy. Over here candy and chocolate is very precious. Please don't worry too much if I'm late with answering your letters. Hope to see you soon, Love from Irving

1944/3/16 Irving to Marie, Anzio Beachhead, Italy (V-Mail, Slide 85)

March 16, 1944 Italy

My dear sister Marie,

As you said in one of your letters it's long way to get home. But I say that God will help us and the day will come. Yes indeed, it's very difficult to wait even one minute, but still we have to. There is nothing it can be done about it. They say, time will tell. Please Marie, don't worry about things that you are not sure like seeing me in papers. I don't know anything about but still you think that I am and worry too much. And I don't want you to worry. Thanks for your letters and I'm hoping in God that he will help me to see you all soon! Remain with my love, your brother Irving

1944/3/16 Louis Schwartz to Hermine, Iceland (V-Mail, Slide 90)

Iceland March 16, 1944
Dear Hermina,

Received your letter yesterday. I was indeed very glad to hear from you again. Also that Irving is feeling well. You don't have to worry much about him. Uncle Sam is taking care fairly well of his boys in the army. Did you write him[?] I expected him to write me even if only a few lines. I'd be glad to hear from him. I'm looking forward to get the pictures promised me. I really didn't have a chance to take any though I've a camera from a friend of mine also films more than three weeks but it was no sunshine here since especially in our free time. I'm going to send you when I take some. Thanks for offering to send me what I used. I really don't need anything right now, but if I do need I certainly will write. Right now I'm expecting to get three packages from Youngstown and New York. I couldn't refuse asking because they wanted to it. I guess I've to close. Write soon. Love, Louis

1944/3/16 Louis Schwartz to Marie, Iceland (V-Mail, Slide 91)

Iceland March 16, 1944
Dear Maria,

Was glad to hear from you after a long silence. I received both your letters the same day. Yesterday. There's not much new here since I wrote last time. It's quite nice here. The weather looks like in Christmas time in Ohio nice and white. I'm pretty used to it by now. I'm in one of the nicest and best camp in Iceland. Hope I'll stay here while I'm in Iceland. You girls didn't write me anything about Dave. Is he in Columbus? Yes I don't know if I wrote you in my previous letters my brother Joe is a corporal and was all packed up ready to leave. I'm afraid it's also for overseas. I hoped he'll stay in the States. But that's army life we've to go where they send us. That's all for now. Write soon. Love, Louis

1944/3/17 Irving to Dave, Anzio Beachhead, Italy (V-Mail, Slide 97)

March 17, 1944
My dear brother Dave,

Here I'm again, you know I'm writing to you more than home. As you see when I get time I think of you. I have written one letter to them yesterday and I will write some more today. That is my 4th letter to you. Now don't get me wrong that I think of you only when I write. I think of you always. I sure would like to be with you, you know there is the best place to be. However the way God wants, that's the way has to be.

Page 290

You know sometimes the best place isn't good, but if you trust in God a small ditch will save you as well as a foxhole. Over here it's like you said it. Where ever you go it's still the same! Love, Irving

P.S. DO NOT WORRY! TILL WE MEET AGAIN!

1944/3/17 Irving to Herman, Anzio Beachhead, Italy (V-Mail, Slide 96)

March 17, 1944
Italy

My dear brother Herman,
I received a letter from you Herman and I'm glad to hear that you are well. However it was a surprise, because you have been listening for so long. Well I hope now you will answer me much faster than before. Since I have been overseas I bet I can count on fingers the letters that you have written to me. Dave writes me 3 to 4 times a week. You know he wasn't like this. I would say make it as a habit and drop me a line. Will you? I'm OK and hope to stay that way. In God I trust, that we will meet again soon in U.S.A. Love from Irving

1944/3/17 Irving to Hermine, Anzio Beachhead, Italy (V-Mail, Slide 95)

March 17, 1944
Italy

My dear sister Hermine,
Just want to tell you my dear that I'm OK. And hope that you are in the best of health. Your letters are wonderful. It does not make any difference in which language you write me. Your English is very good. You know, I would write you in foreign language, but here isn't any interpreter. So I would say that you just go ahead and write me. Your letters in any language is worth to me a million dollars. I'm looking at your picture now, and believe me I'm proud of you. I'm hoping to see you in person soon! Remain with all my love to my sister, your brother, Irving

1944/3/19 Irving to Dave, Anzio Beachhead, Italy (V-Mail, Slide 99)

March 19, 1944
My dear brother Dave,
Just a line to let you know that I'm OK and hope to stay that way. By now you have received my letters. Hope that you are in the best of health. I have received a small package from you. I don't know if I mentioned it to you in my other letter. Thank you for it. A small package comes handy. I'm receiving from home too the same size. I wonder how many packages they sent me, well I'll ask them sometime. Remain with love, Irving

1944/3/19 Irving to Family, Anzio Beachhead, Italy (V-Mail, Slide 98)

March 19, 1944
My dear sisters, Hermine, Maria and brother Herman,
Just a line to my dear sis[ters] and Bod [brothers] that I'm OK and hope to stay that way with God's help. By now you have received my letters I hope you are all in the best of health. I have written to Dave too. He is OK. You know I don't answer all the letters, because when I get time I just write. Please don't worry so much, because that doesn't help. We all hope in God that everything will be all wright [sic]. I would appreciate if you would send me a small picture of you. When I will be able I will send you too. My trust in God! I'll remain with love your brother, Irving

REG[ARDS] TO RELATIVES AND FRIENDS.
ALSO TO DAVE.

-TILL WE MEET AGAIN!

1944/3/20 Marie to Irving (V-Mail, Slide 100)

My Dear loved little brother Irving,

Today is Monday and I'm trying to write to you. Also last week we received your long letter and we are happy to hear that thank G-d you are healthy. All of us are well. I can hardly wait for the minute to be together with you. All of us can hardly wait for that. Yes my little brother, yesterday David called us on the telephone. He is also well. The relatives, Flora and the family, also read your latest letter and they are happy to hear that thank G-d you are well. I wish I could see you, or at least talk to you my dear Irving, I can hardly wait for that minute. I think about you a thousand times. I ask the good G-d to help you with a very lucky return home. I will continue this letter.

Countless kisses, Maria

1944/3/21 Helen Perl Goldstein to Hermine (Book 17, 386-387)

Cleveland Mar 21. 44.

My dear Hermine!

You can't understand the reason for my silence. The reason is that I had a cold and besides that I wanted to see that particular man first, since I know you. So, the thing is this, the man is really very nice, but I think it's called off because he is being drafted. They can call him in any day about his standing. He was dismissed for an uncertain time, so I will stop what I started for you and I will introduce another young man. He is a very nice and serious boy. He was a soldier for a year in the past summer. They sent him home and then he bought a very nice business. Now, he would like to get married. So, I told him about you and he is willing to get to know you. I will send his card in an attachment.

So, decide an exact time when you can come, so I can set up the date ahead. If you can, do it on Passover because I know a business man is busy on Passover and you as well, naturally. Do not follow my example, write immediately. I'm sorry to hear that the Schwartz boys are soldiers and you got a part from that too. But at least here we are fighting for our freedom, meanwhile at home, they slaughter our dear country innocently, wrongfully. Especially what has now taken place I have been just thinking about. I hoped until now, but after all this, all our hopes are just wasted. Closing my lines, kissing all of you, and I wish a Happy Passover!

Helen,

Write me immediately.

1944/3/22 Irving to Dave, Anzio Beachhead, Italy (V-Mail, Slide 102)

March 22, 1944

My dear brother Dave,

It's just another day and I want you to know that I'm OK with God's help. Hope that you are feeling well. I have received those long letters that you have written in November-43. Those letters traveled all over the places where I have been. Now it catched [sic] up with me. Since I have been at this place, I have received about 130 letters. But believe me I didn't answer all of it. I'm keeping those letters, so that sometime I'll get enough time off and answer it. I believe that will be when the war ends. We hope that it won't be long. With God's help everything can happen. Love to you and family from Irving

1944/3/22 Irving to Family, Anzio Beachhead, Italy (V-Mail, Slide 101)

March 22, 1944

My dear sisters Hermine and Maria,

Just received one of the old letters in which you were asking me what I think of giving a picture to the Social Hall. Now it's late to decide, however do the way you think it's best. How are you? I hope that you are all in the best of health. I'm OK with God's help. Since I have been at this place, I have received about 130 letters. I'm hoping to receive more. However I'll have to wait till this war ends. You know I need a secretary to answer all this mail. So now and always I'm hoping in God, that it won't be long that this war ends. Till we meet again! Love from Irving

Reg[ards] to Herman and Dave and relations

1944/3/24 Irving to Family, Anzio Beachhead, Italy (V-Mail, Slide 103)

March 24, 1944

My dear sisters Hermine and Maria,

Hope that this letter will find you in the best of health. I'm OK. I received a couple letters from you and I'm glad to know you are all in good health and thinking of me. Believe me I do too. I also received the Chronicle in which I found Maria's name. It was very interesting to me, to find her advertisement. I also found my name in the book. That doesn't amount very much. It would be more interesting if I was home. I hope that God will help me and it won't be long and we will meet again! Remain with all my love, Irving

Reg[ards] Dave and Herman relatives and friends!

1944/3/26 Irving to Dave, Anzio Beachhead, Italy (V-Mail, Slide 104)

March 26, 1944

Dear brother Dave,

It's just another day over here and I want you to know that I'm OK with God's help. Hope that you are in the best of health. Since you have been in California probably by now you are an actor. On that picture you look like one. All kidding aside you look good. Thanks for your thoughts. Also received a couple letters from home they are fine. How is everything with you? In one of your old letters you're asking me if I need anything. When this war ends I will ask you plenty of?! I'll tell you then I trust in God that he will help me and it won't be long. Reg[ards] to the folks back home. Till we meet again. Your B. [brother] Irving

1944/3/28 Irving to Dave, Anzio Beachhead, Italy (V-Mail, Slide 106)

March 28, 1944

My dear brother Dave,

I just want to tell you that I'm OK and I hope that you are feeling fine. I have received yesterday one package mailed on Feb. 5th and if you enjoy sending them half as much as I enjoy receiving them we are both happy. Hope that you continue sending them always and you'll never know how much I appreciate it. Mail is one of the important factors in building up our morale, without it, it would be much lower. In God we trust and hope for a quick and prosperous victory for all the people, all over the world. In closing, this letter is like turning the page of the book. Till we meet again, Your brother, Irving

1944/3/28 Irving to Family, Anzio Beachhead, Italy (V-Mail, Slide 105)

March 28, 1944

Italy

My dear sisters Hermine and Maria,

I just want to tell you that I'm OK with God's help. Hope that you are all in good health. Thank you very much for the packages, I received four small and one 5 pound package from Dave. It's very sweet of you to send me the small ones, however I think it's lots of trouble. I enjoy receiving packages very much and I hope that they continue to come. The first package that I have received from you was homemade cookies. It took some time to get here, but even if it took a hundred years it would be worth waiting for. I hope that this letter finds you all in good health. I will write more later. I remain with all love, your brother Irving

Regards to all my friends, and relatives.

1944/3/30 Irving to Dave, Anzio Beachhead, Italy (V-Mail, Slide 108)

March 30, 1944

My dear brother Dave,

Just another day I want you to know that I'm OK with God's help. I hope you are the same. I'm thinking of you a lot. I have received your news paper and I found it very interesting. The funnys were in time. What about the news? That happened a long time ago. We have to look always ahead. I hope that it won't be long and we will meet again. I remain with all my love your brother, Irving

March 30, 1944
Italy

My dear sisters Hermine and Marie,
Just another day and I want you to know that I'm OK and thinking of you a lot. I hope that you are all in good health. Please write to me even if I don't write as often as I used to. I'm hoping that it won't be long that we will meet again. How is everything back home? I'll write more later. I remain with all my love, your brother Irving
How are you Herman? Please write me.

1944/4/1 Undated Hermine to David (Book 10, 27-29)

[Dated to sometime before 4/22/44 because Louis Goldblatt has a picture of Hermine but didn't send her one. Louis is the soldier that Helen Perl mentioned in the letter dated 3/21/44]

Dear Dave,
I received your letter and I'm writing a few lines to you so that you should not worry about that foolish thing. I would have sent you the letter, but you are writing so seriously. It is not worth it. I will ask him what it was all about. I can understand it must be a joke, but if the boy didn't like it, it wouldn't be important that he should write, but I don't want you to worry about it. First of all, you have to borrow money and ask for a loan - and you don't have to be ashamed of driving a car because it's America. Whoever is rich today started small before becoming rich. Therefore, it is more interesting than thinking about the past. I was a maid and I'm not ashamed to tell anyone. It doesn't matter if they don't like it. I whistle at him. You know, today you don't find too many honest men. For example, the one in the army asked me for a picture in one of the letters, and I never mailed him one. The only thing I told him was when I get one, I will mail one. Since then he didn't even answer, therefore it was better than if I would have sent one because if he would really be interested then he wouldn't be angry now. That's the way it goes. As I told you before, it is good for entertainment. Therefore, don't worry if you don't like it. I will write again. Until then, kisses and love, Hermine

1944/4/3 Irving to Dave, Anzio Beachhead, Italy (V-Mail, Slide 110)

April 3, 1944
My dear brother Dave,
Just want to let you know that I'm OK, with God's help. I'm hoping that you are well and in good health. For a couple days now that I haven't received mail from you. You probably have written, but I didn't get it. Sometimes it comes in late. I know it's not your fault. However I'm waiting every day to receive something from home. You must forgive me if I'm late with answering your letters, but I'll make up for it when I go back to the good old U.S.A. I'm hoping to see you soon! Love to you and the folks back home, Irving

1944/4/3 Irving to Family, Anzio Beachhead, Italy (V-Mail, Slide 109)

April 3, 1944
Italy

My dear sisters Hermine and Maria,
It's just another day and I want you to know that I'm OK and hope that this letter will find you all in the best of health. It's a couple days now that I haven't received any mail from Dave. I hope that he is all wright [sic]. Maybe our mail will come in tonight and I'll have some letters from him. I have received yesterday a couple letters from you. It was dated March 15-16 and 19th, sometimes get some real old letters, such as like August 29. Yes it just got here. You know it is interesting that after that time and it catched up with me. I'm hoping in God that it won't be long and he will help me to a safe return to the good old U.S.A. I remain with all my love your brother, Irving

Regards to Dave and Herman.

1944/4/4 Herman to Dezső (Book 19, 31-32)

4-4-44.

Dear Dezső,

You're asking that I should mail you the voting application. I was in the office and I was told that you have to write to them to their address and then they'll mail you the questionnaire that you have to fill out and mail back to their address. What's new there? How's your work going? We are working on Sundays. I don't know for how long. Seven days a week for $72 and they take out taxes also from the bond. A few days ago I mailed the military document, however I didn't get a reply. I wonder if they will give me anything. Otherwise I know nothing special. We wish you the very best, Herman

1944/4/4 Irving to Dave, Anzio Beachhead, Italy (V-Mail, Slide 111)

April 4, 1944

My dear brother Dave,

Sorry, I can't be with you at this year on Passover day, but I'm hoping that next year we will be together and celebrate. This year I'm hoping that we will have a new Passover such as it was in the old days. If those things would happen today, believe me the people in this world would realize the things that yet they don't. I know you'll think of me, when you get this letter, Passover will be well on its way. My thoughts are with you. In closing this letter I want to say I'm OK, and wishing you a very happy holly [sic] days. Remain with all my love, Your brother, Irving

My best reg[ards] to Hermine, Maria and Herman

1944/4/4 Irving to Family, Anzio Beachhead, Italy (V-Mail, Slide 112)

April 4, 1944
Italy

My dear sister's Hermine and Maria,

By the time you receive this letter it will be Passover, yes believe me time goes fast. Last year in the same time I have been where I could go and celebrate that day, but today I don't know if there is going to be any celebration. Today as I'm writing this letter I'm hoping in God that we might be able to celebrate another Passover like in the old days. I hope this war will come to an end. Yes, that all people on earth would realize that there is God. God is the only one! Believe me I can't express myself, but I'm hoping in God that He will help me and we will be together again soon. In closing this letter I'm wishing you a very happy holly [sic] days. I'll remain with all my love, Irving

1944/4/5 Irving to Dave, Anzio Beachhead, Italy (V-Mail, Slide 114)

April 5, 1944

My dear brother Dave,

It's another day and I have not receive[d] any mail from you. I don't know why you are not writing or maybe your letters are late. I hope that I'll get some today. You know I'm waiting for a letter every day just like you. I know how you feel when you don't get any mail from me. I hope you are not angry at me. I hope to hear from you soon. I'm OK and thinking of you. My trust in God, that we will meet again soon! With love, Irving

1944/4/5 Irving to Family, Anzio Beachhead, Italy (V-Mail, Slide 113)

April 5, 1944

My dear sister Hermine and Maria,

I have received three small packages from you today. Thanks very much for it. It's very sweet of you sending me like you do. How are you? I'm OK and hope that you are all well and in good health. I don't know why Dave hasn't written to me. I hope he's well. May be he is very busy. As you said, when he doesn't get letter from me, then you are sending the letter that I send you to him. My letters are all alike, because there is not anything that I could say or tell you. In closing, I'm hoping in God that we will meet again soon! With all my love, Irving

1944/4/6 Irving to Dave, Anzio Beachhead, Italy (V-Mail, Slide 116)

April 6, 1944
My dear brother Dave,
I have received today 2- v-mail and one air mail letter. I'm glad to know that you are well and in good health. I'm OK, and hoping in God to stay that way. As I look at your picture I can read your thoughts. You are worrying too much. You know that saying "even if things look dark for you just now, remember a cloud across the face of the sun has no effect on old Sol… he keeps on shining just the same." May God help us! I remain with all my love to you and family,
Your brother, Irving

P.S. Thanks for sending that news real, however it's not me. But looks very much as [illegible].

1944/4/6 Irving to Family, Anzio Beachhead, Italy (V-Mail, Slide 115)

April 6, 1944
Italy

My dear sisters Hermine and Marie,
I have received a couple letters from you today and I'm glad to know that you are all in good health. I'm OK and hoping to stay that way with God's help. I also have three letters from Dave he is well. I'm waiting to receive some pictures from you. I don't remember if I asked you to send me, but if I didn't, so please send me in your next letter. I also received another small package from you. That makes four this week. Thanks a million for it. This is a request to postmaster, I want to have some homemade cookies. That's all at the present time. Show this letter to the P. M. They let you send me a package. Thanks again! I remain with all my love, your brother Irving

And best regards and Dave and Herman also my friends.

1944/4/7 Irving to Dave, Anzio Beachhead, Italy (V-Mail, Slide 117)

April 7, 1944
My dear brother Dave,
Just another line to let you know, that I'm OK and thinking of you. Tonight starts to be Passover, it's not like it used to be a year ago, or a couple of years ago. I guess that's the way it has to be. I hope in God and everything will be all wright [sic]. I sure wish I could talk to you for a while. I hope it won't be long and our dream will come through. Please write me when ever you have time. I remain with all my love your brother, Irving

Reg[ards] to Hermine, Maria, and Herman

1944/4/7 Irving to Family, Anzio Beachhead, Italy (V-Mail, Slide 118)

April 7, 1944
Italy

My dear sisters Hermine and Maria,
Passover starts tonight over here, when you will get this letter it will be all over. That just shows how fast time goes. How are you? I'm thinking of you always. Here it's not like used to be at home at this time last year or years ago. It's a great difference. Maybe it won't be long! I'm OK with God's help. Hope that you are the same. How is Herman? I'm still waiting to get an answer to my letter. I hope he is fine. My best regards to Dave and I remain with all my love, Irving

Reg[ards] to Aunt Helen

1944/4/7 Irving to Family, Anzio Beachhead, Italy (V-Mail, Slide 119)

April 7, 1944

Page 296

Italy

My dear sisters Hermine and Maria,
I have just received two letters from you Maria I'm glad to hear that you are all in good health. I'm OK with God's help. The next few days I'm going to send home seventy five dollars. At the present time I don't need any money. However as soon as this war ends I'll ask you to send me. I'm waiting for the day to come. Believe me one minute is enough of this. My trust is in God. He's the only one who can help us, and guide us to Victory. I have since received v-mail, however I don't remember if it was homemade cookies with it or not. I remain with all my love, your brother Irving

1944/4/12 Irving to Family, Anzio Beachhead, Italy (V-Mail, Slide 120)

April 12, 1944
Italy

My dear sisters Hermine and Maria,
Just a line to let you know that I'm OK with God's help. I hope you're well and in good health. I received a package with candy bars in it. Many thanks for it. It's very nice to receive packages, however I don't like to ask for it. I know that you would like to send me everything if I would ask for it. At the present time I don't need anything. A couple days ago I was asking for some homemade cookies. It does not make any difference what kind it is, because all tasted delicious. The only thing was that it came a long time. Hope that now it won't take so much time. In your letter you were asking me what I'm doing? Please don't worry! God will help me and everything will be fine. I hope to see you soon in the best of health. With all my love, your brother, Irving

Regards to Dave and Herman

1944/4/13 Irving to Dave, Anzio Beachhead, Italy (V-Mail, Slide 121)

April 13, 1944
-A-B. Italy [Anzio Beachhead]

My dear brother Dave,
I'm sorry for putting up [off] my letter writing from one day to the other, but that's the way it goes. I'm OK. I have received a couple letters from you. I'm glad to hear that you are well and in good health. Please don't worry so much! You know that doesn't help. I'll tell you something about the other day, I was in my dug out and I heard some nice music. It's a long time since I heard last. So I stept [sic] out and everything was so quiet that at that moment I thought the war has come to an end. But in the next minute the big guns continued their crush. However the band played, but the war is still going on. I hope in God that he will help us, sooner is better. You know how I felt in the next minutes. That can't be told. I remain with all my love your brother, Irving

Give my love to family back home

1944/4/14 Irving to Maria, Anzio Beachhead, Italy (V-Mail, Slide 122)

April 14, 1944
Italy

My dear sister Maria,
I'm glad to receive your letters and I understand you very well. Sometimes I try to change my letters, but you know every day it's the same. No news at all. The only news that would concern me, that the war has come to an end. Maybe then I could begin and write you all day long and always something interesting. At the time being I just want to say that I'm OK with God's help. I hope that you are well and in good health. Please don't worry if I'm late with answering your letters, but sometimes it's my fault. Because I'm putting up [off] writing from one day to the other. My trust in God! Till we meet again, your brother, Irving

I'll write to Hermine too!

P.S. Write me__ and don't worry!

1944/4/15 Marie to David (Book 8, 37-38)

Dear David!

As you can see it I will try to write a few lines today as well. Thank God I'm well. I hope my lines will find you well also. We got a letter from our little brother last week. Thank God he is ok, though he doesn't know when he can come home, but I hope he will be able to come home soon. It would be about time. I wrote in my last letter that I'm home. I am not working for now.

How are you? Maybe by now you were laid off. They started here as they did everywhere else. But what's important is that the war is ending. Now, take care of yourself wherever you are going or whatever you are doing. I wish you the best of health and luck! And even if you don't feel like it, you could write. Otherwise nothing new. From my heart I'm wishing you all the best wishes and kisses. Love, Maria

1944/4/16 Hermine to Mary Kay (Book 11, 9-10)

Apr 16, 1944
Dear Mary Kay,

Just to let you [know] I am well, and miss you very much. I am sorry I couldn't write to you sooner but you know already about it, so I don't have to worry about that. I have some news for you what Berry, the red haired one, came to me and told me the news about you, and ask me if I know it, but I told her no. She told me the story your brother and her brother are working at the same place. I think her brother is a foreman. Your brother told him and he doesn't know about his sister working at our place so the news came up. They were talking to Iren too about things, but nobody told her anything. I thought I will see you and everybody was hoping to see you now they thought you just didn't want to come up. Please Mary Kay don't you worry about that, but I told you and we wouldn't tell anybody about that baby. Please write to me I will try to answer it. Here I enclose a picture, but hoping I can send you a better one next time. Best wishes and love, Hermina

1944/4/16 Irving to Dave, Anzio Beachhead, Italy (V-Mail, Slide 125)

April 16, 1944
My dear brother Dave,

Just another day and I want you to know that I am OK hope that you are well and in good health. The holy-days are over, however here wasn't any difference between any other day. The first night I was to the services. It was like in the old days! Hope that next year we will celebrate all together. God knows everything. Please write me more often. I'll try my best. My regards to the folks back home, Till we meet again. I remain with all my love, Irving

1944/4/16 Irving to Family, Anzio Beachhead, Italy (V-Mail, Slide 124)

April 16, 1944
Anzio Beachhead

My dear sisters Hermine and Marie,

Hope this letter finds you in the best of health. I'm OK. The other day I received three small packages from you. Thanks very much for it. I know it's a lot of trouble with small packages, but it makes me happy just like if I got a five pound package. Shall we say it last that long too. During the holidays, I was only the first night to the services. That was all. I hope that next year we will celebrate it all together. God knows everything. Please write me and forgive me for not writing you like I used to. I remain with all my love, Irving

1944/4/16 Louis Schwartz to Hermine (Book 17, 131)

Iceland 4-16-44
Dear Hermina,

Received your letter yesterday the same time I had a letter from your brother Irving. I was glad for both of them. He seems to be all right there. Believe I wouldn't mind to be there too. May be some day I'll too. Who

Page 298

can tell maybe we'll be able to visit home, which is not very far away from them. I had a letter from my brother Joe. He was expected to leave on 1st of April to a different camp to be shipped probably overseas too. Now that Easter is over business has probably gone down and you'll have more time for yourselves. Or am I wrong? By the way how did you spend the holidays? Did you go any place to the seder. Otherwise I'm fine hope the same about you. Love and best of luck, Lou

1944/4/18 Hermine and Marie to David (Book 9, 18-20)

[from Maria]
Dear David!
I was in the post office today to find out what was the reason that they did not get the pearl there and here I will attach the statement, that it was sent down and when. They told us to send it back to the office there. Besides that, there is no news here. We just got a letter from our little brother today and thank God, he is well and he wrote that he got a five pound package from you. He is sending his best to you. How are you? We are well. Currently I am working, for how long? I don't know since this job is temporary, but we hope the best. You better write and take care. I will close my lines now. Greetings and kisses. Maria.
You better write!

[from Hermine]
Dear David,
Marcsa already wrote to you surely about everything and so just, I am well. I just packed for my little brother 3 little packages and a newspaper to you. Yes, it is very late already. I cooked dinner for tomorrow and the time ran so quickly. Next time I will send the letter that we got from our little brother. He wrote that the first package was the 5 pound package, which took a long time in coming, but if he would have had to wait for 100 years for it, even then, it would have been worth it. You always make him happy with a package and he is hoping that we will keep the sending up after that as well, because he likes to get a package.
Take care of yourself! Kisses, Hermine

1944/4/19 David to Family (Book 2, 120-124)

My Darlings!
Hermine, I got your letter by plane as well as the simple one. I'm glad that you are all well. I don't know any special news. As far as writing is concerned, I wrote that I work from 6pm to 4:30 in the morning and I'm very tired and I have no patience to write. Next week we'll go back to 8 hours of work. So I will go back to the Graveyard [shift]. I don't like to work for them too much. I will work at night and day also. And I will go to the beach. Oh yes! I forgot, I went to school to study Marine Electric for 120 hours and they paid the cost. Not too much, but I learned enough to set up power anywhere. But it's enough about this. Regarding coming here is concerned, you are not fair. You only have to take half of the responsibility to come here

and to go back. Here you'll make enough money that it will be enough to live. (More than in Columbus). So it's only $50 there and back. But you'll make that here, and you'll see if you like California. You better respond to that! Pardon, I meant you Hermine and Mariska. As far as our father is concerned, I can only say that when the war is over for them, they don't have to come here because there the livelihood is good. People go there from here. For 600 to 800 dollars payment and they want to be able to come here. There will be a problem with the military and they won't have place for civilians/privates. So don't even think about it for them to come here. They will have a better world there and they'll make better money there than here. Many American factory people will go there and produce everything.

You could see the war hasn't even ended, but American companies are going to Cairo, Palestine, Naples, and other [s.t.b. = s a tobbi = and others] places already. The Russians are not far from Ungvár and with a few days passing by, they can be easily in Polyán also. And that will help you better too. Hermine, on Monday I sent you a necklace set. I hope you will like it. I didn't see a better one. The lady said this is the best color for your dress. If it's not good, tell me what kind would be good, OK ?! From our little brother I got 6 letters and I will attach a few here. Don't throw out the 4 letters that I sent home. Be careful because you have here 2 letters also- our little brother wrote that he got the February 5th package where I sent a jug of shaving [cream] for him

and he was very upset, if I send him only ½ of it, he will send it back. At the post office, they indicated that they allow to send 5 pound packages, which I will send to him this week. Thank God he is ok. I will let you know again, if I don't write promptly, nothing happened. I just don't have time to do that. If there would be a problem, you would get a telegram because I gave your address to them. If you don't get normal mail, you don't have to worry. I will close my lines because I have to write to Ignác too and I did not eat yet and its already 1/2 8 pm [7:30pm]. So good luck and kisses to Hermine and Mariska and Herman.
Dave

P.S. Where did you go for movie acting? Ignác said it also, that you look like an actress. You know I'm not even going to Hollywood, I don't care-But if I would be interested, I could get in to work there at Warner Brothers.

[On the side] Here, many people go to Hollywood where they can take a group photo and pay between 10 and $20.

1944/4/21 Irving to Dave, Anzio Beachhead, Italy (V-Mail, Slide 127)

April 21, 1944
My dear brother Dave,
Thanks very much for your three long letters and small package. I'm glad to hear that you are well and in good health. I'm feeling OK, and hoping in God to stay that way. I realize the way you feel about getting letters more often. I'll try to do my best next time. Some times you have time to write, but not in the mood. At present, news the same. Please don't worry! I have received a letter from Arthur and Samuel. They are well. Please write me. I remain with love, and hoping to hear from you the best. My best wishes to Hermine, Maria and Herman. Love from, Irving

1944/4/21 Irving to Family, Anzio Beachhead, Italy (V-Mail, Slide 126)

April 21, 1944
Anzio Beach Head

My dear sisters Hermine and Maria and brother Herman,
It's swell to receive letters from you, please keep it up and write me whenever you can. Even though I'm late with answering it, always remember that I'm thinking of you. I used to write you more often, but today it's the opposite. Yet, I just want to tell you that I'm OK and hoping in God to stay that way. I have received a letter from Arthur and Samuel, they are well. I'll have to take time to write them too.

I remain with all my love and best wishes to you all. I'm hoping to see you soon. In God is my trust, till we meet again! Love from Irving

1944/4/22 Irving to Dave, Anzio Beachhead, Italy (V-Mail, Slide 128)

April 22, 1944
My dear brother Dave,
Writing to let you know that I'm OK and hoping in God to stay that way. Hope that this letter will find you in the best of health. I'm still praying for that day to come, when this war will be over. Boy, won't that be a happy day and then we will all be together once again. Thanks very much for the radio, but I can't use it over here. I know you would do everything for me. Now the only thing we can do, just trust in God and hope that he will help us. I remain with all my love your brother Irving. Please give my love to Hermine, Maria and Herman

[Illegible]

1944/4/22 Irving to Family, Anzio Beachhead, Italy (V-Mail, Slide 129)

April 22, 1944
My dear sisters Hermine and Maria,

Writing you to let you know that I'm OK and hope in God to stay that way. Hope that this letter will find you in the best of health. I'm still praying for that day when this war will be over, Boy, won't that be a happy day and then we will all be together once again. I'm wishing you Hermine many happy birthdays. I hope that next year I'll be there and will help you to celebrate. In closing this letter hoping to hear from you soon. I remembered all my love to you, and Herman and Dave. From, Irving

Here is a friend and says hello to you.

1944/4/22 Louis Goldblatt to Hermine (Book 17, 191-192)

B"H
Somewhere at Sea

Dear Hermine,
This is a very difficult letter to write because I have so much to say and because I haven't written you for so long. My silence has been not my idea. But things have happened so rapidly that it seems like a dream. Just as I was going to answer you and send you my picture I heard my mother had an operation so home I went - expected to visit you but didn't- went back to camp again started to write you and then received my orders to go over-seas but went home for a few days. My mother feels much better now and is only worried about me. I have been at sea for many days and have been kept rather busy as one of two doctors of the many hundred troops on ship and as a censor. So when I have time to write it is dark or too hot below deck. The trip has been really beautiful and wasn't very seasick because I didn't have time to think about it. I shall write you another letter - much longer - but to write to you is a very difficult thing because I have so much to say and it is so hard to put it to words (Maybe I should put it to music). Your very beautiful picture was received quite some time ago and I wish to thank you - It is very beautiful and I appreciate the expense you went through for it and having it colored. Thanx again. As for my picture for you I will write home and have them send you one. I would very much like to hear from you and how things are going in Columbus. How the family is getting along and if your youngest brother is home. Say hello to all for me and keep well.

With Torah Blessings,
Louis

1944/4/23 Irving to Dave, Anzio Beachhead, Italy (V-Mail, Slide 131)

April 23, 1944
Anzio Beachhead

My dear brother Dave,
Please forgive me for not writing you sooner. But I do whenever I can. I'm OK and hope in God to stay that way. I'm glad to hear you are well and in good health. I was just thinking about your letters, they're very sweet and God will help me after this war is over, I'll go down and see you and then we'll talk things over. I'm hoping in God that it won't be long now. Let's hope together that way. Please write me about yourself. Sometimes I forget to answer your questions, but forgive me for it. God will help me and someday I can answer everything that you want to know. Love, from Irving

My love to the family!

1944/4/23 Irving to Family, Anzio Beachhead, Italy (V-Mail, Slide 130)

April 23, 1944
Anzio Beach Head

My dear sisters Hermine and Maria,
Please forgive me for not writing you much sooner. I'm OK and hope in God to stay that way. I'm glad to hear that you are well and in good health and I hope this letter will find you also in the best of health. I have received four small packages, many, many thanks for it. It's very sweet of you to think of me. I feel about you the same. Please write me more often. Whenever I can I will write you too. How is David and Herman? Also received a letter from Arthur and Samuel, but haven't answered them yet. Will you please tell them

that thanks for their letter and I'll try to write them sometime soon! I won't forget them! All my love to Dave and Herman. Love to you from Irving.

1944/4/24 Irving to Dave, Anzio Beachhead, Italy (V-Mail, Slide 134)

April 24, 1944
Anzio Beachhead

My dear brother Dave,
It's just another day and I want you to know that I'm OK with God's help. Today I haven't received any mail from you, but I think I'll get some tomorrow. I received four small packages from my sisters. They are very sweet. I hope in God that we can meet again soon. I wish if I could drop in for a minute to see you and the family back home. As the saying is, there isn't anything that has no end. And this war should come to an end soon. It has been long enough for anybody. Well, till write some more, I remain with all my love your brother, Irving

Please send me a small package.
Love to my sisters and brother and relatives.

1944/4/24 Irving to Family, Anzio Beachhead, Italy (V-Mail, Slide 132)

April 24, 1944
Anzio Beachhead

My dear sisters Hermine and Maria,
It's another day and I want you to know that I'm OK with God's help. I hope you are all well and in good health. I'm waiting to receive your pictures. Boy that will be something. I wish I could send you my picture so that you could see me too. But I guess we have to wait for a while and as soon as I can I'll make some and send you. I'm hoping in God that it won't be long and everything will be OK. Please don't worry! Please write me more often. Till we meet again with God's help. I remain with all my love to you, your brother Irving

Love to Dave and Herman.

1944/4/24 Irving to Herman, Anzio Beachhead, Italy (V-Mail, Slide 133)

April 24, 1944
Anzio Beachhead

My dear brother Herman,
I have received most welcome letter from you. I hope that you'll keep writing me. I'm OK with God's help. I'm glad to hear that you are well and in good health. I sure would like to have a picture of you. If you can send me I appreciate it very much. How is the bicycle? Is it still running? Or by now you have a car? Please write me all about it. Tell my sisters that I always think of them. I hope they feel fine. Please write me about them. I remain with all my love, your brother Irving

1944/4/25 Irving to Family, Anzio Beachhead, Italy (V-Mail, Slide 135)

April 25, 1944
Anzio Beachhead

Dear sisters Hermine and Maria,
Writing you again and I want you to know that I'm OK with God's help. I hope you're well and in good health. How is everything back home? Did you see the Yenkins lately? I have received a letter from them, but never answer it, I'll though. I have seen Fred Yenkins picture in the Jewish Chronicle. He looks good. If you see them tell them that I said hello and also tell them to write me. How is our neighbor next-door? I mean Mr. and Mrs. Walters? Also Mrs. Hason? Tell them I said hello and I would like to hear from them. I hope to see you and them personally soon. I remain with all my love, Irving

My Darlings!

I can't write any special news. This week I did not get any mail from you. I don't know what's the reason for that. Here I'll send two letters from our little brother. You better send them back to me with airmail please! Thank you! Right now I don't have time to write, I'm in a hurry. I wrote two letters to our little brother, too. Dear Hermine, don't send me anymore Sunday newspapers for now. I don't have time to read it. I did not go to my night job. In the future, if you want to send me newspapers, send it to me so I can hear a little bit of the gossip, ok?! What's going on over there? Here there is nothing, right now the weather is cold. You better write to me more often and write a lot. I will also. You too Marcsa, write a lot!

I hope my lines will find you in the best of health! You Herman! How are you? You write to me too, ok!? I will send a newspaper article here, where you can see what kind of ship we are making. I'm also working on it. I will indicate it with a line what area I'm working at. I don't know, if I ever wrote that I go to school to study to be an electrician. So, it's enough about this for today. I don't know any more news. Good luck and all the best. You better take care.- Did you receive from the lady the overpaid rent? If you did not, go to the O.P.A. office and have her pay you back. I hope you'll write! Until then, I wish you all the best! Yes, I was in Hollywood on Monday night the "Blondie" Cavalcade of America, A Song was Born, "Judy Canova" Show. It's pretty good. I will send you here a signature in his own hand from Pat O. Brien [Brón]. You better keep it as a souvenir.! Kisses, David.

[On the ticket:] With this ticket, you can go to the performance/show.

May 4, 1944
Anzio Beachhead

My dear brother Dave,

I understand all your letters and I'm glad to hear that you are well and in good health. I'm OK with God's help and hope to stay that way. Yes, I have received the other day a small package and 2, L.A. paper. Thanks very much for it. The paper is very interesting, however if you want to send me I would rather have life magazine and also some funny paper. Concerning the package, I think the weather is getting hot and the chocolate melts before it gets here. So I would like some cookies instead [of] candy. I'll write in my letters a request to P.M. Please send me some cookies or fruit cake. Many thanks for it Dave, I hope and pray to God, that it won't be long, till we meet again! Love from Irving
Reg[ards] back home!

May 4, 1944
Anzio Beachhead

My dear sisters Hermine and Maria,

Just another line to let you know that I'm OK and I hope in God to stay that way. I just read one of your old letters and you were asking about that Schwarc boy, that I met in Africa. Well yet I don't know what to say, but I think he is better off. As you know he is an M.P. I left him a long time ago. He's still back in a good place. Someone is lucky. It's good for him. I hope I can see him again in the future. How is everything back home? Please write me whenever you can. I'll do my best. I hope that God will help me and it won't be long. I remain all my love to you, Irving
Love to David and Herman

May 4, 1944
Anzio Beachhead

My dear sisters Hermine and Maria,

Just a line to let you know that I'm OK with God's help. And I hope in God to stay that way. I have received ten letters and four packages from you. When I received those 29 letters, it all came in at once. I did have enough time to read them. That is the first [th]ing that I do, when I receive mail. But when it comes to answering it, then it['s] a little difficult. I realize that the small packages are lots of trouble sending it. So from now on I'll make a request to postmaster, and then you won't have to send me the small packages. I'll write to Dave about it too. Please send me a package of cookies or fruit cake. I'm not much of a candy eater, I like it, but at the present time send me only cookies, any kind is OK. My trust in God! Till we meet again! Love from, Irving

1944/5/4 Irving to Marie, Anzio Beachhead, Italy (V-Mail, Slide 136)

May 4, 1944
Anzio Beachhead

My dear sister Maria,

Just a line to let you know that I'm OK, with God's help and I hope in God to stay that way. I received letters from you, but when I answer it, I always write you and Hermine on the same letter. I know you understand me well. I figure it like that, if I can, I write extra, but if not, that will do it. I wish I could be home and talk to you personally, but at the present, we just hope and pray to God that He'll help me. I sure wish that this war would end, it's time now, it has been going on long enough. May God listen to our prayer for a speedy Victory. I hope that this letter will find you in the best of health, my love to you and Hermine, From Irving

Reg[ards] to Herman and Dave,
P.S. WRITE ME SOON!

1944/5/4 Undated Marie to David (Book 8, 1-2)

[Date determined by 3 packages each week, and a 5 pound package. Also, Marie laid off 3x from previous job maybe at the balloon factory and D-day is one month away, and Irving just wrote that he'll request larger packages]

[At the top of the page] What happened with the Army? How is your leg? Is it better?

Dear David

A couple of days have passed and we haven't heard from you. As I see it, you must be very busy because you do not have time to write. In the beginning you wrote more often, but lately you stopped. How are you? I hope you are not sick. Please write at once. Otherwise, I will do the same. I think you might not write at all, but I'll leave it as it is. We received a letter from our brother. Thank God he is ok. Every week we send him 3 small packages, this week it was 5 pounds. Here, otherwise there is nothing new. We are ok. I'm working, but in another place. Where I had been working I was laid off 3 times. Last Thursday, I got another job at the American Education Inc. Press. This is on Front Street where the Kerz Clothes is. It is a very nice place. I'm getting $28.60 for 48 hours, but after the war I think it will be 40 hours. I'm giving out the order for the small newspaper. It isn't hard, I only have to stand and look and read the numbers. At this time I don't know what will be. I hope it will be ok. Take care of yourself. Best wishes and love, Maria

1944/5/5 Irving to Dave, Anzio Beachhead, Italy (V-Mail, Slide 141)

May 5, 1944
Anzio Beachhead

My dear brother Dave,

I received two letters from you, I'm glad to hear that you are well and in good health. I'm glad that you are at home, not like me. I wish you good luck, and I hope in God that you'll stay that way. Do you remember last March? You know when we were together. I have never thought of things like it. You know that song is right, when time comes, you will cry where no one sees it! I guess now it's too late. I hope in God that he will help me to go through it. I have a letter from Louis Schvarc, he is OK. My love to you, Irving

May 5, 1944
Anzio Beachhead

My dear sisters Hermine and Maria,
I have received seven letters from you today. I'm glad to hear that you are well and in good health. I'm OK with God's help. I can't say much about myself. Please don't worry. I can say like you said, I wish I could be home and talk to you. Time will come, with God's help, our dreams will come through. I have a letter from Louis Schvarc, he is OK. I wish I could be with him. However now, after all my only wish is that this war would end and we all could be home. Till we meet again! Love, Irving

My Darlings!
I don't know any special news. The same old everything. I got 3 letters from you this week. 2 from Hermine, 1 from Mariska. Thank you! Maybe I will write more often next week, since I went back to work at night. So I will have a little time for that. I'm glad you like the pearl, Hermine! I sent a very important package and two little packages to our little brother yesterday. You can send as many as you want, but it costs 24 cents for 8 oz. I will send at least 2 per week. Hermine, you wrote, be careful with the electricity! Ridiculous!! Yes, you don't know. You believe that the name is electrician, but we don't even touch electricity, we only install it and when everything is done, there is another crew coming called, "Test crew" and only they work with hot wires. So, no need to be sad this way. Oh! Do you know what happened when I asked for night shift? They wanted to deal with me badly. They scheduled me to do the hardest work. And it's dangerous, also where they build the ships. But when they gave me the report slip, I went to the Superintendent and I told him clearly.

Look, I know I'm not better than the others, but I'm sorry I can't go to work there. Is this a Dr's order? He asked what's wrong? I told him about my legs and that I'm not going to go. But he said this: I see that you are right. So he scheduled me to work at the easiest part of the entire factory, for 157 cents. I don't do anything, just sit. It's ridiculous. But it's ok that way. I'm not the only one who works there. There is an entire team. The job is when the electrical department needs something on the ship, I order it from the shop and I bring it up to the ship. This is the 3rd evening I work here, but they did not have one order yet. My boss says, don't worry about a thing! It's not your concern that they don't order anything. You are there and doing your job. Whoever works here says the same thing. So you don't need to be sad, ok! Let me know, if I should send some kind of fruits. I kiss you until I'll see you again. David
2 letters from our little brother.

May 6, 1944
Anzio Beachhead

My dear sisters, Hermine and Maria,
Just another line to let you know that I'm OK and thinking of you. As you see I always try to write you whenever I can. The other day I got paid forty one dollars and I don't yet, but I might make out a check to send it home. You know here money can't buy anything. So it's no use to have it. If I'll need some later so I'll ask for it. Will write more, I wish you good health, Love from, Irving

P.S. Write me
Love to Dave and Herman

May 7, 1944
Anzio Beachhead

My dear sisters Hermine and Maria,

I can't tell you how happy I was when I received your pictures. For a moment I couldn't believe my eyes, it has been a year now that I saw you last. You know those pictures that I have brought with me are different. Those look like you, but that which I got now, somehow it seems to me that you are worrying too much. Also you lost some weight too. I guess this war gets everybody down. You look pretty, though! I bet if you would see me, you would say, boy! What happened? I guess I have gray hair, all kidding aside. Please don't worry, my trust is God and I hope he will help me. Till we meet again! Love, Irving

I'll write more soon!

1944/5/7 (b) Irving to Dave, Anzio Beachhead, Italy (V-Mail, Slide 144)

May 7, 1944
Anzio Beachhead

Dear brother Dave,
Just a line to let you know that I'm OK with God's help. I have received a couple letters from home, they are OK. Also some pictures too, but the story is the same as yours. They are worrying too much. Just like you. I don't blame them a bit. Please write me whenever you can. I'll do the same. I remain with love, Irving

1944/5/10 Irving to Family, Anzio Beachhead, Italy (V-Mail, Slide 145)

May 10, 1944
Anzio Beachhead

My dear sisters Hermine and Maria,
I just received eleven letters and three small packages from you. It's very sweet of you the way you are writing me. You know I'm doing my best. I always try to write you. Sometimes I think I should just write a couple lines, because you know how it is. Here it's not like back home, if you know what I mean. So now I just want to say that I'm OK and my hope is that God will help me to stay that way. I hope that this letter will find you all in the best of health. I remain with love, Irving

1944/5/10 Irving to Family, Anzio Beachhead, Italy (V-Mail, Slide 146)

May 10, 1944
Anzio Beachhead

My dear sisters Hermine and Maria,
Writing you again to let you know that I'm OK and thinking of you a lot. I hope that this letter will find you in the best of health. I'm still thinking about those pictures, that I have received from you the other day. I think that during a year period a person changes a lot. I mean if you don't see each other during that time. To all this I have to say, this war helps a lot in making changes in a person. I can see that too, that you are worrying too much. Worry! That goes with the picture. Please take care of yourselves and don't worry. God will help us. I remain with the love, Irving

Please write me soon.
Love to Dave and Herman.

1944/5/10 Irving to Family, Anzio Beachhead, Italy (V-Mail, Slide 147)

May 10, 1944
Anzio Beachhead

My dear sisters Hermine and Maria,
The other day I have received a letter from Dave and he was saying he would like to have you go to Calif[ornia]. But he also said that you'll wait until I go back and we'll go all together to look around. Then we will decide. I sure would like to be back, anyplace in the U.S.A. You know I really would like to go somewhere, where [it] is nice and quiet. At the present I'm just hoping and praying to God that he'll help me. I'm hoping that it won't be long till we meet again soon.

I remain with - Love from, Irving

P.S. WRITE ME
(illegible)

1944/5/11 Irving to Dave, Anzio Beachhead, Italy (V-Mail, Slide 149)

May 11, 1944
Anzio Beachhead

My dear brother Dave,
Just another line to let you know that I'm OK and hope that my letter will find you the best of health. I've written you the other day and I think by now you have received that letter. I thank [you] for that package that you are sending. I hope it won't be long and it will be here. It's good to have someone like you, who thinks of me as much as you. Believe me I think of you a lot too. I hope it won't be long now and we will meet again with God's help. I remain with all my love your brother, Irving

P.S. WRITE ME SOON

1944/5/11 Irving to Family, Anzio Beachhead, Italy (V-Mail, Slide 148)

May 11, 1944
Anzio Beachhead

My dear sisters Hermine and Maria,
I have received your letters today and I enjoyed those letters very much. I can't begin to explain [or] to tell you how happy it makes me to receive letters from home. I know that, you are thinking of me. I'll be very glad when the package arrives with the cookies. I hope it won't be long till this war is over and we can be home together. Boy, that will be a happy day. In your letter you said that the Broad Street Rabbi became a chaplain. Yes, we had one here the other day and he came over not long ago. He was telling me that. So now he is Capitan Zeiber. I would like to meet him and talk to him, but I guess he won't be over here. I'll write more later. Love, Irving

1944/5/12 Irving to Dave, Anzio Beachhead, Italy (V-Mail, Slide 151)

May 12, 1944
Anzio Beachhead

My dear brother Dave,
I have written a letter the other day and I forgot to mail it, so now I'm writing you another one. How are you Dave? I hope that this letter will find you in the best of health. I'm OK and hope in God to stay that way. I realize that my letters are always the same, but you know how it is. As you said the other day, write me just a line. You know I was thinking maybe I should draw a couple lines and let you know how I'm. Concerning your letter, it would be very nice to go out with you, but yet we hope it won't be long and God will help me and we will meet again. However as I said one minute is enough from this. I'll write more later remain with love, Irving
P.S. Write me soon.

1944/5/12 Irving to Family, Anzio Beachhead, Italy (V-Mail, Slide 150)

May 12, 1944
Anzio Beachhead

My dear sisters Hermine and Maria,
I just read your letters over and it makes me happy to know that you are thinking of me. Believe me, my thoughts are always with you. I wish I could write you every day like I used to, but I guess that was in the good old days. A person never realizes things only when it's late. Now let's hope and pray to God that He'll

help us and everything will be OK. I'll write more later. Now I'll close for this time I remain with all my love, Your brother, Irving

Reg[ards] to Dave, Herman and relatives

1944/5/12 Louis Schwartz to Hermine and Marie (Book 17, 124-127)

Iceland 5-12-44
Dear Hermina and Maria,
Received your letter. It was swell to see you girls - - your picture.
I'm going to have a few snapshots done in the near future. If they're not too bad I'll send you some. If and when you make some more pictures I'll be glad to receive you again. No! You didn't write that you were doing office work. I'm really very glad to hear that. The more it does not require any physical strength. Please write me more detail just what you're doing. Are you typing, too?? Irving
did not write me since the last time I wrote you. Maybe he'll write me someday - may be…There is nothing new here. My brother Joe
is still in the States near Los Angeles - hope he'll stay there for the duration. It's now 11³⁰PM and it's still daylight. I don't know if I wrote you that in the summer months here is 24 hours daylight a day. Now is about 22 hours. It seems funny before one get used to it. The weather was very nice and sunny yesterday. Today was snowing and blowing again. It must be nice over there now. It probably started the bathing season. Are you girls going swimming? If not, you should. I wish I could but I guess I'll have to wait with that for some time. Otherwise I'm fine. Hope the same about you. It's getting close to midnight so I better sign off. Hoping to hear from you soon. Love, Louis

1944/5/14 Irving to Dave, Anzio Beachhead, Italy (V-Mail, Slide 153)

May 14, 1944
Anzio Beachhead

My dear brother Dave,
Just a line to let you know that I'm OK and I hope and pray to God to stay that way. I have written home also, they are OK. I hope that you are fine and in good health. Please write me and I'll try my best. I hope that your packages will arrive soon. One package is on the way here from home too. I'll ask more later, but at present time I'll have enough for a while. Now I close this time I hope and trust in God that He'll help me and everything will be OK. Love from, Irving

1944/5/14 Irving to Family, Anzio Beachhead, Italy (V-Mail, Slide 152)

May 14, 1944
Anzio Beachhead

My dear sisters Hermine and Maria,
Just a line to let you know that I'm OK and I hope and trust in God that He will help to stay that way. I have received a couple letters from you and two small packages. Thanks very much for it. On your question about entering the army, it was March 16 - 43 and I left home the 23rd of March. And left the states August 23rd and arrived to Africa Sept[ember] 2, 1943. Since then you know where I'm, I hope and pray to God that everything will be OK. I have been over seas almost as long as I have been in the States. That's the way it is. I remain with love and trust in God that we will meet again soon in the best of health. Love, Irving

1944/5/16 Irving to Hermine and Marie, Anzio (Book 2, 117-119)

Anzio Beachhead
May 16 - 44
My dear sisters Hermine and Maria,
Just a line to let you know that I'm okay and hoping in God to stay that way. I have received five small packages and a couple of letters from you. I'm glad to hear that you are all well and in good health. The other day I have written a letter and said that I'm going to send some money home. So today, in this letter I'm enclosing a money order of forty dollars. I hope you'll receive it. If you need of anything, please don't

hesitate to use it. If I need some later, you'll send me. But it won't be long we will get paid again. Money doesn't mean anything over here. I'm glad to see that you really bought something on your birthday. A present that I wanted to get you. I hope that God will help me and when I return home I won't forget you. Please write me and don't worry. I remain with, Love and hope to see you soon! Irving

Love to Dave and Herman.
Irving
I'll write more later.

1944/5/17 Hermine to Gilbert Rosewater (Book 11, 12-13)

Columbus May 17-1944
Dear Mr. Gilbert Rosewater,
It seems rather strange writing to some one whom I have never seen, but through Mrs. Goldstein I feel that I have come to know you. I had planned on coming to Cleveland to visit Mrs. Goldstein, but due to her condition I thought it is better to wait awhile. Since this may be some time I thought it would be nice to have you as my guest for dinner, a week from Sunday which will be May 28. Until I hear from you, I remain, Very truly, Hermina Gluck

1944/5/18 Irving to Dave, Anzio Beachhead, Italy (V-Mail, Slide 155)

May 18, 1944
Anzio Beachhead

My dear brother Dave,
Just a line to let you know that I have received your letter and I'm glad to hear that you are well and in good health. I'm OK I hope in God that He'll help me to stay that way. The other day I have written to Louis Schwartz I have received [an] answer of it. He is doing OK. he is asking me if I have fun on my pleasure time. Yes, plenty of it, you know what I mean. I guess I have told you the other day what I'm doing. I know people don't believe things like that. My only hope is that God will help me to go through this and help me to return in good health to America. I remain with love, your brother, Irving

Till we meet again!

1944/5/18 Irving to Family, Anzio Beachhead, Italy (V-Mail, Slide 154)

May 18, 1944
Anzio Beachhead

My dear sisters Hermine and Maria,
Writing you again to let you know that I'm OK and hoping in God to stay that way. I hope that this letter will find you in the best of health. The other day I have received some old letter which you have written sometime in December. It's nice to think back on the things that you were answering. That was in the good old days. For example you were saying that you are glad that I had a good stove. That was in Africa, yes that was OK. But I remember I had a comment on it. I guess it wasn't too good. Today I guess I would not mind to be back there. Now I remain with love and my trust in God that He'll help me. Till we meet again! Love from Irving

Love to Herman and Dave

1944/5/20 Irving to Dave, Anzio Beachhead, Italy (V-Mail, Slide 157)

May 20, 1944
Anzio Beachhead

My dear brother Dave,
It's another day and I want you to know that I'm OK and hope you are well and in good health. Not much news over here at present and if it would be, you would know before I would tell. Because when you receive

my letters, you have already seen the news in the papers. So I just want to say that let['s] hope and pray to God that He'll help me in everything and then everything will be OK. Now I'll remain with love, your brother, Irving

Please write me whenever you can. Give my regards to the folks back home.

1944/5/20 Irving to Family, Anzio Beachhead, Italy (V-Mail, Slide 156)

May 20, 1944
Anzio Beachhead

My dear sisters Hermine and Maria,
Just a line to let you know that I'm OK and hope in God to stay that way. Have received a couple letters from you the other day, I'm glad to hear that you are well and in good health. From here I can't tell you much about myself. Just hoping and praying to God that He will take care of me and Help me to return to America in good health. How is everything back home? Are you at the same place as you were? I hope that this letter will find you all in good health. I remain with Love, Irving

Please write me whenever you can.

1944/5/21 Bertha to Hermine (Book 17, 15-17)

New York
May 21 / 44
My dear Hermine!
I only write a couple of lines because I had to be lazy a little for a few weeks, until finally I also became envious of those who had a chance to protest with the surgeries, and I let myself go under the knife too. But, thank God, I'm already at home for a couple of days and I feel much better than before when I went to the hospital. Although, I am still weak, I would enjoy the csárdás [Hungarian traditional dance and music] already. I would dance already, but there is no one to dance with. But let's leave this. I'm sorry that it took me a long time to give news about me, but you can also understand that it happened against my will. I got from Irving a letter a few weeks ago, but I did not have a chance to respond. Please write to him not to take it the wrong way, but it was against my will. Although, I promised to him that I will write to him often and I wanted to send a package to him too, but I believe that Jenny Frey will write to him and to you as well, and promised that she will send a package to Irving. I hope you will permit me to write such a short letter, but I can not sit for too long. Although I am getting ahead fast, it takes time until one gets one's strength back. I think I will go away at the end of next month for a week. I will write to you in the near future. I hope my letter will find you all in good health! With love, Bertha,
My husband is sending his best also.

1944/5/21 Irving to Dave, Anzio (Book 2, 270-271)

May 21, 1944
Anzio Beachhead

My dear brother Dave,
Just a line to let you know that I'm okay and have received two letters from you yesterday. I'm very glad to hear that you are well and in good health. In your letters you were saying that you were sending me a couple of packages. Thanks very much for it. Also you want me to ask you for some more. I'll ask for more later. At the time being don't send me anything, because I'm receiving some from home too. Please write me more often if you can. I hope that this letter will find you in the best of health. Not much news over here at present. So I'll close this time, my regards to the family back home. Love from, Irving

---

1944/5/21 Louis Schwartz to Marie (Book 17, 134)

Iceland 5-21-44
Dear Maria,

Just received your letter and I'm answering it promptly. Glad to hear that you received a letter from Irving and that he is well. He didn't write to me as yet. My brother is still in the States near Los Angeles. Hope he'll stay there for a long time though I don't believe it. Now is Sunday afternoon. I just got off guard duty which lasted for a week mostly at night. Now it's raining. It is probably nice over there. I've'nt heard from home either. Hope the next months will enable us to know everything about them. As far as I'm concerned, I'm fine. Hope the same about you. How do you girls enjoy the spring? We had a few nice sunny days last week. I guess I'll 've to close now. So long till I hear from you again. love, Lou

1944/5/22 Hermine to Mary Kay (Book 11, 18-19)

Columbus May 22
Dear May Kay,
It was very nice to hear from you. I am glad to hear you are well. I think a lot about you and read your card. It was very sweet. I could talk to you about many things, but it isn't so easy to write it down, hoping you know me and will understand me. We all like to see you, but maybe next time. How are you Mary Kay? Have you heard about your brother the one [who] is in Italy? We received 4 letters from Irving and it surly makes me feel much better. I am sorry I couldn't answer your letter sooner, but there is so much to do and I am very busy. You know I have a surprise for you. Marie and Lilian and I are taking dancing lessons 2 a week. We like it very much and [are] hoping we will learn. We had a birthday party for our boss Mr. Jaqes. I can't remember how we spell his name. Just like when I write about Betty I am sorry but this is the way it goes, you have something to laugh about! Tell me something about yourself and write me please. If I could write better in English it would be different. I will write some more news next time. Till then, all my best wishes to you and good luck. Love, Hermina

1944/5/22 Irving to Family, Anzio Beachhead, Italy (V-Mail, Slide 158)

May 22, 1944
Anzio Beachhead

My dear sisters,
Just another line to let you know that I'm OK and hoping in God to stay that way. I hope that this letter will find you all in the best of health. I'm waiting to receive some mail today, also I think the package [is] supposed to be here by now. Dave has written to me the other day and sends me a package also. He wants me to ask for something, but I can't, because I don't need anything. To that I'm getting enough packages, later I'll ask a package from you and him too. I have almost everything, such as soap etc. I have plenty. The only thing it's worth asking for, something that a person can eat. I'll write more later. Love, Irving

1944/5/24 Dave to Irving (V-Mail, Slide 159)

May 24, 1944
My dearest little brother Irving

I received yesterday 2 letters from you and I really was happy to receive it. I haven't heard from you [for] over 3 weeks, but I hope I will hear from you soon again! Dear brother, this week I will send you a five # assorted box and in separate mail I will send you plenty of funnies and plenty of magazines, I wish you would ask for before, but it isn't late yet. Please let me know if you want me to have sent some magazine direct from the publisher, or would you care for some good books[?] The folks are OK in Ohio. They have written too, that they haven't received no mail from you, I have sent them one of your letters. I will send you some hard candy and a good fruit cake to you [illegible] I guessed you will like it in my last package I have sent you one cake like you asked for. Brother I am glad that you asked for something and I will see that you will get it too. God bless you, I wish you good luck and a happy return to the USA forever your brother with love Dave. Please write soon. Best of luck to you and all.

PS ask for a package again at least once a week will you please?!!

1944/5/24 David to Hermine and Marie (Book 4, 22-26)

May 23rd 1944

Tuesday evening 2 AM

Dearests!

Forgive me that I didn't write sooner. I'm sorry that the situation has changed and I don't have too much time left to write. At this time I am not working at night. I will work daytime. The difference between the work I was doing and this, is that it was 10 hours a day. At this time, I'm in charge [the parenthetical is written in Hungarian letters] (in charge) on a ship like "Material Control" and without my signature, the ship's electrical equipment can't come up and no one can get anything unless I okay it. The man who is in charge, even he has to come to see and get an okay before he can get it, and it's my job to keep a duplicate order off the ship. Yesterday, the general superintendent told me, "Mr. Gluck, you're doing a fine job. You are a very good bookkeeper." I hope it will be good in the future also. Dear Maria, about the cotton I told you about, I ask you to have a little more patience. As soon as I can I will look around, and if it is possible to get, I will. Be sure I will get it. Last week I mailed you some assorted mixed candy and I hope you received it. Dear Hermine, my vacation is very soon. I will return. Take your vacation when it is best for you and let me know when. And when I will return, I will try to arrange to be there at the same time. I would like to buy a good car and I will come back with it and with five or six people. First I will wait and see what we'll decide. I received two letters from our brother yesterday. He wrote them on May 4th and 5th. I'm sending them to you. In one he asked to send him a package of some cookies and a fruitcake. It's very interesting you know, I sent him three weeks ago a 5 pound package. He did not ask for fruitcake then and I mailed it to him. The poor thing will have to keep the candy from melting even more. I will send him some other items again. It would not spoil in the next 10 days. I mailed him 6 small packages, the shipping was okay. I will mail it in about two weeks and next week again, and therefore you shouldn't. We have time later so he should not get it all at once. This way he gets it later on also. I hope God will help him to be safe. Otherwise, nothing new here. I'm very busy. I get up at 4:30 AM and working until six. Yesterday at 4:30 I was very tired and sleepy. I just woke up. I'm in a hurry to write to you so you will get some letters from me. Thanking you for the cookies you sent me. I'm going to mail some to our little brother. I will tell him that you mailed it and some candy. If he likes it he will not have to give it away right away. Please write what you think I should send for my dearest brother. I hope he is in a good position and safe. Where he is in now they have very bad fighting. It is in Cassino. I really don't know what to write now and I want to write to our little brother. Forgive me even if I don't write often. I hope you will understand my situation. Thank you for understanding. How is Herman? If you need something I will be happy to do it with a little understanding. Los Angeles is just 20 km from here. I don't have the time to see you. Therefore take care and wishing you all the best. Dear Maria, you wrote where you work for school and that you have to stand all day, but you did not mention what you are doing, or maybe you don't want me to know? Why don't you ask permission to sit down and tell them to place you in a place where you can sit? How is your hand? And Hermine, how is your throat? And Herman are you getting something from the government for the discharge? Please write as soon as you can. Kisses, Dave

1944/5/24 Gilbert Rosewater to Hermine (Book 17, 273-275)

11523 Ohlman Ave.
Cleveland Ohio
May 24, 1944
Dear Miss Gluck!
Your introduction was really very good and your name does not sound too strange to me since I [have] been visiting Mrs. Goldstein. After a conversation I also found out that a cousin of yours Schwartz from Nagyrapos [maybe Veľké Kapušany, Hungary] married a girl from my home town. I deeply appreciate for your invitation, and would like to meet you personally, but due to business will it be impossible for me to visit you May the 28th. By my first occasion would like to visit the capitol of Ohio, and also to visit you. Kindly let me know if that would be convenient for [me] to see you some other day or week end. Best regards, G. Rosewater

1944/5/25 Bertha and Mannie to Irving (V-Mail, Slide 160)

May 25, 1944
Dear Irving: I do hope you are not angry with us for not writing you sooner, since we were indisposed with ill health and now everything is coming along fine. I sincerely trust your health and spirits are high and good. Knowing that you are on the go so much, I trust this letter finds you pronto. Irving dear, be patient,

and I will surprise you with a package. Jennie Frye was here and promised me to send you a package and a letter, so please look for same. We have heard from your family and everything is fine. Just you keep your hopes high and above all take good care of yourself. We are constantly praying for you. All our love, Bertha and Mannie

1944/5/25 Dave to Irving (V-Mail, Slide 161)

May 25, 1944
My dear brother Irving!
I have received yesterday 3 letters from you and I really can't tell you how much that meant to me. I really was worried. But thanks God you are OK and I do hope that we see each other. I will hear the same thing from you. You know in the last days the news aren't very [good from] out there, but I do hope that God will help you to return safe home. The folks are OK in Ohio. Please you don't have to worry about us, you see that you are OK and see that you are very careful, think before you act. I am not at home yet, I have a little time left on my lunchtime so I just write to you. You know I am back on days again! I like it better. I hope you don't work at night. Please if you can, let me know what you do. I like my job. It is very interesting. I meet plenty of people, and they are all coming to me for information as I am now on material control, and every electrical job must be approved by me before it can be delivered on the ship. I am proud of it. It is a very interesting job and it is very essential too. It is up to me to see that the men get what they need and the right thing - well it is time to close my letter, God bless you, and the best of luck hope to hear from you soon with love from your brother, Dave

P.S. Write soon.

1944/5/27 Irving to David (Book 6, 161-162)

May 27, 1944
My dear brother Dave,
Just received a few lines from you and I'm glad to hear that you are well and in good health. I'm okay and hoping in God to stay that way. Not much news over here, you know what I mean. The other night I received one small package, thanks very much for it. I hope you are right that this war ends by August. Back home they look it different way, not like when you are over here. You know sometimes it looks like that it will never end. But everything has to come to an end, so let's hope. Say wouldn't it be nice to stop and knock on the door at our father's home? Boy, believe me that will be something. You know every day I'm getting closer and closer, but only with God's help. You know more about every days happening than I do. Please write me about everything. You know you can do it, but I can't. I will tell you when I get home with God's help. I'll close this time and I'm hoping to hear from you soon! Love, Irving

P.S. Write me soon, I'll do the same!

1944/5/28 Irving to Dave, Italy (V-Mail, Slide 163)

May 28, 1944
Italy

My dear brother Dave,
Just a line to let you know that I'm OK hoping in God to stay that way. I received a letter yesterday from you and you were asking me to write on ordinary paper. You know Dave at present it [is] much faster to write on v-mail. It's handy and it's easiest to get. So later when everything will be OK I'll write you a very long letter. Till then just take it easy. Remain with love, Irving

Please write me soon!

1944/5/28 Irving to Family, Italy (V-Mail, Slide 162)

May 28, 1944
Italy

My dear sisters Hermine and Maria,

It's another day and I want you to know that I'm OK and hoping in God to stay that way. Received a couple letters from Dave the other day and he is OK too. Not much news over here at present and if it's going to be you'll know it much faster than if I'd tell you. I'll write you more later. Remain with love till we meet again, your brother Irving

Please write me soon!

1944/5/28 Louis Schwartz to Irving (Book 18, 44-45)

Iceland 5-28-44

Dear Irving,

Received your letter yesterday. It was swell to hear from you again. It has quite changed over there the last few days, for the better. Hope it's going to be kept up with the best of luck to you. I've received letters from two friends who just arrived to Italy. I don't think they are close to you. I had also a letter from your sisters. Tell me Irving don't you boys ever have a chance to get behind the front lines for some rest?! I hope you are allowed to write about it. About myself, is not much to write. We're keeping up the same routine with the rainy monotony, but I don't think I can put up in anything on you. We only hope it won't last long. My brother is still in the States - at least he was when he wrote me last about 3 weeks ago. I've'nt heard from home for ages, but it depresses me the events happening there, but let's hope the best. Please write as often as you can. Best of luck. Love, Louis

1944/5/31 David to Hermine (Book 12, 68-72)

Wednesday

Dear Herminka!

I just got the package. The baked goods are wonderful, I could say, ever since I left, I did not eat so well- And you Herman, thank you very much for the drink-I will send the money to you on Friday- Yes.. Thank you for it! The drink is wonderful! You know, Canadian Club, it is not available for any money here. Yes, thank you! I will not even open it. I will keep it as a souvenir. The other drink is delicious too! It is truly delicious! For that, if I have time I will send you something for it. Until then, thank you! I believe next week we will get back to 8 hours daily work, this way I will have time to write more! Until then, thank you so much - You are a truly good boy Herman! Mariska! You are not working as I saw it. So, come here! I will pay the travel expense for you and I will look for some job so you can work in Hollywood at Lady Esther [cosmetic's manufacturing company]. Do you know who that is? A "Face Creme" factory. So, if you want to come, let me know. That way I will go there to live too. Hermine, what's new with the boy? Write about it. There is no news here. I sent a 5 pound package to our little brother yesterday. He asked for a package in a letter from me. This way I will send another one on Saturday again a 5 pound package. And you know what Hermine, I will put your cookies in it because they are delicious. And you know what? I will send a little Palinka in the medicine bottle. This way there will be no obstacles and I will write it to him in advance so he will know. It will come in handy for the poor guy, right?! Write a lot! Currently, I'm going to Long Beach - Hermine the cookies are very delicious. I am eating from them while I'm writing!

I wrote a long time ago that there is something here that I will send home, when I will have time to send it. I got a letter from little brother on Saturday. He is well. Thank God! So, lots of luck with love. Kisses, Dezső

P.S. Hermine, I will write it to our little brother that I will send your cookies to him because they're very tasty.

1944/5/31 Mary Kay to Hermine and Marie (Book 16, 108-109)

151 W. Fall Creek - Indianapolis

May 31 -1944

Dear Hermine and Maria,

Maria must've begun to think I had never given her a thought, but I do. How can I forget how many evenings of pleasure I spent with you two girls. Your letter of the 22d. came and was I glad to hear from you. Was glad the girls got my postcard - I'd love to write each and everyone at the A.P.U., but I don't want to hurt anyone by writing to a number and excluding the majority. See what I mean, dear? What did the girls have to say about the card? Were they surprised and glad I think of them. Sweet Nadine, I often think of her -

remembering the time she fell off her chair. Is Avalon there and Wanda, too? Mrs. Buchler knew I was going to have a baby - recalling the shower gift she gave me - two babies pictures. Tell her she was right. By the way, Dear, have you told the girls I am to be a mother? If so, how did they act - happy or were they like my two uncles - sad. Aunt Alice said when she told them - they just looked sad. Say, why doesn't Irene answer my letter doesn't she miss me that much? Give her a bawling out. I won't let her hold my little baby if she doesn't be good. Gee, Hermine, I wish you could forget you cannot spell and tell me a lot of news about you and all the girls. Reading about your taking dancing lessons along with Marie and Lillian pleased me - you're doing OK. Keep it up! Glad you hear from Irving. How is Herman - still working so hard - trying to help Irving get home sooner. Tell him I said Hi!

My husband is reading. He is a sweet husband and how I'm going to leave him to go home will be a sad experience. He will come to see me and the baby afterwards if he's still at Fort Harrison. Can you make out my terrible writing. I am writing you like I often wrote to Bill - with a book on my knee - remember. My brother in Italy and yours too must be busy by the sounds of news on the radio. I knew about Mr. Jaques' birthday. I almost sent him a card. If I would have known so many were doing so I would've sent it. Listen, no matter how you spell - write me as I do like to hear from one of the finest girls I've ever met. Your picture I have in my prayer book. See? Bye now! Mary Kay

1944/6/2 Dave to Irving (V-Mail, Slide 164)

[Written in English]

June 2, 1944
My dear brother Irving. (I will send you a big letter Sunday)
I haven't received from you any mail for the last 2 weeks. Please try to write me more often as I said before even you write Hello to me I will be satisfied but write. I am sorry I haven't written to you myself either, but you know I am in a different position. Please write will you! Thanks. This week I have sent to you a five pound package. I have sent in it some candy I hope you will like it, and I hope you will get it OK. The sun don't hurt it. Also I had in it some cookies but they aren't very good, I try to get better ones but I haven't found a place to get them, but I think they are better than nothing - today I have sent you some funny papers and jokes, please say when you will get it. One magazine will be in 2 pieces so make it together you know I can only send you 8 ounces. Please ask in your next letter for more, oh yes, I will send you an other 5# package next Monday 6-4th. I will send you in it good cookies, I received from Hermine some good ones, and they are delicious. I have written to her that I will send you some, sorry but the peaches or plums are too heavy for a small package and I couldn't send you something else also in this package. I will send you something you will like. Best luck, God bless you

David

P.S. Write soon

1944/6/2 Dave to Irving #2 (V-Mail, Slide 165)

[Written in English]

June 2, 1944
Dear brother Irving.
I have just written you one letter, but I decided to send you one more, I hope you be glad to get it. I have written you that I did send you a package this week and will send you an other one next Monday. I hope you will like Hermine's cookies and a little palinkat [brandy] what I will send you in it, please write to me and ask me to send you, you can get and ask for a 5# package a week. I bet you are sunburned. Boy I wish I could see you. Last week I went down to Long Beach to the ocean, I got a little tan skin I been in the ocean for the first time oh boy just like salt but it is very good. You know I am fixing my varicose veins, you hardly can see it. One more month and just the place it will be OK. I am working daytime, I don't know it for sure, but I think in August I will go home for a 2 weeks. Hermine wrote to me that she will have her vacation then, but I am not sure yet. - Brother Sunday I will send you a long letter, till then God bless and best of luck to you, I hope this letter will find you in the best of health. Please write hoping to hear from you soon with love for ever

David

P.S. Write soon

1944/6/2 Hermine to Gilbert Rosewater (Book 11, 15-16) - draft

Columbus June 2, 1944
Dear Mr. Rosewater,
I received your letter and it was very nice to hear from you. I enjoyed it very much.
Since you were unable to come this time maybe we can plan on another weekend. Will you let me know when it is convenient for you to come? When you arrive to Columbus please call me EV6223. Sincerely, Hermine Gluck

June 7-44
Dear Mr. R.,
I was very nice for your invitation but because I invited you once so I like to have you come to my house as my guest for 1:30 dinner. Your celebration was very nice on Decoration Day and I enjoy a nice parade too! This year my girl friends and I were at the lake and we had a good ride, and a swell time. Hoping you can come and I am expecting to see you next Sunday. Sincerely, H. Gluck

1944/6/2 Undated Dezső to Hermine, Marie, Herman (Book 12, 309-314)

[June 2, 1944 - The date is determined from the reference to paying for Canadian Club to Herman on Friday in a letter Dezső wrote on Wednesday May 31, 1944]

Dear Mariska! (Friday)
Forgive me that I did not respond to your letter before, but I already wrote that I was very busy. So, next week on Monday or Tuesday I will go to L.A. and I will look after the rent and permit. If it's available, I will buy it for you and send it. I hope other than that you are well! I am thank God also well. I will write to Ignác now also a few letters. So, you better take care of yourself and don't take any jobs if they don't pay enough. It should be comfortable. So, it is enough for today. Good luck. Write a lot of news! OK? Thank you! I kiss you. Dezső

Dear Herminka!
Forgive me that I'm only writing now. I was very busy and I could not get to respond. I don't know any kind of news. Everything is the same. I hope you are well too! I got a letter from Ignác, it was written on May 21st. He is sending his best. The letter came in its original form as a Vmail. I hope he is well! I will send the mentioned package to him tomorrow. I waited with it to make sure he will not get them all together at the same time. So, if you want to send them too, then write, to make sure he will not get the same. I got my vacation, but I still did not decide what I am going to do. But, if my plan will work out, it is possible that I will leave Wilmington and I will go to San Francisco or to Hollywood. I got tired of the lot of dumb morons from Texas and Arizona and where I live they are all from there. I am not in the mood to move to Hollywood to live and go from there to work. It is 60km daily back and forth. Although, they give enough gas, I don't like to drive that much. So, in my next letter I will write about my decision. For now, don't send me any packages! OK? If I need any I will ask. So, I don't know any news. I wish you good luck and everything good until I will see you again. I don't know when yet. I kiss you, Dezső
P.S. I sent a package with today's mail to your address. There are some silly things in it. For Herman there are two ill [fitting] pants and two ill [fitting] socks, candies for you and a glass set and some small things. I felt badly to take it and throw it out, but if you don't need it, do whatever you want with it.

Dear Herman!
Friday
I am attaching here a 9 dollar check here. It's about the amount of the cost you had to pay for sending the drink. Thank you for it! I hope occasionally, if I will ask for it, you will send it to me again. Forgive me that I did not send the money before to you, but I could never make it to the post office on time. Thank you very much for it! I will not open the Canadian Club. If you could, you can buy another one and put it away. But now don't send me anything, because I don't know, if I will stay here. I have already lived here for 7 months. I already wrote that it is a lousy government town. It is enough about this for today. Eventually, I will write more. Kisses, Dezső

My Dear little brother Irving.

Today is Sunday and after a lot of thinking only a letter can give the answer, or the satisfaction because I feel that I am having fun with you. The news sounds very good on the radio and we hope that you my dear little brother are well and healthy, and you will tell us everything about it. With the help of the good G-d we hope everything will be good and soon! We received a letter from Lajos, he is well and I want to write to him also tonight. Take care of yourself my little brother because you know you are always on my mind. I will send you pastries in a small package. We are well and hope to hear the best news from you.
Wishing you lots of luck and good health.
Kisses from your older sister Hermina

1944/6/4 Irving to Dave (Book 4, 102-109) with note from Dave

June 4, 1944
Italy

Dear Brother Dave,

I have received your long letters and I'm glad to hear that you are well and in good health. I'm okay, with God's help. I hope this letter will find you in the best of health. You're asking me to write you a long letter, so here I go, I don't know how long it will be. Also received small packages and today a big one, with homemade cookies. Boy! I can say this, there isn't anything better than those cookies I got. You know, we get candy, sometimes with our rations. Also receiving from home too. I'm used to it and for a change cookies is the best. Somehow I don't like too much sweetness. Also, today in your letter you mailed me some more small packages and that's because I don't ask you to send me packages in every letter. Well maybe you don't believe it, but you know if I want anything I surely would ask you to send me, because I know that you would do it. However I just can't ask you in every letter that you send me something. If I want to I can, but no one says not to. Don't get me wrong. You know candy especially gets melted especially before it gets here. There's no ice box like you said, that it would be good to put it in. So if I don't ask for anything don't be angry, I know you would do me anything I want. Let's hope together the good Lord will help us and we will meet again back in the good old U.S.A. in the best of health. Forgive me for not writing as often as I really should, but you have to consider things. Sure wish that this thing will end soon, so I could be with you with God's help. My trust in God and I hope He will help me. I haven't heard from Louis Schwartz for a long time. I hope he's okay. There're things that you really don't believe, that's the way it goes. Louis was asking me things that you know like if you were out someplace having fun, dancing: Boy! That's way off. I guess when I get home I'll be dancing with my sisters! You know I'll tell you something, till yet God help me and I hope He will help to return to America in the best of health. When I get home, I want to be a good man! To my knowledge I have not done anything that would be sin, but at home I assure you that I'll do like our father did when we were home all together. I wouldn't know how to thank God that He helped me. I guess after things like this, you begin to think. And think hard! I hope you understand my letter, sorry for not writing it in Hungarian language, but I think the censor will be able to read it over here. I didn't want to have this letter alone to send it to Napoly or to Base censor. Maybe it will be a little difficult to read it, but when read it and if you understand it, then everything will be okay. Well, for now I think I'll close and I'm hoping to hear from you soon. Thanks for the small packages and if I need anything I'll ask for it. I remain with all my love to you and the folks back home. If you want to you can send this letter to Columbus. I'll write to them too. I always try my best. Love, Irving

NOTE FROM DEZSO:

Dear Mariska and Herminka,
I got your letters yesterday. Mariska, I'm so glad to hear that you are all doing well. Here I attached a letter that I know you'll be happy about. Nothing is new, kisses Dezső.
As I can see from Ignác's letter, he is near Naples.
Save this letter very well. I want to keep this.
Thank you, Dezső

1944/6/4 Irving to Family, Italy (V-Mail, Slide 167)

June 4, 1944
Italy

My dear sisters,
Just a line to let you know that I'm OK and hoping to hear the same from you. I have received some small packages and one big one with the cookies. Boy! The cookies were very fine. I'll write you a long letter sometime this week. Thanks very much for it. I have written to Dave also.
Well I'll close now, because I want this letter to go out today. Please write me soon. Love, Irving

1944/6/5 Evelyn Bossetti to Irving (Book 18, 51-53)

June 5, 1944
T.B. Sanatarium

Dear Irving:
Gee, it really was wonderful hearing from you again. I couldn't imagine what might have happened to you. Since I last saw you, I received one letter from you and I answered it promptly. Then no more letters until I got your V-mail! Perhaps the other letters you spoke of were lost somewhere between the two destinations. But everything is alright now cause I know that you are all together and still kicking! Has your brother David gone into the Service yet? I must call at your home to see how everyone is there. I hope that it's alright with you! It would be ideal to be back at the skating rink - - the same night we met. Little did I think that night, that I would see you in uniform and then hear from you miles and miles away from home. I can't figure fate out. When I try to put two and two together and the coincidence of meeting your brother David - then getting in touch with you again. Little did I dream that I'd be writing to you at Anzio Beachhead. Time flies so fast and people do the same thing. A person is halfway cross the country before he can catch his breath. Am I not right Irving?? I must close now and do a little studying - so if you will excuse me, I'll be looking for an answer soon. I'm keeping my fingers crossed and praying that this letter gets to you. Love, Evelyn

1944/6/5 Gilbert Rosewater to Hermine (Book 16, 119-121)

June 5, 1944
Dear Miss Gluck!
Kindly let me know if you will be home next week Sunday, or if that will be convenient for you so I would watch for you in Cleveland. I did not have a chance to see Mrs. Goldstein but hope she is well. How did you celebrate Decoration Day? We had here a nice parade and I was on the march too. Closing my letter and expecting to hear from you.

G.

1944/6/6 Hermine to Irving (V-Mail, Slide 168)

My Dear little brother Irving.
Today like always I'm thinking about you a lot and I'm asking the good G-d to help you no matter where you go. Your progress is making all of us very happy but the important thing is to hear from you soon, that all is well and you are healthy. Don't be surprised that I write this way, but there is so much news, that only your letter can make me happy. Besides, if everything is successful I think it will make you happy that you are going to defend our poor father and brother. Believe me, it's a miracle, and we hope that soon and with luck you can visit them. This will be a miracle, but we trust in G-d. Now write my little brother because I think about you all the time. Lots of luck, kisses Hermina

1944/6/8 Dave to Irving (Book 2, 76-79)

6-8-44
Dear little brother!
I wrote it to you last week that I will write a very long letter for you. But unfortunately only today I can get to it and how long it will be, I don't know yet, but I will send a V mail letter also.

I don't know any particular news from home.- everything is the same, I hope the dear God helped you and you are already in Rome in the best of health. May God help us that it is true. I'm starting to be impatient. Your last letter was written on 5.21 and the battles only started after that. I hope that I will get good news from you shortly! First, I will send the notified package tomorrow and I will send some palinka [Hungarian liqueur] in a little bottle to you…

…as a medicine and when you get it, do not open up the bottle front of anyone. There is a little sticky note on the bottle, skin lotion, if you'll get it and if you need it, then ask for a package and I will send more. Otherwise, how are you little brother? I'm, thank goodness well. Yesterday I sent a Life Magazine. I hope you will get it. I don't know any news right now. Everybody is well at home. They are waiting for mail from you, especially Mariska. If you can, write, ok?

Here the weather is very nice and summery. The sun shines and the air is nice and cold. The warmth is not like in Columbus. So, my little brother may God help you and come here to me as soon as possible. I hope my lines will find you in the best of health. Believe me that I would love to be there by your side so you could tell me about many things. But I hope the dear God will help you and you can visit dad shortly. It's going to be a good surprise for him. Don't you think? Poor little Emil will be the happiest, if nothing gets in your way. If you could do something about Dad, do it. I know you will do anything you can, if nothing gets in your way. Currently there is good news coming from everywhere, but many will not come back ever. In my calculation, if you got into Rome, then I'll feel a little better, because the radio announced that everybody who fought for Rome, will get a medal/award.

…they will get a small amount for guarding Rome.
So, it's enough for today. May God help you for everything good and lots of luck in your new home. I hope there is no need to hide anymore. Please write a lot anytime you can.
I will see you later with lots of love, your faithful brother who always thinks about you with love. Dezső

P.S. Write ASAP ok, let us know the news. Write a lot about Rome, ok? Did you see the Pope?

1944/6/8 Hermine to Irving (V-Mail, Slide 169)

[Written in English]

June 8, 1944
My dear little brother Irving,
I can't tell you how I miss your sweet letters and hoping as soon as you can you will write us. I know you are very busy and now more than ever. The only thing is take care of yourself and God will help you. I will send you some cookies in small packages hoping you will like it and if you need something just let me know. Flora was asking about you and so did Arthur too. They are well and we all are well and in good health. Yes dear Irving, I am working on the same place and they are swell to me. I like it very much there. All the good luck, and best wishes to you with all my love, your sister Hermina

1944/6/8 Hermine to Irving #2 (V-Mail, Slide 170)

[Written in English]

June 8, 1944
My dear little brother Irving.
Tonight on JUNE-8th I think very much about you. I wish we could hear from you sooner, because it is very hard to wait. From May 20th we didn't have any mail. I mean your latest letter was written at the 20th. But like you and all of us we trust in God and we are asking him to help you. Believe me with God's help maybe soon you are the help for our dear father and the family. Would it be wonderful, but I hope with all my heart that I will hear from you soon. Everyday I am looking for your sweet letters. Take care of yourself and good luck. With all my love, your sister, Hermine

1944/6/10 Dave to Irving (V-Mail, Slide 171)

[Written in English]

June 10, 1944
My dear brother Irving!

I have received 3 letters from you this week. In God bless you for it. I do hope that you are in perfect health, and I do hope that you are OK in Rome. I have written you the other day a 4 Page letter. I hope you received it. Yesterday I did mail you a 5 pound box. I hope you will get it soon, I have sent in it a can of plums, a bottle of sun lotion palinkat [brandy] , and some Hermine's cookies, some candies some assorted hazel and peanuts, and one O'Henry bar. I hope that it will arrive safe. I do hope that you have received the package what I have sent you 2 weeks ago! Please ask for more then I will send you some more canned goods. If you will like the lotion let me know and if it does you good I will be pleased to send you some more. The folks in Ohio are OK nothing news. Please rush back home as soon as you can. I do hope to see you soon. Please write whenever you can. I will do the best my self. Please ask for anything you would like to get. I will be most happy to send it to you. God bless you with the best of luck. - dear brother I do hope that today you are in a better position than before. Are you? Till I will see best of luck and love to you till we meet again your brother forever, David

P.S. Write soon

1944/6/12 David to Hermine and Marie (Book 15, 102-104) scan of first page blurry

Dear Mariska and Herminka!
I got your letter yesterday and currently I don't have time to write more. Mariska, I don't like it at all what you wrote...
Mariska I don't know what kind of...
You write about a week ago to send you designs for a pocket book, but I could not find the letter anywhere...
So today I bought for you 8 skeins in black color. I believe you asked me, I believe you asked me for that, and a book in different design. Based on the book, 5 and 6 are needed for a pocket book and 1-2 for a hat.
So if you don't need them all, then send them back, or if you need more, then ask for it and I will send more. It comes in two colors black and brown. So write about this! It is as much as in Helmec. Hermine, if you need more in brown, write it and I will send it also. There were two pocketbooks made here. I asked their prices. It is about 30-35 dollars, but it's not for sale. It's only a sample. So I hope you will be satisfied with it because although it is what you asked for I just don't know how much. So, write about what you will do when you come here. I will not go to San Francisco then. And write if you need more cotton because even here they are not encouraging. I hope Herman you got the check! The package went with express, but if something will be broken, you better report it to the company because there is $50 of insurance on it. I sent a package to Ignác. I hope he will get it! So I wish you good luck! Currently I'm in LA. I'm going to the movies. I have not been in Hollywood for awhile. I'm not in the mood to go.
Kisses, Dezső

1944/6/12 Hermine to Irving (V-Mail, Slide 172)

My Dear little brother Irving,
I haven't heard from you for a couple of days but I know how busy you are. It's true that one line, that you are well would mean a lot to me and I ask the good G-d to help you, wherever you are and wherever you go. Believe me that I don't have a minute when I don't think about my little sweetheart, but with G-d's help if you progress, then you could be the savior of our dear father and brother and we hope, that no matter how hard, there will be peace on earth. Now just this, we are well, wishing my dear little brother lots and lots of luck and good health.
With love, kisses, Hermina

1944/6/13 Gilbert Rosewater to Hermine (Book 17, 392-394)

June 13, 1944
Dear Hermina!
First of all I want to take this opportunity and thank you for your hospitality which I received over your house. I am sorry I did not had a chance to spent more time with you, and had to make a brief visit this time, the reason for that was due to my business connection. I still caught the train on time and depart[ed] from Columbus at 6:25P.M. and made pretty good time, and had a pleasant trip. Arriving in Cleveland I notice a lot of people down town section, mostly of them went to listen to a writer who wrote the book Under Cover. How did you spent your time after I left? I hope you had a nice time. Hoping to hear from you and best regards, Gilbert

P.S. Please convey my best regards to your sister and brother.

G.

1944/6/14 Hermine to Irving (V-Mail, Slide 174)

June 14, 1944

My dear brother Irving.

I can't tell you how I feel today because we received 2 letters from you. I could say it is a real happiness, but now I would like to have some more, hoping you are well in good health. I was thinking so hard and wanted a letter so much, that God helped me, and we are very thankful for it. Your letters were written May 22-28. We will write you again and don't worry dear, just trust and hope and God will help you. We received a letter from David he is well. Take care of yourself and good luck. Best wishes, with all my love to you. Love, your sister, Hermine

1944/6/14 Irving to Family, Italy (V-Mail, Slide 173)

June 14, 1944

Italy

My dear sisters Hermine, Maria and Brother Herman and Dave,

Once again I'm writing you and I want you to know that I'm OK and hope in God to stay that way. Also hope that you are all in good health. I'll write more later and forgive me for not writing like I used to. Roma is a very nice city, not like other places around here. Hope it won't be too long and I can tell you everything personally. Now please send this letter also to Dave. I'll write him too sometime today. Remain with love, Irving

P.S. Write soon.

1944/6/15 Dave to Irving (V-Mail, Slide 175)

June 15, 1944

My dear brother Irving!

I am writing you this letter with the hope that you are OK with God's help. I haven't received from you no mail since May the 21st. Please write to me as soon as you can, I am very worried about you. Oh Brother, I do hope you are all right. I can't think of anything. I see you always before me. I do hope to hear from you soon. I hear over the radio good news from Roma but I haven't heard from you nothing - I can't find any words to write. I am so anxious to hear from you, hoping that you are well and will hear soon from you. - I received mail from home the other day. They are OK. Herman wrote to me that he got one hundred dollars from the government for his army discharge. I don't know if he has written you about, I have written Mary [Maria] to come to Hollywood and will pay her the expenses and I could find her a good job, but she doesn't want to come. They say that they will wait till you will come back home. I do hope myself that it won't [be] very long till I will see you in the U.S.A. and I do hope from my hearts that you will come home safe. Best wishes and best of luck to you and your comrades and God bless you, with love to my little brother, David

P.S. Write me very soon please!!!

1944/6/15 David to Hermine and Marie (Book 15, 139-140)

Thursday 6-15, 44.

My darlings!

What is this?! I didn't get any news and didn't hear about you! Why didn't you write? What's up? You don't write, if I don't write?! I got a letter from our little brother today. Thank God he is well! He wrote it on 5-28-44 'Somewhere in Italy'. Thank God he is well and if the dear God would help on the 28th he was well. So this way today let's hope the best, especially he has to be good. It's possible that he is in Rome. It's possible that he already moved ahead. I will attach his letter. I hope you got the package, I felt sorry for what

I don't need, with Herman's things, but I believe that something in it would be worth it to fix and wear. Hermine there was a book attached "Valentine Gardens" it's a nice place and actors go there. I was there a few weeks ago. You can keep the book as a souvenir. There is an actor's own hand written signature in it.

And you Mariska, if you will come I will take you there. OK? There is no news here. The vacation ended [and] I will go back to work tomorrow. The sun shines nicely, but the air is cold. How's [it] in Columbus?

What's the news over there? Hey Mariska I got your letter where you asked me for 5 skein of cotton, but I sent 8. You surely don't know about the hat, but if you don't need it, you can send it back. But yes, if anyone wants me to buy more cotton, I don't have any time. They can order it directly from the company. The address will be on the package! Write about it, if you will get it. Hey Mariska! I forgot! I don't count on anything for the cotton, but I only ask one thing for you to do, I know you have the liquor ration book. Once in awhile, go and order "Canadian Club (whiskey)" for me and send it to me. I will give you the money for it, taking into consideration that I want to send a little bit of it to our little brother, too. I sent it in a previous package to him in a little medicine bottle. Kisses, Dezső
Hey Hermine, today I found some more of the cookies. Don't send it for now.

1944/6/15 Undated Helen Perl Goldstein to Hermine (Book 17, 378-379)

[June 15, 1944 - Dated by Mr. Rosewater and Sunday the 11th]

Dear Herminke!
I got both of your letters. I did not respond to the previous one because I just sent a card to you the day before. A little after, I heard that Mr. Rosewater can't travel at the invited time because he had fire damage and that made him busy, but on Sunday, that is, on the 11th of this month he will travel over to Columbus. I am truly interested if you had a guest? Because I did not talk to him yet this week. It is good to know that he will come by if he is around for business, otherwise he lives very far from us. And I don't know anything yet. Please write and what do you say about that? I wish it from my heart that you can develop a mutual sympathy and it would be a great party. Although this is your business and God's will! I can't write much about me. I am like the weather, my changing situation is complicated enough. God will help somehow and I will get through the situation. Whatever we had in our home country is still going on and I cry about it night and day. But am I helping it? If my husband is at home he neither reads the newspaper nor listens to the radio. But if he is not at home, I do anything else then always make myself upset. Is it a miracle or is it not? I have everybody over there and they are innocently facing their sad destiny that is waiting for them. But it is better if I don't dwell on this subject further more. What did you hear about the Shvarc boys? If you have an address send it to me sometimes. I would write a couple of lines to them. I am asking you again to please respond as soon as possible. Until then, I kiss you and I wish everything good! Helen

I kiss Mariska separately.

1944/6/16 Dave to Irving (V-Mail, Slide 179)

[Written in English]

June 16, 1944
My dear brother Irving!
Today I had a special good day, thanks God. You know I was so happy that I cried. I received a letter from you dated 5-28-44. Oh Boy was I happy. I do hope that God will help you to stay in the best of health. You know when [I do] not [get] your letter I haven't felt to work even, you with that letter have given me the pep to go work. Oh Brother I am so happy I can't tell you how I feel, and I do hope with God's help you will come back to us. But please be very careful and please ask for anything you wish. I will send it to you as soon as I can get it. Please when you ask for a package I will send you some good cookies and some palinkat [brandy] , if you care for, Brother I hope to see you in person so happy as I was when I received your letter. Please write soon with love your brother, David

P.S. Write as soon as possible?

1944/6/16 Irving to Dave, Italy (V-Mail, Slide 176)

June 16, 1944

Italy

My dear brother Dave,
It has been a long time since I have written you last. First I want to tell you that I'm OK with God's help. I hope that this letter will find you in the best of health. Since then I have received some letters from you and from home too. They are OK. Say Dave, did you get that long letter? You know, you just can't write everything that you would like, however the main thing is that I'm OK and hoping in God to stay that way. The packages hasn't arrived yet. It will though soon. I have received home made cookies! Boy that was delicious! I'll write more later! Love, Irving

1944/6/16 Irving to Family, Italy (V-Mail, Slide 178)

June 16, 1944
Italy

My dear sisters Hermine and Maria,
Just another line to let you know that I'm OK and hoping that this letter will find you all in the best of health. I'm preparing to write you a long letter. I'm sorry I couldn't write you before as often as I used to sometime ago. Yet at present I will have more time and I will write at least one letter a day. I know how much that really means, to receive mail. I also will try to write to Dave. I'll close this time and I'm hoping to hear from you soon. Remain with love your Brother Irving

P.S. Write soon

1944/6/17 Irving to Family, Italy (V-Mail, Slide 177)

June 17, 1944
Italy

My dear sisters Hermine and Maria,
I hope that this letter will find you all in the best of health. I'm OK. Yesterday I have received six letters from you and it makes me happy to hear that you are well and in good health. Also received a package from David, Boy! He is like an old grand daddy. He sends me everything. If I would ask him to send me anything he would do it. However I don't know what to ask for. Candy gets melted before it gets here so I just ask him to send me some peanuts [Written in Hungarian - pinac]. I'll write more later. Love, Irving

P.S. WRITE ME SOON!

1944/6/17 Irving to Family, Italy (V-Mail, Slide 180)

June 17, 1944
Italy

My dear sisters Hermine and Maria,
Just another line to let you know that on July 15th will say "Rosh Hodesh av" and on the 21st will be the date of our year date. Yes, time goes fast, it's twelve years now that our mother died [Written in Hungarian - meghalt]. God let her soul rest in peace. I don't know if I will be able to attend the services. However God knows all this. Someday I'll readjust the things that today I can't. Now don't worry, I will write you soon again. Remain with all my love your brother, Irving

Love to Dave and Herman.

1944/6/18 Irving to Dave, Italy (V-Mail, Slide 181)

June 18, 1944
Italy

My Dear Brother Dave,

How are you David? I hope that you are fine and in the best of health. I'm OK with God's help. You know Dave, you are like a grand Daddy. I just received one of the packages that you sent me. It was dated May-5-44. You really would like to send me plenty of everything. Thanks very much for it. If you are going to be a good boy I'll ask for another package. Send me some peanuts [Written in Hungarian - pinac], but don't send any chocolate, because it gets melted. Over here it's very hot, and I can't keep it. Before it gets over here it's melted. I'll write you more later. Love, Irving

P.S. WRITE ME SOON!

1944/6/18 Irving to Family, Italy (V-Mail, Slide 182)

June 18, 1944
Italy

My dear sisters Hermine and Maria,
Here I'm again writing you to let you know that I'm OK and thinking of you all a lot. I don't remember if I wrote you about that small news paper, but if I didn't, I want you to know, this paper would be good to have, but the letter are very small and it makes it unable to read it. Thanks very much for your thoughts. You know at present place where I'm we have plenty of cherries. How is Herman? Tell him to write me. Did you get that long letter? Please write me soon. Love, Irving

1944/6/20 Gilbert Rosewater to Hermine (Book 17, 269-271)

June 21 - 44
Dear Hermina,
I received your letter and was very glad to hear from you. I wrote you one letter before being in Columbus, but according [to] your letter [it] seems to me that you did not receive my first letter or maybe my letter got lost. Kindly advise me if you received my letter from before? Of course I have mentioned I had a swell time with you but last time I could not spend more time. How [have] you been otherwise? The weather down here was very hot. How is it in Columbus? I did not see Mrs. Goldstein but will see her in a few days. Closing my letter and remain with best regards, Gilbert

1944/6/22 Dave to Irving (V-Mail, Slide 183)

June 22, 1944
My dear brother Irving.
I had yesterday received your long letter and many thanks for it. God bless you for it. It was very kindly from you to write me such [a] good and long letter. I had sent your letter to Columbus, I bet they will be very happy. You know your letter wasn't censored in the inside, just outside was the censor's stamp. Please let me hear from you very soon, and if you can please write me where you are, I do hope you are close to Rome and safe. You know as you see I had moved from Wilmington to Long Beach to 1363 Alamito Ave. Apt-11- I have a one room apt, I make my breakfast and same time I hope I will make my supper too. Please ask for something if you would like to have something - Best of luck. God bless you. Till we meet again, with love your brother Dave

1944/6/22 David to Family (Book 12, 78-79)

Long Beach 6-22-44
1363 Alamitos Ave.
APT -11-

NEW ADDRESS

My Darlings!
I believe you'll be surprised that I live in a new place, but as I mentioned in the past I will move. So, yesterday I got a one room apartment, one room and a little kitchen. It's a pretty good place! I have a new ice box. I had to do something because I already have to be at work at 6 in the morning and there is nowhere

to eat then. I will make breakfast alone and sometimes cook dinner, too. If the two of you girls would come it would be enough for you.

It would cost as much as you pay there. So, I don't know any news. Forgive me, if I don't write correctly, but I will be busy. You know, my ice box is so packed that there is no place to put anything else in it.

It is packed with everything. So, it is enough for today. Isn't [it] beautiful!? I am washing the dishes alone and I'm cleaning my room. Please write a lot! Here the weather is beautiful. Tomorrow after work I have to go to town, which is about a mile from me. And I have to buy sheets and a little pillow and many dishes!

But at least this way I don't live among the drunks there- So, don't forget that I have a new address-OK!? Address 1363 Alamitos Ave Apt #11-Long Beach, California.

So, write a lot. I'm waiting for your lines. I will see you again! Hey Marcsa, did you get the cotton? So, what did you do with that material that I sent in December? You have to crochet from the 4 that I sent. Kisses, Dezső

1944/6/22 Irving to Hermine and Marie (Book 6, 163-165)

Italy

My dear sisters Hermine and Maria,
I have just received a couple letters from you and I'm glad to hear from you. I know how you felt for not receiving any mail from me. You know the other day I said that I'll write you at least a letter a day, but believe me, if or whenever I can, I do. But you know the army, you just can't do what you plan. I'm hoping that this war ends soon, so I'll be able to write you whenever I want. Or wouldn't it be nice being at home, everything would be different. I could explain everything that you would like to know. From here I can't tell you much of anything, everything is the same. I have also received a couple letters from David. He is okay. I'm glad he doesn't have to go and also Herman. You know, one thinks it's nice but let me say, stay where you are and be happy. I hope and pray to God that He will help me and everything will be okay.

Please tell the relations if I don't write them it's not because I don't want to, but I'm very busy. Also tell them to write. Tell Aunt Helen too. What's news back home? Are you working hard? Here is something that I want you to know, you know I wrote you that I'm saving all the letters that I received from home and friends. However I'm very sorry to say that the other day I had to burn all the letters because I didn't have enough room to keep it. This is the army you know. Well I guess I'll receive some more letters, but yet I'll try to answer you and to all who write me. But there is that time again. I sure want to write, because that's the only way to receive plenty letters. And you know I like to receive and hear from all my friends. So please, that will concern you too. Write me even if I'm late with answering it. Well there isn't anything to write about, so I'll close now and hoping to hear from you soon. I remain with all my love, your brother, Irving

Please tell Herman that I'll write later, but he has more time so he should write me first.

Irving

P.S. Love to Dave
June 22, 1944

1944/6/24 David to Family (Book 2, 137-139)

Darlings!
This week I did not hear any news from you. Maybe because of the address change. I must get mail from you tomorrow. I did not get any from Ignác either, only the one that I sent home to you. So I became like a housewife. Today I cooked Gulyas [goulash = meat stew] for dinner. Believe it or not, but it was excellent, it was like you would have made it. It took an hour to make it. Hermine, you know, you wanted to send Stuffed Cabbage to me. So, this is your chance to send it to me. But not the cabbage, only the recipe, to see how to make it. I believe rice needs to be mixed with salt, pepper, onion, garlic, paprika, cooked cabbage,

meat, to taste. These all go to the filling, and into the sauce a little roux/thickening. How do you make thickening? Tomato, a little water and fat. Ok? You only write if it's good.

As I wrote, do not forget the thickening. About the guy, only if you like him. It's your business what you do. But, if he is old then he is not for you! But it is your business not mine. Tomorrow or on Sunday I will make new potato with cottage cheese and buttermilk.

Hey, how does one cook good mashed potatoes -There is one thing I don't know, how do I make the thickening. You can write more kinds. This week I got myself an entire set of dishes and pillows, cases [pillow case], but I still need to buy more stuff. The important thing is that there is food to eat and no need to wait on the line and eat junk. In the past I had to get up at 4:30 am to buy lunch and breakfast. And today I have time to get up at 5:15am and I get to work long before 6am. Although I have to make my lunch at night. So, it's enough for today. Kisses, Dezső

Hey Marcsa! Did you get your permit?

Herman, would you buy a little Canadian Club, if they have?

1944/6/25 Louis Schwartz to Hermine (Book 17, 99-100)

Iceland 6-25-44

Dear Hermina,

Received your letter yesterday. I was glad to hear that you have such a nice job and are enjoying it. I'm only surprised it took me almost a year to know about it. But I guess it's better late than never. In the meantime you're getting more and more experience in it. Sometimes I'm thinking to take up something useful for after the war in my free time and I probably would if I were in the States where I had more opportunity and here we never know when we're going to have off. It's now the second Sunday that I planned to go swimming here in a "hot lake" but it's cold so I have to postpone again. I hope you have it nice there. You girls take advantage of the nice weather and go swimming as often as you can. I know how much I miss it. I'm enclosing some of my snapshots taken in spring but developed only recently. It is going through the censor first you'll have an idea how nice and white Spring is here and how we protect ourselves against the cold weather. Most of the pictures taken aren't back yet. If you girls have some more don't forget to send me. I believe that's all for now. Take care of yourself and write again soon. Love, Lou

1944/6/25 Louis Schwartz to Marie (Book 17, 106-107)

Iceland 6-25-44

Dear Maria,

Received your letter the same time when Hermina's. I was glad to hear that you're feeling well. Now it's Sunday afternoon and it's quite a wind and cold. But I'll go later to town to see a show or something else. I had a letter from Irving a few weeks ago and expect to hear from him again soon, I hope… As far as I know, the conditions have improved a lot lately where Irving is - especially since the second front has started. Hope they will finish it up in no time. Hope and believe the conditions with our folks isn't as bad as we're afraid. My brother Joe is in Texas now. At least he was the last time I heard from him. Now I'm closing - hoping to hear from you again, Love, Lou

1944/6/27 Samuel Gluck to Irving (V-Mail, Slide 184)

June 27, 1944

Dear Irving:

It is certainly wonderful to hear from you so often. Instead of letters being 5 or 6 weeks apart, we are getting them every ten days now. We are getting wonderful and accurate news coverage of all fronts, much better than before. Everyone is well at home. I am dividing my time between school and work. I have only one 2-hour class each morning, and the rest of the time I spend helping my father. There are quite a number of soldiers going to school here at the university. The Hillel foundation has instituted a huge program of entertainment: Records of classical music, parties, picnics, etc. For the overseas men they are planning a program. I don't know what it is just yet, but I put your name on the list, and you may find it interesting, whatever they decide to do. Well, take care of yourself. We all miss you. Love from us all, Samuel

1944/7/2 David to Hermine and Marie (Book 12, 81-85)

July 2 - 44

Dear Herminka and Mariska!

This week I got 3 letters from you and I'm sorry that I did not respond to any of them until today, but I hope that you will understand. If you work 10 hours per day and you need to cook and clean, there is not too much time to write. I hope that you will not take it in the wrong way. So, I will note some of your reports that consider that man on 16 E. Broad St. I have never seen him and I don't owe anything to him. I don't owe to anybody else either, except 57 dollars to one person who worked for me and maybe that person is a lawyer. You could find out what he wants so I can arrange things from here. I have a lawyer there in that case. Find out from the neighbor what he said to him and for that I will teach to him. He has no right to tell stories about some people.

I already let the lawyer know once. If I owe him, then sue me and, if he is after my address, tell him that you know. But he is so shameless and goes to the neighbor for information, to ask my address from the neighbor. Otherwise tell him the Columbus Post office knows the address. So no need to be sad. As far as the recipe concerned, yes thank you I already tried 2x, but not yet the stuffed cabbage. Today I cooked Gulyas and roast, and the roast was in the oven. That will be enough for 2-3 days and [it's] like at home. So, I made a big lunch, but by the time it was done I was full with the smell of it. But believe me I cook well. Everything is delicious. I could not have bought my lunch today for 2-3 dollar. -Oh yes, I even had French potatoes [fries] also, I made it. I just cleaned everything, if you would see it, you would not believe. It's pretty clean. -As far as the job is concerned, if you like it there then good, but here you could make double the money with the same job. But the livelihood is not double like there!

Only the house [illegible, from context maybe 'price'] is higher- Oh, if you are interested in what I did last week where I worked, there were at least 36000 people on 3 shifts and the traffic was pretty heavy with 21 thousand workers barely able to get access and it took me 40-50 minutes to go home. So, this is the main reason why I left it. It was also that they only worked 8 hours and this way there was no money. So, I left there.

-It's been about 12 days - And I left Wilmington and I came to Long Beach to work and to live. It takes 10-15 minutes to go to work and it's about 3 miles from me. And there are no more people in this shipyard than in L.B. [Long Beach]. 2000 people here only to make equipment for the ships. They build the ship in a different factory and this way it is not dangerous. The company I work with is said to be the biggest electrician company, I believe in the entire world. They are working in Europe now also for a Jewish company named "Newbery Electric". So, I wrote enough for today. I will attach a letter from our little brother. Hey girls, if you come here I will give the house to you. OK?

I believe, you will be satisfied with it. It's worth at least $40 a month. Hey! What's going on with the old housewife? Did she give you the money from the garage? Hey Herman! Are you angry at me that you don't write? Maybe you are mad that I sent you that junk. I sent it with the thought that you can use it and it is a waste to throw it out. -If you are mad, then forgive me! OK? If you could do it, you could buy a little Canada Club Whiskey and send it to me just like the other one - But to this address: 1363 Alamitos Apt 11-L.B. Thank you for it in advance! Hermine, if you want, you can send a little baked goods with it, but not too much and only if you have time. It is not urgent! And send it to me with insurance and write on the package that it is [In English] "Glass" Be careful handle with care. [In Hungarian] Thank you so much in advance! Kisses, Dezső

P.S. Now I will write to our little brother also and then I will go to the beach. It's only 3 minutes from here-

1944/7/5 Margaret Hunecke (Buddy's Wife) to Irving (Book 21, 202-204)

St. Louis, Mo
July 7, 1944
Irving Gluck
Company B, 6th Armored Infantry Battalion

Dear Friend Irving,

I hope this letter finds you well. Received your nice letter July 5, which you wrote June 16. It is nice to hear from you again after so long a time. I hope you are getting along fine. I hope this war will soon, very soon be over. Let me tell you, I know what you and all the other fellas are going through. It is hell. It is a dirty shame, but it can't last forever. Each day that passes means one day less of fighting and brings us one day closer to the end of this awful war. Another thing I want to tell all of you fellas, is that you are doing a wonderful job. We here at home are very proud of all of you. Irving, I have something to tell you, so if you are not sitting down, please do so. I think it will be a shock to you. Buddy, my beloved husband, was killed, somewhere in Italy on January 30th. That is what the war department said in the telegram that I received from them on the 18th of March. Somehow, Irving, I can't believe it. I feel that he is alive and oh I pray with all my heart, that he is. I don't know where in Italy it happened, or how, all I know is what the telegram said. I wish there was some way of finding out, some way of securing such information, but I was told I would have to wait until the war is over or someone who was with Bud would be sent back to the States and they would get in touch with me. Irving, I have four pairs of wool socks and a pair of wool gloves that I bought and sent to Bud. They were sent back to me. I have no use for them and would be very glad to send them to you. Please write and ask for them. I can't send anything overseas without a written request. Write, so that I can send them and if you can't wear them, perhaps some of the other boys can. If you would like some cookies or candy, write and ask for them please. I would be very glad to send you candy and cookies. Irving, as I write this letter, I have Buddy's letter with me with yours, and I noticed the similarity of handwriting. Yours and my Buddy's look so much alike. The letter is the last I received from Bud. It was written January 17, 1944. Well, Irving, I will close for now. Good luck, and God keep you safe and well for those who love you. Write again please. Sincerely, Mrs. Margaret Hunnake

4517 Tower Grove Place
St. Louis, MO

[Irving's comments: Couldn't tell anything because of censorship. Bitter battle on that date.]

1944/7/7 David to Hermine and Marie (Book 15, 144-146)

L.B. 7.7.44
Dear Herminka and Mariska!
I got your letters, Mariska one from you and 2 from Hermine. And forgive me that I don't write correctly, but I don't have a lot of time for anything, and if you only get mail from me per week, don't take it in the wrong way. I got two letters from our little brother this week. I will send one here and I will keep one because he asked for a package from me in it. He is asking for peanuts. So, I will buy every kind of peanuts on Sunday so the poor thing can have it. You are writing that it is pretty hot there. Interesting, if you would lie on the sun here, you would get burned in a few hours, it shines so hard, but if you are in the sun you don't even feel it because the air is cold. If I go to the beach on Sunday, there is very bright sunshine, but I could almost freeze. I believe this is from the sea air. Greetings to Herman! How is he?

Hermine, thank you for the cookies! I did not make stuffed cabbage yet, maybe I will do it on Sunday. It takes a lot of work and I'm very busy-I will write how it comes out- There is no news here, everything is the same. So, Hermine about the cotton, why didn't you say that you don't know the address and I went to live away from there. Why should a peasant have the kind that you have, but if he wants it still, (IF YOU WANT IT) then here is the address; "The May Co, 7th + Hill St. Los Angeles. I believe the cotton is 75 cents plus the shipping. But I don't know, if you have it. And I can't go in! Don't forget that I work 10 hours and if I go in to buy it, then I will lose 18.00. So, it's not worth it for you

to order it alone. Tell him/her I'm not there! OK!! Hey, I have a little news- Today, Friday night I went to the temple and guess what happened? I see a sailor looking at me and I'm looking at him-after the prayer I go to him and I asked if he is from Columbus. He answered, yes. Finally, I have an old acquaintance here with his wife. His name: Harold Covel. He and his wife worked for Siff Cuposzeg. I was really very happy. Believe me, I have not been in the temple for a few months and tonight I went. I had a feeling about it. He was only there tonight also, because he had a yahrzeit. So, I have an acquaintance from Columbus, this way. He was also so happy, I can hardly write it down. His wife could not imagine that it was me. Hey, what did I hear?! The Davis girls, you know who? I heard they came here to live. From Columbus to Hollywood - No more already, I am sleepy.
Kisses, many times with love. Dezső
You better write to me. OK?

1944/7/8 Irving to Dave (Book 5, 349)

July 8, 1944

My dear brother Dave,

Just want to tell you that I'm okay with God's help. I received a small package from you, thanks very much for it. I'm sorry I'm not able to write you like I should, but you know how it is. Since then I've been on the move. It's the same everywhere. But let's hope in God that he will help in every thing. Please write me.

Love, Irving

1944/7/9 Herman to Irving (V-Mail, Slide 185)

7-9-44

Written in Hungarian

Dear Ignác,

I know you are surprised that I write so infrequently, but you know there is always something that has to be taken care of. But with G-d's help the war will be over and you will come home and then we will catch up, you know the news from home anyway. Write if you want to and if you have time. Currently I'm working 6 days in the same place. The bicycle is spinning but I have problems with it because I bought the wrong inner tube and it doesn't hold. When the war is over and you come home, we will buy a car together and it will be better than a bicycle. You asked for a picture, I will send one as soon as I have a chance to make one, sometimes I forget. And now take care of yourself, till we see each other again. Kisses, Herman

1944/7/11 Irving to Dave, N. of Rome, Italy (V-Mail, Slide 187)

July 11, 1944

North of Roma

My dear brother Dave,

It's been a long time since I have written you last, however it's like this since we started out I'm on the move. It's not like you thought and wrote me in your letters. Even now I don't know if this letter will go out, however when it does that will be the first to go. During that time I have received some packages from you. Thanks very much for it. Also for the funny books. You know Dave, when I'll see that mail goes out, I will write you a long letter and will try to tell you what I can. I'm hoping in God that He will help me in everything. Please send me cookies. Thanks very much for it. I'll write [illegible]. Love, Irving

1944/7/11 Irving to Family, N. of Rome, Italy (V-Mail, Slide 186)

July 11, 1944

North of Roma

My dear sisters Hermine and Maria,

Just a line to let you know I'm OK with God's help. And I'm hoping to hear from you the same. It's been a long time since I wrote you last, however yet it's not like it used to be. A couple weeks ago I told you that I'm going to write you every day, but look what happened. Anyway when I get into a good mood I will write you a very long letter. Yet at present time I don't know if this letter will go out, but anyway I hope it will. We are on the move since the start of this. So it's difficult to write and even though I would, it still wouldn't go out. I hope this letter will find you all in the best of health. I remain with all my love, Irving. Please send me cookies, such as fig bars you can buy it in [the] store. Love, Irving

Thanks very much [illegible]

1944/7/11 Irving to Hermine and Marie, North of Rome (Book 3, 78-88)

North of Roma

July 11, 1944

My dear sisters Hermine and Maria,

Hardly know how to begin and write you a couple of lines. It's been a long time since I've written you last. First I want to tell you that I'm okay with God's help and hope to stay that way. I wish I could talk to like I was home. Yet I'll try to say a few words, maybe it will sound to you like if I was home and talk[ing] to you personally. You know there are so many things, but you never dream of that could be. During that time I have received some small packages and letters too. Dave has sent me some too. I understand all your letters and realize that you would do me anything that you can and with pleasure. For instance you would like to send me a package a week. Yes that is very good, but who is going to eat it. You know every week, that would be too much. And some time you don't feel like asking anything. You are glad that you are able to write a couple lines. Let's hope and pray to God that he will help me to go through this horrible mess that I'm in. God is the only one who can, and I hope he will help me. Sometimes a person gets like foggy, don't know and don't see anything, because if he would he couldn't stand it. So let's not worry, let's trust in God! He is the one to whom you have to tell your troubles and if you deserve it he will help you. I'm not preaching anybody, just telling the truth. Over here every one begins to realize that maybe that's why is war, God wants to wake the people up. The people have forgotten him. The time is here, yet or never.

Forgive me for not answering all your letters, but I feel like just writing anything that comes into my mind. I hope you will understand me. A couple weeks ago I said I'll be a good boy, and will write home every day. But you know what happened. I'm not the boss! Since we started out, we hardly stopped. You're not always in the mood to write. Even today I'm not sure that this letter will go out, when it does I'll write some more.

You know sis: I'm glad that Herman didn't have to taste this in what I'm in. Tell him that, he can be proud to be where he is. I wouldn't mind to do anything if I could be there where he is. I would work for free during this mess. And I mean it too! Many people don't realize all that, but if they were over here and have a little taste of it, boy! They would learn very quick: I know it!! Now let's hope that it won't be too long and everything will be okay. Boy! That will be something when I get home with God's help. I'll be able to tell you more about myself. At present there is not much I can say, just hope and pray that it will end soon. Once again I'll say don't worry! My trust is in God that he will help me. How is everything back home? Please write me even if I'm late with my letters. But the saying is better later than never! Did you hear from Dave lately? He writes me as often as he can. The other day I received from him a few small packages. And that's because I'm not asking a package a day. What do you say to this! You know he's a good boy too. You know when you are away everything changes. If you know what I mean. I know Maria is the same way, she would want me to ask anything that I need, but I don't need anything. And when I ask for something I want only eatable things. What do you think about this letter? Do you have patience to read all this or maybe you want me to close now. All kidding aside I would like to write more and more to show you that whenever I can I write you and I always think of you.

It won't be too long that the home made cookies will get here, boy! That will be good. Let's see, I'm thinking maybe I should ask for something. What should it be? Please send me cookies. You can buy it in the store and also candy bars. Such as we used to buy when I was home. I think the easiest way to send it would be, put it in a Crisco can and it would stay fresh and wouldn't break. A couple cans would be enough and put it in a box and ready to go. You wouldn't need to wrap every cookie that way. I saw the other day one fellow got some like that. That's all at present. I'll ask some more later. Now thanks very much for everything. Keep on writing me. Let me know about everything. Now I remain with all my love, Your brother, Irving

Hello Dave and Herman,
How is everything? I think you will be able to get out something from this letter. I will try to write more later, at present I'll close and waiting to hear from you too. Write me whenever you can. You have more time to write. I know back home everything is different. Boy! I hope to be back soon and enjoy living. Remain with love, your brother, Irving

P.S. I couldn't find any other paper at present so I wrote on this. I will write more later.

1944/7/15 Irving to Dave (Book 6, 151-153)

North of Rome
July 15, 1944
My dear brother Dave,
I just came back, and I received one of your letters. Thanks very much for it. You know Dave, you are one hundred percent right with concerning your letter. However being as you said, one could not last longer than

a minute. However with God's help, I'm not having anything like that. You know it would be a long story and difficult to say. Please don't worry and every thing will be OK. I'll try to write you every day, while I'm back. You know I have just received a box of cookies from home. It came in just in time. Your big box didn't come in yet. It will though soon.

Boy! It would be nice if I could call you up on long distance. I would connect [to] you and we would talk. If you know what I mean. It's not too bad. Well at present let's hope that it won't be long and with God's help we might be able to do it. So as long as you know it's a long story, but let's hope that everything will be OK. Say Dave, do you remember that girl that I told you I met in Africa? I would like to get a picture of her. I would like to send it to you so you would see it. Boy! She was nice. You know she speaks French and a very little English. Well that's that. How are you there?

I hope you're doing fine. Please write me about yourself. Say Dave, you know Ignác? I heard that he might go for a visit to South. I don't remember the place or the name of it. I know if I could do something I wouldn't let him go. I'm afraid he might lose his job if he goes. I sure wouldn't want that to happen to him. I hope though he stays where he is, and does his job. I think you know, if you have to start everything over, that's too much and it might not pay. But it's up to him. I think you were there not long ago and you didn't like it and so you left. That was before you spoke to Arthur. Do you remember? I'll write more later. Let's hope and pray to God that everything will be OK. Till we meet again, Love, Irving

Yahrzeit is on Friday.

[Note - When he asks 'you know Ignác?' he's referring to himself, that he may be going to France, where Dave was before coming to America]

1944/7/15 Jane Schallheim to Irving (Book 18, 103-104)

July 15th

Dear Irving,
I am surprised to know you are in Italy. Your sister said she heard from you, but didn't say where you were. You certainly must be seeing a lot of action. I sincerely hope this war will be over very soon. As I am writing this letter I can look out into our back yard. It is surrounded by hedges and the roses are in bloom. The sun is shining, and a robin is searching for his breakfast. There is a large field in the back of our yard, and back of that is a house which somehow or other reminds me of a farm house. I feel as if I were out in the country. We are now in the midst of our summer vacation. But I am going to summer school so I can graduate next January instead of the following June. My classes are from 7:30 to 10:30, and then I go to work as a cashier at Eldred Hall Cafeteria Western Reserve University. Some of the customers are so humorous I enjoy working there. It seems that everyone is working from the youngest children up. Many of my friends have jobs in war plants or the Navy department. My mother [Elsie Gluck Schallheim] has just finished a dietician's aide course, and is working in a nearby hospital. There is supposed to be a python, an eight foot snake loose not so far from here. Our water hose in the back yard looks quite a bit like a snake. My imagination is playing tricks on me. Enclosed is a poem you might like. (See PDF of her letter dated 1944/4/15). The very best of luck always, and hope to see you back in the "States" soon. Mother sends her best regards. Jane

1944/7/16 Hermine to Irving (Book 2, 73-75)

Columbus, July 16, 1944
My dear little brother Irving!
We did not get a letter from you for days, but I hope you are well and healthy! I know how busy you are and I understand. Still, it's very hard to wait for your letter to come. I can write the same thing about us that we are all well, thank God. David is doing well also. He must have sent his new address to you, but I will attach it also. I don't even know what to write that you would be interested in. I think that you are in the place where happiness does not interest you. But don't you worry my little Irving dear! God is with us and we only trust him that he will help us.
I hope you got the package from home! I will be in the hurry to send them after continuously. Arthur and Helen are well too. I talked to Helen on the phone this week.

The weather is warm and I really don't like it. The neighbors are wondering about you. The old lady said that she will write to you. Write about yourself asap. I am always promising the photographs, but they are still not ready. We did it with your camera and there are a few empty in it still and it will stay that way because if one of them are home, then the other is not. So you are in my mind and I'll be in a hurry so we can send pictures from it to you as soon as possible. Do you still love cherries and do you speak that language yet? It is very terrible whatever is still going on everywhere, but let's hope that it will not last for long. Yesterday night there was a bond show here and it was pretty good. There were many actors and wrestlers in a military group. So we were there. Herman bought a bond and they gave free tickets. You got one as a gift from the unit. B.B. [B'nai B'rith] are still sending the newspapers to you. I don't know if they can be sent to you.

I could say that is very interesting. There is a lot of news in it from the entire world. Sometimes it is terrible what they do to those poor things. I'm thinking that must be on your mind. To save our Dad and Lajos! It is very hard to wait it out and I'm very worried about you my little brother. You are always on my mind. I'm asking you to write whenever you can. I know that you will do that with out being late. It makes me calm about it. Take good care of yourself and we will ask the dear God to take care of you wherever you go. I will continue in V mail. I will only do it to fill up what I missed. I wish you good luck and very good health. See you later soon. With love,
Hermina

1944/7/16 Irving to Dave, N. of Rome, Italy (V-Mail, Slide 188)

July 16, 1944
North of Roma

My dear brother Dave,
Just a line to let you know I'm OK and I hope that you are well and in good health. I hope you understood my letter. I will write another long letter one of these days. You too don't forget to write. The other night I saw a show, the first show since I left Africa. How do you like that? Well I know back home is different. I hope it won't be long and everything will be OK with God's help. I remain with love, Irving

My love to the folks back home.

1944/7/16 Irving to Family #1, N. of Rome, Italy (V-Mail, Slide 190)

July 16, 1944
North of Roma

My dear sisters Hermine and Maria,
Just a line to let you know that I'm OK and hoping to hear the same from you. Did you receive my long letters? I'm waiting now to receive one like that from you. The other night we [had] a good show, however I forgot the name of it. But you know, that was the first show since I left Africa. I took a box with me and sat on it. It's not like home, with soft chairs. However, I hope it won't be too long and with God's help everything will be OK. I'll write more later. Love, Irving

Reg[ards] to Dave and Herman

1944/7/16 Irving to Family #2, N. of Rome, Italy (V-Mail, Slide 189)

July 16, 1944
North of Roma

My dear sisters,
Just received a couple letters from you and I'm glad to hear that you are all well and in good health. I'm OK with God's help. I just took a ride to a small town, but you know there isn't anything. Whatever you ask for, they'll answer that the Germans took it away. You know how they did when we were together, well it's the same thing now. Or like what [it was] back home with the Gypsies. Mostly the people like candy, chocolate,

cigarette or something to eat. The farmers are doing fine, only the city people was hurting. That was before we came in. Will write more later. Love, Irving

1944/7/17 David to Irving (Book 3, 75-77)

7. 17. 44.
Written in Hungarian

My dearest little brother!
Forgive me for not writing to you any sooner, however I have been very busy. I'm wondering why I hadn't received any mail from you since 6-18-44. This was the last letter from you. Hope that God will help you to have all good things. I don't have any news except everything is as it was in the past. I received a letter from home and thank God that they are well. This is very difficult, to wait for you until you return home, but we hope it won't be long. This week we will have Yahrzeit for our mother. We should have been able to go together to the temple. Hope that God will help you, and the time will come shortly, that you will come home.

Forgive me, my dearest little brother, I have written to you last week that I will send you a package this week, but I was very busy. But now, I will send you the package, please forgive me. I'm still occupied. I want to put a little bit from everything in the package. This week I hope God will help me and I will mail it to you. My dearest little brother, forgive me for my delay, will you! I know that you are waiting for it, and it is difficult to wait. I did not mean to do that. Presently I'm cooking for myself supper, by the time I finish cooking, and clean the place, I'm tired and I am sleepy and I fall asleep. But today, I don't want to wait any longer so now I'm writing a few lines. I wished you would have been here tonight. Do you know what I made for supper? Cabbage. Hermina told me how to make it and it turned out to be very fine. When you come home from Europe with God's help I will cook for you a very fine dinner. I hope that the time will come shortly! My little brother take care of yourself. God will help you to all good things.

Presently I don't even know what to write to you. I can't think of anything special, but I wish you would write about yourself. If you can, my dear little brother, write to me and tell me what you are doing. What are you working on? What is the outlook? Are you working very hard? Please write to me about yourself! You don't write what you are doing, but other people write about what they are doing.

I hope that my lines will find you in good health and that God will help you to return home in good health. You should be a very religious Jewish man when you return. I will not be angry at you because of that. I wish you would be here now, the time will come slowly. There is nothing so bad that the end will not come. Remember the difficulties in Polyán and a great cores [In Yiddish: tsures = misery], but God helped us and we came to America, but you returned to Europe, and with our God's help you will return here to America. God should give you everything good and happiness until we meet again here in America, in the best of health. With much love and kisses forever your brother that will never forget you, and will never forget you for as long as I live, Dezső

1944/7/17 Irving to Family, N. of Rome, Italy (V-Mail, Slide 191)

July 17, 1944
North of Roma

My dear sisters,
Just another day and I want you to know that I'm OK and hoping that this letter will find you all in the best of health. Today, I haven't received any mail from you or from Dave. Sometimes I take your letter out, and believe me, when you say how much you are waiting for my letters to come, it breaks my heart. I only wish I could fly home and talk to you. I know how you feel. I understand you. Let's hope that it won't be long, till we meet again, Love, Irving

1944/7/18 David to Hermine and Marie (Book 15, 160-162)

Long B. 7.17.44
Darlings!

I know you will be surprised that it's been at least a week since I wrote. The reason is that I am very busy. Considering that I work 10 hours per day and my entire [free] time goes to cooking. After cooking, I'm so tired that I'm not able to write. But today I will not leave it, so I will write. Thank God I'm well, and I wish to hear the same back from you. There is no news here. I did not get mail from our little brother for awhile. So, did you get any? Write to me when it was dated. OK?! I continue with cooking. I already cooked stuffed cabbage twice and tonight I had cabbage for dinner. Can you believe that it is good?! It is almost as good as you do, only I'm very tired out. I hope the dear God will help us and this war will pass soon. I truly don't know what to write. I am very tired and sleepy and I want to write a letter to Ignác as well. I hope the dear God will help him with everything good! I can hardly wait for the mail from him and from you too. But you will see, if I don't write very often, but I will work on that, I'll write a letter at least once a week - How are you? Write to me about everything. I get the Jewish paper "Jearzeit" now it will be [printed] on Friday and Saturday. The weather here is excellent. Today was pretty warm. How is it over there? So, I will close my lines for today, God bless all of you with everything good, until I will see you again. Kisses, Dezső
How are you Herman? Why don't you write?

1944/7/18 Irving to Family, N. of Rome, Italy (V-Mail, Slide 192)

July 18, 1944
North of Roma

My dear sisters,
Somehow your letters are late, however it's better later than never, but the last couple days, I haven't received any mail from you. I hope you are all well and in good health. I'm OK and hoping to stay that way. Not much news over here at present. I hope to write you a letter every day. I don't know how long we will be back, but even then I will try to write whenever I can. Please you too write me. I'm waiting for it just like you. Now I remain with love, Irving

Reg[ards] Dave and Herman.

1944/7/19 Irving to Family, N. of Rome, Italy (V-Mail, Slide 193)

July 19, 1944
North of Roma

Hello Hermine and Maria,
How are you getting along? I hope fine. I'm waiting to hear from you. The other day I have written to you about that Hungarian friend of mine. You know he is a good joker, it makes you smile whenever he talks Hungarian or English. There is something in his expression, I'm telling you that he is good. However sorry to say that he got sick the other day with malaria and went to the hospital. He'll be OK. That is his fourth time now. Maybe he'll get a chance to go home. I'll write more later, love, Irving

1944/7/20 Helen Perl Goldstein to Hermine (Book 17, 360-362)

Cleveland July 20, 1944
My Dear Hermine!
I got your letter, in other words, your card. But believe me, I didn't respond because of my busyness or inattention. But that I will feel myself better day by day and I will invite you to me. This way you would have more opportunity to get know Rozevater [Rosewater] better because he is simple and as he said, you were together for a short time, it is hard to judge from that. Although, I can say the best about him. I hope you will continue corresponding by letter. And, if I feel much better so I can have you as a guest, truly that would be the best, that at least you could spend a week here. This way you would have an opportunity to meet with a few others. But what is late will not pass. Let's hope for the best. Ann Riech was visiting by me last week. She said she was in Columbus and tried to get in touch with you, but did not find you. She would like it if I would invite you also and as I understand based on her words that she would like an introduction to his majesty Mr. Rosevater. And of course, I was smiling because I did not want to note that she is a little too late with that. She asked for your address that she will write to you sometime. But, if it's possible do not tell her that you already know each other. So, it will be kind of a surprise when you will come to Cleveland. Thank you for Lajos's address. I will write to him and maybe send him a package. Let him feel that strangers

think about him with love, too. I hope you are not going to follow my example and will respond as soon as possible. Until then, I kiss you and I wish everything good to all of you! Helen

1944/7/20 Irving to Dave, N. of Rome, Italy (V-Mail, Slide 194)

July 20, 1944
North of Roma

My dear brother Dave,
Just a line to let you know that I'm OK and hoping to hear from you the same. I haven't received any mail from you this week. Did you get my long letters? I hope you did and understood it. At present everything is the same, just hoping that it won't be long. You know Dave, tomorrow we will have yahrzeit, but I won't be able to go to say kaddish. Over here, it's not like home. Hope that next year the same time I'll be home and everything will be OK. Now I'll close this time and I'm hoping to hear from you soon. Love, Irving

1944/7/20 Irving to Family, N. of Rome, Italy (V-Mail, Slide 195)

July 20, 1944
North of Roma

My dear sisters,
Writing you again, to let you know that I'm thinking of you. I hope you are well and in good health. I'm still waiting to receive some mail from you. I bet you feel the same way, when you don't get any mail from me. Yet as I'm back, I have more time to think about home and receiving mail. That's the only thing I have - mail. At present I'm satisfied with it. I hope it won't be long and we will meet again back in the U.S.A. Love, Irving

Love to Dave and Herman

1944/7/21 Irving to Family, N. of Rome, Italy (V-Mail, Slide 196)

July 21, 1944
North of Roma

My dear sisters Hermine and Maria,
Just another day and I want you to know that I'm OK with God's help. I hope that this letter will find you in the best of health. You know I have just read a couple of your old letters, that is which I received during our move. That's all the letters I have, because the rest of it I had to burn it. I didn't have any place to put it. Since we started out, I hardly got any mail from you. Maybe it will come in one of these days. News. Nothing over here, just hoping, that it won't be long and I can go home. I remain with all my love, Irving

Love to Dave and Herman

1944/7/23 Irving to Dave, N. of Rome, Italy (V-Mail, Slide 197-200)

July 23, 1944
North of Roma

I

My dear brother Dave,
Just received the most precious gift from you. Arrived on July 21st right on the date. Believe me all those pictures are very precious to all of us. It brought back all the memories, Time goes very fast. During this time many things happened! Yes I do remember everything. Over here you have plenty of time to think about it. Thanks a million for your thoughts! You know Dave, I have decided to send these pictures over to Hermine and she will send it back to you. I know that's the only pictures we have and with God's help, when I get back home I will ask you to reprint it and we all can have one from it. I'll tell you why am sending back, first, I'm afraid that I might lose it, second is, because carrying

continue-

Love, Irving

II

My dear brother Dave,
I hope you'll receive all the letters at once. As I said in my other letter the carrying those pictures in my pocket it's not too good. You probably know that we wear our clothes all the time. When we are back then we try to be more comfortable. I know you understand what I mean. I wonder if you received my letters. I hope you did. You write about it. Will you? I'm OK and doing as I said and with God's help I hope everything will be OK. You know the news sounds pretty good. Maybe it will be over by October. Don't you think so! That's a long time yet. Sooner is better. I have written home today and maybe they will send you those letters over to you too. You here isn't much to write about but I still want you [to] receive letters so I will continue to write. Love, Irving

III

My dear brother Dave,
Like I said if you want to receive mail you have to write. So here I'm writing you and hoping that you are well and in good health. I am OK and hope to stay that way with God's help. You were asking about the people over here. You know I have nothing to do with them. They say that the Germans took everything before they left. The farmers have plenty of food, mainly the city people were hurting. I say it's their own fault. I don't feel sorry for them at all. They had a chance long time ago, but they were asking for all this. It's long way, and a hard way to get there, where I really would enjoy it to be. I hope in God that he will help me! Love, Irving

P.S. My best wishes to the folks back home.

Continue

IV

My dear brother Dave,
This is my fourth letter to you as you see I'm thinking of you always. But when I can't write you and you don't receive any mail I know exactly how you feel. I always try my best. In one of your letters you're asking me, if I received the package with the fruitcake in it. Yes I did and it was very good. That was a long time ago. Yet I don't want to ask for anything, because so many packages are on the way, that I won't know what to do with them. Sometime later I will ask for one. You know Dave, at present everything is OK, concerning that last letter. Also you have to be over seas 26-months before you get to go home. By that time I hope the war will end. I'll close this time with love, Irving

1944/7/23 Irving to Dave, N. of Rome, Italy (V-Mail, Slide 201)

July 23, 1944
North of Roma
Written in Hungarian

Dear Dezső,
I can't even express how much happiness you gave me with your letters and also with your photographs. I received them exactly on the yahrzeit. Believe me, you really gave me a lot of happiness. I will keep them here for a couple of days and then I will send them home and Herminka will send them back to you. I will do it this way because I don't want the photographs to break. I have them in my pocket all the time and you know this doesn't help a photograph. I really thank you for being so thoughtful, but I hope that with the good G-d's help we will see each other again in America. Next time I will write a longer Hungarian letter. Now many kisses, your younger brother, Irving

July 23, 1944
North of Roma

I

My dear sisters Hermine and Maria,

Just been thinking to write you a long letter, so I'll start on v-mail and continue on. The last couple days, I have received a few letters from you and also from Dave. I'm glad to hear that you are well and in good health. I'm OK with God's help and hope to stay that way. You know Maria, over here where I'm the fruit is green, however I ate pretty good pears. Even last night I went out towards the fields and got me some pears and I'm going to keep it for a couple days while it gets ripe. There is a small town not far away and I was up there and got some peaches and plums but it was greenish. Maybe a couple days and it will be fine. I sure would like to stay here where I'm for a while. It's nice and quiet place. That's the most a person can ask for, over here. I will continue, Love, Irving

II

My dear sisters Hermine and Maria,

Here I'm again I hope that you will receive these letters all at once. At present I'm OK and do not worry. However I know you do. This place where I'm at present it's pretty safe. I wouldn't mind to stay here for the duration, but I guess it can't be. So the only thing we can do, to pray to God and ask Him to help me. You know in the last couple days the news sounds very good. I hope they keep moving fast and the Jerrys would give up. Boy! What a relief would that be. I think it won't be too long now. I figure it will be over by October, I hope. Maybe before that, but I don't want to be very optimistic. Sooner is better. I should say it has been long enough now. I don't know how they take that much. But I guess they have to take it or else. Continue.

Love,
Irving

III

My dear sisters Hermine and Maria,

I hope that this letter will find you all in the best of health. By the way, today is Sunday over here. It's a very nice day and my thoughts are with you. It's almost like being at home and talk to you. Here I have my letters beside me, which I received from home last week. Surely I would rather be home personally, but yet it's like I said, you are all in my thoughts. I hope it will be soon and with God's help I'll be home. Not so long ago, I spoke to a couple German prisoners and some of them were real Nazi and some Poles and one Czech. They all had different opinion about the war. They know the[y] lost, but they have the idea of killing more and more men. And the other said they have to because if they refuse to fight they shoot him. Continue

-

Love,
Irving

IV

My dear sisters Hermine and Maria,

Let me tell you that so many things are on my mind, that I wish I could be home and tell you personally. Now let's get back to your letters. In one of your letters you are asking me if I received the cookies with three can fruits. Yes I did and it was very good. It doesn't make any difference what kind of cookies you are sending me. Because they were all very fine. The other day I got two small package with cookies and they were very good. That was on the 21st of July. I was fasting, because of yahrzeit and ate cookies the evening of the 21st. Sorry that's was all I could do, but God knows everything! Continue

Love,
Irving

V

My dear sisters Hermine and Marie,

On the evening of July 21st I have received the most precious gift from Dave. It came in exactly in time. The pictures were taken over here in Europa. One was at our mother's grave. That was when we were out there and we are in it too. The other picture is when she was alive. Let me tell you that it really brings back all the memories. If you think in those things, you just can't stand it. Dave told me, that he wouldn't give these pictures to anyone, but me. However these pictures are very precious to all of us. And over here I couldn't take care of it. You know why; so I'll see and next week I will send it home to you and you will send it back to Dave. I will write you about this. Thanks a million for his thoughts. Love, Irving

VI

My dear sisters Hermine and Maria,

This is my sixth letter I hope that you will receive it all at once. Some time this week I'm going to write you ordinary letters. Also I will enclose a fifty dollar money order. Listen here my dear sis: if you need of anything, please don't be afraid to take it. You know I'm giving it to you with all my heart. You know, money isn't everything. And money can't pay you the things that you did for me. However please accept it from me. You know I have not forgotten you and never will. If God will help to go through, believe me I want to be your right hand. What ever I can I will do it for you. Let's hope and pray to God that it won't be long and we will meet again!
Love,
Irving

VII

My dear sisters Hermine and Maria,

Time goes fast and I wasn't able to send you any pictures of myself. However as soon as I can I will. You know there are so many things yet that I should tell you, but I guess I will have to wait when I get home. Then, maybe it will be more interesting, but today when you are in something, you don't want to talk about it. I'm glad to hear that Maria, you have found a good and easy job. I hope you will like it. I think that you have plenty of worries. Does Herman help you with anything? I hope he does. I'll write him too. Now I'll close this time and hoping to hear from you real soon, Love your Brother, Irving

P.S. Love to Dave and Herman!

1944/7/24 Irving to Family, N. of Rome, Italy (V-Mail, Slide 211)

July 24, 1944
North of Roma

My dear sisters Hermine and Maria,

I hope that you have received all my letters that I have written you yesterday. I'll do like I said, I'll write you whenever I can. However there isn't any news over here at the present. So I just want to say I'm OK and hoping to hear from you the same. I sure would like to be home and be with [you] during your vacation. It reminds me of last year. I can't forget the stuffed cabbage [tóltótt káposztát], boy! that was good. I hope when this is over and with God's help I go home, you will make me some. Won't you? I know you will. Thanks very much your thoughts. I'll write you more later. Love from, Irving

My best reg[ards] to my friends and relatives.

1944/7/24 Irving to Herman, N. of Rome, Italy (V-Mail, Slide 210)

July 24, 1944
North of Roma

Dear Herman,

I was very glad to receive your letter and I'm glad to hear that you are well and in the best of health. I'm OK with God's help. I know you are busy most of the time. Your work is different. You can't compare it to mine. I would say that even though you are busy, you could write me more often. At least once a week. What do you say? You know Herman, over here it's rough. I'm glad that you don't have to be in this mess! I know you couldn't stand it one minute. While I was in Anzio, believe me everything changed for me. You are nervous, but I'm or rather I was one hundred percent recked [reckt - not sure of this word]. Now it's not as bad. It could be better. Let's hope in God that he will Help me to go through it and [I] will be able to return to U.S.A.

Love, Irving

My Dear loved little brother Irving.

Finally I received two airmail letters that I was waiting for so impatiently. My dear little brother I can't even tell you how happy I was to receive your letter. I'm also very happy to know that thank G-d you are healthy. We give thanks to the good G-d for this. My dear little brother, I hope in the future He will also help you. And also my dear little brother, I understood your letters. I can imagine what you went through. We hear on the radio about your every move. You wrote my dear Irving, that maybe you are boring me with your letters, don't even think that. They would never bore me, I could read them from morning until night and besides, you write good letters. And you are right, a human being cannot value things when he is here as opposed to being there and witnessing everything. It is horrible. Countless kisses from your forever loyal sister who will never forget you, Maria

1944/7/26 David to Family (Book 2, 131-136)

Darlings!

I got two letters from you this week. I'm sorry I didn't respond sooner, but the reason for that was because I was waiting for mail from our little brother. But thank God I got a letter from him yesterday and as I saw, you got one too. I hope the dear God will help him with everything good. You know, on Sunday I was getting ready to call you on the phone, but I was afraid that you are going to get scared. Maybe I will surprise you sometimes or on a Sunday. Do you still have your phone? It will cost $2.75 for 3 minutes from here on Sunday and 20% from long distance 70 cents. So it will come out for 5 minutes and include $1.00 more, if it's for the minutes. So, when I will hear some good news sometimes, then I will call you. Yes, thank you for the baking! It was very delicious. And this week I sent a package to our little brother.

...and I sent from your baking to him too. Oh, yes! I hope you are not sending the palinka through the postal service. You know, it's not allowed to send it from there. I must get it this week. After this I will not ask for it anymore. Maybe it will be available here, based on the newspaper probably in about a month, as much as we need. I don't know any news from here. Everything is the same. Today I wrote to our little brother also. Here there is no sunshine this week. I will send the money to the Chronicle this week. To our little brother I attached an article from the Chronicle. Little brother knows the "Greenstein" boy. He is an officer. Maybe he's close to our little brother and could help him. Write what's doing with the Mendlovetz boy.

If you want to, call him up and his relatives, too. Find out what's up with him, ok!

What is the news in Columbus? Where did Arthur go with his family? Hermine, did you get your raise? I'm sure not! So, Marcsa! How much do you make? Did you put any weight on? Do you eat or starve? Do you know what I would like to cook? Paprikas [chicken paprika, stew based with red pepper]. How do I make that? You know, I may try to learn about interior decoration. I will buy books and when the war will end, I would go home for a few months. I could make a lot by advertising "Direct from Hollywood". And [with] a few letters from movie stars, I think I could take on the competition from Columbus. And you know Mariska, if you would come here I would help you to get into a good studio, and you'll learn how to tailor curtains based on the style in Hollywood.

So one more time, if you want to make money after the war, come here and be a good student and if we would go back, you can make as much money as you want. So, I think you should come here and learn how to become a good tailor and you could go to school and learn. So, my plan is to learn well how to do furnishings and room layout based on fashion/style. So, I will assure you, no matter what the situation is, we'll be able to make money, because there will always be rich people. You know, it's simpler to make a curtain here than at home. And it's nicer. So Mariska, this is your chance to make good money. So write about this. Okay?

So, I wrote enough. I like my present place. I was getting ready to write many times to you, but when I sit down I fall asleep. So, if I don't write correctly, please forgive me. Ok? Currently I cook dinner everyday. I got bored with breakfast because I only need a cup of coffee and 2 donuts. The Jewish [Zsido] meat store is so far, the same as for you to Oak St. Hey Hermine, what's up with the housewife and the money? How much do you pay for rent? Do you get the garage? What's going on with that man who was wondering about me? So, Lazarus asked for money again? I don't owe anyone there anything! Thank you for the baked goods and the Palinka! Kissing you with love, Dezső

Greetings to Herman!

Why doesn't he write? Is he angry?

If he will write, I will send something to him.

1944/7/26 David to Irving (Book 12, 87-90)

7.26.44
Written in Hungarian

My little brother!

I can hardly write down my happiness that you gave with your letter to me. Believe me, I was so very afraid that God forbid something happened. But thank God you are well and may God grant you, my dear little brother, if you don't have time to write, only that you are well. My little brother, I did not even care about my job, I just wanted to hear from you so much. But, if you could just write. OK? Thank you! I got a letter from home today. Thank God they are well. They got two letters from you. Poor things, they were terrified so much also. But may God grant that you will come home in health to us. I don't know any news here, everything is the same. You know the girls wrote that Edi Medlovetz, you know the "Duch Coffe" [maybe Dutch Coffee]

boy who came from Eperjes, got wounded in France. I don't know what's wrong with him. I hope little brother that you got the latest package. And this week I sent you a 5 pound package where I sent a little Palinka. If you get it, take good care of it. It says on it that it is a medicine. I hope they will not take it out. But be careful when it arrives, don't get into trouble. OK? I will send different walnut, Hershey Chocolate, some cookies, Hermine's kind! Pinocot Hair [perhaps a hair tonic/styling cream] for hair and so on! And other small things. I hope that you got the book that I sent a week ago. I hope you like it! I don't know any news about me. Currently I work during the day and 10 hours a day. Hey, do you know what I did? Hermine wrote

...how to make stuffed cabbage. So, I already made it twice and you know, it was delicious. You know I cook pretty well. If God will help you and you will come home, I will make you a good lunch (more than one not just one), if you will like it, but God grant it that you could be here with me soon. Right little brother? That time will come too with God's help- I will attach a picture to you where I am in it. It's not polite to send something like that, but I know you'll be happy for it. I was out in Hollywood and they took it there, I had it signed with a green pencil, Johnny Puleo [IMG_0243.JPG in Book 20]- you know who that is. He is your favorite actor from "You're Romantic" you know that little old boy [midget] with a big harmonica. At least the five of them in the team and he is short and he fights.

I know you saw him in person in Columbus. But let's leave this, as you can see the glass in my hand, I thought about you, and I wish you could be here with me- You can see a man behind my back with a smile, I met him by chance, a formal shipyard boss. Hey, little brother, do you remember Izy Greenstein? You were with me once there, you know that girl on Wilson Ave. as I can see it, he is there also near by you. I will attach his address. Go and check it out. It is possible that he could help you out. He works at a hospital. You talked to him. You can find out his exact address. Have you met anyone who you know there? If it's possible, write it that you are with the 5th or with the eighth [army]? You know what I think? So, may God give you everything good and strength until I will see you again. I wish you good health and the best of luck. May God give you everything good with love I kiss you forever, your faithful brother. David

1944/7/26 Irving to Dave, N. of Rome, Italy (V-Mail, Slide 212)

July 26, 1944
North of Roma

My dear brother Dave,

Just another line to let you know that I'm OK, however at present I don't know what the future will bring. In the next few days my address will change. I will let you know what or where to. Now just let's hope and pray to God that He will help me like before. How are you Dave? I hope you are well and in good health. Listen! I will let you later, but please don't worry! Because that doesn't help. Now I remain with all my love. Your brother, Irving

P.S. WRITE ME PLEASE.

1944/7/26 Irving to Hermine and Marie (Book 6, 166-168)

My dear sisters Hermine and Maria,
Just a line to let you know that I'm okay. Hope you're well and in good health. Here I'm enclosing a money order of $50. I hope you will receive it. Also enclosed those -4- pictures, that I mentioned. Listen! In the next couple days my address will be changed, so as soon I find out, I let you know. At present, just let's hope that everything will be fine. To all that we need God's help. I hope that he will help me. How are you all getting along? Not much to say at present, I will write you as soon as I can. It may be better where I go. I don't know yet. I could tell you something, but yet I can't. I hope it won't be too long now. I think I will close now and will write you soon again! Remain with all my love. Your brother, Irving

Love to Herman and Dave
Irv.
July - 26 – 44

1944/7/26 Louis Schwartz to Hermine (Book 17, 109-110)

Iceland 7-26-44
Dear Hermina,
Received your letter a couple days ago and was glad to hear from you again. Tonight I'm switchboard operator in the office also taking calls or giving information if I can. Wouldn't it be swell if I could connect you and have a little chat with you? It's 22 P.M. and I'm not very busy so I'm taking advantage of it [by] writing to you and at the same time practicing typing. I hope you don't mind if I'm using your answer for practice having both the pleasant writing to you and usefulness at the same time. I'm quite out of practice and I'm slow at it. You're probably much better. I've very seldom a chance to type. Yes, I guess you [are] right about me taking up something and [I] am probably going to do it, though you know it isn't quite like in civilian life [where] one can make plans ahead but we never know what the next hour keeps for us. Also for studying one have to concentrate what it is hard to do when living with 10 other boys in the same room. We get to sleep very seldom before 1 A.M. in account of the noise. I still miss privacy. This is the army…I was surprised to hear that you girls didn't go swimming yet. I was a few times and enjoyed it. My commander told me that we can make up allotments if our people live in a country occupied by any of the allies and government gives its share. You know your people are only about 90 miles from the Russian hold territory, so write Irving about it. You can never tell maybe we will be able to use it. He did not write me for a long time. I almost forgot to tell you that my brother Joe was home on furlough for 2 weeks from Texas. He expects to be transferred in the near future. Otherwise I'm fine, hope the same about you. Now I'm signing off hoping to hear from you again soon. Love and best wishes, Lou

1944/7/27 Hermine and Marie to Irving (Book 9, 236-239) mentions photo on mantel

Columbus July 27 -1944
Written in Hungarian

[from Hermine]
My dear brother Irving!
I want to keep my promise and now I will write a long letter to you. We got a letter from you yesterday and I'm happy to hear that thank God, you are well. About us, I could write the same thing too, that we are all well. I will attach a picture here and I know I will make you happy with it. It is not really good because it was taken in the room, but I thought it is going to be good, if you look around us a little. I'm sorry that your pictures are not there, only David and the late Uncle Jónász's picture that we got from Flora as a gift. Also, I packed a 5 pound package for you. There is a fruit cake, candy bar, 2 cans of pears, compote and a sea of things is available. Next time I will bake something and I will look around for fig bars. You know my little Irving, it is not always available, but next time I will send other things as well. I heard the girls mention at

work that they sent a sea of things and it can be done. So, if you want then write it to me and I will send more too. You know my brother, you are right, that it would be better to pack the baked goods in a can, but there is only one problem that there are none. Currently they sell Crisco in a bottle, but I will ask around if I could get it somewhere. Yes, little brother that little black [haired] girl on the picture, is the one who I mentioned was selling the movie tickets in the uptown cinema, and she knows you and David from there. Both of them work here with me and they are nice girls. The [picture] that was taken in the room was taken by Catherina from McNeil [House] who used to come to us at Fenton. She came to visit us and was wondering about you. She would like to write to you sometimes. I really don't know what to write now because nothing comes to my mind. We did not give your greetings over to the neighbors yet, since there is always somebody at our house and we don't go to them. But the old lady is well, but I will tell you a little secret. You know, the girl in the neighborhood who lives next to the Walters, always runs and looks to meet with David and Herman, but since it did not succeed she made a pass at the man and they became very good friends.

But the old lady came here and surely they don't get along. This is only gossip from home, but maybe you can decide what is going on. That is, boys are in short supply. So, the old lady told us, that the man was crying and asking for forgiveness. You know, that they get along over here just like before. But maybe these days no, because like before, they did not even talk. Write, my dear little brother! Ok? I just had a conversation on the phone with Mrs. Hawkins and she said that she sent a little news and she hopes that you like it. You know, she is a nice lady, but she is afraid to spend more than 2 cents! Although, she is a very kind lady. I don't know, if I wrote it to you that a son was just born to Margaret, the soldier officer's wife and she invited me. Maybe my vacation will be next week and then I will visit her. Although, it has been 5 months at least. I will get a week off. August 6-12, but I will not go anywhere. If God will help me, then next year with you! Ok? Now, I wish you lots of luck and take good care of yourself! Herman was in the temple. Yes, it is nice that you paid attention to it and may God help you for that! Kiss you with love! Hermina

[from Marie]
My dear beloved little brother, Irving!
I will be in the hurry again to write you a few lines today. How are you my dear little brother? I hope that my lines will find you in the best of health today! Otherwise we are well. This week we got three airmails from you, which I was very happy about. And I'm very happy to hear that you are very healthy, thank God, which is the most important. Yes, my little brother, here we are attaching 4 pictures for you. They are not the best, but I hope you will recognize us on them! I wish I could see you also! One of them was taken in the room and it's not great, but we will send it anyway. In the meantime you can see our late uncle Jónász on it and David. And your picture was between them and we thought it was in it and I'm sorry that what I wanted to send could not be in it. We will take more next time and I hope it will come out well also. Yesterday we sent a package to you. Now I wish you lots of luck and the best of health. Take good care of yourself. Wherever you go the dear God will follow you and be with you in every step of your way. I kiss you countless times, your forever faithful sibling, who will never forget. Maria

1944/7/30 David to Irving (Book 2, 80-83)

7/30/44
My dear little brother!
I got the letter from you that I was waiting for. Also, the 11 page letter written to home, Hermine sent to me. As I can see you are very sad. But, unfortunately we can't help it. You know little brother I can't understand your letter. What do you think…where are you going? Near to Dad's, or are you coming home or going against Japan. I can't understand, write with more details about it. God help me, is something wrong? You didn't do anything bad. I hope whatever you did will only work out with success. My little brother, with the mail today I sent you a 5 pound package. A little "pinoczot" [perhaps a hair tonic/styling cream], candy and cake and guess what else! You can't even think it, can you?! Maybe you will scold me about it, but I know you like it and I hope it will not get spoiled.

So you will find in it a 2½ pound kosher salami! You didn't think so, I thought of it yesterday, so I sent it. I hope you will like it! If you need anything else, I will send it to you. I don't know any news from here, everything is the same- But I hope the dear God will help and you will come soon in good health. Based on the news the war must end soon. By the time you get this letter maybe you will already be in Polány. May

God give that! My little brother, I don't even know what to write. There isn't any news here. The air is cold. If God will help and you will come home to me, there will be enough space for you too.

I came to live here, you know, 6 weeks ago and then the army promised, if there will be a better opportunity I will be the first one to know. So tomorrow Apt #10 will empty out in the same building, so I will move there. It will cost the same as the present one. But it is nicer and prettier and there is space for 2-3 people. My little brother, you already wrote once about the African girl. Maybe you are exchanging letters with her? Is she a Jewish girl? Do you like her? My little brother, I hope the dear God will help you for everything good. You know, if you would be here, you would see many kinds of things. But, if God will help you and you'll come here, I will take you somewhere where you'll see tons of actors. My little brother, I don't know, if I wrote that Edi Mendlovitz, you know who he is? He worked in the Dutch Coffee. I heard that he got wounded in Normandy.

I don't know what's wrong with him. I'm still a 4f, but I hope I don't have to go. Do you remember, little brother, how much you wanted to go? I hope the dear God will help you and you won't have to fight. So I wrote enough for today. May God bless you with everything good in hope and love. Kisses, your faithful brother forever. Dezső

1944/7/31 David to Hermine and Marie (Book 18, 120-122)

7.31.44
My darlings!
I got the package with the drink today. Mariska, write how much it was and I will send the money for it. I will not ask for more drinks, because it is available here as well. I got a letter from our little brother today. I will attach it here. I can't understand what he thinks, where he thinks he will go home to. If you Hermine can understand it, then let me know. Ok? I can't understand it, if you can please let me know! I don't know any news here. I sent a 5 pound package to our little brother. And do you know what I sent in it? You don't, do you?! 2½ pound kosher salami. I believe he will like it.

I believe he will get it fine because it was a whole salami. I will not send his 11 page letter that he sent back yet because he is asking for more and I want to send it to him next week. You can send without a letter also. Forgive me, but I'm pretty sleepy. Currently I can barely see to write from the sleepiness. So, I wish you everything good and happiness with love. I kiss all of you until I see you again. Kisses. Dave
P.S. Thank you very much for the Palinka and write to me Ok? Little Hermine, if you could please explain Ignác's letter. Ok? So, until I will see you and hear you again. Dezső

1944/7/31 Evelyn Bossetti to Irving (Book 18, 137-141)

July 31 - 1944
U.S.A.

Dear Irving:

Once again my prayers have been answered. I have been praying that I would soon hear from you. It seems like years that I received your last V-mail letter and I was so overjoyed in hearing from you. You can't imagine how welcome your short letter was yesterday afternoon. I think I could shut my eyes and repeat every word from memory. I'm so happy to hear that you are in good health and in one piece. You never can know from one minute to the next - what might happen. I'd give anything to be over there in Italy now. I intend to get there sometime in the not-too-far future. Keep your fingers crossed. Do you suppose my knowledge of the language would help me get there? I hope so. Just call on my anytime, Irving, and I'll act as your interpreter. But I think that you can manage very well for yourself. You are a very capable young man. In my next letter Irving - I hope to have a snap of me in my Cadet uniform. I'm mighty proud of it and don't mind admitting it one bit. I must sign off now to dress for duty. But please write soon and often. Love, Evelyn

1944/8/4 Hermine to Irving (Book 11, 21-23)

Columbus Aug-4-44

Written in Hungarian

My dear little brother, Irving!
We got your letter, the check, and our dear late mother's picture. I can really understand you, that you mustn't keep it with you, you could even lose it. But it was nice from Dave and he gave it to you from his heart. It is truly wonderful that you got it on that day and that you were fasting all day. That is truly a good example and the dear God will help you wherever you go. Also, our dear late mother is guarding you above and we should trust and pray, that everything will go well. Believe me when I saw your 9 letters yesterday, I felt like everybody should know about what kind of a little brother we have, who writes whenever his time allows it. The phone was just ringing and it was Katalin who I worked with at Fenta together. Yes, she was wondering about you. Otherwise, I'm well. Tomorrow starts my vacation, in other words I will only work until noon tomorrow. So, I'm thinking of you and sorry, if sometimes I cause pain to you with expressing my feelings to you in my letters. When we get a letter from you, everything is well then,

[Upside Down]
PS: The mentioned offer as far as the money is concerned, thank you very very much! Next time I will write in more detail.

...but if it does not come- then it causes worry. But I'm asking you not to worry, only take care of yourself. Many times only a little dexterity and attention could mean a lot. It made me happy that you got the package. Especially, that I got it [there] in a good time. I will be in a hurry to send it to you. Poor Flora was worried that she did not send you the package yet, but it is very hot here and it is hard for her. I told her not to be worried because it will be ok [if it arrives] later to you also. The fact that David is a good boy to you, I believe it is because he loves you very much. When he writes to us, he is just writing to his little brother also like to us. I can't forget your letters because they sound like I just had a conversation with you. That money, in other words the 50 dollars you mentioned that we can spend - This way I will enlighten you about my plan. Although, thank God, I have a pretty good job that I love, it is the best from any of the jobs before. And my salary is very good, 25 weekly. The tax is deducted from that. I already buy bonds, this way I can keep living on my own. Even if I don't save a lot, but to take yours away from you, I could not do that.

...since we don't want to take it from you. So, because of that please don't be angry when I tell you that we will only buy bonds from it for you...Also, even if Marcsa does not make a lot, she loves it and later she can have another nice job where she can make more money. She likes the work, but she made more at the other place before, but it was not a steady place, anyway. I can't remember all of a sudden what I was going to write you. But I will be in a hurry next week to write to you. I talked to Mrs. Walters the neighbor, and with the old lady, and they asked to give you their best. Believe me that they truly love you, only they are very busy. They can't get enough people to their store and it is harder for them to work. Yes, I'm only thinking that in your situation that would be nothing, but she knows how it goes. Write, if you can and I will write as well. Now I want to still write to David also. The weather is very warm, but this is the time for that...I got a letter from the mentioned boy also and I have to respond, but in English because Hungarian is hard for him. Lots of good luck and kisses with love. Hermina

1944/8/4 Maria to Irving (V-Mail, Slide 213)

My Dear loved little brother Irving,
Yesterday we received nine v-mails and today a letter with the picture and the $50 check. My dear Irving I'm happy to hear that thank G-d you are healthy, but as I can see from your letters you are sad a lot. Believe me my dear little brother, that I understand you and your letter. Yesterday David sent us one of your letters. And I'm sorry we cannot help you. But I ask the good G-d and we hope He will help you and give you strength and health to survive that horrible situation. My dear little brother I ask you to take care of yourself anywhere you go, may the good G-d be with you and help you every step of the way. Wishing you the best of luck and the best health. Now kissing you many many times, forever your loyal sister who will never forget you.
In the hope of reunion soon. Love, Maria

1944/8/6 David to Irving (Book 12, 92-95)

To Censor!

Written in Hungarian

L.B. 8.6.44
My dear little brother!
I got your 4 page long V. mail letter and 2 other letters from before. I'm glad that you are, thank God, well and may the dear God grant that everything will work out for the best. So, my little brother, I hope that you are right! I heard from many, that the confusion there, will pass. May God grant it. In your previous letter you noted west, as I understand, is the French front - But, may the dear God grant that everything is going to work out well. What is the reason that this will happen? Write whenever you can. Hey, if you send your letter sealed/taped down, they will not open it. They will write it on the cover that it could go. Do you know what I think? My little brother, may God grant that you will come back in good strength and health. Currently here it is nice warm weather. Hey, write it if you need canned peaches? I have a letter from you where you were asking for a package. So, next week I will send one. Oh yes, you know I saw it in the newspaper, that on September 15 and October 15 it will be possible to send a package of "Purini" [maybe Purim] gifts, so I will send a few to you then. Write what you need. Do you need any kind of book to read? Or anything you ask for, I will send. So, would you want a little drink? Write it, if you got it and if you liked it. Ok? I don't know if I wrote this to you, that I moved from room 11 to room 10. It is a nicer and better room with a private bathroom. If the dear God will help and you will come home, then you can come here to me there will be enough space - The rent is the same as it used to be! Little brother, I cooked a good lunch today. I'm sure that you would have eaten it, too. I buy kosher meat. I cooked a roast and stuffed cabbage. I could say that it was delicious. I wish I could send some to you from it! But the time will come when you can be with me - I just wrote to home also. I sent your letters that I mentioned above.

...and your letters from last week also. You know, ever since I came here to live, I don't go anywhere. I am busy with cleaning and cooking. My little brother, write a lot and explain better. It is possible that tonight I will go to the movies. I have not been for a while. I don't live on the beach. I live about [K.B. = kőrülbelül] 1300 [szàm = units / numbers] from the beach! I still work in the shipyard. I wish the war was over and I could leave it! You know I am an electrician, even though I don't know much about it, still I am noted as a Critical Skill and I only can work in the shipyard, in other words at a more prestigious company. If I quit, I have to join the army. So, it is better this way. Little brother, I know well that you are bored at your job, but you can't quit like I do, like it or not, that is not important. The most important thing is, that you know what I think. Currently, nothing comes to my mind. I will write a letter this week again about on Tuesday night. So, little brother, may God grant that everything will work out for you and we can see each other again in strength and happiness.

But soon. It would be nice wouldn't it? So, may God grant you lots of happiness and luck to you for coming home, until then, take care of yourself and like I wrote many times, think 2x before you want to do something. Ok!? Do you remember Feri from Helmec, what he always said? My dear Dezső, "get revenge and make money" ["revspéna and megínt pénz!"] You were also there then, weren't you? So, my little brother, think about it before you do anything also. Think this way: life, life, life and I want to live and that way you need to be careful. Little brother, the dear God helped you to go through on the thorny road and when you already got out to the better destiny, God will help you from everything bad. You should know how to be careful because there are many snipers there and they can't be seen. So be careful! Why am I teaching you about this anyway!? You are a fine soldier and you know all this already. But it's easier, if I write to you about my feelings. I know that the dear God will help you with everything good. I will see you again in good health and happiness. Until I see you back in the good old U.S.A. God bless you with love! Forever your brother, Dezső

1944/8/6 David to Marie (Book 18, 116-118)

Dear Mariska!
I will attach an addressed envelope to my address with a stamp. I'm sending this so you can get rid of the letter that way. You will find more in the envelope so be careful to not get it dirty! Ok? If you will write then please stick a 5 and 1 cent stamp on it. Thank you!

[On top in pencil]
Now the icy rain started to fall, actually it's pouring now. The weather is lousy like in Polyán in April.

Greetings to everyone, you better write a lot. So, if you want mail from me, then you better write to me. Hermine, it is possible that I will send the earrings soon and a needle. You will get them soon. Currently there is none in that color. Do you still like the pearl? And you Mariska! Didn't you get bored yet? Respond immediately, please.

1944/8/7 David to Irving (Book 12, 97-100)

8-7-44
Written in Hungarian

My dear little brother!
I got two letters from you this week, a V. mail and a 2 page letter that I was very happy about. And I hope the dear God will help you with everything good. You know, your air mail was interestingly dated. It was at the camp at Jun 27-and I got it on the 3rd I don't know maybe they dated it in NY. My little brother, you wrote that you got a package that I sent on 5.5. And I sent 3 big packages to you and you just noted in this letter that you got one. Please write if the fruit cake was in this package, if no then I believe that package got lost. Absolutely write it to me, if that was not the one. Ok? Thank you, yes! I will send a package on Monday with many kinds of walnuts and peanuts. Some fine cookies and a little palinka. I hope with the dear God's help everything will work out!

As you wrote it, you are getting closer every day to our father. I am very happy about that. But I'm asking the dear God to help you for everything good. Just take good care of yourself little brother. Ok?! So, little brother believe it or not, you are on my mind every day. What a good little boy you were in Polyán and today from the poor little boy you have become a hero soldier and may the dear God grant it, so I can be proud of you. Little brother I think about what I did to you many times, that I made you work for the money I gave you - Little brother, there are a few pictures when you were a little boy. I take them out many times and I wonder about them. Little brother I will send a picture here where you are in it also. It is in the cemetery at our late mother's tombstone. I know you will take care of it well, and another little picture that the late Uncle Jónász gave me 6 years ago, our dear grandmother's picture, I will send them here to you. I know you will take it gladly, and a photograph when we said goodbye in Helmec. Do you remember?

You know, I only send them to you because I know they will make you happy. Do you remember when you were at Jenkin? One night when there was a big fire. Poor thing you were terrified there, weren't you? And look at you now, you are in fire - but this is how it goes - unfortunately. Little brother write it, if you got any medals. Only, if they gave you any, there is no reason to desire any, but just anyway! I saw those who come home for vacation. They are packed. Hey, how much is the monthly payment there to you? I went to the temple last night and you know, I saw a sailor/soldier. I looked at him and he looked so familiar. Today I went after him and I asked him, if he is not from Columbus. He said yes. Finally I recognized him. I used to work for Shiff on Saturdays on Main St and he was the manager there. He is working here in a Naval hospital and his wife is here too. I'm sure you know him. His face was always hairy and he is a short guy. His name, Harold Covel. They know you. So, it is enough for today. God bless you with everything good with love. Kisses, your brother Dave.

Dear little brother I will send here 4 little pictures. I would not give them out of my hand to anybody, but only to you, so I can make you happy. So I will send them and may the dear God grant that you will bring them back in the best of health. May the dear God bless you on your way with love. Kisses, Dave

1944/8/8 Irving to Dave, Outside Naples, Italy (V-Mail, Slide 215)

August 8, 1944
My dear brother Dave,
Just a line to let you know that I'm OK with God's help. Hope that you are well and in good health. The other day I told you that I'm going to be transferred out from the 6th ARM'D INF. [armored infantry]. Well today I'm back in a replacement center. I was here before I went up front. That was in January. Now I'm hoping for the best. Maybe in a couple days I'll be in able to tell you the way I stand. You just write me of [sic] my old address. I might stay here for a couple days or even months. I'm hoping for the best. I'll write you more later. I remain with all my love, Irving.

My love to the family back home.

1944/8/8 Irving to Family (Book 4, 91-97)

My dear sisters, Hermine and Maria,

Here I'm again to let you know that I'm okay and hoping to hear from you the same. At present I don't know what will be, I'm in a replacement center. A few of us were sent out from the old outfit. Maybe with God's help everything will be okay. The only thing I can do, just hope and pray to God. I wish I could talk to you personally. You know, I was yesterday in Napoli and made some pictures. They aren't very good, however I'm sending it to you anyway. Also a couple for Dave, his are all painted and you have one each that's not. I have made it outside on the street. The sun was very bright. I am not as black as I look on these pictures. Sometime next week I'll go again and make some better ones. On one picture you'll see a soldier I met in this camp. We were together in Napoly. He is new from the states. He is lucky that [he] just came over, he hasn't seen anything yet. I hope that this war ends soon, so I could go home with God's help and in good health. I have been up sweating for seven months. God helped me and I hope and trust him that He will continue to help me. As soon as I came in here I spoke to the chaplain about church services. So this Sunday morning was the first time, that I laid tfilem. There were times that I never thought that I'll be able to do it once more. But God helped me and I trust in him forever. I still couldn't find out what will be the next step. When I left the old outfit I was told that I'll get a break over here. It won't be as bad as it was up there. So I'm now just hoping and praying to God for help. I wish I could tell everything, but I guess I have to wait till I get back home. Maybe it won't be long now. Up there one minute is enough. If you know what I mean. Well I guess I'll close for this time and I will write you more later.

Here I'm enclosing five pictures and I'm sending three to Dave. His are all painted so if you want to, you can send them over to Dave, so that he could see me plainly. I'll send you some more later. Probably he will send you his back to you so you can see it. I remain with all my love, your brother, Irving

August 8 - 44
Love to Herman

Aug: 8 - 44
Italy

Hello Herman,

How are you? I hope fine and in the best of health. I'm okay. I sure would like to be back there where you are. I hope it won't be long. You were lucky that you got out in time, not like me. Now it's too late. But now I'm hoping for the best. Write me. Remain with love, Irving

My new address:

Pvt. Irving Gluck
A.S.N. 35633941
555 Repl[acement] Co[mpany]
A.P.O. 781 – R % P.M. N.Y. N.Y.

1944/8/8 Irving to Family, Outside Naples, Italy (V-Mail, Slide 214)

August 8, 1944
My dear sisters Hermine and Maria,

Just a line to let you know that I'm OK with God's help. I hope that you are well and in good health. The other day I told you that I'll be transferred out from this outfit. Well today I'm back again in a replacement center. I was here in January, before I was assigned to the 6th ARM'D INF. [armored infantry] I think you remember it. Now I'm hoping for the best. Maybe in a couple days, I will be able to tell you how I stand. You just write me of my old address. I might stay here for a couple days or even months. I'm hoping for the best. I'll write more later. I remain with all my love, Irving

My love to Herman and Dave.

[Dated by mention putting tefillin for first time]

My dear brother Dave,

Just a little line to let you know that I'm okay and hope that you are the best of health. At present I'm in a replacement center. I still don't know what will be next. I'm hoping for the best with God's help. I was told that in my old outfit that we'll get a break over here. Just a few of us were sent out from the 6th ARM'D INF.

Now I'm hoping and praying that everything will be okay. Last Sunday was the first time I went to services and laid tefillin. There were times that I never thought I'll be able to do it once more. But God helped me and I trust that he will continue [to] help me. Yesterday I was in Napoly and made some pictures. They aren't very good, but next time I'll send you some better ones. I mailed some home too, they will send it over to you. They are almost all alike. The only thing is that it's not painted. I made it outside on the street and the sun was very bright. I'm not as black as I look on this pictures. I wish I could talk to you personally. I'm hoping it won't be long. Up there, one minute is enough. So let's hope and pray to God that it won't be long till we meet again.

Remain with love, Irving

My new address:

PVT IRVING GLUCK
A.S.N. 35633941
555 REPL CO
A.P.O. 781-r % P.M. N.Y. N.Y.

I almost forgot to tell you, that soldier with me on the picture is from this camp. We went together to Napoly. He is new from the States. Some one is lucky. I'll write more later, you do the same. Love, Irving

P.S. WRITE SOON!

1944/8/8 Undated Mr. Walters to Irving (Book 2, 61-62)

August 8, 1944 [from the body text, August 7th falls on Monday in 1944]

Hell-O There.

That a swell introduction to a letter when you wonder what to say. But here goes - Mrs. Hasson just told me I had not been so thoughtful of you Irving. It's not the writing that says we are not thinking of you here at 42 Linwood Ave because we are ever mindful of the boy who sat on [our] front porch and we all enjoyed a many happy hour together. We here are more and more glad to have those lovely sisters and brother as neighbors and certainly they are a credit to a community. They are getting along swell and don't worry about them. For they know that we here at 42 "L" are at their beck and call. Mother Hasson and Hermina were up town yesterday (Monday, Aug. 7th.) so you know now I am writing this on Tuesday Aug 8th - Weather is rather warm. In fact I am sitting here in the kitchen with my pants and shoes on (that's all). Oh yes! They are putting a new roof on the apartments (that's what they have 6 on Linwood and 6 on Madison Ave. In other words that's where you used to ride the bicycle in the back door. Yea! Herman rides two days and fixes the tires the next day - must be getting too heavy on the tires. And to let you in on something - Maria - has a lovely flower garden out in front of the house. Irving I have just rambled on this envelope but it so happens we were out of writing paper as it was down at the store, but regardless on what I write it's still a note. So from us at 42 Linwood we want you to know that we do think of you and if there is anything on your mind you would want done for those swell sisters and brothers next door, just drop us a line and it will be done. How we love to do something for those we like and love. They won't know where we got the tip as they will not know about this (crazy) letter. So Irving as I said in the beginning we think of you and ask the girls when they last heard from you. So from us here at 42 (Mother Hasson, Mrs. Walters and Me) we send our love and kisses to a real swell guy XXXX XXX

1944/8/10 Irving to Dave, Outside Naples, Italy (V-Mail, Slide 217)

August 10, 1944
Italy

My dear brother Dave,

Hope that you have received my letter with my pictures in it. They weren't very good, however let me know what you think of it. Sometimes it's difficult to make a real good picture, because I want to have it right away and a good picture takes to make a couple days. You know over here I don't know at present how long I'll be. I would not mind to stay until this mess ends. I hope and trust in God that He will help me and everything will be OK. I will write you more later. Remain with all my love, Irving

1944/8/10 Irving to Family, Outside Naples, Italy (V-Mail, Slide 216)

August 10, 1944
Italy

My dear sisters Hermine and Maria,
Hope that you have received my letter with my pictures in it. They weren't very good, however please let me know, what you think of it. Next time I get a pass to town I'll make some more and different kinds. I sure would like to get some from you. If you can send me one of yourselves. News not much. The war is still on. I sure would like to drop in and see you personally. Let's hope that it won't be long and we will meet again soon. I remain with all my love, Irving

P.S. Love to Dave and Herman.

1944/8/11 Hermine and Marie to Irving (Book 2, 46-51)

Columbus, Aug 11-44
[from Hermine]
My dear little brother Irving!
It's Friday today and I would like to make up for something I missed out on this week. Believe me, I know what it means when you can't write because you are busy. Since I was at home this week and it was on my mind that I will write to you, and yet I failed to do it. I hope my little brother that everything is good with you and you are in good health. You are in my mind a lot and I'm asking the dear God to help you, so you can come home to me in good health. I prepared a 5 f[ont] [pound] package, what I already mentioned in the V mail. I hope what we are sending [in reply] to your request is going to be good. The "figbars" look good, but I am afraid that it will be spoiled. If you will get it, let me know how it was. Besides that, thank goodness, I'm doing well only the weather is still warm. It would be nice to have a good rain. We got a letter from Dave too this week and he wrote that he is very busy. I believe it, because he cooks for himself at home. What do you say to that?

He cooks whatever he thinks and it was interesting, he was not sure how at first, how to make a Stuffed Cabbage and he wrote down the recipe [to check] if it was good. If it was good I okayed it for him and really, he knew how to do it. So it's possible that it's useful for him to be alone. Although if he calls us to move there now, I will know for sure he got bored from the cooking and cleaning. Right now, I don't have any plan to go there, but I believe that he would really want it. Poor thing, I truly feel sorry for him because he must work a lot. You know it takes a lot of time. But now I will leave it alone, hoping that you are well and we will hear from you again soon. Miss Walters
called me this week from the store and asked for your address because her husband wrote to you. The old lady is very nice, we were at the movies this week. I also bought a new dress for myself.

You might find it ridiculous, that she should rather go with a younger girl to the movies, and you are right, but she is a very delicate lady and I truly like her. She dresses nicely and I really have a good time with her. Yesterday night a girl visited us. She is on the picture that I sent already to you and it was taken on High St. So the taller girl, the second one, is the one who got married. I really hope that you got the present pictures [and] also what was taken with the girls with whom I work. The little black one's parents originated from Italy and I was in their house. They seem very nice. I was with them twice to Bukeye [Buckeye] Lake. My job seems to be pretty good. Just the way the pictures show you, that they like us, which is very nice. I hope you have somebody there besides the Hungarian boy you mentioned. How is he doing? Did you hear from him? Take care of yourself and don't you worry my little brother-Believe me that does not help much.

I scribbled-scrabbled this much to you, maybe you won't even have time to read it. But still, I would like to write to you. So, there isn't much interesting going on for us at home because everybody has someone in the war, so it causes trouble for everyone. Believe me, if this terrible war would end now, with God's help, I would see you in person shortly, besides that a lot of things would be different. Write what you would like to get from home and I will be in a hurry to send something. You would love to have a huge variety of things. Maybe when you have a rest, you can get ready [for it]. I wanted to send you a smaller jar [of compote] , but I couldn't get it, and it would have taken longer. I thought it's better than nothing. So, now I'm really finishing my lines, hoping to hear only the best. I wish you good luck and health with love. Kisses, your sister, Hermina
P.S. Write whenever you can

[from Marie]
My dear little loving brother!
It's been a few days since we got your awaited letter already. But I hope that you are in a best of health. How are you my dearest little brother? I hope I will still hear the best about you!
We are well and I'm thinking about you a lot and I can hardly wait for the moment when I can see you again. We got a letter from David also and he is well. Only like he said, he is very busy. This isn't new, but I'm not going anywhere so I can't really write to you about anything. We did not go to the movies, since the weather is pretty cold and I was very busy with my work. Yes, my dear little brother, I don't know if I wrote that I changed places, although it has been a few months already. I worked for Desler and in the meantime they gave me meals with salary, but I didn't really like it. So I went over to the Neil House and I like it so much better. First of all, here I get $10.00 more a month and they give me meals also. I'm satisfied here since then and I hope everything is going to be fine from now on.

This is the 4th week that I work here. If the dear God will help me, you'll come home and you'll visit me. This is what I'm waiting for so much. And I'm asking you my dear little brother, to take good care of yourself wherever you go. And I'm asking the dear God to help you in every step of yours. And my dear little brother, I hope you will not go back where you were. [In English] But God bless you and be with you. [In Hungarian] I don't forget you not even for a minute. I wish we would be over this awful mess. I would be happier. Flora and the family are always wondering about you and they are sending greetings. You know who at Fenton, who you also mentioned was there, and mentioned you a lot and just said that she got an addressed envelope [from Polish - kopertat] from you and doesn't understand it since the letter was not in it. But she was very happy that you are thinking of her. We did not get a letter from Bertha for a long time. But now I wrote enough. I will write again next time. I kiss you countless times. Your faithful sibling who will never forget. I wish you good luck. I remain with all my love until I will see you again, Maria

1944/8/11 Irving to Dave (Book 4, 89-90)

August 11, 1944
Italy

My dear brother Dave,
Today is Thursday evening and I want you to know that I'm okay with God's help. I hope that you're well and in the best of health. I just came from services. I'm going whenever I can while I'm here in this camp. The name is different, but the same as I used to be way back in Africa. You know the other evening I recognized a guy, he was in Camp Wolters with me. He just came across. Some people are lucky. If I concern myself I was lucky too. Now I'm hoping for the best. It's time to come. Don't you think so? Every day counts, so I'm hoping for the best. Well Dave, how are you getting along? I sure would like to have supper with you in that cottage. Maybe it won't be long and we will make a date. To all that we need God's help. I trust in him he will help me. Please write me even though you are busy. At present I'm not getting any mail. It takes time to catch up with me. Now I'll close this time and hoping to hear from you soon. With all my love, your brother, Irving

My love to the family back home.

P.S. I'm writing this letter on a table, I haven't written for a long time on one.

1944/8/12 Hermine to Irving (Book 11, 25-26)

Columbus Aug 12 - 44
Written in Hungarian

My dear little brother, Irving!
I wrote a long letter yesterday to you, but I will write today again. There is no V. Mail at home, so I will go to the town and I want the letter to go today. As I mentioned to you this week, I would have liked to send you a letter every day, but the big cleaning took my time away. I'm sorry to write it that way, since you surely will be surprised, how is that possible? I planned everything in my mind, but not everything works out. I asked a black person to help and he could only come when I was almost finished. He cleaned up the windows. Believe me, little brother I'm so happy that they are clean, since it is done already, but I'm sorry that my vacation passed by already like that. Although, I was at the movies this week and I will go again today. I don't know what we will decide on tomorrow, but I will try to write to you every night. I hope that you get a letter from us by then. It is possible that it is late and it is also possible that we write less. Don't worry little brother!

We are all well and I ask the dear God, to help you as well wherever you go. Herman is well too, only I don't know what's the best way to describe it, since he does not write to you. I could tell you that he is lazy or dumb, because otherwise he would write to you. Did you get the little package of [in English] cooked ["cokot"] fruit? [In Hungarian] I don't know, we sent at least 2 or 3 of them to you. Today is Saturday, and I hope that we get a letter from you, too. The mailman just came and there is no letter from you. Maybe later, it is possible. I know that you are busy so we should write to you more often. I got a letter from the boy I met a few weeks ago. He is from Cleveland. His name is Rosewater and currently we are corresponding and in English. Believe me it is hard for me at times. And forgive me that I only write Hungarian to you, but it really is easier. Know only that we are all well, the relatives also. I kiss you with love. I wish you good luck and good health.
I will see you again. Your sister, Hermina.

1944/8/13 Irving to Dave, Outside Naples, Italy (V-Mail, Slide 220)

August 13, 1944
Italy

My dear brother Dave,
It's almost a week now that I left the company and haven't received any mail. I hope that it will catch up with me soon. Time goes fast, however not always. How are you Dave? I hope you are feeling fine. I'm OK with God's help. The news sounds very good and I hope it continues so. Then with God's help I could go home. Believe me, I hardly can wait for that day to come. That year that passed away, seems like a life time. At present the only thing I can do, just keep on hoping that it won't be long, till we meet again in the best of health. Please write me as often as you can. I'll do likewise. I am just finish writing one v-mail to the family back home. I always try to write you and them in the same time. I remain with love, Irving

Love to Hermine, Maria, and Herman

1944/8/13 Irving to Family #1, Outside Naples, Italy (V-Mail, Slide 218)

August 13, 1944
Italy

My dear sisters Hermine and Maria,
Just another line to let you know that I'm OK with God's help and hope that you are well and in good health. It's been a week now that I haven't received any mail. I hope that it will catch up with me soon. Time goes fast, however not always. The news sounds very good. I hope that it continues so. Then, with God's help I could go home. Believe me, I can hardly wait for that day to come. That year that passed away, seems like

a life time. At present, the only thing I can do, just keep on hoping that it won't be long till we meet again in the best of health. How are you getting along? I hope fine. Please write me about yourselves. Did you receive my pictures? How did you like it? If you have some taken lately, please send me one. Now I remain with all my love, Irving

Love to Dave and Herman.

1944/8/13 Irving to Family #2, Outside Naples, Italy (V-Mail, Slide 219)

August 13, 1944
Italy

My dear sisters Hermine and Maria,
This is my second letter to you today. That's because yesterday I didn't get enough time off to write you, and I know, how much it means to receive mail. I hope that this letter will find you all in the best of health. I'm OK and hope to stay that way. I still don't know what will come up. However I'm hoping for the best. I would feel much better if this mess would be over. I just can't take [it] off my mind, I dream about it. I hope that time will come soon, sooner is better. I hope that everything goes along as it is. Then it can't last much longer. I bet back home people are happy to hear the good news. How about us? When it ends, the whole world will be happy, so let's hope that it won't be long. Love, Irving

Love to Herman and Dave.

1944/8/13 Maria to Irving (V-Mail, Slide 221)

My dear loved little brother Irving,
I don't know anything special, but I'm trying to write a few lines hoping that I will hear good news from you soon. My dear little brother I don't know anything special. I only wait very impatiently to speak to you in person here in America very soon. I am asking the good G-d to help you and be with you every step of the way. And I am asking you to take care of yourself everywhere you go. I can't even express myself in a letter, but I understand everything you say very well. I'm sorry I can't help. In person we will talk about everything, hopefully soon. There is no special news here. Everybody is well, which we want to hear from you again. Countless kisses from your forever loyal sister, who will never forget you, Maria
[In English] G-d bless you, Good luck to you

1944/8/14 Irving to Dave, Outside Naples, Italy (V-Mail, Slide 222)

August 14, 1944
Italy

My dear brother Dave,
Hope that you have received my letters in the best of health. I'm OK and I hope to stay that way with God's help. Today is Sunday and [I] have some time off, so I'm writing you. Not much news over here, just it's very hot as usual. I'm sitting and sweating, however this time is not the kind of a sweating like it used to be. You remember the time when I told you. I can stand this, much better than those at that time. It would be nice to be home and go out on an afternoon like this. Boy! I bet we would have all the fun that we want. Well let's hope, that it won't be long till we meet again in the best of health. Love, Irving

P.S. Write me soon! Love to family back home

1944/8/14 Irving to Family, Outside Naples, Italy (V-Mail, Slide 223)

Aug - 14- 44
Italy

My dear sisters Hermine and Maria,
Hope that you have received my letters and pictures in it. Today is Sunday and I have some time off, so I'm trying to write about myself. Not much news over here, just very hot as usual. I'm okay and hoping to hear

from you the same. I have written to Dave also. I wish I get some mail, I would feel much better. It's not your fault, don't get me wrong. It takes time to catch up with me. If I'll be here for a couple weeks, which I hope, then I'll get straight mail of this address. Once if you move around, your mail gets every where, but never where you are. Let's hope! Love, Irving
Love to Herman & relatives & friends.

1944/8/15 Chaplain Samuel Kaufman to Family, Outside Naples, Italy (V-Mail, Slide 225)

Office of the Chaplain
Headquarters 24th Replacement Depot
APO #781, c/o Postmaster
New York, N.Y.

Dear Mrs. Gluck,
I am happy to let you know that I have had the pleasure of meeting your son Irving here in Italy. He is well and happy and is taking a splendid interest in our religious activities. It is our hope that peace and victory will come very soon, and that we may once again turn our faces homeward. May God's richest blessings be yours.
Faithfully yours,
Samuel M. Kaufman
Capt., Chap. Corps

1944/8/16 David to Hermine and Marie (Book 18, 106-109)

Long Beach 8.6.44
My Dearests!
Today is Sunday at 4 o'clock. As of now, I wasn't outside yet. All day I have stayed in. I was busy as I mentioned in my previous letter. I moved into a new place. Where I was before it was #11, and now it is apartment 10, next door. This house is just a one room apartment. The only thing is that it has a private bathroom and a very nice small kitchen. In the wall is a very nice bed. It's much nicer and better, and it is the same price. When I rented out the other one I told them if they will have an empty room like this, I want to be the first to get it. Therefore, I was the first to get it. So, I was very busy. Next week I will paint. The furniture is not bad. If you come over it will be enough for both of you. At this time I don't know anything new. Hermine, I received a card from you. And from you Mariska, a letter. I understood everything. Here I'm enclosing a few letters from our little brother. Thank goodness he is ok. As I mentioned in the previous letter that they are going south. They were at the French Border. Write, even if I don't write often. As you see, I'm always very busy. Hermine, how do you make kugel [noodle pudding]? And hremszlit [potatoes]? Let me know. This time is soup, the Mrs. Gross type. Ready like you used to. Also, stuffed cabbage with tomato puree. I can say that it is very good, and I made roast meat which was also very good, but I didn't eat yet. I'm not hungry yet. I also cooked corn. I bought so much that it will be enough for 2 days. Tomorrow I will have the cabbage and will make potatoes. Oh yes, the meat is kosher. Yes, in Long Beach there is a kosher store around the corner where you can get everything kosher. Now I wrote enough, all silly things, but enough for today. I would like to get a long letter from you. Let me know how much I owe you for the whiskey. You don't have to send it to me. We have as much as you want here. Kisses, Dezső

1944/8/16 David to Irving (Book 18, 78-84)

8.16.44
Written in Hungarian

My Dearest little brother
You gave me my biggest happiness with your new address and your picture. I was so scared because I didn't hear from you and I thought you were surely transferred somewhere else. I hope wherever you are you will stay there at least a couple of weeks, I hope with God's help. I hope in a short time you will be able to come home to us. You know, it's possible that while you're not working they'll send you to school, and when you arrive there you will be officially working. What do you think? Is it possible my dearest brother? Whenever you can, write some new news ok! Here I will wait impatiently for your new assignment. My dearest brother, don't worry even if you are not getting any medal that is ok, no problem. The main thing is that you should

be well. I hope with God's help, from now on He will help you to have the best of everything! I see in today's newspapers that in Hungary they permitted the Red Cross to get Jews out from there. I hope it's [for] our father. Thank God with their [the Red Cross's] help they [our family] will be and are in good health. From home today I received a letter. Thank God they are ok. My dearest brother I can't even tell you how happy I was to receive your letter. The picture is very beautiful. You look as though I see you in person. Dear brother, I am so proud of you - what a beautiful soldier you are. The boy next to you looks like a nothing. But you brother, just like a real soldier, like a captain! God should help you to come home in good health and we will see each other again my brother dear. In a couple of days I will send you a package. I will send some kosher salami just like in the other package, the last one [that I sent]. If you received the last one you will find a little whiskey. Write if it was any good! My brother, as I see in your letter, you wrote it on the 10th and I received it in California on the 16th and I was reading it. It was very fast and good service. At this time, I don't have anything new to write about. I'm still working in the shipyard. It is very difficult and dirty work to do, but it is still better than yours. I hope this war also will end soon. My brother dear, are you going to get the right to vote over there? Why don't you register to be able to get it. I think you deserve it. You should get it! Therefore, my dearest little brother, you know, I wrote enough. This week I will write to you again more. Until then, God be with you. Everything will work out and it will be ok. It will bring happiness too. I'm so anxious to see you, waiting is difficult. Oh boy! If you could come here to see me I would take you anywhere, wherever you wanted to go! To the best places. My dearest brother, God will help you. Everything will work out for the best. Don't worry, you see He is helping you. One more thing. I wrote to you before from Columbus that an old fortune teller woman told me I will go to business here in Long Beach in a big way and you will go there where you are. And our grandmother and grandfather in Polyán, they passed away, they will be next to you and they will help you from the trouble. So don't worry, they are watching over you and God will help you, and all the best will come true. Now I am wishing you all the best and all the happiness. Hope to see you soon. With best wishes and kisses, until we meet again. Your brother, Dezső

1944/8/16 Howell Walters (neighbors) to Irving (Book 15, 89-92)

Columbus X5 Ohio
Aug. 16th 1944
Wed. Nite

Hello Irving:

That's from all of us here at 42 Linwood to you. Mrs. Hasson, Mrs. Walters and myself to you. Our apologies for not writing oftener but it is just one of those things. Mrs. Walters and myself have really been going it. We are short handed in the store as I had to let one of the men go and have not been able to replace him.

Merchandise is harder to get or at least as bad as when you were home and that was bad enough - and demand on better grade merchandise is of greater demand. Just to give you an idea whiskey was somewhat hard to get but now cigarettes which were popular are practically off the market here at home. Don't get the idea we are crabbing (complaining) but it just gives you an idea of what things are here in the States.

Say fellow those are some very nice pictures the girls brought over tonite. Can't say you have changed so much. Seem to be holding your weight, if anything you have grown a little taller.

Just stopped to take a drag on a cigarette and look over at Mrs. Hasson and she was watching me scribbling. Well she is about the same. Eats well, sleeps very good (even snores) so we and the folks at 50 Linwood can't sleep. Well Irving there [is] one thing sure. She and the girls are having a real companionship together. We have had a very hot dry Summer but to nite it has been raining and has cooled off quite a little.

Now you know that Guy "Herman". Well he is still riding that bicycle back and forth. So far it's still doing all right except he lets the air out of the tires so he can blow them up (A windy guy) isn't he.

The girls are getting along alright and seem to be very happy in their work.

So from us three at 42 to you our Love and Best wishes and Lots of Luck.

The folks at 42 Linwood
Mrs. Hasson and us Walters

1944/8/17 David to Hermine and Marie (Book 15, 155-159)

8.16.44

Dear Hermina and Mariska!

Forgive me, that I did not respond to many of your letters, but believe me, I am so tired and sleepy after work, that I am not capable to write. I'm falling asleep. I got a letter from our little brother, you got from him since then. I got 3 pictures from him that I will send to you this week. He sent to you also and if you did not get the letter from him, his address is: 555 Repl Co. A.P.O. 781-R. Thank God he will get a little rest. May the dear God grant that everything works out! Hermine, you wrote that you paid off the bill for the Jewish newspaper, mine and yours. You did not owe to pay for 2 newspapers, only one because I just started to get it now. If you paid 6 dollars, for the newspaper to the address there, from August 1-44 to August 1-45. So it has been paid.

Write to me about this, Ok?! Write to me how much was the Palinka, so I will send the money to you for that and for the newspaper too. I don't know any news. The weather is bearable. It is pretty warm, but it is not like there. You know, my little brother looks pretty good in the picture. He is a true soldier. I hope he will get a good position. I will send a package to him and I will send a little salami in it. I hope it will come in handy for him. You know, if the APO will change, then we can send packages to his new address. I will send peanuts and cookies also to him-Forgive me, if I don't write correctly. Can you see? I am so tired already, I barely know what to write. Forgive me! Ok? So, I will close my lines. It is enough for today! Hey, Hermine go check out the Jewish newspaper on 8-11 and write so you can get information. Please write to me and forgive me, if I don't even write correctly. But whenever I can I will write, until then God will help all of you for everything good! Herman as well! Kisses with love, Dezső

P.S. I hope you will write to me! Ok?!!

1944/8/21 Irving to Hermine and Marie (Book 4, 110-118)

August 21, 1944

My dear sisters Hermine and Marie,

Just a line to let you know that I'm okay and hope you are all well and in good health. Just a year today that I left the United States. It seems to me [as] if it was only yesterday, but as you see time goes fast. When you wait for something to come, it seems to you much longer than [it] actually is. During that time I have been waiting and praying to God to end this war. So as time goes by, I'm still waiting, maybe next day it will end. And with that hope I go on. Please forgive me for not writing you as often like I used to. But I'm still waiting to get a permanent address. When I do so, I'll write whenever I can. The other day I have received a package from Dave. He sent me some cookies that you sent him. It was a very good, only they repacked it and the cookies were broken. At present I still don't know what will be. If this war ends then I won't worry so much. But till then I don't know. In my share I had enough of this. If it ends sooner is better. Like I said one day is enough and when you wait for one day you think it will never come. But when it's gone, then you really know that time goes fast. It can't last forever, that's one thing, so let's hope and pray that it [sic] God help to go through it in good health. Did you receive my pictures? What did you think about it? They weren't very good. The other day I was in town again and made some more pictures, but they aren't very good so I'm not sending it home. However sometime later I'll go again and make more and send it home. I want them to be real good. As I'm still in that replacement depot I should write home more often, believe me it isn't anything to write about it. The other day I begin to write but never got a chance to finish it. Somehow this week I didn't have enough patience to do anything, just what I really had to. The end of this war would solve my problem. Nothing else. Now if I will be home, boy! Let me tell you what I would do. I guess I would go some nice quiet place and forget that, that I ever was in the army. Do what I want, I go where I want to. Well, let's hope it won't be long now. It's been long enough. How are you Hermine? I hope that you are feeling fine. You must also forgive me for writing with pencil, but I think it's much faster that way. I'm behind my tent and writing you. The table is not very comfortable and so my writing is not too good. I hope you are able to read it. Sometime later I'll write you more about things. I guess if I want to, I could write a whole book. Maybe it would be interesting, just for myself because not everybody would believe it. The only time you believe something, when you actually are in it. Well Maria, how are you doing? I hope fine. Please write even though I'm late with answering it. But don't forget that, you are always in my mind.

I think of you both a lot. I hope that God will help me and someday I'll be able to prove to it you. How are you Herman? I haven't heard from you a long time. I hope you are well and in good health. Let me tell you something, that you are and were a smart boy for being out of this. It's not so easy to do it, like you think. I'm glad that you and Dave don't have to go through all this. Let's hope that everything will be okay and we will meet again in the good old U.S.A. in the best of health. So now I'll close this time and remain with all my love, Irving

P.S. I'm going to write to Dave also. My best regards to our friends and relatives. At present I'm not writing anyone, just you and Dave.

Hope to see you soon!
Love, Irv.

Italy
August 21, 1944

1944/8/22 Irving to Dave (Book 6, 169-172)

August 22, 1944
My dear brother Dave,
Just a line to let you know that I'm okay hope that you are well and in good health. Just a year today that I left the good old America. It seems like a lifetime. When you are waiting for something to come, seems to you longer than actually is. During that time I have been waiting and waiting for the end of this war. But till yet I'm still waiting for the best to come as time goes by. I'm ready to go home anytime and forget that I ever was in this mess. At present let's hope and pray to God for a speedy victory. Then all our worries will be gone. The past week I have not written letters home. Somehow I was waiting that maybe I'll be able to tell you something and probably have a new address. But as you see everything is the same. Dave, I have a surprise for you, you know I received the package from you. It contains cookies and the special sun lotion! Boy! That's real stuff! It's like a souvenir. The only thing was that the cookies were mashed but even then, don't worry I know what to do with it. Thanks very much for everything. It's very sweet of you, for all that. Please write me whenever you can even though I'm late answering it. The holy days are coming, I sure would like to be home by that time. But it can't be yet. Well there isn't much I can tell you. They say in the army, if something is not the way you want, see the chaplain! But believe me that God is the only Doctor. So, let's hope and pray for the things he did and hope for the future. That everything will be okay. May God help us for a speedy victory. And I hope to see you soon in the best of health. Love, Irving

P.S. My best regards to the family back home. Please forgive me for writing with pencil, but I guess it's much faster this time.

P.S. WRITE SOON!

1944/8/24 David to Hermine and Marie (Book 4, 20-21)

8.24.44
Dear Hermine and Maria,
This week and last week I received a few of your letters I think I wrote a letter to you also. I hope you will forgive me for not writing as often I should. At this time I am working 7 days 10 hours a day. We are very busy. I hope you will understand that when I come home and get cleaned up I'm very tired. After that I have to cook. I'm busy enough as of now by the time I finish I am halfway sleeping. I hope everything will work out. Here I am sending you a couple of letters from our brother Irving that I just received this week. I hope our God will help him to be safe. I think he's going to be part of the "Occupation troops" to seize the country. I hope he will be able to go to Hungary. I hope our father will be able to get somewhere in a couple of days because the Russians are in Ungvár, which is not too far from Munkacs, therefore don't worry, everything will work out.

How are you, Herman? Why didn't you write, I'm getting very sleepy. Hermine, I still owe you for the liquor that you sent to me. Maria it does not take long to make the pocketbook. You can get 50 dollars for it when you sell it. Why not think about it. If you can make it you can get 2 weeks' wages. I will get the cotton for you but for nobody else! Mariska, if the mailman asked for the address give it to them because they know it anyway. Now I'm closing. Wishing you all the best, many kisses with love until we shall see each other in California. Kisses, Dave

1944/8/24 David to Irving (book 12, 102-104)

Aug 24. 44
Written in Hungarian

My dear little brother,
I got 4 letters from you this week and I was pretty happy about them. Although, may the dear God give it that you could be there until the danger will pass. I'm in the belief that you are not there anymore, rather somewhere in France. The important thing is that there, thank God, it is not that dangerous. You know, if you are still there where you were, I think that there is a good job for you in the view in Hungary. Little brother I still did not send the package yet, but I will send it shortly. Write to me, if you got the last two packages. I will send a little drink also. Little brother, forgive me, if you don't get mail from me normally. You know currently we work 7 days a week, 70 hours. Even if a man does not work hard, it is enough to get up at 5 am and be on my feet all day long.

But it is enough about me for today. I got mail from home, thank God they are well. How are you little brother? I hope the dear God will help you and you will come home soon! And promise me you will come to me here. I will pay for the public transportation also. But as soon as possible! Ok? I will make a very good lunch for you and I will take you in Hollywood to the most beautiful places. Hey! What is going on with your French girl? Did you write to her? Did she write to you? Write about it! There isn't any special news here. The heat is hot enough, but it is endurable. Based on the news you are going well there. I'm sure that by the time you get this letter, Hungary will already be at peace. Our poor father and the family, what could they be doing! I hope they are well-Little brother don't be sad. Everything is going to be successful! You know, whoever I show your picture to says that you are a great soldier! I said the same thing! Hey, little brother are you in the Signal Unit? There is an insignia on your uniform. What do you have to do with them, or what [is it]? Little brother, I ask you again forgive me that I did not write you before, and forgive me if I don't write to every response. But I'm in a hurry to write this letter before I fall asleep writing. Now, I will write home too. I will send a few letters to them. So, it is enough for today-May God help you for everything good and grant that you could come home with luck to us. I kiss you with love, your forever faithful brother, David.
P.S. Forgive me for the bad writing! You know I'm sleepy. Kisses, Dezső

1944/8/24 Flora to Hermine and Marie (Book 17, 351-355)

August 24, 1944
Dear Hermine and Marie:
I had every intention of calling you to say goodbye before we left the city but it seems my preparations for going away took me so much longer than ever before - we didn't leave until about 2 o'clock Friday and arrived here Sunday night. We have comfortable rooms and it is wonderful not to have to think about cooking and keeping house. Some day if we have a cottage here we hope you both as well as Herman and Ignác will spend your vacation with us. The sun has been shining these 4 days, which is quite unusual because most of the time it is rainy and damp this time of year. However we can't get along without our coats - it is too cold for that. I brought up the white dress but it hasn't been warm enough to wear it - I have been wearing the black 2 piece you fixed and the heavy suit will come in handy, too. Marie, I still haven't thanked you, as you weren't home when I called nor the Sunday p.m. I stopped over - I appreciate very much what you have done for me and hope some day to be able to do something nice for you. I have been having dizzy spells until today - when I am much better but the rest will do me good and I am gaining weight. Arthur, Samuel and Jennie are O.K. and send their love. Did you hear from Irving? I hope so and we pray for good news from him. Take good care of yourselves and if you have time write and let us know all about everything. Our address is

General Delivery
Sault Ste Marie,
Ontario, Canada

Love to you from all of us, Flora

1944/8/26 Bertha to Hermine (Book 17, 24-26)

New York
Aug 26, 44
Dear Hermina,
Just a few lines to let you know that we are well [and] hope to hear the same from you. Am glad to hear that you have heard from your brother Irving that he is O.K. How is your brother David? You never tell me a thing about him. Hope he is well and that he is doing well [illegible] Please forgive me if I didn't send you Aunt Jennie's address 'til now, it slipped my memory. I just came across her address and that reminded me that you had asked me for it some time ago. Here:

Mrs. Jennie Gluck
234-04 Seward Ave.
Belrose, L.I.

The only news is that Adolf Frey moved to Mt. Pleasant Pa, where my cousin Fred lives. He is opening a jewelry store out there. I haven't seen the relatives for a long time, love to you all.

Bertha and Mannie

1944/8/29 David to Family (Book 12, 108)

8.29.44
My darlings!
Maria, only this, that thank God I am well, and that's what I hope is not missing from you either. I got a letter from our little brother. I will attach it here, the noted sun lotion that he wrote about was Palinka. I will send it to him again. There is no news here. We work 7 days a week. I don't do anything else. I work and I sleep. Oh yes! I got the pictures and they are good. And it was on the news there, so I wrote about it. Forgive me Ok? Write how much I owe you, so I can send the money home! Mariska, I got a letter from you too. Thank you for it and I hope that my lines will find you in the best of health. Write a lot. I will write whenever I can. Until then I kiss you with love. Dezső
P.S. I'm pretty sleepy. It is 10 o'clock at night.

1944/8/29 David to Irving (Book 12, 110-112) Chronicle Article Greenstein

8.29.44
To Censor
Written in Hungarian

My dear little brother!
I just got your letter tonight. I was very impatient that you did not write. Yes, please even if you don't get any mail from me, but if you could just send me a card, please do. But write to me. I'm sorry that I did not send the package yet, but I will send it this week anyhow. I am very happy that you got the package and the sun lotion came in handy. So, I will be in a hurry to send it to you again. I already got the stuff, but it is too late to go and measure it. But with the dear God's help I will send it to you. I hope with God's help you will come home as soon as possible! The news is really good! Since I think the Russians are not far from Polyán, I hope that our father and the family will be on Russian land soon! There is no news here, everything is the same. Currently we work 7 days a week.

Little brother, the news from home is pretty good this week and I hope, that you will see our father and the family in a month. I hope little brother that you don't need to be in danger like where you were before in the past! I believe I wrote about this, you are at the Signal Camp? What do you do? Write about it! Ok? I got a letter from home yesterday. Thank God they are well. Hey, little brother! Write if you voted or if you will vote. If you want I can arrange it for you, so you can vote. Ok?! I hope that the current president will be elected. Do you also?

So, I will close my lines, right now I'm getting tired and I don't even know what to write. Yes my little brother, Hermine wrote that she got a letter from the Chaplain and he wrote that you were in the temple and thank God, you are well! I will send your letter home to Hermine and the others. So, in the hope that I will see you again, your faithful brother forever. Dezső
I will send a package next month with out asking me.

[Side note:] So, I will send a little drink to you as well.

1944/9/1 Irving to Dave #1, Outside Naples, Italy (V-Mail, Slide 228)

September 1, 1944
Italy

My Dear brother Dave,
Once again I'm writing you to let you know that I'm OK I hope you are well and in good health. I have received some letters from you and also from home. Amount 19 letters, boy! I was glad to receive them. I wasn't able to write you for the last couple days or it's more than a week, but the reason is, that I was busy. But as soon as I get enough time off I will write a very long letter. Thanks very much for the picture, you look very good on it. I'll write more later. I remain with love, Irving

Love the family back home.

1944/9/1 Irving to Dave #2, Outside Naples, Italy (V-Mail, Slide 229)

September 1, 1944
Italy

My dear brother Dave,
This is my second letter to you tonight. Yet I'm writing everything very short, however sometime later I'll write you in detail. In one of your letters you were asking me that in which [army] I was in, I was in the fifth. Today I don't know. Like I said in one of my letters, in that letter you didn't understand me well. Anyway I don't have anything to do with the African girl, however I said that she was born in Paris. So if you remember that letter, you'll get to the point [hinting that he may be sent to France]. I don't want anything to do with them just to go home. Love, Irving

I'll write more later

1944/9/1 Irving to Family, Outside Naples, Italy (V-Mail, Slide 226-227)

September 1, 1944
Italy

I
My Dear Sisters Hermine and Maria,
Can't tell you how happy I was to receive your letters and pictures in it. In the same time before I begin to say anything, you must forgive me for not writing you the last couple days or week. However sometime when I get time off I will write you a very long letter. Those pictures made me feel very happy. I just can't stop thinking about you. I hope it won't be long and I'll be able to talk to you about everything personally. The letters I received were 19 all together with Dave's. I'll write more, Love, Irving

II
My Dear Sisters Hermine and Maria,
Here I'm again just writing you another line to let you know I'm OK. That's [sic] stands for everything. I know sometime you wonder why I always say OK. But that I will answer only when I get home. And I hope it won't be long. Tonight I'm not able to write a long letter so don't worry as soon as I can I'll write you a long one like a megilo [megillah]. But you just keep on writing me always. Will you? Thanks very much. Love, Irving

Love to Herman and Friends.

1944/9/2 Irving to Dave #1, Outside Naples, Italy (V-Mail, Slide 231)

September 2, 1944
Italy

My dear brother Dave,
Today like every day I'm thinking of you, I'm glad to hear that you are well and in good health. Thanks very much for the invitation, by that time, you will be an expert in making rolled cabbage. I don't have to tell you that I would really enjoy eating it right now. But I will not forget it, when I get back with God's help. I feel sorry for Mendlovich, but I guess, although he got wounded, he is still lucky. I don't have to say anymore about it. There were times when I was very close to it - but God helped me! And I hope that he will continue to help me. I'll write you more later, Love, Irving

[on the side] Today is a year since I landed in Africa...

1944/9/2 Irving to Dave #2, Outside Naples, Italy (V-Mail, Slide 232)

September 2, 1944
Italy

My dear brother Dave,
Just another line to let you know that I'm OK and hope you are well and in good health. Not much to say this time, but preparing to write you a long letter. Tonight I have written one v-mail, but I decided to write one more. In a few minutes I'm going in temple. Whenever I can I go, while I'm back. I hope that this war will end soon, so that everybody in this world could rest and be free and happy. I can say that, I had enough of this. So let's hope and pray together and with God's help every thing will be OK soon. Love, Irving

1944/9/2 Irving to Family, Outside Naples, Italy (V-Mail, Slide 230)

September 2, 1944
Italy

My dear sisters Hermine and Maria,
This time I just want to say that, thanks very much for your small letters. Today I have also received some 4 letters. It's a pleasure to hear from you. I wish I would get enough time off so I could write you one long letter. Maybe one of these days I'll do it. I'm glad to hear that you are all well and in good health. I'm OK. That reminds me of the letter that I have written you yesterday. OK, stands for everything. Mainly means that, I'm still kicking. I'll write you some more, but first I want to write you a long letter. Today is a year that I landed in Africa. All my love, Irving

1944/9/3 Irving to Hermine and Marie (Book 4, 43-53)

Italy September 3, 1944
My dearest sisters Hermine and Marie,
Not long ago in one of my letters I said I'm going to write you a long letter. So today here I am trying to scramble something of interest. However let me say this, when I'll get home and knock on your door and speak to you personally, then I'm sure everything will be interesting. But today somewhat I have to polish things. The first thing I want to tell you that I'm okay with God's help, and still hoping for the best. There are some things that I could write about, but I'll have to choose something that keeps me smiling. For example, since I've received your pictures, I feel much better and whenever I look at you I feel like flying home. My heart is always with you. I'm waiting for that moment to come, when, with God's help I return home. There is, still so many obstacles to go through before my dream comes through. To all that I'm hoping and praying to God to continue to help me. There also are things that you think about all the time and no way to help on it. So, I'll say, God is the only one, to whom you have to tell your troubles. My only hope is, as I said in many letters if it would end soon, then I'm okay. Many times I said, it can't go on any longer, but it's still going on.

In one of your letters you are saying that I look tired on the picture. I feel tired, but when I say okay, even though I'm tired, not in the mood, but still in places like here, I'm glad to be in, in okay condition. You will understand me I know. At present I don't know what will come up. I'm still in a replacement depot. However some of the boys I came back with, they were shipped out. Maybe back to the old outfit. My desire is to go home; that's a laugh, everybody feels that way. After it ends, then six more months and then we can talk about going home. Once it ends, I'm not going to worry, because then I'll know I'm okay. And if I can, which I hope I will be able to do to take a trip to see the folks back home. That's the hope I really have, and must do! everything it's possible. I know they are worrying too, however they are not sure that it could be? When they'll realize it and will be able to meet again. I can picture everything. I never thought it will be as it is today. Maybe if I would known that as I know now, everything would have been different. Now after all, I'll say; I'm hoping for the best. It must come or else. Once if you have enough, you don't want any more. That's the way I feel.

In near future I'm hoping to get time off and look your letters over, because in this mess it makes it difficult to think of your questions. Which I want to answer immediately. That's why when I write I'm writing about myself as much as I can. However when I look at it, there isn't anything to write about. Just the every days problem. It's just like back home in one way, but there you choose the thing you want to do and you do it with pleasure. But I don't have to tell you the answer over here.

The other day I have received a picture from Dave too. He is looking pretty good. I'm glad to see him that way, because once I received, way back in Anzio and he just found out that I'm there and sent me a picture of himself. Whenever I look at him on that, he looks very sad on it. I know and knew how he felt, he has the real expression. I tried to tell him not to worry, but I know he did. Just like you. Concerning that, it comes natural. It can't be helped. That place was hot, the hottest in the world. It wasn't a picnic there. Sometimes you can't forget it, even though you are trying it hard. On this picture he helps me to forget things, because he smiles on it. So, even though it's hard to forget things and you keep on worrying, try not to, try to forget. That doesn't help anything. Let's hope and pray that victory will be soon and with God's help we will be able to meet again, back in America.

Keep on writing me whenever you can. It's a pleasure to hear from you always.

Yesterday I received my pay for 2 months. Sometime later I will send it home. I know you were buying bonds, but even though you do, take good care of yourselves and get anything you need. Accept things in life wholeheartedly and willingly, because it's sometimes brief, therefore we must live it as best we can and our health as important as it is pure and precious and must take care of it.

Now I remain with all my love and best wishes to a happy new year. Next year this time I hope to celebrate together, also including Dave and Herman, and if possible our father and family.

With love, Irving

Italy
September 3, 1944

1944/9/3 Irving to Dave, Outside Naples, Italy (V-Mail, Slide 233)

September 3, 1944
Italy

My dear brother Dave,
Just finished writing home a long letter, however I wasn't able to write you too, so I'm sending this v-mail. I'm doing like you said it, just a line to let you know that I'm OK and I hope you are well and in good health. I'm still at Repl. Depot [replacement depot] however I don't know what will come up, because some of the boys who came back with me, they were shipped out and maybe they went back to the old outfit. Listen Dave, did you receive the letter from me sometime in July? Concerning about Ignác, I hope you have it and understood it... That was important... I hope for the best, with love, Irving

P.S. WRITE SOON
[Note- See 1944/7/15 Irving to Dave (Book 6, 151-153). He's referring to himself, that he may be going to France, where Dave was before coming to America]

1944/9/4 Irving to Dave (Book 6, 173-179)

September 4, 1944
Italy

My dear brother Dave,
Have finished writing home, so now I'm going to write you also a long letter. I have read some of your letters over and picked out some questions I will try to write about it. First about being in Roma? Well in our way in May, we just went through and haven't have much time to stay there. However we were bivouacked around Roma for a couple days and some of the boys got passes to go there, but I wasn't the lucky one, because when my time came we moved out. So as you see, this is the army. And when you travel with them you go where they tell you and when they tell you. When I came back to this post, we bypassed Roma again, even though we stayed outskirts of Roma and weren't able to go there. Mostly the rear echelon soldiers have the fun and visiting places. The front line men is always on the move. So, I didn't have the chances to see the Pope. Well that's for that.

Your next question is, if I have a chances to get a furlough? Well that is a big question, but it's very simple to answer. No, I can't, because you have to be overseas for 27 months or more. So my only hope is that when it ends, then I'll get to go home. With God's help. Next one is, if I have any medals? No, I wasn't looking for anything like that. I was looking to get myself back and when time comes to go home. Some people have gotten, but some[one] else is doing the job. But they weren't noticed. It's just like any cases that happens every day in everyday life.

Next one is about me being over here in this post. No, it's nothing like you mentioned the reasons. Here or anyplace, as you know in the army they call it, just another Joe. So when I say I hope and trust in God that he'll help me, because there is no one beside him. However, He'll send someone to look into the case and when you believe in him, you must not fear.

I'm glad to hear that you like my picture and proud of it. Believe me if I just could be home I would be the happiest guy. Maybe someday our dreams will come through. I hope! Next one is about voting? Yes, I have signed up for it, but I don't know if they'll accept it. Next one is, about reassignment? Yes, that's the toughest to sweat out. Some of the boys I came up with were shipped out the other day. Believe me if I think about it, I just can't do anything, just cross my fingers, as they say.

The next one is, if I work hard? That will give you an idea, up there it's 24 hour service. And you don't complain either. Talking about rest, since I came back I got me a cot and sleep on it. It feels a little better, than sleeping on the ground. Up there, if you would have a bed you would feel better to sleep on the ground, it's the idea that you feel safer. It would be a good idea when we used to come back for a rest. But that was only a couple days, so it wouldn't [be] worth it, to carrying just for an occasion as that. How is that back home? That good soft bed! Boy! I bet it's wonderful to sleep on it. Isn't [that] right Dave? I know that you'll [be] angry with me…

About your picture? I was very happy to receive it, you look very good on it. I noticed, that someone is sitting beside you. That's not important, however I sure would like [to] have a glass of that soft drink with you. Let's hope that it won't be long! By the way, in one letter I noticed that you're sending another bottle of such as sun lotion, or is that the same or another one. Because I have received one sun lotion. Write me about this so I'll get it straight. Will you? Thanks, like you say. That's a good idea the way you're doing it. I guess it's the best. With that you distinguish yourself that you are the same Dave as when I remember way back in Polány. Yes sir! Thanks for your thoughts!

Yes I remember Greenstein from Vilson Ave. He is in this camp and he was talking about this in that paper. However that he is an officer, so he has it much better off. I don't know if I'll go to see him. It's not so easy to get help from anyone. Because everybody is for himself. For example when I came in here I went to the services and spoke to [the] chaplain. I thought he'll be able to help me, but first I told him what I want and

I know if he wants to help he can. He said that he'll see. But never did anything for me. So as you see everybody's for himself. He has [illegible] and sent home that I'm okay. That's alright, that's only business if you know what I mean. So my hope is in God that he will help me. I never begged anybody and never will.

Meeting friends? The other day I met a boy he just came over from the States. He was training in Camp Wolters with me. He's a lucky fellow that he stayed back that long. Not everybody is as lucky as him. He also told me about the boys. They're all scattered out. When I came across we were 3 of us from that camp. They were sent out before me. By this time I heard that they went back home. They were badly wounded. I think this war will be over soon. The only thing is, as I said, it can't last forever. Everything has an end. And I hope it ends! Up there one second is enough. Concerning myself I had enough!

Well, David! I hope you won't get disgusted with this long letter, but I really tried to write something that you want to know.

Now in closing this letter I'm wishing you a very happy new year and hope to see you home in the best of health. Next year this time we will be celebrating all together and hope that our father and brother Louis and family will be able to be with us. I remain with all my love to you and the family back home. Give my love to them, when you write them. Love, Irving

P.S. I think we will have services on the holy days over here. I hope to be here at that time. Also today's news sounds very good, you probably know more about. Hope to see you soon! It can be if they roll on.

A note!
I got this stationery from the chaplain's office. It's pretty good to write on it. As you see his name is on it. I have enough to write another letter home, but first I'll have to think of something to write about it. Will write more later take care of yourself and good luck, your brother, Irving

P.S. I don't know if I have told you that I was with the fifth not 8th concerning your question! Remember? Irv.

1944/9/4 Irving to Dave, Outside Naples, Italy (V-Mail, Slide 235)

September 4, 1944
Italy

My dear brother Dave,
By this time you have received my long letter, I wonder what you were thinking about it. It looked like a news round up. Hope that you understood it well. This time I haven't much to say, just want you to know that I'm OK. Hope you are well and [in] good health. The other day we had a good shower, I mean a rain, boy, oh boy it really poured down. I was lucky being in my tent. The rainy season started, so it's good to have the rain coat handy. Well I guess I'll close this time and will write again soon. You write me also. Remain with all my love, Irving

Love to the folks back home.

1944/9/4 Irving to Family, Outside Naples, Italy (V-Mail, Slide 234)

September 4, 1944
Italy

My dear sisters Hermine and Maria,
Just another line to let you know that I'm OK and hope to hear from you soon again. I have received a couple letters from you today. And also looked a couple of old letters over. In one of your letters you [are] asking me if I speak Italian. No, just a few words. I never tried to learn it. I was very glad to hear about the neighbor it's really interesting case as you say! Yes I have received the news paper from Hawkin, but I wasn't able to answer him. So when you call him up, tell him that I thanked for it. If I'll get time to write I will so. The great present! Did you have a nice vacation? Please write me about it. Now I remain with, Love, Irving

P.S. I have written a long letter to Dave also and will write you more later.

1944/9/4 Hermine to Irving (V-Mail, Slide 242)

Sept 9-44
Written in Hungarian

Dear little brother Irving,
We have already received a letter from you that was written on the 3rd. You made us really happy with it. Also, that it came in just 6 days is truly amazing. Everything is fine, I will write you a long letter tomorrow. Marcsa and I are ready to do the laundry now, it's Saturday and I only worked until noon today. Also, I wish you a very happy and pleasant New Year and that our poor dear father and Lajos' family will soon be together in my care. Believe me, you have to worry about it in many ways, but let's trust in God that everything will be fine. The holidays start on the evening of the 17th and I hope you will receive this letter by then. I wish you good luck and good health with lots of love, Hermina

1944/9/5 Irving to Dave, Outside Naples, Italy (V-Mail, Slide 238)

September 5, 1944
Italy

My dear brother Dave,
Hope that this letter will find you in the best health. Just now, I have received a letter from you I want [to] write you immediately. I know you were surprised when you received my pictures. They weren't very good. About that shoulder patch? That stands for 1st Armored division. I was in that division, but with the 6th Armored Infantry. So, that's not a signal unit, but a fighting Infantry. Not long ago I have written you something about what I did lately. When I return home with God's help, I'll tell you more about it. Now I'll close this time and hope to hear from you soon again. Love, Irving

1944/9/5 Irving to Family #1, Outside Naples, Italy (V-Mail, Slide 241)

September 5, 1944
Italy

My dear sisters Hermine and Maria,
Just another day and I want you to know that I'm OK and hope you are all in good health. Not much news over here, just hoping for the best. Some times I don't know what to figure it out. I guess I have to sweat this out. Nothing like being home. Some people feel that they found a home in the army, but not me. In the rear, is OK and they have everything. I mean they have a good job and nothing to worry. So, when I say I hope the best I really mean it from my heart. Well I'll close this time I will write you more later. Next letter I'm going to send home ninety dollars. Now with all my love, Irving

1944/9/5 Irving to Family #2, Outside Naples, Italy (V-Mail, Slide 240)

September 5, 1944
Italy

My dearest sisters Hermine and Maria,
Just received a package from you with home made cookies. Thanks very much for it. I'm going to have coffee to it. I wish I could [invite] you and have some with me. However it will be more fun back home. Hope that the day will come soon. Not much to say, everything is the same. I'm OK and I hope that you are all well and in good health. Please write me whenever you have time. I'm doing my best. I'll close this time and hope to hear from you the best. My love to you, Irving

P.S. Give my love to Herman and Dave.

1944/9/10 Hermine to Irving (Book 11, 28-31)

Columbus Sept 10 - 44
Written in Hungarian

My little dear brother, Irving!
We got your long letter yesterday on Saturday and I was really happy about it. I was also very happy to hear, that you, thank God, are in very good health. I really think about you a lot, but I understand that you think about me even more and you wish to be together with us again, and that this terrible war would end. It goes differently at home here, because we don't see anything about it, compared to what you have to go through. I am terrified only from the thought many times when I go to see a movie about the war, because I want to really see what you have a part in. Your letter is so sweet that you truly make me happy with your lines. The dear God will help you little brother, so your plan will be successful and you can visit our dear father, Lajos and his family. I know that time will come, when you will talk for me too and let's hope that soon it will come true. Since this is my wish for so many years and I know it is also feeding your hope and makes you feel better in the hardest situations. The fact that you were happy for our pictures, we will be in a hurry to send more to you again. We got a letter from Dave. He is well and from Lou also. He is in Iceland and he is well. Flora and the family are still in Michigan and I believe they will spend a little time in Canada also.

We got a letter from them that I believe I already mentioned. You know, to their last letter I still did not answer. I got a letter from Bertha also and thank God they are well also. I know you must be surprised what could be the reason that I'm writing in Hungarian to you. Believe me I would love to write in English, but it takes me longer and I have to respond to many people these days. You could see that even to you, either me or Marcsa write. Herman is very negligent to write, but with the relatives I maintain the correspondence. I am the only one who writes, but everybody likes to read it. Now there is not so much fun around here and the relatives want to know how you are doing and I write, but sometimes it gets piled up and I don't feel like writing. The mentioned boy [Gilbert Rosewater] still writes, in other words we are continuing with the corresponding. He was wondering about you too in every letter. I am corresponding with him in English. Hungarian does not work for him. I got a letter yesterday from him too. He did not like it that he invited me to Cleveland on Labor Day weekend and I still haven't gone yet. He is going to New York this holiday and he wants to spend the vacation there.

The Mendlovitz boy, who was very good friends with Dave. They lived in their neighborhood before they came to America and he has information about us from here also, because he asked from the boy who he is in the military with, somewhere in England. The boy wrote that he knows all of us and he is sending his best. So, I want to pass it over to you as well! Believe me my Irving that you were right in your letter when you wrote that it does not matter if he's still 45, but it would still add to everything just like it- That way! He looks like a nice, smart boy, it is possible that he is like a friend. The Friedman boys lived in the same town also. I only write about all these so you can laugh a little. For example, in his letter he is trying to be gentle and he writes very seriously. And he writes, that there it is 11:30 o'clock and he is in a hurry to go to bed and he wants to send his letter and to mark the date on the letter, when I look at the cover the stamp is for 10:30. So, he either made a mistake or just tried to look very busy. But even something like that counts...!? What do you think? True, Marcsa is laughing, but no need to be like that. But still it is very strange. I don't really know him, but I know, that who I really should recognize, will never be.

So, let's have trust in God and hope that everything is going to be fine. If he would not be interested, in that case he would not write, but still somehow I don't have patience and the years are passing by and maybe it would be better to take it seriously. I will go to Cleveland sometime because Elsie invited me also, now that she found out that the boy invited me, and then I will write my opinion to you. Ok my Irving? I wanted to write this foolishness to you a long time ago, but somehow I'm always in a rush. We are all well and we are healthy and we wish to hear the best from you, too. I wish you a very happy new year and that we could be together in health and happiness soon. Let's trust the dear God, that everything will be good. Now I'm closing my lines and I wish you good health and luck wherever you go. Kisses with much love!
P.S. Write whenever you can. Ok? Your sister, Hermina.

1944/9/10 Irving to Dave, Outside Naples, Italy (V-Mail, Slide 244)

September 10, 1944
Italy

My dear brother Dave,

Just a line to let you know that I'm OK and hope that you are well and in good health. I hope that you have received my greeting. I have sent home also to relatives and friends. I bet even Yenkins will be surprised to hear from me. I haven't written to them for a long time. I don't feel like writing to anyone, except you and home. Not much to say this time. We will have services in this camp. Last year I was in Oran, Africa. I was invited to that French family, if you remember I have written to you about it. I wish this war would end I could go over to see our father and brother and celebrate! Love, Irving

1944/9/10 Irving to Family (Book 2, 314-316)

Sept 10, 1944
Italy

My Dear Sisters Hermine & Maria,

By this time, I hope that you have received my greetings. I have sent to the relatives and friends, however I couldn't find the address of Roth bacsi and his family, so when you see them, please tell them, and give my best wishes to them.

Not much to say from here, this year we will have services in camp. Last year I was in Oran, Africa. I was invited to a French family, if you remember I have written about them. I sure would like to be home at this day, but I guess it can't be this year, however I hope that next year at this time with God's help. It would be nice if this war would end and I could go over to see our father and brother, That would be my happiest moment in my life. We really could celebrate on that day. I hope that it won't be long and we will all be happy again. About a week ago, I have told you that I'm going to send you a money order of ninety dollars. So, in this letter, you will find the money order. And like I said in all my letters, if you need of anything, please take it. Anything I can do for you, I will do it, with God's help.

The other day, I went over to Napolys, but I wasn't able to make any good pictures in a day, or while I'm there, so I didn't make any. But soon as I can I'll make some good ones and send you, Now I'll close this time and hope to hear from you soon. I'm ok, and hoping for the best. I'll write you more later, With all my love, Irving

P.S. Write me whenever you can. Thank's very much. Reg.[ards] Dave and Herman

1944/9/11 Arthur Gluck to Irving, (V-Mail, Slide 245)

September 11, 1944
Dear Irving:

Please forgive me for not writing. Have been very busy and not so well. We are all OK now. The war in Europe may soon be won. You expressed a wish that you would like to see your father in Czechoslovakia and I hope you have the good fortune to do so. It would be a great climax to a great adventure. Do you want us to send you anything? Our love to you from us all, Your loving cousin, Arthur Gluck

1944/9/14 David to Family (Book 12, 125-128)

Thursday evening

My dearests! Until 120
I know you are surprised that this is the second week already that I did not write yet. But this is how it goes, when a man works very hard he does not feel like doing anything. Writing postponed from one day to another and this is how it goes. But I will write today and I will not let this happen anymore. I got more letters from you. Hermina, I got an air mail from you and a card and you Marcsa I got one from you last week. Thank you very much and I hope you will forgive me that I did not write. There is no news here, everything is the same. I got the picture of Irving from you and today I sent you the same that he sent to me in color.

Send it back to me so I will send this one back to you, too. With today's mail was a simple letter from Ignác and I sent an 8 page letter to your address. I'm sure you will be interested about what answers he writes to my questions. I met a guy last week, a German refugee, who I did not see for at least 6 years. He lived in Columbus, then he lived in Cincinnati, and he just came out here. There is nothing new here, everything is the same. Please write to me even if I don't write. And don't be scared if I don't write because I have become a very lazy letter writer now. I sent a package to our little brother yesterday. And I will be ready to send him one every week.

I would like to send this letter by special delivery, but I don't know if the post office is open and right now I don't have any more stamps left. So, I wish you a pleasant and Happy New Year to you! I kiss you with love and I wish that in the new year the entire family could be together in good health. Happy New Year Hermine, Mariska and Herman! And, if somebody is wondering, I'm not sending anything to anyone. I don't have time for that. Unfortunately, we must work. We got a letter from the president and he promised a daily job. So, I kiss you with love in the hope that I will see you again. Happy New Year! Kisses, Dezső

1944/9/14 David to Family (Book 12, 130-131)

My Darlings!
I'm sending here a very long letter from our little brother. I'm sure you will be interested in it also, but please save it and put it away well because I want to keep it. There is no news here, everything is the same. Forgive me that I don't write exactly, but I work 7 days a week. You write that I work so much, you're right, but we will not be ashamed of our ships. We are making transport ships here. I'm kissing you,
Dezső

1944/9/14 David to Irving (Book 12, 114-123) Article Slovakians Rout Nazis Near Kosice.

September 14, 44
Written in Hungarian

My dear little brother!
Forgive me that it has been the second week I did not write to you. Before, I was waiting for a letter from you and the time passed with the waiting and this way I'm writing late. Now, I will be in a hurry to write a very long letter for you.
First of all, I wish you a very pleasant and Happy New Year! May God give you that you could come home as soon as possible and I wish you from the bottom of my heart, that the dear God will help you with every good, and come home to us in the best of health-May God give it.
So, my dear little brother in the past days I got from you at least 4 V. mail letters and a long letter, that I was very happy about. May the dear God grant it that you could stay there until the war ends. God forbid, you have to do it over again what you already went through. I was very glad for your letters. Every day the first thing is to see if there is mail from you. If there is, I feel so much better. Forgive me little brother that I did not write for so long, but I was very happy for your long letter and I thank you very much for your nice report. I hope that with God's help everything will end well.

I will send your letter home with today's mail. You know, my little brother, your air mail gets here faster than the V. mail. The letter that was written on the 4th I got by air mail at the same time. The V. mail was written on September 3rd. You know, they have good service now - Little brother I am very happy that you liked the sun lotion and asked if there is one [coming] in your way. Yes, I already sent that to you 5 weeks ago, Listerine to wash your teeth with it, you know what I mean? I hope you will get it when you will read this letter! Based on my calculation you must have gotten letters 2 times. And, little brother write to me, if they will open the package to check to see what is in it. Ok!? Little brother write to me if you need anything, and when I can, I will send packages every week for the next 4 weeks.

Oh yes! Yesterday I sent to your address a 5 pound package and I sent fruit cake, candy, peanuts, hazelnut and a few [items] bought from a bakery in it. I hope you will like it and I sent a little bottle of Listerine in it, what you know that we use for washing, but you know what's in it. Do not give it to anybody. Ok!? Yes, be careful, little brother, not to let them know because here they are paying attention to that. It's not allowed to send this to there - Little brother write, if you need anything, so I can send it to you. Dear little brother, I would love to give you my bed. I wish you could be here. You know, I would make a special dinner for you from the best of everything.

I hope the time will come soon! May God give it. I can't write too much about myself. Currently, I work 7 days a week and 10 hours a day and then when I come home, I cook and clean. It is enough for a man, right? I would like to write about a lot to you, but nothing comes to my mind. I was in the temple on Friday. I will go during the holidays also. You know little brother, the Russians are not far away from Polyán. I will send a little article here to you about what happened there next to Kassa. Maybe you'll be interested in it. Little brother write if you need more comic books or newspapers. Ok? If I should send you a can of plums or peaches? Or sardines. Little brother write it, if you need anything. Ok!? You wrote that it's raining there. You know, here it did not rain the entire summer.

Like you wrote, it was a year ago this week that you moved to Italy. I hope the dear God will help you that you could come home this year in good health. Little brother, if I were you, I would go to see Lieutenant Greenstein. He is a very nice man. He will be very happy for you. Go to him! Ok? He is from Columbus and you know him. Do you remember, you were with me one night and you talked to him? If he does not recognize you, tell him that you are Dave's brother. You know the letter that you wrote about Ignác is very hard to understand. I sent it home to the girls and they could not even understand it well. So, I will wait until you come home and you will explain it to me. Ok? So, little brother, I wrote enough foolishness. I believe it will be enough already for today. But I will note this, I got a letter today from home. They are well and they are very nervous that you wrote to them too and they wrote that you were very happy about my picture. I wish I could be there with you!

You know, little brother, Izy Greenstein [see 1944/8/29 article] is a druggist and at home he works at the hospital. Go for sure and talk to him! Ok? Maybe he could do something to help. I am attaching a little article here that the Greenstein boy's sister [Leah] gave birth to a child. You can show it to him and give him your congratulations like an old acquaintance. He is married. He also has a child. So, it was enough for today. May the dear God give it that I could see you shortly in person in the best of health. I wish you a very Happy and pleasant New Year with love-forever your faithful brother, who feels for you and is thinking of you with love. I kiss you. Dezső
P.S. Forgive me, if I don't write correctly! Ok? Thank you!

1944/9/14 Irving to Dave, Outside Naples, Italy (V-Mail, Slide 246)

September 14, 1944
Italy

My dear brother Dave,
Just want to tell you that I'm OK and hope this letter will find you in [the] best of health. Have received some letters from home and Hermine says that you are very busy, busy cooking that delicious rolled cabbage. I bet it tastes very good. I would like to be there tonight and have supper with you. How about it Dave? Hope that it won't be long now. I don't know yet, but I think that my address will change again. Just hoping that God will be with me and help me and then everything will be all right. With love, Irving

P.S. WRITE SOON

1944/9/14 Irving to Family, Outside Naples, Italy (V-Mail, Slide 247)

September 14, 1944
Italy

My dear sisters Hermine and Maria,
Just want to say that I'm OK, and hoping that this letter will find you all in the best of health. Yesterday, I received several letters from you and Mrs. Walters. When I get time off, I will write them also. From here again, not much to say, just hoping for the best. I don't know yet, but I think my address will change again. Hope that God will help me and everything will be all right. Hope that this mess! ends soon. Please write me soon. I remain with all my love, Irving

P.S. Love to Dave and Herman and the relatives

1944/9/15 Irving to Dave, Outside Naples, Italy (V-Mail, Slide 248)

September 15, 1944
Italy

My dear brother Dave,
Haven't received mail from you lately, I hope you are well and in good health. I'm OK and still at the same place. In a couple days the holy days will be here. We will have services at this post. However I sure would like to go to Napoly for the services. It would be a little different outside, in a town, but it will be good the way it is. Have to be thankful for all this! Please write me, I know you are busy, but just a line like you say. I am wishing all the best from my heart, With love, Irving

1944/9/15 Irving to Family, Outside Naples, Italy (V-Mail, Slide 249)

September 15, 1944
Italy

Hello Dearest Hermine and Maria,
Just want to tell you again, that I'm OK. Have received a small package from you yesterday. Thanks a lot. Not much I can say, because you know more about everything than I do. I'm still hoping for the best. Another day and the holy days will be here. We will have it in our camp. I sure would like to go to Napoly for the services. There would be a little different, however we have to be thankful for all this. Hope that next year I'll meet with you and will celebrate. I'm wishing all the best from my heart, With love, Irving

1944/9/16 Aunt Helen to Irving (Book 16, 293-295)

Columbus on Friday 15.

Dearest Irvin [sic]! I wish you a very happy New Year! God will protect you. Today I am sending a Hanukkah Box with cookies. I hope you like it. I know it is always a treat for a boy to get something from home. I am so glad to hear that you are fine. The girls showed me your pictures and you really look wonderful - a good looking fine soldier. Everything here is the same no especial news. Take care of yourself. Love, Aunt Helen

1944/9/21 Bertha to Irving (V-Mail, Slide 252)

September 21, 1944
Dear Irving
Wish to thank you for the new year card you sent us, hoping that this year will bring you and all you boys a speedy victory and a happy new year. Received mail from Hermina. She tells me that they are all enjoying best of health. Hope that you are well also and that time shall come that you will spend your promised days with us. All the relatives are sending their love to you and their good wishes. My husband is joining me in good wishes and Love, Bertha

1944/9/21 Irving to Dave, Outside Naples, Italy (V-Mail, Slide 254)

September 21, 1944
Italy

My dear brother Dave,
Just a line to let you know that I'm OK and hope you are well and in good health. I'm still at this post. Have been in the temple, it was very nice. Hope I can be here for Yom Kippur. Have been thinking of you a lot. I'll write you more some time later. Hoping for the best, with all my Love, Irving

Please write me!

September 21, 1944
Italy

My dear sisters Hermine and Maria,
Just a line again to let you know that I'm OK and have received about 15 letters from you. It came to the old address. I don't know much to tell you, just hoping that God will help and answer our prayer. Have been to the services, it was pretty nice. I hope I can be here for Yom Kippur too. I met a couple boys that I knew and I left them in Africa. Today they are OK, they have pretty good jobs. My trust in God that He will help me! I will write more later. With love, Irving

Thursday

Dear Irving,
Mother and I received your New Year's greetings and wish you a happy New Year and hope it will be a happy one for you. School started a few weeks ago, and my program and teachers seem nice. Our French teacher is so human. We love to go into her room after school and talk to her about everything under the sun. We are going to have a school dance band. Believe it or not, it was the principal's idea. The school intends to sponsor several dances and we need a band to play for them. Our regular band director will have charge of the dance band. The members will have uniforms, and we are all anxious to see what the band will be like. When you come back, I should like very much to hear what the schools in Europe are like. I have heard that you learn a lot more in the way of academic subjects than we do. This is my last semester in high school, and in February I will start college here at Flora Stone Mather College, Western Reserve University. Take care of yourself, and keep well. Mother sends her best regards. Jane

Sept. 24, 1944
Dear Gluck
How's the old boy? Do you miss me? You don't have to answer that last question. At the moment it's Sunday morning and I'm lying around on my cot before Church which is at 9:00A.M. This joint is just another Repple Depple [replacement depot]. We are going to drill and we have to start retreat at night. It seems that no matter where you are probably even on the front they stand retreat. Was in Leghorn and it's quite a tour. A lot of your buddies are here. But don't you worry they don't want you up here. They want men. Are you still working in the Officer's Mess? Write and tell me all of the news. Today is my birthday. I feel like I'm 90 instead of 19. Would you go over to the mail tent and see if they have my new address? As I don't want my mail to be any longer getting here. Well Gluck, it's about time to go so I shall close for now. Write soon and say hello to everyone for me. Leo

September 26, 1944
Italy

My dear brother Dave,
Have been busy lately and I couldn't write you like I used to. However I want you to know that I'm OK and hope that you are well and in good health. Tomorrow is Yom Kippur! I'm wishing you the best of luck. Hope that next year we will celebrate it all together in the best of health. My address is still the same. Thanks to God. Trust in God, that He will answer our prayer! With love,
Irving

September 26, 1944
Italy

My dear sisters Hermine and Maria,

Have received some more letters from you and I was very happy to know that you are all well and in good health. Have been very busy lately and I couldn't write you like I used to. I thought that I will change my address, at present I'm still at the same place. Thanks to God for his help. Hope that He will answer our prayer. Tomorrow is Yom Kippur! I'm wishing you all the best of luck, With love, Irving

Love to Herman

1944/9/26 Irving to Herman, Outside Naples, Italy (V-Mail, Slide 256)

September 26, 1944
Italy

My dear brother Herman,

Have received a letter from you some time ago, but I wasn't able to answer you. So today I'm just writing to tell you that I'm OK and haven't forgotten you. I'm thinking of you always even though I'm not writing. Hope that God will answer our prayer and everything will be all right. I'm wishing you lots of luck and see [you] soon in the USA. With love, Irving

Love to Hermine and Maria

1944/9/27 Hermine to Irving (Book 11, 33-34)

Sept 27 -44
Written in Hungarian

My dear little brother, Irving!

It was Yom Kippur today and we went to the temple. Thank God we are all well and we are hoping to hear the same about you. Did you go to the temple? I asked the dear God, and let's trust, that everything is going to be fine after this. Now I will tell you an interesting tale/story. Towards evening, before we got home, I wanted to go downstairs and since at the temple I don't really know the way, I went into the girl's lounges so I can be sure where is the way down. And I asked a girl who was closest to the door. She was very nice and offered that she will escort me. Guess who she was?! Florence...she asked me, if I am Irving's sister, Hermina. She recognized me because she saw me once when she met you. Yes, she was wondering about you too and she had the New Year greetings with her that you sent to her. So, it was interesting. Although, I did not know it was her.

I believe, she has changed a lot or she just completely became a big girl. She will write to you for sure. I told the Roth girls that you wanted to send a New Year greetings also. The Aunt is well, Arthur and the others also. There is a new Rabbi in the Broad temple and girls are singing. It went really well for them already today. Only we could pray very little, even less than at the other one. Although, this one [the Rabbi] just graduated, he is a smart man, but he is still very young. I wrote all of the gossip, but I know that you want to hear about it also. Herman was in the temple too and now he is reading a newspaper that mentions our old home and we hope that everything is going to be fine soon. I think about you a lot. I will send you a package again. Take care of yourself, lots of good luck and health until I will see you again shortly. With much love. Kisses, Hermina
Next time Herman will write.

1944/9/28 Irving to Dave, Outside Naples, Italy (V-Mail, Slide 262)

September 28, 1944
Italy

My dear brother Dave,

Just want tell you that I'm OK and hope that our prayer will be answered. I have been to the services at this camp. After services we had sandwiches and coffee. One of my prayer was answered, I have received two packages, one from you and one from home. Also the lotion is very good! Thanks very much for it. I'll write more later. Till we meet again in the best of health.

With Love, Irving

Please write me

Love to the family at home.

1944/9/28 Irving to Family, Outside Naples, Italy (V-Mail, Slide 259)

September 28, 1944
Italy

My dear sisters Hermine and Marie,

Just want to say that I'm OK and hope that God will answer our prayer. I was to the services at this post. After services we had cheese sandwich and coffee. However I can say that one of my prayers were answered, I received 2 packages, one from you and the other one from Dave. It was very good and came in just in time, the best time! I felt like going home and having something to eat. Dave had cookies in it. It was homemade! Yours was sent July 28, 1944. Thanks a million for it! I will write more. With love, Irving

1944/9/30 Irving to Dave, Outside Naples, Italy (V-Mail, Slide 264)

September 30, 1944
Italy

My dear brother Dave,

How are you Dave? I hope fine. I know you are thinking about me, because I'm not writing you like I used to. But you know I'm busy at present. Even though I'm not writing you, but I'm thinking of you a lot. Hope that it won't be long and God will answer our prayer. Not much I can say to you at the present; just that much that [I'm] OK and still hope for the best to come. I'll try to write you more often, whatever I can. Till we meet again, With love, Irving

GIVE MY LOVE TO THE FAMILY BACK HOME.

1944/9/30 Irving to Family, Outside Naples, Italy (V-Mail, Slide 263)

September 30, 1944
Italy

My dearest sisters Hermine and Marie,

Forgive me for not writing you as I used to. But there isn't anything of interest to write about. So I'll say that I'm OK and still waiting for the best to come. I do hope that God will answer our prayer. That's the only hope I ever had and have. Till yet everything come out all right, so I hope it will continue to be that way. How is everything back home? Please write me more often. I will also whenever I can. Some time next week I'll make some pictures and send it to you. In God I trust! Till we meet again! With love, Irving

1944/10/1 Irving to Family, Outside Naples, Italy (V-Mail, Slide 265)

October 1, 1944
Italy

My Dear Sisters Hermine and Maria,

Tomorrow is Sukkot, and I'll go to the services. Over here it's different as you know, but still we have to be thankful for all this. Have received a very nice long letter from you and I will answer you as soon as I get enough time off to write a long letter. So today I just want to say that I'm OK and hope to hear from you soon again, Best wishes to you all! With Love, Irving

Also Dave and Herman

1944/10/4 Dezső to Family (Book 12, 133-135)

Oct 4 - 44

My darlings!

Forgive me that I did not write for such a long time. I already wrote the reason a long time ago, although you don't write either. Hermine, it's been a week since I got a letter from you and you Mariska, I don't even know the time. Especially to Herman, excellent, I still owe you for the drinks, but I will send it soon. It always stays and this is how it goes. It's been a week since I got a letter from our little brother. I hope he is Ok, with God's help. There is no news here, everything is the same- I hope that you are all well! It is the three of you and you have more chance to write. I went to the temple. It was pretty good. The weather here is pretty good, it's not raining yet, but it will in the next month. I registered myself here to vote. I don't know any news, everything is the same!

For Yom Kippur I made fried chicken. It was pretty good and soup too. I made breakfast with eggs yesterday, it was pretty good. So, although I did not write for a long time, I still don't know what to write. I hope my lines will find you in the best of health. Yes, thank you for the new year greetings! Write to me whenever you can. Ok?! So, I will close my lines, may the dear God grant you a happy new year and grant that the whole family can be together in the best of health. May God grant that our little brother can be with us as soon as possible - In good health. And you take good care of yourselves and Herman, you too! Did you get the Jewish newspaper? (New Year's edition). There is Ignác's name in it twice. So, it is enough for today! I wish you everything good with love. Kisses until I see you again. Dezső

1944/10/4 Dezső to Irving (Book 12, 137-141)

Oct 4 - 44

My little brother!

Forgive me that it has been the second week that I haven't written you yet. The reason, as I already wrote to you, is that I'm very busy. No matter how much I try to write, by the time I get home from work and cook, I am so sleepy I can barely see to write. I hope the dear God will help you with everything good. I'm afraid that you are out on the battlefield. You haven't written either. I hope God will help you with everything good. My little brother, take care of yourself. Ok?! I got mail from Hermine this week, thank God they are well-There is no news.

I hope the dear God will help you for everything good. I went to the temple during the holidays and I will go next week as well to "mazkir" [Yizkor]. I hope you had a chance to go to the temple for Yom Kippur. Oh yes, thank you very much for the new year greetings! May the dear God grant that you could be here with us in the best of health. May the dear God grant it-My little brother, write about yourself more, I believe that you are very busy, but you are in a different situation, not like me, and I can hardly wait for a letter from you. Write whenever you can! Ok? There is no particular news here, everything is the same. My little brother you know, you should have gotten 2 packages already, I sent them a long time ago. About 2 or 3 months ago. It was accompanied by a little drink (3 weeks ago) in it. Write it, if you got any of them, what was sent from home.

I don't think you got any of them. Oh yes, last week I sent two 5 pound packages to your address. There was 2 pounds of fruit cake in one of them and at least a deci[liter] of a little drink, you know what? And baked goods, candy, walnuts, figs, gum and other small things. The rare stuffed cookies and Hungarian candy, some figs, and a one pound fruit cake, accompanied by a little drink. You can't dump it out from it because the hole is very small. This package went on a different name because it's only allowed to send one per week. So this way the house wife who is renting the house gave her name to send it. But I will send this week 2 other packages again. There will be fruit cake in it accompanied by a little drink in it. Little brother, if you need anything write it to me! Ok? Thank you! We currently work 7 days a week. Oh maybe you are interested and I don't even write about it, you know I still have my old car. It is still worth $300 today.

It does not run well, but the wheels are still spinning. You know a junker from 42 is 15 percent more. Yes, a lot of money. When you will come home we will buy a nice one. OK? I'm sure you already know how to drive, but the dear God will help you and I will teach you. Yes, please write a lot and about everything. But I'm asking the dear God not to transfer you to fight against Japan. You had enough of this, didn't you? I believe so. So, I wrote enough for today. My little brother, the dear God will help you and help you with the new year, so the entire family can see you in the best of health again with love and with good wishes. Kiss you forever, your faithful brother who will never forget. Until I will see you again shortly. I kiss you, your brother Dezső.

P.S. Did you get the Jewish newspaper? Your name is in it in two places - last Sunday I sent 2 newspapers to your address. Did you get them? A few months ago I sent every week and you only wrote once that you got it. There is no news. I kiss you with love, Dezső

1944/10/7 Louis Schwartz to Hermine (Book 17, 119-122)

Iceland 10-7-44
Dear Hermine,
Received your letter a few days ago and I [am] answering it by first chance. I believe our holidays included Sukos is about or almost over. It doesn't mean much here, there isn't much time to celebrate. I went to the services to "Kol Nidre" with about 250 other boys from all around this rock, included boys from the Allied nations stationing here. Also a few civilian - German and Austrian refugees. No, it didn't look like holiday in any respect. Hope this was the last one to spend far from home. I received a New Year's card from Irving. I believe he'll be able to visit your folks in the near future as I believe he'll be entitled to a furlough. It's not far from where he is, it shouldn't take more than 36 - hours to get there. If I remember right. It's too far for me. I wouldn't give it for much if I could do it. But who can tell. I don't give up hopes… Our Allies, the Russians 're closing in more every day nearer to them I don't think that our people were too much in danger. After all it was Hungary not Germany. So keep your chin up and let's hope the best. No, I've 'nt heard from them for the last two years.

I don't remember if I wrote you in my last letter that quite a few boys left from here on furlough for the States. It'll take a few months till I get into the quota because there are a lot of boys who came much before I did, those've priority. But I will most likely leave before I get into the quota if and when the war against Germany is won. Otherwise I'm fine, hope the same about you.

It's Saturday night now. We're all in our hut, not feeling to step out because of the rain. We've plenty of rain lately though we had snow already too. How're you? Yes, Hermine Dear. Do you get or visit Arthur Gluck, the last time I remember they were operated on. Write me everything. I believe that's all for now so until next time, lots of love, Lou

1944/10/9 (a) Florence Meizlish to Irving (Book 4, 98-99) page 1

Monday, October 9, 1944
Florence Lee Meizlish
995 Ohio Ave. Columbus, Ohio

Dear Irving,
I was so happy to hear from you again and to know that you're safe. Your card was lovely and here's a wish for a very "happy new year" from both my parents and myself. The new year didn't start so well for my family. My father had a heart attack just after Yom Kippur. He's still in the hospital and probably will be for sometime. He's been getting much better lately though. With plenty of rest and care he should be well soon. Since I've been going to college I have met your cousin Sammy Gluck on the campus occasionally and he used to tell me what you were doing and how you were. He's a very nice person–do you remember Myron Pass? He was home on furlough not long ago and he said he expected to be sent to the Pacific Front very soon. Here's some news you're going to be surprised to know about. During the holidays I met your sister Hermine and your brother Herman at the temple. You know Irving, your sister is very pretty. Herman said he remembered me, but I think he was just being polite. He had met me once before. You introduced me to him at the swimming pool once and the three of us went riding together and got caught in the rain. Do you remember? Those days are just pleasant memories now–they seem so far away. Do you know Irving I haven't ridden my bicycle once since the last time I rode with you! It's been down the cellar all this time. When you come home again perhaps we can ride together once more. A few days before your card came I was thinking about you. I remembered that you had sent me New Year's cards before and I was certain you had forgotten me entirely and that this year I wouldn't get a card from you. Then when your card did come I was very happy because I realized you must have been thinking of me a little to send it. Well let's hope that next year we'll be sending each other New Year's greetings from Columbus, Ohio – USA. Do you

Page 374

realize Irving, it's been over a year since I last saw you!! I've often thought about you and wondered why you didn't write. It seems much longer than a year to me.

1944/10/9 (b) Flo Meizlish to Irving (Book 4, 101) page 2

Your sister said you've been very busy. But still a few lines would be appreciated. You must keep up the morale of the home front, you know!! I met a Jewish boy from Hungary that goes to Ohio State also. He was very much surprised to hear me speak a few words of Hungarian, such as - How are You? - Hello - What is your name? - Do you speak Hungarian? - etc. - Do you remember when you taught me that Hungarian? I told him I had a friend that came from Czechoslovakia and he had taught me. By the way Irving can you speak German? I'm taking it in college and maybe we can speak together in German when you get home. That's about all for now. With love, Florence

1944/10/9 Irving to David (Book 3, 89-93)

October 9, 1944
My dear brother Dave,
It's been a long time since I written you last, however I want to tell you that I have not forgotten you. At present I can't tell anything, just okay and don't worry, God will help all those who believe in him. The other day I got from you two packages. Thanks a million for it. The lotion is excellent, but the salami was packed with the candy and cookies and had a funny taste. The next time when you send me, please send it all by itself. Hermine sent me cookies also. They came in all at the same time. Yeah I also want to tell you I moved from this battalion to another and from there to another. So as you see I'm on the move. Please don't worry if I'm not writing, but I will whenever I can. But you just keep on writing me whenever you can. Remain with love, Irving

P.S. Today I was to say Yizkor.
I'll write again soon. I'm still using my old address.

1944/10/9 Irving to Family (Book 2, 308-313)

October 9, 1944
My dearest sisters,
Have been listening for quite a while, however I'll tell you that I have not forgotten you. Since the last couple of days have been moving all around and even now I'm not settled down. I'm still using my old address, in another part of this Depot. Have been to the service today for Yizkor. I could not be there the other day, when I wrote you, that was the first day of Sukkas [Sukkot]. Anyway don't worry my dearest sis. I'm thinking of you always. I'll write you more later. Here I'm enclosing two money orders of amount one hundred fifty dollars. What ever you need go get it for yourselves. I got full paid the other day. Here you don't need any money.

Yet to say anything about myself. I have received two packages from you. One with fig bars and the other with cookies. Thanks a million for it. Dave has sent me also. They all came in at the same time. Dave had the salami with cookies and candy and everything tasted like salami. I'll have to tell him next time when he sends any salami to pack it all by itself. At present you shouldn't send me anything until I get to someplace that I'll have the address. This way it might get lost. I'll write you more about later. Please don't worry! I hope and trust in God that he will help me. Once again I want to tell you not to worry because that doesn't help. Just keep on praying to God, and I'm sure he will answer our prayer. Now with all my love to you, and Dave and Herman, From Irving

Oct 10 - 44
Italy

P.S. Thanks again for the cookies, it was delicious!!!

1944/10/9 Irving to Family, Outside Naples, Italy (V-Mail, Slide 270)

October 9, 1944

Italy

My Dearest Sisters, Hermine and Marie,
Have written you today a letter, but I decided to write you another one. In today's letter I have sent you one hundred and fifty dollars. I hope you will receive it. It was two money order and both on Hermine's name. I want to tell you that please give in [In Hungarian] he's already looking down [Hungarian - már le nez] some amount from it. May God listen to our prayer. He is the only one, who can and will help. Will write you more later. With Love, Irving

1944/10/11 Irving to Dave, Italy (Book 5, 347-348)

Prvt Irving Gluck 35633941
555 Replacement Company. APO
781-R % P.M. N.Y.
Oct 11 - 44
-Italy-

My dear brother Dave,
Once again I want you to know that I'm okay and hope that you are well and in good health. Yet I'm in the Red Cross writing you these lines. Not much to say, just hoping that everything will be all right. I do hope that God will answer my prayer. Yet everything is okay. It's coming along good. Don't worry, this mass [sic] can't last forever. But don't forget, if I am not writing you as I should I'm still thinking of you always. Now with all my love, Irving.

1944/10/11 Irving to Family, Outside Naples, Italy (V-Mail, Slide 272)

October 11, 1944
Italy

My dearest sisters Hermine and Marie,
As you see I'm thinking of you always, now I'm in the Red Cross and writing you this letter. First I want to tell you that I'm OK and hope that you are all well and in good health. Yet I have written today also. Not much to say, just hoping that God will answer my prayer. Till yet my prayers were answered and I hope and trust in God that He will continue to help me. Please write me whenever you can. The cookies are very good. Will write you more later. My love to you, from Irving

The chaplain has sent you a letter - again.

1944/10/12 Irving to Family, Outside Naples, Italy (V-Mail, Slide 273)

October 12, 1944
Italy

Dearest sisters Hermine and Marie,
Have received another letter from you today and I want you to know that it's really very nice to hear from you and to know that you are all well and in good health. I'm OK also. I bet Hermine, you were surprised when you met the Meizlish girl. Yes I have sent greetings to all whom I know and have the addresses. You know that's the first time that I've sent her that greeting, I also sent one to her father in case she didn't tell you. Just let her dream as they say. I'll write you more later. Love, Irving

Love to Dave and Herman

1944/10/17 Chaplain Samuel Kaufman to Family, Outside Naples, Italy (V-Mail, Slide 278)

Office of the Chaplain
Headquarters 24th Replacement Depot
APO #781, c/o Postmaster
New York, N.Y.

Dear Misses Gluck,

I am happy to let you know that I have had the pleasure of meeting your brother Irving here in Italy. He is well and happy and is taking a splendid interest in our religious activities. It is our hope that peace and victory will come very soon, and that we may once again turn our faces homeward. May God's richest blessings be yours.

Faithfully yours,

Samuel M. Kaufman

Capt., Chap. Corps

1944/10/17 David to Irving (Book 2, 71-72)

10-17-44

Dear little brother!

Forgive me that I did not write for 2 weeks now. You know the reason. This week I got a letter from you and last week also. Yes, I'm very glad that you are not on the battlefield. I hope the dear God will help you with everything good. Forgive me, little brother that I don't write that often. But I plan to write a long letter for you and so it remains to be written. There is no special news here. I'm upset that the salami ruined the baked goods and the candy. But the important thing is that was the salami good? Did you like it? Do you want more? My little brother, forgive me, you wrote not to send you more packages until you ask for them, but I sent 3 packages in the past weeks in different names. In the past weeks I sent to you, I don't know for sure, but at least 7 packages. I hope you'll like them? You will find listerine or other bottles in all of them, but you know what is in it. In the package that was sent yesterday and last week, you will find fruitcake, a package of peanuts and walnuts. I hope you are going to like it! My little brother, if you need anything else, ask for it, ok! Forgive me little brother that I don't write a lot. We are still working next week. You know I trust the dear God, that you will come home.

Hey, what's your opinion about the election? Do you know anything about the voting? I will vote for F. D. Roosevelt. Who do you think is good? My little brother I'll be working on writing another letter to you this week again. Good?! I got a letter from home yesterday, thank God they are well. Greetings to you. So, my little brother, good luck to you. May God give you everything good. With love, I kiss you until I'll see you again. Kissing you, your faithful brother, who will never forget you.

Dezső

1944/10/18 David to Family (Book 2, 140-144)

October 18, 1944

Darlings!

Forgive me, that I haven't written in so long, but unfortunately when one works so much, one doesn't have the time. I got a letter from you Mariska, and Hermine I got yours too. Thank God, I'm well and I hope you are as well. Last week you were not in a hurry to write to me. I did not even get a response to my latest letter. What is the reason? Here there is no news, the weather is pretty good! Today the governor was here, Bricker. I did not see him, but I saw it on the news paper. Yes, whenever the movie will get there, "Wilson" about the former President, you can watch it. It's pretty good!

I saw it this week. Oh, yes! I will attach my little brother's picture. You asked me, if I got our late "mama's" [mother's] picture. Yes, I did. I got mail from our little brother, thank God he is well. He is in different location, but his address is the old one. He indicated that he is at the 3rd place. The important thing is that he is not in battle. He wrote that he got two packages at the same time from me. I sent to him salami and he reported that the candy and the baked goods smelled funny. Poor thing, who knows if he had the heart to throw it out. I sent him in the past 4 weeks at least 8 packages.

I hope he will get them! I sent him in the packages fruitcake, candy, baked goods, hazelnuts, peanuts and in all of them a little bottle of drink. Based on his mail, he will get them normally. He wrote the latest letter on October 9th. Poor thing, he'll have a lot of packages. You sent him too. I sent in many names. But let's leave this alone too. How are you? What's going on over there? How are you Marcsa? And you Hermina? So, how is Mr. Gluck [Herman]? Write to me a lot and about everything, ok? I don't even know which of you, Hermine or Mariska, asked me, if I still have my car. I wanted to change it, but what I want will cost $1300 dollar and for mine they would only give me $300 dollar. That is a lot of money. I'll wait until the world is better.

I don't even know what to write right now. It is 7:30pm and I'm already sleepy. I wrote a letter to our little brother yesterday, but tonight I will write him again. The work and everything is the same. I'm getting bored from it. It would be good if the war would end. It is pretty dirty and confusing. One year's worth was enough of this. So, a lot of good luck and everything good. I hope that my lines will find you in the best of health. And please write to me. Hey, is Arthur asking about me sometimes? What does he manufacture now? Take my little brother's greetings that he sends in every letter to you. So, until I'll see you again. Kisses, Dezső
P.S. Based on the radio, I believe the Russians are there in Polyán..there is a war in Hungary.

Side note: In my opinion, Hungary is going to be the Russian's in two weeks.

1944/10/18 David to Irving (Book 12, 143-146)

Oct. 18.44
My dear little brother! Until 120
Currently I don't even know what to write. I wrote to you a letter yesterday and I promised I will write another one this week, so I will keep my word and write! I am, thank God well and I hope that my lines will find you well, too. How are you? Where do you go? I am very interested about where you are. I hope from the dear God that they will not send you again to danger, but unfortunately this can't be helped. Write about yourself whenever you can. I will write home now to the girls. You know, your letter was here in 7 days. You can be close to the center! Right? Little brother, forgive me, if I don't write so often like I used to, but you at least know that we are in a good place, [in English] but you are in a very dangerous place.

[In Hungarian] All of a sudden I don't even know what to write. I see from today's newspaper that Bricker was here in Long Beach to hold a speech. He is smart. You know this is the biggest port here where the soldiers are and there are a lot of people here from all across America. This is a good advertisement. Everybody writes home to someone and that way his name is going places. As you can see, I write it to you, too. But I think there is no hope [for him] because the old man [Roosevelt] can fight them. You are also for the old man, aren't you? Little brother, I will leave this foolishness [because] this will not interest you. You have a much more important job. The weather here is pretty good, the sun shines and there was no rain yet. You know, I have been in California for a year. Time flies fast, the destiny of life goes also, slowly a man gets old and life will go this way. Like you, little brother, you left as a child and thank God, today you are a real man. May the dear God grant that you could come home as soon as possible in the best of health.

My little brother I'm scared that you will scold me because I sent you so many cookies and fruit cake, but forgive me I could not send you anything else, and I want that whenever you need something, you can have it! I hope you will like it, I sent in it a pound package of delicious peanuts in a plain can. I hope it will arrive to you in good [shape]. Little brother write if they open the package I sent to you to check up. You can see if they opened it. Little brother be careful with the little bottle. Don't tell about it to anyone and after using it throw the bottle away. I hope the dear God will help you for everything good. May the dear God grant it, that you could be with us as soon as possible. So, I wrote enough for today and forgive me

...I'm not used to writing so much so that I can't even write in Hungarian correctly. It does not matter, I don't know any of these languages well. So, little brother, may the dear God grant it that my lines will find you in the best of health and in the hope that it will be only a matter of hours until you arrive home. For the past 2 weeks the radio has reported bombings and war inside Hungary. I hope that our father and Sarolta are already on the side of the Russians. I hope that you will see them soon in person. May the dear God grant it! -Dear little brother, promise if you come home, you will come to me. I will make the best for you. But I'm going to ask you to help me with the dishes. Ok? I don't like it, neither do you. So, until I will see you again. Kisses with love, your forever faithful brother. Dezső

1944/10/20 Hermine to Irving (V-Mail, Slide 281)

Oct 20 - 44
Written in Hungarian

My dear little brother Irving,

I think about writing every day, but believe me, something always gets in the way. Miss McNeil who worked at Fenton was here this week and she asked for the address, she will write to you. I told her that you asked about her. Besides, thank God, we are all well, we received a letter with a check for $150, but we will buy a bond for you. I plan to travel to Cleveland and call Elsie to see if I can stay with her while I'm there. I will write to you again in more detail and I hope you are in good health. I'm sorry that Dave's package didn't work out as you write, you certainly couldn't even eat it. Take care of yourself and see you soon. Kisses, Hermina

1944/10/22 (a) Irving to Family, Italy (Book 7, 46-48)

October 22, 1944 Italy

My Dearest Sisters, Hermine and Maria,

It's been quite sometime since I've written you last. As you know there's always something that has to be done first. Yes I want to tell you that I have received some letters from you and haven't answered yet, but you just keep on writing me and I will try to answer them at once. Before I go farther on, I want you to know that I'm OK and don't worry. My prayers were answered. Thanks to God. I always said and will say, if you believe in God, He will help you. Yet I also want to tell you, that I'm still using my old address. I guess it will change soon. If it does not change this week, then I'll write with my new address. This time I can tell you that if I move out from here I will be a cook, and you won't have to worry as before. Those days are over–. I will write about it to Dave also. All this, don't mention [it] to anyone. Even any relatives. When I return to America, I'll tell you all about it. Now my best wishes to Herman and [I] remain with all my love, Irving

ENCLOSED -6- PRAYERS AND ATTACH IT TO YOUR FAVORITE BOOKS.
[See Book 22, 215-220]

P.S. I'm writing this letter with pencil, because it [is] handier. I hope you will be able to read it. Irv

P.S. Again - I want to tell you that I have received another package just now. Home made cookies, fruit cake and a can of pears. Thanks a million. Before that I received one box of home made and one box of bowtie [bòti] cookies. It was all delicious. I will write you more sometime later. When I'll get my new add[ress] I'll ask for more packages - OK?

1944/10/22 (b) Irving to Dave (Book 6, 180) page 1

October 22, 1944 Italy

My dearest brother Dave,

I know that you're waiting to hear from me, so here I'm. First I want to tell you that I'm okay and don't worry. My prayers were answered. Thanks to God! I always said and will say, if you believe in God, He will help you. Yet I want to tell you that I'm still using my old address. I guess it will change soon. If it doesn't change this week, then I'll write my new address. This time I want to tell you, when I move out from here I'll be a cook, and you won't have to worry as before. Those days are over–. I have written about it to the family also. All this don't mention to anyone. I mean relatives, or friends. When I return home I'll tell you all about it. Now my best wishes to you and the family back home

1944/10/22 (b) Irving to Dave (Book 19, 419) page 2

and remain with all my love, Irving

P.S. I'm writing this letter with pencil, because it's handy that way. I hope you will be able to read it. Irv

P.S. Again - I just received a package from Hermine and Maria. Listen Dave when I'll get to my new addr[ess]. Then I'll ask for something from you. So now thanks a million. Write me again soon. Irv

1944/10/24 Irving to Dave, Outside Naples, Italy (V-Mail, Slide 287) - working in PX

October 24, 1944
Italy

My dear brother Dave,
Hello Dave, how are you? I hope that you are well and in good health. I'm OK and still waiting to move out. However yesterday they gave me a job to work at Post exchange, it's like a grocery store. We give the weekly ration to our battalion. So as you see I still don't know if I stay here, I think that I'll move out. But don't worry, I won't be sent up again. Maybe I'll get the job here or they will send me back to the good old U.S.A. With love, Irving

1944/10/24 Irving to Family, Outside Naples, Italy (V-Mail, Slide 285)

October 24, 1944
Italy

My dearest sisters, Hermine and Marie,
How are you getting along? Hope that you are all well and in good health. I'm OK and still waiting to move out. However yesterday they gave me a job to work at the post exchange, it's like a grocery store. We give the weekly ration to our battalion. As you see, I still don't know if I stay here. I think I'll move out. But don't worry, I won't be sent up again. Maybe I'll get a job here or they will send me back to the good old U.S.A. With love, Irving

1944/10/27 Louis Schwartz to Hermine (Book 17, 84)

Iceland 10-27 (1944)

Dear Maria,
It's Friday morning - just came down to the Depot a little early to start to work and it's not much to do yet, so I'm answering your letter. Received your letter a few days ago and was glad to hear that you're well. Heard in the last night's news that Szatmar - you know the town where Sarolta lives is taken by the Russians and are even getting closer to our folks. I'm looking forward to be able to get in touch with them. You girls will probably do the same. I don't think I'd tell them that I'm in the army. The winter is so far not too rough as yet, we had more rain than snow, but it's in the air and we'll probably get it before long. How is it over there? How're you? I'm fine. Hope that same about you. What do you hear from Irving? Love, Lou

1944/11/3 Hermine to Irving (V-Mail, Slide 291)

Nov 3 - 44
Written in Hungarian

My dear little brother Irving!
As you can see, I am trying to write like this, if only with a pencil. I'm at work and since I didn't write last night, I'm going to write now. Believe me, I think about you a lot and I hope you are well. The important thing is that our dear father may have been released from the great struggle. It may also happen that you can go visit them soon. If God helps, it can happen, and soon. We trust in God and hope that everything will turn out well. Until then, good health and good luck with lots of love, kisses Hermina

1944/11/3 Hermine and Marie to Irving (Book 11, 36-43)

Columbus Nov 3 - 44
[from Hermine – In English]
My Dear Irving!
I told you so many times in my letters that I am going to write you a long letter. Tonight is Friday night and [I] thought about you - Hope you are well and please tell us some more about yourself.
I just mean what you can tell us - because everything interests me. As you know the news is good in our old home town and maybe you will have a chance to visit there, maybe to spend your furlough with our dear father and family. With God's help it can happen, but the main thing is if they are well, we try to help them.

Page 380

Ungvár and Csop [are] taken by the Russians and maybe Bodrogmező, too. I received a letter from Lou Schwartz and he was very glad to have a New Year card from you. There would be many things we could talk about together - but it is so hard to write [them] down. Last week I was visiting in Cleveland - from Sunday till Wednesday and it was swell, and I enjoyed it very much. Elsie is a wonderful person and a real relative. Mr. Rosewater came over - Sunday and Tuesday and took me out. He is nice, but too smart. I think it is because really he isn't just a young boy - maybe 35 - or 40. Elsie likes him - He wants to come over to Columbus again and we will see.... But I mentioned once about the soldier who was visiting here and came back 3 times. He looks like you, but taller and older. And Helen called his mother because she wanted to meet me. Tuesday his father came after me and took me over to his house. Boy.. Irving you should be there. The mother is like a mother!... She asked me why didn't I want her son and maybe I didn't act right. I told her because he is younger and what is the use to bother him. But the truth is that he is only 24 years old. He is a graduated dentist and a Lt in the army. He still goes to school - or is studying. I am sorry but I didn't ask, and never thought he will come back. His mother is a very fine woman and lives in a nice home - she wouldn't let me home to sleep - but I had to because I didn't want to stay. She gave me a very pretty apron for a present. Listen Irving dear - maybe you think I am funny to tell you all that - but you are my dear little brother and just to tell you there are people who are all out for you... When she saw my picture at Helen's house she liked it so much that since then always just talked about me, and wanted to know me better. They are asking about you too, and Rosewater asks about you in every letter. The soldier's name is Goldblatt. You know, Irving, he is a very nice boy, too. He wasn't home, he is somewhere with other boys, they are studying and will come home in about 6 weeks and then he will come to Columbus, too. It would be more fun if you are with us, and we are together. But I will try to tell the stories if you want to know it. I just can't forget the women because, maybe she is the one who is working so hard, and maybe she shouldn't do that....Helen or Mrs. Goldstein in Cleveland is very nice and they have a little girl about 5 weeks old. I think there is everything in this letter. I hope you will enjoy it. Please write to me, and take care of yourself. Good luck and good wishes with all my Love, Your sister - Hermina

[from Marie]
Written in Hungarian
My beloved Irving!
We just got your long letter, which we were very happy about. And I'm so glad to hear that, thank God you are healthy. As I was reading your letter, I was imagining you in front of me and if I would be able to see you, dear little brother. And every word of yours is like I would say it. But we are hoping and asking the dear God that the terrible chaos will end soon, which we are all waiting for so badly. Yes, dear little brother as you mentioned, about the money how much you sent home. I will note here how much there is here, only I'm sorry that currently I can't calculate it exactly, since we opened a safety box in the bank and it is there. And I have it written down here at home, but I forgot to memorize it. What you get from the Army, that $50 and I can't remember exactly how much did they send. But next time we will look it over. And now I will attach the following...

First of all, I will note one by one. I hope you will understand! $50-$100 $100 $50 $50 $25 $50 $25 $50 $50 $50 $25 $25 $50 $100 $50 $25 $100 $100....
the amount equals 1150.00 in bonds. And today we got the $100 check, and the remaining $15 from the past which makes $115.00. I will buy bonds tomorrow for you and I will put the left over to the bank. And now I will go back to your money at the bank. We did not deposit it to the bank since then and the amount is 1183.59. which is in the bank. But you have already more than a year old interest for this, which you are entitled to. We will add it to your left over money, so you will get the interest. I hope that you understood me, little brother. And as far as I know, as many times you mentioned that you sent money, I was watching that and I wrote about it to you. And as soon as we got the money I'm in a hurry to buy it for you. Otherwise we are well. And I am thinking about you a lot. I wish we could be together already. I would be so much happier. And to write the truth, I don't go anywhere my dear little brother. I am very busy with my job.

...and then I come home and I listen to the news and that is it. Sometimes I go to the movies. But somehow these days I don't go that often, not even there. As you mentioned that you would send something to the relatives. I'm thinking that with the dear God's help you will come home shortly and then you will bring something small in person. You will make them happy. But we all know that you are busy and they are at home and they don't have time to write. Then it could be imagined how it is for you there. The weather here is pretty bad. It is snowing and it rained at night. We got a letter from Dave last week and he was well. You know my little Irving somehow it seems that I'm waiting for you just like when you were in Camp Wolters.

And I hope that there is no need to wait for long. Only I'm asking you to take care of yourself wherever you go and don't worry. I'll be in a hurry to write to you and I'm glad to hear about you.

And how it is, it's God's order. And you got to meet that boy there. And I gave more information than we know here. But I wrote so much foolishness here and I hope that you can read it. I wrote about your picture already and I liked it very much and thank you, my dear little brother. And everybody likes it. It is so real. I think that you put on weight. And now I will hope to hear the best about you. And I wish you good luck and the best of health. I will stay in the hope of seeing you again. Kiss you forever your faithful sibling who will never forget. Maria

Take care of yourself and write about what you need, a warm sweater or white sheets. Tomorrow we will send the cookies and we'll do it gladly. Don't be sad and take care of yourself.

1944/11/4 Irving to Hermine and Marie (Book 6, 181-187)

November 4, 1944
Italy

My dear sisters Hermine and Marie,
As the saying is, to receive mail you must write first. So here I'm. Many times I begin to write you, but never able to finish it. There was always [something] that kept me back from writing. But today I said [to] myself, I want and must write home. I have never done it before, but this time I really wanted to tell you something good, but as yet didn't come up, and that's why I have delayed the writing. First I want to tell you that I moved again to another company and you'll find the address on the envelope. However I'm still working in [the] store (P.X.) as I wrote you about it. I don't know how long I'll stay here, but don't worry I trust in God, and I know He'll help me as before. My prayers were answered as I told you in one of my letters. This week I haven't received my mail from you, however I know that you're busy and when you get back from work you're tired and don't feel like writing. Sometimes you have to be in [the] mood to write. I know it myself. Anyway I want to tell you don't worry and take care of yourselves. And I'm doing my best. I'm writing this letter in the store. We were busy yesterday, but today isn't much work. Mostly two or three days work in a week. So, as you see it's not bad, while it lasts. I mean while I'm here. Every night someone has to stay here till nine o'clock. It happen[ed] to be that we were only two of us, and I had to stay here every other night, but today we got one more man to help us. I'm not complaining, as you know anything in the rear it's okay. Do you remember I wrote you about six months ago and said that this war will end in October. But it didn't, so now it's just like before, let's hope and pray to God that it will end soon. That's all I can say. It was enough for me, when I was up there for eight months. Well I guess one day we'll wake up and they'll tell us that the war is over, it will come so sudden that we won't believe it. So let's hope the day will come soon and we all [will] be able to return home.

By the way I want to tell you that don't send me candy or chocolate or anything like that, because as you know I can get as much as I need over here. After all the packages will catch up with me, I'll be able to open up a store. Don't you think so girls? I bet you have sent me so much of everything that I won't know what to do with it. So now I'll wait until I receive all the packages and then ask for more if I need anything. Not long ago you were asking me how many packages I have received. I don't remember, whenever I received one I wrote about it. I just couldn't give you the exact number, but when I'll get time off, I will go over all the letters I received from you and if I recall any of the packages I'll write you about it. Also forgive me for not answering of all your letters, I'll as soon as I get a chance. And I will write you whenever I can, even though there isn't much to write about. It's just the everyday's life. The other day I was in Napolys, I went through places where I'm sure you were, when we were together. Remember? It changed some. Today I could tell you more about it, than that time. However we weren't interesting [sic] in anything over here. As you recall it. All that seems to me like a dream, believe it or not. I'll tell you something I did the day when I was in Napolys. I went into places to find out if we have any communications with the liberated countries, such as Czechoslovakia, as you know, they are liberated by the Russian army. At present I didn't get any answer, but they will notify me if they have. So I do hope that I'll get a good answer and I'll be able to find out how the family is back home. I do hope that they are okay. You know it's not far from here it's just a couple hours by plane, and look how difficult it is... I'll do everything I can for them and as soon as I can.... By the way, I also want to tell you that I met a very dear friend of mine, we met first in Africa and here again. I hope to invite him to our house, when we return to America. He is married and lives in New York. I could tell you a lot about him, but wait till we return home.

Nothing else to say about myself, just that I'm okay and will try to write you more often. Please you do the same, and write me about everything.

I want to tell you something Hermine, and don't get me wrong. You have wrote me about that boy friend, well I'll tell you the truth, before you have wrote me about it, that was way back, when I was in Anzio. I played a card, such as fortune-telling, well as you know I don't believe in anything like that, but somethings came true. It came like this, that someone in the family was going to meet someone interesting so far my fortune card is doing very well, but tell me are the wedding bells going to ring?! If so I'm afraid I will have to respect fortune-telling cards in the near future?

I have enjoyed writing this bit of chatter hope that I will hear from you all very soon. I'm feeling well considering my lonesomeness for you all, With love, your brother, Irving

Please give my regards to Dave and Herman.
Also to our friends,
Irv

PVT IRVING GLUCK 35633941
547 - REPL Co.
A.P.O. 781-R
% P.M. N.Y. N.Y.

1944/11/5 Irving to Dave (Book 3, 99-101)

Nov 5, 1944
Italy

My Dear Brother Dave,
The days have passed and I have failed to write you. However I thought that I'll be moving out from here and I wanted to write you with my new address. But as you see I just moved over to a different company. At present I'm still working in the store (PX). It's nothing like home, but as you know anything in the rear it's okay. As you know I have been up for eight months and that's plenty for me. Now I hope and pray to God that it will come to an end soon. Do you remember Dave, that about six months ago I wrote you that it will end in Oct? Yet it's Nov. and it's still on. However I still keep on hoping and praying. Maybe one morning will wake up and they'll say that the war is over, and it will come so sudden that we won't believe it, until it's proved.

The other day I went to Napoly and that day the news sounded very good for the Russian front so I went into a place to get some information if they have any communication with liberated countries, such as Czechoslovakia. But at present they don't know it. However they promised me if they find out anything they will inform me. As you know the family is liberated by the red army. And when I get the answer, I'll do everything I can. It's just a couple hours by plane, and how difficult is to get there! Many times I wished that we could be there first, but I guess it's okay as it is. By the way before I forget it, I want to tell you about that old man that you mentioned in one of your letters. Yes I wrote him to... I guess in one way he is a good man not like the other as you know. I hope he gets it.

Yet I'm writing this letter in the store (PX). The time is seven forty five. Every other night I stay here till nine o'clock. By the way I want to tell you not to send me any candy or chocolate, because I have as much as I need. When I'll get to my permanent place then I'll see what I'll need and I'll ask for it. If and when I get all the packages from you and home I'll be able to open another store I guess. What do you think Dave? I know you don't believe it, that's why you are so kind and sending me whenever you think of it.

Not long ago I met a very good friend of mine, first I met him in Africa and here again. Believe me Dave I could write about him a whole book, but wait till we return and tell you all about it.
Have written home also and now I'll close this time and will write you more often. With love, your brother
Irving

Please you write me soon again

1944/11/11 Western Union Telegram David to Hermine - will call (Book 7, 266)

1944 Nov 11 8PM
Long Beach Calif

Hermine Gluck
50 Linwood Ave (Columbus Ohio)

Will Call Evergreen 6223 Sunday 11AM Your Time

Dave

1944/11/12 Helen Perl Goldstein to Hermine (Book 17, 323-325)

Dear Herminka!
I was glad to hear that you had a good time in Cleveland and that you had a nice trip.
We are, thank God all well. The baby is already starting to smile when she is happy. I'm interested, if you are corresponding with Rosewater? But most importantly I'm interested about how the other case is shaping out. Write if you have time. I am watching excitingly the European happenings. Maybe we can hear something about our loved ones. My Hermine, I was so happy about your unexpected package. I can hardly tell you. But why did you give such a big job to yourself? The cookies are excellent. Thank you very, very much! Yesterday Mrs. Goldblatt was my guest and I offered the cookies to her too. I told her that I got them from you. She liked it very much. I did not have a chance to ask her because I had more guests. So, I'm asking you to write about everything. I hope my mediation will be successful, because I would be very happy about it from the bottom of my heart since they are both very good boys. So the rest is up to you and God. I don't know any particular news that you would be interested in, so I close my lines. I kiss you with much love. Helen
P.S. I'm sending my best to your siblings.

1944/11/13 Undated (a) David to Hermine (Book 15, 148-149) pages 1-2
[Dated by voting in Presidential election]

Monday 13.

Dear Herminka!
Forgive me that I did not write for so long. The reason is that I would love to write a very long letter and it gets postponed [in] this way. I get up at 5 on the morning and when I get home I cook and I put the house in order. There is time about 6-8 o'clock and when I sit down to write I fall asleep. Tonight I will not let this happen and I will write. Hermine, I got 3 letters from you [stating] that you did not get a response to Mariska's letter, but now I will make it up to you. It is possible that I won't write again for at least two weeks. Currently I work 7 days a week - So Hermine! I can only note to your letter that you have two male acquaintances, one of them is young, the other one is old. Which one do you like? So, do not forget! If you did not get married until now, do not look for foolishness. You are not in Polyán! His mother likes you. Ok! But you will not live with his mother, you will live with him - So, the money is not everything. If the boy loves you, do not count on that. Helen Perl must have told him already how old you are! So, think it through, you better not jump into it too fast. If you waited until today, you can wait until the war ends. If the boy was sent to the war and you are his wife, what's going to happen, if he will come home with one leg or eye? Will you still love him then? So, you are smart enough! You can deal with it the way you like it. The way it is better for you - your destiny is not mine and you do it the way you see it's good for you. Considering that I would not like it if somebody would butt into my business. Yes, I got an air mail from you today. and noted that the boy knows Mendlovitz, which boy? And where is Mendlovitz? And where is your boyfriend? I did not write to him, I was getting ready to [send] him...

1944/11/13 Undated (b) David to Hermine (Book 15, 135-137) pages 3-5

Page 384

...a package, but it got delayed. Currently, it is possible I will send a package to Italy. Hermine, find out if the Red Cross could do something about our case because based on my calculation, the Russians are already in Polány for a long time because Munkacs, Miskolc they are all invaded already - And it is possible that you could write through Russia and it is possible that the Russian Consul could do something in our case - So I don't even know what to write. The weather is very delightful, the rain is pouring and it is cold. The weather is pretty much like in Polány in the fall. The fire was where I worked at first, there is a storage at least 500 meters from there - From the current location it is about a km. But I did not hear the explosion because in the factory it is so very noisy that nothing can be heard at all. [Probably the Berth 233 Explosion, October 21, 1944] So, I don't know any other news here. I did not get the package today yet. It is going to be here by tomorrow!

I went to vote. I voted to Roosevelt. Who did the Mr. vote for? Listen to me! If God will help me I will call you next Sunday on the phone here at 5 and by you at 8 at night. If I will not work on Sunday then I will call you before, but we will surely work, so it is possible that it will be later. I will do the connection, then it will be possible that within 15 min or could be 1 hour [to connect] and I will talk for about 5 to 10 minutes. Write down on paper what you want to ask about. OK? Oh yes! I got a letter from Ignác about two weeks ago. He wrote that he wrote to you too about it, but asked not to tell anyone. Noting about him, he noted he worked in a central ration house where they give meals to the soldiers and he indicated that he will not write his new address until he goes to a permanent place. He told me not to be scared because he will not go to the battlefield because they scheduled him to be a cook. This way, he will only work in the kitchen. And he said, if he will not go there, they will send him home! I'm thinking he is on his way home since he did not write for awhile. But don't tell anything to anyone about this! So you better write to me and forgive me, even if I don't write. I don't have patience anymore to write. I will write to little brother too tonight. If he will come home that way the letter will come back at least. He asked me not to send packages to him until he asks for it! So, there is no news, only that there is rain night and day. I wish you everything good and kiss you until I will see you again. Kisses, Dezső

1944/11/13 Undated David to Marie (Book 15, 132-134)

[Dated by similarity to previous letter]

Dear Mariska!
Forgive me that I'm just responding now to you and you wrote 2 letters to me already. I will note before I forget! Be at home on Sunday night between 9 and 10, I will call you on the phone - and to Herman say hello. Yes, I owe him money, but I have no time to go to the post office and I will get a bank check one of these days. So, I'll send it by check.
So Mariska, I can only write to you about your job! I don't like it, but the important thing is that you do. You know, it is possible that our little brother will come home soon. He can not go to Polány already because the Russians are there. The only thing you have to be careful with is that nobody should start with you. There are a lot of vagabonds there, so be very careful, take care of yourself.
There is no news here. It's raining, that's all. Mariska! Please send me the cloth shoes that I left there. You know which ones? The one that you can pull into the other one, if it is there still - Yes, thank you for it! You know it has to come up because there is a lot of rain here. Herman asked me in the last letter, about how much is a heater. The price is 1.95 with tax he could say that is 2 dollar. I paid that much for it. But if Herman wants to give it cheaper then that is his business. Today he can not buy it anywhere because it is not available. But, if he will sell it, the money is yours not mine. So, do whatever you want with it. OK? At our shipyard there was a show. Rudy Wally was here and his band/team. But the first show got cancelled because the rain arrived.

What do you say about the voting? I voted too. What is Bricker [Governor of Ohio 1939-1945] doing now, poor man. Mariska, on the radio there, on Sunday at 11 there is a pretty good program/show W.C.O.L. or W.B.N.S. Its name does not come to my mind. Oh yes! "External Light" a radio program. It is pretty good. You will like it. Write some news, if there is anything there - There is no news here. If this movie will be there go to watch it. It is called the "Lonely Heart" It is very good! Forgive me because I wrote more to Hermine than to you, but I am pretty sleepy. But I want to take this letter to the post office, so you will get it on Wednesday, but it is possible that you will get it tomorrow because I will send it special delivery - So I wish you good luck and everything good with love. Dezső
P.S. Greetings to Mr. Herman and he should write too! Is he working? How much does he make?

Nov 13. 44

My dear little brother!

Do you wonder why you did not get a letter for so long? I don't need to explain in details, you know it as well what it is like when one is being busy. How come that I did not get any news for 3 weeks from you, that is, a letter? I hope you are well and I hope that my letter will find you in good health! Or maybe my little brother, you are on your way to come home! As I can see, if the dear God will help and you will come home, you will know how to cook also - Isn't that beautiful!? One day I, and the next day you, will cook. I wish you would be here. You would like it too, wouldn't you ? But surely me myself too. Currently, it is raining here pretty hard - Now the weather is very rainy here, as hated as it was in Polyán in the fall. You know based on my calculation, the Russians already are in Polyán because they were already in Csop 2 weeks ago.

Forgive me little brother that I write so badly, but I am in a hurry because I wrote to home too and I want to send them. On the weekend I will write more to you. I hope until then I will hear good news about you. I wrote home today that I will call them on the phone. You know, it's been a year that I'm in California. Time flies, doesn't it? So I wish you good luck and everything good with love, I kiss you until I will see you again. Kiss you with love, your brother, Dezső

[In English]

Columbus Nov 14-44

My dear brother Irving:

We received a long letter today from you and boy! was I happy! Believe me it was swell to know you are well, [and] in good health. You know how much we are looking for the mail, and we are happy if we find one in the mail box! But we know that too - in the army is different and many times you just can't do it, and believe me, we can understand it. You are right about us too, sometimes I want to write and then somebody will come in, and gets so late that I just can['t] do it...But I love to write you Irving - my letters aren't very good, but I don't have much passion to write and I have a lot to write to keep it up with everybody. You know I am the only one who does that. To talk about something else - is your letter! The fortune card and the [wedding] bells are funny! And I will let you know about everything. They, because I have 2 now, didn't asked me yet, and if they would - it would be the same, because we have to know somebody very good to decide about that. The dentist wants to come about 3 weeks from now, and he is a fine boy but young. The other is a nice boy but 40 years old! He writes to me but I just keep it up, it can't hurt. Everybody is asking about you and Flora too. We all are well, and will close now till I write again. Good luck and best wishes. With all my love, Hermina

November 14, 1944

Italy

Hello Hermine and Marie,

Today is my birthday I want to thank you for your kind wishes and hope that next year at this time, we will celebrate together in the best health. Also received three packages one was a birthday present. Thanks a million to you all. It's very difficult to bring up the past year, so I just want to say for all that, thank God for helping me through and I hope that this coming year will be a happy one, and with God's help we will meet again in America in the best of health soon. I also want to tell you, that some of the boys I met, lately, also enjoyed the cookies, they said "I would like to meet a girl [who] can bake like that." Well thanks again I really enjoyed them.

However, good as the home made cookies were, please do not take the trouble to bake them again, unless you have loads of time to spare. The cookies you bought, which were enclosed in the wooden box were excellent, not quite so good as the ones you baked yourself but good, nevertheless, and very much appreciat[ed]. So the next time you want to send me cookies the bought ones will more than do. Honestly, the ones you bake yourself are better, and I only mean to save you the trouble of baking, when it is possible to buy cookies nearly as good as the ones you baked.

This time forgive me, because of writing with pencil, but it's much faster this way and this paper isn't very good to write on it with ink. The other day I got me a pen and a watch, boy, it looks very good. As you know, some time we have this articles in the store. This time I was lucky enough and got me all that. It's a Schaeffer pen, and it's nice looking, next time I'll write with it. First I want to get some good stationary. It's a very beautiful watch, water proof and shock proof, it cost me only $21 dollars. The pen cost $4.15. At home it costs much more. I'll close this time and I'll try to write to you soon again. I hope to receive some more mail from you, I guess you must be busy, but don't forget to write me whenever you can. My best wishes to Dave and Herman, relatives and friends, With love, Irving

November 16, 1944

My dear sis,

Here I'm again, I was not able to send this letter out on the 14th however they say, it's better later than never. Today is the 16th. I'm okay and hope that you are all well and in good health. I hope to hear from you soon, Love, Irving

1944/11/14 Marie to Irving (Book 9, 270-271)

11-14-44

Written in Hungarian

My dear beloved little brother, Irving!

We just got a long letter today from you that I was very happy about. And the thought makes me very happy that thank God you are healthy and I hope that my lines will find you this way continuously. Otherwise, we are well too and we are all hoping for the best. And I think we can hear about our dear father since the Russians are there since then. And my dear little brother as you wrote about the package, I hope since then you got from it and you like it. You just ask for whatever you need. I think about you a lot and I could hardly wait for your letter. I ask the dear God to stay with you after this too and help you in every step of your way. Take care of yourself wherever you go. God bless you!

There is no news here, the weather is warm already. But I think it's warm there and I'm happy to hear that you are at your current place and I hope you can stay there in the worst case scenario until it gets better, and I hope that it will be shortly. Yes, that you mentioned about your friend, little brother. I already know about him, I remember you wrote about him. As you can see, the destiny is like that, when you don't even know it. And I can imagine what it means to the both of you. I hope that the dear God will help you both and shortly you can come home together to us in the best of health. We are pretty busy, like usual. And I will be in a hurry to write to you again. [In English] Good luck and God bless you! [Continuing in Hungarian] I wish you lots of good luck and the best of health. I kiss you countless times, your forever faithful sibling who will never forget. In the hope to see you again, write again. Maria

1944/11/17 Louis Schwartz to Hermine and Marie (Book 18, 127-129)

Iceland 11-17-44

Dear Hermina and Maria,

First I want to thank you for your swell package you sent me which I enjoyed a lot. It was really unexpected but it was fine. I also received your letter which was a little late, mail is quite irregular lately due to the weather conditions. That'll explain why I didn't write sooner. Yes, you're right Ungvár is taken and I'm sure Polyán is taken, right now they're close to Budapest. I've an uncle who lives in the same block with the "Keleti Pályaudvar" [the main railway terminal in Budapest] which is a very important place. They must be living through a hard time.

I'm trying to make up allotments for my folks and I'm promised they'll get it too. They'll put it in the bank and deliver it when they can. Did you write Irving about it? Or did he write you? It's too bad I can't contact them through the "Red Cross" while I'm in the army but I wrote my Aunt to do it. If you write please ask them about my people - maybe you'll hear from them sooner. I know it'll take a few months till we'll be able to hear from them. As far as myself. I'm fine hope the same about you. I'm enclosing a couple pairs of moccasins. I don't remember seeing it in the States but it's very popular here. The ladies wear it on the coat buttons. I'm also sending it to my cousins. Hope you'll like it. This was a very quick letter. My time is limited now and I don't want delay answering it so please excuse me for the bad handwriting. Hope you'll be able to read it. Best of luck, Love, Lou

Write again soon!!

1944/11/18 Irving to Florence Maizlish (Book 6, 194-197) - draft

November 18 – Italy

Dear Florence,

I feel somewhat ashamed for not having answered your most welcome letters sooner than I have because it contained so much interesting news. I complement you for keeping me well informed of the things I am most interested in. I was indeed sorry to hear of your father's illness but trust he is his own self again. My New Year started very satisfactory being taken from the front lines one week previous but now I am slowed down in a Repple [replacement] Depot. Being here isn't bad at least I know that I am safe from enemy attack yet I am not satisfied until that one big day arrives when I can stand on my own two feet on Ohio soil and reminisce of (Do I remember?) the fun we had and the days to come when we can go swimming and bike riding again. However I never once forgot about the moral on the homefront yet the Krauts kept me so busy supplying me with punctuation in [the] form of lead that I hardly believe you would care to read such trash. So pleased to learn you are attending Ohio State and that you enjoy your course. Sometimes I think I will take some sort of a course when I return. Although I believe I will be able to converse with you in German. Study hard though and here hoping for a happy Thanksgiving With love
I.

1944/11/19 David to Herman, Hermine, Marie (Book 5, 187-191)

Dear Herman!

I'm writing just a few lines for you too. You ask me why I'm not writing to you. I'm writing to you in every letter I send. I always give my best wishes to you, but you never acknowledge it. Why don't you have the time or are you too busy working hard? You know I'm working 68 hours per week. Besides that I am cooking and preparing my meals and cleaning my home too. You go home and everything is ready. I don't have the time to write. I think it is up to you to write to me. I'm sending the money that I owe you all. I'm thanking you for waiting for a long time for it. With kisses, Dezső

Sunday 19 – 44
Dear Maria!

It was only a couple of hours ago that I spoke with you on the telephone. I'm sorry we didn't speak with you all in more detail, I forgot that before 10 o'clock you're not happy if I call you. I did not know that here it was 8 o'clock. When the woman answered she asked who is calling? When did I place that call? I told her yesterday therefore she didn't answer therefore it was very low. I heard you did very well. Therefore forgive me that I called you at the wrong time. I'm fine. No news here. Everything is the same. I will call you again when our brother comes home. But I won't call from here. It will be when I can talk without interruption. Here I'm mailing one check in Herman's name. I will send something that will be easier to cash in on your name. I'm sending $20 that I owe to Hermine. Maybe $4.50 for one bottle of drink and you also $4.50 and for new paper $3 and to mail it also about one dollar altogether $13 and also for today the price of the telephone. I sent for that $7 if it costs more please let me know. I'll send you whatever I owe you. Here there is nothing new. The weather is beautiful. The sun is shining at 11 o'clock, the same time as when I called you on the phone. I made chicken goulash and it came out very good! I'm sorry I can't do better, but I think I did very well. The cookies are very good. At this time don't send me any. With my love, many kisses, Dezső

Dear Hermine,

Forgive me that I couldn't speak to you properly. You know already why I didn't because I wrote you already in my letter to Marie. Please I'm asking you to write. If I don't write don't be angry please. I will try to write regularly to at least one of you whenever possible. Hermine you were telling me about the boys. Please, I ask you to write a long letter all about them. Which one do you like? Do you have any idea what you want? Please write more how you feel about it. Is it serious? I do not remember what you told me before. You have said that you are going for dinner at Arthur's? On the telephone I mentioned a good friend of mine who is here for the duration, a Yugoslav sailor, that will go home in a few weeks to his country and I asked him to do something for our father. Therefore when he leaves I will write you about it. I wrote enough. With all my love, Dezső

1944/11/19 David to Irving (Book 2, 67-70)

November 19, 1944
My dear little brother!
I got your letter that I was waiting for. I'm glad to hear, thank God you are well, and that after that everything will go well. Little brother, you mentioned in your previous letter that you met a man in Africa and now in Napoly and you could write a whole book about this. Hey, who is he? He must be an official man. I got a V letter from you this week, that you wrote on October 11th. They sent the entire letter with a note that the ink was running all over and it's not good for V mail. But the important thing is that you are OK. My little brother write more often. Good? I understand what it's like working in a big business with a lot of help and you are everything, and the boss too, for 55 per month pay. But let's leave it alone, you know this without me telling you! You wrote that you took action on our father's behalf and that the Russians took over there. Based on newspapers they occupied Csap, Ungvár, Munkacs and around Pest. But it doesn't say anything about our town. But you must know about this better, little brother. One of my acquaintances a Yugoslavian sailor will go home next month and he promised that he will help with our father.

You, my little brother, if the situation gets better, I believe you will get vacation days and you will be able to see our father and the relatives. Why didn't you talk to the Rabbi about this and ask his opinion about this case. But, let's leave this alone too. You know better what to do in that case. -I called them on the phone today. (Herman, Maria, Hermina). They are well and they will write to you. I sent a telegram to them yesterday, that I will call them. They told me they are invited to Arthur today, I don't know, if for lunch or for the afternoon. Hey, did Hermine write to you that she has two male acquaintances in Cleveland? One of them is kind of like Herman. He has his own business (or store). The other one is a dentist and she was at their home in Cleveland. His mother likes her pretty much, but I'm sure she wrote to you about this. There is no news here. The weather is nice today all day.

So, my little brother please take care of yourself, God forbid, something would happen. Little brother, if you need anything just write it to me and I will send it to you. Ok?! Today is Sunday afternoon and the lunch is done. I prepared/made it. There is Goulash and roast. I would like to give you some, too. But I hope that soon it will become true. Today I wrote home that if you will go home then call me. Ok?! So, my little brother, I wish you everything good and happiness until I see you again. I kiss you with love forever. Your brother who will never forget. Kiss, Dezső

PS: Remember? Our father used to write to Bacsi [Uncle Jónász], forever your faithful brother, who will never forget - So, good luck, happiness and come home quickly, my little brother. The old man is the winner, no wonder! God is good, isn't he? You know, the Nazi has a big mouth and his people are almost nothing. Kisses, Dezső

1944/11/20 Hermine to Irving (V-Mail, Slide 298)

[In English]
November 20, 1944
My dear brother Irving!
We received a long letter from you it was written on Nov[ember] 4th. It made all of us very happy to know that you are well and in good health. I enjoyed your letter very much and really I had to laugh about your saying about the bells. Believe me I don't know much, but it is nice to have a few friends-and maybe later we can tell more about the whole thing. I am glad you have a play card because it is fun. Dave called us yesterday from California. He is well and we were at Arthur's house yesterday and they celebrated a birthday party. Her [sic] sister's birthday. We were there for dinner. Take care of yourself. Good luck and all my love, Hermina

1944/11/27 Irving to David (Book 6, 199)

Italy

Dear Brother Dave,

I know it's a surprise to you to hear from me, because I have been listening so long. However cheer up! Here I'm enclosing a couple pictures of myself I hope you'll like it. They aren't very good. One, big one and 2 small ones. I have sent home also, and negatives also, they will be able to make some more prints and on better paper. Not much news from here. I'll write you again soon. Remain with love, Irving

What do you say to my greetings? Please write me soon.

1944/11/28 Hermine to Irving (Book 11, 47-49)

[In English]
Columbus Nov 28-44
My dear brother Irving:

I told you so many times about my long letter I want to write, and tonight I am really trying to do it. It isn't as good and nice like yours, but you can understand it. Believe me I think and talk about you very much, all our relatives and friends are asking about you. If we get a good letter from you, then everybody is happy.

It was about 10 days ago that we received mail from you, but maybe we will have some mail again. David is well, and called us long distance from California. Aunt Jennie's son [Emmanuel] the oldest one was here in Columbus Nov 16-17th, he came over and took us out for dinner - Maria and I and he is very nice and was talking about you. He said Hello especially for you, and he was in [the] army for 3 years and just got discharged a couple weeks ago. Bertha wrote a post card and told me she mailed a package and Flora mailed one to you too. What are you working and I am glad you like your job.

I received a letter from Louis in Iceland and he is well and [would] like to be with you, and he thinks you will have a chance to visit our father and the relatives. Our brother Lou and his family - I have them always in my mind. Hoping they are well, but if you can have a furlough then you can tell them everything. I was at the Red Cross a week ago and mailed a message to Louis' wife Ethel. You know Irving, Louis in Iceland tried to tell me that our father should get money from the government because you are in the army. He did already talk to somebody and told me something that they will put the money in the bank and they will mail it to his parents as soon as possible. He can't write from the army and he thought if you would go there because it can be possible now, then you would find out about his parents, too. Tell me Irving dear? Would you like to go there if you can? Tell us something about yourself and write us more often. I mean when you can. The people here in Columbus are very busy buying the presents [and] it is hard to do anything because it is too crowded everywhere in stores.

We would have a lot to talk personally, but it is difficult to write it down. I am working at the same place and like it very much. The weather is getting cold, but we didn't have snow yet. We have our coal and they fixed the furnace, too. Herman is working, but I have to talk to him because he never writes to you. That would be something if he is there, nobody would know a thing about him, he has all the letters and so it is too much to write. Many times we thought he shouldn't see them and then he would write.

I will try to be regular with the writing and hope to hear about you. Take care of yourself and good luck to you where ever you are. My best wishes and love, your sister, Hermina

1944/11/28 Zolar (Fortune Teller) to Hermine (Book 16, 176-177)

ZOLAR
33 West 60th Street - New York, NY
Telephone Columbus 5-1094
November 28th, 1944
Hermina Gluck
50 Linwood Avenue
Columbus, 5, Ohio

Dear Friend:

Under separate cover you will receive your Giant Horoscope for the coming year. May I take this opportunity to thank you for the confidence you have placed in me. In answer to your first question, there is nothing indicated in your chart at this time that would lead me to believe that you will hear [from] your family in the near future. I am afraid that it will be quite sometime before you get any news from them. In answer to you second question, I would advise you to concentrate your interests on the older of the two gentleman you ask about. He seems to be very fond of you. There is nothing of a serious nature shown regarding the other gentleman. There is a marriage indicated for you but it does not seem to take place during the coming year. Thanking you for your valued patronage, I remain, Sincerely your friend, ZOLAR

1944/11/29 Dave to Irving (Book 4, 16-17)

Tuesday, November 29, [1944?]

It's been two weeks since I heard from you. What is the reason? Why didn't you write? Why don't you write? I'm very worried. I ask you to please write how are you are. Thank goodness, I'm fine, which I hope to hear the same from you. You mention that our father's area was taken over with the country. As I know, it is the Hungarians that just took over. Going towards Budapest, around the Latorca, near Homonna and Nagy Mihely and Sataralya and around Ujhely. In my view the area around Helmec was taken over. This is enough for today.

Please write. I received from home some mail yesterday. They're well. I hope you also received the package I mailed to you. Please let me hear from you if you receive it. What are you doing? Are you still in business [the PX]? I hope our God will help you with all the best. I hope you will not have to go through whatever you already went through. I hope everything will work out for the best and very soon you'll be able to come home. My dear brother, I'm wishing you all the best with all my love and kisses, your loving brother, who never forgets about you. Dezső

P.S. My dear brother, please try to write as soon as possible, even just a short letter, just a few lines. Please excuse me, I'm getting very tired and sleepy, but I want to be sure you will hear from me even a few lines, kisses Dezső

1944/11/29 David to Hermine (Book 18, 86-91)

Tuesday

My Dearest!
Hermine and Marie
I received your letter and I'm trying to write a few lines right away. From your letter I understood the situation there. Also you Hermine, understand that you are smart. You should do whatever is good for you. And you Mariska you should look out that Hermine does not make any mistake. As I am reading the newspaper, they occupied Battjánt and are going up to the rural areas of Pest and from Ungvàr to the Latorca toward Homonna and Terebest. In my view they are close to Polyán and as of now they are still Hungarian. The new report they are 15 miles from Sátoraljaújhely. Therefore in my view and the current situation, Leles and Polyán, Helmec, Boly, Perbenik, Solmoha [maybe Salamon], Boly are still in Hungarian [territory] and they are very close to Russia. They took over many places that you can see on the map. According to the news the Russians are standing in that position. They are around the Hungarians. That's enough for today. Did you receive any letters from our little brother this week? I didn't hear from him. You know, I'd like to go home for 1 week, but it's 3 weeks, since it would be 2 weeks of traveling and that would mean about $300 dollars. This time leave it as it is. When our little brother comes home then we will learn more about it. Hi Mr. Gluck, we could buy a good 42 car there very reasonably. Here there is nothing new. At this time the weather is very nice and now I'm getting sleepy. Today I made liver. Believe me I'm getting tired of cooking and I hate doing the dishes. I'm eating alright, but washing the dishes I don't like it at all. This is enough for today. Please write a little about everything. Hey Hermine, what is the lady doing? You mentioned she is working? What is Arthur making? Just write, Kisses with love, Dezső

1944/11/29 Irving to Dave, Outside Naples, Italy (V-Mail, Slide 305)

November 29, 1944

Italy

Hello Dave,

It's better later than never, so here I'm. I want to tell you that I'm OK and hope you are well and in good health. What do you think about those pictures. They weren't very good, but I want your opinion. I'll make some more pictures next time and send it to you. If you have one that you took recently please send me one. I'm still working [in] the same place. This time it's different work though. Please write me and I'll do the same. With love, Irving

1944/11/29 Irving to Family, Outside Naples, Italy (V-Mail, Slide 303)

November 29, 1944
Italy

My dear sis[ters], Hermine and Marie,

Just want tell you that I'm OK and hope you are all well and in good health. I have sent you some pictures yesterday, I hope you'll like them. Don't be afraid to tell me what you thought about them. By the way I want to tell you that I have sent New Year's greeting to Walters, Hawkins, and McNeil. She worked with you at Fenton. That's about all this time and I'll try to write more often, OK? With love, Irving

1944/11/29 Irving to Herman, Outside Naples, Italy (V-Mail, Slide 304)

November 29, 1944
Italy

Hello Herman,

How are you? I have read one of your old letters and decided to scamble [sic] you a couple lines. So here I'm. I'm OK and hope you all well and in the best of health. Not much to say from here. I want you to write me more often. I sure like to receive mail, but as I see, if I don't write nobody writes me. Please let me know how everything is with you. I'll write again soon. Love, Irving

1944/11/30 Irving to Family #1, Outside Naples, Italy (V-Mail, Slide 306)

November 30, 1944
Italy

My dear sisters, Hermine and Maria,

Here I'm again I want to tell you that I'm OK and hope everyone is all right. About two weeks now, that I didn't have mail, however the reason was that I moved and waited that I'll move again. Till yet I'm at the same place and really working. Thank God, for all that. A year ago I never thought that I'll be around at this time. I try to forget things, but it's not so easy… I'll write again soon, Irving

1944/11/30 Irving to Family #2, Outside Naples, Italy (V-Mail, Slide 308)

November 30, 1944
Italy

My dear sisters, Hermine and Marie,

Again I want to tell you that I'm OK and hope you are all well and in good health. I have been busy the last couple days, as you know I'm working in the store (PX.) This time really working, not like a year ago. Well let's hope always for the best. I have ask[ed] Dave to send me some salami, and now I'm going to ask you to send me some cookies, OK. Thank you very much Sis. I'll write you again soon, remain with love, Irving

1944/12/1 Irving to Dave, Outside Naples, Italy (V-Mail, Slide 311)

December 1, 1944
Italy

My dear brother Dave,

Just another day and I want you to know that I'm OK and hope that you are in the best of health. It's quite sometime since I heard from you. I hope you're OK. I haven't much to say, but I would like to hear from you soon. Today it's raining outside and I'm writing this letter in the store. It sounds pretty good, doesn't it? Well my best wishes till I hear from you again, With love, Irving

1944/12/1 Irving to Family, Outside Naples, Italy (V-Mail, Slide 310)

December 1, 1944
Italy

My dear sisters, Hermine and Marie,

Just another day and I want you to know that I'm OK and hope that this letter will find you all well and in good health. Sometime this week I'll try to write you a long letter, even though there isn't much to write about. I wish if you could write me about everything. About myself I can't say much, just Thank God that I'm OK. That's the only word for it. I'm waiting to hear from you soon again, Remain with love, Irving

1944/12/2-3 Irving to Hermine and Marie (Book 4, 71-86) missing page 9

December 2, 1944
My dear sisters, Hermine and Marie,

I just came back from Saturday evening services and I have decided to write a couple lines. First I want to tell you that I'm okay and hope you are all well and in the best of health.

You know there's so much I would like to talk about but that can be done only when I get home so today I just say what I can. However if I don't write like I used to don't worry. Thank God that I'm in the rear. Tonight after services I met a fellow his name is David Kornfield, lived in Eperjes, Czechoslovakia. He knows Rosewater also Mendlovits. This man Kornfield worked with Rosewater for a lumber company, some kind of a salesman. That was in Eperjes! And if I remember good they went to America together. This fellow lives at present in Scranton, PA. I have inquired as much as I could about Rosewater. Rosewater is about thirty-five and he's said that he knows him very good. As I said before they worked together. He also told me that he was discharged from the army after three months in the service. He has education as it is over here and he also told me he is from a good family and has two sisters. They lived nice over here. I asked him what was the reason as being discharged, well he said, you know he is not a young man… that answer hit me, because I'm only 23 and feel like sixty. That's that. Thanks God for all that, the way it is. It could be worse.

Sometime tomorrow afternoon I'll see him again. I told him if I can help him in anything I'll do so. He has been overseas 16 months. Worked in a hospital and today as far as he knows, he is just a replacement. That's something that back home you don't know what it is. Well let's hope for the best. Also he has received a letter from Mendlovitcz that he was wounded and also that he has returned to his outfit. That means he wasn't wounded seriously. God be with him! It's rough! The only time you know it if you are in it. Boy believe me it's enough for anyone. Things that you can't talk about. Just let's pray to God, he is the only one, who can help all of us. I trust him as ever!

Not long ago I met a couple boys in this camp and we come together whenever we can, everyone is busy here. In the army you always meet different fellows and new friends. I hope to meet them when we return home.

Before I forget it, please say hello to Rosewater from David Kornfield. I told him that I'll write about him.

In one of your letters today you're asking me if I received a package of cookies and the caramel, yes I did received [sic] it. I must have forgotten to write about it.

You know Hermine and Marie, I feel sorry for not writing to Louis Schwartz. I should have written: for everyone, our friends and relatives. However till I will write them, please tell them I'm okay, but busy. Also tell them, even though I'm not writing to them, I'm thinking of them. And that's the best I can do from here.

I'll continue this letter tomorrow, the time is 11:00 PM. The lights just went out.

Back again it's early Sunday morning I want to mail this letter soon, so I'll continue a couple more pages. Maybe you are disgusted now with reading a letter like that. Well how are you this morning? Did you sleep good? I hope you did. It's getting cooler around here. Since I left the good old US I slept once on a soft bed, Believe it or not, my back was aching from it. I wasn't used to it. With a couple rocks I slept much better, as you see I was so much used to it. As yet it could be better, but it could be worse, and it was before: I bet you are listening to the radio this morning, yes I was too, for a while, but every day it's the same thing. What are you going to have for dinner? Maybe I should take a plane and drop in there! Wouldn't it be swell. I know you would treat me as a real guest. And after dinner we would probably go to the show. What do you say? As I'm sitting here all by myself, I can hear you saying That's right Irving, let's go…

Hope it will be soon.

By the way, are you going to write me a letter this afternoon? You say, you will! That's fine. I will be waiting for it. Thanks a lot Hermine and Marie. If not you I could wait for a year until Herman would decide to write me some news, the happening of the home front. Let me know about everything, that doesn't make any difference in which language you write I understand you well. Many times I thought maybe I should write in foreign language, but I'm so used to writing English that if I would have to write in Hungarian, I bet I would have some difficulties. Believe it or not, it's over a year now that I haven't written in any other language, but English. I'm not perfect in it, but I guess it will do it. Also Marie, you must forgive me if I answer you in English all the time, but it's much faster to mail, or send a letter from here in English. You just write me the way you want to, that's okay with me.

Now I want to tell you that in this letter you will find a money order of one hundred dollars. And I'll say like in many other letters if you need anything please be free and take

…

Missing Page 9

…

I get back again to tell you something, I have found the address of Mrs. Janny Gluck and Janny Frye now Mrs. Weinberg so I sent them Hanukkah greetings. I wonder what they'll think. It comes to me now that I didn't send any greetings to Eigner, but it's not late yet. They haven't written me since I left the States, well I don't know, maybe I should forget it too. What do you think Hermine and Marie? Back home they don't know the score as we say it.

Now while I'm at it and feel like writing so I'll just continue okay. Do you think I should? I heard you say, yes! Okay, I'll find something to write about it. In one of Marie's letter I find that the Chaplain has written another letter. Yes, the reason is that I was there and told them about that mistake that they made, so he decided to write another letter. That was correct, wasn't it? He knows me like a coin. That sounds good, well whenever I can I go to the services and that's why, that's the only time we come together. This type of services that he makes, you have to get used to it. You know we are not home, that it could be the way you want to. This is the Army, we hope it won't be long and next year I'll be home and going to the services with you and tell you the difference between it.

Before I'll close this letter I want to tell you to write me in any language and I know you can express yourselves much better than I can. So please write me about everything and let me hear from you soon, with love, Irving

P.S. Say hello to our friends and love to Herman and Dave, from Irv
December 3, 1944
Italy

Sunday evening
Dec 3 - 44
My Dear Sisters Hermine and Marie,
Just a few more lines to let you know that I spoke to David Kornfield this afternoon and I want to make a correction about Rosewater, he went to America before Kornfield. Rosewater has a clothing store in Cleveland. By the way his first name is Gilbert (Geza) Rosewater. He also has another brother in the US.

His father is still over here. Listen Hermine, if you want to know something just write me and I'll try to find out from him. All this what I have written, I guess you knew it before, but it's interesting to meet this fellow over here. Please write me about everything, will you? Okay now I would like to know something, I want to check up if you have received these money orders which I'll mention here: in January I have sent a P.T.A. MONEY order of 20 doll. That's the one that I don't remember for sure. The rest of them are Jan 4-44 $60.00 Feb 27-44 $70.00 Apr 6-44 $75.00 May 16-44 $40.00 July 26-44 $50.00 Sept 4-44 $90.00 Oct 5-44 $50 and another Oct 5-44 $100.00 Dec 1-44 $100.00 if you could check on this money I really would appreciate it. If any of this didn't get there I'll be able to inquire about it with your help. Thanks a million to you. Also there is something I would like to know, how much money I have in bonds, and in the bank. All this I'm not checking up because I'm afraid or something, but just the curiosity, that I would like to know. Listen your letters are not open like mine, so don't be afraid of anyone, even though it's personal. But in my case this is the army. Write me soon will you please. Thanks again…

Listen, I also want to know if you need anything, and you want something from here, if I can I'll get it for you. Sometime when you get more time off, I want you to write me what I should get to send to some of the relatives some kind of a souvenir, I know they want things like that. Actually there isn't anything that you couldn't get back home, much cheaper than here. Here they soak you for everything. Anyway I want your answer before I'll get anything. For myself I have plenty souvenir from Italy… I don't want anymore. I just want to take myself home. By the way, how did you like my pictures? Please write me soon and wishing all the best. Love, Irving

Time is 10 PM

1944/12/4 Irving to Family, Outside Naples, Italy (V-Mail, Slide 314)

D[ecember] 4, 1944
Italy

My dear sisters Hermine and Maria,
I hardly know how to begin my letter as you see it: Time goes fast. A few years ago it was different. I or rather we worked on not to be in it, but everything is up to God. I hope he will not fail me. Please do not worry for not writing to you often. You know how everything goes. I met some old friends of mine. It's different now. Some of them are fine. Were thinking of me a lot. Well now I'm thinking of you all and hope to see you soon. Please tell Dave and Herman to write me. They have plenty of time. Please tell Flora many thanks, for the pen. I remain with all my love to you, your little brother, Irving

1944/12/7 Fred Yankin to Irving (Book 7, 11)

Frey-Yenkin Paint Company

December 7th, 1944
Dear Irving: It has been a long time since I have written you simply because there hasn't been too much to say. You fellows have had a lot of experience and we just go along doing the same job day after day. Nothing much new. We got a letter from Uri the other day in which he tells us he is on an aircraft carrier in the Pacific, He is a Radar Flight Officer and goes up in the air in a bomber. He tells me he likes the work but it is pretty dangerous and no doubt it is. His wife and baby are back in Columbus living with her folks and I see them occasionally. Irvin Kohn, who you might remember working in the warehouse is in the Merchant Marine and has been across the ocean seven times, visited Russia, Siberia, India and a lot of other places. He has changed a great deal. Whenever he is in the country, which is about every 60 days, he comes to Columbus to visit us. Henry Johnson was in a week or two ago. He is stationed down in Florida and has gained 30# since he has been in the Army. He likes it well enough but he told me he is always broke because the Army sends most of the money to his wife and four kids. He was given two stripes a couple of months ago but decided to turn them back in because of too much responsibility. Ray Chittum is in India and we hear from him pretty regularly. You probably remember Bert West Jr. who used to come over to the place. He was paint manager at Cussins and Fearn, A nice, young, tall, good-looking fellow. He went into the Navy as a Lt. (j.g.) as a flight officer. He was in the Navy about a year and was taking a trip from his base in Georgia to some place in New York and ran into a storm and was killed and left his wife and three babies.

It was very sad and we all felt sick about it. Art, Al, Andy and everybody here, Abe, Ben and my Father and the girls all send their love to you and we hope that you come back to us real soon. Sincerely, Fred Yenkin

1944/12/7 Undated Dave to Irving (Book 16, 207-208)

[Dated by 5 pound salami sent on Dec 14, alone, because the previous salami ruined the cookies. Also, has to be after July 1944 because Dave moved to #10 then. The other salamis that he sent between July and December were smaller. Irving writes on Nov 30, 1944 that he asked Dave for more salami]

My dear little brother!
Today is Thursday morning. There is no news. I just got ready to go to work. I will write at the beginning of next week. I hope my lines will find you in the best of health and may God give you the best of luck in the future. If it will be successful to send your letters by the post office, I will send a 4 or 5 pound salami in a package. So good luck until I see you again. I kiss you with love forever your brother, who will never forget.
Dezső

D. Gluck
1363 Alamitos Ave.
Long Beach, 6
Apt #10
California

P.S. Write me first, you shouldn't wait until I write. Thanks, kisses, Dezső

1944/12/7 Hermine to Irving (V-Mail, Slide 317)

[In English]

December 7, 1944
My dear brother Irving:
Received 4 letters today 3 V mail and one air Mail enclosed the pictures of you. Boy is it wonderful! I tell you the truth the big ones are very good and I am happy to get one because it is just like you. Otherwise we all are well and we'll try to write to you again. I know your friends will be happy to get the Christmas cards. Take care of yourself with God's help hope to see you in a short time. Good luck and good health with all my love, your sister, Hermina

1944/12/10 Hermine to Helen Perl (Book 11, 76) unfinished

Columbus Dec 10 - 44
My dear Helen!
Against my will and still a little late, I will respond to your dear letter. I was glad to hear that you and the baby are well, thank God. I guess by this time she could be very cute because she changes everyday and truly, if God will help, she will laugh very soon.

1944/12/10 Hermine to Irving (V-Mail, Slide 31)

Dec 10, 1944
My dear brother Irving!
Every time I think about you, I think to let you know through my letters. I was so happy to get your good pictures and I showed it to all our friends, but Flora and Walter didn't see them yet, because we are busy on Sunday just seldom go anywhere. I know you know all about our work, and when you get back with God's help will try to do it different way that we could go somewhere with you. We all are well, hoping to hear the same, I want you to know, all the girls who saw your pictures like them very much. I will write you again, love and good wishes to you, Hermina

1944/12/11 Hermine to David (Book 11, 57-58)

Columbus, Dec 11-44
Dear David!

Page 396

Just today I received a 10 page letter from our little brother, and last week a few pictures. Thank goodness he looks very well. He mentioned that he sent you some also. Did you receive them? Some of them we can enlarge later. He sent home the film also. This time he wrote a very interesting letter. I would mail it to you, he wrote to you also. He wrote it would be very nice if he would be able to come home for dinner and after to go see a show in the movie. He knew that we would make him the best and he would have the best and would enjoy it. Also he wrote about information about the Cleveland man, the Rosewater friend I used to see, because he met a young man he used to work with before they came to America. Like they say, the world is big, you never know who you meet and where you meet unexpectedly. You never know, even [among] strangers you also still find some one you know or someone from the same place. Otherwise, he is ok. Also, we all of us are ok. Here it has been snowing all day. Afterwards it was muddy. Our little brother sent a $100 dollar check home. We will get him a bond. I'm going to write to him also a long letter. Write, and take care of yourself. I received the newspapers, and thank you. Now kisses, with all my best wishes and Love, Hermina

1944/12/11 Hermine to Irving (Book 11, 51-55)

Columbus Dec 11 - 44

My dear little brother!

We got your 16 page letter and also 2 letters and the greetings for Hannukah. I know that you know how I feel when I get a letter from you, especially a long letter is very interesting and that thank God you are well. That makes me happy. Yes your picture shows that you are a real man! And not a little boy like Marcsa wrote. I just said that maybe Irving does not even like it. Is it true?

It is very interesting what you said based on the boy. You wrote that the world is big but the home is too small in it. But still in the big world the bad brings people together, therefore you can get more information than me here. When the time comes I will write, if the boy sends his best, but I just wrote to him today and I sent a letter to him, so this way I could only write it next time. Yes, I heard that the Mendlovitz boy got wounded also, but it was not severe, he feels fine. Gilbert Rosewater asked me to ask from my relatives, so I called them and they gave me the address that Dave asked for also and his Aunt said that he is well and his wound was not severe.

You know little brother, it is interesting what you are writing, for example about the lunch that I would cook and what would we do if you could fly home, and that we would make a big party. Well, you got that right. But, even if we would go to the movies, before that we would have to talk a lot and we could tell you everything. Yes little brother because on Sunday I baked kugel, stuffed cabbage and made spaghetti with meat balls. You must be surprised that all of them are almost the same meals. The thing is that they can eat whatever they like. Marcsa loves the cabbage and since she eats the other meals at work, this way she needs this. I learned how to make Italian spaghetti. Believe me, little brother that I love it, and if God will help and you come home, I will make it for you too. Ok? I cook on Sunday and there will be food for a few days and no need to rush when I come home from work. I wish I could send you a little strudel, but it's not allowed, only what is dry and stays fresh. Yes, thank you for the offer that you gave me, that I can use it, in other words I can take whatever I want. I can only write this to that, thank God, we have everything. I have money even if I don't save a lot, but I earn pretty well

...for example 2 weeks salary including 2 Saturdays are in it I get overtime and this way I made 57 dollars and I will buy bonds, it will stay 46 dollars, since from this paycheck I do not need to pay for rent and I don't need to buy anything. This way I will put at least 20 dollars in the bank. And from the next paycheck there is a 6th war loan now and I want to buy an extra war bond. So, thank God I always manage it that way so I have left for everything. Recently I bought a dress that I need so if somebody comes, I should have it. Girls spend money more easily. You can see that chair I got on the picture. It is in the room and if I clean it up I will enjoy it. And we fixed the pillow that you sent me from Texas and it is there on it and everybody can see it and then they are wondering about you. So, we are thinking about you too whoever comes in. Tomorrow I'm counting on buying a box of cookies, if it's available, because before Christmas the people buy everything. But I will look around so I can send something good to you and I will bake sometime and don't worry because that is not a big deal for me.

You know Irving that I have been in the bank and the old lady was wondering about you and sent her best. Tonight I took your picture to the neighbor to show it to the old lady and she was very happy about it. She said that she wishes you would send her one too. It's true, I said that you sent the film home. If she wants it, you can offer it. I did not offer it to her. It's up to you if you want to give it and I didn't promise. She said that maybe her son wrote to you. She did not mention if she got a Christmas card. Other than that, I don't know any particular news. The snow is falling all day, but it turns out to be water and there are puddles from it. If you want a good warm scarf for your neck, then you can have the girl make it for you. Flora and the others are well, but they don't come here only once a year. They call us more often to see if we are well. And how are you? I just wrote to Bertha and I should write to Aunt Jenny because I got their address and it always stays here. You were wondering about what to send to the relatives. I don't really know what to tell you because everything is so expensive at home. When there will be something small that can be sent in a letter, it would be nice.

For Lajos in Iceland, I sent the same package like for you with the caramel candy. When he got it he responded that he was very happy about it and he air mailed two pairs of little shoes made out of fur that I wear on my coat and it was nice of him. So, I think that it is not necessary, but if you want, only a little thing. They would be surely happy. Or maybe they would be happy for a picture also, if you want I can have it made for them and if you want to the lady it would be even better. Maybe we could tell them that you sent the [film] plate home. I will close it with this, I will write again and until then I kiss you with much love. I wish you good health and lots of luck! Hermina

1944/12/11 Marie to David (Book 8, 40-41)

12-11-44

Dear David,

Today is Monday. I'm in a hurry to write to you. Hoping my letter will find you in good health. It is quite some time that we didn't hear from you. You are becoming lazy to write. We received the newspaper and you received the shoes. Otherwise, we are ok. As of today, we received a letter from our little brother Irving, and it's a long letter. And thank God he is well. The only thing is that he is very busy. He sends you his regards and kisses and is asking you to write to him. He is going to write to you. Otherwise, nothing new here! Today it started to snow. Also, our little brother mentioned he received a package from you the same time that he wrote to us. That was 12/3 and now you should write also. Here there is nothing new. Be careful wherever you are going. Now I'm wishing you good luck, and the best of health. Many kisses. your sister, Maria

1944/12/11 Undated Marie to Irving (Book 9, 267-268)

[Dated by mention of New Year, the photo, snowing, David in California, present place = maybe the PX, the long letter, so 1944. Also Hermine wrote two letters, one to David one to Irving on the same day and it's reasonable that Marie did, too]

My dear beloved Irving!

We have not gotten any letter from you for a couple of days already. I hope that my lines will find you in the best of health! We are well. There is no particular news here. Today it is snowing. And how is it there? Yes my dear little brother, do you need any warm clothes? Write it and we will send it to you. And I hope you will get the mail from us! I am only asking you to take good care of yourself wherever you go. [In English] God bless you! [In Hungarian] I am thinking of you a lot. [If] only we would be over with this terrible confusion, which is what we are all waiting for with such difficulty. It has been just enough of it. We are asking the dear God for [your] lucky return shortly. The relatives are well. The lady was wondering about you. I gave your best to her. We got a letter from David and he is well. He just got a letter from you, which we are all waiting for with such difficulty. I understand you my dear little brother that you are the same way too. Only I am asking you now to take good care of yourself. Wherever you go, I wish you good luck, and the best of health!

I'm thinking of you a lot and I wish you could be home already! But let's trust in God and hope that He will help! I love your picture that you sent and also the others love it as well. And also my dear little brother, if it can't be another way, at least you could keep your present place. I can understand you very well my Irving. And also as you mentioned, you got to know your friend who you got the information. But now let's hope for the best! Once again, take care of yourself and I am asking the dear God to follow you in every step of your way. And if you could, then write a few lines my dear little brother. Now I kiss you countless times. Your forever faithful sister who will never forget. Maria

And I wish you a very happy new year! May your every wish come true! May we be together in the best of health shortly! With love M.

1944/12/13 Herman to Irving (V-Mail, Slide 318)

[In English]

December 13, 1944

Dear Irving,

I received your letter and I am happy to hear that you are fine with God's help, and I hope to hear the best in the future. I know you are wondering for the seldom writing. I know the girls are writing everything happening here at home. I haven't no special news to write you. Everything is the same. I work in the same place on the same job. Since yesterday [it] is really winter here. I am not using the bicycle very much. I'm getting tired to peddling it. The most I was riding only in the summer time, now very seldom. I [should] sell it and buy a race bicycle or maybe a car would be better. Rosh Hashanah I was to the religious temple. Yenkins ran to say hi. He came over and asked me about you. And said hello to you. I am a member to the Broad Temple. I have to close for this time and hope to hear the best from you. Love, Herman

[On the side] If you need a help to read just ask me up.

1944/12/13 Irving to Dave (Book 5, 350)

December 13th, 1944

Enclosed is one picture to my brother Dave.

From Irving,

Italy.

1944/12/14 David to Irving (Book 12, 148-152)

Dec 14.44

My dear little brother, Irving!

Did you get a package from me? This week I got 3 letters from you, a picture and a Hannukah greetings. Thank you very much! May the dear God grant that in the next holiday, you could be home in person in the best of health. Yes, thank you about the information about the Mendlovitz boy. If you can write to him or maybe write his address to me. How are you doing with coming home? Do you know anything about it? I hoped that after your long silence, you will walk to my place nicely one day. But it looks like my thought did not work out. Little brother, write a lot about yourself! Oh yes, I forgot to write that this week on the 12th I sent a 5 pound package with salami. There is nothing else in it except salami. I sent two kinds. I had to cut one of them in two pieces so it could fit into the box. I hope it won't go bad. My little brother, if you need anything just ask! Ok? I would love to send anything you need - Here there is no news. But they are currently drafting those who don't work in an essential factory. They will call in ages between 26 and 32, currently I am lucky because I am in this factory. The weather here is pretty good. I still have my car. Right now nothing comes to my mind to write about. I bought a new outfit for myself this week. The one before was very old already. If you can, write where you are or how far you are from Naples. So, I can't think of anything. Yes this week I signed up for the B. Brit [B'nai B'rith] here in Long Beach. The president noted that I am a visitor from Columbus.

Little brother, this happened only once in my life that I got applause. After the wealthy gentlemen came to shake hands with me and the first thing was to ask what kind of business I have. My answer was surprising because I answered that I work in the shipyard. They thought as a visitor I must be a millionaire. But let's leave this. You can see how wealthy they are, they bought a hundred thousand dollars worth of bonds in about 2 hours. I don't really know anybody except by sight. I know the Rabbi pretty well. I'm going tonight. The house [hàzóhoa] wants me to become a member of the temple and organize a group that will help the temple. My little brother, did you know if I would have money like they have here in Long Beach, there would be opportunity now after the war to open a kosher store? You know there are at least 3000 Jewish families. There is a shop where they cook both kosher and treif [unkosher] meat.

The religious Jews get the meat from Los Angeles. You little brother, as a religious boy, you would keep the store closed on Saturday. I'm telling you, you could be rich. True, you should know how to handle it so the meat can be kosher. Yes, someone could be hired to do that. I'm telling you little brother, if you like this thought, this is the future, if God will help and you will come home. So, I wrote enough for today. Forgive me about the many foolish things that I wrote. May the dear God grant that you could come home as soon as possible. I kiss you with love, your forever faithful brother. Dezső

P.S. Please write to me whenever you can and a lot and about everything. So good luck [Saying: szerencse fel szmét = good luck up]. I kiss you again with love, Dezső

P.S. The pictures are pretty good. Thank you so much for them! May the dear God grant that soon I can see you normally. Kisses with love. Dezső

1944/12/15 Irving to Dave (Book 6, 200-204)

December 15, 1944
My dear brother Dave,
I was very happy to receive your most welcomed letters and 3 packages and all the three, arrived in good condition and as you have described me in one of your letter. The Fitch and glycerin is very good, arrived in time and from here I'll say thanks a million for everything. There was [a] hundred different articles in these packages. It's swell, of you that you really think of me with everything and I know that you would send me anything I want, as yet I have everything, thank God. About myself I don't have much to say, just thank God that I'm okay, and even though that word means a lot, but I'm glad to say this way. I hope that this mess ends soon, it's not as easy to return home as you thought. I prefer to stay here until it ends, but I would like to have it end as soon as possible. Please write me more often, I know you are busy, I would like to stop in and help you out with your work, but that's only a dream and I hope that it will come true. I have received some mail from home and they are okay, however complaining that you are not writing them as you used to. They understand that you are busy, but even then a letter from you means a lot. I like to receive letters just like you and I guess everybody is and feels the same way. So please write me and to them too. I hope that it won't be long when I'll be able to call you up and even stop in to see you. That day will be a happy one. In this letter I'm enclosing a picture of myself just to refresh your memory. I also have sent home, they aren't good, but I'll send you a better one next time. Okay? That's about all the news from here, it's raining mostly. I bet in Ohio it's cold, there was something in today's paper about it. You know Dave it's almost a year that I have been in Italy as soon as I got in here I was up in a hot spot. I would like to send an article home from our Stars & Stripes, but I have only one so I want to have it with me. But if I can get another so I'll send it home. It's a very good article about my outfit that I was in. You probably read all about it but you never noticed it. I'll show you someday okay. Thanks again for those packages and I'll ask for more later. Now I'll close this time and hoping to hear from you soon. With love, Irving

P.S. How did you like the pictures that I sent you before? Please write about it, and if you have one made recently please send me, okay
Irv.

1944/12/15 Irving to Hermine and Marie (Book 4, 66-70)

December 15, 1944
Italy

My dear sisters Hermine and Marie,
I have just mailed a package and contained 2 bracelets and a ring for Herman, besides this one patch that was issued while I was with my outfit. I hope that you will like it, when you receive it. Please let me know when you'll get that. I'll tell you how interesting it is with these people, they always ask for double prices and you don't know how much it's worth, they naturally get as much as they want. However I have done a little different. I decided to practice up with the Italian language. Yet I have begin to speak some, so they understand me and I try to understand them. This time I found this bracelet and I begin to talk the style they do and I told them in broken Italian that I know the prices, I have been here before and I don't want him to overcharge me. So the Italian said, when were you here, so I said when I was little, "because you speak the lingo I'll give you for the same price as for an Italian" he said. It's interesting the way all this things goes over here. I found if you speak the language where-ever you are it always comes handy. I guess when I return to America I will have to practice all over again. Please let me know how you like it. By the way in

this letter I'm enclosing another picture of me that I took while I was in town. That's just to fresh up your memory. There isn't much that I can tell you about myself, just waiting and hoping for the best to come. Hope that our prayers will come through soon. That's about all I have to say for myself. I went to the Red Cross to find out if they received anything from Czechoslovakia, but they haven't received anything yet. So I just hope that I'll get some good news one of these days. I received two letters from Dave and also three packages and now I'll try to write him a couple lines. He is okay, but busy and that's why he isn't writing as before. In one of your letters you are asking me if I need anything, at present I have everything thank God, however if and when I'll need anything I surely will ask for it. I'll close this time and don't worry, take care of yourselves. I'll write you again soon, my best wishes to you all with love, Irving

1944/12/16 Irving to Family (Book 4, 64-65)

Hello Hermine, Marie and Herman,
Hope that next year we will celebrate Hanukkah together in peace and in good health and happiness. With love, Irving

1944/12/17 Hermine to Irving (Book 11, 60-61)

[In English]

Columbus Dec 17-44
My dear brother Irving,
As always I think a lot about you and tonight I decided it to write a long letter to you. Maria isn't home they have a big dinner for the employees at work and tonight is the Christmas party. Herman is at home, but as always is too lazy to write. We received a letter and a telegram from David, he is well and doesn't like to write so sends a telegram, just like Herman. But he is really very busy house cleaning and cooking gives a lot of work. Tell me Irving, did you know Lieberman whose father is working for Brier the Butcher shop? This man knows you and I showed him your picture. His son is 20 years old and was in France and Belgium and now in Germany. He had all kinds of money and things his son sends home from there. I hope with God's help everything will work out just fine with you. You know what I really mean! So let's hope OK. sweetheart. I said to the girls at work, do you want to see something? Some of them know [it's] probably a picture! Then I said that is my sweetheart, they said I didn't know Hermina that you have a sweetheart! I just laugh[ed] then told that's my little brother, and you know they just laugh[ed] because they thought you are tall and a big boy! Otherwise we all are well. On Saturday I had to work all day and maybe on New Year's day, too. We are very busy, many girls went with their husbands, you know how it goes, and if they can I don't blame them.
Elsie from Cleveland is coming home for the holidays and Flora wants us to come over, too. I wish you could have a good dinner with us, but I will try to send a package this week again. The weather is pretty good, not too cold. Take care of yourself. Love, Hermina

1944/12/18 Private Leo Seide to Irving (Book 18, 68-69)

Dec. 18
Dear Irv,
Haven't heard from you in a long time. I hope this letter finds you in the best of health and in a better position than you were. In fact, I hope you're either going or gone home. They claim that a lot of you boys are going home and brother, I hope that you're one of them. From my address you can see I'm rather a busy boy and I don't care to stay around here much longer. So see what you can do for me in the way of ending this damn war. How's your family? Fine I hope and in the best of health. Are you still working at the Mess Hall? It was a swell job and I wished I could have stayed there myself. Please excuse the short letter, I'll try to do better next time. Write and let me know the latest news. Your buddy, Leo

1944/12/19 Marie to Irving (Book 9, 241)

12-19-44
Written in Hungarian

My dear beloved little brother, Irving!

We got a very long letter from you last night. And today a V. mail, that I was very happy about and I'm very happy to hear that you are in good health. Thank God. Believe me little brother that I can understand you very well and I know what it means when one is waiting for mail and doesn't get it. I'm sorry if sometimes I'm late with the writing even if it is against my will. But believe me my little dear Irving, I did not forget about you and I will be in a hurry to write to you. As I can see you changed [addresses] again. But we hope and ask the dear God to help you and he will be there with you in every step of your way. And my little brother, you are right that Herman is too lazy to write. But he can hardly wait for your letter, he read that one. We are otherwise well. I wish we could see you already. I can hardly wait for that moment that we could be together again. There is no news here. I only ask you to take care of yourself wherever you go! God bless you! But I hope that you will come this way. I wish you lots of luck and good health. Now I kiss you countless times, your forever faithful sibling, who will never forget you. Maria

1944/12/20 Helen Perl to Hermine (Book 14, 158-160)

Cleveland Dec 20, 1944
My dear Hermine!
I am very surprised that you did not respond for so long. I believe that you are very busy with work and with housekeeping. It is not a small job, but I hope you will get married and everything is going to be different. When I got the package from you, Rosewater was just here and he ate from it, too. Mostly we talked about this and that until I brought up the subject, that is, what does he think about you. I got from his statement that he likes you, but you do not know each other well yet. You should insist that he should go to you, even though I would like it if you would come to Cleveland. Maybe it will be successful to introduce another one, a third one to you. Since I already, thank God, feel better. This way I'm in a better mood for everything. The baby is beautiful and what is important, she is a very good child. She sleeps through the night like a grown up. She doesn't even wet the bed the entire night.
She is already laughing and babbling, she fills up the house. She was barely 7 weeks old when she started to cry. The doctor saw her three weeks ago and said that she developed well physically, like a 4 month old child. Thank God I am very happy that it was successful to lose weight. Mrs. Goldblatt was here on Sunday and she said that she got a letter from you and did not respond yet because her son does not want to hear about marriage yet. If there is an opportunity that opens up for you to get married, he would keep you away from it with the uncertainty, he would not like that, but he likes you a lot. Her heart is breaking in her sadness, if you could not be her daughter in law. She said that. It is childish of him. The children here can not be influenced by the parents. Write a response as soon as possible. I'm interested, At Christmastime you are my guest, come over here. I kiss all of you. Helen

1944/12/20 Irving to Hermine and Marie (Book 4, 54-63)

December 20, 1944
My dear sisters Hermine and Marie,
I'm back again with a couple more lines to let you know that I'm okay and still kicking. I received a couple letters from you and it makes me happy to hear that you are well and in good health.

In many different letters you are asking me to write about myself. It's not much I can say, just that I'm hoping for the best and please don't worry, with God's help everything will be alright.

On Saturday evening I was at the services and had a little party, it was interesting, here you will find a copy of the program. The services are just like in the Broad Street temple. I always meet different people there, however in the army they come and go. I'm used to all that, let's hope that soon we all return home in the best of health. I spoke to Kornfield and he has written to Rosewater that he met me. It was really interesting of meeting him. What did Rosewater say to all that? Did you mentioned about meeting his friend over here? I bet he was surprised too. Please write me all about it.

How did you like my latest picture? I'll make some better ones when I get to Napoly. I'm glad that you did like the big ones that I sent you in the first letter. When I was in town I was looking at those places where we have been together for that short vacation. Since then everything changed. That time if you remember we were talking about staying here if not this mess, just for a good vacation, about 3 months. Today I feel much different about all this. Back in the U.S. you can find the best places you want for enjoyment. Time goes fast and when I get home I guess I'll have to learn everything all over…

I haven't been able to get any information about [Lewis] case, neither about [mim]. The reason is that I have to straighten out certain things before I can or want to bother with this. I know it can be done, but I figure to wait till next payday.

How is Herman getting along? I bet he is just as lazy as when I was home. He is industrious only at work and thinks of himself only, but not in writing a line. I guess he feels this way, maybe he will learn or somebody will teach him, he thinks that he can live by himself, maybe, tell him that I said hello and waiting to hear from him and I mean it! Okay sis. I really can thank you for the letters that you are and have written me, because if not you I don't know where I would be. Dave used to write more often, however I can understand that he is busy and when you don't write I know that you must be busy otherwise you would write me. That is all a GI want[s], mail from home. I know that you are in a safe place, but beside the point, whenever you can, please drop me a line will you please. Thanks a million.

Just last night I received the mentioned package from Bertha, it contained a fountain pen, a can of pineapples, chocolate bars and some more small articles. It was very nice to think of me. I will write her some time later, please don't mention anything to her in your letter. At present I'm busy I don't know when I can sit down and write her, so a couple days probably I'll be late. I'm behind of answering letters already, but if they know how things go, they will forgive me, I'm sure.

You know I haven't written to Louis yet, if he has more time to write, I think he should. There is plenty reason for not writing, but when I can I will. As yet I want to write to Dave and that will be all for now, With all my love, from your brother Irving
Till we meet again!

1944/12/20 Sgt. Tony Novak to Irving (Book 18, 47-49)

France 20 Dec 44
Dear Irving:
Received your Christmas Greeting a few days ago. Thanks a million for it. So far am getting along quite well. France is not such a bad place to be in. I'd much rather be here than in Italy. Everything out here is much cleaner. By the way how are you getting along by this time? How about some first hand information? Would very much like to hear from you. Say Irving, I saw Ernest Selig - you remember him don't you? He happens to be with the 45th Division and likes it. He does clerical work and holds a corporal rating. He asked me about you and I'd told him that I last saw you in Italy. Not much more to say for now. Will wait to hear from you. Wish you a very Merry Christmas and a victorious New Year. As Ever, Tony

1944/12/21 Irving to Dave, Naples, Italy (V-Mail, Slide 322)

December 21, 1944
Italy

My dear brother Dave,
Must forgive me for not writing you as often as I used to, I always say I'll, but there's always something it comes first. I moved again, you'll find my new address above. Please write me and whenever I can I will also. I'm OK. Please don't worry, everything will be OK with God's help. I was at this place a year ago for a couple days. Now the situation is different. I'll write about it more sometime later, With all my love, your brother Irving

1944/12/21 Irving to Family, Naples, Italy (V-Mail, Slide 321)

December 21, 1944
Italy

My dear Sis, Hermine and Marie,
Here I'm again and want to tell you that I'm okay and moved again, my new address is above. I was here at this place a year ago this week. Now it's different, I hope in God that He will help me. I will write again soon, don't worry! Remain with all my love, your brother Irving

December 21, 1944
Iceland

Dear Maria,

Just received your swell package and also your letter. I'm answering it promptly I want to thank you for it and tell you how much I enjoyed it. It took a little long to get here as it usually does, but it still arrived in time, a few days before Xmas. Chanuka past without even me knowing it when it was. One boy told me yesterday about it. That's army life. You probably celebrated it even if in different conditions. Maybe we'll do [it] too [in] some of the coming years. Did I tell you that my little cousin from Youngstown one of the Eigners is studying in Columbus College. He is one of the swellest kids you ever met. What do you hear from Irving. I wish he'd write me sometimes. As far as myself I'm fine hope the same about you. Love, Lou

Columbus Dec - 23 - 44
[from Hermine, in English]
My dear brother Irving,

Since last week we didn't get any mail from you, but I am just like you reading your older letter, like the 16 pages letter. It is long and very interesting. Today is Saturday but we aren't working, so I want to write to you. We all are well and hoping to hear the same about you. Thursday evening McNeil came over and was asking about you. She likes your picture and the two big ones are so sweet. You know what she said, "Bless his heart. He is sweet!" So you can see she likes you, too. But everybody thinks the pictures are very good. Flora and the family didn't see it yet, not Aunt Helen either. Otherwise everything goes on their regular way. The Rosewater didn't answer my letter yet, but I didn't write to him for two weeks, so he isn't in a hurry. He is too smart and was asking me when I could come to Cleveland again, and I told him that not in the near future and it is his turn. Not because he is the right person for me Irving, just you know how that goes. He is probably a good boy and is working out his business the way he can and thinks too much of himself. It is good to have somebody if nothing else but a letter once in awhile, but he is too busy and that is about all. I don't know but Elsie thinks he is a nice boy. It was really very interesting to hear the information from you and from overseas, but the world is too little, because people get together like that, and have somebody they both know. About his army life he said 1 year but Herman is the same way. As you know they don't like to tell or talk about it. I think there is time, and I can wait - it is not a hurry and maybe somebody else will come and be better, but just to write to him, He is smart, because he is old too. The years are flying and we can't stop them. You know Irving dear, I want you to see the one I decide and I think I would wait for you! What do you think Irving? Boy when the time comes, and we will see you with news from our father and family. Maybe you can hear from them soon[er] than we at home. Or if everything is over, and you can go and see and we all know, you are the one who will do all you can. Maria is working today and Herman is going too. The weather is pretty good not too cold. I will try to write some more again. Take care of yourself and good luck best wishes with all my love, Your sister, Hermina

Regards from your friends.

[from Marie]
Written in Hungarian!!
My dear beloved little brother!

Today is Sunday and I'm in a hurry to write to you a few lines. How are you little brother? I'm hoping to hear the best from you, otherwise we are well too and we think about you a lot. And my dear little brother, as you wrote in your letter, that you are in a hurry to write and you want to be a good boy. My dear little brother, I know that [you try] the best, that you are a very good boy and it's not your fault when you don't write, but I can understand you well. I'm asking the dear God to help you as soon as possible, so we can be together in the best of health. But beside this, I'm asking you very much, little Irving, that take care of yourself and [look] to your health as well. Wherever you go the dear God follows you in every step. You don't leave my mind, not for a minute. We listen to the radio and hope that a better world will come sooner than later. Although it can't be written down how hard we wait for that, together with you little brother. Yes, last week we sent you a few little pictures, I guess you got them already by now. I wish I could see you. I'm waiting for that moment when we meet again. But I'm asking the dear God to help in every step. Also, I'm aware of your other address change. I can imagine, dear little brother, you also have the prospect of being without mail, like it is for us to be with out mail. Like usual, there is no news here, the weather is warm. We got a letter this week from David also and he is well too. Yes little brother, we got the package last week and there was a 5 pound package sent and we will send one this week also. And as you mentioned, little brother that you would like to eat stuffed cabbage. Believe me little brother I can hardly wait for that moment so I can give you your favorite meal that you like so much. Let's hope we don't have to wait for long.

If I cook something like that, you are always on my mind because you like it. And that I wish it would be so good, if you could be here too and you could eat from it. I hope that I will hear the best about your address. I will wait for your letter very much after this. I write to you my little brother correctly. Only in the past I sent you air mail letters, as I think that it takes more time for you to get it. But now little brother, I wish you good luck and the best of health. [In English] And take care of yourself! God bless you! And I hope to see you soon in the best of health. [In Hungarian] I will write next time too. I kiss you countless times with much love your forever faithful sibling, who will never forget. How is the Hungarian friend? Give my best to him. I kiss you again countless times, your faithful sibling, Maria

1944/12/25 Hermine to Irving (Book 11, 63-66)

Columbus Dec 25 - 44
My dear little brother Irving!
Today is Christmas eve and I hope you had a good dinner. With us [it's] as usual, Marcsa worked today and Herman went to the movies. It's been two days that it is raining, but it is totally changed at night, now it is only snowing. So it turned out to be cold. I don't even know what to write first because you know better that we could discuss many things together about things, but currently only trust in God that He will help all of us and soon we could see each other. About the boy from Cleveland, as I mentioned this a few days ago to you too, that he did not respond to my letter. I got his letter yesterday, where he wrote that he can't promise, but it is possible that on Sunday or on next Sunday he will come over to Columbus. You know they take the mail on Sunday before Christmas. And 10 minutes later, the phone rang and the boy was here. You know, it is better to know about it, but it doesn't matter because one is fine either way.

So I had an unexpected guest. I told you that the Kőenfield boy sent his best to you and he [Rosewater] asked me to give his best to the Kornfield boy. He did not mention that they worked together only that he knows him very well. This time he pulled himself out of it and as a matter of fact he cannot be mocked because he tries everything and after all we all had a part in many of these things, which he was not used to. And the best thing is, maybe to forget what has passed. Do you know what I think about the job, my little Irving? Believe me whatever will happen the decision isn't easy, plus he is smart too and does not talk the way I believe him! Other than that I got another letter from the other boy's mom. If you could see, my little Irving, what kind of letter she wrote to me! She is head over heels for me. But she is only a mother! But still it's a little fun - But I will leave the gossip and let's talk about something serious or let's go back to the letter way. We are all well. Thank God and let's hope from the dear God that He will help all of us. How are you sweetheart? Write more often

...if you can and I will be in a hurry to write as well. I'm out of V. mail, this way I can scribble more foolishness to you because there is enough paper. Flora and the others liked your picture very much and everybody I showed it to did, too. You know, I am very proud of my little brother! And they say on the picture you are smiling just like someone who is proud of himself or of the uniform. So, it makes me happy and I hope you look like you do in the picture. As far as the replacement goes, you are right, that they don't even think about it at home what it could mean, but believe me, even if they do, let's trust that everything is going to be fine. Right now, it's only better than other places, but they could send you to another place, if they would need you. I also heard that you could be entitled for a holiday and then they could bring you home. This way let's hope and ask the dear God to help you, even after that. Write about yourself and take care of yourself and ask for whatever you need or ask for a package more often!! It did not go [out] for a long time or [it was] a very small amount. Take care of yourself and I wish you lots and lots of luck and I stay with love. Your loving big sister, Hermina

1944/12/25 Marie to Irving (Book 9, 243-245)

Written in Hungarian 12 - 25 - 44

Dear beloved little brother, Irving!

It has been the second week that we did not get any mail from you. I hope that my lines will find you in the best of health. We are well and I can hardly wait for your letters. Besides all that, my little brother, I can understand you, that you could be very busy - I can imagine. I hope that the dear God will help you and I ask him to stay with you in every step of your way. I hope, my dear little brother that you could be there at least at your current place and that soon you could come home in the best of health. We got a letter from David last week and he is well. There is no particular news here. The weather is rainy today. Yesterday was snowing. But I'm really asking you to take care of yourself wherever you go and do not be sad. I think about you a lot. I wish we could see you already! I'm waiting for that moment so much. Although, I can understand that you feel the same. Now I wish you lots of good luck and the best of health. I kiss you countless times forever your faithful sibling, who will never forget. Maria

1944/12/29 Western Union Telegram, David to Hermine - illness (Book 7, 267-269)

1944 Dec 29 AM 9:22
Long Beach Calif Dec 28

Miss Hermine Gluck
University Hospital

Very sorry to hear your information Please do what you think is best. Will write soon. Am well Hoping you will be the same Love

David

1944/12/31 Irving to Dave, Naples, Italy (V-Mail, Slide 325)

December 31, 1944
Italy

My dear brother Dave,

Just a line to let you know that I'm OK and hope to hear from you the best. At present I'm still in a Repl Depo [Replacement Depot]. Waiting for a new assignment. This time I might get to be an interpreter or translator. At present I don't know what to write you, at this place I'm not able to write like I thought, so please forgive me and if you have time please drop me a line and I'll try my best. My best wishes to the new year, till we meet again with all my love, Irving

1945/1/4 David to Hermine and Marie (Book 2, 145-154) sea trials

Jan 4, 1945
Dear Herminka, until 120

Forgive me that I didn't write you in so long, but if you would be here you would see what the situation is. You would see that I'm right. So first, thank you for your letter where you inform me about the situation. You wrote in one of your letters that you are better. I dreamed that they will do surgery on you. But it's better this way because I'm more relaxed now. But may God give us that after this everything is going to be successful, and we can see each other in health and strength again. And God help us that years from now we will not hear any bad news about each other anymore. Please take care of yourself and don't work for awhile.

I could have called you on the phone, but I didn't know if I can talk to you because Mariska wrote that you were very sick. I hope that the dear God will help you and everything will work out after all this. Oh yes! If you want me to talk to you on the phone, write it to me!!!?? So, I'm hoping all the best. Yes, Mariska wrote that there were only private rooms. This way it's better that you were not sharing the room with anyone. Write about everything. Ok? Write who went to visit you, ok!? Yes, Herminka I need insurance like yours. I need to pay for a combined room for 2 or 4. But here for you, you only need to pay the extra fee.

Write how much it cost for the doctor and etc., and I'll work to reimburse the amount or pay it directly. But definitely write it to me. If I send the money, it's not charity, only a little help. If you would be in my position, you would pay this as well. Does the gentleman in Cleveland know about it? What did he say? Was he to see you? Did he buy you something? If you let me know that he did not get anything, (flowers or anything) he's just a moron and it's not worth it to waste time on him. You know Hermine, there are enough honest guys out there for your age and it's hard to find girls like you.

It's not the way you are thinking over there. There are no men these days, except those with faults and sickness. But it's not urgent. No matter how rich he is, I don't even know what, if he was sent home from the military that means that he is over 38 and pretty sick, and that's not for you. So "whistle to that" [do not give a damn]. See, with me what happened with my eyes and legs, but I was not enlisted to the military. But whoever was in and was sent home, has some kind of problem. If he will start to speak with ease, ask him why he was sent home? That's not a shame and you have the right to know the truth. But, if he's smart and will not tell you, tell him not to bother anymore, you are not interested in someone who keeps a secret about this.

So, it's enough about this, right? Write how you feel, and please, yes, about a suitor, do not listen to anyone, only to yourself. Remember your Uncle Lajos in Polyán...
There is no special news here. The sun shines nicely every day, [and it's] not raining a lot. The water is so nice I'm going to bathe in the water. Yes, about me, the company I work for has many contracts for ship making. So, this is the second week since I was moved to another factory in Wilmington where I lived in the past. So, I have to get up earlier in the morning and I come home later at night. This is how it goes.

My job is better now that I do the Hood Scale [Húgy Scale = maybe the binnacle], which is, one could say, one of the worst. It is on a kind of structure that controls the ship and the speed indicator, it has the sea direction on the compass [gyrocompass - similar to Arma Mark 7 or Sperry]. So, everything is important. I will work on a little box tomorrow that is 22 cm tall and 10 cm wide. It's spherical and there will be at least 100 wires in it. Naturally covered with colored material, this way one can tell which one is what. So, it is enough for today (this is a secret what I'm writing). We call it I.C. Inner Communication here. Oh yes, next week the ship will go out for testing, to tryouts. Probably from 10:00-15:00 o'clock. We will go out to the sea and on the sea, also probably from 100-150 km or maybe farther.

That is when the ship is done and we will test it before the Navy takes it over.
This ship is a passenger ship. It looks beautiful. So, dear Herminka, I wrote to you about a great deal of foolishness that is enough. Please write a lot. I did not get mail from Ignác this week. Kisses Hermine and may God give you everything good and all of you, that my lines will find you in the best of health. I kiss you with love and I wish you much luck and everything good. I'm waiting until I see you again in hope and happiness. Kisses many times your older brother. Dezső
P.S. Please write a lot ok?!

Dear Mariska!
I got your letter and I thank you very much!
Please write me after this also and write about everything and take care of yourself ok?! I wrote everything in Hermine's letter. Thank you very much for Ignác's new address, I don't have it yet. I will write to him also. So, I hope that you are well and, that Hermine is already at home. And you Mariska, if Hermine doesn't write the cost then you write it to me! Ok? If you don't write it, then I will not write also, not even as much I wrote before. How much was the surgery? Also, write about everything. Also, about Sir Herman Gluck, and tell him, if he wants to change his job, then he does not need an "availability ticket" because he is an ex-soldier and he can change it whenever he wants. I kiss you with love until I'll see you again. Dezső

1945/1/4 David to Irving (Book 15, 10-11)

My dear Irving!
I was very happy to get your letters. I can not even write how much your picture that you sent made me happy. I'm sorry that I don't have one, but I will send one. I hope the dear God will help you and you will be home before [I do] and you will see me in person. Ok!!
I don't know any particular news. Everything is the same. Currently I work for the same company where I used to, but I was transferred to another factory in Wilmington where I used to live. Currently, I still have my car and it's running well, better than when I got it. Do you remember my little brother, the first day when we sat in it, how courageous ["corezos"] I was? I could not drive it and I wanted you to do it. Can you forget

it? I will send a package to you next week. I know somebody at the post office, so it will be sent to you without asking! The weather here is excellent. The sun is shining, only the nights are cooler closer to the mornings. My little brother write about that situation that was written in the Stars and Stripes. Ok?! I'm interested. Otherwise, how are you? Mariska wrote your new address. What do you do now? I hope they will not send you out to the battlefield. Write about it. Ok? Mariska wrote that you were there a year ago, it's around [K.B = körülbelül. = approximately] North Africa. right? Write a lot. I have not heard from you in a long time. Please write Ok?

Forgive me that I write so badly, sorry I can't write better. I'm so happy that you got three packages. I hope you will get the rest as well. How was the fruit cake? Did you like it? Do you need more? It looks like they will call up the 4F's. It is nonsense to call [them up] and the newspaper says they want them to work for soldier's pay in the factory. Imagine, one will make 120 in the shipyard, and the 4F just 15 or 20¢, isn't that crazy? If so, I will leave my job or I will say that I'm sick. I don't know if it's going to be true or not yet. It is in today's paper and it's crazy how many people they have even today. We don't know what to do with them and [they] need more! Why? They don't even know what to give [them] for work. I think they want everybody to wear a soldier's uniform and there will be no work that way. Believe me it is nonsense what they do.

I work 10 hours per day. 8 would be enough. They steal from these and that is nothing. And today they need more people.[?] I hate to hear this on the radio as well, because I know that it's not true. But let's leave this too. How are you? Write a lot! I hope you will be able to read my lines! So, my little brother, I think that our father and family are already under the Russians. Did you hear anything since then? What can we do? Did you ask around? If you could, please write whatever is possible. Ok! Forgive me, I'm closing my lines now. I'm getting sleepy. Be in a hurry and come here, so I will not be alone. So, I will kiss you with love. In the hope of seeing you again. Your forever faithful brother, who is always thinking of you and will never forget. May God grant me to see you in good health again.
P.S. If you could do it, just write ok!! Kisses, Dezső

[Side note:] I got mail from Hermine. Thank God they are well. They send their greetings.
Kisses, Dezső

1945/1/4 Hermine to Irving (V-Mail, Slide 331)

[In English]
January 4, 1945
My dear brother Irving,
Sorry I am writing to you with a pencil but, just in a hurry you know how it goes. I am well and so are the others Maria and Herman. The weather is getting better but, it was too cold last week. How are you sweetheart? I am so glad for the bracelet you are sending us, it is really wonderful and the pictures are swell and I really mean it that you are just a swell and good brother, and doesn't forget about their sisters and the family. All my love, Hermina

1945/1/4 Private Earl Wetzel to Irving (Book 14, 14-15)

Jan 4, 1944 [he meant 1945]

Gluck
Well how in hell are you? Fine I hope. I have been going to write for a long time but never got around to it. I wrote and asked around. Heck to look up my razors hone and strap but I guess he's too busy to look it up for me. He was supposed to take care of it for me. Now I want you to find it for me. It's in B. Co[mpany] some place. Please don't forget. I'm in the hospital again, the same thing as before and a few more aches and pains for good measure. If I find out for sure if you are still around I'll send you your five dollars I owe you. I also owe some other guys some money and I'll send it too. I have never forgotten you, nor Anzio either. I don't think you will either. Don't forget now. That's all for now, more next time. As ever, Earl Wetzel

1945/1/5 Hermine to Irving (V-Mail, Slide 334)

January 5, 1945

My dear brother Irving:

I am just looking at your picture and it seems to me if you were just out somewhere. With God's help everything will work out all right and maybe very soon we'll see you. Hoping that our father and the family are better than they were and maybe one day you will be a great help to them. I will write some more. Till then good luck and best wishes to my little brother all my love. God Bless you. Love, Hermina

1945/1/7 Dezső to Hermine and Marie (Book 1, 125-127)

Jan 7, 45

Darlings!

I don't understand what you did today? Between 2 and 5 pm Columbus time, I called you all on the phone. There was a connection, but your phone was always busy! So, I just cancelled [after] 3 hours here and it's five or 6 o'clock there. I called the University Hospital person to person and I gave EV 6223, if Hermine will not be in the hospital. Based on my calculation, Hermine is at home because they did not connect me to the hospital! So, I hope you are well, just better take care of yourselves. Especially Hermine! You better rest and write how much was the cost, ok?!

There is no news here, everything is the same.

I don't know if I wrote it, but two weeks ago I got a picture from our little brother. Thank goodness, he is ok. So, I'm three times as hungry and I will go to eat. The sun shines, the weather is so summery. I'm not in the mood for cooking. I already got bored of it. Yes, it's a lot of trouble. So, good luck and wishing everything good to you Hermine and Mariska and to Sir Gluck too. Kisses with love, Dezső

P.S. The lawyer's name who I gave the documents is Harry Goldstein. He is in the phonebook. Herman can call him. As I saw he is at home. I saw his name in the Jewish newspaper and Herman can find out from him what's going on with the documents. Maybe his wife knows also who his substitute lawyer is. So, (Howard Benny Peres). My lawyer is Harry Goldstein. I kiss you with love, Dezső

1945/1/10 Irving to Dave, Naples, Italy (V-Mail, Slide 335)

January 10, 1945

Italy

My dear brother Dave,

I want to thank you for your thoughts and packages. I have received 2 packages from you and it's very sweet of you to think of me. I wish I could have written you before, but even now it's OK Someday! I begin and write you a long letter, first I want to have a permanent add[ress]. Till then just take it easy and I hope it won't be long till we meet again. With love, Irving

Please write more.

1945/1/10 Irving to Family, Naples, Italy (V-Mail, Slide 369)

January 10, 1945

Italy

My dear sis[ters] Hermine and Marie,

How are you? Again want to tell you that I'm OK and hope to hear from you the same. Other day I received a couple packages from Dave and from aunt Helen. It's very sweet of them to think of me. I'll have to write them too if I get time. At present I don't need anything, thanks very much for your offer. Please forgive me for not writing you, I will do my best and write again. With love, Irving

1945/1/14 Irving to Family, Naples, Italy (V-Mail, Slide 370)

January 14, 1945

Italy

My dearest sis[ters] Hermine and Marie,

I have just finished a letter to Dave and decided to drop you a line again and to let you know that I'm OK and have received a couple letters from you today. It was written in Dec. 22nd. As yet I have[n't] received any mail to this add[ress]. It should come in anytime. I'm glad to hear that you are well and also received not long ago a letter from Herman, but haven't answered yet, I will soon. I was sorry to hear that about waiting to receive mail from me, but by now you already know the answer. Will try to write you again. With love, Irving

1945/1/14 Irving to Hermine and Marie (Book 6, 205-214)

January 14, 1945
Italy

My dearest sis. Hermine and Marie,

It's Saturday night again and I'm able to drop you a couple lines to let you know that I'm okay and haven't forgotten you even though this year I have not been a good writer, but this is the army for you. I know you will understand me, to that, many of times I have begin to write you but never able to finish it. I'm sorry I'm not able to explain it in letter, but someday and I hope it will be soon I'll tell you personally. You know the facilities aren't very good for writing, sometimes I'll go over to the Red Cross and try to get a seat or a table to write on, but that place is always packed and you really have to be the first one to be there then you'll be able to sit down and write. To that you need patience because when you sit down you must concentrate if you want to write and in a place like that I just can't do it. Now I just can tell that I do hope you'll forgive me.

The other day I received some letters from you, and two packages from Dave one from Flora and Aunt Helen, I'm not finished yet?! Well, before I'll tell you I know you will be surprised, because I was. A package from the Meizlish girl. A 2 pound box of fruit cake and one box of candy. How do you like that? Well don't say it, just write it down and let me know what you think about it. Okay?

Now I want to give you some information what I did the other day when I was in Napoly. I have decided to buy some kind of a gift for the relatives, because I know they'll like it and it will come in for them very good. First I bought a very beautiful cassetta cigaretta case (a cassetta for cigarettes) This one I'm going to send it to Bertha in New York. It cost me $12.50 but it's very beautiful. She probably will write about it to you, when she'll get it. That will do for them and I personally think that it [is a] very nice gift. It has a bronze top and engraved is a [kastély] castle of Roma. The second package is going to the Meizlish girl. I figured that I must send her something, so I got a beautiful small table cloth and has the Volcania [volcano] on it. It's all hand work. Probably you will see it, she will tell you, I hope! I still didn't finish it. I'll have to get something to send Arthur and family and Aunt Helen. That will be next time when I'll get in town. I have written to all and thank[s] for the package. My letters aren't so good this days, because everything comes up when I want to sit down. You know it's not like home! I'll have to write Dave a long letter, today I wrote him a v-mail only. You can say it again, Irv, you are a bad boy! I know it my dears, but you must over look things this days. You will? Aren't you. Thanks for it. Just please don't follow me, if you can, please keep on writing me whenever you can. Okay, thanks a million.

Here in this letter enclosing a money order of $80 dollars and hope that you will receive it in the best of health. If you need any thing, please don't be afraid to use it. Next month I'll get my combat pay. I'll get some $80 dollars back pay. It's not much, it's not like home, as I said before. Let's hope that God will help me, and all of us that this war ends soon and can get back in good condition and one piece! The other night I met another fellow from Ungvár and he married a girl from Homonna, so I have decided to ask you if you remember those girls that were working for Lajos bácsi in Lelesz. If you know their name please write me about it your next letter. I'm sorry my memory is so poor that I don't remember any of those names.

Now again something about myself, it's not much I can say, just waiting for a new assignment. I hope that I'll get a good job. It can be five different things, but the best would be to get an interpreter's job. That means I would go to Budapest. That really would be something. It's nothing like hoping! Maybe my dream will come true.

Now please forgive me the way I'm writing, that at present place, that's the best I can do. Sometime when you'll get to send me a package, please enclose some stationery, maybe that will help me to write better. About those pictures to our neighbor, I don't know how would be the best. Maybe I'll wait a while and I'll get my awards and then make some new pictures and if they will be good I'll send them okay. I'll try to write you whenever I can and also tell Herman to write me and I'll do my best. I'll write to Dave and Louis sometime this week, With all my love to you from Irving

P.S. This chaplain at this depot will drop you a letter that I was at the services.

1945/1/14 Marvin Reznikoff, Chaplain to Family, Italy (V-Mail, Slide 371)

Chap. Reznikoff's Office
7th Repl. Depot
APO 372, % PM New York
Italy, January 14, 1945

[Typed]
Dear Miss Gluck:
Your brother Irving attended religious services at this Military Shteebl. He is well and in good spirit. That you miss him sorely, I've no doubt, but if your faith in God is strong enough, you will soon behold the day of his return.
We are very proud of him here. Be the excellent soldier he is. May the war end speedily and all your cherished hopes swiftly come to pass. [Handwritten] Thumbs up now!
Cordially,
Marvin M. Reznikoff
Chaplain, AUS

1945/1/15 Irving to Dave (Book 6, 215-219) pages 1-4, 6

January 15, 1945
Italy

My dear brother Dave,
Just want to tell you that I'm okay and I'm sorry for not writing you sooner, but this is the army you know, and I'm not doing the planning. Anyway please forgive me for not writing you. First I want to thank you for both packages, I understood it and I can say that you are a smart boy. I don't mind to admit it a bit. And the Listerine comes very handy over here. You know I want also [to] tell you that I have received a package from Flora, Bertha, Aunt Helen and guess who! The Meizlish girl! Please don't be surprised but that all came in at once. From the Meizlish girl I have received 2 pound fruit cake and a box of candy. It was very nice of her to do that. Don't you think so Dave? I want to tell you that since being over seas I have written her 3 times. And you know I have been [very fortunate to be] over here almost 2 years in luck [mazúldikesír

= מזלדיקשיר in Yiddish]. So now don't say anything just write it down and let me know what you think.

Also I want to tell you that the other day I was in Napolys and bought some gift [s] to send to the relatives. I have just wrapped up a very beautiful cigarette case (cassetta) and I'm going to send it to Bertha and a table cloth to the Meizlish girl as a souvenir of Italy. To the rest of the folks I'll send the next time when I get to go to Napolys. You know Dave I haven't forgotten you even though maybe you think I did, but it will come a day that I'll be able to prove it to you. At present place I'm waiting for a new assignment. This time I might have five different things to do. I'm just hoping for the best and that would be if I could get that interpreters job. I remember you writing about it not long ago, but that time I didn't know what might come up. I can't tell you anything yet, but let's forget the past and I hope that the Almighty will help

1945/1/15 Irving to Dave (Book 19, 429) page 5

me and all of us to return home in good condition and in one piece. Now my Dear David, don't forget to write me because I enjoy hearing from you. I'll say it, like you, sometimes I'll go crazy if I don't get any mail and when I do I feel happy and even the c. ration tastes better. So please let me know how you are and take care of yourself and I'll try to write you again soon. The only trouble is that the writing facilities aren't so good around here. Sometimes you have to be in the mood to write and even only a line like you used to tell me. Well Dave, I guess I'll close this time and hope to hear from you the best, and best wishes to you to the new year and I hope I can be with you at this time next year! With love, your little brother, Irving

P.S. Forgive me because I'm writing with pencil that's the best I can do around here.

1945/1/16 Dave to Irving, (V-Mail, Slide 340)

[In English]
January 16, 1945
My dear brother Irving!
I have received your letters from Dec[ember] 21. 31. and many thanks for it. I hope you're fine, and I hope the new year will bring us more happiness and a Victorious war ending then you can come back to us safe and with good health. May the Lord bless you. Many thanks for your new year greetings it was a pleasure to receive from you.-the family in Columbus are OK. I just received mail from them, nothing new at home just as you know it too. You boys there make history as you know it too. Till I see you soon, hoping the best luck to greet you where ever you are, but please be very careful whatever you do! Promise… thank you! Thanks for your timely photo, please when ever you want some thing just ask and I will be glad to send it to. With love, your brother, David

Please write soon.

1945/1/16 David to Hermine (Book 16, 241-246)

Jan 16 1945
Dear Hermina and Mariska!
I read your lines with happiness. I was very happy to hear that, thank God, you are feeling better. Forgive me that I don't write conscientiously, but you are on my mind always! I'm only asking you to take care of yourself. You better take care of yourself! About the company, it is nice of them that they pay you- about the girl from the neighborhood, she has the right to get paid from you. Write how much you pay to her, so I will send it to you. Do not take it from her for free! She can't say she worked for free for the Jews. So, there is no particular news here. The weather is pretty summery during the day. The weather is so nice, we can work in short sleeves. I believe that there are more people traveling here than there.

But let's leave this.
Yes, write it when you will find out how much you owe to the doctor, ok!? I am well, thank God. I hope my lines will find you in the best of health. I will attach a card that I got from our little brother yesterday. Thank God, he is well. Last Friday, as I wrote before, I went on a boat trip out to the sea, at 11 o'clock. It was pretty good. My stomach did not really like it, but nothing happened. It was interesting, we were calm on the boat, but there was another escort ship with a cannon and an airship, in case the Japanese would come they could "kenjék" [lubricate?] them well.

Anyway, if there is an enemy submarine near by, there is a type of machine like a Radio that picks up a signal where it is. So they are out of luck. Also, it not only picks up the signal, but it takes a picture of it too. And see it moving. Do not tell this to anyone! It is a secret. I only say that they pick it up with "radar." On the boat that has that, there is a guard constantly and nobody can go in to that room, only those who have a special permit to work with it. Hermine, if you'd like me to do it, I will send anything you ask me to send to you. Please! Californian orange, figs, walnut, hazelnut, grapes, tangerine…etc. Absolutely write to me what to send!!! OK ?
I'm waiting for your response to that!!
I don't really know what to write. I understand you about the boy. Believe me, Hermine! You didn't lose anything. And do not rush [into] anything. The situation is crazy today [and] nobody can be trusted. There are plenty of girls here too, but to find a nice one...Where could one do that? Do you know? I don't!!! Today everything is business. So, don't be sad. There will be a better world! If things will turn serious with you,

keep that in mind. If you get married, you want to live better and not to suffer. The man should have a good livelihood and should not be stingy because then you will only fight and won't live your life.!!! If somebody is not attentive, I'm only thinking, a kind of man who only lives for himself and the other party is only for his help. So, whatever you will do to me, it doesn't matter. But think about this, If you waited until today, then don't rush anything. Here in America, a divorce is nothing! And believe me, I have found enough Jewish guys here, and I saw who and what they are. And I could not find anyone worthy. To say it better, only "gyork" [maybe jerks?]. The boy who has a business, that's worth something. Definitely not a 5+10 cent or second hand [business]. No!? Forgive me that I write that way, but I don't want, God forbid, something to happen because then only God can help it. Yes, I am 3000 km away, but by plane it is a short time.

So, it is enough for today. Write a lot and about many things. I want to write to Ignác and Mariska too. Yes, thank you for the birthday wishes. It just came in handy. I appreciate it.
Kisses with love. Dezső

P.S. You know, those girls who get married today are only the bow legged ones. Yes fat, ugly, those who are afraid of the future. The majority will think about it until the war is over. No! You have time! So, I wrote enough for today. Kisses, Dezső

Dear Herman! Until 120 years!
Only couple of lines. So, here I will write only shortly.
Forgive me, but I only write it, maybe you forgot. So, I will remind you! You know, you should contribute, not divide the cost in 3 parts. You know, we don't live forever. You know, the proverb! One tomorrow God will save you, but you better be a good boy. You know for the good you get good and for the bad you get bad. So good luck up! And write! Kisses, Dezső

[On the top right side] Write the birthdays. I don't know any of them.

1945/1/16 Irving to Dave, Naples, Italy (V-Mail, Slide 338)

January 16, 1945
Italy

My dear brother Dave,
Just received the first letter to this letter from Marie, and I'm glad to tell you that they are OK. I know that you have written me too and probably I'll get it tomorrow or next day. Anyway I hope that you are feeling fine. About myself I'm OK and I would like to have a little chat with you, but I guess will have to put this aside for a while. Nothing else to say at this time just let's pray that God will continue to help me and all of us. Please let me hear from you soon and take care of yourself with love, Irving

1945/1/16 Irving to Hermine, Naples, Italy (V-Mail, Slide 372)

January 16, 1945
Italy

My Dearest Sis[ter] Hermine,
I know that you have written but I haven't received it as yet, maybe I'll get it tomorrow. How are [you] Hermine dear? Hope that you are well and in good health. I really would enjoy to have a chat with you, I guess you feel the same. But will have [to] put this thought aside for a while. I just spoke to a couple old friends of mine, I met them just a year ago, sorry I can't tell you more about it. Let's pray to the Almighty that this war should end soon. Please don't worry take care of yourself and my love you and best wishes, Irving

1945/1/16 Irving to Maria, Naples, Italy (V-Mail, Slide 337)

January 16, 1945
Italy

My dearest Sis. Marie,

Your letter was the first to arrive to this add[ress] and I'm very happy to know that you are well and in good health. Marie dear, at present I don't need anything, however a box of cookies I will accept from you. You know anything eatable it comes very good. Otherwise winter underwear or scarf I have as probably you have seen in one of those pictures I have sent you. Nothing else to say this time, just take care of yourself and don't worry just pray that this war should come to an end. My love to you and best wishes, Irving

1945/1/17 Bertha to Hermine (Book 17, 28-29)

[In English]
New York
Jan 17 / 45
My darlings!

I hope my letter will find all of you in good health. I just got home from the post office. I sent Irving a 5 pound package. I sent writing paper in the package. I hope he can use that V. mail paper from here. It is only 9am. I am only thrilled because the post man didn't read the letter I handed him. He just looked at the address and stamped the back of the letter. Here I am hoping that he will get it and important, I also am hoping that he will be able to go to visit our folks in Hungary and that with God's will, he will return back to the States as he left. No extra news that would interest you kids. I [have] been having a cold for the longest time and can't get rid of it. I started to take [an] injection for it and some kind of "vacagen" tablets [vaccine for bacterial respiratory infections]. It seems to help me and am hoping that I get rid of it. Please do write more often even if it is a few words. With best wish and Love to you all,
Bertha and Mannie

1945/1/17 Helen Perl Goldstein to Hermine (Book 16, 239-240)

Cleveland 1945 I 17.

My dear Hermine!

I could not imagine what was the reason for your silence. Rosewater was over the other day and he wondered if I heard anything about you these days because he was by you at Christmas and a few days later they did surgery on your appendix. Also he said that you are already feeling better, thank God! I was so shocked and grateful for this, I could barely come to my senses. So I'm asking you with my lines, if you don't mind, please let me know about yourself or ask Mariska to write for you a few lines. I hope I will hear that everything is good. We are all well, thank God. The baby is so sweet [and] she is getting sweeter. She likes to play, to eat and does not cry. She is a good kid. I don't know any particular news. Ann Rich will visit you in the winter when she travels through to visit her sister. Did you get any news from home? I did not hear anything yet. Let's hope for the best! I'm waiting for your response. I kiss all of you. Helen

1945/1/17 Hermine to Irving (Book 15, 7-8)

[In English]
Jan 17 - 45
My dearest brother Irving,

As always you are with us in our thoughts and, the only way to let you know is if we write a letter to you. We really should write to you more often but maybe it is laziness or maybe because there is always the same thing in almost every one of them we write to you. Flora was visiting here today because she was at her father's house and I gave her some of my milky gingerbread [tejès kalacs] I baked. It was really very nice and good too. With raisins and cinnamon. If you are at home I bake a big one just for you. Maybe I made you hungry with my little story and I am sorry but, hope it won't be long now. We received a letter from David and he is well but busy and, enclosed one of your letter in it. He knows we are always happy and glad to have a letter. I am well and so are the family at home. There isn't much news here only about 2 weeks ago Rosewater was visiting here in Columbus and also he wrote to me since - but I don't know how he will feel from my answer to his letter. I told him that no business - So that's [sic] is over I hope and, probably you feel much better now. Otherwise everything is the same old story, busy at home and not many places to go, only the picture show. Maybe on my vacation I will go some where - maybe till then you [will] be back. Received a letter from Bertha, Elsie, and Louis Schwartz from Iceland. He said there he doesn't know anything about VE day, but hoping to be back some time maybe soon. I was so happy to learn about the letter you sent to our family back there. Wishing we would get good answer real soon. Tell us more about yourself and, we wish you all the luck and good health to you. You know Irving dear, that girl never called or asked about you. We thought maybe she will if she will receive the gift - from you. So I close now and take care of yourself. My Love to you, Hermina

1945/1/17 Irving to Dave, Naples, Italy (V-Mail, Slide 339)

January 17, 1945
Italy

My dear brother Dave,
Back again with a couple lines to let you know that I'm OK and hope you are well and in best of health. Hope that you are still working at that position, don't forget even though sometimes it's hard or you might be disgusted, stay there and take care of yourself, I don't have to tell you anything else, because you remember and know what I mean. Hope that this war comes to an end, and as you know I would like to stop in and see you in Calif[ornia]. Best wishes and love, Irving

1945/1/17 Irving to Family, Naples, Italy (V-Mail, Slide 373)

January 17, 1945
Italy

My dearest sis[ters] Hermine and Marie,
It's raining again and this is called the Sunny Italy, one day it's raining and next day the sun shines. I can picture the way we used to be some years ago standing beside, beside the fire site and looking through the window, it was a small town, but still a happy one. The people are different, they are doing their every day's work and they live and enjoy their life. As Petőfi said, it's better a piece of black bread at home than white in the land of others. Hope the day will come, when we can enjoy ourselves again. Love, Irving

1945/1/18 Bertha to Irving, (V-Mail, Slide 344)

January 18, 1945
Dear Irving!
I am glad to learn that you received the parcel and that you are well. Hoping that you will not let me wait as long for mail as you did this time. I mailed you a box of assorted things and the v-mail writing paper if you can make use of it. I also received mail from Hermine. They're well, the weather outside here it is quite cold, it's real winter. I spoke to Jennie Frey the other day and she sends you her love and best of wishes and that goes from us too, take care of yourself with love to you, Bertha and Mannie

1945/1/18 David to Marie (Book 16, 248-250)

Dear Mariska! Until 120!
Forgive me, but I'll write this letter briefly. This is the last year left for our little brother in war and I will write V-mails from now on. Yes, thank you for your letter and please write, even if I don't write promptly. Ok? I wrote everything to Hermine already and please take care of yourself and Hermine, you too. And write about Herman also. Ok! Don't kill yourself with a lot of work! You know it's not worth it, because then you have to give more to the doctor! I hope you will write a lot again. Forgive me, if I don't write promptly. Ok? Write about what is going on over there. Did you see that girl who was with me? Not to you now, but to the hospital. Do you remember she got the perfume? She went to look at Hermine. It is enough for today. I kiss you with love. Write a lot. Dezső

The letter for Hermine is for you too!!

1945/1/18 Irving to Dave #1, Naples, Italy (V-Mail, Slide 342)

January 18, 1945
Italy

My dear brother Dave,

Again received 2 packages from you today and thanks a million for it. I can tell by that, that even though you are busy, but you are still thinking of me. Many times I'm reading your old letters over and over again and I feel happy about it. I also realize how busy you are, but believe me I'm very glad to know that you are in a good position and a safe place. Any thing back there is OK. Even sometimes a person gets dissatisfied, but remember it could be worse, that's the way I feel. Will write you again. With Love, your brother Irving

1945/1/18 Irving to Dave #2, Naples, Italy (V-Mail, Slide 343)

January 18, 1945
Italy

My dear brother Dave,

I hope that you have understood me in my last letter. Sometime ago you told me in one of your letters, so the other day I saw an article in the paper and I am referring to that. When you get time please drop me a line and let me know about everything. About myself I can't say much just one of these days I'll get my new assignment and hope that [God] will be with me and help me. Hope to hear from you. With love, Irving

1945/1/18 Irving to Family #1, Naples, Italy (V-Mail, Slide 377)

January 18, 1945
Italy

My Dearest Sis[ters] Hermine and Marie,

I want to tell you that I just received 2 more packages from Dave. He isn't writing, that means he must be busy. I figure this way, during the time he would write me, he sends me a couple packages. And on his packages it's always more food! He really knows what I want, anything eatable is fine. He has some good taste about it. Just ask him, he will tell you more about than I could. I'll write you another v-mail and tell you an interesting story, till then, love, Irving

1945/1/18 Irving to Family #2, Naples, Italy (V-Mail, Slide 374)

January 18, 1945
Italy

My dearest sis[ters]

Back up again with that story. This time I want to tell you about a package I got from Flora and family. It contained a fruit cake and toilet articles. It was very nice of her to send me all those, however some time ago Samuel was asking me if I need anything and he mentioned toilet articles only. At that time I told them I don't need anything in that line. That went on quite some time. So as you see anything eatable is OK. That's all for this time and I hope to hear from you soon, with love, Irving

1945/1/18 Irving to Family #3, Naples, Italy (V-Mail, Slide 378)

January 18, 1945
Italy

My dearest Sis[ters] Hermine and Marie,

I wonder if you have received some of my letters that I have written about those money orders that I have checked and wanted to know if arrived home or not. If you didn't get it, please write me about it, will you please. Just the other day I mailed another money order of eighty dol[lars]. I hope you get it soon. No news at all, just stopped raining for a moment. That's good enough isn't it? Well I'll close this time and I'll write you again soon with best wishes and love, Irving

1945/1/18 Irving to Hermine, Naples, Italy (V-Mail, Slide 376)

January 18, 1945
Italy

My dearest Sis[ter] Hermine,

Angry? I'm not I know that you must be busy or your letters are a little late. I hope you are in good health, I'm okay. Just got 2 more letters from Marie. She is sweet, she always writes me whenever she can. Sometimes she says in her letters that [she is] sorry for writing with pencil, well on a v-mail [it] doesn't make any difference and to me anyway it's OK until I hear from you. Say Sis. Do you know when is Dave's birthday? I'll try to send him something in the near future. I hope to hear from you. Love, Irving

1945/1/18 Irving to Marie, Naples, Italy (V-Mail, Slide 375)

January 18, 1945
Italy

My Dearest Sis[ter] Marie,

Happy to tell you again that I received 2 more letters from you today and glad to hear that you are well and in good health. It just stopped raining over here, I bet back home it's snowing. I think it's much better if it's cold and stays cold, because here it's just raining and when the sun comes up or shines it feels like summer in Columbus, but if you have a cold you can't get rid of it. It takes quite some time before you do. Please don't worry Marie, take care of yourself and my best wishes and love, Irving

1945/1/19 Hermine to Arthur and Flora (Book 11, 73)

Columbus Jan 19-45
Dear Flora and Arthur,

In this note I wish to express my thanks for your kindness and for the nice things you showed me regarding my illness. The flowers were beautiful and I enjoyed them very much. Your visits and everything else you did for me I appreciated very much. Many thanks again, With all my love to you all, Hermina

1945/1/19 Hermine to Friends (Book 11, 78-79) draft

Jan 19, 1945
Dear Friends,

Thank you so much for the beautiful flowers. The colors were lovely and I have never seen a prettier arrangement. They gave me many hours of enjoyment. I also appreciated the nice cards and calls regarding my illness and many thanks again, Sincerely, Hermina

My Dear Flora,
I take this opportunity and want to thank you for the nice thing you…

1945/1/19 Hermine to Irving (Book 2, 55)

Columbus Jan 19-45
My dear little brother Irving!

We just got a letter from Dave today. He attached your letter to it. I was very happy about it, but besides this I was waiting to get one from you as well. I know how busy you are and it would be great, if you would get the translating [job]. I guess, since the last time I saw you, you learned to speak many languages. And, with God's help you'll be home and you will teach me too. Ok? Although it's true that one can do without those, but it's good to know them also. About us, we are doing well and we are all healthy. The weather is pretty cold. I got a letter from Elsie and they are only coming to Columbus next week, because until now they were very busy. Her daughter did her exams and she will go to university in Cleveland to study. So, she has a big daughter and she will be our guest. Helen Perl invited me to visit her, but only in the Spring. The [guy] I mentioned, Rosewater, visited me, but I believe I will not hang on that case for too long. I don't care. You little brother, will get a good woman, will you not? Do you ever play chess? I always thought that it's hard to learn, but it goes pretty well. And it's very interesting. I am writing in a hurry to you. Until then, good luck and I wish you good health! With much love, your older sister, Hermina.

1945/1/19 Hermine to Mr. and Mrs. Walters (Book 11, 75) draft

Jan 19, 1945

Dear Grandma Mr. and Mrs. Walters,

Thank you so much for the beautiful flowers. They were such a pleasant surprise and enjoyed them very much. The colors were lovely. They gave me many hours of enjoyment. I appreciated your visit and hope to see you again. Thanks again. Best regards, Love Hermina

1945/1/19 Irving to Dave #1, Naples, Italy (V-Mail, Slide 347)

January 19, 1945
Italy

My dear brother Dave,

Again a couple lines to let you know that I'm thinking of you. The other day I have received a package from Louise Gill, I think I know what you meant with it. However the hand writing is different, anyway she has a pretty handwriting. Thanks again for the package. I have written about you home and told them how thoughtful you are. Everything came in good condition. In your next package will you please send me white almond and honey face lotion, that's very good after shaving. Hope to hear from you soon and take care of yourself with best wishes and love, Irving

[Note: I don't know the name Louise Gill. Perhaps there was a limit to how many packages could be sent by one person overseas and Uncle David sent an extra package using a pseudonym. - Sherwin]

1945/1/19 Irving to Dave #2, Naples, Italy (V-Mail, Slide 349)

January 19, 1945
Italy

My dear brother Dave,

I'm still waiting for your letters to come. I know you have written me this changing add[ress] cause the mail to come much longer than if I have a permanent add[ress]. Now I don't know how I'll make out I might change add[ress] again. This is the army for you. That will really teach me when I return home with God's help to stay at home and settle down. Yes I know what you are thinking of, but I don't mean it that way. I'll tell you all about when I return with God's help. Till I hear from you. With love, Irving

1945/1/19 Irving to Family, Naples, Italy (V-Mail, Slide 348)

January 19, 1945
Italy

My dearest sis[ters] Hermine and Marie,

Hope the news will continue to be good, at least we'll have a chance to go home this year. It's almost 2 years since I left home and during that time I saw you only once. Time goes fast, you realize it only went it's gone. I can almost say that I was in the States as long as overseas. Well, thank God for his great help, let's forget the past and hope that everything will come out all right. Hope to hear from you soon and take care of yourselves. With love, Irving

1945/1/19 Irving to Hermine, Naples, Italy (V-Mail, Slide 346)

January 19, 1945
Italy

My dearest sis. Hermine,

I was the happiest tonight to receive mail from you. I didn't know what to think why you haven't written me. I thought maybe you are angry or something. But today I know that you are well and in good health. I'm happy and will be happy to do anything I can for you and the family. I do hope that God will continue to help me and all of us. And anything I can do I will. The next few days my add[ress] will change again I think but don't worry, when I get to a place that I can drop you a line I will. Please take care of yourself and my best wishes to you. With love, your brother, Irving

January 19, 1945
Italy

My dearest sis. Marie,
Another letter received from you and I'm very happy to know that you [are] well and in good health. Sometimes I wonder what you think about me answer[ing] your letters in English. I bet sometimes you feel like telling me that why I'm not writing the way you do. But I can tell you why it's that way. First it goes faster and second is, while I was with my old unit, it was the best way of writing home and now I'm so used to write English that I think I couldn't begin to write any other way. So please forgive me and continue to write me any way you wish. Best wishes and love, from Irving

1945/1/20 Arthur Gluck to Irving (V-Mail, Slide 352) - Hermine's Illness

Arthur Gluck
178 East Frazbee Avenue
Columbus, Ohio
January 20, 1945
[Typed by his secretary]

Dear Irvin: [sic]
You no doubt know by this time that Hermine was ill and had an operation for appendicitis. I want to assure you definitely that she is o.k. now and you have no need whatsoever to worry. She was at University Hospital and one of the best surgeons operated. She had every care that she needed. We were glad to know that you may be able to get into the interpreting service. That may give you an opportunity to get into many interesting experiences. You may even be able to go into Hungary and Czechoslovakia and it would be a great adventure to be able to visit with your father. Moreover, if it would work out, you should take in all the historic sites. It isn't very likely that after the war you will be able to soon take a pleasure trip to see the old war area and while you get a chance to take in ancient historic places, you should do so. Sam has been turned down by both the army and the navy and he doesn't like the idea of being a 4-F, but he can't do anything about it. We all trust and pray to God that this war will be over soon and we all send our love to you. I am as ever your loving cousin, Arthur
ag/mr

1945/1/20 Irving to Dave, Naples, Italy (V-Mail, Slide 351)

January 20, 1945
Italy

My dear brother Dave,
How are you? I haven't heard from you for years, why don't you write me. Please drop me a line if possibly you can. I hope you are well and in good health. Just today I received a letter from Fred Yenkin, they are well and [in] good health and waiting for me to go back to them. You know Dave, it's almost 2 years since I left them. Time goes fast. Let me hear from you. Love, Irving

1945/1/20 Irving to Family, Naples, Italy (V-Mail, Slide 350)

January 20, 1945
Italy

My dearest sis[ters] Hermine and Marie,
Received a package of fruit cake from the US Army Mothers of St. Louis, MO. It's a long story behind this, anyway I met a fellow [Buddy Hunecke] and we became friends. Later his wife [Margaret] got a notice from the "War Department" so she wrote me again and told me what has happened. [see 1944/7/5 Margaret Hunecke (Buddy's Wife) to Irving (Book 20, 202-204)]. And in one [of] her letters she asked me if I need anything so I should ask for it and then she'll send it to me, but I never asked for anything. So this time

through this organization they sent me this package. I'll write them also tonight. How is Dave? Haven't heard from him. Love, Irving

[My Dad read the letter that he is referring to from Margaret Hunecke on Veteran's Appreciation Day at SHS - Sherwin]

1945/1/21 Hermine to Irving (V-Mail, Slide 355)

January 21, 1945
My dear brother Irving:
I can't tell you how happy I was, when we got 2 letters from you. One of them is a big one, it took only about 6 days to get here, it was wonderful. It was nice you received 5 packages in a short time and I was surprised to hear about the Meizlish girl's package, but I think it was very nice of her. I am glad you will send her too something. Listen Irving dear that really doesn't mean anything because a boy can change his mind even when it is serious not like that, you know what I mean?! When I talked to her in temple she was very happy and showed me the New Year card. Maybe she will be very glad but won't call me or show it to me. I write some more. Love, Hermine

1945/1/21 Irving to Dave, Naples, Italy (V-Mail, Slide 354)

January 21, 1945
Italy

My dear brother Dave,
An other day and no mail from you, why don't you write me Dave? I'm waiting for your letters and waiting every mail call, but no mail. I do hope that you'll write me soon. Are you OK? Please let me hear from you. I'm OK. Have written home also, they are fine. Not much I can say, just I was pretty busy today. I'll write you more soon. Please take care of yourself and I hope to hear from you the best soon. Love, your brother, Irving

1945/1/21 Irving to Family, Naples, Italy (V-Mail, Slide 353)

January 21, 1945
Italy

My dearest Sis[ters] Hermine and Marie,
Just a line to let you know that I'm OK and hope to hear from you again soon. I was pretty busy today, but I said to myself, I must write to my darling sisters to let them know that I haven't forgotten them. Yes, believe me that's the way I feel about it. I wish I could drop in and see you, but it will be much better when I return home with God's help and stay there! Then I'll be satisfied, but not till then, so let's hope that it won't be long. Love, your brother, Irving

1945/1/22 Hermine to David (Book 11, 81-88)

Columbus
Jan 22, 1945
Dear David,
I was very surprised that unexpectedly you have called us, but I'm sorry that our conversation wasn't successful. I hope that in my next letter, I will write the things that I could not answer you now on the telephone. I hope you have understood me this time, because I have surely spoken very loud to you, but it was difficult for you to hear me. The main thing is that, thank God, I'm well. I haven't been in bed much today, even though it's good in bed. However, that way I won't be strong. Even if I'm a little bit tired, it's better to be up. It's 3:30PM. I was only with Herman and Maria. Maria was cooking. There is plenty of food, I only have to heat it up. I plan to call the doctor. One of these days I will have to go to see him, so then I'll know how much he will charge. I think that maybe he would not have to take out the stitches because it appears to be disintegrating, but I'm not sure. Do you know that this Dr. Reel is a very famous doctor. He does not say a word, he is very serious, just his work is the most important thing. He was Flora's doctor, but for her the stitches had to be taken out after surgery. Flora said that he would not let it be there so long.

Wednesday will be four weeks since I was operated on. Thank God that I'm well. It will be a couple more weeks before I can go back to work.

There were visitors, especially from work. The secretary is a fine girl, and I'm a very good friend of hers. She was here and told me that the President of the company, when he found out that I was in the hospital, they were told to find out if I need someone he would send a person from work. Thus, he is a fine man. The girl told me discretely that his wife is Jewish and that they are very happily married. He asked the girl to find out if I need anything she should tell him. He will be of help. When I return to work, with God's help, I'll thank him.

Oh, yes, we received 2 letters from our little brother. One is a very long letter. Thank God he is well and will write you also. At this time he sent a V-mail only. He sent a handkerchief to Herman because Dec 16th was his birthday. He received 2 packages from you, one from Flora, and from Aunt Helen, and from the Meizlish girl. What do you say to that! 5 packages in one week. He was very happy for the packages. He mentioned in the last letter that we can send him and we can mail them anytime if the same postman is in the office, but not when he is not there, because it would not be good.

I have written a lot of things, so now I don't know what else to write that would interest you. Oh yes! I don't know if I should write to my dearest Irving that I was sick. I'm afraid that someone will write to him and it won't be me, and he'll be offended that I did not tell him. If not that, I would not even write it to him, but the thought that someone [else] has written it. What do you think? Do you think that someone has written it to him? Tell me - write to me - ok? You asked what you should send me? Really I don't know, because we can get it here, and it costs you money. If you think that it's worthwhile, oranges would be very good. It stays a long time, but only if it doesn't cost you too much!

Hey David, don't take this young man seriously, since he won't come towards me. After the 2nd time he called on the telephone, he wanted to speak to me, I briefly said that I'm well and hung up on him. He must have gotten offended, but Maria said to him that I can only talk to him for a minute. I wasn't interested [and] if he would come over I would tell him that. It's true, he finally did not say that I'm likable. The best thing is to forget the whole thing. His purpose was to succeed. It's forgotten, it's not worth it. If the war ends, that doesn't mean that [just because] the war will be over there will be more selection of boys. It's all the same. There'll be more vain girls! What do you say to that?

Here, I'm enclosing one picture that I have made a few weeks before, that is, before Christmas, because the other fellow's mother wrote to me and asked for a picture. Not that her son would be of interest. I know his mother likes me a lot. She is a fine lady. Some time I will send you information as it relates to him. So, you'll write me if you like it? My hair is dark in the picture. It's difficult to recognize me. It was interesting that there were a lot of visitors last Sunday evening. The person from Norway with her 3 year old son. When she saw the picture, she began to laugh and looked at me "Oh Hermine" everyone was laughing. They thought that I colored my hair because it changed completely. It could not have been so bad because the child recognized me immediately. If it could be the same for me now it would have been good for me to travel on a ship. I have plenty of time. Everyone who worked there went on the ship? Write when you can, and take care of yourself and relax. Kisses with love, Hermina

1945/1/22 Irving to Dave, Naples, Italy (V-Mail, Slide 356)

January 22, 1945
Italy

My dear brother Dave,
How are you Dave? I hope you're fine and in good health. I'm OK just came back from town and want to drop you a line. I met a sailor from my home town and [he] will drop in to see Herman in [the] near future. I still haven't heard from you, hope your letters will catch up with me soon. I hope that the Russian[s] keep on the move. I'll close this time, take care of yourself and let me hear from you. With love, Irving

1945/1/22 Irving to Family #1, Naples, Italy (V-Mail, Slide 379)

January 22, 1945

Italy

My dear sis[ters] Hermine and Marie,
How are you? I hope fine. Just came back from town and want to drop you a line. I'm okay. Met a sailor from home town and will drop in to see you in near future. Nothing new, hope that the Russians will continue their drive. Then it wouldn't be long that I could knock on the door. Boy oh boy! That would be nice. Let's hope for the best and hope that our dreams will come true. With love, Irving

1945/1/22 Irving to Family #2, Naples, Italy (V-Mail, Slide 380)

January 22, 1945
Italy

My Dearest - Hermine and Marie,
How does it feel to receive mail? I know it's very good so that's why I'm writing every day. I know when you come home from work the first thing you do [is] check the mail box. That's right. So when you do that, I want you to find a letter or two there from me. How is that? It's fine. Yes I'm happy, because I'm able to write you. Let me hear from you soon and remain with love, Irving

Give my love to Herman

1945/1/23 Gilbert Rosewater to Hermine (Book 16, 229-230)

Jan 23, 1945
Dear Hermina,
I want[ed] to call you last week, but I was not sure if I [would] find you [at] home. I also was expecting some mail from you but I did not receive any. Therefore today I decided [to] write you a few lines. First of all, would like to hear how you are getting along after your operation? I hope that's all right. With what are you spending your time? I suppose with a lot of reading, listening to the radio, etc. How is the weather in Columbus? We have here a lot of snow. With best regards, Gilbert

1945/1/23 Irving to Family, Naples, Italy (V-Mail, Slide 381)

January 23, 1945
Italy

My dearest Hermine and Marie,
Hope that you are well and in good health. I'm OK, haven't heard from Dave [for] quite some time, hope that he is OK. He must be pretty busy or maybe his letters are misplaced. Nothing new except that I have received a letter from Fred Yenkin and [he] wants me back to work. I told him in my letter that I hope to knock on the door in [the] near future, especially if the Russians keep on the move. I hope that they do. Till I hear from you again soon, Remain with love, Irving

1945/1/24 Evelyn Bossetti to Irving (Book 18, 63-66)

January 24 - 1945
Mt. Carmel

Dear Irving:
You can't realize how happy I was to hear from you again! I had been waiting for quite some time and just keeping my fingers crossed. I only hope that everything is alright by the time this letter gets to you and for the rest of the horrible affair! The only other word I got from you was your Season's Greetings from Italy. I was hoping that it would have been a letter but it was only a card! At least I still knew that you thought of me. I spent three months at Children's Hospital [Mt Carmel Hospital - see photo Class of 1945] receiving my training in Pediatrics and really liked working with the children there! Then I got a 10 day vacation which was spent very enjoyable! I really painted the town and the outskirts in the most fashionable colors of the day! I was out every night and never hit home before 2 in the a.m. I guess you might not think that is very nice but I did have a very good time! One of the boys I know, was home on a furlough and we did have

loads of fun. I'm so glad that my prayers had something to do with your luck! I did remember you in my prayers always. I prayed that I would hear from you soon and heaven help me! I did! I must remember to thank the Good Lord for that and to keep you safe always. Your description of the life over there "a living hell" doesn't quite emphasize it in the least! I know I've haven't seen it or even feel it but I have a pretty good and vivid imagination. But that will not stop me from wishing I were there to be of some assistance. But give me a little more time and then we will see what uncle Sam will want me to do. You see, I passed my Army Physical the middle of January and came through with flying colors! Irving - shall we set a meeting place over there somewhere?? All kidding aside, Irving, - - It would only be short of a miracle if we should meet! But remember, I shall be a <u>Second Lt.</u> Can you feature that!! I can hardly believe my ears or eyes when I hear it or see it! I have some "Coke" and carmel lain in my room. Irving - would you at least join me in spirit!?? I'd love to have you in my company. There are a few chores that need tending to so I hope that you will excuse me - Write soon - Love, Evelyn

1945/1/24 Irving to Dave, Naples, Italy (V-Mail, Slide 358)

January 24, 1945
Italy

My dear brother Dave,
Hope you are well and in good health. Nothing new, no mail from you, and you know I'm waiting for it everyday. Maybe it will catch up with me soon especially if you have written me. I hope that you did. I got a letter from Fred Yenkin and he wants me back, so I told him that I hope to knock on the door soon especially if the Russians keep on the move. I hope they do. I'll close this time and hope to hear from you soon. Love, Irving

1945/1/24 Irving to Family, Naples, Italy (V-Mail, Slide 382)

January 24, 1945
Italy

My dearest Hermine and Marie,
Another day and another line to let you know that I'm OK, but haven't received any mail today. Hope you are all well and in good health. I'm waiting for some of the old letters to catch up with me. One is a very important one, if you remember I was asking in that letter if you have received the money orders during the last year. Now I'll close this time and hope to hear back from you soon. My best wishes to you and Herman. With love, Irving

1945/1/25 Irving to Family, Naples, Italy (V-Mail, Slide 383)

January 25, 1945
Italy

My dearest Hermine and Marie,
Was very happy to receive six letters from you and happy to know that you are all well and in good health. By this time I'm sure that you have been getting mail from me. I've started to write you from the 15 of Jan[uary] and since then I hope to keep up dropping you a line every day. That's only for you. Tonight I hope to get enough time off, so I could answer all your letters. At present not much to say. Just I'm OK. Hope to hear from you soon again. Remain with all my love to my Sis[ters], Irving

1945/1/25 Selective Service to Dave (Book 7, 56)

SELECTIVE SERVICE SYSTEM
Columbus, Ohio

January 23, 1945
Dear Sir,
In reply to your telegram of January 23,1945.

You are in Class IV-F as a result of being rejected at the Induction Station on March 16, 1943 because of Varocosities marked right leg and thigh. You have this Local Board's permission to enter the U.S Maritime Service at this time and it will be necessary for them to file DSS Form 42 with this office as soon as you are their employ. Sincerely yours,
Mary F. Krivicich
Clerk.

1945/1/26 Irving to Dave, Naples, Italy (V-Mail, Slide 360)

January 26, 1945
Italy

My dear Dave,
Time goes and no mail from you, this year I haven't received any mail from you. I'm lucky that Hermine or Marie tells me that they received mail from you and you are very busy. I can understand that you are busy, but even then I would like to get mail from you. Hope that you are not angry at me. How are you getting along? Please let me hear from you as soon as you can. I'll close with love, Irving

1945/1/26 Irving to Hermine and Marie (Book 4, 122-135)

January 26, 1945
Italy

My dearest Hermine and Marie,
In this letter I'll try to answer your 14 V mail letters and possible two air Mail letters and to that one message to Herman. How do you like that? I'll try my best. The other day I told you that a fellow will stop in and see you in near future, probably by the end of February. Not much really to tell you, just as I'm saying in my every day's letter that I'm okay and would like to stop in and see you. It could be if the Russians will keep on the move. I'm glad to know that you like my picture, sometime later when I will get my awards I'll make some new ones. What did Flora talk about me after telling her that I have received her package? I hope I didn't mention anything that you couldn't tell her. A couple days after, I have written her or to the family. I hope to get something for them. The prices are very high over here. They think that we can't get anything like that back home. You really have to pay for everything. I wonder what Bertha will say about my present to her. I have already told you that I sent her a cigarette cassetta. It's beautiful. I was planning to send the same kind to Flora only with a little slight design. Today the prices are higher than last week were. So it goes. And to aunt Helen I don't know what I'll send, but will try my best, if you have any suggestion, please do so. I really would like to get something from Czechoslovakia; there I know, I'm sure I could choose something good for anyone. What do you say to that? I'm still waiting for that assignment. I hope just like you that it will come through.

I have written to Louis Schwartz a few days ago. I'm glad to know that he's okay. Did you receive my small package yet? I hope you did. Over here they call it "kemijó" [cameo] the prices are from $5 to $50. By the way I want to tell you that I left that work. If you remember that I work in the PX. Whenever I move or change my address I'm in a different place. Down here it's better than up there. About the weather, here it's sometimes raining and sometimes the sun shines. We had once snow. That was a blanket of snow, just covered the ground. It's a funny type of place isn't it? It doesn't matter much now as to me. It can't be worse as at times it was! Yes last year at this time until August and even September. It can't be told, but you know what I mean. Let's try to forget all that even though it's hard for me. Now let's hope the best. Haven't heard anything from the Red Cross about my father or family. It would be good to get in touch with the Russian consul they could do more than anybody else. When I get to Napoly again I'll see what I can do.

At present I really don't need anything. Just now I received a box of cookies from you. The same type as Aunt Helen sent me. I'll use the box to send a package home to Flora if or when I get them something. I'll write more about it, when I'll get the stuff to send. Thanks a million for your thoughts and I try to be a good brother as you say… and anything I can do for you or the family I surely will do it without fail. I just need God's help and everything will be fine.

I'm glad to hear about Dave that he is okay. I haven't heard from him quite some time. I wrote him though since I begin [sic] to write you. Maybe his letters are a little late. It could be, because I have just received 2 air mail letters from you and it was written December 22. However I'm still waiting to get some more old letters from you. Because I haven't received that letter in which I wanted to know if you have gotten my money orders. I hope that you got my letter. About Herman I want to tell him that I could have used him in helping me at that store. But don't worry about it. Just stay where you are! Also Dave, tell him that I said so! And mean every word of it. You don't know what's what! So just stay out of it and don't think that you are the Superman. I know m[e]n like that, but today they aren't. So take care of yourselves and my best wishes to you all and I hope to knock on your door in [the] near future. I'll try to answer your 2 air mail letters also one of these days. Hope to hear from you soon again. Love, Irving

P.S. Forgive me for writing with pencil, but this way it's much faster.

1945/1/27 Irving to Family, Naples, Italy (V-Mail, Slide 384)

January 27, 1945
Italy

My dearest Hermine and Marie,
Yesterday's letter was only 13 pages and at least I should have written three more then we would have been even. However today I'll try to continue with writing you a couple lines. First I want to tell you that I'm OK and hope that you are also well and in good health. Tomorrow I will go to town and try to get something for Arthur and family. Will tell you more about it later. Please let me hear from you soon again. Best wishes and love, Irving

1945/1/27 Irving to Hermine, Naples, Italy (V-Mail, Slide 385)

January 27, 1945
Italy

My Dearest Hermine,
Just a line about your letter of the Dec. 25-44. It's very difficult to explain myself clearly in a letter, however at present that's all we can do. You asked me about going home, well you have to have 32 months overseas. The best bet is if the war ends soon. At this place I have a job while I'm here. I have just written to Dave an answer of his letter. Please tell [him] to stay where he's and do the way it's best. Let me hear from you soon. With love, Irving

1945/1/28 Hermine to Irving #1 (V-Mail, Slide 364)

January 28, 1945
My dear brother Irving,
We received about 11 V mail letters from you last week, and it was swell to know that you are well and in good health. Also we received a small package with the necklace and the ring. It is very pretty and we like it very much and, thank you with all my heart and hoping you can see it soon wearing them. Maybe you will get a furlough and boy that would be swell! Where would you like to go? Maybe to see our father and the family - If it is easy! With God's help everything will work out all right. Love, and best wishes, Hermine

1945/1/28 Hermine to Irving #2 (V-Mail, Slide 363)

January 28, 1945
My dear brother Irving,
I want to thank you for the pretty gift you sent me. The letters made me happy too. We got one from the rabbi, told us about things we know for a long time, that you are a very good boy and a good soldier. We all hope with God's help everything will work out. Maria and I were at Arthur's house for Friday dinner. Elsie and daughter were in Columbus and it was nice to see them. They are very nice and asked me to come to Cleveland sometimes. David is well and so are we. I will write some more tomorrow. Till then, best wishes and love, Hermina

January 28, 1945
Italy

My Dearest Hermine and Marie,
Back from town and want to drop you a line and let you know how I made out. First I bought a very beautiful cigaretta cassetta for Flora and Arthur and a billfold for Samuel and a handkerchief [for] Jany [sic]. I hope they'll like it. Also I got a nice present for Aunt Helen. It's a beautiful handkerchief. She or rather they will show it to you I'm sure. Next time I'll get something for Dave. Best wishes and love from Irving

January 29, 1945
My dear brother Irving,
Just a few lines to let you know we all are well and hoping to hear the same about you. As always I am expecting mail from you, and we really had last week. The necklace is very pretty and we like it very much. Maria mailed a package to you, hoping you will like it too. Louis wrote from Iceland and is well, I will write to him and tell [him], you think about writing to him. How are you Irving? Do you have your shopping done. Will you tell me if the girl will answer for the present. Take care of yourself. Love, Hermina

[Class I-B = Available for limited military service]

Jan 29, 1945
Italy

Dear Dave,
Can't tell you how glad I was to hear from you. I have been writing you almost every day since Jan. 15. Hope that you have received it by this time. Tonight I'm trying to write you again a couple lines with pencil, because it's much faster this way and I think that the main thing is that you can read it and understand me. I hope so any way. Yes Dave I haven't forgotten about you and when we were together trying to drive your car. I was not thinking about that. Today I wouldn't be able to drive not even as good as I did at that time. That's the way it is. Dave dear, you really are a mind reader! I was reading the same thing as you in your paper. You have written in your letter about it to me. I can understand the whole situation and the same thing it's all over. I wish I could be there and talk to you..

I always wanted to ask you Dave, how do you feel? How is your hand, leg and nose? Does it still bother you? Please write me about it. Dave, do you remember what you told me once in your letter that it was in the papers. Well remember that and I'm sure that they don't want you. However in their point of view they want everybody. Also remember that I don't want you to be in it. I wish if you would have the paper in your hand like Herman then you could tell them to blow it, you know what I mean! Don't worry Dave just let me hear from you please, OK? Now I want to tell you something Dave, I haven't told you before. And that's between you and I and when you'll write home if you want to tell the family and just the family! It's up to you and I'll wait to hear from you…I'm limited service, reclassified as class B…

Please don't ask any questions and remember what I told you before. And that's why I'm here and back. I came back in August. This will make it clear for you. This time when I get a new assignment it will be noncombat job. Tell me Dave, do you remember that letter I wrote in August? If you got it, please read it over…yes everything changed, the other night I told Herman off, and told him to tell you. He is the type who talks too much and wants to be in it. Maybe like you said once, that I asked for it. Well that's why I want you to stay out of it, whatever you do. I have my lesson. The saying is that everybody learns for himself. And I did, as you know. Well Dave, I want you to write me about yourself and more often please. I trust in God that He'll help all of us. I could begin to write you a whole book, but the best thing is to forget it. Let's hope that it won't be long, when we'll meet again in the U.S.A. The other day I was in Napolys and made some pictures if it comes out all right I send one to you again. On this picture you'll see my combat badge and European campaign ribbon with 2 stars in it. One star is for Anzio and the other before the bridge head. That's all for now, Let me hear from you soon, my best wishes and love, Irving

P.S. Let's hope and pray till we meet again, Love Irving
Give my love to family back home

1945/1/29 Irving to Family, Naples, Italy (V-Mail, Slide 387)

January 29, 1945
Italy

My Dearest Hermine and Marie,
Another thing I want to tell you that I have made some pictures and next time when I'll get to Napolis I'll get it and send it home. I have my combat badge and the European ribbon with two stars in it. One star is before we made the bridgehead at Anzio and the other one is for Anzio itself. If it comes out good I'll have it made as large as the ones I sent you the other time. Will write again soon. Love, from Irving

1945/1/29 Private EH Nagy to Irving (Book 5, 28-32)

Jan 29th - Italy

Hello Irving,
I believe I fell short on my promise to write you immediately as I recall it's been sometime since I pulled out from your neck of the woods perhaps even by now you have moved. If you have I trust it's been home. By chance you're still in the same spot are you working in P.X. yet? How is Lt. Mathews and Joe? I have often thought of you all please give them my regards. I received word from home that they received the letter you helped me with in Hungarian. They were so pleased with it that even yet they speak of it and asked me to thank you for your help. I'm sure if I had been around you all this while I would now be able to write it halfway decent. If you don't know it you made a hit with my folks so if you get a chance to be east even if I'm not there stop in, the town is yours for your stay. Have had several letters from Finger and he's doing very well for himself. If you are still at the same depot and if the gang is there, Red Miller and the rest, give them my hello. Now just a word about my good fortune. I'm with a grand outfit and doing the work I like. Perhaps Lt. Matthews will be amused to learn I'm with the Special Service and with a Quarter Master Group. Also I'm working with a Jackie Vikes. He will remember him because Jack put on quite a few shows boxing to be exact for the depot. My friends have been writing me saying that soon there will be a big demand for P.T. back in the States. Sure would like to hitch my wagon to one of those deals. The only hitch is it's being worked through Washington. I really enjoyed spending these few moments, drop me a line when you get a chance. Your friend, Erv
P.S. excuse the odd size paper.

1945/1/30 Irving to Family, Naples, Italy (V-Mail, Slide 388)

January 30, 1945
Italy

My Dearest Hermine and Marie,
Back again on v-mail as you see I'm trying my best. I want you to get mail from me and so a v-mail a day comes very nice, doesn't it. My letters aren't long, but at least I know that you hear from me, and as you do when you come home from work the first thing is, you look for mail. And so there it is. One of these days I'll drop you a long letter. Till then, take care of yourselves and best wishes. With love, Irving

1945/1/31 Elsie Shallheim to Hermine (Book 16, 232-234)

Monday

Dear Girls:
It was nice seeing you both. However, we really didn't have much time together. I would have enjoyed my trip to Columbus if Flora would have been well. However, I see that she is a very sick woman. It worries me a lot. In regard to your affairs Hermine with Mr. Rosewater, it is hard for me to tell you what to do. I'm really afraid to advise you because I may not advise you correctly. If you think you do not like him maybe

it is best to drop the whole matter and not write to him anymore. Maybe your girl friend in Cleveland could tell you what to do. If you have an opportunity to meet someone else here in Cleveland, you are welcome to stay at my home some week end. In marriage one has to give and take and learn how to say I'm sorry, even if you are not in the wrong, to make it a success. Would you care to write this in your next letter to him? "My friends have been very kind and considerate to me in my illness. I have always admired those two qualities in an individual." I wish I could help you Hermina dear, but it is a hard thing to do so in this matter. Take care of yourselves. Love, Elsie

1945/1/31 Irving to David, Naples, Italy (V-Mail, Slide 389)

January 31, 1945
Italy

Dear David,
Have received a long letter from Dec 14 and a vmail from Jan 16. The address makes the difference. However I'm glad to know that you are well and [in] good health. By this time I hope you received my long letter too. Some time next week I'll send you a picture, before you get it, I want to tell you that it's not so good, I think I have too big of a smile on it. Let me hear from you again soon. Love from your kis őcsed [little brother], Irving

1945/1/31 Irving to Family #1, Naples, Italy (V-Mail, Slide 368)

January 31, 1945
Italy

My dearest Hermine and Marie,
Another day and another $ Dol[lar] we say, but to you another line to let you know that I'm OK and thinking of you always. I got some mail today from Dave, Arthur and Flora and some buddies of mine. So that means I'll have to begin and write tonight to all these friends and relations. You know I'm glad to do it, if I have the time. I'll drop you another line later, my best wishes and all my love. From your kis őcsed [little brother], Irving

1945/1/31 Irving to Family #2, Naples, Italy (V-Mail, Slide 367)

January 31, 1945
Italy

Dearest Hermine and Marie,
Just finished one letter to a friend of mine, he is [in] France. It's a nice place he said and likes it very much. However I would rather be home. By the way I want to tell you that I made the pictures and I'll send it home sometime next week. It's as large [a] picture as the ones I sent you the other time. However it's not so good, because I have too big of a smile. If you think it's good enough, then you'll give one to the neighbor at 42nd OK. Best wishes and love, From your kis őcsed [little brother], Irving

1945/2/1 David to Hermine (Book 15, 84-87)

Jan 31. 45
Dear Hermina!
Only a few lines so I can write something since there is no news here, everything is the same. I am very happy that, thank God, you are well and I hope to hear the best in the future also. I'm sending you a check for $50 that is for the doctor for your discharge. Don't cash it until the doctor says how much it cost. So the money won't go yet and do not sign your name until then. But absolutely write how much your cost was. There is no news here. Everything is the same. I got two letters from our little brother yesterday. Thank God he is well. I still have his old address. Oh yes, we talked on the phone and I will send money, 60.00 - next time. You asked me if everybody went on the ship who worked on it? No, only those specifically allowed on the ship, about 1000 people work [on it] and at least 50 went and at least 50 big dogs [important people] and ship officers. I will send the staff description about the trip [USS Crittenden].

Right now it is raining. Already the time is about 10 o'clock in the morning over there. But you know, I would not mind, if the war would end. I already wrote to the shipyard, but I can't quit because I am a critical man, so working isn't terrible, so be it. So I'm closing my lines for today. I wrote enough. I still want to write to our little brother also. At least to write a two page letter. So I will write again at the beginning of next week. Waiting for everything good until then. Kisses, Dezső.

P.S. Herminke, your picture is beautiful. Whoever I showed it to, loved it. Send one to our little brother. Herminka, you write to him. It is better if you write something like this to him.

P.S. Herminke, only your bank can cash this check in because this is a personal document and it is from out of state. Herman can cash it in also. Ok? Kisses, Dezső

1945/2/1 David to Irving (Book 16, 204-205)

Feb, 1 - 45
My dear little brother!
Forgive me that I haven't written to you in so long, but believe me that something always comes up. I hope you will understand and you will forgive me! Right? Yes, thanks for your letter and I'm sorry that you did not get a letter for the new year. I wrote a few lines last week. I hope you received it! It was a V mail letter. So, here there is no news, everything is the same. It started to rain today. The weather is like at home as fall approaches. What do you know about our father and the family? As I heard they will be joined to Czechoslovakia again and President Benes is getting ready to go home. I hope our father and the family are well! Believe me that I don't even know what to write. There is nowhere to go this year only work and work. I just wrote home. Thank God they are well! You know, as I understand it from the letters, I believe that they have become smarter. Mariska wrote a letter, it truly surprised me. Poor things, too bad they are not rich. I wrote to Hermin about the Presov boy. As I understand it, he is a stingy kind of friend. I wrote her to be careful and do not rush into it. I believe that she already wrote about this. So, forgive me, I'm getting very sleepy. It is already 10 o'clock at night. So, tomorrow morning I will write a few lines to you.
Until then, Kisses, Dezső.

1945/2/1 Irving to Family, Naples, Italy (V-Mail, Slide 392)

February 1, 1945
Italy

My Dearest Hermine and Marie,
Just another day and want to tell you that I'm OK. Hope that everything is okay back there. Haven't heard from the Red Cross as yet. How about you? If it ends soon, then I'll see what it can be done. But till yet not much I can do. Please let me hear from you soon, my best wishes and love to you, From Irving

1945/2/2 Fred Yenkin to Irving (Book 7, 14-15)

[Typed]
Frey Yenkin Paint Company
251 North Sandusky Street
Columbus, Ohio

February 2nd, 1945
Dear Irving:
We were awfully happy to receive your letter and have been wondering why we did not hear from you. I see your cousin Arthur Gluck quite often and he tells me that he hears from you occasionally. We hear from all the other boys quite often. Uri is out in the Pacific on an aircraft carrier. Ray Chittum is in India. Irvin Kohn is on a Merchant ship in the Atlantic. Henry Johnson is down in Florida and that's about all I can think of at this time. There isn't much news around here. Everything is going along o.k. The Government keeps putting out a lot of orders and restrictions on our paint materials but we seem to be able to fool around and keep everything under control. We have had snow since the 22nd of December - more snow than we've had for years. But as long as everyone can keep going we don't complain. Everyone at the office and plant are pretty good. Art has had a few teeth pulled and has been off work a few days but is back today and seems to be

getting along fairly well. Andy keeps the warehouse going and under his thumb at all times and always seems to be able to find enough paint to fill the orders. There isn't anything else new. Let us hear from you, and we sincerely hope to see you soon. With best wishes and regards from everyone. Sincerely, Fred Yenkin

FY:an

1945/2/2 Hermine to Irving (V-Mail, Slide 393)

February 2, 1945
My dear brother Irving,
We received 5 letters again this week, and I am happy to know you are well in good health. It is swell you got some mail from me too. The package you mentioned from St. Louis it was very nice but it is really a sad story, and I am sorry to hear about it. How did she get your address and where did you meet him? Was he Jewish? Did you get the new job. Tell us - will you! It is cold out today and have snow, too. Take care of yourself and with God's help everything will be OK. The news is very good. Best wishes and love, Hermina

1945/2/2 Irving to Family, Naples, Italy (V-Mail, Slide 394)

February 2, 1945
Italy

My Dearest Hermine and Marie,
No mail from you today, I hope that tomorrow I will hear from you. I'm OK nothing new. I'm hoping that one of these days the war would end. Please write me about yourselves and let me know about everything. Sometime next week I'll write you a long letter and mail my picture, my best wishes and love, Irving

1945/2/3 Irving to Family, Naples, Italy (V-Mail, Slide 395)

February 3, 1945
Italy

My Dearest Hermine and Marie,
Just received my pictures and sometime next week I'll mail it home and I hope you will like it. If you want to give any away to friends or relatives it's OK with me. I'll mail the negative too. But don't forget to tell me what you think of it, OK? Thank you. Let me hear from you again and remain with Love, from Irving

P.S. Give my love to Herman

1945/2/4 Irving to Dave, Naples, Italy (V-Mail, Slide 397)

February 4, 1945
Italy

My dear brother Dave,
How are you getting along? I hope fine. Nothing to say today, just I'm OK as usual. I have been writing home almost everyday since Jan 15-45 and so I'm just beginning to get mail too. Did you get my long letter I hope you have and understood it. Please let me hear from you and best wishes and love to you, From Irving

1945/2/4 Irving to Family, Naples, Italy (V-Mail, Slide 396)

February 4, 1945
Italy

My Dearest Hermine and Marie,
Not much to say just I'm OK as usual and hoping to hear the best from you. As yet I don't need anything however if I don't bother you much I would like to have another box of cookies. Thanks a million for your thoughts. Please write me more often if you can. My best wishes and love to you from Irving

Page 430

February 5, 1945
Italy

My dear brother Dave,
Back again with a couple lines and not lies! To let you know I'm OK. Hope to hear from you the same and the best. Nothing new that would be of any interest. I'm doing my best. I wasn't able to write to Mendlovitz, but [will] as soon as I get the add[ress] from that fellow of Eperjes. By the way Dave I might get to see him personally. You know what I mean. I'm hoping for the best. Some of the boys I met they'll go there and may be see him. So let's hope and will write you again soon. With love, Irving

February 5, 1945
Italy

Dearest Hermine and Marie,
Another line till I get some more time off and will drop you a long letter. First I want to tell you that I'm OK and hope that you are all well and in good health. The other day I received 4-V-mails from you, but I'm still waiting and hoping to get some more. I mentioned in 1 of my letters sometime in Dec. about if you have received a letter in which I ask you if you got the money orders through out the year. I had all the date[s] on it. If you didn't get that letter please tell me so. Love, Irving

[from Maria]
My dear loved Irving!
We did not get mail from you today, but I hope that we will get one tomorrow again.
How are you my dear little brother? We are well again, which is what I'm expecting to hear from you, too. We got a letter from David yesterday and he is well. He said that he wrote once to you, also. I hope he kept his word. Although supposedly he is very busy and does not have much time to write. Here there is no news. Only I can hardly wait to see you again. But I hope the dear God will help my dear little brother and soon you will be able to come home in the best of health, for which I can hardly wait. I'm asking you to take care of yourself. May God watch you in every step of your way wherever you go.

I think of you many times and I mention you a lot. I only ask you not to be sad and take care of yourself. I hope that everything is going to be ok, with God's help. The weather is very cold. Otherwise, we are very busy. But besides all this, I haven't forgotten about you my little Irving and I'm in a hurry to write to you exactly. I hope you will get my letter even if it's late. I wish you good luck now and the best of health. I kiss you countless times, forever your faithful sibling, who will never forget. And G-d bless you, and be with you. With love, Maria

[from Hermine]
My dear little brother Irving,
Since I have been getting ready to write a detailed letter to you, I did bring myself to it today. I know it will be a little surprising, but I hope you'll forgive me. So, to cut to the chase, I will admit that I had surgery for appendicitis on December 27th. Thank God I feel amazing. I would have written to you before, but you would have just been worried. I did not want that. As I said, I'm ok and I hope I can go to work soon. So, I wanted you to hear it from me, not from somebody else, like about my tonsillitis. I hope you will be glad that I'm over it. I mentioned it to David, what the doctors said, but he only knew about it after, also.

The symptoms came back three times, so it's better this way. I was in the University hospital and Flora was with me for 3 days and Marcsa also. And you are smart my little brother, because you knew there was something going on, since you only got a few letters from me for a couple of days. But since then, I was in a hurry to make it up to you. I would have written to you sooner, but I don't go anywhere so this way everything is the same. I would have gone to the movies already, but it's very cold. So, we were only at Flora and the family for dinner, which I wrote to you also. I got a letter from Dave. He is well. He sent me a check for 50 dollars and asked me how much was the cost. Yes, it is very nice of him, but you know, I had hospital insurance, so it did not cost a lot. I was in a private room and everything was fine. The same doctor did the surgery, who did it on Flora and he is pretty famous, the most famous in the city. Besides this, they also sent me my salary from the office.

So, it worked out well this way. I'm only writing all this so you don't worry, because everything is fine. And, if God helps me soon and, if the weather is good, maybe I will go in next week already. Since I made you think with my letter, I will attach a picture to bring a smile to your face. I had it done before Christmas and everyone says that it's pretty good, although it was developed very dark and it changed my hair color also. Write what you think, ok? I sent one to David and he loves it. He said it is a success. So, I wrote on it, to my little brother as a souvenir, but believe me I meant, my little brother, but it came to my mind, if you would show it to someone, they will think I'm some kind of old-maid, and you are my little brother...! But you really are to me. Write about yourself. Write, if they will move you, also.

...while I was sick and in the hospital my acquaintances were very nice. Flora brought me flowers and her siblings did as well when they were at home. Mrs. Walters (and others) also sent a beautiful bouquet of flowers. From work they bought me candies and all kinds of little presents also. And finally from my little brother a beautiful necklace...! You can see now that it came on time, when I thought about you so much. I will tell you, the happiness that you caused with your letter, since I had plenty of time to read it and there was mail everyday from somebody. You wrote so faithfully also. Later there were [only] a few, which proves that one can sense it many times if there is a change in the air. I hope you will be happy and will not be worried. I'm at home and I'm enjoying the good radio programs. But surely it makes me think. Mc Neil visited many times and would like to send a package to you with home made cookies. She asked me to tell you to ask for it and she will send it...Take care of yourself and don't be worried. With love, Hermina

1945/2/6 Irving to Family, Naples, Italy (V-Mail, Slide 400)

February 6, 1945
Italy

Dearest Hermine and Marie,
Just a couple lines to let you know that I'm OK and thinking of you. I will mail you my pictures tomorrow and one for Dave. I mailed a couple handkerchiefs to Aunt Helen. I hope she'll like it. Please let me hear from you and let me know what you really think of my pictures. Best wishes and love, Irving

1945/2/8 (a) David to Irving (Book 16, 198-202)

Feb 8. 45
My dear little brother!
Forgive me that I'm not writing properly the way I used to. But I hope you understand me and you won't mind. This week I got at least 5 V-mail letters from you. Yes, thank you for it and may God help [us] to hear the best about you after this also. I understand from your letter that you want a little face lotion. If it will be possible, I will send a 4 pound salami and a cologne. If they will take it though since you only asked for cologne. But, if that person will be there, who I know well, then it will be successful. That person already told me the last time that they will do it for me. I hope the dear God will help you with everything good. The news is that the Russians are at least 30 miles away from Brussels. I hope it will end soon! May God give that. There is nothing new here. My dear little brother, forgive me, if I don't write correctly. I'm not in the situation like you are. You don't have to worry. Promise! Ok? Thank you! As you can see, I can't even write, I am so lazy to write. I barely even started and I'm falling asleep already. This is how it goes now. How much I used to love to write in the old times. Right now it is not raining. The weather is pretty summery. I'm surprised that you did not get mail from me. Even if I don't write a lot, but I do write every 10 days to you. I hope by the time you will read this letter you will get more letters from me!

Oh! Do you know what I made for dinner today? Guess what? You do not know, right? Hungarian Goulash. It is not delicious, but it is edible. I wish you would be here too! Yes, I'm happy that you, my little brother, are waiting for mail from me. So, I will work on that [by making] this letter at least 5 pages long. Ok? Sorry, if I fall asleep until then. And I'm very happy that the packages I sent have arrived and you liked them. I got a letter from home. Hermina and Mariska wrote also. They wrote that they liked the necklace that you sent very much. Oh, my little brother! Promise me that you will not send me anything, just what I'm asking from you. So, listen to me little brother, anytime you can and will have opportunity and you will not be busy and will not be so lazy, like I am, (I know that you are not lazy) so please do this request for me. Regardless, if you don't get any mails from me, you [can] always write a few lines. Ok? This is the only thing I'm asking. Yes, sometimes send nothing else except your letter to me and mail. Ok? Forgive me for my long introduction, but I want to write to you and there is no news that I can write about. What I know, you don't care about there. I'm still in the shipyard. I'm starting to get bored of it, but what else can I do?

Forgive me, that I'm writing in such a silly way to you. Hey, little brother! Do you get the Chronicle from Columbus? Why don't you write to them? They all write to them. What do you say about Hermine's photograph? Isn't that excellent? It is, isn't it? But, it is enough about this for today. I wish everything good from God for you and may God give us hope that we will see you as soon as possible. I kiss you with much love your forever faithful brother, who will never forget. So, good bye! I kiss you with love, Dezső

P.S. I want to write to home as well tonight, but I'm so sleepy. I can hardly write. You can see it from my writing.

1945/2/8 (b) David to Hermine (Book 18, 37-42)

Feb 8. 45
Dear Hermine and Dear Marie,
This week I received a letter from Hermine and 2 letters from Marie. I thank you both for them. I don't know annoying special. I'm sending this letter by special delivery so you should get it on Sunday. I know you are waiting very hard for it. Even though I don't have anything special to tell, I'm very happy the check arrived home in time in a few days. I will send you another one. Please forgive me for my writing, but I'm very sleepy. I just finished a 5 page letter. I'm surprised that you didn't get any mail from me even though I don't write often, but I'm writing sometimes that I'm ok. I have become very lazy to write. The time is 9 o'clock. You can see from my writing. I hope you will be able to read it. I repeat, if you don't hear from me don't worry, nothing is wrong. The only thing is that I'm very lazy to write. I don't have any patience to sit down and write, I'm telling you the truth. If a person gets up in the morning at 5am and works all day then you get exhausted and lose your appetite from everything. But, I hope this war will end and soon, and everything will work out for the best and we would not have to work as hard. Hermine, if you are going to work, be careful and don't work so hard ok? What's new with the guy? Did you hear from him? And you Mariska? I forgot to thank you for reminding me to take care of myself. It is very nice of you, that word means a lot to me. You know if a person is looking out for you or [if they] could care less. Many things could happen and I want to thank you very much for caring so much. At this time, there is nothing special. Write about yourselves. How are you at home with the coal and water situation? What do you mean no water? For example, there is no water running out of the tap or the gas is down? What it means, let me know. Write what you mean, ok! There is a lot of water and enough gas! This winter only 2x was I using it for heating. Right now I am in short sleeves and the window is open. It is very nice outside. This is enough for this time. Wishing you the best of health and good luck. Wishing you all the best and to Herman, too. Please write even if I do not. Love and kisses, Dave

1945/2/8 Irving to Dave (Book 6, 220-223)

February 1945
Italy

My dear brother Dave,
Just finished writing home and now I want to drop you a line. At present I'm still here and maybe sometime later I might know if it will be like I said to you in my letter the other day. Even if it would be please don't worry, everything will be okay. I trust God that he'll continue to be with me and help me and all of us. This afternoon I received a package with salami from you. Can't tell you how glad I was to see it, boy I already have eaten from it. It's delicious!!! I'm going to get some bread and I hope to get some pickles. I bet that makes you hungry too.

I have written to Hermine and Maria, about this, and I bet after reading my letter, they'll have to go and get some salami. I'll say it again that's delicious and thanks to you a million. You know Dave, I received a letter from Bertha and she mailed another package for me. I'm telling you that she is really sweet. I mailed her a cigaretta cassetta. I hope she'll like it. I also mailed one to Arthur and family. Received mail from them too. You know how Arthur is with his big mind. Well I don't have to tell you, you know it. I'm sure… he thinks of something like that, after the war he said, you might want to travel and see the battle area. I didn't write them yet, but maybe I should tell him that I'll buy the ticket for him. I'm satisfied with that what I saw, and furthermore I don't want anything to do with it. I just want to forget it as fast as I possibly can. I'll tell him something in my letter or maybe, I'll skip everything and just tell him that I'm okay. What do you have to say about it? It's, if you are in something and you know how it looks. so after that you want to forget it. Here in this letter you'll find one picture and I know you'll be surprised. I don't have to tell you why, because you have already seen it. It's my mustache! Please let me know what you really think of it, okay? Thank you. Listen Dave, if you have a small picture that you made recently, please send me one. I still have your big picture that I got from you in Anzio. That's a place that I'll never forget…

Well that's about all for this time and I'm hoping to hear from you soon. Best wishes to you, and hope to see you soon. With love, your little brother, Irving

P.S. Thanks again for the package. Love, Irving

1945/2/9 Irving to Family, Naples, Italy (V-Mail, Slide 401)

February 9, 1945
Italy

My dearest Hermine and Marie,
Hoping that this letter will find you in good health and hope that you have received my long letter with pictures in it. I'm very anxious to hear from you. Not much to say just I would like to get a good assignment. Hope this war ends soon. How are you getting along? Please write me about yourselves. Hoping to hear from you soon and best wishes. With love, Kis őcsed [Little brother], Irving

HAVE WRITTEN TO ARTHUR AND FLORA - 2 AIR MAILS

1945/2/9 Private Rudy Matson to Irving (Book 18, 55-56)

9 Feb 1945
Dear Friend,
Pinch me if you can reach me. I don't believe it. Yes, 'tis true. Regret that I did not get your A.S.N. but perhaps it will not delay this letter and will reach you in good time. The above address was written several times this evening before this 1 note materialized so it should be correct - mine I mean. Thank Shorty for me and I thank you for your effort in securing that contribution the last night I was there. The best of luck to you Irving. How's the salami? Is that spelled correctly? Rudy

You are a pvt [private] are you not?

1945/2/10 Irving to Family, Naples, Italy (V-Mail, Slide 402)

February 10, 1945
Italy

Dearest Hermine and Marie,
Last couple days there was no mail from you or anyone. I guess my mail is misplaced again as usual. It always has to happen to me. Well, they say, maybe tomorrow I'll have more luck. Nothing new we [had] a little shower today. That's rainy Italy. I'm still here and waiting for the best. I hope that God will continue to help me. How is everything back there? Hope fine. Tell me Hermine and Marie, what size gloves you wear? Don't forget to write me, best wishes and love, Kis őcsed [little brother], Irving

1945/2/11 Irving to Family, Naples, Italy (V-Mail, Slide 403)

February 11, 1945
Italy

My Dearest Hermine and Marie,

Hello there, how are you today? Hope fine. Nothing from here just I'm OK. The salami that Dave sent me is very good and I got some pickles too. Boy! It's really good. In one of my letter I asked what size gloves you wear, I would like to get you and mail you, but with out the size it's no use to get any, so please let me hear from you soon. With love, Irving

1945/2/12 Irving to Dave, Naples, Italy (V-Mail, Slide 405)

February 12, 1945
Italy

My dear brother Dave,

How are you Dave? I hope you're fine. Haven't heard from you quite sometime, however I have received the package with salami and I got me some pickles to eat. Boy oh boy! It's very good, thanks to you a million Dave and I appreciate it very much. Please write me about yourself and about everything. Nothing new, just waiting and hoping that everything will come out all right. My best wishes to you until we meet again soon and good health. Love, Irving

1945/2/12 Irving to Family, Naples, Italy (V-Mail, Slide 404)

February 12, 1945
Italy

My Dearest Hermine and Marie,

Just another line to let you know that I'm OK and hoping to hear from you also. At present I'm still here, but as you say Hermine, my number will change again, maybe I'll get closer to Lew Schwarcz, or some place, I don't know yet. Don't worry I'll let you hear for me whenever I can. My best wishes and love, kis öcsed [little brother], Irving

1945/2/13 David to Irving (Book 16, 210-215)

Feb 13, 45
My dear little brother! Until 120!
I was very happy about your 8 page letter. And yes, I'm very glad, thank God, you are well. Also, with God's help, you will not go out to the battlefield in danger. But dear little brother, for that question you better give information as soon as possible. I promise I will not mention this to anybody, without your approval. Ok? So, you wrote that you are in since August and you are currently designated to class B. But in your letter you informed me that you still can't drive a car, like in [1]940. This is incomprehensible to me. I hope, God forbid, nothing happened.

...and you wrote that you will write home too. So, this is my response. And, if you want for me to write to you, I accept the same from you, exactly. You write the truth and fact and don't just play me. I want the truth!! I am going crazy with your letter. I don't understand the reason. Please write the entire case to me immediately. Ok? Based on my calculation, as I can see on the picture, thank God, you are well and your writing is good! Only one thing I can't see. I hope, God forbid, you did not get shell shocked, God forbid. But, if it's something like that, please write it and also [write] how bad is it?

I promise you nobody will know anything about this. But I expect the truth from you. But I will note this, if you don't write it to me, I will find out anyway. You know, I know where to turn to get information from Washington. They know everything there. So, little brother you better write it. Ok? Based on my calculation, by the time the letter arrives you will be home already. I hope they will send you home. You had enough already. But, if you will be there, please absolutely write everything to me! Ok? So to home I will note this shortly. May the dear God help you to manage to get a good position, where you don't need to get close to a battlefield. Just an easy job. And I will note, they should not say it to anybody that you will not fight with a weapon. Write what you want about this to them. About me, only that I still work at the shipyard. Don't be worried about me. I'm not afraid. They will not take me. There are enough young men. But they don't want anybody to leave their current job. Do you understand? But I wrote enough for today. There is no news here. My little brother, I'm sorry that I write so badly, but I have no patience to write.

Write the reality of the situation. Oh yes, little brother, I mailed an approximately 3½ pound salami in a package to your address, but if it's moldy just wipe it down, you won't have any problem with it. Ok? And a little bottle of Vida Ray [brand of skin lotion] that is very good to use slowly. I hope it will get there ok. Don't forget it is for the stomach and not for the face. And a can. Imagine, I saw a cheap one this week. And I really liked it. So, I will send it to you also. You know what? Gefilte fish. Kosher! I hope you will like it also. So, it is enough for today. May God give you everything good and the best of health. I will see you later. Kisses, forever your faithful brother.
Dezső

[Note on the side] I got a letter from Hermine, thank God they are well.

P.S. My dear little brother!
I can hardly wait for your photograph. I hope that you are well with God's help and you feel good. But we have to thank God that it has succeeded also. My little brother, do you get the Chronicle from Columbus? And the B. Brith news paper? I became a member also for [it] here in Long Beach. There is no news here. Everything is the same. Based on the radio today, the Russians took over B. Pest [Budapest]. Thank God our father (and the others) are already on the Russian side. I repeat, forgive my bad writing. I hope you will be able to read it. My little brother, please don't be sad about me. I'm fine. You just take care of yourself. You know, if God forbid something would happen, God save us from that, the girls and me would be lost. I only live for you anyway.

[Note on the side] I want to see you, so take care of yourself, yes. I will see you with love. Kisses, Dezső

1945/2/13 Dezső to Hermine and Marie (Book 1, 121-124)

Feb 13, 1945
Dear Herminka and Mariska!
Currently I don't know any news. Everything is the same. Yesterday I got a 7 pages long letter from our dear little brother. Thank God he is well, and he will have a picture done again. If it will be good, he will send some home as well. On the picture there will be a European Campaign medal. and 2 stars will be on it. One for the Anzio Beach Head, the 2nd for something else "Brigy hegyért" [Bridge Head]. So the important thing is that he is well, thank God. He noted to me in writing, that I should write it in Hungarian to make sure you will not show it to anybody. I should absolutely write it to you not to mention it to anyone! Not even to the relatives.

What I'm writing now, he does not want you to know, and [he wants you] to think that he has not even been on the battlefield. So, here we go with good News!!

I hope you will like it. And I repeat it, do not tell anybody, ok?! Promise me! Thank you!! So, my little brother, in the past few days was able to get a good position, that means, they will not take him out to the battlefield, but rather to an easy service, that means it's for limited service. For example, like an office job, phones, or kitchen duty. But not on the front line, that means they assigned him to class B service. That is why he does not want anybody to know about this.

...and do not say anything about what he did. So, you better be careful and not to tell anything about this. So, the important thing is that our little brother will not be fighting anymore, based on his current position. Oh yes! A few weeks ago he met with a pretty famous man, who he recognized when he went to America. And I believe, that he helped him. But this is enough for today. There is no news. It is not raining. I sent a package to our little brother 3 1/2 pounds of kosher salami and a little bottle of Palinka. And guess what, you don't know, right, kosher Gefilte Fish in a tin can. Yes, I will send you also from it. So, it's enough for today.
I kiss you Hermine and Mariska as well. Write a lot. Until I will see you again. Good Bye, Dave

1945/2/13 Irving to Family, Naples, Italy (V-Mail, Slide 406)

February 13, 1945
Italy

Dearest Hermine and Marie,

Hello there, how are you getting along? I hope fine. Today I have received eight letters from you and thanks a million. I'm sure you'll receive more mail also, because I have written every day a couple letters since Jan 15 – 45. However maybe in the next couple of days I won't be able to write you, but don't worry. I'm hoping for the best, Till we meet again soon. Love, Irving

1945/2/14 Irving to Family, Naples, Italy (V-Mail, Slide 407)

February 14, 1945
Italy

Dearest Hermine and Marie,

Thinking of you as you see with a couple lines and hoping that you are well and in good health. I hope my prayers will be answered, as yet I'm still waiting but any time now. Please don't worry I'll let you hear from me whenever I can. Hope to call you up soon. Boy! I hope my dreams will come true. Nothing else to say. My best wishes and love to you, Irving

1945/2/15 Bertha to Irving (V-Mail, Slide 410)

February 15, 1945
Dear Irving!

We are happy to hear that you are OK hoping that you continue to do so I hope you will get a chance to visit our family in Hungary now that the Russians occupied the country. Thanks Heaven. I wonder if they are alive. I want to send you a parcel again. Don't know what you need most. Don't hesitate in telling me in your letter. Keep well and take care of yourself. With best wishes from all of us. With love, Bertha and Mannie!

1945/2/15 Irving to Dave, Naples, Italy (V-Mail, Slide 409)

February 15, 1945
Italy

My dear brother Dave,

Hope that you have received my letters and understood it. In the next few days my add[ress] will change. I'm hoping for the best. Whenever I can I'll drop you a line. I wish to call you up. Boy! wouldn't that be fine. I'm sure it would. Let's hope and pray to the good old Lord and hope that our prayers will come true. My best wishes and love to you, kis öcsid [little brother], Irving

1945/2/15 Irving to Family, Naples, Italy (V-Mail, Slide 408)

February 15, 1945
Italy

Dearest Hermine and Marie,

I wonder where? Like in the song they used to sing a few years ago as I remember next few days will tell, but don't worry and keep on writing me and I hope it will catch up with me if not here, maybe? Never can tell. Let's hope and pray and I'm sure the Lord will help us. Will write you again soon…Love kis öcsid [little brother], Irving

Give my Love to Herman.

1945/2/16 Arthur to Irving (Book 4, 139)

Bonded Scale and Company
Columbus 7, Ohio

February 16, 1945
Prt. Irving Gluck
A.S.N. 35633941
432 Repl. Co.
A.P.O. 372
% Postmaster, New York

Dear Irving:

We have had a very cold winter in Columbus, and in fact the only thing I can remember to compare with it, is the winter of 1917 during the first world war. We had a lot of snow and no thaw. That has meant a water shortage in Columbus. That sounds funny I know. However, today we have it much warmer and I wouldn't be surprised that Spring is on its way. It may be that you will be able to find a way to be in Czechoslovakia at the old home town and see your relatives this Spring and Summer if the war turns for the better and I am sure that it will. The girls are in good health and everybody is in good spirits. We are working long hours at the factory and labor is awfully hard to obtain and everybody seems to be buckling down to do their bit to get the war over with as quickly as possible. With love to you from all of us, I am Your loving cousin, Arthur Gluck

1945/2/16 Bertha to Irving (V-Mail, Slide 411)

February 16, 1945
Dear Irving!
Just a few lines to tell you that we've received the most beautiful cigarette box you sent us. Accept our courteous thanks for your kind thought. Hoping that you don't deprive yourself of things and that you spend your money this way. I would appreciate if you can send us only a few lines that you are well. This will make us happy. Hope to hear from you real soon and that you are well. With best wishes, Love Bertha and Mannie

Regards from the relatives

1945/2/18 Hermine to Elsie Schallheim (Book 16, 236-237) - draft

Columbus Feb 18 - 45
Dear Elsie,
I am sorry for being late with my answer to your nice letter, but I wanted to tell you about Mr. Rosewater's answer to my letter. He is as always, and doesn't care to understand it. You are right it is hard to decide, but I will wait a while till I will answer him. I received a very nice Valentine card from the other boy, and he wrote on it a very nice little note. He said this was the best he could think to start corresponding with me. Otherwise I am getting along just fine and hope to go to work tomorrow. How are you and how is Jane? Thank you so much for the few lines you wrote - and I will wait till I have a chance to do it - or maybe will really drop the whole matter. Writing can't hurt and I will see how things work out. Maria and Herman are well and we all hope to hear the same about you. Our best wishes, and Love, Hermina

P.S. Thank you again for your nice invitation.

1945/2/19 Helen Perl to Hermine (Book 2, 203-205)
[Date written is the 12th, but mailed on the 19th]

Cleveland, 1945. Feb. 12.

My dear Hermine!
I got your letter and I was glad to hear that thank God you are having a good time and it is better to work these days. I am responding with a little delay, but the reason for that is because I wanted to send that person over who we talked about. We are a little late because he is already a happy fiancé. As far as your opinion is concerned, I don't really know what to tell you about Rosewater, other than what I said before, that he is a particularly good one who is diligent, and besides he is a handsome young man. He has a very nice store and he will make a good husband, which is good! Sweetheart, don't think that he will not find a girl here in

Cleveland. Many are fond of him. I don't want to talk you into him, because you have to love him. As far as Goldblatt is concerned, Mrs. Goldblatt was by us the other day and she said she wrote to you, but her son does not even want to hear about marriage yet. So my little girl, now I have informed you about everything, and you do the way it is the best for you. We are, thank God, well. The baby is cute. She does not cry, plays, and sleeps. She eats or is breast fed and I think she will sleep through the night without interruption like a big kid. And she likes dressing. It is so beautiful to see. She looks at her little hands from both sides to see what I gave her to put on. I made for her little dresses. Around the neck and around the arm I embroidered with different colored yarn each and every one of them. She likes those little dresses. If I dress her in one color or designed dress, I could say she truly is a miraculous miracle. She notices immediately and starts to pull it off of herself, and complaining, hm, du, du, du, bu, bu, bu. Her father wants to eat her, he loves her so much, although poor him, he spends very little time at home, because the Spring season is coming. He is mostly on the road, but I bragged enough about my big daughter. I will close my lines waiting for your response. I kiss all of you. Helen

My husband sends his greetings, as well as the lady who is with us.

Respond

1945/2/20 Irving to Dave, France (V-Mail, Slide 413)

February 20, 1945
France

My Dear Brother Dave,
Just a line to let you know that I have arrived to France, Marseille. I'm OK, hope you are well and in good health. You can continue to write me to my old add[ress] till I get assigned. It will be pretty soon, I hope. I was sea sick one night, but later I got over it. I thought that this ride would take me to the U.S.A. So, as you see, I'm hoping for the next one to take me back home. Let me hear from you, With Love, Irving

1945/2/20 Irving to Family, France (V-Mail, Slide 412)

February 20, 1945
France

Dearest Hermine and Marie,
Just a line to let you know that I have arrived to France, Marseille. I'm OK, hope you are all well and in good health. You can continue to write me to my old add[ress] till I get assigned. It will be pretty soon, I hope. I was sea sick one night, but I got over it. I thought that the ride would take me to the U.S.A. But as you see, I'm hoping for the next to take me back home. With Love, Irving

WRITE ME SOON

1945/2/22 Irving to Dave, France (V-Mail, Slide 415)

February 22, 1945
France

My Dear Brother Dave,
Another line to let you know that I'm OK and have been in town, and now I'm thinking of you with a couple lines. This place is much nicer than where I was before. As far as I'm concerning, I don't know I'm going to do, but next few days will tell. I'll let you hear from me again soon, With Love, Irving

1945/2/22 Irving to Family, France (V-Mail, Slide 414)

February 22, 1945
France

Dearest Hermine and Marie,
Just a line again that I'm OK and have been in town and so now I'm thinking of you. Here everything looks much better than where I was before. However I'll have to start learning French. I knew some when I was

in Africa, but since then I forgot what I knew. As far as I'm concerning I don't know what I'm going to do, the next few days will tell. I'll write again soon, Love, Irving

1945/2/22 Louis Schwartz to Irving (Book 18, 131-132)

Dear Irving,

It was nice hearing from you after a long silence. Hope for your sake that you'll get what you [are] trying to. So for myself I just tried to get in touch with my folks through the Red Cross after my relations tried without success. May be you'll be able to see them in person before I'll hear from them. I hope to get a 30 days furlough this Spring going home to the States. You can imagine how I'm sweating it after staying here a year plus a few months. My brother Joe was transferred a few weeks ago to an embarkation camp ready to be shipped and I just got a letter from him telling me he'll most likely going to stay there for 6 more weeks. I'm glad for the break he is getting. There is nothing more to write about myself. I'm fine though life is quite dull here. Drop me a line when you have a chance. Notice the change of the address. Love and lots of luck, Lou

1945/2/25 Hermine and Marie to Irving (Book 2, 57-60)

[from Marie]
My dear beloved little brother, Irving!
As you can see, I'm in a hurry to write to you. How are you my dear little brother? I hope that my lines will find you at your best. We are well and thinking of you a lot. What you mentioned in your letter about yourself, as I can understand, you just tell me, that you are well, since I know you can't do it otherwise. But, I'm asking you dear little brother to write to me how you really feel. Although, I can understand you and I know you have enough there. I wish we would be over with this terrible war! You know my little Irving, that navy man was not here yet, but I hope he will keep his word! I'm only asking, my little Irving, to take care of yourself very much wherever you go. And, we are asking the dear God to be with you and follow you in every step of your way. As you mentioned that you would like to surprise us and call us, I wish it was true. We are all waiting for that so hard along with you, together, in the best of health.

There is no news here. Nothing special. We got a letter from David last week and he is well. I sent a package to you yesterday. I hope you will receive it and you will like it! And tell us what to send next time as well. Your picture that you sent us before came out well. But, if God will help, we will see you in person. When you will be home and I can see you, then we can talk about everything with each other. My dear little brother, I'm only asking, whenever you can, write, even if it's only a few lines. I am trying to write promptly also after this. But, we'll hope after this we will not have to go through things and places anymore. And we are hoping that it won't last for long. Although, even a minute is too much about that. But, now I'm asking you not to be sad and take care of yourself. I will not forget you, not even for a minute. The relatives are well. Aunt Helen is wondering about you and sending her greetings. I am wishing you now lots and lots of good luck and the best of health. I am kissing you countless times, your forever faithful sibling, who will never forget. I will stay in the hope that I will see you again. Your forever faithful sibling, Maria

[from Hermine]
Dear Irving, my little brother!
As I mentioned in my last letters, that we got a few V mails and a letter with your picture that you mentioned, which we were very happy about. Thank God, you look good on it, just there is something my little brother, that makes me worried. It looks like you are keeping something from us. Whatever it may be, I would like to know and I'm asking you to be honest. The boy you mentioned was not here to visit us yet. But I hope he will come! I'm waiting for him so much, but even they don't know when they can come. So, I'm just waiting and hoping he will talk to me about you -we are very interested in that. Believe me, that I don't even know what to write to you because you wrote that the picture will tell it all - but believe me it is hard to judge from a picture and the mustache is a bit unusual. Whoever I showed your picture to before, told me that you have a mustache, but I could not believe it. I thought it is only a shadow. I am well, thank God and I hope I will hear the best from you too.

Last week I worked and it feels good to work after resting. I hope you got my letter with my picture already and you understood the case and you are not worried. Maybe I shouldn't have written about it to you, but it is better if you hear it from me and not from somebody else. Write, my dear little brother about everything.

I hope you are in good health! Write! Ok? Since, you are a sweet little brother and I want you to write to us everything! Ok? Currently, there is no special news. It is really great that David is sending good things to you. I would love to send also, but you can't even get kosher - stuff here. We have the bakery at Lazarus and they don't have it in overseas packages, what I sent at first and you liked very much. And last time I baked for you, I will try that again. Take care of yourself and don't be worried! Everything is going to work out. Write! I wish you could come home so we could be together again. And that terrible war I wish would end. Good luck and good health! With love, Hermine

1945/3/6 Irving to Dave, France (V-Mail, Slide 418)

March 6, 1945
France

My Dear Brother Dave,
Just a line to let you know that I'm OK and arrived to my new post. I became a Military Police. Well I guess I'll be pretty busy and won't be able to write you as often as I used to, but I'll try my best. Above you'll find my new address. Please write me whenever you can. I hope that your letters will catch up with me one of these days. I have been in Dijon and [censored] it's [a] very nice place. Well I guess that's all for now and hoping to hear from you soon. With Love, Irving

1945/3/6 Irving to Family, France (V-Mail, Slide 417)

March 6, 1945
France

Dearest Hermine and Marie,
After a long journey I have arrived to my new post, I became a Military Police. I guess I'll be pretty busy and won't be able to write as often as I used to, however I'll try my best. Not much to say, just that I'm OK and hoping to hear from you soon. Above you will find my new address. Please write me whenever you can and let me know how you are. I hope that your letters will catch up with me one of these days. I have been in Dijon and [censored] it's [a] very nice place. Well I guess I'll close this time and hoping to hear from you soon. With Love, Irving

1945/3/8 Louis Schwartz to Hermine (Book 17, 136-137)

3-8-45
Dear Hermina,
Was sorry to hear that you weren't feeling well and you had to go through an operation. Which explains that I didn't receive any mail from you for some time. But I'm glad that you [are] feeling better now and you're probably completely well by now. I hope. Yes, Irving did write a few lines telling me about his plans, and I'm almost sure he's going to get it, they need boys knowing how to speak several languages. It's also a big chance for promotion. I'd probably have done the same if I were in his age. Today I had a little disappointment. I found out that I wasn't getting my furlough in Apr[il] though I didn't expect it much but still I did hope, now I've to hope getting it in May. It's only one month but it's a long time when one is looking forward to it and wouldn't like to get another disappointment. I believe I wrote you girls in my last letter that my brother Joe was going to stay in the States as he hoped. Now I had a letter from him telling me for certain he is going to 've it for permanent. He'll try to get home for a weekend when I get home. It's probably nice there now that spring is getting close. I believe dear Hermina you should take advantage of it and get a lot of sun before you start to work again as I know you won't have much time after you get started. Or do you work already? I'd'nt be surprised if you did as much as I know you. They're some signs of Spring here too, as we [are] having plenty of rain and mud but winter may come back again. One can never tell about this climate. Otherwise I'm fine, hope you [are] feeling the same. Take care of yourself and let me hear from you real soon. Love, Lou

1945/3/9 David to Hermine and Marie (Book 15, 164-169)

[Dated by mention of Doublemint and Dentine gum. Envelope's postmark has month beginning with 'M' so March. The 9th is a Friday, but he was tired so it may be a mistake.]

Saturday, the 9th
Afternoon at 6 o'clock

My Darlings!
Forgive me, but currently I only will write a few lines. The reason for that is I work 7 days and 10 hours daily. It is 70 hours work plus 1 hour traveling. That could be 77 hours. So, you can see there is not too much time left. Oh yes! I forgot. I have a new job. Where I was before they only work 5 hours per week and it is very hard to live from that in California. The work is already done there on the new ships. And this way I took a new job at another shipyard where they fix junk boats. The one that just arrived returned from the other side [Japanese?]. In other words, we work with any kind of ships. It is like, we would work at different families.

There are many boys from Ohio, but they can't write home that they are here and neither can I, since they are here today and tomorrow they will be already on the way to Columbus. I did not see it, but others come from Cleveland every day. But let's leave this. Next week, if I will have enough time, I will send to you the good old chewing gum, Dubblemint and Dentine. I can get these on the ship. But don't tell strangers where it's from, but you can offer it. But I will note Hermine! One can not take this and if you will offer it to someone, they will love it. Also, I can get cigarettes, as much as needed. Although, all of these cost 3 times more. But it is worth it. I can put a few packages of gum in the mail to you -Write it, if you need. I will send Hershey too, unless you could get it there. So, it is enough for today, darlings.

I also got two V. letters from our little brother yesterday.

My little brother, thank God, is in good place. In France, at a summer vacation place in Marseilles. He is closer to home- U.S.A.-than he was in Italy, and I hope that he will come home soon-Forgive me, that I'm writing with a pencil! OK? It goes faster this way. Herminka, to you only this, that in your case, you do everything the way you like it. Arthur, Flora, the dear God knows who, your case is nobody's business and you will do whatever you will see is right. And, if the boy will talk seriously and you will love him, you will have time to discuss the case then. But I will note, if something goes seriously, the first thing to have is the truth! Promise! Ok? Hey, look at the Dispatch and you will see that

things happen on a daily basis, where the boy is younger. I already wrote it in the past, if I ever will like someone, it will not matter, if the person will be 10 years older. But, even if she is older, that doesn't matter. The important thing is that she can take care of herself and can handle his youthfulness. There are women these days who are in their forties and they look 25-30. So, that is what counts, not the age! It's rather how you are feeling. But I wrote enough for today. In about a week I will write again. Until then, I kiss you with love. Dezső

Now to Ignác, and to Mr. Herman too. Write to me ok? Greetings to Mariska too! Kisses, Dezső

1945/3/11 Hermine to Irving (V-Mail, Slide 419)

Mar 11 - 45
My dear little brother Irving!
Today is Sunday and so I want to write you a few lines because I know how hard it is for you to wait. We are all well and busy as always. That bad Hermann is sitting here next to me, he doesn't even write that instead of writing to you, he's having fun - and eating for Passover - it's not Passover yet, but we love it - anytime. Take care of yourself, my dear little brother - I hope you will have time to worry and take care of yourself - I hope that we will meet in person soon. We also hope to hear from our dear father and family soon. Hugs and good luck with love, Hermina

1945/3/14 Hermine to Irving (Book 9, 250-251)

Marc 14 - 45
My dear brother Irving,
I was very happy to know you are well, it was swell to find your letter when I came home from work. Tell me Irving dear, how do you like your new job? It seems to me you are OK - for it, maybe a little hard work. I wish we could see you. Yesterday I talked to Flora and she told me about your gifts you sent them - and

they like it very much. It was very nice of you to do it - she said. Hoping you received my letter and a picture enclosed in it. How do you like my picture? I am well and busy as always. The weather is very nice this week- just like Spring. Do you like it there? There is probably many new and nice things to see - but maybe the war changed that - Aunt Helen just called us and was asking about you. She received the present you sent her. And was asking for the address and I have forgotten [to] give it to her, but will call her tomorrow. We received a letter from David and he is well and busy and said hello to you. Rosewater told me in a letter that the Mendlovwitz boy is back in the States. Also another boy sends his regards to you. I mentioned it to you but you never answered - maybe didn't receive it. The soldier I met. The dentist from Cleveland. I told you he is like you - because he is a very good boy and I met his mother when I was in Cleveland. I am writing to both boys, but it is nice to receive mail - even if we are home. Take care of yourself and don't worry! I will write again. Till then, good luck and all good wishes. With all my love. Your sister, Hermina

1945/3/14 Marie to Irving (Book 9, 247-248)

Written in Hungarian 3-14-45
My dear beloved Irving!
We got a V. mail from you and I'm glad to hear that thank God, you are healthy. We are well too. I'm thinking of you a lot, my dear little brother. We hope that this terrible war will not last for too long. Although, I can understand it very well. I wish we could be together already. But let's hope that the dear God will help us after this too. I understood your address, my Irving. It was erased a little in the letter.

I just talked to Flora and she mentioned that she got a package from you. It was very nice and she liked it very much. She will be in a hurry to write to you, too. Otherwise, everything is the same. We got a letter from David too and he is well also. He sends his greetings and kisses to you. He wrote to you separately also. The weather here was pretty nice today. We are getting closer to Spring. I'm asking you again my little brother to take care of yourself.

...wherever you go or whatever you do. I can imagine how busy you are. Besides all this, even if it's just a few lines, please write. My dear little brother, I will be in a hurry and write to you also. If you need anything, write it and we will send it immediately. Yes, my Irving, did you get the latest package that I sent and the letter also, where I wrote about the money in detail? I hope you did! Also, my last letter. I will be in a hurry to write.

My dear little brother, I can't write anything particular. Herman is well. Did you get Hermine's picture? Next time I will have one done also and I will send it to you. I told you we got yours and I liked it very much. Now I wish you lots of luck and health. And that you could come to us soon. We ask the dear God to stay with you in every step of your way. I kiss you countless times, your forever faithful sibling, who will never forget. I hope to see you soon.
Maria

1945/3/15 Hermine to Irving (V-Mail, Slide 420)

March 15, 1945
My dear brother Irving,
I read over your letter we received yesterday and try to write some more for you. We mailed an air Mail letter too - this morning. Hoping it will find you [in] the best of health. I am well, busy as always. Hope to see you - maybe in a short time. Please take care of yourself and don't worry. Do you need anything we could send it to you. Tell me Irving dear what did you really mean with that you are and look different - I understand but hope you are well. Love, Hermine

1945/3/16 Irving to Dave, France (V-Mail, Slide 421)

March 16, 1945
France

Dear Brother Dave,
Just a line to let you know that I'm OK and hoping to hear from you the best. By this time you have received my letter in which I told you that I'm a policeman, well, what do you think about that? Please let me hear

from you and write me often. I don't know how I'll make out about the holy days, however it has to be, as it comes. Let's hope that next year with God's help, we will celebrate it together, Best wishes and happy holidays to you! With love, Irving

1945/3/17 David to Irving (Book 16, 217-219)

3.17.45

My dear little brother!

Forgive me that I did not write in so long, but I was in the belief that you are coming home. But as I can see what happened [we] still need to give thanks, even if your work becomes busy. At least you don't need to be out there on the battlefield. I feel better since you wrote last time that you were scheduled for limited service. I was worried that God forbid, something happened. But now I can see that you are being assigned there, so this way at least I know that you are a man. Currently, I don't know what to write. If you need any package, just ask for it and I will send it immediately. If you need good chewing gum, for example: Double mint or Denton, ask for it and I will send it. I could successfully buy a box last week. You know the censor erased the place where they wrote where you are or were. I only know about your old places that you were in Varsailles [sic] and you went from there. I don't know, currently the weather is nice here. I believe that you are close to the French Riviera, right?

As I heard the Mendlovitz is at home somewhere in a hospital. You know, I saw it in the Jewish paper. Breir the kosher businessman died a few weeks ago in his store. Poor thing, he was only 40 years old. It was early. Hey! Do you know who got married? I saw it in the newspaper. The Greenstein girl, the one we were with in the night club one night. Remember? I don't know any news about me, everything is the same. I was officially taken as a member last week at the B.B.Brith, if you know the ceremony how it goes. Hey little brother! Do you know what I did this week? I don't care, but I will write it. You know my car became very sick. It did not want to work well. It's going to be the fifth year since I bought it. You know, I can't buy a 42 because it takes a high priority and the 41 is already old and it costs $1200 and the 38-40 is about $1000. So I took it to a garage where they will fix it completely. With either a new engine or they will overhaul it to make it as new. This will cost about $150 and they will make it as new, fixing it from every problem it has.

But this way, I will have a new car. Currently it is in good condition. It is worth about $600. I bought it for $339. Do you remember? Today I could've gotten $300 for it. But let's leave this alone for today. It's enough about this. Passover is getting close. I'm officially invited to a house, but I don't know if I will go. Currently the weather is beautiful outside. The sun is warm. My little brother, I'm asking you to write whenever you can. But I'm afraid that after your training, they will send you to Germany. And those kinds don't really like humans. But let's leave this alone for today. It's enough. I don't know any news. Everything is the same. Forgive me, if I don't write correctly, but you are on my mind always. So I'm closing my lines. I hope the dear God will help you with everything good! Until then, I wish you everything good. Good health and happiness. I hope with God's help everything will succeed! Good luck until I'll see you again. Kiss you with love forever, your faithful brother, who will never forget. Kisses with love, Dezső

1945/3/17 Undated (a) Florence Meizlish to Irving (Book 15, 2-5) pages 1-2

[Dated by her having received the gift that Irving mentioned he would send earlier and last day of finals, which was March 17, 1945]

Dear Irving,

Well, I've just completed all my finals at school and I now have a ten day Spring vacation in which I can do all the things I've wanted to do for a long time. The very first item at the top of my list is a letter to you. So here goes!

When I go back to school after the Passover I'll be starting my second year of school. How time flies! It seems as if it were just yesterday that I started college. I don't think I've ever written you what I'm studying here. I'm in the College of Commerce, and a major in Retail Merchandising. Just think when I graduate (If I ever do) I'll be all ready to step out into the business world. But that seems such a long way off! Wonder if I'll make it!!! I really wanted to study music, but Ohio State isn't a very good school for music and I thought I'd better take up something that would be of use to me in the future. Besides I'm studying piano with a private teacher. I'm taking popular music but later I intend to take classics too!! But enough of me!

What about you!! It seems as if I have you and several of your friends running around in circles wondering what my little insignia stands for. You wrote that one of your friends, a very intelligent person, said it was a cat and that it could stand for a lot of things - Welllll - that interests me - sooooo - I think I'll withhold my explanation of what "it" is for just a little while longer, that is, until your friends give out with his interpretations. Let me know what he says. By the way Irving - what do you make of "it"? As I said before, I think I'll keep you in suspense for just a little while longer. Mean little devil, aren't I??

I received your package not long ago. It was very sweet of you and the gifts were really lovely. I looked up the place marked on the sea shell "La Spiagalla" [Italian - "The Beach"] on the map but couldn't find it. I also looked up the name "Ricordi" on the back of the charm but couldn't find it on the map. Is it the name of a town or does it mean something else - you must have done some traveling.

1945/3/17 Undated (b) Florence Meizlish to Irving (Book 4, 100) page 3

While listening to news broadcast recently I heard that the men with the 5th Division in Italy are going to be issued 30 day overseas furloughs to come home. Are you affected by this in anyway? I received a letter from Myron the other day, the mysterious Orient so he says of India, that's where he is. Well my friend, that's about all for now.– More later. Always, Flo

1945/3/17 Undated (c) Flo Meizlish to Irving (Book 17, 207-212)

[Date determined by vacation, has to be Spring break which began March 17-18, 1945 since in the next letter written a few days after she mentions the thank you for the package she sent back in January.]

Dear Irving,

I'm really determined to make good use of my time during this vacation. And what better use could I make of my time than by using it in writing to you. You remember Shirley, don't you? Well, she went to the hospital last night and was operated on this morning for appendicitis. I just talked to her mother and she said she's fine. As a matter of fact she's lying in bed just blabbering away and wanting someone to talk to her. My father had all his teeth pulled and since his heart attack last October, he's lost 28 pounds and he really shows it. He looks wonderful though and feels fine. He's watching his weight carefully now and eats sparingly - he has to - with no teeth. Shirley kids him about his teeth. Every time she sees him she calls him "old toothless." During my little vacation I'm going to read all the books I've wanted to for a long time - I just bought a very good book - "A Guide for the Bedeviled." by Ben Hecht. It's on the subject of Anti-Semitism. I also bought an album of records - "Rhapsody in Blue." I also intend to listen to all the music I can. Oh yes, Irving, did I tell you that I too am writing a book and this vacation will give me a good chance to work on it. The title - "On Such As We" - A lot of the experiences are going to be taken from my life. And you know Irving - I'm patterning a character in my book after you. Imagine me turning authoress - And imagine you, a character in a book. Oh yes! such is life. Don't mind me, I'm in a very silly mood as you must have gathered by this time! But I am serious about the book. I suppose by now you're wondering just how much I've changed since we last met. Ah, my friend, I have changed very, very much. The last time I saw you I was still very much in the adolescent stage. Now that I've come out of it and grown up - it's brought about quite a change in me. I know this must sound very silly on paper but it is very, very true. Several people have remarked on how much I have changed. For the best I hope- but then others are better judges of that than I am. I've changed in other ways, too, I doubt if you saw me now, you'd know me. Well, that's enough of this crude scribbling for now. I know this is a very messy letter, but really you have no idea how wonderful it is not to have to sit in a classroom and hand in every paper correct down to [the] last quotation mark. So I think I can take it for granted that you'll forgive this messy scrawling. Until next time, As ever, Flo

1945/3/18 Hermine to Irving (V-Mail, Slide 422)

[In English]
March 18, 1945
My dearest brother Irving.
Today is Sunday evening and we were at the neighborhood show. It was a good picture but it was raining and we had a walk coming home. But it was so nice like a real spring day when Maria and I left home. You remember when we were together on your furlough and started out it was raining hope it won't be long and

we'll be together again. We all are well, hope to hear the same about you. Take care of yourself and don't worry. Good luck and best wishes, with all my love, Hermina

1945/3/18 Undated Marie to Irving (Book 16, 227)

[Dated after 3/15 because Marie mentions that she will send a picture. Since Hermine mentions the rain in the last letter, and that she took another picture, this seems like a good spot to put it.]

Written in Hungarian

My dear beloved little brother, Irving!
It has been already a few days that we did not get a letter from you. But I hope that my lines will find you in the best of health. We are well and thinking about you a lot. And I hope the dear God will help you after this too. Yes, my Irving as you can see I can hardly wait to see you again. And that is why I decided to come to visit you. I hope you will recognize me in it. And I hope that we won't need to wait any longer to be together here, where it is the best, in America. There is no particular news. The weather is still cold. Now, I'm asking you my little brother to take care of yourself, wherever you go. God bless you! And I wish you good luck and health. Now I'm kissing you countless times. Forever your faithful sibling, who will never forget. With Love,
Maria
Please write your opinion about the picture.

1945/3/20 Irving to Family, France (V-Mail, Slide 424)

March 20, 1944
France

My dearest Hermine and Marie,
Just another line to let you know that I'm OK and hoping to hear from you soon. This week I have mailed a P.T.A. money order 11,500 franks, which will be paid out as $272.01¢. If you need of anything please help yourselves and the rest of it put in the bank for me. You know Marie, I have [not] received that letter in which you have written me the amount I have. It might come in one of these days. Nothing new just hoping to hear from you the best. Since 17th of February I have [not] received any mail, now I'm waiting any day that it will catch up with me. Will write you again soon. With all my love, your brother Irving

Give regards to Herman and relatives. Irv

1945/3/21 Undated Flo Meizlish to Irving (Book 17, 214-217)

[Dated by being a few days after Shirley's surgery]

Dear Irving,
I'm sitting here in Shirley's room keeping her company. She's feeling fine now, she was going to write you a few words but she's still a little weak. So she said to say hello and give you her best. Her mother just came in and brought her some mail from her boyfriend. I told Shirley that when she reads that letter her temperature will go up to 105. Just as I said that the nurse came in to take her temperature, but it was normal. So I told Shirley her boyfriend must be slipping. Naturally she didn't agree. We have to be careful what we say in front of her because she can't laugh, it's painful for her. Tomorrow she's going to sit up and walk a few steps. She smiled and said "Gee, I feel just like I've had a baby." Irving, I remember you told me you were in some way related to Alma Gluck, the opera singer? Well, there's a very famous book out now "The Valley of Decision" by Marcia Davenport who is the daughter of Alma Gluck. And in her book there is quite a bit about Czechoslovakia. Do you know of her? I went horseback riding yesterday and Ohhhh Irving, am I sore to-day. I had the most horrible, and dumbest horse around. All he wanted to do was gallop through the mud and run through bushes and under low hanging trees. I was almost knocked off twice by low hanging branches. My whole outfit was splashed with mud, I even had it in my hair. But am I sore- It takes me a half an hour to sit down - Go on - laugh!! Well, this is just a short letter, I know, but this is all I have to write about. More later. Flo

P.S. It was very sweet of your tent mate to write me that short note - in your last letter. I'm glad you all liked the box.

Thursday, March 22 '45

Dear Irving,

I was looking through a magazine just now and came across an article on Else Lasker Schneider, one of the greatest of all Jewish writers. One of her most famous poems was also printed. While reading it I immediately thought of you, when you read it you'll see why. I'm sure you'll like it as much as I did, it's very lovely and very timely, even though it was written many years ago. It was originally in German and this is the English translation.

A thousand years old is the Temple in Prague, dusty and gray is it's old age, and the old fathers closed its gates.

But now their sons go out to battle, the broken star of the Synagogue is awakened and it blesses its young Jewish knights.

Like a star of good fortune it rises above the Jewish city of Bohemia, of the purest gold like the stars in the sky, and again, beneath its glory, mothers are praying.

I think that is one of the most beautiful pieces I have ever read. Don't you agree? There was another little saying of hers that I also enjoyed very much -

"Nicht Hebraeerin der Hebraeer willen, aber Gottes willen."

"Not a Hebrew for the Hebrew's sake, but for God's sake"

Tuesday, I have to go back to college, this vacation has been so wonderful I hate to think of going back. But all good things must come to an end. I shouldn't say that because I do like school very much - I guess I'm just lazy. I like to loaf around - but then who doesn't? My father said last night - "Babe you're getting awfully lazy lately, aren't you?" I said, "Yes, daddy, I guess I am." Whereupon he answered - "Look you're even too lazy to deny it" So I said, "Sure if I deny it, I'll just have to argue with you over whether I am or not - and I'm just too lazy to argue!!" Terrible aren't I?? Well Irving I think I'll sit back now for a while and wait for you to answer a few of my letters. By the way, have you figured out my little insignia yet? Flo

1945/3/23 Hermine to Irving (V-Mail, Slide 425)

[In English]

March 23, 1945

My dearest brother Irving,

An nother [sic] day and so I write again hope you are well in good health. We haven't have [sic] any mail since you told us you became an M.P. You are probably busy but I miss your mail so much. Did our mail go after you, or maybe you didn't get it yet. We are all well and so is David too. Herman is working now. I came home and had to cook but it was good - fish. On Friday evening - you are with us if not personally, but in our hearts and thoughts. Don't worry and take care of yourself. Good luck and best wishes. Love, Hermina

1945/3/25 Hermine to Irving #1 (V-Mail, Slide 428)

March 25, 1945

My dearest brother Irving,

Today and always I think about you hope you are well. We haven't have [sic] mail only 3 V mail since you are in France. You are busy but we miss the letters so much. Otherwise we all are well and hope you received my picture, tell me if you liked it. Don't worry I am well and take care of yourself. With best wishes and good luck to you. I will write more tomorrow! We had cleaning for the Passover holly [sic] day. Hope to see you soon. Love, Hermina

1945/3/25 Hermine to Irving #2 (V-Mail, Slide 426)

March 25, 1945

My dearest brother Irving,

Today we received the so long waited letter and I was happy to know you are well. Also the 3 pictures you mailed to us. They are very nice and it looks like [a] painting. We saw those places when we were together hope next Passover we'll all be together again. Did you get any mail from us lately and the picture I sent you. Take care of yourself and God bless you. Love your sister, Hermina

1945/3/25 Hermine to Irving #3 (V-Mail, Slide 427)

March 25, 1945

My dearest brother Irving,

I just wrote a letter to you but want to write another one. Wednesday evening is our Passover holly days starts and we'll miss you and pray for you and all our dear ones. Hoping next year you and our dear father and Louis will be with us again. So don't worry and God will help us. Take care of yourself and don't worry. I think your new job is better than before. Good luck and best wishes. My writing is terrible but I am in a hurry. Love, Hermina

1945/3/26 Irving to Dave, France (V-Mail, Slide 429)

March 26, 1945
France

Dear Brother Dave,

It's been a long time since I've written you last, however don't worry I haven't forgotten you. I got a few letters from you the other day, but I didn't answer it as yet, but I'll as soon as I get some time off. As you know on my new job, I have to stay clean at all times and that takes up my spare time. I'm stationed in a nice town, it's not bad. I'm hoping to see you soon, With all my Love and best wishes to the holy days, Irving

1945/3/27 Irving to Family, France (V-Mail, Slide 430)

March 27, 1945
France

My Dearest Hermine and Marie,

It's been a long time since I have written you last, but don't worry I haven't forgotten you, I have to stay clean at all times. That takes up on my spare time. Yet I'm stationed in a nice town, it's not bad, I'm hoping to see you soon, with love, and best wishes to you and to the holy days, Irving

1945/3/28 Marie to David (Book 9, 7-8)

3-28-45
Dear David!

It's been a few days since we got a letter from you. But I hope that my lines will find you in the best of health! We are well. We just got a letter from our little brother yesterday. Thank God, he is well. I hope that the dear God will help him after this also. Otherwise, everything is the same. Yes, I already wrote to you about the citizen[ship] papers. They just called me in to the first interview. You know, it is just before the holidays and I could barely get witnesses since the ones I listed could not come. Flora called and moved it to another day. Otherwise, it was moved to Saturday. Today will come one of her girl siblings. You know, Flora, me and Hermine sent our papers in at the same time, but they called us in separately. And they did not call Hermine in yet. Now I hope you will have a nice Passover celebration. The weather here is pretty nice now and it's warm. We are busy today also and I'm pretty busy with work also. You better take care and watch where you go, and write! They talked about it yesterday that the war with the Germans ended, but unfortunately it was not true. Let's hope that yes [it will be]. Let's hope that it won't last for too long which we have been waiting for so hard. Now I'm closing my lines and I wish you everything good and lots of luck. Until I will see you again. I'm sending my best and kisses to you, Maria

Hermine and Herman are well also.

[In English]
March 29, 1945
My dearest brother Irving,
I am sorry for not writing to you more often but the time goes fast and there is so much to do. Especially before the holly days. I started the house cleaning and it is really a big job. But tonight just like always you are in my mind and to let you know, it is a good way to write and I feel better too. It isn't as used to be when you were at home because Herman is working - and if the war is over and you are with us we'll do it like before. We all are well and don't worry! Take care of yourself. Love, Hermina

March 29, 1945
My dearest brother Irving,
I was very happy to receive a V mail letter from you a couple days ago. I think it is nice for you being a police man and I hope you like it too. Take care of yourself and tell us something about yourself. We all are well and we are busy with our Passover holly days. Herman went to the temple this morning but is working now. I am working too but this is a different place and have to do it. Flora likes the gifts you sent them and thank you for the pretty pictures you sent us they are real pretty and I like them. I will write you again. Till then good luck and best regards. Love,
Hermina

[In English]
March 31, 1945
My dearest brother Irving,
Hope you received some mail from home till now and also my picture what I sent to you. How do you like it? I wish could talk to you - boy would that be swell! But we hope the time will come in soon. The news is good and the only thing is that you take care of yourself and don't worry about [a] thing. We at home have everything we need we all are well. When [the] day will come and you are with us again then it will make us much happier. Let's hope it won't be long, and this war is over. Good luck. Love, Hermina

April 1, 1945
My dearest brother Irving,
We received a V mail letter from you a couple days ago and I am happy to know you are ok. Hope you are well and like your new job. I think it is good and wish [I] could see you as a policeman. Everybody thinks it is very nice. Otherwise everything is all right and we all are well. Today was Easter was a very nice day but it is raining now. Is the climate different there from the others you [have] been? Do you speak French yet? Hope to see you soon. Take care of yourself and don't worry. God bless you! I will try to write to you more often. Love, Hermina

April 6, 1945
My dearest brother Irving,
We received a V mail letter from you yesterday and we are very happy to know you are well and we also are glad to know you like your new job. It is hard but God will help us all. So don't worry to take care of yourself. Maria and I were at the show last night it was my birthday and I thought it is nice to do that much. Hope to spend time next year together with you. Good luck love and best wishes, Hermina

April 6, 1945

My dearest brother Irving,

As always so on tonight I want to write a few lines just to tell you how much we think about you. We all are well, hope to hear the same about you. I showed your picture in the bank to the lady you know her, and likes it very much. I think they all are good pictures. I cashed the check and put it in the bank for you. I will write again tomorrow. Till then good luck and all good wishes to you. With all my love, Hermina

1945/4/9 Undated Dezső to Irving (Book 1, 211-217) - dated from Benes return to Kosice

My little brother!!

I know well, that you are angry at me!! But please forgive me!! Ok!! I'm sorry that I can't be beside you! But I did everything to be where you are! But this is how it goes, if you want to go, nobody needs it, but if you don't, they will take you. My dear little brother! I'm repeatedly asking you to forgive me for my long silence. But I hope the dear God will help you and you will be here with me shortly. My little brother, I learned one thing since I'm in California, that is, don't believe and trust in anyone. There is no one in the world today who can be trusted.

Little brother, I don't know how many pages this letter will be, but currently I only want to write and write. The time is 3:30 in the morning. Don't be scared! I'm currently still working the evening shift. And it's 2 o'clock in the morning, sometimes 4 o'clock in the morning, when I go home from work. Currently, my dear little brother, I would love for you to be here. You know I got bored from the entire everything. That is why I took the night shift. Here in California, a Jew or a goy [non-Jew] can't be trusted, it's the part of the world that's the hardest that can exist on the Earth. Did you know?

I was in the temple today. I went Saturday night also. But, this is the way I like it. Everything is only a Purim Spiel [a Purim story, make believe]. Dear little brother! Come home. I miss you so much. Sometimes, I would like to get to know someone, but there is nobody. It would be good if you would be here, and sometimes you would deal with me. My little brother, man lives like a machine, especially like you do, as well! Say it! That's what it is!! Isn't it?! But what can we do, if God will order it that way, it can't be helped. Little brother, I saw it in today's paper that President Benes went home to Czechoslovakia to Kosice. I hope he will help!

But I think the Jews are looking for trouble for themselves. Jews are in Long Beach. There are 3000 Jews supposedly and you know, there were barely 9 Jews in the temple...! That means that Judaism will pass away and only the name "Stinking Jew" will stay! I can't understand the situation. But I want to sleep and I will continue the letter tomorrow. I'm sleepy. Until then I kiss you from my heart forever. Your faithful brother, who will never forget you. I'm writing this from my honest heart. Currently it's 4 o'clock on the morning. I will continue tomorrow.

My little brother I will continue tomorrow!
Until then I kiss you from my heart.
Your brother Dezső

Sunday

It's only a difference of a day and my writing is a little better. I'm not sleepy, I just woke up. The weather is nice, it's completely summer. I wish you would be here also. My little brother. Write to me, if you need a package. I will send it to you with pleasure. Only ask me, OK? Maybe I will go to Hollywood today. I have not been there in at least 1/2 a year. If I will go, I will send the letter tomorrow and I will write what happened. Until then, I'll still write a few lines.

Write my little brother what kind of food do you get and what kind of apartment do you live in? Do you have a decent bed? Or do you still live like you used to live sleeping on the floor...? So, I believe I will go to Hollywood. So, I will continue the letter tomorrow. Until then, lots of luck and everything good. Today I looked over my letter from yesterday, I saw how ugly I wrote, but I would not have the patience today to write it over again, so that's how everything is. I hope you will forgive me for that. Ok!? Kisses, Dezső

Monday noon, 12:30pm. I just got up (woke up), so I'm writing a few lines and I will finish the letter so it could go today. So, yesterday I went to Hollywood with the Leadman I work with and his wife. I went to the Palladium, you're surely listening to the music from there. I went alone, but you know, there are so many people, you can't see individuals, only soldiers and sailors. There are many people [hardly a few]. I was there until 11:30. It takes an hour to go home. Currently, there is a curfew in the entire America. Everything has to be closed at 12 o'clock. So, an hour after midnight, I was in bed already. It's not worth it to go there. There are too many people. So, little brother, if God will help and you will come home, I will go everywhere with you. So, I will close my lines. I'm hungry. I'm going to eat something. I'm hungry. Yes. I fixed my car, had it overhauled and he said it's like new. So, I kiss you with love. Your faithful brother forever. Dezső

P.S. I just got a letter from home. They wrote that they got mail from you. I got a V mail letter written by you on 3.26.45. Yes. Thank you for it. Write to me little brother whenever you can.
Kisses, Dezső

1945/4/9 Hermine to Irving #1 (V-Mail, Slide 443)

April 9, 1945
My dearest brother Irving,
We received one V mail letter from you a couple days ago and we were very happy to know you are OK. We miss you a lot and I wish we could talk personally. Hope it won't be long now - till we meet again. Do you need anything just let us know so we could send it to you. The weather is nice our house cleaning is almost done. Louis in Iceland thinks he'll get a furlough soon. Flora likes your gift very much. Good luck and best wishes with all my love, Hermina

1945/4/9 Hermine to Irving #2 (V-Mail, Slide 442)

April 9, 1945
My dearest brother Irving,
It is an nother [sic] day and we are thinking a lot about you so just a few lines to tell you all are well. It is late our teacher just left and, it is nice to receive mail - then we should write more often to you too. David and Herman are well too. I will write more tomorrow hope to hear about you and take care of yourself. Good luck and God bless you. Love, your sister, Hermina

1945/4/10 Hermine to Irving (V-Mail, Slide 444)

April 10 - 45
Written in Hungarian

My dear beloved little brother,
Believe me, it is very difficult to express one's feelings and our monotonous letters can and do get boring. As much and often as we are with you - of course in our thoughts and in our hearts - somehow I can't find the words in writing. That's why I'm asking you, my dear Irving, don't worry and we hope to see each other again soon. Forgive me because my letters are always so messy, but I know you understand and now good luck and take care of yourself. Kisses with lots of love, Hermina

1945/4/10 Irving to Dave, Germany (V-Mail, Slide 446)

April 10, 1945
Germany

Dear brother Dave,
Hoping that this letter will find you in the best of health. I'm okay and as you see I'm on the move again, I'm writing this letter from Germany. Have received some mail from you and from home, but as yet I wasn't able to answer it. Yet I'm pretty busy. However as soon as I get some time off, I'll begin to write you like I used to. I hope you understand me. Nothing much to say, just hoping for the day to come, when they'll call it quits. I would like to drop in, in Czecho[slovakia] and that's the only time I'll be able to do it. Here the air force has done a good job, I think that this people learned this time. Well I'll have to close this time, Will write you again soon. Please keep on writing me. Thank you. With love, Irving

1945/4/10 Irving to Family, Germany (V-Mail, Slide 445)

April 10, 1945
Germany

Dear Hermine, Marie and Herman,
Back again with a couple lines to let you know that I'm OK and hope that you are well and in good health. I'm now in Germany on the road to Berlin… Hoping that one of these days the war will end and then I'll be able to go to see the family in Czecho[slovakia]. Let's hope for the best. I received some mail from you and Dave before I left France, but I'm very busy and not able to write like I used to. However I'm thinking of you always. By the way, I want to tell you that I have received that long letter in which you have marked my bonds and amount I have. Thanks very much! I'll send some more soon. Now I'll close this time and will write you again soon. Love, Irving

Please write sooner.

1945/4/10 Undated Irving to Flo (Book 14, 222-225) draft by PFC Joe Sklar

[draft by Joe Sklar, see handwriting and language (azzever, and c'est le vie) in 1945/6/26 PFC Joe Sklar to Irving (Book 18, 134-135). After Shirley's surgery]

Hello Puss,
Your letters finally have caught up with me. As you see by the return address I am now a Military Policeman. No cracks! No matter what you might say about the MP's it's at least a cleaner, and definitely much safer, life. I'm at least back in so called civilization now, with baths, hot chow, etc.. Of course, I liked it much better in France. I met some nice families there, but here in Germany with this no fraternization policy, there's very little to do except work and sleep. I used to get a kick out of watching the so called super race making with the garbage, but even that palls on one and my thoughts are only on returning home. Oh well, it shouldn't be too long now. I hope [to] see you soon. Well, Puss, I see you've drawn up a nice ambitious program for yourself in school. That's exactly the way I like my women. Well read in all the Arts and Sciences. Let's concentrate on that retail merchandising course though. Who knows, perhaps some day we'll open a little candy store on some busy little corner together. And if you're a good little pussy cat and get good marks in all your classes and get to know all the angles, why then I'll be able to go to the ball game every day. And at night when I get back tired from a rough day, why then you'll be able to soothe me with some of that sweet music you're now studying. I'll be highly honored to become a character in your book, but you had better send me the proofs before the publisher gets them. There are certain lurid events in my past life that I shouldn't care to make public just at present. Let's keep them just between you and me. OK? So you say you've grown up and changed. Well, my little "kötzile" that's just a natural process c'est le vie! Me too baby. How about a picture of them terrific metamorphoses so [as] I can enjoy some of it, too. That's a direct order! I'm sorry to hear about your father going through so much, but since you say, he looks and feels fine, I guess it's all for the best. Here's hoping he keeps that a way. Say hello to Myron for me. You might tell him that I'm sweating out that mysterious orient, too. I hope I get a chance to get home before I find out if it's true what they say about the Geisha girls. Say hello to Shirley too. I hope she doesn't put on too much weight after the appendectomy. Incidentally, did she ever marry that guy she was going out with? So long now toots old gal, take care of yourself and don't work too hard. Above all, keep smiling. Give my very best to your family and take a little for yourself. Azzever [sic] Irving

1945/4/11 Marie to David (Book 8, 48-50)

4-11-45
Dear David!
Received your letter. I'm very happy that thank God you are ok. We are ok, too. Last week we received a letter from our little brother and thank God he is ok, too. The only thing is that he is very busy and doesn't have much time to write. There is nothing new that he can write. I hope God will help him with good luck and he will safely return to us in good health. I wish the war would be over soon. Otherwise, everything is the same. I'm still busy with the school for the citizenship papers. We were called in and we are still waiting that they will call us in again. I hope everything will be ok and we will get the citizenship papers.

First I had a problem with it because everything was recorded that we were Hungarian. When I went in I told them we came from Czechoslovakia. Meanwhile, they said that they would not accept Hungarians who came out during the war. Then I took in my papers and I explained to them what happened. Now she said not to be afraid. Today she would do it so that everything would be fine. I hope so and that there will not be any problem. Take care of yourself and write. The weather became very hot yesterday, otherwise nothing new. Wishing you all the best and good health. Love, Maria

1945/4/15 Jane Schallheim to Irving (Book 18, 94-98)

April 15
Dear Irving,
This week I've had vacation so I'm catching up on my mail. College started eight weeks ago and this is the first breathing spell we've had. College is really wonderful in spite of all the homework. In between classes a group of us go over to "Haydn Hall" for milkshakes. I'm gaining weight which makes my mother very happy. Mother and I went to Columbus near the end of January. We saw both your sisters. They looked quite well. We have to take five subjects in college so I'm taking English, French, Political Science, Biology and Anthropology. Our French professor is wonderful. She was born in France and dresses in the French style. Anthropology is my most interesting subject. We study about the lives and customs of our primitive contemporaries the Crow Indians, the Aztecs and Polar Eskimos. Last week in biology we dissected an earthworm. What a mess! In a few weeks we shall dissect a frog. We were so shocked to hear of President Roosevelt's death. The stores and theaters have been closed in his memory. Monday I saw "A Song to Remember" a movie about Chopin's life. The music was superb. I do hope you will have a chance to see it sometimes <u>soon</u>. The war situation looks brighter and I hope you'll be home real <u>soon</u>. Mother sends her best regards. Jane

1945/4/15 Hermine to Irving (V-Mail, Slide 447)

April 15, 1945
My dearest brother Irving,
Hope you are well in good health as we are too. There isn't anything new but we can hardly get over President Roosevelt's death. I know you over there feel the same way. But don't worry dear the new man is [a] good man and hope everything will work out well. Tell me something about yourself. Flora and the relatives asking how you are and Elsie never mentioned anything about you but always asking how you are. I will write some more - take care of yourself. With all my love, Hermina

1945/4/15 Irving to Hermine and Marie (Book 6, 224-230)

Germany
April 15, 1945
My dearest Marie,
Thanks a million for your letters and I'm happy to know that you are well and in good health. As I said to Hermine that I have received 30 – letters from you and her, but as yet I'm not able to answer you in detail. However I'll try my best. Like you say, even a line from you it helps me a lot. Well nothing specially new, just as being in Germany it means that we are closer of getting home. It's closer every day that I'll get to go see the family back over here. Believe me I have been sweating it out as well as you. I know how you feel. But what can we do, this is war. Thank God that everything is as it is, because it could be worse. I heard about Pres. Roosevelt, I feel sorry for him that he had to go. I can say this, that he was a great man. I voted for him... well, that's the way it goes, when time comes, you must go.

Thanks very much for your letters Marie and I really enjoy hearing from you. Whenever you get time please do drop me a line. Just now I have received a package from you with homemade cookies. It was mailed February 12, 1945. Thanks a million for you and Hermine. How is Herman? Tell him please to drop me a line. And you Marie, please take care of yourself hoping to hear from you again soon and the truth about yourselves. With all my love, Irving

Germany
April 15, 1945
My dearest Hermine,
Can't tell you how happy I was to hear from you. I've been thinking of you always but never able to write you. This new job really keeps me very busy. However today I just couldn't stand it any longer. So I'm

going to write you a few lines. First I want to tell you that I have received 30 letters from home since I have been here. It's really wonderful to get them, however you will have to forgive me for not answering of all your letters at once, but as soon as possible I will answer you everything in detail. The picture is very good and I have compared with the one I brought along when I came over and it sure changed. Well it's that way, 2 long years and that's enough for everybody and especially the way everything had to happen to you. If I think of it, I just can't stand it. However thank God that everything is OK now… Please write me whenever you can and please tell me the truth about yourself. About myself nothing new, just as I said I'm very busy and don't get time to think about myself. However I'll say it again, please don't worry and everything will be fine. About my picture that you were asking, my eyes are OK and that spot must be on the paper. The other picture with the badge, if you like the picture and want to enlarge it, it's okay with me. The badge is for being in combat as Infantryman.

Hope to send you another picture soon again as a military policeman! How do you like that? Sometimes it's interesting work, but besides this I wish I could be home and see you. Hope that the time is not far off. Before I return home I sure want to see the family over here and I hope to get permission to see them. My dearest sister Hermine, I want to tell you if you need of anything, please use the money that I sent home and let me hear from you how you are and please take care of yourself. So please forgive me this time for closing this letter, but I'll write you again soon. With all my love, your little brother, Irving

P.S. Again want to say about your picture that you look wonderful kánahare, and as always with love, Irving. I'm wishing you a happy birthday…

P.S. Here I'm enclosing a picture I've taken when I arrived to France. I'm with a French boy on his bicycle. Love, Irving

Please give my love to Dave, I'll write him also soon…

1945/4/16 Arthur Gluck to Irving (V-Mail, Slide 123)

[Typed]

April 16, 1945
Dear Irv:

We were all shocked Thursday afternoon when our great President passed away. Sam heard first over the radio and rushed upstairs screaming "My God". I wondered what happened. He broke down in tears and said the President had died. I truly believe that he has set such a wonderful example that the ablest people in our country are united to see that the lasting peace in a better world will result out of this war. We are glad to know that you are in the M.P. service and I wouldn't be surprised if you wouldn't have an opportunity to get a leave to visit your father in Czechoslovakia. I hope that he and the rest of the folks are o.k. Jennie has been ill in bed for six weeks but she is well now. I have had a siege of sickness myself. We are all much better and look forward to a speedy conclusion of the European end of the war. Your sisters and brother Herman are o.k. They are getting along fine. With love to you from us all,
Your loving cousin Arthur Gluck

1945/4/16 Bertha to Irving (V-Mail, Slide 449)

April 16, 1945
Dear Irving just a few lines to tell you that we are well, hope to hear same from you. It is a long time since we got word from you. Please write if your time permits you even if only a postcard. Mannie sends the second package to you this week hoping that you will receive the contents. Enjoy it in case you are in need of things don't hesitate to let me know and I should send it to you. With our love and best wishes, Bertha and Mannie

1945/4/16 Hermine to Irving (V-Mail, Slide 448)

Apr 16 - 45
Written in Hungarian

My dear little brother Irving,

I hope you received our letter that we wrote to you recently. I'm also interested if you got my photo? Thank God we are fine. And I hope to hear from you. We can't wait for your letter, write when you can. Marcsa went to bed and Herman is not home yet. It's raining, but I hope it will pass, it's not very pleasant. Kisses, Hermina

1945/4/16 Irving to Dave (Book 6, 231-234)

Germany

April 16, 1945

Dearest brother Dave,

I have been trying to write you a long letter for months, but there is always it must be done first. And even today I just want to say that I'm OK hoping that you are well and in good health. Since I have been in Germany, I have received about 30 letters all together. So you can see I'll need plenty time to answer them. I'm kept pretty busy and that's why I'm not writing. To one of your very important letter I can only say don't worry, I know that you are on the right track, but you know you can say what you think, but here is different. Before all that happened, you remember I told you that I met a very good friend of mine and so everything was fine. I'll have to write him also one of these days. So the best thing I must say, we must forget the whole things as yet. When I return home with God's help, I'll tell you about everything. Well, now about myself, nothing new, just hoping that soon I'll be able to get to see the family back home. Hope they are well. I'll be saving some money over here, when time comes so I'll have it ready. Now Dave I'll close this time, and please, don't worry! Hoping to see you soon with all my love, your little brother, Irving

P.S. Here is a picture I've taken in France with a French boy.

1945/4/18 Flora Gluck to Irving (V-Mail, Slide 450)

April 18, 1945

Dear Irving:-

It has been a long time since we received your very beautiful gifts you certainly would have deserved a much quicker acknowledgment and thanks. It seems very inappreciative when we think of all you go thru and yet you think of us and take the time to send such a lovely remembrance. I hope you will forgive us if you believe how much we do think of you and pray for your welfare and safe return. Illness not only of myself but Jennie and Arthur kept me from writing, Thank God we are all well now. Your sisters and brothers are well. I was witness for Marie and Hermine when they applied for their papers and saw them about 2 weeks ago. They are fine - They keep us informed about you and we are always anxious for the latest news. We hope very soon that u [sic] will notify us of your speedy return. Thank you again on behalf of Arthur and the children. Loads of love, Flora

1945/4/22 Hermine to David (Book 8, 52-53)

Columbus Apr 22-45

Dear David,

We haven't heard from you in a long time and hope that you're in good health. We don't have any special news. We haven't received a letter from our little brother Irving in a couple of weeks, but he's definitely busy. I wrote to a Jewish association in New York if I could find out something about our dear father and family. I haven't received an answer yet. How are you, David? Do you work? Here I also read in the newspaper that the work in the shipyards will slow down a lot. What will the many people do? You might as well go to another job where you want to.

The important thing is to have an end to the horrible war and bring our little brother back healthy. I want Herman to write to you as well as to Irving - but he is very lazy to write letters.

We are busy, especially learning what one doesn't want, but the teacher said you knew very well everything [even though] you really only learned for a couple of days, so I hope we will learn, too. I don't even know if I wrote to you that President Roosevelt's death was so depressing that you could barely stand it, but hopefully the new President will take good care and continue to help the Jews. Take care of yourself and don't work too hard. Kisses with love, Hermine

1945/4/24 Irving to Dave, Germany (V-Mail, Slide 451)

April 24, 1945
Germany

Dear Dave,

Just want to tell you that I'm OK and thinking of you always. And planning for quite some time to write you a long letter, but I'm pretty busy and not able to do it. So yet just a V-mail. Hoping that you are well and in good health. Have received mail from home they are OK. Please write me about yourself and if you have a picture that you took lately please send me one. Now all my love to you, till we meet again, Love, Irving

Undated 1945/5/1 Marie to Irving (Book 9, 244-245)

[Dated by warm weather, war not over yet, new address - probably Spring / Summer 1945]

Written in Hungarian

My dear beloved little brother!

It's been a week that we got mail from you, which I am very impatient about. But I hope that my lines will find you in the best of health. Otherwise we are well, my dear little brother and let's hope that the dear God will help and soon we will be over with this terrible confusion. I wish it would be already so we can be together. I'm waiting for you so much, so we can be together. I miss you so much, my little brother. How are you anyway, my little brother? If you would have a chance, I would be so happy if you could send me a picture of you. Although, I know that you are very busy and I can understand you. But it has been enough time since the last we saw each other and I would love to see you. But I ask the dear God to help you as soon as possible, so you can come back to us in the best of health! And I'm asking you my dear brother to take care of yourself, wherever you go. And the dear God should follow you in every step.

I think about you a lot and we know everything from the radio. But let's hope in the dear God. There is nothing particular here. David is well too. The weather is pretty warm these days. I think that is the case where you are now. Today is Saturday and I don't work and I'm counting on going to the movies. And also, I'm in a hurry to write to you as well, with the hope that soon I will hear news from you. And also your mentioned new address. Please my dear little brother, don't be worried. I can understand your last letter very well. I wish I could help. But I know that it is all useless because we are far enough from each other. Although, I only meant in distance. But unfortunately I can't help you with that either. I wish you good luck now and the best of health. I will stay impatiently until we see each other again. I kiss you countless times your forever faithful sibling, who will never forget. Good luck and God bless you. Love, Maria

1945/5/2 Irving to Family, Germany (V-Mail, Slide 452)

May 2, 1945
Germany

Dear Hermine and Marie,

Back again with a couple lines to let you know that I'm OK and hoping to hear from you the best. Some time ago I told you that I spoke to a high ranking officer and told me that he'll call you up or drop you a line. Please let me know if he did. Nothing else new except everything looks very good in Europa. Hope that pretty soon I'll get to go to see the family. I'm saving for the day. Please write me and let me hear from you. With love, your little brother, Irving

1945/5/3 Private Earl Wetzel to Irving (Book 14, 9-12)

May 15, 1945 [misdated?]

Gluck,

Well I got your letter dated Feb. 1. that's been quite some time ago. But as you can see by this letter I am back in the States. I didn't know you left the outfit. It will be a long time before you get this letter and when you do I'll be out of the Army. I get a discharge in about a month or so. So you write me a letter to my home address 1817 Liberty St. La Crosse <u>Mr.</u> Earl Wetzel (No PVT.) Give me your home address and I'll come and see you some time no fooling. I think you will be home soon as you're no good over there. You always were too jumpy, how did you get out of the 6th Inf.? You didn't get hurt did you? Let me know. I still like my Vino just a well but now I can drink beer, that's better any way. I bet you would like to be back on <u>Anzio</u> that was such a nice place quiet and peaceful wasn't it? Well, that's about all for now as I'm running out of paper. More next time. As ever, Earl Wetzel

P.S. Don't write so fast next time. I could hardly read your writing. Was there some 88s around? Ha Ha.

1945/5/8 Irving to Family, Germany (V-Mail, Slide 453) V-E day

May 8, 1945
Germany

Dearest Hermine and Marie,
Just a line tonight to let you know that I'm okay and happy to hear the real news, that's "it's all over," The V-E day is here. Thank God for all his great help, helping me to go through this horrible war. Many times I have given up hope and said that's not possible to go through it, especially way back in Anzio, that one place I'll never forget, and now that it's really over, I'll sit down and say a prayer. I wish I could be back home and celebrate with you, but yet I don't know what will come up. I would like to go to see the family over here. I hope I get a pass to do it. How is Herman? Tell him to write me. I'll try my best, Till we meet again, With all my love, Irving

Please write soon

1945/5/11 Hermine to Irving - Victory in Europe (Book 16, 221-222)

Columbus May 11 – 45
My dearest brother Irving,
I told you a long time ago about my long letter that I want to write to you and till now always just the V mail. It is faster I thought and, we can mail to [you] more V mail letters and you probably get tired of them too–they are all alike–main thing really is that we all are well in good health and now that Victory in Europe is won we are thankful to God for helping us, as much and we hope and pray will help us after that too. Maybe you'll get to come home soon, but I wish you would have a chance to go and see what happened there, because you could help better and would tell us about them. So let's hope now and, take care of yourself. Don't worry about us we are well. I am feeling just fine and thinking a lot of you. We received some letter from you and a long air mail letter, also a V mail yesterday and we are happy to know you are well. You probably saw many things interesting, nice, but not so good or sad things too. We know about it - only from the pictures, and it isn't as in real [life]. The main thing is now that take care of your health as much as you can and, don't worry we all are well and looking for your arrival. The V-E day brought our thoughts closer and our hope that we'll see you real soon. The long dreamed dinner and after that, the show can come true. I wish I could go to see our dear ones and that would be a real dream then, you know what to do. I wish I could but I tried it and no answer- maybe we'll get some soon. Benes is in Prague now. We can say there were times we never thought that will be again. So let's hope God will help us and, good luck to you wherever you are. David, Herman are well. Love and best wishes, your sister, Hermina

1945/5/13 Irving to Dave (Book 6, 242-244)

May 13, 1945
Germany

Dearest Dave, (unto 120 years!)
Just a few lines to let you know that I'm thinking of you and hoping that you are well and in good health. I'm OK and keep myself busy, no place to go except when working and plenty to do on my spare time. Just finished washing and cleaning and I'll have some pressing to be done. Have to stay clean at all times. As you see that takes care of everything. I don't mind it, because I like to stay clean. The point system is out as you probably heard about, according to that it will be quite a while before they'll send me home. When I go home I want to stay there. Let's hope in God and everything will be OK. Not long ago I spoke to a person about getting a pass to see the family in Czechoslovakia and he thinks I'll get to go there, however everything

takes time. If you have any suggestion, please let me know. Have received a Chronicle [for] the first time since I left Italy. I guess it will catch up with [me] now as I am settled down. Also received 2 packages from Hermine and Marie, with a fruit cake and cookies. Now I don't need anything Dave, but if I will, I'll ask you to send me. OK. Thanks a million…

I wish I could be there as you have described in one of your letters, it can't be long now, hoping that God will help all of us. Well Dave, nothing else to write except it's hot here, but I guess there is the same way. You know Dave, the only time I was to the services, when I was in Nanzy + Toul. I worked there before I came to this place. Well, keep writing me and hoping to hear from you the best, with my love, Irving

1945/5/13 Irving to Hermine and Marie (Book 6, 235-241)

May 13, 1945
Germany

Dearest Hermine and Marie, (unto 120 years)

Just finished reading your letters and now I will try to write you a few lines and let you know that I'm OK and hoping to hear from you the best.

In every letter you want me to write something about myself, well my dearest, nothing much I can say just I'm pretty busy and that's why I'm not writing you like I used to. Here the work is okay and when I finish doing my work I cleanup, press my clothes, and have to stay clean at all times. I don't mind. I feel that way, if I can stay clean I'll stay so, and if not, well it's OK that way. When I get to work I have my shoes polished, just like back home my civilian shoes. The work is interesting and it [is] better than many other things in the army except in civilian life. However about that I can't talk much, because the point system, doesn't come close to me. So I'm still as before, hoping that God will help me and everything will be OK. As soon I find something out about going to see the family in Czechoslovakia I will let you know. I have spoken to a person and he said that in near future there will be passes for that purpose, so then I'll get to go. But in meantime I'll see what can be done. However it's very difficult to do anything yet, because everything takes time. If you know something or want to suggest me, please let me know. Now I'm quite far away from Czecho, however by plane it would take me about 4 – hours to get there and that's not much, if I have the pass. Hoping that God will help me to go there.

Say dearest, have you received your papers yet? I hope you have. I bet you had to study a lot to get them. Please let me know about that. When I got it I really had a tough job ahead of me. But now thank God that it's over…

Here we are having nice warm weather and the country is beautiful and it's a shame that this people can't be satisfied what they have, and like it, and live like a peaceful nation.

Have started to study French, but now I don't study anything, because here you can't talk to this people. There are plenty Polish people and sometime I say a few words to them and that's about all. Where I want to go [Czechoslovakia] I speak that language, that will be enough, don't you think.

Haven't heard from Dave and Herman for quite sometime, please tell them to write me. I know sometimes you feel tired to sit down and write a line, you really have to be in a mood to write. Anyway, please tell them I'm waiting to hear from them soon.

Dearest sis, I want to tell you I don't know what I could send you from here, so I want you to buy something for yourselves and charge it to me. Here I have started to save some money when they say go! I'll be ready if you know what I mean…

How are you? Please let me hear from you and tell me everything about yourselves.

On the holy days I have been once to the services and that's all I could do, that was when I was in France. I worked in Nancy and Toul it was good there, but this is the army and always on the move.

Talking about pictures you have never said anything about my picture with the mustache. By this time you know that I've taken my mustache off. What do you think about this. I'll try to make some pictures again if I'll get a camera somewhere or borrow one. I'll see what I can do. I was looking at your pictures and 2 years really changed all of us. However we have to be thankful the way everything is. I would like to see you in person, let's hope for the best! Please write as often as you can and I'll do my best.

Dearest Hermine, tell me where do you work and what are you doing, and how do you like your job? And tell me how do you feel? And I want you to take care of yourself, don't work hard, that doesn't pay. And you Marie dear, I want you not to worry, and everything will be fine and take care of yourself. Sometimes I say something and I shouldn't then when you are worrying, but don't do that. About my furlough, when that will be I don't know. I hope Marie that you are right, but the way I feel when I get home and want to stay there.

Haven't written to anyone since I came over from Italy except you, and somehow I just postpone it, but one day when I'll get more time off I will write them, the meantime tell them that I said hello.

I have told you not long ago that a big shot will call you or drop you a line, did you get anything yet. I hope you have. I'll see him again soon. He'll be back I guess by the time you get this letter. I wish I would get the opportunity to speak to him, he is the one what he says goes and I would like to go to see the family and with his name I could go anyplace.

That navy guy never dropped in to see you or did he? Let me know if so.

The other day I have received two packages, with cookies and candy and fruit cakes. That was very sweet of you to send me. Thanks a million, and I know you want me to ask for some more, but yet I have plenty of everything. Thanks just the same.

How are you with Rosewater and that young Lt. Let me hear from you please. OK.

Oh yes, Marie, I want to tell you that the bonds were stopped sometime last year and don't worry about it. Please say hello to Miss McNeil! and tell her that I don't know what happened to that letter and she must forgive me for not writing her, but I'm so busy, that I don't know what to do first. Tell me did you enlarge the picture with the combat badge? I have been planning to make some more pictures quite a while, but when I'll I don't know, hope soon… about that picture you saw in the papers, well that was taken of one of the boys from this outfit. At that time I left and those two boys were there, so they were the lucky ones. That's a good one isn't… now please keep on writing me. Let me hear from you, with all my love, Irving

My love to Dave and Herman

1945/5/13 Marie to Irving (Book 16, 468-469)

Written in Hungarian 5-13-45
My dear loved little brother, Irving!
Today is Sunday and I'm in a hurry to write to you. Hoping that my lines will find you in the best of health. We are well and thinking about you a lot. I hope that you can spend your time more relaxed. I'm thinking that you could be very busy today. But I hope we can get closer to our goal. It's been a couple of days since we got a letter from you. From David, we did not get a letter for a few days already, but as you know him well, he is not the best at writing. The weather here is very nice, only cool. Forgive me dear little brother that my letter has a monotonous sound. Maybe I already bore you with it. But I hope that with God's help, I can personally make it up to you! Now I'm asking you again, wherever you go, take care of yourself. God bless you! I wish you lots of luck and health. I kiss you countless times, forever your faithful sibling, who will never forget. With love, your sister, Maria

1945/5/15 Hermine to Irving (Book 16, 225)

Written in Hungarian 5-15-45
My dear little brother, Irving!

It has been few days since we got a V-mail from you. We hope that currently you are in good health also. There is no news here, only we are waiting to see you again shortly. The way the papers and the radio are calculating the points, I believe, you also have to [calculate]. You must read the papers and listen to the news. How are you my little Irving? I believe that you see a lot of nice things, but a lot of things that are hard. Let's hope that the time will come and everything will be fine. The important thing is to get news from home and that they are all well. You were wondering if the person you mentioned [General Wilson], wrote or looked for us. Nobody wrote to us here and that boy from the Navy was not here either. The one that you mentioned already a long time ago. Many times we are trying, but with no success because, you know, it works differently at the military. David, Herman are well. Today it rained, but yesterday the weather was sunny and beautiful. I don't even know what to write that you would care about. I wrote to Bertha too and she wrote that she sent a package to you. Take care of yourself and don't worry. I am well and feeling good. Good health and good luck! Kisses with love, Hermina

1945/5/17 Irving to Dave, Germany (V-Mail, Slide 454)

May 17, 1945
Germany

Dearest Dave,
Haven't heard from you quite some time, I'm hoping that you are well and in good health. I'm OK. Since I've been over seas, this is my first letter that I can seal it myself without anyone reading it, censoring mail was stopped and from now on I'll be able to write you whatever I want, and if it will be of any interest to you. I was examined again yesterday and I'm hoping to see you soon. I'll write you a long letter in the near future. Love, Irving

1945/5/21 Irving to Dezső, Germany [Uncensored] (Book 5, 333-337)

Germany
May 21 - 45
Dearest Dezső live to 120.
It has been two years now since I've written in a Hungarian. Up till now I couldn't have written in Hungarian. [In English] On May 16, 1945 they stopped censoring mail and so from now on [In Hungarian] I can write about everything, whatever I want. At this time I may write to tell where I am and what I'm doing and so forth. Therefore now I can tell you that I'm in Mannheim Germany. I'm working in this town. I live in a regular home as a military policeman. This is better than as it was in Italy as an infantryman. I could write you about a lot of things, but slowly I'm going to try to write a few pages.

As a policeman I have a lot of responsibility. I must know the laws up to date. The average soldiers do not like military policeman. [In English] It is interesting work, there's always something new. [In Hungarian] One must be like a detective, you have to find errors. You can imagine how it is. True, you can be a good man, they still won't like you either. To me it doesn't matter, if someone does something wrong, you must punish him. In France it was much better. When I finished my job I could have gone anyplace I wanted to, but here is no place to go. Here I put in more time, more hours, than there.

I hope that in a short while I will get my freedom to visit our father. The captain said as soon as he finds out something he will advise me. [In English] So let's hope it won't be long now. I'm about 600 miles from Bodrogmező, by air.

Not long ago I told you that I met and spoke to a big shot and he was going home. Well, [In Hungarian] He is a two star general. I am taking care of him and one afternoon before he was going home he spoke to me and asked for my home address and promised that he would write to my sisters Hermina, [In English] and he said with a smile "I'll tell them that you look lousy" I hope he did. [In Hungarian] In few days he will return and I hope that once again I'll have a chance to talk to him about other things. However, I can only speak to him if he talks to me. He is the person that this territory in Germany is under his command. His name is General Wilson. I hope you understand me. What do you think of your little brother as a military policeman? Please write to me about it. On May 16 - 45 I was to a doctor for examination who would decide when I can go home. As you know, everything is destined for a person. I hope it won't be long that I could tell you because I know that you would like to know. But those that trust in God will not be disappointed.

Please write to me. I remain with kisses to you, your little brother Irving, who will never forget you. Love, Irving

P.S. My best regards to Hermina and Marie and Herman. Love, Irv.

1945/5/22 Hermine to Irving (Book 16, 224)

Written in Hungarian

Columbus, May 22, 1945

My Dear loved Irving, my little brother!

I have been getting ready to write to you and it always gets postponed. Currently, I'm very busy with the citizenship papers. We are being called to the interview tomorrow, and I hope I will get the residency and I will be an American resident. I have been waiting so badly for that, but it came too. The important thing is that everything will be fine after that, too and we can hear from you and the others as well. There is no particular news here. There was a lot of rain this Spring and it is enough of it. Let's hope and trust that everything will be fine. Take care of yourself and don't be worry. Did you hear about when you will get your turn so can visit us in person? I think [it will be] soon. That person who you mentioned, still did not call and did not write a letter. If he promised it to you, he will do it for you. Aunt Helen, Arthur, Flora and the neighbor was asking about you. Kissing you with love, Hermina

1945/5/22 Major General Wilson to Hermine and Marie (Book 22, 98-99)

[Typed]

War Department

Headquarters, Army Special Forces

Washington 25, D.C.

22 May 1945

Misses Herminia & Marie Gluck

50 Linwood Avenue

Columbus, Ohio

Dear Misses Gluck:

When I left Germany for a short trip to the United States I asked members of my staff to give me any messages they would like delivered. Private Irving Gluck asked that I write you and let you know he is in good health and feeling fine. Lack of time and press or work prohibit a personal telephone call so this greeting will have to suffice.

Sincerely,

Arthur R. Wilson

Major General. USA

[Handwritten]

All I can say

That is the zone

1945/5/23 Marie to Irving (Book 16, 466)

Written in Hungarian 5-23-45

My dear loved little brother, Irving!

It has been a few days already that we have not heard from you. I hope that my lines will find you in the best of health. We are well and thinking about you a lot! I hope that the dear God will help you after this, too, and we can see each other in luck and health again. There is no particular news here. The weather is still cold. And how is it there? I guess you must be busy. Thank Goodness for that too. Aunt Helen was here on Sunday and she is well. She sends her greetings to you and she would love to see you, like all of us as well. We hope that we will not have to wait for long. I'm just writing a letter to David. We did not get any letter for a few days, but like you know, he doesn't like to write either. Now, my dear little brother, I will close my lines. Only I'm asking you again to take care of yourself wherever you go. God Bless you and good luck after this too! I kiss you countless times, your faithful sibling, who will never forget. Love, Maria

Dearest Dave,

I can hardly write how long it's been since I got news from you. I hope you are well. I'm, thank God doing well. I could write that, as for me, it's possible that I will go home very shortly.

I don't know, if I'll go to Polyán first or to America. If God helps me and everything will go well, and if I go to America, then I will be out of the military. Judging from the doctor's tests they have to send me home based on the present classification. I will thank God, because I could only thank him. You know Dave, when God will help me and I go home, I will tell you everything. I got 3 newspapers from you today, and I thank you for that. When I will be able to, I will look through them. Here we get the Stars and Stripes newspaper everyday, just ordinary news. We only have to work, like you said in one of your letters. However, my job is clean and we just worked until now, 12 hours per day, and I'm on walking patrol and walking is enough. But all this is not as bad as it was on the front [lines]. A couple of days ago we began to work less hours. That is the way. Well Dave, I hope that you are well and you will write and until then in the hope that I will see you again. Kisses, your little brother, Irving

1945/5/27 Irving to Dave #1, Germany (V-Mail, Slide 456)

May 27, 1945
Germany

Dearest Dave,

Hoping that you are well and in good health. The other day I have written you a long letter and hope that you have received it. Nothing new since then. On that going home business, it might be in the next six months. Sooner is better. But as yet nothing came down about it. You know the army, you don't know what will come up from one minute to the other. I'll believe everything when I'll shake hands with you. Now with all my love, Irving

1945/5/27 Irving to Dave #2, Germany (V-Mail, Slide 455)

May 27, 1945
Germany

Dearest Dave, until 120

Just a line to let you know that I'm OK. Today [for] the first time in five years I was able to write to Czechoslovakia, I just found out that we can write there, so I have already mailed my letter and hope to hear from them real soon. May be you could write them also. It shouldn't take long to get an answer, when I do I'll let you know. I told them that I hope to stop in and see them soon. Now my love to you from, Irving

Please write me.

1945/5/27 Irving to Family, Germany (V-Mail, Slide 457)

May 27, 1945
Nemetország [Germany]
Germany

Dearest Hermine and Marie, until 120

Happy to say that, that the first time in five years I was able to write to Czechoslovakia. I have just found out that we can write there, so I have already mailed a letter and hope to hear from them real soon. Maybe you could write to them also. It shouldn't take long to get an answer, when I do, I will let you know. I told them that I'll stop in and see them soon, I hope. Now all my love to you. Your little brother, Irving

Give my love to Herman tell him to write me.

1945/5/28 Hermine to Irving (Book 4, 136-137)

[In English]

Page 462

Columbus May 28, 1945

My dearest brother Irving,

We received a nice long letter from you last week and we were very happy to know you are well. It is really wonderful that our God is with us and helped us till now. Hope everything will work out all right. M. G. Wilson wrote to us a short letter written on a typewriter and also a few word that he saw you and, you are well. It was swell to receive it and, was very nice of him. Maybe I will write and thank him for his kindness. I have a very good news for you that, I became an American citizen today and I am an American! It is swell but poor Marie wasn't called in yet, because they didn't get the paper back from Cincinnati. But there is another class and in a short time she will be called in too. So don't worry Irving dear everything will work out all right. Otherwise I am well and still working at the Telephone Company and they are very nice to me, also like my work too. You should see me–I am really an office worker and, doing very important and interesting work. I had company yesterday unexpected Mr. Rosewater–came over from Cleveland and was asking about you and his friend in Italy but told him you aren't there anymore. Believe me Irving dear it isn't good if we have somebody and, if we don't have the right one–because I don't think he is the right one. The young Lieut. that was funny you wrote about it. But you were right he is young. He writes to me and is stationed in Oklahoma as a dentist in a hospital. He asked me to come to his mother's house for my vacation– but I am not decided about my time what I am going to do, but was very nice for inviting me there. So till next time good luck and best wishes to you with all my love. Your sister, Hermina

1945/5/29 Marie to Irving (Book 4, 138)

Written in Hungarian 5-29-45

My dear beloved little brother, Irving!

I'll try to write a couple of lines again. How are you my dear little brother? I hope that my lines will find you in the best of health. We are well. I'm thinking a lot about you. I hope that the dear God will help you after this also. We got your long letter last week, my dear little brother and a V-mail. I'm so happy to hear that you are well. And yes, my little brother, like Hermina wrote to you, she got the citizenship papers yesterday and she had the interview. You know, like usual. And as you can see, for me, I have to wait, since my paper did not come or it is late. But I hope I will get it the next time. Everybody got it, except me. There is no reason for it. They must have made a mistake. Now, I will leave this too. I wish I could see you. I already started counting, if you my little brother will be in the [news]paper, but unfortunately I did not get my goal. I'm asking you little brother to take care of yourself, wherever you go. God bless you! And lots of luck and the best of health. I kiss you countless times. Forever your faithful sibling, who will never forget. Maria

1945/5/30 Hermine to Irving (V-Mail, Slide 460) - Gen Wilson

May 30, 1945

My dearest brother Irving,

Today is Memorial day we were not working - but Herman is even today. It was a very nice day and hope you enjoyed it too. We received that letter from the Major General and [it] was very nice of him. I wish [I] could answer him because that would be nice- but you know my English…Otherwise I am just fine and hope you aren't worrying about it because that is the truth. Maybe our wishes will come true and we'll see you in a short time. Let's hope [for] the best, with all [our] good wishes and take care of yourself. Love, Hermina

1945/6/4 Marie and Hermine to General Wilson - written by Mr. Walters (Book 22, 101-102)

Columbus 5 Ohio
June 4th 1945

Arthur R. Wilson
Major General U.S.A.

Dear Maj. General Wilson:-

We wish to express our appreciation for the lovely note from you, relayed from our dear brother Irving. It meant more than you will ever know. We realize you are pressed with urgent necessities to matters pertaining to your responsibilities and we do thank you for the time given in sending this message. We wish you everything good - health, happiness, and the best of luck. Sincerely, Herminia [sic] and Marie Gluck

June 11, 1945
Germany

Dearest Dave,
Have been waiting for your letter, but never arrived, so here I'm again and let you know that I haven't forgotten you. I'm OK and hoping that in near future I can drop in and see you soon. In next couple weeks I'll let you know how I'll make out. I don't know if I will get to go to Czechoslovakia, that also will come out in that couple weeks. So please don't worry if I'm late with my letters, Till we meet again with all my Love, Irving

June 13, 1945
Dear Hermina and Mariska!
Forgive me that I have not written for a long time, but I already wrote to you that even if I don't write to you, you can still write to me. This week I got mail from our little brother. Thank God, he is well and he wrote that he wrote to Czechoslovakia to our father and the family. He hopes that they will get these letters from him. I wrote a letter to him tonight and I wrote a letter to our father and asked him to send it. So, I can't write any news. Everything is the same. There is no news here. I got your letters and I'm asking you, even if I don't write, you can still write to me. If you don't write anything important, send it anyway. Nothing comes to my mind, but still, I would like to write something. I will continue tomorrow morning. I will remember something by then. I'm writing this letter from work. It's time for us to go home. It's 4 o'clock in the morning. It's about time. I will send the letter by special delivery, so you will probably get it on Sunday. I hope I will get good news from my little brother. How are you? I'm well, thank God. I hope I will get all the best from you. Heck, it's 4 o'clock in the morning. I'm going home.

Currently it is 2 o'clock, I don't know any news. Everything is the same. The weather is pretty nice! I went fishing last week at sea on a little boat from 6am-6pm. I didn't catch anything, because I got sea sick. I threw up everything I ate. It was just as bad on it as if I would have been on a big ship. Otherwise, if I would not have been sick, everything would have been successful. Everybody caught something, except me. And I was the only one sick on the boat. But you know, as soon as we got to land, I immediately felt better and I was hungry as a wolf. I don't know when I will go again. So, I don't even know what to write because I don't go anywhere. I was in Hollywood on Sunday and I ate in a Russian restaurant. They informed us that everything will be Russian and there will be Russian gypsy music. But when the music started everything was Hungarian, even the musicians were Hungarians. They were pretty good musicians. They know how to play the csardas [czardas=Hungarian traditional folk music+dance]. But that's enough about this for today. There is no news. What's worth writing about, you can read in the papers, anyway! Yahrzeit [for our mother] will be on July 10th and the 11th during the day. Write a lot, ok! You can write too Mariska! I kiss all of you with love. I'm wishing the best of health. Kisses, Dezső
P.S. Write to me. Currently I'm going out. I will work 6 nights from 6pm to 4am. There is enough work. Kisses, Dezső

[In English]
June 16, 1945
My dearest brother Irving,
We received a letter from David and [he] enclosed one of your letters written to him. He told me that he wrote a note to our dear Father [and] he mailed it to you. I will try that too if it is possible. Hope you are well and in good health. The cherries and other fruits sound very good but don't worry Irving dear we have everything at home - and we are happy to know you have some too. So take care of yourself and let's hope in the best. Love, Hermina

Written in Hungarian
6-17-45
My dear beloved little brother, Irving!
It has already been a week that we did not get a letter from you. I hope that my lines will find you in the best of health. We are well. I'm sorry my Irving, but it happened against my will that I did not write as I usually do. I will try to become a better writer from now on. Here, there is no news. Particularly the weather is cold now. We got a letter from David and he is well. He is sending his greetings. And how are you? I thought you must be very busy. I hope that the dear God will help and we can be together again in the best of health. We are all waiting so badly for that. I hope since then you heard about the family. We can't really write from here yet. Next time I will look into it, if we can. Now, my dear little brother, I'm asking you to take care of yourself, wherever you go and that the dear God follow you in every step of yours. And I wish you lots of luck and good health. Now I'm closing my lines and greetings. And I kiss you countless times. Forever your faithful sibling, who will never forget, wherever you go. And take good care of yourself, wherever you go. And I hope the time will come soon so I see you again. With love, Maria

1945/6/19 Irving to Dave, Germany (V-Mail, Slide 468)

June 19, 1945
Germany

Dearest Dave,
Haven't heard from you for quite sometime, I hope that you are well and in [the] best of health. I'm OK, and as you see on my above address, it has changed again. This time I'm hoping that everything will come out fine and with God's help I will return home in [the] near future. Not long ago I said that I'll be home in the next six months, but yet it might be sooner. I have high hopes that God will help me and all of us. Well Dave, nothing else to say, just hoping to hear from you soon. My best wishes and love, Irving

Please give my love to the family back home...hope to see you soon? Irv.

1945/6/23 Hermine to David (Book 11, 90-92)

Columbus Jun 23-45
Dear David,
I hope you are ok and well. This week we received a letter from Irving and he writes that he hopes that very soon he will be able to be with us in person. I hope it will come soon. As of now, we did not hear anything more about when he is able to visit the family. We hope it happens soon that he would be able to look around and be able to help them if it's possible. I'm in a hurry. I want to mail this letter. Maria will write tomorrow. I'm going shopping now. With best wishes, Love, Hermine

1945/6/24 Emil Schwartz to us - 1st letter after liberation (Book 3, 259-261)

Mailed to:
Hermina Gluck
50 Linvood Avenue
Columbus 5, Ohio

1945 June 24
Emil Schvartz
Kralovsky Chlumec
Ceskoslovensko

Dear Hentsuka, Mariska, Mendu, Jichak. Until 120
Before I begin to write to you, I will introduce myself to you. My name is Emil, your cousin. Márton Schwartz Bácsi's son. I know you because you came to our home when you went to America on the farewell evening. I will now tell you about my dear parents and brothers and sisters. On 1944 April 4, they dragged us to a concentration camp. We thought it would be altogether as a family. On May 10 they marched us to a railroad box car. We were 94 of us in the one cattle boxcar. There was no air and no water in the closed boxcar. After four days of travel we arrived in Auschwitz the famous (extermination) [Yiddish: far nichtungs

= פֿאַרניכטונג=extermination] camp. They have driven us from the train and immediately we stood in line. It didn't take more than 10 minutes [and] they have separated us. As I looked back I saw my dear mother and children on the other side and my dear father, Hersu (Puju) and I on another side. Poor Magda cried. Without saying goodbye we have not seen each other after that. Within two days they took all three of us in a transport to Austria to a concentration camp [Mauthausen]. We worked there for three months. Within that period Hersu was taken with a sick transport. From that point there was no news of him. My dear father couldn't take it any longer. Two days before Chanukah he died in front of my eyes. This difficult event one cannot imagine. At that moment I have lost my desire to live. I knew that my mother was burned at the gas chamber in Auschwitz. But I didn't want that from our family no one should return home. After that I began to suffer. I don't remember the exact time when we were freed. Before being freed and during that time I was very sick and very weak. I was bedridden with typhoid fever [flek-tifuss]. Later I was taken by the Americans to a hospital and in one month I became well completely. With the first train transport I came back home to Helmec. I am staying with my cousin [Batyamanal] Zoltan Pollak, I'm sure that you know him. From Lenke nenni's [Lefkovits] family Hersu, Hentsu, and Jidesz survived. From the Pollak family, only Zoli remained. We were together with your Lajos in Auschwitz. There he volunteered for masonry and there's no news of him from that point. I do not have any more to write. I would ask all of you of one favor, if you can secure or send me a visa, because I am under 17 and have no one, no relations alive.

My birth information is as follows… Schwartz Emil, 1929 August 13 Király Helmec

Out of a pure heart and kinship, an embrace from your cousin. Schwartz Emil

P.S. I'm enclosing two pictures in this letter.

1945/6/25 Hermine and Marie #1 to family in Europe [war just ended] (Book 3, 419-426)

1945 June 25
Columbus, Ohio

[from Hermine]
Dear beloved father, Lajos, and Etelka!
We have been waiting for years for the moment that we would hear from each other. I hardly can find words to express what I feel in this particular moment. I hope that all of you are in good health. We are thankful that our good God was a special God to our loved ones, and that he cherished our life and kept it alive for us. It's very difficult to wait for a reply from you, but as soon as we get one we will do everything possible that we can help. How is my brother Lajos? Believe me there wasn't a minute that we didn't think of you because you may have been in the worst danger. How is Etelka and those dear children? I wish to help them if God has helped you to live through this terrible war then I hope he will give peace after this so that the people can live. How are our grandparents grandma? Grandfather?... And Uncle Marton bacsi and those dear children? Uncle Lajos bacsi and Aunt Etel neni? Write about everything and as soon as the moment arrives immediately we shall help with whatever we can. I'm keeping the packages as of now and I'm waiting for the moment that I could mail them to you. I don't even know what to write to you first.

I'm well. I'm working for a telephone company in their office and Mariska works in a hotel as a cashier. Herman is working in a factory. Ignác is an American soldier [and] is in Germany. He wrote that he would like to go there to look around to help you if it's possible. We hope he'll succeed. He wrote last week that he has written everything also. Thank God he is well. I wish he would be able to go through so that our dear father would see him, a golden young man, 'kanahare.'

Dezső went to live in California. There the climate is always warm and he likes it quite a bit. We didn't go because I and the rest of us want to help our family to perhaps come to America. This way Arthur would be able to help more so if we need to. They are well. Bertha as well. I received a letter from her. How are Miksa Shon and Rezsi with their families? The Szurti relations? I will write again. Take care of your health for the children and to all love, luck in good health.

I'm sorry that at the present I can't send a small package of edible things in the post office, but as soon as I can I will immediately!..... I wish Ignác would succeed with his plans. It would be wonderful, everything would be well. Once again, I repeat and ask God that he should give strength to all of us----- to maintain us in the aftermath of this horrible war. I would send it immediately, but I don't think it's possible. Please don't worry about us. We are all of us well and in good health. Thank God, Dezső is also well. Do you have food to eat? And at home? Write!! With love and kisses to our dear father, Lajos, Etelkat, Emilt, Lenket, Miklost,

Gyulat and Zolikat? Marton bacsi's and Lajos bacsi's families----- and also to our dear grandparents, Hermina.

Our address is;
Hermina Gluck
50 Linwood Avenue
Columbus 5, Ohio
U.S.A.

[from Marie]
Dear beloved father, Lajos and Etelka,
I don't know how to start this letter. First of all we are well. We think of you dear father a lot and the whole family. These terrible years that you had to live through. I hope that God had a special thought for our dear family. We did not forget you and not even for a minute whom we have left behind. My dear father how are you? Please take care of yourself. We are going to try everything to help you as soon as possible. And you dear Lajos, how are you and your family? I can't even imagine what you had to go through. It is a miracle of God And I hope that God did not forget to help further. How are our grandparents? Poor people, what they had to go through. Also dear Uncle Marton bacsi and family, Uncle Lajos bacsi and family. We are waiting for the minute to be able to hear from you. Our little Ignác is in Germany as an American soldier. We received a letter from him in which he tells us that he also wrote to you. He will try everything to help you. He is a very dear young man. I would be very happy if our dear father could see him. Hope that this letter will find all of you in good health and hope to hear from each other. At this time I'm asking you father and the family take care of yourselves and your health. And a lot of kisses always, your daughter and sister, Maria

1945/6/25 Hermine and Marie to David (Book 9, 68-70)

6-25 45
[from Marie]
Dear David,
I'm sorry that I'm a little late to write to you, even though you are not the best either. At this time nothing new. We are alright. It's been a couple of days since we heard from our little brother. He was ok as I think he will come home in a short time. He did not write when. The weather here is very hot. All at once it has become summer. Please take care of yourself and write. Wishing you best of luck and good health. Best wishes with love, Maria

[from Hermine]
Dear David,
This time only a couple of lines because it's getting late. I wrote to Father because I was asking at the post office and was told now we can mail a letter with regular mail. It cost 5¢ to mail it. If it is heavier then it would cost more. Don't be angry because I'm writing only a note. I washed my hair also and it is getting late. I'm working also and I'm very busy. Write about yourself. How are you? Also write about everything. Take care of yourself. Kisses and love, Hermine

1945/6/26 Hermine and Marie #2 to family in Europe [war just ended] (Book 3, 427-430)

1945- June 26
Columbus Ohio

[This is the second letter to Europe]

My dear loved brother Lajos and Etelka,
After long, long years now we can begin to write letters and I hope that all of you are well. It's God's miracle if some of us are alive, and well. Now we are hoping the time will come shortly that we could be of help. I only found out yesterday that I can send you a letter. We have mailed you a letter yesterday addressed to our father. We hope that all of you are in good health. We would like to hear good news from you, if you have lived through it all in this horrible war. Believe us, there wasn't a minute that we did not think of you and also those innocent children, how much they have suffered and were hungry. All of us will try to do

anything possible, and Arthur as well, to help as soon as possible. I know that with nice words you cannot fill an empty stomach, but at this moment we cannot do much more. I will write to the rest of the relations and am hopeful that they are existing. We are informed about everything. If you lived through it then will continue to trust God that he will continue to help. I'm sorry that I can hardly find proper words to express my thoughts, because for years we have not been writing and I would like to write so much about everything. All of us are well and in good health. Irving-- that is Ignác, is an American soldier. He is in Germany and he looks forward to go to your place to look things over, if he has an opportunity. He is well and hope that he can succeed. Wish you good luck and good health to you and our dear father and your children and the rest of the relations. Kisses with love, Hermina

Dear Lajos and Etelka,
Yesterday we mailed a letter to our father, hope that you have received it. We are well and I hope that these lines will find you in the best of health. I can hardly wait for the moment that once again we hear from each other. Kisses to you all, individually many, many times... Maria

[Note - This letter was returned by the Post office, as was the first letter, because the service was suspended.]

1945/6/26 PFC Joe Sklar to Irving (Book 18, 134-135)

June 26th

Hello Irv,
Don't let that return address fool you. I'm still in Marseille sweating out some sort of transportation. Here's the dope briefly! We got here, were processed, but no boats. So they get us rations to go to Le Havre for a tub. So then they changed their minds at the last minute and we're going by plane. I was happy as a lark yesterday when I heard it. But today the Air Corps decides I need a yellow fever shot because we're going to stop off in some damn place in S. America. So I get the shot and I find myself quarantined for 10 days. I guess when the 10 days are up, they'll decide to send me home by 2 man submarine. Oh! Well! C'est la guerre. At least I'm on orders anyway. How's everything back in the company? Let me know! Give my best to anyone who might possibly want it. Did you get that furlough to Checo [Czechoslovakia] yet? Be good. Azzever [as ever] Joe

1945/6/28 Roth Family to Hermine, Marie, Herman (Book 14, 112-113)

June 28, 1945
Dear Marie, Hermine, and Herman:-
Papa Roth [Flora's father] wishes us to thank you for the lovely flowers you sent him while he was in the Hospital. It was very kind and thoughtful of you and he does appreciate it. We all hope that Marie is feeling much better and soon will be perfectly well. With love from us all -
the Roths

1945/7/2 Hermine to Irving (V-Mail, Slide 471)

July 2 - 45
My dear little brother Irving,
We haven't received a letter from you for a few days, I hope you are in good health. Thank God I'm all right. It would be great if you could really be with us and I am very much ready to see you again. I wrote 2 letters to our dear father and Lajos. I will write whatever we get, and if you get an answer, write about everything. Take care and write as soon as you can. I kiss you with lots of love - see you later. Hermina

1945/7/6 Hermine to Irving (V-Mail, Slide 472)

[In English]

July 6, 1945
My dearest brother Irving,
It is quite a long time since we've heard from you. Hope you are well [and] in good health. Maybe we'll see you soon - I hope everything will work out all right. We are all well and as I mentioned to you that I wrote

to our family back there so the letter came back today. Have you heard anything yet. Let us know and take care of yourself and good luck to you. All my love, Hermina

1945/7/8 Hermine to Irving #1 (V-Mail, Slide 473)

[In English]
July 8, 1945
My dearest brother Irving,
We haven't heard any mail from you for a couple weeks. Hope you are well - We thought maybe will see you soon. That is why I don't write as often as before. We all are well and love to see you. My letters came back I wrote our dear Father. Have you heard anything yet? Take care of yourself. Good luck and best wishes. Love, Hermina

1945/7/8 Hermine to Irving #2 (V-Mail, Slide 474)

[In English]
July 8, 1945
My dearest brother Irving,
We haven't received mail from you today hope you are well in good health. Maybe you will be home soon. Let's all hope for the best and for the happy day. Everybody wants to hear the news if you have enough points to get home. Take care of yourself. Good luck and God bless you. With all my love - your sister, Hermina

1945/7/15 Irving to Dave, France (Book 3, 435-439)

1945 July 15
France
Written in Hungarian.

Dearest Dave, it's more than a month since I have heard from you. I hope you are well and in good health. I've been very busy so I couldn't write to you. I must mention that I didn't write to anyone because I just couldn't do it. Since my address has changed so is my work. I was working in a German prison camp. My job was to transport prisoners from Germany to France. Therefore I wasn't in any one place particularly. I was in Paris for a few days and now I'm back in Paris but for a different activity. I'm hoping now that I'll be on my way homeward. If the Almighty will help, then next month I'll be home, I won't believe it until I arrive home. I'm hoping for the best. It appears I'm not succeeding in visiting our father. Their excuse is that there is no communications. So it is. It's not easy to do anything here. When I get home as soon as possible, if I can, as soon as possible, I will return I will do anything that I can for our family. I wrote to our father, but I didn't get any reply. We must hope and believe in God, that everything will be well. David I hope that the almighty will help me and as soon as I arrive home I will send you a telegram open. O'K.? Now David don't write to me until I will write you again. I hope that this week everything will be successful and then in a short while we'll see each other again. Now, many unnumbered kisses, your little brother that will never forget you. Irving

[In English] Please give my love to the family back home and relatives and friends. Irv

1945/7/22 Hermine to David (Book 11, 104-106)

Columbus, July 22, 1945
[Aunt Marie incorrectly wrote the date below it as April 25, 1945]

Dear David,
I'm sorry that I'm responding a little late to the telegram-but it is very hot here in the past [few] days and somehow the feeling did not want to come to write. It really surprised me when the phone rang at such an early hour, at 7:30am. When I first heard the ring, I thought I got news from Irving or he is calling us on the phone. But besides this, I was happy to hear from you that you are well. I believe that you are busy, particularly if you work 7 days. But when you don't write for such a long time, we think that there is something wrong with you, and you are sick.

It is possible that our little brother Irving can come home soon because we did not get a letter from him for about 4 weeks. The letters that I wrote to home came back. Did you go fishing since then? Or you didn't have time for it? Do you still cook at home? Currently, there is no particular news here. There will be a picnic for the company on Monday afternoon, but I don't know if I want to go. Maybe I will go to the movies instead. You must have heard that the Captain Eddie R[ickenbacker] film will be shown in Columbus for the first time and I'm very excited about it. There will be only regular prices and this way we can go too. Write if you can, and take care of yourself. Kissing you and wishing you good health. With love, Hermina

1945/7/22 Hermine to Irving (V-Mail, Slide 479)

July 22, 1945
My dearest brother Irving,
We haven't heard from you for a long time but we hope you are well, or maybe on [the] way coming home. That is why we didn't write to you as often as before. We all are well and looking for your arrival. Let's hope it will be soon and that you can stay with us. Take care of yourself and God bless you. Good luck and best wishes. Love, Hermina

1945/7/22 Irving to Dave, France (V-Mail, Slide 481)

July 22, 1945
France

Dearest Dave,
A few lines again to let you know that I'm OK and hope that you are well and in best of health. Nothing new, since I have told you that by next month I might be home, however as yet it's like [a] dream. I'm hoping it will come through. I know the army, so I will believe it when I get there. I haven't received any mail from you quite some time, however don't write me to this address; here today and some other place tomorrow. Till we meet again with all my love to you from, Irving

My love to the family back home.
I'll try to write.

1945/7/22 Irving to Family, France (V-Mail, Slide 480)

July 22, 1945
France

Dearest Hermine and Marie,
Just a few lines to let you know that I'm OK and hoping that you are well and in best of health. Nothing new, since I have told you that, by next month I might be home, however as yet it's like a dream, hoping that it will come through. I know the army, you can't plan anything, because I'll believe it only, when I get there. I would love to have some mail from you, but please don't write to this address, because here today and some other place tomorrow. Now all my love, from Irving

Love to you until we meet again give my love to Dave, Herman, relatives, and friends.
I'll try to write you more often. Irv.

1945/7/29 Irving to Dave, Outside Paris (V-Mail, Slide 482-484)

1945 July 29
France

Dearest David
It's very difficult for me to write this letter, since in my last letter I wrote that shortly I'll be on my way home. However, as it appears to be, I hardly can believe that they'll be sending me home this year. I could write a lot of things about everything, but that wouldn't be satisfactory to me. When we returned from Germany to France they said that on the 23rd we will be on our way homeward. The 23rd came and went and nothing from nothing. On the 25th I signed the papers and everything was completed. They asked me

where I will be spending my furlough. I am again in a different place and it appears that they're going to assign me. I will continue this letter. With love, Irving

Continuation of the above letter.

July 29, 1945
France

Dearest David.
Here I'm continuing the above letter. I mentioned before that I'll be going to a new assignment and I'll be here for a few months. This is the way it is, and this is the Army! As I said before, I believe something only when I see it and when I get there. I wish I could stop by and have a talk with you. I could talk to you about a lot of things, but now all we can do is hope that God will continue to help me and all of us. If I have to stay here I hope to be assigned to a unit real soon. There I could receive mail, but to this address I can't because I don't know how long I'll be here. Yet, I'm in the replacement depot near Paris. I'm going to continue this letter. Kisses many times your little brother Irving

Continuation of the above the letter.

July 29, 1945
France

Dearest Dave,
Back again hoping that you are well and in the best of health. I am okay. As I said, I'm near Paris. Maybe I'll get an M.P. job in Paris. It wouldn't be bad, I think. Anything is better than to stay here. As soon as I get assigned I will try to get permission to visit our father and family. You know Dave, it is very difficult to do anything in the Army. They do what's best for them. It's a long story, I will have to make it short. Don't worry! I hope to see you soon in the best of health. With all my love Irving.
P.S. Please give my love to the family back home. Irv.

1945/7/29 Irving to Family (Book 7, 41-42)

July 29, 1945
France

III
My Dearest Hermine and Marie,
[In English] As I said before, if I can't go home yet, I hope to get assigned to a unit real soon. Then at least I'll be able to receive mail. Yet I'm in a Repl[acement] Depo, near Paris. Maybe I'll get to be an M.P. in Paris. It wouldn't be bad, I think. Anything is better, than stay[ing] in here. [In Hungarian] As soon as I get a new job, I will try again to visit our father and family. You know, it's very hard to do anything in the army. They do whatever is best for them. [In English] It's a long story, I'll have to make it short. Don't worry! Hoping that you are all well and in the best of health. Hoping to see [you] soon in the best of health. With all my Love, Irving

P.S. Please give my love to Dave, Herman, and Relatives. Irving

1945/7/30 Irving to Dave, Outside Paris (V-Mail, Slide 486)

July 30, 1945
France

My Dearest Dave,
Back with a couple lines and let you know that I'm OK and hoping that you are well and in the best of health. As yet nothing new, I'm still waiting and hoping that's about all. However as soon as [I] find out something I will let you know.

How are you and everything back there? I hope fine. I wish I could hear from you. Maybe in the next few days I'll find out what will become with us. As yet I guess no one knows. Everything is undefinat [indefinite]. Let's hope and my best wishes to you with love. Irving

Give my love to the family back home.

1945/7/31 Irving to Dave (Book 6, 245-246)

July 31, 1945
France

Dearest Dave,
Just a few lines to let you know that I'm OK and thinking of you, hoping that you are well and in good health. I'm still waiting for something to come up. As I told you, nothing definite yet, so I still have high hopes that I might go home. And if I stay here in Europa, I will try everything to get to see the family in Polány. I'm hoping that they are well and in good health. I have saved some amount for that occasion.

Well, I will close this time, I will let you hear from me more often. With all my love, from your little brother, Irving

P.S. Please give my love to the family back home. Irv

1945/8/1 Hermine and Marie to David (Book 11, 94-95)

Columbus, August 1, 1945
[from Hermine]
Dear David!
I know you are surprised as well that we rarely write. It is not because I don't want to, yet it still stays [unwritten]. Thank God I'm well and I hope you are as well. We got a letter from our little brother that I will attach here. Today it rained for the big celebrations. If you could see how the city was decorated to the delight of Captain Eddie [Rickenbacker], but there was no parade because of the rain [World premiere of the film was held in Columbus, his hometown]. What is important, which I mentioned many times to you, is that it makes me so worried when you don't write. But believe me it's true. I believe that you are very busy, but I'm afraid that you are sick and that is why you don't write, but we have the right to know. However, we hope that you are well. Elsie was here on Sunday with her daughter. We got a letter from Bertha as well. She wrote that a man called her from New York to tell her that he was with Irving and that he is ok. We can't know for sure when he will be arriving home, but let's hope the dear God will help us. The girl's name from Lelesz who was in the concentration camp, Schwartz Lenke and I can't remember who she could be. Hey David, really, why don't you write it to me, if God forbid, you are sick?! Write 2 lines. Kisses with love, Hermina

[from Marie]
Dear David!
I'm sorry I didn't write to you for a long time. It looks like I'm taking an example from you. We are well. There is no particular news. I hope that my lines will find you in the best of health. I hope that the dear God will help my little brother and when he will be home he will not have to go to Japan. Now I'm hoping for the best and you should write about yourself. I will write again next time. Watch where you go and what you do! Now greetings with love, Maria

1945/8/1 Irving to David, France (V-Mail, Slide 489)

August 1,1945
France

Dear Dave,
I hope that my few lines will find you in good health, I thank the almighty I'm well. As of now I haven't heard anything new. I hope that shortly something good will come. I know that you're also impatient, but as you can see that's the way it is, especially in the Army. One day they say one thing, and the other day

they will do something else, therefore, I don't believe anyone until it happens. Please take care of yourself. Best wishes to you, I remain with love, your little brother, Irving

My love to the family back home. Irv.

1945/8/1 Irving to Family, Outside Paris (V-Mail, Slide 487-488)

- France -

I

My Dearest Hermina and Maria,

Just a few lines again to let you know that I'm OK and hoping that you are well and in good health. [In Hungarian] My letters sound the same everyday, but unfortunately, I don't go anywhere. I'm at the camp all the time and I don't have the patience to go to the village. Paris is thirty kilometers away and I would like to go there and only five people are allowed to go there daily. You can imagine that out of several hundred soldiers, it will take a long time until it's my turn. By the time it is my turn, I will be assigned to a different location. This is the situation. I would like to send something home for your birthdays, I will continue the letter. With Love, your little brother Irving

- France -

II

My Dearest Hermina and Maria,

I hope that you will receive all my letters at the same time. Yes, as I mentioned I would like to send something home. But it looks like I will not be able to do that. So I'm asking you Herminka and Mariska, buy something in my name and I am sending, rather I will send home some money and take it out of it. Wishing you a happy birthday, [In English] even though I'm a little late to yours Hermine, but please accept it from me anyway. And you Maria, I think that this v-mail will get there by the 16- of this month. No I haven't forgotten it! I will write again, With all my love,

kis őcsetak [your little brother], Irving

Please give my love to Herman and Dave and relations. Irv.

1945/8/5 Helen Perl Goldstein to Hermine (Book 14, 162-164)

My dear Herminka!

I know you don't know what to do with the reason for my silence. Believe me, it is not because of my whimsy nor my negligence, that I did not write. The reason for it is that I am very busy. The apartment is big and I do everything alone. The lady who lived with us got married and moved out before Shavuot. At the beginning, I really missed her, but I got used to it by now, and I feel so much better alone. The child is cute. May God hold her, [along] with others. She does not cry, only babbles, and is starting to take steps. A true companion in my free time. If you would come to me now, you would find yourself more at ease than before. I was at Mrs. Goldblatt and family and they all wondered about you. Her son Lajos is on his way to the fighting in Japan. I did not see your other boyfriend since the winter, so I don't know anything new. You should write about all of you. Did you hear anything about the people from home? Where are the Svartz boys? I became an American citizen on July 23rd. Maybe now, if I would hear about people from home, I could help more easily, but God knows if any of them are alive. But let's hope for the best. Where is your little brother? Write a lot about everything. Don't follow my example. Until I see you again, kisses to you and dear Mariska. Helen

I am sending pictures about us attached here that did not come out the best. The child messed up daddy's hair.

1945/8/7 Hermine to David (Book 3, 145-148)

[In English]

Columbus August 7, 1945

Dear David,

We received your letter yesterday and all are happy to know you are well and good health.

I know you are very busy but maybe you don't know that the letter before this one was dated June 17. We are busy but, I don't like it very much. Because, just work and that isn't much– to stay home so much. So talk about something better that is swell so we have a telegraph today from Irving from France, they just called today and read it to us on the phone. He is thinking of us is well in France. If we'll get it, we'll mail it to you. Sorry the last time I left out the letter I mentioned we'll enclose from Irving but it is not so bad because he sent one to you too. Also we have three more v-mail yesterday and at present he isn't sure if he be able to come home soon. Maybe it is better this way so, we hope God will help us and everything will be alright. Otherwise I am just fine and unexpectedly started to write my letter in English, not very good but if I have more time can do it better too. You're asking me about the boys. Yes Mr. Rosewater doesn't come anymore. I wrote and told him so because he was serious and wanted to come back-but no business!! I just heard from Helen Perl in Cleveland that the other one is on his way to Japan-I sent him my picture was asking for it but didn't get answered yet. I will write some more again till then good luck and best of health to you. Take care of yourself and write! Love, Hermina

P.S. I will write to Bertha again sometimes and I had a letter from her last week. I don't know if I told you about it. A boy call her in New York was overseas with Irving and just got back. Irving is well. But he said the transportation does it why Irving isn't home yet.

1945/8/7 Irving to Family Telegram Paris (Book 4, 120-121)

1945/8/7
Western Union
Visiting Paris. Thinking of you. Love. Irving Gluck.

1945/8/7 Maria to Dave (Book 3, 142-144)

Dear David!
We received your letter and we are happy to hear that thank God, you're well. We got a letter from our little brother also and thank God, he is well too. He is sending his best to you, too. He doesn't believe he can come home soon, but he will write again. Now I will get back to me. You know, that I worked in the Neil House as a cashier and I was very busy all the time. I was there for 7 months. I did not miss a day. I liked my job, only I did not like my boss [female]. Meanwhile I did not feel well and I went to the doctor. The doctor said I have to stay home for a few days until I'm better. And that it's important that she has to give me lunch time. She said she will not give it to me, and I must go to work, otherwise she doesn't need me to go back at all. This is how it happened that a few days became a few weeks. But now I feel completely better

and I can go to work. And you know, this is the second week I have been looking for a job and I was not able to find a proper one yet, until today. Since they know I can sew, and they say that is the best because I learned that, but I don't want to sew. One can not be a cashier just anywhere for anybody. And where one would like to go, they will not take her/him. I can tell you this much David, I was a perfect cashier. In two hours for one lunch for 300 people and even more. And most of the time it came out [exactly] to the penny. But the doctor said that I cannot do this job. This is where my knowledge stops. And please do not worry because I'm fine now. I did not want to write to you because I know you would have been worried. That would not help anyway. Don't write this to our little brother. Good luck and good health. I kiss you with love, Maria

1945/8/11 Irving to Dave, Chamarande (V-Mail, Slide 491)

August 11, 1945
Chamarande, France

Dearest Dave,
First time in two months I have received mail from home. I was very happy to hear from them, they are OK. Thank God. Hoping that you are well also. As for me I'm OK and have been trying to do something so I could go and visit the family in Polány, but from here nothing can be done. Here again I signed my papers as going home and as they said the boat is waiting for us, but I don't believe it until I get there. So that's the way I stand. Let me hear from you and best wishes. With Love, Irving

1945/8/11 Irving to Family, Chamarande (V-Mail, Slide 490)

August 11, 1945
Chamarande, France

Dearest Hermine and Maria,

Have received 6-vmails from you tonight. Thanks a million for it. Have been reading some of the old letters I received from you and still have them. Especially tonight, I didn't know what [to] do, just didn't feel like doing anything. God really helped me and answered my prayer, as I said I was really happy to hear from you. I told you the other day to continue [to] write me, however yesterday I signed my papers again and [they] told us that the boat is waiting for us, but I will believe only when I'll be on it. I'll write you again, hope to see you soon. With love, Irving

1945/8/15 (a) Irving to Dave (Book 5, 360-361) pgs 1 and 3

August 15, 1945
Dearest Dave,

Again on my way to America. We were told today that we will form a packet and get ready to go back to America. So here everybody is from Ohio, Indiana and Pennsylvania. With God's help we will leave this camp on 20 – 45 and will go to Le Havre, and from there we will sail to the Promised Land. That's the way I stand and I'm hoping that everything will be okay. And they won't change any orders, hold us back.

1945/8/15 (b) Undated Irving to Dave (Book 19, 428) - page 2

I think that we'll make it this time. However, I don't believe it until I get there! So let's say if and when I get home I will call you and in the meantime I'll try to write you whenever I can. OK! That's all this time and take care of yourself. Remain with love, your little brother, Irving

P.S. I have written home also. Give my love to them also when you write. Irv

1945/8/15 (a) Irving to Dave (Book 5, 360-361) pgs 1 and 3

P.S.

Dearest Dave,

I don't know if I have told that I have tried to go see the family, but promises that's all I got from them. So you see how everything is in the army. Will try our best from the U.S.A. and I hope to return as a civilian and whatever I can I will do for them. Till we meet again. Love, Irving

1945/8/15 Irving to Hermine and Marie (Book 4, 140-143)

August 15, 1945
My dearest Hermine and Maria,

Again I'm on my way home to America. That's with God's help. We were told today and moved to another company. Here everybody is from Ohio and Indiana and Pennsylvania. So now as they call it, we are in a packet and we will travel home together. From this camp we will leave August 20, 1945 and we'll go to Le Havre and from there will sail on to America. That's the way I stand and I'm hoping that everything will be okay. And that they won't hold us back, like the other time. I think that we will make it this time. However I don't believe it until I'm there! So let's say, if and when I get home I will call you, and in the meantime I will try to write you when I can. Okay sweetheart! Take care of yourselves and give my love to Dave, Herman and relatives. Also to Mr. and Mrs. Walters and Mrs. Hasson. Love to you all, your little brother, Irving

P.S. I don't know what to tell you, because I have tried to go to see the family but only promises, that's all I got. I hope that I can return from America and as a civilian. Then will help them and meantime will try to send some messages to them. Well, I'm hoping that they are well. Best wishes and love to you all, From Irving

1945/8/16 Hermine to David (Book 11, 97-98)

Columbus Aug 16-45

Dear David!

We didn't hear from you for a long time therefore I'm writing now and hoping to hear from you. People all over, everywhere, are very happy because this horrible war is finally over and V-J is here. I had 2 days off and heard that all over people were let off. And how are you? Do you think you will be laid off? I hope everything will work out alright with you, too. Please write. We received a letter from Irving last week. He mailed his address where you can write to him. I read in the newspaper that lots of people already left California and are going home. Therefore, it should not be difficult to get a job. They will need more kinds of work and they will try to change over to different factories to create jobs for civilians. I don't have anything else. Last week Flora and the family left to Michigan for the holiday. I still have one week vacation. I hope our little brother will come home soon in good health. Here the weather is beautiful. Write as soon as possible. With my love and kisses, Hermine

1945/8/19 Hermine to Irving (V-Mail, Slide 492)

[In English]

August 19, 1945

My dearest brother Irving,

Today is Sunday and I want to write to you and to answer some letters I received. Hope you are well and maybe on [your] way coming home. I wish it would be true. I am well and have a week vacation coming to me but I am saving it - so when you come home could stay with you a week longer.

Flora and family left for Michigan for a few weeks - but we spend our vacation just at home. As the war with Japan came to an end so the people have gas - so it is easier to go on a trip. But I don't even have a car! Maybe you'll have one - Will you take me with you Irving? I know the answer! I will write again. Till then good luck and God Bless you. Wish all my Love, Hermina

1945/8/20 Irving to Dave (Book 5, 351-352)

August 20, 1945

France

Dearest Dave,

Hoping to see you real soon and best wishes to you. I'm okay. With love, Irving

1945/8/24 Irving to Dave, Camp Lucky Strike (V-Mail, Slide 495)

August 24, 1945

Camp Lucky Strike

France

Dearest Dave,

Just a line to let you know that I'm at Camp Lucky Strike and from here I'm ready to take off. This is the last stop before going home. I can't tell you when, or how long will be here, but I hope when you get this letter, I'll be on my way to the U.S.A. Nothing new around here except it's windy and cold and when the sun is up it's hot. Here the food is good and get plenty rest, in other words, doing nothing at present. And as we say it, sweating it out. Take care of yourself and I'm hoping to see you real soon. In mean time I'd let you know what I can. Remain with love, Kis öcsed, [your little brother], Irving

P.S. Please give my love to the family back home. Irving

1945/8/24 Irving to Family, Camp Lucky Strike (V-Mail, Slide 494)

August 24, 1945

Camp Lucky Strike

France

Dearest Hermina and Marie,

Page 476

Just another line to let you know that I'm at Camp Lucky Strike and from here I'm ready to take off for my journey. This is it. This is the last stop before you go home. I can't tell you when or how long will be here, but I hope when you get this letter, I'll be on my way. Nothing new around here except it's windy and cold and when the sun comes up it's hot. Here the food is good and get plenty of rest, in other words doing nothing at present. And as we say sweating it out. Take care of yourselves. And hoping to see you real soon, in meantime I'll let you know how I am and what I can. Please give my love to Dave and Herman, relatives, neighbors, and friends also. With love, kis őcsetek [your little brother], Irving

1945/8/25 David to Hermine (Book 2, 199-202)

6/25/45

Dear Hermina and Mariska!

Currently, I don't know any news. I got your letters, where I can see that you are all well, thank God, and I hope that my lines will find you in the best of health! Currently, I don't know any news. Everything is the same. I'm currently working. The work was going to end and the factories laid off 1/3 of the workers, and we were going to work 40 hours. But we are working again 60 hours. Almost every shipyard works 40 hours. Next week we will work 60 hours again and then 48 hours for about 2-3 weeks and then 40 hours - But then I will go. I hope that we will get back pay 11.6/hr daily.

I will probably get 7 months that will be about 200-250 dollar. But when will they give it to me? I don't know. There is plenty of work. But the Union doesn't want to work that many hours. They want us to get 40 hours worth of money, so we could make a living from it. Did you hear anything from Ignác? I hope he'll be home soon. Do not forget to let me know asap! Ok? I don't think I will go home. Here there is more work to be found. What could I do there? Nothing. To work [there] for $30 a week and where [would I work]? [Doing] what? For who? Since I'm here, it's just as good as at home. When one is poor, it doesn't matter where one lives. At least here, one does not become cold during the winter. But we'll see what the future will bring.

The important thing is, that our little brother is coming home. And then we will see what will be. Does Herman still work? He should get a job as a service man, if it exists! Currently, I don't know what to write. I'm writing this letter from work and I don't have another pencil. I hope you will be able to read it! Currently the difference is that one has to know the work better and, if one does not know it well, then they will deal with that person easily. I don't know if I could get into Columbus as an electrician. If yes, I could make pretty good money. But I feel badly leaving this town. Shortly many will go home and it will be better to find a proper place to live, and if the work situation will be better, then you can also come out here. The air and the weather is very nice! So, it is enough for today. Kissing [you] with love. Write! OK? Dezső

1945/8/29 Irving to Dave, Camp Lucky Strike (V-Mail, Slide 497)

August 29, 1945
Camp Lucky Strike
France

Dearest Dave,

Again a line to let you know that I'm OK and hoping that you are well and [in the] best of health. As you see I'm still here. We were supposed to be on our way to the US by this time, but that's the army for you. When you get this letter I think and hope to be on my way home. Just now I was over to the Field Director at the Red Cross. I wanted information about the family back home in Polány. He said to try and <u>write</u> to <u>International</u> <u>Red</u> <u>Cross,</u> <u>Geneva,</u> <u>Switzerland.</u> Take 3 copies and write <u>Missing</u> <u>Persons,</u> and under that, put the <u>names</u> and <u>add</u>[ress]. It will take time to hear about them, but that's the best he can do. I'll try it and if you want to try it also. Or write to American Embassy in Czechoslovakia. Hoping to see you soon. Love, Irving

1945/8/29 Irving to Family, Camp Lucky Strike (V-Mail, Slide 496)

August 29, 1945
Camp Lucky Strike
France

Dearest Hermine and Maria,

As you see my dear, I'm still here at this camp, and still sweating, until I get home. We were supposed to be on our way by this time, but that's the army for you. Any way, when you get this letter I think and hope to be on my way to the US. Now I want to tell you that I'm OK and hoping that you are well and in best of health. Just now I was over to the Field Director at the Red Cross. I wanted some information about the family back home in Polány. He said to try and write to the International Red Cross, Geneva Switzerland. Take 3 copies and write Missing Persons and under that put the names and add[ress]. It will take time to hear about them. But that's the best he can do. I'll try it and if you want to try it also. Love to you and Herman and Dave, Irving

1945/9/2 Irving to Dave, Camp Lucky Strike (V-Mail, Slide 498)

September 2, 1945
Camp Lucky Strike
France

Dearest Dave,

I wish I could have celebrated with you today, because it's the day I landed in Africa 2 years ago, it looks like we will be here for awhile. We were postponed a few times, and now it's been said that sometime this month we will be on our way home. That's the way it is. It would have been nice to be home at the holy days and celebrate together. Well, maybe next time... At this camp we might have some kind of a services or maybe I'll be on the high seas, on the holy days. I'll write or let you know all about. Also I wanted to postpone my New Year's greeting, so that I might have greeted you in person, but now as I can't make it, so I'm wishing you a very happy New Year, and may God help us and unite us, real soon in [the] best of health. Also hoping that our Father and Brother and Family are well and will hear from them the best in [the] near future. Take care of yourself and Lasunu Tajvu Tikuszani [L'shana Tova Tikateyni - Happy New Year]. With all my love, kis őcsed, [your little brother], Irving

Give my love to family in Columbus, Love, Irving

1945/9/3 Marie to David (Book 8, 56-57)

September 3, 1945
Dear David,

We got your letter and are glad to hear that you are well. We are well too. And we got a letter from our little brother and he wrote that he is on his way to come home. We hope that he will be home soon with God's help. Otherwise there is nothing new in particular. I currently have found a job at the A.P. company as a cashier and checker. Currently I'm going to school because I have to study. They pay for the classes for the time being. In probably about a week, they will put me back to the normal job. That place is in Bexley [Bekszli]. They have a store there and I will work there. I hope that everything is going to work out well. The boss looks nice he/she is from England. Currently I don't work there. And how are you? Write about yourself. And I wish you good luck and a very happy holiday! I hope my little brother can be home by that time. Now, take care of yourself and write. The weather here is pretty nice right now. I'm sending greetings from the heart and kisses to you with love, Maria

1945/9/10 Lucille Flicker to Irving (Book 19, 404-407)

[Inside a New Year's greeting from Aunt Jennie]

9/10/45
Dear Irving,

We were glad to receive your letter of Aug. 11, 1945 and learn you are well. We are looking forward to your return to America and coming to see us. Our telephone number is Hollis 5 - 8898W. As soon as you get here, telephone to us and we can direct you how to come here. With the best wish - that you'll be home soon, I remain, Sincerely, Lucille (Gluck) Flicker

1945/9/18 Hermine to David (Book 11, 101-102)

Dear David,

I'm sorry that I'm just writing you now I've tried several times, but it always remained. I was happy to hear that you are well, but I hope you told the truth that you're okay. We have received a letter from Irving and the letters of V-mail were returned and so we trust in God that he will shortly be at home. Yesterday we were in temple and Aunt Helen was there. I invited her for Sunday evening, for dinner. I prepared chicken. I must tell you that in the past few days I was very busy and that's why I neglected writing. We have not received any letters from you, but hope that the money sent to you was received in time. I don't know whether you thought of sending it like that, but this way was the only way you could receive it by that day. This is what I want to write to you, but don't worry about me mailing it to you, because I'm happy that I was able to save the $50 for you as I always planned to give it to you, because you need it also. The balance you have time if you have it. I hope that you're working so you don't miss out on anything. Herman is not working presently, but he can use a little rest because during his vacation he worked. He's looking for daytime work. I don't know what else I can write to you. Arthur and his family are at home already and they are well. The new Rabbi is good and speaks well and it seems like he's a smart man. I will write you again. Till then, take care of yourself. Write to us. I wish you good health. Love and kisses, Hermina

1945/9/19 Private Bill Chapman to Irving (Book 14, 1-3)

P.F.C. Bill Chapman
35545410
921 Ord. Ham. Co.
A.P.O. 887

Sept 19 - 45
Paris

My Dear Friend,

I received your letter just a couple of days ago and I was very glad to hear from you. I was surprised to hear from you and above all, from Camp Lucky Strike. I am feeling pretty good but I have been losing weight and I'm really sick of this country at the present time. We have been moved around so much since coming to Paris. We went to HQ and from there we went to the 460 Ord. Evac. Co. Gentry went to the MP's. Has been transferred twice since he has been in the MP's just to another company is all. While I was in the 460, I wrote to you boys while you were still in the 19 Depot. How long did you stay at the Depot after I left? I'm now in the 921 and where next, I don't know for sure. The old men have already left and they keep bringing in men from the 13. Some of them only have a mere 4 points so it looks like we will be going back to the Depot or something. I'll be home by November any way. I hope. I guess this is all I have to say for now. I hope nothing changes our plans so I hope to be seeing you soon. So till we meet, be good, good luck and God bless you. Hope to be seeing you soon. Take it easy. As Ever, Bill

1945/10/2 Irving to Dave, Camp Lucky Strike (V-Mail, Slide 500)

October 2, 1945
Camp Lucky Strike

Dearest Dave,

Hoping that you are well and in best of health. I'm still sweating it out at camp Lucky Strike. They were telling us that there is no transportation. And from here every day other units were and are going home, except us. And now some of the boys are getting reassigned, so now I don't know what they plan for us. Yet I have no address. I will let you know if I get reassigned. If I do I will try to go and see the family in Polány. Please don't worry! Hoping to see you real soon, With love, kis őcsed [your little brother], Irving

Please give my love to family in Columbus

1945/10/2 Irving to Family, Camp Lucky Strike (V-Mail, Slide 499)

October 2, 1945
Camp Lucky Strike

Dearest Hermina and Maria,

Hoping that you are well and in best of health. I'm still sweating it out at camp Lucky Strike. From here every day someone is going home, except us. They were telling me that there is no transportation. And now some of the boys are sent back and are reassigned different part of the country. If I get reassigned then I go and try to do something about going to see the family in Polány. As yet I have no add[ress]. As soon as I get one or something, I'll let you know and I will have some sort of a story..I hope…Any way, please don't worry! I also will send some money home. If I'm not going home, I bought some souvenirs and will send them home also. I hope to get an address or something. I have waited long enough here. Please give my love to relatives and friends. Don't worry! Take care of yourselves. Love, Kis őcsitek [your little brother], Irving

PS Give my Love to Herman and Dave

1945/10/4 David to Hermine and Marie (Book 2, 185-189)

October 4, 1945
Dear Hermina and Mariska!

Forgive me that I did not write for such a long time. Although I wrote, actually I told you on the phone, that I will write. Ok? But I did not write, I was waiting for the report that our little brother came home. But, as I got the news from the paper, they are just starting to come home this week (Sunday). Based on my calculation, when you will read my letter, you will get news from him too. Thank God, I'm well. I'm still working, although it's not worth it to work for $35 when you get nothing for $20. But that is the way it is. Please do not be sad, even if I don't write. You know how I feel about writing, but that's the way it is. Please write to me as soon as you can. I promise [to write] as much as I feel like writing. If you felt like that, you would never write. I don't know why, but when I start writing the letter, I want to finish immediately.

How do you like the new time? Is it better by you than here? We have daylight here at 7 o'clock [in the morning] and it gets darker earlier than in Columbus. It seems like today the sun will not shine. The air is cold. Yes Herminka, thank you a thousand times for the favor. I will deal with this next week with you. You Mariska, forgive me, if I don't write to you separately, but take it as though the entire letter is for you. This way you will read less foolishness in a letter. I met a few people from Columbus who I worked with in 1940. I did not recognize them, but they even knew my name. That is the way it goes! It seems like there will not be too many unemployed in California. They will do many things and they will open factories. So, it is better here than in Columbus. I hope that Ignác will like to be here. You Hermine and Marcsa, you could get a job anytime, there are enough of your kind [of job], with a little money.

What does Herman do? He has nothing to be sad about? He gets $20 a week and he does not need to work for it. He should go to school and study something. Maybe I will do the same, if we won't get a raise. But I will leave this for today. It was enough. I hope my lines will find you all in the best of health. Until then, I wish you all the best with love. Dave

P.S. If our little brother got home and he is there, while he is reading the letter wish him all happiness and good health for the home coming. Until I can see him in person, may God give everything best for him. Kiss him with love, David

1945/10/10 Customs Declaration to bring P-38 Pistol (Book 4, 119)

Certificate of Retention and Customs Declaration
(Strike out portions inapplicable)

1. I certify and declare that the following items of government property were purchase by me and are my personal property.
NONE
Irving Gluck
PFC 35633941
2. As his commanding officer, I certify that the above named has, by the authority of the theater Commander been authorized to retain the following items of captured enemy material, and has evidenced to me his right to possess the items of British, Canadian, Russian. And I further certify that the provisions of WD Cir 155, dated 28 May 1945 (allowing only one pistol per man) has been complied with.
Captured Enemy Material 1 - P-38 - German

Allied Government Material

Gabriel Bourga
Capt. C.I.
Date 10-Oct. 45
3. The following Customs Declaration will be accomplished in all cases. In addition the Customs Declaration tag will be accomplished and affixed to the container.
CUSTOMS DECLARATION
I declare that all items herein consist of personal and household effects either taken abroad by me or acquired abroad, for my personal use, except the following:
(Here list items or write "No exceptions" as appropriate)
NO EXCEPTIONS
Date 10-Oct. 45
Signature Irving Gluck
Rank and ASN P.F.C. 35633941
Type of Container B - Bag
No of tag

1945/10/15 Hermine to David (Book 16, 4)

10/15 - 45
Dear David!
I know that you are surprised, [and wonder] what could be the reason that I have not been writing to you. We got your letter and I'm glad to hear that you are well. I'm sorry that my last letter was so serious. But believe me, when one is angry, one does not care about anything. Herman is not working yet, but he must find some good job soon. How are you David? Do you work? The weather here is pretty good and the day was very nice today. In the City Hall there is an exhibition and I went to see it. Maria already wrote everything about our little brother, Irving. So, let's hope that we will see him soon. Although, it makes me impatient that we did not get any letter from him in about 4 and a 1/2 weeks. Otherwise, I'm well. I hope you will write and soon. If I get to know anything about our little brother, where he is and when he will arrive, I will write to you. I will end this with that and I wish you good health. Kisses with Love. Hermina

1945/10/19 American Embassy (in Prague) to Irving - Missing Persons (Book 7, 247-248)

American Embassy
Consular Section
Prague, Czechoslovakia
October 19, 1945

Mr. Irving Gluck
50 Linwood Ave
Columbus, Ohio

Sir:
The Embassy has received your letter of August 30, 1945, concerning the welfare and whereabouts of various persons. Immediately an investigation was initiated through the District Office of the National Committee at Leles. An answer has just been received as follows:
"Jeremias Gluck, Lajos Gluck, Miksa Schőn and Joseph Lefkovitz, former residents of Polany, were interned during the Hungarian occupation of the country and taken to Germany. Not a single one of them returned as yet. Gyorgi Gerenyi, resident of Polany, the neighbor of the above mentioned persons is alive and is well. He is supporting his family of eight members from proceeds of land on which he works. Finally we wish to inform you that there are residing in our district near relatives of the above mentioned persons, namely Marton [Emil] Schwartz, 14 years of age, residing at Královsky Chlumec, son of merchant Martin Schwartz, who has not yet returned, and Ignac, Manci, and Rosalie Klein, residents of the town of Leles. No person is able to give any information regarding the fate of the above mentioned persons and no details are available. However, information gathered in connection with similar cases leads one to believe that the above mentioned persons may have been killed by the Germans."

While this information is apparently authentic, the Embassy cannot vouch for its accuracy. A letter addressed to Mr. Jeremias Gluck at Polany by this office was returned by the postal authorities with the statement that he does not reside there. It is suggested that if you wish to write to any of the above mentioned persons still residing in this country, direct air mail through your local post office is the most expeditious means. Very truly yours,

For the Ambassador:

John H. Bruins,

American Consul.

1945/10/21 Irving to Dave, Lucky Strike (Book 2, 259-260)

France
Oct 21 1945
Camp Lucky Strike

Dearest Dave,

Hoping that you are well and best of health. I'm OK and on my way home on a Victory ship the name is Frederick. After being here at Camp Lucky Strike for over eight weeks, I guess it's time.

Well, don't worry, I'm hoping for a happy landing. Till we meet again, I remain with love, your little brother, Irving

My love to the family back home in Columbus

P.S. I'll call you when I get home to the U.S.A. Please don't worry and hoping to see you soon. Love, Irving

1945/10/21 Irving to Family, Lucky Strike (Book 7, 43-44)

France
October 21, 1945
Camp Lucky Strike

Dearest Hermina and Maria,

Hoping that you are well and [in the] best of health. I'm OK and hoping to see you real soon. After being here for eight weeks I think it's time. I will tell you all about [it] when I get there with God's help. I'm going on a Victory ship the name is Frederik. Hoping for a happy landing in the U.S.A. Best wishes and love, your little brother, [kis őcsétek], Irving

Please give my love to Herman and relatives and friends.

1945/10/23 Welcome Aboard SS Frederick Victory Ship with Newsclipping (Book 22, 134-135)

W E L C O M E   W E L C O M E

Welcome aboard the good ship SS Frederick Victory. We feel sure you will never forget the name because it it the ship you have waited so long for to "Come in." You can rest assured that it is as much a pleasure for us to be instrumental in taking you HOME as it is for you to be going. We are going to try to make this as pleasant a voyage as possible considering the crowded conditions and the lack of certain facilities which can be found only ashore. We do have the following aboard and they are yours for the asking: Magazines, games, hobby craft kits, cards, library books, athletic equipment, musical instruments, phonographs and records, moving picture shows, and a pretty complete supply of PX supplies which will be on sale (watch the bulletin boards for time and place). We have also a transport Chaplain who will do his best to help you in any way he can. He has a supply of religious literature and items such as Rosaries, Mezuzahs etc. Don't hesitate to call on the Chaplain. Last but not least we have the best chow that ever graced a mess kit. (this includes FRESH MILK)

The permanent Army Personnel aboard the Transport consists of five officers and eight enlisted men, Captain Ervesun, Transport Commander and Lt. Koop, Assistant Transport Commander, will be handling your bed and board and those wonderful PX supplies. Lt. Mallen, Transport Services Officer and Sgt.

McHugh his assistant will cater to your recreational needs. (We've got poker chips too) Chaplain Walker is the man we told you not to hesitate to see. Lt. Belt is the medical man who has the pills for that certain feeling.

The Transport Commander's Office is located off the troop mess opposite the library. Don't worry about the location of the PX; we give super service; the stuff is brought to you. The Transport Services Officer will be hiding behind his books and supplies in the library and storeroom which is located right smack in the troop mess. The Chaplain's Office, and the Infirmary are located conveniently near each other in hatch number four, both for your spiritual and bodily ailments.

Here's a couple of friendly tips:

Keep your valuable in your possession at all times. (YOU"D be surprised how things get lost aboard ship and how rarely they're found.)

BE CONSIDERATE of your fellow passengers. It pays dividends! Clear the mess hall as soon as you are thru eating. Give the fellows waiting a break. The sooner the mess hall is cleared, the sooner the library and movies can function.

It takes approximately nine days to get home. They can be nine pleasant days if you co-operate.

WANTED IMMEDIATELY:

By the Chaplain - - Assistants, Catholic, Jewish and Protestant. Song leader and Organist. (see the Chaplain at once! A reward awaits you.)

By the Transport Services Officer - - Barbers, and musicians. (Report to library.)

NOW LET'S SEE SOME OF THAT CO-OPERATION!
THANK YOU
The Ship's Complement

[Newsclipping Above on first page]
The following Columbus members of the armed forces were listed as returning to the United States from overseas assignments: **Aboard SS Frederick Victory Docked at New York Nov 1**
Pfc. Lawrence E. Hessinger; T/Sgt. Charles Davis; Pfc. Glen H. Wilson; Pvt. Lindsey L. Johnson; Pvt. Russel E. Merchant; Pvt. Marion Vincent; T/4 William T. Schoch; Pfc Irving Gluck

1945/10/26 Bertha to Hermine (Book 4, 87-88)

[In English]
New York
October 26, 1945
Dear Hermina!
Am hoping this letter will find you all in best of health and also that you can tell me good news about Irving that he is in the States. Jennie Frye called me over the phone last night and sorry to say that she got word through Jack Eigner's daughter that Etelka Klein from Szürty and her husband were the victims (of the war) and left three children. I can't go into details about as I am almost nuts thinking that what must of happened to our sisters also. I have written to the World Jewish Congress in Sweden, hoping that I find someone out of the family.
October 30, 1945
I couldn't continue this letter on the day I started as Lea Rosztyo got a letter from her brother Sandor and she lets me know that since Rezsi and Marcus were they haven't heard a word from either side of them. Hitler sure made a good job of the world. In case you do know something please don't hesitate to write and tell me. It's better to get over with. I intended to visit my relative Fred, the only thing kept me back, didn't want to miss seeing Irving in case he docks in New York. I do hope that Irving will get here safe and well. With best wishes and our love to you all. Bertha and Mannie

1945/11 Undated Marie to David (Book 8, 5-6)

[Undated, but probably Nov 1945 since she mentions that Irving wrote that he will come home (see letter 1945/10/21 Irving to Family, Lucky Strike (Book 7, 43-44) and that Louis Schwartz wrote that he will come home (see letter 1945/11/4 Marie to David (Book 8, 59-61))]

Dear David!

As you can see I am taking the example from you. We got your dear letter last week and I am happy to hear that thank God you are healthy. One cannot even know what to think, that I did not hear from you for so long. Even if it is a few lines, you should write. I can't say that I was such a correct writer in the past weeks, but I can say that at night it is too late when I get home and I am busy when I am home also, as usual. Otherwise I am well. We did not hear from Irving until today. He mentioned in the last mail that he will come home. I hope that the dear God will help him and he could be home with luck in the best of health. I can hardly wait for that moment. Otherwise there is no news. I am only asking you to write and we will be in a hurry to write too. Now I wish you good luck and the best of health. And take care of yourself wherever you go. I kiss you with love. Marie.

Herman is still home currently. The weather is pretty cold. We got a letter from Lajos Schwartz also and he wrote that he will come home. Or he is already at home. I don't know. We got the letter returned that we wrote to our little brother and also from others too. And I'm thinking it could have come back sooner. And you should write about yourself, but not a year later. Now lots of luck and I wish you the best of health! I kiss you M.

1945/11/4 Hermine to David (Book 11, 108-109)

11/4 - 45
Dear David!

We did not get any news from you for weeks - although I'm learning from you too and it's going well for me - I'm sorry, but I did not write before because I wanted you to see how hard it is to wait. You are busy, but I'm thinking that you are not writing the truth and are just concealing things! Although, I could not stay quiet anymore since you did not talk to our brother Irving and he called us twice tonight already. Thank God he is well and as soon as he arrived to New York, he called us on the phone. And oh boy! Was that wonderful to hear his voice!

Currently, he is in PA and with God's help, he is planning to come home on Thursday. He asked if you have a phone? He wanted to call you and said that he sent you a telegram. Today I was preparing to stay home to cook so I will have everything at home since he could be home tomorrow, but our brother Irving said he had a very good lunch and I do not have to worry about it.

I know you would love to see our little brother too, and to be here when he arrives, but the truth is that Long Beach is far. Besides that, I'm well. I'm getting a week's vacation time when our little brother arrives. Lajos arrived home from Iceland and last Monday night, he was in Columbus, but only at 11:30 at night and he only had half an hour, so we only talked on the phone. But he said he will travel this way soon and then he will have more time to visit us. His brother is at home already from the military. Lajos was wondering about you and he thinks that everything there must be very nice and it is agreeable. The weather was pretty good until now. Nice sunny weather with little rain and it was not too cold. In other words, there is only a little coal left in the furnace because there is no need for that. I hope you are well and we will hear good news from you. I wish you good health. Kisses, with love. Hermina

1945/11/4 Marie to David (Book 8, 59-61)

11-4 45
Dear David!

For the past week we still haven't heard from you. We are ok. Finally, I can tell you a little news. Our little brother arrived in New York on Friday night at 6 o'clock and he called us 12 o'clock. Thank God he is ok. He told us he hopes that he will come home in a few days. I'm having a hard time waiting. I wish he would be home now. I'm hoping that he will not have to go back. Also, Louis Schwartz came home too, and last Tuesday evening he was going through and he called us also. He has been home for a couple of days. I hope he was also discharged. His brother is already at home. Otherwise, nothing new. The weather is not bad.

How are you? I hope my letter will find you well. It seems you must be very busy because you still aren't writing to us. Irv sends you his best wishes and yes, Herman is still not working. He still isn't getting any money. There are always excuses so that they would not have to pay. There isn't too much work, especially in a better job. Are you working? Be careful wherever you are going and whatever you are doing. I'm wishing you all the best and good health. I hope you have enough time to write. I'm closing for now wishing you all the best with all my love, Maria

1945/11/6 Klein (Ignác, Manci, and Rohcsi) 1st letter after Liberation SURVIVORS (Book 3, 227-228)

[This letter has been written by the Klein girls, my brother Lajos's wife's sisters.]

1945 November 6
Lelesz

With love, dear Herminka and Mariska.
Unfortunately, we have taken the letter you wrote to your family into our hands, but I believe regretfully that in America you know more about everything than we do here. We were taken in 1943 [she means 1944], one week after Passover, on Saturday, to a concentration camp in Ujhely. It was here where poor Etelka from Helmec gave birth to a little boy, Smaje, but the little boy died there in Ujhely. It was a good thing for that little boy.

When they were transporting us from Ujhely, your dear father, Patyu [Uncle Marton] along with [Uncle] Lajos bacsi were taken away together, but we remained there for a few days. It's regretful that we only saw them in Ujhely.

My dear Hencsukam, God gave only to those that came home the strength to be able to survive one and one quarter years of misery. There, in the concentration camp at Auschwitz, they separated people that they considered to be strong. Rohcsi and I were together from the first moment, and from there they took us to Nuremberg. We spent time there during the heavy bombardments. In February they brought us near to Pilzen, where we were freed on May 5 by the Americans.

My dearest, it's unfortunate that in Polyán the only person that survived is Malvin. She is in Sweden, because those that were weak were taken there to recuperate.

Malvin writes to us. Lenke nenni's [Lefkovits] two daughters are there, too. Hersu is at home and just one single child of Patyu bacsi [Uncle Marton], Emil, came home. The Pollak girls all died from typhoid fever [flek tyfusz]. Zoli [Pollak] is back home by himself, alone. The Braun family all died. Tuci Lefkovics is back home by himself and now he is getting married to Edit Weiss. Médi, Mityu and their father are at home. Etyu Moskovits has a relationship with one of them. Etyu is in Homonna. The 3 Slanger girls and Marie are living in Uncle Lajos bacsi's house. From the Frida family, Hetyu and Arsu survived. Hersu and Yentu Zinger survived. The 2 Stark boys are at home and of the 3 Stark girls, Lenke and Irene, who are in Sweden survived, but Helen died. From the Reisman family only Szerénke and Miki survived. Miki already got married to a Kaposi girl. Szerényke is living in Karleszbád. As it is in Lelesz, there are only 22 Jews left that survived from several hundred. Majsu Frőlinger survived, but poor Berti with his son both died. Their daughter Lili is also in Sweden. We have received several letters from the two Klein girls.

I was wondering why you have not written to us. The situation here [in Lelesz] is very bad. The non-Jews are very bad and they are not willing to return anything to us. For example, your father left a watch with Gerenyi and we asked for it. They replied that they'll give it only to Dezső because that is what your dear father said to them. Therefore you should write to them.

Ignác was declared to be the trustee of your property. The fields were not plowed or seeded when we came home. Now Ignác has given out the fields to be seeded. The furniture is at Ivanyo and Ragany. They took it. There is no law to make legal decisions, therefore nothing can be arranged. We found in our house only the furniture. Everything is very costly here, therefore no one can be considered as poor, only unhappy, because very few of us remained.

My dearest's, it's impossible to write down what we have gone through. The Feuereisen girls [returned], with the exception of Nelli, their parents, and little Majer who are missing. Zseni did not write yet. My dear

Hencsukam, I believed that at least little Emil would come home, but the little Elike [Lenke] died after we were freed. In other words, the old, the children, the pregnant women, no longer exist. This is the German culture. Here is a new sidra [chapter].

My dear Hencsukam, now I know how strong a person can be and how much one can take. I have no patience to write. To all of you with kisses and love, Ignác, Muncie and Rohcsi

1945/11/9 Irving to Dave Telegram Discharge (Book 5, 358)

Dated Columbus Ohio 2:14P 11-9-45
To Dave Gluck
apt 10 1363 Alamitos

Dearest Arrived home. Discharged everyone well. Love, Irving

1945/11/10 Irving to Dave (Book 6, 249-250)

Columbus, Ohio
November 10, 1945
Dearest Dave, (unto 120 years!)
Home sweet home they say, well here I'm home in Columbus and out of the army. I'm discharged. So I wish I could talk to you or see you but will have to discuss what we'll do. Here in Columbus, I have visitors, and I'm busy almost all the time. Hermina is at home for a week she has her vacation and Maria is working anyway. I can't tell you how happy they were to see me, but so was I. I'm really happy to be back. You know I haven't heard from you since May. In a way I haven't had an address and couldn't write you either. Well I guess I will have to forget the past and start a new life over. Listen here I will enclose a very small picture I made yesterday so I can send it to you it [is] not so good, and I hope I can see you in person. Listen write to me and let me know how everything is with you. Take care of yourself. Yet you can write about everything you want there is no more censoring like it used to be. I would like to show you my discharge papers, but when I'll get my copy I will send you one to show it to you. Well Dave take care of yourself and I will write you now more often. Remain with love, Irving

P.S. If you have a telephone number please send it to me and I will call you. Okay. Write soon. Love, Irv.

Hermine, Marie and Herman sends their love to you.
Please write soon

1945/11/14 Bertha to Hermine (Book 2, 84-86)

Mount Pleasant PA
November 14, 1945
Dear Hermina,
Forgive me for not answering your letter sooner and to tell you our excitement we had when Irving called us and came to see us in New York. Hoping that he is home with you by now, he is a proud kid don't let him go to work for a while. He should take a rest for a while. Mannie and I asked him to come to New York for vacation and to bring you with him. He promised to do so. I'm spending a few weeks at present with my brother [cousin] and family. I haven't seen Fred for a long time. We almost surprised you kids last Sunday and then when we changed our mind as I was afraid the trip would be too tiresome to make in one day so we called it off. Hoping that you and all yours are well with best wishes to you all. Fred and family are sending their love. I remain as always, Bertha

1945/11/26 Irving and Hermine to Dave (Book 6, 302)

Nov 26 -45
Columbus, Ohio

[from Irving]
Dearest Dave, until 120!

Here enclose you'll find some souvenirs from me, a pair [of] gloves I have taken from a German prisoner between France and Germany, and bracelets from Paris also a billfold I bought there. So I will write you more next time and here you will find some pictures of me they aren't so good, but you let me know what do you think about it. All our love to you and write us when you can. Love, Irv.

[from Hermine - in Hungarian]
Dear David,
It is late tonight therefore I will write only a few lines to you. I hope you will like the cookies. I'm fine and will write more soon. Kisses, Hermina

1945/12 Undated Marie to David (Book 8, 26)

[Undated, probably beginning of December 1945 since Irving is home, Hermine is still in Columbus, and it is snowing. By the following year in Dec 1946, both Marie and Hermine are in NY]

Dear David!
I'm sorry that I did not write to you for such a long time, but I hope that my lines will find you in the best of health. There is no news here. I am very busy with my work and also at home. And how are you? Do you work? Although it has been a few weeks that I got a letter from you. I don't know any particular news. Little brother already wrote about himself. The weather is pretty cold. There was a big snow last week. I think that the weather is nice and sunny already. And now, I wish you a happy New Year and lots of good luck. I am sending my best with love and kiss you with love. You better take care of yourself wherever you go! Write! Maria

1945/12/2 Irving to Dave (Book 6, 251-252)

Dec 2nd 1945
Columbus 5, Ohio

Wishing you a happy Hanuka!

Dearest Dave, until 120
How are you Dave? Hoping you are well and in [the] best of health. I'm O.K. and have been thinking what to do to start the future. As yet I can not decide. There are so many things that it would be good to do, but who knows if I will have patience to it. First it would be nice to go to school on government expense and I could get 65 doll[ars] per month plus pay for the school. And also I spoke to Yenkins and asked them, what they got for me. So I would have there some future. At present he says, if I want I could work warehouse or factory and [in] about 3 months later I would work in store for a year and when I know the business I could or would have one for myself and they naturally would help me with it. Well Dave, that's that. Besides, maybe I would get another job some where. But I guess at Yenkins I would have some future. What do you think about this? It's nice to go to school, but there [are] plenty smart people and [they] still have to work just like anyone else. Well I don't know Dave, but if you have something in your mind, please let me know. The whole thing gives me a headache. You might say what I haven't been thinking of that before, well to that I can say only, I never thought I'll get home and I figured, when I do, I will have plenty [of] time. Oh yes! [In Hungarian] Now I remember you writing to write in Hungarian. Many times I don't have the patience to write, but for your sake so, I will try to write often, and in Hungarian. I want to see you, but I still don't want to go. If I decide what I'm going to do, I'll be better able to write to you if I go there or not. Take care of yourself now [in English] and write me soon. Love, Irving
Everyone is well!
P.S. Write me about yourself and social activity…

1945/12/5 Helen Perl Goldstein to Hermine (Book 15, 179-183)

Cleveland Dec, 5.

My Dear Herminka!
I know you don't know the reason for my silence. Believe me, it is not because of negligence, but somehow I am always very busy. I can't even write down how much. In the past days, the child was sick many times. First with a cold, and then with a sore throat, and then she got smallpox. You can imagine what I went

through. Now, thank God she is well. She is already walking, that is, exactly at the age of 1 she started to walk. She talks full words already also. She likes music very much and she has a good ear for music. She copies things from the original like she is a wonder. Not to speak out loud, but a sweet kid. Her father loves it when they ask him in any language whose child could she be, only her father's. He would take the eyes out of the person who would say she is mommy's daughter. My Herminka! Did you hear anything from the old country? I did not yet. But some of my girlfriends heard sad news from there. There are some families who got wiped out completely. Where those who were found, they are sick with their organs just like with their body. I heard that the Shvarc boys are at home also and that Jozsi is counting on going home to look around. I wish we could go as soon as possible! Maybe we would have more results from that as opposed to corresponding with them by letter. Please send me your addresses. There is no particular news here.

Mr. "R" [Rosewater] was here last week. I acted like I didn't know anything and I asked him what's new. He answered that he got a letter from you, the letter in which you cancelled on him. By the time he said he was not even about asking you yet, he already got a basket [you get a basket when someone refuses your offer, usually when someone is proposing could get a basket if the answer is no], so there is nothing to talk about, if you are not interested. How are your brothers? Your little brother might be at home already! Or maybe he will succeed to get to his place of birth. When are you coming to Cleveland, my Herminka? Come for the Christmas vacation. Bring Mariska too. You can be our guests now. There is plenty of space.

I get together with Goldblatt and the others very often. Lajos is in Japan as the camp clergy. Now I really don't know what else to write. My husband is away for the entire week. He will come home on Saturday night only. It would be so good if you would live here. Oh! Anus Reic got a letter, his parents and sister are alive somehow. A French soldier helped them to escape. He lives in Columbus. I'm sure you will see each other. I will close my lines now until I will see you again as soon as possible. Kisses. Helen
Greetings separately to your siblings.

1945/12/9 Irving to Dave (Book 6, 253-254)

Columbus, Ohio
Dec 9 - 45
Dearest Dave, until 120
Here I'm again and want you to know that I have been thinking of you and hoping to hear from you soon. Hoping that you are well and [in the] best of health. I'm feeling fine, Thank God. At present I would like to hear from you an answer to my letter in which I have said that I don't know what to do. I can go to school for 4 years on government's expense. At present they pay only 50 dol[lars] a month. I will let you know how I'll come out. Well nothing to say except here I enclose an article of a Cohn girl that you knew. She is getting married. I spoke to her mother. That's that real religious woman. I'm sure you know her. Listen Dave, I want you to write me whenever you can, and I'll do my best. At present Hermine, Marie are here and will write you a few lines. They are waiting to hear from you, just like me. Herman is well. He isn't good in writing, as you know. I will ask you to drop him a few lines, so then he'll get to think a little and then might start to write at least once in [a] while. He began to work this week at Went Bristol Co. It's a drug store. They don't pay so well and works 48 hours for $27.00 Well that's that. Now let me know about your self and write me a lot. OK. Best wishes to you. Love, Irving

[In Hungarian]
P.S. After I finished writing my letter then I thought I should have written it in Hungarian. However it is much easier to write English because I have become accustomed to it. Write to me frequently in any language. I remain with love, your little brother, Irving

1945/12/10 Mrs. Sandor Kosztyo (Ilonka Török) and Sandor to Hermine (Book 18, 225-229)

Dated 945 XII/10
Dear Herminkám!

We received the letter that you mailed us, which I was very surprised when I saw the mailing address. Dear Herminkám, I'm sorry that I can tell you an answer to your question. I have a very sad answer. Neither your dear father, nor your brother and his family have come back. We don't have any information about what happened to them ever since they took them away. We did not hear anything more about them. About Shŏn, unfortunately we only know that there was a young man here in the first half of October. He told us that he was the son in law of Mr. Shőn's brother. All he knew was that Mr. Shőn and his son Tibi died, and about the others [he knows] nothing. From the Lefkovics family no one, only Olga's husband Ignácz Klein is in Leles. I heard that Malvin wrote to Ignác but we didn't speak to him. We don't know for sure if it's true or not. The young man who was here told us he is Miksa Shőn's relative. [They?] agreed and he rented the farm and the house. We don't bother with [them] if our best neighbor did not come back. I didn't want to bother with new neighbors. I don't care. Dear Hermine, if it would not be too much, I would ask you a favor. If it would be possible to speak with Bertha or write to her and tell her what is happening here. If it is possible to do this for us, that is, to rent us the "belhelyet" because it was her father's property. Then we would be able to buy it. Nobody can do anything on their own, and we are afraid if we have a really bad neighbor, there will only be a dispute, we are trying to prevent it. We have already written all this in a letter to your Aunt, but it seems like she never received it because there was no reply. If you receive my letter somehow let me know, I really don't want you to say we didn't answer because we're really happy to answer even if you hadn't sent a stamp to answer, even then we would write. If I write something wrong, don't be surprised because I have two beautiful blonde daughters [and] both of them are near me and they also want to write, but they are too young. From my heart, I'm wishing you best wishes to you all.

Mrs. Kosztyo Sándore né
Single Name - Török Ilonka

Dear Herminke!
You wrote to us asking about your dear father and your brother Lajos and his family. I'm sorry we can only write what we know. In April 1944 they took them away and they did not return. If someone would be able they would be in Switzerland or Sweden. Maybe they are in a war sanitarium there. From Ignác Klein you can get more information because he has more information than others from everyone. Mr. Shőn's relation who was here has taken care of the property. He is, according to Ilanka, the son in law who was a lawyer. I don't remember his name. I remain with friendly wishes from a far distance, best wishes for the boys also.
Sandor Kosztyo, Polány

1945/12/11 Hermine to David (Book 11, 111)

December 11, 1945
Dear David,
I'm sorry that I didn't write you sooner but I also became lazy, because I have someone I can depend on - on Irving, as you know..... I can say that I'm well and hope that you are also. Are you working yet? Herman began to work, hope that he will like it, however the wages are not great. Presently there isn't much work, therefore one cannot be selective. Did you receive the package? As of now we have not received any replies from Europe. We hope that shortly we will be lucky and succeed. I don't remember if I've written to you a few weeks ago, that we mailed via air mail a number [of letters]. All the letters to our father and to Gerenyi, Kosztyo and Deak, to the mailman Janos Bácsi's address. We have enclosed international stamps, so that they would reply to us. We received a letter from Lajos Schwartz and he wrote that his sister and her two children are staying with Ferinel Garanyi. He did not write about anyone else. Etelka from Terebes and her husband do not exist, only the three girls. We hope to hear news, until then, kisses, Hermina.

1945/12/11 Margit and Ica Gereny (from Bodrogmezo) to Mariska (Book 1, 119-120) pg 1-2

Bmező [Bodrogmező] 1945
XII, 11
Dear Mariska!
Herminka, Ignacz, Hersmendu and Dezső

I got your dear lines and I was very happy, because I could not wait to get them. Many wrote from America already and I thought, if you are alive, you will write. It felt very, very good for the entire family. We are all alive, only I miss my poor son, Gyuszi, he died. Everyone has their own cross to bear. [Hungarian expression, everyone has his own problem]. Then a daughter was born, Gabriella. She is already 3.5 years old. Etelke [Gluck] has a little girl also, Kornelia. They are the same age. Let's get to the subject, even if it's very difficult to answer. I'm asking all of you to be strong and trust in the good God. He could still help you. I will be able to give you more answers [in the future] than I can now.

They took your dear father and Lajos with his family in the beginning of May to Kiralyhelmec with an official notice. In other words, my husband with the carriage took them away. They were there for a few days and then they took them to Ujhely. We don't know anything about them since then. Nobody came [back] here, except Ignácz Kláyn [Klein]. Nobody else came to the town, but we are always waiting for them. It's very bad for us also. The good old neighbors. We helped them so much. My husband at dawn got the carriage ready and took food for them. To send it that way, because he carried them in his heart. We got used to Etelka so much, and needless to say Mr. Gluck bácsi

[This line is written by a child] I kiss all of you many times. Ica

1945/12/11 Undated Margit Gereny [neighbor] to us (Book 5, 276-277) pg 3-4

When the information came in from Mr. Gluck [that you arrived to America] I was very happy about the news. My children are now in a good place. The only thing is is that I feel very badly about Lajos and his family. He doesn't care about himself, for him it doesn't matter. Therefore, don't worry, because you make him very happy with the knowledge that you are safe. I'm still waiting for them because time has passed, he was supposed to be at home. They'll come home last. I'm also hoping and struggling. About Dezső, where is he? I have not heard from him for a long time. He sent something from somewhere to Lelesz and to his family here. The authorities were asking, but the truth is, I'm always waiting for you to come home and come to us as if you were going to arrange the little things. I can write so many things, but not before I will receive an answer from you. Then I will write about the others. Ignác [Klein?] got angry at me because I didn't give him what he asked me to [the watch?]. But you just write to me and then I will answer again. Margitka is in a new position at the post office. Ica is home. She wants it too but she can't go now. We've been through a terrible world war, I don't even like to talk about it because we're so nervous you can't tell. I'll write about it later if you write that they leave the letters alone unopened. I didn't write only to Hermine, but to everyone else. Ignác himself and Hersmendú [Herman] didn't write. And they have to write a lot with Dezső because they are so good. You can kiss the whole family with love. We are also crying. It is just very difficult for us. I'm kissing you because I miss you a lot, Margit

[Margit Gerenyi] the neighbor from across the street

1945/12/17 János Szmolyák (Postman) to Hermine (Book 18, 250-255)

Dear Herminka, and all of the other sisters and brothers,

I hope my letter will find you all in good health. I ask God that all should be well. Dear Hermine, I received your letter which I was very happy to get. I want to thank you for remembering me. I'm writing right away without delay, but I feel I would like to tell you some good news about your dearest Father and all your family. I don't know anything about them now. In the Spring of 1944 all the Jewish population was taken away, but to where we don't know. Nobody knows. As of now, no one returned here. Some have returned to some other villages. To Leles, some of the younger boys, girls, but the oldest and the women and children have not. The ones who come home they looked well and healthy. Dear Herminka, we lived through a horrible nightmare that still continues. Even now it would be difficult to believe what we went through, it's even too much to write about. Even what comes next we're waiting to see how it will work out with the situation. We still don't know. I just wanted to tell you all that I'm still continuing to work as I was assigned, but it is very hard and tiresome, and it is a very difficult task to do. I also wanted you to know that my family came back. We are well, but we don't know if my son and the oldest grandchild are dead or alive! There are many other people who did not hear from their family. Now, I'm closing my letter. I'm wishing you all the best to you all dear Herminka, Mariska, Dezső, Herman and Ignác. Some other time I will write more or hope to hear better news. I'm sending my best wishes to you all, the whole family. Please write again. I'm waiting. I remain, Jànos bacsi

1945/12/18 Private Paul Imhoff to Irving (Book 15, 51-53)

Dear Irving:

I became a civilian Nov. 8, 1945. Last week I bought a motorcycle and this Spring I'll try to take a spin up to see you. I'll write before I come though -

Always

Your friend,

Paul

I was glad to see you are now a MR. instead of an MP.

1945/12/19 Mrs. Deak, neighbor in Polyán, to us (Book 3, 375-378)

[Mrs. Deàk, was a very good friend to our family and her daughters went to school with my sisters. Their father was in America, married an American girl. She was like an actress, she arranged shows in the school and was a very fine person. Their father had TB and died from it. The children have gotten the same problem, according to my sister Maria, and as you will read in this letter, that Mrs. Deàk wrote, that the whole family was wiped out by that illness. We have other letters from her that tells their story.]

1945 December 19
Polány, post Lelesz,
Ceskoslovensko

My dear children!
Please do not be insulted by my salutation, but it happens to be a wonderful feeling to say these few words, children, because I cannot tell that to my own because they aren't alive. My dear children, I received your letter and it found me in good health and I hope that you are too and it is my wish to you from God. I regret that I cannot answer your question. I cannot reply, because of the situation, because of the sadness and to write it down is impossible and I cannot do it. My dear children, I will inform you that your dear father, that is the whole community of Jews, were told by the Germans that within one week's time they were to report to them. Every family should take along one pair of underwear and clothing, shoes and food packaged for themselves. Anything of that which remained at home they [the Germans] took an inventory of everything. They took all the Jews from the Helmec region to Ujhely and a week later a few of us took them some food while they were there, after that when they were taken away, we did not see them again. I was in Ujhely after that, but I didn't even go to the place where the Jews were, so I didn't meet them anymore. [Miksa] Shon came home once for food and we have collected about 8 loaves of bread, eggs, and bacon. He couldn't talk to me when I was there, but he has written a letter from Ujhely to me. Shon expressed his sorrow that he could not meet with me. This was the last thing and from there we did not hear anything from them.

In Lelesz, many people came home. Ignác Klein and his two sisters and Veiss's daughter came back. There are more men that came home in Lelesz. Unfortunately none of our people have returned. Malvin Lefkovics is in Switzerland [she meant Sweden] and wrote that should be coming back home in the spring. She's communicating with Icuval [Ignác Klein]. There are still others coming, but as of now I said that your father definitely went to your place in America. We hope and trust God that Shon will return home. And God forbid that if they do not come home then they may have been destroyed. I beg you to accept God's will because you can see that you were taken away from the hands of monsters and he saved you for the sake of the next generation. Just love each other as brothers and sisters and ask God to help you and take care of you from all bad things and unfortunate events.

My dear children, you cannot know and imagine how destructive the days were that we lived through. We have envied the dead. We do not know from day to day what tomorrow bring us. The men folk were taken by the Russians and as of today they are there. It has been already a year that a few of them came home and many have been destroyed. From 70 men only one third came home and they were not soldiers, they were civilians. There are some families that lost three from their family. We have gotten, all of us, from the bad things, but more likely we deserved it. The whip of God has come upon us. Why is God's hand [upon us]? Because we are bad and we are not willing to improve. My dear Herminka, you asked me about Maríska and Anùs? They're well, because they do not shiver whatever the situation is. Let me now say about my fate. In 3 years I have buried six that have died. My dear mother in one year and then my Grandfather and then Icsa, Anùs' little daughter died 2 years later, this was in November. And on February 16 Anùs, and on February 25 Mariska. Anùs died in one week on Monday and the second week Mariska on Thursday and with all this I had to struggle with. The mother has to bury all her children and now I am alone in this miserable role and waiting when the wind will grab me also. You can imagine how orphaned I am. Trusting in God that he will watch over me, if not He, I would also be destroyed. He arranged for me a small thing that I can lean upon. From Agard, my nephew's wife passed away and left 5 children and 2 years ago he brought here a 4 year old little girl, and now she is 6. If God would help me so that I can raise her, at least I wouldn't be at home alone. I would have someone to speak to. It's for sure our situation is very difficult. I hope that God will help me. My dear children don't be angry that I brought this up about myself with my problems, but I did that so that you could take an example from me that you too should accept what God has brought upon us. I am asking you please write about yourselves a lot and just write. My relations did not give a living sound of themselves. I'm closing these lines with kisses to all of you and God be with you, Mrs. Deàk.

P.S. The furniture from the house is at Ivanyó. Puskár lives in the house.

1945/12/20 Pauline Riley (Private Boyd Riley's wife) to Irving (Book 15, 55-58)

Graer St
House 55
Kings Mountain, NC [illegible]

Hello Irving
Just a note [to] let you know I got the card which you sent Boyd, he not got home yet. I been think all day where you met Boyd but I guess in the army some where. Last letter I got he said he might be home soon. Boy I really hope, so far it been 21 month since he been home. I guess you are married too. Well me and B I been married 9 years only he been in the army 3 of them. I hope it won't be that long, any moment. Well, when B I get home I will tell him about the card. I guess he will write you. Boys we are have snow. We had 3 this year. I be look for a ans[wer] tell me how you met Boyd.
Boyd wife
Pauline

1945/12/21 Private Earl Wetzel to Irving (Book 14, 5-7)

Dec. 21, 1945
Irving
I was sure glad to hear from you, but why in <u>hell</u> didn't you write some thing or have you forgotten how? I got out of the Army June 6. I was discharged out of a Hospital in Ky [Kentucky]. I got $69 a month of pension out of them. Do you remember that I owe you some money? It's either 5 or ten dollars. So when you write, and be sure you do, tell me and I'll send it to you. At present, I'm not at home. I'm at my uncle's about 62 miles from La Crosse. I would like to see you and one of these days I will, don't forget it. Then I will start giving you hell again. How would you like to be back at Anzio in that little hole of ours. I'll never forget it. Wasn't that <u>hell</u>. It's coming over the news that Patton's dead, isn't that too bad. He sure was a good man. You know that we were pretty lucky and some times I think we would be better off dead. Well that's all for now. More next time. As ever, Earl Wetzel

1945/12/27 (a) Hermine to David (Book 11, 113-114) page 1

Columbus 12/27 - 45
Dear David,
I think you don't know what to think that I didn't write to you in such a long time. Believe me, there is always something that comes up, or maybe it could be laziness, too. I was at home 3 days on Christmas holiday. It went by so quickly. We had delicious chicken and were thinking of you. I don't know if I mentioned it before that Mrs. Walter's mother is in the hospital. It is 12 weeks tonight. Irving and I went to visit her. She is better, but she doesn't know when she is going home. Otherwise we are all well and hope you are, too. The weather is very cold the last couple of days. Last week it was snowing heavily, but today it is like Spring. Don't laugh at me, I'm just joking. How is everything there? Write you lazy [man]! Ha Ha. Oh yes, I mentioned that I filled out [forms] at the Jewish Agency - in Europe -

1945/12/27 (b) Undated Hermine to David (Book 19, 421) page 2

Lajos from Szürte asked me to find out about his too. So, a few days ago I got a reply that they found his brother-in-law in Germany. He can write to him but only through the association. There are at least 3200 Hungarians in that town still. Poles and other nationalities. And I sent 4 applications in. The entire family was named out on it and this way now we will also get some news. I also mentioned that Lajos' brother Gizi found two children and they live in Garany. As soon as I find out something I will write it to you. Write about yourself. And I'm truly telling you that you are even lazier then I! I wish you a happy new year and lots of luck. Hey, would you like to see Irving our little brother? He is just us mischievous as he used to be and we are always fooling with him. Kiss you with love. Hermina

1945/12/27 Irving to Dave (Book 6, 301)

Columbus, Ohio
Dec 27 - 45
Dearest Dave,
Here again letting you know that I'm O'K and still loafing and hoping for some good ideas, maybe you got some good ones for me, I hope. Well nothing new around here, just once in a while I get disgusted, but holding my temper and say, let it come, as it is. I have mailed my papers in and when that comes in, I'll start going to school. That's about all the news this time, will write you more later. Let me hear from you. Everything that was in the package was and is yours!! Write me whenever you can, Till we meet again, Love, Irving

1946/1/8 Hermine and Irving to David (Book 11, 68-71) mistaken date

Columbus Ohio
Jan. 8 - 46
[from Hermine]
Dear David,
Every day it was in my mind that I will write you and yet I didn't write because I was so lazy and didn't have a chance. It is Friday evening. We received a letter from the American Consul in Czechoslovakia, too. Irving asked them to help about the family when he was in Europe. He wrote to them for help in locating our family there. The Lefkovics' answered about this that our dear Father, and Lajos our brother, and Uncle Marton, and Shon Miksa were taken away by the Germans. Since then they haven't heard from them. It is horrible. How can a person live with that knowledge. I can't ever forget, not even for a minute the horror, how can a person live with that? And those beautiful children, who knows what happened to all of them? They don't tell exactly what has happened, but in a similar situation they probably finished them just like others. I hope to God that it isn't the truth. God forbid. It's horrible even to imagine or even to think about it. However, I still try to think they might be alive and will come home, or maybe someone will find them alive. We must trust our God. Uncle Marton's youngest son is in Helmec. He came back and they wrote he is 14 years old and they call him Marton. I don't remember his name. He may be the 3rd son in the picture you took when you came to America. Also, [the] Kleins - Manci, Ràhcsu, Ignác are in Leles. They wrote that we can write to them

in a regular letter. I sent an international letter today to the young son, and Manci with stamps enclosed so they should let us know what they need the most, and we will mail it to them. I'm not going to wait for the answer. I want to mail them a package of food with clothing. You can send 11 pounds for each and for the other one also. It is horrible, but we hope for the best just like Lajos from Szürte found his brother in law. Maybe I hope they might be able to be found. We must hope. The Gerenyi family also wrote that they are 8 in the family and they live from the farm and they are ok. The letter [I] sent was to our dear father's address and they wrote back with all this information that I wrote you before. Write about yourself and how you are. We are all well. We received the package. Do you need the suitcase? I will mail it back. We put up the curtain and thank you very much. With all the best wishes and love to you with kisses, Hermine

[from Irving]
Dear David, until 120
Hope you are well. I'm O'K and going to school. Will write more later. Take care of yourself and write us more often. Love, Irving

1946/1/8 Private Boyd Riley to Irving (Book 15, 43-49)

Kings Mt, N.C.
Jan 8, 1945 [misdated - should be 1946]

Hello Gluck

How is everything going with you these days? As far as myself, I don't hardly know yet for I haven't been out of the Army long enough to say just yet. I got my discharge on the second and I just been home for about five days. I guess that you have been home a long time? Did you come home when we were in Lucky Strike to Gautier. I went from there to Dieppe France and stayed a while. From there to Brussels Belgium. Stayed about a month and from there to Marseille France. Stayed about fifteen days and went back to Antwerp Belgium, and from there I come to the States. It sure is good to get back to the States. I thought that we would not make it for we sure did have some storms and the scariest part we got about a thousand miles out when the boiler on the ship blew up. We sure did have a time. I got back to Paris and fought the Battle of Pigalle. Say, while thinking of it Marseille is lots worse than Pigalle. Have you been there? I was with the 400 MP Military Rail Service. It sure was worse than the 67th. Have you writing to Bill yet? I tried to locate him while in Paris but I could not find him. I guess that he is home by now. How do you like civilian life? I guess that you got your old gal back. I don't think that I will ever ask about the one that I had before I went to the Army. Well I must stop for now. So hoping to hear from you soon. A pal,
Boyd Riley
55 Church St.
Kings Mt.

1946/1/9 Private Clayton Potts to Irving (Book 14, 149-152) MP at Mannheim

Germantown, N.Y.
Jan. 9, 1946
Dear Irving:
Was wondering Xmas if you were discharged or not. I received your card the day after I had sent mine. I was glad to hear from you. I was discharged Oct. 26 Camp Atterbury. Up until now I have been taking life easy and how good it seems. What are you doing with yourself? Remember how we used to walk guard at Mannheim. How good it seemed to be home on the holidays again. It was my first in four years. Well Irving when you get over this way you are welcomed at any time. Let's hear from you soon. Sincerely, Clayton

1946/1/15 (a) Manci and Rocsi Klein [Etelka's sisters] to Hermine and Marie (Book 3, 231-234)

Lelesz, 1946 I - 15
[from Manci]
With Love to [you] Dear Girls and Ignacz,
Your precious letters brought happiness. I have already written to you a long letter. I have gotten your address from your communication directed to your dear father and I took it from the postman, Smojak bacsi. I don't know if you received my letter, did you? There I have written everything in detail. Dear Hencsukam, I don't have the strength to write about this suffering. I would like to forget everything. I said it many times that it is better for those that died. We came home, all three of us, as you have seen on the list. I thought when we come home, we would slowly become more like ourselves [and] it will be without any worries and we would be able to live. My dearest, think of that, when we came home besides the furniture we found nothing else. Imagine, being there one and a half years and we lived on beet soup, and yet our bodies desire good food for energy and well-being. You can get everything here, but we do not have money. As of now we have received American help, but now we are not getting anything. My dearest, I'm cooking kosher. We have received from Rezsik Klein a package weighing 2 kilograms. In the package there were food products.

Dear Hencsukam, if you are able to, please help us monetarily. Rozsi will continue this letter. I'm awaiting your reply. With kisses and lots of love to you all. Manci

[from Ròkcsi]
Dear Herminke and Mariska.!
I was very happy to receive the letter. I was by myself in the room when the postman delivered it. I began to read your letter and I burst into tears crying. Dear H. you could have seen those golden children as they were waiting that you and Marcsa will send things to them. It is unfortunate that those poor children and my poor sister after all the suffering and how well she brought them up and lived for the children and now especially she would have enjoyed them. It is like a dream in front of us. Mancie has already written to you about how we live our lives. Now I'm going to write to you about relatives. We were going together with Lajos bacsi. Your grandfather died here at home in 1942. It was a good thing since he was buried. Your grandmother and my mother were together in Germany, but they do not have a monument. You are asking,

Mariska, about Marton bacsi from Helmec. His little son is at home and lives with Zoli Pollak in Helmec. His name is Emil, and his Jewish name is Avruham. He is a beautiful, big fellow like you Ignác. He comes to visit us. At Zoli's he is well taken care. Lenke nenni's [Lefkovits] son Hersu also exists. I have written to you about all the relations. At this moment, in Shon's family no one exists. There are two girls from Szürte at home. I do not know them. Herminke, why is it that you do not write about Dezső and Hersmendu? Are they soldiers? Our Ignác is writing to you about the problems in Polyán. Dear Ignác, I wish you would have come home to visit. Dear Herminka, I would ask your help. If you remember Tuci from Asvany his father lives in New York. We do not have his address, perhaps you could advertise it in the papers that his nephew survived. He's a very gentle young man and he's by himself. There is no address and the poor thing came home alone. You are asking about Lenke Schwartz, Lenke Slager and Moric. They are at home. I'm writing this with a broken heart, Mariska, and nothing will heal it. Regretfully, we are poor and unhappy. Please write to us about everything. The address is Márton Klein, Tisza Ásvány. With lots of love and kisses to all of you your loving relations, Ròkcsi

1946/1/15 (b) Undated Ignác Klein to Hermine (Book 4, 422-425)

[dated by being first letter he wrote in reply to Hermine. Also, Rokcsi mentions in her letter above that Ignác will write about Polyán]

Dear, beloved Hencsu and Mariska,
We were very happy to receive your letter. Unfortunately, I can't write anything good to you, after all this horror. Dear girls, I can only write about the family. Whoever hasn't given a sign about their life until now, unfortunately no longer exists. Dear girls, you asked about the home and the land. The home is in bad shape. There is a poor peasant that lives in it and I rented the land out. Your dear neighbors stole everything from the home, and even from the barn. They stole everything. They even want you to send them dollars. They would have taken the house too, if it would have been on wheels. Unfortunately, nobody came home to Polyán. Malvin is in Sweden already. I sent to her already to write to you. Dear girls, you asked me what do I live from. Unfortunately, there is nothing to do and I have no money either. Dear girls, I bought two horses in the past. I helped Lajos out. So, I'm asking you now to please help me out so I can buy two horses for myself in order to succeed because now I'm very poor. I live together with the girls. They unfortunately don't live, they only eat. Unfortunately, we have neither clothing nor shoes…

…I have nothing, so please, if you can help me out, I will never forget. Dear girls, the furniture is there all over at the gentiles [Gojok]. They don't want to give it [to me], so please do me a favor and send me an authorization [so they will] give it back to me. Not even a pillow is left. Nothing. They took everything. Your best neighbor, who you would not even think of [doing this], the Simon family. They are very nice, they stole plenty from you. Pista Ivanyi isn't better and the Csarosz family, I can hardly write to you what bastards they are. They would kill us too, if they could. They can hardly take it, that a few people came back. They would have been happy if nobody came home at all. Believe what I'm writing in this letter. I don't even have enough money to send this letter to you. So, if you could, please help me out. If you could, it would come in handy for me, because now I'm here without anything. Why didn't you mention [anything] about Dezső, only Ignácz? I will not write more, I'm waiting for your response. I remain with love, your relative, Ignácz

1946/1/15 (c) Undated Malvin Lefkovits to Hermine and Marie 1st after war (Book 5, 183-184)

[Dated by Ignácz Klein mentioning in the letter above that he gave Hermine's address to Malvin]

My Dear Herminka, Mariska, and the boys!
I know and am wondering when did you receive our letters. I want to tell you about my life which I hope maybe you already know. I'm alive. I remain all alone, the only one left from my family. You can't imagine my position. What kind of days I live. The Swedes are forgetting everything very fast, like it never existed. They don't want to know anything and they don't care. But we cannot forget when all of us were taken together with our dearest parents. All of us were taken to Auschwitz, but when we arrived there we were separated from each other. Even my dearest family was also separated from each other. One side one and the other side the other. My dear Elike was with me, but she died also when we were liberated. She lived through and suffered so much. She lived through all that you cannot even imagine what we went through, the horror a human can endure, the suffering. What we went through a human can not take. No one can even imagine the torture. A person can not even imagine all that. I lost 35 kilo. It is only God who can know what we do and how we were able to survive as many of us that did. You don't believe it. I feel we would be

better if we had not survived at all. The pain of what we went through and go through now, it's unbelievable. And to live with that now. How are you? I thank God I'm okay. I got your address from your relation in Lelesz. My dearest, you cannot even imagine how lucky you are that you didn't go through all that horror and torture, all the suffering, whatever we all went through. Dearest, write to me all about yourself, maybe one day we might have a chance to meet again in person and we will be able to speak with you in America. I received this week a letter from Rezsike Vinkler and she asked for my birth information. I was so bitter by what they said since it was such a surprise. Do you think something will come from this or not? For you already know that I don't think I'm lucky, and so because of such an unfortunate pattern, I do not have another person in the world. Everyone has someone, but unfortunately I have no one. From Lelesz I get a letter sometimes, but they don't tell me anything about themselves and they don't tell me anything good either. Please just write to me. I will wait for your letter and will count every day restlessly to hear from you. I hope you will not let me wait too long. What are you doing? How are you spending your days? Please write at once. All of you. Many kisses, with my love to all of you. Malvin

Give my best wishes to the boys and tell them they also should write. I'm waiting for your letters.

1946/1/15 Private Irl Harris to Irving (Book 15, 37-41)

Albany, California
January 14, 1946
Dear Irving,
Thanks a lot for the card you sent. I was both surprised and glad to hear from you. You must have gotten back to the States shortly after I did. They certainly stalled us a long time before I finally got back. I left the 67th on June 14th and was sent to the 472 M.P.E. G Co. We moved four times within two weeks and then finally went back to France - to Troyes, to be exact. I stayed there from July until the 13th of September, when I left on the long journey to the States. First I went to Cheims, then to Chateau Thierry and then to Camp Philip Morris at Le Havre. We sailed from Le Havre on Sept 30th and arrived at Staten Island on October 8th. We then went to Camp Kilmen and stayed until October 12th. On the 12th they got us on a C49 and we flew to Camp Beale here in California. Four days later I was given my discharge. I loafed from October 17th until the 12th of November and then started to work. I'm working for my old boss only he is the [illegible] not a pretty good offer so I'll string along with for him for the present. The future can be mostly good if I get the break and I have two other jobs lined up if I [illegible] need them so I'm not worried. I certainly had a lot of trouble finding a car to buy. I loaned my Buick to my sister when I entered the service and when I got out she didn't want to sell it back to me, so after a lot of searching I found a '40 Ford and bought it. By the latter part of next year the new cars should be plentiful and then I'll probably want a new one. I don't like a Ford - but had to take this one or pay $1,400 or more for a heavier car - so naturally I took the Ford! This is more than enough about me. How are you and what have you been doing? If you find time, drop me a line. I'd like to hear from you. Say - believe it or not, but Capt. Thomson and Lt. Helms sent me Christmas Cards! They were the last persons I expected to hear from! Several of the old gang of the 67th have written me, or sent cards. All of them but Billy Chapman were civilians when they wrote. Billy sent me a card that came a couple of days ago - and he was still in France. That surprised me, for he joined the 67th in Algiers - so he piled up several points with us. Probably by now, though - he is on his way home. Well- this is it for now. If you have the opportunity, drop me a line. I'd like to hear from you. If you ever get to California - be sure and look me up. Always a Friend, Irl

1946/1/16 (a) Aunt Jenny to Irving (Book 7, 284-286) - missing last pages

[This letter may be missing the scan of the back of the first page]

Jan 16 / 46
Dear Irving,
I was indeed surprised and pleased to hear from you and learn you and your sisters and brother are well. It also gives me a great deal of happiness to learn of your safe return home and your joy in being a civilian again. I hope all your prayers in the future will be answered. Now as for me and mine - first thank you.

[missing last pages]

1946/1/16 (b) Undated Aunt Jenny to Hermine (Book 7, 287-289) - missing page 1

[At first I thought this letter belonged to the one above, similar paper and ink, but it was written to someone other than Irving at the same time, probably Hermine. Since she's telling about those killed in the war, the war just ended and it had to be before June 1946 because by then Hermine is in NY and there would be no need to write. It also is contextually the same as what would be the continuation of the letter above]

...hear from you more often. I am kept very busy, since it is a problem to get help and so expensive. Thank God I am fine, but Lucille hasn't been so well since you saw her. Only now she is trying to regain her strength after losing a baby she expected in March. She was in the hospital in August and again in November. She is feeling much better thank God. She has a darling daughter - 2½ years old. I understand David is in California. Where is your other brother. You don't mention him. What is he doing? Is Irving working? Have you made any inquiries through any of the organizations about your folks back home? Bertha has, and got the information that her folks are all gone. Also Jennie Frey has heard that her father is gone, but through some organization who made inquiry for her, she has heard from some cousins on her father's side. They are safe but in want. She is in communication with them and is sending packages, but hasn't heard yet whether they received any. I do hope you hear as good news as you possibly can and that it won't be as bad as you think. It is time for lunch and my pen is running dry so goodbye for now. Let me hear from you. Love to you one and all from all of us. As always, affectionately, Aunt Jen

1946/1/16 Istvanne Toth to Hermine and Marie (Book 18, 202-213)

Monday
Polány 1946 January 16th

My dearest Hermikám and Mariskám and all the rest of your family,
How are you all? We, thank God, survived the terrible ordeal that we have gone through. It was such a nightmare and a horrible ordeal that we went through and lived through, it's unbelievable. It took all our strength. We hoped in God that our life will get better. Dearest Herminkém and Mariském, I was thinking that you too will have the same thought about me that I was [thinking] about you ever since I moved to Polány. Yet, what I see is that you don't even want to remember, the only thing you are interested in are just those Christian friends that you write to. Believe me dearest, that maybe they don't even think about you, and not even a minute goes by that I don't think about you all. I cannot even write about how I felt in my heart when your dearest Father and dearest brother and his family walked down the yard. For me to see that, when I was staying with your family. I was like your own family if you would remember. I was treated as one of your dearests, no different. Your dearest Father, when he was getting ready to be taken from his home, he gathered all of your pictures from each of you and held them up to his heart and pressed [them to it] and started to cry. He told me I will take my children's pictures with me at least as long as I am alive I will see them and look at them, but the other pictures with the album he gave to me that I should take good care of it. Believe me dearests, there isn't anything greater than to take a look at your pictures. Dear Hermine, when your father and family left they were first in Helmec. While they were there I took food to them every day. After that they took them to Ujhely. There I took them whatever I could, anything. When I went there to Ujhely I went in the morning, but it took me all afternoon to find them because there were so many people, it was almost impossible to find them. I was doing it for them. I almost died there because I was so upset about them, believe me dear Hermine and Maria. If you would have seen the beautiful children that Etelka had. Even in a picture you couldn't look better than they were. Your dear father was aggravated with them a lot while Lajos was in the Army. Poor Etelka always encouraged me to stay. They will soon be able to send a package from America, they'll send it to us, [and she said] she will give from it for me also, because I did a lot of good for her. But she certainly didn't [get that], poor thing.

Surely sweet Herminka and Mariska, if you could have seen how we prepared those children, we sewed clothing suits for them because it was not allowed to take any, and we are without clothes because it is still very expensive for people with big families like mine. So, I can't buy any because I have to buy food. I can't afford it. My sweet Herminka and Mariska, believe me I would be able to write so much to you or talk, only I wish you would come home. When your father and the others left they took everything, only the furniture was left in the house. But nobody knew who took them when the Germans came in. There were many of them at your house because it was empty. They were baking cookies in the oven. They wanted to cut the furniture up to put it on the fire for heat. But Ilon and Juczi felt sorry about it, they took the wood to the soldiers, so they wouldn't cut them up, but it was not enough. So, they threw the many dirty clothes together for an entire day and Juczi and Ilan always did laundry for them, so they will not cut the furniture up because we thought that Etelka will come back home, so at least she could have the furniture. But until now we don't know anything about her yet. So, my dear Herminka they took the furniture from all over in the town.

So, we took your two beds also and Etelka's mirror. I thought, if they happen to find their way back home, it would be here. My dear Herminka, Ignacz is always asking money for it, that I should pay for it, but I know it well that I deserve it better because Ignacz, you know very well that you hardly love them. Only he and the two girls came home and he wants your belongings, Mrs. Lefkovics', along with Hermine's. Although, I told him that when your dear mother was sick, I went in the morning to milk [the cow] and I ran home to boil the water and I took that to her waist or to her back. Even if I don't pay to Ignacz, I deserve it just like he does. So, write it to me darlings, if you want me to pay him for it. Write to me, if the boys are there where you are. My sons are always wondering about Ignacz and Hersmendu. They always promised the goat to them, but they still didn't get it. Write to me darlings a letter already about all of you because you are all to me like you would be mine. Dezső can't even honor me with a single letter now that he is doing well, but when I was angry at you, I left him there and went to bake him cake on Saturday.

Dear Herminka and Mariska, I'm letting you know that poor Margit also lived through a very difficult time in Budapest with the big bombings. She was just very lucky with whatever party she had because that was what she got. Poor her. She was a real bride in Budapest for six months. Since her fiancé was a soldier, she doesn't know anything about him. They took everything. The only thing she took was what she was wearing. She came home because she was very afraid what will happen to her. She always wanted to [return]. In February it will be a year since came home. Well, I have enough grief to buy clothing for a family with two big girls, but Margit got married in a village near Kisvárda two months ago to a farmer. They met on the bus in Agardon. He's a nice boy. The only problem is that I don't have much to do with it, because I can't even afford the expense. I don't have a loan [to give], but they're asking me for it. She is waiting that maybe there will be found some relation who would help her go to America, but she has no one. Dear Hermine and Maria, God help you all if you are able to send some old clothing, women's or men's or shirts, please send it to us if it is possible. It doesn't matter how old it is. At home, everything is good. Ever since the war we can't get anything. Now I would say we are barefoot. They give shoes only to those people who have protection. Therefore, if you are able to help us, do something good. Dearest Hermine and Maria, somehow we will appreciate you and we will do something too. I know you can do anything, whatever you want to, if you want to! Dear Hermine and Maria, please write to me about yourselves. If you got married, and the boys, did they get married, and also what kind of job do you have? I feel very badly that you wrote to so many people and for us you were not able to write, not even one letter to let me know how you are. Don't be angry because I write to you as I do. I can't wait until you will write first, but I waited until maybe you would remember and write to me, but I really could not wait any longer. I have never forgotten you and always remember you all! Please write, don't be silent. I'm waiting impatiently for your letter to Polány. If I find out about the Shőn family I will let you know. At this time, we don't know anything. Also about Lefkovic, so far I don't have any information. But I want you to know we never had any problem with anyone. Therefore I'm not writing at this time any more. I think you will be angry for writing to you as I do, disturbing you with it. But at least I write to you because your dearest father can't. We are wishing you the best, and kisses to all of you. The only thing is that when you receive my letter, if you find time, please answer me. Yes, I will be waiting for it. Best wishes and kisses from Margit. When you write, then Margit is going to write. God be with you. I will never forget you. With love, Mrs. Istváne Tòth

1946/1/16 Jolán Ragány to Hermine (Book 18, 243-248)

Polány 946 January 16

Dear Hermine,

First, forgive me if I disturb your privacy. Thank God we are alright, which I am wishing from God that you are the same. Dear Herminka, I think you will not be angry at me because I'm writing to you. I liked you very much when you were here. I think you will remember me? I'm very sorry that Etelka and Mr. Gluck didn't come home. When they were home I was always there, up to the last day when then were ready to leave, they needed something and I was there even then because Etelka was a very fine woman. I really loved all of them very, very much. I think that Etelka wrote about me, too.

Dear Herminka! I believe you know what's going on here at home. I'm sorry we couldn't help. I should write to you about [something] that I can't stand. Do you know Dear Hermine, my heart was aching terribly to see Mr. Gluck because I was with them all the time. You remember when you were at home, I came to see you, do you know whom I'm talking about? I hope dear Hermine you will not be angry that I'm telling the truth and I write whatever I know. I don't want you to hear it from someone else. Do you know Hermine, when the Germans came into the village they went into Mr. Gluck's home. They wanted to chop up everything to make a fire of anything that you had there. I felt very sorry that maybe the Gluck family might come home, and they will not find anything there. We went over with Iványo. We asked the German soldiers. We were happy to give them something else, or we will help them too, but then they have to stop. So we were washing their clothes for 2 days, as many as they were, all of them. After that, one closet of Mr. Gluck I brought over and 2 beds, Etelka's also. Therefore, dear Herminka, I don't want that you should believe we did it for any other reason than we just wanted to save them for Gluck bacsi's family. I wish that God would bring them home and I would give them back everything. Those people who have come home, they are here for a long time. I'm very sorry that they didn't let Etelka and Mr. Gluck come home. We trust our God. I hope you will answer me. And how is Mariska, Ignác, and Hersmendel? I'm asking you Herminka if or when you receive this letter, will you please answer me because I am waiting impatiently for an answer to it. At this time I will stop writing. I remain with all the best wishes. Also send my best wishes to all your family, with many kisses to you from Elza Török and many, many kisses, and kisses to the hand, I remain with love,

Ragàny Jolán

Pólany

1946/1/19 Hermine to David (Book 11, 116-119)

Columbus Jan 19 - 46

Dear David,

Now only a short letter. I'm trying to write letters to Manci and Malvin. I'm mailing [them] to you so you will understand the situation that went on or is happening there. It is horrible even to think about it that maybe someone will come forward, one of our family, God only knows. But we are still hoping. I don't want to believe or give up hope. This week I mailed 3 11 pound packages to Helmec, Leles, and to Sweden for Malvin. We sent food and it will come in handy for them. If I could help, but what can I do. If we will get some answers then I will write them, and if they want something I asked that they will let me know what it is. It is true we cannot do too much, maybe food or some of our old clothing. I hope that maybe Etelka will come back even though I can't believe that is possible. Our dearest father gave his watch to Mrs. Gerenyi. Therefore he knew! He knew what to expect from them, those robbers. Even I know you can't expect anything from them, even then I can't forget even for one minute. From their letter I understood. Our grandfather wasn't alive. One of Uncle Marton's sons, the last one born, was given the name Smaje, our grandfather's name. Bertha received a letter and she doesn't know more. We wrote to our father's address sometime in November. They gave it to Manciak and they answered to that. Write about yourself. How are you and what are you doing? You know how your letter is signed…it seems like you are driving a car. So be careful and try to rest so you will not fall asleep. Be alert. I received the newspaper. It's very interesting, but I have no desire. Gizi from Szürte and her sister and 2 children, and Helen Perl's 2 brothers, she doesn't know about or has heard from them. She wrote to Louis and Ernő Eszemji and is asking for their relative's address. Love and kisses to you, Hermina

1946/1/19 Irving and Marie to Dave (Book 6, 291-292)

[from Irving]

Dear Dave, until 120

Again a line to let you know that I'm thinking of you, and hoping that you are well. Hermine has told you all the news there is, so from me that's the only thing I can say. I'm back in school and very busy, and I would like to hear more about yourself. Please write more and I will try my best. If you have a little snap shot please send me. O.K. Thanks Pal! Now take care of yourself and let me hear from you. With love, your little brother, Irving

P.S. Happy Birthday, a Happy Birthday Dear David, A happy birthday from us all. With Love…

[from Maria]

Dear David!

I'm sorry I did not write for so long. But I'm very busy with my present job. Yes, we didn't get a letter from you for a long time as well. I hope that my lines will find you in the best of health! I think Irving already wrote about the news. It is very terrible [from] whoever stayed alive. But I will leave this too. Otherwise there is no news. I don't go anywhere. But I have some hope that maybe we can hear about somebody. We wrote to Malvin Lefkovics, too because we got a letter from her. And now you should write too. I hope you will not take my example. Since our Irving is at home I have to admit the truth, I am waiting for him to write. Although, he is also very busy with studying. It's pretty hard, but I hope that the dear God will help him and everything is going to work out. Now I wish you good luck and the best of health. I kiss you with love. Take care wherever you go. Maria

Send the attached letter back.

1946/1/22 Malvin Lefkovits to Hermine and Marie (Book 3, 251-258)

1946/1/22
Goteborg, Sweden
Malvin Lefkovics

Dear girls with my love!
I received your wonderful letter. I can't even tell you how much happiness and love you have given me with your letter. It brought me life and hope, so that I do not feel that I am alone even though we are far away from each other, but I feel very close to you dear girls. I received from my great uncle two letters, my father's brothers, in America. I would like very much to be there with them, but regretfully it's not so easy. There are too many difficulties, so I do not know what will be because they have not sent me the papers. You girls have been asking about your family. I regret I can't write to you anything except that it's better if you don't inquire because until then there is hope and a person is happy because hope feeds you.

Dear girls I thank you very much for your observation, but you know I'm not a demanding person and I accept things as they are, especially now and hope that the creator will help me.
I'm going to work, but I do not know when since I have to see the doctor and go through an examination. Perhaps at the end of this month, after going through the examination, then I can go to work because the camp will be dissolved and everyone must help themselves and earn their upkeep. This is also a problem for me: how to start a new life without anyone and anything. Nonetheless, I must start a new life.

I received a letter from Lelesz and they told me that they received letters from you. They tell me in their letter not to return home because I will find nothing there. I have no one and as you know, when a child dies the relationship does also. It's true that when I received a letter from Ignác, he says he is not forgetting me, but I know my dear, that you can understand me. I recall many beautiful evenings we have spent together, walking and speaking about everything, but I hope that after this, if not in person at least by letter, we will not fall behind because the present letter made me happy.

My dear girls, you asked me if there is any one that I may have information about. From Helmec, Lenke's daughter Hencsu and Jidesz are also going to America. And from Lelesz, the Frőlinger girls, Irene and Lili, and also Lenke Stark are going to America. They are waiting for the ship. I believe you remember them. Rozsi Hausman from Agard is here. I just received a letter from her and she asked me for your address.

How are you my dearest? I thank the Creator that I'm well. Please write a lot about yourselves, about everything, because everything about you interests me. Did you write, my dearest, to Polyán? They truly do not deserve it. We also gave the gold jewelry and other things to Gyula Szabo, and yours also was there, and she said to Ignác that it isn't there. If I go home then she will account with me. Believe me my dear it does not pain me because I have greater pain that can't be healed.
You are not writing about your work. What are you doing my dear? Do you know anything about my Uncle Vilmus [Sofier]? If you can inquire about him because then he would write to me. What does Bertus Gluck [Bertha] say regarding to the bitter happenings when you get together? Please give my regards to her. I do not know her address, if I would know it, I would write to her.
We get every day 50 Filert [pennies] pocket money and I arrange it so that I'll have it for letter writing. I'm happy that I can and have someone to write to. At this time I will not write more. My regards to the boys and all of you. Kissing you many times with lots of love, Malvin.

Please write to me immediately my dear girls and I want to thank you very much for the package and I hope that I will be able to do what you are doing for me, even though today I'm a beggar. As above

P.S. I was dreaming with my mother this week as she told me don't be afraid my child you will have everything. She cannot even rest there because of me. That pains me a lot.

1946/1/24 Emil Schwartz [Helmec] to us Columbus (Book 3, 404-406)

Kral. chlumec 1946 January 24

My dear cousin Hencsu.

I received your letter and I'm replying at once. Last time I wrote a letter but I put in the wrong number instead of 50 I wrote down 59, I hope you will receive it. In your letter you are inquiring about your parents. We have not received any news from anyone and they must have perished like my parents. In my last letter I wrote to you and told you how it happened, that great disaster.

I thank God, I feel fine. I'm here with my relative Zoli Pollak. I'm sure you know him. He takes care of me like a father. I have everything, clothing, shirts and underwear. In other words, everything and it's enough. Thank God I'm well and in good health. I sent you a picture, as a remembrance, it appears that you didn't receive it yet. I know everyone who is in Lelesz. It is regretful that at Uncle Lajos Bácsitol, no one remained, only Etyu from Paloc, probably you know him. Please do not send any packages because I have everything. I would like to see you very much. Please write to me and tell me if any one of you got married. I remember all of you, Mariskára, Dezsőre, Mendura, Jichukra. Because you did not receive my previous letter, so I introduced myself, [what] my name is and [who I am to] you. Tomorrow I will be traveling to ex-Germany and from there to Palestine, I would like to get there with God's help. Please write to the following address, they will forward it to me. Once I get there, I will write you again with my new address. I will once again write the address, because I'm not sure whether you received it previously. Truly, I thank you very much that you have not forgotten me. With a true, pure heart and kisses to all of you with the love of kinship, your cousin Emil.

Address in Helmec
POLLAK ZOLTAN
KRÁLOVSKY HLUMEC
CESKO-SLOVENSKO

P.S. As I wrote above, Zoli will forward the mail to me. When I get to my new place I will give you my address once I arrive there. Write a lot to me. I'm very happy that you did not forget me. Once again if and when I'll be in Palestine I will let you know and I'll write you a lot. You, Hencsuka, I kiss you separately, because I always loved you when you were in our place. In my last letter I sent you two pictures, but I'm not sure whether you have received it, so I'm enclosing another one.

1946/1/31 American Embassy Prague to Irving (Book 19, 116)

American Embassy
Praha, Czechoslovakia
January 31, 1946
Sir:

The Embassy has received your letter of January 17, 1946 in which you acknowledge the receipt of the Embassy's communication concerning the whereabout and welfare of your relatives and request assistance in obtaining information regarding the status of your family property, situated at Polany, near Leles, Czechoslovakia.

The Embassy has addressed a letter to the District National Committee at Leles with the request that it be furnished with whatever information might be available or obtainable regarding the property in which you are interested. As soon as any information is received by the Embassy it will be transmitted to you. Very truly yours,

For the Ambassador:
Paul M. Dutko
Chief of Consular Section

Columbus 2/4 - 46
[from Hermine]
Dear David!
We got your letter and I'm just trying to respond. I will attach Malvin's and Mrs. Gerenyi's letters. We also got letters from Janos, the postman, Mrs. Deak, and from Sandor Kosztyo. I would send them all, but it is hard like this, so I will send them some other time. Although, it is about the same thing and surely did not give too much consolation. I got a letter from Malvin tonight again and she is healthy. One of her father's brothers is in America and she got a letter from them. They want to have her come here, but they did not send the papers to her. I'm sending with this Uncle Marton's son's picture that he sent in the letter to us, but send it back to us, ok? Although, if you want one of them, you can take it. From the Agardi girls one of them is in Sweden. The rest of them, Bela Stark's two daughters, the 2 Floringer girls, and 2 of them are Lenke nenni's [Lefkovits] daughters. They are waiting for the ship and they are on their way to America. About me, only that I'm well-I'm doing my job and that is it. I will ask what can we do about Emil and if it will be successful, I would want him to come out. I told this to Arthur and he said he will think about it. I will respond to Gerenyi too, but I will not write about the watch and you can write to them also. We can not send the letter anymore because poor Gyuszi' s son is not alive. So, you should write to them. You asked me what's going on with the boy- I did not get any letter from him, but his mother wrote to me and the boy is in Japan as a chaplain - in other words rabbi - on Saturdays-And if they need him for all dentistry work also. He is very busy-I responded to his letter, but I did not get a response. This way I did not write to him anymore. On Saturday I bought an 8 Cubic gas refrigerator. It cost 272 dollars and in a few days they will ship it home. I want to make up 2 more packages. I will send it to Manci and the others and to Emil and the others. Malvin is pretty happy that I will send one for her too and I wrote to her that I want to write more letters tonight. Write to me. I kiss you with love. Hermina

[from Marie]
Dear David!
We did not get a letter from you for a long time already. But I hope that my lines will find you in the best of health. We are well! Hermine wrote about all the news we had already and it is very terrible even just to think about it. If we could get Uncle Marton's little son out. But the question is, if Arthur would give a guarantee. Currently I don't know anything exactly. And I am very busy. Mrs. Gerenyi wrote to us pretty nicely, but even that can't help this. Surely she couldn't do anything more. Now you write too and take care of yourself wherever you go. I will write again next time. I will close my lines and I wish you lots of luck and the best of health. I send my greetings and kiss you with love. Maria
Otherwise here there is no particular news only it is cold, but that is not news.

1946/2/4 Manci Klein [Etelka's sister] to Hermine and Marie (Book 3, 229-230)

Loving Dear Herminke and Mariska
We have received your letter with happiness. I have written to you quite some time ago, but I do not know if you have received it. Did you receive it? We've all replied to your dear letters but we did not mail it by airmail. I don't know if it will arrive to you. I want to tell you that at that moment, my dearest, as I was going to the post office, I met Emil, Patyu bacsi's son and I gave him your address. The following week he left to Palestine, if he can get out from here I don't know. He will be going with several other individuals together. He more likely will write to you from there. Mrs. Lenke's [Lefkovits] son went to Sweden to visit her daughter. What can I write to you, my dear Herminka, [except that] it's a miracle that the good God left these few Jews [alive]. After all this suffering, since I have suffered for my Jewishness I want to continue to be Jewish. I keep cook kosher.

My dear Herminka, thank God that I feel much better. You know, my heart was so nervous before, and now after the bombing of Nürümberg, even Doctor Adler did not believe that I would be able to survive it. Now I see how strong a person is. The doctor said to me that there is no ailment, I only need rest. My dearest, if I tell myself that only three of us were born, then I will have peace of mind and in my heart. I've gained back weight now to be 58 kg.

If monetarily I would be able to write to you more frequently, I would love to. But this nation's public [K. = kozseg = village] stamp costs 2 koronas in the post office and for a very thin air mail letter the post office charges 25 Kc [Czech korona]. We have received a package from Helen Klein with food products. Here one can purchase that also, but clothing is very costly. My dear Herminkem, I'm asking you if you have any used clothing that you don't use, please send it to us because I have heard that used clothing can be sent and I know you're a smart girl and I leave it up to you. At this time, Ignácz is not doing any business and conditions are not good and everything is very costly. Living requires and demands its share my dear Herminkem. Do you know that at times I am a very bitter and I do not have anyone to complain to. I will return to the point where it is written that whatever will be cannot be avoided. I don't have the desire to go to America, if I would be younger then yes. After so much disturbance I desire a peaceful life because if 10 people come into a house, I feel like I'm in the concentration camp. Here, it is the season to get married because there are so many widowed man, but I'm not going to at this time. Do you remember my dear Herminka that I always had difficulty making a decision. And yet, you did not select someone? My dearest, I do not want this letter to weigh a lot, so I will close this letter on this page. Ignacz and Rozsi will write to you in the near future. I'm awaiting your dear reply as soon as possible. Kisses always with lots of love to you, Manci

Lelesz, 1946 II / 4.

1946/2/14 Helen Perl Goldstein to Hermine (Book 16, 189-190)

Cleveland Monday - 1946 -14
My dear Herminka!
I know it is not nice of me that I start every letter with an apology, but you know how fast time goes by each day that I realize it is already 12 or 1 o'clock at night. Since I do everything on my own and even putting the fire for the house is something [I do] and my husband is not here. I even take the child to the basement with me. I am afraid to leave her alone upstairs. By the time I supply the fire, she always makes a mess on herself with coal. She looks like a little chimney sweeper. My Herminka, I'm writing news for you. I got letter from the old world and so far I have two [younger] brothers alive. They were there, but only stayed for a few days. They went up to Czechoslovakia, where, compared to the conditions, they have it good there. One of my 2 brothers, Berna, do you remember? He got a spice store from the government and he wrote that it is going very well and I should not send anything because they have everything. My little brother wrote down the entire list of names who came back to Szürte. Unfortunately very few, only 28 people. From your dear relatives, other than from the Kleins nobody, but the other Klein, Majer, his kids all came back, Emanuel, Ignác, and Frida. From my siblings, my sister and my parents were also victims. But I will not write anymore. I'm waiting for your response as soon as possible. I kiss all of you, Helen

1946/2/14 Hermine to Louis Goldblatt (Book 11, 129-130)

Columbus Ohio Feb 14 - 46
Dear Louis,
Your pretty Valentine card and note received. I was quite surprised since I had not heard from you for so long. I have been looking for that letter and your picture you said you would send to me last August, but I never received them, and couldn't understand why. If you aren't going to send me your picture I wish you would please return mine. As you say it seems like years. It would have been so nice to have heard from you if only a card. Yes, so much has happened since I wrote to you and a word from you would have helped so. I have heard news from my family and as yet we don't know what became of them. In the German occupation in 1944 all my family were taken to concentration camps and never heard from them since. One of my little cousins is back 16 years old and as he said in the letter it was very terrible. There isn't much hope as he says but we just can't give up. Are you on your way or are you stationed there? They say Hawaii is such a beautiful place. Please write me about it. I suppose the weather is pleasant there. We have had a rather mild winter, not so much snow and ice this year. The past few days have been very bright sunshine, but the temperature is around 25. However it was pouring rain today. I am sure Spring is coming. Hope it will not be so long until I hear from you again, Hermina

1946/2/21 Rozsi Hausman to Hermine and Marie (Book 18, 318-323)

[This letter is from my brother Lajos's wife's cousin.]

Älmhult [Sweden] 1946 II 21

You'll be surprised from whom you're getting this letter, I don't want you to think too long, I will introduce myself. I am Rozsi Hausman from Agar. I'm your Etelka's cousin. I'm sure that you remember me. I got your address sometime ago from Lelesz, but with my bitterness, I placed your address somewhere. Today accidentally I found it. I immediately sat down to write to you. I thought, perhaps, it would be easier to express myself, to pour my heart to you. I know when we got to together we understood each other. Now, I will tell you my unfortunate life. I think that you know that we were six siblings— four girls and two boys, and my dear father and my brother's six children and my sister's three beautiful children, together we left from home. Unfortunately in a moment they deported all of us to Auschwitz and as soon as we arrived we were separated from my sisters and my dear father and brothers and family. We hoped to meet the next day. I was there in Auschwitz for 2⅓ months. From there they took us to Dauchau. I was there 4½ months. This was somewhat acceptable. From here they dragged us to Bergen-Belzen, regretfully it was a death camp. Here they did not give us food or clothing. They threw us together with 1000 people in one block where we were sleeping on the ground one on the other. Due to hunger and tiredness and from unsanitary conditions typhus broke out between us and people began to die. It became common and we too were waiting for that every moment that it will be our turn to die. It seems that we needed to suffer! We dragged ourselves until Friday, April 15, 1944. The English freed us. As for us it was unfortunately late because those that were alive were all sick. They brought us to Sweden to recuperate. Until July 5, I was in the hospital and I was released a few weeks ago. Let me say in good health. I feel very lonely and unlucky, because up to now I was thinking that it would have been better to be dead. Due to the good God who helped me to improve my health, so now I'm thinking to whom will I go home, because I did not hear as of now from anyone. I think you understand my situation and my misery and bitterness. At home we were very happy. I was very happy amongst my family and now it's an empty house and it's a waste. I'm unable to write more. I do not have the strength, personally, maybe I annoy you with the bad information. Do not feel badly. I'm by myself and it feels good to write to someone. The only conversation I have is by writing to you. I'm very interested about your way of life. Write about yourselves. Perhaps you have gotten married and Dezső also, and your two younger brothers. What are they doing? In other words, please write about everything. I will close my lines. I wish the best. I'm waiting for a reply. Hope to hear from you. Hearty wishes to all of you, from the past acquaintance. Rózsi

My address:
HAUSMAN ROZSI
HVITA KORSET
ÄLMHULT, SVERIGE

Send me some pictures of yourselves.

1946/2/22 Irving to Dave (Book 6, 289)

Columbus Ohio
Feb 22nd 46
Dear Dave, until 120
Please forgive me for not writing you before, but since you know I'm going to school, I'm very busy. However, one day Hermine wrote you a few lines and I have also written some, but it was accidentally left out. Any way, I want to tell you that I have not forgotten you. At school I have lots of studying to do. When this quarter is over, I'll write a long letter and let you know more about everything. So now let me hear from you and best wishes and take care of yourself. Love, your little brother, Irving

1946/2/22 Marie to David (Book 6, 290)

II / 22 / 46
Dear David!
It's been a couple of weeks since we got a letter from you. And I'm sorry, but I want to say that we didn't write to you either. But somehow time goes by and there is no time for anything. As usual. How are you, David? You should spend more time writing. Write about yourself. Otherwise we are fine. Yes I met last week with a friend who works for Lazarus. I don't remember her name. The one who gave me perfume. She was interested in you. She just said she got married and showed her little son, it's true he was in a photo. And she invites us to go to her. She no longer works and is a housewife herself. Her brother had married the girl who works for Jenkin with that black hair. You know who I mean. But leave it at that. Otherwise,

everything is the same. We have not received any mail at this time. And how do you do with work? And as our younger brother writes, he's very busy. The truth is he is constantly learning. Because it's hard enough to learn. Now I wish you good luck and good health. And you should take care where ever you go or what you do. And try to write. I'm closing my lines now. And greetings from the heart and a kiss with love. Maria

1946/2/23 Hermine to David (Book 11, 132-135)

Columbus Feb 23 / 1946

Dear David,

Since we are not writing to you very often, therefore now you are writing even less and we hardly hear from you. Thank God we are all well. We haven't heard from them at home in Czechoslovakia. Last week Arthur received a letter from one of the Kleins from Szürte. He writes his name as Herman. I think it may be Henrik from Ujhely. He writes to Arthur that he lived in Perbenic in 1939 and Uncle Jónász sent him a guarantee to be able to come to America. I think it must be Lipot and now he lives in Budapest. When he came home from the concentration camp he came back with his wife and 2 daughters. Now they are all staying in Budapest with him. He is the only survivor from the 8 sisters and brother, they all perished. He is asking Arthur that he should help him. Anything would be very good because he has nothing, no furniture. I'm going to send them a package also, but I'm so busy and have little time. I will write tonight to them. Helen Perl received a letter that her two brothers survived and are in Szürte. Only 28 people of Szürte survived in all. Uncle Isidor's brother's children all survived and returned. One of the Perl sons is in Czechoslovakia. He has his own business and writes that he doesn't need anything. I don't remember if I wrote to you before that little Emil from Helmec wrote that we should not send him anything good because he would like to go to Palestine if he can't come here. He went to the former Germany. Maybe from there he will be able to go there [Palestine]. Otherwise, nothing new. Our brother, thank God, he is doing very well studying, but he is working very hard at it. Flora invited all of us to have dinner tomorrow with her sisters and Aunt Helen. Herman doesn't feel like going. You know brother, the Lieutenant sent me a Valentine's card anyway. He writes that he is very sorry. He would like to write to me more often. At this time he is in Hawaii. I should write with his mother. He wrote that he is listed as the camp priest [rabbi]. That is the reason he is so busy. If he doesn't write then I'll blow the whistle on him. From New York I received a letter from Bertha and Aunt Jennie. Bertha is asking me to go to visit them for a couple of weeks. Helen in Cleveland also wants me to visit them. In California it would be much nicer, but Irving would like to go there. What do you think? But I should not tell you that. It's supposed to be a secret or just a dream. With all the best wishes and love, Hermina

1946/2/27 Louis Goldblatt to Hermine (Book 17, 182-187) with photo

27 Feb '46   B"H [baruch ha-Shem]

Dear Hermina,

Thank you for your very prompt answer. I hadn't received any mail for about 2 months but then all of a sudden a ship full came in and I was very happy. Your letter added to that happiness.

About my picture - I took pictures before I left the States and they must have 20 or 30 of me at home. I had written for Mother or someone to send you one of me. I am sorry but don't be angry. I am enclosing a recent snapshot until you receive one of me from home.

It makes me feel very bad that I had not written anyone while in Manila but there was so much for me to do and not enough time. I could write a book on my activities. I tried to help many of the Jewish families with food, clothing and any way I could besides their teeth. If I wasn't working nights in the clinic I was running around doing things for our group of orthodox boys. I helped found a Friday nite and Shabboes minyan. By Shabboes I mean all day. Never in my life did I have such an enjoyable time - religiously and socially. We had such wonderful times at our few orthodox Civilian homes - eating, singing, etc. It was a job to get ice, food, go shopping, bartering, stealing for our Sudas [meals]. But with G-d's help everything turned out wonderful. I left many Mothers, Fathers, brothers and sisters in Manila and part of my heart. Manila [is] all in ruins, [with its] high prices and discomforts had something not even beautiful Hawaii can ever reach or have. The people - true Yiddishkeit [a real Jewish feeling]. The Jewish Chaplains were against the orthodox men and I as the only officer to take an interest became their leader, Gabi [gabbai] and Schamis, and Chaplain.

My words are not very expressful but I can't convey what a situation existed. I made so many friends but at the cost of my old friends. There were times I didn't even write home for weeks. There was no alternative for me and my every minute was not my own. I was foolish enough to go overboard and forget myself but I enjoyed every second of it and it certainly changed or affected me - besides losing 30 lbs [pounds]. I know now how things were with all of you at home. News from Europe - we had 600 refugees in Manila and every day the news brought sadness and occasionally happiness. There were cases where Kaddish was said for people but yet they like came back from the dead. Stories, we have heard and seen but we can't comprehend them because they are beyond our small human imagination. In spite of all, HOPE! should never die but the tragedy arises in some of these new found cadavers where life is worse than death. Here I must stop my sermon before I too begin to cry tears because each time I think of us as Jews and our people and what menschlichkeit [good upright behavior] the world shows toward us, my heart cries.

Yes, Hawaii is to be my station - for how long no one knows. Regulations read that I will be in the Army for another year - but who knows that either. I am not worrying just hoping. Hawaii is beautiful - the weather ideal, sunshine plentiful and scenery beyond description, but everyone is trying to make a sucker of someone else - and regardless of the good there is the bad. Even a bowl of cherries has seeds in it.

Incidentally there is a boy in Columbus Irv Covel or Kovel - he lives on the south side somewhere if you have a chance call him and give him my regards, address and request that he write me.

Hoping this letter brings Spring to Columbus (can't spell any more) - maybe it should be Ohio. Regards to all the Family

And hoping to hear from you also. With Torah Greetings, Louis

1946/3/1 David to us (Book 2, 180-184) Japan China Bank Note

3.1.46

Dear Herminka and Mariska and Ignác!

I don't know any particular news, everything is the same. It is an unfortunate that I don't write more often, but you understand the reason. Especially you Herminka, you know when one works 10 hours per day, you really aren't in the mood or have the patience to do anything that way. So, I don't even know how to start. I got a letter 3 weeks ago from Lajos Schwartz, but I just wrote a response to it. I will attach it here to you. The weather here is excellent. I wish you could be here. Ignác could go to school here. Job opportunities are better here than in Columbus. The weather is better also. So, why couldn't you come to live here? What is in Columbus that you can't find here? Currently, I did not write to Polyán yet, as I heard it on the radio, there is inflation there. The dollar is worth a couple of thousand Pengo-You know Herminka, I thought it would be a good idea for you to write a letter to the American Consul in Hungary with this request concerning Jeremias Gluck's children Lajos, Emil, Lenke, Hersu whose property is in our name, that is, Herman, Ignacz, Hermine, Mariska Gluck. You are the current, closest [relations] and nobody else can be entitled to our late Grandfather's property, for example, Ignácz Klein and his siblings also, and you want to maintain your rights, you are the closest relatives, so too with Uncle Lajos' legacy, as I think that the "Slanger" family [misspelled - Csallag = család] deserves it. Also, what is going to happen to Uncle Marton's son and his wealth? Currently, there could be a few smart people and get everything for themselves. I will return to Ignacz Klein's stewardship/guardianship. I will be working on formally reviewing this. God forbid, he will use up all the crop and then take the land from underneath it!! So, I don't know any news. I will send the requested letter back separately by regular mail. Also, I will attach a couple of international stamps and a couple of American stamps ["hajuget" = missspelled] and a Japan China note [money]. I got it from a boy.

...it is worth at least 50 cents! So, currently I can't think of anything else to write about. Oh yes! Forgive me that I still did not send you the money. I will open a checking account next week and I will send it. I'm so lazy to get up during the day, I believe I wrote that I'm working at night. Oh yes, currently there is a bus strike in Long Beach so business is better than it used to be. So, Ignacz! Why don't you write? You promised me, you already forgot, right? Although, I got a few lines from you this week. Mariska! Forgive me also that I don't write to you separately, but I became a very lazy writer. I don't know why, but I don't have any patience at all to write (Herman). I kiss all of you with love. Dezső

P.S. Write to me, if you want to come here - You could buy a nice house here. But first it is important for you to come.

1946/3/11 Margit Gereny to Marie (Book 18, 215-220,223) pages 1-4

Polány 1946 III/11
My dearest Mariska!

I received your letter which really made me very, very happy because I was thinking you must have received [mine]. 2 months have already passed by since I received your answer. A few days ago I dreamed of Mr. Gluck and Lajos. Mr. Gluck said I was a very happy neighbor because I had 5 children, except Lajos. He told me when we spoke together that not even one day goes by that he doesn't think about you all. Because we are very distressed, I thought that you might come home. Dear Maria, about 5 weeks ago there was a really big storm and the building with the straw was demolished. It is my duty to tell you what is happening there. You know, Ignác Klejn took everything to Lelesz. He is there now and he has the power from you. That is not a problem if it is true. I'm writing to you so you should know about what is happening here and you should not be angry at me. When they came back Rozse came over and she was looking around as though we would be thieves at the Gluck's. She is mistaken and I told her so. And she left. Ignác is bothering me, but I'm asking you to ask me. In my heart Mr. Gluck has five children in America and you didn't write. Dear Mariska, before they left, Etelka brought over her earrings and Mr. Gluck's pocket watch with the chain and the pipe. She told me I should keep it here as a remembrance from me to you, that is what I have from you. That is what he left us. The earrings they took. The watch and the chain, when with Gold's help and if we are still alive, Dezső [asks], then we have it. Is that the reason you are angry at me, that I didn't give my watch to them, the one that my friend your father gave to me as a remembrance? But know this, they are trying to get everything from all the relations that they know, but I don't believe that is all. Please write to me if I should give it to them or not because they have everything from you. Did you give the power to them to do whatever they are doing? They are saying Dear Mariska that you did give them that paper. Dear Mariska, just write to me. Believe me, I'm very happy to read your letters every week, but don't wait for my letter, just write to us. I think that we are all together. Please, the boys should write also. I still didn't hear from Dezső. I'm sending kisses to him also, with all of you. Just write a lot. Wishing you all the best and kisses, your loving neighbor Margit

Dear Herminka, I received your letter and I was saddened that you did not answer. I didn't feel it just now. I wanted to have our relations continue even to always hear from each other, not just me, but my children also. I think we deserve it from each other. When Ica saw that the Gluck girls write she teases that I am happier than [if it were] even my own brother. She said why and I told her we know them and I love them, but we're just corresponding, but with God's help, if they come home any of them can come to us anytime and be welcomed like my family to stay with us like my own from the heart. I would tell them whatever I know, everything, about them. I assure you that when my husband took them, even the policeman told us they must have been very good people because everyone cried for them. Mr. Gluck loved everyone. Dear Hermine, when Ignácz left, no one helped them. Now everything is fine, it will only improve. My husband and I went to the orphanage in Helmec. I told them, if you believe in God, take down some clothing to Etelka's children. They got 5 pairs of clothing and shoes. Etelka asked me how I got them. I said others and for you. She started to cry a lot. Don't cry, it's important that you have it. I am sorry Herminkem, it comes to my mind that we can't buy anything. We still can't buy clothing and shoes. We have to give up food because we have no one to help us. I will mention one thing, I have a jacket

1946/3/11 Undated Margit and Ica Gerèny to Hermine and Marie (Book 18, 263-268) pages 5-6

so from it I get a blanket and a winter coat, but what could I have done? Now we take the fur off and it will be good for Spring. What can I do? I just wish it would be something more decent. With two grownup girls you need so many things, how can I buy it from his pay. He can't afford the clothing and the food and stocking, but what should I do there are so many problems. Is this life? I am a mother. Ica is big and growing. On the 27th of the month she will be 12 years old. I also have a little girl. This I have written to you before. She will be 4 years old in June. Gabriella is a very sweet little pancake, beautifully developed. She says to write and give my kisses to them. Don't take it as a complaint, it's just easier to know with your home that it was hard then, but it's much worse now. I'm not in the best of health. I survive [with] a leaky heart valve and anemia. It is enough. Both. We must believe in God that he will help. Dear Herminka, just write a lot. I could also write six pages because it feels so good to write about myself. Lots of kisses to you all. [My husband] Gyuri bacsi also greets you, and asks if he could do better could we be there? Herminka, write about yourself. Kisses to all of you and the boys also. Just write.

[on the side] Don't write to Klein

[from Ica]
Dear Girls!
I'm happy to grab a pen to spend a few minutes with my loved ones. When I received your letter, I was happy to hear from you after so many years later, and you remembered. It's been a long time since you left. I have been a grown up ever since. Before the war I finished middle [school], but unfortunately I can't use it yet. I would like to study further, but the circumstances are difficult. We went through a terrible ordeal. The horrors of the war have greatly devastated us all. Because of that I would like to continue my study, but now I am a young woman. My dear mother cannot even get me the clothing that I need. The war stripped from everyone everything. Thanks to that, I'm stuck too, but it's ok. We are happy to have whatever we have. I just hope we don't have to fight more because I could not live through it. With lots of love, waiting to hear letters from all of you. I have one request. We don't want just a letter, but some pictures. We would love to see you. If it is not too much for you. We would be very happy to see you all. Many kisses, all of you, your little neighbor. Ica

[On the side] The boys should write also because I expect a lot just about them, too.

1946/3/12 Malvin Lefkovits to Hermine and Marie (Book 3, 415-418)

[Malvin Lefkovits was my Godfather's daughter.]

Mölndal [Sweden] 3 / 12 1946
Loved, Dear Girls,
I have received your letter which always brings me happiness and I'm happy to read it because I feel like I'm with you at that time, I'm sorry that it's only in thoughts. Dear girls, I don't know what I deserve from you, that you are so dear, that you think of everything for me and probably you take from yourself with that...., but I really don't want that, because I am also working now. I can't save much from the income. I am getting 50 Kronan weekly wages and it costs me 25 Kronan per week for an apartment. It is a very tiny room. The only thing that fits into it, is one bed and a tiny table and that's all. Two of us are living there. However, in April we are going to get a larger room and that will cost us more, but it's not a problem because it's so uncomfortable when I get up in the morning I'm more tired than when I go to sleep in the evening. I'm not accustomed to the work, it is a bit difficult, because I'm not as strong as I was at home. It's clean, very clean, only thing I found the paper...... is difficult, I just realized that I'm complaining, please don't take this as a complaint.

I received a letter from Bertha. She is inquiring about her sister Mariska and family. I told her that she went with my parents and I haven't heard anything good. I didn't explain it to her whose daughter I am, I believe she knows and there was a dollar in a letter and she asked what would I need.

Dear girls, I believe that Marton [Schwartz's] bacsi's son left already. About two weeks ago I wrote to Helmec to Hersu and he said that in his next letter he will know more about it and will let me know.

How are you? I thank the good creator I am well. If it will be interesting to you I will write to you how it happened in our sad days. My dear Herminka please write. I'm very happy that you're interested. It is unbelievable that anyone would be interested. Accept my humble thanks for everything. Please write because I am not the only one who reads it, but the girls in a factory also. I am very proud of such a beautiful letter that I received from you. I'm working in this shirt factory. And until now I found the language to be very difficult to learn. Now I will have more opportunity to learn because I am among Swedish people, but I do not have patience for anything. Mariska I'm not satisfied my dear, because you did not write enough. I haven't received any letter from Lelesz for more than a month, they do not write. I communicate with Rozsi Hauzman. It is unfortunate that she is not completely well. She is at a Hungarian camp in a beautiful place. They take them to interesting places. I have written about everything to you. My best regards, many times, to the boys and to you with kisses and love. Malvin

My dearests,

I also send my best regards to you even though I do not know you. I speak to Malvin a lot about you. Many kisses to all of you. Enga, from the camp

1946/3/14 David to Hermine (Book 16, 359-360)

3.14.46

Dear Herminka!

I got your picture yesterday of our the little brother, which is excellent! He looks pretty good on it. How are you? Why don't you write to me? You do the way as I do. If I could I'll get the nylon stockings. If you don't write the number for you and Mariska, it is hard to get them here. But they promised me a few nylon's, so write the number! Ok? How is our little brother? Why doesn't he write? Since he came home he wrote to me only once a couple of lines. He always promised that he will write. Why doesn't he write? Tell him to write! Herminka, I will attach here a 50 dollar check. I am sending this made out to cash. The phone conversation, based on my calculation, will be a 100, so I will send another 50 soon. Greetings to all of you! I kiss you and write to me about our little brother. OK?! There is no news here at all, everything is the same. Write to me Mariska also. OK? Best, Dezső

1946/3/18 Bertha to Hermine (Book 16, 313-315)

New York

Mar 18 / 46

Dear Hermina!

We are glad to hear that you want to spend the vacation with us, but in July most people will go away. My husband is taking the last week of July also, so if you could do it, try to manage to take your vacation either before or after. The people you know also will be in a hurry to leave town because in the summer the heat is terrible. May is a nice month and June also. I hope that you can come in those days or in August, although that is a hot month too. Not much of the fashion is what it is in Columbus, a few printed dresses and a costume is enough already, what you can put on and everything has to look good on you. I am very curious about you and to see you. If you could spend at least two weeks here in May. As far as I know, you can find your acquaintances in the town still. I talked to Rezsi Winkler and she would love to see you. They rented a room in the mountains for the entire summer. I got a letter from the late Zsiksan's brother's daughter and she wrote that she rented the house out- the house and the land also and I asked Kalman's son to look after everything. Friedman Boske [short for Erzsebet] is a very smart woman, I can see it from her letter because she is not in a hurry to argue. She wrote to Zseni that she found a sewing machine. She took an old horse and would like to sell it. I believe that Friedman and the others took care of it. Don't you think they are entitled to it? I wrote to Malvin Lefkovitz and I even put a dollar in the letter too. As soon as she responds I will get a package. I will send one for her. How old is Patyu's son [Emil] ? Write to me first because it feels good to read your letter. Give my kisses to the dear relatives. With love, Bertha and Mannie

1946/3/20 Hermine and Marie to Dave (Book 5, 303-305)

Columbus

March 20, 1946

[from Hermine]

Dear David,

I know you're wondering why I'm not writing more often. Believe me I am always writing, the only thing is I have more people with whom I'm corresponding. Therefore time passes by so quickly, we don't even realize it. 50 D[ollars] received and Ignác paid for the phone call. Therefore he doesn't want to take the money back and you only owe me $20 because that fifty was yours. Therefore you don't have to mail it to me. But if you still want to, then I will save it for you. How are you? Are you working hard? Today we received a letter from Gerenyi and Malvin. Also, if you remember back, Regus from Agarde's sister-in-law, Rezsi, is in Sweden. I received a letter from her. She is still sick. This is what Malvin wrote: she's planning to come to America. From Leleszi, two Klein girls got married and they are the ones who will bring them out. Nylon hosiery would come in handy, because we can't get them at all. Even Rayon is impossible. I still have two pairs. Nylon for me 9½, for Marie 10, and if it can be thinner, the more beautiful [it would be]. Thank you in advance. What are you thinking? The company sold the business where I am working and we'll be working only in April and May. They gave us a $.05 increase and 2 weeks vacation, and 2 weeks to stay there all the time. It's true, they want us to transfer to the Bell company to stay with them. I hope it will work out. Bertha called me a few times to go to New York. I wrote to her maybe it will be possible this summer that we'll visit them. Oh yes! I received the guy's picture. Would you like to see it? Maybe in June we'll go to Bertha. It will be very nice. You will get us the stockings by then and I will be very happy to pay whatever it will cost. I will write again. Until then, many kisses and love, Hermine

Mrs. Gerenyi wrote that as of now she did not hear from you. If you want to, write to her. That is true, they are all complaining. They're very poor. Our poor father gave him the watch because he helped them several times. But she gives it to you because she knows it's very valuable to you. Therefore, maybe it is true. They are gossiping about Klein. At this time I don't want to do anything because Irving wrote to the American consulate. In the near future I will write more. And now, love

H.

[from Marie]
Dear David! Received your letter and was very happy to hear that thank goodness you are well. I'm sorry in the past I've become a little lazy to write, but it seems we are all very busy, otherwise I'm fine. Nothing new. Hermine told you all about everything. We received letters from Europe. And it seems all over they need help. It is very sad and painful that we could not help our family. Dave as you mentioned, the stockings are impossible to get here. We haven't been able to get any for months. Since I'm not working in the city, I don't know when they will get any in. And when I will have time to go in, then nothing. There are a few people that already have a few pairs. Fortunately, when summer is here it will be easier. I want to thank you very much because you didn't forget about us. We are very happy to pay you, but now I will leave it. I want to wish you good luck and the best of health, but be very careful wherever you are going and please write. Kisses and love, Maria

1946/3/21 Irving to Dave (Book 5, 353-357)

III / 21 / 46
Dear Dave, until 120
It's been a long time since I have written you a long letter, but as school is over for a few days, so I want to write you at least a half a megillah. How is that? First I want to tell you that I'm OK and have finished one quarter at the Ohio State in Commerce College. My grades were OK, however the final grades didn't come in yet. It will be out one of these days. However, in the first midterm in speech I got a B-minus and second time C-minus. [Continued in Hungarian] So, you need to get at least two or 3s in speech. Although, it was very hard. You know the book has at least 350 pages and it was filled with such words that you can't even find in the dictionary because it was filled with Latin comments and it was necessary to know everything. For example: I needed to know where the voice is and where is it produced, and how the human body works. For example: it had to be noted that voiced Lingua-Alleolar Latteral and words that I never heard before. The other subject was Psychology, there I had to do speed reading and to have that kind of skill. For example: I had to read 150 words in a minute and write about what I read. I got a B+ the first time and the second time an A-. This way I think I will get 2-A's as my final grade. The third subject was English. They did not give a grade from this like the others, but I think I will get a 3 [it's a C] from it. The hardest thing was that everywhere my English vocabulary is not enough, but I hope next time everything is going to be better! And now you can see why I didn't write to you. I spent my free time with the dictionary, because it was a must. Although, I will be like this next week also because the school year starts again. Now I will take English, Economics, Speech and swimming. You know Dave, [continues in English] I would like to see you this summer, but at present I don't know what I will do. Till then, why don't you send me a small snapshot. Well Dave, I would like to write you a lot, but I don't know how to begin to tell you. First I want to know if you remember the Meizlish girl, well don't worry. She got married. Any [way], she waited until I got back. Wasn't it nice, hah, hah. Here in school you meet plenty others. I met one from Cleveland, she is not Jewish so don't worry. Anyway, it's lots of fun. Well Dave how are you standing? Did you meet some nice girls there? I bet you did. All Hollywood stuff. Well, you should be able to choose a real good one, one of these days, and with plenty of money. Oh you don't want money. All kidding aside, how are you doing there? Just working. Well, Dave let me know about yourself, and I'll try to inform you as much as I can. Everyone is well, Maria, had a cold, but now she is coming along fine. Herman likes to read your letter, but is too lazy to write. Hermine is writing you, I guess she is our secretary. I used to be a good writer, but today I write only when I have to. How is business over there? It's very hard to get into something today. I would like to

get me a nice car one of these days. How is your car? Running good. If I'll get one this summer, then I might drive there as you did, will talk about that later. Well, Dave I will close this time, but I want you to write me even though I'll be late in answering it. Let me know about everything, so will I. Forgive me, because I'm writing with pencil, but my pen isn't so good, so until next time. Take care of yourself, best wishes from your little brother, Irving

1946/3/22 Rozsi Hausman [SWEDEN] to Hermine and Marie (Book 3, 398-401)

[This letter is from my brother Lajos's wife's cousin.]

Vikings Hill [Sweden] 1946 III 22
Dear Herminka and Mariska,
Received your letter yesterday and I was very happy that you have not forgotten about me and that you replied to my letter. You cannot imagine how it feels in this strange country to read the letters from old acquaintances. I can say as a person by herself to communicate in a letter, therefore thank God, there is hope because I had mailed an advertisement today in a Hungarian American newspaper in which I was searching for my family relations. So few of them who know me from home have written to me. However I would like to have a real letter from my dear family, but unfortunately to this day no news has come from them. This week I received a letter from them in Lelesz. Unfortunately, they do not write anything favorable about my brother which has been my hope so far. My dearests, as you can see from my letter, I am no longer in Älmhult because that camp has disbanded and now we have come to another camp near Stockholm. This is a beautiful place, everything is very nice, but unfortunately for me there is no beautiful. This week I went to Stockholm for an x-ray. We remained a few of us in the capital city. It is nice, but to me I was not interested, not even a little bit, but only my own loved ones were in my mind. I do not want to make you sad with these bitter things. I don't know if I have written to you in my previous letter that I received an affidavit from America, and God willing I will also get out of here, but I do not know yet when it will be my turn. At this moment I have a place and I can wait here, but for how long I don't know. Beside writing, I'm getting accustomed to it and also I'm sewing and from that I earn a little money. I have mailed more packages to Lelesz to Manci and in Budapest I have one uncle [nephew]. I received information from them that they received the package and nothing was missing. I was very happy. It wasn't much, but some food items. There it is very costly and they cannot secure it. I believe now that they would like to send us to work because the Swedes do not want us to be kept here. I've written enough. Once again, I thank you very much that you were so sweet and have written. I thank you very much for your best wishes and for the 2 stamps. Write again, with plenty of information about yourselves and about your American lives at home. I wish you all the very best. Dearest, give my regards to your dear brothers and relations not knowing them. Kisses with love, Rozsi

P.S. My address is:
Rozsi Hausman
Vikingshill
Saltsjö-Boo
SVERIGE

1946/3/26 Emil Schwartz to Hermine and Marie (Book 4, 395-398)

III/26 Kiralyhelmec

My dearests, until 120
I don't know how to start my lines since I'm sure it will be a big surprise to all of you that I'm writing from Helmec. Specifically, I started to go on this trip on the condition that I will be together with a good friend of mine. Since this did not come true, I came back. I was very happy to get your letters, where you wrote that you sent a package, but it did not arrive yet. I'm asking you very much to send me cigarettes! So I can offer some to Zoli, since he deserves it because I'm here with him for a year already! I have nobody to ask anything from. You are the only people I have left from the big family. I really feel ashamed that I'm asking for help from you. Since what we had for us, we only had it. I was being robbed to the last cent. I came home to an empty house without furniture. I'm sure you will understand my situation. I also got pants from the Lefkovics girls in Sweden. I didn't even ask and still, they sent it. I was ashamed to ask from you also, but you wrote to write if I need anything. So, I guess you will definitely help me out. I will figure out approximately the most important things that I will need. For example 1 pair of size 42 shoes for the summer,

since I've been wearing a pair of boots this past summer, and a suit for the winter, if it's not a problem for you. Here, Zoli gets things from the relatives. There are 4 people from America that send packages and letters every week and they include $10-$20, but they are not even his relatives. If I get the package, I will write immediately. And I'm asking you, if you will send a package, it has to be sewn up in a bag otherwise, they will steal ¾ of it. It's possible to put the money into the letter, this way I can get it. I am thanking you for everything in advance. I will close my lines in the hope that you all are in good health. From the bottom of my heart and with a relative 's love, kisses, your little cousin, Emil

1946/3/26 Irving to Dave (Book 6, 293-294)

III / 26 - / 46
Dear Dave,
Just a few lines, while waiting for the next class to begin, to let you know that school started and I'll be very busy for another three months. However do write me even though I'll be a little late to answer your letters. Here in Columbus, it's raining almost every day. How is it there? Maybe it rains and the sun shines at the same time? Do you like it there? Do you plan to stay there? Please let me know about everything, so will I. At present I'm taking economics, English, speech, and physical education. Some of this are very difficult. Oh yes, I have received my final examination grades and are 2 B's and one C. [In Hungarian] So I had two doubles and one triplet. I hope the good God will help me and now this quarter I will be better. True, I always think it's worse. The important thing is that it turns out well. I only have a few minutes to go before English language school, so write and take care of yourself. I say like you used to write when I was in Italy [In English] My best wishes, hoping to hear from you soon. With love, Irving

Maria said if you can get nylon stockings, then 9½ is good for her.

1946/3/26 Istvanne Toth to Hermine and Marie (Book 3, 385-388)

[This letter was written by Mrs. Istvanne Toth who used to work for us milking cows and helping whatever needed be done in our home as I remember as a child.]

Polány 1946 March 26
My sweet and loved Mariskam and Herminkam. How are you? Thank God we are well and in good health and we wish you also. I do not know how to begin this letter my sweet Herminka and Mariska, because I always felt towards you as part of the family. I mailed you a letter in January and you were not answering me. I do not know whether you have received it. Sweet Mariska and Herminka in my last letter I wrote to you that when the Germans came in, your home was full of soldiers cooking at the oven and they wanted to use the furniture for firewood, but my daughter Ilan told them that she would bring them firewood from us, because she was very sorry to have them use the furniture as firewood, from then on every day we gave them fire wood. They were doing the washing. After they left, we brought the furniture, the beds and Etelka's mirror, to our home. If you would have seen it today, you would have destroyed it. As you know, due to old age they are full of holes.

To understand it, Ignácz [Klein] came and wanted to take it away. I felt very sorry, but we have watched it and I was thinking that someone hopes to come home from your family, so that they would have it, but Ignác [Klein] wanted to sell it to Puskár for a calf. My dear Herminkam and Mariskam, if you believe in God tell him not to take it away from us. The furniture has no value. He is not as desperate as I am. As you know, when you needed anything I helped, I went to your place without any concern about whatever I had to do. My dear sweet Heminkam, I would ask one more thing, if you can help, please send us some used clothing for men or women. Everything is well here, however, here you can buy only with bacon, fat and flour, but we do not have it because a very sad thing happened to us. On February 25, my husband Pista,

suddenly died at two o'clock in the afternoon. He came home from the village, wanted to lie down because he had pain in his legs. He fell asleep and in the evening at eight o'clock was dead. I am in this difficult situation and with 7 children. The burial costs me one thousand Kronin, but I don't know what I will use to pay for it. Because of that, my dear Herminkam and Mariskam, if you can afford it, and if you believe in God, do something good for me because God will return it one thousand times if you do good with the poor. Margit got married in October near Kisvarda. She also said that if I'm going to write to you, I should tell you that you should send her baby clothing because they cannot buy anything there and she's expecting in

July, and she needs it. Please write to me, tell me if you received my letter, if not then I will write to you everything again that I wrote in that letter that you did not receive.

I should have mailed it to you via airplane, but I didn't have enough money. My dear if you believe in God, do something good for me please, leave the two beds for me. You know it just seems very weak because it's already fifty years old. Perhaps one day one of my children will go out there, [and] she's going to pay you for it. My sweet Herminkam and Mariskam, write to me about the boys. Were they soldiers? I would like to see you. I'm very bitter because your father gave me your album with pictures and I watched it like my own children, so I would have it as a remembrance. Once I was going to Helmec and Ignác took it. If I would have been at home, I would not have given those precious pictures to him. I will close this letter. With respect from my whole family. Reply immediately if you can, Istvanne Toth

1946/3/28 Hermine to Louis Goldblatt - drafts (Book 16, 260-261, 264-265)

Dear Louis,
As you see I am quite a prompt writer with my answers, but I like to get mail and that is the only way to expect them. I enjoyed your very nice letter and the stories about your experiences and can understand now how busy you really were. Thank you for the snapshot I think you worked real hard to lose so much weight. Hope you will gain it back or would you like to be in style too?
I wish I could write Hungarian letters to you so I could do much better. About myself just that I am very busy also. At present we received more letters from Europe from friends and my sister in-law's two sisters and one brother are there and a cousin of ours with his family. So I am busy sending them packages and writing letters to them. Two of my girlfriends are in Sweden, one of them is from my hometown and they need a few lines to make them feel better.

[END OF DRAFT]

Dear Louis,
As you see I am really quite prompt of answering your letters so this time

[END OF DRAFT]

Dear Louis
Received your very nice letter also the snapshot it was very nice to see you and thank you very much for. I enjoyed your very interesting letter and the stories about your experiences. As I understand now you were more than busy to lose so much weight. Hope you'll gain it back soon, or do you like to be in style too?

I wish could write in Hungarian could do so much better. About myself just that much I am very busy also. At present we received more letters from Europe from friends and my sister in-laws two sisters and one brother. Also one of our cousin in Budapest with his two daughters and wife. Keeps me quite busy to answer their letters and we are sending them packages. Two of my girlfriends are in Sweden and one of them is from my hometown. Our mail means so much to them because they are all alone. It is probably better for me to all those happenings there and who knows what happened to our dear ones. I just can't find enough words to tell you how I really feel. Only thing we must have is our hope that they might come back. I shouldn't bother you with my stories but I know you'll understand me. I wonder if you could tell me about those refugees-what nationalities they were?

I tried to find your friend Corel but there's only one and didn't have anybody in the service. Here I am sending an address in case you don't have it maybe you could write they don't have a telephone. I called more Kordell but without the right answer I was expecting. I don't know if I told you my brother is back from overseas and goes to school now. Hope you are well and we'll hear from you again. Till then with all good wishes to you. Hermina

[END OF DRAFT]

My dear Father and brother with those sweet little children and I almost have to give up hope. It is very hard to do it - but what can a person do? I shouldn't bother you with my stories, but now I know you'll understand me. I wonder if you could tell me about those refugees - what nationalities were they. Somehow I want to believe it that maybe they will get back. I am very sorry for not finding your friend the Corel - but please could you send me his full address because under that name is only one, but they didn't have anybody in the service but Kordell - are many others and [I] called a few of them, but with out any luck. Hope you give the address so [I] could call him. I don't remember if I told you about my brother is home from Europe and at present is going to school at the O.S.U.

1946/3/28 Hermine to Mrs. Goldblatt (Book 16, 255-258)

Columbus 3/28 - 1946
Dear Mrs. Goldblatt!
I got your dear lines and Louis' picture. I was very happy. I could say that the picture came out very well and he looks the same on it just as I saw him the last time in Columbus. I'm sorry if I caused a little misunderstanding, but I wondered what could be the reason that you promised me his picture, but did not send it to me. Although to be wrong is human nature, and the situation is even more interesting that way. As far as your dear sibling's case goes, it is too bad that they decided that way and did not use the opportunity to migrate to America. But poor you, unfortunately don't know, what could be better. And for us it can only be hoped for in the fate, which is almost impossible, but what could we do other than try to comfort ourselves. Until this day, from our family only a little grandchild came back [Emil] , our dear late mother's sibling's child. We did not hear news from him, but he mentioned about his calculation that he is not counting on going to Palestine. Also, another cousin of ours, from our father's [side], suffered with his family throughout the terrible situation and they live in Budapest [Lipot Klein]. He was raised in Szürte and Helen Goldstein knows them too. So, there [they] are 8 siblings and out of the entire family only they are the ones who exist so far.

So, for that we have to accept what our destiny brought to us. We sent many packages and many letters because I know very well that it helps some people recover, since they feel so alone. Many times I can hardly believe everything that happened and it felt good to hear that at least Helen's two siblings came back. I'm only writing about all these, so Mrs. Goldblatt you will not be worried because after all, we can't change anything about it. It is very hard and only the dear God can give strength to bear this. Besides them, I am doing well also. My brother goes to school at the O.S.U. which he loves so much. My cousin [Bertha] invited me to New York, so I'm counting on going there to spend my vacation.

There are many relative of ours that live there and we only met when we arrived to America. I guess it will be very nice and I promised that I will go. Tonight I was busy cooking, particularly the stuffed fish takes time, but we all like it very much. We got the gas refrigerator a few days ago, that we waited for so badly. I am very happy about it and we finally got it. The weather is nice, but it also brings the spring cleaning. I didn't even think to write so much, but somehow there were few letters [to write]. I will close it with this and thank you very much for the picture. I wish good health and am sending my best to all of you. To Mrs. Goldblatt separately, with love, Hermina

1946/4/1 Undated Malvin Lefkovits Godfather's Daughter (Book 3, 383-384)

[my Godfather's daughter from Polyán. Writing from Sweden. Dated by Rezsi Hausman hearing from Uncles in America. She mentioned advertising in letter 1946/3/22 and Emil returning to Helmec after saying he's going to Palestine]

Dear loved girls!
I received your dear letters to which I was very happy, because it feels great when I receive letters from you, and I cannot even write my feelings down. Your pictures are very good. You're so lifelike, for that accept my thanks. Also the dollar that I received, many thanks my dear Herminkem. Believe me you should not enclose money, because for me the letters are very precious. You may have been taking it away from yourself and that I do not want. Dear girls, write about Emil [Schwartz] it could easily be that he is [alive] because he must have gone with his father and such a child as he must have gone to work. And a child like he must have survived because his head was down and this made me very happy, but you're not telling me where they found him. Dear girls I cannot write any news except that after being freed, the Jewish agency and the Red Cross arranged a nice evening. First it was a prayer to God and they said kaddish three times. My dear, you can imagine what it was after that, everyone cried their eyes out. Everything was very nice, but in the atmosphere it was not. My dear Herminka, I want to thank you for your kindness that you're willing to help on my behalf. I would enclose the address of Rezsi, but she doesn't write to me and I don't want to make

her write, since I don't want anyone to be forced to write. I will enclose my uncle's address and be so good to go see him because I have written to him a lot how sweet you are and how much you have helped me and

now he knows you all. Imagine that Roszi [Hausman] from Agard was found by two American uncles in the newspaper and has already received a letter and photos from them. Now she has someone. She was just as unhappy as I was. And now they want to do anything to help her to go to America. As of now, I don't know whether I will be able to go because my papers were returned, therefore I don't have much hope. Last week I spoke to the Hencsu from Helmec and she said that Marton bacsi's son [Emil] returned to Helmec. They too are sending their regards to you. Dear girls, please write to me because I'm waiting and it's very difficult. Can you imagine someone to be all by herself like I am. Tomorrow I'm planning to go to the city to the consulate to inquire what will be with me. How am I? I am well thanks to the creator. The weather is getting warmer. I will not write more. Many kisses to all of you with love, Malvin.
The address for Ignác bácsi:
Ignác Lefkovits
1325 Lafayette Avenue
Bronx 59, New York
P.S. My best regards to you also, Malvin's camp friend. [Illegible - perhaps Olga].

1946/4/3 Bertha to Hermine and Irving (Book 16, 251-253)

New York
April 3 / 46
My dear Herminka!
Forgive me that I postponed the response for so long, but the business did not allow me. Although I don't even know how, but time is running so fast, by the time I look around it is already night. But let's leave this. The thought makes me so happy that you decided to spend some time with us in June. The first weeks will be fine. We are also counting the days so we can see you. I got a letter again from the Freidman's. They got our letter.

...and also the 5 dollars that my husband put in the air-mail. I just finished that 3 "tinen" an important package to the Friedman and others. I will send it tomorrow morning by the Post office. I hope that they will get it. My dear Herminka, these Freidmans are very nice people, especially the man, and he encourages me not to give up hope and Magda could be somewhere and he is looking for the little girl in every resort "well I hope", you know who they are waiting for in New York with the Stark girls from Lelesz - their father named Samu (?) They called him Bella. I talked to Rezsi Winkler and she is very curious to see you. I hope my letter will find all of you in good health! With love, Bertha and Mannie

Dear Irving!
Glad that you made up your mind to study. Good luck to you. Mannie would advise you to take up a business course. Will write you real soon. Excuse for cutting it short. With love, Bertha and Mannie

1946/4/3 Hermine to Manci, Rezsi, and Ignác Klein- Draft (Book 16, 310-311)

Columbus, Ohio 4/3 - 46
Beloved Manci, Rozsi and Ignác!
I got your letter and I am just responding to it. Yesterday we got a letter from Emil from Helmec where he wrote that he came back to Helmec. Also, we got a letter from the Jewish Association where they informed us that they have found a Emil Gluck who on December 22nd 1945 went through Vienna with 8775 other people. So, my hope is that he is our poor Lajos's son, Emil. I wrote a letter to them today also that the Association will forward, hoping that soon we will get more news about him.

I'm sorry that I still don't know anything to write about the money. The thing is that there is not much I can do currently. I hope that we have found little Emil and then, of course, the Association will help to bring him here. Also, Emil could not go to Palestine and this way we need to help him too because neither he nor we have anybody else. So, I hope you will understand it and now I will say that I will not forget about you, but unfortunately I can't send that amount to you soon.

I sent a drink last time that was very valuable and I hope you found it. Believe me, thank God we have everything and we are working. The prices are high, and the household costs a lot - but what's important-it's not like I want to complain, but I want you to understand the situation. Since we came to America, Mariska is not so healthy, but she must work. The doctors can't find what's wrong with her, but the trouble is [caused] in big part, by our dear family and our Ignác being in the war. So, she can't help much. Ignác goes to school and cannot work. So, he gets as much [as is needed] from the government so it is enough for him. As for me, I try my best, but it's about everyone and I have to help out everybody a little. I will write more some other time to you and I hope you will get the packages for now. I wish you a healthy Passover and let's hope that some members of the family could be found. Believe me my Manci, one's age does not matter here and I wish I could help you to come here! What you could earn would be enough for yourself. I will try to ask around to see if I can do anything in your interest-maybe some rich family could get papers to you. Hermina

1946/4/3 Margit, Lipot, Lulu Klein to Hermine and Marie (Book 18, 184-189)

[from Margit]
Dear Relations!
We received your dearest letter which I cannot tell you how much happiness it gave us to hear from you all. I don't remember too much about you other than Mariska and Dezső. Sometimes she used to visit us in Perbenik. We talked about you all the time. How smart you were to leave the country just in time when you did. We remained here cruelly battered by fate. You can say you took part, because there is no news from those nearest to you. It is also a terrible tragedy in our family. Only a few of us remain. From Lipot's sisters and brothers, he is the only one who has come back. From Etelka's cousins who lived in Terebés only 3 daughters came back. Arthur wrote that they are helped by Eigner. Lipot also sent a letter to them. I also want to write you about that. Dear Hermine, I felt very, very happy to read your letter, how much you care and want to help us. I do not want to tell you that we are okay and that we don't need any help because the situation isn't that rosy. Lipot wrote in the first letter how brittle the situation is. We were left without anything.

Unfortunately, he came home late from the deportation like an excavated skeleton, in sickness. He was already in the hospital a few days later and he lay for months with pleurisy. He is already, thank god well, but he is still under care and he can't put stress on himself. We are suffering like this now unfortunately, because had he come home in health, maybe our situation could have been different. For now, the most important thing is that we are together. Those who came home healthy could arrange their things sooner. You can get everything here, you just have to earn a lot to live in the most modest way. For example, we are still at the point where we can't buy candy and meat because they cost a fortune. But at the same time, Lipot needs to eat well. I will not even mention the clothing and we have only the furniture that we borrowed, but we are alive. I only write all this because it feels good that I have somebody to talk about this with, to write it in a letter. I want to ask you darling, that whatever you do for us, do not cause struggle with it for yourself. We don't know about your financial situation.

...and that is why any kind of help comes in handy. God forbid, it would get you into a financial burden. That is why Lipot turned to Arthur with his request. He thought he has a better situation to do something for us. Many have already received complete packages - nothing was taken apart. I wrote enough about us, I would like to know what do you do? Are you satisfied with your destiny there? Lipot responded to Arthur's letter. I am writing to you so we can send you both letters today. Your letter came after 5 weeks. If the package arrives, I will write immediately. Is your brother Herman there also? I only know about Dezső and Ignác. Write all of you, it feels good to read your letters. I kiss you countless times, all of you, with love. Margit

[from Lipot]
Dearest Cousins!
My wife wrote all about everything. I can't stand not to write at least a couple of words. I would not feel happy if I don't write to you, it makes me very happy this way. If only I could just be able to talk to you in person at any cost, even just a few minutes, it would make me very happy. Please write a little bit about all of you. Kisses to all of you hoping you are all ok. Best wishes, your relation, Herman (Lipot)

In the future, when you write or send a package, send it to the address below:

Súrányi Miksa letters
to Klein Herman
Budapest
Reiter Ferencs utca 58

1946/4/5 Private ? Julius Contz to Irving (Book 14, 109-110)

Hello Irving

What are you doing the most of all was nice to hear from you. Did I even write to you about Moyer, you know the red head that done one kp [kitchen patrol]. He was killed did you know? Well, until I meet you, J.W. Contz

1946/4/12 Hermine to David (Book 11, 137-138)

Columbus 4/12 - 46
Dear David!

We did not hear from you for a long time, but we hope that you are well. Although I did not write to you for a long time also, but believe me I am very busy and I have a lot to write always. This week we got a letter from the Jewish association through whom I sought ours and they wrote that they have found a Emil Gluck and instead of '31 they have his birthday in '32, and he's Hungarian, but it was written that he was born in Budapest. He went through Vienna on December 22nd, and there were more than 7 thousand people of all nationalities.

I wrote a letter to him, about who I am in detail, so that even if he does not remember it could come to his mind. We got a letter from Emil in Helmec also, but poor thing is asking help from us because he has nothing -no clothing- no shoes. He did not go to Palestine- I'm amazed that last time he wrote that he has everything and I should not send anything. Although, he lives with the Pollak boy and he is getting married now. It could be that he was very proud and did not let Emil write it to us. I sent 5 dollars to him. Now I want to send some clothing to him. Manci and the others are writing too, but poor things their situation is very terrible. Gerenyi and the others also wrote at least two weeks ago and I would like to respond to them also. Mrs. Ivanyi wrote also, her husband died and she was begging us to help her because she is so poor- I wrote to her that I can't do it because there are others who I had to send things too. But now I talked to a Catholic girl who works where I do and I told her the situation and I asked her if she could help this lady through the church. She promised that she will talk to the priest, maybe I need to go there also, but she was a good lady to us and I would like to do as much as I can.

I had an interesting case last week, I got a letter from the Goldblatt boy. who was in Pearl Harbor when the water was flooding and wrote to me that he has a friend in Columbus. His name is Korel-Covel - he did not know his name nor his address. So, after a week long search I called one of them, Covel on Lockburne Ave and he said that it is him, plus he also knows you because you worked for him in the shoe store and when he was a soldier in Long Beach you went together to party and that you have taken a picture together. So, he is some friend of this boy from Cleveland. Also he became a "Kpt" [Captain - Hungarian "Kapitány"]- this is the boy I'm corresponding with in letters. The Covel boy was wondering about you and was pretty happy that he could write to the boy because he did not have his address. I will finish with this. Write!!! Kisses, Hermina

1946/4/12 Manci Klein [Etelka's sister] to Hermine and Marie (Book 3, 379-382)

[This letter is written by Mancie = Margita Kleinova]

Dear loved Herminke and Mariska!

We have received your dear letter which contains official papers, however I replied already to you and it may be crossed with your letter. I hope that you're going to receive it. Dear Herminkam, on April 10 we received the package that you mailed us with groceries, nothing was missing from the package, more likely the other will be coming also soon. We want to thank you very much for everything. It was a very appetizing package. Lots of packages are coming, but not like this for anyone. My dear Herminkám, of the things collected in America which we have already gotten, I can only use them as dust rags. I don't know where the better things are taken out.

My dear Herminka, we are preparing for Passover which is to me most depressing due to the fact this holiday reminds me of how we were in that nice position 2 years ago. I didn't even feel like going out to the street. Etyu and I stopped at the end of a backyard. I would have gone out of this world [how] I felt as I saw everything. At the present, I could sit in peace, but I don't have with whom. A person can stand so much.

Ignác at the present is not at home my dear Herminkam, that's why he's not writing first. I want to thank you for the things that you have sent him. We have gotten matzos, but only 5 pounds. We are going to add to that potatoes. They charge 65 Kronin for one kilogram of potatoes.
I gave your addresses to Etyu, he was here. He will get married after Passover in Homonna. He looks quite well. After they are married they plan to travel outside of the country, and from there it will be easier to go to America.

My dearest, next time I will write to you much more, but at the present I am busy. Róhcsi's finger is painful. Wish you all the best. With lots of love and kisses to you all, Manci, Rózsi, and Ignác.
Lelesz, 1946 April 12

1946/4/16 Manci Klein [Etelka's sister] to Hermine (Book 3, 235-238)

Dear Herminka with love,
A few days ago I've written to you in a letter that we received a package which has had food products. I also want to inform you Herminka the coats and everything that was in the package has arrived and are very beautiful and it fits me perfectly and I have used it on Passover. Anyone that saw it admired it. The blouse and the light dress is good and fits me well, but the black dress is tight. The shoes are good, and I'll repair them because it is very difficult to get shoes here. My dear Herminkam we thank you a lot, all of you, for everything. Emil sent a message that he too got the package. Dear Herminkam I have another question and I will turn to you. As I have written to you before that I feel fine and I have regained the weight that I lost in the concentration camp. But I must tell you, I cannot sleep at night and I would like to go to Kassa to a doctor, to examine me with an x-ray so that I could find out if there is anything else that may cause that problem. Perhaps after that I may be able to rest and relax. I cannot ask from Ignác therefore I am turning to you Herminkam, if you can afford it, please mail me in the letter $10. I'm sure it will arrive safely in the letter. Please don't be angry my dear Herminkam that I disturb you and I'm asking you because I do not have anyone that I can turn to. I know that you're all busy. What are the boys doing? And how come that you are not writing about the watch? Why are you leaving it with those damn peasants, they are all so bad. Dear Herminkam, please write, it is a great feeling to read your letters. Wishing you all the best of everything in good health. With kisses and lots of love, Manci.

1946/4/18 Emil Schwartz [Helmec] to us Columbus (Book 3, 407-410)

Kralovsky Chlumec
April 17

My dearest!
I received your letter which brought happiness with it. Together I received both packages one came from you Hencsukam, and the other came from Arthur Gluck. Thank you very much to all of you. The letter came in unopened. You wrote that I should contact the consulate in Prague. I did not write there at this time, because I would like to go to Palestine, with Zoli. Thank God, I'm healthy and I hope to hear from you as soon as possible and in the very best of health. You wrote that you are going to mail another package. I want to thank you in advance very much. I'm waiting for it. Clothing will be very handy. As I wrote to you before that nothing was left over in this world and nothing in the store, not even the furniture. I hope you understand me.

Summer is coming and it's nice and warm and I spend my time in the sun. After Passover I'll likely be going to learn dentistry. I'm asking you please write to me more in detail about everything. How was Passover at your place? Here not so well, because I have been thinking of the past [and] of the last Passover in which my poor father has done all of the way. You wrote that you are going to send some cigarettes. I will be very grateful because I'll be able to make Zoli happy. He smokes a lot and the cigarettes here are not the very best. I received a letter from Sweden from Hencsu and from Jideszku they are also interested to know what you're doing and how you are. Don't be surprised by my handwriting because my hand is a little bit nervous and it's shaking when it comes to writing. I will be writing to you on the typewriter next time. At this time, I'm forced to write with a pen. I have nothing special to write about. I'll close my lines with the hope that all of you are healthy. Kisses to you, my brothers and sisters. Emil

P.S. Zoli sends his regards. He cannot write because he is in business and he doesn't have time. Kisses, as above.

1946/4/18 Irving to Dave (Book 6, 284-286)

April 18 / 46
Columbus, Ohio

My dear brother Dave, until 120
One really does not know how to strike the pen to write a line. It has been quite some time since we have heard from each of us. Yes, time flies and we keep on being quiet writing and that's all. As from my point of view, it is hard to begin, but one can only say it can't be helped. To bring the story to a point, it is really my turn to write you, but it seems some people do not know how one is occupied in the present school situation. The only thing there is "studying" so my time is taken up with that. As time goes on I'm thinking of you and the family as a whole and somehow one does not or can not take off a few minutes for pleasure or writing. And especially this quarter I'm so occupied that from 6 A.M. till 11 and sometimes 12 P.M. [sic] and I still have work to do. In this case there isn't enough time to do all the work that is necessary. Finally today I have finished a couple examinations and begin to write you and Hermine and Marie. To them I have done the same, just listened. Yes, some one thinks well why doesn't he write? To tell you, it seems to me that I could go there faster than take out time as during these study periods. Well, now I want to tell you I'm sorry that all this happened, but hope that you will understand me. As you know the pressure in school is very high and we must, or some of us, must, do the best to go on with the University policy "learn or get out." Thank God, as yet, God was with me and everything is OK and hope it will be so _ _ _ in [the] future. Now hoping that you are well and please write me and again I want to say if everything will go on well maybe in September I'll see you. Oh yes, I want to mention that Herman went back to work to Arthur and he became in charge in the supply room and doing well. How did you spend the Passover? Here we were at Mr. Roth's place the first evening and the second evening we were at Arthur's. Everything was fine. Once again Dave, please forgive me for not writing you. Please let me [hear] how you feel and wishing you the best. With love, kisses, your little brother who will never forget. Irving

1946/4/19 Manci, Rozsi, Ignacz Klein to us (Book 4, 414-417)

My loved sweethearts!
We read your dear letter with happiness. Purim has just arrived. I'm so glad that I can write in detail. Since we are interested in your well being also. My dear Herminka, you are very sweet, that you think about us so much, but I did not think that a thing like that should be sent through the postal service at all, because the difference is too great. Here they give 220 korona for one dollar. And it arrives in a letter for everyone, no matter how much they put in. I think you are such a smart girl, [send] only what you can afford and it's up to you. We just got a letter from the Jaski sisters. They sent $10 in the letter. We used it immediately to have a [pair of] shoes made for Rozsi, because shoes are very expensive here. One sole costs 1000 korona. It is so expensive. My dear Herminkém, you wrote that they take the best items out of the packages. But that's not true, because we got a package from Rezsi Klein, that cost 11 font, and everything was there in it.

My dear Herminkém, Ignacz just travelled away, therefore he can't write to you, but since you are wondering, he said that I should write to you, that he could buy two middle sized horses for $100. My sweethearts, Etyu from Homanna who was waiting, just got engaged with a relative, with the Moskovits boy from Ungvár. I'm sure you will know who that is. I always thought that Moricz Schlanger will marry her! Moricz still did not get married. He has responsibilities. Hersu Braun is just getting married, also. He will marry a relative of Stark from Agard. Everyone needs to get married. They are already having Yentu Singer's documents done, and Patyi will go out to Palestine. [As for] me, sweethearts, I do not wish to go to America. If I would still be as young as you are, but I feel I would not be so happy there either, after all this loss.

In turn, Petofi [the poet] has a saying, "Everybody has to be happy once."

My sweethearts, I take everything the way destiny orders it, because now after the deportation, I have experienced more. I made peace with everything. Thank God, I'm healthy. You have a very nice job, my Herminkém. I would take such a job like that too. My sweethearts, we thank you very much, but the aforementioned Laci, has sent a telegram to me. We were very happy because poor him, he was left alone. His father, for sure, will have him taken out now. Zoli Pollák is engaged to Tobi Komáromi's daughter. They really wanted to catch him for Médi Veisz, but it did not work out. Ignac does the right thing in that he is studying. We wish him lots of luck. How come you are not sending pictures to us? I would love to...

...see you. I would send one, but for now, I can't do it. I already wrote about many things, so you will have something to read. Thank you for everything. And write about all of you. I will visit little Emil, if I will be in Helmec. Very well. Kisses to all of you with love. I wish you everything good. Manci, Rózsi, Ignácz Lelesz, 1945 IIII 19

1946/4/23 Eta Moskovic to Hermine and Marie (Book 18, 157-162)

[Our Grandmother's maiden name was Moskovic (Haia Schwartz) , so they are related from there]

Humenné 1946 IV 23.

Dear Hermina and Mariska!

It has been such a long time and finally I was able to get your address. This week I was able to hear that you wrote to Lelesz. I'm sorry, but there isn't anyone in Lelesz. No one came back. So now I'm staying here in Homoná. I was in Leles when I came back from the camp, but was there only for 2 weeks with my younger brother Hersu. I met him there. He also lives here now. After Purim I was in Leles a 2nd time and the Klein girls were very nice and gave me your address. Maybe you will not even remember me. When you went to America I was a young girl. I'm Aliznak's youngest sister and Lajos was staying here. I still can remember you very well. Maybe you heard that I got engaged, and with a relative. My fiancé is from Ungvár, Majer Leib Moskovits' son. With God's help we will get married. We also would like to go to America. My greatest wish is to get away from here. After so much suffering, even now it must be said it was not worth staying alive, especially here. We still have lots of trouble. By 8 o'clock in the evening we must be home from the city. I will correspond more diligently about everything. I would be very happy if you would send me an answer to my letter. I would also be happy if you would write me more details about everything. Also, how are you living? What are you doing? Did you get married yet? I hope you will answer me very soon because I am waiting. I would love to get a letter to read with good news about you all. Many kisses to you all, Eta

My brother sends his regards.

[from Herman]
As a relative whom you have never met, I greet you warmly. Herman Moskovits

1946/4/29 Bertha to Hermine (Book 16, 267-268)

New York
April 29 / 46
Dear Herminka!
You will surely be understanding that I left your lines without a response for awhile, but my activity did not let me. First we were getting ready for a wedding and by the time we shopped for everything, believe me, we got tired. The wedding was done by this month on the 20th. I could say that it was held at a very elegant place with a fancy serving and everybody was very elegantly dressed. I can't write it in a letter, I can't explain it because it would take a very long time. I am very happy to hear that you are in good health. As far as we are concerned, we are also well. We went to visit the two Stark girls. They are well and they, and everybody who knows you, are very curious to see you already and I am just counting the days (weeks) until the time [comes that] you could be here with us. Give our kisses to the dear relatives, accept our thanks...

[In English]
For you good wishes to the Easter Holyday with best wishes to all with Love, Bertha and Mannie

1946/4/29 Istvánné Toth (Ilon nenni and Ilonka) to Hermine and Marie (Book 18, 191-198)

[from Ilon]
Dear Hermina and Mariska!

I'm asking your apology if I bother you with writing to you. I just wanted to write to you what happened when we were not at home, the little gal Erzsi [Klein?] came over and was rude and nasty. She took the album and all the pictures that Mr. Gluck gave to us when they were going away. Even though I had them and was watching them, and took care of them with my heart so that when someone will come back they should have it. And to show, I took care of it for them. And now she took it because she wanted to have it because we were so happy whenever we looked at those pictures. How beautiful you were, both of you, what you sent to your father from America, Dezső and Hersmandu, also your relative from Helmec, and your dearest mother. Everything, whatever was in it, your pictures, you looked so beautiful. Ignác from Leles complains that they have nothing. Don't believe that because whatever they had the neighbors gave back to them. It is a good excuse for that is a good reason. I don't want to gossip, the only thing I want to tell is the truth. For me, I don't buy this for nothing. The only thing I can see is how Ignác operates. They have so much clothing for sale and shoes. They are selling everything. Now they are doing very well. They never had before [so much]. Ignác sold even the furniture, yours also Herminka and even what Etelka had, too. They had so much money. They are talking about even putting your house for sale just like he would own it himself. Even though you are alive, thank God, beautiful Hermine and Mariska. Please dear, be so kind to send us some women's clothing if you are able to. Now I will close my writing. Many kisses to all of you. Ilonka

[On the side] Sweet girls, time went by so quickly. I'm 22 years old.

[from Ilon nenni. It appears to have been written by Mrs. Toth on behalf of Mrs. Ilon. The handwriting matches Mrs. Toth's but is signed Ilon neni]
Monday Polyàn 1946 April 28th

Dear Hermine and Maria,

I received the long awaited letters from you and they both found us well, and this is what we wish all of you from our heart. Dearest, when I received your letters I was so happy to hear from you and felt so happy that you did not forget us and remembered us. I would have been even happier if you wrote to us about your dear father and your brother. Please believe me there isn't a day that goes by that I don't remember you and think about you all. Dearest Herminkam, I'm very happy that you assured me that some thing will come around to help us, but we don't have anyone who can help us about anything. You have forgotten us. But believe me dear Herminka, that our heart is broken because of our sorrow that whoever has someone in America they are very happy because they are helping their relations. We have no one who would even think about us. Dear Herminka, you are writing that you don't know anything about the furniture. I don't know what to say dearest. Ignác and his family whatever was theirs they got back, and whatever you had also, they got back. Every piece. Ignác went with a police man wherever or to whoever took something. He found them and took it to your home and sold everything at a very high price believe me. Dearest, they have all your belongings. Your father was always angry with them, especially with Ignác. Understand only one thing, he sold even what belongs to [your brother] Ignác.

They got everything back. Some of these people have nothing. They are selling them in the yard on your property. You can buy clothing and pairs of shoes, but it is very expensive, 5 hundred korona for one pair of shoes. The dresses are also very expensive. Dear Herminka and Mariska, do you know what they are doing? They sold everything, even the house is for sale! Excuse me, Puskár and Horvyak live there. Yes, Puskár is boasting that he will buy the house. I'm not sure if he will. If you would see it, knowing your room, you would die from seeing the condition it is in. How beautiful it was before and now. Dearest, talk to your aunt, maybe someone can help us to get help. If God willing, sometime one of us goes there, they would do and show you that they will appreciate whatever you did for them by one hundred percent because you know, I don't have bad children. I have 4 boys and 2 girls at home. I have the 3rd daughter living at home. Margit got married. Believe me, I have plenty of heartaches. My situation in [the past] 5 years [was such that] we were not able to buy anything. Now, even if we can get it, it's [just] food. I get only what we need because here we can't get any job where we can make some money. Now I'm closing my letter. Best wishes to the boys. Write about everything a lot. For me it is good if I hear from you. God be with you. Just today Andras Tóth died. Gerenyi already knows. I remain with love, Ilon neni

Polány 946 IV 29

Dear Herminka!

Received your letter and we are all well, which I hope you are okay too. I ask God for you, too. Dear Hermine, don't be so bitter. God is good, you have to trust him. A person who is alive has hope. Poor Etelka always used to say that. We are all saddened by this Dear Herminka because they were so nice to us, just like one family. I especially was with them all the time and Etel néni was very good to me. She never gossiped and she was a very smart woman. I told her if I had any problem because she understood me. I know dear Herminka that it hurts you that you don't have any news of your dearest father and your brother and family as of now. People are still coming back and maybe they can still come back. Don't be so bitter. God is good and you must believe that he will help. That is true. Dear Herminka, I just want to let you know about the furniture which we had here. Ignác Klein from Leles took away everything and sold it here in the village. He came with 2 policemen and we were forced to give it back. Can you imagine Herminka, we were not able to buy anything from him because he wanted such a high price that it was impossible. One closet that Mr. Gluck paid for, he was asking from us 1000 korona. He sold it to someone else for 400 korona. He didn't want to know that I should have been the first to buy it because I was always there at Mr. Gluck. I'm not saying it to "throw it up". I used to help Etelka a lot because she was very busy with the children. Also, the Leleszi princesses never came to help them. I didn't deserve that I should buy it for my money. Now they are big shots. I hear you send packages to the Leleszi girls and they are selling it. Herminka, don't think that I'm just saying it or guessing about it. 2 pair of shoes that you sent them they sold for 500 korona. Ask about it. Your dress and skirt that you sent them and more dresses, they told me it is for sale. We can't afford to buy it from them. You should not tell them that I told you, even though I don't care. They can't write anything about me. I told you the truth about me. Ignác says that you sent them the authorization. If it is true they would have it. We would never sell it and he sold everything that was good. I would give it back with my heart to whomever comes back and to help them with everything. God help me, even though we are not rich, whatever we can [we would do] even though we are poor. Boszike is grown up, a young woman of 19. She was a little girl when you were here. I wasn't even married. Now I'm at home. I was very lucky. When I was ready to get married, my boyfriend passed away. I hear that it was because a bomb shell "exploded" in the officer's building. Poor Etel neni. She liked him very much. We corresponded for 3 years. We were friends. In the meantime, I had a little girl. She will be 2 years old in May. She is a beautiful little girl. I also trust God that he will help us. I was so sad, even now I feel I'm writing in my sorrow. You can't even believe it, but now I will stop writing. Herminka, please write to me again soon. I'm waiting, and it is very difficult to wait. With much love to your whole family, and kisses, Jolany

[Upside down] Mr. Török sends his regards to both of you and will write.

Dear Maria!

I'm very happy that you are such a nice person as I'm reading your letter. Don't be angry that this time I am writing only a short note. Next time I will write more to you. Therefore, you write more Maria for me. I love all of you. I hope you will remember me. You did not get married? And Herminka, you too? Mrs. Gerenyi felt very badly that you didn't write to her for a long time. It takes 2 months already to get an answer. Please write to me sooner about my letter that I sent previously. Send lots of regards to all of the family and I separately send lots of kisses with love. Jolany

I'm waiting for you

Columbus 5/3 - 1946

Dear Bertuska!

This time I'm responding a little late to your dear lines, despite thinking about you so much and that I want to see you again-which is getting close now. I hope you are well and thank God we are well also. The Passover celebration passed by and the fact that our Irving was with us made the fun even better-Unfortunately, there are many other people living in our thoughts that are constantly with us.

We got a letter from Budapest a few days ago - Lipot Klein from Perbenik lives there and as I wrote this the last time to you, that they survived, in other words-they suffered through their hard times. Arthur wrote to them as well and I think he will have them come here.

I also got a letter from the Jewish association with whom I did the search for our little ones. They notified that they have found a child Emil Gluck who would be the oldest son of Lajos-and in December 1945 he went through Vienna, with more than 7000- of all nationalities. So, I wrote to the notified address that they will send to him. I'm hoping and trusting in God, that it is truly him- The year was correct, only the place where he was born was different. Mistakes could happen everywhere, that is why I wrote it, so I can be sure and I could get news from him. About myself, I still don't know the exact day when I will arrive to you, but I will notify you.

1946/5/3 Rozsi Hausman to Hermine and Marie (Book 18, 143-150)

Vikings Hill 946 V/3

Dear Herminka and Mariska!
I received your letter which I was waiting for impatiently. I was happy to hear from you and to prove it, as you can see, as soon as I received your letter I sat down immediately to write to you. My dearest, you cannot even imagine how it feels to be all alone in a strange country. To hear from someone, an old friend, gives some hope in life. I will be honest with you. It was very difficult to write the first letter because I was afraid you might tell me or think that I wanted something. As you see from my first letter, thank God I don't need any help because I always make a living and I will be able to get whatever I need. Thank God, I can even help others. This week I [prepared] 3 drd [Hung. darab = piece] of 1 kg packages with food. I just mailed them to 3 girlfriends in Agárd. I also told them what you wrote, that God will always help and he will give it back [to us] if we give to a good cause by helping others. I will tell you what happened, something connected to me. Before Passover I had a very difficult problem. I didn't want to go through a holiday eating treif at home or eating hametz with making a bracha [blessing] on non-kosher food. Here there is a place in Sweden that is not too close to me, only 350 km, and it costs lots of money, but it is what I wanted. Therefore our God helped me and it was good enough and he protected me, and it came out OK and most people went there. I was very happy because it was just like I used to have at home. The only difference was at home my dearest love, my family, were together and happy for the holiday, and here I was happy that I was able to keep the holiday. It is sad that with so much pain, as you can imagine, the good God helped, and besides that, here too I was happy I had this place. By the time I returned, there were 4 letters waiting for me, all from America. They were from my dearest father's brothers, and one from one of his children, one of my cousins. You can imagine when I finished reading those letters - in a way I could not even think. I wasn't able to find words. It was only a letter. I never knew about them. I only knew that my dearest father has a brother in America, but they never wrote to them and I was looking for them. A few girlfriends went out from Agárd. They also went through the Hungarian registration list where they put my name. They answered immediately. I must tell you that I'm very happy they wrote because they write beautifully and it's interesting, they would like me to be there as soon as possible with them. I think they are still my Aunt and Uncle, they are not strangers, and maybe they want to make up for what they missed in the past. Even they would forget all of that. If I would only hear from my 2 brothers with the news that they are alive I would be very happy. Like you have heard from your dearest Emil, whoever hears good news like that I am happy. I hope the dear God will help that it should be true. From Leles, I'm also waiting to get some mail. Oh yes, from Leles the Stark girls, Lenke and Iren left to America last month on the 26th. They wrote me and they are very happy because they went to their brother. I'm waiting for their pictures. I thank you very much for the dollars, but it isn't necessary to send it to me. And now I'm closing, with lots and lots of love and kisses to all of you, a lot
Ròzsi

1946/5/4 Louis Schwartz to Hermine and Marie (Book 15, 237-238)

5-4-46
Dear Herminka, Mariska and boys!
I can barely remember the last time I heard about you. What are you doing?? I think I already wrote it to you that our Gizi got married to Lajos from Garany and they live in Garany. Our Anci got engaged with the Karpat Abrahamovits' youngest son, with Meier. Our Erno is still in Szürte, he has failed to cross the border yet. How did you spend the holiday? We had a very nice Seder. The first night was with a lot of guests, but of course the next day we started again at our daily jobs like normal. We barely knew that it was Passover. This is America! There is no news otherwise. The great season before Passover has past. Now I am not that busy.

...although in the store there was enough work on Saturday. I write this before closing because I don't want to postpone it to another week. I wonder, if I could find a proper place, I would make myself independent, but of course this is only a plan and a hope, but I am hoping. And you Irving, what do you do? Do you work or [are you] just studying? Write to me what you do. I have to finish my lines. Write to me! Kiss you all, Lajos

1946/5/5 National Council of Jewish Women to Marie re Citizenship (Book 17, 389-390)

Columbus Section
National Council of Jewish Women

May 5, 1946
Maria Gluck
50 Linwood
City

Dear Friend:
We wish to congratulate you upon your recent graduation and tell you how proud we are that you are now a citizen. As a reward, we are extending to you a year's free membership in Council. We hope that you will be able to attend our meetings. With all good wishes, I am, Sincerely,
Florence P. Lieverman
Corres. Sec'y [corresponding secretary]

1946/5/7 Lipot, Erzsi, Lili, Margit Klein [Budapest] to Hermine and Marie (Book 3, 392-397)

[from Lipot]
Budapest 1946 May 7

Dear loved Herminke and Mariska!
We have received the package that was sent in February, we thank you, everything arrived in accordance with the list. I don't know who packaged it, but they must have learned how from your mother. In the front of me there is the right hand of your mother and her heart, whom I knew that she did everything with a pure heart with complete giving and I see that you are 100% her descendent. Loved Herminke and Mariska, you did not write about the boys, especially Dezső. You did not mention anything about what is with him. I hope to hear the best thing. The package that you have mailed on March 5th, has arrived. There are situations that it can arrive in one week and you can be at ease that the shipped package was not opened nor the letters. I regret that I am still in the doctor's care and I must rest a lot, but according to the doctor, I am improving and I recognize it. In my last letter I gave you a new address but I remained here in the same place where I lived. Therefore mail anything to my old address. If you have sent me anything to my new address, it will not matter because I will receive it a few days later. With the hope that my lines will find you all you in the best of health. Lots of regards and kisses to all, individually, from our family. With love, Lipot
The forwarding address is;
Klein Herman
Budapest
Dohany U[tca]. 36. 2nd. door.

[from Erzsi]
Dear Herminke and Mariska,
I can't write down how happy it made me with your packages. This is the first package that we have received from America. We thank you very much. Everything was very nice and it came in handy, but we cannot wear the clothing because we are fat. We are not as skinny as you, but with a little repair all will be well. The sugar, it means a lot here, it's like gold, you can't purchase it. Because of that, everyone here is starving and nervous. You can purchase everything here, but it's very costly.

Do you remember us? More likely only as little children. Now we are big girls, who have become working ladies. Both of us are going to work as sales ladies, however you can't make a living from this. Now I'm learning English and I'm doing quite well. You probably know English well. What are you doing? How are you? I remember Dezső, but the other brothers I do not remember. I would like to get out of here and go somewhere. You can't imagine how our little family, thank God, is all together. We can't write it down to tell you the story. It can't be done on what we, and our people, have gone through. The best thing is to forget.

In the near future I will write again. Write to us frequently. You don't realize how much happiness you have given us. If a letter comes from America, our father brings it to us in the business, because he knows we are happy with it. As [soon as] the package came, father came to the business to tell us. He didn't want to wait till the evening until we get home. I'm asking you to write frequently because it takes a long time to communicate. If you can, mail us some pictures of all of you, we will also do the same. Many, many kisses to all of you, Erzsi

[from Lili]
I also send my kisses to you. Lili

[from Erzsi]
If you see Arthur and meet him please give my kisses.

[from Margit]
Budapest 1946 May 7

Dear Herminke and Mariska,
I want to thank you very much for the items in the package. I can't write down how good your attentiveness felt, every piece of clothing comes in handy. Even if it can't be worn, it can be transformed to anything. Erzsi and Lúlu are also shorter. We were happy for the sugar, cocoa, and the tea. We do not buy these items because from day to day the prices are going up and up, a person becomes confused. I would like very much if you would write about Dezső. I remember him quite well. He is a very nice, vibrant, young man. Probably he hasn't married yet? I did not know Ignác. What are you doing? What is each of your occupation? Do you get together with the relatives frequently? It would be wonderful to speak a little bit in person and to discuss it. Mariska, you promised that you will write frequently, now you ought to do it.........
Many, many kisses to all four of you, with true love, Margit

1946/5/9 Irving to Florence Meizlish's mother - wedding invitation (Book 22, 267-270)

May 9 / 46
Dear Mrs. Meizlish,
I regret that I will be unable to attend Florence's wedding on May 19 / 46. Please give my best wishes to Florence and her husband for all the happiness that life can bring. Sincerely yours, Irving Gluck

1946/5/10 Hermine to David (Book 11, 140-144) pages 1-2

Columbus 5/10 - 1946
Dear David,
As I was waiting a long time to hear from you, I finally received [your letter] and I am answering now. I received your package and the stockings are beautiful and thank you very much. I didn't think it will be difficult to get it by you. If I knew I would not bother you with it. As you mentioned you would be able to get it, so I took the opportunity because I could not get it here. I asked at Lazarus. I told them I will pay cash, but even then I can't get them. I could not get them anywhere. Here in a couple of days both of us are getting one pair. I will give it away to some one. It will be very good for me also. I plan to go away, too, if God will help me. If it will work out then in the beginning of June I plan to go to New York for about 2 weeks. I will write from there, too. In this month we will finish work and they promised that they will give me a job at the Bell company [and] will place a few of us there. Today it is Saturday. I was working all day because we have to get ready for the other Company sooner and they will be able to take over. I could go anywhere, in Long Beach also, for the same company because they have offices there too. Tomorrow will be a big day because we have to put up the wallpaper. The paper is ready. We just have to put it in water to make it wet and paste it on the wall. I hope it will work out. It is pink in color. On the card it is very beautiful with a small design. I will paint the ceiling. Therefore, I always have a job. It is enough to be busy. Otherwise, I'm fine. I'm wondering why don't you write. If we would not write to you for a couple of months then you would not write. About Emil Gluck you didn't understand because I told you about our

brother Lajos' son Emil. I think he was born in 1931 but on the paper that the organization sent me it was dated that he was born in 1932. This is correct. Also they write he was born in Budapest, it could be Bodrogmező and they can be mistaken, I hope…

1946/5/10 Undated Hermine to David (Book 19, 425) page 3

Emil from Helmec would like to go to Palestine, if it would work out. We didn't hear from Manci for a long time. Emil wrote that he already received 2 packages. One Arthur sent to him. Last week from Budapest we received an answer from Lipot. Arthur wants to bring them out. At this time Arthur is sending them 2 packages every week. Maria and I also sent them 2 packages. We are corresponding with Malvin and the girl from Agárd. They are asking about you in their letter. Bela Stark's 2 daughters who were in Sweden arrived to New York. Bertha wrote to me that she went to visit them. Write about yourself because I write to you about everything, but you never answer. Or maybe you don't even read it…? I will continue tomorrow. You could write a few lines to Emil in Helmec and Lipot also because they are always asking about you. Thank you again very much for the stockings. With kisses, Hermine

1946/5/15 Margit, Lipot, Lulu Klein to Hermine and Marie (Book 18, 177-182)

Budapest 1946 V.15
[from Margit]
Dear beloved relations!
The same day that we mailed you the letter in which we mentioned that we received the package from you, we received the 2nd one in which you mailed out on the 16th. This came in a shorter time. I must say we were very surprised it came from you again. As I was taking it, I felt humbled by the contents, not because it came in a perfect condition, and it did come in a perfect condition, but how nice it is of you and to feel that you are such a warm and caring person. Even in the letter, it shows what a caring person you are. Have you received any mail from us? Every evening we are hoping to get your letters faster. I count every minute. Arthur's letter took 2 weeks. He also sent a package with food. We thank you so much for what you are doing to help us. Maybe, possibly it can or will get better. Please write a lot about yourself. Everything interests us. Did you hear anything from the Schwartz children? Until now it is very sad, but we didn't hear anything more from the family. Hope all of you are well. Best wishes, and many kisses to all 4 of you. Love Margot, Lipot, Erzike and Lulube.

I found some stamps in the package. I don't know if they got in there accidentally or if you sent them to us.

[from Lipot]

Dearest loved Herminka and Mariska,
Please don't take it wrong that at this time I only write a few lines. I do not want to mail a letter without a few lines. It is difficult for me to write sometimes. I would write the same thing that my wife did. The latter page is very nice. Next time I will write more. Kisses to all of you. With best wishes and love, Your cousin, Lipot

Address:
Klein Herman Lipot
Budapest
Dohàny ù 36. II 2 apt
Hungary

To Arthur and his family, shalom, kisses, we greet you with love

1946/5/16 Emil Schwartz [Helmec] to us Columbus (Book 3, 411-414)

My dearests, until 120
I received your dear letter and it made me very happy, especially the pictures. I was very happy to see it because I remember the good old world. Thank God I'm a healthy [and] hope to hear from you all. I have difficulty with my leg and I have gotten flat feet and I need an insole in my shoes. More likely I will be

going to Kassa to make a new pair of shoes. Don't be scared. I can walk normally, but I can't walk too much because that pains me. This also keeps me back from traveling. The marriage of Zoli will take place on the 19th. He's marrying the Komarom's Rabbi's daughter. I gave your regards to him and the same to you from him.

In reference to the packages, here the girls are getting a package weekly in sewn bags. This way, packaged properly and strong, they will not open it and you can send new merchandise. In the first place I want to thank you for the packages. It will come in very very handy especially the clothing. Clothing is more important than cocoa, etc.. But cigarettes okay. Don't take it in a bad way that I'm writing to you what can be and what cannot be done, because I think it would be better for you, and for me, that you are sending what I need. We have plenty of food here and that we are not missing, like shoes etc. You write in your letter that there was five dollars in it, but the envelope was opened and was empty. This can also be helped if you mail it express, or guaranteed, or a different way. All I know is that they get everything here. Yes! Perhaps stick the stamp to the area where it's closed. The best bet perhaps is to insure it. I thank you for everything in advance. I'm closing my lines with the hope that you're well, in good health, and you will reply. With a pure heart, kisses to all of you, individually, your nephew. Emil

I'm writing here a letter to Arthur. Please Hencsukam, be kind enough to give it to him.

Dear Arthur bacsi,
Before I begin to write to you, I want to introduce myself. I am Emil Schwartz, Uncle Gluck's nephew. Thank you very much for your package that you sent me. It was very nice of you. I am very grateful to you for it. The package arrived in good condition. As my cousin Henscu writes that you would like to help me to take me out to your place. It is very nice! If it doesn't become too difficult for you, then I would ask you to send an affidavit. My dates are: Emil Schwartz, birthdate: 1929 August 13 in Kral. Chlumec. I'm very grateful to you in advance and thank you. I remain your relation with love and regards to you. Emil

1946/5/19 Elsie Schallheim to Hermine and Marie (Book 14, 154-156)

Sunday

Dear girls:
How are you getting along? I've been thinking about you all. I do hope things about Europe are not as bad as you think they are. Have you heard anything in regard to your Father? I'm glad that Irving is going to school. What is he majoring in? How does he like it? Are you girls satisfied with your jobs? I do hope you all have been well. Jane studies hard. There are three more weeks left of school. Do you see my folks once in awhile? I suppose Flora is rather busy because Jennie will be confirmed soon. At the present time I will have some people living with me. A teacher from Case College and his wife. She teaches too. They rent out a room in my home and have kitchen privileges. It's nice having them for two reasons. First they pay well and second they are lovely people. I've had them here since August. I wish you girls could have a chance to meet some nice young men. Take care of yourselves and love to you all. Elsie

1946/5/21 Hermine and Marie to David (Book 16, 123-126)

[from Maria]
Dear David!
I'm sorry that I did not write for so long to you, but here work got busy somehow in a way that I did not have enough time to write. First of all, thank you very much for the nylon stockings. What I did not even think about, is that it will be so much work for you. It appears that there is a shortage of it everywhere, but this is going to be enough for a while. It is a lot of money for you to pay for it, even though they are all very beautiful. Otherwise we are well. There is no particular news, our little brother as you can see, is very busy also with the exams, which are pretty hard. Also, we got your letter last week and I'm glad to hear that thank God you are healthy, just take good care of yourself and write. I work currently where I was. Now I'm sending my best and kiss you with love. Maria

[from Hermine]
May 19 -46
Dear David!

Our last letter was sent a little late because we were pretty busy. Thank God, the room is organized and it looks pretty great. Currently we are very busy with work, but it won't last for long, until the 26th. If God will help then around the 1st I'm planning on traveling to Bertha. I hope I will get a job by the time I get back, otherwise they will place me at Bell since they promised that. Although, I can look around before at others as well. So, I'm hoping - and how are you? You never write about yourself. It's true that I don't want to write myself either, but I have to. I got a letter from Malvin, Rozsi from Agard and from Etyu Moskovits. That poor little girl who stayed with Uncle Lajos in Lelesz, Aliz's younger sister from Palocz. She wrote that she is engaged with a boy from Ungvár and she is together with a brother in Homonna. According to what she wrote, she just had her wedding today. There is no particular news here. The weather is not really nice because this month it rained everyday. How's the weather by you now? I'm afraid that by the time you have to go to New York, they will restrict things and then you will have to stay home. I don't remember if I wrote this to you that I wrote about our Lajos's Emilke, that his birthday was written in at 1932 and he was born in 1931. I hope that it is truly going to be him - I wrote to him and they will search for him until they will find him. I will finish with this. Write a lot! Thank you the stockings and I kiss you many times. Hermina

1946/5/25 Hermine to Pál Lengyel (Book 11, 146-147) draft

Columbus, Ohio 5 /25 -46
Very Honorable Notary!
We have been notified by the American Consul, that our sweet father Jeremias Gluck's wealth goes to Hermina, Maria, Herman, Ignác, Emil and Lenke's name. Ignác Klein is the appointed one to take care [to be the guardian] of our property. So, we declare that by this appointee there is no permission granted to sell anything without our given permission. We have control over it. We are all American residents. Our property cannot be taken away by anyone and in any way. I'm kindly asking you to provide some information regarding this matter, which we will be grateful for. We would like a statement about everything that belongs to the persons named above and also that we pay to Ignác Klein to bear the title of guardianship and we want to pay the tax from the crop and we are waiting for further clarification. With excellent respect,
Hermina, Maria, Herman and Ignác Gluck

1946/5/26 Irving (written by Hermine) to Ignac Klein - draft (Book 19, 120)

May 26 - 46
Dear Ignác!
I tried to write to you on many occasions already, but I am very busy. I think Herminka and Mariska have already written about everything. Now leaving my busy schedule, I would be interested if you could give me a little enlightenment regarding our assets. We already received several more notices that you put the house for sale. I really don't know what's the truth about it and what isn't - but all I know is that in all cases you should be aware that without our consent you will not be authorized to sell it in any case. Likewise, as American citizens, the state is very strict, and our rights can be upheld even more strongly. I hope you can understand and that you will provide the necessary information. Thank you for your effort in advance and I am still sending my best to all of you. I can hardly wait for your response. Ignác

1946/5/28 Bertha to Hermine (Book 16, 192-194)

New York
May 27 / 46
My dear Hermine!
I'm sorry for my silence so far. I hope I will confess the reason. If you let me know when you will leave from Columbus, and which station will you arrive at in New York, maybe Penn Station, but it doesn't matter, one is just as far as the other, then I will wait for you. I am only waiting for the time so you could be with us. I hope I will be at home when you will arrive, since my husband has to leave for business on Thursday. This way I will have the chance also to travel there with a very good acquaintance. I will be back on Sunday night, since I don't know when you will come and I don't like to stay alone in the apartment. Until I will see you again. We kiss all of you with love. Bertha and Mannie

1946/6 Undated Louis Schwartz to David (Book 17, 189-190)

[Undated but probably just after May 28, 1946 since Louis mentions the strike]

Dear Dezső!

Hermina sent me your address at my request. My cousin [older and male] was getting ready to go to California a few weeks ago for a vacation, but due to a lack of hotel reservation he had to cancel. I thought they could have visited you if...but looks like we had to go to a different place, to the south. Now that I have your address I can use the opportunity and write to you a few lines. I'm sure you know, that I changed. I went back to my old job with my older brother who came home a little earlier. Also they probably wrote it to you that from our beautiful family only three of them: Gizi and Helen's two kids survived the Fascist hell. They write often and we are sending many packages to them. Dear Dezső, I would be happy if you would write to me in detail about how you are - What do you do? How is your general situation? Many came from this region to try their luck in California where supposedly the conditions and possibilities are much better than here. What do you think? Is it possible to start something with a little money? I would like you to write everything that you know about yourself etc...I'm writing this letter in the store because of the strike. [Business] is going very weak, so I have time to write this way. But I will close my lines. I hope to hear from you soon. Kiss and write. Lajos

My brother sends his greetings.

1946/6/5 Private Paul Imhoff to Irving (Book 15, 76-82)

June 3, 1946

Hello Mr. Gluck:

As I wrote in my salutation I wondered just when you became a civilian once again. Maybe you beat me? I got my discharge Nov. 7, 1945. Shortly after I last saw you, that grand old 67 M.P. Company took off for Rheims, Fr. I took one of the motorcycles and the ride was really swell. After lazing around Camp Cleveland for about a month the drivers took the jeeps, trucks, and cycles down to Marseilles and then came back to Rheims by train. That trip was a great one too. Then the Company went to Marseilles and we were just there a few days when the Jap war ended. After being taken off of shipping orders 3 times or so, we finally made it and sailed for the good old U.S. We came in New York harbor - up the Hudson to Camp Shanks. From there I went to Atterbury and then home on a 45 day furlough. (I needed 4 points when I first hit Atterbury) When I returned from my furlough the critical score had dropped 10 points and so I was discharged. At present I am on the night shift here at work and as I am running an easy job on the press I decided to write you while the press worked for me. This fancy stationary is all I could find handy here in the shop. About the 3rd week of July, I expect to go to Cleveland and could go through your fair city and stop in to see you. If you are still in Columbus and will be home around the 3rd week in July - drop me a line and give me the directions to your place. If you won't be home I'd still like to hear from you! What I mean to say is that I'd like to hear from you regardless of the fact that you may not be home when I could stop in to see you. Remember Lt. Henderson? He married a French girl and stayed in France. Because I got back to riding a cycle while in our M.P. co, I had the yearning to get one once I got out of the army. So - I now have a cycle which was in the army at one time too. It is exactly the same as the one I rode to Marseilles. Well I have to get to work now on another job so I'll sign off for now. Hoping to hear from you. I'm just your old pal Paul

My address
3001 Henshaw Ave
Cin. 25 O

1946/6/6 Pál Lengyel to Irving (Book 3, 243-246)

Lelesz 1946 June 6

Mr. Ignác Gluck

Columbus 5,Ohio

I wish to advise you and reply to your letter that the properties of Gluck were given to Menyhert Török of Polány and became his property during the years he used it. The rental was paid to the War office and according to the present time you cannot get it back. In such situations where government changes properties that were left behind, the government takes care of and declares management so as it turned out to be that Ignác Klein, the closest relation was declared to be the manager. The manager has no right to change its ownership, just to maintain it and must account with its income and you cannot worry about it that he can sell the property. Also you don't have to worry that he will pocket the income because he has to report and account with it. He got the properties, but you should be relaxed and not worried. To return the properties to you, as American citizens, it will be very easy to do that. Please turn to the Czechoslovakian consulate regarding it. And if you're not happy with things as they are, you could now change from Ignác Klein to whomever you want to. You must send an authorization to do that. If you wish to get copies of the properties from the official book you must secure it. At the present time it is very costly, but as far as you know what you have had approximately. The complete properties are all those properties that when you left to America are here. If you intend to sell the properties then you need a copy. If you trust me, I would secure it, but you must send me to cover my expenses, then I will be glad to secure it for you and mail it to you. I will do it gladly because the old Mr. Gluck bacsi [and me] we were very good friends.

I also wish to advise you that said building is very neglected. The building for the hay and straw was destroyed by a strong wind. I'm sure that in this regards Ignác Klein will write to you in detail and you can trust him completely. He has also suffered quite a bit in the concentration camp and doesn't feel like wanting to create any problems. He was declared as a manager by the Kiralyhelmeci district office and he gets no payment for that.

I believe that with this communication I have provided detailed information about the properties. If you need any other information please turn to me and I will be glad to give you complete information on everything.

My best regards to all of you wholeheartedly
Lelesz, 1946 June 6
Sincerely,
Paul Lengyel

Address: Lengyel Pál, Lelesz.

1946/6/8 Hermine to Irving, Marie, Herman (Book 11, 149-151)

New York 6 / 7 - 1946
My darlings!
Maybe it is time to write a letter to you, but really the time passed by very quickly here. I was in town today, Mili Winkler's daughter took me, so she can introduce me to the town. We were in the Radio City Music and actors were playing too. It was very beautiful, the movie and the actors as well. We went to a famous Swedish restaurant for lunch and then on the bus, where the top was open, in other words the bottom part of the bus was like in Columbus, but on the top, it had seating and it was very pleasant, [it runs] that way from 10 am to 5 at night. I got home at 5 at night. So, everybody is very nice. Tomorrow we are going to the temple with Bertha for a belmicva [batmitzva]. Jenny Frey invited me for dinner at night and to the movies. On Sunday I will go to a Hungarian picnic, where there will be only Jewish people there and I'm counting on going to Jenny on Monday. I already talked to them on the phone and she was very happy that I'm here and that I can speak very well in English.-She wondered about everybody and is sending her best to all of you. I already sent two cards to you. I hope you got them! Bertha and the others want me to try to find a job here because they pay much more money here and I could get a good job with this experience. Currently I did not go after it yet, but maybe next week and then I will see what will be.

If it works out, then whoever wants to come here, can come and we will see. Although, for our little brother it would be very hard because of school. It would be very hard to leave from there. So it is that nearly every girl has a better future here. If you could see Malvin Cimerman, what a majestic woman. She got married and the oldest Stark girl got married too. We will see, if I will get a good job, that will decide it. Although, it is true that here everything is so expensive. My Irving, I got your letter and thank you for the address! How did your exam go? What's going on Marcsa? Did you go with Flora and the others? Were you there? The brown suit would have come in handy, but it's not a problem. Today I was in the gold dress and in the gold coat. It was very warm. I'm sending my best to Aunt Helen, Flora and the others, and the Walters too. I am also writing to Dezső although I'm in a hurry because Bertha's husband will be home soon and we will have dinner. They are very nice and I'm having a good time with them. If I got something good in a letter, send it to me. How is Mr. Herman? He is also a good boy. I'm kissing you, Hermina

1946/6/11 Hermine to Marie and Irving (Book 16, 389-391)

Long Island - 6 / 11 - 46
My darlings!

I arrived yesterday to Aunt Jenny and they were very happy to [see] me. Bertha accompanied me for awhile and our aunt's daughter Lucille waited for me at the crossing and we went together to her house. They live beautifully in a little town, that is, it is as quiet as in a village. The little grandchild is a very cute baby. Our aunt was asking about you separately. Yesterday I came out [here], but maybe I will go back to Bertha tomorrow. Yesterday I went to look for a job - but there is no result. I went with Bertha, so I gave them enough work, but her husband would love me to stay - now I'm writing this letter in the garden, on a hammock [with] only [the paper] in the hand with just a book underneath and that is why it's not that great. Aunt Jenny wants to call a few offices, so she can enquire about a job. She just came to tell me that where they sell comptometers, they teach how to use them for free and they would like me to go in tomorrow and they would teach me how to use the adding machine - and then they will place me. So, I will find out tomorrow, what will be. More importantly, I met a Hungarian boy at a picnic last Sunday and he took me out to the movies yesterday. He called me here and on Thursday he wants to take me out again. The most interesting thing is that Dr. Hajos in Columbus is the uncle of this boy. The boy's name is Hajos also. Although Bertha's sister-in-law introduced me, and she was in good terms with [him], he only just came back from the military where he was for 4 years...He is an optometrist and a poet. He writes poems - yes dear and a good looking boy, but started seriously because he was afraid that he will not meet me again and that he will not impress me since his family has a different style. Right now, to go out with him does not matter, and it does not have to be serious. Yesterday Jenny Frey talked to Emil's uncle, Lefkovits from Helmec and he did not know that our uncle Marton's son [Emil] came back and was very happy and he will do anything to bring him out. I forgot his picture at home and I'm asking you to immediately send one here by air mail so his uncle can see him and I hope he will have him come out here. The good Lefkovits girls were afraid to tell him, so maybe he will not have them come out here. I will not write anymore now. If I get a job Mariska and the boys can come too, but only whomever wants to, of course. It is also possible that I will not get a spot. Write about everything. I kiss you. Hermina

[Side note:] Did my little brother pass the exam? The relatives [send] kisses to everyone and the relatives.

1946/6/15 Hermine to Marie and Irving (Book 16, 427-431)

New York 6/14 - 1946
Dear Marcsa, Irving and Herman!
I already wrote a letter to you and two cards, but one of them came back because I forgot to address it. Right now, I don't even know what to write because I don't know what will be. Bertha would like it, and the other relatives too, if I would stay here and look for a job here in New York. Although I went to a few places, but without much results. I'm still expecting to go to work. The hardest part is I can't go myself, so I have to look a little for it. I got little brother's letter and I just wrote a card to the lady and to Arthur and to the others and to Dave. You did not reply to me, but if you will not answer to this, then I will really stay here!

Is that ok little brother? You know Mariska that the relatives would love to see you, too. I still did not go to visit everybody because I don't have time. I'm counting on visiting the Stark girls tomorrow. I already wrote that at the Hungarian picnic I met a very good looking boy, who is very handsome and nice, but it seems that there is always an excuse when finally I find somebody. Bertha and the others like him a lot and so does Zseni and the others. He called me on the phone everyday and since Sunday he looked for me 3 times. He asked me out on Saturday and Sunday. He is an optometrist.

...and he writes poems and he paints pictures beautifully and he makes watches, or that is his hobby - he is good at many things- and of course he's a relative of Dr. Hajos, that is, his [the doctor's] sibling's son. Although, the way they talk, they laugh at me that it is a problem that his aunt is Christian-It is not important to show this letter to others because I just write in confusion, there is everything in it. Mariska and Irving, what do you think? Is it worth it to keep the friendship with him? Aunt Zseni said that I really don't know our family because there are cases here too and because of that I don't even know what to say.

I'm curious if I got a letter from Louis? You wrote about that official letter that Arthur mentioned. Write it to me and then I will go to the Consul too and I would send a letter through them. Do not forget to send Emil's picture to my address so I can send it to his uncle. I guess he will help him to come out here. Bertha and the others are going on vacation soon, but they want me to stay and if I get a job you can come also. Of course it is hard to get a house. Currently, I don't know what to say and I'm very worried. If I really go back maybe we will never be able to change my destiny. They pay more here, if one can find a proper job. Although the boy already found one for 1 dollar an hour in the office at the company where he works.

Although, he is not making glasses in the factory - but I am looking for something else, if it will work out. So, Ms. Mariska and little brother, you can write the response, if you want to come here later. Of course, it would be better in California, but you can easily get company here because there are a lot of acquaintances and Hungarians. So, I think it is worth it if it will work out and then Mariska would have a friend too - something that perhaps will never happen in Columbus! [This is] what I know from experience - it worked out for me so well. So, we can bring the furniture here. Maybe, even to sell it. Two weeks is enough for me to see about the tradeoff, what I lived through for 6 years. I'm sure that I will get a job. I even thought that maybe I will stay for two more weeks. I should write to the Bell [Company] that I will be a little late and that maybe I should not miss it. Hey Marcsa! Write if you want to leave Columbus. If yes, than it would not take long for you to come here. Herman would be glad for the opportunity to get rid of us. If he would want, he could come also - Although, we would not buy a house - So, respond! Kiss you, Hermina

1946/6/20 Undated Marie to David (Book 8, 3-4)

[Dated by Hermine in NY, may stay there.]

Dear David!
It has been a few months that have passed by since we have heard from you. Hoping my letter will find you in good health. As I see it, we learn from each other. Soon we will forget how to correspond with each other. We are ok. Hermine mentioned before to you that she is in New York. As we can see it, the relations would like her to stay in New York. At this time I don't know what she will decide. I think it would be much better if we could stay there as it would probably be a better future there, otherwise we have to wait and see. And how are you, Dave? What are you doing? I can't imagine that you are so busy that you don't have any time to write to us, not even a word, since you don't have to cook at home. Please write about yourself. If you remember, Hermina wrote to you in a previous letter about one young man whose name is Covel. He knows you from here and California, too. About 2 weeks ago he called us and he was asking about you, and if we heard from you. What do you think because he sends his regards. We were ashamed to tell him that we haven't even heard from you. He asked us that if we hear from you we should call him because he would like to hear from you. Otherwise, nothing new. Are you still working where you worked before? I really wasn't happy about that job. I'm closing for now. I want to wish you all the best. With kisses. Maria
Take care of yourself wherever you go and write about yourself.

1946/6/23 Undated Hermine to Irving (Book 10, 23-25)

[Dated by reference to going to visit with Milli Winkler and Lengyel's letter, 3 day holiday maybe Shavuot]

My dear little brother Irving!
I got your letter with the check, that is, with the money order. The gift will be sent to them by railway express in a few days. I could say that it is a very nice gift, but I hope I am not in trouble, that maybe I gave you a big expense. Yesterday I went with Bertha to visit Milli Winkler and Rezsi and this way we spent it nicely. A real "Polyán"!
Besides this we are well, thank God we are healthy. How is Herman? Maybe he is angry at me because he does not find it worth writing even a line.
When did you see Arthur and the others and how are they? Tell me little brother, how is Jenny [Arthur's daughter]? Surely she is a big girl already! Believe me that I started to write and somebody always comes in and they talk so loudly that one can't write. What did you do for the three days holiday? As you can see I had to stop with the writing. I will write about everything, but I am trying to finish, so I can send this letter. Write about yourself and about the studying. Until then, take care of yourself and eat. Don't get weak because I know that you neglect it since you are very busy with studying. Did you write to Pál Lengyel? I would have written already, but I don't have his letter and I would want to respond to everything exactly. Write about everything. I kiss all of you with love. Hermin

1946/6/30 Hermine to Marie and Irving (Book 16, 383-387)

6/30 - 1946
Dear Maria!

I got your letter and I am already responding to it. I can imagine how busy my little brother Irving could be with studying, and I will forgive him-but Mr. Herman, looks like he is a big Mr., that he does not want to write. What is important, that you are well and thank God I am well too. I would like to write a few letters, but I don't have time even though I don't do anything besides work. Sometimes I help Bertha, but she does not let me do anything. Now, of course she will be going to Canada tomorrow and this way I will cook for myself - sometimes. Today I was at Jenny and they took me to the beach, although I did not bathe and they don't go to the water, but it was very nice.

She made delicious dinner and yes, she is nice just like her husband. A simple Hungarian boy, but a very good man and they live beautifully. As far as my job goes, I like it. Currently I work 37½ hours for 5 days a week from 9 to 5:30 at night for $30 - but I will go to school at night, so I could learn how to use the machine for all 4 types of use and if I will take the exam, I will make more money - but someone who can understand it well could get $45 and $50 for a week. So, I hope it will work out. I don't work hard, but I want to show that I can do it and I understand the job.

The woman who hired me, she just believed what I said to be true, even though I did not have any kind of certification now. So, when you will come Maria, it will be good for you to ask a few lines from your boss, so he can show and prove that he was really satisfied with you. But I will leave this too. Today Bertha wanted me to send you a telegram, that you should come here for your vacation. Although, I did not see that as good because you are not prepared and, if they are not at home and I am at work, you are on your own and you would not know what to do alone. If God will help, we will see in the Fall, how everything shapes up by then. One thing for sure, that it is better here than in Columbus. Of course, in California it would be better and healthier for you, but before we go there, we must come here first. Do you know why? Because here there are a lot of acquaintances and we can meet with them and then the good will come. I already met three of them and I keep the friendship with all of them. I met a Polish boy and he is a gentleman. He took me to the most elegant places for dinner and to the movies. The next day he took me boating for 2½ hours and he brought food with him that he had wrapped in a restaurant. So, the time spent was great. Mannie and their friends just came home. They will play cards and Bertha went out somewhere. Tomorrow Mannie's sister will come up to me to sleep. Last week there was a couple here for dinner, they are in really good terms and they are related to Mannie. So, they wanted to introduce me to one of their acquaintances. We met in the park last week, such that Bertha and the others and the couple and the boy and me, the 6 of us were there. From there we went to a beautiful Hungarian party place. That man is Hungarian, at least 43 years old, and he is a perfect gentleman. Of course, he said he would love to see me again, which I promised him. I know he is a nice man and he can't hurt me because he takes me to the most beautiful places and they know him.

Yes, I told them that I don't want to take advantage of him, but it does not matter to him - so it will be as it comes. Of course, as I hear that the Polish boy is rich too, but his only problem is that he is too short. The third one looks old - so there is always something. They tell me that I could be 25 years old and he is too old for me. Bertha and the others only laughed at it because they know the truth. I write a lot of gossip here, but just to have something to read. No need to gossip it to strangers. If you would have seen the third man, Maria! He was like an actor. Ugly, but a gentleman and very polite.

...you can see [people] like him in the movies. Bertha's husband likes him so much, that he promised him if they will come back from the vacation, they will take that man out to the party place. Hey Maria, don't be sad, whoever I know, they all want to introduce a boy and if you will come you will have one too. My dear little brother, about the business, I can't respond because I haven't had the opportunity to look into it further, I don't have a chance. I would like it, my little brother, if you would be with us also. Herman doesn't lack much and can't wait to get rid of us. Write to me! OK? Do you work hard? Why does David not write? Maybe he is angry that I didn't go there? What did you give to Lina?

I will give the money for everything and I will send the check back, I just don't have that type of envelope. I will write to Ms. McNeill also. I would like to write to Europe as well and I will send money, we could send most of the clothing because we don't want to bring it here. Did you sell the ice-box? Will that pay off the payments? Write about everything. I already got the weekly paycheck on Friday. I just want to buy a dress for myself that I can wear to work. Everybody likes my dresses, especially the small dress that you have as well. It looks like a better dress. Aunt Helen kisses you all also. With love, Hermin

July 4th

Dear little brother! Until 120

I got your letter. I'm sorry that I did not write for such a long time, but I am so lazy to write that I can't even imagine what's happened to me. I am not able to get myself to write. You know I work at night, and in the daytime I am so sleepy that I don't even know why am I such a lazy letter writer! I don't know any particular news, everything is the same. Thank God, I am well, and that's what I hope I can hear from you, too. I got a few cards and letters from Hermin that she wrote from New York writing that it is possible she will stay there, but I did not even write to her. So, I will write to her too in this letter a few lines. Maybe she came home, but if she is in New York then please send it to her. Ok!! The weather here is excellent, everything is so nice here that one cannot ask for any better. I don't know any particular news. Please write to me even, if I don't write.

Even if I don't write correctly, don't take my example Ok? What's new in Columbus? Do you go anywhere? Do you still go to school? I really don't even know what to write, nothing comes to my mind. What does your dear brother Herman do? Did you hear anything from Polyán? Did you write to the Consul to look around in Polyán? Find out. It is for your own good- Do you know that a dollar is worth 100,000 Pengo in Pest or more - I did not write to anybody yet - If you write to the Consul, find out if we can get the gold watch from Gerenyi - in other words - send it there - Currently I don't know any news. I kiss you with love until I will see you again.

Your brother [older], David

P.S. Write, do not take my example. Ok! Do not buy a car now. It will be cheaper in at least two months. Kisses, Dave

July 4th

Dear Mariska!

I know very well that you are the one who I owe with the most writings. I hope you can forgive me for that. Ok!! How are you? You work hard don't you? If Hermine will stay in New York, then you should go as well. You know there is a bigger and better future for girls there than in Columbus - There is nothing interesting here, everything is the same. Thank God I am well, [and that's] what I hope to hear back from you. Although, it is true that I am a very lazy letter writer. I'm sending my best to that boy who was wondering about me. What is his name? I don't know all of a sudden (Kovan). If you see him, you can tell him that I saw that family where he lived. They are well. Currently, I don't know anything else. - Write to me and then I will write to you also - Did you get [any] letter from Polyán? What do they write? Did you hear about Emil Gluck from Pest? I'm waiting for your lines. I kiss you with love, Dezső

P.S. Send my best to Mr. Herman Gluck! Don't forget to write. Ok! So, take care of yourself. Do not work too much. Leave some work for Mr. Herman also. He loves to work anyway. Kiss you, Dezső

VII/7/46

Dear David!

We got your letter and I am in a hurry to respond. I'm glad to hear that you are well, only that is not an excuse for being a bad writer or that the writing does not come to you. I know this well, I can say the same thing, since I don't have patience to write. But I also know, if it feels good to get a letter, then I have to write it too, even if it's hard. Otherwise I am well. This week I had my vacation although I only spent it at home. And as you can see, Hermine stayed in New York and she is already working. I'm sure she wrote about this to you too. She likes the job. Currently she is at Bertha's. They want me to go there too. Now, I don't know how it will be. Maybe in the fall. Currently, Irving goes to school and he is having a hard time with studying. So, he does not have a lot of time for anything. After summer school he will have some. I hope that everything will work out. And since you mentioned about the Emil from Pest, you did not really understand [the situation]. About this Emil, we only know that he traveled through Germany in December 1945. He is 13 years old and [named] Emil Gluck, but his birth place is not correct. We think that it could be a mistake, but since then they don't know where he is. He was with a couple of thousands. And now the Jewish community is searching for where he went and what happened with him. It could be our little Emil easily, but who knows if they will find him or which side of the Earth he is at.

We wrote to the unit so they can search further, since we want to hear about this more. But currently we don't know any news. We hope that it is he who we are looking for and that the dear God will help him, and we can hear about him from Polyán. We got letters from many and from the goyim [non-Jews] and they all wanted something and when they found out that there is nothing in sight, then they did not respond. I also mentioned to you that Uncle Marton's little son Emil stayed alone and he is in Helmec. Arthur said that he wants to have Zoli Polak come here. And as it looks like Emil does not seem in a hurry somehow. One of them is asking in a letter that he wants to come. As it seems, poor thing, he himself does not feel good there, this is why he is not in a hurry. But now Hermina talked to the uncle in New York and he did not know that the child is alive, he only knew about the two Lefkovics girls and they are being brought here to America already. And let's hope that he could bring more. We got a letter last time from the girl from Paloc, who lived in Lelesz at Uncle Lajos and she wants to come here also with her husband, since she just got married at that time to a boy who is a relative in Ungvár. Now I think I wrote enough and I hope I don't have to wait for months for the response. Take care of yourself wherever you go. Why do you work so many hours? The weather here is warm enough. We got a letter from Hermine and she could not imagine either, why you don't write. And now I will attach your letter to her. She is already working and she likes it. Now I wish you everything good and kiss you with love, Maria

1946/7/14 Hermine to Marie and Irving (Book 11, 153-157)

7/12 - 46
Dear Maria and Irving,
I got your letter but I am only responding now because I'm always getting ready to write and then I leave it. As I wrote already, I will go to the comptometer school. I talked to the teacher and she said that 10 nights are enough for me, and then I will get the $33. I hope that the exam- in other words, they will try me and they will see how well I work on the machine. As of right now I like it and the girls tell me that I work a lot because they only play on the job. I went with 2 girls for lunch today and I dined with them. I had my payday today. They pay me every week and this was already my 3rd check. I only worked 3 days last week because it was a holiday and we got Friday off- but I still got the paycheck for the entire week. It is not a lot, but I hope I could get more later.

Otherwise, we are well and I hope that you all are. What's important is that I'm writing this letter while I'm working because there was nothing for me to do, and many of us write or read a letter. It's hard to get used to it because I could not do that so far. So, that I can have a little discussion about something else too. So I will get to it. First of all, as I wrote it about the holidays, in other words, for 4 days I was at Aunt Jenny. I got to know many relatives because there is always someone coming to her. They live in a beautiful place outside of the city, and it is like in a village, but it is very pleasant and they don't let me do anything, only rest. Although they do everything on their own. Lucille's little girl is very cute and I will attach her picture here. On one of them there is me, Aunt Jenny and her grandchild Jo Ann. On the other one Lucille and her child and Aunt Jenny.

We had have many takes, but they were not successful. I even have a picture of the sailor, but it is not good and I don't want to go out with him anymore because he is a miser and I am not interested in that at all. Especially when he would seriously think that it would be good for me. The boy is pretty handsome, but he makes himself to be hated by his behavior. Last night, the second boy I met came up to Bertha + others to visit me and he wants to take me out on Saturday - If something will not come up - But he will call me on the phone. This boy originated from Poland and he is very modest and he looks very cute. As much as I know him. The trouble is that he is short. Bertha's sister-in-law introduced me to him. He took me to the most beautiful place for lunch last time-to a kosher place and to a beautiful movie, where actors play too.

The girl says that he is a very wealthy man. He is being placed as a watch maker - in other words, his job is to install the clock's structure to the case and they pay well for that. He only does that work and not fixing. So, it was enough about this gossip also. I would like to send a check home, but I did not get a chance to go to the post office yet. I don't even know where there is one. I would like to put a few packages together and I will send the cost - Only clothing because when the house will fall apart, what will we do with our stuff. Did a letter not come from Mannie + others? Did Arthur send the letter by the lawyer to them? Bertha suggested to me to hire him or write to Bozske Kramer's husband, who lives in Helmec and then he will look into it and it will not cost anything.

I will see what your response is and then I can write a few lines to him. Maria, how are you? Are you not sick? Do you work hard? Do you cook a lot at home? All these questions that I wanted to ask many times already. Jenny Frey invited me yesterday night for dinner, but I did not go and I called her on the phone to tell her - since the boy came to us. Jenny is a very nice woman with a good heart and she is just like her husband and shows me that they like me very much. The relatives don't agree together and all have something to tell about the others, but I only listen (quietly) and this way I make them happy with it. I still did not visit the old uncle Gold nor Emanuel, Aunt Jenny's son, who was in Columbus.

I would like you to send a few things for me here. It is not important yet, I will write about it next time. I'm counting on writing to Emil in Helmec, but I did not hear anything about the uncle since then. I got a letter yesterday from Lajos from Youngstown and he really wanted me to write to him about everything in detail - He would like to go somewhere too. Jenny Gelatin wrote to me a response to the card that I sent to her- you know the one?- who knows how to sing and worked with me. Lillian will come for the money don't worry about that! She is not worried that you will not give it back. I will continue sometime soon at night because I could not finish at work.

The boy did not say when he will call me on the phone at what time and this way I can't go anywhere, although I wanted to buy a few dresses for myself that I can wear for work. It's interesting that Bertha has expensive clothes, and yet she likes mine and so does everybody else. I don't know the stores here yet very well and I can't go on my own to shop. Jenny Frey keeps the store closed this month and she would love to come with me. I will call her tonight and I will find out what would be the best. I'm sorry that I only write a card to my acquaintances [in Columbus], but I don't have time to write a letter, but you give my best to the acquaintances.

I wanted to clean tonight, but the black lady came because Bertha wrote to her. Hey Marcsa, your stuff that I brought here I could give you the money for it because it is not worth it to send it back to Columbus. Bertha+ others will be back maybe tomorrow or on Sunday. They want me to stay with them until the Fall. They don't accept money for it and this way I can't take it away from them, although her husband does not even want to hear about it. I am doing well particularly. I brushed my hair up and everybody likes it this way. Did you write to anyone in Europe? A letter came from Malvin here, but I did not open it up. It came to Bertha's name. A letter from J Mintontal and her mother came and she feels like I'll be back in the fall. Here everything is so expensive, but it is still worth it because there is an opportunity to get to know someone. How is Herman doing? I am angry at him that is why I don't write to him.
Kisses, Hermina
[Upside down at top] Irving dear, write to me!

1946/7/15 Flora to Marie (Book 16, 379-381)

Sunday July 14
Dear Marie:-
I have been thinking a lot about you and hardly can believe that three weeks have already passed since we came. I had intended doing a lot of painting and varnishing but haven't felt any too well so nothing has been done. Also we are still waiting for the plumber, the electrician, the carpenter and a man to cut down the trees and clear the grounds - Help is just as hard to get here as at home. What is the news about Hermine? Has she come back yet or is she planning to stay in N.Y.? And what are your plans? First of all, I hope you are feeling well and taking care of yourself. Please drop me a card and tell me how you are - and Irving and Herman -
Jennie and I miss Arthur and Samuel very much. We do like it here and it would be perfect if all our family could be here together. We hope some day you will come too. Love to all of you, Flora

1946/7/18 Hermine to David (Book 8, 62-65)

7/18 - 46
Dear David,

I received your letter from home. I'm happy to hear that you are ok. I know you are always very busy, but even then you still can write a few lines. It is true that here is not the same as in Columbus. Time passes by very fast. Therefore, we stay behind in our writing. Now I'm writing at work because I don't have anything else to do. It is very hard to get used to because I was never so lucky. I'm going to school to learn how to divide, for which the company pays. The woman told me that about 10 nights will be enough, just 2 evenings every week and then they will give me a pay raise. That is true, they are going according to how fast you are. Otherwise, I'm ok. I have seen lots of nice places and I met lots of people. There are a few boys, and Hajòs is very stingy so I got disgusted with him. I'm not going out with him, but he calls me on the telephone. So don't worry David, it doesn't go so easily. Whomever I meet wants to introduce someone to me. Yesterday evening they wanted me to meet a Rabbi's young son. He was at Bertha's home and can you imagine Bertha told him how religious I am. Can you imagine she wanted me to meet a Rabbi? It is true, he was very modern. Don't get scared. Everyone is trying to be helpful. Don't laugh at me for this, I'm just mentioning it to you because I had a good laugh about all this. You know Bertha had a couple for dinner and they also wanted me to meet someone. We were 6 people together and the man was about 42 years old and rich. He was very fine and very smart, just like a real gentleman. The place where we were was a Hungarian place and it was very nice. As I'm writing it seems like I wrote to you before about this. I don't remember for sure. I'm not writing as much as I used to, and still I mail out so many letters that I don't remember to whom I wrote to and about what. I write so many silly things and you don't even write. Lipot from Budapest wrote that they received it and are asking about you also. Last time Jenny Frey spoke to Lefkovic, who is Uncle Marton's brother in law, he told her that one of our Marton bacsi's younger sons came back to Helmec and imagine that Lenke neni's daughters are corresponding and they never told him that he is alive. I mailed 2 pictures and he promised that he will help do whatever he can on his behalf. I hope Malvin Lefkovic's uncle will come to visit me. He looks like Adolf bacsi. Now I'm closing and you write, too. Best wishes, the relations send their best wishes, everyone is asking about you. Kisses, Hermina

1946/7/21 Hermine to Marie and Irving (Book 11, 159-165)

July 21 - 46

Dear Maria and Irving,

I was getting ready to write to you, but somehow it still remained [to do]. Yesterday Mannie talked to some good man, who will be a professor at the Ohio State University and will be going there in August. So, we talked about changing apartments with him. He has a 3 and a half bedroom apartment and Mannie gave the address and one of them will be going there to measure the house. So Mariska, for that reason please get it together a little bit so you will not be ashamed. I know that you, poor girl, have enough to do, but still it could work out that we will get an apartment and this way Irving could come too, and Herman if he wants to. It depends on if ours would be good for them. Theirs is an elegant place, but since they are not able to get an apartment at all in Columbus, it could work out that way.

Although, it would be possible to give the ice-box, to transfer it, over to them. Bertha and her husband said that if this apartment would be too expensive for us, then they would go there and they would give theirs to us because this one would not be too much for us. This way, maybe we could bring the furniture here. So, I think it would be good if my little sweetie would be with us also - "I just can't live without you" I know he is glad to see me here, but my little brother could be with us. Maria, write about everything. Here in the A&P store they pay more also and until then you could go to work there until you find something else. My job is so far so good and I hope I will get the raise...

...after I do the exam. I do pretty well with the division and I have to go 6 more nights to the school. Yesterday I went to the movies, the company gave me tickets for two people to go. They played a beautiful movie the "Searching Wind" the story was good, but the performance in person was not the best. It is interesting that I met with a Hungarian boy and I gave him the other ticket and we went together to the movies. I don't know if I wrote about this, but I met him last Saturday. Bertha's sister-in-law talked to her friend and gave him the address, but at least two weeks ago. He was afraid to call me. Who knows how fat I could be, but they took a chance and both of them came over. The next day they took me to bathe in the ocean, because the other boy has a car - otherwise, I liked his friend better than the one this girl wants for me. So, we will meet on Wednesday after school. Yesterday we went for dinner together and to the movies. Today he will take me to bathe [swim]. Last week I bought a little dress with green and white stripes and a colorful striped play suit with a skirt, which is really beautiful. Yesterday I got a bathing suit, light blue with a design that develops in stripes. I got flat shoes also, it is a light sandal shape. So, it is a must, if one wants to go out because everybody is like this with this and I can't spend too much money because they don't take money from me, and they don't even want to hear about it, that I'm looking for an apartment at somebody else. But Bertha + others want me to save the money for a nice winter coat. I had to put the money in the bank, so that $60 is in the bank.

So, I want to send a package for the kids - to Emil and to Lipot + the others. What did Manci + the others write from Leles? Or maybe they did not write yet? I wrote to Lipot + the others and to Emil, but only a simple letter because I did not have a stamp. I'm getting ready to go to the post office, but I don't even know where it is. That is why I did not send the check yet because I wanted to send a money voucher. I owe you for the stuff that I brought here and they were yours. You can't even imagine how nice Bertha is + the others and the rest of the relatives also. They want Mariska to be here as soon as possible. Maybe it would cost too much to bring the furniture here, but maybe it would be worth it. Write if the man came to see your house. I send cards for many [people] in Columbus and a few letters. Lillian was here for the money. I wrote to her a letter too. I would like to write to Lina also - what do you think, maybe I should give her something? So, I am well and I really mean it, that this boy is very nice and he is a delicate boy, but he is not really religious either. Currently I only go out with two of them. I already cancelled the other one, because he was really a miser. The second one is a Polish boy, he has at least 30,000 dollars, religious also and a delicate boy, short - only he is very quiet and he gets on my nerves. He took me on Thursday to a Jewish place for dinner and he always takes me to the most beautiful places. [In English] Hey Maria, hurry and you will have one too! OK? [In Hungarian] Write about everything. What's going on with Mr. Herman? He did not write to me yet either! What a big person! I must have committed a big crime against him! How is the studying going? [In English] Don't work too hard. Love, Hermina

[In Hungarian] Aunt Jenny + others think that it is best for you to finish school and you can learn about business anytime. It is very hard and it is on my mind a lot. What do you think, my little brother? Write and don't worry! I kiss all of you many times, Hermina

I'm afraid to send the check home to be stolen – Even though I bought a big couch and didn't get it.

1946/7/24 Hermine to us (Book 2, 167-170)

7/24 - 1946
Dear Maria, Irving and Herman!
It has been a few days since I wanted to write you about everything in detail, but somehow time goes by pretty fast. Last week I looked for work and today was my first day at work. I work in the Paramount Movie's office and it seems that I will like it. The pay is like in Columbus and the work is similar also, but I will go to school to learn how to work on the machine well, and then I will get so much more. Although, here everything is more expensive, but everything is more available. I did not believe that I really will stay, but perhaps it is better when one starts it, because if not, we would have enough time to get old. So, I hope it will shape up somehow. If God will help, then Maria will come in the Fall and here a cashier gets a big paycheck. My little brother, I don't even know what to respond to you to your letter because it is very hard - but maybe it would be good while the old man is alive because then his sons will not take care of you. I will write about this in more detail. I will ask Mannie. Believe me, that it's already 3 weeks today since I arrived here, but I was always busy and...

I did not go to the relatives yet. I would go next week. Bertha + the others want me to stay for the vacation and her sister-in-law will come up to me to sleep. I was at Aunt Jenny and at Jenny Frey. I was there for dinner many times. She is very nice and gave me a black hat. We took pictures, but I did not bring them to get them done yet. Bertha + the others took me to the movies on Friday. On Saturday a boy took me out who I got introduced to by Mannie's sister, or I met him through her. He is a very nice boy and he took me boating on Sunday.

It took at least 2½ hours to get there and we had like a picnic there. We took food and we went back with the boat again, with the big boat, at least 100 people fit on it. So, here it is easier to get together with a group. Tonight was very warm and we went out to the street and a Hungarian woman wants to introduce some acquaintances. So, it is not about that a decision needs to be made immediately. What I mentioned about the sailor boy, it is only for fun, that he took it a little too seriously, of course. But don't be sad my little brother, it is not going to be that easy and I don't want to hurry to be steady with anybody and I told him it's because if I go with him I can't get to know others. So, it is not necessary to tell this gossip to anyone. The Bell Telephone Co. would be good maybe to call on the phone, that now I'm staying here longer and then they would not wait for me - because they are surely counting on me. Also, in that office where Lillian sent me to ask for a job and maybe it would be better to call him up on the phone, that I'm staying here for a certain time and they should not count on me. It would be good to find out how long was my homeowner's insurance paid for. Maybe later it could be transferred here. Just not yet. If we could, bring the furniture here, if not, we have to sell it. I know that it would not be possible to leave my little brother Irving, but he can come also if he wants to and Herman can't believe that he is done with me. It sounds heartless to say it to myself, but I know everything and I don't need

...much explanation to see how other's live their lives. Please give those few cents or dollars to Lillie for the shower that they will give to Lina and for such a gift that it could be split, or a wedding gift of 250-300 [dollars] would be needed, but I don't even know what to say. If you buy anything then I will send half of the cost. If I get a room then I would because it is very hard to carry the bed back and forth at Bertha's. Although, they don't even want to hear about it.

I was getting ready to write a letter to Aunt Helen and Arthur, but now I really will. I did not even write to Malvin in Europe and to anybody at all. Tell me Maria, will you write for me? Louis wrote to me. I wrote a card to Helen and to the boy's mom. Malvin's uncle came to visit me. He looks like Adolf bacsi from Polyán. It is already 11:30, I have to go to work at 9 and until 5:30. I'm sending my best to the Walters + others and I still have the tickets and I don't know how am I going to use it yet. Write and take care of yourself. I should help to pay our costs. Did David write to you?

[Side note:] Thank you for the nice letter-I will write again. I kiss you with love, Hermina

1946/7/29 Hermine to Irving and Marie (Book 16, 372-373)

7/29 - 46

My darlings!

I know you must be surprised that I did not write for such a long time. I got your letters and it is natural that even if it would work out well, you could not decide that fast. I don't even know what to decide, how would be the best. Next week I will finish the school , in other words the studying, and then they will transfer me. So, for that reason I am uncertain. I did not want to plan for you to come here. Although, I know they are satisfied, but the salary is not enough - But they promised that they will pay more. I am writing with a pencil and in the hurry, because I left my pen at home, in other words, my little brother's pen. I am at lunch now.

We are pretty busy at work today. About myself, I don't know what to write, because I could write so much gossip to you. First of all, I got 3 dresses on Saturday, one of them is pearl- elegant, $12.00. The other one is with little colorful flowers on a white background $5.00 and a custom made one. Mannie likes it a lot. I still live with them, although I am ashamed of it even though I'm home very little. When I go to school , I always eat out in the city. In the boy case things are the same. I met a boy accidentally - a Hungarian boy - he came home from the military in Feb[ruary] - a very cute Hungarian boy and he comes often to visit me - otherwise, I only know him for two weeks, but he is still interested.

Yesterday we went to bathe with him and with his friends - Yes, I don't know how to swim. Bertha's sister-in-law wanted to introduce me to the other boy's friend, but it did not work out. We were on good terms because the boy's friend has a car and he brought his younger sister, and she brought her friend also. So, the time we spent was a lot of fun. Next time I will write how interesting it was to get to know this boy. I went to the movies with Bertha + others on Friday, and on Saturday the Polish boy took me out, [the one] who has a lot of money - if you are interested in this. The boy is kind but stingy. It's in vain because he barely talks.

Gossip - gossip goes to you - do you like it? It is not important to tell anyone what I'm writing you about. Mariska, what was the problem? Do you work a lot? But you shouldn't, because you can't take it. It would be good, if they could transfer you here from your job until you can find a better one. You could work for that company. The suit and the coat are very nice and I guess it looks good on you. I will write again, until then I kiss you with love, Hermina

I'm sending my best to Aunt Helen and to the neighbors. Maybe it would not be bad to rent the house out to Mr. Zur, because Herman would not be able to keep it and it's not life. Nor is it worth it for someone to ruin the furniture.

1946/7/29 Margit, Lipot, Lulu Klein to Hermine and Marie (Book 18, 164-169)

Budapest 1946. VII. 29
[from Margit]
Dearest relations!
Mariska we received your letter and now I'm pleased with you and I forgive you. I will whisper the truth to you, many times I also would like to go to America rather to write to you. Even now you are asking too much. I should answer. How did you feel at Bertha's dear Hermine? It is very good to rest up so you can start a new job. I remember that Dezső was always very much in style. I hope he must be a nice man by now. Why didn't he marry yet? It is true he is a young man and he still has time. And you, how are you with love, such perfect girls as you are, is it difficult there to find what you are looking for? I would like to hear from you all the best. Erzsikem is already in Slovakia for a couple of weeks. She is looking around. I hear it is very difficult to settle down and make a living. Too many people lost their jobs. Lipot now has an infection from the injections that he was getting, if he gets better he will see what he wants to do. Arthur and his lovely family must already be home. We still don't know if they have any children. They write very warm letters even though we have never met them. They are such caring people and care for us. We wrote them in our past letter that we received 5 packages with food and clothing. We received them in good condition. It is possible to let them know in a polite way that it is not worth it to pay the postage? On the other hand, don't mention it because Lipot told them already. Today we will mail [this letter] by airmail [with] a special delivery. Please write long letters regularly. I like to read. With lots of love and kisses to all of you,
Margit, Lipot, Erzsika, and Luluka

[from Lipot]
1946 VII/29
Dear Hermine and Maria!
I think that by the time you receive my letter, Hermine will have come home from New York. I remember when Bertha went to America in 1914 with our Uncle Julius. We never corresponded with her. It was difficult to correspond. The only thing we do is just send our best wishes to her. I am interested if she had any children and how are they doing? I'm sorry that I'm still not feeling well. I still have to think about what I want to do. I hope that in a short time I will be able to do something. Until then it is very difficult to manage our life. Please write more often about everything. Don't wait for an answer. It takes so long for a letter to come. In the meantime we forget when we received the last letter. With best wishes to all of you individually, and love, Lipot

1946/8/3 Hermine to Marie (Book 16, 362-364)

8/3 - 46
Dear Maria,
I got a card from you today and I'm glad to hear that you are well. Unfortunately I don't write many letters, but this week I wrote many letters and that is why I wrote little to you. Now I'm getting ready to go to the post office, so I write, so that I could send it immediately. Thank God I am well. I still have two nights from the school to go to and then I will find out if they are satisfied with me, but I would like to make more money. I will go tomorrow with Zseni outside in nature - to the water and she'll bring food and we will enjoy a great picnic. I don't know what to write about the package, what we could send to Emil. You can send the winter coat to him and the big part of the clothing also - because I only sent a small amount last time. His uncle does everything for his interest, but I'm sorry I did not hear about him since then. Bertha sent a package to Lipot + the others and now she will send two suits for them again. So, they can be given to Emil.

The black and brown winter coat that was ours can be sent to Lipot + the others. But my beige coat too and the 2 red suits, if you think for Manci + the others would need them, then do what you think is best. I would like you to send them your letter. I writing [to tell you], it is not important to send the letters to me at your expense. I don't write as much as before, because now I don't have time and I'm sending it as a simple letter. Now I'm in a hurry to the post office and Bertha wants me to go with them at night to her sister-in-law.

I don't know if I will go yet. I bought beautiful little dresses cheaply and Mannie likes them too. Do not buy a winter coat because we can buy them from the factory by Bertha more cheaply. Write about everything and how you feel. My little brother Irving, how are you? Don't you want to come here? I will talk to Zseni tomorrow about what she knows about Lefkovits, maybe since then she got another letter from Emil. I'm sending the money, in other words the check, so you can pay for my insurance and for what you have already spent on it since then. I will write in more detail again, but now I'm in a hurry. I kiss all of you and Aunt Helen. With love, Hermina

1946/8/5 Malvin to Hermine and Marie (Book 4, 418-421)

Dear, beloved girls!
I got your dear letter. You cannot imagine how happy you made me with your letter. I read it many times. It feels so good to read it. I feel like I am with you, but unfortunately only in my mind. Dear girls, I got the package, I can hardly find words to thank you. So, I will do it the easiest/simplest way. Thank you so much and accept my appreciation. I don't even know when will I be able to reciprocate your kindness. Dear girls, I already started a new life also. Imagine, how far I have gotten. I started to work in a paper mill. The work is not that hard. I hope I will get used to it. However, I feel like I am a beggar on the street. Do not think that it's because I need anything. I don't write it because of that, only that I miss the most that which is not here. Believe me, I become hysterical many times wondering why I am alive or who am I working for, since I'm so lonely. I still didn't get my documents. It is also going very hard. Looks like my luck is just like that. But I get myself over everything. I will just get through my life somehow. It doesn't matter to me anyway. Dear girls, How are you? You wrote that you are very busy, but at least with a job you like, and for the sake of a good job, one can work willingly. Dear girls, you write if I can remember these people you write about, but I remember just fine. When you came home...

..from Szürte, you talked to me about them a lot, my dear Herminka, and you are not following it's example either, you did not respond [about] some good looking man, but you don't want to admit it, you could just tell me, because I am still who I was. Dear girls, I have a request that you have to do for me. Send me pictures. I would love to see all of you. Send [them to] me as soon as possible, at least this kind of wish of mine should come true. One more time, accept my appreciation for the package. I can't forget your kindness, just write me as soon as possible, and about everything, because I'm interested in everything. Oh yes, you asked me, about Rozsi, what she would like to do. She would like to emigrate to America, also. Her documents are already here, if you can remember, Makszi, her family member, from Lelesz. There were two girls, and she already got married in America, and they sent the documents to her, and, if it would not work out for me, then I will have no other alternative but to go back to my old house, because I don't want to stay here. This is not a life for me here. Convey my appreciation to dear Ignac, because he did not forget about me, and I wish to him much luck in [his] studying. I understand that he went through a lot also, as much as we did...when we will ever meet, I will tell you. I will not write anymore, because the landlady wants to go to sleep, so I must finish. I kiss you countless times with love, Malvin
My address did not change yet.
Greetings to the boys.

Lefkovits Malvin
Barhemsgatan 14 Mölndal I

Please send me Bertus' address [Bertha's], I don't want to ask for anything, except, if I write I will find consolation there. Although nothing can console me anymore.
Write. Kiss
As above

1946/8/9 Hermine to Marie (Book 2, 171-175)

8/9 - 1946
Dear Maria!

I got your letter this morning and I'm responding to it already. Tonight I'm at home. Bertha + the others called me to go with them to the movies, but I had a little work so I did not go anywhere. Tomorrow I'm planning on going on a boat trip. We will be leaving sometime around noon. It is supposed be very good, but I heard on the radio that it will be raining tomorrow and I don't know how it will shape up this way. I already went with this boy on a boat trip. This is the Polish boy. He is a nice guy, although he is short. He can't be taller than I am. Yes, he is a nice guy, he talks very little and I often think that it might not even be worth it to continue the friendship with him even though he takes me to the most beautiful places for lunch or to the movies. So, they say he is not a poor boy. It was very interesting yesterday night this boy called me first and Bertha picked it up, when she told me - she said - [Written in English] "Hermine one of your boyfriends wants to talk to you." Surely, this boy could hear that and he asked me which boyfriend am I talking to. A half an hour later the other guy called me and Bertha told me again - [Written in English] "Hermine, another one!" And he heard that too.

...because Bertha wanted it that way. Although I tell them that I go out with others, too. In other words, both dates wanted me for Saturday so I had to cancel one of them. What do you say about me having had many dates since I am here? Of course it doesn't mean that I have to marry them. Don't be scared! I had an interesting case with the Hungarian boy. Once we went for a walk with Bertha, it was when I came here, and of course they presented where I was from and that I don't have many acquaintances yet, and they promised that they will introduce me to a very cute boy. They told me what he looked like and his name was Pista. So, I was not in the mood [to meet] him, since his name was very rustic. A couple of days later the lady called me, that her son has a girlfriend already and it would not be worth it to look for another one. So 3 weeks have already passed and Bertha's sister-in-law talked to some Hungarian boy who she goes out with sometimes, and she told him that I just came here and I don't have a lot of acquaintances, but the boy was afraid that he will be disappointed and he did not call me for a few weeks. Finally someone called me and he said who gave him my number and that he will come with his friend to visit me. And so it happened and his friend, in other words the noted boy gave the address to his friend, and later we found out that this boy is the same guy who the lady wanted to introduce me to. So, New York is crazy enough!?!

When I go to bathe, I always go with someone who knows how to swim. Pista's - in other words in English - Steve's friend has a beautiful car and they take me to the most beautiful places. That time I went with both boys and his sister came with her boyfriend the last time and the place is such that you can see the bottom and licensed ambulances go there - in case there would be trouble anywhere. So, don't worry, because I am only on the side and they take little babies there to bathe also and children 4-5-6 years old. I write about so much foolishness for you here, but I promised and now I had a little time. I will take my exam sometime next week and I talked to the teacher and she said I can go for a few times until I get better practice at it. Yesterday they gave me an assignment that took one and a half days to do and it came out exactly, which I am happy for. I'm using the machine right now, but they want me to take the exam from the class -because until then they will not give me a raise. I wrote to Emil + the others. I will [write] to Manci + the others also. Did Flora + the others come home already? No need to tell them this foolishness. I got a letter from Malvin also. Bertha will send a package to Lipot + the others. A female coat for Margit and 2 beautiful suits for Lipot. I guess the black coat would be good for Manci. The beige coat is yours, maybe it would be better to [send it] to Pest and if mine is good enough, then that too. And the red suit also. The two blue coats will be good for us still to go to work. Maybe the beige coat would be good for you. I will write with more details again and maybe for Mrs. Deak we will send from the children's clothes to other's addresses, so we will not be in trouble because of the others. My little brother, a little vacation would be good, but if you will go, David will not let you come back.

...and until you come [back], what will Herman do? Maybe it would be good to sell the furniture to Mr. Zur and the apartment the way that the boys will live there, because little brother would just go broke and the boys would not be able to keep it clean - because that isn't that easy. I think it would be good for little brother to get rest, but he should write to me if he will make a decision. Maria, don't worry and don't work too hard. When you will be here everything will be different. We are not going to get rich, because just to get out will be [only a] maybe, but still it will be better- in a way. It's true, I don't want to leave my little brother there, especially the way they want him to [be]. As of now, they aren't able to manage, and it wouldn't look good to leave them there. Although, I don't care about the others...Do you know how old they think I am? 24-25. So, I know the truth and I don't care about others. So, tomorrow [will be] the entire day – that is, I will come home late. Maybe I will prepare lunch to take with us. The boy brought some the last time, although he had it prepared in the restaurant. Maybe on Sunday I will go with Steve somewhere because he will call me on the phone. I was at Jenny Frey on Tuesday for dinner and they called me on the phone and on Wednesday I was in school and the other one called me. I am pretty busy. I will send money and I would like the brown suit and black pocketbook, the crocheted one, and the shoes, the nylon, the beige skirt, the pink and white blouse, my flat shoes. Look over what's worth it to send. My little brother, I wrote to you about that foolishness also, and I will write separately soon. Take care of yourself. I kiss all of you many times, with love, Hermina

Lajos wrote that he will come over for a weekend to visit me.

1946/8/10 David to Marie (Book 2, 19-22)

Aug 10.46

Dear Mariska! Until 120

I got your dear lines. I was very glad that thank God you are all well. Forgive me, that I don't write punctually, but I have become a very lazy letter writer. I just wrote to Hermina a letter also. There is no news here, everything is the same. It is very hot, but it is more bearable than in Columbus. Here the heat is drier than in Columbus. So, I haven't written in so long, that I don't even know what to write. There is no news here. I am well, thank God. I work and I sleep mostly. Please write to me, even if I don't write. OK? How are you? What do you do for work? Are you where you were? How's Mr. Herman? Did you get a letter from Hungary. Hey, does Polány belong to Hungary or Czechoslovakia? I really don't know. You know, I did not write to anybody yet. I don't know what to write and they will all just be asking I'm sure.

I would like to write to Gerenyi + the others, God forbid they will sell the watch. They surely want money for it - write what should I do. OK? How is little brother? I hope he is well. I wrote to Hermine that it would be good for you as well to go there, you would have a better future there than in Columbus. Here you just work day after day, but in New York you can have a better future than where you are now. Here you have nobody, but there you have the relatives. So, if they will call you, you should go. Don't be sad about Herman and Ignác. They will live, even if you will not be the maid. Especially Herman, a little school would not hurt him. Ignác in turn, when he will finish school, he could go to New York or could come here, or you could all go to New York. I believe that Herman would be so much better in New York. Bertha would make a man out of him.

At least he could learn how to go into business. In Columbus he definitely does not do anything else but work and sleep. He does not go anywhere, so he will not spend his money, that is very good! But a man needs to live also. We don't live forever. So, he should do what makes him feel good. It is his business. I wrote enough Maria. I kiss you with love, Dave

P.S. Write a lot to me and about everything. OK? Kisses, Greetings to all who are wondering about me.

1946/8/14 Marie to David (Book 9, 13-16)

August 14, 1946

Dear David!

We have received your letter that we have been waiting for, thank God that you are well. We are well. Here, there is nothing new. My little brother has just received a card from the University that if he does as well, then he can qualify for a scholarship. He is a very good student. If he receives this notation a few times then he would get a year free education. There aren't many who receive this notation. Presently, the course that he's taking is difficult. With all of that, he has not yet decided what would be best to study.

You are asking about Europe. We wrote the American consulate and they gave us information, but they themselves can't do anything. We also wrote to Lelesz, to the district office a few weeks ago. We received and letter from Lengyel, he was the district officer when we were at home. He wrote that the state took the property, but for the management it named Ignác Klein. He said that he [Ignác] is not going to get paid, but he must report the income to the state. And he also said that we must, as owners, write an application so that we can receive our property back to us. There is some law that we could receive our property. He recommends that he would send us the complete information that we may need, if we pay him his expenses. He notes that he'll do it because he was very friendly with our dear father. He also said that the house is in very bad shape. He also wrote that during the past three years Menyus Török used our property and we can't do anything about it. I mailed that letter to Hermina, maybe she would talk to the consulate and could take care of the situation because, as it is, one doesn't know how to begin. We wrote to Gerenyi and received a reply and [she] complained, and hoped to receive some packages from us. All of them complained [gossept] because he [Ignác] wanted to take back all our property from them. Mr. Lengyel also said that he will not do anything that would not be approved by us. We weren't in a hurry to send packages to Mrs. Gerenyi. Since then she did not write to us. Perhaps, I think you should write to them and don't mention anything, however you should ask them what happened to the watch that our dear father gave to them. And [write] that you would very much like to have it whichever way. Then you would hear what they have to say. Mrs. Gerenyi said that Manci was asking for the watch. It would be better if they would have it instead of the goy [non-Jew]. David, perhaps to you they will not lie, and I don't believe that they'll also ask for packages or big money.

We received a letter from Mrs. Deak that her two daughters died in one week namely, Anus and Maris. She took in a girl and asked us to help her because she feels a lot of emptiness. Ivanyo wrote that her husband Pista died. She too wants something. We wrote to them that we have others that we have to help, and we are unable. Once again she asked, but now I did not reply to her letter. Presently, we are mailing some packages to Manci Klein and also to uncle Marton's son. We also sent a package to Lipot in Budapest. He lives there with his wife and two daughters. We do not know anything about the others, more likely they do not exist. I'm going to close at this time, since I have written to you a lot of silly things. About myself I don't know what to write. Presently I am at home. I don't even know how to get started, because my little brother is here and I don't feel like leaving him here, since he wants to keep up the house. I hope everything will turn out well. Please take care of yourself, regards, love and kisses, Maria.
Herman is not a good writer as before and the best from Irving.

1946/8/16 Hermine to Irving (Book 16, 275-279)

8/15 - 46
My dear little brother, Irving,
I know you are surprised, that I'm writing so little to you, but when I write to Maria it is for you too. Somehow there is always something that takes my time away. I still go to night school - and the boys! Maybe it is not even worth it to be so busy. Last time I wrote the foolish letter, where I wrote everything together. For example, about the two boys and that Bertha wanted to scare them or to make them jealous, and this way she totally scared them away. The Hungarian boy asked me to go with him on Saturday night and I already promised the other one, so this way he got offended and he did not call me since then. So, it is what it is. But it happened many times [before] that when he called me and I could not go with him because I already promised others. Don't worry little brother, they already want me to meet somebody else, and the Polish boy still exists. This is a short boy and very modest and he barely talks, but very delicate and polite, a good boy, and they say he has $50,000. It is possible, and the boy takes me out quite often, but I don't know if it is worth it - to have him go - although it doesn't matter, as I say - If there is no horse, the donkey is good - I'm thinking about fun.
I don't even know what to write because I would like to write to you so much. How are you with the studying? Do you have a girlfriend? Or are you just studying all the time? If you would want to travel to California, it would be good, but write to David to see what he says - because many times there is no place to sleep - maybe he would have a space for you - Write to him. OK? I got a letter from him and he is well. He wrote that he wants to write to you too. He is very busy because he works at night. Bertha prepared a 40 pound package today for Lipot + the others and she sent a 2 pound package on Monday for them. Also one last week that was with food. These were all filled with clothing. She sent two beautiful suits and a good woman's coat also. Besides this, I forgot the most important things, what I wanted to write many times to you.

What do you think, how would be best to deal with our apartment? I know it would be good, if it could stay the way it is, but who will keep it clean for you? In the meantime, if you would keep it, it would look like the girls betrayed all of you. Herman does not mind that, but I don't want to do that to you. Many times I think that it is not worth it, because we could live in Columbus somehow, since we have a house. Here it is not available and I don't want to stay here for too long. Bertha and Mannie said that I could stay here until Christmas. Mannie's sister will get married this fall and I would get that room too - there is room here for 10 dollars a week and food from 26 and the clothing is difficult. Although, I have to get a raise soon. That is why they want me to save and buy dresses and a winter coat. It is very nice of them, but many times it does not work out well like that because people are capricious and you need to know them, the relatives don't stick together so much, but I don't want to get involved into this business.

Over 11 pounds could be sent only to Hungary. I don't even know who it would be worthwhile to send the coats to, because Bertha will send more to Lipot + the others. The black maybe to Manci and the brown also to Lelesz - the light coats maybe send to Pest and the red suit as well. The handbag and what it's worth, you can send - in other words Maria will package it - the question is, how much will it cost. I will pay the cost also. Write to me little brother and I will write too to you. This letter is for Marie also. In the drawer, in the kitchen, in a box there are Christmas cards and there is Mary Kay's address in it. I would like you to send it to me because I did not write to her yet. Zseni will come from Columbus for vacation here. Today I got a letter from her - the one that sings nicely - Kisses to all of you, Hermina

1946/8/19 Hermine to David (Book 8, 67-73) pages 1-3

8/19 - 46

Dear David,

I received your letter and I'm answering you now. You are right what you are seeing. I am a very good writer because I write promptly, but still I'm behind with my answer. Tonight I went to school. I didn't have to, but the teacher told me if I wanted to, I can. She called me on the telephone. Most likely the manager will call me in to take a test. My writing is not the best because I'm in a hurry to finish this letter. Saturday evening we were visiting Uncle Gold and family. They are ok. They were asking about you. They say that the Uncle is 93 years old, but Bertha thinks that he is older, and he still can remember everything and is very smart and speaks well. The only thing is that he can't hear too well and we have to speak louder. One of his sons got married. Also, Jenny Frey's brother which I think you knew about before. Otherwise, we are all well. I'm still with Bertha, which is not easy. They don't take money from me, at least for my expenses [they should]. I hope to find a room so when Maria comes, she can come also. I don't know what would be the best because the boys want to keep the apartment. I don't know how it will work out. What do you think? What would be the best? It is very difficult to make a decision. I received a letter from home and Marie wrote that Irving received a letter from Ohio State University that Irv is in a position to get a scholarship. I don't know if he will go there, so I can't tell you for sure. About my job, it's not too bad. The only thing is that I don't get much money at this time. The work is the same as it was at the telephone company. The only thing is that here it involves more money at Paramount Pictures so I think the movies were made for this company, and they rent out the films to whomever wants it, all over America and in Canada. My work is to check the reports to see if it was entered in the books correctly, and to see if there is any error to be corrected. Once in three months they give us a ticket to see a movie. And here there is the premier showing before it goes to the other places [theaters]. Otherwise, I'm ok. On Sunday I was on a Hungarian picnic with Bertha and her husband, and his, Mannie's relations. It was very nice. I met a few Hungarians and more came to visit Bertha. Yes, they are well to do. Here they don't talk about money like in Columbus. It seems like it is easier to get rich here. They have guests tonight, too, and they are playing cards. This way I am able to write letters, even if they're not the best, but at least I am writing. I received some letters from Manci, and Malvin, and the Rozi from Agárd, and Lipot from Budapest. Also from Uncle Marton's younger son, Emil. Gerenyi also and the Deák family. From the Ivonyi family and the Ragány daughter also. Naturally, they all want packages. What can you do? Deák is telling that her daughters are not alive. The only thing she has is a young girl, a friend who lost her family that she adopted. She is asking that we should send her something. They all want something. Therefore, what can we do. It is true that she did lots of good things for us, and was very nice to us. Bertha sent to Lipot a package 3 pieces - an 11 pound one and a 40 pound package. It goes to Hungary. You can send packages. We also received from Lengyel the notary a letter. He replied to our letter that we mailed him. He wrote that our property is now in the State's hands. As citizens we would be able to get it back. The American Consul advised us that we should get a lawyer who is doing this kind of work. Also, if we want a land registry statement, he wrote that he would be happy to help us if we are willing to pay for it. We don't have to worry because no one can take it from us, and they can't sell it either. Also he wrote that we should not worry about Ignác Klein because he has enough and will not cheat us out. For the work that he [Ignác] is doing to help he doesn't get paid. He has to report everything to the State. Bertha wrote to the Czech Consulate what the lawyer recommended and told us...

1946/8/19 Hermine to David (Book 19, 423) page 4

... that we also have to hire a lawyer. Malvin wrote that Olga and Zoli Lefkovits from Pólyán are alive and Zoli is in Palestine. Malvin's uncle visited me and he looks like Adolf bacsi. I don't know if I wrote to you that the two Stark girls came to America, at least 10 weeks ago.

Jenny Frey talked to little Emil's uncle Leftkovits and allegedly he promised that he will help. About Emil Gluck we did not get any news yet. Although, may the dear God grant it that he will be found. Write again too and next time I will write again to you. I got a letter from Youngstown and Lajos wrote that he will come sometime to visit me. Poor Maria has enough work, but until it is not in words, we have to wait until somehow my job will shape up also. I would like to get more money. Don't work too hard and write about everything. Take care of yourself. I kiss you with love. Hermine

1946/8/20 Hermine to Marie (Book 16, 409-414)

8/19 - 46

Dear Maria,

I'm writing from work now because today I'm not that busy. I sent a letter to David also today. I am well, also the relatives are as well. I went to visit the old Uncle Gold and his family on Saturday and he was wondering about you and about the relatives. They say that he is 93 years old, but he can remember so well - when I went in and I told him who I was - he said, he remembers when the 4 of us arrived. I went to a Hungarian picnic with Bertha again, where there were many relatives, and she introduced me to many. The Hungarians come to the house also, who are on very good terms with Bertha, but only the very rich people. They don't even want to hear of it that I would go away, but I asked her to look for some nice and cheap room. They say, that I would not be able to live from that money. They want me to supply myself with clothing, because here one needs many more things. Although, it is true that Bertha has a very good heart - but poor thing, she is just as capricious as her dear father was. She says whatever she wants, to whomever, and she can offend people, which she regrets. I should not write this, but I don't write it so you would tell anyone. She does the same to her husband, and yet forgets about it - I already know about her whims and I don't even mind them. Maria - it would not be good with her because both of you would say something to each other. It's true, they are working to catch me a good...

...guy and then it would all be a pleasure. Somebody even promised that they will introduce me to a very delicate American man - As of now, I did not see him yet, but if I meet him I will write about him. He just came home from the military - otherwise, in secret I will tell you, that he will come up for dinner to Bertha's on Friday - Mannie invited him. He's a designer- I don't know if I wrote it correctly - that is the job that he does. But Mannie asked me not to mention it to you either, so this way you should not write about it either, if you will write to me. He could be about 37 years old and an American man. The people who recommended him to me were at the house to see me and they are very rich people. If you will send a package and there are men's things, then send them to Emil.

Bertha sent beautiful things to Lipot and the others, three 11 pound packages and a 40 pound one. Some of the winter shirt things could be put in also. Maria, don't work too hard and I hope it won't take too long to get a proper room and then you can come too. Send me Mary Kay's address. It's on the back of the Christmas card and it's in a box in the kitchen drawer. Are Flora and the others at home already? My Irving, write to me with more details about when is the scholarship - or maybe that is already valid for the Fall? Where will you go to spend your vacation? And you Maria? Will you go somewhere? Or are you working now too? And I'm not with you so there is no one to make it dirty. Right? Mrs. Hawkins wrote and Miss McNeil and Jenny, whichever you are interested in. Mrs. Minton and her daughter and Lillian and the girl with the red hair who I worked with at the Telephone Co. did not respond yet, so if you will talk to them, give them my best.

Vera wrote also and Mr. and Mrs. Walters wrote a card from California. Bertha was at the Czech Consul and they told her that she needs to hire a lawyer who will deal with the case. The American consul suggested that too so maybe that should be done. The telegraphic statement would be good also, but how can money be sent there? When one does it in a letter it is not certain that they will get it, and they could deny it. I did not send the 10 dollars to Manci and the others. Maybe I will send 5 and to Emil too. Now I put in 1 dollar separately in an envelope - If they will get this, then I will send it. My letter gets filled up with a lot of foolishness. Oh yes, I had a haircut and I had a perm done that cost 10^{25} cents, but it looks pretty good. You will have time to get it done also here. Don't buy a dark blue dress for yourself because they wear that in the fall, but in the winter they don't. Don't buy a hat, because you can buy it from Jenny, which is the most beautiful and it is cheaper. I wore the dark blue hat once. I never wear a hat only in June when I came here. Don't buy "Lag" shoes either because they don't wear them in the winter. I will finish with this. Write a lot

- you too my little brother! You don't miss me I know. Maybe it even came handy?? So, take care of yourself. I kiss all of you with love, Hermine

Herman is very proud and lazy too, although until now I did not think he is that much!!!

1946/8/21 Margit, Lipot, Lulu Klein to Hermine and Marie (Book 18, 173-175)

Budapest 1946 VIII.21

Dear Mariska and our other dearests!

We received the letter you wrote on July 18. We also received a package which you mailed on May 29th. I was surprised because you didn't mention the package in your letter. Thank you very much. Dearests, I can't even tell you how happy we were. I didn't believe, as I remember all of you well, how nice and caring people you are. Only a mother can make such a package as you carefully sent and mailed to us. What is the reason that Hermine remained in New York? Do you also plan to move there? Is it easier to get a job? Then the boys will go there too? It's very nice of you even telling us that you hope to see us again. It is a warm feeling. I wish we would be that close! I'm sorry it doesn't go quickly. Until we receive the affidavits it will be a difficult time to get the permit to leave the country. At this time, there isn't any chance in the near future, and the money [is an issue] but with hope it will start slowly. As I mentioned before, Erzikam is in Slovakia. If with luck she is able to settle down, then we will go there also. Maybe it will be easier to make a living. If we decide [to go] we will let you know at once. Today I will write to Arthur. We just heard that he has a grown up daughter and a son. They must be very nice children. Please write more often. I admit I'm lazy to write. Many kisses to all of you. To Hermine in New York also send our kisses. With all our love, Margaret, Lipot, Luluka

Erzikém from a distance also sends her kisses

1946/8/21 Marie to David (Book 8, 75-80)

8/21/46

Dear David!

As you see, I do not wait for your letters. I'm trying to write to you. We are ok and we hope to hear the same from you, too. First, Irving asked me to ask you what is your opinion. He is going to finish exams and he is thinking that he would like to visit you. The only thing keeping him back is that he only has 4 weeks vacation and it's a little too much of a trip to drive such a long drive. He would not have too much time there to rest and then he would have to be back in time for the Fall semester when school opens up. He wants to see you very much so he can't decide what is best, and resting would help him very much. He is waiting to hear what you think. Right now he is waiting because he was studying very hard. He is hoping that he passed his exams with good grades. If we are well, with God's help, then next year he would not go to school. Then he would have more time to do whatever he wants to. I hope you will write as soon as possible because he is waiting for your answer. Yes, I forgot to mention in the previous letter that in Polány Czechoslovakia, it is the same as it was before. Did you write to Gereny? About myself, there is nothing new. I'm not sure when I will go to New York. Here, the boys want me to go, but I don't know because it will be very difficult and a hardship for them, even though Herman doesn't care either way. This is the situation at this time. It will be very difficult for our little brother to leave him here by himself. In any case, when you think about it, he can come anytime whenever he wants to come to us. I received a letter from Hermine also. She is ok. She also feels it would be much better for all of us if the boys would come there, too. We can't change it too much, everyone has a reason. I'm still working at the A.P. I don't like grocery stores. I don't think I would go to work in another grocery store. I hope I will have better luck next time. What are you doing? Still working so many hours? That isn't the best. You need time off for yourself. Otherwise, everything is the same. The weather the past couple of days has been cold. You can wear a coat. Dave, how are you managing at home? Are you still cooking at home? Write down everything, we are waiting for it. Irving also will receive from the government 3 years vacation money that has now been approved. As of now, I wrote about everything. Now I'm closing my letter wishing you all the best. With love and kisses, Maria and Irving

Herman loves to read your letter, but he doesn't like to write, not even to Hermine either.

1946/8/26 David to Marie (Book 2, 159-164)

Aug 26. 46

Dear Mariska! Until 120!

I got your precious letter and I'm in a hurry to respond to you. Yes, I'm glad to hear that thank God, you are all well and I hope my lines will find you all in the best of health again. I got a letter from Herminka last week. Thank God she is well also. She would like you to live there also. I repeat, that your future is in New York, not in Columbus. You could earn good money in California as a tailor, maybe you could have your own sewing business. But as for a girl, your future is in New York and not in Columbus or California - Yes, I'm in a hurry to write, so it could go today, so forgive me if I don't write in the best way. So, as far as little brother concerned, I can only say that it depends on him. He does what is the best for him. I would like to see him very much. I wish I could be there with him.

But for him to come on the train for five days and another five days back, is not for his nerves. He should fly, yes it is only a 10-12 hour trip. But it is a waste of money, to go and come on the plane it is about 200 dollars or more, on the train it would be silly and he would be on the train for hours, it is about 150 dollars. It is not worth it to spend that much for 10 days to stay here. For that matter there is nothing to see here in the summer. Hollywood is on vacation and every better place is on vacation. But I repeat it, I would love to see you very much, so may the dear God help me that way. I wish I could be with him, but he should not spend 300 dollars to come here. That would be a sin, when the poor thing only gets 50 dollars per month. But in my opinion, if he thinks it's good, he should do it. He should go out to Lake Bakaj and rent a room for a week and he could go fishing and swim there. But if he goes, he should not bathe in the free water, only in the swimming pool and he will feel very good. He could go to dance every night and also to skate, there is an ice rink there. But I repeat, he should take care of himself. And he could go to Cleveland, there are Hungarians there too and he could meet with girls and it will not cost too much. But tell him, don't be a sucker, that he will spend so much money. So, I think it will work out better if he goes to Cleveland and maybe Youngstown also, but if he comes here I can get vacation days as long as he stays here. But to bring him to companies here in Long Beach, everybody lives for themselves like in Columbus. I don't know anybody in Los Angeles nor in Hollywood, so if he comes here it will be only me as his entertainment - But here I will write a few lines to him. Dear little brother, believe me I would like to see you, but after a long hard study you need a rest and not a long trip like this. I hope you will understand me, that I am right.

Right now you need a good rest, or if you go, take Mariska with you. Not Herman! This way they would pay your cost too! Hey, dear Mr. Herman Gluck, next time if I will have lots of money, I will pay you for the writing - so that you will write to me. You should write how much you charge for the words. OK?! Currently there is no news here, everything is the same - little brother you know if you want to go to school maybe you need to transfer here and to Los Angeles also, but if there is, then wait for later, until you can get a new car for yourself and then you will come out here and you can see the Grand Canyon, which is pretty nice, and many other things, or maybe I will surprise you sometime, I will go home to Columbus. But let's leave this for today, I wrote enough. So, take care of yourself - thank you for your letter and also thank you for you Mariska, that you wrote that Polány belongs to Czechoslovakia. I will write shortly to Gerenyi + the others.

I'll tell you if they can send the watch here, then I will recommend something for you to send them. But I will not send anything to anyone. Write to me when you will find out about some news. For example like about Emil Gluck also - Right now the weather is nice and cold here, it's good to sleep in it - little brother I hope I will have an opportunity to find an apartment later, so if you will come, you will have a nice place to stay. The current place is pretty good, but if I could live in a better place, I would have more acquaintances - But it is enough for today, I will close my lines. If you write to Hermina, write to her that I will write to her this week also. I did not have time to go get the photograph, so I will only do it on Wednesday when I have a day off. I will go get it and I will send one to you. I am attaching a little one here, it is not good, but it looks like me. So, with love I kiss you until in the hope that I will see you again, you and little brother, and Mr. Herman also. And in case somebody would be interested about me, I'm sending my greetings to them as well. With much love, David

1946/8/26 Undated Dezső to Irving (Book 2, 23)

[Dated by advice to come to CA or NY, the photo he will send, letter to Mariska above]

Dear Little Brother!

I'm sorry that I did not write for so long, but I became such a lazy letter writer. Although, you don't write a lot either. I hope my lines will find you in a best of health. There is no news here. I hope you are doing well with school and get excellent [grades] in everything. You know, I would love to see you here. I would love it if you could come out here. But I believe that you would rather be there. I don't even know what to write now, I wrote everything in Mariska's letter (about foolishness). Little brother, I don't think you'll be interested, but believe it, the girls are in New York and not in Columbus. Hey little brother, I heard that as long as you are in school and not working, you can get unemployment 20.00 for 52 weeks and the normal monthly support. You are entitled for that and also, sign up for the 2½ vacation money that the President signed up for. In the past you wrote to the American Consul. Did you got a response about the Polány property? Write a lot! Currently I have to close my lines because I have to go to work. I kiss you with love. Your brother, Dave

P.S. Greetings to Herman. Yes for him too.

[Side note:] P.S. Next week I will send you a photograph. Kisses, Dave

1946/9/1 Undated Hermine to Bertha New Year's Greeting - draft (Book 2, 190)

[Dated to 1946 because only Hermine writes, so Marie isn't in NY yet, and that she left Columbus, and she mentions about their help]

[Note in Hungarian on top] I sent them a New Year's card and I wrote this for him

[In English]
Dear Bertha and Mannie,
Just because I left Columbus I wouldn't miss sending you my good wishes to a very happy new year. And also this is the only way I can think to thank you both for your kindness and, everything you do and have done for me. Let's hope that my story will bring some happiness to us all - so that we might spend some happy days together. Love to you both, from Hermina

1946/9/2 Hermine to Irving (Book 16, 366-369)

9/2 - 46
My Dearests!
I got the letter and the package last week already, but I am just responding to it. The coat and the suit came in handy already, but it is so cold out here already, that soon we will need a winter coat. So, I am well and I don't go to school, although I would like to go more. Lajos came on Sunday and we went together to Coney Island. More people came together and he will stay for a few days. I just got a letter from Emil from Helmec, and he got the letter from me, where I put a dollar and also the package that was sent using Maria's name with food. He asked me to send only clothing. Sports clothing and shoes, also he asks for socks - his undergarments are all ragged - His uncle still did not write to him. He is pretty shameless - but I will look after it and I will look his address up to call him. Besides this, he is well and currently he will not go anywhere until he learns dentistry. Maybe I will send shoes from here - somebody promised to Bertha. So, a few shirts too to put in the package maybe. From the one that you got Maria paid the cost and if you don't take it then buy cigarettes and send them to him because if he will sell them there, he will get a lot of money for them. Lajos told me that there is a place where they send cigarettes and it's cheaper and they send them to Europe - I will look into this. I don't even know what to write because I'm still here, but that is not good and they want me to stay awhile longer because the money would not be enough. It is true, but there is no room yet. I will look into it in the newspaper already. Oh, Lajos' aunt got married, so they will need the room for them.

How are you little brother? What is going on with the exams? Have you decided about the vacation ? Believe me Maria, that I know what you have in Columbus, and that you work hard. I don't even know what to write because it would be the best if you would know also what is up. I don't even know what to do with the house because the boys want to keep it, that is not coming out good. Write too about what you are doing. Bertha said that we should send to Mrs. Deak - so put a little package together and the warmer things would be better. I did not even write to her yet - I don't know what to write - When you will write a response I will write then. If Mrs. Gerenyi finds out, she will be mad.

It would be better to send it on somebody else's name, that others will not know who sent it. Bertha + the others left from home, I am just by myself. Lajos called me yesterday, to go to his aunt with him, but I don't want to - I was there on Friday night. I'm very tired because I went to bed late. I went with a Hungarian boy to the movies on Saturday, who I met at the other picnic. All of them have a bad habit and so do I - so, if it is not the way it should be, it is not worth to waste time on it. I already met with so many, but I'm not interested. The one who Mannie called for lunch, has not called yet since then, although he is an important man, I'm sure he is not impressed by me! But that's the way it goes. So, I am always busy. Many times I would go somewhere everyday and then there is nothing. Tomorrow, Bertha will have guests and I don't like to stay home because I don't play with cards. Maybe I will go to Jenny. I don't know for sure yet. I would only like that if there would be somehow a room for me. Bertha is happy that I am with them - but in another minute she is moody. I should not write this because she does not let me work at all and I don't pay, not a cent, and when she is in a good mood, then she is very fine and if she would want it, she would not have to keep me here.

I wrote to Mr. Kalman's son, to deal with our case, so he can get our wealth back from the government. We are just listening to the news on the radio and it gets on a person's nerves. I will finish with this now. I will write again. Greetings and kisses to all of you and the relatives.
With love, Hermina

Dear Irving my little brother!
Write a couple of lines about what you think would be best? Believe me, that I'm thinking of you a lot, but somehow to write, I'm in a hurry, so I write together to all of you. What is going on with school? They want to strike here and there will be a little break shortly at work. I still did not get a raise, but I already told them. I will wait a few days and I will see what will be. Little brother, write to me about yourself and about everything? Do you make it from what you get from your paycheck? Are you all in good health? I would like to write to David too - but I will do it some other time. Miss McNeil, if she is wondering, greetings to her. Take care of yourself. I kiss all of you with much love, Hermina

1946/9/3 Undated Irving to Dave (Book 6, 247-248) after summer session at OSU

[dated by David's description in letter 1946/8/26 Undated Dezső to Irving (Book 2, 23) and that Irv doesn't have a car yet See 1947/3/21 Hermine and Irving to David (Book 9, 22-23)

Dear Dave, Until 120
It was really sweet of you to give a nice description of a journey that I planned for sometime. However, in that case I hope that I will be able to get a car for next summer and see you then. Now, I do hope you will forgive me for not writing you as a couple [of] years ago I used to. However, today it's a little different, but now you should drop me a line, as you are still away from home. Oh yes, here I must [add] home is where ever we make it. Please don't worry. In school I had a tough summer, now it's over so will write you more later. Love, Irv.

1946/9/8 Marie to David (Book 8, 82-86)

9/8/46
Dear David!
We received your letter. I was very busy so I'm sorry that I didn't have the chance to answer your letter. I'm happy you are ok and hoping you will stay well always. As you mentioned, our little brother is also thinking that way because he would not have too much time to spend with you. Therefore he decided not to go at this time. Poor thing. Right now he is very busy and doesn't have much time to socialize. About myself, I don't know what to write. We are ok. As you see, I'm still in Columbus but for how long I don't know. I received a letter from Hermina. She is ok. She will look for an apartment. I hope somehow it will work out. It is very difficult to decide how it would be better. Here I want to mention something, but I don't want you to mention it to Herman that he should find out. First, as you wrote asking why doesn't he write to you? About this, it is very difficult to answer. He doesn't write to Hermine in the same way either. When we get a letter, he also likes to read it. A better way to say it, I don't even know what we can do. The situation is not getting better, it is getting worse. I'm not writing this to you to complain, but somehow we have to get help before it is too late. I know that here they can't do much. I'm worried what will happen. He hardly can wait. How can I leave and know that. I can imagine what will happen. He still doesn't feel well. He went to a neurologist, but he's still the same without any improvement. We can't even talk about it [with him]. When we speak to him, he can't help himself. That is the problem. He really needs help. Therefore, I'm writing to you about it. Maybe there would be someone who is able to help. The problem is that for a couple of months

he is not eating at home. You can see that not eating causes his problem. I can't say that he looks good. You can see that he is very nervous. Therefore, when I leave from home I can't watch him any more to be sure he is safe and I can't help him. I know you will say Irving is here and he will help him. I can't say how much because the situation is very bad, and there is no result. Maybe it will help if he is alone, then there wouldn't be anyone here to interrupt him. I don't even know what to say. When Hermine was here it was the same. Maybe I should not even write to you about this. I hope our God will help him so he will be able to function. Otherwise, there is nothing new to write. Don't mention what I told you. He would be very upset. Write him a letter and he will feel better to hear it. Maybe he will take the pen and will write to you. Take care of yourself. I hope you will answer me, not weeks from now. I will write to Ignác Klein in Leles, too. They are asking why you are not writing to them. Best wishes, and love, Maria

1946/9/10 Hermine to Irving (Book 11, 167-171)

Dear Irving,

I was very happy about your letters and I know, that you are smart boy and I wish you good luck with your studying after this also. I would like it very much, if you could have come to visit me, and it would have come in handy to you at the same time. You are right, that I can't calm down about you staying together with Herman that way. I hope it will shape up well, but it would be good if at least once a week someone would clean there for you. Besides this, everything is fine and if it comes to that, maybe it will be easier. That is why it is best to keep our apartment.

..because in the meantime if a person changes his mind, there is somewhere to go. Tell Maria not to worry, when she will be here, she will like it. Right now, I don't go on a lot of dates because it's not worth it if it's not like one would like. They say here that I am terrible - but now that I'm here, I'm not in a hurry. For example, I met a boy who has lived in America for at least 20 years and he does not speak - the words need to be pulled out of him - and the Polish one is the same - and I always regretted it - because why does he take me out, if he can't talk. Bertha + the others blame it on me, that I should talk and keep him in the conversation. Although, it is true that sometimes I am very serious, but I don't mind. You asked about Steve. He is a good boy and he was nice, but as I wrote, Bertha mentioned that there is another boy - in other words, I already wrote this to you, about the announcement on the phone, that it did not make the boy feel good and then on a Saturday he wanted a date, but I already promised to somebody else who called me before and that is why he got offended. I don't even mind because he was younger than I and he wanted to see me so often that I did not have time to sleep and in the meantime I had a date with somebody else too. So, surely many times I had at least 4-5 dates too for a week - but this week I didn't have any and I don't even mind.

As far as the man is concerned, the one who Mannie brought home, he was a very cute man, but for him, of course he needs an elegant, intelligent woman. He makes at least 300 dollars a week - of course he took me out once - but he did not call me up since then. It is better that way because I found out that he was a divorced man. Don't tell these things to anybody. I already met many of them, so I got bored of them.

Write about everything - I wish you and Herman a Happy New Year. Which temple are you going to? My writing is messy, but I'm in a hurry. Kiss all of you, with love. Hermina

1946/9/12 Hermine to Marie and Irving (Book 15, 215-219)

9/12 - 46

Dear Maria,

I got your letters and I'm in a hurry to respond to them. Although I don't know a lot yet because I'm still looking for a room, but it is very hard to find. Lajos' aunt gave me an address where I will go on Saturday to look because the woman is not at home. Otherwise I'm well. Yesterday night I went to sleep over with Mannie's sister. This is the girl who stayed with me when Bertha + the others were on vacation. In the city she has a room and I wish that ours would be that pretty and clean - but what is it worth! Partially maybe it would be better, if we would keep the apartment in Columbus - because if it doesn't work out, then it could come in handy. What is important is who will keep the house clean? The way it looks, how long can we wait, but don't worry Maria because as soon as possible, you will come here. You don't want to go some place else because the apartment situation is like that everywhere.

I got a letter from Manci + the others from Lelesz and they are well. They wrote that they were very happy to [receive] your letter and he was in Kassa and the doctors helped him and thank God he is much better already. I put a dollar in the letter and they got it. I got a letter from Emil and he got it also and now I sent 5 dollars to him. I hope he will get this too. Although, I did not mention about that because you know how it goes. Now I would like to send 5 to Manci, since I promised them a long time ago already. I will go on Saturday to buy a coat or a dress from the factory by Mannie and this way I get it cheaper. I still don't know what I want, but I will see - maybe I will get a suit. I'm sorry that...

[On the side, up side down:] I would like it if you would buy a coat here!

after all this time I did not send a birthday gift to you. Blouses would be the best to buy, which I could also buy by Mannie, and one can get a good one for [the price]. So, if I will know what kind I need then I will have them bring one for you too. Besides this I owe you so much for sending the packages and the insurance. Write to me how much it is and I will send it to you. I have so much to write, that I don't even know where to start. I am asking you not to worry, if you can't take the work, leave it there, even if it's about two weeks. You could get a place somewhere else. I know how it goes, but what can you do. Unless, what else, if I go back, so I would maybe go back this way I'll wait for a week and try what we can.

Lajos was here at least for a week. He came with one of his friends in a military Jeep. We went to see many things and it was nice. The only trouble is, that almost the whole thing was serious - because I went with him to visit his aunt and they brought it out because he is too serious to me. Also [we went] to Newberg to another aunt of his and they all asked me to stay there or go for the weekend. So, the time was spent this way. Another aunt called me for lunch - but I didn't go. If she will write, I will tell her my opinion. Now just that, if you buy a dress with one color, that is becoming for you. The 2 suits are enough and it will be good with the blouses. I guess the clothing is cheaper, and buying a pair of shoes here is very expensive and they're barely available. Buy something beautiful, the price does not matter rather that it is pretty and it looks good on you. At work I wear a simple dress and it does not have to be expensive, but buy it ready made and don't let it wait for you to sew it for yourself.

The beige coat will come in handy for you and you could spare the good one with it. I don't need the winter coat [sent] to me - I will write to you when to send it. Where do you get that amount of money that you are paying for everything and for my things that you don't miss the spending. So, write how much it was. Oh, yes, do you still have the phone? Who is paying for it? Poor little brother could have a problem - because he can't help like he would like to. If he did not go anywhere then he should rest at least and eat as much as he feels like. What do you cook these days? Does the refrigerator come in handy? Herman is surely angry that he has to pay, but tell him that now he could get more for it and always get the price for it and the money would be certain. Take care of yourself and don't worry, eat, don't worry about the boss! Write, kisses with love, Hermina

My dear little brother Irving,
I was very happy for your letter and at least you can rest a little. Take care of yourself and eat. I am well and today I had a test about how I'm doing my job and the woman said that it was good. So, I'm entitled to the raise - if I don't get it tomorrow, I will go to talk to the boss. This place only promises, but they don't do anything. The workers want to strike when they [the owners] don't expect it. Bertha just said that I should write to Malvin's older brother, who lives not too far from here. Maybe he could rent the apartment out for us because his wife died and he wants to give up the house. I thought I will send you a bow tie in Marcsa's package, but it is still just a promise. Write to me and I will write separately and more too - until then good luck. I kiss you with love. How is Herman? Why doesn't he write? Hermina

1946/9/17 Hermine to Marie (Book 11, 172-173) missing pages after pg 4

New York 9/17 - 46
Dear Maria!
I already got two letters from you and one from our little brother Irving. Tonight I am alone at home and this way I have time for more writing. After work, Bertha and her sister-in-law came with me to buy a suit. I have found a beautiful one, which the factory price is 41 dollars, but in the store it could cost 75-80 dollars. I got the winter coat at the same place also last Saturday. It's claret in color and the length is 3/4 long. Its back is fuller and has a high neck with three buttons and with full sleeves. The fabric is so fibrous like the beige coat was, but that is more delicate and a softer material. I can wear it with any color. It's harder to choose something than one thinks - It cost 45, but it would definitely cost 80. It's without fur. The suit is

brown - but very beautiful. So, it is enough about this - otherwise I'm well. I'm still interested in the room and I hope I will find one. The important thing is that you, Marcsa don't be worried because as soon as it is possible you will be here and I hope - it will work out. It is possible, that Bertha + the others will go somewhere for the holidays, but it is not certain yet. About the job, I still don't know much, but I already took the exam, which I passed, but I still did not get a raise.

But I talked to the woman in the office and she said not to worry because they are very satisfied with my job. Mannie said that I need to stay there at least for three more months - so it will be good for a guarantee. So, I need to work there, even though the pay is not good. I hope you are healthy and you don't work too hard. I wish you a happier new year and that we could hear good news about each other. I will write to McNeill also. But I don't have the patience to write, since I have to respond to more letters. I just wrote to Mary Kay. I did not write to Mrs. Deak and to Manci. Emil from Helmec asked me for a pair of boots, sport clothing and at least a few pairs of socks. So, he wants a new one - but where can I get it from? Bertha said that they promised clothing for him, so maybe I will send some. There is still a pair of military boots and they are good for him too. There is no need to send to Pest any because at least 5 packages went. If you get a letter from Szatmar, write, because Bertha can hardly wait for it. The man where I bought the coat from, asked if he will give you one when you come, and he promised me that I could buy the same suit for you too, because it is loose and my size would be good for you, too.

1946/9/19 Marie to David (Book 8, 88-89)

9/19/46
Dear David!
As you can see I am in a hurry to write to you again. We did not get mail from you for a long time. I hope that my lines will find you in the best [of health]. We are well, there is no particular news. We got a letter from Hermine, she is well also. Only she is very busy. As it seems, it is hard to get a house there too. And it is hard to decide what would be the best. And how are you? Do you cook for yourself at home? You could write about yourself a little bit. We did not hear any particular news since then. I'm just getting ready to write to Emil from Helmec. And yes, what I already mentioned last time that as [both] the notary from Lelesz and the American Consul wrote, that we need a lawyer, so we can get our rights back. In Europe for the properties, I don't know what Hermine decided, since she talked to the Consul in person. Now I'm waiting for the response. We got a letter from Mancie + the others last week and they are already better. They wrote that Cousin Sarolta's daughter from Szatmar is alive, but I don't know where she is, and which one it is. I don't know if I wrote this to you, but Lipot is wondering about you also, and they are surprised that you don't write to them.

I did not write to Mrs. Deak because I don't even know what to respond since I should send a package to her and I can't do that because then I would need to send to the others also, otherwise it would not end well. I sent several packages to Lelesz already, [and] for Lipot + the others and also to Emil in Helmec and they already got them. Last week I sent a few also to them. Yes, I'm not sure if I wrote this to you, that in Polány the [neighbor's] son, Sandor Klein, went home also and he is well, and in the meantime they thought that he was not alive, and also the Weiszer boys, who they did not even hope. So, this way we can hope, too. Maybe, if the dear God would help our darlings. But now I think I wrote about everything. And I hope that shortly we can hear the best about you, like about all of us. And write. Now I wish you a very happy and joyous holiday. And take good care of yourself wherever you go and whatever you do. Our Irving will continue the letter tomorrow, since it is too late. I will write next time. I wish you everything good and give my best with love. Maria

1946/9/23 Hermine to Irving and Marie (Book 16, 404-407)

Dear Irving, it came to my mind that I promised you that I will write and today the weather is good for that. I don't go anywhere and outside the wind is just blowing. Otherwise I am healthy. I'm planning on going to the temple on Yom Kippur. Where did you go for Rosh HaShana? What's up with the studying? When does registration start? Oh yes, little brother send me pictures of yourselves because the relatives and the acquaintances want to get to know all of you. I was at Mili Winkler's last week and she would like to see all of you, and is sending her greetings to all of you. I'm sorry that Maria could not come, but I hope I can see you soon. Believe me little brother, that I can't even think about what it is going to be when we are not going to be with you. Your apartment is going to be so cold, that even with the heating you will freeze or

God forbid you load it up - I am almost scared when I think about that, and that is why it would be good to have the furnace checked out, so that it won't be a problem - when the heating season starts. Buy coal - So I think there is a lot more! How is Herman? He is bad enough, if he is not capable of writing a few lines. Little brother, you write to me about everything and

you know, that it is hard for a person to make a decision - because somehow it goes hard. I don't even know what will happen, if I don't get a room, because here as it is - I can't do it for long. It is too much for me, that it is for free and that I am at someone's expense. I know, if they did not want it, they wouldn't have done it - but maybe they thought that it would be easier for me, and they would be able to marry me off. But it does not go that way. Miksa and Berthy Floringer's daughters came out here from Sweden when I came here and last week they got married to some relatives, two bachelors who came here years ago and the girls could be about 23 years old. So, it goes like this. I still didn't call Emil's uncle because the phone number isn't theirs and Zseni still didn't look for it for me. Tell Marcsa not to send more packages to anyone. And if I will get one from someone, then I will send one to Emil. Of course, it won't be new, but he can think whatever he wants. I sent $5 to Manci and the others, and that is all. I can imagine how much money went for the shipping - write it to me and then I will send it. Now I will write to David also. I kiss you and Herman with love. Hermine

New York 9/28 - 46
My darlings! On Saturday I promised that I will write a short [note] again. So, I will continue now. Thank God, we are well and I hope you are as well. I still work at the same place, but I'm planning on leaving them because they still did not give me the raise. Besides that everything is the same. The weather was really fall like today, it was raining and the wind almost tumbled the house over. Mariska, how are you? It goes without saying that I believe how tired you are. I don't even know what's going to happen with that room. Somebody promised me after the holidays, but it is not certain. I called a few of them today that were advertised in the newspaper, but they already rented it out. They say it happens already when we want to call them. I already owe a lot of money for the insurance again, but I am afraid to put money in the mail, so maybe I will go to the post office on Saturday. Soon I will need a winter coat - but there is still time, when I will send the money and then I want the hats too. If I get the mentioned room if it would be shortly, you could come. What did you think about [this] that I left after work [to find another job] - it was not proper, but Mannie is very educated, [and said] that if I couldn't go other times, then I will never have a job. Well the dear God will help me - but if I will quit, I will have more time to look around, because it is not worth it to go for nothing - because they hardly give a raise. So, it goes like this. Did you get the vacation for the holidays yet? What do you eat, when barely anything is available. What did you decide about the apartment? It should be kept, but they need to hire someone who keeps it clean and for our stuff that we don't use. We should pack everything together. I can't even imagine what's going to happen if there won't be anyone to organize the apartment.

When I know anything exact, I will write. Oh yes, Maria - you are surprised that I don't write about the boys these days - but really there is none here right now because I don't have the patience for anyone and they notice that. The last one was a very cute boy, a butcher, who wants to start his own business, but he was so quiet, that only the anger eats me up, if I have to spend a night with someone like that. I just got a letter from Youngstown, from the boy who was here with Lajos. He is a cute guy and very smart - although he is German, he speaks English beautifully. He just came home from the military. So, it is how it is. Lajos' aunt asked me to visit her because she wants to talk to me. I will write more next time.

[Upside down Page 3] I will send 5 dollars as a test. I hope you will get it. For the apartment cleaning I will send you the rest. Write how much.

[Vertical Note on spine of Page 2-3] Send me the black, brown and claret hat.

[Side note on Page 4] I kiss you with love. Hermina.

1946/9/28 Hermine to Marie (Book 16, 419-425)

New York 9/28 - 46
Dear Maria,

I'm just now responding to your letter, although I should have done it before because you can hardly wait for it. I had so much to write, which was also the reason why I did not write to you. The important thing is that thank God, I am well. The holidays went nicely, but I did not go to the temple although I would love to go for Yom Kippur. Now it is Saturday morning at 11 o'clock and later Jenny Frey, in other words after her husband, I'm going to Mrs. Weinberg to the store. I wanted to buy a hat, so I could have one, if I need one and when she made (fix) it, she did not take the money for it. Her store is very good, but she is working hard and her husband is a very simple working man. But they are happy and that is important. About my job, I only know that they did not give me a raise, but they want to give it as they said it last week. I really hated them only because they make it seem that they are so small - but it is a very big company - and it is so for the sake of Rose's son [unclear]. Some places where they were looking for workers, I went - because Mannie thought that it is a good place. They wanted to hire me in one place, where I would start with 33 dollars, and there I was able to bring it up and I told them why I want to leave my job here, and [they said] that would not happen with them. If you could see, that there isn't much to see on the tram here for the holidays, and in Columbus during this holiday traveling - if I know it well.

So, I will go in on Monday and if they will not give me a raise I will leave them because these people will give it to me, in other words at the new place - in a big department store. Besides that, there is a 20% discount if I buy anything. Write about yourself and how everything is and what's with your work. Don't worry and don't torture yourself about this also, because I hope there will be a room. You could buy a coat maybe if you come here - of course only if it's not after the season. I did not get a letter from David- I got one from Mrs. Gyuri Gerenyi and yes, the letter is full of complaints. She thought that we got angry at her, that the girls from Lelesz were mocking them. The watch got a little rusted and she thinks that her husband would deserve it better than the Kleins, so it goes that way. I did not write to Malvin, to the girl from Agard, or to Mrs. Deak yet. You don't need to write too often because it is not worth it. We got a letter from Lipot + the others, and they write very well and that one of the girls is in Czechoslovakia and if it will be successful to get their place in order, they will go to live there, too. As far as sending packages is concerned - don't send to anyone anymore - because Bertha and Arthur will send to Lipot + the others and from us too and it is enough. As I heard it went to Lelesz too - I talked to one of their cousins, Jaszi Csendor's sibling on the phone, he says that they sent a lot of money and packages, but as I heard they are liars and it is possible, that it is not true. From Mancie + the others I got a letter - the two girls wrote what a nice letter they got from you. Mrs. Gerenyi wrote that I was telling everyone - see how many people there are looking at you.

So, even if it's not true, but enough about it. Also, they [Ignác Klein] were at the notary to announce that our brother got 30,000 korona [dowry] and maybe they want to get it back. Now I will leave this, because I'm in a hurry because Bertha wants to buy a hat, too. I will write tomorrow again. I want this to go today. My Irving sweetheart I wanted to write separately to you - but I'm in a hurry to make sure it won't wait because of me and if I stay here there will be nothing to do here. I wish Happy New Year to all of you and to Herman also. I kiss all of you with love. Hermina

Mrs. Gerenyi is asking if we want to sell the house.
Bertha got a letter from Kosztyo and he offered 1000 dollars for her house - his sibling would give the money for it.

1946/9/29 Hermine to David (Book 11, 175-178)

New York 9/29 - 46
Dear David,
It's been such a long time since I have heard from you. I hope you are ok. I'm still here. The problem is that we can't get an apartment. I would like to have one so Maria would be here. It is very difficult for her. From myself, I don't know what to write. At this time, I'm still working with Paramount Pictures Company. In a short time I'm planning to leave them because elsewhere I can get offered more. I spoke to them [another company] and they would pay me as much. As of now, I'm waiting. I've been here for 3 months and they should have given me [a raise]. 2 months ago they already promised it and I still didn't get it. I don't know for sure if I will stay here or not. How are you? Are you working hard? Why don't you write? I don't write often. Now I received from Gerenyi a letter. She is asking for your address. They are full of complaints. She is asking me to write to them because even they can be kicked out. I don't know. What do you think about that? I wrote to Kalmán's son, the lawyer, if it is possible that he can help us to settle the problem. From the Government we can get our property back. We didn't hear from Pál Lengyel for a long time. We received a

letter from him and he told us not to worry about it because no one can take it from us or sell it without our consent. We would like to have an official report for all our property. He wrote back that if I mail him the money for the expenses, he would be happy to help. Here I don't know what to do. Sandor Kosztyo offered Bertha 1,000 dollar for the home. So they would pay her in America and Gerenyi wanted to know if we would be interested to sell. It's true, that until we get it back from the Government we can't sell it. Please write what you are thinking. What would be the best thing to do? Gerenyi writes that the Klein girls wanted to get the watch. They told them that because it got wet, it was a little rusty now, and Mr. Gyuri bacsi deserves it more since they wanted to have it also. I wrote to them before that they should not give it to anyone. She also mentioned that the Klein girls reported to the lawyer who is in charge with them legally that their sister gave money [a dowry] when she got married [to our brother Lajos] and they would like to get it back. What do you think about that? Maybe it could be a lie, too. Now I'm going to close my letter. I am wishing you a healthy and Happy New Year and write. Best wishes, with love to you. The relatives are sending best wishes, Hermine

1946/10/3 Hermine to us (Book 2, 191-193)

New York 10/3 - 46
My darlings,
I got a letter today from Marcsa and I am in a hurry to respond. Bertha + the others are not at home and this way I have a lot of time. I can imagine what the situation is at work when the cold comes and it is already cold, especially when the door is open. So the thing is this, that Malvin Leftkovits' uncle said that we can live with him, that is, if you will be there too. This man's wife died a couple of months ago and [he's] an older man [and] has a 3 and 1/2 room - but I'm afraid that he thinks that I will cook and clean. If we can't get the room that they promised to Bertha, this way maybe we should try to give up the apartment. He wants that Malvin should have a home when she comes. But as much as we want it, it takes so much to pay for the room. So, you Maria and Irving write more too, what do you say about that, because it can't be like this for too long and then the only thing that's left, is to go back. If it would be available, but I don't have time to look after it, and they dismiss me on the phone easily. So, one of these days I will go to look at the apartment
…

…and then you could also come soon. Now I had a little situation at work – that is, I will quit, if they don't give me the raise and they promised that they will give it in two weeks. So this way it doesn't matter. My pen is so bitter – that is, the little brother's pen. Maybe you are mad at me little brother that I confiscated it for myself. Bertha is corresponding with Boske Kramer and with her husband. They have a baby. Two of her sisters are alive. It would be good if our little brother would be here with us. Write to me little brother what's going to be when you are going to be alone. What do you study and how's everything? I will send a tie here maybe it is not even [good] for now. I think it is elegant. It could be worn still. Did you get that 5 dollars that I put in the letter? Manci and the others sent me one of their cousin's address and I called him/her last week. I talked to him/her and they invited me tonight to visit them on Sunday. And I promised that I will go. Here everyone is well and [they] are sending their best to you. How's Mr. Herman? He is a big man, but he still hasn't written!! Little brother, did you buy some clothes for yourself? Here it is $1 for a pound of butter. Happy New Year to all of you with love! Hermina

1946/10/3 Malvin to Hermine and Marie (Book 4, 391-394)

Dear, beloved girls!
I got your dear letter, that has arrived a little late, but it's ok, what is delayed won't pass [an expression]. I got the package and accept my appreciation for it. Dear girls, the dresses are too tight on me, but I will try to do something about it. Looks like you are all very pretty. I will promise, no matter how fat I get, I will not mind. Dear girls, this week we moved to a bigger apartment, and now we are cooking alone for ourselves and we do the cleaning for ourselves, too. This way we are busy, but it's better that way since I don't have time to think. Dear Herminka, you asked an opinion about [the people of] Polyán. What do you think, all of them were great. They would have hidden every Jew in a spoon of water. If they could only see how they succeeded. They were all happy about our misfortune. How are you? I already waited so long to get…

…pictures, but I was disappointed. I hope it will be in the next letter. Dear girls, this week I got from America the affidavit, but the question is, if it will be good. I took it to the consul and only after 14 days can I get an answer. I can hardly wait for the result. On March 16th a lot of people from us went to America. They are already happy. Dear girls, I wrote to Bertus. I don't know what could be the reason, but she did not respond to my letter. She just wrote that I should write to her about whatever I need. But I did not ask for anything and she did not respond. I'm very curious why she did not write. Dear girls, in my next letters, I will write about our unfortunate life, because this week I was very sick. I did not even work, and I still don't feel well. Due to this, I will write more next time. But respond immediately, because it feels good when a letter comes. I kiss you countless times, both of you. With love, Malvin

Greetings to the boys.

1946/10/7 Hermine to David (Book 11, 187-188)

New York 10/7 - 46

Dear David,

There is no news from you, so it seems that I must write. I'm well and there is a room, it is for rent and yesterday I talked to Marcsa and Irving on the phone and Marcsa will come here. If God will help us, she will be here on Sunday. Although it comes out really badly that my little brother will stay there. I can't even feel sorry for Herman because he is a bad boy, he did not even write a line yet, since I am here. It is already the 5th month and it was just enough for Bertha + the others also. But now I will also have at least a room. It is $12.50 for a week and it is at a lonely old lady who keeps a Kosher house and I am allowed to cook, so it is good enough. The neighborhood is not bad, of course - there are a lot of Hungarians. It is a central place. The room is very clean. So, now it is going to be hard for Marcsa until she learns how to orient herself. But Bertha wants her to be with her for a few days. So, we our hoping that it will work out. I quit, but the boss called me in and asked, that I should be patient for a little while and I will get the raise and that I should stay. So, it is the way it is. And you, how are you? Do you work hard? You could send a little photo, the relatives would like to see you too. I was at Rezsi Winkler's yesterday. Last week I was at Mili's. There are a few acquaintances that I did not even go to visit yet. Hey David, in case you have some old clothing, things you don't need anymore, send them to dear Uncle Marton's son, who lives with Zoli Pollak in Helmec. Write about yourself and I hope you are well.

I wish you a happy New Year to you. You could at least write a card sometimes. We got a letter from Lipot + the others from Budapest and they are well. They wrote from Lelesz that our Cousin Sarolta from Szatmar's youngest daughter is alive. So, next time I will write too, but I would like to get an answer also. Kiss you with love, Hermina

1946/10/7 Hermine to Marie and Irving (Book 11, 180-185)

New York 10/7 - 46

My dearests,

I don't even know where to start, especially now when Marcsa is already getting ready and you little brother Irving, stay on your own. Although, maybe on the one hand, it is better, but it could be that you will neglect yourself, but it is true, that because of the school it is better maybe if you will stay - The important thing is that you will take care of yourself. Marcsa write what time will you leave and I will wait for you on Sunday. It would be better if you could travel at night because then on Sunday you could look around already - since I work on Monday and Bertha said that she would like it if you would stay with her at least 2 days and you could get to know New York. Of course it will work out somehow. Maybe it is not even worth it to bring summer dresses. You can bring those later and this way your luggage would be easier. You can also bring your beige coat, so even the home dress would be good because it is good for home. The house coat - is simpler so you can even wash it. I don't even know what to write what you should buy because you can buy that here too. Maybe it would even be worth it to bring my winter blazer or the boys can send it with the post office. I hope Marcsa you will like it and of course, hopefully we do well in New York City, in the meantime at most we could just go back. Although Herman is wrong, if he thinks that it is better for him in Columbus, because they pay better for boys here and you can earn more and he could be a bigger man. There are streets where we could go to live too, where there are many Hungarians and when he goes out to the street, he could meet with someone easily. Don't think that I want an apartment because I don't really miss it - but he could have a better life too. Yesterday I was at Rezsi Winkler's and at the cousin of Mancie Klein + others from Lelesz, who is Samu Csendőr's daughter. So, if it should not be concerned, that what's going to happen with the household. I wish I would be somehow already, but this way my head is in a thousand directions. Marcsa, you can also bring our albums and it is important that the boys will carefully close the house up, so nobody will take our stuff out, what we have there, because I don't want it to disappear. Maybe it would be worth it to hire someone who would keep it organized and would cook. For example, Mr. Zuhr and his family. It is possible that we could agree about something and write [to me] little brother, what do you think. But of course you need a room and to get a pull out bed for his son, and that would not be bad. Write what you think. Until you write about it, don't arrange anything about this case. What do the relatives say that you are coming Marcsa? Hey little brother, what would be the best to do with the insurance? Maybe transfer it here?

Put the bank book away and take out its number, so that we will have it separately. Also, what do you think, is it ok if the bond has a different address? What's going on with the ice-box? Who is going to defrost it and keep it in order, so it won't get rusty? I'm going to miss the radio, but it is possible that I will buy one. We could cook at this lady. So, if God helps me, I will go on Sunday. How did you fast? I fasted well and I went to the temple. Besides that I'm well and I hope you are as well! Marcsa, don't worry! On the train, the conductor will tell you when you get to New York. Write what time you are coming on Sunday and I will wait for you. Mannie says that it's not worth it to send a suitcase, so no matter how junky it is, just bring it and the rest can be put into a box and sent by the post office. The relatives send their greetings. It is already the 5th month that I'm here. Don't worry Maria, everything is going to be fine and you boys take care of yourselves and eat. I kiss all of you with love, Hermin

[Side note:] Did the 5 dollars and the tie arrive?

1946/10/8 David to Herman (Book 12, 154-160)

Long Beach, 8 October 1946
Dear Herman!
Another year has passed again without getting a line from you - One year. What is that? Nothing - A man only lives 70 years - it does not matter - So, the New Year is here and I am myself a bad letter writer also. But I decided to write this letter to you. I repeat, if you don't want to write to me, it's fine! I'm not going to get offended about it, but write it to me, so I will know. So, I am writing here the following, I want you to remember this as long as you are alive!! Take this from me like from a sibling, either if you want it or not it is fine either way, take it and throw this letter away, no one will know what I wrote to you. I did not even mention what I'm going to write to you. I only noted that I will write separately to all three of you. So, here I will start my thinking about you.

Dear Herman - You lived in Polány just like me - You remember very well our dear late mother - and you remember very well when the auto brought her dead body home. Who did you go to to cry? To me. You were sick, who took you to Ungvár with a bicycle? I took you. Who worked so that you could become healthy? Me! Who did you go to with your complaints, with your troubles? To me! But you already forgot about that, right? I don't write this to blame you, I just want you to bring out your good thinking and do what I will ask you to do - We were in Polyán, 4 brothers and 2 sisters, and Lajos' children and our dear father - We lived in the "coresz" [trouble] and unfortunately, you know it well, that we lived on bread and milk for days. It was good, if we had them. I successfully made it through so that I could come to America. I was working night and day, that you could come out here - which finally worked out - but you know well, if I did not come, then this way couldn't have happened - But thank God it worked out.

We came to America. So, what happened? The war came. Our sweet father, Lajos and the boys and Lenke, Emil who you loved very much. Where did they go? Only God knows. It is possible that they are alive, or not. But we are here, 3 boys and 2 girls, siblings. That is all, nobody else! Do you understand? Nobody else!!! This is the entire family!! My heart is breaking when I think about this. And here you are and you can't even write a letter. This life the way you live there is not a life. Like siblings, poor Ignác what he went through and with God's help he came home and today you live like complete strangers - This is not life - Listen to me and take my word, I promise, that while I am alive, I will never write to you and don't even want to hear about you, if you don't do what I am asking you to do. I will note to you, I am serious about this and I'm not kidding -

You, like me, I know it well, you are [obsessed with] the thought that you are sick. This has been already for at least 15 years. You talked yourself into this, which has gone to your mind totally. There is nothing else in your mind except that you are sick - So, do this - Go and search for the best doctor and go to him weekly and have yourself examined well, not for 20 dollars. And ask to be under treatment - And you will see, if you take that out of your head that you are sick, you will be so much better. The important thing is that you should eat like a man! Do not starve! That is why you are sick, because you don't eat - So, I'm asking you, also that Mariska is there with you, poor thing her life is grievous. Believe me, she is sick too and she works and when she comes home, she has to clean and if she wants to eat, to cook also - and she has nobody to turn to like a sibling. And I know it well you are like a cat that is with the mouse. But I'm asking you to do the following...

You know we don't have anybody in this world, only the five of us, and look how we don't live like siblings. Why? I don't know. So, I'm asking you to do the following-
1. Write something to this letter to me, immediately after reading it.
2. Go to a good doctor and do the way he wishes.
3. Eat at home like a man and don't spare it from yourself. You know we don't live forever. We only live once.
4. Watch it, so Mariska will not be so sad, don't be cross with her always. Poor thing, she loves you so much and she worries about you, in a way that she makes herself sick. Although, poor thing is only sad about you, more than about herself.
5. Look that Irving is coming like a sibling. They don't ask money from you, only for the love of a sibling.
6. If you will keep these above, you will see that you will be better and you won't be sick - think about our poor family. Doesn't it break your heart when you think about them?

Yes, I'm asking you - you know for writing a letter, if somebody would have paid me 20 dollars, I wouldn't have done it. But I can't imagine how it is possible for a sibling to live in a situation like you are in. Take my word and don't be so angry in America, in other words, [you're] not in Polyán. You can eat here whatever you want, not like there - there you didn't have money nor clothing. Here you have anything you need. Please take my word and have a good heart for Mariska and Ignác. Also write to me and to Hermine too. I wish you a joyous and healthy New Year. I will attach two pictures here. I hope you will not throw them out! If you don't want to keep them, then just throw them away. Ok? I'm waiting for your lines with a note, if you don't write back to me to this letter, you will never hear about me again in this life and I won't be interested in your destiny at all. Greetings and I kiss you with love, your sibling, David

1946/10/8 David to Irving (Book 2, 176-179)

Long Beach 10-8-46
Dear little brother, until 120!
I read your letter with happiness and I am pretty glad that thank God you are well and that you are doing well with school. I hope it will work out to get through with your plan. May God help you with that. Also I wish you a very Happy New Year and that the dear God may grant that you can have everything good in the future and that you shouldn't even need to hear about what you went through anymore - As far as your letter goes, I will answer your questions here - I am pretty happy that you and Mariska at least understand each other. I hope after she goes to New York you can be with them later also. I'm asking you, poor thing, to be happier than you were until now. I hope Herman will be there too, so Mariska will not be sad about him when Hermine will leave. Although, Herman knows it very well, what is good for him is good for others as well. I am really proud of you little brother. You really know how to write in English and I'm happy that you have a type writer, something you wished to have, I know, for a long time.

You know, if you will take it to a store and have it cleaned, then it will write like new. I am glad to hear that you are interested in medical science. The important thing is that you need to love it and then everything is going to work out. It is interesting you know, last week everybody was rooting for Ohio State, so they can win the game that it worked out. I was rooting for them too, since you go to school there, too. Although, I was not at the game, I only listened to it on the radio. You know, I don't really desire to commit myself to writing and here we go, tonight I wrote already at least 14 pages. I'm not even sure if I didn't write the same thing twice. I will write to Lipot, but I won't send anything to him and he only wants help, not me. Write my greetings to him. Although, I don't even know his address. About me, I can't write anything, everything is the same. I work at night from 5 o'clock to 3 in the morning. By the time I get home it is 4 o'clock in the morning. So, this way I sleep during the day and because of that the letter writing stays for the day also. It is warm and I don't want to write, maybe I am lazy.

I wrote a letter to Herman too, I hope he will not get mad at me, why I wrote to him. I hope he will behave and will do as I wish. Little brother when you get a letter from Polyán, be careful what you sign. God forbid, someone will deceive you. So I will close my lines. It is enough today. I wrote enough, I don't know any news. I am free tonight. I did not work on the holidays and the New Year's wish is in the Ohio Jewish Chronicle. I don't know if you saw it. Watch under GL. I hope that my lines will find you in the best of health and that soon I will get good news about you - I will attach two pictures to Mariska and I will send them, and about 3 to Herman as well. I will send bigger ones to you. It is already done, I am just too lazy to go to the post office to send it. I kiss you with love, my forever faithful little brother who I would love to see so much. Kisses, David

P.S. On Sunday I will buy the Columbus Dispatch. They are selling it here. I kiss you with love, David

1946/10/10 Hermine to Marie and Irving (Book 11, 190-192)

10/10 - 46

My dearest,

I am writing in a hurry a few lines at work and I hope you will get it before you leave. First of all, the umbrella would be good if you would pack it, and sugar, crisco, and powdered soap or only the lumpy ivory soap, pack them too because they are not available here, currently. You can pack from the brown sugar also and don't give it to anybody because if you don't need it, then it will be good for me. So, you need to make a big package already for yourself, but later maybe it will be better to get things. The insurance and medical insurance would be good to transfer to Bertha's address or to give them that address of that New York office, then we could pay the amount in. Write the time when you will arrive, and then I will wait for you. Just don't run away from there, wait for me and then we will go up to take our stuff to the apartment. Don't carry the packages, instead send them and I will pay the cost. So, don't be worried Maria and you little brother, manage it so it will work out for you too. What's going to happen with the ice-box? Who is going to keep it clean? I kiss all of you. Hermina

Bring a few wire hangers because we don't have any and it is not even available. I did not see any, just the expensive ones.

The new address:

H Gluck % Weisman

784 704 St, New York, Bronx

Dear little brother,

Separately a few lines and I don't need to write that I can't imagine leaving you there. I hope that in the meantime you will think about it and you will come over also – that is, if you will find it good. It's true, that you might be better off in California - well for me too!! But right now we will try this first for awhile. I kiss you with love. Hermine

How's Herman? That bad boy should write!

1946/10/14 Hermine and Marie to Irving (Book 15, 233-235)

10/14 - 46

My dear Irving!

I'm writing a couple of lines in a big hurry before going to work. Marcsa has arrived with luck, but I have a big aggravation because I called that woman at night, that we want to go in to live on Sunday morning, and imagine this, she rented the room out to somebody else. She said that I didn't call her up and didn't know if I needed it. I even gave her the money - One week rent and if we are going there the rent will start. I guess, there was somebody immediately and she rented it out. Today in the morning she sent the money back by the post office. I went on Sunday to a house - in other words after a room, but even if they promised when I get the turn to go there, they will give it to somebody else, since many don't want two girls. Maybe we'll get a room, even if right now we wouldn't be together. Rezsi Winkler will give a room for one girl - until we get another one and one of us would stay at Bertha. Bertha will talk to Lefkovits today. It is possible that we will both be going there. Don't worry, there will be room, but it came out badly because it is not comfortable for us, nor for Bertha. Otherwise, we are well. I got free tickets from the company yesterday night and we had to use it.

In the meantime, Marcsa has already seen it with you Bob Hope - played and [other] actors too. She will write to you also, but yesterday even at lunch time, I was on the phone. I thought that maybe tonight we can get into one of the places. Take care of yourself and eat and you, little brother, don't worry. I kiss you with love.

Hermina and Marcsa

1946/10/15 Undated Marie to Irving (Book 15, 222-224)

[Dated from previous letter Marie's arrival to NY from Ohio and next letter Hermine finding a place]

My dear Irving!

I know you are surprised that I had you wait for so long for my writing. You know that the reason is that I did not know what to do. Since I arrived Hermine waited and somehow it came out that [regarding] the room they promised to us, they changed their mind in the meantime, and they did not [want to] rent it out. And when I came here I did not know what to do, but we were at Bertha's in the meantime. Finally today we have found a place and Hermine just went there to live. She will write to you in more detail. And now, I am hoping my dear little brother that you are well! I am well and I am thinking of you a lot. I almost went back, but now I hope that the dear God will help and everything will work out for the best! Yes, my dear little brother, if you can do it, please buy the sugar. Two 5 pound, [there's] a stamp in the book, since here it is not available at all and shortly I will send the whole thing back, if it is available there. Now I will ask you to take care of yourself and don't be sad because everything will work out. How are you doing with school? Did you talk to the teacher? Did you talk to Flora? I will write more next time. Otherwise everything is well. The weather is pretty nice. Now I will close my lines and I will write again next time. I wish everything good to you! I kiss you countless times with love, your forever faithful sibling. Maria

Just take good care of yourself and eat and write! M.

1946/10/22 Hermine and Marie to Irving (Book 15, 230-231)

New York 10/21 - 46
[from Hermine]
Dear little brother Irving,

I was getting ready to write many times, but now I will not leave it anymore. I hope you are well and thank God we are well, too. Yes, I'm happy that at least there is a place and we don't have to be at the relatives. Although Bertha has found the place and this way she deserves a thank you. We are at an old lady and she is a very delicate woman. I hope it will be for later too. She wants us to feel at home. We don't pay a lot - Relatively [speaking] because it's 35 dollars for a month and we can cook and she even lets us use the dishes, since she keeps kosher too. But now, my problem is still big because of you. I'm asking you to take care of yourself and eat, because God forbid you get sick. Also Herman should come to his senses already, since he is not a kid anymore. It would be great if someone could go in sometimes to clean, because even the furniture is going to get destroyed by the dirt and it is not something we should throw away - You little brother, eat normally, and I am only mentioning the cleaning because I know how Herman is and it would be a waste to destroy beautiful rooms like that.

Believe me that I would be happy if that furniture and apartment would be here. I will leave this too now and I want you to write about yourself in detail. How is school going? What are you studying? Did you get the tie? I would like you to send us that package where the sugar is next week only because I want to send the cost for it. Right now there is no particular news here, but I will write again. Take care of yourself and I kiss you my Irving with love. Hermine

[from Marie]
My dear beloved Irving!

I know you think that I forget about you and also about the neighbors, the Walters. First of all, until I did not place myself at least with a room, I did not even know where to start. This way at least there is somewhere to live. About me, only that I am well, and I wish to hear the best back from you. Currently everybody is busy and I didn't have time to go anywhere. Now I'm starting to look for a job and I just heard that I need a letter from my boss. I'm getting ready to write to him now, too. I hope he will have as much dignity to send it. And how are you my buddy? I miss you very much! But I hope that the dear God will help you and everything will work out! What's going on with school? How are you progressing? Did you talk to the teacher? Write about yourself and I ask you very much to take care of yourself and eat. I will write next time again. Until then I kiss you with love. Your sibling, Maria

Greetings to the relatives and to the acquaintances! Did you take out the money for the phone? I will send it next time.

1946/10/27 Hermine and Marie to Irving (Book 15, 226-227) missing 2nd page

10/27 - 46
[from Hermine]
My Dear Irving little brother!
I was very happy to [get] your letter. Bertha + the others brought it to us. We live in the neighborhood and believe that the dear God ordered this for us to come to her. Although at first she only wanted to give a bed for one of us, but slowly after a talk she gave it to us both. Although we sleep with her in the same room - she is a very nice and clean lady. Her family must be talented people. Now we are getting ready in the neighborhood for a movie, but I wanted to write this letter for you before.

[from Marie]
My dear Irving!
We got the letter you sent and thank you for the information. I'm glad to hear that thank God you are well. How did your studying go? I hope you will be successful after this also. I am well. I'm looking for a job, but I don't know what it will be. You know my Irving, that I did not write to anybody yet. But somehow it is always remaining [to do]. Since as you know, a letter in English is hard to write and Hermine does not want to write. I will only send a card to the Walters today. I know that is not nice to have them wait for so long, but everybody is busy here right now and I can't say that I have been in many places. I was at Aunt Zseni on Saturday. She is well. And now I will close my lines and kiss you countless times. With love, your buddy, Maria

1946/10/29 Sanyi Klein to Ignác (Book 4, 430-433)

October 29th

Dear Ignác!
I received a small note that was included in Ignác [Klein] bacsi's letter. I was very happy to know that you thought of me. Dear Ignác, don't be angry that it took a long time to reply to your letter, however I wasn't at home. I also was waiting for Ignác bacsi to write to you and I would also enclose a few lines. They did not write to you, therefore I'm in a hurry to write a reply to your letter. I know how difficult it is to wait. However, I do not know, but I am sure that you are waiting for my few lines also. Dear Ignác, otherwise I'm well and in good health. What I've gone through in four years, it's not even good to write about it, but the main thing is, that I do not have any problems. I worked two years in a labor camp and two years in Russia. From there I was lucky enough to escape. At this time, I'm living with Majsu and Smaju Fröhlineg, in Lelesz. I'm sure that you know them.

How are you? What are you doing? What is your occupation. Write to me about everything.
How is Hersmendu doing? Are you living together? Tell him to write to me also a few lines.
I'm closing these lines. My regards to the girls, Dezső and Hersmendu, and to you individually from far away. Your true friend, Sanyi

Wish you all a happy new year and that I could wish for myself also. fin Sanyi
My address:
Alex Klein
Leles
Ceh Slovakia

1946/11/1 Hermine and Marie to Irving (Book 16, 320-325)

10/31/46
[from Marie]

Page 562

Hello my buddy,

I'm sorry that I did not keep my word and I don't write the way I thought, but somehow [In English] (I am so disgusted) [in Hungarian] since I don't work, but I am still busy. First of all I thought when I come here it will be easier to find a job, but as you can see, it is just the same way, as usual. As I already mentioned that there is no result about a job. First of all little brother, I'm starting with [the fact] that here they don't believe that one understands the job, since at a better place a cashier needs to get an ID. And last week I wrote to the boss in the A&P to send it to me. You know, Mr. Worgana. Even until today I did not hear [anything] about it, but in the meantime I was in the unemployment office many times. Again this morning and I was so annoyed. You know last week they sent me out to a very nice hotel and everybody said that I have to get $40 per week. And there I should have worked until 10 o'clock at night. They couldn't have paid a lot and this way I did not know what to do. Today the lady who sent me out to that place was very offended. She blamed everything on me. She said "who do I think am I that I think I should look for a job as a cashier when I don't have any experience and that only the dear God knows what kind of job I did before." So, you can imagine how I felt myself.

And somehow I have the feeling that they asked for information from Columbus and I think that they couldn't give me what I deserved. That could be the only reason. And as it seems, I will not have a job in another way, except if I get the reference. And that is the only one thing I would like you to do for me my dear Irving. Please call Flora and ask what can we do, because if it does not go nicely, it must be gotten in another way. I think if Flora would do me this favor, to call them on the phone, and then she could find out what is going on. Also from the Neil House. I'm sorry that I have to bother both of you with something like this, but I don't know what to do. I know that it is not nice of me that I did not write to Flora, but I did not write to anybody. Since from [just] a few days [after arriving] all I do is go looking for a job. I could say I travel completely alone from one place to another, because everybody is busy and I did not want to leave it for the last minute. But I hope I will be able to get those papers. Now I go back to you. How are you my dear little brother? What do you do? Is your work hard in school? How are you doing? I got a letter from Flora and I will write to her [one of] these days. What's happening with the phone? I did not forget to send the watch. I will do it. Did you go in about the transfer to underwrite it over to us here and the other insurance. The book is mine. Hermine's is next to my bank book, when you will underwrite it in New York then you need to send those two books here to us.

So, it could be paid here. Otherwise, how are you little brother? I am well and I think about you a lot and I'll be in the hurry to write to you. Somehow I thought I will have better luck here. But I hope that in time it will come to me too. Currently I don't have acquaintances. I was at Bertha's today. She is well and she thinks if I get a reference from there then I will get a job. I will ask you now not to worry and to take care of yourself wherever you go. And do you eat, that is, do you have time for it? Write to me about yourself. And thank you for the small things in your multi-page letter. And don't worry, just take care of yourself. Give my best to the relatives and acquaintances. Also, to Mrs. Hassan and Mrs. Walters. I will write a card for them today. Now I kiss you countless times with love. Maria

[from Hermine]
My dear Irving,

I'm thinking of you a lot, especially today while I'm making dinner. I'm making soup with kneidal and meatballs with spaghetti. What did you cook for Saturday? I'm only kidding, since it's not missing for you. You just go out to eat, and everyday - at least a good dinner once a day. How are you little brother? What does Herman do? I hope he will learn what it is. How is the studying going? A letter came from Flora + the others and she said that she wrote that they are all so proud of you. When did you see Aunt Helen? Believe me little brother that we live with a very fine lady and the family is terribly nice also. The lady said, if you want to come for Christmas, then she would be happy too and you could sleep at her daughter's. Write - Kiss you with love. Hermina

1946/11/9 Hermine and Marie to Irving (Book 16, 327-331)

[from Hermine]
My dear Irving,

The week passed by and I did not write to you yet, like the way I wanted. Thank God I'm well, only I became negligent to write. Almost like Herman! Well, if you would be with us, it would be so much better, but this way we need to think about you too, that how busy you are. It makes me glad that at least you can make a good lunch. Write about yourself and how you are doing with studying? Do you still have the telephone? Does anyone come to visit you. Is it nice of Flora that she never calls Herman at least for pennies? When did you see Aunt Helen? Marcsa is getting ready to write to many, but that means that I have to write in English, but I don't have patience to write. It has been already the second letter from Malvin and now I must to respond to her. Still to Gerenyi + the others I should write, but it is not worth to do it in the case that is concerned about our property. I wrote to Bertha's relatives again because the Feirezen boy did not promise that he could help.

So, this is the continuation and shortly I will finish. Tell me my Irving, do you still have the package for Emil from Helmec? In case there is something left from the money, then send the package to him and as much as you will pay over [what there is left] I will send it [to you]. Did you find out about the insurance? Maybe it should be paid already also. Write and I kiss you and Herman, too. Hermina.

[Vertically on the left side] Write if you want me to send...

[from Marie]
My dear Irving,
I'm sorry that this week I did not write a card to you, but I hope that my lines will find you in the best of health. We are well. We got your package and letter and I am happy to hear that thank God we have a woman to cook [you]. I can imagine that everything was delicious and that you could be a good housewife. I'm only asking you dear Irving, that take care of yourself and eat and don't be sad. God is good and let's hope that everything is going to turn out fine. Yes little brother, what's going on with the phone and with my hospitalization? Did they ask for the money? You know [regarding] the Blue Cross, if you could, tell them to send it over here since it would be easier to pay from here and I should not keep it in my head so I will not forget. Also, the other insurance that I already wrote about. This way I have to bother you my little brother. Also, there is no sugar available here and Bertha wanted us to buy one for her from there and that is why we needed that much sugar. But now there is enough for now. I have two stamps here. I think if you can get the sugar there, then I would send the stamp home, since if that much sugar will be here, we will run out of it. And this way you...

...you could get for yourself or if you don't need it, then there will be time then to send it here when we will need it. And if you want, write if you want the book and I will send it with the stamp. But I will leave this too now. I will get back to myself. As of now, I did not get the paper from the boss, but I found a job this week. I don't know if I'm going to like it. It is at a very busy restaurant. I will start to work on Monday. In the meantime I will look for something else. I will write about this more next time. And then I could send my debts. And how are you? What's up with the school? Have you decided what you will take next? Write about everything. How's Mrs. Hasen and Walters and the relatives? Now I wish you good luck and the best of health! I kiss you countless times with love, your forever faithful sibling, who thinks about you a lot. Love, Maria

1946/11/10 Louis Schwartz to David (Book 14, 75-76)

11-10-46
Dear Dezső,
I know how surprised you will be when you will get my letter. But I hope this time you won't have me waiting for your response, instead you will respond immediately.
I'm seriously getting ready to give up my work. Indeed, halfway I already did, because I don't work all the time. Partially because the business in our profession has dropped significantly and my brother's son works in the same business too. They can work without me. I don't want to be a burden, so I only go to the store when I think there are enough jobs for me. I planned to make myself independent, but I looked after it and I came to the conclusion that it is very hard with the limited capital that I have. I'm seriously considering the thought of going to California, where I hear there are more opportunities, as in getting a job and etc. I would like you to write your opinion, what do you think about it. If I could get an idea on how much I could make and what I can do. I know it is hard to answer a question like this, but you can give me a little clue. Although I have a multimillionaire cousin [male and older] in Los Angeles. I don't think that I will find him before I get a job - if I get one. Otherwise no news here. I'm sure you know that I met with Hermina when I was in New York. I would be happy if you would write everything about yourself. What do you do? How

do you like it there? A lot of people went there from our town. Are there only factory jobs there or can we get other jobs as well? I'm waiting for your answer as soon as possible. Kisses, Lajos

1946/11/14 Irving to Dave (Book 6, 256)

November 14 / 46
Columbus 5, Ohio

Dear Dave, until 120

Just a few lines to let you know that I'm O'K, and thinking of you even though I'm not as frequent a writer as I used to be. This time, I'm still busy except it's a little different manner. To give you just a few hints, this week I had three midterms and believe me it took some time to study for it. However, at the end it turned out to be fine. But you can see that my time at present is more occupied than ever before. Although don't get me wrong, I'm not complaining, I just hope that at the end something will become of me. It's a hard way ahead, but as you see time flies very fast. It's been a year that I have come home to America. In a way, I feel lucky that I'm so busy and don't have time to think about anything else, because of the past as you know very well. Well, now I believe I have told you some of the things that is on my mind, so now, tell me about yourself. How are you? Are you working on the same job as before? I sure would like to see you. Well, I hope that next summer it could be done. If only the prices of the cars would come down a little, then I could get one, and take a round trip to see you, and the girls in New York. I have received a letter from them yesterday and they are well, and Maria started to work this week, although she does not like the place very well and hopes to find a better position in the meantime. Here in Columbus everything is the same, still smoky and dirty in a way. Herman as yet is at work, he is still the same. Well, I guess I will close for this time and hope to hear from you real soon. Love from your little brother, Irving

1946/11/18 Hermine and Marie to Irving (Book 16, 333-338) maybe missing last page

11/15/46
[from Marie]
My dear Irving,

We got your letter and it makes me happy knowing that thank God you are well. I'm sorry that you had a problem with the boss. That is an old thing that he is so insolent. And he purposely does not give it. He thinks that this way at least he can take his revenge. He hoped that I will invite him like he said, and since I did not invite him, he has an excuse. But my little brother don't be sad. God is good and we hope that he will help us too. I can't write a lot about me. First of all, I'm well and right now like I wrote, I found a job as a cashier and in the meantime they are fixing the place. So, probably I will start the job next week. And I hope the best for us like [I hope] about you. And also I was in the labor office, but I did not get a check from them, since they will send it to me from Columbus. And how are you little brother (my little buddy)? I'm sorry I did not keep my promise, but not because I don't have time, I have plenty of that, only I don't have a lot of patience since somehow it was nowhere. But now it will be somehow. I'm only sorry that I still can't send my debt to you, but I haven't forgotten it. What's up with the phone? Did you take it out or does your brother help to pay for it? Write about yourself my dear little brother. Do you study hard? I would like to listen to you since I have the time for it. What would you say...

Now take my best wishes and proceed with the best of luck. I think about you every day in good health and still I respond with a delay. I would have wanted to celebrate your birthday and you being at home for a year. But I hope that next time our wishes will come true. And as you mentioned what a good cook you are. I believe that because when you do something it is done well, but I hope you don't do the dishes! That is, you didn't take over my job. I'm only asking you to take care of yourself and don't work too hard. Here the days are going very fast. I called Aunt Jenny on the phone and she was wondering about you and sending her best. And also the rest of the relatives. We see Bertha many times, since we live close by them.

Everything is fine. I'm just waiting for Hermine [to come] from work. In the meantime I'm in a hurry to write to you. Although I know she will write to you also. Did anyone call me? You know I did not write to anyone yet. Not even to Miss McNeil. I don't have patience to write in English - you know very well that I'm not a good English writer. And Hermine is busy and does not have patience and doesn't have time to help me. So I don't go too far with my time this way. It is possible my little brother that I bore you with my letter, but somehow I would like to talk to you so I will write it down. I'm only asking not to be so sad and take care of yourself and eat. You can send the insurance to our present address. Now I will close my lines and I wish you everything good and kiss you countless times with love. Also greetings to Flora and the others. Love, Maria

And to Aunt Helen and the others.

[from Hermine]
11-17-46
My dear little Irving,
First, I hope that you spent your birthday nicely, and I'm sorry that I could not go out with you on a date. I bought the tie at lunch time, but I hope you will like it. It goes very well with grey and I did not want to buy a red one. It is not a big present, but we'll make up for it. Ok?? Now I want to write to Mrs. Deak and to Mrs. Gerenyi. Jolan Ragány wrote to me again, but now I am letting her know that I am not a millionaire. I still did not get the raise, but I joined the union and they promised that they will deal with it, so I can get it shortly. I hope they will get the job back, but now they are fixing the inside lunch area and it is not done yet, I can't start to work. I saw Bertha yesterday and today there was rain, and this way I did not want to go anywhere. It was nice of Arthur that he offered money so warmly, in case it's missing. Say thank you to him for us. Thank God that it is not missing so far.

Now I paid for a monthly ticket 35 dollars and that is why I did not send for the insurance, but I will send it on Saturday because it is surely too late. Although, they keep it for a month. Did you find out about the hospital insurance also? Maybe it would be best to give Bertha's address for the insurance. If I would have time, I could take money out of the bank around noon, but I think it is maybe not too late. It's not like I would want to be late for Herman, but in case it is already expired, he could give a few dollars to you also for that. And then I would send it immediately. Tell him not to be worried about the ice box because he will always be able to get the money

for it. There are two medications I think will be good for him. One of them is a laxative and for me Bertha gave me the name and the other is good for a stomach bug and you have to mix it with a little palinka [Hungarian drink]. It is pink. She asked at the pharmacy how often should one take it. I could say that it was very good for me. At work I went to the doctor because it was burning in my stomach and I took it and it stopped immediately. He can buy both of them, but the pink one he should ask about in the pharmacy. Who is cleaning the ice box? Write about everything in detail.

1946/11/22 Hermine and Marie to Irving (Book 16, 340-344)

[from Hermine]
My dear Irving,
I wanted to write a long letter tonight, but still it will be short. Thank God I'm well and I hope that you are well, too. I got a letter from Helmec today from Bertha's relative who is dealing with her case too, and he promised that he will deal with ours also. I only need to send an authorization that they need to prepare in the Czech office building. I would like to go next week so it will be settled upon as soon as possible. Of course, don't be scared because the authorization is not about selling and I will do it in a way so it will work later also. About me only that I'm well. I have a date tomorrow night, but on Saturday I have [another] one…that is something! Although, I will only be seeing him for the second time and that is why I did not write about him, because when I write about it, it does not work out. But he is a very nice, cute boy and he will take me for lunch and to dance -imagine that- although, I am not really a good dancer. He will take his friend and his girlfriend too. So, the four of us will go together. Write about yourself in detail and don't worry. Hey! Sunday is a secret!! Ok!? Kisses, Hermina

[from Marie]
My dear Irving,
We got the letter that you sent on Monday, which we were very happy about and I'm so glad to hear, that thank God you are well. We are fine also and I could say that I am working. After all that struggle I have found [a job] and I hope I will like it. Do you know what is the Empire State Building? In that store, in other words, in that building, there is a shoe store. [They have] very nice help and they only sell better shoes. Its name is Coward Shoe Company. They have more stores and I work in the main building as a cashier. Although it is pretty hard, since I have to do bookkeeping work also. And what we get from the Post Office goes through my hands too. I hope that everything will work out. I have been working for two days already

and I'm doing well. Yes, and now I will go back to answer that question you asked me. You know we were at a dance, we can go anytime in the season, and I met a guy there too.

And I know, that you won't believe it, ever since I'm here that was the first one. And he wanted to take me out on a date, but I don't want to go with him since it's not what I want. And you know he called me again since I'm here and it was the first time I had a date with him. I don't want anybody to even know this because they would not believe it and it's not important for other people to know. You can see now why I didn't write about him, but I will leave that too. I want to hear about you. How are you? My little brother, what do you do? Are you doing well with your studying? Write about everything for me. And also take care of yourself. You know my Irving I'm a little ashamed that I didn't write to Mrs. Walters and the others, but I don't have patience and now my hours are long in 6 days and they pay only 32 dollars to start, and in two months I will get 35 dollars. It is not a lot, but they don't pay more here. 44 hours a week. How are Flora and others? Give my best to everyone. Take care of yourself. Write to me and I will write too. I kiss you with love. Maria

Bertha will travel to Florida on Sunday for at least 4 weeks.

1946/11/24 (a) Undated Hermine to Irving (Book 16, 301-304)

[Dated by Marie in NY, Bertha to Florida]
[In English]

Dear Irving,

I promised a longer letter so here I am writing you one now. I am alone because Maria has a date I mentioned about last time. The funny thing is that we don't have it on the same evenings and that means that often we have to stay home. You know Irving, I had a nice date last night and believe me he is different than any other I met before. He is a Polish boy who came to this country 5 years ago and that was my 2nd time that he took me out. He took me to a very nice dinner. His boyfriend with a girl friend was also with us. After dinner we went to a German night club and he is a very good dancer and we danced very well. Hope he'll call me again but you know that we never can tell. Sometimes they are funny about that and it is hard to understand. Mannie's sister knows him well and through her he called me. So this is that. At present I don't go out much, but sometimes it just happens that I could go out more often. Well that is enough.

Tell me something about yourself, but please don't tell about all my stories to anybody this is just for you!! I wish I could talk to you. Don't you think it would be nice to go home for the Christmas vacation and clean up the house. Tell me how is everything. What needs cleaning? I know how it is and it is very hard for you and I think of you a lot - but what can we do. If we keep it nice maybe that is all we could have all our life and it isn't worth it. So let's hope that it will work out everything just the best. Believe me this old lady where we live is just like a good grandmother and many times we call her that. She puts our breakfast on the table and I never had as big a breakfast as what I eat now. We buy everything and cook here and thank God we have everything. The best cheese and poppy seed rolls are available [turós és mákos tekercset lehet kepni] and you can't get that in Columbus. Would you like to come to New York for the vacation, Christmas or New Year's? If yes you let me know -boy! I'll fix you up with a nice date - O.K.? You'll have a place to sleep too!…Bertha left this afternoon to Florida and will stay there about 4 or 5 weeks. Jenny Frey stopped here to visit us. She is sweet. Yesterday I went to a factory where they make dresses. This old lady's daughter-in-law gave me the address - so I couldn't get anything for myself, but got a gray dress for Maria - for 10 dollars. It looks beautiful on her and it would cost about 25 dollars in a store - it is mended in a small place, but it is hard to tell - so I was happy to get that. Tell me did you buy anything for yourself? How is everything with you? How is school? Otherwise I am fine and hope to hear the same. You need not worry about Sanyi [Klein] because I talked to his relatives and they told me that they are sending him money and everything. The 2 girls from Lelesz got married, the Srol girls, and they are rich so they can help him better. Bertha received a letter from Malvin and she is asking for money because she needs it very badly, but she didn't answer yet and wouldn't for a few months probably. We received a letter from Lipot and they received Bertha's packages and it fits fine the suits and also the things for the girls. Tell me everything about you both and I [would] like to send the money order to pay the insurance but I hope [to] make it before they close. I wanted to do it Saturday but was too busy. So take care of yourself and write to me. Please go out and eat so you would not get sick. I am with you always. Love and best wishes to you both. Hermina

1946/11/24 (b) Undated Hermine to Irving (Book 10, 148-149) last page 2 sides

[Dated by similar paper and ink, late birthday present, going out with many people]

Let us know what size shirt you and Herman wear. It is time that we should send you the belated birthday gift. How would you like to call us maybe on Monday evening when we both are home and we'll pay the charge!! The telephone number is Cypress 9 - 4769 Hermina Gluck Please call it doesn't cost so much and we'll pay with the bill. O.K.!

[On the side] Don't tell about this boys, the friends, to anybody!!!!

1946/11/28 Marie to Irving (Book 16, 281-284)

My dear Irving!

I know you are surprised that I became such a bad writer. I was already getting ready to write, but somehow something always came up. First of all, how are you my dear little brother? I am very happy to hear that Walter is such a fine boy, and you are right that you go with him, and if you talk to him tell him that I send my best and I'm sorry that I did not have a chance to invite them before I left. And you my little Irving, or my buddy, take care of yourself. I know that you study hard, but take care of yourself. Is it warm in the house? Is there coal? Just be careful with it. And what's going on with your other schools? I hope to hear the best about you. Yes, the curtain is not really black, we should have it washed, not just give it to them, but tell them to clean it nicely, especially those in the first floor rooms. How's it going with the cooking? I just hope that your brother Herman won't forget that it is for him too, and that he should help you. How is Mrs. Heszon and Walters? If I would know English, I would have written to them.

But this way I'm just postponing it. Now little brother let me write about me. First of all, I'm well. As I mentioned about that boy, that I met him. You know that on Thursday it was Thanksgiving Day. That boy invited me to go with him for dinner to his siblings since he has more siblings and he wants me to be there too. And he thought that it's no big deal and I will go, since he is a very nice guy. And only for fun. It was a three hour train ride and I spent the day very nicely. I met his family, that is, his siblings. And since then he took me out on Sunday, too. And now I don't even know what to do because he is very serious now. And I would not like to take him seriously. First of all, he looks from 40 to 43, but I did not ask how old he is. And then, he is not even beautiful. He is a little taller than I am. So this way I know that he has a store. I'm only writing this since the boy is very serious. And one does not even know what would be the best. I did not want to let it go that far, but now I don't really know how it will be. The relatives say that it does not matter that he is old. And the boy is very serious. He is only afraid that I will leave him. I wish you could be here my little buddy. I only write about this because I know you are interested. Write to me about yourself and next time I will too. I kiss you countless times with love. Maria

[Side:] Greetings to Flora and to her family.

1946/12/1 Hermine to Irving (Book 16, 297-299)

12/1 - 46

My dear Irving,

I got your letter and thank you very much for your effort, that you dealt with the insurance. I sent 5 dollars in my last letter and I will attach the rest here, that is, 2 dollars. It makes me happy knowing that you are good with the studying and also that you go sometimes to Flora + the others at least for dinner. It is not nice that Herman is behaving that way, and it is not polite, if he would do that also. If they call him he should finally go then and he shouldn't live in the forest. Believe me, if here in New York somebody would live a life like that, they would think he is really sick, even the relatives. This is his sickness, because he does not go anywhere, only being sad and what could be the end of that? This empty problem goes to the nerve of a man that he would not spend 2 cents. I'm sorry that I am writing this to you, but why would I write to him, since he would not even read it. Believe me, that for us it is just a waste that we did not come here before. It's not like it would be so easy here, but at least a man can feel that he is alive and he is not completely forgotten with his question. It is very hard to find good company here, but it is very different from Columbus. Last night we went to dance and it cost us 2.50 dollars for the two of us, but at least one can meet with someone. Well, this is the way it goes!

Marcsa is not at home. She left at 10 o'clock in the morning. The man she mentioned took her to Radio City Music Hall and it is possible that he will take her to dance at night. Looks like she wants to decide seriously, but he's a little old. Although he looks very loyal and he introduced his family too on Thanksgiving. One of his siblings took them for lunch, where the family was together. It is not important to mention to Marcsa that I gossip about that, but I am just telling you little brother. I know you are interested in everything. Currently I have someone, but it's only for fun. One that I wrote about, is a very cute guy, but we only meet rarely. I'm sure he thinks it costs too much. Last Saturday it cost him maybe even $2- So this is how it goes. Write about yourself. We are sending our best to the relatives and to the acquaintances. Tell to Mrs. Hassen and Walters that we are sending our best in our letters, and we are wondering about them. Write about the cooking and the cleaning. Should I go to clean? To clean the curtains. Write about everything and now I wish you good health. I remain with love, Hermine

With love to Herman also.

1946/12/3 Hermine to Irving (Book 16, 286-288)

New York 12/3 - 46
My dear brother Irving,
I sent a letter just today, but in the meantime I called the Slovak office where Bertha had the authorization done. They said that I need the resident papers also. So, without those we can't do anything. I'm thinking that maybe it will be on all of our names and maybe I will need your signature as well. For now, only send my resident papers by registered mail. Maybe you can take a picture of it like we did with the military papers. You have one too because here there is no place to keep it yet. So, please send it to me, and then I will have the letter written to Boske Kramer's husband. He is a lawyer - or to Miksa Shon's sibling's brother-in-law- I got a letter last week and if he will get this authorization, then he will take care of it. This only has the effect of getting it back from the government. He also mentioned, which I already spoke about it, that who would be the caretaker because everything is very neglected. Until now, Ignác [Klein] wrote nothing about this case and how everything is going. So, I'm thinking that they will do something about that, too. Maybe that lawyer would take [care] of that case, too. I don't even mind if it will not go well for Ignác, since he never even brought the case up. Last night I finally found Emil's uncle from Helmec and I told him that Emil complained that he does not even write to him. He confessed to that and he said that he was waiting for Emil to write. Now he promised that he will write and will send money too, which I hope he will. Otherwise I'm well and you write to me about everything. If you want to come for the New Year or for Christmas, I will be very happy. Write it. Ok? I kiss you with love, Hermine

1946/12/11 Hermine and Marie to Irving (Book 16, 346-352)

12/12 - 46
[from Hermine]
My dear Irving,
I have not heard from you for a long time already, but I hope you are all well. I know how busy you are and because of that I forgive you. We are well, we still work at the same place, but it is possible that I will change. You know, that they promised a raise for 5 months already and they did not give it yet and I can get more money at other places. I was trying to write this letter at lunch, because there is always something that comes up at night and the writing stays. I'm interested [to know] if you got the 5 dollars in the letter, and the 2 dollars in the other for the insurance. What's going on with the phone? Do you still have it? I wanted to have it transferred where I live and after a year I can get it. So, I should wait for a year after it. Bertha wrote from Florida and she is well. Her sister-in-law will get married and we got an invitation from her - It is going to be on January 5th. I don't know if we are going to go yet. Did you get a letter from David?

It's been awhile since we got news from him. Since I'm here he wrote two letters and we have to get used to it - but I hope he is ok! Little brother write about yourself and about everything because I'm interested. Is there coal and is it warm in the apartment or maybe you didn't even make fire in the furnace? How are Flora and the others? When did you see Aunt Helen? What new [things] did you get for yourself - since I left? Believe me little brother that I'm lucky partially that I'm buying clothing in the factory and this way it is cheaper. The old lady gave me three addresses again and there if I tell them that she sent me, then they will sell to me. If you could see how much that lady loves us, you could only laugh. [In English] "Mine children" [In Hungarian] she says about us- when she mentions us to somebody and there is no one like those two girls- she says. You know little brother - she gets the breakfast to the table everyday because she is afraid we won't eat. So we are lucky that we got to this house like this. I think about you a lot and I'm sorry that we left you there. It is possible that because of this maybe we can have more hope for the happiest future. Write and kisses with love, Hermine

[from Marie]
My dear Irving!
I haven't heard from you for a long time already. I hope that my lines will find you in the best of health. We are well and I'm thinking of you again and I'm writing this letter from work. I'm just thinking how busy you must be, since you are getting ready for your tests. I hope the dear God will help you and you will be successful. Hey my buddy, how's everything with all these, or are you feeling yourself well? Did you buy coal? Although, here the weather is beautiful and I guess [it is] there too. I mention you a lot, but I know that all that is not enough. Somehow, I don't even know why, the time goes by so fast that by the time I realize [it] I didn't write to you. I can imagine how busy you must be. I am continuing this letter from home. When I got home I found a card from you, which I was very happy about, and it makes me happy knowing that thank God you are healthy. You were wondering if I got the check from the A&P store that you sent me. I thought that I wrote this to you, but if I didn't then I am sorry, since it was on my mind many times. I got that and the insurance...

..the book, otherwise, how are you my little brother? My dear I know that you think that I forgot about you, but that is not true. Have you decided what you are going to take in the next semester? What is going on with Walter's teaching. Give my best to him. And also to the relatives. We have not heard about Flora + the others already. And how is Mrs. Hesen and Mrs. Walters? I'm sure they are angry at me because I did not write to them [or] Mrs. McNeil, but I'm sorry, Hermina is pretty busy, so she does not have a lot of time for anything. I don't have a lot about myself to write. Currently I already wrote about my job, where I work and now they transferred me to the Empire [State] Building and I am there.

I will attach here the stamp for the candy, there is one in it what is necessary to buy in this month. I am a cashier for the same company. It is a very nice place and I also like the job very much. I'm only saying as an example. I was there completely by myself two weeks ago, and I took in $5000 last Saturday, what I never did before and I made it out until the last penny. The entire week is not as busy as on Saturday. But I hope it will be successful after this also. Currently I am alone at home, since Hermine got invited by a lady, because they are introducing a boy to her. She will write about this next time. She already has acquaintances. For me, that boy who I mentioned before, I was out with him again, and this Saturday we expect to go to a big Hungarian party. We will go there. I will write about this next time. Just take care of yourself. I kiss you countless times, your forever faithful sibling. Maria

[Vertical on left side note] Number 51 is good candy
[Vertical in middle note] It is not available here, so buy it, but not necessary to send it now.

[from Hermine]
My dear little brother Irving,
I will write a few lines in Marcsa's letter. I hope you are well. We got your card yesterday and I wish you good luck with the exams. I don't know if Marcsa wrote it to you, that the check from where she worked - the one you sent to her, she got it. I will also write to David a few lines and give it to him. [Regards] to the relatives and to Walters + others and whoever is wondering about us. I would like to give you a little gossip to you - Because I know it [continues in English] would be a lot of fun. So let's hope that we'll see you soon. If not for Christmas, but we will see you. Maybe I'll go to see you OK? Take care of yourself and don't work too hard. Did Herman get that medicine? Or did he like it? Well, I have to sign off because it is time to go back to work. Love to you both, Hermine

1946/12/16 Private G.R. Hubbard to Irving (Book 15, 64-65)

Burgaw, N.C.
Dec. 14, 1946
Dear Gluck,
I should like to hear from you some time. I am teaching agriculture here. Have been here since March. Best wishes to you always,
Sincerely, G.R. Hubbard

12/16 - 46
[from Hermine]
My dear Irving,
I'm thinking of you a lot and I know how hard you study and that you are very busy. I hope you are well. Do you have good heat by you? Write about everything to me. Bertha got a letter from Iren from Szatmar in which she wrote that she stayed there alone without her family. And I wrote a letter to her and she responded to it. Poor thing, her life is very hard and bitter, that she is alone and she had to live through that. She would like to be with us, but she did not write or ask anything at all. I hope Bertha will have her come here. Besides that I'm well and I will write again. I will finish with this. I kiss you many times with much love. Hermine
P.S. I would like to have that resident paper sent as soon as possible so we can deal with that case. Kiss you.

[from Marie]
My dear Irving,
I am sorry again that I did not write for so long, but I hope that my lines will find you in the best [of health]. We are well, but now I work at night before the holidays and it is 10 o'clock by the time I get home and this way I am always getting ready to write, but it stays. And how are you? What's going on with the exams? I hope everything will work out. And write about yourself also. Did you get a letter from David. I don't even remember the last time I heard about him. I hope...

...he is well. I just thought about it, that there is Hanukka now so I will check it over at night. How are the relatives? Does Mrs. Walters, Mrs. McNeil come to you since then or surely she is angry. Otherwise here everything is the same. I was at the dance on Saturday with that guy who I mentioned, that he is very serious. But currently I don't know how it will be, since I'm planning on giving up on him. I will write more next time. Only take care of yourself my Irving, and write to me, I will also. I kiss you countless times, your forever faithful sibling, Maria

1946/12/26 G. Rudolph Hubbard to Irving (Book 2, 165-166)

Burgaw, North Carolina
December 26, 1946
Dear Irving,
Thanks for the note and Christmas greeting. Oh! I have been back since February 19. I was out as a free man on February 25. During the past summer I went to North Carolina State College for nine weeks. I am teaching agriculture. Have had rather good luck since I have been out of the army. Was successful in getting a 1946 Plymouth and I am rather proud of that automobile too. I have had a good Christmas and am hoping that you did too. Write me when you have time. I'll be looking to hear from you. Sincerely,
G. Rudolph Hubbard

1946/12/27 (a) Hermine and Marie to Irving and Herman (Book 16, 354-357)

[New Year's Greeting Card]

My dear Irving little brother,
Forgive me that I only write so briefly, but I will write a letter tomorrow. I will arrange the documents that I will send home because you have to all sign them too. I wish you good health and everything good with much love. I kiss you, Hermina

1946/12/27 (b) Hermine and Marie to Irving (Book 16, 398-402)

12/27/46
[from Maria]
My dear Irving,
I got your letter that I could hardly wait for, which I was very happy for and it makes me happy knowing that thank God you are well. We are well and we mention you a lot. We wish you could be here with us. But I hope the dear God will help and your plan will be successful and that you could come to us, too. Otherwise,

I would like to introduce somebody to you. What do you say about that? My little dear brother, you know I already wrote about this, but now I will start again. First of all, when I came to New York, like I wrote, I met a guy. His name is Irving and he is a very fine boy. He is not beautiful and allegedly he is 38 years old. He has a store in wholesale and he sells goods in bulk. Since then he takes me out all the time, in other words we go together twice a week. I did not want to be serious with him, but somehow I don't even know, how it would be the best. I would like you to meet him. Although, he is very serious and a very fine boy. And a business man. Allegedly, he would do anything to make me happy. He is always wondering about you. Now he took me for Christmas at one of his siblings to a big party. I was there with him before to another sibling of his and they are very fine people and they keep a kosher kitchen and they are all with good manners. One of them has a fur coat store and has a factory and for the rest of them also…

…they have a very nice store, and this boy wants to open a store also, when he gets married. As it appears it is God's destiny and it will be the way he orders it to be. Finally I had a case, one of Hermine's boyfriends took her out for Christmas and he has a good friend. At the same time that boy wants to take me out. He is a very nice guy and he is not poor either. Somehow it came out when he called me to go out I already had a date with the other one. So, I could not go with him. This way it got cancelled, because when one only looks to have a date, then he will let the serious one go. Yes, my Irving, only so you can laugh a little.

…we met these boys on time and as you could see my boyfriend is Irving and Hermine has two boys whose names are Irving. So this is by chance, if two of them walk in they don't even know which one is being called. As it appears the dear God knows how we ([In English] love our Irving) this way he gave us others with that name. But my dear little brother, I'm asking you to take care of yourself and don't be sad and I hope that soon you can come to us. Write to me what you think about all this. And now I'm wishing you a very happy and lucky new year. May the dear God help you in every step of your way. Dave still didn't write. I kiss you countless times, your faithful sibling, Maria
[In the middle of the first page] I don't work at night anymore. Love to you.

[from Hermine]
My dear Irving,
I glanced through Marcsa's letter and as I can see, she wrote about everything in detail. There would be a lot to talk about, but in a letter it goes completely differently. But so I could cut to the chase, only a few words about Marcsa's boyfriend. You know little brother, the boy is a very nice boy and very fine. He does not look young, but maybe he even brings the stars down for her. He takes her to better places and to his siblings also. I don't know what to say because it is totally up to her. Yes, it is not that easy to find a nice man.

Last Tuesday I had a date with a boy, but the boy wanted Marcsa to go too on a double date with his friend. That could not happen because the one she always goes with would have gotten offended. So, it happened that because of that it got canceled for me too. He is a very fine boy, but he only takes me out once in two weeks, and this way one doesn't even know what to think. Later I have found out that this boy bought a house with one of his siblings for 42 thousand dollars. He is very rich, I know the boy too. But this is the way it goes. I had a Hungarian boy too who was rich and cute, but he was a big moron - why should I start with someone like him - and this way slowly I got rid of them.

I have a few acquaintances but maybe it isn't worth a thing. Otherwise we are fine. I'm still working at the same place and I still did not get my raise. I got a week's paycheck as a Christmas present. Bertha's husband travelled to Bertha in Florida and they will come back next week. Bertha's husband's sister is getting married on January 5th, where we are invited also, and the both of us will go. I already got the present yesterday.

…It is a dish that is very beautiful and it is enough for four people. Marcsa is going to sign the document and to authenticate it, then I will send it to you also, and I will write to you what to do with it. Write my Irving - and did David write to you the reason that he is not writing? I hope he is not sick? We think about you a lot and Herman too, although he does not deserve it. All the things we did for him, we should deserve it. Maybe it is better that way, that we came to this realization in time. I kiss you with much love, Hermina

[On the side] I wish all of you a very Happy New Year!

1947/1/3 Hermine and Marie to Irving (Book 11, 194-198)

1/3 - 47

[from Hermine]

My dear beloved little brother! I got your letter this morning and I already wrote a little note, that I attached with the official documents and I will send them with the post office. So, now I want to write a detailed letter and I am truly sorry that I wrote so rarely to you in the past. Although, I wrote a lot, but I was behind with the writing. This way a lot of letters did not go out to you. The thought makes me happy that thank God you are well. We are ok as well. But I got news for you! I have a new job. The company where I worked only promised a raise, but did not give me one and I told them that I will not stay then. Although they sent me to school where I learned a lot, but they wanted to get the expenses out of me. So, one morning I left them and I got another job on the same day as a comptometer operator. I get 35 dollars. It is 5 dollars more a week. They tried me to see what I know and as of now they were very satisfied. They sent me to a doctor's exam yesterday. I will start to work on Monday at 9 o'clock. This is New York's biggest department store. This way I will also get a 20% discount if I buy anything. So, it is pretty good. I have to work 40 hours and 5 days.

I hope everything will be fine because I hated the other place so much, that even the air made me sick. I learned a lot from them, but they employed me as a clerk and they did not want to place me as a comptometer operator. I am going to a wedding tomorrow. Bertha's husband's sister is getting married - as I heard Manny would have come home yesterday and that Bertha is not coming. She always shows who she is. I got a very nice present for her. She invited Marcsa also, although she does not know her. This way together we will give her a dish set for 4 people to set the table. It is very nice! I got it for 8 people and I kept half of it for us. This lady is old and she does not have a dish set like that and if a boy comes here, we need it so he could at least drink tea from something. On New Year's eve we went to a party at Zseni's with Marcsa and her boyfriend. I am so sorry that you were so alone. I know how it goes and believe me that I am like that also, but somehow there is no time to think about that here. Currently there is no need to go to Europe because we can't do anything that way. The person who I will hire will take care of everything well. I believe and trust him. If he will not like Ignác [Klein], he will appoint somebody else. Ever since he [Ignác] has been taking care of it, he did not even write to us about it. Therefore he does not care about it and this way he will appoint somebody else. That is, he will arrange it the way it is going to be good. It will not cost a lot and let's hope that somebody will come out from the children. Somehow I don't even care about the property, but still it has to be taken care of. There is some new tax on the property, but we can't let it be neglected.

Now I will write to Fenicky also. When you get the document back from Cleveland send it to him. I would like a phone because it is not good like this! You know last week there were almost three boys meeting at our place on Friday night. Luckily, I went to the door and sent them away because the boy next door, who I met a few weeks ago, was here. So there is no phone and this way they think about visiting me. I told that I am busy and he left this way. So, it is possible that he will not even come back. But this is how it goes. Last week there was someone who was truly serious and he had plenty of money also, but he looks like a moron and too ordinary. I don't want anyone like that. I don't care what you will say about that. He wanted a date at Christmas and I told him I was busy and I already had a date and this way it stayed that way.

Marcsa told me that you don't like it when I talk about the boys like that. Believe me, that they were all nice guys, but not real. This neighbor is a very nice guy also - He went to Florida now. He will be there for three weeks. He always came here and he wanted to take me to his siblings. He only did one date. When he comes, he takes me to the movies or to his siblings. I don't want that either because I don't know why he wants me to spend my time with him. One can always go out somewhere and get to know someone, but someone who is serious. I just want to say that from the many dates there is none left now. Although, it happened before too and later will happen again and in the worst case scenario the neighbor will be home soon. Do you still have the phone? What's going on with the apartment? Is it warm? Is there anyone who does the cleaning sometimes? How is Herman? What is going on with David that he is not writing? It's his birthday on January 11th. Write again. I kiss you with love, Hermina.

[from Marie]
Dear little brother, Irving!

We got your letter, which could hardly wait for and I was very happy about it. The thought makes me happy, that you, thank God, are well. I am thinking of you a lot as well. I can imagine how everything goes in Columbus. I hope the dear God will help you and your plan will work out successfully. Take good care of yourself and don't be sad. And yes, my Irving we will send you two scarves, that my friend Irving gave me to send to you. He also deals in that. I hope that you will use it, too! He would like you to be here also, since I mention you so much. I just told him that you will surprise me sometime. It just came to my mind, you know that paper that they sent from the A+P, a statement of the tax income. I put it somewhere, and I can't find it.

I have to tire you out with this. If you would be so kind to call him, in other words to ask for the statement from the boss, so we could have it because the tax needs to be paid soon. I hope that he will give it again. If you will call the boss on the phone, if you don't remember his name I will send it here, Mr. Morgan. I'm sure he will give it out and if he will say that he can't give it, then ask for the address. But as far as I know, he has to give it again. I'm sorry, but this is not my fault. I thought that I put it away, but I can't find it. I hope that I will be able to get it again. I'm sorry my little brother that I always bother you with something. I also will send the money for the hospitalization next time and as they said, they will send it over, and when and until when it was paid? Thank you very much in advance, my dear little brother. I hope I can give you a kiss soon in person for it! (how about that) Is it all right with you? All my love to you. Kisses with love, Maria

1947/1/4 Hermine and Marie to David (Book 8, 91-94) working as comptometer and cashier

1/4/47
[from Marie]
Dear Dave,
I don't know what I should write to you. Ever since I'm here, we didn't hear from you. That is a long time. I hope my letter will find you well. I know you don't like to write, but I hope you will get the pen and sit down at once to write to us immediately so we shouldn't worry about you. I promised myself if you do not write to us then I will not write to you either, but I can't keep my words. Therefore, I'm asking you again, please write. Are you working? We wrote many letters. We just received a letter today from our little brother in which he also wants to know what happened to you because he didn't hear from you for a long time. While he worries also, you know you aren't helping by being silent. I can't believe that the reason you're not writing is that you are that busy. I know from myself. I do not write either and I'm also busy, but because we are a family, brother and sister, we like to hear from each other and we are concerned about one another. It doesn't matter, you should write even just one word that you are ok, even just once a month, even 2 words you should write. Therefore, now it is up to you whether you desire it for your side. I wrote to you before that I'm working in a store as a cashier. As of now I like it, only the weather is not so good. Otherwise I'm getting used to New York. Bertha has been in Florida for about 4 weeks. I don't know how long [she will stay]. The relations are ok. Now I want to wish you a happy birthday and a happy New Year. We should hear from each of us the best all the time. Please take care of yourself. Our brother Irving is worried about you, therefore don't forget to write to Irv, too. With this hope, that I will hear from you soon, I'm closing my letter. Kisses with lots of love, your sister. Take care of yourself wherever you go. Please write. Maria

[from Hermine]

Dear Dave,
I can't imagine the reason that we haven't heard from you for such a long time. Are you well? Please, I ask you to write as soon as possible. Don't be lazy to write to us. God forbid, even if you are sick, you should let us know because we are concerned about you. If something is wrong and we don't know, we can't help you. Please be smart and think. Just like you worry about us, we do the same. We are happy to know all about you the same way [you are to hear about us]. I'm fine. I have a new job as a comptometer operator. I'm getting $35 in a store where 17 dozen people are working. At this time, I like it. Write about yourself. Many kisses, Hermine

1947/1/4 Hermine to Irving (Book 19 53-54)

My dear Irving!
We got your letter this morning which I want to respond to in detail. I will send this letter as registered mail to you. One of the letters which we both signed are needed to be signed by you also. Maybe it would be better to ask Mrs. Fleming because you need to sign it at an official place and then send it to Cleveland to the Czech Consulate for authentication. I will attach 4 dollars and the letter with a reply stamp, so he will

send that back to you and the money is for the cost, that is, for the authentication. Then when the document gets back to you, you can send it to this address:

Bela Fenicky

Kralovosky Chlumec

I will write to him too and I will notify him that we will send the documents soon and the bond and to mention to him the rights in the Varalja forest. The notary in Lelesz would not have arranged it and he only would have taken out only the land register statement to us, if we think we need it. I did not respond to him yet because I don't have any writing to do to him. I talked to a lawyer here and it would cost so much more than at home. Don't worry, this individual will be good and he will take care of it. I attached my resident papers.

[upside down top of page 2] I also enclose a copy of the document and put it with my civilian paper. Kisses, Hermine

1947/1/7 David to Irving and Herman (Book 12, 162-165)

1-7. 47.

Dear little brother! Until 120!

Forgive me that I did not write for so long, but I really don't have any reason for that, maybe just that I have become very lazy. I really don't know why, but I can't make myself write. How are you? How is studying going? I hope everything is going well and everything worked out. What do you study now? Do you have company? How is Herman doing? Does he do the cleaning? Who is cooking, you or Herman? What's new there? Do you go dancing? There is nothing particular here. You know, I am well. Currently I work at night. It is possible, if it's going to work out, I will leave L.B. [Long Beach], but I don't know what to do yet. Maybe I will go to San Francisco or some other place. I will ask here tomorrow. You know I don't like to be at the same place for too long. It's been three years that I have been living here. There is nothing here except a little town, although the population is about 300,000. I don't like Los Angeles, nor Hollywood. That is a city only for actors. You only need to have money. I don't really know what to write. I have not written for so long, that I don't even know what to write. I just wrote a letter today to the girls also. I hope they are well! I'm asking you to take care of yourself too. OK? Don't rush anything! Think carefully about what you want to do and stick to it. Currently, the weather here is very beautiful. The weather is very summery here. I would like it if you could be here. Lajos wrote that he wants to come here to California. I don't know if he will come. My little brother, I really don't know what to write, nothing comes to my mind. So I will close my lines for today. I will be in a hurry next time to write more, and more often. I wish you everything good with love! I kiss you, forever your faithful older brother, Dezső

P.S. Write to me even if I don't write properly. OK? I will write a few lines to Herman. Please give it to him. OK? Thank you! Kisses, as above

Dear Herman! Until 120!

Forgive me, that I did not respond to your letter, but I probably wrote the reason already, that is, I have become a very lazy writer. Please write to me! Yes, thank you for your letter and it was very nice of you that you wrote to me. I'm asking you to eat like a man and don't starve and see to it that Ignác is eating as well. God forbid, the two of you would starve. I wish you everything good and a Happy New Year and good health. Please write to me again, I will appreciate it very much that sometimes you write to me too. I kiss you with love, your faithful brother. Dezső

P.S. Write - write if you are still there at Brixtol?

1947/1/7 Sanyi Klein to Ignác (Book 4, 426-429)

1947 1st month 7th day!

My dear friend Ignác,

I received your letter and I am in a hurry to reply. I am thank God healthy and I wish you the same. I understand from your letter that you too have been a soldier. Unfortunately I went through a lot of difficult situations, however let's forget about it. If I want to write about this to you then I could write a whole Megillah. The main thing is that I'm at home and in good health. My dear friend, you're asking about your family, I regret to tell you that I came home late. The only person I know that survived from Polyán is Malvin Lefkovics, however she remained in Sweden. Otherwise I know of nothing more. Dear Ignác, what do you say to it that I want to go to Palestine if I can. If you write to me again we'll be in Nagy Mihaly. If you write please write to me at the old address since they're going to mail it to me anyway namely, the Frolinger boys.

And then I'll send you my address. You're asking how the people react, most of them are afraid because these Hungarians are trying to be well-behaved. On Saturdays when I go to Polyán they are always inquiring about all of you. They're asking how you are, but I do not trust them. I believe I've written enough. With regards, your true friend from faraway who thinks of you a lot. Sanyi.

Individually my best wishes and regards to your relations and those that I know. Sanyi

1947/1/12 Hermine to Irving (Book 11, 203-205)

New York 1/12 - 47

My dear little brother Irving!

Today is Sunday night and I did not go anywhere, so I thought about you. I got your letter already and I wrote to Mrs. Goldstein - this is Helen Perl from Szürte - who wrote. This way on a day like this [you] will be my guest. Otherwise, I am fine. Marcsa is not at home now - what we wrote many times, she has a boyfriend who is truly serious. We should call it steady, because she only dates him. [Bertha] is going to Florida this Tuesday and she will be there for a few weeks. Did you and Herman get the scarves? They are so beautiful, aren't they! Write which one did you take for yourself. I was at Jenny Frey last night for dinner and last week Bertha's husband invited us for dinner to go to talk to them a little - since he only just came home from Florida, but Bertha stayed for a few weeks. Oh yes! I have a new job in a department store as a comptometer operator and they pay 35 dollars to start. I like the job and at least 11 thousand people are working at this company. It could be the biggest store in the world.

We got a letter from David a few days ago and he had his birthday on the 11th of this month. Thank God he is well. He wrote that he has just become a very negligent writer, just like me. Now I wrote to Malvin Lefkovits also because it has been a while since she wrote. I should write to many others, but I don't want to. Currently, I don't even want to go on a date, if it's not someone that one can like, then what for?! Well, this is what it is. You know little brother, Marcsa's boyfriend would like to give the ring already, but she does not know what she wants. I can't tell her because it depends on her. The boy is a pretty good boy and he works for himself. I guess he has a storage [business]. He also said to Marcsa that he knows how sad she is about the boys - especially about our Irving and because of that he would like you to come here too and he will arrange it so you can go to school here. You know that's only gossip so I will tell you, so he is a good boy...otherwise a man. He could be around 40. I will write to you more and I will try to write more often. Write about yourself and send my greetings to Flora and to Aunt Helen and I'm sorry that poor Flora is sick. Write about it. Write about everything. Good luck with studying! What do you study for? Write in detail.

[Bottom of first page] I kiss you and Herman and you with love. Hermin

1947/1/20 Hermine to Irving (Book 11, 121-124)

1/20 - 46

My dear little brother Irving!

I know your opinion [and] what you think about me because I have not written for this long, even though I thought about you a lot. Well, I hope you are well and Herman too. I got a letter from Dave last week, but I did not respond to him yet. How does Flora feel? Write little brother because I'm so worried about her, who knows how she is. She always works so hard. Guess what my little brother, that the Goldblatt boy from Cleveland called Mariska last week at work - Mannie gave her address - then on Thursday night he came up with his mother to us, and when I came home from work they were already there, so I made dinner for them. I just made them stuffed cabbage - but my cooking was not a big success. You know little brother, if you could see him, not to jinx it, but he became a very nice guy since I saw him. They were here yesterday for lunch. I invited him and Mariska's boyfriend. Louis' mother travelled back on Thursday night. She was here for two weeks already. Although, I have a date with him today and I know that [he] will have something important to say. Right now I am only gossiping to you, but I hope that I am right. You know little brother, if it will work out, and the dear God wants it too, then maybe I can go to Columbus soon. Ok? Did you get that document that they are asking for in this office? I did it for the sake of our case and my resident paper was in it too. Also, the package where the two scarves were. Write about everything. I will write again soon. I wish you good health and greetings to the relatives. I kiss you with love. Hermine

1947/1/20 Jane Fabianova Postmaster to Dezső (Book 7, 51)

[This letter was written by Jane, the postmaster from Lelesz, to my brother David]

Hnúšťa 20 I 1947

Dear Dezső and all of you!

You will be surprised receiving my few lines. I do not know your address so I mailed it to your uncle's address. I am alive! I believe you and your family are, too. Write as soon as you can a lot about everything. Presently I'm at home, in my beloved country. The outrageousness of this war. I spent my time in a foreign land, however as soon as I could, I came back home. Dezső, I lost everything, but thank God I'm alive. My mother, my brother, and father died, Aunt Mili and more, although I haven't arrived to that point. Please write, my address is on the envelope. My regards and love, Jane.

I do not know English, but you do not know Italian. IO PARLO MALTO BENE IN ITALIANO. [I speak Italian very well.]

1947/1/20 Marie to Irving (Book 6, 28-30)

1/20/47

My dear Irving!

Now I have a little time, so I'm in a hurry to write to you. I'm sorry there has to always be an excuse. We are well which I hope that my lines will find you the best. Otherwise how are you my buddy? [In English] I miss you very much, [In Hungarian] but I hope that the dear God will help and everything is going to work out fine. For example yesterday we had company. I don't know if Hermine wrote about it. Louis Goldblatt, you know from Cleveland, who asked for our address last week. He called on the phone on Tuesday, that he is here with his mother and they want to come to visit us. So they came up to us. Louis looks very good and is a very intelligent, fine boy. Also, my friend Irving was here too. This way we invited both of them for lunch on Sunday. In other words for yesterday, and everything worked out. There was only one mistake, that you could not be here, which is what we all wanted. Also, Hermine is busy again tonight, since they will go somewhere. And I want the letter to go as soon as possible. Now I will get back, my dear little brother to Irving. I don't even know how to present this whole thing. I started many times, but I still don't know how it will be. First of all, he has serious intentions and he is waiting for my answer. But as it seems, it is very hard to decide. Everybody likes him, but he is not good looking, although he is very fine. He is about 40 years old and I don't know even know what else to say. Probably if he would be a different boy, I guess then it would be like that too. But I will leave this too. I don't want to bother you with this. Hermine will write about hers to you next time with more details. How's everything with you? Do you still take help with/for money? Otherwise is it still hard what you study? I can imagine how busy you must be. Otherwise, what is the news at home? What did you decide about the school? How are Flora and the others? We have not heard about them. And how about Aunt Helen? How are the neighbors? Did you hear from the boss from the A&P? Now I hope to hear the best from you! And I'm asking you to take care of yourself and don't be worried! And eat! I think about you a lot. Now I wish you lots of luck and good health. I kiss you countless times, your forever faithful sibling. Love Maria

1947/1/22 Marie to David (Book 16, 129-131)

1/22/47

Dear David!

We got your letter that we were waiting so hard for, and I'm happy to hear that thank God you are well. We are well and just like you wrote that you are very busy, I am becoming a negligent writer. I am just writing to little brother too. I have not heard from him for a couple of days. I know that he is very busy, especially now that he has to take care of the house. I hope that the dear God will help, and your wish will come true. And now I will get back to the acquaintances. I thought I already wrote about this. Berthuska went away to Florida for two months already and it is expected that she will stay there for one more month. And this way we miss her.

Besides that Mani, her husband will come to visit us. Hermine and I live with an old lady. Her family is also very nice. She was wondering if we have acquaintances. When I came here I met many and in the meanwhile I had a boy who started to think seriously. And since then, we kept being friends. First of all, I know this about myself, how it would be good. I only know that what one is looking for one can't find it. For example, this boy, his name is Irving. He is a very nice boy, his family is a very good Jewish family and are business people. He took me out already in the first week to them and to his siblings. As for him, Irving's appearance is not beautiful at first and he is 39 years old. Supposedly he has a business selling wholesale goods. A poor thing he can't be, but I don't know exactly.

Although, wealth doesn't always count. And this way supposedly everybody has a good opinion about him. But right now, I don't know yet. It will be as the dear God arranges it. But now I will leave this too. I am writing this letter from work and I'm in a hurry to finish. Hermina is well and I leave it up to her to write about herself. The weather today is very cold, but this year there was not much snow. And now I hope that you will respond. Take care of yourself. I hope to hear the best about you and kiss you with love. Maria I like my current job.

1947/1/22 Undated Marie to Irving (Book 8, 23-24)

[Dated by mention of A+P papers and David's letter]

My dear Irving!
It has been a couple of weeks since we got mail from you. I hope that my lines will find you in the best! We are well, only like usual we are very busy. We got a letter from David this week and he is well also, just like he wrote, he has become a very lazy writer. And how are you my dear little brother? Do you work hard? How do you do with studying? And what do you eat? I can imagine how busy you can be. How's everything with the rooms? Do you have to clean alone? Or your brother helps? I hope you have time to rest and eat! I am asking you my dear brother to take care of yourself. Is there heat in the house? Yes my little brother, what's going on with the hospital insurance? Did they send it here and when? Also, what did they say at the A.+ P. Will they send the statement again about how much I made there? I hope they will send it! Yes my little brother, did you get the scarves and do you like them? Write about everything my buddy.

Did you see Walters the neighbor? You know I did not write to them even until today. I'm sure they are angry. I'm sorry, but time goes by such that there is no time for anything. Plus [it needs to be] in English. You know how it goes. I hope that Flora is better! Also Helen! She never wrote to me, but as it appears it is my fault since I did not write to her. And Mrs. McNeill. I seems that I became a lazy writer, too. There is no particular news. I guess Hermina already wrote about everything. I am writing this letter from work and I'm in a hurry to send it with today's mail. Now I'm asking you my buddy to take care of yourself and don't study too hard. At least you should have time to eat. Now I kiss you countless times, your faithful sibling who thinks about you a lot. Lots of luck and the best of health. Write. Love, Maria

1947/1/27 Marie to Irving (Book 6, 24-27)

1/27/47
My dear Irving!
I got your letter last week, which I was very happy for. And I'm glad to hear that you are thank God well. Thank you very much that you were so nice that you wrote that letter to me and I just signed it. I know that others would not even think about what you did. I don't even know how can I be here without you my little brother. Many times it would be good if you would be here and we could talk in person to each other. But I hope you don't have to wait for too long…

[Note on bottom] And how's our brother Herman? Is he still the same?

…that I can see you again. And also my dear Irving, as you mentioned about Mrs. Walters. That is a fact and it is real. That doesn't always matter. I mentioned about you to her so many times that she would like to get to know you. I was invited to a party on Saturday to one of Irving's siblings. And everything was very nice, as usual. I have met with more of his siblings and at times like this the entire family gets together. Currently I can't write anything exact to you yet. Besides I am writing this letter from work and this way I don't know if Hermine will write. But I think she will write to you also, just like I do. And as you wondered about Hermine's boyfriend also. It is very hard to know. As it seems, it is not sure if there will be anything about it. Louis is still here. But I will leave this to Hermine to write about this. Otherwise, everything is fine. Bertha still did not come home yet. Yes, my Irving, how much money do I owe you with for the hospital? It would be about time to give it to you. And I would like it if they would send it to us here, but as it seems, they are not in a hurry with that. I would have looked after it but it has a different name here and I don't know exactly if that is the association and I'm just waiting for them to intervene. Now my dear little brother, I'm asking you to take care of yourself and don't be sad. Write about yourself and don't be sad. How are Flora and the others? Did you see them? Do they wonder about me? Did you mention Irving to them? I'm sure they are surprised. But this is how it goes. Everything is God's order. And the way it comes is the way it will be. How do you do with school? Do you study hard? I am currently not that busy. Did you hear from Lipot and the others? I write like David writes. I became a very lazy writer. I am ashamed that I did not even send a card for anyone. Now I will close my lines and I wish you everything good and lots and lots of luck. And I kiss you countless times, your forever faithful sibling, who will never forget. With love, Maria

1947/1/30 Hermine to Irving (Book 11, 207-209)

My dear little brother, Irving!
It was not nice of me that I did not write to you for so long, but I thought about you even more. I would have a lot of writing to do and if God will help, I will write again on Saturday night. Yesterday I was free and this way I should work on Saturday. It has been seven weeks already that the Goldblatt boy was here with his mother and since then we met a few times. He was here yesterday afternoon also and today at lunch time he came to me where I work. Well, the thing is this, the boy is a very nice and cute guy. What will turn out I can't predict because as I heard, the girls are all over him. Also, his uncle would like to have him marry his daughter. Louis told me. He also told me, if I want it, he would take me with him to Palestine because he would like to go there to study and the government would pay for it. So, if it's true, he wants me to go but it can't be built on that. He will come back on Saturday night.

..and he said that he would want to come back for Purim. What do you say about that my little brother? Believe me, that he is the type of boy -not to jinx it- who is hard to find. I have never seen him look the way he looks, so to tell you the truth, I like him, but still it does not go that easy. My little brother what do you say about that? Although, he could change his plan a hundred times.

Marcsa is well also. Tonight she worked longer because she went to work later. The boy came home with her. He wanted to drink coffee and the little donkey brought milk and cookies - she was afraid that it will cost them. I scribbled some foolishness here, but the company is here and it is not allowed to write. I wish you good health and sending my best to Herman as well and I kiss you with much love. I still did not respond to David. I am sending greetings to the relatives and neighbors too. Greetings, Hermin

1947/2 Undated Irving to Dave (Book 6, 257-258) - at OSU

[Dated by letter 1947/1/20 Jane Fabianova Postmaster to Dezső (Book 7, 51)]

Columbus 5, Ohio

Dear Dave, Until 120
Have received your letter and I was very glad to hear from you and to know that you are well, although I would like to hear from you more often. As for myself I know I should write you more often, too, but as yet I'm still so occupied that I don't know if I'm coming or going. I have to sign up for the Spring quarter. I do not know what to do. That is, I should decide what I'm going to major in. Till now I have taken different courses and in one college I have enough hours to begin and study for specializing. But if I stay in Commerce, well I do not know what to follow. Say Dave; Do you think I should become a (1) Psychologist, (2) Speech correctionist, (3) Businessman, (4) Radio announcer, etc. or what? As I stand I could follow in to be a historian, lawyer, etc. but most of these profession is teaching and they say, some people in the University, that I would be a good teacher. Although their income does not amount to much. Let me know if you have something that you could suggest. Now otherwise I'm OK, but have plenty to study, and that takes all my spare time. Just received a letter from Hermine and they are well. They also are slow in answering letters. Hermina's boyfriend, that is, the Captain from over seas is in New York and his mother was there also. Maria has a boyfriend also. I don't know if they have mentioned anything to you or not, but that's that. How are you coming along? Here you'll find a letter enclosed from Janka Fabian[ova] the post office girl from Lelesz, Czechoslovakia. It was mailed to Arthur's address. She says that she was "külföldön"

[abroad]. At the bottom of the letter she says that she can write in English, and you can't write in Slovakia and then she writes in Italian that "I speak very well in Italian." So that's that. I mention that so just in case you did not or rather might not, understand her thought. Let me hear from you real soon, my best wishes to you. With love from your little brother, Irving

P.S. Also another letter enclosed as a birthday greeting. That goes from me, too

1947/2/2 Hermine to David (Book 11, 215-220) Goldblatt to Palestine

2/2/1947

Dear Dave,

I wasn't planning to delay writing my answer to your letter, but I wanted to write more details to you. I was very happy to hear from you and hope you are well. We are alright, but sometimes it's almost impossible to think. In the letter, Maria wrote about the boy who is serious and would like to marry soon. The boy is very nice. He looks older than he is. Manny told me if I give him the name he will find out and the address and everything. At this time he is traveling. He sells wholesale clothing to business people. As I understand it, the clothes he sells are in storage. I'm sorry, but I don't know if it is legal or not.

About myself, I don't know where to begin. It is too much for nothing. Sometimes too many dates, other times nothing. 2 weeks ago I had a big surprise. The Cleveland boy, Goldblatt, called Marie and one night he came over with his mother to visit me. It's only been a couple of weeks since he came home from Japan and he came here for some kind of business that he wanted to take care of. The mother probably wanted him to see me. They were already here when I came home from work. I prepared dinner and the same day in the evening the mother left for home. I was in the city with him a few times. He came up to my new job. What is important is that he is a very fine person.

He looks very nice. He was in the Army uniform. He was discharged a couple of days ago. One opportunity he told me about is that he is planning to go to Palestine to go to school because the government there will also pay for the expenses if I would go with him as a new bride. He is already a dentist, but he would like to learn (talmud yeshiva). He is very religious, I know for sure. A better person, you cannot find if you want to. Here is where I stand. One of his uncles where he was staying for a couple of weeks would like to get this boy to marry his daughter. This is what Louis told me. Therefore, I don't know what will be. Last night he went back. I hope to hear from him. Otherwise everything is the same. Bertha didn't come yet. Maybe she will stay for a few more weeks. I could say that I was introduced to all kinds of men. So far there is always something. There was one who was serious minded, but I wasn't interested. Now I have a man in my neighborhood. Sometimes he comes in. He just came home from Florida so he can't be poor. I met his sister also. He speaks real Hungarian. He eats pork like a non-Jewish goy and I can't stand that. Otherwise he is a nice person. He likes to (blabber mouth) gossip, even when you are not interested. I'm sorry, here we are just existing, but it is not best that the boys in Columbus are alone. Poor Irving is working hard at school studying. Herman doesn't write a word to us ever since we are here. I hope he is ok. Please write to us about yourself. I would like to hear from you. I will try to write more often to you. The woman where we are living is very nice. She is like a grandmother to us. I wrote to Bőske Kramer's husband. He is a lawyer in Helmec about the legal authorization from the government that we can get back our property. If he approves then he can help us to get back our property. Ignác Klein never mentioned anything about that. Therefore, I don't care about his opinion or what he thinks about it. Many kisses and wishing you all the best. Love, Hermine

1947/2/2 Hermine to Irving (Book 11, 211-213)

2/2 - 47

My dear little Irving,

I am alone tonight because Marcsa is not at home and the lady has gone to lay down. I wrote a letter to David too and I hope that you heard from him also. Thank God I am well and Mariska also. This afternoon her boyfriend came and he stayed with his brother for dinner. It looks like they like her and the family is a very nice Jewish family and I can say that he comes more and more often to her. As it appears he has the intention to get married, which I can't say anything about. It is totally Marcsa's decision. As we mentioned, he does not look young, but he is a very nice man and he likes Marcsa very much. About me I still don't know much, but Louis said that if I would go to Palestine with him, then he would take me with him. He also said that he lived with his uncle while he was here, who would like to have him to marry his daughter. So, now the case is this.

I hope I will hear news from him, like he promised. He went back home to Cleveland yesterday evening. He came to me at work on Thursday night at lunch time and he said he will come back to New York soon. He would like to go to Palestine to study because the government pays for it. It would take 3 and a 1/2 years. How are you and how do you do with the studying? Write about everything because I am interested. I'm sorry that I did not write to you for so long, since I think about you so much and talk about you a lot. I would love to see all of you already, even the little malicious Herman. I guess, it can't be known what will happen with Louis and maybe, even if it's for visiting [him], but I could spend some time with you. Looks like there are many after him and whomever is clever will get him. If he is really who he is showing himself to be, then anything should be done to win this man over. Currently I am only gossiping, but it feels good sometimes since I don't do it so often.

I am truly sorry and I am ashamed of it about how everything ended when you came home and we left all of you. I guess many will judge me for that, but it can't be explained for everyone because it is not easy. It is too bad that we could not do it and I hope it is not too late still. As it appears Marcsa has to make a decision fast and I can only hope that the boy will not change his opinion. I mean Louis. He also said that he does not know yet. It is possible that he will stay here and he will study or he will work. The point is that even he himself does not know what he wants. Well, he will write, I hope. Write about everything and take care of yourself. Do you eat normally? My little brother write about everything. Now I will close it with this, with much love. I kiss you! Hermine

I'm sending greetings to the relatives and the Walters, Mrs. McNeill also.

[Upside down] Why doesn't Herman write?

1947/2/11 Marie to Irving (Book 6, 16-19)

My dear brother Irving,

As you can see I will try to write to you again. Hoping that my lines will find you in the best. We are well. We received a letter from David last week and he is fine and mentions that he has not heard from you for a long time. And we also received a letter from Emil from Helmec stating that he would like to receive a package with shoes and a shirt as soon as possible. He can use everything. I don't know if we mentioned this to you that we got a letter from Aunt Sarolta's daughter a couple of weeks ago. She's alive, which Bertha was also very happy about. But it is very difficult for her as well as for everyone. Otherwise, no special news. The weather is pretty cold here. I already thought it wouldn't be winter and I washed [and put] it all away. And you dear little buddy, how are you? Are you studying very hard? It's cold there, dress warmly. Did you find this sweater? And take care not to go crazy. And I haven't heard from you in a long time. But I hope my lines will find you in the best of health. Write about yourself and everything you hear about everything. Now I close my lines and wish all the best and kiss with countless love. Maria
Forever your sister who will never forget you

1947/2/19 Marie to Irving (Book 6, 11-14) pages 1-2

My dear brother Irving,

We received such a long-awaited letter, which I was very happy about. And I am happy to hear that thank God you are healthy. I didn't know what to think about why I hadn't heard from you for so long. I know you're very busy. And besides that my buddy, do you know what I was most happy about? That God will help and shortly (I could hold you in my arm). I wouldn't mind if you were here now. My first wish is that you could be here with me. (Sweetie dear, you remember). I haven't seen you in such a long time from now on I'm going to just count the minutes so please my little brother dear take great care of yourself. And I hope you pass your exam. And if you need clothes or shoes, don't buy them there, and if you're here, you can buy them here cheaply. You know my little brother dear, you have a pajama in your drawers which is new, look to keep it clean and bring it for yourself. Otherwise, how are you, my dear brother? Poor Flora is definitely angry that I didn't write to them. Here nothing is special. We're fine and Bertha is coming home next week. I've had a hard time waiting to go home. And when I went home last night from work, Hermine wasn't there and the old lady told me there was a letter from my sweet heart. But what a letter and Hermine told her how you will come to us. And so until next time I write, I kiss you countless times with love. Maria
Again, I write from work, hello to everyone.

[Dated by Saturday being February 22 and the letter 1947/2/19 Marie to Irving (Book 6, 11-14) above has 2 pages]

Yes my little brother dear now is the time of the year on Saturday that we came to America and I hope that the good God will help us. And to hear the best from one another. And that your wish may be fulfilled. Although we could celebrate together, that is, we could, but I hope you don't have to wait long. Just take great care of yourself and don't be upset. And as you can see, your brother Herman hasn't changed. And he could be a good boy. Again, I kiss you countless times with love.

1947/3/4 Hermine to David (Book 11, 240-241)

3/4 - 47
Dear David,
We received a letter from Irving and in it we found out that you are sick. We hope by now that you are all well. Take care of yourself. It was enough for you. Do you need something? Let me know and I'll mail it to you. I thought that something must have been wrong and that's why we didn't hear from you. You explain that it was because you became a very lazy writer. I always answered your letter. As of now, I don't have any more to tell about the guys. I hope my little brother will come to visit us for his vacation on his time off. On Saturday evening Bertha came home from Florida. She was there 3½ months. This is the 2nd week that I'm at the new job at the Warner Brothers company. I must say that this is the best job. I like it very much. Write more about everything and about how you are. Until then, wishing you good health, with love and kisses, Hermine

1947/3/4 Hermine to Irving (Book 11, 231-234) undated but with envelope

My dear Irving!
I have been getting ready to write to you for a few days, but I only started now. First of all, I want to tell you that I have a new job. I hope that I will stay with this now. It happened that I had a day off on Tuesday and I thought I will look around to see what I can get and they tried me at the first place I walked in and they hired me. The next day when I went to work, and told them I'm leaving. My boss did not want to believe me and he said that if I am leaving because I want more money, they will give it to me also. So, last week I already was at my new job and I liked it a lot. I work at the foreign service accounting. It is a very nice office and at least 35 of us work there and for 37 and a 1/2 hours I get 37^{50}. Last week I worked 3 and 3/4 hours overtime. The company's name is "Warner Brothers". It is like Paramount used to be where I worked before. Oh yes! My little brother, what did you decide about coming here? I would like to see you very much, but arrange it the way you like it.

What's going on with the studies and what did you decide on what you want to be? We got a letter from Flora and we were very happy about it and I'm sorry that she doesn't feel the best. I went to visit Bertha tonight. She just came home last night and if you could see how black she got in Florida. How is Aunt Helen? Do you talk to her sometimes? Give her my greetings. I just remembered that I did not respond to the Klein girl's letter from Lelesz for months already. I wrote to Malvin too, but it looks like she did not really like my letter, since she did not respond. Today it's raining all day and I did not want to go anywhere. Write about yourself little brother and about how you are making out with the work. Do you cook something good still? Maybe better things than I usually cook. You are in my mind a lot and I wish you could live with us! Boy! It would be good, but I don't think it would be worth it for me to go back because somehow it is hard enough anyway. I met with so many boys, but still nothing came out of it. I got a letter from Cleveland and I did not get a response to my letter. I wrote to David also. When did you hear about him?

Write my little brother about everything and I wish many good things and to Herman also and hoping that soon I will hear about you. With lots of love. I kiss you, Hermina

1947/3/4 Undated Hermine and Marie to Irving (Book 10, 49-50)

[dated by David not feeling well and having surgery]

[from Hermine]
My dear little brother Irving!

I can't imagine what could be the reason that we did not get a letter from you for so long. I even wrote to Dezső, and he did not respond either. I only know from your letter that he had an operation. Today we sent the letter to him like to you, but as I came home from work there was no letter anywhere. So, I will not leave this anymore. Be good and write immediately because if it would have been possible I would have called you today. I hope there is nothing wrong, but write because I want to know. It is still before dinner and I'm writing in a hurry, so I can send it with the post office before they close. I heard here that everybody has to be vaccinated against some kind of sickness. And how's everything by you? I probably have to do that at work with the doctor. We are well, only worried about the letter. I hope you are all well and Herman and David also! Ask about the vaccine and if you have to get it you should go too! I wish you good health with love! Hermina

I kiss Herman also with love. He should write too!

[from Marie]
My dear Irving!
I know you are surprised, why I'm writing this letter. But I am very impatient, what could be the reason why we did not get a letter even today. How are you my little brother? Or did you hear about David? Write immediately. We are well. And I hope to hear that about you as well! How is Herman? I kiss you countless times with love. Next I will write again. Maria

1947/3/5 Marie to David (Book 8, 102)

3/5/47
Dear David!
We just got a letter from our little brother yesterday, where we read that you were sick. I hope that my lines will find you in the best of health. You had enough to deal with, but I hope that the dear God will help you and everything is going to be fine. It is very hard that we are so far away from each other and I can't go to visit. You just take care of yourself. We thought that there was something about you, since you were silent for so long. Otherwise we are well. Currently I can't write anything about myself. Also, Hermina probably wrote about everything already. I did not see the relatives for a long time, since I am busy working 6 days. I wish you the best of health and I kiss you with love. Take care of yourself and write. Maria

1947/3/5 Marie to Irving (Book 6, 9-10)

My dear brother Irving!
We received your letter yesterday, I was very happy. It makes me happy to know that thank God you are healthy. I'm just sorry to hear that poor David is sick and that was just enough for him. No one was allowed to visit yet. And you little brother dear, again, please take care of yourself and don't get overwhelmed with learning. I hope you will succeed. I'm writing to David right now. I somehow became such a bad writer that I don't even write to anyone. And I don't have time to visit relatives here either. I don't see anything new now. Now I close my brief lines. Otherwise, kissing you countless times with love, just be very careful wherever you go. Maria

1947/3/10 Hermine to Irving (Book 11, 243-245)

My dear little brother, Irving,
Today it's Sunday night and I got myself to write a few letters. I hope you are well and if it will work out, we will see you soon. Do not worry about how it will be, because when you come here you don't have to go to the relatives. You could sleep in a hotel also and I will try to find out if you could sleep at the Y.M.C.A. This way it would not cost a lot. When your plan works out, in other words when you will know when you come, then let me know and the room can be arranged. How are you little brother and Herman? I wrote a letter to David last week and I hope, that he will take care of himself and he feels better now. There is no news here. I like my job and at least it feels easier to work there. Mariska is not at home. She went with the boy this afternoon and I did not want to go anywhere. Berthuska came last week which it is possible that I already wrote to you. They live in the neighborhood, but it does not feel [right/good] to go over there often because they have guests all the time. Last night I was at Zseni and she would like to see you too already. I got a letter from Malvin yesterday and she wrote that she will go back to the Czech Republic for 3 months and Olga Leftkovits, Adolf bacsi's daughter, will send the tickets to her. As she wrote, it is out of the question

that she could come to America for a year. Write my little brother and give our best to the relatives and acquaintances. I kiss you with much love. Hermine

I am also sending my best to Mr. Herman and kiss him.

1947/3/21 Hermine and Irving to David (Book 9, 22-23)

3/21/1947

[from Hermine]

Dear David!

Although, I did not get a response to my letter yet, but I write anyway hoping that you are healthy. I will write about news that will surprise you - our brother Irving came to visit us - he arrived last Saturday and he will go back on Sunday. Today he is at Aunt Jenny, because he wanted to stay with her at least one night so he could meet her son as well. Believe me, that we were so happy to see him. Otherwise, we are well, and I hope you will write soon.

Today we got from a letter from Pest from Lipot's wife and she was wondering about you too. Lipot is not really healthy. He is in the hospital because he has pleurisy and did not get better completely. He wrote that his oldest daughter got married to the youngest Stark boy at Perbenyk. The oldest Stark boy, the dentist, who you also have known, married Sari Winkler, that is, Dezső Weisz's daughter from Lelesz. Bertha got a letter from Iren from Szatmar and she wants to have her come here. Besides this, nothing comes to my mind all of a sudden.

But, I will write to you again. I like my job very much and Irving was up there and saw what a nice office I work in. I only deal with the European cases and the office has a big department. I am in Foreign Service Accounting department. So, I will close this with this. I wish you good health and luck! I remain with love, Hermin

P.S. Write about how you yourself feel.

[from Irving]

New York

Dear Dave, until 120

Just returned and found Hermine's letter, so I want to add a few lines. Hope that you'll forgive for not writing you about my trip and also for not answering your letter. Here life is different, however, one of these days I'll get me a car and on my next vacation I'll go to see you. Well talk about it. O.K. now I would like to ask you to write me anyway, that's even though I'm late in answering, but you must remember that I'm thinking of you. Now wishing you good health and a Happy Pesah with best wishes and Love from us all. Your little brother, Irving

Herman is well, but lazy to write.

1947/3/25 Hermine and Marie to Irving and Herman (Book 11, 247-251)

3/25 - 47

[from Hermine]

My dear little brother, Irving,

I think about you a lot since you left from New York and I hope that everything is ok and you arrived luckily. How was your trip? I did not go to Jenny Frey, but I called her on the phone and Aunt Jenny also. They already forgave us for not going on Saturday and I didn't blame you - that is, I didn't [put the] blame [on] you for not going. Guess what little brother! I got a letter from Cleveland and Louis wrote that he will be in New York soon and that he is getting his documents arranged to go to Palestine. I did not realize that the paper's corner is missing. I would not have written on it if I would have known, and now I don't want to rewrite it. Also, last night Irving the neighbor came in and was wondering if you went home, because he would have come on Sunday, but he did not want to bother us. This way he took me to the movies. Too bad that you are not here because maybe tomorrow I will get two tickets from where I work to one of their movies. Oh! I remembered that despite my great desire, I did not take you to the movies. I wanted to, but I didn't give you the money and I don't want to offend you by sending it to you. I will write you more soon until then, take care of yourself and I will stay with love. I kiss you with love, your older sister, Hermina

Greetings to the relatives and to the acquaintances.

Dear Herman,

Do you know that I still did not buy the ink that would be good for the pen? And because of that, I am only writing a short letter. The pen set is beautiful and I really thank you very much! Even if you don't write, but still, I think, that you love me, if you spend that much money on me. So, you could write sometimes a few lines and believe me it does good for everyone. When it's getting warmer, come here for a few days and I know that you would like it and it does not cost a lot. I will write more next time. The pen is out of the ink. I kiss you with love, Hermine.

[from Marie]

3/26 - 47

Dear little brother Irving,

I just came to work and so I'm writing to you. We received your letter this morning, which I was very happy about. And since you left, I miss you so much. All the same as you say that if we hadn't finished we wouldn't have finished at all. But all in all, I'm sorry I couldn't even talk to you because there was always something. The couple of days have passed without being noticed. Otherwise, I'm happy to hear you were lucky to come home. And as you mentioned, you go to school early at 8 o'clock Oh! I remembered, that Hermina wrote this letter last night and we only got the letter this morning. If you would have seen Mrs. Cuglar, that even she misses you. Besides that my little brother, we will write about the Passover dishes next time because we forgot to tell about the cooking. Also the recipes that you will need for Passover. I kiss you again countless times with love. Maria

And forget about that letter that I mentioned to you which you would help me to write, since you have enough problems without it. But thank you little brother for it.

[The second letter from Marie to Irving is only a repetition about how much she misses him since he left. Wondering about his well being and school, health...etc]

1947/4/3 Undated Hermine to Irving (Book 10, 66-67)

[Date determined Hermine and Marie in NY, from mention of Passover the following day, Irv at school, Emil's letter mentioning a suit, Manci's letter]

My dear little brother Irving!

I have been trying to write to you for a few days and even now [I can] only write in a hurry at lunch time. I hope everything is fine by you! I am only worried about what you will do on Passover and what you will eat. So, I thought that I will [send] a few recipes to you. Maybe you will be able to make it for yourself. So, you need to make the potato hremzli, boil the potatoes with the skin and when it has cooled, peel and grate it, and stir in the eggs one at a time, so it will be soft. Salt must be added to it, and Passover flour [matzo meal]. Not too much, only so it will keep the potato together and when it's done, it needs to be fried in hot fat [oil] so it will be enough fat in the pan. It is best to fry it in a flat pan. You can cook meat soup and cook kneidlach [matzo balls] in it. You just have to make it in the same way as for baking, just put more Passover flour in it - so it will not fall apart. Potatoes with liver - so [you] don't starve - and write about everything. You recognized the milk dishes because there is only one pan and the tea spoon in in it. Otherwise me and Marcsa are well and we will write more shortly. Thank you to Herman for the pen and I wrote this letter with that already. Oh yes! The boy from the neighbor comes again and he was wondering about you, too. I'm sorry my little brother, but it is at night already and I am finishing writing at home. How is the studying? What have you decided? I already thought about you studying to be a doctor. It would take a long [time] and maybe it is hard for your eyes. What did they say about your coat? Or what did you say [about] where you bought it? I'm planning on buying a suit for myself and [for] Marcsa tomorrow. Tomorrow night we are officially going to Bertha's seder. I guess you will be officially [going] to Arthur's - Or not? I only called once to Aunt Jenny since then because somehow the time runs so fast at lunch time that I don't have time for anything. I'm sorry, but I still did not respond to Flora, but I am counting on it shortly. I wrote to Elsie in Cleveland. Yesterday I got a letter from Manci Klein and last week from Emil, but he asked me to send him fabric for a suit. There are a few pieces that I will send to him, but remnants. I would write to Herman too, but now it is late. I wish you a happy Passover to all of you with much love! Hermina

[On the Side] I'm sending greetings to the relatives too.

1947/4/3 Undated Marie to Irving (Book 8, 293) - before Passover

[dated by handwriting, ink, paper. It's possible that it could also be 1949/4/11]

My dear little brother Irving!

I'm sorry that I have to write so briefly, but I'm in a hurry to go to work. But I wanted to write to you too a couple of lines. I am well and I hope that my lines will find you in the best. First of all, I wish you a very nice Passover holiday to you. And take care of yourself. I think Hermine already wrote about everything. Now I will close my lines with wishing you everything good. And I kiss you countless times your forever faithful sibling. With love. Maria

1947/4/11 Marie and Hermine to Irving (Book 8, 104-108) Marie breaks up with boyfriend

4/11/47

My dear little brother Irving!

I don't know what to do with the fact that I have not heard from you until now, but I hope that my lines will find you in the best. I know my little brother that you are busy, but you have never done this before, that at least you would not write a word, except if there is a reason for it. I am very impatient already, since I am not a good writer as well. I am not waiting from you to write first. I write to you. Also, about David. Did you hear about him? How is he? We wrote a few letters to him and he did not write yet. I hope he is ok! I am getting ready to write to you for a few days already, but there is always something. Besides that, this week I looked for a job, since I left my old job on Saturday. Luckily, I have found another one on Wednesday. I will start on Monday. First of all, I hope I will like it. It is at a famous Jewish restaurant. 6 days of work for $35.00 and they give a kosher meal twice a day. It sounds good and I hope I will like it! Otherwise about me, I am well. And the boy, Irving, I don't know, if I mentioned it to you, but it has been a few weeks already since I gave up on him. I am home today, since I will only start work next week. And you my little brother! How is your studying? I hope that you got a proper grade! Write about everything my buddy. Or is it still hard to study? I can believe it. Now I wish you lots of good luck and good health. I kiss you countless times with love. Maria

[Hermine's letter is similar to Maria's except she mentioned that she will go on a date with the neighbor.]

1947/4/12 Hermine and Marie to David (Book 16, 16-17)

[from Marie]

Dear David!

I can't imagine why don't you write. I already wrote many letters to you and we did not get a response. As our little brother mentioned, you were sick. I hope you are feeling better since then! I am asking you to write immediately about how you are because I will wait for it. And I hope that my lines will find you in the best of health. We otherwise are well, there is no particular news. We did not get a letter from our little brother either, about which I am very impatient, but I think he is busy studying. Are you working? It is possible that you need to rest still. I hope that you will write immediately. Until then I wish you good health and take care of yourself. There is no news here. The weather is starting to get warm. The relatives are well, but I am very busy and I don't have time to visit them, except Bertha because we live close to her. If we don't go, then she comes over to us. They are wondering about you. Now I will close my lines and I wish you good health and lots of luck. And I kiss you from my heart with love. Take care of yourself and write, even if it's only a few lines. Maria

[from Hermine]

Dear David!

I can't imagine what could be the reason that we did not get from you nor from Irving any news. I hope you are well and will write a few lines. Believe me it is also hard for me to write because I don't practice it enough. The lady who we live with does not know English well and when we come home from work we are always with her. So, this way I am going backwards with the English language. She is very good to us and it is very hard to find an apartment. I don't want to look for a house. How did you spend Passover? It must have been hard for Irving + the others also. If God will help, then it would be the best if one of us would go home to deal with the apartment. That is, to sell the furniture because it is giving them too much work, and we don't miss it either. Today the weather is very nice and the sunlight feels good. Yes, I'm asking you to take care of yourself and write about everything. I wish you everything good and good health.

With much of love, Hermine

[The first letter, from Marie, has no new info]

[from Hermine]

My dear little brother, Irving,

I still did not get your letter that I can hardly wait for, but I hope that there is nothing wrong! God forbid! I also wrote to David and he did not respond yet. We are well and I went to the temple yesterday to say yizkor. I already thought about writing this for you, but still I always forget. We don't know anything about our dear father, but as they wrote, we know what is going on. I would like you to talk to the Rabbi and see what he says because we know how the situation is and maybe we should talk to the Rabbi. He might add to say kaddish since at least it would help because this way they are only just being forgotten. Lajos can be more trusted [to return] even more because he was younger. My Irving, it is very hard to even write about this, but it was on my mind so much. Write, if you find out something. Herman, you should write too. Don't be so bad. I will write shortly again. I already started to write today when the neighbor came in. Last night I had a date with him. He took me to the Rokxy and I saw a very good show - and he is always wondering about you too. I did not respond to the European letters, but maybe I will write to Ignác Klein about the property because whoever we sent the documents to, did not respond yet. Love to you both, Hermina

[Typewritten]

Dear Dave, until 120

I was very happy to receive those few lines and I should say that you should do that more often. Because I'm quiet, and not writing, you should not follow my example. First, you know that I'm always busy, as I'm going to school, and believe me not loafing around. I sometimes wish I could loaf a few days, but if I would, I would not get those checks coming every month. Well Dave, I want to thank you for your lines and I hope to write you more sometime after this quarter is over. Oh yes! I bought this typewriter. It writes well, only I will have to get used to it. Nothing new. Hermine has probably written you more, and take care of yourself till next time, Love, Irving

[Handwritten]

Saturday afternoon

Dear Dave, until 120

You know Dave, I forgot to enclose the letter from the young woman from Lelesz [Jana Fabianova] , so here it is in this letter and hope that you will forgive me for it. But there is always something so that one can't help to overlook things as such. Nothing new, but waiting to hear from you the best. Herman just came home from work and feels lazy as usual to write. Till next time. Love from your little brother, Irving

[from Marie]

Dear David!

I don't know since when I heard from you, but it has been a few days. We wrote to you since then many times and you did not respond to us even until today. How are you? Write about yourself immediately because you know very well, that we are impatient about you as well. How are you? Are you feeling better yourself? Take care of yourself and write the truth, how you are. I don't even understand how could somebody be such a lazy writer. How would you feel if I would not write to you about anything? Or maybe you want that? Besides that, are you feeling better? What do you do? About me, I am well. We just got a letter from Irving. Thank God he is well, but he studies hard. As he wrote it, there are many students in the school and they are trying to get rid of them. They find every mistake they make, so they can kick them out, but he currently is proceeding well. How's your leg? Write about everything and don't neglect it. We did not hear anything from Europe. But I will leave that too. And now take care of yourself and write immediately because you know well that I am impatient about you. I wish you good health and good luck. We kiss you countless times with love. Your sibling, Maria

[from Hermine]

Dear David!

It is useless to wait for your response to our letter. Nothing has come from you yet. I hope everything is ok and you are feeling well. We just got a letter from Irving today, and surely we did not know what to do with his silence. Since he went home he only wrote two letters to us, but thank God that he is well, only he is busy with the studying. As our little brother wrote, Herman has a great job. He went back to Arthur and it sounds great because he has no boss. If he is not entrusted to a supply room then he is the time keeper for 50 people. It sounds good and I hope he will like it. I am well and I still like my job. The weather is starting to become nicer. Bertha was over today to visit us, too. We see them often. The relatives are still wondering about you. I wrote a letter today to Emil from Helmec. He asked me to send new fabric for a suit, not a low-end one, because it could come handy to him. I wrote him that I unfortunately can't do that now. First of all, it would cost at least 18 dollars, if a low-end one is not good, I am sorry. Sometimes I send him a little money and I talked to Lajos' uncle to help him because he has nothing. So I will finish with this and write! I wish you good health with much love. Hermine

1947/5/1 Undated Marie to Irving (Book 8, 17-19)

[dated from phone strike and Hermine mentions that she was at Bertha's in the letter dated 5/4]

Dear brother Irving,
I'm sorry the week is gone and I didn't write for you, but I was busy this week. I hope my lines will find you the best. We are fine, and you, I think you must be studying hard. We got a letter from David last week and he is well. I am writing this letter again from work, so I know I'll send it today. No special news. Bertha was with us yesterday. Mannie is traveling and Hermine went there to sleep. Zseni left on Wednesday, but I didn't see her and she's already mad about it. The phone company is still on strike so we couldn't even call the aunt. Somehow I don't have time for anything. That is, I work for six days and after work I don't really want to go anywhere. Don't think Irvingkem, that maybe I'm going with a boy because I don't have time. All I can say is that I haven't been with them since you [illegible]. But let's leave this. And how are you with everything my dear little brother? I hope to hear the best from you. It has been raining here for three days. How are the relatives and Miss McNeil? They are definitely angry that I don't write. Unfortunately, I can't help it. Now take great care of yourself little brother. And don't forget to eat too. I know you're angry that I'm writing that to you. Now I wish you good luck and the best of health. I'm closing my lines now. Heartfelt greetings and kisses countless times with love. With love, your sister who will never forget you. Maria

1947/5/4 Hermine and Marie to David (Book 16, 1-2) image cropped left side

5/4 - 1947
[from Hermine]
Dear David!
We were very happy to get your letter because we did not know what to think since you did not write to us for so long. We did not get a letter even from Irving for a few weeks. We did not know what to think. We got a letter from Irving last week and he wrote how busy he is. Poor thing studies so hard, but let's hope that it is with success. About us, only that thank God we are well and we are always very busy - Mariska works 6 days, but the important thing is that it is good enough and she likes it. I was thinking that we have a few things, which if it would not be too small, I would send it to Miss P. [most likely Jana Fabianova]. I could not go to look around yet. If I could buy some nice pieces, so it will not cost a lot. I will try it on one Saturday. Send her address to us. Write about yourself, about how you are feeling and write a little more often. I like my job very much and I hope it will be that way after this too. It is possible that you would like it here also, but I don't know if you would know that. They say that once you have lived in California you would not be able to live here. [missing left side of letter]
I like it and if I would know that it would be easier... then I would like it better. But they have a job...because it is a kind of house...that needs to be cleaned, so I will finish with this and I will write again shortly. Now take care of yourself. I wish you good health I remain with love. Kisses, Hermine.

[from Marie]
Dear David,
We have received your kind letter and I am glad to hear that you are well thank God. We are also well. We got a letter from our younger brother and he is very busy. Otherwise, there is nothing special. How are you? Write about yourself. I saw Bertha yesterday and they are fine. Take care of yourself. I work six days and it

takes up all my time. I have been working in a Jewish restaurant for three weeks now as a cashier. Right now I love it and here I get so much more food. Now I want to kiss you in good health. Love, Maria

1947/5/4 Hermine to Irving (Book 11, 253-255)

My dear little brother, Irving!

I am responding late against my will to your letter that I could hardly wait for. How happy we were to hear about you, you can't even imagine. We got a letter from David also and thank God he is well, too. I'm glad to hear that you are doing well with the studies, and I hope that you will succeed with that even further. I would like to go to night school as well. Maybe a little study would help me, too. My writing is so slow because my pen is barely working on the paper. I don't know for what reason. I was at Bertha's last week and she showed your letter that you wrote to her. It was a very nicely written letter and always when they talk about my little brother, they can see the happiness on us. Last time I was there with Irving the neighbor, and he already asked if I want to go out with him in the afternoon. So, he comes to us very often. Last night I went to a temple with Marcsa to dance, Temple Emanuel on 5th Ave. This is a rich person's temple and we could see in the crowd the problem, that there were mostly young boys. I met two boys and they asked for my address. One of them was very elegant, believe it or not? He spoke a type of English that I could barely understand

...every word. It is possible that he is at least 30 years old. Well, we will see. He told me he will call me at work because he would like to meet me. Also I got a letter from Cleveland, from Louis. It's possible that he will come to New York on the weekend, but before he will come, he will write. This is how it goes. We still don't have anyone so one could say that we don't have to sit at home. Marcsa met someone also, but he is young. It has to be tried many times, until one can meet someone nice. We wanted to go to visit Aunt Jenny, but it started to rain and it's not worth it to go there that late. Besides that, everybody is well. Mannie's legs hurt and he was in bed, but because of the phone strike I can't call them yet. I bought a beautiful coat last week. It is very beautiful. It is a deep pink color. I will write more often. I bought post cards yesterday so I can write a few lines at least to you. I am glad that Herman changed his job. I hope he will like it! Take care of yourself and write. Give our greetings to Flora + the others, to Aunt Helen, and also to our acquaintances. Louis wrote from Cleveland that he was in Columbus about 2 weeks ago. He called you on Tuesday afternoon because he wanted to get to know you, but nobody was at home.

[on top] Mr. Kugler says hi.

[on side] I kiss you with love, Hermina

1947/5/9 Irving to Dave (Book 6, 287-288)

May 9 / 47
Columbus, Ohio

Dear Dave, until 120

Believe me Dave, I was very delighted to receive your letter and I only wish that I would get a letter a day from you. However, probably that is not possible especially in America. Somehow the people are always in a hurry and lazy to write and so, sometimes probably we feel that way. It's a conditioning, that's all. Well one thing is, we'll have to try our best as you said once, "life goes on so fast and we hardly hear from each of us" These words still stand out to me. Incidentally you mentioned this to Herman in one of your letters sometime ago. So today I repeat it back to you and please take out time and keep on writing me. Let me know about yourself more specifically, because I want to hear from you the best of everything. I have just written a letter to Hermina and Maria and they are well, however, they too slow down with their writing. So, now I want to say that I'm O'K, and still have more examinations, but in about three weeks the vacation will be here once again and I'm waiting for it to come. I don't know if I should go in summer school or get a good position if I can. What's your opinion of it? It's hard to decide on what to do or in what to specialize. Time will tell. Now I want to say that take care of yourself and if you can please drop me a line and write me about everything and about yourself. Best wishes to you from your little brother, Irving

The relatives are well and asked about you.

1947/5/10 Marie to Irving (Book 8, 122-124)

5/10/47

My dear brother Irving,

I'm sorry this week I haven't written to you, but time goes by so fast. I hope my letter will find you well. We are fine. I can imagine how busy you must be. About myself, there is not much to tell, everything is the same. I'm writing this letter from work. I have a minute, but as I see it, it will be very busy today. My dearest brother, how are you doing in school? I hope everything will work out for you. I can imagine how hard you are working. Just take care of yourself my little buddy. My dearest brother, if you have time to look for my white hat. If you think it is worth it, send it to me. I know it is too much trouble to mail it to me. It is up to you. Otherwise, what's new over there? Did you see the relatives? How are they? Here by Bertha, they are ok. We plan to visit our Aunt. I hope I have time. The weather looks nice, but it's cold. Yesterday I went to see a movie. The name is "Duel in the Moon" and when they will show it there it is worth seeing. It is very beautiful. I know you will like it. It is a very famous picture here. Maybe you have seen it already? My dearest brother, I'm closing now because I don't have more time. Wishing you all the best. Good luck and the best of health. Many kisses with my love always loving you, who never forgets about you. Always, forever remember you lovingly, Marie

Write my little dearest friend. With regards to whomever asks about me. Will write soon.

1947/5/10 Undated Hermine to Irving (Book 11, 276-276)

[dated by Louis not yet in NY, waiting for letters from Louis. Also, waiting for Irving's letter which she gets on 5/13]
[In English]

Dear brother Irving and Herman,

I know you were surprised to the long distance call but I was glad you were home. I know you are busy with school, but I am looking forward to your letter. About my problem I can't tell you much because everybody tells me something else - so I can see the best thing is to decide for myself. We'll see what kind of letters he'll write and what does he have to say to me. So when I hear from him I let you know. You see these things come pretty hard to both of us. For me to leave you and for him all the expenses. Don't worry about it yet because I am not going yet. We'll see how things can work out. Tell me all about yourself and also Herman should write too. Give our regards to relatives, Aunt Helen, and friends. Hope to write you sometime soon. Take care of yourself and let me hear your opinion. With all good wishes and love, Hermina

1947/5/12 David to Irving (Book 12, 167-169)

5-12-47
Dear little brother! Until 120!
I got your dear lines and I was very glad to hear that, thank God, you are well and that you are proceeding well with studying too. You asked me what to do, to stop or not. You know, in my opinion, it would be better if you would study. I believe that the government will still help you with studying, otherwise why don't you ask Arthur what to do? He knows better what you can do and what you can do with what you studied. Currently there is no news here at all. The weather is excellent. It is pretty nice summery weather here. You know nothing comes to my mind currently. Oh yes, you didn't even write about the bond. Considering the Miss's [postmaster's] letter. Why don't you write? Please send me the letter. I asked the girls to buy something for her and I will pay for it. How is Herman? Who does the cooking and the cleaning? You know if you don't keep the house kept up, you could get evicted, based on the law. I hope that Herman helps you with the cleaning! I also hope that he is not sleeping in a dirty bed like he used to do. Currently I don't even know what to write. Thank God I am well and I hope to hear the same from you too soon! Write about everything and you should know, that I am interested.

Currently, I'm writing this letter from work and in a hurry. It's possible that you won't be able to read it, that I'm in the hurry and my pen is not really good. There is nothing particular here, everything is the same. What do you do with your free time? Do you have many acquaintances already? You can definitely find a lot of acquaintances in school. Do you go to the B. Brith congregation? I belong to them also for about 3 years. The Jewish people don't stick together here as much as in other places. Sometimes I go to the temple and meet with a few acquaintances, that is all about it here. Currently I close my lines, I can't write anything else. Please write about everything. I will be in a hurry to write a response as soon as possible. Write about everything. You know well that I'm interested in everything, especially if you write about yourself. So, I'm asking you to write to me and I will write as well about everything. Ok? So, I'm closing my lines for today.

In a few days I will write again with more details. Until then, I kiss you with love, your forever faithful older brother, Dezső

P.S. I got a letter from the girls this week. Thank God they are well. Mariska has a new place [job]. I kiss you with love

1947/5/13 Hermine to Irving (Book 11, 257-260)

May 13 / 47

My dear little brother,

I wanted to respond to your dear letter immediately, but still it remained. I want you to know how happy you made me with your smartly written letter. It sounded like some big scientist to me, like a middle aged person who could have given that kind of enlightenment. Believe me, it was well put together and what's important is that you leave the decision up to me, the way I see that it's the best. Now the status of the situation is that I responded with a yes with the hope that everything is going to be fine. The important thing is, if God helps, it will be - and no need to be afraid of why I gave up on it. If we will understand each other - when he will come to New York, then we will talk about everything and if God will want it too, then it's worth to go with him anywhere. He is a good and gentle boy and I am not afraid that I can't be happy with him.

It's not about his beauty, but he is a good boy. He is counting on going to Columbus and absolutely will want to visit you. He wrote that he knows well that I talked a lot to you about him and this way it will be hard to stand up for himself. But he could say as much, that he will try to be good. I got a letter from Flora as well and she wrote very smartly - I want to respond as soon as I know something for sure. I got a very nice and smartly written letter from Louis and I want to respond to him too today. I wrote to David also and I know he will be mad about my decision, but why did he leave if he loves his siblings? I will write more elaborately later, now I will finish with this. I will write with more details. I love your letter and I will keep it - whatever will come out of this case - but it's worth it and I am very proud of my little brother. Greetings to Herman, Flora + the others. How's Aunt Helen? Walters + the others, Miss McNeill. You never write about Mrs. Hassen? Write, Ok? Until then, I kiss you with love. Hermina

Greetings from Kugler and Bertha + the others also.

[The second letter has no new info…]

Dear little brother Irving,

I have this letter ready as of Sunday but today I wanted to write to you more. Last night Bertha came over. I answered that I will finish more with my writing for you. We are fine. Today is a beautiful day. I hope you are okay. We were happy for the special delivery letter we received on Sunday. Kisses to both of you and to the relatives, Hermina

1947/5/13 Marie and Hermine to Irving (Book 8, 130-136)

5/13/47

[from Marie]

Dearest brother Irving,

I'm sorry that I'm not writing more often. If I write today, Hermine wants to write, therefore we delay the letter and it is late. Now I'm trying to mail it now. We are ok. We received your letter Sunday. We were all so happy that we wanted to read it all at once. We were very happy that you are ok, thank God. Herman finally paid up for the refrigerator. Otherwise, what's new over there? I can imagine how busy you are. Just take care of yourself. As you mentioned about your vacation, Irving dear, it is a big problem. It is true that going to work is not enough! And just for any job, it is not worth it. If you can get a good job that is different, or if you are studying, that is a bigger, more difficult job. You need some time off, but that my dearest brother, you know what's best. I wish I could see you soon. Just be very careful. I'm wishing you the very best. Good luck and good health. Many kisses, love forever, your sister forever, Love, Maria

May 13 / 47

[from Hermine]

My dearest brother Irving!

I promised that I will write to you tonight and I want to keep my word. I'm sorry that I have become such a lazy writer. Believe me, I'm thinking of you all the time. Here, there's nothing new. The weather was very hot today. Maybe we are not used to it. It makes me happy that you are ok. We received a letter from David last week. He is also ok. I know how busy you must be with studying. I wish I could give you information. It would be nice to go to summer school, but you need to think about how hard it is without even a vacation. When did speak to Yankin? Just to work for 2 months is not worth it because it won't help too much. Studying instead is more worthwhile. It is also time to decide what you really want to do, or study further. To be a doctor would be good. Even if everything works out, even then it is very hard work. Believe me, I know how hard they are working, especially when young, day and night 24 hours a day have to be ready to go somewhere. I didn't speak to Mannie about school. We don't see them so often because they always have company. When Bertha is alone then she comes to visit us on Saturday. She was here on the 11th. She also comes over in the evening. I will write to Helmec, and to Lipot's family. I would like to write to Sarolta's daughter also. Believe me my dearest brother, I neglected my writing. I received a letter from Lillien from Columbus. She will come here to NY for a vacation. She plans to visit me. Also, I spoke with Aunt Jenny last week. She mentioned that she heard from you and she will write you. Until then, she sends her regards. How is Herman? Is he still so lazy to write? It is a shame. I did not write to Flora. I started a few times, but it's not easy to write, especially in English, so I stopped many times. Please give them my regards, and to Aunt Helen, too. I wrote to the neighbors a long time ago, but they never answered. Also to Mrs. Hawkins. Maybe they will call you. Give my best wishes to them. She also wrote to me some time ago. I do not have patience to correspond with friends or otherwise. If they ask about me, give my best wishes. You know what to say. How is Arthur and his family? For them, remind them about us also. I will write soon to you. Until then, many kisses to you and Herman. Hermine

1947/5/13 Marie to Irving (Book 8, 125-127)

My dear little brother,
I'm sorry that I kept you waiting with my letter. I am well and I hope my lines will find you in the best [of health]. And how will you spend your vacation? Have you been anywhere or do you work? My little brother I could talk to you better in person, but I will try it in letter. I know my little brother that you are the best, like gold, and you try to understand everybody. As you wrote in your letter, Hermine is absolutely right. I said the same thing, but why is it so hard for others to understand this? But my Irving, you try to understand everybody, even if it's too hard. I can understand very well and I think the same way. I don't know anything particular about myself, everything is the same. But now I will get to the point about Hermine. She got a letter from Louis this week and I think that probably she will go with him, unless she will change her word. To tell you the truth, I don't know what to say to you, my little brother. We went to visit a family last week, Louis' mother's best girlfriend. They live here and a few years ago they lived in Palestine and they are getting ready to go back again. They love it so much there and their kids live there even today.

They came from Hungary also. They know Louis very well and his mother, too. They say that with a boy like Louis you can go anywhere gladly because he knows how to find a livelihood, because he is a certified dentist and on top of that, he is a very fine boy. He considers everything well. Besides that, they say he could get married for money. Any girl would marry him gladly. But as we can see, it is God's will. And we will hope that everything will turn out for the best. There are different types of people and it is easy to talk. I only know that Hermine loves him and she will not listen to anyone. Louis just wrote that he is planning on visiting you. Also, he will come to New York. He writes very nicely and he is a very fine boy. As he wrote that it is very hard for him, that he has to take Hermine with him from me because he knows how hard this is to all of us. And I am asking you my little brother to take care of yourself and don't be sad. Don't work too hard. How did your exam go? Yes, we got a letter from David and if you could see how he writes and no matter what, he says she should not go. Although, I am just writing a response to that and maybe he will be angry at me because he does not want anybody [for her]. Nobody is good enough for him. Take care of yourself my little brother. I wish you lots of luck and the best of health! With lots of love and all the best. Love, Maria

1947/5/15 Undated Hermine and Marie to David (Book 9, 4-5)

[Louis will call before he comes to visit]

[from Marie]
Dear David!

I think you are angry, but still I am in a hurry to write to you. I hope that my lines will find you in the best [of everything]. We are well. There is no news currently. Everything is the same. And I will mention one more time, that nothing goes the way we want it. You should know this on your own. We did not even get mail from our little brother either. I hope he is ok. As always, he must be fine. He must be busy. Poor thing, he studies so hard. But I hope that with God's help everything is going to work out for him! And what are you doing? Do you still work a lot? I work more than I should also, but this is how it goes. I started this letter at work, but I will finish it at home and Hermine wants to write, too. She just went to Jenny Frey and I don't know when she will be home. The relatives here are well, but I don't get together with them much since I am very busy, and when I could go then they are busy. Now take care of yourself and write, don't be such a lazy writer. Greetings from my heart and I kiss you with love. Your sibling, Maria

[from Hermine]
Dear David!
It is useless to wait for your letter, we can't hear anything from you. I hope you are healthy! We are thank God well. We are getting ready for the holidays and we only went for shopping today because tomorrow the stores will be closed. However, Mariska will work tomorrow, too, that is she works 6 days a week. I have a very good job in an office, where there are only four of us girls. I always worked at a place where there were 40 people working. My salary is not so bad, but I could have gotten 43 dollars at another place, but I could not stay there for more than a week, because there was a big draft. This is how it goes. There is always something. Other than that, everything is fine. How are you? Why don't you write? Maybe you are mad at me? I understand and I'm asking you not to be worried because I will not rush and you can trust me on this. If God ordered it, then let's hope that everything will be good. It is possible that Louis will not want to go to Palestine. Currently I don't know anything because he is planning on coming here. It is possible that he will come for the weekend or for next week. He wanted to call if he is coming, but from this house I gave the lady's daughter's number but it has been two days since they went away from home. So, now I don't know if he will come. Don't be mad. Don't be sad, but write! I kiss you with lots of love! Hermina

1947/5/27 Marie and Hermine to Irving (Book 8, 138-141)

[from Marie]
My dear little brother, Irving,
I'm sorry that I neglected writing. The reason was that I was waiting until we know something certain to write. But as you can see, it is still uncertain. First of all, we are well. Hermine's boyfriend was here from Cleveland and now he is talking seriously. I will leave it to Hermine to write to you about him. He wants to go to Palestine in my opinion, he wants to go. If she wants to go that is up to her. Currently

...there is another boy who met me, but there is always something. That is why it's hard to make a decision. She will write more elaborately about him to you my little brother. Otherwise about me nothing in particular. I am very busy as always. But my buddy, don't think about that boy!! And how are you? Do you study hard? Did you make a decision about what you want to do? Take care of yourself. Yes, my dear little brother we got a letter from Manci Klein from Lelesz. She wrote [asking] why did we pass the case over to that person, when he was the [one] appointed. We regretted even that small benefit from him. And everything has to be accounted for anyway and he can't even take his own house back until they get the statement, so the person truly does not exist who is the real owner. But I will leave that too, but it is very painful for him, since his sibling [Etelka] brought money [as her dowry] to us and at least he could have that much profit from it. And this way we gave it to strangers. But I will leave this too. Now I will ask you to take care of yourself and don't be sad. Everything is going to turn out for the better, we hope. I wish you lots of good luck and good health! I hope you had a nice Shavuot! What did you do? Did you go anywhere? Now my dear Irving, take care of yourself and write! I kiss you countless times forever. Your faithful sibling, who will never forget. Greetings to everyone who is wondering about me. Love Maria

[from Hermine]
My beloved little brother!
Now I will write briefly again. I will write with more details about everything tonight. I hope both of you are well! Thank God I am well also. Last week Louis was here, like you also wrote it, and his intentions are very serious because he wants to get married and go to Palestine in the fall. I did not give a response and he has to get it by Jun 15th at least. I will write with more details and now I kiss you, Herman and the relatives. Hermina

5.27.47

Dear little brother! Until 120

Today only a few lines. Last week I told you I will write again. I know it's a little late, but I'm still writing. Last week, one of my neighbors who went to Columbus, Ohio told me that she is connected in Columbus. She used to work there. I asked her to look you up or call you and give you the message and she will tell how you are looking (want a package, she has a business). Sometimes I buy some clothes from them. Maybe she will tell you some stories. She will tell you whatever you want to hear (silly things) and it is up to you what to believe or not. I just asked her to call you on the telephone and give my regards. At this time, nothing new. Last week, I went to [unclear]

Oh yes, I told her she should tell you the situation, what's happening, and if you like it here then you can come here and go to the university here. At this time, nothing new. Everything is the same. With all my love and best wishes, your brother, Dave.

Today I wrote to the girls also. Herman, how are you? Why don't you write. Best wishes. As above

5/30 - 1947

My dear little brother Irving,

I promised that I will write, so now finally I sat down so I can write about everything in detail. Although, it is not easy to write about everything. So, the thing is this, I was so busy in the past and with a big problem so I did not have a head for the writing. As you wrote, Louis came to visit me. Of course, [it was] a few days after he arrived. I don't know what was his reason, because he wants to know the truth, he could have come in person to find out, if we are not here then we went somewhere. But many times it is better just to leave things alone and not to push it. So the thing is this. He is going to Palestine and he came to find out from me if I want to go with him, like he already mentioned that to me. I did not give him an answer and I presented to him that he did not treat me the way I deserved and because of that I thought that he already forgot about the whole thing. Of course, he responded that he was not sure about what he wants and after a lot of thinking he came to the conclusion that if I want him, then I should give him an answer as soon as possible and we put the date down to Jun. 15th, when I will make a decision with an answer. And until this day I still don't know what it's going to be, because he has a good idea, but it is not easy for him even if he would get married. The woman should have a couple of thousand dollars under her name, that he would arrange also, as well as the traveling expenses. The government pays for his travel, his school in Palestine too. And his plan is that he could get out there because he would have a much better future there.

He only takes on the school, so he can look around in the meantime to see what would be the best for him. His brother is going with him. He is also a dentist. He thinks he can get into the Hadassah Hospital, where until now there is no dentist yet. He has a plan that he could provide a good livelihood, but it is about the decision that needs to be made. It is either a yes or just to give up on the whole thing. I think it's very hard to decide because I like him, even if he did not treat me the way another man would have done, since he did not write to me normally. Other girls would not care about that as long as she gets what she wants. So, the time is short and I have to give an answer. Many find it ridiculous. Many have every desire to go there. I wish I could think and make a decision! But what, I don't know. To leave Maria and all of you would be hard.

...and it is hard because until now I did not have anybody who I had a hard time to make a serious decision about. Although, he knows that I am older than he is by two years, but the difference is really 5 years. My little brother, what do you say? Write it to me. He said that if we would like it, we could also go. He is an American citizen. So, if he would not like it, he could come back anytime. I also know that the start would not be easy with him, but I think the future with him would be easier. No matter that he is younger, but maybe even if he would know that, it would not matter to him. [In English] Well, dear Irving! What could you tell me to make my decision easier? He would leave with the boat the 1st of October to Palestine and that means if I let him know he will plan further and get papers ready. That means business and I don't have a head to use it. So what do you think about it?

[In Hungarian] So, it could be a little more confusing adding to all this, that Louis' [Schwartz] uncle from Youngstown introduced a Hungarian man to me a few weeks ago, and ever since then he wants to spend every Saturday afternoon, night and Sunday with me. He did not go away for the weekend because he did not want to leave me here. Although the man is a very sensitive and intelligent gentlemen. He is a very good boy and he thinks seriously that with time, I will marry him. But the thing is that he is 43 years old, and besides that, his eyes are very weak, since even he said that he wears many kinds of glasses and adding to that he has sinusitis - it means, that in case he would move to a different area maybe it would go away. But that maybe is silly. I am just afraid to get into it, although a woman who he likes will have a good life. He is a foreman in a paper factory where they make papers for store window decorating and for package wrapping. He makes 80 dollars a week. So he is very honest and told me everything, although he only knows me for few weeks. I told him that between me and Louis the thing is that I can't make a decision whether I should leave the country or my siblings. I asked him not to come steady because I would not want to hurt him. Otherwise I don't know it yet because I don't really know him yet. He is willing to spend his free time with me hoping that he will succeed. He said he will be so good to me, even if I don't want him, I must love him. Don't laugh! But the neighbor just got so envious because I am very busy these days when he would want to take me out. [In English] That is that. A person can get crazy with all that business. So now my little brother, I am looking forward to hear your opinion. Tell me about yourself and Herman. Want to write to David, too. I'll write again. Received a letter from Louis. Will write to Flora too. Please write me soon. Love, Hermina

1947/6/1 Hermine to Irving (Book 11, 268-269) Goldblatt's ultimatum to marry

New York 6/1 - 1947
Dear David,
I received your letter and was really happy to hear from you. I was thinking of writing you a big, long letter to tell you about my problem. Something I don't know how would be the best to solve it. I wrote to you many times about the Goldblatt boy from Cleveland, the dentist. Well he was here again and he wants to get married and go to Palestine. I have to give him an answer by [this] month the 15th. I asked him to stay but he wouldn't and he wouldn't be happy anyway because he made up his mind and he almost [has] his papers ready. So he wants to get my answer. If I go, he has to plan further. It isn't as easy for him either. If he gets married he has to have or the woman has to have about 3,000 dollars on her name. So if something happens, there would be no help needed from the English government. He has some good ideas about Palestine and I think he can work it through, too. He goes as a student and the government pays his traveling expenses and 4 years [of] school. His brother is going too and already has a job there. He could get into Hadassah hospital because they don't have a dentist yet. So many other things that I just can't write it down, but in time he would have a chance to see. If he doesn't like it there, he can always come back. So the time is here now and is very short too. I know your answer already, but don't just answer, but think a little and figure it out so - because it is serious. I'm working all right. I can always have a job it is true. Just last week the [company] laid me off - I know why too. Because I became a member of the union and they found out that I get as much money as the girls working there 2 or 3 years. Don't worry, but I have two jobs for tomorrow. I don't know which one I'll take yet. The only thing is that it would be nicer to have it a little easier. Years go by and it is true I met so many boys already, but it didn't work. A few weeks ago I met somebody who is 43 years old. The Youngstowner Louis' uncle introduced him to me. He is a very intelligent man and means it, too. He told me already about his plans but I can't think of that. Has a nice job - makes 80 dollars a week. He could make a nice living and looks like a real American gentleman. He is a different type altogether. He enjoys operas and concerts. From a nice family that's also Hungarian. He is the nicest I met - but his eyes are pretty bad. I mean if he tells the truth. So he told me how many sets of glasses he has. He is very good and believe me any American girl would want to have somebody like him. But do I want to start out like that? I just tell you this to get the idea that it is not as easy as we think. As I am writing you this, Maria and Mrs. Kugler are talking here and maybe I don't write the way I like to. This man is coming every day this weekend and [I] didn't go away because of that. I told him about Louis that he wants to go to Palestine. So please answer me soon. I don't know exactly what my answer is, but I know we could get along - Louis and I. I want to hear what Irving has to say and you, too. Tell me about yourself and let me hear from you. Love, Hermina

1947/6/3 Marie to Irving (Book 8, 143-147)

6/3/47

My dear little brother,

I wish we could have talked more on the phone, but the time goes by so fast, one doesn't even realize. As you can see, I'll try to finish it in letter. First of all, my little brother (about Hermina) you know she has a big problem and she can be understood. First of all, she knows Louis as much as it's possible. But as it appears, it took Louis a long time to make a decision, since he did not know Hermine well either. But now that he was here, he decided that he loves Hermine also and if she would go to Palestine with him, then he would get married. It is very hard to give the answer to that, since Hermine loves him. And that one is very hard because she would leave us here and she knows that it is not so easy to leave us. She does not know what to do yet. Louis would get married now only on the condition that she is going with him to Palestine. And she loves him so much, that she can't give up on him. First, it is very hard to find somebody else like him. We have been like this for awhile and I can see how everything is. I myself don't know how it would be the best my little brother. It is true that currently it is not that easy there since you also know what is going on, but let's hope that everything is going to turn out to be better. And if she will give up on Louis now, then it is possible that she will be resentful always. And you know little brother, the relatives here can see that she loves him and so they say that she should go. Since both of them are residents in America, if they want to come back, then they can come back anytime. Now he says that he goes to study in Palestine and the government will pay for his expenses and he will get 100.00 "lárt" [lirot] a month for the tuition. If Hermine will go with him he has to have $3000 under his wife's name and he has to pay for her expenses as well. He will do that, which means something, since he will not get married only out of pity. But now the question is, will there always be someone who will invent something? Somebody just said last night, that perhaps he does not go to study, since it is not true that the government will pay 100 lárt [lirot] so he can study in a foreign land. Plus he is a dentist. They are scaring her so she would not go. Besides that, my little Irving, you know if it's true, he can go to school for four years. And what do you think about that?

My dear little brother, do you think he is lying?

I can't believe that he is not telling the truth, since he has no reason for that. Besides, nothing matters if they love each other and as it seems one can't know what would be the best. I can only say that the sadder she is, the harder it gets. I will leave this too. And how are you my buddy? How did the exam go? I hope to hear the best from you! I can imagine how hard you studied. You know, we called you on the phone because we could not wait any longer [to know] what you say about that because if you will say that (it is alright, Hermine), then everything will be easier. Since the people here are just talking and they don't think about it. They think and hope, that the dear God will help and everything will turn out for the best. Besides that, I can't say anything particular about me. Since you were here too my buddy, I could say that I did not go anywhere, not even to the relatives. First of all, I am very busy since I leave at 7 in the morning from home and I get home at night after 6, six days a week, so I don't want to go anywhere.

My opinion about Hermine is, that if she truly loves him, as I can see it, then it's best if she leaves with him. Otherwise, it will always be on her mind. You don't have a problem, now you will have more. I'm sorry my little brother that I can't help you, but believe me, that I think about you a lot, and I hope that the dear God will help you with everything. I know that you are wondering if I have a boyfriend. I note that I don't have one yet. I am not really in a hurry and I don't even mind it yet. At least I have time to sleep and rest, even if not too much. Otherwise, what's new over there? I started to write this letter from work, but I will finish it at home. For now, I wrote enough already. Yes, last week we got a letter from David and he is well and he said that he will write to you too. Now take care of yourself and don't be worried. We hope that God is good and will help. Also, I wish you good luck and the best of health. I kiss you countless times with much love. Your forever faithful sibling, who will never forget. Love, Maria

Greetings to all the relatives and acquaintances.

Is Herman still as lonely as [he was a] long time ago?

1947/6/11 Hermine to David (Book 11, 271-272) to Palestine with Louis

New York 6/11 - 1947

Dear David!

I am just now responding to your letter, although I wanted to write immediately. It's true, as far as your letter is concerned, you completely misunderstood the whole thing. I understand, and partially you are right, that I should not go to Palestine to leave the siblings here, especially Marcsa. But as far as Louis [Goldblatt] is concerned, it is a different situation. First of all, he is from a very fine, nice Jewish family, and young - of course, not really the way you think. He is 28 years old or could be 29 also - I don't know for sure. Although, he is younger than I am, you know by two years - So next time he will come, I will have a chance and will tell him. But it does not matter for him - because the year [difference] would only matter if I would look like it. Also, he could [bring an additional] 3 thousand dollars with him [if he were] to write it under the woman's name.- in other words, if I would go then he knows that I don't have money and this way he should have it. Although, if others would have the same skill as he does, they would know how to furnish everything here, too. But he has different plans. I thought about what you wrote about going to a foreign place with him and then he would leave me there. Believe me, if it really comes to it that I will go with him, I don't need to worry about things like that. I can say this much, that it is too bad he does not want to stay, but I think that he would even deserve it for me to go with him to Palestine. As much as I know him - I'm not afraid of the bad and if he is planning on coming here, then we can talk about everything in more detail. I can say this much, that as many...

..men that I have met in a week, I don't even want to spend time with them again. All kinds and ordinary people. Don't think I just went out with anyone. Of course, many American girls never have a chance to meet someone. Wherever I went everybody was trying to introduce somebody to me. But here is Marcsa and for her it goes totally differently, even though she is a pretty girl and she looks good now. So, all I am trying to write is that if everything will go well, I will go with him to Palestine, and then I will write to you in detail. But right now I don't know yet even though I responded with a yes. I think I would not be able to find more of that kind, because he would not even look at me. The important thing is that we should understand each other and only be happy.

He's an American citizen and if he does not like it he could come back anytime. Besides that, he gets 100 dollars a month if he goes to school, and even more if he gets married. This way, in the worst case scenario, he would go to school for 1 or 2 years. It will not be like in America. Well here too, if I don't work seven days a week, what am I going to live from? If I go with him I can be happy forever, something I can't find here and I can't throw it away. Don't say I am in love with him because I like him, but I can see the difference and he belongs in our family. If God will help, everything will work out, and everything will succeed, then Marcsa and the boys can come too. What do I have in America besides my siblings that I can feel sorry for? Flora + the others said also, that if I like him then I should go with him - because I wrote that I don't know what to do. Our Ignác wrote a very smart letter, like a middle aged educated man would have given me enlightenment - I wish you could read how intelligently he wrote. I will write again. With lots of love. I kiss you, Hermina

1947/6/11 Marie to David (Book 8, 149-152) about Hermine to Palestine

6/11/47
Dear David!
I know you are surprised that I did not write until now to you. We got your letter last week and as I can see, you don't understand the situation about Hermine. We are well and I hope that my line will find you in the best. And now I will start with the case. First of all, as you write it, that Hermine should not go to Palestine and that she should leave the other boy. I already know that it's true, but have you thought of that this could go on forever and they always end up at the same thing? I know that you know women, and you want us to have the best. This is a fact and real and it would be great. But unfortunately it is easier said than done. Don't forget that we are not children anymore, and if you are afraid from everybody and find excuses, then it will never end. Now we don't make decisions so easily. Do you think a rich young boy is only waiting for us? We are not enough for them. They can buy girls for themselves, whatever they want, and with money on top of that. And in America, it is only by luck and the way the dear God orders it. I could write more about that. For example, I'm almost 30 years old and I would be ashamed if somebody would know that I have been here in America for 7 years, and I did not have a date. It is nothing for you, but believe me, it does not feel good to me.

And a person does not live forever and needs to have some fun, too. Although, it is true that just the opposite comes true and that can't be helped, since when one thinks that it is the best, one could be disappointed too fast. I came to New York. I thought everything is going to be different. Maybe I will have more luck. Although, first we went for dancing to get to know boys and in the meantime I wrote already to you about this, a few months ago, that I met with an older guy. That happened and he wanted to get married and I thought this case through, before I left him and this way I saw it better how I was with him. This is how it was. That has been a few months already. I had my first date with him. And since then nobody else. I live with myself like in Columbus. I went dancing since then many times. I came home because not even a dog looked at me, because I don't go after the boys and they don't notice me. Now first of all, I am elegant and if I am alright, that way everybody can see that I look good. I work in a Jewish restaurant. I already wrote about it, because I think there are better people who come there and everybody can see in me who I really am. This way everybody is complementing me, but I still don't have any luck. And this is the way it is. I don't write this to complain, only for you to see what life is here and everywhere else. And now I will get to Hermine.

She met many of them. Yes all kinds, poor, rich, young, old and also it's been three years since she met Louis from Cleveland. Since then they corresponded in letters, even if not too often, but they kept their friendship. First of all, he is an licensed dentist when he was overseas. He was the only dentist in the hospital and he must be good. Besides that, Hermine knows his family. It is a very fine family. They only have two children [boys] and both of them are dentists. And as for Louis, he is a very fine boy. He is not a nobody and he thinks a lot about Judaism and he does not work on Saturday. This is why he wants to go to Palestine, because he knows he can keep all that there. He is a very serious boy. He is very considerate about his life. So, if he takes Hermine with him, I believe he knows and understands what that means for us. And adding to that I will tell you one more thing, that I know will surprise you. The fact that Hermine loves him also, and whatever she does when she has a date, she always thinks about him and cannot give up on him. She does not leave us here easily, but still thinking it through, that is the only solution because if Hermine does not go with him to Palestine, then she would not get married and then Hermine will never forgive this to herself.

...and if somebody loves someone as much and gets married to him, she will go with him wherever he goes because she can't live with her siblings forever. I know you are mad at me because I write that way, but I hope you will try to understand me. It is just as hard for us to decide about her leaving, since we know it very well what is going on over there. But besides all this, he is American born and a citizen. In case he will not like it there, then they can come back anytime. And it is better if you are not being so sad about this because you can't help this. For example, there is a family here who we met through Louis and we were visiting there. The woman is Louis' mother's long time friend. They have known each other for a long time and they are also from Hungary. They said that they lived in Palestine for years and their kids are still living there and they are planning on going back. They also said that Louis is very smart and he knows what he is doing. To go with a boy like Louis she does not have to be afraid wherever she goes with him. They will find a good livelihood everywhere with him. As far as the money is concerned, he knows it well that Hermine does not have any, especially 3000 dollars. He could get married with his money with any girl. Any girl would get married to him happily, if she would not go to Palestine. Now don't be sad. God is good and will help everybody. Take care of yourself. Write! Kisses with love, Maria

1947/6/15 Irving to Dave (Book 6, 299-300) - Hermine said yes to Louis

June 15, 1947
Columbus 5, Ohio

Dear Dave, until 120
Sorry to wait to answer your letter, but in a way I wanted to get you a full report about that California girl, which was supposed to call me and tell me something about you and about California. However, when she was in Columbus she called me, but I was just before the examination and I couldn't go and meet her. She mentioned something about some fishing trip and she said that when she comes back to Columbus at the weekend she would call me and will tell me all about it. But sorry to say I waited for that phone call, but never came. I tried to find out if she returned, but I didn't know her name and through her room number I was not able to locate her. So that's that. And as you see this was one of the reasons why I'm a little late in answering your letter. Now I want to say that the exam came out fine and hope to continue good work. During the vacation I worked a few days, and in a few days, that is, on Tuesday school starts again and will be busy for a couple months. You know I'm ready to major in something, but what, I'm not sure, well maybe I'll know it one day. As yet I just consider to get a better knowledge about the world in which we live in. Since I don't have any good air mail paper, I'll close this time but will write you real soon. Hoping that you are well, and drop me a line when you get a chance. Oh yes, by now you probably know about Hermine, she answered to Louis with yes. That is, Louis asked her to marry him and she said yes. So wishing them lots of luck and happiness. How do you stand? Let me hear from you, my best wishes to you and if that girl went back you may tell her that I was waiting for her call. Now, remain with love, your little brother, Irving

Herman is as he was, too lazy to write to you

1947/6/18 Hermine to Irving (Book 11, 274-275)

New York 6/18 - 47

My beloved little brother,

Tonight I'm already writing the third letter. So because of that, I am writing in a hurry again. I have neglected the correspondence, so this way I just responded tonight to Flora to her letter, too. Today I got a letter from Louis and his mother, and they are both writing very nicely. It looks like David is mad at me because I wrote that if everything goes well, then I will go to Palestine. He is planning on coming here soon and then I will know more. If I will know something, then I will write to you. Until then, write to me about everything, and about yourself especially because I am interested. What's going on with school? What did you decide with the studying? How is Herman? Give my best to the acquaintances and to the neighbors. Write in detail. I kiss you with love. Hermina

1947/6/18 Marie and Hermine to Irving (Book 8, 154-160)

6/18/47

[First letter from Marie does not have anything new, only about Hermine's situation with Louis and other repetitions of Irving's study and well being.]

My dear little brother Irving,

It's useless to wait for mail from you or from David. I guess, that you are busy with studying - but then why doesn't David write? I guess he did not like my letter to him and he'd rather not respond because of that. The thing is that when I wrote to you about Louis, I wrote to him too. In his response, he did not even want to hear about it - therefore, he has found out about my opinion and he did not like it. Tonight I went to Berthuska and her husband bought a car and she did the exam just now, but she doesn't know if they will give her the license. Otherwise we are well and currently I don't know anything special. I got a letter from Cleveland and Louis is planning on coming here soon. It is possible that he already has been by you since then - If yes, then write about it! Ok? How is Herman? Do you know that it has been a year already on June 6th that I came to New York. Time flies so quickly. We were at Aunt Jenny on Sunday afternoon and they are well. The little JoAnn is well and very cute and she was wondering about you. Jenny Frey is going to Florida with her husband for at least 4 weeks. How are you my little brother? What did you decide about school? I wrote to Flora, but when I write to her I am always in a hurry and I don't have a lot of patience to write and it is not the best this way. If I want it to be correct, it would take an entire night to write a good English letter. Now I will continue with a pencil, it hardly works from the finger and I will take it up there where they are making it and I will show it to them - what could be the reason. Forgive me little brother that I am always writing so messy. Write about everything and I kiss you until then with much of love. Hermina

How is Herman and Aunt Jenny - I am getting ready to write to her too.
Write, kisses.

[The last letter, also from Marie, is only a repetition.]

1947/6/21 Jana Fabianova Postmaster to David, Irving and Herman (Book 14, 82)

21.VI.1947

Dear Dezső, Ignacz and Herman!

It is making me feel really bad, that neither one of you responded to my long letter, that I wrote on March 9th. I sent them both with airmail, one to Ignác here, the other one to Long Beach to Dezső's address. I was expecting a response from both of you for Easter. "Perche non scrivere Lei "? [Italian - Why don't you write?] Unruly bad boys!!

I'm worried for Dezsert [Dezső] very much because he is sick. That is making me uneasy because I hope that he isn't. It's a joy when one hears good news. Write to me gladly, both of you. I'm waiting for it impatiently. I'm sending greetings to the girls too and I wish you all the best. With love, Jankica

Jane Fabianova

[Left side note] post madnizikre Hanusta C.S.R. [Czechoslovak Soviet Republic]
ohr. Rim. Sobota
[Right side note:] Ignác promised that he will send a picture and it did not come either.

1947/7/5 Irving to David (Book 16, 14)

July 5, 1947
Columbus

Dear Dave, Until 120
Hoping that you are well and in the best of health. It has been quite sometime since I have heard from you
and also as I have received letter from New York, Hermine and Marie write the same thing. They are waiting
to hear from you. So, how about it? Please let me know how you are and if you're very busy with your work,
well, even then drop me a card or anything!
Thanks very much and hoping to hear from you real soon. I'm O.K. and studying. Herman is OK too. Arthur
and family are in Canada. So this is all for this time, Best wishes and love from your little brother, Irving

1947/7/8 Hermine to Irving (Book 18, 270-274, 278-279)

7/8 - 1947
Dearest brother Irving,
We were very happy to hear from you! It's Sunday about 9 o'clock. We still haven't heard anything from
Dave yet. I hope he is ok. Thank God, we are ok. The holiday was ok. I was by myself because Maria was
working Friday and Saturday. Jennie Frey wanted me to come to their home. I didn't go because if Maria
comes home at night she would be all alone. Maybe in a few days Louis will come to visit you, too. Maybe
he was there already. At this time I can't say too much about it. Bertha received the new car. It is beautiful.
Bertha can't drive it yet. I'm very upset that Herman is not happy with his work. Don't forget that today it
isn't easy to get a job. I know he knows it. He should do whatever he thinks is the best. You are busy enough.
I know how busy you are. I understand. He should buy a ready made postcard and mail that if he doesn't
feel like writing a letter. I was thinking about what would be the best to make it easier for the both of you.
With the home and so much work, and the expenses. I was thinking it would be very nice for 2 boys who go
to college to rent our room. You can get more than just the rent that you are paying. You can tie up the stuff
so no one can get to it. The only thing is that you are working too hard and that would help out at least with
the expenses. It doesn't mean to do it right now, but you could clean up and it would be worth it and rented.
At the university they would recommend someone. Maybe 2 nice young men and they would be happy to
pay the rent for the rooms. I wrote to Helmec to Fenicky about the property at home. Oh yes, how to make
pickles. First you have to peel them. Then wash it. The 4 sides of the grater on the one side where lines are
on it, not the potato grater side, and slice it on that side. Put just a little salt on it. Slice onions, and put it on
the cucumber. First in a thick, round slices. After you put on a little salt, squeeze out the juice with your
hand from the pickle and the salt. Then when you finish this, then you put on a little water, a little vinegar,
a drop of sugar and stir it up all together. After that it is ready. Just put it in the refrigerator. It will stay one
week and will not spoil. #2 You can make iced tea. Boil the water. First boil it and you can put the tea bag
in the hot water then you can add sugar and lemon to taste. You can make it light. It is very good in hot
weather. When this is ready put it in the refrigerator to cool off. Now you have iced tea whenever you want.
It is very good. Irving dear, you should try grapefruit and orange juice mixed. How healthy it is. You should
have it every morning. My heart aches that you might get sick. You have to take care of yourself. You are
no longer babies, so you need to take care of yourselves. I know everything is expensive, but you must eat
because you cannot neglect yourself. Sometimes, you can make even a can of salmon with radishes and raw
lettuce like they sell outside. I love it with tomatoes and you don't have to go hungry. Let me know how
you like my recipes. Another time, I will send you more. I don't know if you like it (Betty Crocker) with
pea soup is good. You can buy it in a paper box and it is vegetable soup. You can add the soup dry to hot
water. You have to stir it in with the hot water and add a little salt and a little oil or margarine. You can
make 4 plates of soup from it. I like it very much. I will see - maybe Maria or I will go to see you sometime.
Love to you both, Hermine

1947/7/11 Undated Hermine to David (Book 10, 1)

[Dated by Bertha's new car]

Dear David!

We did not hear from you for a long time, but I hope you are well! We are also busy with nothing. As a matter of fact, I am only busy with school and with work. I just wanted to call Zseni. It is possible that we will go there tonight. No date! I did not see Bertha for a few days already, but they bought a car and now Bertha is learning how to drive. Otherwise we are well. I kiss you with love. Hermina

1947/7/12 Hermine to Irving (Book 11, 279-280)

[In English]

New York 7/12 - 47

Dear Irving,

It is Saturday evening now and I'm home so I drop you a few lines. Hope you both are fine. Maria went to a movie but I didn't because I'll have company tomorrow and I have some things to do. Louis is coming or maybe he is in New York already. Received a letter from him from Washington D.C. His brother is here in New York and called me last week - maybe he'll be over too. So as soon as I know something I let you know. I tell you the truth I don't know myself what would be the best. Anyway this will tell now. The only thing is that sometimes I feel it will be terrible for Maria if I would go - on the other hand if we are together very seldom get along and I believe you know it too. Sometimes I feel she'll be maybe better off alone. She is nervous and nobody can tell her nothing. It's true that she doesn't have anybody since the one you met. Well he wasn't for her. The one I told you he is very nice man and intelligent. I used to go out with him but when I told him off he told me that he thinks Maria is also a very nice girl and maybe she would go with him but I believe he is a little old for her.

Also the neighbor Irving would take her after I told him that I have somebody but she don't want to hear about it because I used to go out with him. He used to stop at the window and he asked her for a walk she wouldn't go - and I believe it isn't right. She doesn't have to marry him and just to go out he is a nice boy and treated me right and there is nothing wrong in it. She is the same as before. So I don't know what to tell you but she said if I go she wouldn't stay here.

Well that's all for now - please dear don't get me wrong. I just felt like that now so I wrote it down. Let's hear from you and I'll write too. What about Herman and David - how are they? Jeanne and husband left for Florida today. Best wishes to Aunt Helen and to you both. Love, Hermina

1947/7/12 Undated Marie to Irving (Book 8, 28-29)

[Dated from Louis to NY and Jennie Frey to Florida]

My dear little brother Irving!

Just a few lines again that I am well and I hope that my lines will find you in the best also. How's everything by you? How do you do with studying? I guess it must be hard in the heat like this. Besides that, you study so hard. I hope that everything will work out successfully! I can't write anything particular about me. Everything is the same. We got a letter from Lipot and the others yesterday and poor him, he may be very sick. He has been in the hospital for seven months already and it is possible he will stay there longer. His wife wrote that the doctors don't encourage them with anything. They only say that it takes time and they are hoping. As it seems, poor thing has enough. And he wrote that Arthur sends packages and money properly. It keeps the life in them. No need to mention to Arthur that he wrote it to us about the money. I will leave this too. Yes my little brother, as David wrote that we should send a package to the mail lady already. He has it wrapped for a few weeks, but it is still there. David does not write to her because she is waiting for the package. I will not neglect it anymore. Yes, I'm writing this from work because I am not really busy and I'm thinking of you. Now my little brother, take care of yourself and as much as you could do, try to rest too. I myself don't know what to do, everything is so uneventful. I am talking about myself. Hermine's boyfriend Louis will come tomorrow. And she will write about this to you properly. I am just asking you my dear Irving, not to be worried and take care of yourself. I will write again. Jenny Frey went away today with her husband to Florida. Bertha is well. I don't know if Hermina mentioned to you that Bertha and [her husband] got a beautiful new car. Although, I did not see it yet. Now I will close my lines and I wish you my dear Irving, good luck and the best of health. I kiss you countless times with love. Maria I'm sending greetings to everyone.

And what does Herman do? Is he still lazy to write?

1947/7/17 Marie to Irving (Book 8, 168-170)

July 17 / 47

My dear little brother!

As you can see I am trying to write to you again a couple of lines. We are well, which I hope my lines will find all of you in the best. Otherwise what's new by you my little brother? How are you doing with studying? As I can see it, you are still in summer school. I hope everything will work out. Yes, my dear little brother, have you heard about David? We did not get a letter until this day. Hermine wrote to him that she will go to Palestine. I hope he is ok. Other than that, what I mentioned in my last letter, that Louis will come and now he is here. I was waiting to find out something certain so we can write it to you, but I will leave it so Hermine can write about it. I only know this much, that it is probably going to happen with God's help. Louis came here on Sunday with his brother and they stayed here for lunch. And dear little brother, I can say this much, that Hermine loves him very much and she would not forgive herself if she didn't go with him. This way I will hope the dear God will help both of them. I myself could not believe that she loves him that much, but life is like that. Bertha and Mannie like him a lot. His brother will go with him too to Palestine. And they say if they will not like it, they could come back anytime. Hermine showed us the letter where you write about what she should do and they liked it a lot, but I will leave this too to Hermine and she will write correctly about it. Although Louis is going home tonight, and I don't know if I should wait with this letter until she will write, since I would like to send it to you today. Besides that Lilian and Ernie will come here on the 20th, you know, Hermine's girlfriend with her husband. You know who I mean? The one from Columbus. And also, Lajos Schwartz will come too from Youngstown. Other than that, everything is the same, only it has been raining all week long. I don't know any details about me either, everything is the same. Now I hope that I will hear from you soon. I wish you the best! Take care of yourself, my Irving dear. I will close my lines and send my best wishes and kiss you countless times with lots of love. Greetings for everybody and write, don't be sad. Your forever faithful sibling. Love, Maria

1947/7/20 Hermine to Irving (Book 11, 282-285)

New York 7/20 - 47

My dear little brother,

Today, Sunday afternoon I sat down to write a couple of lines because like you, I am very happy for your letters - also it will bring a little happiness to you. Thank God we are well and I hope the same from you too. Last Sunday Louis arrived. He spent Saturday in Washington. He and his brother, who is also in New York, came to visit us on Sunday for dinner. So, the thing is that now he is arranging the passports, the traveling and the other things. Right now I only know that he is planning on getting married soon. He said that in a couple of weeks he will come back because now he is here until the 9th and he had to go back because of the business. He had to go back to Cleveland. He needs to buy a car and maybe he will come with the new car. He did not mention anything about the engagement yet, only asked me to tell him what kind of ring because I know better how it goes with that. Well, for me the diamond does not matter. There are many who only get a wedding bend. So, this way based on him, he will arrange it when he will find out about this. It surprised me because he asked me if I wanted a big wedding! What do you say about that my little brother? I can hardly believe it, but many people told me that they like him very much.

Not his colorfulness, but his goodness. Believe me my Irving, that he is a very sweet boy and I am not afraid with him that I will be betrayed. I hope that the dear God will help me and everything will work out! It is possible that we will go in October, but maybe only in February! So, I will just tell you, in case Louis will go to Columbus, don't mention that you know about it because it is only just talk and he does not know how it will be the best. Don't tell it to anybody because he has only told me. I will not tell either. Louis just mentioned to me not to tell anyone. It is not important to let anyone know about this. If I told it to the aunt or to Bertha, then you know how it goes? They like to explain everything. As a matter of fact, I thought that it is better if I will write it because this way it won't be unexpected. Although, if I will know it exactly I will write to you. He was in Columbus again last time, but only for a short time and you were not at home when he called you on the phone. At yahrzeit, we did not even light a candle for our dear late mother. Dezső is angry for some reason, since he hasn't written in so long. I want to write to Aunt Helen. You can mention it to her, but only that it is serious and that I answered yes. In case Louis will go there, then I made you two years younger. I have only spent 2 years on him and next time I will tell that, too.

We went to Bertha and Mannie the other night and Mannie likes Louis and we wanted to go to Aunt Jenny, but they were very busy - so then we will go some other time even though their opinion doesn't matter.

Don't mention what I wrote to you about Maria because she would feel bad about it - about the boys - but many times I can't help it and she behaves like I wrote, which I shouldn't have written. I wish I could do something, so it would be easier for her, but I don't even know what will happen if she will stay alone. What do you think, Irving? Besides that, she is well also and let's hope that everything is going to be fine. Write about everything and don't be worried, my little brother! Take care of yourselves and I kiss all of you with love. Hermina

1947/7/25 Marie to Irving (Book 18, 276-277, 280-281) Bertha bringing Iren to America

July 25 / 47

Dearest Brother Irving,

Again a few lines that I'm ok and I hope to hear the same from you. I'm very impatient because it's been two weeks since I heard from you. I think you must be busy also. I heard from our brother Dave. It is his fault. We wrote him more often and he still doesn't try to write to us or understand. He thinks we all have to listen to him, but he can do whatever he wants. I believe that at least he should write to you. Are you studying hard, Irving dear? You know, Lillian from Columbus is here visiting. Otherwise, what news is from there? Bertha and the others are well. Did you hear from Flora? Is Herman still working there? Please write, my dearest little brother. I think you might have exams and that's what is taking all of your time. I wish you all the luck and the best of health and take care of yourself. Many kisses and all my love as always forever, your sister Maria

Dearest little brother,

As you can see, I'm continuing to write. I started at work and I doubt that I will have a chance to mail it to you sooner because it happens that today is Sunday and I'm working. I received your letter and I'm reading it now and I was very happy to realize that you are well, thank God, but school takes all your time. My little brother, what are you planning to do on your vacation? Are you going somewhere? I hope you are not planning to work especially hard. I hope that Aunt Helen is not angry because I'm not writing to her. That is the way it goes. At this time, nothing special. The weather here today is warm. Oh yes, how are the Roths [Flora's family]. Are they staying at the relatives? If they come for a visit, then they will not be able to stay here. I think I mentioned before to you that Bertha is bringing aunt [cousin] Sarolta's daughter [Iren]. Maybe she would not have to wait too long because they are trying to help from here. Now I'm closing. I'm wishing all the best and good luck in everything. Many kisses, with all my love forever, your sister who never forgets you. Take care of yourself, give my best to whoever asks about me. Love, Maria

1947/7/26 Marie to David (Book 8, 172-173)

July 26 / 47

Dear David,

As I can see I should follow your example too. But still, I can't not write to you. We are well, and I hope my lines will find you as well in the best of health. I cannot imagine how somebody like you David can talk something into yourself so much. How would you feel if we do as you do and would not write to you at all? And we would wait for the better luck. That is very old fashioned. You do what you think is the best for you, but I will note this much, if you will not be in a hurry to write a few lines and will make others sad, then I will take it easy too and I will not be in a hurry to write. But I will leave this too. We did not hear from our little brother for a few weeks, but at least I know about him that he is very busy. There is no particular news here. And I hope to hear the best about you. Take care of yourself. I wish you good luck and the best of health. I will close my lines. Greetings from my heart and kisses to you with love. Your sibling, Maria

I did not send the letter yet, so I will attach a few lines more. We got a letter from our little brother and thank God he is well, only as I mentioned, he studies hard. He just wrote that you did not write for a long time to him either. This way I will hope that you will change your mind and will write. Take care of yourself. But I wrote enough for today. I'm sending greetings and kiss you with love. Maria

1947/7/26 Undated Hermine to David (Book 10, 6-7)

Undated [from the content and reference to Louis and Palestine, and the delay in Marie sending her letter, it seems to belong with this letter from Marie dated 1947/7/26 Marie to David (Book 8, 172-173)]

Dear David!

It has been a couple of days since Maria wrote this letter and did not send it, so I can write too and then it can go together. I hope you are healthy and you will think about it and will write. Even if you are busy, you could write a few lines. Although, it is true, that you can get out of writing easily because there is no advantage to it. But many times even without an advantage one could make some time. I know that it does not feel good that I am writing that way, but it does not feel good to me either that you don't write. We put together a package for the post lady [Jana] , but I heard that the post office is not open in the afternoon. In this way we can send it only on Monday. We are sending beautiful things, I am just thinking that our clothing is very small. However, every piece is excellent. Maybe later there will be more so we will send once again, but until then we will send this. I don't know what to get from the used clothing store and if somebody would come with me then I will try that.

I should have done it before, but I was also busy with my own job. I did not want to send money to the [employment] office until they find me a better job. Now I have a pretty good job. I could have gotten 6 dollars more for a week and I was there for 8 days, but I could not take the draft. This way I get 37 dollars, but they are very satisfied with me, until I'll ask for a raise, but then I don't know. Otherwise, thank God we are well. Louis was here two weeks ago. I don't know what will be, but it's not worth it for you to get mad at me about that. It is possible that he will not even go to Palestine. Currently, I don't even know. So write as soon as possible because I can hardly wait for it. Write about yourself and I wish everything good with lots of love. I kiss you, Hermine

1947/7/28 Bertha to Irving (Book 17, 43-44) - Bertha's scheme

New York
July 28 / 47
Beloved Irving!
My lines will surprise you, but I got two letters today from Iren from Arad [Romania], where I can only make out great sadness from them. A few weeks ago we sent two hundred dollars for her. She said that there they want to pay $50 in value. This way, so I can get to the point, I don't have too much hope that we can have her come here. Even if I have the money, I can't send it to her. I already tried every club/agency but it is impossible. So, I would like your opinion about what I am thinking. I know that this is the only way for her to get here. The thing is this, that to my inquiry I got an idea, that if the X.G. would want her, [he'd have] to write that he wants to have this woman come here because he is engaged with her and wants to marry her - By the time it would come to that, he would not need to marry her, which means, that you Irving you would only need to do the documents [stating] that you want her come here. I hope I did not scare you away with my lines, but I am assuring you, if it would work out, you don't need to be afraid of any inconvenience. If Iren would arrive with your endorsement, I will take this trouble over and every cost will be our problem. You don't even have to see it and in the meantime, so we can comply with the state law, since you regretted this and you found some reason and you will not get married. I know that this can be taken care of. The State will not investigate it. Believe me, my Irving that it is very hard for me to talk to you about something like this, but I know that you are a smart boy and you will understand me. I don't want to deceive you or to pull you into something like this. So think about it! My Irving, if you could do this big favor for me, you should inquire about this too before you would give me an answer to my letter. You can inquire about the documents at the Veteran's Administration. Kiss you with love, Bertha and Mannie.
I hope you are well!

1947/7/30 Marie to Irving (Book 8, 174-178)

My dear little brother, Irving!
As you can see my buddy I am writing again a couple of lines, although I know you will be surprised about why am I writing. First of all, I hope that my lines will find you in the best of health. We are well also. But with this letter I am in a hurry to write to you because I just found out what our cousin Bertha is speculating about. That is why I am in a hurry so she will not talk you into anything. First of all, Hermine was over last night and they talked like always and they brought up that they tried to bring [cousin] Sarolta's daughter here. They just found out that they can't do anything. It is very painful for them since Iren, Sarolta's daughter, is sick and she needs a doctor and she has nothing for clothes or food. They sent money to them somehow and by the time she got it she barely received half of it. So, there is not too much hope for anything. They thought that they will find a boy for her, who is an American citizen and would bring her here like a wife, maybe then she could come here quickly. But as I just found out, it is not enough. Nowadays, it takes

a soldier in Europe to marry her and as a war bride she could be here in a few weeks. This is the only solution. And you my little brother know it well, that it is very hard to find...

[On the crease] Because you can help them? Don't listen to anyone, no matter what they say, and don't do anything like that. I kiss you countless times. M.

...even for money. But as they state it, no need to get married, just a promise is enough. When she comes here they can just change their mind. The boy doesn't need to marry her and the government would not send her back when she is here already. So, this is how the case is standing and there is no other way and as I heard they want to ask you for that purpose. You already know that because they wrote to you last night. First of all, do not mention this to Bertha+others that I told you about this because they did not tell me. Since if they would tell me, I would not mind if they would be mad at me because I would tell them what I think. They told Hermine not to tell me about this because they are afraid of me. She knows that I would not let it happen. And she asked Hermine to write to you to do it for her. She was almost crying because she is all worked up about it. And now I am writing here about my opinion. My dear little brother, do not care about them, even if they get angry. Write it to them that you are very sorry that you can't satisfy their request, but this is the kind of thing where everybody should look out for themselves first and you are fighting for your future and you would appreciate it if they would choose somebody else. If you could be there to help in other ways, then you would be glad to do it. But you don't think about [doing] this at all. And don't be afraid of her if she is not ashamed of herself. My little brother, I know you are smart and don't listen to anyone. You have enough problems and nobody would do us any favors. Our cousin is there too, and we would like Iren to be here too, but no.

I will attach a couple of lines here again, what I forgot to mention to you. First of all, they should be ashamed of it to write something like that to you. Don't think, my dear little brother, that anyone will do anything for us. You know, since I am here, they did not introduce me to anyone yet. But don't you mention this to them. And if we meet a guy then they will ruin it because she likes to talk and she thinks that she does good with it, but she already ruined it. I am not writing this to you to complain, just that you should not be afraid of them. Yes, my little brother, I will continue my letter here. Bertha came in and I could not continue. She already left and she is trying to be nice, but she did not mention anything to me. Now little brother, I hope that you will understand me and I wish everything good. Hermine will write tomorrow since it is already late and I want to send this letter today. She is well too and sending her best. Now, my little Irving, take care of yourself and don't worry. God is good and let's hope that everything will be fine. I kiss you countless times with love. Maria
Write, because I'll be waiting.

[Upside down, top of page 4] – Take care, and don't worry. Love, Maria

1947/8/1 Undated Irving to Bertha (Book 17, 39) - draft response to request to bring Iren to America

Columbus, 5, Ohio

Dear Bertha,
In regard to your letter it is very difficult for me to come to a general conclusion since I know the situation in Rumania and the other occupied countries. However, since I must touch upon this point or situation which is closely interrelated with your proposal, that is, the present urgent help which is necessary to bring Iren to America. First I would like to point out that the situation over there is very complicated and by no means could be analyzed on a few pages. However, I do want to point out that there are at present, difficult as it may be, is not as one might think, that is, in respect that the minority groups are not prosecuted [persecuted]. Therefore, the urgency of your proposal could be overcome by some other method or means by which Iren could be helped. For example, a few weeks ago three people came from Europe by using tourist visas and now it will be possible to remain in the United States. So I would think that could be done also in the case of Iren and the more complicated factors left out since I feel that I'm unable to comply with your proposal. Although I know the situation and I wish to help, but by not with the mentioned proposal. A proposal as such is more than just a signature. It involves into a complicated psychological factor, therefore I hope that you will understand and see my reasoning. I remain with best wishes and ...

1947/8/5 David to Irving (Book 17, 37-38)

Aug-5-47

Dear little brother! Until 120!,

Forgive me, that I am just now responding to your letter- I have become a very lazy writer, and I don't even know the reason why. I just can't talk myself into writing. I just wrote to the girls. I got a letter from them yesterday. Here there is no particular news, everything is the same. It is very hot. It is possible that I became a lazy writer because of that. How are you? What do you do? Do you still study hard? Does Herman still like the new place? I think that Arthur is in Canada. I saw it in the newspaper. I also saw that the neighbor, Roth, brought some Hungarian family out here. Do you know them? Did you hear anything from Polyán? I did not write to anybody. You know, currently nothing comes to my mind so I can't write about it. Oh yes! I wrote to the girls. It is possible, if they think that I could get a job there, that I will go to New York. What do you say to that? The situation here is very nice, but there is no future here. I don't know if I am serious about that yet. But you know well, that I don't like to be in the same place for too long. You know, here the Jews only live for themselves. They don't care about anybody else. I am not in the mood to go back to Columbus, you know. There is nothing there either. It is impossible to get a good job there and they pay nothing. But I don't know what I am going to do yet in this case. My little brother, I don't even know what to write to you. There is nothing particular to write about here. I don't go anywhere, this way there is nothing to see and to write about. So, I will close my lines for today. I kiss you with love in the hope to see you again. I kiss you, your forever faithful older brother, David

Write. OK?

1947/8/5 Hermine to Irving (Book 11, 290-292) not marrying Louis but got check from Flora

[In Hungarian on the top - Do not read aloud to anyone]

Dear Irving,

Haven't heard from you [in] a long time, hope you all are well. It's too hot here in New York and I believe it is in Columbus, too. Are you going to school yet? Please let me know about everything! You know that Bertha never talks about that business to me and didn't tell me about your letter either. To me also happened something and I was very nervous about [it] because [I] received a letter from Flora about two weeks ago and I didn't answer it, but last Friday I received another one wishing me good luck and a check of $25 for a wedding present. Believe me I was upset for that because she could wait till I tell her and she knows I wouldn't do anything without letting them know. Well the way things are, maybe there would be nothing of the whole business so I wonder if you told them about something? Don't tell about this letter to them please because I wouldn't tell any more from nothing to you either. When he was here he talked about it seriously, but I believe he doesn't have as much money as he needs and I told him I don't have either - so he would get married if I stay here and he would go alone - but I wouldn't do that. So that is that! That is life for girls - and it is not so easy to get the right guy! Don't worry - and take care of yourself. Received mail from David about 2 weeks ago. How is Herman? Till next time, Good wishes and love to you both, Hermina

1947/8/10 Marie to Irving (Book 6, 7-8) pages 1-2

Aug 10 / 47

My dear little brother Irving!

Today I'm in a hurry to write a few lines to you again. First of all we are well, which I hope I will find you in the best again. I think Irving dear you must be very busy since the exams are now, but I hope that it will be successful. We just got a letter from David yesterday and currently he understands things about Hermine. But I think that you could have written to her about it, and so could I, that she can't do anything but accept her fate. My dear Irving, David writes if we think he could come here, that is, he is asking our opinion, if he should come here. He got bored living there already. And if yes, he will come. But this is the next one. First of all, he wants to get a house because he does not want to live with anyone. I don't even know what to say about that, since you my buddy know very well, how it is. I know him and even if he has changed I don't want to go back to a household because it would be again as it was before. We should look at the other side. It would be better for him here since he does not have any acquaintances.

This way I don't even know what to say about that. And you my little brother, what do you think about that? If he would want to take a room out for himself then it is completely different. But I don't want to live together like [it was a] long time ago. And the other thing is, it is not that easy to find a house. It is hard enough to find a room, but that is not so hard. I will leave it to Hermine to write whatever she thinks is good. I don't know if you should mention it to David that I wrote about this, but I'm sure he will write about this to you. Take care of yourself my dear little brother. And don't be sad and I wish you lots and lots of good luck and the best of health. Yes, Bertha was here since then and she told Hermine that she feels better now, since she hopes you will do what she asked you for. And she asked Hermine about that, if she got any letter from you. She said no. Hermine said to [her] that she should not to be so sure of it, since she knows that you will not do that. And because of that she got offended. And now she says the license would be necessary. And it could be taken out also by marriage. Hermine said to that, everyone should do it for them self and she should not count on you. And you my little brother don't be afraid.

1947/8/10 Undated Marie to Irving (Book 6, 5-6) pages 3-4

for she would not do such a thing. When I'm there, she doesn't even bring it up. I don't even know why she was afraid to tell me. I didn't do anything to her. But you know that I wouldn't let her fool you. Because she doesn't have a mind, if she had a mind she wouldn't ask for such a thing. As though you didn't have any other problem [to deal with]. Forget it my little brother and don't be fooled. Write to her what you know is good, you know, my buddy. She thinks you're so good that you'll stop running in a minute. Nobody does anything for me either. But now leave it. You just take great care of yourself. And don't be upset, God is good and we hope he will help you. Now I kiss you countless times with love your forever sibling. Love Maria

1947/8/15 David to Herman (Book 12, 176-178)

Wilmington
Thursday afternoon 6 o'clock

Dear Herman!
I have a little time today, so I can write to you also. How are you? As it seems we work the same shift. Did you like the medication? If it is not good and did not work, write to me. OK? I think it's good! I use it too. I have a little favor to ask of you. I hope you will do it. Here in California the whiskey is not rationed, but only a person can buy it who is a good buyer of the company. There is rum, cognac, and vodka here. Those are available as much as you need, but I don't like them. So, if you would be so kind and do this favor for me, I will send you a little present. So, buy on your name or on the girls' name 2 bottles of whiskey. Canadian Club or 4 Roses or other better whiskey. If it is not available there in one place, then there will be at another place. I hope you will do it. I did not think about a small bottle, rather 1/4 [a quart] or 5 "tett" [maybe a fifth] and wrap it up well in a lot of paper so that it won't break and if Hermine wants to send a pound of pastries that she bakes, not store baked, take it to the Railway Express on High Street. There is one about 3-400 N. High St, next to the uptown theater and address it to this address: D. Gluck 435 Neptun, Wilmington, California. But not with the post office!!! It is not allowed to send it with the post office. Express it is allowed. I will send every cost to you. Thank you so much! If you don't want to send it, write it. Ok? I hope you will write! Dezső

[On the reverse in Herman's handwriting]
Canadian Club
4 Roses or something else better.

1947/8/17 Marie to David (Book 8, 180-182)

Aug 17/47
Dear David!
We received your letter and were happy to hear that thank goodness, you are ok. Therefore, I could say the same thing. First, to get a job is always difficult, it doesn't matter where. I think it would be a little easier in New York than it was in Columbus. The biggest problem is to get a room. That is very difficult, and you don't have much choice, first come first served. Otherwise, nothing new. We received a letter from Irving last week. Thank God, he is ok. I'm sorry that I'm just mailing this to you, I didn't have the time sooner, so I'm just mailing it today. I hope my letter will find you in good health. Take care of yourself. Do whatever you think is best for you. You have to decide. No one can advise you because look how lucky we are, and

if you are healthy then you have everything. I'm closing my lines now, wishing you good health and good luck, with my best wishes and love, your sister, Maria

1947/8/18 Hermine to David (Book 11, 294-296, 298-299) tries to convince Dave to come to NY

New York Aug 16 / 47
Dear David,
Finally received the letter that we could hardly wait for. I was very happy to hear that you are ok. We are ok, too. In the last day it's been very hot here. I'm not working today. It is Saturday. Maria works 6 days a week and it's enough. I would like to tell you something good if we approve for you to come here. About this I can only write my opinion. In a big city like New York it is always easier to get a job than in a smaller place. It takes time. I think you would be able to get a job easier than in Columbus because you have more opportunities and we have here a larger Jewish population so it's easier to get a job. Also, we can get all of our clothing, even coats, at wholesale. I buy them there for much less than otherwise. In Columbus, I wasn't able to. There we have to save our clothing. For the boys, it is more difficult. They are not children. For them, it is not worth it to stay there for long. It is true that for Irving, he has to be there for school. Here expenses are greater, especially for a boy if he wants to go somewhere, everything costs more. What is more important are the rooms, which are impossible to get, even one room is difficult. Where we are is good. Why? Because where we are she is a very fine, elderly lady. She keeps kosher and we are allowed to cook whatever we want just like we are in our own home. Every morning she makes my breakfast. She doesn't want me to be late or leave without breakfast. Everything is good, but I wasn't used to it. If I could get another nice room, then it would be better, but even that would be more difficult because we are 2 girls. Some people won't take us because they feel it is too much trouble. We understand very well. This woman is so nice to us, 'like my own' she says about us. Her family is very nice to us also. This isn't very helpful to you, and I cannot write more or give more information. I heard that where Bertha lives, [someone] in her building just bought a home so she is going to move. It's a 3½ room apartment. Many people signed up who are waiting for that apartment. This person will give $500.00 just so he will get the apartment. He will get it because it is very difficult to get one today. This is what you need just to begin with. Maybe you need to exchange in Columbus if you have an apartment there, but I'm not sure even then it would be worthwhile because the upkeep is very expensive. I hope you will write soon. Maybe for the boys it would be ok. Until then, with my best wishes and love, Hermine

1947/8/18 Hermine to Irving (Book 11, 301-303)

Aug 16 - 47
Dear little brother Irving!
We got your letter last Sunday and you made us very happy with it. I was getting ready to write since then, but the heat was so terrible that one had no mood to start it. We also got a letter from Dezső and he is well, too. Thank God he is writing that if we think, and there would be apartment available and we can get proper work, then he would like to come here. I don't even know what to write to that because it is possible that he would like to come here even if he would have a hard time to get a job, and we can't even dream about the apartment, but he does not want to live with anyone. Where we are is great because the lady is as good to us as though we would be her relatives and that is excellent. But it is not comfortable because we don't even have a separate room. We will see what it's going to be because I would not like to stay here for too long. In case it will not work out with Louis, since the way the situation is now, there is nothing to build on, but it will be the way it should be. It is not worth it to kill oneself over that. Oh yes, Bertha did not mention anything about your letter and was wondering from the lady, if we got a letter from you, and she said no. The letter was very serious because it was serious and this way you ended it. It was for the best. But you can tell me only, little brother, if anyone helped you with the letter because it was very good sounding English. You gave a great offer, that she should bring her out here as a visitor - I hear that she is still looking for someone who would undertake the case. Don't worry and take care of yourself. How are you with the studying? Write about everything. There is no special news here. The heat is terrible these days. I would like to go for a boat ride with Marcsa tomorrow where we would spend the day and get out for a few hours. I wish you would be with us and the bad Herman too. It would be good to go to you in Columbus for the holidays, but I don't know yet because to tell you the truth, I would like to buy a winter coat first. But we will see. Until then, I wish good health for the both of you. I'm sending my best to Aunt Helen and to the acquaintances. We got a letter from Flora. They are well. Next month on the 15th they are planning on coming back. Love, Hermina

1947/8/18 Undated Marie to Irving (Book 6, 3-4) - part of a letter from Hermine

[dated by "being over with her now" which I think is referring to Bertha's plan vis a vis Irene]

Dear Irving,
Yes, I will add a few lines. And as you can see, I am sending this letter late against my will. I don't want to write anymore. But again, I will write to you separately. With this letter, I waited for Hermine to write in it and it stayed because of it. We have received your letter and I am happy to hear that thank God you are healthy, but we didn't say [that we received it]. Bertha writes to us what she wants to see and I haven't even seen her [Iren?] before, but don't be upset my buddy, you're over with her now. It's just what you need for your learning. I know buddy, that not everyone can do what he wants with you. Now good luck and best health. And take care of yourself. Kissing you countless times with love. Maria
Here are the letters. Love, M.

1947/9/2 Irving to Bela Fenickecho (Book 19, 126)

[See 1947/9/3 Belo Fenicky to Irving PROPERTIES (Book 3, 247-250)]

Sept. 2nd 1947
Columbus, Ohio

Mr. Bela Fenickecho
Kralovsky-Chlumec
Czechoslovakia

Dear Sir!
It has been more than a few months since I sent you the authorization so you can get our wealth back from the government. The time is passing and you did not give any response, therefore I will ask you to respond immediately to my letter and I will attach a stamp for you to send the letter. Also, we will pay back your cost and effort. I will stay until I will hear from you again. Irving Gluck

1947/9/2 Irving to Dave (Book 6, 303-305)

Sept 2nd 1947
Columbus Ohio

Dear Dave, until 120
Just to say that everything is O'K and hoping that you are well and will hear from you soon. Here in Col[umbus] not much news except the transportation will be different, such [as] buses instead of street cars. Col[umbus] is growing, but still nothing important that would reflect to something that would make one stay here. However, all American cities are alike. Well, I guess I'll think about these things later, that is, after the school days are over. By the way, I have received to this address several letters from "The New York Merchants Credit Ass'n Inc" As you'll see I have the letter inclosed here. As I note from the other letters, they are asking for some amount that you owe them. Just to give you a tip - there is a statement that I heard some time ago and that is, if one owes to someone for eight years and didn't pay a cent on it, the balance is erased, but if the individual pays even a cent on the account, that, naturally they'll collect, maybe you know this already. Well let me hear from you and best wishes from your little brother, Irving

1947/9/3 Belo Fenicky to Irving PROPERTIES (Book 3, 247-250)

Dear Sir!
I acknowledge that I'm somewhat belated in replying to your dear letter. You must know that in Europe after this horrendous world burning event, Jewish life is somewhat more difficult as is earning a living as a lawyer. Due to the situation and letter writing, we do not have any time for that. I want to advise you that everything I could have done up to now I did in your behalf, but your relation Ignác Klein from Lelesz created a difficult road and I want to go against him because all the methods he is using is with deception. As of now he has not paid any taxes and monies that came in together is for himself. He bothers with the property until he sees an income, but does not repair the building. And I want to inform you about other

things. I will tell you that I want to sell my own property, because the only person that can hold any property is one that does the work for himself. I will also advise you that the best thing is to sell it. There was a man from Lelesz whose name is Hornyak who was here and he is willing to buy it. His offer, in the present situation as it exists, is 9000 Czechoslovakian Kronen for one Kat. Hold. [katasztralis hold = 0.5755 hectare, where 1 hectare = 2.471 acres] because here in Hungary the land is not being taken with respect, because they are waiting for the occupation by the Hungarian government. I advise you that one of you should return to Europe soon. I would be more than happy to help you to with regards to the legal affairs. Accordingly, while you're making a decision, I will be glad to help you and with my time I'll do my best, but I cannot commit myself, because I do have too much work at this time, and I could not do justice with your property, as I would like to and as I wholeheartedly did in the past. I want to tell you that I would be very glad to share my service, but I'm asking you not to question that as if I would not do anything because I do it without personal interest but like a brother that would demand but I must tell you that nothing can be finished here. I would like to ask you to please write to me regarding to Emil and Lenke Gluck's relationship with you. My dear relations, please give my regards to the rest of your family and from all of us, heartily regards. Please also write to me that all four of you are United States citizens. My advice to you is to sell the properties. As I'm writing to you I did the same with mine. Whatever decision you make it's up to you. Please let me know. My heartfelt regards to all of you, Fenicky

Král. Chlumec 3 September 1947

1947/9/9 Hermine and Marie to David (Book 16, 9-11)

Sep 9/47
[from Maria]
Dear David!
A few weeks have passed by again and we did not hear from you. I hope that my lines will find you in the best of health. We are well. There is no particular news here, everything is the same. The relatives are well. We got a letter from our little brother [Herman]. He has a job now. Have you decided what you will do? I hope everything is going to turn out well. First of all, I wish a very good holiday to you and an even luckier and happier new year, and that we can hear the best about each other. Did you hear recently from the post lady? We did not write to her. I became a bad writer too. I should have responded to many letters to Europe and I'm still not writing yet. When a person works, the day goes so quickly that I don't even realize it and everything stays [undone]. But I will leave this too. Now again, take care of yourself and I wish the best of health. Now I will close my lines and I'm sending my best and kiss you with love. Your sibling, Maria
Our little brother wrote that he will write to you too.

[from Hermine]
Dear David!
We did not hear from you for a long time, but I hope that you are well. Currently there is no particular news here. I just hope that the boys will come from Columbus to visit us. We wanted to go to them, but it would be better if they would come now, which I can hardly believe. I started to write and Bertha came in and they took me for a car ride. It's not like I would wish to go after [all], but I can't say no to her. So she tries to please me and I don't even appreciate it. They will travel for Rosh HaShana. Write about yourself and if you are willing to visit New York? You know what you could do here! Get a rich girl - maybe! Let me hear from you. Till then, Love Hermina

1947/9/21 Jane Fabianova Postmaster to Hermine (Book 14, 84-86)

Hnušta 21/9 - 47
Dear Herminka!
Today the 21st I received the package that you mailed out on August the 6th. I was very surprised and happy to receive it and am thanking you very much for everything. It came just in time. I can use it as it is very nice. It's good material that [for me] it is impossible to get. For me, everything has disappeared, but the terrible horror, to trust someone again, I can't even think about. I'm fine. I'm working in an office, which I am happy about. Dear Hermine, please write when you receive my letter. How are you all? And what will be with getting married? You were beautiful young ladies before you went to America. Write a little and send some pictures. Dezső should write and send a picture. Also you answered the first letter, but after that you never answered. I thought that you got angry forever. First I was worried because I didn't put on any

stamps. Also on another letter that you never answered. I felt very badly and was hurt. If you are interested, please let me know. Therefore, I send my best wishes. The flower dress is beautiful. Tomorrow I will stop to have it taken in a little and one of them I will let out to make it a little bigger. On the others there was nothing that needed to be altered. It's just a small alteration. You wrote Hermine about remembering. I really can't even write how happy you make me with them. Once more, I'm thanking you for the package you sent me. It will be hard to wait for a letter. Please Dezső should write also. I'm worried and hope he is well. I'm worrying about that. He was a very good person. With love and with the best wishes to you all. I'm very anxious waiting for your answer. I wish I would have it now, Jan kice

1947/10/1 Hermine to David (Book 16, 19)

Oct 1 - 47
Dear David!

I hope you are well, since we have not heard from you for awhile. We are, thank God well, especially now that our little brother Irving was with us this week. I guess he had a good time. Otherwise we are well and I am attaching here Miss P's [Jana the postmaster] letter and I'm truly glad that she received the package we sent so soon and that she can use it. Although every piece was good, they were only tight and she wrote that it is good for her and it does not need so much fixing. How are you David? When do you plan on coming here? If you come here, I will introduce you to a cute girl, who Irving liked also. Accidentally the girl saw your picture and she liked it very much. If you are interested, then I will get a picture and I will send it to you. OK? I know you don't need help, but I only thought about her. So, I will write it to you. The relatives are well, but I have not seen them for awhile. I went to Bertha's last night. She lives about 5 blocks from here. Write - until then I wish you lots of luck and everything good. I kiss you with love, Hermina

1947/10/3 Irving to Hilda Goldberger - draft (Book 16, 459-460)

Oct. 3rd. 1947
Columbus 5, Ohio

Dear Hilda,

Hope that you will permit me calling you by your first name since it's more [convenient] that way and also it makes me feel as if I have known you before. Although, as it happens it has only been a matter of a few days that we met. However, all in all, time flies fast. Maybe because of the pleasant memories that I brought home from "The Center of the World" as you recall the movie philosophy. However, I must say that the journey home was much shorter, because of the pleasant thoughts that you too have helped to contribute during my stay in New York. And thanks to you.

Finally, school began for me also and just to mention that we, at the O.S.U. have only 25000 students. The size of some classes [is] unmentionable. However, I can not complain because in most of my classes there are only forty-five persons, which is considered to be the minimum.

Well, I presume that I have cause[d] you much trouble already in having you read my scrambled writing, so I'll close this time and let me hear from you, too. With best wishes and Sincerely, Irving

1947/10/3 Marie to David (Book 9, 10-11)

Oct 3 / 47
Dear David!

I don't even remember exactly when I heard from you. I hope you are well! I guess you don't want to write, but it would be about time for you to respond. We already wrote many letters to you. I hope you are not sick! Even then, a few lines would not cost any money. There is no news here. I thought that Hermine already wrote to you that our Irving was here last week to visit us, and thank God he is healthy, just very busy. He does not even have time to think about himself, or what is worthwhile to study. And this way we only hope that everything will work out well. And what are you doing? Yes, we mentioned the last time that we sent a package to the post lady from Lelesz and we got a response from her this week, that she got everything and she can use everything. But now I will close my lines and I hope that I will hear about you. Take care of yourself wherever you go and write and don't be such a lazy writer. I'm writing this letter from work and I will hurry to send it. I'm sending my greetings and kiss you with love, Maria

Oct 3 / 47

My dear little brother Irving!

I'm sorry that I had you wait with my letter, but this week I was very busy. But now I will be in a hurry to write. I was very happy to [get] your card. And I'm happy to hear that thank God you are well. I'm just sorry that you are so busy with everything. We all miss you here my little brother. The house is pretty empty my buddy. When you left I went to the movies and Hermine went with that boy. Also, she will go this week with him. I think she already wrote about it to you. Mrs. Kugler's family is well. They wondered about you. I did not talk to the relatives since then. Yesterday Hermine signed up for school and she will go twice a week. Although, I will not go, this way she will go alone. I would like to study too, but right now it's enough for me to work six days because I can't help it. I hope I will be able to do that later. And how are you my buddy? Do you study hard? I hope to hear the best about you. Yes, what's new there? What did the relatives say? I'm sure they were surprised that you were here. Did anyone see the suit? Do they like it? What is going on with the neighbors? I know my little Irving that I have a lot of questions for you. There is no particular news here now. We still did not get a letter from David. I hope that he is well! I am planning on writing to him too. Now I wish you lots and lots of luck and the best of health. And take care of yourself. If you could, my little buddy write too and I will be in a hurry to write to you next time with more details. Now I will close my lines and I'm sending my greetings from the heart and kiss you with much love countless times, your forever faithful sibling. Maria

I am writing this letter from work and I want it to go today.
Take care of yourself!

Oct 8, 1947

Dear Irving,

I was very happy to hear from you and derived a great deal of pleasure from reading your letter.

It is a shame you were unable to stay any longer in New York. I would have enjoyed showing the city to you - and to myself, also. I really hope that you will come and pay us another visit very soon. It will give us a chance of becoming better acquainted. School also continues for me and since this semester I am only carrying a limited program I find it quite easy. Hunter College is one of [the] places I would like to show you. You cannot possibly imagine how different it is from a larger university such as you go to. I think I better close this letter now as the bell has rung and I must go to my next class. Hope I shall hear from you very soon. As ever, Hilda

Oradea [Romania], 1947 October 8

Dear Irving,

I was glad to read your letter, and I did understand it. And just because of that, I will try to respond to it. I am very clear about Bertha's love and great generosity. To be honest, I'm a little embarrassed to face all this goodness, since I can't give you anything in return for it, but please believe me, that it is not a whim, what I want to get. Moreover, if I would know that I have to live in Cuba, I would not even go. The only thing I wish for, and I'm sure I will get it, is to get to Aunt Bertha and I could live in a family environment again, so I can belong to someone, something I have missed for a long time. To get to Paris is illegal and is absolutely impossible. Even if I would want to get to the Czech Republic, even then, I have to pass two borders to escape. That equals certain disaster. It's not that I am afraid of it, since in Germany for an entire year I was faced with that. The fact that I survived there, is a total coincidence. Therefore, fear is not what will hold me back, rather the struggle to be without anything and to wait for months, among strangers, for that I'm very tired about and I'm lonely also. It would be possible to get a passport to Paris legally, but this would cost a fantastic amount, something I did not even write about yet, because I don't want the impossible. There is only one way to get out - if you heard about Alex Schwartz - the way he got out. Because, if I get the visa, and the immigration status also, then here without a doubt, with those documents, I would get the passport within 5-6 weeks. And in a short period of time, I would be in Paris and from there everything would go the way you already know. I hope that you were be able to understand me, and I would like to note, that if you heard anything in reference about me, then it's not cowardliness on my part, to get held back. I hope you will contact me some other time with a letter again. I'm closing my letter with a greeting and a wish for everything good in the new year. Iren

1947/10/8 Irving to Pál Lengyel (Book 19, 128-129)

October 8, 1947
Dear Mr. Lengyen [sic],
I would appreciate your help, although I have not replied to your previous letter. I am attending the university and have been quite preoccupied with studies. Here then, I must refer to the properties. The "Prehlaska Majetku", which refers to the consulate general's application for the declaration of properties / Czechoslovak Law Number 134/46 and necessary instructions should be mailed to Bratislava by October 31, 1947. This must be done if we intend to retain our property rights. All four of us have sent this information plus that of Emil and Lenka's to Bratislava. However, no details of individual real estate were available; therefore I have given your name to supply this information. Any expense will be reimbursed. It's true that no one can confiscate these properties; however we have no choice in such matters. About six months ago, Bela Fenicke of Kralovsky-Chlumec, was authorized by us to attend to the matter on hand - - to our knowledge he has accomplished nothing. Therefore, Mr. Lengyen [sic], I am asking you to help us - - so as to prevent the confiscation of our properties. Herewith, I am including stamps for reply. Please advise the following address - - - "Berna sprava Bratislaba - - mesto, Bratislava, Czechoslovakia." According to my knowledge these papers must be in the office by the thirty-first. For additional information they will turn to you. I'll conclude with best wishes and hope to hear from you soon. My brothers and sisters all send their best regards. Many thanks, I. Gluck

P.S. I have just mailed a letter to Bela Fenicke, in which I declared that the authorization has been rescinded. Also to the Leleszi land office that our property and father's property have been included in the report.

1947/10/9 Hermine to Irving (Book 11, 305-307)

My dear little brother Irving,
Now I will try to write a couple of lines - since I became a student as well at Roosevelt High School. I go twice a week, on Tuesday and Thursday. If you would be here too, you could help me with my schoolwork. [In English] I'm taking English and History. How do you like that? Well, I hope to learn something and it was really quick because one of the girls in [the] office told me that I speak much better already! Just for a joke!! I'm enclosing [these] 2 addresses and please write to them maybe that will help, too. I'm glad you went to that lawyer and only hope it will work out well. Bertha asked me to write to Lengyen [sic] in her business also, but I will some of these days. Tomorrow is school again and Saturday night I have a date with that fellow I met at the dance. He's a pretty nice guy! Did you hear from David? We wrote to him but didn't answer yet. Did Hilda answer you? Please tell me all about it O.K.? If I'll have a chance will get some nice neckties, but only on Saturdays can I do that. Everyone sends their regards and especially Mrs. Kugler. She was very nice when you were with us and she is really very sweet! How is Herman? Regards and best wishes with our love to you both, Hermina

1947/10/12 Irving to Hilda Goldberger - draft (Book 16, 442-443) planet of oneness

Oct. 12, 1947
Columbus 5, Ohio

Dear Hilda,
I have just finished "The Planet of Oneness," a philosophy discussed in a form of utopia, which is due Monday. The whole analysis is based upon a free world, economically, politically, and socially, in which mankind can survive. To form new theories, I have searched from some of the social prophets, like Amos, Hosea, Isaia, Jeremiah and many others. From Plato to Lord Keynes, the British economist. Finally, it seemed after seeing what they had to offer to nations, I have decided to include new points and stimulate mankind as a whole, forgetting about selfishness and pointing to the present century, in which the atomic power made us to behave, and as a result we became the "Planet of Oneness." To describe nations, I assumed as if I were sailing into the Land of Dreams and describing the past history & destiny of mankind. So as you see Hilda, this is one way to spend time in a city as ours. Analyzing the present and visualizing the future.

However, to come to the point, I have enjoyed hearing from you. Your letter gave me pleasure to write my report faster so that I might give you some insight the way I have spent this weekend. So, I'll close this time and hope that you'll let me know too, how did you spend your weekend. Sincerely, Irving

1947/10/14 David to Irving (Book 12, 180-183)

October 14, 47
Dear little brother, Until 120!
Forgive me for my long silence, but unfortunately I can't give you any excuse except that I have become a very lazy writer. And this is all a cover. I don't even know how to start it. I just wrote to the girls also. Thank you for your letters very much and for your new year greetings from New York. I wish I would live closer so I could go too, but by airplane the trip costs 250 dollars and the train is about 5 days and at a night - This is a long trip like that. The important thing is, that thank God you are all well. I went to the temple during the holidays. Did you go also? To which one? Here there is a normal (religious temple). But let's leave this for today. How did you find yourself in New York? I heard that there is a girl who you love very much. But the fact is, the way Hermine wrote, that she saw my picture and she likes me too - So here the situation is shaky - right little brother? How old are you? 35? But let's leave this girl.

How are you? What do you do? Who cooks for you? What does Herman do? Did you get "Mustering out Pay"? If yes, how much? Write about everything. Ok? Hey, if the mail will come again from Benny Howard from Newark, Ohio, you know who that is? (For Work man), then you just write on the letter (not live here). Like you wrote, I don't think that he can do anything and it has been 8 years already, as I think, and I only owe 40 boxes to him. And he wanted to deceive me, so this way he can go to hell. And today he asks about 60 dollar, so he should go to hell. My credit is in Long Beach, if it's known and it does not hurt at all to comment about that (No Information about settling the case). Maybe, if I would go back to Columbus, it would not be to my advantage. If he would take the 20 dollars, then I would pay it off to him anytime. But let's leave this for today. Do you know what I was thinking? Don't you want to go to Alaska? If yes, I would go with you too. Currently you could get 160 hold [160 acres under homesteading act, Bureau of Land Management] of land for free from the government, as an ex G.I. You need to sign up for it from October 15-January 1st. I can also sign up after January 1st without being a veteran.

It's farm land and currently they are farming in the neighborhood nearby. Many go from this place from (Washington State), it only takes 3½ hours to get there by plane. This is not new. It is a fact. The request should be sent to Washington to the Interiors Office (Krug [Secretary of the Interior]). Write it, if you are interested and I will write about it in more details. Oh yes. After 6 months it is allowed to be sold and the cost is about 17 dollars. You know, if you are not interested, I think I will go out there. The cost is about 60 dollars from Long Beach. The weather is like in Polyán. Right now the daylight lasts for about 15 hours. Nice, right? There is time for everything. If you are interested, then I will write about it more. So, I can't even write anything else for today. I wrote enough. I kiss you with love your forever faithful brother, who will never forget you. I kiss you with love. David
PS: Write. I hope you will be able to read my lines!

1947/10/15 Jana Fabianova to Dezső (Book 5, 366-367)

Dear Dezső!
I'm writing very randomly, but I'm still writing because Herminka wrote to my address last month on the 22nd. I got a package from her and I want to thank you too because I was really happy for it and all the clothes are very good. I've already altered them all and they are all fine. Thank you very much for this. Dezső, I just can't understand one thing, that you don't write at all. And why don't you write?!!! The only letter I got from you was full of a lot of kindness and really good familial-blood love, as you wrote. I feel like I did not write anything to deserve this eternal silence. I waited and am waiting for the promised photo as well. You asked me too, but like this I can't send any either. "Ejnye, ejnye" [Hungarian warning usually used for little kids] You've become such a stepbrother. There was a time when every night I dreamed of you and it was unsettling that God forbid you were sick after you had that operation in the past. Ugly bad boy really.

If something were ringing in my garden, as my dear brothers would love to say, I think he wasn't writing because he was angry at my request. Dezső dear, write to me by air mail when you receive the letter and I will really ask you for something. In addition to the swallow material, what do I need now if you mentioned it? I want to see if you smile or if you are angry. Yes, I wanted to get a little fine wash soap, a bar or two of white American soap, or two shirts you no longer wear. We'll sew blouses from it because I have been dressed in my father's beautiful shirt since I came home. Lemon extract under the sign "Lemon Juice Powder" and a nice trench coat or cellophane like rain cloak. Get what you want. Would that be very modest of me? Right? Helen now has some caps and hats on hand that they don't wear, fine material, and I'm buying it here. First of all, however, I am waiting for a par avion [air mail] with elegant photos and then I will also send mine. You will recognize me by my teeth. They are intact and milk white. The truth is that you could also send a good toothbrush because this wooden handle is always red. Gizi is with me now. Do you want to write par avion [air mail]? I can only greet you with brotherly love and hope illness does not hinder your response which I have a hard time waiting for. Janakuca

My photo is here waiting to be sent. Ready to write right away.

1947/10/18 Marie to Irving (Book 6, 84-88)

Oct 18 / 47

My dear little brother Irving!

We got your letter yesterday, which I was very happy for. I am happy to hear that thank God you are healthy. But as far as your being busy is concerned, I think that your every minute is being counted. Also, [about] the attached letter [from Fenicky?]. He will not undertake that case and if he is really that honest then before he decides anything he has to notify us. But he did not do that. And the other thing is, that if he did not want to take it on, then he would have to say what he wrote today, that he is very busy and has no time to deal with that. I think my dear little brother, that what you started to do is the only thing that can be done. Since it isn't possible to sell it and it is not worth it also.

First of all, we have to take our rights back from the government and only then we can sell it. It is not worth it to go home. But in my opinion, the way you started to arrange it so we can control it from here, that would be the best. And with the notary's help.

Yes my Irving, last night Mannie and Bertha were here. They saw the letter and you know that the case is good for them, too. Now they are telling us to tell you to give the copy to whom you are writing to. They can do the same by themselves, although we can't say anything. But it will come the way it is. And you should do the best you can. They say the best would be to go home. I did not want to say why doesn't *she* go home. They will do the way they can. But I will leave this too. We got a letter from David and as always he is very busy, even today. He is sending his greetings. We are well, even if we don't write too often.

But you are on my mind a lot. And I hope, that everything will work out for the best. Take care of yourself and take time to eat. And don't be sad too much my buddy.

As you are wondering about me, currently everything is the same. There is no particular news. We went dancing since then. You know with that girl who came to us with Mrs. Kugler. And as always I was the left over. But I've almost gotten used to it. Even if it's hard for me. Still I go so at least Hermine can get to know somebody. The boy that she met when you were here, she has a date again, if he will come. But so far he kept his word exactly and he looks like a very nice boy. At least Hermine says that.

I think he is a cute boy. He is not rich, but that does not mean anything. I hope we'll have a chance to get to know others. And as you wrote my Irving, that you are corresponding with that girl. I know that you know my buddy, that you can do and I think, that you will write an appropriate letter. And that does not mean that you need to go if you don't like it. You can stop doing it anytime. Now my dear Irving I wish you lots and lots of luck and the best of health. Now I will close my lines, sending my greetings from the heart and kiss you countless times with love, your forever faithful sibling who will never forget. Love, Maria

I'm sending my best to everyone.

1947/10/19 Hermine to Irving (Book 11, 308-310)

10/19 - 47

My dear little Irving!

I will attach here Fenicky's letter. I don't even know what to respond to it. We should not offend him, because it looks like he did what he could, only it's too bad he did not let us know about it. Ignác Klein is very rude, but Fenecky should not [bring a] lawsuit against him. We could not sell our little property and it

would only be worth it if they could pay the money here for it. I saw an article in the newspaper here that in Szolnocska, the county estate is for sale. Also, there is a letter from Iren from Romania and she wrote to Bertha that she is not even sure who she wrote the letter to. How are you my little brother? I thought that Herman decided to write himself because his name was on the envelope. How is the studying going and the correspondences? There is no news here. I will write more next time. We got a letter from Dave. He is well and now I wrote a reply to the post lady. I kiss you and the relatives with much of love. And Herman!
Hermina

1947/10/25 Irving to Hilda (Book 6, 333-334)

Oct. 25th 1947
Dear Hilda,
Since I realize the situation in which you were in, I can not, but to forgive you for not answering me immediately. Although, the same situation might be reversed and perhaps there should be a mutual agreement about things as such, Don't you think so Hilda? I'm also glad to hear that you had a swell time and enjoyed the football game. Sometimes it's not necessary to know the rules and regulations to have good time. I mention that because there is a good story about one who hears and knows not (this doesn't have anything to do with the Whig or Know-nothing party) but perhaps I shall wait and tell you in person, since it would be more interesting that way. Now to be a little more serious, I surely would have liked to be there and help you to pass the time. However, as yet I can not determine when that will be, but let us hope that it won't be long. Let me hear from you again, I remain with best wishes, Irving

1947/10/25 Marie to Irving (Book 6, 104-106)

My dear brother Irving!
Again, I try to write a few lines that we are fine. And I hope that my lines will find you in the best of health. What's doing with the studying? Yes my little brother we have the papers you sent. I hope everything will work out. And as soon as you write that you correspond with a girl Irving, it doesn't matter when, you can do it the way you see fit. It's just true, it is very difficult for you to leave. But we hope for the best. What about Walter and the teacher? Are you in good shape? I'm sorry I have so many questions for you. Yes, that boy has already been stood up because it's not worth it just go out with them. It's already Saturday and I'm trying to send the letter today, so Hermine can't write to you. I don't know where we're going in the evening. Since then we have been dancing and everything is old. The family is fine. We received a letter from David last week and he's fine, but like everyone writes, he is a lazy writer. He does not write exactly about coming here. How is Flora there? The neighbors? Now I wish you lots of good luck and the best health and take great care of yourself. Eat too. Now I close my lines and greetings and kisses from your sister, forever with countless love. Maria
Hi to everyone. Is Herman still working for Arthur?

1947/11/2 Hermina to David (Book 11, 323-325)

November 2, 1947
Dear David,
We were so glad to hear from you and to know that you are well. We are also well and the days are almost the same. Our work keeps us busy. I am a working 5 days a week, but Maria works 6 days. I started going to evening school. I like it only it is pretty hard. From next week on, it will be 3 times a week. Hope it will help to improve my English. Otherwise, everything is alright and the weather here is almost like in California. It was very nice until now, but it is getting colder. We bought our beautiful winter coats last week and they are really very pretty. Mrs. Kugler's daughter took us up in a wholesale house and we could buy real nice coats for less money. You wouldn't believe how nice these people are to us, I mean Mrs. Kugler's family. Anyway, if our home would be here that would be a big difference. But, at present we don't even need it. Who would clean and work? We miss that, but there isn't much we can do about it. We meet quite a few persons but not much to talk about - not even in New York. For a man is easier here because there are plenty of girls and probably nice girls too. The girl I mentioned last time is a very pretty girl and she is my friend, that is how Irving met her. She has a nice position, but I don't believe she has money. [In Hungarian] If Bertha would not be the way she is, maybe she would know a nice girl who would be good for you. It is not worth it to start with her! If you are here it would be easier, however I don't know how difficult it would be to find a position for you. Write about yourself. Did you write to the post lady yet? I replied to her letter,

however I don't have patience to write. For months I did not write to Lipot, and then in the last letter they wrote that he has been in the hospital for 8 months already. Like this, I can't help so what can I write. I did not get a letter from Emil from Helmec for a while. I send a few dollars to him sometimes. I gave up my correspondence with the others, it's not worth it. I kiss you with love. Hermina

[On the center fold] I received a letter from the little lady from the post office [Jane]. She wrote before she received my letter. I'll send it to you.

1947/11/2 Hermine to Irving (Book 11, 316-317) first time voting

[In English]

11/2 - 47

My dear brother Irving,

We were very happy to hear from you and I'm sorry for not writing you more often. As you know, I'm going to school and next week will start 3 times a week instead of twice a week. I registered, so Tuesday is my first time [that] I'm going to vote not only in this country, but the first time for me that I ever voted. I asked the History teacher and I gave him the list, the one they gave me when I registered and in class he explained how it works and it was very interesting not only to me, but to the others, too. We'll have exams in [another] three weeks. It would be nice to be smart, but to me is still different - only I would like to be good - just like my little, big brother Irving! Really I couldn't think of such things because he works so hard and I'm taking it easy! But my good news to you is that we bought our beautiful winter coats through Mrs. Sofferman's cousin. He works 16 years in that place and never takes up there anybody, but gave us the address and believe me, we bought the most beautiful coats there. It costs plenty, but I wish you could see it. Will try to make snapshots in them later. How are you Irving? How is Hilda? What does Herman think of your suit, you never mentioned it. If he wants one we'll get it for him! Dave said he would be interested in a nice girl but with money. That is possible but only if he is here and looks around himself. If they have money they like to know what does he have. What kind of business he is in. Otherwise, everything is the same. That nice young man you met made a few dates - was very nice but one time I received a card from him telling me he is sorry can't come this weekend but he is in bed with a cold [and] made a date for the next weekend and never showed up. Just for you so you would see how it works. Well, it doesn't matter there are many more like him so it isn't worth to worry about them. How is Herman? Do you have heat in the house? Please have the furnace cleaned so nothing would happen and don't put too much coal in it. Did you have mail from Europe? Let me know. Please write. Love, Hermina

1947/11/3 Marie to Irving (Book 6, 78-80)

Nov 3 / 47

My dear brother Irving,

I'm sorry to write late, but I hope my lines will find you in the best of health. We are well. Hermine wrote to you yesterday. And I think she mentioned that we bought winter coats. And although as you could see my buddy it's wholesale, but it's something beautiful. Like a dream. And even mine because I didn't bring it home. Mine is gray and white fake fur is on the collar and continues to the front and is very beautiful. Hermine's is beautiful brown with a new cut. But leave it at that. And how are you Irvingkem? Are you studying hard? I just talked to Mrs. Klein and she said she got a card from you and she was very happy to bring it and said she would answer you. Mrs. Kugler also received it and she asked me to write to you to thank you for writing to her. And she says hello. And so does her daughter. Now my little brother dear take very good care of yourself my little brother dear. What about those papers you sent? Otherwise, what's up with you? I didn't get that letter from the girl here again. The relatives I saw are fine. I haven't heard from David lately. I hope to hear the best. Just take great care of yourself and don't get upset and try to eat properly. You are greeted and kissed countless times with love by your forever sister. Maria

Hello to everyone

1947/11/8 Irving to Hilda (Book 6, 335)

Nov 8th. 1947

Dear Hilda,

With the hope that you will forgive me for not answering your delightful letter immediately. However, as you recall previously I have mentioned that sometimes I'll be a little late, well, this is it. To sum up the past week I can only say that I was very busy. By being busy, I simply mean that I had four exams and all happened to be on the same day. Therefore, I need not go any further, since this should be no news to you. Exams are first if one like it or not. Now to mention something about my spare time, that is, if I have any? Well, sometimes I do, and sometimes I don't. When I do have free time, I usually spend it at the Hillel Foundation (it's a university club) or going to lectures like for example last week, we had an excellent speaker his name was Dr. McDonald. He is the President Truman's representative to the Anglo-American Palestine Investigation Committee. His subject was "Palestine and the U.N.". Believe it or not, he was good. You have probably read some of his books. Well, as you see at present this is one good way of spending time. Next time I'll try to give you a longer report. Finally, to mention it would have been swell to be in New York to answer your Halloween invitation. Thanks for your thoughts, maybe next time. Incidentally did [handwritten] you have a nice time? Please write me all about it. Now, I hope that everyone is well and best wishes to you, Irv

1947/11/15 Pál Lengyel to Irving (Book 19, 131-134)

Dear Mr. Gluck and family,
I have received the letter which you sent me. My advice about the properties is as follows. I have not received anything from Bratislava; however, if I receive anything then I will attend to all your desires to the fullest extent. In fact, the mere failure to report the property tax on the property application [Slovak – "prihláška majetku"] does not result in the confiscation of property, only a rather heavy fine. Thousands of such foreign applications [Slovak – "prihláška"] must have been submitted to Bratislava and it will take a lot of time to process them. So I think I will be waiting a long time until they contact me with the answer. I have already taken the necessary measures in advance so that there are no surprises if they ask for details. Through Ignác Klein, I have requested copies of the land register that exist on the books at the office. Because this tax administration office [Slovak - DaNová správa] usually gives short deadlines, there would be no time left to obtain the documents. The documents have not been sent yet, but they promised that they will be soon. They have advised me that they will be costly - - - however this poses no problem because Ignác Klein will pay it from the rent. I am very surprised that you don't know a great deal about your properties. However, if you had read my previous letter carefully, then you should have known that your property was declared as abandoned property and that the National Administrator [Slovak - národny správcát] has authorized none other than Ignác Klein , your dear brother-in-law, who just came home from Germany at that time. Therefore, Bela Fenicky of Kiraly Helmec was never your agent and can't take any action on the matter. Ignác Klein, as an ex officio appointee of the national administrator [Slovak - národny správcát, Hungarian - nemzeti gondnok] / the district's administrative commissioner [Slovak – okresná správna komisiának, Hungarian – járási intézöbizottság] owes a settlement, but I don't know, and it's not very important whether he has settled or not, because the national guardianship lasts only until you decide to act otherwise. If you want to stop the national guardianship of your property here, send someone a power of attorney written in Slovak and witnessed by the nearest Czech-Slovak consulate, that is, authorize someone to manage your properties. Then, based on this power of attorney, the district office [Slovak - járási hivatal] will be stopped from acting on your behalf by the national administrator [Slovak - národny správcá] and the person you authorize will manage the property. In this matter I have spoken to Ignác Klein who has indicated that he will write to you. He told me that he manages the property. He also rents them out - - and he will certainly use the income he receives for his own needs. You yourselves will certainly not be troubled, because if nothing else, you must know from the newspapers how much suffering the Jews went through, and now they came home with nothing. The economy hasn't even started, let alone run, so one has to make a living. He will not expect this from you and will reimburse you what he may have kept. He has also declared that he claims the share of his sister's 2 children from the Gluck properties. You know what he's doing, so please make a statement on the matter, either directly to him, or in a letter to me. Ignác claims that he has already written to you about this, but to no avail. It would be a shame to take the matter to trial, because if it is true that she invested the dowry brought there in the property, then he will definitely win the lawsuit. It would be good to repair the house as well, because it is in a very dilapidated condition. If it's not thoroughly repaired, it will soon collapse. I believe that in this short letter, I have written quite clearly about everything that is important. It is up to you to act in your own behalf. If it will be necessary for you to make decisions in regards to the properties, I will give you additional information. Until then, best regards, Pál Lengyel, District Notary Officer

1947/11/22 Marie to David (Book 16, 6-7)

Nov 22 / 47

Dear David!

I don't even remember who didn't respond yet. I only know that I did not hear from you for a long time. I hope my lines will find you in the best of health. We are well, only I have become such a bad writer, too. I hope you will be in a hurry to write also. Have you decided what you will do yet? I know the air there is very healthy. The weather here is not really good. I think it would be better for me to be in a warmer place, since here I catch colds easily. Every winter I have to get a shot against the cold. I cry, but I don't know what I want to do myself. Otherwise, we don't have company here now, because it is very hard for girls. Wherever you go, there are always more girls than boys. I am truly surprised about you. In the world a boy like you could get a girl easily and you could find good girls too. It is easier for a boy than for a girl. It would be good for you to look after this seriously. I don't think it would be so difficult. It is hard to ask, but then it comes naturally. But I will leave this too. Take care of yourself. We got a letter from Irving last week and he is very busy with studying. He is sending his best to you, too. Now I will close my lines with greetings and I kiss you with love. Maria

Take care wherever you go. Write. Herman is doing well, too. I'm writing this letter from work and I want to send it today. We got a letter from the post lady about two weeks ago. She is well. I don't know if Hermine sent that letter, but if she did not then next time I will send it. She asks us to send something to her again and [she writes] how she used everything that we sent to her. But I will leave this too for today.

1947/11/24 Hermine and Marie to Irving (Book 6, 22-23)

Nov 22/47
[from Marie]
My dear little brother Irving!
I'm really sorry for neglecting my writing so much. It's not enough that I don't write to anyone else, I also rarely write to you. I hope that my lines will find you in the best of health. We are well. I did not heard from you for awhile. I guess you are very busy. Do you study hard? Hey my buddy! Do not think that I forgot about your birthday. First of all, even if it's late, I wish you lots and lots of luck and may the dear God help you after that also in every step of your way and also in the best of health [so] that we can hear the best about you. Take care of yourself. Do you have time to eat? I know, my dear little brother that you don't like my questions like that. But take care of yourself as much as you can. What is the news in the school? How are you doing ? How is your friend Walter? I can't write anything particular about myself. Everything is still the same. We were to dance a few times since then, but did not have any result. We hope that everything is going to be somehow. I don't even want to go anymore. I will leave that too already. Hermine wrote to Flora this week. Did you hear anything from Europe? I did not write there, I don't even know since when. My time goes so fast somehow that I don't even know how. I saw the relatives last week. Jenny [Zeny] Frey is well too. Have you heard from David? I am in a hurry to write to him a few lines, too. I am writing from work. Currently it's not that busy. Now I will close my lines and wish you everything good. I'm sending my best from my heart and kiss you countless times with love, forever your faithful sibling. Love, Maria

[from Hermine]
I will attach this letter that Julis Bolsi wrote to me. As I remember they sued our father for some reason - but I don't remember what was the reason. Maybe you remember better. I kiss you! H[ermine]

[from Marie] Write my buddy! that you or I will try to write again

[from Hermine]
My dear Irving,
I am upset about it that you sent a check, but I know you will be mad if I were to send it back. So, thank you for it! I gave half of it to Marcsa. I am planning on sending a package tomorrow. One of them is Herman's, the other one is yours. If it's not good then send it back. I will exchange it. I'm not writing which, choose the one you prefer. I will write again. I kiss you with love. Hermina

1947/12 Undated Hermine to Irving (Book 11, 200-201)

[1947/12 from mention of Fenicky's letter which was sent in 1947/9/3 and Julis Balsi's letter]

Dear little brother Irving!

We got your letter and the papers and if the office is open, then on Saturday I'm counting on going there. First of all, I will go to that Slovak office and maybe I will write it in Czech like Lengyel the notary wrote and have it signed that way. I talked to Bertha too and she suggested that we can get the papers from the consul and we should write in Czech the same as what you sent to us. Until I go there I won't know anything, but I will be in a hurry to get this done as soon as possible. I want to write to Julis Balsi also tonight. We sent the article to David and we hope that he is well. We, thank God are well, and I hope you are, too! Aunt Jenny is always wondering about you, but I did not call them this week yet. Bertha is here now. I talked to her about Lengyel's letter and I think that Fenicky's letter was official and surely he did not understand what it was about. I guess the documents will give explanations and they were put together pretty well. As soon as I find out something about it, I will let you know. My little brother, believe me, if we take the situation seriously in regards to school work, I don't know what to write since I like it, but after work it is very hard. Plus, I did not go to school for many years and they are expecting me to know everything in English. I will have to go for a couple of times and then I will see if I will continue. I don't have much patience for it my little brother. How is Arthur and the others? I wanted to write, but maybe just give out our greetings to them. Also to Aunt Helen. I wish you everything good with much love! I kiss you. Hermina
Happy New Year to you both! Love.

Oh yes! I don't even know how you can devote yourself to studying?! It is very hard! Good Luck!

1947/12/22 Marie to Irving (Book 6, 33-35)

Dec 22 / 47
My dear little brother Irving!
We got your letter which we could hardly wait for and I'm happy to hear, that thank God you are healthy. And now I hope that you are resting. And don't look for a job at home, my little brother because you can use some rest. I hope you have success in school! Don't be sad my buddy. And also, I am happy Irving dear that you like the package and that everything is good and you like it. But it is a present from us. Do not forget that you gave something to us too. You just wear it in [good] health. Yes my little brother, what's going on with that girl? Are you still corresponding? I hope to hear the best from you. Now my buddy I will get to the case. As you can see, as the notary writes, Ignac Klein could have worked with him. We just talked to Mannie and he said that it would be best if you would go to the Veteran's Administration office and since you were a soldier and you could not have done anything either then as an American resident, they could help you. And that office should write on your behalf to Washington. Because otherwise there is not much you can do because the notary is able to charge you the amount he wants. And the way he writes that he already wrote to us once, that our property is listed as abandoned property. That's not true either because he never wrote that to us. It is his fault because he knew very well that we are alive. And Ignac [Klein] demanded his share. As I mentioned, only from here

could you do something about it. And Hermine will write about it. It would be the best to sell it if we could. Because many are dealing with it and this way it could go to nothing. And my dear little brother, do as you see best in this case. And those documents that the notary is asking for, we already sent them to Miksa's relatives and that is why he can sue them. And this way at least he will pay for the cost from the wealth. That man seems to do whatever he can do. Now I will leave that too. Now I can't write anything particular about me. Everything is the same. We have not heard from David for a long time. And as far as Arthur's factory is concerned, he is lucky that besides all that [happened] nobody was in it, that is, the fire was at night. It is important that it was insured. I hope to hear the best about you and take care of yourself. You know my dear little brother, I mentioned it last time, that I will go to a Hungarian party. We went with Bertha, but as always there is no result. Everything is the same. I have to work as you can see during the holidays. Hermine does not work. I kiss you countless times with love, your forever faithful sibling, who will never forget. I wish you lots and lots of luck. I'm sending my best to all of you. Love, Maria

1947/12/24 Jane Fabianova to David (Book 7, 101-105)

Dear Dezső!
Now, I'm keeping you waiting with my lines. It's not like I want to though, but I was waiting for the package, that [should have] come in the middle of the month. Today is the day before Christmas, and I'm still waiting for the "dear Jesus" to bring the package that I am waiting so hard for. It felt very bad that you didn't write anything to me through all these months. But now, when I'm reading your long letter, I am doubly happy.

Dezső you are truly nice, and you are as good as a sibling. Thank you very much for everything you sent. If it doesn't come today, then I will send this letter, and if the package will come in later, then I will send a different letter immediately, because I will not postpone writing anymore. If I get the things that you wrote about, I will be truly happy. No way would I give anything to anyone from it, since it's impossible to buy anything, and if it is, then it's the cheapest merchandise. You need a voucher even for that, and sometimes [the merchandise] is very rare. Imagine that there aren't any stockings anywhere, not even for the winter, and if someone can get one cheaply, it's 800 korona a pair. Dezső, if it would be possible to send anything, then please send 2 nightgowns and 2 slim silk camisoles. They are so beautiful from America, like a dream. A flowery Italian [design] or from poplin or something like that, just beautiful, and a raincoat, without an insert. I am sending here the fabric and the color. This sample is American. If the package will arrive, I will write more. I am sending here my picture. It was made in June 1944. I have nothing newer, but there isn't much of a difference, just my hair is longer. The thing that can't be sent in a letter is lemon powder for tea. You sent me 2 packages a year ago, but there is nothing left and it's really good in the tea. Otherwise I'm good. I hope you will write before spring. I am writing to Herminka and Mariska today also. I truly can't forget your goodness, that you helped me out from such big trouble. Dezső, from those things you sent, I could supply myself with clothing in the right way. If it could only be here already. I truly appreciate everything because if you could only see how I came home. I was ragged with only one dress, with only one bad pair of wooden shoes, pale, starved out, and sick from the misery. But, thank god, now I am healthy, you supplied me nicely with these packages and even with this pretty, nice camisole. I will be alright. And I am smiling again, like in the picture. Greetings with much love, Jankica

[from my] mom also
This is the color and this is the fabric.
The raincoat is long in the back…not a rubber coat.
Neck is 105 cm it has to be big and with a belt.
On the front, 2 pockets and a button-up hood.
Here is the fabric sample...

1947/12/25 Ruth Balbach to Irving (Berlin) (Book 16, 433-436)

Dear Irving
It's been a long time since we've heard from one another. We've been waiting for a letter from America that hasn't arrived yet from "Irving Berlin. " Now, I will try to write you and I hope that it will reach you in the best of health, which I can also say we are in ourselves. My husband is home since the 13 July 1945. At the moment he's studying in Karlsruhe at the Technical University. How are you? I hope you are alright. Unfortunately, I can't say the same thing about us as you probably know the situation in Germany. The living conditions here are so bad that you can't imagine or believe it unless you live here in Germany yourself. We all hope that in the new year the situation will get better. Dear Irving, how is William Chapman? Is he at home, too? He visited us one time in July 1946 and both of us were very happy. Now I would like to ask you something, too. Dear Irving, please send me the pictures that you took of us, I would like to save them and please send a picture of yourself, too. I hope that my letter will reach you and that you won't make me wait too long for an answer. I will now end this letter. Sending you many warm greetings, Ruth, Heike, Parents and Toni.

1947/12/26 Hermine to Irving (Book 11, 327-331) about Ignác Klein lawsuit

12/26 - 47
My dear little brother Irving,
We got your letter and we were very happy for it. I'm sorry to read that Arthur's factory burned down. I hope that at least he had good insurance. I hope that he will get the value of the damage back. But what will he do? Will they try to build another one? If everything got destroyed, then Herman does not work. I hope he will find another job for himself! I'm planning on writing to him too, but something always comes up. This is why it gets delayed always. Give my greetings to them and to Aunt Helen and that I was sorry to hear about this. So, that I can respond to Lengyel's letter, I don't even know what to write, because I still have his previous letter, where he wrote that we should trust in Klein because after his suffering he won't give his wealth to anyone else. He had enough trouble already. Also, that the state appointed him to be the guardian and no one can take it away from them and now he wants to do this conspiracy with him. He wrote that he already wrote to us, that if we don't deal with it, it will be turned over to the government. Since he

and everybody knew very well that we are here and they only wanted to keep quiet about our existence so that maybe it could be his. I will write about everything to you in detail. Now I will take some time for the lunch topic, so at least I could write a few lines to you. I'm afraid that it will not matter much what they will do. It is possible that Feneky would have done more than anybody else, because he already mentioned that Ignác [Klein] is suing him, because he took everything for himself from the profit. It would be best if we could sell it and get rid of them, because they only have an interest in the profit. Manny, Bertha's husband said that you should go to the veteran's administration and tell them about the case. Maybe, they will give you enlightenment. What did you hear from Washington? When did you talk to the lawyer? What is your opinion considering the case? I'm planning on writing to David and to you too and then I will send back a letter to Lengyel. I want to read it again. Write about everything and take care of yourself. Love to you both. Hermina

Side note: Wait with the response until I write to Lengyel

1947/12/26 Undated Hermine to David (Book 10, 3-4) pages 1-4

[This date 9/55? is written by Aunt Marie on the top when she was organizing the letters, but there is no envelope and it is wrong since Aunt Hermine mentions the article about Arthur's fire]

Dear David,
It looks like you are not interested about our well being, because if you would be, you would write to us a few lines once in a while. Although I could not do that to you and even if we don't write often, but we do write to you. I don't even know where to start this letter. Irving attached a letter to us that was written by Pali Lengyel from Lelesz. Before we came to New York, we wrote to Lengyel about our properties, that we would like to get it back from the government and that we are American citizens and they can't take it away from us. Then he responded that the state appointed Klein to be the guardian and that we should trust him because he will not take somebody else's property after the big struggle he went through. Now Ignác [Irving] wrote a letter again and asked if he [Pál Lengyel] can secure all the papers from Bratislava, then we shall pay him for his effort. When Irving was here in the Fall, he got the papers that we had to fill out and sent it to Lengyel. Like Lengyel wrote, it was only sent in because of the tithe tax and the failure of taking that action could cause a penalty. So, he promised that he will do what he could. But he wrote that we are considered to be disappeared and Ignác Klein was appointed as trustee because we did not act about it. The property was declared an abandoned property. This way he surely has taken all the profits. When some people wrote about this to us, Ignác from Lelesz did not mention anything. We sent an authorization to Fenecky, to Boske Cramer's husband from Szerdahely, who also dealt with Bertha's case. He was also a notary before the war and an expert in the case. He did not write to us for months. This way our Irving wrote to him a very stern letter, to which he responded that even if he did not write to us, he arranged things in our case. As a matter of fact he even sued Ignác Klein because he lied and kept the profit from everything. Since then we did not hear anything from him. I don't even know what would be the best. Irving is dealing with the case. I'm asking you not to do anything. Only if you have any idea, then let me hear from you and also tell it to Irving. Please don't write to anybody else because it would mess the whole thing up. So write to me and I could write in more details, but I can't [now] because I don't have any patience.

1947/12/26 Undated Hermine to David (Book 11, 297) page 5

Also, write about your well being and about what you are doing or what do you do? How's the weather? Here there was big snowfall last Friday, so the traffic stopped. There was 26 inches of snow. I will attach an article that Irving sent to us. Arthur's factory burned down. What I hope is that it was insured! I would like to write to him too, but I don't have time. This week I went to Bertha every night because she is alone. Her husband is in Florida. Write about yourself - we are well. Kiss you with much love. Hermina

1947/12/29 Marie to David (Book 8, 192-193)

Dec 29/47
Dear David!
It's been a long time ago since I heard from you. I hope that my lines will find you in the best of health. We are well, there is no news. It has been a few weeks since we heard from our little brother. Thank God, he is well. No particular news. I thought that you read about the snow around here. The traffic stopped, but today the buses already started to go. Otherwise, no news here. The relatives are well. Mannie is away to Florida

for a few weeks. Me as it seems, I am always busy, although I can't say that we go out a lot. That is still the same here. It is still not easy to meet anyone, but it will come as it should be. I think Hermine already wrote about everything in more detail. I started to write this letter at work and I want it to go out and that is why I write on paper like this. I hope that you will be in a hurry to write a few lines. Take care of yourself wherever you go. Now I will close my lines and send you my greetings and kiss you with much of love. Your sibling, Maria

I wrote to our little brother too in the previous letter. He is sending his greetings also. And he said that you did not write to him for so long already. He is very busy with studying and I wish you a very happy and lucky new year!

1947/12/29 Marie to Irving (Book 6, 20-21) - say Kaddish

Dec 29 / 47

My dear little brother, Irving!

It has been a few days since I heard from you. I hope that my lines will find you in the best of health. We are well. Surely you heard about it too what a big snow we have here. The entire transportation stopped, only our subway works. Business is stopped too. I am working, but there is no savings. I have to be here. Today the bus started to go and the rest of the traffic. But I will leave this too. Mannie travelled away last week to Florida for a few weeks. This way Hermina slept there. I don't like to sleep at other places. I was there for dinner too. Also, we went for the movies together. But other than that there is no news. I worked on Christmas. And how are you my buddy? How are you spending your vacation? I hope you will try to rest. I guess you are working hard at the house. Take care of yourself my Irving. Is there heat at home and do you have coal? I think about you a lot my buddy. How's everything with the girl? Did you hear from her or do you correspond with her. Write about yourself my buddy. Yes my little brother, I will note something here. I [may have] already written about it, but if I did not then it is the following. I talked to a Rabbi last time here about our father [and] about what we have to do. We should not neglect it. There are thousands of others like this. He said if they are alive, then we would have heard about them already. And to encourage ourselves is not good either. If the case is really like that, then it is better to say kaddish because if we [continue to] hope, we aren't doing them any good. And the rabbi said that we should choose a day as we see fit and keep that same day for yahrzeit. In a case like that there is no need to sit, but Kaddish can be said. And everybody can be taken [into account on] the same day. Write my little Irving what do you say about that. We can't neglect it. And then David needs to be told to say kaddish also. At least we can help poor them with that. But I will leave this too. And write my buddy. I have not heard about David for a long time. I hope he is well. The relatives are well here. I'm sending my best to everyone. And you my buddy, I'm sending my best to you from my heart and I kiss you countless times with much love. Your forever faithful sibling. And I wish you a very happy and lucky new year and I hope our wish will come true. Hi to Herman and everyone. Love Maria

1948/1 Undated Hermine to Irving (Book 10, 101-102) - fire at Bonded Scale

[Dated from reference to Arthur and the insurance, presumably from the fire]

My dear little brother Irving,

I hope you are well, since I'm waiting for your letter in vain, but it does not come from you. Although, I can only wait for one from you because Herman is not interested in things like that. We are well. Regarding the documents, I was only waiting for you to notify me if they were signed - because if you want to have them signed, then it is not worth it to spend money on the authentication until then. So, please write what you want. I think the note about considering Lajos' children could bring some inconvenience. And if the dear God would give it, that they will be found, then we would give it back to them anyway. So, write about that. Did you write to Lengyel already? I would like to help you, but I don't even know what to write to him. Also, I did not write to Arthur and the others yet because I don't know if I should offer if it's necessary. I will give my debt to him in small amounts. Write considering this. God forbid, but poor man, he might need it. I hope he will get an insurance [payment]! Write, and I kiss you with love. Hermina

1948/1/3 Undated Hermine to Irving (Book 10, 57-58)

[Dated by reference to going to Czech consul, it being closed, and noting about Emil and Lenke]

My dear little brother Irving!

This morning I sent a letter to you, but as I thought the case through, the way the documents are being written, if you remember what you wrote about Emil and Lenke Gluck's property, you wrote that they could be somewhere and they still can be found and they heard about them in 1946. I thought that it is also good because Klein and the others can't demand [it], and we want to keep their share for the children. I only wish it would be true! But in case we will not hear about them or about their existence, it will make the situation harder with the property, since it will be impossible to sell it and their share will not be separable from the rest and this way it will be hard to sell the rest. The buyer will not want to hear something like that. So, I will see what should be changed about that. I will wait until maybe you will respond. I will see what they will say in the office. I guess it would be best to translate it to Czech. I wanted to go today at lunch time, but the office was closed. Besides that everything is well here and I hope with you as well! Oh yes! If you could call the hospital – that is, to call the company, that it was transferred here and they sent the documents to the company where I work and they will send the money to them because the insurance was sent to them too. I work for them: Goodfriends Department Stores 505-8th Ave. Love to you both, Hermina

1948/1/4 David and Dorothy to Hermine and Marie (Book 12, 189-190)

Jan 4, 1948

Dear Hermine and Maria,

I know you will be very much surprised receiving David's letter concerning the news of our forthcoming marriage. It is just a bit sooner than we had anticipated, but inasmuch as David's birthday is on the 11th, we felt that we would have a double celebration. We are being married on Jan. 10th in the evening by an orthodox rabbi, in his study and with us will be several of our close friends. On Sunday the 11th, we are having a small reception at my apartment in Los Angeles, sort of an open house so our friends can come in and celebrate with us. My address there is 712 N. Hobart Blvd, Apt 300, and of course on that date my name will be Mrs. David Gluck. My only regret is that our loved ones will not be there with us. You see, I am from Chicago, Ill., some 2000 miles away, so time and distance will undoubtedly prevent their being here with us. The same I suppose is true of you, as well as Irving and Herman. We are hoping that soon we shall be able to obtain an apartment, and, I trust, one large enough so that you can come out to visit us. I am looking forward to that day with great enthusiasm, and I hope it will transpire in the not too far distant future. I have heard so much about you girls, that although we have never met, I really feel as though I know you. Just as soon as we have a permanent address, we'll let you know, so that we can correspond regularly. I know that David has neglected writing to you, so if you will permit me, I'll just take over and let you have all the news. In the meantime, my best wishes to both of you for a Happy, Healthy and Prosperous New Year. Your "future sister" Dorothy

1948/1/4 David to Irving (Book 22, 205-210) - marriage to Aunt Dorothy

Jan 4. 948

Dear little brother!

I read your precious lines gladly and I am very happy that thank God you are well, and everything is going the way you planned. I got a letter from the girls this week too and I got the newspaper article about Arthur. Thank you! Currently, little brother I did not give you a definite answer to your letter, but I will write a little news which I believe will surprise you. So here it goes, Hold the horses! Believe it or not, but it happened, that is, it will happen. On Jan. 10th at 6 o'clock in the evening, I will get married with a very cute little girl by an Orthodox Jewish Rabbi. I know you will be very surprised. But if you will see her you will give your blessings. She is a very smart and loyal girl and she comes from a very good family. I will get married on January 10th. So, you know that my birthday is on the 11th and I decided it that way, so I will have a real birthday. So I can inform you better, there will be no kind of ceremony, only for the closest. On Saturday night, it will only be us and the necessary witnesses. The reception will be on Sunday afternoon, where there will be 25-30 officially, but nothing will be special. I would like it if you could be here, my little brother. But right now I don't wish it and don't even want you to come. Eventually, if I will get settled here and I will have a proper place, I will invite you here, but before that, I have to find a proper apartment. So, I know that my lines will surprise you, if you want, you can tell this to Arthur and the others also, but that is up to you. Right now, I live at the old place, but in about 2 months I will get a normal place and I will live in Long Beach. If you think that I will not get your response until Friday night, then write a letter to this address: David Gluck 71R N. Hobart Blvd, apt #300, Los Angeles 27. California.

P.S. I forget, try to remember in the care of Dorothy Pinkus 712 N. Hobart Blvd apt 300 L.A.

My little brother, I will ask you for something. If you want you will do it, if not, then that's fine too. Currently I have a lot of expenses. If you want to help me out, it would be great. I will give it back to you in 2-3 months. But please don't write about this to anyone, not even to the girls or to nobody else. Ok? So, if you can send me at least 200-250 dollars - which I will probably pay you back shortly. I don't want them to know the truth about how much money I have. They asked me, but I didn't tell them, and the bonus has to be paid here too, so I can get a nice house. I want to be certain that I will have enough money, that is why I'm turning to you. I know it very well, that you will send it to me. You don't need to send it in a hurry. You will get the letter on Tuesday afternoon - maybe on Wednesday. If you go to the bank and if you will send a [Cashier's check] then I will get it on Friday with special delivery. But please don't say anything to anyone, not even to Herman. Ok? So, little brother, I hope that everything will work out for the best and I hope you will not take this the wrong way, that I am turning to you for money. But I know that you will do it. It is possible that I won't even need it, but I want to be sure that I have money for everything. Eventually I will send pictures too. Now I will write to the girls too. So, I wish you the best. I will stay with love, your forever faithful brother. David.

P.S. If you cannot send me money, please write to me with special delivery, so that I could possibly get it from other places. I kiss you, David

Dear Herman,
A few lines to you too. I am well and Ignác will tell what I wrote about myself. Kisses, David

1948/1/4 Dorothy to Irving [1 week before wedding] (Book 2, 14-15)

January 4, 1948
Dear Irving
Although I don't know you, I have heard so much about David's "kid" brother, that I already feel very close to you. I hope in the not too distant future, we shall have the opportunity to meet each other in person. No doubt David's letter to you will come as a complete surprise since you perhaps have just come to consider him as a confirmed bachelor. However, after January 10 he shall have a "ball and chain", and that is me. Seriously, we are both sorry you and the girls won't be with us, and am sure nothing would please us more. Shortly after the wedding date, we shall take some photos and send one to you, so at least you will have an idea of what your "sister-in-law" looks like. Also, we hope that we shall be able to obtain an apartment soon suitable enough to enable us to invite you for a visit. Believe me, I shall look forward to that day. In the meantime, I know you will rejoice with us in the news. Extend my very best to Herman, whom I too look forward to meeting. Love, Dorothy

1948/1/6 (a) Irving to David and Dorothy - Draft Wedding Congratulations (Book 16, 186-187)

Jan. 6, 1948
Dear Dorothy and Dave,
After I have opened your letter it was indeed a surprise to find a strange page included. However, soon enough I found out what it meant. I really am rejoicing with you about the wonderful news. I want to congratulate you Dave and to you Dorothy, my best wishes of everything today and always. As for the wedding, I'm sorry that I couldn't be there but [the] time will come that we will meet in person. I'm very glad that David told you quite much about me and I hope that you will not be disappointed one day. I thank you already for your very nice invitation and it's always a good feeling to have a brother and sister-in-law who are looking forward to see me. I wish you lots of luck in your apartment hunting. I understand that it is just as difficult as all over the United States. As I'm not as curious as women are, I would like anyhow to see you both on a photo as a married couple. We, Herman and I, will be thinking of you on January 10th, 1948. Since it's Saturday we will have plenty of time to celebrate with you at home. Once again, best wishes and lots of luck to you both and may God bless you. Love, Herman and Irv

P.S. As I'm not so experienced in buying presents, please let me know what you could use for your new home.

[In Hermine's handwriting on the bottom] - very good, Love, Hermine

1948/1/6 (b) Irving to Dave (Book 6, 255)

Jan 6, 1948
Columbus, Ohio

Dear Dave,

I have practically answered your letter, which I'm sure, you'll find enclosed. However, here I just want to add a few more lines. First, you'll find $250.00 enclosed. Secondly, once again congratulations and best of luck as well as a very happy "birth day." At present, school keeps me quite busy, therefore, I'll have to cut my writing short. But will write more later. However, let me hear from you more often. I have written to New York also - Hermine and Maria are well. Hope they'll follow your path soon. Flora, Arthur and family wishing you the best of everything. Now, I remain as ever your brother, Irving

P.S. Herman probably will write, too. Mean time, good luck and good health

1948/1/6 Hermine to Irving (Book 2, 1-3)

1/5 - 48

My dear little brother,

I called today the Czech office because I went there on Saturday, but it was closed. So the woman who I talked to said that she would like to see the copy of what we sent to Fenecky last year [1946/12/26 Power of Attorney to Bela Fenicky (Book 19, 122-124)] so she could give the proper information. I told her that I just want to translate it. So, write what you think? I sent the copy home to you and if you have it then send it to me by air mail. This way I will get it by Saturday since I will go there on Saturday. How are you? We are well, thank God. I just wrote to Emil in Helmec. He has not written for awhile and I sent a package last week. Now I want to send 5 dollars. Really boys, maybe you could write him a few lines.

It is not nice that a child is alone. At least once a year Herman should write also and he could put 5 dollars in for him. Basically his father took out a loan so he could give us a loan, so we could come here. I will write this to David, too. He should not forget this. Other than that, Maria talked to a Rabbi about what happened in Europe and he said that we should choose a day that we would set for the yahrzeit. Based on the cases, there is no hope to find anyone who stayed alive. So, it would be better to accept the fact that our poor father does not exist. For him, it would be better if you would pray for him. This is important, so my little brother, ask the Rabbi about that and let me know. Let's not neglect it because it is worse...

Write

I kiss all of you with love. Hermina

1948/1/7 Hermine to Irving (Book 10, 83-84) David getting married

1/7 - 48

Dear Irving,

A big surprise isn't that - David is getting married. I wrote them tonight. My English is not too hot and it took me so long that it is late already, but I want to write a few lines to you, too. I like to send a telegram to wish them luck and to congratulate them. Hope I will be able to do so because the Western Union wants to go on strike. Oh, yes, in my next letter to them I like to find out what should I buy for them as a wedding gift. What do you think and Herman? Does he think of giving him something? I thought a silver set would be very nice the 4 of us could do it...! let me hear from you. Here I'm enclosing her snapshot they asked me to send it to you. I'm going with the paper [to the Czech consul] this Saturday. Please write! Love to you both, Hermina.

Did you talk to the relatives?

Herman is next!!!!!

[In Hungarian] My little brother, the name Dorothy and then David should be paragraphed first

The letter is good

Even if you send the letter, send a telegram with just a few words to congratulate them. I'm writing again, but now I'm in a hurry, I brought your letter with me in the morning, so I'm only hastily continuing to answer your letter.

1948/1/8 Marie to David and Dorothy (Book 8, 195-196)

Jan 8 / 48

Page 626

Dear Dorothy and David!

I'm writing as soon as I can, what a surprise your precious letter was. But besides all that I am very happy to hear, that David, you finally made up your mind. And I think that you have found what you were looking for. First of all, accept my best wishes, lots and lots of good luck and a very happy birthday! I'm sorry that I'm writing in Hungarian, but it is the easiest and David please translate it to Dorothy. I am only sorry, that I can't be the first one to congratulate you and to wish you good luck in person. And thank you to both of you for the precious invitation. I hope that I don't have to wait for too long [for us] to get to know each other. I think Hermine wrote about everything in more detail. I hope that after this we can hear about you more often. There is no news here. We are well, and I would like to hear the same back from you also. We got a letter from Irving last week and they are also well. They send their best to you. Now I will close my lines and I wish everything good and the best of health. I kiss you and I am sending our best with the biggest love. Maria

I'm writing this letter from work so it could go as soon as possible.

1948/1/19 Dorothy to Irving and Herman [9 days after wedding] (Book 2, 16-18)

January 19, 1948

Dear Irving and Herman:

Many thanks for your congratulatory wire and it was nice to know that although you weren't with us in person on that all important day you were with us in spirit. I can truly say we had a lovely wedding ceremony, and our reception turned out beautifully. My sister surprised me by coming to California for the wedding, so you might well imagine how thrilled and happy I was. I really hadn't expected her, so that was an added thrill. We have finally obtained an apartment, and it will be ready for us this Thursday. We can hardly wait to move in and get settled, so we can start our housekeeping. It is a furnished apartment, not too large, but very cozy: living room, bedroom and kitchen. We also have an inner door bed so we can accommodate weekend guests (that, of course, does not apply to you boys if and when you would like to pay us a visit, in other words no time limit for you)! Seriously, the place is cute and I know David and I will have lots of fun fixing it up. The address is 918 Main Ave., Long Beach, so now you can write us there. We are both fine and very happy, and hope this finds you well too. Keep us posted about everything, and we, in turn, will do the same. Love from, Dorothy and David

1948/1/28 David and Dorothy to Irving (Book 12, 185-187)

Jan. 27, 1948

Dear Irving,

It looks as though David wasn't kidding when he said to me, "You take over the correspondence for the family." Not that I mind, except I wonder whether you wouldn't like a line or two from David himself. However, I have discovered that in order to keep informed of your well-being and activities, I shall have to keep it going - so please bear with me. We both enjoyed your letter so very much Irving, and I wish you could have seen the pride in David's eyes when he read it. Believe me, he is proud of you, and talks about you constantly. I can well imagine how busy your school duties keep you, but as you so aptly put it, one must work for anything worth attaining. David and I moved into our own apartment last Saturday and are just about organized. Although the place is furnished, there are always so many things to be done. However, things are now taking shape, and in a day or two we can really relax and enjoy it. One thing, I have made a startling discovery. David is by far a better cook than I am. Now I can take lessons from him. Really he puts me to shame in a kitchen and that's bad. His potato pancakes are really a masterpiece. Perhaps some day soon you can taste them. Nothing much more to write about at present, except you have our good wishes for success in your studies. Let us hear from you again, real soon. Love to you and Herman, Dorothy and David

[Note from David in Hungarian at the bottom]

My dear little brother,

Only a couple of lines for today. Thank God I am well, Dorothy is as well. I hope my lines will find you in the best of health, too. I kiss you, David.

1948/2 Undated Hermine to Irving (Book 10, 69-70)

My dear little brother Irving!

[In Hungarian] We were very happy for your letter, thank god you are in good health! We are well too. I wanted to write to you more, but tonight we had the Union meeting and the time got a little late. So, next time I will write with more details. I hope they will agree with the company because if they don't, we will strike. The Union is demanding 5 dollars. [In English] Will let you know. Otherwise we are well and at present just that I thought of getting for Dorothy and David a silver set. It would cost about $115 or more - I wish she would tell us. Maybe a nice dinner set would be nice, too. So what do you suggest? The only thing is that maybe her family will give that. So I let you know and if it is all right I'll find it out and then I will buy it here...I'm angry because David didn't even mention that he missed us at his wedding. He didn't write at all. She sounds sweet and I answered her. About your girl - maybe she felt you don't get serious enough to spend time corresponding. Don't worry [you] will find another one when you'll come again. How is school - the exams? I know [it's] good because we have a very smart brother! Kanehare! [Yiddish - without the evil eye] Will write soon. Love to you both, Hermina

[On the side] What do you know regarding the documents?

1948/2 Undated Marie to Irving (Book 8, 8-9)

[Dated by mention of Julis Balsi and David's wedding]

My dear little brother Irving!
We got your letter last night that we could hardly wait for. I was glad to read that thank God, you are well, which I hope that you will be after this, too. Last night I also wrote a letter to you but I did not send it since I had to make changes on it. We are well too. And it is interesting the way you write in Hungarian already. I got used to you writing your letter in English. It doesn't sound great anymore, you are right about that. I understood your letter my Irving, what you are thinking, but I can give you the same answer. If you would be here too, surely it would be better and there would be an opportunity to get to know someone. It is very hard this way to find the proper place. Wherever we go there are only very young ones and even if there are older ones among them, they don't even notice us, and I get bored sitting around. I can't say that Hermine has had more luck recently. She is also this way with this. And because of this I don't even care. I know that you believe that we should not give up hope, but it is what it is. It is harder for girls these days. And as you wrote that this year is good to get married. Although, I believe it, but it's got to be [with] someone. And thank you my Irving for the information. Only you take care of yourself and eat. We got a letter from Julis Balsi yesterday and she was wondering about the house again. She wants us to write the price for her. She seriously wants to buy it. Yes, my Irving this Saturday Mrs. Saferman's son had his engagement. You know who it is I think, with that girl who you knew also. The lady's grandchild Marven. Now I think I answered everything. Yes, the sister-in-law. I don't know what to say. I know this much, she must be very smart, if she could get David. She is writing smartly and tries to become friendly. But just between us, I think that we expected David to write a couple of lines after the wedding, since none of us were there, but it seems he does not really want to write. I hope that they will be happy, that's most important. Now I will close my lines and kiss you countless times. Love, Maria

Take care of yourself. Why doesn't Herman write now?

1948/2/16 Hermine to Irving (Book 10, 86-88)

2/16 - 48
Dear little brother Irving,
I am writing a couple of lines early in the morning before I go to work. Since I wrote in your last letter regarding how much would be your part to pay for the gift, I got annoyed. I was thinking that maybe I did not even think how much you would want to chip in on this and I got an expensive gift. First of all, I thought if you would like to chip in that much money, it is more than I thought for our part and this way I almost got it from the two of your parts. That is why I bought separately other things for our part. So, please write only what you think about this because if it's too much for you, then I will return the smaller things and we will also give the utensil set because on this Saturday I would like to give it to David - in other words, send it to them. But write about it because we can still help in case you don't want to chip in that much. Although, it would be a beautiful present. Write it. I kiss you with love. Hermina

My dear little brother!

Page 628

I only want to [add] a couple of lines from work because I want to send the pictures to you. There are a few that aren't the best, but I hope you will like them! Especially one of them came out very good of me. [In English] I must admit it. Will write again. Love, Hermina

1948/2/17 Jane Fabianova to David (Book 7, 89-92)

Dear Dezső!
The package on January 28th arrived untouched. Truly beautiful things and I am very happy. There are only a few that need to be adjusted, and some of them need no adjustments. I can't write down my happiness, I am fully supplied for awhile. Currently, I'm well. I'm taking a course, and on March 27th I will be home again, because I don't want to stay here. I'm getting ready to go near Polány also for 2-3 days. I will write in the afternoon. Now, I'm only writing in a hurry, lots to study. It's so good that I learned French, at least it is not hard now. I wonder, how long does it take to get this letter, as I know it, at least 14-16 days. How beautiful the orange trees look at this time. California is beautiful – a dream world. I can't even write my happiness, thank you very much for your goodness. On the other side I'm sending my exact shoe size. Dezsőke, if you ever send anything, then stockings, because there aren't any stockings. The shoes and the neckbands are very good. It's good for the winter, even if it's large. The winter stockings and socks are good too. The sweatshirts are very beautiful also. How could I have gotten to put all these together. How could I do something good for your goodness? How's the little Ignác? Is he studying to be a doctor or an engineer? I'm sending greetings to Herminka and Mariska. When I'll be home, I will write again. With a true sibling love
Greetings
Jankica

I don't even wait for your lines for a moment, because I know that you are a "little lazy."
Send cookies and canned goods, coffee and tea too for when I go home, because we don't have those at all. Tea, coffee, cocoa, or chocolate, are just a dream here; if there were any, then they would only give 10 dkg [decigrams] for little kids [in exchange] for vouchers. There were lemons in January, but not now and I haven't eaten an orange for 7 years, nor cocoa. Now I've heard that it will be even for adults, but I don't know. [In the drawing of a shoe insert] if this will go into the shoe, then it's good. This is my exact shoe size.

1948/2/26 Hilda Goldberger to Irving (Book 17, 255-257)

Feb 26, 1948
Dear Irving,
I am very sorry I haven't written you for such a long time but a million things came up after I received your last letter. It came just when I was getting ready to study for Final Exams. I don't have to tell you what that means. After Finals came intercession. I got about three weeks off and since I was so disgusted with school, work and New York in general I decided to pay my aunt in Tallahassee, Florida a visit. I asked her if it would be all right with her if I came down and she said of course. So without another thought (I might have changed my mind) I went down to Florida for two weeks. I had a wonderful time there. Please don't ask me if I have a sun burn because I don't. It is too cold in Tallahassee in the winter to go swimming so I didn't get sun-burned. When I came home I had to register and then school started and here I am. Does that explain my laxness in writing satisfactorily? I hope so. I didn't mean not to write for such a long time but you know how easily things like that happen. How is your progress this semester? Mine isn't too bad. I don't have any first hours (classes start 8:40 for first hours). Four times a week I start at 9:45 and the other day I start at 10:50. Not bad, eh? I finish the day at either two or three o'clock four times a week and once at five - that I do not like. The courses I am taking aren't too bad. I have three major courses (Home Economics) and they are Nutrition, House, and House Furnishing. I also have an Education course which I am minoring in. The other two courses are English Lit II and Home Nursing. Sounds interesting, doesn't it? Like fun! I guess that is enough for now. Please answer soon, As ever, Hilda

1948/3/2 David and Dorothy to Irving and Herman (Book 12, 192-193)

March 2, 1945
Dear Irving and Herman:

I can't begin to tell you how thrilled and delighted I was to receive your very wonderful gift. I understand the girls bought it, and believe me they couldn't have made a wiser choice. The silverware is beautiful and it is exactly what I had been wanting. I was so excited with it, I couldn't wait for David to come home so that he could see it. Thanks a million to both of you. Now that I have service for 12, what would be more fitting than to have you all for dinner? I hope some day that will be possible. David and I are both fine and have settled down to a completely domestic life. It is about 9:30 p.m. now, and here I am writing letters, while David is relaxing near the radio, reading the paper. He told me to write that he is very tired - otherwise he would add a few lines. Some day soon I'm going to corner him and make him sit down and write to you personally. The girls write that the weather has been extremely cold in New York, and it's hard to believe with all this beautiful weather here in California. The afternoons have been so warm, we are able to discard our wraps and just go walking in a suit. I want to write a letter to the girls tonight too, so this will be all for now. I hope this letter finds you both well, and again accept our sincere thanks for your very wonderful gift. Write soon. Our love to you both.

1948/3/15 Undated Hermine to Irving (Book 10, 92-94)

[Date determined from mention that David's wedding gift received and note from Dorothy a week prior]

My dear little brother,
We got your card and the thought makes me happy that you, thank God, are all well. I know that you are very busy and because of that I forgive you if you don't write too often. I only hope that otherwise everything is ok for you! Last week we got a letter from David's wife in which she wrote that they got the wedding present and they liked it very much. They are thanking you very much and it was something that they just needed. However, only Dorothy wrote, which I hope she did to you as well, since I wrote the card in all of our names. So, please write if she wrote about that. Also Marcsa wrote in a letter that you sent money for me to buy it for you, too. Otherwise, I am well which I hope to hear about you too. I am asking you also, not to forget about eating because if you will get weak now, you can't get your health back later. So, don't think about how you also have to save because eating is very expensive, and you should not look at how much dinner costs, rather what kind of nutrition you get out of it. I don't want to preach, but I am afraid that you totally forgot about this because I am not there with you. How are you otherwise and the relatives? Give our best to them and write a few lines little brother whenever you can. Until then lots of good luck! I kiss all of you with love. Hermina

How many months do you still have to go to school?

1948/3/23 Hermine to Irving (Book 22, 201-203) - Truman, Palestine, strike

3/23 - 47 [The year is incorrect. It should be 1948]

My beloved little brother!
I was very happy to get your letter because we have not heard from you for so long. The thought makes me happy that thank God you are in good health and that you got a letter from Dorothy. I was afraid that she wouldn't write about it - but to be honest with you, it is not nice of David at all, that he does not think that we are worthy enough to mention the gift. It is not about the value of the gift, but it would have contributed, and I can write as much, that it would have been good for a bigger gentlemen [and] I think that it would have felt good to hear from him what he said about it! Otherwise how is everything with you? We are done with the big cleaning, that is, the painting and poor Herman has to fix the wall and other small things after that. Although, if I could hire someone for a day, they could at least refresh the apartment. I will leave this now and I will get to us. I had a big surprise last week when Bertha's brother Feri [Fred] was in New York. We were invited by Bertha and the others to spend the night with them. He is such a fine and nice man and he wanted to hear about us in detail. I am attaching his picture here and I tell you that he looks so much better in real life and he is a very fine man. I told him that I will write you that we met them, that is, his wife and daughter, who is also a very nice girl. They asked us to visit them this summer in Pennsylvania where they live. If you have a chance you also should visit them. I will continue with this, that everything would be good, if only the good God would grant that something good would come out of this terrible and demanding life because the rumors are so cruel that there is nothing to think about - the rumors about Palestine and Pr. Truman. Unfortunately, they still did not get their lesson and they didn't learn enough. Let's hope that something will develop. Tomorrow night there is a big get together for Jews, where there

will be important people from Palestine and everybody will participate. On the radio, they are calling all Jews to go and see and hear the Jews' protest, and see if that will help. Aunt Jenny and the others and Jenny [Frey] and others are well. I kiss you with love and Herman. Also the relatives. Hermina

1948/4/6 Hermine to Irving (Book 10, 96-97)

Apr. 6 - 1948
My dear little Irving!
It's been a long time that I haven't written to you, although we did not get news from you for a long time. The important thing is, that thank God we are well. Mrs. Kugler was sick, but she feels better now. Otherwise there is no particular news, except that I thought there is a new guy! But in the meantime he forgot about calling me. My Irving is a man at work. He is only here for a year in the country and he is the son of a multimillionaire. He knows the relatives from Munkacs and the entire family. Although I had a little cough and cold, he called me many times on the phone and it is possible that he got scared that there is something wrong with me. To hell with it. It was ordered that way surely, but it is too bad because he is a gentleman and he looked very gentle. Although, if it would have been true, then he would have been smart enough to come back. So it is enough about this. I will write again. Until then I kiss both of you with love. Hermina
When will you come to New York?

1948/4/13 David and Dorothy to Irving (Book 12, 201-202)

April 13, 1948
Dear Irving:
We were so glad to receive your letter and know that all is well with you. It certainly must have been pleasant to get away from your grind, if only for a few days and I know it did you a world of good. As for ourselves, we are fine and enjoying splendid weather. Up until a few days ago it has been rather cool, but now the afternoons are typical of sunny California. I am leaving for Chicago the 25th of this month, and will arrive there on the 27th. When I bought my ticket, I inquired whether that particular route would take me through Columbus, but I'm sorry to say it does not. I am taking the El Capitan, a fast streamliner, and that gets me into Chicago in 39¾ hrs. Once there, I intend to stay about 3 weeks. If it were possible, I would not hesitate to make this stop-over but as it is I too don't know how I can. Once in Chicago, if an opportunity presents itself, maybe somehow it can be arranged, but that remains to be seen. I shall take your address with me, and if I can do it in any way, I'll let you know. Also, here is my address in Chicago - just in case you can arrange something:

%J. Pinkus
4237 W Grenshaw St.
Chicago 24, Ill.

We received a letter from the girls last week, and were glad to hear all is well with them. It's a shame we are all scattered by distance, but then again, that's life. Nothing much more to report at this writing. I do hope in some way it will be possible to meet you and Herman. In the meantime, write soon. Love to you both from David and, Dorothy

1948/4/13 Hilda Goldberger to Irving (Book 17, 251-253)

Dear Irving,
I know I am late again, but gosh I am so busy. On top of all my regular work, my mother has been sick for the past four weeks. She had the Flu and got up out of bed too soon and had a relapse. Back to bed she went. She is a little better now but is very weak, due probably to her having taken sulphur. How have you been? Did you enjoy your Easter vacation? I spent mine staying at home with my mother. I also had to study for two Mid Terms - one in Nutrition and the other in English Literature. The Nutrition was a corker. Some of the questions I never even heard of. My teacher said she doesn't really expect us to know all the answers. She took the questions from the Teachers Exams which didn't help any. Last night I went to City Center and saw "Madame Butterfly." It was beautiful - but, oh so tragic. I don't know too much of the music so I really didn't appreciate it as much as I should have. I started this letter in my Education Psychology class. All we do in class is read aloud from the textbook. I am fully capable of doing that at home myself. That class is so darn boring. I don't know how I'll last out the term. I guess that's all for now. As ever, Hilda

1948/4/20 Undated Marie to Irving (Book 8, 31-32)

[Dated from Dorothy's trip to Chicago and her letter about it, and Hermine wishing Happy Pesah]

My dear little brother Irving!

I started to write already many times a couple of lines and it always stayed, but now I am in a hurry to write. I hope that my lines will find all of you in the best of health! We are well and this week we got a letter from David and the others. Dorothy will go to Chicago on the 25th and she can't promise that she will come to visit us since she is very far. She wrote that if she will not be too tired from traveling, [then maybe] since it will take 20 hours to come from Chicago to New York. This is why she does not know yet, but she will see how it will be and she will let us know then. She would be very happy to come to visit us. And I guess she wrote to you also since then. My Irving, what did you decide? Write my dear Irving! How is it going with studying? I hope to hear the best about all of you. And what does Herman do? There is no particular news with us. Are you working hard before Passover? I'm thinking of you a lot my buddy. I would like to help you, but it is not enough that all I can do is only promise. How are Flora and the others doing? Aunt Helen? I'm sending greetings to everyone. The relatives here are well, but I haven't seen them for a long time. The weather will warm up and then I will be more willing to visit them. About myself everything is the same. And you my Irving, when will you have a vacation? Before summer school or after? Write my buddy! And take care of yourself and eat. And don't work hard, even if it's necessary. I wish you lots and lots of good luck! And the best of health! Greetings and I kiss you countless times with love. Your forever faithful sibling, Love, Maria

[Hermine writes]

And we wish you a very happy and festive Passover holiday!

I'm sending my best to everyone who is wondering about me. Hermina

1948/5/5 Dorothy to Irving (Book 12, 204-206) - miscarriage

Wednesday, May 5th

Dear Irving:

Here I am in Chicago after a not-too pleasant trip in. I left California in apparent good health, but suffered an internal hemorrhage on the train about an hour away from Chicago, and had to be taken to a hospital. I was released from there last Thursday and have been home and confined to bed ever since. I am feeling lots better now but still rather weak and need plenty of rest. However, I am getting the best of care at home and by the end of this week I hope I shall be able to go outdoors and give Chicago the once over.

I spoke to David several times since I got home, and as a matter of fact he called me last nite. He's just fine but a bit lonesome. Now of course, Irving, any plans I might have had to come to Columbus probably won't materialize, but if you can possibly see your way clear to spend a week-end in Chicago, you would be very welcome to stay at our home. Please let me know if you can. I imagine I will be in Chicago until the end of May. Not much more to write, except it's wonderful seeing and being with my family - my only regret is that David isn't here with me. Let me hear from you soon. Love to you and Herman - Dorothy

1948/5/6 Hilda Goldberger to Irving (Book 17, 248-249)

May 6, 1948
Dear Irving,

I was very glad to hear from you. Thanks for not taking as long as I did to answer. I am glad to hear that you are coming to New York. You will arrive here right in the middle of my exams. My last exam will be on June 14, Monday. I certainly want to see you when you come here. Do you like the beach? The reason I ask that is because I expect to go out to Rockaway June 11 for the entire vacation. You must be taking your final exams pretty soon, now. Well, good luck in them. I hope you get all A's. That's all for now. As ever, Hilda

1948/5/8 Hermine to Irving (Book 10, 99-100)

[In English]
5/8 -48
Dear Irving,

All this week I was thinking of you and still I'm writing only today. At the firm they gave the vacations this week, and my turn would be in June because we are unionized so who came first gets first choice. Anyway mine will be from the 14th in June so, if you'll come we could have a very nice time and the same goes for Herman. If you think that you both could come please let me know so I could plan on that. Maria would take time off too. Also, in the fall I will have one more week on my expense and then I'd like to go to Col. [Columbus]. Maria will get a vacation but she wants to go to see you later in Cols [Columbus]. Otherwise, we are well nothing new just as usual…Received a letter from Dorothy and I answered her already because she wrote me that [she was] coming home to Chicago [and] one hour from Chicago she got ill and had to be taken off the train and taken to a hospital. She is home now and at least her family could be with her in the hospital, too. In a way she was lucky. She probably wrote to you also, because of that now she would be unable to do so much traveling so she wouldn't come to New York. Last week I wrote a letter to Arthur and Flora. I wonder if they told you about it. I'm sorry but I just can't sit down to write and concentrate on it. Well, I did my best that is what anybody can do. How is school and everything else with you? Please let us hear from you and get ready if you can so everything would work out right. Tell Herman he doesn't need so much clothing [so] that shouldn't keep him back. Shirts and a few of them so if that is nice he looks good. If he needs [a] suit he [can] get it here. Take care of yourself and please let me know about your plans. Regards to the relatives and best wishes to you, With love, Hermina

1948/5/13 Margit Klein to Hermine [addressed to Herman] (Book 18, 259-261)

Budapest 1948.V.13

Dear Hermine,

We received your letter and we were very happy to read it. Don't be angry that we are just answering your letter, but I thought we will be able to write together with my husband. I'm sorry but he is not able to write any letter at this time, therefore I'm going to write. Maybe you heard the terrible news about it from Arthur, that again he got sick, terribly sick. The doctors did not tell me how sick he is until now. All this sickness is connected between when he is speaking he doesn't or can't tell clearly and he gets dizzy. He also has double vision. Maybe they didn't know what it is for sure and now have become panicky. Now I know the truth. Unfortunately, a tumor in the forehead. They can't operate here. The medication that you mailed which we received, even that will take time. We thank you very much, even the doctors were helping him. We were waiting for the time a t.b.c. [unclear] continuation that it will get better, and now it is worse than ever. The situation is bad. Arthur wrote that in his factory the work is very helpful. I wrote to him 2 letters [addressed] in his name which I never received an answer. I hope he received them. In one of the letters I mailed Herman's picture. Also, I know that his daughter lives in N.Y. We are corresponding with them. What is Dave doing? Is he still unmarried? You know that Erzsika got married. Now she has a baby whom they named Zsuzsi. Lili is with me. She doesn't know what she wants to be. In the last letter Arthur wrote that Irving was going to the University? In the last letter [he wrote] that in May he is going with his wife to a clinic. Did they leave? We hope it will help him. I didn't write yet to Arthur about Herman's sickness. If he is there, would you please tell him because he knows everything and he is waiting for every letter. He is always asking. Arthur doesn't write often. Now I'm taking the letter to the hospital so that he would write at least best wishes because he doesn't know what is his sickness. I just assure him that I just answered your letter, so you understand what is the situation. With love and kisses to everyone separately and to Arthur and his family. Margaret

1948/5/17 Hilda Goldberger to Irving (Book 17, 244-246)

May 17, 1948

Dear Irving,

I was very glad to hear from you and as you can see, I have reformed and am answering comparatively quickly. I certainly am sorry I could not see your play ["A man must marry"] , although if it was in German, I am afraid I would not be able to understand very much. I never studied German in school. Sometimes my grandmother talks to me in German. I can just about get the gist of what she is saying. With my Home Economics Major I don't need any language at all. Most of the other girls have to take about two years of the language they started in High School or a new language. In High School, I took two years of Spanish and four years of French.

About your visit to New York - there is a phone in the house where I'll be this summer but I don't remember the number. I'll probably be able to tell you that in my next letter. The address is:

171 Beach 66 St.
Rockaway Beach, L.I. N.Y.

I think that is right. Yesterday, Sunday, my House plan was supposed to go on a picnic. However, because of the cloudy weather only a few of the girls showed up. We, the hardy few, went anyway. We were not in the park 15 minutes when it started to rain. We were planning to have a fire and roast weenies (small frankfurters) but the rain called that off. After finally deciding to go home we got on the wrong trolley and found ourselves in Yonkers. By the time we got home, we were absolutely drenched. We all went to my house and I supplied all the girls with clothing. It was lucky that we still have some of my brother's clothes left in our house for the fellows. Regardless of the rain, we had a nice time. That's all for now. As ever, Hilda

1948/5/22 Dorothy to Irving (Book 12, 208-209)

May 22, 1948
Dear Irving:
I just received your letter and am answering quickly. I feel fine, Irving, and the reason I haven't written sooner is because I was waiting to hear from you as to the exact date you expected to be in Chicago. Now that it is definite, we all shall be looking forward to seeing you on the 9th of June. Please let me know what train you will take, also the station you will arrive at, and the time. I will try to be at the station to meet you, although I am wondering how we will recognize each other. What do you suggest? I could tell you what I will be wearing and perhaps in that way we won't miss each other. In any event, please give me the above information. As to my going on to New York with you, I have been giving it considerable thought, although as yet I don't know definitely if it will be possible. I'd like nothing better than to meet Hermina and Maria, believe me. What train are you taking to New York? Have you made any definite reservations? Write me soon and give me all the "dope." Until I hear from you, regards from all to you and Herman. Love, Dorothy

1948/6/3 Dorothy to Irving (Book 12, 211-213)

June 2, 1948
Dear Irving:
This is certainly a coincidence. I had just finished writing a letter to you when I received your special delivery. I had started worrying about your delay in answering my last letter. However, I assumed that it was due to the fact that you were busy with finals, etc. I will be at the bus station to meet you and feel sure that I shall be able to recognize you. From the picture I have of you I think that there is a strong resemblance between you and David. As for me, I hardly know how to describe myself. I have sort of auburn hair and am about 5'4½" tall. I don't know what I'll be wearing since that will depend upon the weather, but if it's cool I'll have a green coat on. My sister may be there with me, and she is slightly taller than I and has dark hair. I just know I shall recognize you without any trouble. We are eagerly looking forward to your visit Irving, and shall be anxious to hear about everything. All is well with us and David, too. So, until next Wednesday when I'll see you in person, regards from all. Love to you and Herman, Dorothy

1948/6/4 Undated Hermine to Irving (Book 10, 9-10)

My dear little brother, Irving!
We got your letter today and I'm responding from work. I got a letter from Dorothy and she wrote that it is not certain she could come since she is still under medical care. So, I don't want to talk her into it and then she will get sick. So, if she wants she is truly welcome to us. Otherwise we are well - I'm sorry that I did not respond to David yet nor to his wife, but I will. Oh, yes when you arrive to NY you can try to call us on the phone. We have a phone, but we can't use it yet since this is a new challenge. The phone number is Cyprus - CY9-4769. By that time it could be connected already. Be careful with your travel and do you think it won't be dangerous with a bus. Maybe it would be worth it [by train] even if the train costs more. Arrange it the way you think it's the best, but write as soon as you will have a chance. I just wanted to call the Y.M.C.A. today. We don't know anybody here who would have an empty room. Mrs. Klein is in the hospital, and I just remembered that I should have sent a card to her. Bertha's husband is away for business. Tomorrow I will ask what can be done. Maybe you could do it by phone because I don't believe that the office is open on Saturday. Also, it takes more time than you think to be able to travel that soon, but I will inquire about that. I started to write at work and I will finish it at home, but I'm in a hurry because I have a date tonight.

But I still want my letter to go. Herman is a big donkey because if he would come, we would just invite him [to go with us]! At least he would have a chance to see how others live. If he does not change his destiny [now] then when will he? And who will look after him? If he would come here we would introduce girls to him and at least he could be a man like anybody else. He could do that and somebody would be happy to get to know him. He should not live like a dog. We know better that there is no one to take care of him. If it would be so easy for me, I would do it too, but it is easier for him. So, tell this to him my little brother also. I kiss you with love. Hermina

1948/6/5 Hilda Goldberger to Irving (Book 17, 241-242)

June 5, 1948
Dear Irving,
This will have to be a very short note because I am in the middle of studying for my finals. They start Monday, the 7th and end the 11th. The schedule was changed slightly. We will probably leave for Rockaway the 13th or the 14th of June. If you come into New York later than that you can call me. The phone number is Belle Harbor 5-6709. I still don't have a phone in the city. You know how to get in touch with me here though. Hope your finals weren't too difficult and that you have a nice time in Chicago. Hope to see you soon, As ever, Hilda

1948/6/17 Undated Anne Pinkus (Dorothy's sister) to Irving (Book 12, 290)
[Dated by Irving visiting Chicago to meet Dorothy in June 1948]

June 17th

Dear Irving:
The Pinkus family received your lovely gift for which many thanks. You really shouldn't have done it. It was, as I told you before, very nice having you as our guest and we all hope there will be a "repeat performance" in the not too distant future. I'm sure we would all enjoy that. All here send best wishes to you and your sisters. Thanks again, Anne

1948/6/18 Undated (a) Dorothy to Irving (Book 12, 196-199)
[Dated by Irving visiting Chicago to meet Dorothy in June 1948]

Friday

Dear Irving:
First, permit me to thank you for the very lovely gift which you sent me. It was very sweet of you and I shall think of you every time I wear the hose. Also, I'm sure David will love the ties which you sent him. They are in perfect taste and I know he'll enjoy wearing them. My mother was thrilled with the towels, and it was so thoughtful of you to send them. Your package arrived on Wednesday, the day I returned from the hospital, but I couldn't acknowledge it immediately, due to the fact that I didn't feel very well and couldn't write. I fully intended writing you yesterday, but during the nite on Wednesday, I twisted my back and suffered severe strain. I had to be in bed all day yesterday lying on a heating pad and swallowing aspirins to try and alleviate the pain. Today I feel a bit better, although the pain is still there. The doctor has ordered me to stay in bed until Monday, when, I hope, I shall once more be up and around. My hospital jaunt wasn't too pleasant, but thank goodness it is over. I'm happy to report that my brother is home, too, and that all his tests and x-rays proved perfect. The Doctor has concluded that his condition is apparently due to too much acid in his system and now it will just be a matter of watching his diet. We are all thankful for that. Irving, your letter was enjoyed by all of us. I read it aloud to all, since you allotted a paragraph to each member, which was so sweet of you. Anne got a kick out of your reference to her hair, and Mother was happy you enjoyed her meals. I don't have to tell you how much we all enjoyed your short stay, but am sorry it was at such a time when we couldn't go "all out" to entertain you. I hope we shall have another opportunity to make up for it.
You didn't mention whether or not you enjoyed your train trip. I hope the "Manhattan" had no ill effect on your well being - or did it draw you to the club car for a reinforcement? Don't forget I shall be waiting to hear all about your future plans; also let me have your reaction to your date with your New York girlfriend. You know I'm interested in your social life, too. In the meantime I'll keep a sharp outlook for "the" girl. That's about all for now. Even writing tires me a bit and I shall have to get back into bed to rest. Please write

me soon, won't you. Thanks again for your sweet remembrances. Have a good time and lots of fun. Regards from all at home. Love, Dorothy

1948/6/18 Undated (b) Dorothy to Hermine and Marie (Book 2, 4-5)

Friday

Dear Girls:

Thanks so much for your letters. I enjoyed reading them and they came at a time when I really appreciated them. I am back home again, but a bit on the weak side. To add to my discomfort, I have wrenched my back and have to be in bed again for a few days. I got home on Wednesday afternoon and sprained my back that night. The doctor says that a few days on the heating pad will help a lot, so that's what I have been doing. I find it a bit difficult to write, so please forgive me if this letter is a "shortie". I have written to David and Irving today too, so this will be my quota. I did want you to know that I am home again and that I had received your letters. I am sure in a few days I'll be up and around again. Have a nice time and I'm sure you will. Regards from all. Love, Dorothy

1948/6/24 Marie to Irving (Book 8, 206-207)

6/24/48

My dear little brother, Irving!

We got your precious card and I'm very glad to hear that thank God, you are well and that you arrived home with luck. We miss you here and too bad that you could not stay longer. Yes my little brother, how did you decide with the school? I hope you will take time to rest! Did you get Dorothy' s letter? What do you say about that? Now I'm planning on writing to David also. I have not heard from him for a long time already. As it seems, Dorothy still did not go home yet. Louis Schwartz called me last night on the phone and he is here with his brother. His nephew arrived to America, but he is still on Ellis Island. Why? I don't know. But this week in a few days they can take him out. Hermine talked to his brother Joe and he asked for your address since he travels often around that way and he would visit you. Otherwise there is no news. The pictures are ready. They are not really good, but I will send most of them. What's new by you? Write our little Irving! The weather since you left is still rainy. Today it is starting to get sunny. Next time you come my little buddy, you should come so you can stay for a longer time. Although, I guess you could not wait to leave from here, could you? There is no particular news here. Take care of yourself and don't be sad. Rest as much as you can. What is Herman doing? Why doesn't he go for a vacation somewhere? It would be good for him, but he does not believe it anyway. Now, my little buddy, I'm closing my lines and I wish you lots and lots of luck and the best of health until I see you again. Greetings from the heart and I kiss you countless times with much of love. I'm sending my greetings to everyone. Love, Maria

1948/6/25 Undated Dorothy to Irving (Book 12, 295-296) the week of the 30th

[dated by Irv back in Columbus after visiting briefly in NY]

Friday

Dear Irv:

Thanks for your post card. I didn't expect you would be back in Columbus so soon. Are you going to summer school after all? This is just a short note to let you know that I'm feeling fine now and all is well with the rest of us. Also, I'm happy to inform you that I am leaving Chicago this coming Wednesday, June 30th, and I'll be back in Long Beach on Friday, July 2nd. Now you can write me a nice long letter there and tell me all about everything. David asked me (after he heard from you) whether you and I schemed to bring up the subject of his English. He was able to detect something that suggested that question. I denied it in my letter, but I do honestly think that he would take anything from or do anything for you. I'll start my campaign when I get home. Until I hear from you - all at home send their very best regards. Love to and Herman. Dorothy

1948/7/7 Undated Dorothy to Irving (Book 12, 298-299) - first week of July

[Dated by Hermine's next letter that Dorothy is back in California and Dorothy still in Chicago in previous letter, and that she arrived on last Friday]

Wednesday

Page 636

Dear Irving:

It feels good to be back here again and in the swing of things once more. I arrived last Friday and stood the trip very well, although I was a pretty tired girl when I finally got here. David, of course, met me at the station and he was home with me for a few hours before going back to work. He is well, and didn't even lose an ounce while I was gone, so maybe that doesn't say much for my cooking. Anyhow, I guess he was glad to see me after my long absence. Now that I am here there isn't too much to write about. We haven't done much, except having company over and passing the time. The days are quite warm here but the evenings are grand. Now tell me all about what you are doing and if you are really relaxing and taking it easy. I was surprised at your short stay in New York - thought you would be there longer. What plans do you have for the balance of the summer? Write me about everything. I'm going to drop a line to the girls too to let them know I'm back. I'm feeling fine now thank goodness and all is well in that direction. So much for now, Irv. Love to you and Herman, Dorothy

1948/7/8 Hermine to Irving (Book 10, 107-108)

7/18 - 48

My dear little brother, Irving!

I'm sorry about writing so rarely, but we don't even hear from you that often. I hope you and Herman are well! We got a letter from Dorothy and her travel was nice and she wrote that she is waiting for her sister and she'll be with them for 6 weeks. Therefore, I am interested if you decided yourself about what you are going to do in your free time? If you can, you could come here anytime! Yes, if it works out then Marcsa will go away on 7/23, for two weeks, as I already mentioned to you in my last card. You could have used a little rest also. I have not decided either what I want to do with that week in which I want to take off. I already have my home and it is better this way! Jenny Frey and her husband went to Florida and they will be there for at least 6 weeks - they went by car. The relatives are well. We got a card from Arthur's wife, which she wrote from Canada to us. We got a thank you letter from your friend after he arrived home, where he thanked for the hospitality that you gave him while he was here. He wrote very nicely and that he is proud of you and that you are his good friend. I am also attaching an address to you that Joe gave me when he was in New York, he is the brother of Louis from Youngstown. And that person is a very good friend of Joe and he is in charge of some kind of Union. So, if you need some kind of information, he could get it only from his good friend. But I know that it is not important to you. So if you want to, just out of friendship, you can give a greeting and you can call him. I did not get a letter from Emil from Europe yet, and I'm still only getting ready to visit the Lefkovits girls. We went for the movies and it was pretty good. While we were there it was a big shower and we did not even know about it. I will close it with this and I am asking you to write about everything. About the sewing machine I only know that it cost at least 40 dollars when Marcsa bought it. As I heard there is no available sewing machine here and it is expensive. I think we can get more for it. But do as it is best for you. I will write again. I kiss you with love. Hermine

1948/7/8 Undated Marie to Irving (Book 18, 301-302)

[Dated from July 4th, and type of paper that it's written on, and Irving is still in school and Marie in NY]

My dear little brother Irving!

I can't even write down how happy you made me with your letter, which we got on Sunday already. Also, knowing that you are in good health thank God, makes me happy. We are well and you are right about our letter writing. As it seems there is always some excuse for all of us, although, we should not neglect it. And my dear little brother, I can imagine how hard you are working. It's not enough to study, but cooking there also. The truth is that you can eat better this way. Besides that, the relatives just [asked] me why you don't rent to somebody there. For example, a boy who goes to university and has no place to live. You can rent to him there and he would have enough [for the] expense. He can help you out with cleaning. I know it's not that easy, but still, you should make it easier for yourself somehow so you don't have to work so hard. Otherwise how are you getting along with the studying? You know I already thought that it is easier that you can eat better. For the money you pay there you can eat better. I hope my dear little brother that everything will work out fine. And you just take care of yourself and don't be upset. Otherwise I am well. There is no new news currently. We did not get mail from David for a couple of weeks either. We write to him too. How is Mrs. Hasen and Walters and the others? Maybe they will get home? I just thought about 4th of July and on Saturday, like usual, we had to work at a place like that, but it was not busy. Yes my dear little brother, I will attach here how to make that cucumber [salad]. First of all, peel it, and then cut it to thin circles with that peeler that we have. Cut an onion and salt it together a little and stir it over. Then you squeeze out its juice and pour a little water on it and put a little sugar and vinegar in it, pepper, and stir it over so it will have a little taste and then you can eat it already. And Hermine will write the other recipe for you. Now I will close my lines and I kiss you countless times, your forever faithful sibling. I wish you good luck and the best of health. Love, Maria

1948/7/9 Irving to Dave and Dorothy (Book 6, 306-309)

July 9th, 1948
Dear Dave,
I need not repeat myself in stating my illusions, but we live in assumptious [sic] world and we believe that if things remain the same we are going on well. But remember as soon as things change we find ourself [sic] falling apart. Trembling on our feet. Therefore, from me or from the world this little analogy can be simply realized and understood. Now then I firmly believe that you were happy to see Dorothy - your wife, home again. She is a wonderful person. I haven't changed my mind on that. The world around us changes, but that remains as I have previously expounded. Between you and I, tell me the truth, are you still proud of your "little" brother after finding out so many things. I assume that you were full of questions when Dorothy arrived, weren't you? Let me hear from you both. With loads of luck and love, Irving

Dear Dorothy,
With my humble apologies for being somewhat behind time in replying to your welcomed letters. Sometimes it's very difficult for one to determine oneself to write. This time I must sympathize with this reasoning. since this was the experience with which I have been struggling. But now, as you see, I'm back in the groove. This habitual motive must be discontinued, because it's a bad policy. Therefore, I shall assume that forgiveness will be granted and things will resolve - all for the best. Today we should have the second "Manhattan" since it's the 9th, which reminds me of Chicago. It was indeed a great day, but there will be days like that because we shall meet again soon. By the way, I'm working on that project and as soon as I'll come out with results I shall let you know. By this time I'm with the assumption that you are in California and well - in "tip top" shape. I'm sure that David was glad, in high spirit, and his mind is at ease knowing that you are there with him. It is said that life is very complex. Nothing can really contradict that statement. Therefore, I shall refrain and say that it is as complex as we make it. With the belief that everything will be as you both want it and luck will turn to our and your side.

[The page that's marked "II" seems out of place and may not belong to this letter, but it is on the reverse side of the letter to David" and seems to be part of the draft to Dorothy]

... I shall try from some other angle if possible. We shall see. One shouldn't give up the ship without a fight. Who'll do the fighting? It depends upon the side of the fence you are on. Maybe a fight is lost before it starts. - it's complex. New York treated me well while I was there. However, to relate a specific point which entails into a personal affair - the date with the New York girlfriend has been canceled. Reasons were allocated through our friendly bird... I'm glad that you are interested in my social life, because I'll know that you'll keep a sharp look out for "the" only one... we have taken some pictures in New York and I'll send some over to you as soon as I'm able to obtain the reprints. That I hope it won't be too long. A personal discussion could eliminate some of the brevity of these scrambled lines, but as I stated previously that there our possibilities and in near future I shall fulfill. I remained with best wishes to you and David, till next time, from Irving
P. S. My regards to your folks back home

1948/7/16 Aunt Helen to Irving (Book 17, 259-260)

Dear Irvin!
Will you please meet me on Tuesday about 2:15 in Hills Rest. If you can't come don't call me at the Hotel only at my home MA 1002. I never leave before 1 ish. I will be in Hills anyhow so if you [are] not able to come it wouldn't matter so much. Love, Helen

July 16

1948/7/17 Undated Dorothy to Irving (Book 12, 301-302)

Saturday

Dear Irving:

Since the sequence of our letter-writing has been slightly broken, I'll write you and make a fresh start. Many thanks for your special delivery, which we enjoyed very much. To get David to write you personally, even in answer to your specific questions, is almost an impossibility. When I was away, he naturally had to write himself, but now that he can once more rely on my taking over, that is that. I'm afraid it's a lost cause in that direction. I know you will understand fully what I am trying to put across. Life once more is assuming its normal routine and already it seems as though I have never been away. I receive letters from home regularly, and all are well. They do ask me to remember them to you. My sister is planning to spend her vacation with us, but she as yet is not certain of the exact time she will be here. The days are lovely here, and I have been taking advantage of them, soaking in as much sun as I can. I'm getting the start of a nice suntan too. What are you doing to keep yourself out of mischief? Did you have pictures developed that you took while in New York? We are anxious to see them, so send them along when they are ready. There isn't too much more to write about. We are both well, which is the most important thing. We received a letter from the girls last week, a nice newsy one. So, let's hear from you again real, real soon. Love to you and Herman. Dorothy

1948/7/23 David to Irving (Book 12, 215-217)

July 22
Dear little brother! Until 120!
There is no particular news. Thank God I am well, which I would like to hear back from you too! Forgive me, that I did not write for so long! Currently I'm out in Bakersfield City. The company I am working for opened up a store and I will be here for a few days to help with the decoration. This is about 140 Km from Long Beach. The temperature is 110-115 during the day. This is a very warm town. I believe that I will be back on Saturday to Long Beach, but I will be back again about next month on the 5th or the 6th for at least for 3-4 days. And Dorothy is going to come with me then. The trip takes about 4 hours by car. It is now 11 o'clock at night and the air is still warm. The company pays the cost for the hotel as well as for the food bills. So, I wrote enough for today. Please write to me shortly and a lot. Write what you are going to wear when you come to California. Ok? So, I wish you lots of good luck and everything good. I am with love. I kiss you. David.

1948/7/29 Dorothy to Irving (Book 12, 219-221)

Thursday

Dear Irving:

It's always nice hearing from you, and we especially enjoyed receiving the snapshots you forwarded. Hermina also sent us the snaps, so now we have two sets. They're very nice and now I can see what the girls look like. So, your aim is now to be a capitalist! Good for you. However, when you make your first million, don't forget to send us the secret of your success, so we too can enjoy and reap the "capitalist's" harvest. Seriously, keep us posted on the progress you are making. As for your dancing lessons, that too I approve of. Now when I see you again, you can give me some pointers and perhaps we can become a dancing team. I'm sure you are getting a kick out of it, and I know it will prove beneficial when put to use. Now you can be the "life of the party" and be much in demand. We are leading a more or less quiet life, but then in Long Beach that is the thing to do. I have joined a women's charity club just recently and have discovered some nice girls as not too far-off neighbors. The club does some very nice work and it feels good to be a part of it. Weather still is gorgeous and I'm enjoying every bit of it. David tells me he wrote you while he was in Bakersfield. I believe he will have to make another trip there next week, and this time I will go with him. So much for now. Keep us posted on everything. Love from both of us to you and Herman. Dorothy

1948/8/8 Undated Dorothy to Irving (Book 12, 292-293)

[dated by 1948/7/23 David to Irving (Book 12, 215-217) in which David mentions going back to Bakersfield on the 5th or 6th of August]

Sunday

Dear Irving:

Just a line to let you know that David and I are in Bakersfield. David had to come out here for a few days so I came along too. The drive here was beautiful. We started out a 5 o'clock this morning and arrived at 9A.M. David had to go right to work and after checking in at the hotel I decided to drop you a line. Bakersfield is an extremely hot town, but most all places are air-conditioned so it isn't too bad. The room at the hotel is quite comfortable and I'm enjoying it very much. I shall give the town the once-over after a little while. Sorry your venture is not working too well, but as you say we can attribute it to the uncertain conditions prevailing at this time. I had hoped you would make scads of money from the start, but then I'm sure things will take a turn for the better (I hope). We received a card from Maria while she was on vacation, and also a letter from Hermina. They are both well. So much for now. Keep us posted on everything. Love to you and Herman from us. Dorothy

1948/9/19 Herb Baum to Irving

Dear Irving:

I am sorry for two reasons. First of all the tardiness of my writing to you and second my regret that you were unable to visit with me. I shall not leave for Chicago until this coming Friday so I once again extend an invitation which requests your presence possibly during the early part of this coming week. I have been corresponding with Renee and if her letters are at all representative of her true feelings she likes me a good bit. I wish that I could believe all that she has told me in the letters that I have received thus far but I am just a bit cautious since I realize that a girl might very well do anything. I plan to visit her during the coming quarter sometime and will be sure and call you when I do make this trip. Our experience at State I feel was of advantage and interest to both of us. We learned from each other Irving and this I feel is as it should be. It is difficult for one to find himself in such a complicated world where no one has the answers as far as what sort of purpose a man should have to his existence, what his function should be in relationship to his fellowman. I think that you have finally found some sort of pattern to your existence. You have discovered that far more important than the incomplete cause of the individual is the cause of society. Thus you have undertaken a study of the economic aspects of our civilization, its strong points and its weak points, always keeping in mind that your job is to bring about the progress of society. To me, this is one of the ways by which I can also attain personal happiness. Another is of course the discovery of a good girl that you can have for keeps. There is a possibility that I have found her but only time will tell. That's about it for now Irv, let me know about what you plan to do about making this visit that I spoke of above.
Sincerely, Herb

My Chicago address 6042 Ingleside, Chicago

1948/9/23 David and Dorothy to Irving (Book 12, 223-224) drapery business and won store lottery

Sept. 23, 1948
Dear Irving:

Sorry for the delay in writing you. I meant to allot a day for just such a purpose, but something always comes up and I keep putting it off. First let me tell you we are both well and getting along fine. Here's news which I know you will be happy about. David has gone in for himself in the drapery business. He doesn't have a store for himself, but is associated with some upholsterers, who have been in business here quite a few years. David handles the drapery department, and they work together. This has just happened about 2 weeks ago, and it will take a little time until he gets going. Also, we have bought a car, which is very important in his business, as he is out a good deal making contacts, selling, etc. I am enclosing a business card which he just had printed. We hope it will work out successfully. Another thing, and this I just can't get over. Yesterday was my birthday and what a birthday I had. I went to a grand opening of a furniture store and they had a radio broadcast from there, prizes etc. in honor of the occasion. Tickets were passed out for prizes of all kinds to each person who came in. I filled mine out, listened to the broadcast and left before the drawings. I was so sure I wouldn't win anything, I never gave it a thought. Some time in the afternoon I received a telephone call from the store informing me I won a $300.00 laundromat and to be there for the presentation. I called David all excited and he went with me. The newspaper photographers were there and they took pictures of David and me standing in back of the laundromat. I'll send you a copy as soon as it comes out. As it happens I can't use the laundromat in my apt., as it is too small for such a big thing. I believe I'll take a credit slip, or perhaps trade it in for something else. Wasn't that wonderful? To think it happened on my birthday!! We celebrated by going out to dinner and a play after that. Tell me more about your plans for coming out here to finish your schooling. I'm going to write to the girls tonite too, so will make this all for now. Write again soon. Love to you and Herman, from David and Dorothy

1948/9/23 Hermine to Irving (Book 15, 193-194)

9/23 - 48

My dear brother Irving!

I can't understand why are you all so busy that you don't even have time any more for dropping us a few lines. We received one letter last week and that is all. I wrote to Dorothy and David but they didn't answer me yet. It's a few weeks already since I heard from them, too, hope they are well and also you, too! How is Herman feeling? You never mentioned that. Hope he is well and maybe one day he'll let us know how he is. I went over to Bertha's tonight and she received a letter from Zsiga - she wrote to him and he lives in Helmec. He wants to take care of the property and Bertha wants to send him the necessary papers. Otherwise everything is well with us and I hope to hear the same about you. Let me hear from you, Until then, best wishes and Love, Hermina

1948/10/6 Aunt Jenny to Irving and Herman (Book 16, 393-396)

Dear Irving,

Thanks for your kind wishes, and your thought of us. It was indeed a pleasure to hear from you. I hope this year brings you all you wish for yourself and your dear ones. Lovingly, Aunt Jennie and Lester, Lucille, Howard, and Joanne

1948/10/6 Undated Hermine to Irving (Book 15, 185-186)

[In English]

New York 10/6 - 48

My dear brother Irving,

As much as I thought of writing you still it is just now that I set down to do it. Hope you're well both of you. We are well, too and had a nice holiday. I had four days rest! A real vacation! Believe me Irving we missed you - Mrs. Kugler and even Mrs. Klein mentioned that to us. I wish I would be able to invite you both for the Holiday dinner. What do you think of that? Just wrote a letter to Dorothy and told her that when Irving is finished with school we might go to California. Asked her about rooms and positions. She might even get scared that we want to go but even if we do we wouldn't live with them. But the truth is that especially Maria has colds one after the other when winter comes. Maybe if she would be there that wouldn't come to her. I like to wait for a while but it is not much here - or I could say that nothing keeps me or nothing holds me back to New York. We have everything Thank God 100% improvement in everything since we left Columbus. I mean personally - we don't have a home but at least see things differently than there. The only thing worries me that you have all the work and probably neglected with your eating. Irving please let us know how are you and everything? What does Herman think. Tell him to look around and find a nice girl than he can have the apartment or you too Irving, we would give it to either of you! Don't get angry or make fun of it because I mean it!! On the other hand believe me Irving it isn't worth it to live in Columbus. You can't even have nice friends, but in New York you could Irving. It is much easier for a man to get around. Received a card from Arthur and family. Mrs. Kugler was very happy to hear from you and told me to tell you that and thanking you and also she is wishing you a very "Happy New Year." Let us hear from you and about everything. Herman is a "Bad Boy" Herman is a "Bad Boy" I'm singing this so he should know that I mean it. Maria went to sleep so she'll write separately. The relatives send their regards to both of you and to the relatives. Please write and regards to Mr. Zuhl and wife also Happy New Year to them. Tell him - will you! Love to both of you, Hermina

1948/10/25 Hermine to Irving (Book 10, 116-118)

[In English]

10/25 - 48

My dear brother Irving,

It is a long time since I heard from you and never answered you yet. Hope that you both are well and had nice Holidays. It was very nice of Mr. Zuhl and his brother-in-law to invite you up for supper. Just remembered his brother-in-law as I was reading your letter. You see, it happened a few years ago when we went to night school in the Shontal Center that Mr. Zuhl introduced him to us. He was single at that time, and he roomed at this woman and her husband who then was getting along all right, and between time he fell in love with that woman and she divorced her husband and this fellow married her. That is the story behind it - that is why I never paid much attention to him! Don't mention that about this to them - but I like you to know just in case you were not told about yet. That is enough already so let's go to something else. I haven't heard from Dorothy and David [in] quite a long time and I hope I didn't scare Dorothy with my questions about California as I told you about it too. I mentioned that if you could come too or want to come then maybe next year we might go out there and she never answered. As you know Maria has so many colds when the cold weather arrives that it is really not worth it to stay here but that doesn't mean that we would go to live with them! Oh, well - why worry about it - if not Long Beach, Florida is good enough. How are you and Herman? Have you seen Aunt Helen or Arthur and his family? Tell us some good news about yourself. How is school and what is that degree called you'll get first - please let me know because I want to know! Bertha received mail from Zsiga who lives in Helmec and was asking about us and what would we like to do with the property. He is taking care of Bertha's now. Also he wrote that Ignác Klein worked that he could get the children's property, but the law refused it to him. So what do you think Irving? Maybe he would do something so we could get it back. Irving tell me about you - where do you eat your meals? What do you cook at home. Do you still want to keep up the apartment. I write and it is if I would talk to myself. Nobody answers to my questions. I know you are busy but I like to hear more about you. I'm one who tells everything and maybe that is why I don't get [an] answer. Well, Irving dear - take care of yourself and Herman too. Maria is sleeping already and she is well, too. Let me hear from you. Love, Hermina

1948/11/2 Undated Hermine to Irving (Book 16, 290-291)

[dated by Election day]
[In English]

My dear brother Irving,
I wrote you a few lines yesterday and I am not so sure that you received it before voting - but it really doesn't make much difference because nobody knows what is good and each person does the way they think is best. Just now we have the radio on and Maria is all excited about who is going to win the Presidency. As I mentioned it yesterday, that we received a letter from Dorothy and her answer to my letter is that if we decide to go to California she thinks Los Angeles would be better for us because she thinks they have more Jewish people and also young people. In Long Beach they are mostly couples and not so many Jewish people. So that is a pretty good answer and this way she doesn't have to have the worry that we'll move in to them. But she mentioned also that David will write more concerning our problem. Dorothy also wrote that her sister is there and she was very busy since, but now she is going home soon. [She] asked about you and wants to hear about you and wrote that we should tell you to write to them. Otherwise they are well and everything is all right with them. We are also well and quite busy as usual - with nothing! You mentioned about the graduation that you [would] like to have us. All right Irving - we will go - but don't worry about money because if we go there is no need to pay it back - so don't worry! How is Herman? Believe me Irving, I shouldn't even ask because I don't know if he is interested to know that I want to hear from him. Lots of luck to the studying and hope that it will work out well for you. It is a hard job, but you can do it - so good luck sweetie! Do you have a girl friend? Tell us about it! Best wishes and love, Hermina

1948/11/10 Marie to Irving (Book 6, 98-101)

Nov 10, 1948
My dear brother Irving,
I'm sorry to reply to your letter just now, but I hope my lines will find you both in the best health. We are also well. And I think of you. And yes, my little brother, as you write, if you graduate from school with the help of the good God, how do you want us to go? If God helps you, just write when and let us go on our own expense. And I don't know why you keep writing that you owe us. You already gave me, remember when we bought our coat, you sent [at that time] what you owed. And I'm going to visit you, so it's worth it to me so much. And I wish you the best of health and lots and lots of good luck, and for all your wishes to come true. Just take care of yourself little brother dear. I know you have a hard time learning and you don't have much time to relax. What do you say my little brother about President Truman, I voted for him, too. We hope he will try to improve the situation. If not good, at least better than the others. We hope we will not be disappointed. How is Herman? We have no special news. I kiss you countless times. Love, Maria

Regards to everyone. David is fine.

11/19/48

My dear brother Irving,

I hope our lines will find you both in the best health. We're fine too and it's just about time to hear from you. How are you my brother and how do you do with your studying? And what does Herman do? Here's nothing especially new. About the relations, I haven't seen them in a while, but I'm fine. And how is Flora? Have you seen Waltor since we left to live here. Have you heard from David? It's been a couple of weeks since we've received from him, but have yet to respond. As you can see I am not the first lazy writer. I write to you, my brother, if not much, but more often because you don't want to answer to anyone else. With us, time is still quite good. Currently at work it's quite slow, not very busy. And that's how I try to write to you. But I'm sorry I'm writing such a monotonous letter but there's no specific news right now. Hermine isn't writing right now since she had someone for her this week but you can't know how he is. On Saturday, she found out that there is always someone, but not all that she wants, but I hope that it will come even if it is too late. Now I kiss you with love countless times. Love, Maria

[on the side]

Hermine says hello. Write my buddy

Dear Irv,

This is a much delayed note of thanks for treating me so kindly while I was in Columbus. I shan't forget it. Sorry that I was able to spend such little time with you Irv but you understand my position I'm sure. I'm really in love with Reneé Irv and my actions are so governed. Tell me truthfully Irv, what do you think of her. You have had ample opportunity to see her and talk with her and you must have opinions. Please tell me the truth and no holds barred. Does she appear intelligent?

I'm having a difficult time with "Price Theory." I've read Stigler, which isn't assigned of course, for they assumed that you have mastered it. Haven't done anything but study of course. I'm getting sort of tired Irv and would like to take off a quarter some time. If things work out OK I will have the course requirements for the PhD in about 5 or 6 quarters. That's all for now Irv. Sincerely, Herb

P.S. Please write

6042 Ingleside

Chicago

Received the notes. Thanks

[In English]

11/23 - 48

My Dear brother Irving,

I mailed a card to you today and enclosed in it a necktie. I hope you'll receive it and will like it, too. I'm sorry that we both forgot about your birthday. I'm quite busy and I just didn't realize that we missed it till this morning. But even if it is late but we wish lots of luck to you. We both are well and the weather is also wonderful - as I wrote to Dorothy tonight almost like in California. David and Herman could or should shake hands. As much as I try to write to everybody but as soon as I stop everything stops and I can't expect mail from no-one. Aunt Helen never writes to us - maybe she is angry for only writing her a card but I just can't do it!! Aunt Jenny was asking about you both and also the other relatives. I never went out to Aunt Jenny since you were here but [would] like too. When we'd like to go she is always busy! Let's hear from you Irving and take care of yourself. Regards to relatives and friends. Love, Hermina

Nov 28, 1948

Dear Irving:

Well, it's just about time that you came across with a letter. Being 2 months late in replying just doesn't seem like you, but I'll just have to accept your excuse of having your nose to the grindstone again. However, don't let it get you again to the point where you just aren't interested in anything else. Didn't your summer relaxation teach you that you must have a little let-up from the steady grind? I don't mean to be "bossy," but I just feel that you work too hard. I'm happy to report that all is well with us and we are feeling fine. We received a letter from the girls on the same day we heard from you, and it was nice knowing that all is well with them too. I don't have to tell you how wonderful it was having my sister with me for a few weeks. However, it was all over too soon and now it seems as though it was all a dream. I do miss my family so very much. To get back to you, what's new with your studies. You haven't written much about what you are taking this semester and if you have changed your mind about your ultimate goal. We are interested, so let's hear about it. Thanks for your good wishes for my birthday - and no matter how late, they are always acceptable. Tonite is my letter-writing nite, and I have 3 more to go. So, this will be all for now. Please write us again soon, and I don't mean in 2 months. Love from David and me to you and Herman. Love, Dorothy

1948/12/2 Hermine to Irving (Book 10, 124-126)

My dear brother Irving,
Just a few lines because it is late already. I wanted to write and just then Bertha came in and I had to stop writing. Hope you both are well because it is a long time already since I heard from you. I thought of calling you up to Lindseks, but just then I thought that before Christmas you are probably busy with exams. Let's hope that both of you are well and please drop us a few lines when you have a chance. We have a real winter here since Saturday and plenty of snow, too. How is it in Columbus? Do you have coal or a warm room? The only thing I like you to watch that you shouldn't over heat the furnace. Otherwise we are well. Take care of yourself. With love to you both, Hermina

1948/12/14 Dorothy to Irving (Book 12, 229-231) ate in Hungarian restaurant

Dec. 13, 1948
Dear Irving:
We were just going to mail the enclosed card but on second thought I decided to write a few lines to enlighten you. We had dinner at this Hungarian restaurant yesterday, a charming place with delicious food. They had a gypsy violinist playing old Hungarian music, and naturally David was in 7th heaven. He spoke to Mama Weisz, and before we knew it we were sitting at their table, about 10 in all. They were all conversing in Hungarian (except me) and David found much in common with them. This Edith who wrote a few lines is a lovely girl of about 19 or 20 who just recently came over from Hungary (about 14 months ago). We thought it would be fun to send you a card with some of the signatures. So much for that. We are fine, and enjoying somewhat of winter weather. It has been cool, quite cool for the past few days. My sister writes that it's about 19 in Chicago, as I know I shouldn't complain. What's new with you? It's your turn to write, you know. Don't let's wait 2 months again. Love from both of us, Dorothy

1948/12/22 Undated David and Dorothy to Irving (Book 2, 40-41)

[Dated by David mentioning it's been 6 years since he's seen Irving, and by Dorothy mentioning that it is winter and before New Year]

Thursday

[from Dorothy]
Dear Irving:
We received your letter and were happy to hear from you, as always. Of course we understand that you are busy, but a line or two telling us you are well is okay. We are "enjoying" winter weather in California, and I mean it is really cold. What with cold weather and plenty of rain, it is almost like being back East, except of course, no snow. David is working late tonite so I am catching up on correspondence. Perhaps I have given the impression that David has gone into his own business. He hasn't, Irving, but what he has done is this. Formerly he had been working for a furniture store doing drapery work. Now he is doing this drapery installation on his own. In other words he works for a few stores, charging them by the hour. When they have draperies to be installed, they call him and in this way he is not confined to any store in particular but can work for anyone. Also, he is connected with an upholsterer who has a shop in Long Beach, and David takes care of any drapery orders this man may get. They split any profit on this type of work. Eventually,

Irving, David hopes to open a drapery shop of his own, but this takes money and thus far we are not able to do this. So you see, the above is what I meant when I said David was "on his own." As for his writing you in person, he should of course do so, but you know what it is for him to write. I always preach to him about it, but it's one of those things. We heard from Hermina last week and finally David wrote her himself. She too sailed into him for not writing and it did the trick. By Jan. 1st we will be moved to another apartment, a larger one than we have now, and we're quite happy about it. Our new address will be 1152 E. 1st St., Apt. 202, so please send your mail there. We don't know anyone who has a wire recorder, Irving. I wish we did so we could take advantage of your records. So much for now. Have a nice holiday, and our best wishes to you for a Happy and Healthy New Year. Love, Dorothy

[from David]
Dear little brother!
I just got home and I so I write a few lines to you. Currently there is no particular news here, everything is the same. I wrote to the girls this week and I invited them here, if they want to come here. I would like them to come here! You know it has been 6 years already that I haven't seen you! You know you could live here also and you could go to school here. You could live better here than in Columbus, Ohio. I think you can change your school...So, I truly don't know any news. I believe that Dorothy wrote about everything already. I hope I will see you soon in person! What does Herman do? Where does he work? Did Arthur open his factory? How does the business go for him? How are you otherwise? Who cooks for you and who is cleaning? Write about everything ok?! I kiss you with love until I will see you again. Your forever faithful brother. Dezső

1948/12/30 Hermine to Irving (Book 10, 128-129) no xmas gift for Marie

12/30 - 48

My dear brother Irving,
This week past by and I never wrote to you. Hope you both are well and it was wonderful to get your letter. We are very happy to know that you are only very busy because we were worried already. We received a letter from David and Dorothy. It was quite a job to make him write. They asked us to come out there if possible for Jan 11th when they have their wedding anniversary. Just wrote to them too that at present time we want to wait here in N.Y. Whenever we would decide it would be with the boys! I really don't know if that is the truth because I don't know if Herman would be willing to go there. We'll see - but maybe N.Y. would bring some luck to us. I will send them a card to congratulate them on the anniversary and on it also to wish a Happy Birthday to David. I'll try to write more real soon because this is on my lunch time and I believe you can tell that! Let me hear from you and real soon. You didn't tell us if Arthur and family is going for vacation or going to live in Mexico. Best regards to them all and to Mr. Zuhl and wife. Take care of yourself and dress well so you wouldn't catch a cold! The weather is bad last week was very cold this week it is raining! Had a very nice bonus for Christmas 2 weeks pay! Maria had gifts but no money because the excuse is that Jewish people don't believe in Christmas. Love to you both, Hermina

1949/1/6 Carabel Kortkamp to Irving (Book 14, 122-124)

1583 Mistletoe Dr.
Cleveland 6, Ohio

Dear Irving,
New Year's or there about is such a good time to do things which one has been planning and so here is the note I was going to write to you. But this note is coming now only because your address just wouldn't turn up no matter how madly I tried to find it. Then over Christmas vacation, I finished unpacking my trunk (yes actually just finished it!) and like looking for buried treasure, there the looked for - but seemed forever missing - address was - and following thought with action - the note! So what are you doing now? How's school - madly working? And dancing - have you been down to Jimmy's? But I'd like to hear this first hand. I'm going to be in Columbus Sat. Jan. 8 why don't you give me a buzz at Wa-6-1253 Sat. about 8 p.m. It would be fun to talk to you. Sincerely, Carabel KortKamp.

[Note: Carabel Lee Kortkamp became the bride of Michael Hakeem, Friday evening at the First Presbyterian Church in Pataskala. The former Miss Kortkamp attended the University of New Mexico and was graduated from Ohio State. Hakeem is a graduate of the University also and is now doing graduate work in the School of Social Administration. The OSU Lantern. Nov 30, 1942]

1949/1/12 Hermine to Irving (Book 10, 131-132) worldwide yarhzeit and kaddish

New York 1/12/49
Dear Irving,
I was waiting to hear from you but so far no news and I hope that both of you are well. I mailed a card to Dorothy + David + congratulated them also wished a Happy birthday to David. I don't remember if I mentioned that they asked us to come to California if possible for their anniversary so we could celebrate together. If I remember well this was the second or maybe the third letter since David got married. My letter must have impressed them because they answered me as soon as they got my mail. My answer to their letter was that at the present time we want to take our time to stay a while and if you too decide then will let them know. Sometimes I wonder maybe it would be better but everybody thinks New York is the best place for girls - so we feel that the best thing is to stay. Tell me Irving about yourself and your graduation ? When is that going to be and how is everything with you? How is Herman? Did you have a nice vacation - is there anything new you like to tell us!... I almost called you up because for the Jan 11th all Jewish people who lost somebody were asked to keep it as a day for the people that were lost in Europe and I didn't know about it until Saturday night and then I thought of calling you but because David has his anniversary I changed my mind. We waited long so we shouldn't put [it] on the same date. So Irving please let's make a date for that and real soon - because it will be easier for them. You know that very well that there is no hope so if we can't have them back anyway - at least we should set a date and you boys should say kaddish so they, our loved ones, should at least rest in peace. We don't have to sit not even an hour, but to lite candles and to say kaddish. Please mark a date and write to David too so all of us should have the same day. This is on my mind so don't let it go any longer. Tell me how is everything with you. Oh, yes about the Meizlish girl or the young married woman. There is nothing wrong in going up to their house, but it isn't important. There are times when a nice friendship can be kept and it is always nice to have friends, but somehow I wouldn't care to do it. Everybody sends their love to you both. Love, Hermina

1949/1/18 David and Dorothy to Irving (Book 12, 233-235) new apartment

Jan. 17, 1949
[from Dorothy]
Dear Irving and Herman:
Many thanks for the very lovely anniversary card. It was sweet of you to think of us, and we were so happy to receive it. I am a bit late in acknowledging its receipt, but really these weeks have been busy ones for me. Getting settled in a new apartment is quite a job, what with cleaning painting, etc. However, things are starting to take shape now, thank goodness. One thing, though, we have very noisy neighbors upstairs, and that's the only thing that's spoiling our enjoyment. Sometimes it feels as though they are walking on our heads. I just don't know how people can be so inconsiderate of others, but that makes the world I guess. The weather here is starting to return to normal, after a real session of snow and rain. Looks like we'll have to come East for the winters instead of the other way around. I suppose the papers really wrote it up big - snow in sunny California. It was a thrilling sight, though the snow really didn't settle on the ground at all, not in Long Beach at any rate. My folks called me on our anniversary, and of course that's always a thrill talking to them. My Dad hasn't been feeling too well, and I am trying to get them here for a visit. I do hope they'll come at least for a couple of weeks. We heard from the girls last week, and all is well with them. What's new with you Irving? Still grinding away I suppose. Everything here is fine, and outside of a cold, which we both shared, we are feeling okay. Well, Irving, maybe next year you can see your way clear to visit us on your summer vacation. Any chance of that? Nothing would please us more. Write soon and let us know how everything is. Love to both of you from us, Dorothy

[from David]
Hello Irving and Herman! Until 120!
How are you two boys doing? Hope you both are fine and in good health! Hoping to hear the best from you. Please give my regards to everyone. Wishing you the best of everything, with love, David.

P.S. I am fine too!..

2/7 - 49

My dear brother Irving,

I can't remember when we heard from you. Hoping that you both are well, only busy as usual. It seems that we always find something to make us busy. If I have to prepare my supper I wouldn't mind if only I could invite you up for supper, but after supper time the evening is almost gone. Hoping that maybe a day will come when everything will be different. Friends I have some, but nothing serious yet. I met a fellow in an Hungarian ball who is a friend of Emil Mendlowitz and knows him from Europe. He is 38 years [old], a tall, dark fellow and I saw him, but he'd like to come more often and means it for good - but he is an ordinary fellow like his other friends - so I have to find a way to tell him off. Don't tell that to Mendlowitz because I'm not interested anyway. I met another fellow also at a dance, but he is about 42, a lawyer. A very fine person who takes me only to kosher restaurants for dinner and [I] saw him a few times. I have the feeling that he might not be able to settle down. He has an office downtown, but he is not the type who wants to show up - and is a very plain person, but intelligent. To me it seems he can make a living but would never be rich - maybe it is funny but I wonder if they make out to get along! How do you like that. Don't get me wrong Irving because I'm taking it this way, but it is nothing to talk about it too seriously! But just in case - I can't help thinking that way! He is doing all right as he always tells me how busy he is, but I wouldn't know how to judge him. He only told me that he doesn't want a rich girl whenever he decides to get married. He is originally from Poland, his parents are in Canada. I met some of his nephews when they were in New York. Also, he has a brother and sister here. One of his brothers is a children's specialist. Well that is all for now. He is somebody and here I'm the one who doesn't know - just in case! Will see and I hope he'll call again. You know we can't never tell! But I go to more dances again and also Maria too - Would be nice if you could join us and Herman would be able to find nice girls - believe me!! He should learn to dance and come here for a few weeks. He would meet girls and it doesn't even cost much money - just a ticket for himself. He is silly for not trying to do something when there are only a few decent boys and so many girls wherever we go. A girl hardly has a chance even for a dance. Does he want to live all alone for all his life - I don't believe that. You Irving I can't say much because you are studying, but you also should look around and let us hear from you. Love to you both and please write all about you. Love, Hermina

2/8 - 49

My dear brother Irving,

It seems like ages since we heard from you. Every day I am looking for mail, but you probably do the same. Well, that goes like that - I know that you are busy with your studies and maybe we should do some more writing to you. The only thing is that we or perhaps I should say that I'm a poor writer, and try to get out of it if possible. There isn't much to say - everything goes as usual. Nothing new - pretty busy with school and business. Not much new socially either - but what I wrote to you - you never answered me anyway - maybe you are not interested to know all about it as I tell you almost everything in detail. You see because I can't tell you anything wonderful so I think those little things might give you some idea of our life and the things we do. Haven't heard from Dorothy yet, but hope they are well. It would be nice to go there for a vacation and I'm trying to talk Maria into that. We are also planning for June when you'll graduate - If God helps we'll come then. Let us hear from you and Herman should also write. How is he? Is he working? When did you see the relations? Aunt Jenny's daughter-in-law has a new baby boy and I visited her when she was in a New York hospital. They are very happy because they have a little girl already who is in one age with Joann. That is Aunt Jenny's oldest son's family [Emmanuel]. They moved to New Jersey a few months ago. Jeanne Frey is pretty well, but her husband isn't working for awhile already, but as long as Jeanne is - no worries for him! Her business is alright, but she works very hard. Bertha was here last night. She is just like before. Haven't seen Mannie for a long time. Don't have time for them. Let us hear from you if you have a chance - Mrs. Lindek never called us - or is she back already? Tell us some good news about you and how you're doing there. Love to you both, Hermina

Regards from Aunt Jenny and all. Love from Maria and Mrs. Kugler

Sun:

Dear Irving:

I bow my head in shame for not having written to you Irv and I cannot nor will not attempt to give any excuses. I just didn't that's all, and I'm sorry. Reneé tells me that you were over to see her and have called. She thinks you're an awfully nice guy and I of course agree. Yes Irv, I have taken the decisive step, first engagement and then marriage. I don't feel as if I could have met a more intelligent, sweeter girl anywhere. She's so understanding, and so like me, at least as far as fundamental values are concerned. I guess it was almost "inevitable" that this should be the result of such circumstances. I've been in love with Reneé for a long time as you so well observed but this is the first positive manifestation of it. She has probably told you about our marriage plans, the fact that she will work while I finish my PhD. As I see it Irv we are only young once. Life is short and one may as well enjoy this short life as much as possible. There must be an integration of study and other things, namely family life, and more so than anything, that which we all search for and long for, love and appreciation. Reneé is as anxious for me to get my PhD as I am, she too is interested in growing and developing, so we shall grow and develop together rather than apart. We are similar in many respects and yet we are different and this difference must be retained. There should be no insurmountable problems between two relatively intelligent people able to adjust to each other and to life in general. Marriage is really an experiment in human relations based on biological factors and spiritual unity. Not sure about the wedding Irv, but I would like you to come. The University of Chicago is such a wonderful institution Irv that I can hardly emphasize the importance of your coming up here. I realize now how inadequate Hayes was and also James, etc. Here you have the top men in the country who go through an analysis so much more rigorously and thoroughly. I've learned more economics in these 2 quarters than I could ever to hope to learn at State. I got 3 B's last quarter. A's just aren't to be had up here at least not by me. I got a B in that Prime Theory course also, but boy did I work. How did you come out? Grades I mean Irving. I'm taking courses in State and Ideal Finance, Monetary Policy, and Price Theory this quarter. By summer quarter I'll have all the courses required for the PhD exams and will take one or two of them. I'll still be around here for quite some time. When Reneé and I are settled here and organized it would be nice for you to come up one weekend. Be more than happy to have you and I mean that. Well Irv that's all for now. I'll answer your letter more promptly this time. Sincerely, Herb

1949/2/15 Undated Hermine to Irving (Book 10, 113-114)

[~1949/2/15 From Dorothy's letter on 1/11 and mention of the yahrzeit date that hasn't been set yet, but it will be by 1949/4]

My dear little brother Irving!
We were very happy to [get] your letter and it made us entirely impatient that we did not hear from you for so long. Thank God we are well, too. I started to go to school , one night per week. Vocabulary Building and English. I hope something will work out by studying. I have found your comment interesting considering that maybe it is possible that I must go besides the school or next to the school. It does not mean a lot, but it is better than nothing. I bought a very good dictionary, but if you could use it then I will send it to you because to me, a smaller one would be good too, but this is a very good book Roget's Synonyms - I don't remember if I spelled it correctly. Write if you can use it! Besides that, David's wife wrote to us on 1/11, but we did not respond to her yet. Regarding the yahrzeit, that is why it would be better if we would choose a day because it would be about time for us, and we know that to hope that they are alive is useless anyway. So, I'm writing again, I want to choose a day, and write what day you think my little brother. It really does not matter because we don't know when it happened exactly. I know that our father is entitled to that and also to our Lajos. We are making the situation easier, as we think. I will write to Dezső also and I am asking his opinion, if he does not respond then we will give him the day and we will leave the rest up to him. About the house, the best thing is only if we can do it, that is, to sell the furniture so at least you will not have trouble with that. I think that you want to give up the house before you would decide, but I think that even if you would sell it then they would still give you time to deal with it in that case. Write your opinion and if you can see that it is better, we have no problem with you selling the furniture. It is not worth it to ship it here or to California until we decide that we will go there soon. As far as the boyfriend is concerned, I will write about that some other time because I am on my lunch break and the time is up! I will write again shortly. I kiss you many times with love. Hermina

Herman should take care of himself because he does not work. He should eat because without it there is no life. You can't forget about yourself. Eat on time so you can study.

1949/2/21 Irving to Herb Baum (Book 6, 328-329) - draft

Feb 21st 1949
Columbus 5, Ohio

Dear Herbert,

Prior to your arrival and calling Saturday, I began to reply to your welcomed letter. I needn't reiterate that how glad I was to hear from you and see you, especially knowing that you have made the decisive step. When I've 1st learned about your engagement, for a moment it was difficult to believe it because the attitude that you have shown toward marriage at this time. However, your choice was practical. The search to enjoy life spiritually (and through marriage) is important. The conclusion arrived at by you (that you two can grow and develop together) is possible and it's wise, because the adjustment in general is simplified, which might be more difficult to do in later years or in late marriage. The pleasure will be mine to observe your wedding, my presence will depend upon the probable developments, but inform me about your plans. There are only a few institutions like Chicago University it's undeniable. However, there seems to me questionable of being able to attend it. Partially due to financial reasons. This can be met though if I would switch plans. I shall comment upon this more fully in person, before final plans are made. Before concluding at this time let me repeat that the B's you get shouldn't matter because you'll get accustomed to it. I have. In the practical world there are other important problems that matter of which you are quite aware. Therefore, as time goes on, before you'll realize it, you will have attained your primary goal - education. Thanks Herb, for the invitation and also for the pleasant evening. Until I hear from you again, my best wishes and thanks for the pleasant evening and invitation to Chicago, I shall try to fulfill it. Sincerely,

1949/2/28 Marie to Irving (Book 8, 241-242)

2/28/49

My dear little brother Irving!

I am in a hurry to write again a couple of lines. We are well and I hope that my lines will find you in the best of health. It has been a few days since we heard about you, but I hope that you are healthy. Do you study hard my dear Irving? Just take care of yourself. There is nothing particular here. Oh yes! Aunt Jen's son, you know the oldest son [Emanuel] , just had a baby girl, very cute you also will be delighted along with her son. You can imagine how happy they are with God's help. Otherwise the relatives are well. The weather here is not very good. It is snowing. Yesterday the weather was beautiful. How is it by you, my little brother? You know my little Irving that on the 21st it was the 9th year since we came to America. How did you celebrate it? I worked and Hermine was on a date with the boy. Otherwise there is nothing particular, currently everything is the same. Just take care of yourself my dear Irving! Write a couple of lines. David and the others are well also. Now I will close my lines and I kiss you countless times with much love, your forever faithful sibling. Maria

1949/3/9 Marie to Irving (Book 6, 1-2)

3/9/49

My dear brother Irving,

We haven't heard from you in a long time. I hope both of my lines will find you in the best of health. We are fine and as you can see my dear little brother, I will try to write to you. Are you still studying so hard to learn? I hope everything will work for you Irving dear. For myself, nothing special. Hermine wrote to you last night about everything. Have you heard from David? We haven't received a letter from them in a couple of weeks. How are the relations? He wrote about the same time as Aunt Helen and Flora. The relatives here are fine. My dear, have you decided what you hope to do? Will you continue at this school ? Or do you already have an idea? Write my little brother dear about everything. It would be good for you too, to go relax somewhere. Do you want to go to California? Now I close my lines and a heartfelt hello. I kiss you countless times your sister forever with love. Love Maria

1949/3/17 Marie to Irving (Book 2, 32-33)

3/17/49

My dear little brother Irving,

I'm trying to write a few lines again. I hope that my lines will find you in the best of health. We are well and it felt good to hear your voice my Irving. Hermina tried to call you many times only we did not know if they will call you over. First of all, we did not know the phone number either, so it was hard to find it. But what is important is that we talked to you. How is Herman? He doesn't have time to write? He would have a chance now and he could go to David and he could try. Maybe he would have more luck there to get a job. He could get unemployment there too. We will see how everything will shape up here and we are planning on going there too.

And you little brother? Do you plan on going to school continuously? Write, my dear Irving.
We would love to see you. It would also be better for you to be in a bigger city than in Columbus. I can imagine it would be harder to get a job there than ever. It is not easy here either, but still there are more opportunities. I will leave this too now and I wish you good luck and the best of health and take care of yourself. I kiss you countless times with much of love. Maria

1949/3/19 Hermine to Irving (Book 2, 34-35)

March 19, 1949
My dear brother Irving,
I can't tell you how happy we were to talk to you. If I would know it is so easy to get you we would try it a long time [ago]. I only hope that you didn't get scared when they told you that NY is calling. Hope that Herman is well and if he is smart he wouldn't worry because here too there are plenty of people without jobs. What happened to Arthur's business that they let him go? Does he at least collect the money from the US employment office? I hope to get my increase maybe next week. The union was trying to reach an agreement for an increase but as I learned just this week were they promised. I only hope that next week I'll get the pleasant surprise! Also the backpay with the beginning of January. Yes Irving - As things are today I believe we are lucky to be here at least we don't have worries about these things. Do you remember Leona? That is the girl in our office you met there on a Saturday when you were looking for me. Well, she is getting married next Saturday and I'm invited too. I hope to go because it is in our neighborhood. Since yesterday we have a real winter here in New York. How is it in Columbus? Haven't heard from Dorothy for a couple of weeks. Happened to mention to them that we might surprise them this summer. Everybody thinks we should try to go there because it is so beautiful out there. Maybe Maria will go if they will answer to our letter. For a vacation it is quite an expensive place because the traveling is very high. Will see how things work out. We both are well. Take good care of yourself and Herman too. My best wishes and love to you both, Hermina

P.S. Regards to our friends and relatives

1949/3/30 Frey-Yenkin Letter of Recommendation for Irving (Book 22, 228-230)

March 30th, 1949
To whom it may concern:

Irving Gluck was employed by our company from 1940 to 1943, in several capacities. We found him to be a man of excellent character, honest and very dependable, and we would not hesitate to recommend him to anyone for employment, in any position which he is capable of handling. Yours very truly,
Frey-Yenkin Paint Company,
A. Yenkin

Dear Irving:
Following up our conversation, I'm enclosing a letter of recommendation. I don't know whether I've covered everything you want me to say and if not, please let me know. With kindest regards and wishing the best of luck, I am Sincerely yours,

FREY-YENKIN PAINT COMPANY
A. Yenkin

1949/4/5 Marie to Irving (Book 2, 44-45)

4/5/49
My dear little brother Irving,

A couple of lines again [to say] that we are well, thank God. And last night we got your precious letter which I was very happy about and I'm happy to hear that thank God you are well, which is what I hope to hear about you again. Now my dear Irving, I will get to [tell] about Herman. Like Hermine wrote to him also. There, in Columbus, it is very hard to find a job. I know that about myself too. And if he is a smart boy, then he will do like Hermine mentioned also. He will not pay for it because that is not a life the way he lives there. If he would be here, he would have more benefits and he could get a job faster. In this world, it is hard everywhere. They don't pay anyone, except one who wants to work. This way everything can turn for the better. And about you my dear little brother, I am very sorry that you have to study so hard, but I hope that the dear God will help and everything is going to work out successfully. Also, my dear Irving, if God will help, you will graduate and it will be easier for you too. You can more easily make a decision about where you would like to go. We are hoping that it will work out with God's help. And my little brother, the way Herman decided himself to come here, I will help you pay the rent and expenses there until we will make a decision. And my Irving, don't be sad. If Herman is smart, then he will bring out his best thinking and he will behave because this life the way he lives is not a life. If he would see other boys like him, [he would know] how different a life he lives. The years are passing by very fast and we are not getting any younger. He would like to be young, but it will be too late. That is why it would be better if he would think about himself today before it's too late. Now I am asking you my little brother not to be sad and take care of yourself. You know that we can't do anything about anybody. Now, I will close my lines and send greetings from my heart. I kiss you countless times, your forever faithful sibling. Take care of yourself. Love, Maria

1949/4/5 Undated Hermine to Irving and Herman (Book 10, 52-55) - Herman not working

[Dated by Hermine's $5 raise]

My dear Irving and Herman!
We got a letter from you this morning and I'm trying to respond to you during work. As far as Herman's welfare is concerned, he is entitled to a check. Even if they sent it out after working, but he doesn't like [the work], then he will find some excuse, then they can't force him to accept it until he finds a proper one, but he is entitled to it. He should go to the employment office and talk to someone in a higher position or at the information. He should inquire what he can do about this case. As long as he pays it and now that he does not work, he is entitled to get it. What would he do if he would not have money? He still needs to live! So, he should go in and try until he gets to his goal. He should tell them there that he wants to work, but he does not like that kind of work or he does not like the hours, or that he wants to improve his situation not to go backwards. So, he can say all kinds of excuses. Only he should not say that he does not want to work. I know individuals who were sent out to 15 places and when they were sent out they came up with all kinds of excuses and they are still getting the money until today. He should go someplace else, but no one can force him to take a job he does not like! If he wants to, he should arrange it so he can get the money and he should come here in the meantime and he should collect and maybe he would get a job. I guess it would be good for Herman to come here. It is possible he could get a job where I work. He could do better here anytime and little by little he could build himself up. I would love to help you Irving to pay for the rent while Herman stays in NY. If he would like it, then you could give up the house because it's not worth it to keep it there. Thank God I earn $45 a week and I will get a raise around Friday. I don't know if it will be 2.50 or $5.00 yet. So, I think it is not worth it to stay there and if you want, Herman, come over here and we will help you to find a job. If Irving would want it, then he could take a young couple in to rent the apartment out. He could get good money for it and he could leave a room for himself. Write a response and I will write again. Jenny Frey's husband also does not work, but you Herman, could find some place. Come and try it. You can eat with us and it will not cost a lot until you will find a job. And don't be upset. You could live better than in Columbus. And you could have a chance to get to know people. Kiss all of you. I ask for a reply. Hermina

1949/4/7 Dorothy to Irving (Book 12, 237-239) - pregnant

April 7, 1949
Dear Irving:
We were so happy to receive your letter and know that all is well with you. My only excuse for not writing sooner is that I have been quite busy. You know my mother was with us for 6 weeks, and believe me we were on the go constantly. She left last Friday and now I can go back to a more or less settled routine. I'm really tired after chasing around so much, and just taking it easy feels good. Sorry to hear that you may be forced to vacate your apt. Are apartments hard to find now? Out here there are plenty available now, and it

seems like old times to walk along the streets and see "For Rent" signs hung out. Rentals however have not come down in spite of this condition. The people who were so noisy above us moved out last week, and I'm keeping my fingers crossed hoping the new tenants will be more considerate. Well Irving, I'm hoping that in late October you will become an uncle. I'm keeping my fingers crossed, in view of what happened last year, and am taking every precaution to be careful. I hope I'll have better luck this time, as there is nothing that David and I want more. I'll keep you informed of course. The weather here is beautiful now and a welcome relief after the "unusual" winter we've had. It's been 80 [degrees] for the past few days. Nothing much more now. I'm waiting to hear from the girls - it's been some time since they've written to us. Everything else is fine. Please write and keep us informed of everything. Love to you and Herman, Dorothy

1949/4/11 Hermine to Irving (Book 10, 151-153) saying Yizkor on 2nd day Pesah

4/11 - 49

Dear Irving and Herman,

Just a few lines this time because it is late. I was visiting tonight at the Gold Family. [I] went there after work because Uncle Gold died last week and I didn't go to the funeral so I had to go to see them. They were asking about you and Joe called up the Rabbi and told him the way we are with our yahrzeit. The Rabbi said as long as we know that they were taken away on the second day of Pesah we should have the yahrzeit on that day. So Irving and Herman we go for Yizkor and you say kaddish on that day. Received a letter from Dorothy and she also said that David wants [to know] it when [and to] tell him so I'm going to write to him too. The Rabbi also said that we could keep the second day of Pesah every year - that means on the same day - but if we want to, we can find out about the date when they all were taken away and have the yahrzeit on the same date. That is the day when we say Yizkor. Please lite a candle too. Our Father's name is Yiddish Hebrew Jermije. His father I think was Avram Mendel {Hajem libe} Our grandmother Haje and will have them all on that day - You say Yizkor only on the yahrzeit. Otherwise we are well. For the first seder we are invited to Brooklyn to Mr. and Mrs. Noti. How is Herman? Is he going to come here? I got my increase, $5 instead of 2.50, what the union wanted them to give. Here everybody has a better chance and he would have a chance, too. He should get the money and I hope he does. Please let me know! I'm going to write to David too! I wish I could invite you for seder but it is not easy. Please let us know what you like to do with the house because it doesn't pay to stay there to save the things. Wishing you a very Happy Passover Holiday. With Love, Hermina

Mrs. Kugler sends her regards

1949/5/7 Marie to Irving (Book 8, 248-250)

5/7/49

My dear little Irving!

We got your letter that we could hardly wait for, which I was happy about and I am happy to hear that thank God you are all healthy. We are well also and I hope we will hear the best about each other after this too! And also, as you wrote my dear about the studying, that is up to you. Today it needs to start from new. Hermine is sending her greetings too and kisses you. She will write. About the studying, in my opinion, you don't know if you will like it yet (to be realistic). And in the meantime, you could lose these two years. In other words, as you wrote, that if you would continue this, then you would get the diploma in two years. I believe my dear Irving that it is very hard to decide. And I would also understand it if you want to study to become a Rabbi and it would not cost you anything. If you will continue the present [course of study], then you would have to pay and that is hard too. I think that if you are already in it, then these two years will pass even if it will cost you money, but if you like it, then it's worth it. So, my dear Irving I only think that studying is not an easy job. And it is up to you now. I wish you lots of good luck whatever decision you make, and also about the work you mentioned. Maybe it is necessary to know how to speak and write perfectly. I hope that it will work out for you, my dear Irving. Yes, my Irving. Write to us when you will take the exam because we need to know the exact time, so we can be there [at graduation] on time. Now I will close my lines and I wish you lots of good luck and the best of health to both of you. I am sending greetings to Herman too and I kiss you countless times with much love. Love, Maria

1949/6/16 Hermine to Irving (Book 10, 164-168) - Emil to Israel, Lipot Klein died

My dear little brother!

We read your letter with happiness, only I am very sorry that we can't be a part of the celebration. It must have been beautiful and you didn't write anything about that to us. Accept with love our good wishes and [we] wish you lots and lots of good luck in the future as well. It was against my will that I could not be there. I hope you will forgive me for it! How are you otherwise? I understand from Dorothy's letter that she would want the best for all of us, but somehow I would not like to go [in] to a business like that. Maybe it's the best but I don't know what kind of response I could give to that. First of all, if you already got this far with studying, you can get situated easier. And Herman, if God forbid something would not go the way he wants it, he could not stand it. Although, that's the way starting out goes for others too, and many times an idea can be the best business in the future. So, surely there is something in the case and surely the business promises [to make] good money, but I don't know what to suggest. What does Herman think? What does he do these days? And how do you spend your vacation time? I did not know that Arthur rebuilt the factory! The business is good surely, but then why did he let Herman go? As far as I am concerned, I don't want to deal with a business, rather [In English] to catch a nice boy! You know Irving, I met a nice young girl about 21. She works in our office. She is very sweet but a short girl and if you'll come to N.Y. I [would] like you to meet her. You see she has lots of friends and she is the daughter of a well to do family, but we are all very good friends and I told her already that I have a sweet brother but he is tall. I haven't heard from Dorothy for quite a while, but I'm glad to know they both are well. I wrote to Emil in Helmec and my letter came back with the note that he left to Israel. Also received a letter from Budapest [and] Margit wrote that Lipot is resting now that he past away in April this year. He suffered a lot so it is better this way already. Why didn't Herman come to the telephone? Shame on him! How is he feeling now? I talked to somebody and [they] told me that sometimes too much acid will make the stomach ache and [he] has to watch what to eat. No heavy greasy or can fruits or vegetables, lots of milk, but not ice cold as he drinks that. Why is he so afraid from people? He thinks that one person living all alone can be happy or will ever be happy - that is no life and a right minded person wouldn't want to live that way. Love to both of you, Hermine

1949/6/20 Undated Irving to Dave and Dorothy - draft, after graduation (Book 6, 337-343)

Dear Dorothy and David,

Immediately after the graduation was over, several friends and relatives invited me to be their guest. Thus, this is my first real opportunity to respond to your welcomed call as well as to your letter. Believe it or not, the commencement, which marks the seventy fifth year of the Ohio State University's history, was one of the greatest. We have had almost 2,500 graduates. This includes some Dr's and some M.A.'s and the most were BA's and BS's. It was interesting to note that only one Dr of economics and one MA of economics was from this amount of graduates. From my college there was 10 economics, from over 400 students. Thus, the ratio was not bad. Will this mean more opportunities? That's supposed to be so, but all remains to be seen. Speaking of opportunities and business. During our conversation last Thursday evening as well as in your letters, you have indicated the probable achievement in the business world. This question of business has been, to a great extent, discussed with Herman and I have also given some thought to it. The question I have raised was that, what is it that I want to do ten years from now. If so, what is the immediate problem before that goal can or could be attained. Then further, I superimposed the question, what is the real motive of business. Many times we are forced into doing things that we seldom want. Then again, the question why I'm hesitating to become a business man. I could go on [and] raise more questions than the probable answers would suggest. But any one kind of reasoning I have not come to the definite conclusion, but one thing is certain that even though life is short, there must be ways of doing something in order to bring forth a mutual cooperative society in which the past decade will be a dream and never again will they lift sword against one another. Why were these conditions that caused so many innocent people to lose their life. Was it because of their deeds? That is full of doubt, but one can only think of today that as the economic conditions well indicate that most of the trouble starts from economic reasons. Thus, a business venture at this time as I see it is very questionable because I would like to have a different approach to life than as I have pictured it in the past and future business world. Today, a small businessman can not develop as was prior to the 1890's, the development at that time could probably be justified, but looking the year over with its struggle that brought to humanity many times without real cause, except the economic struggle, the struggle for power and authority and thus, today the trend is toward the lifting of this economic struggle and putting it to the cooperatives of society. Today to thrive to build up a business seems all right for some, but the trend is such that the struggle that it takes in building up a business is not worth it, because today the trend is that we are a mixed people. That we are more and more becoming less and less of the owner class. To return and become specific about the problem of business venture. Herman as well as I would suggest that if we would have capital in cash, that is, if the market, in which we have our liquid assets, would be at the level of getting out or able to get a return for invested liquid assets, then it would seem fair to help you out in order that your desire and business venture could be fulfilled. But under the prevailing market, the probable effect of getting out from the market would mean a tremendous loss. Thus, at this time we must wait and see. To the fact that you have someone that would be a silent partner seems to be the solution and if that is what can put your ideas forth, it seems logical to follow. Although, the probable business predictions as you know must be understood in order that you'll [have] a profitable business without silent partners. That's as time goes on one needs to be able to realize your future goals. This time, lots of luck and best wishes and love

1949/6/26 Hermine to Irving (Book 19, 431-432) - broke ankle - pages 1-4

New York 6/26
My dear brother Irving,
We were very pleased to receive your letter. It is a very well written and beautiful letter. I agree with you on the subject concerning Herman. I wish I could help to solve the problem but only he could do so and I wish he would try to see the other side of life. Money is really wonderful but just like any other thing in a normal way. We also received a letter from Dorothy and told us about the business they are or hope to open maybe on the 5th of July. I hope it will be with great success, also how sorry they are for not being able to attend your graduation. Well Irving dear, I want to tell you that I'm sorry and very much so, but now I['ll] tell you that I had a little accident. I fell and twisted my ankle on Marvin's wedding, Mrs. Sofferman's son's wedding, but that wasn't all because a bone was a little bit fractured and I had to have a cast on. But now the cast was taken off last Saturday and I'm well again thank God so I thought I better tell you so you wouldn't feel that I ever would neglect you like that, not to go after all our planning. Don't worry now because I'm all right now, but I'm not working yet and the doctor said next week I might go in - it happened the 26 of May and the funny part is that I wrote to Dorothy that I'd love to visit them, but don't want to fly. So that shows that when something has to happen it can happen anywhere. The doctor said I better go back to work for a few weeks and then take my vacation, so it seems I'll take it sometime in August. The weather is absolutely terrible and that is why my writing is in such a scribbling. I would love to see you and maybe you could plan to have a vacation with us in the mountains. It is not too expensive! Irving dear, don't worry because I'm well but have to rest with my foot for one more week.

1949/6/26 Undated Hermine to Irving (Book 10, 146-147) pages 5-6

I took an attorney [and] hope to have a case - but not much hope for that. I get paid from the union 15.00 dollars a week as compensation so don't worry Irving I'm OK.! Somebody suggested that you could sub lease the apartment. That means to sell that with furniture and everything and then we could get our money back or maybe make money with it. But you would have to talk with the landlord and give him some money too but then you could easier get rid of the apartment if you like to give it up - forgive me for my writing and spelling but I'm perspiring, it is very hot here. Bertha and husband are vacationing in Canada. Jean Frey has a fractured arm. [In Hungarian] There are plenty of people here with this disease, it's somewhat like an epidemic! [In English] How is Herman now? Regards to Flora, Arthur and family. Tell them how sorry we are that we couldn't see them either! Let us hear from you and take care of yourself. Love to both, Hermina

[On the side] Mrs. Kugler sends her regards

1949/7/5 Hermine to Irving (Book 10, 170-172)

New York 7/5 - 49
My dear little brother Irving,
We were very happy to get your letter, I am only sorry that you are disappointed in me. I promise you, that I will not do that, and am hoping that I am not in need, besides you couldn't have helped me, only I would have scared you, which I did not want. Thank God I am well and I am already walking a little and everything is well. I was at the doctor on Saturday and he said that my bone is already healed. If God will help I will be able to go to work soon. Right now, I am still walking with a cane for support because the muscles are not flexible yet, the way they should be. It will take a little time. Do not worry because there is nothing wrong and I have enough money also, thank God. Thank you for the offer and I would like to see you, if it would be possible. We welcome you anytime you can do it. There is only one big problem with New York, that the heat is terrible and I thought because of that, if you could come to the mountains it would be nice for you. Although, I will go sometime in the end of August and Marcsa maybe by the end of July. In case

you want to come, then you can. We welcome you anytime. Write about yourself and also about your work. Did you find a good job? How is Herman? We got a card from Dorothy announcing the opening of their store. I did not write to them yet, but maybe I will send a telegram. I will wish good luck to them. It is hot today and I hope it is cooler by you. How are the relatives? Jenny [Arthur's daughter] must be a big girl already! I would have loved to see everybody already, but I hope it will work out soon sometime. I will write again, until then I kiss all of you with much love. Hermina

Maria is at work still, that is why she did not write. When do we have yahrzeit for our dear late mother?

1949/7/11 Marie to Irving (Book 8, 261-262)

7/11/49

My dear little Irving!

I am truly sorry that I did not write to you for so long, but it was against my will. Now I will be in a hurry to try to write. I hope my little Irving that my lines will find you both in the best of health. We are well. As far as Hermine is concerned, thank God she is better. Today was the first day that she went back to work. The doctor said that she could go. It has healed, but she is not allowed to put weight on it yet. It will take a few weeks until it will be healed perfectly. We had a very good doctor. And my dear Irving, as you wrote in your letter that you could not understand why we did not tell you about it before. We did not want to because I know you would have gotten scared and you could not run here to look after her and I was waiting for her to get better. When we called you I was afraid that you will notice that something is up. And I could not leave her here so I could go alone. Although I would have liked to be with you, my dear little Irving. But now my little dear Irving, let's hope that we all will be in the best of health. Just take good care of yourself. And Herman also could have thought about it better to take better care of himself. And you my Irving, what do you do? Do you work hard? Take care of yourself also. And my dear little Irving, if you are planning on coming to New York then write to me and I will take my vacation on July 23rd for two weeks. I don't know how Hermine will arrange it yet. But don't be sad now my little Irving and take care of yourself. There is no news here otherwise. I did not write to David for a very long time. I am planning on writing now. I hope that their business will bring good luck to them. Health is more important. Now I will close my lines. I hope that I will hear the best about each other. Eat and take care wherever you go. I'm sending greetings and I kiss you countless times with much love, your forever faithful sibling with love. Maria

1949/7/13 Elsie Schallheim to Irving (Book 14, 133-137) OSU Graduation

3496 Blanche Rd
Cleveland Hts. Ohio
July 13, 1949

Dear Herman and Irving,

Jane and I wish to extend our best wishes to you, Irving. How does it feel to graduate from College ? I suppose you are now busy trying to get something that you will like. What are you plans? Jane graduated in Feb. and is now working for the Ohio State Unemployment Bureau. She had to take a Civil Service Examination. I wish you boys lots of good luck. If sometime in the near future you would like to come to Cleveland some weekend let me know. Jane will try to make some plans for you both. I have an extra bedroom so you boys would be welcome to stay over for the week end. Cleveland really is a beautiful city. Take care of yourselves and Jane joins me in sending her regards. Your cousin, Elsie Gluck Schallheim

1949/7/16 David and Dorothy to Irving (Book 18, 7-8) new store opening

July 16, 1949

Dear Irving:

Seems like I must always start with an apology for my laxity in writing, but we have been so busy there wasn't a chance. Seems like everything once started just kept on going, and now that the store is open and running we can relax a bit. First let me tell you we both enjoyed talking to you on the phone, although it already seems like ages ago. We are wondering what you are doing now though - Anything new in your plans to work in the State Department? Keep us informed about what transpires as you know we are very much interested. I am enclosing pictures and clippings of our store, which I am sure will be of interest to you. I must say our store is beautiful and we have had favorable comments from all who have seen it. We know your advice, as far as going into business at this particular time, was given after due thought and deliberation, but we also felt, we, being on the ground floor, could see great possibilities in this particular line. At any rate, we took the chance, and so far haven't regretted one single step. I only hope things go along at this tempo. Everything is a gamble and I for one always said "nothing ventured nothing gained." As I wrote you, I did not favor the idea of bringing in an outsider in the business, even though the couple I wrote you about were more than willing. So I wrote home explaining the situation, and my Father approved it by loaning us the money. Now it is up to us to prove that our ideas were well founded and we shall do everything possible towards this end, and success. David regrets very much that Herman at least can't be in it with him as he could use him in the store to great advantage and be together at the same time. David has employed a man under the G.I. Training, and he is working for us, along with 2 women. Other than the new store, there is not much to write about. I am feeling fine, and although I'm not too active in the store, I am here to help whenever I can. It won't be too long before I'll just be a housewife again, and soon a "Mother." That's about all for now. Please write soon and let us know all about everything. Until then - Love to you and Herman from Dorothy and David

1949/7/18 Undated Hermine to Irving (Book 18, 27-30) off crutches

My dear little brother Irving,
I'm sorry I neglected my writing. Thank God I'm Ok. Last week I went back to work. As of this week I threw away my crutches. I'm walking quite well. The only thing is that it is still a little swollen. I hope that both of you are Ok. I would like to hear from you. I wrote to Dave also and sent him a telegram, but as of today I haven't heard from him. I would love to see you my little brother, if you could come to see us. The only problem is it would cost you a lot, [but] to tell you the truth, the mountains would be good for you. They have very nice hotels and lots of girls, all kinds. I would love it that you would meet someone nice, a young lady! What do you think about that? My God, you would have a wonderful time there. A man, especially a nice young man, is very rare to find. Therefore, let me know if you want to come. Please let me know. Maria will go on Saturday for 2 weeks and I will take mine some time in August. Write about everything because I'm interested in how everything is and what you are doing. How are you spending your days? How are you doing with the job? Or maybe you are already working. And how is Herman? When have you seen the relatives and Aunt Helen? If you see them or the other acquaintances, give my best to them. Bertha was here a few days ago. She told me that she wants to bring Iren from Szatmar out from Roumania because it would be easier to go somewhere. But poor thing, should couldn't go too far because they arrested her and now she is in jail for already a couple of weeks. As soon as she left her home she received the paper to go to Palestine. They are also working on going to Canada. Maybe she will be able to go there if someone will be able to help her. Bertha is working on that. Otherwise with us everything is Ok. If you want to come, please write to let us know when, ok? Many kisses with lots of love to you both, Hermine

1949/7/26 Hermine to Irving (Book 10, 174-176)

My dear little brother Irving!
We got your card and letter and we are glad to hear that both of you are well. We are well also. Maria called us on Sunday morning on the phone and she is well. She went for a two week vacation on Saturday. I hope she will have a nice time! Oh yes! I still don't know where I will go. I guess that maybe I will go for a week and I will take one week some other time later to go to Columbus. If you could come that would be great, but I know that it is hard for you to make yourself go. As I told Maria too, that at least she will rest and it's worth the money. I just talked to Aunt Jenny - Lucille just had a little girl. She was wondering about you and Herman. We got a letter from Dorothy and David. They wrote a few lines too. Also they sent two pictures. Dorothy is in it too with David. And this is the only picture they finally sent after so much asking. Although, they are pretty busy. I hope the business will work out because I can say that it looks beautiful. The important thing is to be successful. I want to write to them also. Oh yes! There is Yahrzeit. The candles need to be lit on Wednesday, tomorrow night, that is, on Tuesday we need to light the candles for our late mother. Although I wrote about this to you, but you forgot and did not respond to it. I hope David did not forget! What's new by you? Write Irving! Write about everything and about Herman also. [In English] Believe me I would love to go with you for a vacation! If not this year - let's hope that in the near future. I think that will be the best if I go for 1 whole week to see you this fall. O.K.? I'll [find] out from my boss! Otherwise everything is well, my foot is well too! So let's hear from you both real soon. How was your short trip to your friend? Love to you and relatives. Hermina
[on the side] Mrs. Kugler sends regards

New York 8/9 - 49

My dear little Irving,

First of all, thank you very much for the picture which came out very well, you only need to put on a couple of pounds that are missing, then our little Irving would be very good looking!! We also got your other letter where Herman wrote two words, too. Although it was nice of him that he admitted the truth, that he was forced to write, it still felt good to read it and it would not hurt if he would make himself stronger and would write more often. If God helps me, I will go on vacation for a week on the 20th and I will bring you for a week - but later in September or October. Otherwise I am well and my leg is okay too and I hope you are healthy as well! Marcsa came home on Sunday and she looks like a gypsy she is so black. When do you plan on coming here, Irving? Write it and whenever you come we will welcome you and you can sleep at Mrs. Sofferman's because she has two empty rooms. What's the weather like by you? Here we can hardly take the heat. Dorothy wrote it as well, that it is very hot by them too. They sent us pictures too and the newspaper article also. The business is beautiful and I hope it is good too. Write about everything and until then, I kiss all of you. Hermina

1949/8/15 Undated Marie to Irving (Book 6, 91-92) - maybe Hermine just started dating Eugene

[dated by Marie just coming back from vacation and Hermine going on vacation on the 20th]

My dear little brother Irving!

I know you're wondering why I haven't written you just a card in so long.

First of all, as I wrote to you my Irving, that I was on my vacation. And time flies there so much, by the time I realized it myself, I was already at home. So I did not even write to anyone.

First of all, about myself I am well and I spent my vacation very nicely. Although, as usual, there were not many boys and most of them were young. Like everywhere there are more girls than boys, and it goes well for whomever is the cleverest. I was here last year too and then I met a few boys. They even took me home and they promised they will call, but I did not hear from them even until today. So this is the way it goes. The way it comes is the way that it will be. One only needs luck. I was there for two weeks. And now I will get to you. First of all, we got your picture where you look really good and the picture is beautiful. But now what is the most important, I wish you lots of luck and the best of health. I hope that your wish could come true! Just take care of yourself! How is Herman? What does he do? Believe me my dear Irving, it is worth it to go somewhere, even for a few days. The air and everything else helps a lot. It almost makes one feel better. If Herman would try it once, he would not spend his time the way he does. As long as one can live, one should live. And what did you decide my Irving? Did you hear about the jobs? Write about yourself. I can't write anything particular about me. Yes, I studied tennis in the country and I like it so much. But at home I don't have many occasions to practice because it takes two to play. I haven't found someone yet so I can't go and the season is almost already ended.

Yes, Hermine thank god is better and with God's help is planning on going this Friday on vacation for a week. She is going to a different place. Currently I'm sure she wrote that she met a very nice boy a few months ago. They see each other every week. But I don't know how it will work out because both of them are slow, especially Hermine needs more time to decide. But let's hope, that with God's help, everything will turn out for the best. Now take care of yourself my dear little brother and eat. I will write again. You write too. Now I will close my lines. Sending my best from my heart. I kiss you countless times with much of love. Who will never forget. Maria

1949/8/18 David and Dorothy to Irving (Book 12, 244-247)

Aug 18, 1949

Dear Irving:

I finally got 'round to acknowledging receipt of your picture. We think it's very nice, and thanks a million for sending it. David certainly made sure everyone here saw it, and it's something to see - the pride in David's voice when he says - "My brother." We are fine and keeping busy. Right now I am at the store alone, and David is out on a job. This is the dinner hour and always slow, so I can catch up with my letter writing. We received a letter from Hermina and also one from Maria who was on her vacation. Nothing much more. Time is going fast. We were already approached by the Rabbi to get tickets for the High Holidays so that won't be long now - Sept. 23rd, a New Year, and that means Summer is practically gone.

Of course, I keep pushing the time too - for a good reason. I see a customer approaching so I'll cut this short for now. Let us hear from you often. Love, Dorothy and David

1949/9/15 Marie to Irving (Book 2, 36-39) maybe dating Eugene

9/15/49

My dear little brother Irving!

I'm sorry that I made you wait for my letter, but I hope that my letter will find both of you in the best of health! We are well also and we got a letter from David and thank God they are well too. They are sending their best to you too. Although I wrote to them, it was in Hungarian and since Dorothy can't read it and David is very busy, they don't even write [to say] if they got it, but I hope they did. That is why I don't feel like writing, but the important thing is that they are well. I can't write anything particular about myself. I am busy like always. I'm thinking about what I should do, so I can change a little bit in this uneventful life. I went to play tennis in the summer as I mentioned to you already and I liked it very much. The only problem is that they stopped that too, since the season is over. I met a few boys there, but I knew them there only for as long as we played. There is no time to continue, but if the dear God will help me, by next time I will know, that is, I will understand the game. I'm already doing quite well this year. I will leave this too now. I would like to hear from you something good. How are you my dear brother? Have you decided if you will go to school ? I hope whatever you decide will be for the best! And what does Herman do? Is he working? Yes, my Irving when do you plan on coming here? I know that it is not easy for you, but I can help you too. We will pay your expenses because you know my dear Irving, I would love to see you. I hope I will have a chance to see you! Hermine, with God's help, is planning on visiting you. She is well and wrote to you. I'm sure she wrote about it, that she is going out with a boy for a few months. We can't know how it will work out. It is hard to decide. I trust her. The way she will decide will be good because it's not good to get involved. The boy is very good and he is in business. Whatever you talk to him about regarding business, he knows the answer. He is as tall as Hermine. He was here last night and comes twice a week and he calls her on the phone. I think that if he would not be serious he would not be so proper, but I'm sure she wrote to you about this! My dear Irving, just take care of yourself. And whatever you decide, may the dear God help you, and [stay] in the best of health. Now I wish you lots and lots of good luck! And I kiss you countless times with much love, your forever faithful sibling who will never forget. Love to Herman and the relatives. Maria

1949/9/30 Aunt Jenny Gluck to Irving and Herman (Book 14, 139-142) New Year's wishes

Dear Boys,

Also good health, and may all your wishes be fulfilled. Thank you for remembering us. Let us hear from you. The children all join me in sending our love and best wishes. As always, Lovingly, Aunt Jen

1949/10/2 Marie to Irving (Book 6, 89-90)

10/2/49

My dear brother Irving,

We have received your long-awaited letter which I was very pleased and happy to know that thank God you are well. And as far as school is concerned, I believe you are very busy with studying. But what is important is to hope that the good God will still help and you will end up richer. This is so, Irving dear, every beginning is difficult no matter what profession you choose. But don't be upset Irving dear. I can't write anything special about myself. Happy New Year, and we thank you too and may all your hopes come true. Also, we received a letter last week from Dorothy and they are thankfully fine. They will also write to you. You know, Irving, I wrote you a letter this week and forgot to tell you that I'm sorry I write to you so rarely, my little brother, dear. Now, let Hermine review her writing for you because then she can report more accurately. The boy I mentioned has serious intentions, but they hope that with the help of the good God, everything will come out good. The boy is very good. If it develops, she will write to you about it. And so Irving dear, as you mention winter sports and dancing, that is very good. I know Irving it is good, but I have no luck with the number of times I went to dance. But now leave it and take great care of yourself Irving dear and Herman. Write. Greetings from the heart and kissing you countless times with much love, your forever faithful sibling, see you again. Love, Maria

1949/10/10 Western Union Telegram Frederic Jerome Gluck Birth announcement (Book 7, 265)

1949 Oct 10 AM 12:47
Long Beach Calif
Herman and Irving Gluck
50 Linwood Ave Columbus Ohio

Your nephew Frederic Jerome weighing 7 lbs 12 1/2 ounces arrived Thursday morning by Caesarian therefore delayed. Letting you know all well now. Briss will be next Thursday. Mother and baby fine. Love, Dorothy, David, and Jerome

7 12 1/2 Briss

1949/10/12 Hermine to Irving and Herman (Book 3, 174-175)

New York 10/12 - 43 [misdated]

Dear Irving and Herman,
First of all, mazel tov Dorothy has a boy. We received a telegram from David and we hope she is doing all right. I also received a letter from Aunt Helen and I want to write to her - maybe tonight. Elsie's daughter came in last Saturday from Cleveland and I saw her yesterday. She is sweet. If everything is well I expect to go to see you one week from this Sunday. I will probably leave Saturday evening and arrive Sunday - but I'll let you know just when for definite. Please Irving don't prepare or do anything, you'll do it when I get there. I'm looking forward to see you and Aunt Helen. I don't know what is the reason that Flora never wrote to us. The news with Samuel surprised us but I don't want to know until they'll let us know - so if they didn't tell you don't say anything. I don't know what should we send to the baby as a gift? Maybe I'll send some money. Will write again, love to you both, Hermina
P.S. Please write. Maria sends her love too.

1949/10/18 Hermine to Irving (Book 10, 186) visiting Ohio

10/18 - 49
My dear little brother Irving,
I read your letter with happiness and if God will help, I will see you shortly. I will be leaving on Saturday night at 7:30 and I will arrive on Sunday morning at 8:00 to Pennsylvania station. Maybe it is a little too early for you to come out to get me, but you know that I am happy to see you again in advance. It is already too late. I have to start to work so I am in the hurry. I also think we will talk about everything in person. I got a letter from Dorothy. They are well. We are also well. I kiss you with love, Hermina and Maria

1949/10/25 Marie to Irving (Book 6, 102-103)

My dear brother Irving,
I will try to write to you by letter if I cannot be there personally at the moment to speak to you. How about it Irving dear, about Hermine's surprise [In English] it is a good surprise. [In Hungarian] Even better, it just came out that I could go to you for at least a couple of days. Otherwise nothing special now. We got a letter from David yesterday and thank God they are fine. And they are very happy to hear about Hermine from you and wish you all the best and like Dorothy writes you had a double surprise and how happy they were to talk to us. And what are you doing Irving dear? How are you progressing with learning. Write about yourself. Here the weather is currently cold and it is starting to be fall and I hope you have better weather. Now I'm closing my lines as I'm starting to be busy, but next time I'll continue. From the heart and kisses with love, and love, Maria

Hermine says hello to you and everyone. Mrs. Kugler will also welcome you.
And yes, what did Herman say to you? At least you saved him the trouble of writing a letter because you told him everything in person, didn't you Herman?

1949/10/29 Marie to Irving (Book 6, 93-94)

My dear brother Irving!

We have received your letter which we are very pleased with and it makes us happy that thank God you are healthy, which I hope to hear from you again. We are also well, and with God's help she plans to travel to you on Saturday night. I think the train will leave from here at 7:30, but I think she has written to you about it. I'm sorry, Irving, dear, I can't go right now, but I hope I'll see you soon. We also got a letter from Dorothy and thank God she feels better and little Jerome is also "kane hare" very cute. And what are you doing? How are you doing with the studying? I hope everything will work out for the best. Just take great care of yourself. I can't write anything special about myself. Everything is the same. And Hermine will speak about herself in person. Now you also write about yourself and next time I will write again and be careful where you go and work hard. Currently, I am closing my lines in the hope of seeing you again. Hello from the heart and kissing you countless times with love, your forever faithful sister who will never forget. Love, Maria

I also send regards to our relatives and acquaintances

1949/11/1 Hermine to Irving and Herman (Book 10, 188-189) mentions Eugene

New York 11/1 - 49

My dear little brother Irving and Herman,

I'm sorry why I could not write to you immediately, but I wanted to write in more detail and last night I was so sleepy, that I could not write. First of all, my travel was very nice. I changed trains in Pittsburg and it was faster and more comfortable, so I arrived by 10:40 to N.Y. Eugene was already waiting for me at the station. I know that you don't want me to go to visit you and the reason is all kinds of excuses. But I still say that I had a wonderful time with you. I talked to Eugene and he also said that it would be better for Herman in New York. So only in short, it depends on him completely and he should do the way he thinks is the best for him. What's going on with the apartment? Did you find anyone? Write about everything and I will soon also. I'm sending greetings to Lindeck and the others. How do they spell their names? Send it to me because I want to write a few lines to them. Also, to the relatives. I told it to McNeil and to Eugene about the record and he is waiting for it already. I just talked to his mother and she was pretty happy that I called her. Maria is well and I am writing from work, but she can't write.

Write about everything and I will reply to it. I kiss you with love. Hermina
Greetings to Mr. Zuhl [Hungarian neighbors] and his family.

1949/11/1 Marie to Irving (Book 8, 267-268) Hermine engaged

11/1/49

My dear little brother Irving,

I am trying again to write a couple of lines. Thank God we are well and Hermine luckily arrived home. She will write to you also. Right now I am trying so it will get to you as soon as possible. I am very happy to hear that thank God you are well and Hermine was very happy to spend those few days with you. As I hear it, you my Irving study very hard. I am only asking not to hurt your eyes. You should go to a good eye doctor. If you would be here I now have a very good eye doctor. In his opinion my glasses were too strong. I think so, too. Hermine is sending her greetings to you and her kisses to all of you. As you can remember when you were here, I started winking and now I am not winking anymore and I feel better with these glasses. It's possible that you study too hard and that is not good for the eyes even if they are in the best condition. Take care of yourself my little brother. Write about everything. There is nothing particular about myself. Hermine wrote everything about herself that I know. There is nothing particular. Currently everything is the same. Her fiancé is a very smart boy. We hope that with God's help everything will turn out for the best. And how are you Herman? Yes my Irving, I am planning on visiting you in the next year. David and the others also. I have not decided it yet, but when everything turns out to be better, I will decide it. And what do you look forward to? It would be better for you to start to move out of there. Now my dear, little Irving, I'm sending my best and kiss you countless times with much love your forever faithful sibling, Maria

Write about everything and take care of yourself!

1949/11/8 Hermine to Irving (Book 8, 270-272) Helen Lefkovits marriage

New York 11/8 49

Dear Irving and Herman,

We received your letters and I'm sorry for not answering you sooner. I hope you both are well and so are we. Herman, I hope also that you'll keep up the good work and will write us some more. Just now Helen Lefkovits from Helmec called me. You remember I wrote you about it that they came to America about three years ago and the younger is getting married in December and wants me and Maria to come to her wedding. I never met them since they are here but expect to see them next Tuesday and will eat dinner with them. Otherwise everything is well with us. Eugene and I were visiting Aunt Jenny's house last Sunday night and stayed there for dinner. We had a nice time with them. How are you both? Have you found somebody to rent the house? Please let me know about everything because I'm very anxious to hear from you. Haven't [written] to Dorothy and David yet and to anybody in Columbus except Elsie in Cleveland because she congratulated me. Aunt Helen told her the good news of my engagement. Maria is well and she'll write separately because I want to mail this letter. Irving I hope you don't work so hard with your studies and eat when it is time to eat. You too Herman and don't forget. Remember me to all my friends and I'll try to write to them real soon. Did Samuel get home yet or have you seen them yet. Write me about it. With all good wishes and love from me and Mrs. Kugler and Aunt Jenny and family, and Maria too. Love, Hermina

1949/11/14 Hermine to Irving (Book 10, 193-194) Lefkovits wedding

New York 11/14 - 49

Dear Irving and Herman,

I received your letter Irving and as always we are happy to hear from you, but we are sorry to hear about Herman. How is everything now - is he all right? That must have been more than enough and I hope he is well by now. We both are well and so is Eugene. He is very busy with his business but looking always for something easier to do. So far we didn't get anything as far as an apartment, but we are looking for that, too. Wrote to Aunt Helen last night but I still have some more writing to do. I wonder if you could send me Ms. McNeill's address because I'm not sure that I have it. About the apartment - maybe we made the mistake that we had in the ad young couple - maybe elderly couple or just couple would be better. Did you try it in the Jewish Chronicle? That wouldn't hurt! Let me know about everything and also about your studies. What happened with the writing of the book [thesis]. Please tell me about it when you have a chance. I visited Jeanne Frey last Saturday and they were asking about you and send their regards. Wrote to Dorothy and David but haven't heard from them yet. The two Lefkowits girls called me yesterday - you remember I told you they live in Brooklyn with their uncle. Lenke Lefkovits's daughters from K. Helmec. The youngest is getting married Christmas evening and they want us to come to the wedding. Also, we are going to meet them tomorrow night, the first time since they came to this Country. Maria is well and she'll probably write soon. Take care of yourselves and let me hear from you. Love to you both, Hermina

1949/12/1 Hermine to Irving and Herman (Book 22, 281-282)

New York 12/1 - 49

Dear little brother Irving and Herman,

I hope you are both well despite the fact that we have not heard from you for so long. We got a letter from Dorothy this week and they are fine. We are fine too and I wonder if you expect to come here this month. Write that you are coming and when. What about the house? Have you ever taught someone? I imagine it wouldn't be easy, but it would be great. I wouldn't worry about spending the winter in a cold house. At least the steam could be done in our room and you could go in there to sleep. [In English] Will you Irving do something about it. [In Hungarian] I write again soon and kiss you in the meantime. Hermina

As you can see, I will continue my letter and in the meantime we received a letter from Dorothy and some photos of little Jerome, which are cute, but you know it was done in the house and so you can't really see it, so it definitely looks different. I think they sent you and I am only sending one, but if you didn't get it, we'll send the rest. What's up otherwise and what about learning? You must be writing a book. It's great if you can do it, but I don't even know how you do it! I hope you'll forgive me for the bad writing, but there's always some excuse. How is Herman? Is he also coming to N.Y.? Please write, kisses with lots of love. Hermina

P.S.
I still didn't write Arthur and Zuhl. I'm sorry but I'll say hello to them soon.

1949/12/2 David and Dorothy to Irving (Book 12, 249-252) Freddie eight weeks old

Dec 1, 1949

Dear Irving:

It's been ages since we heard from you. How about a letter letting us know what's new? We were thrilled about Hermina's engagement and hope she'll be very happy. You must have enjoyed her visit with you - she wrote us all about that. I'm enclosing a snap of the baby taken in our apartment with a flashlight camera. He was 8 weeks old yesterday, and is already quite a boy. His hair is turning light, and I do think he'll be a blond one of these days. He weighs a little over 11 lbs. and is getting bigger every day. Who he looks like is a mystery at the moment - doesn't resemble either of us very much. Shall I say he's a lucky baby? The postman is due here any minute and I want to get this off to you, so I'll make this a "quickie." Let's hear from you real soon. Love to you and Herman. Dorothy

1949/12/7 (a) Hermine to Herman (Book 2, 24-31) come to NY #1

New York 12/5 - 49

Dear Herman,

We received your letter this morning and as you see I'm answering you now. First of all, whenever you decide to come you can and you'll have a chance to see it for yourself. I'm not promising that you'll get right away something what you want but I think it will be much easier here than in Columbus. If you decide [to,] you should come soon because after Christmas [it] is harder to get jobs, but anyway you don't lose much. 1 this: You could tell the people you work for, that you must go to N.Y. and [have] to take off 2 weeks - and you can look around, and if you don't like it, you didn't lose your job. 2, or this: If you decide to come to stay the best is to get papers from the US unemployment office that you left your job because you are going to live ^stay in N.Y. Then it is much easier to get a job here and get the money from the US unemployment. I think even if you wouldn't make much for now, but you have a much better chance here and can work yourself up to a better job. As for Irving, he should talk to the Landlord and tell him if he would let him sell [sublet] the apartment with the furniture he gets part of it. Just how it works I don't know but I think it works better if he could do that would be the best. Also, if you belong to a Union you should talk to them and they can transfer you to N.Y. When you are here the Union could also help you to get a job. If you let me know when you come then I could make an appointment with a Jewish employment office, but it takes 2 weeks to get an appointment. If I know when you come then I call them before you are even here and by the time you come you are registered. They got the job for Maria and me too - without money. If you come you don't have to carry all your belongings, Irving could send it to you later, but bring what you need because first you have to find a place to stay. I think you could stay in the YMCA and in the meantime you have time to look around. When you come, Irving should wait until you are sure you like it here then he should get rid of the apartment. It doesn't pay to keep it for one person. Hope you both are well and will let us hear from you. Let me know when you plan to come. If you come Saturday or Sunday we can wait for you at the station or anytime in the evening we would come to meet you. Irving dear, what do you think about that! How are you? Are you coming to N.Y. too? Believe me that wouldn't be bad. Maybe you should try it! Good luck and best wishes. Love to you and regards to Arthur and family, Mr. and Mrs. Zuhl

Hermina

[In Hungarian]

Marcsa [and I] talked about it and we think that if there is a chance for you to get a bonus, then it would be worth it to wait until after Christmas. I will go tomorrow for dinner to Eugene and I will ask him what he suggests. Marcsa thinks that now whoever gets hired before the holiday will be fired after. So it does not really matter if you get your presents. Here they give five days from the Union. One year's money and 5 if it was taken as a sick day and one can stay out longer. When I talk to Eugene I will write again. If you would wait until after the holidays then they would give you 2-3 weeks' vacation and if you like it better here, then you will write to them what you've decided and you want to move here. I would like you to come, but if I would have known about it, it would have been better for you to come a few weeks before.

I will write again soon, but until then, do not quit your job there! How long did you stay away from your job? No need to rush and I don't want you to have a problem. Be well! Love to you both! Hermina

New York 12/7 - 49

Dear Herman!

I already sent a letter to you today, but I promised that I will write, so I'm trying to keep my promise. I talked to Eugene about it and he recommended that you should come here, but it's not worth it to leave the other [job] before Christmas. We think it would be best that you should do as I have already written. They are willing to give you two weeks unpaid vacation in January and then you will have time to look around. If it's about me, I am not afraid, but since it's about you, I am afraid that you will have excuse. That is why I suggest that it is more certain that way. So you will not stay with out a job. I guess this is the best way, and as much as I would like for you to come immediately, I think that the holidays are so close, that if you won't find anything immediately, then between the holidays there will not be too much of a chance. So try what I wrote to you already. You will come in January and if it is something that you don't like, then you will have the place to go back to. But I know and I hope, that it will not happen. You are bad because if you would have come when I was there, maybe it would be somehow by now. I don't want to promise you, but I know that you could get a job like you have now, and you could also learn a skill on the top of that, and then you can open a business. Until then you can't start anything. I hope you will come. Write what you think about it. There is nothing to be afraid of because if the beginning is hard, you will like it later. How's my little brother? Hey Irving! That means you! What's new? Write in detail and don't be worried. Arrange everything, so the hand will be warm. Herman write! We kiss both of you with love. Hermina and Maria

1949/12/7 Undated Hermine to David (Book 10, 12-13)

[dated by Dorothy mentioning on 12/21 that Hermine "sailed into him for not writing" and this letter fits that description. Hermine also mentions that Irv hasn't written and he's busy studying. It may belong somewhere else.]

Dear David!

Now I can find your silence very interesting and I hope that there is nothing wrong with you! Although even then, you should write about yourself. It has been a couple of weeks since you called me and you promised that you will write the next day. I wrote to you since then, but you did not. I thought about sending you a telegram, but if you don't need me and you can't even write, then why should I force you?! Believe me that the nerves bring me to this writing because everybody makes me angry. We have not heard from Irving. The letters are coming back everyday. Herman does not work and every small thing makes me nervous, that I should just go somewhere, so I don't make anybody nervous. Believe me that I don't write this to tell on people, but somehow it gets on my nerves also. As I wrote about the money, I sent it already. Don't be worried! It is yours and I have some too, thank God, even if there is not a lot, but it's as much as I need. I hope you did not wait with the writing because of that? If you don't work, you could have written that too! But I will leave this, because you will be angry at me too, like Herman. I wish Irving would be at home! I would be happier with that much. Write, if you want and if you don't wish to receive a letter from me then it does not matter....

I kiss you with love, Hermine

1949/12/14 Warren Howard to Irving (Book 7, 16-19)

Hello Gluck,

I remember you well Gluck from those days on Anzio. Houy, Dewey and I lived in one dug out. You kind of over a little ways from us. I'm working on air craft assy [assembly] at Westinghouse, generators, alternators, control, panels. It's probably all Greek but after you work for so long they are very familiar. I don't write much anymore as you can tell by this scribbling. I hope this Christmas card finds you OK in good health. I remember how I felt on Anzio when not receiving any mail for a number of months then getting a Christmas card with no writing in it so now whenever I send one I usually write a little. I saw your address in the 1st Armored Division Association bulletin. Good luck to you and drop a line and let me know how you are. Your old friend, Howard

1949/12/15 Undated Hermine to Irving and Herman (Book 2, 109-111)

[dated by mention of previous letters to Herman urging him to come to NY]

Dear Irving and Herman,

We wrote a few letters to you, but so far no answer yet. I hope you both are well, and that Herman isn't angry at me because I told him how I felt about his coming to N.Y. After I mailed the letter I thought maybe I did the wrong thing. I want him to come and even if it takes time, but I think he shouldn't worry. What I told him was only because I was afraid that he couldn't get something at this time - because if anybody takes him now they would let him go after Christmas. Also that he might get some bonus on his present job. Let me know Herman when you expect to come. If Irving comes for Christmas maybe you would like to come with him. The only thing you must be ready for a couple weeks before you get something. On the other hand - that shouldn't bother you either because you never had a vacation. Well, Irving you let me know what you think and if you are coming. Believe me I want him to come, but because this season is not the very best I was afraid of Herman. If he doesn't care to lose a few weeks he can come any time! How is school and the book [thesis] coming along? Do you still study hard? Have you seen Mrs. and Mr. Zuhl? I'm ashamed for not writing to them yet, but I will. Aunt Helen wrote this week and told us that she saw you at Arthur's house. How is everybody and how is Samuel? Regards to all. Have you seen Miss McNeil? Regards to her too. Let us hear from you real soon. If you both can come, let us know when. Love to you both, Hermina

1949/12/16 Marie to Irving (Book 8, 277-278)

12/16/49

My dear little brother, Irving,

I'm sorry that I kept you waiting for so long with my letter, but I hope that my lines will find both of you in the best of health. Also, my little Irving, as it seems you are studying very hard and I think that you don't even have time to eat. And you Herman, I hope you are well. As Hermine also wrote to you in reply, I can write the same thing, that wherever we go today, it is hard everywhere and it would be best for you to take a few weeks off and come over here and you will see how you like it. It is hard to get a job everywhere. You only need luck and I don't care if they say that one has no chance to get a job. I know that it is like that, and it was always like that. I learned here that [we] must look through a lot if we want to get to our goal. And I know about myself that everybody tells me why do I work so many hours? They don't pay me if I stay home. If I would follow everybody [and do what they say] I would regret it later. I can say this much, that I would not get as much money in other places. And they are very fine people and it is the best job [I've had] until today. I would not leave them that easily. I only write this Herman since I know, that if you would not get a proper job immediately, that you would not have patience. And when I came here I did not get a job for at least five weeks. And the second time, I got my present place [of work]. And if one truly wants to work, then one will go after it as long as he can to find one. In the beginning, it won't be the best place. And because of that, I could say that this best one costs a fortune. You can try and at the same time it will be good as your vacation, too. But I will leave that. And you my little Irving, do you plan on continuing the studies? Write about everything. We are well and I will write again. Take care of yourselves. I kiss you countless times with love, your forever faithful sibling. Love, Maria

1949/12/29 Elsie Schallheim to Irving and Herman (Book 14, 144-147)

3496 Blanche Rd
Cleveland Hts, Ohio
Dec 29, 1949

Dear Irving and Herman:

How are you boys getting along? I really didn't get a chance to talk to you very much at Flora's reception, Irving. However, I understood you to say that you would try to be in Cleveland during the school vacation to see if some employment might be available for you. If you are still contemplating coming here, you are more than welcome to stay at my home while you are making serious investigations regarding the work you would like to get into, Irving. How are you feeling Herman? We missed you at the reception. Do you hear from the girls? How are they and when is Hermina getting married? Take care of yourselves boys. May the New Year bring you both happiness. Love, Elsie and Jane

1950/1 Undated Margit Klein to Arthur Gluck (Book 19, 48-49) - draft translation only

[This letter was translated by Irving, and the original letter and the final translation were probably given to Arthur. It could be dated to any time after Lipot died (1949/6/16) since she doesn't mention him]

Klein Herman (Margaret)

Budapest, Csaky u 32.IV.4

My dear relative Arthur,

I received your dear letter and the nylon. Accept our sincere thanks. Your help means a lot to us because without it, not even the cost of keeping the home could be covered. You are a very good hearted man dear Arthur. I wish you from my heart that you always will be able to do good for others. Hope to hear from all of you the best. I haven't received mail from Hermine and Mariska for quite some time. I believe they are well also. Isn't Mariska married yet? Finding a husband doesn't go easy for anyone. My daughter from Czechoslovakia was supposed to visit me with my little grandchild. However, she didn't get a passport. I want to see them, but for us, that can't happen. There are however those who get passports. How is the weather there? Here we have it much colder than during the past year. I don't like the winter temperature because I'm always cold. Before Christmas I worked in a store as a saleslady. I was glad because all that I earned during this month came in very handy. They were satisfied with me. I hope they'll call again when they'll need helpers [salesladies]. Write dear Arthur because you create happiness with it. Kisses to you, together with your dear family, with lots of love

Heartiest regards to Mr. Roth

1950/1/20 Hermine to Irving and Herman (Book 10, 199-200)

1/20 - 50

Dear Irving and Herman,

We were very happy for your cards and that you spent your time so nicely in Cleveland. I know that Elsie is very nice and she does anything so she can help you. It would be great if your plan would work out and you could get a proper job. If you can't, then you can still come to New York. Even if it takes time, but I guess, that it could work out. You had enough of Columbus already. In case you would come here you would not need the car because it is easier to go by train anywhere. Also, there is no place to park in the city and a garage is very expensive. I don't think they would allow it in front of us to park there permanently, but if you would still want it then maybe where you will live they will allow it. If you will need one later you can buy another one, a bigger one! So I should get to myself. So only this much, that if God will help, we are planning on getting married in February and we still did not decide it for sure. We would like to get an apartment, but it is still a promise, since it did not work out yet. If we will not get another one we are planning on moving to a furnished room. Many say that it is easier to get one once we get married. So the important thing is that I would like you to come here, but I will write about this more definitely. I don't think we will do anything else besides the wedding with close relatives. I did not even write to David about this. They would like a few relatives to participate, but there is no one who would arrange things for us. This is the simplest and cheapest way.

Maria does not write because she strained her right hand and the doctor said that she can't use it. Don't be worried because there is nothing else. Herman this is for you too. If Irving is not in Columbus, then send it to him to Cleveland. This letterhead is also our co.[company] and I'm writing it from work. Many greetings to Elsie and the others too. Write about everything. And you Herman, how are you? If you need Maria, then she will go there and will help you to arrange things with her. You write too. I kiss all of you with much love.

1950/1/28 Elsie Schallheim to Irving (Book 14, 118-120) job advice

3496 Blanche Ave.

Cleveland Heights, Ohio

Jan 27, 1950

Dear Irving,

I have been thinking of you. It was very cold when you left. I do hope the heater gave you enough of warmth. Try not to get discouraged. I spoke to the gentleman you saw at the Jewish Vocational Service. He advised me to tell you that it would be nice to keep in touch with O.S.U. Placement Service. I know you haven't gotten any results from that source. If you should consider teaching, I know some one here, a Jewish man teacher at the college who might be able to make some good suggestions to you. Should you care to meet him I could ask him over. Getting a Master's degree in teaching would bring a steady income. However, I hope you will soon get some light on the path you decide to follow. Jane and I hope things won't be too hard for you in finding yourself something that will give you happiness. Tonight Jane started a course at Cleveland College. It's a course dealing with Freud. She takes it from 6 P.M. to 7:30 P.M. I'm glad it isn't too late. Monday she starts a tennis course. How is Herman? You and Herman are more than welcome to come to Cleveland when you feel lonesome or want a little change. Take care of yourselves, Your cousin, Elsie

1950/2/1 Hermine to Irving and Herman (Book 15, 174-177)

Sunday evening

My dear little brother Irving,
I am attaching here Maria's papers so the money can be sent to her.
We are well, and I hope that you and Herman are as well. How angry I am with Herman I can hardly tell you. The reason is that he does not want to come to my wedding. Everybody is wondering about him and they can't imagine what could be the reason that he is not coming. It can't be the money because I know that he can afford it. So, I hope Irving you will come, and if you are coming with a car then be careful. I would feel better if you would come with [the] train. Bertha came home three weeks before [she planned to] because of my wedding. She has been in Florida for at least 6 weeks. It looks like a cousin is better than a sibling. Herman please make up your mind and come! I'll be looking for you and so is Eugene and Maria, too!! Love, Hermina

[From Eugene]

Dear Herman and Erving [sic],
I'm looking forward to meet both of you as my brother-in-laws. Hermine is telling me that Herman might not come. Is it true, Herman? I can't believe you would want to miss meeting the family! I'm sure you will both enjoy being here. Your brother, Eugene

1950/2/1 Private Leo P. Duffy to Irving (Book 14, 115-116) - missing last page

Feb. 1, 1950
Dear Irvin,
I know it's late answering this letter of yours. Been kind of busy you know how it is when you work swing shift in a steel mill. You don't have much time for anything. It's sleep and work. Just wrote Brown a letter. You know he lost a brother overseas. He also was wounded. Well it's over with. But no matter how you try you can't forget things like that.

1950/2/3 Jane Fabianova Postmaster to David (Book 7, 54-55)

Dear Dezső!
On January 30, I received a large package without any loss in it. I was very happy and very surprised. Everything is very beautiful and everything is useful. The clothing came in just right. There will be some for my mother also. One truly did not expect such a gift, not even a closer relation would have done it. I'm fully clothed and my mother also. It came just in time. I don't really know why I deserve this. The shoes are fantastic. They are just the right size, and I'm very happy with them. This pair of shoes is very stylish. I'm very happy with it. The medication cream is excellent and I gratefully thank you for each individual item. With regards to Hermine, Marie, and you.
Jane.
Bátka [Czechoslovakia], February 3, 1950

1950/2/4 Hermine to Irving (Book 10, 134-135) wrong year - will marry Eugene

New York 2/4 -49
Dear Irving and Herman,
We received the long awaited letter from you and you should know that it gave us much happiness. First I thought you got yourself a position in Cleveland and you are too busy to write, but anyway we are very glad that you found something. Are you traveling with the car? Let us know all about it. How is everything there. Do you expect to come to my wedding? You never answered to my question on that! I would want to have you here very much! Both of you, and I hope that you'll be able to come. The date is set for March 5th. So far we have to make plans and if everything works out then that is the date. Tomorrow we are going to look [at] the temple and make other arrangements. I wrote to David, too. Tomorrow I'll know more about it, but

I wanted to write to you tonight so that you would know at least that much. We plan to make an afternoon wedding and would wear a color dress - not white. As soon as I know more, then I [will] let you know. How is Herman? I thought that because he is the older he should walk me up to the chuppe! What do you think? Otherwise Irving, but I know Herman so I know his answer!!! You may tell to Arthur and Aunt Helen. I will send them [the] invitation just the same, but I don't think they'll come. In a discrete way you might even find out if they expect to come. It would be nice, but we'll have only a sweet table, and for that maybe it wouldn't be worthwhile. Anyway, for you I know it is too much expense, but it would be wonderful and at least you would meet Eugene. He always asks for you and if you're coming. Let us know real soon. Love from us all and from Mrs. Kugler. Hermina

1950/2/8 Hermine to Irving and Herman (Book 10, 202-204)

New York 2/8 - 50
Dear Irving and Herman,
Here I'm again and have more to tell you this time. First of all, the date of our wedding is set for the 5th of March and we want you to be there. I made up my mind that no excuses should be accepted! How do you like that! I'm not having a white dress, but I think it will be nice. It is going to be in the temple and after the chuppa, will have something to eat, too. I hope you both decide to come because otherwise it doesn't pay to have anything at all. At least you could meet Eugene. I hope the answer is yes. I also wish David could come, but for that there isn't much hope. Let us hear from you as soon as possible because we want to know. Eugene is always asking about you and he also wants you to come. How is everybody and how are you and your work coming along? Herman, if you don't come I'll never talk to you!!! You need only a suit with a white shirt and you are all dressed. Irving you could wear the suit you bought here in N.Y. I'm inviting all the relatives and Elsie, too. We are planning to have about 80 people if all come. Maybe Elsie would come with her daughter. Also Aunt Helen or Arthur with his wife and daughter. You see Eugene's mother wants to have a wedding so it will be for the family. Lots of love to you both, Hermina

1950/2/15 Undated Marie to Irving (Book 8, 282-283)

[Dated by mention of Hermine's wedding]

My dear little brother Irving!
I'm sorry that I did not write for so long, but as I mentioned it was not easy. But thank God today it's alright already. One more week and then I will be able to go to work. I hope I will go back where I worked. And you my Irving, how are you all doing? Also, as you wrote that you are planning on coming on the 26th. It does not matter if you come before, at least this way you will have time to look for a job. I hope that it will work out even if it takes time. It costs money there too, but at least you will see if it's better here. And Herman will see until then and he could come to the wedding. We got a letter from David too, and they are well. They can't come and Elsie and the others will not come either and wrote that you were there. Otherwise, how are you? I hope you are well and you take care of yourself! And my dear Irving, take care of the suit so it's going to be nice and clean and the white shirt. And when you will come here bring another suit also so you don't need to put [the same one] on always. Otherwise everything is fine. We will talk about everything in person. Now I will close my lines. And I am sending greetings from the heart and kiss you countless times with much of love. I will stay in the hope to see you again. Maria

Hermine is sending greetings to both of you and we were very happy that we could talk to you on the phone. I wrote enough for today and take care my little brother. I kiss you again. M.

1950/2/20 Undated Hermine to Irving and Herman (Book 10, 47) - will Herman come to Hermine's wedding

[dated by Monday sometime just before the wedding on March 5]

Monday evening

My dear little brother Irving and Herman,
I hope that now Herman made a decision that he will come here too. If not, then I can say that it is not nice of him. Even strangers judge him, not just me. I understand that he does not want to spend the money, but still it should maybe mean something to him too. One does not live forever and he will not take it with him anyway, so from now on there's no need to save on something like this, or on food. Unfortunately, I can't

write any more lessons down. It is too late already and I could not even find normal paper. Maria and the lady went to sleep and I did not want to make noise to find some. I wanted to write to you little brother, when you come then bring your winter coat because it became very cold suddenly and I was afraid that you will not find it to bring it here. Besides that, we are well, but we are busy a little bit. We will talk in person. I hope it will work out for you to find some job! Come on over and at least you can look around. How is Arthur and his family? And Aunt Helen? I got a present from Elsie and a letter also. You don't have to mention this to the relatives! I kiss you with much of love. Hermine

1950/3/15 Irving to Herman (Book 6, 319-321)

Dear Herman,

How are you? I wanted to write to you several times, but everything remained. So now a few lines again that everything is fine. As for work as an economist, the outlook here is bleak for now. But besides that, I might get a job in a few days. Don't ask what, but I'll write about it. Yesterday I almost got a job for $55 five days. The headmistress was a big dog and so it didn't work. At the place in May, there is a prospect that they will start calling me to work within a few days. In the meantime, I'll keep looking to see if there's anything else. If I succeed, I'll write to you and then we'll make arrangements and you'll go out too. Here a shipping clerk gets $30 to $40 according to the newspaper. It all depends on experience. There will be time to talk about that later. You can write too. If I work soon, I will send you money for my debt. If you need money now, sell the six and a quarter shares that expire at the end of this year (I was thinking about Texas Eastern). I will write again. Otherwise, everything is fine. If I have work, it will be much easier for you. [In English] Till next time. Irv
P.S. Hermine and Maria give regards to those who ask about them. Hermine & Maria send [their] love to you. They said that you should eat well and be careful of yourself. Write! to them!

1950/3/17 Herman to Irving, Marie, and Hermine (Book 18, 315-316)

3/17/50
Dear Irving, Maria, and Hermina,
Received your two letters, of which I don't know too much. Do you know when you will return with the car? If not, I don't want to know. Your check has arrived and I will mail it in a letter with this $25.00 to get for you [something]. You must sign it. Maybe I can also sign your name for the taxes because maybe I'm paying $76.00 in taxes. I gave $200.00 and for the Drs only 5%. I'm suing. What news is there? How are you Maria? Hermine give my regards to Eugene. Until I hear from you again, with best wishes to you all. Herman

1950/3/20 Jane Schallheim to Irving (Book 14, 190-195)

Jane Schallheim
3496 Blanche Avenue, Cleveland Heights, Ohio

Sunday

Dear Irving,
How is the job situation? Are there any good prospects in New York? Business at the Unemployment Compensation Bureau has decreased somewhat. That should be an encouraging note for job hunters. How was Hermine's wedding? We received a letter from Aunt Jennie saying that Hermine was a beautiful bride. She is a very attractive girl and must have been a lovely bride. I understand the ceremony was Orthodox. Most of the weddings I have attended have been reform or conservative. Few of my friends have had Orthodox ceremonies. I took a short course on the "Influence of Psychoanalysis on Contemporary Thought" at Cleveland College. Our class was small, and we had the opportunity to express our own opinions on Freud and his doctrines. We discussed many subjects from the psychological aspects of the atomic bomb to the psychological aspects of sex. We were hoping the College would offer an advance course in psychoanalysis, but it couldn't be arranged. I saw an excellent Jewish actress perform last week. She is Celia Adler, and she presented a series of monologues in English and Yiddish. It was an experience to watch her. Every gesture, each inflection was expressive. Fortunately we sat near the stage, and so we could see every change of expression and hear each word. There have been several excellent war movies in Cleveland lately - "Twelve O'Clock High," "Battleground," and "Three Came Home." "Twelve O'Clock High" is one of the best

movies I have seen. Dean Jaeger, one of the actors, was voted "best supporting actor" at the Academy Award banquet. Mother is busy with her teaching which she likes very much. Spring Vacation is coming soon and she will have a week off from classes. How is Herman? Let us know how you are getting along. Love, Jane

1950/3/24 Hermine to Herman (Book 10, 206)

New York 3/24 - 50

Dear Herman,

I read your letter this week and so I'm writing to you. I'm sorry you weren't here with us and we wished you would. My wedding was very nice and you would [have] enjoyed that, and to meet your brother-in-law. Irving probably will tell you more about it when he'll see you personally. I wish he could find a position then he would be able to stay in N.Y. Then you could come, too. So far he tried and it might come through yet. He doesn't have much more patience to wait. Tell me about yourself. Remember us to the relatives. Let us hear from you. Take care of yourself. Love, Hermina and Eugene

1950/3/28 Herman to Irving, Hermine, and Marie (Book 14, 293-294)

3-28-50

Dear Irving, Maria and Hermine!

I attached a letter here and a check to be signed. I don't know how to send it back in a letter, maybe yes! You should send it registered. What's new? It is hard to find a job. What's going on with the car? Is it still running? What is the reason that it is not going uphill? Did you get enough gas? When you get to the top it is already late, but as I know, that is a different gear, backwards and it brings more power to it and many people do that, but I don't know how safe it is. Nothing particular. I am a very frequent writer. With love to all of you! Herman

1950/3/29 Herman to Irving, Hermine, Marie (Book 14, 291)

3-29-50

Dear Irving, Maria and Hermina,

I forgot to mention in my last letter about the car loan. Here it has to be done by April 1st. Now if you will take it out there, I don't know how long it will be good here. Mr. Andrew Zuhl wants to buy a car and they had a tune-up job so I went out too with them and I saw a car that [he] wants to buy, a 46 Nash "Jekarba." He got it for $750. It is 100% inside and out it looks A1. In the meantime, a few days ago I was telling him that I will sell the house with the furniture. And tonight he came that he has two who would take it over with the furniture. If they need it, but I said that I don't know it yet. In the summer the rent is at least $36.00 while I am in Columbus maybe it's worth it to have a big house so I can run around in it. But I would like to know.

Until I will see all of you again.

P.S. If there is somebody to sell the car [to], you can for about $500. If you would see what a beautiful car then, it is only $700, for a 6 seater. With love. Herman

1950/3/30 Irving to Herman (Book 6, 313-318)

Wednesday evening

Dear Herman,

I received your letter and the check in it today. It's really good that they handled it so skillfully. You also cleverly sent it to me. Since I wrote to you in my letter yesterday, so now I just want to write a straight answer. FIRST, day by day, people think that something will come up, but [there's] still nothing. It's still hard to get a job here. Even a street sweeper must have experience, so you have to seize the opportunity. More than likely, every week you have to turn right or left. Here, the relatives and Hermine and Marie would like to stay here and have you come over. If I had it, we could make arrangements, but until then I don't believe in anything.

Where I live now, I am already making arrangements so that after the holidays (as you know, Passover begins on Friday night - the first night will be on Saturday) there will be a room in this building that is suitable for two. But never mind it all because if there isn't a job, it doesn't matter here or there. Yes, the census papers. If you can, please get them out and note that I am unemployed and looking for work [In

English] (looking for work). [In Hungarian] What newspapers did you mention that came to me? Read more about them. Did I get anything from the Federal Government? You know, I made out papers that I want to enter as a tobacco inspector. If only it would work out.

Today again, finally, the market is stabilizing and I hope it will go up. You may want to sell something. Be smart and earn some easy money. I don't even have a hard time making money. Until today, there was no one interested in the car. Here the dealers promise two hundred or so $; May the devil take them away. You know, if I have to hold a sign, you'll have to buy it - Ours comes in at almost $13. I hate money, but it has to be. Write about everything. I was just writing to my neighbor and to Zuhl. I still need to send to the Hudsons and to you. How are you otherwise?

How do you feel? Aren't you afraid alone in that big palace? Are you interested in someone? Was Hilda there? What do you get for my History? It's easy for someone! The poor beggar is still struggling and perhaps hoping, but I'm starting to run out of trust. You can imagine that here in such a big city how difficult it must be to get a lousy job. [In English] Well, we will see. Now, be good. Hermine & Marie are well. [In Hungarian] They work and struggle for their daily bread. It is true that they claim that this is life and as an example, the gifts that Hermine receives, she would not have received them in Columbus. It's easily over $500. If necessary, write to me and I will send you some money.

Dave's wife wrote that he is fine. [In English] Till next time, with love, Irving

Now it's morning - Thursday, and I was inside the Y.M.C.A. and from here I was sent to the labor offices. I hope to get something. If I live here, I can help you find a job - it really costs money. If I lived here, the room would cost $1.25 a night. I will write again as soon as I have some good news. Eat well and write. - a lot!
Irv

1950/4/1 Irving to Herman (Book 6, 277-283)

Mar. 31, 1950
Dear Herman,

Yes, we are all glad that you have become such a frequent writer. Your letter sounds like someone who deals with it all the time. Just remember to write about everything and often. I will now turn to the situation. Today, Friday, I went to work. Yes, this place is a kind of printing house and I went because for now, if I am hired, then I will have something to live on and I will be able to look for other things. The American - US Employment sent me here. I note that I don't know if they will hire me. I was the first to apply - It's true,

they already know me quite well in this employment office, and as far as I know, they won't send anyone else here; then I'm lucky to have a good job. The boss said that they give $45 to start and then give a salary increase based on merit. It's like a government job - [as] a true private agent. Its name is "National Health Council," here, if I get in, I get a weekly allowance, a vacation, one week the first time and 2 weeks the second time. You have to work five days. 9 in the morning until 5 in the evening. If the person is sick, they will pay for that as well -

because they give it every year, I don't know how many days, but you can take off and they pay for it too. So, now the situation is that if there are no other applicants who would understand more about the work, then I would have a job for myself. I don't want to fry the fish in advance. I hope that from this point (Friday at the end of the day) they will call me on Monday. You know, you have to lie a lot, then you can go for something better. So I'll let you know as soon as I work.

I just received two of your letters and I want to reply to them. First, I'll sign and cash the check here. So you will find the deposit of $25 in the letter. Now the problem with the car is, as I mentioned in my previous letter, the "clutch" - the one that is pushed down with the left foot when you want to change from first, to second and third, is completely worn out. And so, if I can't sell it, I'll have to have it done.

Yes, car prices are very low. I could get more privately, but not more than possibly $300. I would have a hard time getting more. I haven't taken out the car sticker [the registration] yet. I know it has expired, but if

I stay here, I'll have to take out a New York one within 60 days. And if nothing works out here and you have to go back to Columbus,

there's definitely a couple of days before you have to change the plate. Now I'm waiting to see what happens. If I get this job or the next one, I'll have money and I won't sell the car, so I'll do it and I'll take out the license plate. I'm not going to sell the car on the spot, because if I'm here and when you come too, I'll have to go out for a temper tantrum. Now the only important thing is to get a job.

Regarding the house, I think it would be good to sell it or rent it out so that they would get some income. If anything, I still want to write more about this. As I imagine now, if I get a job here, after the holidays, I will have a room and both of us could sleep in it. So if I'm working and you go out, the thing there will be -

we will deal with what is yours and mine. Hermina was told that they don't need the [ice] box that is there, right Hermina, she said that if her husband bought a house, she would accept the refrigerator as a gift. So, this is still just an idea. A room here will cost you $25, but as I mentioned,

two people can live in it, and you won't have to worry about anything. Now, since I'm not sure when I'll have a job, I can't say for sure, but in addition, here you can go to more places after work sooner than in Columbus, so there is more to view. To get back to letting or selling the house, if I have time and

while you're leaving, it would be nice to get a room - to keep and then it would be good for you for the time being and you would get the lease. So you don't have to struggle with that. Even if I had to go back, that one room would be good for now. It is true that the young couple who wants to rent it out does not need to know this.

If I were to go back, it's still possible that I'll be called to work as a tobacco inspector. I will write more as soon as I can. If you are the one making the arrangements there, do your best. I repeat once more, if I have a job here, I will write to you and take immediate action to improve your situation.

Now thank you for writing such a letter. Write a lot about everything, like I do. Take care and don't be lazy and eat properly. I will write more later as soon as I talk to Hermine and Marie. They also work - hard. Marie's right hand is still weak and it is difficult for her to use it. [In English] Till next time best wishes to you from Irving
P.S. Regards to all. WRITE. WRITE…

1950/4/6 Herman to Irving, Hermine, and Marie (Book 14, 296)

4-6-50
Dear Irving, Maria, and Hermina!
I am attaching here the check from the Tax Audit and the rest of the documents too. And, I also sent the F.H.A. papers for examination on 4-13 in envelopes to Columbus. What is new is that I just paid the pig who took the money over. I paid it on the 5th and 5 days cost 70c more for overcharge. For a month they took $1.82. "Eaffa" [unclear] is sending his/her best. It is 8 o'clock in the afternoon and there was in a way a good day in the market. My television is pretty good. Although I bought it from the RC. D.T. starting to get stronger, but it will take a couple of weeks until they will declare the second quarter Div[idend] There are other papers, maybe I will send them one of these days. There is a big $12.00 estate value tax application. I have to go to the court house and where I should be going I could find out, of course when I will have time. How's everybody? With Best Wishes. Herman

1950/4/7 Irving to Herman (Book 6, 310-312)

Dear Herman,
I received your letter today and I will reply. Now I'm just going to write briefly, because I'm feeling a bit lazy. I worked today. I got a printing job here. The payment is $1.05 (a dollar and 5¢ until I finish the job), but the highest is 1.25 for an hour. If I have to work with another machine, it's $1.45 an hour. But that's not the future, because it's fifty or sixty dollars. So the thing is, wait to pay for the house and I will be able to write to you more next week. Maybe if I don't get a better job I'll go back to summer school. Until then, I'm looking for a few dollars here. If a good job comes in from the state or is still coming, I would go there.

Otherwise, there is nothing new, I have done what I was told. I hope it will be good for a while. What do you say if I take out a room here for $25 a month for the two of us? Do you think you would like it? And instead of [being] there, we would give [ours] out for a couple of months or until we don't need it. So [In English] till next time. Write! My best wishes, Irv

P.S. [In Hungarian] It will be possible to write longer on Saturday. If you need money right now, give Texas Eastern the bill they sent out.

[On the left side - In English] Hermine & Marie & all send their love to you!
[On the right side of page 1 - In Hungarian] Did you get the $25 I sent? This week!

1950/4/13 Marie to Irving (Book 8, 280-281)

4/13/50
My dear little brother Irving!
I'm sorry that I waited to hear from you before I write, but now I will try to write to you all a couple of lines. First of all my dear little brother, thank you for the telegram, where I was very happy to hear that you have arrived with good luck to Columbus. I hope that your neck does not hurt anymore! Write about everything. First of all, yesterday night I called Hermine immediately and she was very happy to hear that thank God you arrived, which I know Herman was the happiest about, that he could see you again. Now we talked to Mrs. Shafferman and to Mrs. Kugler. They miss you also my little brother. Mrs. Kugler misses you for breakfast and Mrs. Shafferman misses you for the night. And I miss you for dinner. I don't even cook for myself. As long as you were here, at least I cooked, too. Hermine misses you too because she has no one to run down to look after her because it is so far from me. As a matter of fact, everybody misses you. But now what's important is that the exam will be successful and what is even more important is that you can get a good job. And now take care of yourself. Herman as well, and eat. We are well. I will write again next time. I am sending my greetings from my heart and I kiss you with love. Love Maria
Eugene called the man and he was very surprised that you would take a job if you didn't plan on staying. It's not worth feeling badly about that, it was not for you.

1950/4/24 Marie to Irving (Book 8, 285-286)

4/24/50
My dear little brother Irving!
We got your letter and I am very happy to hear that thank God you have arrived with your car with good luck. I can imagine how much you enjoyed the traveling/road. And I can imagine also that Herman had such a surprise because he did not think that you will get back so well also. I hope it will have a good result, that is, that your exam was successful. I hope that you don't have to wait for [the results] too long. We are well. Hermine is also. I saw her on Saturday night and Mrs. Kugler, too. I didn't see the relatives since then, but they are well except Aunt Jenny's son Emanuel had surgery. I didn't see him yet. Now I wrote about everything. And how are you and Herman? What do you do? Do you eat? And you my little brother, do you work on anything? Are you trying to put on weight? Write about everything. My hand is a little better. Now I will close my lines and am sending my greetings from the heart and kiss you with much of love. Love, Maria
Eugene, Hermine, and Mrs. Kugler are sending their best for the both of you, too.
And as you write my Irving, that you will come to take him/her/it to the fresh air. Alright then. I will count on you. Now take care of yourself and write.
I kiss you again M.

1950/4/26 Hermine to Irving and Herman (Book 10, 208-211)

4/26 - 50
Dear Irving and Herman,
We received Irving's letter and the money order. It was wonderful to hear from [you] and we hope that [it] will work out [for] the best. I can't tell you how much we miss you, especially me - on lunch time!! I'm sorry I couldn't even invite [you] to my house — but you know how it is. First of all, I don't even have a home and because I never know when Eugene gets home — so let's hope by the time you come back to

N.Y. I'll be able to make up for that. I know you understand, but it hurts me that I did so little for you. How are you and Herman? Have you seen the relatives since you went back? How are they? Here I'm enclosing some snapshots which we took in Atlantic City. You saw them, but Herman didn't and if you see the relatives you'll be able to show it to them, too. Received a letter from Dorothy, but never answered her yet. I'm going to. Forgive me that I didn't write to you before, but I think of you just the same. Try to gain weight, not to lose it!! The same goes for Herman, too. Let us hear from you. With love from us both, Hermine and Eugene

P.S. Mrs. Kugler, Mrs. Sofferman and Maria missed you very much. Eugene didn't call the man in the U.S. employment office - you should write!

1950/4/28 Marie to Irving (Book 8, 288-289)

4/28/50

My dear little brother Irving,

A couple of lines again. We are well, and I hope that my lines will find you all in the best of health. Also my Irving, I got your letter and I think that you got mine at the same time. And as it seems you still did not get that job, we hope that you will have better luck with it. And besides that, what do you do? Do you have enough money so you can eat? Or you forgot that you must eat? And you Herman, how are you? What do you do? As it seems you got lazy with writing again. Yes, my little Irving, I wanted to ask you already if you wrote to that man where you worked, or did he send you the money that you were entitled to? I did not get anything here and I am surprised if he sent it to you. I saw Hermine yesterday and she said that she wrote to you and otherwise they are well. She will come to us today as usual and they send their best, both of them. I talked to Jenny this week and she was wondering about you too and she is hoping that it will work out for you. Otherwise about myself, I am well also. Mrs. Kugler and her daughter are too. Only if you remember her daughter-in-law, Szedi, you know, the one who lives in the neighborhood, her father died yesterday. He was very sick. Other than that, everything is the same. Just take care of yourself and eat and write. Now I will send my greetings from the heart and kiss you with love. And Love, Maria

Hermine and the others are sending their best and kiss you. Write.

1950/5/10 Marie to Irving (Book 8, 291-293)

5/10/50

My dear little brother Irving!

I got your letter and I'm glad to hear, that thank God you are well. About myself I can also write that we are well, including Eugene and Hermine. Yes our little Irving, first of all, as you wrote in your letter that you still did not write to that company where you worked. I believe that you have to write to him because otherwise he will not send the money to you. Write to him that you are sorry that you had to leave him, but would he be so kind to send you the money? Then he will do that for you for sure because you need to sign it surely. Now as you mentioned again that we should buy a farm. I don't know about that. You can see if it's worth it or not and you know better how would be the best because we can't tell about this to anybody else. Our Irving, what do you eat if you don't work and don't have the money? Should I send it to you? Write about everything. And Herman, what does he do? Does he work? And do you eat enough? I can imagine what you do! You fast more than eat. Yes, my little brother, your girlfriend called on the phone about two weeks ago and she was wondering about you. You did not write to her? I told her to call you some other time, but ever since then she did not call. Now otherwise everything is the same. How are the relatives there? I hope to hear the best about you, just don't forget to eat. Yes, my Irving, are you are planning on going back to school? Mannie and Bertha were wondering about you. And Aunt Jenny, Mrs. Kugler, and her daughter, too. They are well. Now take care of yourselves and write. My greetings from the heart and kiss you with much love. And Love. Maria

Write again and greetings for everybody, too.

1950/5/18 Marie to Irving (Book 8, 296-297)

5/18/50

My dear little brother, Irving!

We got your latest letter and I'm very glad to hear that thank God, you finally got a job! Even if it's not what you wanted, it still sounds good. I wish you lots and lots of good luck and the best of health. Let's hope that with time you will find the kind of job that you like. For now, you just take care of yourself and don't worry, everything is going to be fine and you will like it. First of all, it is a clean and a responsible job, and it will be easier to find another one after this. And you Herman! How are you? What do you do? Write! I don't know anything in particular about me. My hand is better now, but not completely. And yes, my little brother we got an apartment for Hermine, and with God's help, they will move in in August, until then it will take time until they will buy or find furniture. Otherwise they are well. The relatives are well too. And how is Arthur there and our Flora? When did you see them and Helen? I'm sending my best to everyone. Now I wrote about everything and I hope to hear the best about you. And yes, my little brother, the most important thing is that you only work 5 days, that means a lot. Now take care of yourselves, and eat and write. Did you get the check? I sent it to you. I'm sending my greetings from my heart and kiss you with love. Love Maria

Hermine and Eugene send their greetings.

1950/5/29 Hermine to Irving (Book 10, 213-214)

5/29 - 1950

My dear Irving!

We were very happy to get your letter, especially for the good news. You just didn't write where you have to go to accept the job and what you will have to do. When you will know about it, let us know. Let's hope that everything will shape up for the best. Only the beginning is hard, but there is no reason for you to be worried. I know that you know how to help yourself. What do the relatives and Herman say about all that? We wish you good luck and we hope that everything will work out! I have very good news, too. We have a 3½ room apartment on Long Island. I would like you to send the quilt, that is, the 2 dunna [fluffy] blanket that you used and you should buy the red blanket. I want to have it changed to a blanket anyway. I don't know how much one would weigh in Kg, but you don't need it anyway. So send it and I will give you the cost. Also, the Prudential bond, the W Bonds, and the citizenship paper, too - so my documents, but in a way that they will not get lost. And maybe it would be good to write down the B.'s [bond's] number in case they will take it away, so we would have it. Whenever you have time for it, no need for it immediately. I am writing this letter from work because now we are not that busy. We did not get a letter from David and the others for a long time. I will write. I hope they are well also! We kiss both of you with love. Hermina and Eugene

1950/5/31 Marie to Irving (Book 6, 43-48)

My dear brother Irving,

Sunday I got your letter as I was going [out]. I was very happy. And I am happy to hear that thank God you are well. And that your work is at least clean and not so hard as far as public work is concerned. We hope, I hope and wish good luck to you Irving dear at this time to improve the situation. The only question is if you will be called in by the state and if you really will know about this job because they think you really understand it. And God forbid, you leave this job, too. Now we just hope you will get there. It's a very good job and we hope everything will go well. Now write about everything and, as soon as you know more, about your work. Above all my little brother dear, I wish you a lot of good luck and the best of health. How is Herman, how are you? Write about everything. Hermine is also well and very happy to hear your results and we hope to hear the best from one another. We're fine. I saw Hermine yesterday and they send greetings. We haven't heard from David since long ago. I hope they're fine. Otherwise no special news. Yes my brother, did you get the check? I sent it to you two weeks ago and also this week I will send you the shirts too. I'm sorry that I didn't send it for so long. But now I close my lines. Greetings from the heart and kiss you with love and love to you both, Maria

I send greetings to everyone and Mrs. Kugler also sends greetings to you.

1950/6/13 Marie to Irving (Book 8, 303-304)

6/13/50

My dear little brother Irving!

We got both of your letters last week and it makes me happy that thank God, you are well. We are well, too. As you can see my Irving, I try to write to you. First of all, as you wrote, that you want to send money to me. Do not hurry, you have enough time with that. When you will have the new job and you will have more money than now, then you will have time to send it. You are still good for now. It would be better if you would get places now somewhere close to here. And do you know my Irving, that you will be able to do the job? And you Herman? Do you plan to stay there alone or will you go with Irving, too? Write about everything. And take care wherever you go. And don't forget to eat. OK? Have you heard about David and the others? We already wrote many times and it has been a long time that we did not hear about them. Let's hope that they are well. We are only very impatient about them. You know my Irving, if God will help, I am planning on going to visit David and the others. I am taking my summer vacation now and I am planning to go for about 6 weeks to California. What do you say about that? Wouldn't you or Herman come? I wrote to Dave about that, but I did not get a response yet. I still have time to talk about that and I hope that everything is going to be fine and my plan will work out. Also, I wish you lots and lots of good luck and the best of health to both of you. Here otherwise everything is the same. The weather is bearable. One day it is warmer than the other. How are the relatives there? Is Arthur better? I'm sending greetings to everyone! Also, Hermine and Eugene are sending their best and kiss you all. And I'm separately sending my greetings from my heart and kiss you with love. Love, Maria

1950/6/13 Undated Hermine to Irving (Book 11, 311-314) - Lefkovits wedding

[1950/6/13 Dated from Lefkovits wedding on 1950/6/12 mentioned end of letter 1950/6/2]

My dear Irving!
Last night when I came home I have found your letter here. We were at Lenke Leftkovits' daughter's wedding from Helmec. I don't even know how to tell you how happy we were for your letter. I think it's for the best if you give up the house and both of you will come here. It is not worth the fight the way you struggle. Although, it is not a small task to have everything brought here for you, and you should sell the rest. If you think that you can arrange it, then it is OK. If not, then Maria would go to Columbus to help. The important thing is, as you wrote it too, that it is not worth it to live like this. As far as the job is concerned, we should find something. If those who just came here can settle down, then I am pretty sure that it will work out for Herman and for you as well. Although, it is a little different for you because you have a place where you want to stay. So, in my opinion you should come, even if you can't find what you are looking for immediately, you can get a job and in the meantime you can search for what you want. Here you could have more of a chance than anywhere else. In a big city like this there is a bigger perspective than any other place, and if you will not go to Dezső, then come here. I'm pretty sure it will take time, but even if it will be slow, it will work out and it is a big business city. Here I think, even if there are many without jobs, at the same time there could still be work for others. Even if it costs money because you will have expenses, but you have that now also and this way there is not much you can lose. I am sure that you will eat better for the [same[money. Marcsa just called me on the phone and she thinks that way too. So, write it when you want to come. We want to give up the house no matter what. Whatever they give for it, it doesn't matter. Write it how you decided. It is not worth it for one to stay there and struggle. If you want to go to school then you can do that in other places too. I got a letter from Lipot's wife, that they don't have anything to live from and she is asking for junk clothing that she could sell. If you would have time to put together a few packages with men's clothes, then I would send money to the money sender. They would get good money for the military clothing and you have no need for that. You don't want to bring all the junk and rags here, at least it would be worth something for her. I would pay at least $10 dollars and I would make them happy. If you my Irving would want to do that and would have time for that because I could only wish from you to do something like that then. If you want it and made a decision then write it and I will send the address and the money. I will get back to the wedding again because I met with relatives there. If you remember the little Etyu from Palocz, who stayed at Uncle Lajos' from Lelesz, she is here in America. She was with her husband together at the wedding. Her husband is a relative also. A cousin from Ungvár. So, they were very happy and they also gave us the address for Etyu and Hajnal from Homanna and I want to visit them sometimes. I only know that if you will settle down in NY you will like it. Here at least one can live around the people and it would be better for you to get friends. I wrote enough now and it is for Herman also. Write immediately! Until then, I kiss you with love. Hermina

1950/6/24 Marie to Irving (Book 8, 299-301)

6/24/50
My dear little brother Irving!
I am writing a couple of lines again that we are well, which I hope to hear back from you. I have not gotten a letter from you for a long time already. How's everything? Did you hear about your job? And you Herman, how are you and what do you do? What do you plan on doing, if you my Irving will go to that other job?

Does Herman still want to stay there alone? Write about everything. Last week I got a card from Dorothy and she is in Chicago. She is visiting with little Jerome at her parents, and about July 4th she is planning on going back home. I have not heard about Dave for a long time. About me, there is nothing particular, everything is the same. And Hermine and Eugene are well, too, they are just very busy. As I mentioned, they are looking for furniture because they don't have a lot of time since they are leaving the apartment by August 1st. They got the [other] apartment. And with God's help, if they are already organizing, then everything is going to be different for them, too. There is a lot to do until then. Let's hope that the dear God will help them, and everything is going to be fine. The relatives are well and they were wondering about you. And how is everybody there? Write about everything. And take care of yourself wherever you go. Also, [take care] with the house. Eat. It would be better if they would place you here in New York, my little brother. Let's hope that with God's help everything will work out for you, too. Don't be sad. Now I will close my lines and I'm sending my greetings from my heart and kiss you with love. Maria.
I'm writing this letter from work again and I want it to go [out].

1950/7/4 Marie to Irving (Book 6, 51-52)

7/4/50
My dear brother Irving,
Again, a few lines that we're fine which I hope to hear from you the best. I haven't heard from you in a long time, but last week Dorothy wrote to me and mentioned that you probably expect to go visit them. I hope your plan succeeds and you will come home happily. And if you were, write about everything and [if] Herman was there, I think you went by car. At home right now there is nothing special. Everything is about the same. Yes, my dear little brother, what about your work? Have you heard about it? Write about everything. Hermine and Eugene are fine. I still worked today and as you can see I think of you. Yes, we got the money, but we still had our hands full. But then Hermine will write to you. Today I think they went somewhere. Jean [Frey] is going to Florida tomorrow by car and Bertha hasn't seen me for a long time. Aunt Jennie was fine. I talked to them yesterday, but as you can see I still haven't had time to visit them. If you were here now, we could go for a ride and it would have been much more pleasant to me. And how are the relations there? Regards to Aunt Helen and Flora and everyone. Now my little brother dear, take great care wherever you go and don't forget to eat ok. Now I close my lines. Greetings from the heart and kissing you countless times with much love forever, your sister. Love, Maria

Hermine and Eugene send kisses and greetings to both of you.
And also to Herman. Love, M

1950/7/7 Hermine to Irving (Book 10, 216-219)

July 7, 1950
Dear Irving and Herman,
I'm very sorry for neglecting you like that, but I asked Maria to write for me, too. Believe me we were very busy with shopping for our home. Thank God we bought our bedroom suite and also the sofa and two club chairs for the living room. The other stuff isn't bought because we'll have to see the rooms first. We expect to move in sometime in August. I hope Irving when you'll be here my apartment will be set up so you could see it. We received mail from Dorothy but I didn't even write to her. She mentioned that you might come up to see them. I hope you did. Please tell us about them especially about the baby! How long were you in Chicago? Maria wrote to them that she might or want to go there for a vacation. We are having one week on July 14th and expect to go to the mountains. I'll get one week later - then I'll stay and do some work in our new home. How are you and Herman? How are the relatives? I mailed a wedding picture to you - a big one. This way you'll be able to show it to our relatives - if they are still home. Mrs. Lindeck wrote to me and I regret that I couldn't answer. The same goes for Miss McNeill. Please tell her that I'm always asking for her but will write her too. We see very little of our relatives in N.Y. Eugene is still busy and we have only one Sunday when we can go somewhere. Have you heard from your new position yet? How is your present place? How does Herman feel? When is he taking a vacation? Let us hear from you both. Love from Eugene and Hermine

1950/7/12 Undated Marie to Irving (Book 6, 53-54)

[Dated from Marie mentioning on the 13th that she wrote the day before and that Hermine is going on vacation]

My dear brother Irving,

Just a few lines that we are fine which is what I hope to hear from you. I no longer know what might be the reason why you haven't written to us for so long. I haven't heard from you in such a long time that I don't even know the exact time. As Dorothy wrote that you would probably go to them in Chicago, I hope you had a chance and everything was fine. I think you must be very busy, but you're not used to being such a lazy writer. And you Herman, what do you do? Write immediately. And you Irving dear, have you heard of this work of yours and are you still working in this place? Write about everything. With us nothing special, everything is the same. Hermine and Eugene are fine [and are] now going on a weekly vacation. I just hope the weather gets good. Currently, it has been raining for 3 days. So I am glad to send this letter as soon as possible. Now I close my lines and greetings from the heart and kisses with love countless times. Love, Maria

Be careful where you go and eat. And write right away, ok

Hermine is also sending greetings and love.

1950/7/13 Marie to Irving (Book 8, 306-308)

My dear little Irving,

We got your letter, which we could hardly wait for and I was very happy about it, and I am happy to hear that thank God you are well. I wrote a letter yesterday and I hope that you got it. Last night I took your letter to Hermine and they were very happy about it and about your picture, also. Otherwise we are all well, which I hope to hear from you back. Hermine and the others are going on a vacation tomorrow for a week. And with God's help they will move in August to the apartment. They already got the furniture, although there are a lot of things still missing, but slowly they will move in soon. As you wrote about the ice-closet, that you want to send it, Eugene just said that it comes with the apartment and it's not worth it to bring it here. You will be better off to sell it there, as well as what you don't need. Now about your job. My Irving, I don't know if it's worth it to go to school. It is very hard and the second job that you mentioned is not that important. The government one sounds good, but it is up to you, my dear little brother, what you want. It is very hard to go to school, but you know better what you want. And now I will get to something. You know the situation from all sides is not really nice. It is enough so because of that you have to arrange it so you will have a bigger insurance. So you don't need to go farther. You know what I think? You must be smart and arrange it in a way you think is the best. What does Herman do? Do you plan on leaving the apartment? It would be good if they would place you here. And let's hope that the dear God will help and everything will turn out to be good. Also, about Samuel [Gluck - his marriage was annulled] I am very surprised how a smart boy like him, would fall into [something] like that. But as they say, it is better now than later. About me, as I mentioned my Irving, that I am planning on going for a vacation to California, probably in the Fall. I did not decide on the exact time, but if everything is going well, with God's help, this is my plan. I hope that until then you will start with your new job also. It would be great if you could come with me, too. Now I will close my lines and I'm sending my best from the heart and I kiss you with love. Hermine and Eugene, too. Love, Maria

1950/7/19 Irving to Herb and Renee Baum (Book 6, 336) - draft

July 19, 1950

Dear Reneé and Herb,

Just a few lines to let you know that the complete tour was excellent. As a matter of fact I hope to make another journey in the near future. Thinking of Chicago and Cleveland, I believe that both cities are very pleasant. Somehow a change, away from Columbus, rejuvenates a person. Plus, the pleasant day with you is also a memorable one. I have enjoyed it immensely. However, I regret that I wasn't able to see you, Herb, before my departure, but I hope to see you again as indicated above in the near future. To you, Reneé, I wish to indicate that I enjoyed speaking to your family. They are swell people. I hope to be in Cleveland, again, probably this weekend. Well, till next time, I remain with best wishes to you both, and if you see Ann, my hello to her from me. Good luck, Irv

1950/7/20 Marie to Irving (Book 6, 37-40)

7/20/50

My dear little brother Irving!

I received your long awaited letter and I'm glad to hear that thank God you are all well. Also, as you mention my Irving, that you went to the third job with the exam. I know that there is no reason to sue them at all. I'm sure the rest will come too, only it takes time. But what is more important, the situation today is very bad and I am very sad about you. As you write it my dear little brother, that until today as we can see, the dear God helped, but let's hope that he will be with you after this also and he will help you in every step of your way. Because of that, if it's possible, choose the job where there is a better prospective. Try to be smart. You know what I think. It was enough that I mentioned about this in my past letter, but you did not really understand me because you did not respond. What does Herman do? Write about everything. My Irving, the way you write, [you think] that I will go to [stay in] California. I am only planning on going to visit. And as you mentioned, that they could transfer you to Texas. Why do you want to go so far? If you can choose, it would be best if you would come here and maybe, if it comes to that, you can come here. Or if you like that job where you working at and there is a future in it, then do the way you see the best. The only thing that is important is that the dear God will help you not to come to that [the draft]. God forbid you have to go there again where they are fighting. Write immediately to me. Otherwise we are well. Hermine and the others did not come home yet. They will be home with God's help on Sunday. I talked to them on the phone and they are well. They are sending their best. Did you hear about Dave? We did not hear anything from him until today, since Dorothy went back. I hope they are well! Yes, I still want to know what they say now that they call in the reserve solders for 30 "min" years. God forbid that they are counting you or Herman in to that. Write about this to me. I can't even think about that. Yes my little brother, last Sunday was our yahrzeit for our late Mother. I hope you did not forget to say kaddish. If yes, then maybe it is not late even today my little brother. Now take care of yourselves wherever you go. I'm sending my best from the heart and kiss you countless times with much love. Maria

Yes something came to my mind, what is going on with the stock that you have. I hope you did not lose on it. God forbid. Be careful with that too and don't be sad about me my Irving. I have enough money. You just be careful with that too because it comes hard for you too. Now I wish you lots and lots of luck and the best of health! Love, Maria

1950/7/28 David and Dorothy to Irving and Herman (Book 12, 262-265)

July 27, 1950

Dear Irving and Herman,

We received the package yesterday containing the adorable gift for the baby, and please accept our thanks. It is perfect in color and style, and I'm sure the baby will look darling in it. My trip home was uneventful, and your nephew behaved beautifully. That's the beauty of traveling by plane - before he got a chance to become bored we were already home. The flight to Chicago seemed to be smoother than the one coming back, and I understand the time of day has a great deal to do with it. At any rate I was glad when we landed and were on good old terra firma. Since I've come back we've made a move and are now living in a house instead of an apartment. It certainly is more satisfactory for all concerned, and especially for the baby. We have a nice back yard and front lawn where I can put the baby for an airing without having to run up and down stairs. We have 3 bedrooms, so if and when you come to pay us a visit you can have a room to yourself. That's an invitation. Our new address is 3242 Maine Ave. I wrote home and relayed your message to all. They always like to have you, Irving. I'm going to cut this short as David would like to add a few lines. I feel fine and hope the same goes for you. Write again soon. Love, Dorothy

[In Hungarian]

Dear little brother! Until 120!

Forgive me that I have not written for so long, but you know how busy I am, so I don't have time to write. I hope you feel good and Herman also. I am also, just like Dorothy and Frederick Jerome are feeling good too! Why don't you come here? Currently, there is enough space for your visit. How are you otherwise? I hope that they will not call you in again! Please write it to me asap. I hope that you did not sign up again as a <u>Reservist</u>. Also write it what kind of government job did you take. The way things are currently, it is necessary for you to get a good salary. Here in Long Beach the situation is good, that is, business is good. They are building an entire city here with 17000 houses and a business center about 2 km from my business. Also, where my business is, there is an entire road being built. Also, they are building at least three factories. I hope that the business will go well for a while! It is enough for today. Kiss with love, your older brother, Dezső

1950/8/1 Marie to Irving (Book 6, 57-59)

8/1/50

My dear little brother Irving!

I got your last letter and I'm glad to hear that thank God, you are all well! We are well also. Sunday I was at a bathing place with Hermine and some others. The entire family went, but as you also know my Irving, that it means a lot to me because it is far and we went with a car, which I don't like. I thought about you that you would like this so much. In the summer there are many places where you can go to look around. Hermine likes to go too. Yes, my Irving as you mentioned it now, that you are not in the reserves. At least it makes me feel better. But now what is most important, is that it should pass as soon as possible. God forbid it will come to that, that they will call you. I know very much that one person does not plan on it. Every single person counts to their family. But it is the way it is. We can only trust the dear God. Let's hope, that we are not wrong! Otherwise everything is the same. Currently it is very warm, but in has started to rain. This way I hope the air will get cooler. And how's everything by you? I hope to hear the best about you! And my Irving, what's going on with the work? Did you hear anything about the others? Write about everything my dear little brother. How are the relatives? Here everything is fine otherwise. And how is Herman? Write about everything. And take care wherever you go, especially with the car. Do not go too fast! Yes, and it was also the yahrzeit for our late mother, that is, on the Jewish [calendar] Rosh Hodesh Eriv [evening], that is, it's the first day of the new [month]. And for our dear father and the family it is on Passover on the second day when we light a candle and say Yizkor and you have to say kaddish. I'm only writing this again because I thought that you thought that now [was the time] to [say it] for everyone. I will leave this too. Only take care of yourself. And don't forget to write! Hermine and Eugene are sending their best also. And I kiss you countless times with much of love. Your forever faithful sibling. Love, Maria

1950/8/22 Hermine to Irving (Book 10, 227-232)

New York 8/22 -1950

My dear brother Irving,

I'm very sorry that I couldn't speak to you when Maria telephoned. We went to a wedding Saturday night. It was very beautiful and we enjoyed it a lot. Maria probably told you the reasons that I'm not prompt with the letter writing. It seems that I'm always busy. When I get home I have to prepare dinner and especially now Eugene works late. They are remodeling the store inside and in a couple of weeks the front, too. The landlord is giving them a new front, but they take care of the inside. The apartment we still didn't get yet, but we hope it wouldn't be far for getting it. Dorothy sent us the Baby's picture and he is very sweet on it. She also told me [that] through David I might be able to get material for drapes and lamps. All that would be wonderful because we could save something on them. We bought the bedroom suit and living room furniture. I don't know if I ever mentioned that to you but [I'm] always in a hurry [and] probably forgot it. Otherwise we are well and still live in the same house. She is a pretty nice woman, but I wouldn't mind going from there already. How are you Irving? Maria told me that Herman has his vacation. It is a shame that he is so stubborn. Even if it costs him money he should try to change and it would be high time already! How long does he think this can go on, and what is he living for. For whom is he saving his money. I assure him that he can't take it along. If I were him I would try to have some enjoyment until I'm able and not the way he lives. First, he should be well, and I wouldn't suffer either. It doesn't pay because it is more fun to be well and healthy. If he would come to N.Y. most doctors are good and he goes to Kantor and Kantor again. It is no life. I wish he would make up his mind. As for you, I still think it would be better to get rid of the home. If you decide [to], then when Maria will stop off she could help you. If you have something you could store them until you need it. I mean clothing or your books. Maybe Arthur would permit you to put it in the basement or ceiling? [In Hungarian] In the attic. [In English] If you feel [that] you [would] still like to stay there, then maybe you should try to advertise for an older Jewish couple. Then they could take care of the house. Even if only enough money to spend [to cover] your expenses and keep up the home so she would prepare a meal and clean the rooms, try it please. I must tell you, I worry about you and just remember that what would happen if we would stay there in Columbus. No future in it - maybe if your jobs are so wonderful, but it is cheaper to be healthy. So please Irving, try to figure out and don't struggle in that home. We pay $10.00 a week and do working and washing. If you can stay in a room together then you have only $20.00 each and your food - but that is cheap because you have a warm room, and clean, too. So please do something because the cold weather will come and you can get sick without heat in the home. Well that is enough of that. Please don't mind me because I'll like to help you some way. If you decide to come to NY even then [it] would [be] good. It is expensive until you settle down, but it pays believe me. Herman too - could spend a few dollars to try. This is the time, not in December. Why didn't he come for a vacation to NY to see if he likes it or not? I have this powder he should try. 1. teaspoon in a glass of water after meal. If it is good, I'll send him more. Have to close now, Love to you both, Hermina and Eugene

1950/8/22 Marie to Irving (Book 6, 35-36)

8/22/50

My dear brother Irving,

Again, just a few lines that we are fine with my hope that my lines will find you in the best of health. Hermine was so glad I called you on the phone, she was just sorry she couldn't talk to you also. I told her about Herman. It's enough to make you feel sorry for even that little pleasure from our mother's years because it is not [living] how he lives at home. I write this from experience. It does a lot to see at least sometimes [during] the day you go somewhere [and then] to see when you go back so you would feel a lot better. And so, even now, not asking to take a few days and eat. We also have a very good doctor here and he could help him too. And as you say Irving, man will not live forever and will live as long as he lives. There will be no poorer age and money is not everything. But if you want to think more and come. But now Irving dear I was very happy to talk to you. And that otherwise everything is fine. Yesterday I saw Hermine and Eugene. They are well. They each send special greetings. And I know very well that it is so very difficult for you, but I hope the good God will help and soon I can hear good news from you too. You just take great care of yourself. I hope Herman thinks about it and will let it go, and try it and see that it gets better. And also what I mentioned on the phone is that if God helps and if you don't come here by then, then if I go to California with you, I'll stay with you and it won't cost more. For now, we hope to hear from you about the work. Hermine said maybe you could write to them at the public place and ask when you could plan on it. Now I close my lines with heartfelt greetings and countless kisses many times with a lot of love. Love, Maria

Take care of yourself, ok my buddy

1950/9 Hermine to Irving (Book 10, 78-81) – Labor Day

[dated from mention of being on vacation through Labor Day and reference to the wedding Hermine went to on Saturday night see 1950/8/22 Hermine to Irving (Book 10, 227-232)]

My dear little brother, Irving!

I got your letter, but I'm sorry that I'm only responding just now. I'm still on my vacation, that is, I get two weeks plus Labor day. This way I will only start to work on Tuesday. On Friday we went away for the weekend and we spent it very nicely. Because of the wedding we can't go away, otherwise we would have gone for the entire week. I hope everything is fine with you also and with your job. Write what is new by you! Yes, I am attaching Emil's address here and I used the blue envelope's address, but it's the same on both. I hope you will be able to read it, I re-wrote it on purpose for you, so maybe it will help. I'm sorry that you could not come for a few days, but many times one can't help it. Yesterday I went to Mrs. Kugler and I saw Maria, but she is working, so I could not spend too much time with her. She says that she is far, but I got used to it and here it's like we would be in the country. When are you coming to see it already? Anytime, but I would like to see you. I read Maria's letter too and if Herman wants to come, then he should not wait for too long because it is easier to get a job in the Fall than in the Winter. Forgive me, because my writing is so messy, but I have an appointment, so I'm in a hurry and my letter has ink all over, but I don't have time to rewrite it. I want to buy a lamp shade. We already bought the lamps. Let us hear from you. Love to you both. Hermine and Eugene

1950/9/6 Marie to Irving (Book 6, 41-42)

9/6/50

My dear brother Irving!

I have received your long awaited letter and I am happy to hear that you are well, thank God. We are fine too and I was late in answering because I wanted to give you an exact time for my trip. But as you can see today, I don't know definitely, but I hope I will get it. I mean, I went in yesterday to make a reservation to go to California, but since I stop in Columbus, they have to make a reservation from here to Chicago and also to Columbus. And it takes me 10 days to get the answer because they have to know the exact number

Page 680

to start there. They did it until Columbus, so that if I get that train in Chicago, I'll leave here on Saturday night, September 30, and then I'll write the exact time and I'll get there and go to California on Sunday. I hope my plan will succeed with God's help. Don't do anything for me. Just take care of yourself. And what is Herman doing in his spare time? We thought he was coming, but as you can see, he's not used to it. What about Arthur and the relations, are they at home, that is will they be? And Aunt Helen? Write Irving dear, about everything. And take great care of yourself wherever you go. Now heartfelt kisses countless times with a lot of love. Until I see you again [In English] soon. Love, Maria

1950/9/12 Pollock Paper Corp Letter of Recommendation Irving (Book 22, 232-233)

September 12, 1950

To whom it may concern:
This is to certify that Mr. Irving Gluck has been employed by the Pollock Paper Corporation in its paper mill office at Columbus, Ohio as a production clerk. He handled all production time cards, inventories and office records as well as other duties. Mr. Gluck was a conscientious, steady, sober and painstaking employee. He left our employ for a change to fields more suited to his academic background, which is extensive in educational and cultural fields.

W.A. Johnson
Pollock Paper Corporation
780 Frebis Avenue
Columbus, Ohio

1950/9/13 Hermine to Irving (Book 10, 221-225)

My Dear brother Irving,
I read your letter which you sent to Maria and we all are happy to know you are well. Maria called you, but I'm sorry that I couldn't talk to you. Maria is all excited now about her trip to California and to see you in Columbus. If you remember I was there last year and [it] was also in October - this year Maria expects to see you. I know that one week goes by very fast. I wish we could have some arrangements about that. I keep on lecturing continuously about that and you might not like the idea, but I would like to get you out of there. It seems to me that you are afraid to move, for that I can't blame you but wonder if it pays. I feel that way - even if it is hard [in] the beginning, but on the end you're better off. I would very much want you to be nearer to us. I don't mean to be selfish, but that's how it is. If God will help us and we will get our apartment, at least you could come over to us. At least you could have my Hungarian cooking once in a while. Where today you are all alone - I must tell you that I don't like [it] at all. That is the reason that I'm bothering you so much. [It's] the only medicine for Herman too! [It's] the only thing that can save him from his illness. Since Maria is in NY she is a different person and I hope California will even be better for her. Believe me it doesn't matter where you are, but only if you take care of yourselves. Life is too short so you should look out for yourself. Have some fun, too. Oh boy Irving! Some nice and wonderful girls are looking for boys like you!! Believe me there is [a] better chance to catch fish in a big body of water. Take that from me. Herman, too. I wouldn't give him only six months, he wouldn't even want to leave a place like NY. You don't have to be rich to be happy, and little by little things work out. I know Irving how you feel about it and I don't blame you - you had the real experience in N.Y., but you should know that is only the beginning. You would do much better later on for that I'm sure! Here I must close this letter and we wish you both a very happy New Year. Forgive me for this letter for writing as I do, but in case you decide, Maria could help to arrange things now when she'll be there. Love from us both, Hermine and Eugene

1950/9/15 Marie to Irving (Book 8, 310-315)

9/15/50
My dear little Irving!
I got your letter, which I was very happy for and I'm glad to hear that thank God you are well. Plus the surprise with the car. The car is beautiful. I am very pleased with it. First of all, I wish you lots and lots of good luck and the best of health for the new year for both of you and that every wish of yours will come true. Do not forget to drive carefully!!! Now I will get to the traveling. First of all, the way you wrote, my dear little Irving, that you would come to get me and would take me to California , it is very nice of you.

And I know that you would do it. But it is impossible for me to take such a big road trip with my car sickness. Only an hour is enough for me to get sick in the car. So, as you can see my dear Irving, it is better for me to travel by train. It takes 3 days and 3 nights from here and plus I take a Pullman because not everyone can travel and I am one of them. Now I will get back to the apartment. As you mentioned that you would rent it out and you would leave a room, it is a very good idea. There is only one thing though, that then it is still hard to start because the house still needs to be dealt with. The other thing is the way I thought I wanted to go to Columbus, but only to see you. I don't have any other things to do. And that is why I'm in a hurry to send this letter, so you will get it as soon as possible. I believe that it would be better. Last night I made our reservation and I got the tickets and I got it so I will leave on September 30th to Columbus and October 1st I go to Chicago and California. I arranged it from work that way. And I thought, if you think, both of you come here [to N.Y.] and you can deal with the house there [in Columbus] in a way so you could stay here and it would be that week for me that I would have spent in Columbus, then I could stay here with you and I would help you and if you would come now, we would have three weeks together. And even if I will leave, Hermine is here too and it would be 100% better for you here than in Columbus. And it is a miracle that Herman came to his senses and because of that it would not be worth it to neglect it. That is the one of the reasons why I am happy for the car, too. At least Herman has an opportunity to look out to the world. Plus, there is nothing you would feel bad about leaving behind in Columbus. When you decide yourself that you will stay here, then you will go look for a job until you can find one. And here, even if it's hard, there are more chances than there. When there is no apartment to be sad about, then if one of them does not work, the other could go until he finds the one he wants. And you asked me, if I am planning on staying in California. I don't know that yet. Now I bought a round-trip ticket to come back and I took off two months from work. In case the outlook is better, a young crowd, and I would get a good job in California, and I would like the place, then maybe I will decide myself to stay there. And also, if you want it nothing holds you back. If you don't like it here, then you can try it there. For you, for boys it is easier to go there with the car. You have time, although it is a big trip even for you. And if you want we can meet there in California. It is very hard to decide to stay there since I do not want to leave Hermine alone here. But if we think about it on the other side, the dear God helped her and she is married. So she is not alone then, and now I have to look after that too. Maybe I would have more luck there. And that is why I write it this way even if it's hard, but we must try. It is not worth it to sit down and to be sad about what's going to be, but we have to help ourselves, the way we think it's the best. And now it depends on you. I will only note this, if you decide to come here then write to me immediately because then I need to change my ticket straight to California. So there will be no need to run around because of me. Yes, my dear Irving, I called you on the phone last night, but nobody answered. I thought maybe Lindek and the others are not at home. But I will call you again tonight. In case I can't get you, then do me a favor, and you call me immediately at night. The number is CY9-4769 cypres 9-4769. It is on Hermine's name and ask for me on it "person to person" and tell [the operator] that they should charge it to me. I will pay for it because I don't have too much time and I need time if I want to speak. Although, it is true that everybody thinks that it is good to go with a car because you can stop at night and stay at a hotel and look around everywhere. For those who can travel, it is nice. If you my Irving, plan on staying there, then it is different anyway since one can take a trip, but just because of me it is not worth it. If I will decide to stay then two months is not enough time there to look around. If I would know that I will stay there then it would be better. But I don't know what to say anyway. Thank you my dear brother that you thought about me with this. And now I will close my lines, sending my best from the heart and kiss you with much of love. Maria

I showed your car to Hermine and to everybody and everybody liked it. But now what's important is that you should have lots of luck and health. I already wrote enough and I will close my lines. Hermine sends her greetings to you. Love, M.

1950/10/3 US Embassy Prague to Dept of State re. Property Claim (Book 19, 140)

Unclassified
Foreign Service Operations Memorandum
To:Department of State
From: AmEmbassy, Praha, Czechoslovakia
Subject: American Property - Case of Irving, Herman, Maria, and Hermina Gluck
Reference: Department's Operations Memorandum dated March 9, 1948

Pursuant to the Department's Operation Memorandum under reference the Embassy requested the Czechoslovak Ministry of Foreign Affairs that the present legal and physical status of the abovementionedclaimants' property located at Polany, Czechoslovakia, be investigated and that the Czechoslovak authorities be notified about the American interest involved. In reply to the Embassy's repeated requests that action be expedited, the Ministry has now furnished the following report:

"The real property owned by Ignac, Hermina, Herman and Maria Gluck, located in the cadastral area of Plant, District of Kralovsky Chlumec, consists of 7/9ths of a house with yard and of landed property covering an area of approximately 3 hectares. Since the year 1945 Ignac Klein, a resident of Leles, on the basis of an authorization given him by the Local National Committee under Ref. No. 1946/45 of November 15, 1945. Ignac Klein is using part of the property himself and collects the rent for the use of the remaining part of the property."

In the event that the claimants have not yet arrived at a settlement with Ignac Klein, it seems that they may desire to engage the services of a Czechoslovak attorney and instruct him to take the necessary steps on their behalf. For their consideration, there is enclosed a list of attorneys practicing at Kralovsky Chlumec and Kosice who are believed to be capable of handling such matters. While due care has been exercised in the preparation of the enclosed list, the Embassy cannot assume any responsibility for the professional standing or integrity of the persons whose names appear on the list.

Enclosure

1950/10/5 Hermine to Maria (Book 10, 234-236)

New York 10/5 -50
Dear Maria,
We received your letter and I don't blame you for liking your trip. It was really beautiful in there. Also Irving's car must be so too! The main thing is now to arrange something to make it easier for the boys. I think the idea is very good. If they could lease the apartment for the money they could get a nice room and no work - they could save money yet. Just that if they would rent [it] to see nothing should be left there - no linen - just the furniture and curtains or bed spreads. I thought of that only because if you don't have enough they might want to make you buy it and if you have any they steal it. We don't get any linen at all and pay for one room $10.00 Let's hope everything will work out for you and the boys. Let us know how everyone welcomed you there? I'll write more next time because I'm on my lunch time and I want you to get this letter before you leave to California. Please Irving, you write to me, too. I hope you enjoy Maria's cooking and everything is all right. Let me hear from you all. I was very busy lately because of the Holy days. We went to my mother-in-law for dinner. Last night I made dinner at home. How are you Irving and Herman? I would love to see you too. Is Herman as skinny as last year when I was there?! He better put some weight on. We all are well and hope to hear the same about you. Everyone sends Hello and Helen Frank, too! I haven't heard anything from Dorothy. I wish I would know why! Hope they are all right. Tell them we think of [them] even if we don't write as often. Regards to her family in Chicago and our love to them in California. Best wishes and love, Hermina and Eugene

P.S. Let us hear from you when you get there!

1950/10/9 Marie to Irving (Book 9, 263-265) on the train to CA

Santa Fe Super Chief [Amtrak train]

My dear little brother Irving,
As you can see, I am writing this letter from the train. I hope you will be able to read it. I wish you could see! Herman, if you could see the train. It looks like armor, the entire thing is something beautiful. I can't even write it down. I arrived to Chicago on our time 3:45 and they were already waiting for me and I had to go. I had dinner there and they were very happy for me. I only had time to eat and leave. He took a cab and took me back to that station. But now only a few lines, that it was a very nice trip and I met a Californian woman, who is nice and helpful. Take care of yourself when you go with the car and give my best to everyone. Next time I will write more. And you try it as well. Now I will close my lines and I kiss you countless times and kiss you with love. Maria
I wrote to Hermine too, I only hope you can read it.

[from Marie]
My dear little brother, Irving!
Only a few lines, I hope you got the letter from the train and I hope you were able to read it. I arrived on Tuesday morning at 8:45 and Dave came to me, but he did not really recognize me immediately. I just saw him from a distance and he still looks the same. I could say that he was very happy about me. He did not even know what to say. Then he took me home and there Dorothy was also very happy. Now I will talk about the child, he is like gold, he could be eaten up. And how are you? What's going on with the house? Did you sell the furniture? I hope yes! You know my Irving, Dave has a very nice store here. He is making upholstery too, but it is not really worth it. He thinks if you would be here, you could work with him and if not, then other jobs are available too. In my opinion, my dear Irving, I think that you should not stay in Columbus, not even for a government job. If you want, it would be worth it to come here and look around. I know you would like the weather here and the car would not cost a lot, if you could come as long as I am here, if none of you will like it then you can go back. Maybe I would make myself in New York not in Columbus. You could use a vacation and since you worked with Arthur, you could learn something here too. Yes, the apartment here is beautiful and Dave said, if you have $100 to pay [a deposit], then you can buy an apartment and you could rent it out also. The rent is cheaper here than in New York, but it's up to you. If it doesn't work out, then in the winter, like you said you can go to a warmer area. Now I will write to Hermine too. I will look around and I will write about everything in detail again. If the furniture can be sold then it's worth it. Write about everything. I'm writing this from the store. I can't help him much, but you little brother could do more for him, I'm sure of it. They live very nicely, but I don't have patience to sit and wait. Dave said if you would be here, it would be better, because we could go together to look around. I talked about your car here, which comes in very handy. He has a car too in the store, but a different one. I'm closing my lines and sending greetings to all of you and kiss you with love. Maria

I'm sending my best to everyone and tell me what you think about everything.

[from Dorothy]
Wednesday

Dear Irving,
Since Maria is writing you, I thought it would be a good idea finally to drop you a few lines too. I hope you will understand how little time I have for letter-writing when I tell you I am now working at the store every day. I have a lady coming in to take care of the baby, which of course is a necessity. At any rate that's why I have neglected my correspondence shamefully. I don't have to tell you how wonderful it is having Maria here. I would have recognized her anywhere since you resemble each other so very much. She is very sweet and already I feel as though I have always known her. I was so sorry to learn that you lost your position, and hope it won't be long before a better one will result. We are all well and things are pretty much the same. I'll enclose this with Maria's letter. Love to you and Herman from all of us. Dorothy

P.S. Write soon.

1950/10/17 US Dept. of State to Legal Aid Clinic OSU re. Property Claim (Book 19, 142-143)

October 17, 1950

To: Mr. Harold R. Black
     Legal Aid Clinic
     The Ohio State University
     College of Law
     Columbus 10, Ohio

Reference is made to previous correspondence concerning the property interests in Czechoslovakia of your clients, Irving, Herman Maria and Hermina Gluck. The Department has now received a report regarding this matter from the American Embassy in Praha and a copy thereof is enclosed for your information and that of your clients. While due care has been exercised in the preparation of the list of attorneys attached to the enclosed report, neither the Department nor the American Embassy at Praha can assume any responsibility for the professional standing or integrity of the persons whose names appear thereon.

Francis E. Flaherty
Assistant Chief
Division of Protective Services

Enclosure:
Copy of a report, dated October 3, 1950 from the American Embassy at Praha

1950/10/20 Legal Aid Clinic OSU to Irving (Book 19, 147)

October 20, 1950
Dear Mr. Gluck:
We have just received a communication from the Department of State enclosing a report received from the American Embassy in Prague regarding the property in Czechoslovakia in which you were interested. We tried to locate you through the registrar's office on the campus, but were unable to obtain any information from them so we assume that you are not in school this quarter. For this reason we are writing to you about this matter. At your earliest convenience if you will call at our office, we shall be glad to give you the information we have received. Very truly yours, Legal Aid Clinic, M.L. Daehler
[See 1950/10/3 US Embassy Prague to Dept of State re. Property Claim (Book 19, 140) and 1950/10/17 US Dept. of State to Legal Aid Clinic OSU re. Property Claim (Book 19, 142-143)]

1950/10/21 Hermine to Irving and Herman (Book 15, 196-202)

New York 10/21 - 50
Dear Irving and Herman,
We received your letter with Emil's letter enclosed. I'm very happy at least he gave some news about his whereabouts. He seems to be different and I really hope that he learned something about being independent. It is hard to tell what would be the best thing for him. I would say we should try to get him out here. Then again as soon as he gets here he will be taken to the army. I called the Lefkovits girls, Lenke nenni's daughter and told her about it. She is going to talk to her uncle. In the meantime, I don't know what would be good. Do you think it is all right to talk to Arthur about [it]? Would he be kind enough to help him get here [and] get papers. I will write to Emil and ask him what he thinks [he] would like to do. Received a letter from Maria and Dorothy and so far, she likes it there. Also mentioned David would like you to come. It is hard to advise, but if you feel you want to try, it can't hurt. If you don't care for it you can always come back, especially now that you have such a beautiful car. Lots of luck to you and don't forget to be careful because it is still dangerous. With the job you expect from the government if you leave the address at the post office you would get it wherever you stay. They send it after you so it doesn't pay to stay just for that. Who knows how long you might have to stay there. Maybe you could even join him in business. If he thinks it is good and you see it for yourselves, then I think it's all right. How long can Herman work the way he does? He doesn't have any other enjoyment out of life besides his work and that is not enough. It is high time to do something about it and you should know he depends on you. He wants you to make up his mind for him. If you [would] rather come to NY it's fine with me, but you should do what is better for you. I must say that so far, everyone likes you in N.Y. Mother and Mrs. Kayn even [have] girls for you. If you come, they want to fix you up. About ourselves, only that we are well, we miss Maria and so does Mrs. Kugler. She is very nervous and doesn't know why. I was there today and go there every Saturday and must eat with her dinner. She is the most wonderful person to know, and loves you and our family! She even loves Eugene. We are still with Mrs. Saks, but expect to move next month and hope this time it will happen. It's high time already because even our furniture is ready and we try to put off delivery on it and how long can we put that off. But we saw our apartment and it is very beautiful, and so is our furniture. Oh yes! Tell us about yourselves and your apartment. Could you rent it to someone? To lease it or sell it. Would you please measure the refrigerator how wide it is. We don't get a refrigerator in our apartment and we'll have to get one, but I don't think yours would go in. It's too big. Eugene thinks that it doesn't pay to bring that here. You are better off to sell it. That should not keep you back. How much do they want to give for all the furniture? You try your best and that's all anyone can do. How are the relatives? Remember us to them, and to Miss McNeill, too. Love from us both. Hermine and Eugene

[from Maria]

My dear little brother Irving!
I got your letter and I'm glad to hear, that thank God you are well! It's just hard the way you write, that there is still no news with the house, that is, [no] result. But now I will get to the point. First of all, I still don't work, but now I will look for it this week. And then I will be able to write more exactly to you. Although David thinks that you will be able to get a job. In my opinion, while I haven't looked around and don't work yet, I don't know what to write. But if you want, you should wait for a few days and by then I will write to you again. You just be all right with the house. And if you want to try to come, even if you like it or not, it is not too late to come to New York. At least we will see where it is better. Now I wrote to Hermine also. And I hope it will come out good! Just take care of yourself. I will write with more details. I'm sending my best from my heart and kiss you. Love, Maria

[from David]
Dear Irving!
Just a few lines. So I will give you information about the situation here. You can get as many jobs as you want in the factories. For example, "Douglas Plant" and LTG. What kind of job, I don't know. Maybe you can get into their experimental plant business. Now it is before Christmas, too. It is very hard in downtown Long Beach for Mariska. There isn't the same job as in New York, since there are no restaurants here. L.A. is much better. And tell her if she will stay here, you should come here too because it is not really good to be alone here. Also, it is so much easier to get a job for men than for girls. So if you will come out there are enough jobs, if it's important. I am in a hurry to send this letter that is why I'm not writing more. What they are writing about now is not that there are no jobs, but that there is a shortage of men. Kiss you with love, Dovid

My dear little brother Irving,
A couple of lines again, that I am fine and David is as well and [so is] his family. I hope that my lines will find you in the best of health also. What do you do little brother? Is there any result with the house? I still can't write much about my self, but last week on Thursday I started to look for work. Also, yesterday I was in a few job offices. Since being a cashier isn't in need here, and even if they need them, they don't pay them well. Here they pay less for a job like that. And in the government office there is nothing at all. Right now I'm waiting because the money office promised that they will look into it, which I hope will be successful. And what did you decide? If I would get a good job, then I would stay here because the weather is beautiful. I like that and then I would probably go to live to Los Angeles. Yet, it is also hard because we don't know anybody there. Here in Long Beach there is nothing for young people. There is nobody socially for young people, not even a girl. I don't like this area for that reason. Also there are more jobs in Los Angeles. We will see what will be. I hope everything is going to work out well! In case I would not find a proper job here then I would have to go back to New York soon. Although David wants me to wait with it [and work] with him in the shop where they make the curtains, but I don't want to work for him nor to wait. It is good until we share a situation together. No matter how good that is, I like to work for strangers and it is better for him too, if a stranger works for him. Right now, I don't even know how it would be best. We will see this week how it will shape up. Now you take care of yourself too and write about what you are doing. I hope you can get rid of the house. Yes, my Irving! What's going on with the stock? I hope everything is fine! Write and my Irving, do me a favor and give my best to everyone who is wondering about me. And if you want to, send Mrs. Walters' address, because I could not even write a card for her yet. I am just writing to Hermine too. Otherwise everything is well. Frederik Jerome is very cute, if [only] you could see him now. He is starting to walk and talk. You could eat him up. David is very busy in the store. And I can say that I can't help, because I don't understand it, and as I mentioned, it is better to work for strangers. It is better for him, too. Now I will close my lines and send my best with love and I kiss you with love. Maria
And you Herman what do you do? Don't forget to eat!

November 6, 1950

Bonded Scale and Machine Company
2176 South Third Street
Columbus 7, Ohio U.S.A.

Dear Irving:
I had expected you to drop into the factory and further discuss those items that were discussed the last time you were in. I want you to know that I am always willing to help and while I am rather vigorous in my criticism I feel that is the best way to be of help. You are always welcome to come in and in fact if you don't, I will feel disappointed. Sincerely, Arthur

1950/11/9 Hermine to Irving (Book 10, 238-240) - 36-19 167th Street

My dear little brother Irving,
We got your letter today and I was happy that finally you got a job. I hope it is going to be good and everything will work out for you! It would not hurt to learn diamond grinding. In New York, for example, it is hard for them to get a job. Mrs. Soffermen's son learned it and could not get a job. So, it is worth it for you only for the reason that you could get from the government a paycheck for three months. They would give $400 for an apartment that comes with the ice closet. It is not enough, but if that is better for you, if you don't need to [be] worried about the house, sell it for as much they give for it. Yes, including the ice closet $400 is not enough. We did not get a letter from Maria this week, but it looks like she doesn't even know what would be best for her. Now I only write briefly and I will write more next time. We will move to our new home on Sunday. The address is 36-19 167th Street Flushing, L.I. New York. As of next week you can already write to the new address. You could maybe rent out the apartment. Oh yes, my little brother, would you send me my war bonds? If you can't do it, Herman can do that, too. Please do it. If you could see what a beautiful apartment we got, you would be happy too. It is already painted. Only a little paper work left. Love you both. Hermina and Eugene

1950/11/19 Marie to Irving (Book 6, 66-69)

My dear brother Irving,
As you can see my little brother, I'm on an expensive planned trip and my trip is very pleasant. I only regret that it came out that I couldn't give you a quiet time to come to California. I'm sorry, but I thought it better if I decided that way and I hope you understand. If you want to come out to California, it may depend on you that you will love it and you will certainly be better able to get a decent job.

It's 3pm on Sunday afternoon

And if you want to come to NY, that's good too. I don't want to talk you in to it. I'll write more about everything next time. Just take care of yourself. David and his family are well. They took me to the train. It is very difficult because the child was already very used to me in the house. And I can't write how very cute he is. Now take care of yourself. How is Herman? Kisses with love. Love, Maria

1950/11/26 Marie to Irving (Book 15, 23-26) - returned from CA

My dear little brother, Irving,
I hope you got my letter which I wrote from the train. I know you are surprised that I decided myself to come back, but I thought it through and I thought this is for the best, because I could not find a proper job. Besides that, commuting from one place to another is very hard and it is not enough that the climate is good. Also, the two months passed by and I had to go back to work. And I don't want to look for another job. Long Beach is very beautiful, but only for families, not for a single girl, because there is nothing there. Los Angeles would be better, but the commute is very far, and living there alone is very hard since I don't know anybody there. Also, for my job I would have gotten $30 and they take off from this, so nothing remains. I'm sorry, but I could not be without a job anymore. David didn't let me work while I was there, so I did not do anything. Two months were enough for my vacation. I thought about it and from every single angle I saw it is best to come back. As you can see, I did not regret it. My trip was very nice. I arrived on Wednesday morning at 9:30 to NY and Hermine waited for me at the train station with Mrs. Schaffermen. As you can see I live here again at 1941[Walton Ave.]. I will go back to work on Monday. Yes, my dear Irving, I am thinking that it would be the best for you too in NY because here even the food is better than other places

and here to come and go is easier. Wherever you want to go for 10 cents, you are there. But if you want to go to California to try, it is up to you. I don't mind. You can try it and if you don't like it, you can come back. I just tell you that I don't recommend staying with David or working for him. He works very hard and his wife works at the store also. He has a lot of expenses, so nothing is easy, but that is what it is with everyone. When one wants something, one needs to work for it. Dorothy is very nice, and the baby - he is like a candy. He is so sweet and smart. And yes, my little dear brother, if you write to David and you mention the name of the child, then write Frederick Jerome, both names, because it is his name, but don't say that I wrote this to you. I will leave this too and I hope that my lines will find you in the best of health. You would be smarter if you would not spend the winter in that house. You should get out of there as soon as possible. It would be better, you would be healthier. You will have an excuse in the spring too. The only problem is that you want too much. If you are smart, you will figure it out and you will do something with it. I don't know anything particular about me. We are all well and so is Hermine. I was there yesterday to see them. There is still work with the apartment and not all the furniture is there yet. I am sending my greetings and I kiss you countless times. Love Maria

Herman should take care of [himself] wherever he goes and you as well.

1950/12/4 Marie to Irving (Book 8, 323-324)

12/4/50

My dear little brother Irving,

I can not imagine why are you not writing? Since I came back I wrote to you. I hope you are well! Also, my little brother, the letter that you sent last time to California, David sent this week because I was already not there. I am well, but somehow I am always busy. What do you do my Irving? Do you work or do you go to school to study about that jewelry job? I hope to hear the best! Also, what does Herman do? I am only surprised about how silly you are to live in the cold house like that without heat. God forbid, one can easily get a big problem and can suffer forever. Instead of leaving that place, you suffer with that house. Believe me my little Irving, it is not worth it to stay there for the winter. You can come here any time you want to, just write it to me and then you can come. Hermine and the others are well too, but I can't go to see them often because they live very far from me. I hope that everything is going to be fine just take care of yourself. I will write again next time. Otherwise I am well. I am in a hurry to send this letter as soon as possible. I will attach here that statement that you worked at this place. They sent it this week. Now, I send my greetings from the heart and I kiss you countless times. Love, Maria

Write and eat! Ok?

1950/12/5 Hermine to Irving (Book 10, 242-246)

12/5 - 1950

Dear Irving and Herman,

I'm writing you both, but I really should write only to Irving because you Herman never write to me anyway. I guess you don't care to do it and I don't want to force it on you, but don't you think it would be the right thing at least once in a while. You think it over and I'm sure you will feel the same way. Eugene wants to know why doesn't Herman write to us. You should also know that you are the only one Eugene wrote if you remember it yet. Well, Herman, could you make up your mind that [it] is wrong what you are doing and from now you'll be a good boy and will change just a little - bit - OK? I'm sorry Irving for my lecture I'm giving for Herman, but it seems we all are so busy that we never even bother about these things that are so important. That goes for my writing to you, too. It seems we are too much occupied and try to get by without writing letters. We think of you a lot, and you know that, but I can't just write at times. As you see I'm on my lunch time and [it] is a must to let you hear from us. We are well and the apartment is coming along very nicely. Maria is in a pretty good disposition. That's why I would suggest for everybody to have a vacation once in a while. It costs her plenty, but it was worth while. She learned something. She was on her own. If she meets someone, she is able to keep up [the] conversation because she has something interesting to talk about [that] makes people listen. All that goes for Herman again. Your problem is on my mind and if I were you, I would do it differently. It is too bad that it is not the best time to change because after New Years is too slow in business, but I feel the beginning is hard so I would spend money until I find something to do, and even if I lose money, I would feel that is an investment for my betterment just as much as opening a business. Even then with all your investment you or no one else can tell how it might work out. That's why I believe young people should have a different life than you at [the] present time have, and that goes from

Eugene, too. Do you think for me was easy? I hope to tell you not. I started with $30.00 and I was wonderful they told me. They kept me there with promises for 8 long months, and on the end they laid me off because I asked for a raise, but I was promised after 2 months I'll get 5 dollars - so that shows you must take a chance. They sent me to school. I improved with my work and Irving knows how I worked myself up to the present position. Helen Frank and I are considered the [In Hungarian] best workers. [In English] That shows you must invest to get somewhere. Irving, I know you know the whole thing about this, but I'm writing mostly for Herman. You too could try here as much as in Columbus. If they call you from the government for the job it could be sent after you. I met Maria last night after work and she is well. She can't just run over to see us because it takes about 1:45 to travel from the Bronx to our house. Please Irving, let us hear from you and I'll try to answer you. Our love to you both and to the relatives and friends, too. Love from us both, Hermine and Eugene

1950/12/5 Undated Hermine to Herman (Book 10, 34-35)

Dear Herman,

I know my brother Herman is a lazy character and he really doesn't care how we are, but I can't help it. Here I am with a few lines. I surely hope you feel well and whenever you want to talk to somebody you should sit down and write to me. You remember when I was your friend, besides that I'm your sister. Don't you need anyone anymore? What is the reason? Are you such a rich brother that it wouldn't be nice to associate with poor people any more?!! Hm?!! You let me know will you! Believe me, I'd like to see you happy and I wish that for you, just as much as for myself. Believe me, I'm sorry that I don't write as often as I used to, but today I'm busy. To keep a home and also to go to business is just enough for me, but I love it. My husband is wonderful, my home is beautiful. It is worth everything. I wish you should get a nice girl as I got a nice boy. Thank God for that. Please sit down and write me will you, Love Hermina

1950/12/10 Undated Marie to Irving (Book 6, 60-61) after Marie returns to NY

My dear little brother Irving!

I got you letter, which I waited so hard for, and I'm happy to hear that thank God you are all well! But I can tell you my dear Irving, that you are a very childish. I can't imagine why you sent me that $50. Do you think that I wrote because perhaps we need the money? You are so silly! I only wrote this since Hermine wants to buy the band she needs, but not because we want your money. First of all, I don't think that you owe me that. And if so, you take your time to give it back. And I want you to not forget, in case you need anything, write it and I will send it to you immediately. I'm trying to send this letter today and I'm writing it from work. I don't know anything particular about me. I am well. Also, I saw Hermine yesterday and she sends her best. Oh yes, my dear Irving, since I came back to NY I got a raise of $3.60 a week. And as you can see [in English] it was worthwhile to come back. [In Hungarian] Now you are right about it that Herman has to decide on his own, he can't blame anybody else because it is hard to start everywhere. But with God's help everything will work out well, but he has to help himself too. And about you my dear little brother, I know that it is very hard to do the work that you do. And surely it has no big future. But as it seems, nothing is easy in this world. Especially in this world. But let's hope that the dear God will help us and everything will work out. And thank you for the money and for the band. Hermine got it. And you have time with the present. And I can give her the money, just write how much and I will give it to her. Write how much and don't spend every penny on debt now. Take care wherever you go and write. Are you going anywhere for Christmas? I am working now. I kiss you countless times with love. Love, Maria

1951/1/11 Marie to Irving (Book 6, 74-77)

1/10/51

My dear little brother Irving!

Here are a few lines again that we are well, which I hope my lines will find you all in the best of health! What do you do? Is it worth it for you to work so hard my little Irving? I believe it isn't because you need to take care of your health as long as possible. It is not necessary for you to earn so much money. Even if you need that money, you shouldn't work so crazily. Take care of yourself! And you Herman! What do you do? Do you eat? There is nothing particular here, currently everything is the same. I am very busy too and additionally I became a very lazy writer. Yes my Irving! Did you talk to Miss McNeil? You know, I lost Mrs. Walters' address again before I would have written to them. I am very sorry that I did not even send a card to them. Since I came back, I did not even write to the relatives either. If you see them then please tell them my dear Irving, that I am very busy. And I'm sending my best to everyone who wonders about me. I wrote enough foolishness already. Just take care of yourself and don't forget to eat! OK my buddy and you Herman. Write! Now I will close my lines. I'm sending my best from the heart and kiss you countless times. With love. Maria

...and I also wish you a very happy New Year and lots of luck and the best of health to both of you! Love,
1951/1/23 Marie to Irving (Book 8, 317-318)

1/23/51

My dear little brother,

I don't even remember the exact time when I heard from you, but I do know that it is about time to hear from you. I hope my lines will find both of you in the best of health! How's everything by you? You must be very busy! But that doesn't matter, at least you could write a card. It is the best for you, and don't laugh at me, because I am truly thinking that it is about time for both of you to get married. The same for you, my Irving, as for Herman. There is no need to wait today until you get old. As long as one is young, and there's no need to be rich, only then could you know what life is. You could have a warm bedroom and you could eat normally, because it is not a life like this. Especially for a boy it is easier in this world since there are more girls. How is it there? Are there any girls? Do you go out with anyone? If you would be here, you could have better opportunities. I hope there will be good news about you in the future! Take care of yourself! I am well. My situation is completely different. It is so much harder for a girl, but with God's help, that will work out, too. I talked to Hermine on the phone. She is "alright" and she is already not working. I'm sure she wrote about this to you, too. It is about time for her not to work. It is not that easy to be two places at once. But with God's help, let's hope to hear the best about all of us! Take care of yourself with love and I kiss you with love. Maria

1951/2/7 Marie to Irving (Book 8, 320-321)

2/7/51

My dear little Irving,

I got your letter that I was waiting so hard for and I'm glad to hear that thank God you are well. First of all, I wish you lots and lots of luck in your new job! I hope that the dear God will help you to be successful with your job! I hope it is what you want! You deserve it after waiting so long. Write about it and about everything. And how is Herman? What does he do? Yes, my dear Irving, as you wrote that you were very angry about the house. I believe that. But I can only say, that it is not worth it to dwell on the past. As you can see, there is not much that can be done about it. If I were you, I wouldn't destroy my nerves with that because it's not worth it. Sell it the way it is, one by one, for as much as they will pay for it. I know you will not get much for it, but there is no other choice, unless if you want to live that life. I think you would be better off if you would rent out a nice room and you would know that there is somebody who takes care of it and it is clean. You would have a whole different life. Tell me my Irving! Do you eat? Don't be sad that they don't pay a lot these days. With time, every job can be done. The only important thing is that you like it. Yes, my Irving! Last night Jane, Elsie from Cleveland's daughter, called me. She is here, you know, and she just told me that she is going to Columbia University for a year because she wants to be a teacher. I did not see her yet, but she said that she already started it for 6 days. I got a letter from Helen too and she also said that she is planning on coming here. I'm sure just to visit. I did not respond to her yet, but I will. It would be good for her, too. Now about us. I am well and I saw Hermine and they are thank God well. They send their greetings to you. Take care of yourself wherever you go. And eat! Herman, why don't you write? Yes, my Irving! Do you still have your car? Write about everything. I kiss you countless times with much of love. Maria

1951/3/2 Emil Schwartz to us, Israel (Book 3, 307-309)

March 2.51

My dearests,

It is said that when a man's stomach is full, he is in a better mood. I don't how much this applies in actuality, but I am in peace with my stomach and I feel great. That is to say, because of the package that you have sent me. I know you will be surprised to learn it has been a long time ago that I had anything as good as I ate today, namely meat. It has been two days since I received the package. I do not remember when I was so happy for anything as a gift. Hencsukam, don't believe that I have a big stomach, but when a person is over-hungry then nothing is a miracle, isn't that the truth? It was very satisfying especially because I know that you have sent it with pleasure. I've also received the letter with the photographs. Hencsukam, I cannot express your beauty and stature that you have. With pride, I took your picture and said to my friends that I also have someone for I am not alone. You children will not leave me alone, will you? Your husband is very good-hearted and blessed. I can say to both of you you're a good couple and you should be happy (amen). How do you live? Please write to me about everything if it doesn't become difficult for you. Don't be angry that I will make this letter short, but today I worked 10 hours and I am tired and it's a little late. Once again, I thank you for the beautiful and lavish package. I will be eating from it for a while. In conclusion, good luck and happiness to you both. Kisses to all of you, lots and lots of love. Your cousin, Emil

1951/3/12 Hermine to Irving (Book 10, 248-255) help support Emil

New York 3/10 - 1951

Dear Irving,

I'm sorry for not writing sooner but I hope you received my postal card I sent you last week. We are well and I met Maria last night. She is well too. I call her a few times a week but she thinks our home is too far for traveling so she comes very seldom. It's true but we couldn't help it and it is only about 15 minutes for Eugene from the store. That means a great deal that I don't have to spend all evenings in the kitchen. Maria told me she received a letter from you and that everything is well with you. Whenever you decide to visit us you're welcome. I don't know just when I'm taking my vacation this summer but I'm getting two weeks and I thought of staying in N.Y. We are close to Rockaway Beach and there are so many other places to go. So even if you come now, but maybe you could plan on coming again when I have my vacation then I could spend more time with you. Eugene takes off only one week but he has plans and we'll see. His brother got a good position and it is worthwhile to examine it. As you know he sold his store because that was too hard for him. He studied tailoring and sewing. Then he got a job for a place where they rent dress clothes for men. That means for wedding, graduation and so on. Today that man opened up a new store and Milton is his manager. He started with $75.00 and in June he'll get an increase. A business like that is good. I thought it would be good for you both. We'll see later. The owner is a professor in one of the N.Y. colleges, but he is a wealthy man. So Eugene thought of getting rid of his store if it is possible and start something where he makes money easier. That is I'm just telling you about this, but so far is just talk and don't mention this to anyone because it is just something we try to figure out and [is] not serious yet. How are you both? Let us hear from you. How is your work Irving? Did Herman get an increase yet? Elsie's daughter goes to college in N.Y. She came to see Maria, but so far I haven't had a chance because we just couldn't make it. I [would] like to have her come up here. She asked Maria for that already. Received a letter from Israel from Emil and he tells me about life there. He needs food. I'm enclosing his letter and you decide. I think we all should send him some food so he would have enough to eat. I think we should take him just like our brother. He is alone. He is our dear Mother's brother's child. Irving please forgive me, but I think Herman too should try. We [are] planning to send another package, but that's not enough because even if he has money there is no food enough for everyone. You see, Eugene figured that out for about $12.00 dollars he made up and sent a good package. That [was] mostly meats. Kosher canned meats, a fish. That is [at] cost. So if you want me to make the package I could do that. He is allowed to receive only to a certain amount, but we could find out so that he should have food. I tell you the truth I'm afraid to write about this to David because he doesn't have much. The business he owes money. That means [he] works with someone else['s] money. We give charities - so we should help our own. He feels lonely and a few lines would cheer him up. Don't have to tell no business just a few lines. He doesn't ask for anything but in his last letter and that was food. Please let me hear from you both. Herman, please would you do it for me. At least one package he should get every month. I'm willing, Maria is also - so let's try it! O.K? Love from us both

I did not tell to Eugene that I'm asking to do this deed.

P.S. If we look at the truth, our dear uncle Marton bacsi gave a few koronas for our spendings, this way we owe him. So, we should give it back to his son, that is, to send him food.

1951/4/10 Marie to Irving (Book 8, 325-327)

4/10/51

My dear little brother Irving!

As it seems all of us have become very lazy writers, but it [also] seems that I have to remind you to write a line sometimes. I hope to hear the best from you. Also, Hermine told me that she wrote to you too, but you did not respond yet. My Irving, you were always a good writer, but now you got lazy too. At least a couple of lines even if you are lazy. You can at least do that. Otherwise, how are you? And what do you do Herman? And you my Irving, how are you with the girl? When did you see her? Write about everything. About me everything is the same. I saw Hermine and they are also well and they send their greetings. Somehow it appears that we are very busy too. The relatives are well. I saw Bertha last night. And how is everybody there? Elsie's daughter Jane is still here. She called me on the phone. She was at home for a week. Otherwise everything is fine. And how's everything with the house? I hope you found some good solution, because it is about time. How's the weather there? It has been beautiful here for a few days. It is a true Spring. Now I will close my lines and I am sending my greetings from the heart and I kiss you countless times. Love, Maria Take care wherever you go and whatever you do and write immediately. M.

1951/4/15 Irving to Steffi Goodman (Book 6, 330-331)

April 15, 1951
Dear Miss Goodman,
It was a pleasure to receive your letter and thus to make your acquaintance. I do not know what my friend stated in her initial letter, but I believe that the points must have been well taken. I'm blond with blue eyes; 6' tall; and like good books, music, as well as sports. At the present I'm employed by the U.S. Government. I graduated from the Ohio State University, in the field of economics. In order to improve our friendship I assume that it would be feasible to enclose a snapshot at our next correspondence. Looking forward to hear more about you. Sincerely yours, Irving Gluck

1951/4/19 Marie to Irving (Book 8, 329-332)

4/19/51
My dear little brother Irving!
I got your letter which I could hardly wait for, and I'm glad to hear that thank God you are all well. I don't understand that you work at night. It is no surprise that you are so sad, but you should not be that way because we hope that God will help and with time you can improve, that is, in the meantime you can get another job. But the way I think my little Irving, you still live the way you did and that kind of life is not good for you. The only solution would be if you would start again in another city, where there are more young people and [live] in a clean apartment, where you can live your life, but not in Columbus. It would be the best in NY. Maybe you could submit a job application here for a government job. It is hard here in New York also, but I still think there are more opportunities and you would not get bored of life so easily. Boys like you should not talk yourself into this. You must control yourself. I could talk about myself like that also, but many people are like that with their life. What is important is to take care of yourself and eat. And at least you could work and eat together. It is good for you. Just take care of yourselves wherever you go. Otherwise I am well. My hand is better also. There is nothing particularly new. I just got a letter from Dorothy this week. She is sending her greetings to you too. Also, I saw Hermine and the others last night and she is very sorry that you sent that money, since you also might need it. She will write, too. When God will help, you will get married also. We will give it back. And until then, if you need anything, let me know my buddy. Yes my Irving, what's going on with that girl? Have you heard from her? I hope you could come to NY sometime to see us. It has been just a year that you were here at Passover. Now I have to go to Hermine's mother-in-law for two nights. Hermine and the others are going to be there, too. And how are you? Have the relatives called you? It would be good if you would be here. Even if we eat out, here it's still easier. Let's hope that the dear God will help us and everything will work out for the best. Yes, my dear Irving, I will note something to you. If you write to Hermine, don't mention that I mentioned to you about her, but write for the both of them because it does not come out good that you don't write to Eugene. He might think that you don't like him or you are angry at him. He does not write because Hermine writes in his name, too. And Hermine would feel good about it, too. I am writing this on my own because I know that you don't really want to write it, like we are all like this with that. I hope that your wish will come true and the secretary will write to you. It's never too late. Otherwise write about everything. If you respond to the letter, what kind of job you are doing? I hope it is an office job and it's not too hard. I still work where I was and right now the business is not too good. Everything is very slow now. Let's hope that it is going to be somehow. It will come out good. Now I will close my lines and I'm sending my greetings from the heart and I kiss you countless times with much love. Maria
Also, I wish a happy holiday for the both of you! And don't forget to write and take care of yourself.

5/2/51

My dear brother Irving,

Received your last letter. I was very happy to hear that thank goodness you are both ok. We are well. I saw Hermine yesterday evening. Everything is ok, just busy. How are you doing with your work? I hope you will not have to work this summer at night because it is not easy to do it. Otherwise, what's new with the home? What is your plan? Will you get a vacation this year? I don't know what I will decide, if I will go anywhere. Write about everything. About myself, it is the same. The relations are ok. Have you seen Flora or Mrs. Walters and family? My dearest brother Irving, you mailed the address to me in California and I lost it before I had a chance to write a thing. As of today I didn't send them a card yet, but if you see them tell them why I haven't written to them. I'm sorry for that. I don't have too much patience either to write. Oh yes, what happened with the girlfriend you mentioned in the previous letter? I hope to hear the best from both of you. Take care of yourself wherever you are going or whatever you are doing. I'm closing now wishing you all the best with all my heart and lots of kisses. Love, Maria

Received a letter from Dorothy. They are also well.

May 16, 1951

Dear Irving:

A thousand pardons for my neglect in not answering your letter sooner. My only excuse is lack of time. As you know I am down at the store every day, and when I do get home there is so much to do that the evening goes by with nothing accomplished as far as letter writing is concerned. Can you believe this? By the date above you will see when this letter was started. It is now Tuesday the 22nd and I am again going to attempt to finish this letter. Writing from the store seems an impossibility - always an interruption. Well, I'm happy to report we are all well and going along in the usual way. Business has been slow, as it seems to be all over the country. We hope though it will change soon for the better. You write you are working now for the Government, and I understand from Maria that Herman is also employed there. Is the job what you were looking for, or hasn't that come as yet? In what capacity is Herman employed? I sound like a census taker, but I do hope it's what you both want. My sister Anne was here visiting with me in March and naturally it was wonderful having her. I had hoped Dad would come too but that was wishful thinking. I was tempted to go back with her but I felt it was still too cold back East to take the baby. Incidentally your nephew is getting quite grown-up. He is starting to get a nice vocabulary and points out many things that catch his eye. Too bad you all can't enjoy him with us. I owe both Maria and Hermina letters but I hope they understand how difficult it is for me to write. We think of you all believe me. Love from all of us, Dorothy

5/18 - 1951

My dear little brother Irving,

[In Hungarian] We were very happy to [receive] your letter [and] that thank God you are all healthy and that you have opportunity to save a couple of days for a vacation. I know you know how much I do want to see you. Although I know you would like to visit David as well, so it depends on you, and do what you feel the best. David would like to see you too, but right now it is impossible by him, unless we are going to them. In the last letter [from them] Dorothy wrote that it is possible she will visit her parents in the summer. It is uncertain yet, but if it will work out, I would like you to come to NY. If not, then maybe I will go to Chicago because I would like to see the baby already. Although I don't want her to know that, and if she can't come to us only then would I go to Chicago. So, don't mention that to them. [In English] It will be a surprise. I'm happy to know you are working especially when you both can travel together, but I don't like night work. You have to do it, but what about Herman? How does he feel? Does he like his present job better? What does he do? Please let me know! Otherwise, everything is well with us. I saw Maria a few times this week. She met me at my business place. I also had her here for Sunday dinner. You know I made a dinner for the family - My Mother-in-law and Eugene's brother and family, Marie and Elsie's daughter Jean [Jane]. They said the dinner was good, but you know how that works out. I know you would like my cooking, but we are too far from one another. Last summer I couldn't even do that in your honor. Take care of yourself and let me hear from you again. Oh yes! News the latest!! is that Lester - Aunt Jenny's son is engaged. [In

Hungarian] That is, he got engaged. [In English] I spoke to Aunt Jenny and they are all very happy for him. Haven't seen our relatives for quite awhile. I might stop by at Jean Frey's tomorrow. I'm busy with myself and don't have too much time to go visiting. They were here a few times but Bertha and [her] husband only once. Her niece [Irene] arrived to Israel.

[On the side] Lots of love to you both, Hermina and Eugene

1951/6/2 Undated Hermine to Irving (Book 15, 188-191)

[Dated by Lester will marry in August]

New York 6/2

Dear Irving,

Received your letter and we were very happy to hear from you. It seems that now it will take a while before we'll see you, if you take your new job. Hope you'll like it. I never cared for night work. What about Herman? Is he going to keep working at night? On the other hand, is the new job more satisfactory to you? It pays only then. I imagine you started already so good luck to you. I wish you both could be here in N.Y. I couldn't talk you into it - but it is a better future. Every beginning is hard and takes a while, but after you [are] settled, it is much easier to improve. As you experienced it already so no need to tell you what it takes to start. I know that I disappointed Herman once when he wanted to come - New York is all right, but not in Nov, Dec, Jan, and Feb, so if you want to get a job you have to try in the other months of the year. In the above mentioned months you can be almost sure not to find a good job. I also explained to Herman he should be willing to pay out some money before he can make some - and he got scared from it. This time I can only tell you that you try with Arthur and if you like it, alright, if not you'll try something else, but not in Columbus. I explained that before and I still feel, here you can do better than in Columbus. Life and living can't be compared so you think about it. To me Columbus compared to N.Y. is like Europe or Polyán to Columbus. If I would know that before, I would tell you to study | accounting | very good field for it. Pretty late to tell you now. So don't worry, things will work out. I'm taking my vacation on the 20th of August. If Dorothy comes before I still would take off a few days. I would love to see you. Even my mother-in-law tells me my brothers should come closer to us instead of going to other cities. So I think she is all right. Hope you both are well and drop me a few lines again. With lots of love and good wishes, Hermine and Eugene

P.S. Lester [Gluck - Aunt Jennie's son] is getting married Aug 19. Hencsu Lefkovics from Helmec is also getting married June 12.

1951/6/28 Hermine to Irving (Book 10, 257-260)

New York 6/28. 51

Dear Irving,

Please forgive me for not writing you sooner. I didn't forget you, but somehow time goes by very fast. I hope you both are well and that your new position will work out satisfactorily. I sure hope so. I still think it would be very nice to have you here with us. I know it is not too easy, but if possible it is nice. How is Herman feeling? If he is smart he wouldn't suffer in case he isn't feeling well. He should go to a doctor. I don't trust Herman. If someone is ill then they'll do almost anything to get well. So if that's the case, come for a vacation and [we] will find a good Dr. for you. Just so happened that I'm writing this letter in the office. We are pretty slow so the manager didn't care what I'm doing. He saw I'm writing so I told him I must catch up with my writing. I don't know how to explain, but I tell you that I think of you, just my time is so limited that I never have a chance to sit down and write. My vacation starts in the 20th of August - maybe by then you [will] decide to come to N.Y. If Dorothy decides to come to Chicago then for a weekend I would go there to see her. Let us hear from you and I try to write you real soon. Love from us both, Hermina and Eugene

I see Maria quite often and she is well, too. Love, Hermina

1951/7/3 Marie to Irving (Book 8, 339-340)

7/3/51

My dear little brother, Irving,

It seems like time passes and we don't even notice it. I am in a hurry to write a couple of lines. I have not heard from you for a while. I hope you are well! And you my little brother, do you still work for Arthur? How do you like it? Do you work hard? I hope that everything will work out well. And what does Herman do? Does he still work at night? He needs to look after [himself]. This is not a life that he works at night. Also, what's going on with the house? Do you still live there? It is about time to look for another apartment or room. I am only surprised that you did not get bored with this life. I can't write anything particular about myself. We are well. Hermine and Eugene were by me on Sunday and they are well, they are just very busy. Yes, my Irving what's going on with the vacation? Will you take it? You should take some this year and go to some good place where there would be a little life at least. Right now I don't know if I will go anywhere. Write about everything. And how is Flora and her family doing? Yes, my dear Irving, do you still have your car? In case you would go somewhere, be careful! Take care, now I will close my lines, sending greetings from my heart and I kiss you countless times. I kiss you with much of love. Love, Maria

The relatives are well here. Lester is getting married on August 14th. I did not see the girl yet. I was officially invited to her engagement, but I didn't go. Bertha is going to Canada for a few days…This is the only news.

1951/7/21 Hermine to Irving (Book 10, 262-264)

New York 7/21 - 51

Dear Irving,

I read the letter you wrote to Maria. I'm glad to hear you are well. As you know, we are busy, that's the reason that I don't write so often, especially to you. We expect to take one week vacation and it would be nice if you could come, too. Even Herman could offer that much. You see that [it's] important just as much as eating and sleeping. I'm worried that you don't take care of yourselves. Hope everything is well with you. Received a letter from Dorothy and she probably told you about the good news. Well, I thought I'll see her this summer in Chicago but maybe next summer. How are you and your car? Do you still like it? Instead of a car, I have my apartment and I wish you could see it. I love it. It's beautiful. But my dear Bertha was here only once for 15 minutes. She must be jealous - - I met Marie last night and she is well. My mother-in-law is away for vacation and so is my sister-in-law, too. They are always asking for you, two different people told me I should let them know when Irving is in N.Y. I guess they have some nice girls for you. I'm sorry for not writing to the [Columbus] relatives, but will try one day. Tell them how busy I'm. How come Flora and the family didn't go away this year? Let us hear from you, Love from us both to both of you, Hermina and Eugene

1951/8/30 Hermine to Irving (Book 10, 266-268)

New York 8/30. 51

Dear Irving and Herman,

Here I'm again with a few lines. I hope you both are well and aren't working too hard. My vacation is almost over, but I still have an extra day. I'll be coming back Tuesday with the old routine. But I think it is wonderful to be able to work especially, if you divide your time with some relaxation. I miss you Irving - I hoped you'll be here for a few days, but the main thing is to be well and maybe soon you'll come to see us. I wrote to Dorothy and David and have some more corresponding to attend which, I neglect all year around. I was quite busy this week. I went shopping with my mother-in-law. We still have some more shopping to do. You can't always get the things you have in mind - not even in N.Y. Especially if you want to get [it] in a moderate price. So far we have very beautiful things. Irving I wish you would see it. I also have a wonderful husband, too. My mother-in-law is always asking for you and said it would be nice if we all could be together. They are plain, honest people and, they like me very much. I hope and wish that you meet a nice girl. New York has some nice girls too and [you] only need a little time to get to know them. I'm almost sure that is what Herman should get. If he would meet a nice girl and she would make a good home for him. What can the future be for an old bachelor? I hope he wouldn't want to become one! You? I'm not worried! but you deserve the best and can get one too. So I would suggest to pick what you think is just right. I'm not a preacher but it seems I'm doing some preaching so don't mind me. I feel I'm just talking to you. You know we could do even better if we could get together. I don't have Arthur's home address please send it to me and I'll try to write them a few lines. By the way, did you get an invitation to Lester's wedding? It was nice and cost plenty of money, but I think ours was nicer. That is just between you and me! I called Maria today and went to see her last week to Mrs. Kugler. She is very happy if I come up there. But I [would] like Maria to find a place for herself. It was enough of it already. It pays to look around she might have better luck some other place. We can't afford to sit down and wait. Time is precious and the past will never come back so every minute should be enjoyed at least. The same goes for you also. We can't say that [it] is easy because we all must work, but isn't it better to know that after work you're free and [can] do what you enjoy most. I would say it is a men's world and just anybody can get around and you are all alone! If Herman could find a job I bet in six months he wouldn't want to move anywhere! God forbid - I'm afraid to force the issue - So do what you think, to me all start[ing] is hard but on the end you're better off. So long and take care of yourself. Let us hear from you. Our love to you both, Hermina and Eugene

1951/9/21 Marie to Irving (Book 8, 342-344)

9/21/51

My dear little brother, Irving!
As it appears, you have become very lazy with writing, too. I hope you are all healthy! What do you do? Write immediately. There is nothing particular about me, everything is the same. I am well, but as always I am very busy. I got a letter from Dorothy yesterday and I thought that you also hear about them. Otherwise, everything is well. I saw Hermine yesterday and thank God they are well too. They send their greetings to you. How about you, my Irving? Do you still work at Arthur's? And what does Herman do? Does he still work at night? Write about everything! What's going on with the house? Do you still live there? Take care of yourself wherever you go. I hope you will not forget about eating! How's the weather by you? It is a real summer day here. And now I wish you a very happy New Year! And I hope that we will hear the best about each other and [we should] be in the best of heath! Now I will close my lines, sending my greetings from the heart and I kiss you countless times with love. Maria

1951/10/16 Hermine to Irving (Book 10, 273-275) mentions Emil

New York 10/16 -51

My dear little brother Irving!
I got your letter and I was very happy about it. The poem is very touching and thank you for it! Eugene loves it too. If it entertains you, then it is time very well spent. I already knew that you are a very talented boy, there is only one problem, that you still did not find people who would appreciate it. That is why I am preaching to you because I think it is too bad for every day wasted. The important thing is for you to be satisfied and then I will be happy, too. I thought that Herman already made up his mind, but for him it is a big deal. Others go every 6 months or once a year to travel to see the world. It can't hurt, it just could cost a few dollars. What is important is that you are not angry at me that I'm preaching about it in every letter of mine. [In English] I mean well, that's the most important thing. Hope you both are well and will let me hear from you. I just wrote to Dorothy and to Emil in Israel. Maria & I sent him $15.00 through an organization and he can buy whatever he needs in Israel. I hope it works out for him, then I would like to send some shirts and underwear. Whenever you decide to give him something I could take care of it because there is a great need of food. So many people suffer from hunger and there isn't much they can do about it. Now I'm waiting to hear from him and then I'll send him a package. He is a fine boy and we must help him just like our brother, especially with food. I'll write you again, but let us hear from you. Love, Hermine and Eugene

1951/11/1 Emil Schwartz to Hermine, Jaffa (Book 3, 268-272)

1.11. Jaffa

Beloved Hermine,
Your long-awaited letter has arrived with a check on October 27. I can't remember when I was so happy. I was happy for both the letter and the check at the same time. I'm surprised that you haven't received my previous letter Herminkem or my New Year's card. I mailed them to you about two months ago. I hope that during that time that you have received them. Did you? I do not receive cash for the check immediately because there are hundreds of people receiving checks at the same time. Everyone gets a number and then it takes about two weeks before I can receive the cash, including the package also. After 10 days I'll go to the bank and by then, my number will come up. Now I can tell you, concerning this it's much better if you send me a package because here they ask twice as much as what it costs you there. I know this because my neighbor [a woman] gets packages weekly from her uncle, either a check or a package. Here our fellow Jews work according to the black market. Therefore Hermine, if you shop there for $15 then you could send me almost double what I could get here. The only difference is that the check comes in fast, whereas the package comes very slowly. Hermine, I hope that I may reply sincerely to your question regarding the beddings? If

I'm too forward with my letters you should caution me that I am being rude (you have the right to tell me). I am sorry to tell you, but it's best that I tell you the truth about my bedding situation. If you saw it, you wouldn't believe it that Patyu-bacsi's [Uncle Márton] son is dressed so poorly. I don't want you to misunderstand me, so I'm going to explain why I don't have [anything decent to wear]. I don't like to write about this, because I would like to forget this ugly incident, however, I would like you to see why exactly I have this problem with clothing. As you know Hermine, after the concentration camp I was freed and I was by myself. My cousin Zoli would have been my guardian because I was underage. My poor father, before he died, told me where he buried gold, silver, and dollars in a small place in the ground. When I returned from the camp, I found some items [of what he had hidden]. I discussed everything with Zoli. At that time he was an upright individual (he was not yet married). We decided that we would convert everything I found into dollars and I'd put it away until the time comes that I needed it. That's the way it was. As you know, I've studied dentistry and I was living from that money. I didn't have any need for anything from what Zoli had. As a young man, I felt relaxed one hundred percent because of my little wealth, but regretfully I trusted him too much, and I had to pay for it. Zoli got married and he completely changed. It would have been of no concern to me if he would not have done what he did. Before my immigration [to Palestine], I went to him and asked him to please give me my money because I would like to buy things before I go to the new country, where I don't have anyone, and a person should have some money with him. He replied that he was very sorry, but he can't give it back because there's nothing left. I thought for a moment that he was merely teasing me, but after he explained that he had to keep up his house and had other expenses and he used a lot from mine and the money disappeared and he himself has only a little left over. I don't know what other people would have done, but I turned around and I left him. Regretfully, because of this, I was penniless as I left home, and I know now what it means to buy every piece of clothing and bedding. This wouldn't be a problem if it wasn't so costly to secure it here. [In Israel], everything is obtained according to points. I can't afford to get it for a decent price [and] I can't pay the black market price. My dear Hermine, you can see that despite my situation, I am not envious. Don't take this that I'm complaining but it's somewhat true as the saying goes, that lightening always strikes the same place. Therefore, my dear Hermine, if you want to help me, I will answer your questions regarding sizes that I wear. They are the following: my shirt size is 39, my pants size is 44. I have shoes. I looked at my socks, but my socks don't have a size marked on them. I don't know how it's called, but one wears it under the regular shirt, [in America] it may be called Trico. Here you can't live without it because it's very hot and this will be excellent because it absorbs sweat. I don't know where to get it at the market here. I don't have the courage to ask you for all of this, and I'm ashamed of myself, but I want you to know it's a must to have it, what can I do? Also, if it's not too difficult for you Hermine, then if you really want to help me, send pillow covers and bed sheets. All of these please send them to me if it does not cause too much difficulty for you. I can't over emphasize what it would mean to me. But you, Hermine, probably can see that I'm not asking for these things lightly. I will let you know what I bought with the check and how much money they gave in the exchange. I believe that you'll be interested to know. In advance Hermine, I am not hungry because I'm satisfied just by thinking of the good meat in the package. It's time for me to close this letter because I think you will get tired of this long letter. Hermine write, both of you! I'm waiting impatiently for you to write. Please tell Eugene to write to me, even if it's only to send his regards, but please write because if he doesn't then I'll think that I'm creating difficulties for him. Maria, I always put you as an afterthought in my letters, but please don't take it that way. I'm a little bit tired and I'm unable to concentrate for another letter so this letter naturally speaks to you, too! In any event, I am very grateful to you Maria, and thank you for the package and its contents, the good G-d should pay you! Kisses to all of you and true love, your cousin, Emil.

1951/12/28 Private Paul Kalinchak to Irving (Book 15, 70-74)

[Enclosed note from Hermina]
Irving dear - maybe you know who sent this Christmas card to you with all good wishes - so I enclose the address - maybe you [would] like to write to him. Love, Hermina

December 27
Pontoye, PA

Dear Irving,
It was such a pleasure to receive your card. I apologize for not sending one. But in any case, best wishes for the New Year. This winter I am at school again - working on my Master's degree at Pennsylvania State College (Art Education). Last year I taught grades 6-12 in a public school in a suburb of Cincinnati, Ohio. I

expect to return there next year, although not to the same school. I have enjoyed my work at Penn State. Viktor Lowenfeld is head of the department there. He is just about the leading man in art education today. Formerly from Vienna he came to the US about 1940. He is a very fine person and I have acquired much from him. How are you and your work? Perhaps when I return to Cincinnati we could meet somewhere for a weekend. I would enjoy seeing you again. I believe it was 1943 when we met at Shenango, PA or was it at Canastel, North Africa? I am not sure. I met so many different people that year. If you have the opportunity, write a few lines. I would enjoy hearing from you. Sincerely, Paul Kalinchuk

1952/1/19 Hermine to Irving and Herman (Book 10, 280-281)

New York 1/19 - 52
Dear Irving and Herman,
Several weeks passed by since we heard from you. We hope everything is well with you. Have you received those books I sent you? We bought them when we were in the country last summer. Dr. M. Banks lectured there and everyone liked him. We thought it's good. Ever since, I meant to mail them to you. Beside that I thought of Herman and his illness. You see as I'm studying that he might have ulcers. I hope not! Even then he can take care of himself. The main thing is to watch his diet. His diet should be warm milk, sweet cream, cooked fruit, toast, soft boiled eggs. Don't get hungry. Don't eat raw fruit or vegetables or greasy food. No juices either. When you feel better then after breakfast drink juice. You see [a] nervous stomach will cause that. I'm writing you this because you never tell us how you feel and I know you must suffer. When I had my accident 2½ years [ago] I suffered from stomach burn[ing] and ever since I'm thinking of that diet. I think I mailed you some powder to take but you never even answered if you tried it or not. Let me know then I'll get it for you. Thank God it never bothered me since. By the way my case came up and they want to settle for $1,500, but half of that goes to the lawyer and Dr. bills. Herman warm milk when you have [heart] burn is like medicine. Haven't heard from Dorothy [for] quite a while. I hope they are well. The weather wasn't too good and [I] surely hope they are well. Otherwise we are well. In a couple of days I'm leaving my job that means I'll have more free time to write and to fix up our home. When are you coming to N.Y.? Please little brother let us hear from you. Everyone is asking for you. Take care of yourselves, with lots of love, Hermine and Eugene.

1952/2/1 Undated Hermine to Irving (Book 10, 277-278) sent shoes clothing to Emil

Dear Irving,
I received your letter and the 20.00 dollars. Thank you very much. I'm going to send him the package. We mailed one about two weeks ago so I'm sending one in about 1 week. We sent him clothing and shoes. I hope it will fit him. We are going to send food in the next package. Eugene likes Emil and wants to send him packages, but I mentioned it to you because this way he can get more. No matter how, but one person wouldn't do the same. Thank you both very much. Maria sent him a syrup which he got very fast and then he buys what he needs more but he wrote as you'll see in the enclosed letter that he is much better off with the package we are sending him. Eugene pays wholesale so it costs me about 12 dollars for 20 pounds, that means something he'll really enjoy. Otherwise we are well and busy as usual. Hope you both are well, too. I'm writing from business again so I'm short, but will try to write you again. Let us hear from you. Till then, our love and best wishes. Love, Hermina and Eugene

1952/2/21 Emil Schwartz to Hermine and Eugene, Jaffa (Book 3, 262-267)

Jaffa March 21. II / 52
Dear Hermine and Jenő [Eugene]!
I believe I can explain my long silence. About two months ago I received a letter from you Hermine and it arrived just as I had to report to military service for five weeks. Every year one has to go for [army reserve] duty. This causes problems because after you finish the service [reserve duty], you lose your job because by the time you return they usually hire someone else. Therefore, I'm unemployed now and I'm looking for work every chance I get. Unfortunately I haven't been able to find a job. I hope that in a couple weeks I will work. If I don't get the job to drive a taxi, then I'll have to look for something else. This is what happens when you're employed, but you're not your own boss. The main thing is to be healthy and everything will turn out okay somehow....I almost became bitter because of my misfortune, but when your beautiful package arrived - I can't find the words for what you've done for me. My dear Hermine, you can't imagine it. First of all, everything, every piece, each item individually is beautiful and fits me perfectly. It's [all] very good

and beautiful. I need it as desperately as one needs a piece of bread. As I opened the package, I tried every item on. Each [thing] you sent fits as if it was measured to my size. Hermine, I must mention the shoes separately. Whoever bought the shoes must have good taste. It has to be a man, most likely it was you, Jenő. I'm not trying to exaggerate, but everyone who saw them, admired them. For the bed sheets and pillow covers I made a separate holiday because I have been sleeping in a bed without any sheets. What I had has disintegrated. I don't want you to think that I'm exaggerating, therefore I'm not going to detail the rest of the items, but the fact is, every piece is very valuable to me. In the first place, the economic conditions here in this country [Israel] make it impossible to buy it. If you can, you have to be a wealthy person, only they could afford it. For example, with the income I would receive from one day's work, I could not purchase even one necktie from the three that you sent me. I can tell you something even nicer. The issue is I could not have purchased it here at all because it's impossible to find it here. If you could, you would have to work for a whole week, and then there would be no money left for food. Therefore one must be resigned from even walking in these magnificent shoes...Unfortunately, it is very sad to be in this country now. I'm sure you know the situation. I don't know where this will lead us to. The only thing I'm certain of is that there's no future here for an individual. I don't know my dear Hermine, perhaps I'm in a bad mood, and because of that I'm writing everything! I only know that from day to day it's more difficult to make a living (not only for me but on average). Think of what it means to stay in line for a loaf of bread for hours before a person gets one. I know that you won't believe this situation and I hope you'll never have to know what it means. We've become accustomed to not eating meat for months. Whatever we can get we are happy with and those that never ate anything good may think that this is an exaggeration. The situation is such that we don't know how to solve it. Every evening we are waiting for a miracle to happen, but it just doesn't want to come. Let's not discuss whether this is true, because I believe we are little people and we are unable to help with this. With regards to myself, the problem is that I can't afford to get a room. They ask fantastic prices for a very small room that I'll never be able to buy. I take from my mouth a few pennies so that I can save, but this is not life for a young man. I would like to get married Hermine, because it will be easier for two people to get through this problem. As I wrote you before there is a young woman that I would like to marry, however as wrote you in the past, I don't have a place to live and because of that, we are unable to get married. This is the reality here, it's a miracle to be healthy. Regarding this Hermine, I have one thing I'd like to ask you if you are not going to get angry at me. I'm sure you know how important it is for a man who wants to be a groom to get some gift for this young woman. I would do it, but without money I can't buy anything. If you have something that you don't wear Hermine, like a white night gown, you know what ladies want. I hope I'm not making it difficult for you, but please do it for me. You would help me tremendously with that. And if you have any nylon stockings, or clear ones, even if they have a run in them down the side, that's no problem, they can fix it here. Even if it's used, it's no problem either, because whatever you have can be worn. This young woman is pretty like you. I'm asking you for used items hoping that it will not create a problem for you. If Jenő has any used clothing that he doesn't need or use, I'll be glad to accept it. Forgive me for being very forward, but this is due to necessity. To conclude, I have tried your patience with this long letter. I promise next time I will write a shorter letter. Hermine and Jenő, I want to thank you for your good deeds and G-d should repay you for them. I have been so occupied with myself I just discovered that I didn't ask how you are and how life is with you? I would like to hear some good news from you and the family. Please write everything about all of you. I'm waiting for your lines as soon as possible. Lots of love and kisses to all of you, your cousin, Emil.

P.S. Everything arrived perfectly as you have written it to me. There were some changes, as I noticed, there may have been a necktie. I'm curious what was the paper that was included before they changed it. Please let me know Herminkem.
It was a good idea to wash all these things. Kisses as above

1952/2/28 Hermine to Irving (Book 22, 284-288)

My dear little brother Irving!
Forgive me that I did not write to you until now. Although, I truly did not want to neglect my response. It is true that I am very lazy. Politely, the reason is that sometime in the beginning of September with God's help, you will become an uncle and Herman as well. Therefore I have plenty of time, and I have an excuse. I did not write this news to Dorothy yet. If you do write, don't mention it. I want to write it in person, so I will not offend them. [continuing in English] Maria was here last week and calls me quite often because I have a telephone. I don't do much traveling now so who ever wants to visit us are welcome. Eugene is quite busy. He is always wondering why do you have to stay in Columbus - My Mother-in-law feels the same way.

They would like it if my family is closer to us. They left to Florida for a few weeks. We never heard from Emil yet we mailed two packages - He never wrote about the package we sent the clothing - hope he'll get it all right. It should be there by now. We still have some money left from yours so later on we'll make up another package. If you want to send it's alright. Sometimes it takes a while till Eugene finds time to make it up and especially to take it to the post office. So whatever you like, do. Do you still have your car? At least that gives you some pleasure. Please be very careful with driving especially in Ohio. I understand you had a cold and probably icy winter. Let us hear from you and I'll try my best, too. Oh yes, Emil's address is

Emil Schwartz
BISVIL [Hebrew 'for']
c/o Zahava Braun R293 B5
Jaffa Israel

Otherwise everything is well with us. I listen to the radio, mostly live a lazy life. As soon as I feel like traveling we want to finish up our home. First of all to get a television set. I'll write again till then, our love to you both. Give my love to the relatives and some day I'll write to them, too. Love, Hermine and Eugene

1952/3/15 Undated Hermine and Eugene to Irving (Book 18, 4-5) before Passover - missing pg 1

[This seems to go here in 1952. Before Pesah 1950, Hermine wouldn't be writing to Irving because he was coming to NY for Hermine's wedding, 1951 they were sending food packages, by 1953 Hermine would sign Linda]

Page 2

I'm going to make up a package with women's clothing this week and we like to send him a few things for Pesah. On second thought I figured out that if you want to send sometimes, I could do it so that I get those papers to fill in from the post office and then Eugene could send the package with the boy to the post office. So Irving, it's up to you how you want to decide. I know only that they suffer plenty. Eugene likes him and now he wants me to send him rubbers and a rain coat. So as soon as [I] have a chance for shopping I'd like to do it. How are you both? Let us hear from you and about everything. Emil's new address is Emil Schwartz, Jaffa, R. 293 M. 10, Israel. That's all for now. I'll write again. Remember me to the relatives. Is your apartment warm? Get rid of it already. You don't need to save the furniture. You may even sell the sewing machine. We are going to buy a new one! Take care of yourselves. Let us hear from you. Love, Hermina and Eugene

1952/3/18 Hermine to Irving (Book 10, 283-284)

New York 3/18 - 52
Dear Irving,
We received your letter and as you know we are always happy to hear from you. Hope the business you have planned will work out all right. We sure wish you lots of luck. The only thing we were thinking that a business of that sort might be for down payment. As Eugene said in N.Y. that's the most popular way of buying and would be pretty hard otherwise. Let us know what you have in mind in arranging your business. The main thing is to try and I don't blame you and lots of luck little brother! I just wrote to Dorothy and Maria heard from them last week. Dorothy wrote that David thought Frederick Jerome sings Hungarian. That must be something to hear. Maria is all right, calls me quite often. Haven't seen the relatives for a long time. Bertha and Jeann Weinberg calls me once in a while. That's all for now, but will write again. Take care of yourself and when Herman decides to come he should do so. Love to you both from us, Hermina and Eugene

1952/3/19 Sam Fried to Irving (Book 17, 335-340)

Pardes Hanna [Israel]
March 19, 1952
Dear Mr. Gluck,
Received your letter of March 4th with pleasure. I owe you many thanks for you have come to my aid. Help to us is very important since we at the present live in the world's greatest impoverished place. If dear Arthur and you would not be thinking of us, then it would be an impossibility to exist. In the previous letter the

Page 700

picture indicates the home in which we live. If my dear wife wouldn't be with me, then I couldn't have held out till this time. During the past six months I aged ten years and lost 12 pounds. I cannot get accustomed to the food here. The tent furnishing is from the following: 4 wooden horse upon which 2 boards rest; upon this 2 straw sacks, and 4 light covers. My coat is the pillow. My wife's coat is an additional cover; 2 tin plates; 2 spoons; 2 forks, and 2 cups. The evenings and mornings are very cold. We have a lot of rain and wind at the present, so at times it rains in and the wind hammers the sides of the tent. In the past we had a flood that crippled traffic for 4 days and many homes were destroyed from it. All our hope was with Mr. Benozer. He promised to relocate us, but it has been now 7 months without any result. I don't know if I can trust in him any longer. Here the people promise everything, but fail to keep their promises. Their mentality is different than it was in Europe. Shortly, I'll look up Mr. Benozer again, and since he may not be able to fulfill his promise, I'll look for another solution because here I can't stand it any longer. He promised me without asking for his help, but he has not done anything in my interest. Dear Mr. Gluck, I want to inform you that I received the 4 addresses of scale buyers, also the catalogues. Further, I want to inform you that I have examined the scales of Gantz Shemial Kibbutz and they were in excellent shape. Benozer gave me the address. I would like to know if this is your manufacturing, since the insignia is The Elect Scale Co. serial 229600. 2 plates split of which I have written previously to Arthur. Please inform me if the parts will be sent. Forgive me for such a lengthy letter. Every move will rest upon the fulfillment of my responsibility. Thank you for Mr. Schwartz's address. I'll visit him at some occasion. I'm awaiting your reply with heartiest regards. Sam

1952/4/6 Undated Marie to Irving (Book 6, 111-114) before Passover - blue border

[Dated to 1952 because of the blue bordered stationary that Marie uses again in 1952/4/30 Marie to Irving (Book 6, 70-73) missing last pages - blue border]

My dear little brother Irving!

I can't imagine why I don't hear from you. I hope you are all well! Write immediately. I am well and also very busy like everybody else. Although, it is true that before we realize it, time goes by quickly. Otherwise how are you, my little brother? It is not worth it to work too hard. I hope that you take time to eat. What does Herman do? Does he plan to come here? I won't believe it until he will be here. And how do you expect to stay at home? It is going to be hard enough for you, too. But you know better how it will be best. I hope that with God's help everything will work out for the best. How are the relatives? Flora and the Aunt [Helen]? Where will you be for Passover? Did they invite you? I don't know what I am going to do yet, if I am going to go somewhere. I am working and this way it is very hard to even go to Hermine. She wants me to be there with them, but I don't know yet. I talked to Hermine yesterday and they are well, but like everyone they are busy with themselves. Plus they live very far from me. Mrs. Kugler is well and her family is sending their best to you and also to the relatives. I talked to the Aunt [Jennie] and she was wondering about you too and sending her best. Otherwise everything is the same. I'm sorry that I am not writing anything special. Now take good care of yourself and don't forget to eat. Hermine and Eugene are sending their best from their heart and kiss you with love. Love Maria

1952/4/24 Hermine to Irving (Book 10, 286-291)

New York 4 / 24 - 52

Dear Irving,

It was so wonderful to hear your voice over the telephone. It was almost like seeing you personally. We hope it wouldn't be long before we do have a chance to see you. Sorry Herman wasn't there to talk to us, but he wouldn't do it any way. Boy I would love to fix him up. I mean marrying him off! I spoke to my mother-in-law and she has a girl for you. I thought maybe we could ask her if she is interested to correspond then you could write to her, but Eugene thinks I should meet the girl first. So I guess he is right. You see, he was introduced once to a girl on a blind date by Mrs. Noti and when they wanted him to meet me he wouldn't do it, and had quite a time to make him come up to see me. With the first girl he was very much disappointed so that's what he thinks is best. He said you deserve the best and I agree! I also spoke to Eugene's aunt and she is always asking about you. This time she again told me that if you'll come she would like to introduce you to a nice girl. That is that! Otherwise everything is as usual. Eugene is busy, but I'm home most of the time. I don't like to travel, every one is quite a distance from us. Now that we have the telephone I get a couple of calls every day. That informs me about some of the family. Bertha and Jeannie Frey call me. Some of my friends and Helen Frank from the business I used to work. Aunt Jenny wouldn't make a call it costs money you know. They are disappointed because I didn't have them over for dinner. I asked them once last summer, but they wouldn't come because I asked Bertha and H and Jeanne and H. They are like fire if they get together. None of them was here for dinners. You see when I went to business I hardly had time for it. I thought it is easier to have them all together and no one would feel hurt that they weren't the first ones to be invited. Since I'm home Aunt Jenny never called - I called her twice. She told me they'll come over whenever I want, but tell them when. That means I should have something nice. I feel that as far as they are concerned I come first. Now I want to take care of myself and not worry about relatives. Don't you think I'm right? If they come they are welcome. I meant to write to the relatives, but didn't do it so far so please remember me to them. I try to keep busy at home and time really flies by very fast, at least if you could be near to us well, we could get together. Let us hear about you when you have a chance. I want to write to Dorothy yet. Don't work too hard! Even if business didn't work out at least you tried. I wrote a long story this time you might even get tired reading it. Oh, yes, Bertha's niece from Israel, Sarolta's daughter [Iren] expects to be in Canada some time in May. Take care of yourself and drop us a line if you'll get a chance. Love from us both, Hermine and Eugene

1952/4/30 Marie to Irving (Book 6, 70-73) missing last pages - blue border

4/30/52
My dear brother Irving,
As you can see I try to write a few lines. I hope my lines will find both of you in the best of health. I'm fine. And you made me happy by calling and I was able to talk to you for at least a few minutes. You shouldn't neglect writing because you become very estranged from someone else unless you write a page [once in a while], just like you talk about David. We must not look at his example. You know he would never write because he has no patience for it. Luckily, Dorothy is like she is, at least she writes. But it's hard enough for him because he has to go home and be in the store. You should write to him, too. When I was there David was angry that you didn't write to him. I told him why - he wanted you to write to him, when you didn't write to him either. And besides all that, he expects you to write to him. And I think the smarter one lets go. But let me leave it at that. And take great care of yourself with your car.

1952/5/10 Dorothy to Irving (Book 12, 274-275)

Thursday

Dear Irving:
I'm visiting my folks and will be here the month of May. Any chance of your coming here to see your nephew and me? I'm returning to California on June 1st. All here are well, I'm happy to report. Hope this finds you and Herman OK, too. Please let me hear from you. Love, Dorothy
All send regards to you.

1952/7/23 Tonti and Bill Zuhl to Irving (Book 16, 78-80)

7-23
Dear Irving!
We were very happy for your letter, since we are facing a big problem to see what to do. I will refer starting from the time when they left. At that night there was an interest to look at the car. Of course, they did not want to give more than $100 for it and even that they wanted to finance. Although, I agreed with them to pay it over four weeks, but then I should get $125 for it. They promised to come back the next day, but we did not see them since then. There was a couple of interested [people], but they did not even want to hear about it for that much. Now it is Sunday 20:00 o'clock [8pm] we posted another advertisement. There was a old Jewish man who came early in the morning. He was looking for one for his daughter and said that they will call us, but that wasn't even true. To tell you the truth, I thought that I will not be able to sell it. There was not really anybody serious. Finally there were two boys coming who wanted to give the $100 for it. The problem will come now. Should we give it? Should we not? I thought that would be the first opportunity, maybe we should not let it go. I took the money from the boys and of course we held back the car until we write the title over. I thought in the meantime I can ask you, if you want to give it for that price or not. If not, I thought I will use it as an excuse that I could not write it over, since there was no authorization officially authenticated. All this happened on Sunday afternoon and on Monday morning we got his letter where he leaves it up to us how we will do it with our best knowledge. And I don't know, my dear Irving, if I did it right or not. But I thought this is a sure thing, who knows if there will be another serious buyer or

not and I sold it. Although at the signing over there was an obstacle, that it was not authenticated by a notary, they did not want to sign it over, and the boy wanted to take his money back already. But last night we found somebody who got it done. Now I don't know if Herman will be satisfied with the price, but believe me we could not get more for it, nobody else wanted to give even the $100 for it, like this boy. We will send the money over with today's mail. Yes, I did not give the spare tire. Maybe we could get something for that also. I'm glad you got a cheap apartment, I am very sure that you will get a good job too, it only takes patience. Maybe you already got one by now. Surely we miss you, but it is important that you will get to your goal. Nothing important has happened to us that is worth mentioning. The heat is terrible. I guess it could be hot there too. Otherwise how do you like your new life? Write dear Irving about everything and take care of yourself! Lots of love and greetings to all of you. The Zuhl family.

1952/7/28 Roberta Gluck to Irving (Book 17, 236-239)

Wed 7/28/52
Dear Irving,
The Friday that I came into N.Y. with my sister I was unable to contact you. I did leave a message, I presume it was with your landlady that I was in the city, but that I was leaving that same day. I am sorry about that. We came home last Tuesday, and I find I have been on the go since. Four days I spent at Penn State with my roommate, and since, I have obtained a part time job for the remainder of the summer working in a drugstore here in town. There aren't too many weeks remaining before I return to school - - - of which I am very anxious. I do miss my school friends - - that is having people who think as I do to converse with. By now I hope that you are settled and know just what you are going to do - as far as a job is concerned. I realize it can be quite frustrating not knowing just what you are going to do. Good luck to you - And Irving, thank you very much for being so considerate and driving me to Lakewood. I certainly did appreciate the effort involved. My regards to your sisters and brother. Yours truly, Robbi

1952/8/15 Sam Gluck to Irving (Book 14, 328-331)

This is the first chance I have had to write, and now that I have a few moments, perhaps we can bring each other up to date. Please excuse the handwriting and the paper, but you can well surmise conditions here. I have to snatch a few moments when I can. First of all, my mother tells me that you have a good job; I'm anxious to hear all about it. Frankly, I'd also like to know what the salary is - and this now comes to my side of the story. I am awaiting notice from Columbia University as to whether or not I'm admitted to the graduate school in philosophy. Frankly, I want to go to school only if I cannot get a job before hand. I've struggled over and over again, as you know, trying to come to a solution to my problem. The academic career is a sound venture to embark upon except for two things. One is the four or 5 more years of "marking time" before I can even start to stand on my own feet, and the other is the fact that the only independence from certain other things is real and complete independence. From what my mother read to me of your letters, you sound as though you are happy in your decision to leave Columbus and Bonded. I think it is the right thing for me to do, too. When the break comes it must be quick, complete, and permanent. Four more years of school will not accomplish that. I've been learning some very valuable things about the job situation; I'm afraid that my scattered qualifications and lack of deep experience in one single thing will be a handicap, but _____ well _____. I would be grateful for any help or suggestions you have. If I'm admitted to Columbia my idea is to go to N.Y. immediately and just find a room as a student, near the University. I will make all arrangements, but will not pay fees until the last day in hopes of finding a job. If I don't, at least I'll be putting in my time properly. Also, I'll be able to keep in touch with opportunities much better if I am in N.Y. I've got a few very slim contacts, but I plan to contact the best employment agencies, and - if there is one - the city or state bureaus. What do you think? Hopes of landing a job close to $6000.00 per year are - I suppose - ridiculous. Can you get me Jane Schallheim's latest address? Give my love to all the family, and write me soon. Sam
Box 566
Columbus, 16, Ohio

1952/8/15 Undated Irving to Samuel Gluck - draft reply (Book 6, 262-270)

Dear Samuel,

Upon return from Clairmont Terminal - a receiving and shipping point for the Atlas Contractors in New Jersey, I found your letter. It is indeed a pleasure to hear from you and the decision which you are about to make. It is true that some difficulties lie ahead of you, but if you are determined to solve your problem, then you ought to make a sort of checklist in regards to the advantages and disadvantages that do exist. On this matter, my opinion is that you ought to be diplomatic, since the sudden break that you state which "must be quick, complete, and permanent" cannot be regarded as a wise move. One is unable to read into the future with much accuracy. Life as you know is a bitter struggle throughout. We at times think that the grass is greener on the other side of the fence. It is true that a change must be made due to the fact that other important matters of life must be fulfilled. One of these, the social, is an important one. I think that one can accomplish this end here more so in favor of our desire, than in a small city as Columbus. To attain happiness, in accordance with Schopenhauer, one may attain that goal anywhere, since happiness to him means absence of pain. But truly, happiness is gained by having peace of mind. To land a good job, with the probability of growth in valuable experience and monetary return, takes plenty of time. Therefore, I'm not attempting to discourage you, but merely indicate an observation that can happen. By now you may have received a favorable reply from Columbia graduate school. That may not solve the intricate problem, but it seems to me that you'll gain contacts there, plus your time will not be wasted. [The] accomplishment will be immeasurable in terms of knowledge - the asset that no one can take away from you. It will also give you a good opportunity to solve your social problem. To sum up the whole situation, I sympathize with you. But I wish to remind you that try to be diplomatic. Try to indicate that your departure is due to social (progress) problem that must be solved. Thus, you'll leave the region with a clear conscience. My present assignment is helping economically gain that goal. I'm getting $60.00 for 40 hours, plus all benefits. Paid holidays, 2 weeks vacation per year, 2 weeks sick leave. Probably periodic increases in wages. To elaborate further upon securing this job, [it] was a simple sort of thing. Although it involved in filling out application forms daily for weeks with other companies, employment agencies, private, gov't. During this process I gained enough insight as to how and what to say in my application and interview. Your qualifications with the amount of experience can be interpreted by prospective employers in various ways. Some employers prefer individuals with broad backgrounds, but they may think only in terms of one who is capable to learn and accept new ideas. Usually in a new organization you get a training period. Thus I wouldn't worry about that problem. Secondly, if you intend to enroll in Columbia, if you are unable to get a good assignment, then being here you'll have all the opportunities to make contacts and to land a job which may give you the remuneration of $6,000/year. All depends on luck. But, be prepared to take something less with a good org[anization], until you find what you really want. To avoid living from the bank account. Let me hear from you. If at any time I can be of any help, with best of my ability, I'll do so. I remain with love from us all

1952/8/20 Katelin (Tonti) and Bill Zuhl to Irving (Book 16, 41-43)

8-15

Dear Irving!

We will forgive your long silence, because of the result you achieved. In six-seven weeks [you've taken] a couple of steps from zero. I could say that happened quickly. After all, they have a lot of money to pay for Capitalists. Just go ahead my little boy! I'm proud of you, unless you will not be a capitalist to the blood, and especially if you will forget your hard worker friend. Currently I need $20,000. I believe that you will not have to strain yourself to send a check. I'm not being very demanding, am I? But maybe I will ask for more later, if you don't charge too high interest. You know, it is a good feeling to know that we have a relative close to the capitalists, maybe we'll even get into it with time. So, I already put your house for rent. If once [again] you will come to us we will welcome you at the James Rodon. I already looked up a house for $30,000 that is why I need the $20,000. Well you might think that poor Tonti lost her mind, but I know that it is polite to correspond with a person, who from today to tomorrow could be...? (important in business) But, let's start seriously. First of all, we are very, very happy that you got a responsible job, and experience for the future. I know it is not polite because it is personal, but still I will ask. What is the monthly salary? You know that good Tonti is interested in everything. This will be alright. Now let's hear something about the social situation. I hope you got good results in that field, too! How many dates did you have already? This is also a personal case too since you know I have a very curious nature. I want the truth. Is it every week someone else? Blond? Brunette? Or maybe red? There is a selection there, I think. Our poor friend Weiss and Bill are so envious of you. Did Herman get a job already? He never writes anything. How are his sisters? I know they are together again. I think Bill will have a vacation in September. He will visit you sometime. I have no idea when. The entire family is sending greetings. The Czigany "100" send kisses in the hope that when he will grow up he will be driven into Wall St. I'm sorry that I wrote with pencil, but my pen is broken. With lots and lots of love and with greetings. Tonti and Bill

Herman should write because Tonti is upset!

1952/8/25 Roberta Gluck to Irving (Book 14, 207-211)

8/24/52

Dear Irving,

Just three more weeks and I shall be off for school. That is just about sufficient time for me to sort and gather my belongings ___ and what a mess that is. You see, for the past three years at school I have been accumulating papers, books, clothing and all sorts of odds and ends. This summer was the first time that I have brought everything home with me - the reason is that I shall be at York, PA for the first eight weeks of the term and was not able to store my belongings as usual in the dormitory. This is really very good because now I have no storage space at home and must discriminate between what I shall and shall not use. There are mountaineers living near us who are really in need of clothing. I took one small load to a family in the mountains and Irving, you can't imagine how appreciative they were. These people living in the mountains are very, very poor that whatever I gave them will be of use. I know that some of these people must believe me absolutely crazy - I've simply been knocking on doors and asking if what I have could be of any use to them. The expressions on the faces are wonderful - and I've met some very interesting people. This is one experience I shall never forget. I seem to have just been rambling - I'm sorry. The job that you have obtained will as you say provide important experience for you - the more experience you get the better for working your way to where you want to go. Shortly after I started to work I got sick and was in bed for a week with an infection in my ears and throat. Because of this I had to discontinue working. Anyway, now I have been doing a lot of things that I don't always have time to do: practice the piano, read, and do some sewing. This actually means more to me than the experience I could obtain working in a drugstore. Very soon I shall be independent and will be working. Are you still living at the apartment that you had with your brother? I noticed that the return address is different. As I have always said, it is difficult for me to correspond when I know someone very little. And I don't believe you can really know another person through writing. For me it is necessary to see facial expressions and mannerisms. I would rather not correspond, but when you're near Mt. Pleasant, please do stop. I would like to see you - and when I am in N.Y. I shall certainly try to talk with you. My regards to all. Yours truly, Robbi

1952/11/3 David and Dorothy (Book 12, 277-280) - with 4th anniversary advertisement

Monday

Dear Irving:

We received your letter with the pictures enclosed. Thanks so much for sending them - they are darling. I wondered if they had come out. The one of Freddie with the hat on is too precious for words. Please, Irving, do send me the negatives. I know my family would be thrilled to have a set of pictures too. We have worked pretty hard getting ourselves moved into our new location, but are finally settled. The store is much larger than our other one, and our merchandise is therefore much better displayed. I am enclosing a picture of the exterior taken by one of our local newspapers. We have a lot of parking area in front of our store, which means a great deal when people have to shop. Next door to us is an appliance store, and they opened the same time we did. Maria tells me you are working, but did not say what you are doing. Anything interesting? Also, is Herman working too? Things are a bit quiet, but I imagine election time has something to do with it. I sure hope there will be a big buying spree after that is over. Other than the above, there is nothing much new. We are all fine, which is the important thing. All is well with my family in Chicago too, I'm happy to report. We are having Indian Summer in California now. It's just beautiful. Hope it lasts for a while. And so, that is all for now. Let us know what's what with you boys. Our love to all of you, and write soon. Dorothy

1953/5/25 Atlas Construction Recommendation for Irving (Book 16, 25-26)

May 25, 1953

To whom it may concern:

This is to certify that Mr. Irving Gluck has been employed as an expeditor by the Atlas Constructors in its home office in New York.

He supervised and directed shipments and delivery of materials, such as heavy equipment, spare parts, processed foods and medical supplies to job site overseas. Contacted vendors, manufacturers and transportation authorities; kept abreast of regulations relative to marking and packing; prepared weekly status reports. Supervised one or more stenographers or typists in preparation of letters and forms required in the work. Maintained office records as well as other duties.

Mr. Gluck was a conscientious, reliable and trustworthy employee, and I can recommend him highly without any reservation to any position he may apply for.

Very truly yours,
ATLAS CONSTRUCTORS
Diego R. Blasi
Chief Expeditor at Atlas
Business Manager for Galiana Construction Corp.

1953/8/4 Marie to Irving (Book 16, 74-76)

Dear Irving!
I'm sorry that I did not write until now, but I was waiting to hear some news so I can write. First of all, the place is very nice. I don't believe that there is another place like this. Yes, my Irving I got your letter yesterday and I'm happy that thank God you are all well. I hope you will get the check so you will not have to wait for too long. I hope that you will be home by the time I get back. Don't be sad and take care of yourself wherever you go. Do it the way you see best. And now about myself as I wrote, the place was very good. The road was beautiful. There were 5 girls and a man. We left at 5:30 and we were here at 2 in the afternoon. The only problem we had was that it was raining. Yesterday was beautiful weather. [In English] I enjoyed it very much. [In Hungarian] There are plenty of boys and girls here, but it takes time until one gets to know someone. [In English] I met lots of people and I really want to enjoy it very much. [In Hungarian] Right now, I don't know any particular news that would interest you. There are plenty of girls here my age. I will write with more details next time. I will write to Hermine. I only wrote a card for her. I will not write to others. If anyone is interested about me, send my greetings. [In English] I send my regards and give my love to Hermine and Eugene. And take care of yourself and don't worry and remember me to Mrs. Kugler, too. Love to you and Herman. Maria

1953/9/16 Marie to Irving (Book 9, 150-155)

9/16/53
Dear Irving!
This morning I got a special delivery letter and I'm glad to hear that everything is fine.
First of all, you got two checks here and yesterday I gave them to Herman because I thought that if you will come back, you should have it. I called Herman on the phone this morning, but he just left from home, so I'm sorry that I could not send it to you. He will probably come tonight and then I will tell him where he should send it to you. I don't know if you will get it on time, that's why I wanted to send it this morning. Also, you have a card, I think it's from a girl, but I did not open it. You have one from David, too. That is all the mail. Otherwise, this is all the news. Right now, I am waiting for your decision and then I can decide for myself, too. Herman was by me yesterday and he is waiting every minute for when you come back, as usual. He does not like the room. He wanted to get out of there already. He wants an entire apartment. I told him to do whatever he wants. In the meantime, he looked for another room, but I will leave this too. Now about you. I got the telegram also, and the other letter too. I did not write because I did not know how long you will stay there since you mentioned in your letter that you have an opportunity for a good job. If you like the work and it is a good salary. And here also, if here is something worthwhile then you don't need to be sad. Everyone does whatever they want. Especially, if it's to your advantage. First of all, I wish you good luck and the best of health, and a very happy New Year and I hope that all your wishes will come true! No need to be sad about your clothing, no need to come back for that. When you get your job, you will see if you like it and then there will be enough time to send it. And Herman will find another place. I will go for your stuff anyway. We can leave it at Hermine's until then. I hope it will be good for him! Now he will have

a chance to use his own mind. Oh yes! In your last letter you mentioned that you would go to Florida.. Irving! Don't you remember what everyone is saying, that it is even harder there. I hope you will consider that! Let me know, in case you don't get the check on time from us. And Irving, I hope it will not be late to cash the check, since it's already been here for a few weeks. Take care wherever you go and do the way you see best. No need to be sad about other things. Hermine and the others are fine. I was there for the holidays. They are sending their greetings to you with best wishes and love.

Maria

Herman just called me. I did not know what to do with your check because he says that you will not get it until Friday. I told him to send it to you, and they will forward it to you there. Or, if you will come back here then they can still send it back. He will send it with air mail. He gave up on the house today already from the 1st. If you will not come back until then, take care of yourself!

Love.

Greetings to Mr. and Mrs. Zuhl and the others too!

1953/9/26 Marie to Irving (Book 9, 206-207)

9/26/53

Dear Irving!

I'm sorry that I did not write before. I got your letter yesterday and also the other one as well. I'm sorry that I could not write before. First of all, I'm glad to hear that you are well and I hope that you like your job! You didn't write anything about that. It must be hard that there are no girls there for you. You can't go on dates. Although, you have a chance to save money, but you don't need to save money on your food. You should eat a little so you could put on a few pounds. At least you should have that much advantage from it. Have you heard from the girl in Cleveland? What's going on with her? Did you give up on her already? As I can see you are corresponding with the girl from New Jersey. It is going to be easy to decide how you want it. I wish you good luck and a very happy New Year! May all your wishes come true! [In English] And be well and take care of yourself. Let me hear from [you about] everything. [In Hungarian] As you mentioned, that you will come if you will have enough days, let us know when. About Herman, he waited for you so badly at first, that you will come back. And because you did not tell him immediately, he did not like it. But I told him that [in English] he doesn't have to wait for you, if he wants to move I shall take your clothes, and when he heard that you made up your mind to stay [in Hungarian] then he changed a little. He will calm down. So, ever since then he comes every night to me. Yesterday he said that if he will not get a job then he will leave NY. I'm pretty sure he thinks he would go to you. Besides that, everything is fine and I'm looking for another place for myself, but right now I am still here because one can't rush that. I am planning on looking again tomorrow. I was at a place today, too. A 1 bedroom apartment, but I did not like it so I did not talk to them. I talked to Hermine. They are well and send their greetings. Oh yes! Herman is staying at that lady's because she gave it for $30 for a month. How long? I don't know. [In English] Take care of yourself and with best wishes and Love. Maria

1953/10/9 Marie to Irving (Book 9, 145-148)

Oct 9/1953

My dear Irving!

I'm sorry that I did not respond to your letter before, but time passes before we know it. I hope my lines will find you in the best of health! First of all, on Saturday night I will move to another place. It is not what I wanted, but right now I'm going there. How long? I don't know either. I will share a four bedroom apartment with an elderly lady. I will not even change my address yet because I will see if I like it there and then I will change it. Until then, you can write to my job address c/o Ratner's 103 2nd Ave. I will get it this way or you can send it to my old address because it is not too far from me. My new address is 1898 Harrison Ave, near to Burnside. Apt 9D c/o Mrs. Kreitzer Tele TR8-5719 I will write if I will stay there and then you can write to this address. But for now, wait with it. Herman came to visit me last night, but he is the way he is again. I need to beg him to come and he says he will not even come to the other place. I can't do anything else anymore. The way he wants it is the way it shall be. He told me if he will get a job, he will move to the city too, so he doesn't have to travel so much. I just talked about it. If you don't need it you have to get rid of it. So, you don't have to carry every rag with you. I told him that I will write to you. Whatever you don't need write it to him, so it will be easier for you to carry things. But I will leave this too. Otherwise everything is fine and don't be sad about the packages. Take care of yourself wherever you go. Write about everything.

How are the girls? Have you heard about them? Also, you mentioned that you will give me money. Don't be silly! I don't need anything. And I did not give you anything and you don't have to, either. That's just childish. Just buy whatever you need. And don't forget that you need to eat and put on weight! There is nothing particular about me. I started to write this letter three days ago already, but now I'm in a hurry to send it to you. My dear Irving! If you will come to New York, write when. I hope everything will turn out for the best! And you are right about that too, that you don't need to work there for years. Just until you will have enough experience and then you can get a job anywhere. Now take care of yourself and don't be sad. With my best wishes and love to you. Let me hear from you. Maria

1953/10/10 Hermine to Irving (Book 10, 296-298)

New York 10/10 - 53
Dear Irving,
We received your letter last night and as you see I'm answering already. I'm also enclosing a check that you received. Herman came over last Saturday to pick his mail up. He is alright. I think it's a good idea to leave him alone for a while. Without wanting to change he'll be forced to do so. Otherwise we are well. Maria is well also. She probably told you about her moving tonight. It seems pretty good besides Herman found it for her. In case she wouldn't care for it, still there are always more places and it will be easier to change. Linda is doing fine. She talks to daddy on the telephone. She thinks I always talk to Daddy when the phone rings. She loves cake. She grabs it from me and as fast as she can she puts it in her mouth. Haven't heard of David and family. Hope they are doing all right. We can imagine you are lonesome. After New York in a small town any one would feel the same. Your girl is nice and I'm sure you can see the difference between the two now. Remember us to her too. If you feel you want her she could come over sometimes to see Linda. It's a beautiful day today so I want to get out. That's why my writing isn't so good and I guess a few misspelling too. Let me know. Let's hear from you again. Love from us all, Hermina, Eugene and Linda

1953/10/18 Michael Conley to Irving

Voor Clarenburg str. 7 Bis
Utrecht, The Netherlands

Holland-America Line

Mr. Irving Gluck
% Mrs. H. Solomon
36-19 167 st.
Flushing L.I. New York
U.S.A.

18 October 1953
Dear Irving

I am now back in Utrecht after having spent two weeks in Heidenheim with Ilse, meeting her parents and relatives and traveling by bicycle and bus over the land side of Ilse's Heimat. I want to come to know her home land as well as she does and I have already made a substantial beginning. This is a world of beauty. One must see it to believe it. It is unfortunate that you can not come and see it while peace reigns in Europe. Your last impressions of Europe could hardly have called forth thoughts of beauty.

However this beauty is not absolute. My first impression of Germany was of the extensive rebuilding, and this impression was gain[ed] as I looked at the cities from a train window - a position of observation from which little accuracy can be expected - and then I was involved in Ilse's home which lies in a beautiful valley, unaffected by the war. At that time I had not seen the city of Stuttgart, the capital of the state of Württemberg. This city, the largest in the state, is not beautiful. Here the savage cruelty of war still leaves stark signs of its uncompromising bestiality. Beauty is a matter for the smaller towns and the provincial dorfs. Here the rolling hills and mountains, sheltering the many farming communities, is in truth a fairy land, but in the city, in Stuttgart all is hard and mean. The facade of hollow buildings still thrust up into the sky as monuments to a defeated Germany. And I think the fact of defeat is more clearly present in the minds of the city dwellors [sp] than among the farmers. The latter can see no war when they look across their fields or into their towns. Such minor destruction as occurred in a few of them was quickly repaired.

The miracle of rebuilding, I will still affirm. The progress that has been made is substantial. Along Königstrasse, the main street of Stuttgart's down-town, little destruction is apparent, but one must only go behind this row of buildings to find broad islands of destruction which have been hidden behind the neon signs. And in one section of the city even this attempt at "cover up" proved futile. There, to the north stands square mile upon square mile of goast [sp] city. There, life is dead and the rooms that are occupied can only bring hard thoughts to the minds of the occupants.

One of the most saddening of experiences is to visit what is left of the Neue Schloss - the new castle, built in the nineteenth century. The floor plan, broadly speaking was that of a double "L" with the two bases joined. This formed a great rectangular court yard before the front doors. The great wings of the building were extensively decorated with figures and the whole gave a majestic impression of formal beauty which is to be associated with the architectural styles in use a century before. Inside the building consisted of a series of over three hundred rooms, each highly decorated and containing irreplaceable period furniture.

This much one can learn of what the building must once have been, from observation and explanation. But this is only a hint. Through the great windows, one now can see the sky above and to the right, through a broad doorway, one sees the great pillors [sp] of a hall, some of them holding up no more than the air above them, while others lie broken on a floor of sod. I made this visit to the new castle in the after noon of a day that had been made dark and cheerless from a heavily overcast sky. The whole effect of building and sky seemed to heighten the sence [sp] of despair which must lie in the hearts of many people,
However, I don't know if despair is the correct word for typifying the attitude of the people. Indeed, beauty does not exist here, but the rebuilding program is proceeding, and I have seen some excellent results of that program. Stuttgart now has several buildings that may be classified as sky scrapers. A very modern department store has been built with escalators and all the other gaggets [sp] to be found in America and a local newspaper, the Stuttgarter Nachrichter, has built a building over 30 floors high. The ultramodernism of these buildings in design is most interesting and certainly a radical departure from the kind of buildings which were destroyed in the war. Where previously very steep roofs were the, rule, now absolutely flat roofs are the mode. I don't see how a people so accustomed to the former type of architecture can accept these new buildings. One German who did not like these buildings said to me, "They are to [sp] modern. They are more American than America. Soon Stuttgart will no longer be German."

I am sorry that I was unable to meet you in New York city. Wherever this letter reaches you, I wish you success in your new undertakings.

Sincerely,
Michael

My address in Utrecht in the Netherlands is Voor Clarenburg 7 BiS. I will be at that address until Christmas time when I am going to join my wife in Heidenheim. That address, in case you don't already have it is, Fam. Fr. Benz, 14a Heidenheim/Brz. Hurdenstrasse 18, Württemberg, U.S. Zone.

1953/10/19 Marie to Irving (Book 9, 229-234)

10/19/1953
Dear Irving!
[In English] I received your letter and was very happy to hear from you. [In Hungarian] And I'm sorry my Irving that I only write so rarely to you, but until I am settled I will have no time, even to write. The thing is this. [In English] I moved, but it is only temporary [In Hungarian] because I thought that Herman will come like before. And even if I didn't like the place, I would have been at home, because she allowed me to cook here and he could come whenever he wanted. But Herman changed his mind. He does not want to come here. Ever since I am here, he hasn't come at all, except when I moved in. And that boy! He is hopeless. He does not even call me on the phone. And I called him once before. You never saw anything like it. How angry he was, that he does not even want to talk because I called him. Instead of talking to him, he was arguing. I asked him if he is coming on Sunday, he said he will not. Yes, he likes the house and the place where I live. He is angry because I'm looking for something else. Yesterday I wanted to go down to the

YWHA, to find out what's there. I said I will be at home until 12 or if he wants I said he can come at 4. And I came in at 1 o'clock...[In English] I was surprised Herman was there ready to come up. In a way, I was very sorry that I had to go away, but I couldn't help it because I had to be there in time. He wouldn't come with me and he wouldn't come back either, so I was aggravated. First of all, if I know he comes I would prepare something for him. He has plenty of time to come back if he wants to, and I don't want to stay in the house and wait if he doesn't come. And so, between him and the house I'm disgusted, and he said he wouldn't come. So this is the case. [In Hungarian] But don't be sad. I'm sorry that I'm writing this, but he is the way he used to be. The only thing would be good, if you would give him money to get more stocks....He already wanted to get a loan to buy them. He does not know anything else. He was angry at you about that also, because you called him and it cost money. Yes my Irving, as you mentioned about the phone call, I'm sorry but I will not even go to Hermine and the others either because I don't have patience and time until I get a kind of room that I want. Hermine's hand is still not the way it should be, but she says that the doctor was not good because he dried her hand out too much. Now take care of yourself...Yes, I was in the Y and they have an age limit of 26 years of age, so now I am looking for something else. You don't need to mention what I wrote to Herman...[In English] Otherwise we are all well and hoping to hear from you the same and take care of yourself. [In Hungarian] Otherwise what's going on with the girls? Have you heard from them? Write about everything! I will also write to you. [In English] With best wishes and love to you. Maria

1953/10/20 Dorothy to Irving (Book 12, 282-285)

Oct 30, 1953
Dear Irving:
We received your letter and always are most happy to hear from you. I've wanted to write you so many times, and my only excuse is forgetfulness. Time goes by and one doesn't realize how long the span. True I've been in Chicago for a while and since I've been back it's always something - busy here or there. I'm getting just as bad as your brother when it comes to writing. I'm also glad that you take the initiative and write us without standing on ceremony. I'm happy that you like your new position and wish you good luck. The important thing is to enjoy your work. Things on the West Coast are very quiet as far as business is concerned. One would think that at this time of year, so near to Christmas, that things would be on the upswing, but so far there seems no indication of people spending money. This is a general thing out this way affecting all types of business. Undoubtedly other parts of the country are feeling it too. Our store number is listed on the letterhead, but our home phone is Long Beach 396536. We would be most happy to hear from you, even as you say, for a few minutes. Who knows - about visiting the East - although we are not contemplating a trip - strange things happen! I received a letter from Maria today telling us she had moved. I assume Herman will be staying with her. Is he happy living in New York? We are all well here. Wish I could say the same about my Father. He's been ailing for a while now, and of course that was my main object in going home - to be with him. Our visit did a lot to perk him up, and needless to say just seeing his grandson meant so much to him. Yes, Freddie is quite a boy. Forgive the long delay in writing you. David and Frederic Jerome join me in sending our love to you. Write again soon. Dorothy

1953/10/26 Hermine to Irving (Book 10, 300-302)

New York 10/25 - 53
Dear Irving,
As always it was so wonderful to hear from you. Sorry that I didn't answer your letter sooner. It isn't much new here because we don't go much. You know how important a car is in N.Y. It is also very difficult to travel with a baby. Herman surprised us Saturday. I was on Northern Blvd. with the carriage and my mother-in-law was with me too. I look up and there he was. Just so happened that Maria also came in the evening and stayed over night. She doesn't like her room at all. Herman is like always, it is all a waste of time. It goes in on one ear and out on the other. Thank God he stayed for dinner. It was a hard job to make him do it. Milton [Eugene's brother] is going to open his store in about 3 weeks. He told them already that he is leaving. You received a letter from your friend from Europe, but I think Herman took it. I guess he is going to mail it to you. We miss you and Linda does too. She just loves everybody. She talks and says Hurry! Come! If she wants us. When she has to go! She doesn't want to stay in the room by herself that means I have to let her cry or be there with her. She likes cake and you should hear her ask for it. Flora and Arthur were here one day to meet Jenny at the boat coming from Europe. They called me up. Have you seen them lately? What about Aunt Helen? Let us hear from you again. Love from us all. Hermina, Eugene, and Linda

[On the side] If you can, collect a stamp for me

1953/11/1 Irving to Michael (Conley?) (Book 6, 275-276)

11/1/53

Dear Michael,

It was a pleasure to receive your letter dated 18 October, 1953 regarding your activity and observations of the present Europe with its progress of rebuilding from the impact of war. It's regretful that the people of the 20th century had to experience such conflict that almost lead to the destruction of civilization. This regressive action is probably one of the failures of evolution. It seems that before progress is attained, some sort of set backs comes forth. The development of the "atomic bomb" for example, came about by the intensive research to improve the destructive ability of the ordinary bomb. Your observation points to the fact that the latter was powerful enough to eliminate cities with its population. The aftermath of war ought to warrant [warn] humanity of the consequences of another conflict. Thus, it is necessary to invent a mode of progress without the means of the past. It ought to be realized that peace and good will toward all people, at all times, is essential for survival. In essence, representatives of nations ought to learn to understand the fellow nation-states; its problems, since it affects all, in order to attain happiness and justice for all. Forgive me for not being in New York to meet you and Ilse, but I remained in Ohio. At the present I'm in Portsmouth, as a buyer for the Atomic Energy project. Thank you for your kind words regarding my undertakings. Let me hear from you again soon. Also let me know if you need anything that I could send you. I remain with best wishes from all of us, to you and Ilse, as well as her family. Sincerely, Irving

1953/11/7 Marie to Irving (Book 9, 106-110)

11/7/53

My dear Irving!

I got your letter and I'm glad to hear that, thank God, you are well. I'm sorry my Irving that I did not have a chance to take your call. Right now I'm still where I was. How long? I don't know it yet, since now even the weather will hold me back. I hope that everything will turn out for the best. And for you my little brother it must be hard because you can't even eat the way you should. Plus, it must be far away from your job. Don't be sad about me my little Irving, everything is going to be fine soon. Take care of yourself and try to arrange it so it will be good. Oh yes! My Irving! Do you know who called? The Hungarian girl, Hilda. And she wanted to know where you are and if you go to school. I told her that you are somewhere in Ohio and you are working, but I did not give her your address. I'm sure she was ashamed to ask for it because she saw that I don't really want to give it to her. She talked so timidly that I could barely hear what she was saying. I asked who is calling and is there any marriage. She said no. So I said that I will write to you that she called. And I know that much about her. Besides that, I'm glad to hear that you get along with the girl, because you can get to know them well this time. And since you mentioned the girl in Cleveland, she thinks that she is a somebody, otherwise they will run after her. And she surely expected that you would marry her immediately. That's not good, because even if you would marry her, she would always want to be the center of attention. And that is true about a NY girl, that a solid girl could be smart if she can hold on to you. And she knows how it is. It is not that easy in this world, it is not what we want. Let me know what you decide. She would surely go to you even to there. And that would be the best for you. Then you would have somebody who you could talk to. You would not be so lonely. Take care of yourself and lots of luck to you! And I hope that all your wishes come true with bigger luck! She could get a good job there too, surely. Now, take care of yourself and let me know about everything. By Hermine, they are all alright. They send their greetings to you. And my Irving! Write to Hermine too because she said that you don't write to her. I saw Herman this week. I don't know if he works and in a small place like that it is pretty hard. Since then I did not see him, but he was fine. But you know, it's a problem because at the last minute he doesn't get the job that he wants. When I told him not to wait for the last minute, he didn't care [to listen]. He should do as he pleases. Oh yes, my Irving! If you want on 11/16/53 at night on Monday from 8 to 9:30 you can call. Where I live the phone number is: TR8-5719 or if you can't call, then write [to tell me] when so I will be at home. Don't be sad about me. Otherwise everything is fine. Just the weather is suddenly winter. It is pretty cold and it snowed, too. It is raining also. Last week it was real Spring. With my best wishes and love. Maria

1953/11/10 Hermine to Irving (Book 10, 304-306)

Dear Irving,

I just can't imagine the reason you don't answer my letter. I hope not because I asked for the stamps. You see for a minute I thought of collecting stamps and I felt you might get mail from different places and you could save it for me. It wasn't too serious so you just forget about it. Or is it something else? You better let us hear from you. Eugene meant to write too. It seems he is always too busy. Maybe one day he'll do it. This time I'll make it short because I want to take Linda out. She is getting too smart and wants me to be with her all the time. Maria calls me quite often. She is all right. Herman called me too. He doesn't change easily. We haven't heard from Dorothy. I sent them pictures of Linda and also a record player for Frederic Jerome about a month ago. People are sure funny. Sometimes I wonder how anyone could do such things. OK Irving. This wasn't meant for you. Take care of yourself. Love to you from us all. Hermina

1953/11/18 Marie to Irving (Book 9, 216-221)

11/18/53

My dear little brother Irving!

[In English] It was very nice to talk to you and hear your voice again. And also received your letter and was very happy to hear that you are well. As you mentioned [In Hungarian] my Irving that you got something from the girl and you talked to her also on Sunday. Was she happy because you called her? What did she send to you? I'm not asking you because I want to be nosy....What did you send her? It would be about time that you would give something. Although, it is true that you don't really have time. When you will come to NY, I'm sure she will be happy that you will come! I hope to hear the best about you! Only take care of yourself wherever you go and whatever you do. If the weather will be bad then you will be smart and will take the train. This way you don't have to be worried about how you will have to go back. Right now I will stay where I live because it is hard for me to do what I want. It is expensive enough. And [I] must go to [a different] one. This place where I live is only bearable. You will see. The lady is very refined. She wants Herman to come more often....[In English] He comes on Sunday. I can't call him because he is angry if I do. [In Hungarian] And that is why I don't know how he likes the work. The only thing I know is he likes it because he drives a new car. He drives a type of car that I don't like. He says that there is no better available. As I can see he may have long hours. Although, they said that they only need to work until 5. But this is how it goes at a small company. That is why it is better to work for a larger company. Let's hope for the best! The only thing good about it is that at least he started to work. There is nothing particular about me. I am well. And Hermine and the others are as well. Although, Hermine was upset because you haven't written and neither has David. Now take care of yourself wherever you go. And write about everything. Jane Shallheim wants to know how you are and what you are doing. [In English] Probably she expects to hear from you. [In Hungarian] I told her that you are busy. I saw Mrs. Kugler this week. Oh yes! My little Irving, you should write to Mrs. Kugler at least a line because she doesn't really like it that you did not write to her. She was wondering about you. She did not say anything that I left her because I don't live too far from her and I can see her many times a week. The way it is, they know that it is for the best and it is better to change after so many years. I will write again next time. Oh yes! My Irving, it was in the newspaper that whoever had family in Europe that were destroyed, they should report it and they will get money for it accordingly. I don't know what is true about this. So, you find out what is true about this and [In English] you let me know. With best wishes and love to you. Maria

[Note in Irving's handwriting]

1. Was Lee happy? As to why I called?

2. Necktie

3. I sent her a necklace

4. Herman says that nothing better is available because the welfare is up to date and that he wants a job that is good. Although, now one can get a good job before the holidays.

4. Jane's address

5. Bertha

6. Mrs. Kugler

7. European family problem - Where did you read it?

8. May be - room - She would let you have it for $30

1953/11/30 Hermine to Irving (Book 10, 308-310) - Misha born, David closes business

New York 11/30 - 53

Dear Irving,

I'm ashamed for neglecting your letter. I meant to write but as usual if it is nice out I want to go out with Linda. Especially now that the days are shorter and colder. It's mostly before noon that it takes me all afternoon to catch up. At present I'm waiting for the painter. He was supposed to be here this morning then 1:30 P.M. So far nothing happened so here I'm writing you. Everything is well with us hope you are well, too. We are very happy to know you expect to come to N.Y. It's a good idea to come with the train. Let us know when you come. We were at Milton's house for Thanksgiving dinner, Maria too. Herman wouldn't go. Received a letter from Dorothy. She told us in the letter that they had to give up the store, liquidate the merchandise. Now Dave is thinking of getting into the restaurant business because they wouldn't need much money for that. As far as I'm concerned that's not for him. Emil's wife in Israel gave birth to a Boy Mazel tov!! I went to a doctor with my hands and he put me on a diet and in one week it's almost gone. I'm going there tonight again. I can't eat fats, butter, egg yolk, milk only skimmed milk, no ice cream or any cream at all. That's what I miss the most. That was about 10 days ago. Maybe that will be only till it heals up entirely. That's all for now. Love, Hermina
Where were you for Thanksgiving dinner?

1953/12/3 Marie to Irving (Book 9, 112-114)

12/3/53
Dear Irving!

I just received your letter and was very happy to hear that you are well. I was wondering why I didn't hear from you. I thought that you must be very busy. First as you are asking about Herman he was over to see me Sunday and also Monday evening. He is alright except you know he has some different problem. About his job the only thing that he likes is to drive the car, but not long enough. Only a short distance and he wouldn't mind to do it all the time and then he has long hours so he told me Sunday he will leave them. I told him it is better now than later because it's easier to get a job now. The other thing you are asking if he goes out or if he wants to meet people. Oh yes, you have a very good case! I'm afraid he will never change. He is still the same. Otherwise about the room. When you write to him, you could tell him maybe he should tell the woman that you will stay with him while you are in the city. So far as I know, he will stay there until you will come and then he plans to get something different if he gets a better job. I told him that last week he should stay there until you come. So I think you will be able to stay with him. The woman seems nice to me, but you can never tell with people. Oh yes Irving dear, I'm very sorry that I have forgotten about your birthday. First of all I want to wish you a very Happy Birthday. With all the happiness and good health and [that] your hopes and dreams would come true. About the girl, you know best, but she seems very sincere and I'm sure that she means business too. To make a big trip like this for such a short time she must be very proud of it too!! So let's hope for the best. You could tell her she could call me. It is better when she calls, than [if] I would. Otherwise we are all well. Hermine and the family and the baby. She is a real angel. She started to talk. You should hear her, but you will see yourself. Till then take care of your self and let me hear from you. Hermine just got a letter from Dorothy. They had a hard time to try to save the business, but they failed. [In Hungarian] So everything has to be auctioned off. And it may be enough for the poor. Because one wants more and in today's world it is [In English] almost impossible to be in business unless you have plenty of easy money [In Hungarian] Now I don't know what he will do. In today's world, having a good job is worth more than having a business because at least you have fewer headaches, but I'll leave that too. Hermine got a telegram. Emil also had a son born. Sends greetings to all. All our best wishes and love, Maria

1954/1/4 Marie to Irving (Book 9, 116-118)

[In English]
1/4/54
Dear Irving!

I got your message in person from Lee. I was happy to hear that you are alright and arrived safe. I was waiting for your letter, but so far didn't get any. We are all well. Hoping to hear the same from you. You know Irv, yesterday I met Lee downtown and had dinner together at Glickstern's. I enjoyed it very much. Lee is a very nice girl. She must like you, too and [she] also told me about Samuel. She met him with you. As you mentioned to me too, you know Irving, he must like Lee too, because I don't know if Lee mentioned to you, but Samuel took her out for lunch that time he told her all about his past. So Lee said she doesn't know what to do about him. She thinks he is maybe too well (educated) and hard to find the type of girl he should have. But I thought that if she knows a nice girl she could give the number to him and the rest is up to them. And he wanted to know how did you meet. And Lee is smart. She told him to ask you. That was a good answer because he doesn't believe in a dance. Probably she told you about [it]. But Irving dear, if she did not mention about this thing, then tear this letter and never even mention that I ever told you anything because if you will mention this then I [will] never tell you anything more. Because it is not nice to talk about. So did you hear from Samuel? Hermine told her that he is a nice fellow and if she knows a nice girl then she could give her number to Samuel and the rest is up to them. I think he must of liked Lee, because he was so (confidential) to talk about himself. Or maybe this is the only way he could keep the (conversation) some people they don't know nothing else just that. Maybe that is his trouble. But as I said Irving dear, don't ever tell anyone about this. It is between you and I. But now you have enough (gossip) and take care of yourself and let me hear from you with best wishes and love, Maria

Hello to Herman and Lee

[On the side] Did you call David, let me know.

1954/1/8 Irving to Samuel Gluck - draft (Book 6, 261)

1/8/54

Dear Samuel,

It was a pleasure to be able to see you while in New York City. I only regret that we had but a few minutes to talk about things…I would appreciate to learn, Samuel, about your opinion regarding Lee. Your general observation in conversation, personality, etc. Your knowledge about me would warrant a good appraisal of my selection of the proper mate. Your true opinion is appreciated. I hope to hear from you at your earliest convenience. I remain with best wishes to you and a very Happy New Year. Irv

comments

1954/1/15 Marie to Irving (Book 9, 138-143) - trouble with Bertha

1/15/54

My dear Irving!

I got your letter and I'm glad to hear that thank God you are well. I hope that my lines will find you again in the best of health. First of all, thank you that you offered to correct my letter. If you can, you could only write the words down, so I will learn or remember more easily. And thank you very much for it! I always write in a hurry from work, even to Dorothy. I'm sorry that she has such a hard time reading my letter ([In English] but if I would wait until I know how to write correctly in English, you and Dorothy would have to wait for a long time. That is the reason I don't care and write the way I can.) [In Hungarian] But now everything is good otherwise. I spoke to Hermine and Herman too. They are well and send their wishes to you. They will write as well. Last night I talked to Lee and you know that I was ashamed because her father picked up the phone and I don't know their names and did not know how to address him. So I only said that I want to talk to Lee. And I just told Lee that I did not know that it was her father. I told her that I am sorry, but I did not know it was him. I called her because she wants me to go with her on Sunday to see a play. I don't know if I will be able to go with her since it is possible that I have to go with the boy. Although, about the boy [I can say] only that the sooner I will give up on him, the better. I talked to Aunt Jenny and she was glad to hear the good news, and maybe you should write a card for her. Yes, my Irving, about Bertha. Her niece is here from Canada. And you know that I don't talk to her [Bertha]. But now that the girl was here, I had to go to her. But as always, I got so much from her, that it will be enough for awhile again. You know that her niece got married, and there are boys here who she knows from Canada and they did not tell me anything, but made a double date with me. They told me that no one will be there and no need to dress up. It was very bad weather. When I went there, they told me they want to go to a night club. You know, to make a big trip like that again and I did not have time to even take a breath. When I got back to them it was too late already. And running and everything else, and that was not even enough because she argued with me about how badly I looked in my clothes and coat. You know my Irving, that I was dressed nicely, but I will never do it again. To add to that, if you could have seen the boys! The one I go out with now is so much better. Junk. So little. So it was not worth it to go through all that trouble. I can find a better one for myself. No need to mock me because I don't laugh properly or don't dress the way they want. So that's the end, but don't be worried about me. I am old enough to take care of myself. What's the news by you? Write about everything. And my Irving, take care wherever you go and take care of yourself and dress warmly. Now I will close my lines with best wishes, and love to you from all of us. Maria

1954/1/15 Sam Gluck to Irving (Book 14, 325-326)

January 15, 1954

Dear Irv:

Have wanted to write before, but have been really snowed under with work. I will answer your questions as best I can, but remember, only you can decide. First of all, I like her very much and am much impressed that she is honest and genuine and she loves you very much. She seems very sweet and a genuinely loving "marrying woman". What I said is true, had I met her I would have wanted to date her. Whether or not she would be for me might not turn out to be so, as in many respects I am an old man and very settled, while she is young and would be happy with someone like yourself. Though you have been through many worse things than I, and are older, you are fortunately unaffected by them. But I certainly would have given her a big try myself. Yet, having been through my own experience, I always have vague and undefined reservations. I did not see a single flaw I can pick in her manner, appearance, attitude, anything. She seems to be really terrific and meant for you; and you seem to be ok for her. Of course, it was only the first time I saw her. We talked at lunch. She "pumped" me a little about you. Her questions all centered around whether you had had many boy friends, etc., when I knew you; whether you went around with the boys, etc. Maybe she was fishing in a nice way to see if there were any "roving tendencies". I told her that I really did not know much about your social life at home, except that you often spoke of close friends who were family people, and that we do not go around together. Also told her that I was more or less of a homebody, and that all the family was generally that way. Not the type to run around. Perhaps she was a little anxious about sexual experience, which of course would be a natural thing. She is, I am convinced, quite healthy on such matters. By that I mean that she has high values and is well balanced, but would certainly be the kind to keep her husband, and only her husband, well contented at home. Actually, I cannot say how things will turn out. Only you can judge that, and no one can be certain. But I do not see a single thing wrong with her in the little time I spent with her. She appears to be someone who is used to work, and would stand along with you. Exams are two weeks away, and I hope to be home by March 1. Sam

1954/1/27 Marie to Irving (Book 9, 134-136)

1/27/54

Dear Irving!

I have not heard from you for a long time. I hope that everything will find you in the best. Lee spoke to me and I saw her too. She said that she spoke to you and mentioned that you made a change in your new job. I hope you will like it and that it is not a hard job! Write about everything. Take care of yourself wherever you go and when you drive the car because as I hear it, there is plenty of snow there. Here over the past few days it is warm enough. It is like Spring time. Besides that we are well. There is no particular news about me. I gave up that boy. Nothing from nothing. Oh yes my Irving, as Lee mentioned, that next month she is planning on going there to visit you, but only for three days. That is better than nothing. It is not a lot of time. Traveling takes up the entire time. Do you know what Herman says? That Lee is a little fat. You could see that she is very refined and a good girl also. She is not a spender, who likes to spend on dresses. One can see that. [In English] But you can always help her too to pick the right type of clothes. You know my Irving, as I do it too. I have to buy a dress that makes me bigger and for her she should get one that makes her look skinnier. For example, she should not put on a big heavy skirt because she will look like a little fatty. Maybe that is why Herman said that she is fat. But my Irving, you should not mention this to her. God forbid she would get mad about it. When you have an opportunity or if you will buy clothes for her, then you should look for ones in which she would look skinnier in. She is on a diet now as well. And make sure she will not gain more weight, but that is very hard. Now don't be sad and take care of yourself and don't be so lazy to write. I'm sending greetings and kiss you with love. Herman is sending greetings. Love, Maria

1954/1/28 Hermine to Irving (Book 10, 312-314)

New York 1/27 - 54

Dear Irving,

As always I have to excuse myself again for neglecting my answer to your letter. As always it was so wonderful to hear from you. Especially to see you even if only for such a short time. Your girl is a very nice girl and we wish you both all the happiness. She calls me some times and I know from her that you are well. Hope you like the new job. Lots of luck. We are well and so is Linda. As soon as she saw I took the pen - she cried for one also. I have to give her paper and pencil. She has a record player and she knows which 2 records are doggie and Poki little doggie. She can turn it on already. As you see she keeps me busy thank God. It wasn't nice outside today so we didn't go out. Bertha's niece [Iren] was here from Canada. She changed so that I would never recognize her. Otherwise everything is as usual. A couple of days ago we got our television set, a table model. Philco 21 inch. When do you expect to come back to N.Y.? Let us hear from you when you have a chance. Eugene sends his love too. So till next time all our love to you and a kiss from Linda. Hermina

1954/1/30 Marie to Irving (Book 9, 128-132)

1/30/54

My dear Irving!

I got your letter and I'm glad to hear that thank God, you are healthy. First of all, I wish you lots of luck on your new job and I hope that everything will work out for the best! I talked to Lee last week and she said again today that she will call you on the phone. Since you mentioned it, my Irving, if I liked the theater? I'm sorry my Irving, but I did not go. I was very busy and it was very cold, so Lee went with somebody else. I hope that next time we can go together to the movies. It is hard for me to plan ahead. I wrote a letter this week and I hope that you got it. Yes, my Irving! Did you write to Dorothy? If not, then you should write, even if it is just a few lines. I thought that you called them and I wrote to them about you. They were very happy to hear the good news about you. Now I will get to what you mentioned, that you will send me a watch. That is very nice of you and thank you very much my Irving! But I am sorry, I can't accept it from you, except on the condition that I will pay for it! Otherwise, if it's possible, cancel the order. You have enough to pay for these days and not to worry about me. It is good enough that I can buy a watch from a wholesaler by you. So, only send it with that condition and write the price to me [and] I will gladly send it to you. Ok, my Irving? And write about everything. Oh yes, also you asked me what I think, if it's good about the wedding. First of all, my little Irving, it depends on the girl, is that what she wants. But I don't think that they want a big wedding. The girl pays for the cost and she arranges it the way that is best for them. You have to pay for the music and the flowers. It is possible that Lee does not want a big wedding, but her parents want it for sure. You have to think this through. The only thing I know is that I would not make one too big, but that depends mostly on the girl. First talk to her and then we will see what would be best. I talked to Hermine about it and she said that. Besides, why do you care what others think? Whoever wants to give anything will give it. This way or another if they will not want to give then they will not give. Make a decision about when you plan on getting married. Let me know my Irving. And write about everything. And take care wherever you go. Herman and Hermine send their greetings. Herman will send the papers to you. And thank you very much for the English words! I just don't have time to practice, but I will practice shortly. Now I am in a hurry to send this letter. As always, I am writing from work. I don't even have time to look over what I'm writing. Take care wherever you go and the way you drive that car. With best wishes and love. Maria

1954/2/13 Marie to Irving (Book 9, 120-126)

2/13/54

Dear Irving!

First of all, I can't imagine why you are not writing. I hope you are well! I wrote two letters to you last week and it's been the second week that I did not hear from you. I know that time can go so [quickly] that before you realize it, it has been another week already. First of all, my little brother, I got the watch and it is very beautiful. Thank you very much and I hope you will send me the bill because I don't want you to pay for it. Right now, you have enough expenses. My dear little Irving, as I mentioned about the income tax [papers] we will send yours. I don't know what Herman will do with his. It is not worth it to send mine there because they will do it here for about 3.00 dollars. Now the case stands this way. First of all, don't be scared because it is not dangerous and he is already fine, but Herman had an accident. [It happened] when you left from here in NY on Monday night. So where he works, the shelf where they put the papers, the screw got loose and [the shelf] fell over in a way that luckily, as he tried to run away from there, it only got his leg. Although, it was enough too. So, [In English] he got a broken leg. [In Hungarian] He was very lucky. His bosses took him to the hospital immediately and he has been there until today. It is going to be the seventh week on Monday. His leg is already in a cast and he can probably go home soon. I am writing about the income tax paper because if he will go home these days, then he will give it to me and I will send it to you. [The boss] will pay the compensation because it happened there and he was going home and his boss called him back to look at what he will do on Sunday. It seems I can't relax for one minute. On one hand, the more they keep him in the hospital the better because at least he eats normally and there is someone who takes care of him. It is not that easy at home. But you know Herman, he is always upset. He is even upset about paying the rent, since he is not at home. And that the hospital costs too much. And he should not be there and so on...! You know that the relatives did not even go to him. He could lie in there for who knows how long [before someone] from them [would go] to look at him, if I would not go. I see him always. I come and go for him. And Hermine and Eugene were there and Lee was also there too to visit him twice. [In English] You know Herman does not want anybody to come, but when they do come, he likes it. I asked him to write to you and he doesn't want to, so I have to tell you all about it. [In Hungarian] I did not want to write to you about him because I knew you will be upset and I told Lee not to write about it either because you would have only gotten scared. Now everything is all right. The cast just has to stay on for a few months probably. The lady where he lives visited him and she will help him. Herman [thinks he] does not need anything. He thinks that he could live alone in this world. Now at least he can see that it is not the way he thinks. I will leave this too and don't be upset because everything is fine now. He wrote to you last week. Did you get his letter? And yes, about the stock, he also said that I should write if you saw it because I think the Braizer merged with another company and maybe it is going to be better. Did you see that my Irving? Oh yes! Samuel found out from Lee that Herman is in the hospital and last Sunday he was there too, which is very nice of him. Although, he was not there for long, but he is planning on going again. Otherwise, everything is fine. Hermine and the others, as well. Everybody sends their greetings. And best wishes and love. Maria

And take care wherever you go and the way you drive your car. And write about everything. Did you write to David? I did not hear from them for a couple of weeks already. And write even if it's [only] a few lines. How do you like your new job? I did not hear from Lee this week. She will probably call me today. Yes, the lady where I live came home this week and she was there too for a week. She also wants to visit Herman. I saw Linda last week, if you could see her, she's so cute you could eat her.

1954/2/20 Marie to Irving (Book 9, 98-100)

2/20/54

My dear Irving!

I got your letter that I could hardly wait for and knowing that thank God you are well makes me happy, and I hope to hear that again. First of all, we are well. Herman is getting along alright. He is still in the hospital, but he is already walking. I told him he should write to you, too. I saw him last night. Now he is waiting to go home. First of all, I want this letter to go immediately because I'm sorry my Irving, but I was not able to find your income tax papers. I went last night alone and I looked over that briefcase and there was also a bigger folder and there were two papers in it, but the income tax paper was not there. I am very sorry my Irving, that I left this to the last minute. If you could, you should call them and if you want me to, I can go ask for a duplicate. I hope it will not be late. I don't want you to waste more time, and it is not worth it to spend your time looking for it because I looked every piece over and it was not there, unless you put it someplace else. I hope they will give you another one! So you won't have trouble with them ask for a special delivery. Write immediately what I should do because you don't have a lot of time for it. At least I would have known before Lee went to you, but it's not worth it to be upset about that. Even if it costs money, my Irving, it would be best if you would call them on the phone, then they will send it to you in time surely. Write how everything is. I will tell Herman tomorrow, to write all together and if they want I will send it to you to state it. They state mine here and thank you my Irving for it. I did not want to bother you with that if it's possible. Now I hope that you enjoyed the holiday. At least you have been together for a few days. I talked to Lee and when she comes back, she will call me. Take care of yourself wherever you go. Write about everything. What did you decide with Lee? Oh yes, my Irving we have a lawyer for Herman. We are hoping that everything is going to be fine. Love, Maria

1954/2/23 Hermine to Irving (Book 16, 115-117) - wedding plans with Lee, Hermine pregnant

New York 2/21 - 54

Dear Irving,

We received both of your letters and we were very happy to hear from you. I was also happy to talk to you over the telephone. I believe that you know about Herman. The main thing is that he is well and doing alright. We got him a very good lawyer who took care of a compensation case for Eugene's uncle. His specialty is compensation. So don't worry he'll take care of it. Eugene's uncle had some trouble with his arm. He got $7,000. So we know he knows his business. We thought Herman would write [a] long time ago, but as you know Herman. He is quite lazy for that. With all the bad luck he had he was lucky because, he at least is covered with compensation. He doesn't have a hospitalization and you know what happens if that happens on the street or somewhere else. As I understand Lee is there for the weekend and that is really wonderful. Hope you work out all the problems according your belief. As far as I am concerned it follows like this. It doesn't pay to make a big formal wedding - bigger the wedding more ceremonies and bigger expense. Flowers for decorating, liquor, music, and probably other expenses belong to the groom. Flowers might cost hundreds of dollars. So I can't advise you because that's up to Lee and her family. A nice simple wedding is nice and all brides like it. I don't believe in inviting too many people, lots of girls, rather pocket the cost of that and use it for the house. I really think the best is to talk to Lee. She knows about all that and I'm sure she wouldn't want too much expenses. Our wedding was only an afternoon wedding with about $65.00 for flowers and the caterer cost about $250.00 and yet [when] everything [was] added up [it] cost $500.00 or $600.00 I think you do get back lot of things in gifts. Besides gifts we received a few hundred in cash. She probably wants a white dress and I wouldn't like to dress formal. Beside you better hurry up because I [would] like to be there, too. To give my news away, Linda is expecting a little sister or brother sometime in July. So I would love to be there. O.K.? Wrote to Dorothy and they know you're getting married. Let's hear about your plans and decision about the whole thing. Don't work hard and relax. Even if Lee would go to Ohio to settle down for a while I don't think it would pay to furnish a home. Because as we know that's temporary. I hope there is something that you get out of my letter. Let me hear from you. Oh, yes. We like to watch television, but Linda doesn't care too much. She likes commercials, dancing, and singing. We'll close this time, lots of luck and best wishes. Hermine

1954/3/18 Marie to Irving (Book 9, 102-104)

3/18/54

Dear Irving!

It appears that we are writing with a delay again to each other, but I hope that my lines will find you in the best of health. I was waiting that I will hear back from you. Herman got your letters and he is getting along. He has to go to the doctor on Monday and then we will see what will be. If everything is fine then maybe they will take the cast off or maybe they will put a smaller one on. Otherwise everything is well. I am well. Hermine and the others are as well. I just talked to her, she sends her greetings. Besides that, I will go to visit Herman today. Although he is so stubborn that he does not listen to anyone. So, I will leave him to do whatever he wants. He is not a child! Oh yes! I talked to Lee on Sunday. She called me on the phone. As I was talking, she mentioned that it would be good if you would be here at least for a few days because she is alone and she can't arrange it alone and make decisions about it. Which I agree about that too because she is very right. And she said that she would like it if you could come for Passover for the entire week. It would not be a bad idea. It would be the best. She did not want to talk you into it, but she would be very happy to have you here. It seems that is the best way. And one can't save all the time even if one wants to. First of all, it would be good if you would come to her for Passover and, if the dear God will help, if you decide then about the wedding you can take your own time off. They allow it in cases like that to take off a few days or a week. Even if you lose those few dollars then it is worth it also because now it is just as important as later. And this way, it is possible that you can arrange it for less and you can save for that there. And it isn't like you have time to do it some other time when you will be able to. Do the way you see it's best. I send you greetings and kiss you with love. Love, Maria

Take care wherever you go and let me hear from you. With best of wishes to you.

1954/3/20 Dorothy to Irving (Book 12, 287-288)

Thursday

Dear Irving:

It was nice hearing from you, even though it was the shortest letter you ever wrote to us. We have heard the great news from Maria, and are real happy for you. Needless to say, we wish you the best of everything always. Maria writes that Lee is very sweet, as I know she must be. Do you have a snap[shot] of her we might see? We certainly would like to be kept informed of everything. As for us, things are going along fair. You were undoubtedly informed that we have gone out of the lamp business (polite way of putting it), and now have a restaurant. This present venture is a rugged one as far as work is concerned. David is working harder than he ever did, putting in hours particularly. I have been going down on Saturday and Sunday to help out. The place is open 7 days a week and David is down there every day. Seems like every business we go into is more confining than the previous one. We are all well, and that's the most important thing. Freddie is getting to be a big boy, and will be starting school in September. I'm ashamed to say we haven't taken any pictures of him recently, so you can see how much he's grown. However, I expect we will this summer. My Dad is not at all well and hasn't been for some time now. He had an operation recently and now has to go again shortly. I spoke to the family on Monday, and they will know in a week just when he has to enter the hospital again. Naturally we are all quite upset about his condition. I know you're a busy guy, but how about a nice, newsy letter telling us all about yourself, your fiancée, etc. You now we are interested in anything concerning you, even though our correspondence has been neglected lately. You will have to forgive David not writing, but you know him, and believe me when he gets home at night he's so tired he just flops into bed. Love from all of us to you. Dorothy

1954/3/25 Marie to Irving (Book 9, 223-227)

3/25/54

My dear Irving!

I got your letter last week and I'm glad to hear that thank God, you are well. And I think that you got my letter as well. As it seems we thought the same because when I write to you, you respond to me at the same time. Lee called me last Saturday and we were going to meet, but we couldn't because her sister-in-law left. If everything is going well, then I want to go out (this weekend) together somewhere. I will call tonight about her plans. If she has nothing else to do then I will see her. [In English] I know you would like to be with us, too. I wish it [would] be possible, but sometimes we can't help it. Just we got to try to make the best of it. [In Hungarian] Yes, Irving dear I was with Herman last night, [In English] he is getting along. He called the doctor and he has to be in a cast for two more weeks. We hope that everything is going to be fine, but he makes his trouble worse. For example, if I bring something to him then he just yells why do I bring anything to him because he can buy it too. And the lady begged him to say what he wants or she would have shopped for him anything. Do you think he wants it? He is so proud or afraid that it would cost even a cent, I know. And what does he eat? I don't even know. I only know it's a lot of nothing. He, as always, only needs one kitchen and maybe he is doing this because I did not want to rent a room with him as he wanted it. So, this way he does not want it because he still mentions it, even today, that there is a three bedroom available which would be cheaper than the way we live. And as soon as he gets better he will go there. But I don't want it for myself. And he can do whatever he wants. He was happy to hear from you. He got the cookies and he would have called Lee already, but he is worried that he has to speak to her mother. You know, he does not like her. Besides that, he already asked me when will it be Passover because he thinks that you will come. He does not say anything, but I know he is waiting for you to come here. Oh yes! I just got a letter from Dorothy and she was very happy to hear from you, but you did not write enough. And you know, my Irving don't wait until Dave will write to you because he works very hard, night and day. Dorothy's father is very sick. So there is enough for them too. Now, take care of yourself and write about everything. And don't forget to eat. Hermine and the family are sending their greetings. Now I will send my greetings. I kiss you with love. Maria

I will send a check here.

1954/4/2 Marie to Irving (Book 9, 203-204)

4/2/54

My dear Irving!

I got your last letter with your photograph, which I was very happy about. And I'm very glad to hear that thank God you are well. I hope that my letter will find you in the best of health! Out of all [the photos] this is the best. I saw the rest. They were at Lee's. But those are not really good. I have one that I took when we went to Hermine's and I think that is better than the rest. I will attach it here to you anyway. I hope you will like it! She looks better in it. Lee called me last night and she is ok and told me that she did not get mail this week from you either. I hope everything is fine. You know my dear Irving, as I mentioned in my last mail that I will meet with Lee. So she came. She met me on Saturday afternoon at work. I introduced her to my boss, Mrs. Sternfield - you know her too - Do you remember them? So, I introduced her to them. They liked Lee very much. [In English] They think she is very beautiful [szép] and very lovely. Anyway, they liked her. [In Hungarian] After that we went to eat at Gluck Stern. We went to Radio City Music Hall from there, which I enjoyed very much. [In Hungarian] I think that Lee [In English] told you all about everything. And she is a sincere and honest plain girl. [In Hungarian] And she looked very good. She was nicely dressed. [In English] and she missed you very much. [In Hungarian] I hope that [In English] it wouldn't be very long and we could be together again. But with a car to come it is a very big trip. [In Hungarian] And I don't know if it is worth it because you need four days to travel and you will be exhausted. But take care of yourself and write about everything. [In English] And be careful how you are driving with the car there, too. Oh yes, I saw Herman, Hermine and family this week. They are all right sends there love to you and also Dorothy. She was very happy to hear from you. And Dave he is working very hard. [In Hungarian] I know that it is not easy for him because it is a very hard job. And Herman [In English] he is getting along. [In Hungarian] I hope that they will take the cast off next week and then it will be better for him. It would be about time already. I don't know anything particular about me. Everything is the same. [In English] Take care of yourself. With best wishes and love to you from all of us and [In Hungarian] from me separately, Maria

1954/4/19 Marie to Irving (Book 9, 209-211)

4/19/54

Dear Irving!

I'm sorry that I kept you waiting for so long with my letter, but I hope that my lines will find you in the best of health! And I hope that you are not working too hard! As you mentioned, you started to sell. That itself is enough work. You need time to rest, too. How are you otherwise with the eating? Did you gain any weight already? At least a couple of pounds. Write about everything. I talked to Lee last week and she was alright. We were going to go look at dresses, but it rained that day so we didn't go. Since then, before the holiday, she was busy, but I hope we will have a chance to meet soon! Last night I was at Hermine's for the second seder and Herman is there for the weekend, too. He does not want to stay any longer even though [In English] he is having a wonderful time with the little Linda. You should see her (kane hare) She is a big young lady. She knows everything. She even talks Hungarian! I could eat her up. Oh yes, my Irving dear [In Hungarian] I almost forgot that Hermine told me that you called her. [In English] I was very happy to hear that. And that Herman was there, too. At least you had a chance to say hello to him. [In Hungarian] Besides that everything is fine. [In English] I'm fine. But as you are asking about the social life. I'm sorry to say that at present everything is the same, no excitement. And it is not an easy job. And as you are asking if I met Lee's family. As yet, not yet. Only I was talking with them on the telephone and they wanted me to come and meet them. But I guess it will wait until you will come here. And [until] then you take care of yourself. And let me know when and how you are coming here. If you will drive, then be careful don't run, take your time, it is better to be slow and safe. And now take care of yourself and let me hear from you, too. With best wishes and a very happy holiday. Love, Maria

Where were you for the seder? It would have been nice if you could have been here, too.

1954/4/20 Marie to Irving (Book 9, 213-214)

4/20/54

My dear Irving!

I'm writing a couple of lines again, that we are well. I hope that my lines will find you in the best also. Although, it is true that it's been a week already since I heard from you. I hope you are well my little brother! You are upset about others, but you don't take care of yourself. I called Lee last night and she is well. She is waiting to see you already very much. I don't blame her because we are waiting for you to come here soon, too. Only that is very hard. Have you made a decision my Irving? Maybe it would be better by train because it would be at night and you could rest in the meantime. Also, I don't think that it would cost a lot. I think it's worth it because you would spare your health. If you would have somebody to come with you, it would be different. It is easier for two. Oh yes! My Irving, I will meet Lee this Saturday again and she would love to be together with you also. She is a very fine girl. She is true and does everything willfully, not because she has to. I don't know what we are going to do yet. I hope it's not going to rain on Saturday! Otherwise everything is fine. About Herman there is the following, he was at the doctor yesterday and he is well. There is no reason why they can't take the cast off of his leg, but this doctor is not in a hurry to take it off. He must be waiting until it's completely healed so he won't have a problem with it later. Whomever he puts a cast on keeps it on for 4 weeks, no matter what kind of break they have. So, he still has to have it on until May 9th. He will take the cast off then. The doctor told him that in advance because he did not want him to be upset to have it on for so long. He started to tell him at the beginning and he saw that [In English] he got all excited so he figured he is better off this way. [In Hungarian] Now it is important that [In English] it won't be long, another couple of weeks and then he will be all right. He is a little nervous like always, but otherwise he is all right. [In Hungarian] He is getting the money from the compensation and if he would want that much, he would have no trouble at all. [In English] With best wishes and love, Maria

4/26/54

Dear Irving!

I got your letter and as you can see I'm trying to respond immediately. First of all, I'm very happy to hear that you are well, thank God. And I hope to hear that from you again. We are well too and everything is the same. No particular news. Yesterday I was at Hermine and others [In English] and they are alright, except Hermine is very busy. The baby keeps her busy all the time and you probably know that Linda will have a little brother. And she doesn't have the time to write. And now Linda wants company. You will hear how beautiful she speaks, even Hungarian. Yes, as you mentioned Lee wrote to you that we will meet next Saturday. Yes, we did after work. I met her at the Radio City Music Hall. And I enjoyed it very much. And also she brought me a beautiful collar. She crocheted it herself. [In Hungarian] Which I am wearing right now on the sweaters. You will see it when you will be here. Besides that, I just told Lee that if you are coming on Saturday I will be home. And I want you to come to me and stay over at night because you can be with Herman also and no need to run back so far. And we will eat by me. And then [In English] you will have the whole week to do everything you want to. I will be at home Saturday when you will come. Telep[hone] T.R. 8-5719. Address 1898 Harrison Ave, Bronx near Burnside. And Herman is alright, too. [In Hungarian] And as you wrote my Irving, if it's possible to [find] work? And now I will get to the point as you mentioned, my Irving, How is the work situation. It is the way as always. We have to decide first what we want. And what is better for us because only living to work is not worth it, no matter how much one can make, unless if there is some joy coming out of it. Working only for the money is not worth it because the money goes away one way or another. And that depends on you my Irving. I can't live like this anymore. If one can have a good future in it then it is worth it, but only a simple job for one. But we will discuss this. Life is too short, so one has to live in it too. Take care of yourself, Love, Maria
Till I see you.

5/15/54

Dear Irving!

I just got your letter which I was very happy about and I'm happy to hear that everything is well. I talked to Lee yesterday and they are well. Her sibling is here. When you left he/she came. Thank you, my Irving that you called me on Sunday night even if I was not at home. I got your messages. The lady told me that you called me. I was at home about 10pm. I'm glad to hear that you were smart and did not go home with the car at night in bad weather like that. I talked to Hermine and they are well also. I saw Herman too. He is a little bit better, but it takes time. He was at the doctor's on Thursday and the doctor said that the bone is healing, it just takes time until it's completely healed. It is possible that he will have to have a bath for his leg because the warm water is good for it. He is always afraid that they will rush him to go back to work, even though it's not true. I told him that until he is completely better, they can't send him back because he could say that it is still hurts. No, he doesn't need to neglect his leg because of that. But I will leave this too. Otherwise everything is fine. Just take care wherever you go and whatever you do. And write about everything. You have time to look for a room and maybe you will find a cheaper one. I'm sure it is hard, and it takes time too, but I hope you will find what you want. The trailer is not the best, but you will see and you will do the way that is best for you. I am glad that you take the vitamins. I hope they will be good. I can't buy any vitamin. I have some too and I tried, but I stopped more than once because it is not good. I wish you could gain weight from it! I already gained weight since last week. Now, take care of yourself and write. And rest. How are your eyes? And don't be upset. Lee told me that she would not mind if you could be here again. Best wishes and love. Maria

May 25, 1954

Vinnell Co., Inc.
Subway Terminal Bldg.
417 Hill Street
Los Angeles, California

Attn: Mr. A.J. Kirkland

Gentlemen:
I am very interested in the possibilities of employment with your organization as Purchasing Agent, or Chief Expediter. My experiences are in expediting and buying for contractors of CPFF basis. I would appreciate receiving an application for employment at your earliest convenience. I remain, Very truly yours,

I. Gluck
1810 Highland Avenue
Portsmouth, Ohio

1954/5/25 Marie to Irving (Book 9, 191-196)

5/25/54
Dear Irving,
Received your letter and was very happy to hear from you, and that everything is alright with you. Last night I spoke to Lee, too. She called me. [In Hungarian] and she said that she got a letter from you and does not know what to do because as she mentioned, you want her to go [In English] half way to meet you on the weekend. [In Hungarian] She thought you were kidding at first, but now she can really see that you want this. Now she would like it too because it's not so bad by train. She can rest there too. It is true that you should not go with a car because the weekend is very busy, especially [In English] the roads outside of New York. But if you want to, do as you like. But be careful!! [In Hungarian] And take care wherever you go and whatever you do. Besides this Lee surely mentioned that we were at Hermine's on Sunday. Lee enjoyed it very much. If you could see Linda, how cute she is and how much she loves Lee. She already knows her too. She went to sit on her lap. I can say this much my Irving, that she is a very refined girl. I know that she is honest. [In English] and she means it when she said she likes all our family. [In Hungarian] There was a Hungarian boy by Hermine's mother-in-law, but he can be dropped too. He thinks that this is still Europe. He thinks that the girl will support him. [In English] He was afraid he will waste his money, so he wanted to know everything the first evening. And if I have any money. I told him no - and that's all. I bet he is like Herman, and who wants that. So, it is gone with the wind. [In Hungarian] And the rest of them did not call me. I don't pay attention to them already. But I will leave this too. [In English] About Herman. He is getting along. [In Hungarian] I saw him yesterday and I told him to write, but he is so lazy. He doesn't know what to do with himself. And he doesn't want to write until he can stand on his feet, but that takes time. It hasn't been so swollen. And don't be worried that he will sign anything. I told him that, and so did the lawyer. The most important thing is that his leg gets better. Hermine and her family are alright, too. They send their greetings. Also, were you in Columbus? How are the relatives? And thank you that you thought about me to give greetings to everybody. Also you asked me if I plan to go on a vacation or not? Right now I don't know if I will go anywhere. I will see. Wherever I go a better place costs more. And this year I bought the coats. As you know that too. So, I have to save somehow. And [In English] this is one way to do it. [In Hungarian] Write about everything. And thank you for letting me know about everything. Oh yes, Lee wanted me to go over to her on Sunday, if she does not go to you. I wanted to go if she does not have other plans, but I told her I have time to go some other time. [In English] We have plenty of time. [In Hungarian] And eat. Don't forget about that. [In English] Best wishes to you and Love, Maria

1954/6/2 Hermine and Eugene to Irving (Book 10, 316-317)

[from Hermine]

Dear Irving,
As you see this is a very short letter. Thank God we are all well and hope to hear the same from you. I'm sure you had a wonderful time with Lee. She probably told you I was so busy on Friday when she called that I could hardly talk to her. We also had a nice weekend. Lot of company yesterday and today we went to a park with Linda and we had the most wonderful time with her. She really enjoyed it. Will write you soon again. Let us hear from you. Love, Hermina. Maria and Herman are well also.

[from Eugene]

New York June 2 / 54

Page 722

Dear Irving,

Having a two day holiday I'm taking advantage of it and answering your letter. In reply to the appliance I was interested. It seems that here in New York, retail competition is big enough so that a consumer has the better deal. I'm enclosing the catalogue you have sent to me and a circular from a local retail outlet. This will explain what I mean. About my new venture I have nothing yet. I'm still studying its possibilities. Have you heard from Scot Homes? Hermina, Linda, and I are fine. Hope to hear from you soon. Love from all of us, Eugene

1954/6/5 Hermine to Irving (Book 10, 318-320)

6/4 - 54

Dear Irving,

Here I'm enclosing a snapshot of Linda. I know you'll like it. We think it is pretty good. She is getting bigger and smarter every day. One night we were laughing about something when Eugene was holding her in his lap. All of a sudden she looks up and smiles saying "Funny!" That Linda! Hope you had a wonderful weekend with Lee. She called us, but I was so busy that I couldn't talk to her. I'll call her up some night. I know she understands. Today is Friday - Linda is asleep yet so I'm taking a chance of writing. That's all for now. Love from us all, Hermina

1954/6/5 Marie to Irving (Book 9, 173-176)

6/5/54

My dear Irving!

I'm sorry that I did not write this week, but the time passes somehow before you know it. Although, I did not get a letter from you either this week, only I got your card from Washington. [In English] I'm happy to hear that you are alright and you enjoyed the weekend. [In Hungarian] Lee called on Tuesday, but I was not at home. [In English] but I got the message. [In Hungarian] ...and really she called me at work. But I didn't speak to her for too long. We will meet probably today and maybe we will go to the movies, then we will have more time to talk. How are you otherwise? I hope to hear the best! What did you decide? Did you find something? Write about everything and take care wherever you go. There is nothing particular about me, everything is the same. About Herman? He is like he used to be. He is lazy to write. Last night I went to see him and he is a little bit better, the only problem is, as always, that he is angry and I can't talk to him. I can't call him on the phone because then I don't hear anything except arguing about why I did not call him! And to go there he shouts again about why do I go? Whatever I do, no good comes out of it. Do you know that he is angry because he is looking for an apartment and he only talks about that. He lives like an animal and doesn't even eat like a human being. He has no kitchen where to cook and he would like to have a home. And he does not tell me to go with him, but I know he wants it. And I told him that it is only possible, if he gets married, otherwise I have to live my life, too. I don't want to bury myself alive. He blames everything on me and he doesn't care what's going to be with him. He thinks that he does everything for me. I told him that he can do whatever he wants, I don't hold him back. He does not want me to buy anything for him. He does all this on purpose. So I don't mind, but I will leave this too. Do not write about this. I asked him if he wrote to you...but he does not have patience. Now he will be better so he can look after it and he will buy what he likes. I don't know what to do with myself. What more can I do with him? He is not a baby that I could have him sit on my lap and tell him a story. He will not do the right thing anyway. He says that I am dumb so I shouldn't talk. Do not write to him about this, he would choke me for it. I will leave this, too. [In English] Hermine she is alright. [In Hungarian] Oh yes! Lee just called me and I will meet her tonight. Now take care of yourself wherever you go and don't be upset. Let's hope for the best. Did you put on a few pounds yet? [In English] With best wishes and Love, Maria

1954/6/23 Marie to Irving (Book 9, 81-84)

Dear Irving,

Received your letter in which I was very happy to hear that you are alright. I thought that you must be busy because I didn't hear from you for a long time. I spoke to Lee Monday evening and she told [me] you called and everything is alright and that is the most important thing, to be well. Otherwise we are all well. I saw Hermine and the family yesterday. They are alright except it is getting very hot for Hermine. The last couple of days [were] really hot days. But we shouldn't complain. This is summer. Soon it will be cool, too. Time goes by, before we know it. And know also about Lee, as you are asking from [me] she probably told you all about everything. Last Saturday we went downtown to Glicksterns for dinner and her mother came along too. So finally we met. It seems that she is a very nice woman and how she said she is in love with you and she loves you very much. And you know Irving dear what I said. The girl who gets him probably was praying very well because he is a very good boy and he will be a good husband. They shouldn't think they are somebody and somebody is nobody. So the mother said he is getting a good girl, too. I said I hope so. That's the reason Irving picked her to marry. So far it seems they are honest, sincere, and very plain people. But the only way to really know someone is when people live together. But it is up to them both to make a good and happy life together. And I'm sure Irving dear you will do [your] best. We will talk more about everything. And whenever you come let me hear from you. Call me up. [The] telephone [is] TR.8 - 5719. And take care of yourself and be careful how you are driving with the car there, too. Hoping you have a very pleasant trip. And let me hear from you. Till then with best wishes and love as ever, Maria

1954/7/1 Marie to Irving (Book 9, 178-181)

7/1/54
Dear Irving,
Received your letter and was happy to hear that you are all well. And everything is alright with you. And as you mentioned about changing your plan. I'm glad! Because the traffic would be very big and you will enjoy it much better the following week. So let's hope everything will work out for the best. But the only thing is, I don't know if it is worth it to come with the car the way you mentioned because you wouldn't have much time left. It is such a big trip. But you know that too. And I hope that you will do what's best for you. I spoke to Lee too and she is alright. She told me that she spoke with you! And also I called Herman, too. He received your letter. Otherwise he is alright, he gets along. He comes to see me sometimes. I also spoke to Hermine today. They are alright. Everyone sends their love to you. And please take care of yourself on the weekend, how you are driving, or wherever you go. About myself, everything is alright. But it looks like I will have to take my vacation in July. No definite date yet, but the only time I can take any time [is] in July. So I will see and then try to make some arrangement. It depends on if Hermine will need me. And if yes, I should be at home. That is all at present. But I'm closing for now with best wishes and love to you, Maria
And don't worry and take care of yourself

1954/7/15 Marie to Irving (Book 9, 166-169)

7/15/54
Dear Irving,
Just a few lines that everything is alright. And it was nice to hear your voice. In a hurry I didn't know what to say. Just that you will be back later. You heard that too, because I know how you talk. And I was happy that you arrived safely. I spoke to Lee and Hermine. They are alright. Lee was on the beach with her mother, and it was a very hot day yesterday, but today is a little better. Now about myself. I made a reservation at the Pine's new hotel in South Fallsburg. I was there about 6 years ago. It is just for a rest. It is a small place. If everything is alright, then I have the reservation for this Sunday, then I will go there. The Levovich Pine View Hotel, South Fallsburg. I will let you know when I will be there. And don't worry. Take good care of yourself. I could come to N.Y. anytime it is not too far. I will have a good rest there. Otherwise nothing new, everything's the same. Let me hear from you whenever you can. With best wishes and love, Maria
And please keep up the good job and gain another 10 pounds. Until next time. Love, M

1954/8/3 Marie to Irving (Book 9, 161-164)

Aug 3 / 54
Dear Irving-kém,
[In Hungarian] I'm so sorry that I didn't write. [In English] But I'm sorry. I was thinking of you every minute, but was too lazy to sit down to write. The truth is, I wanted to tell you something good. And with this waiting, time went by without anything. Before I knew it, it was time to come home. First of all, I'm fine and had plenty of sunshine and rest. I met people, but they are married or too young. I knew that before I went there so I wasn't disappointed too much. I needed the rest, too. Just to get away from the city for a while that helps. I met a very nice girl there. She is a little older but very nice and I hope to see her in the city too. I met others too who want to see me in the City. They had some fellows there too, but they were babies and for that I didn't bother because it isn't what I wanted. Then I met a chazzan from Kassa - he is here for six years. And he sings on the radio, too. So as you see I met people, but not the right one. I still

have to look around. So we still have to look around. But don't worry, time comes for everything. But now, how are you getting along with everything? Let me hear from you. And take care of yourself. Oh yes, I spoke to Lee and she told me that you called her and everything is alright. And we are going to see Hermine Wednesday. Also I spoke to Herman. He called me last night and he is alright. He might come over tonight. Otherwise everything is alright and take care of yourself. I had beautiful weather and now take care of yourself. With best wishes and love, Maria

1954/8/8 Irving to Marie (Book 16, 139-143)

8/8/54

Dear Maria,

I'm glad to hear from you, and to know that all is ok with you. Did you enjoy your vacation? Tell me more about [it]. I hope that you met interesting people and that you gained a few extra pounds. The fresh air, proper breathing helps anyone to vitalize the health. I, personally, would not have gained any weight, if not a daily five minute exercise and canned milk that I drink. Thus, as you see that it is essential to eat properly and get some physical exercise. Also, I'm taking "unicap" vitamins, once a day. So, all in all, I'm going to maintain my present weight, without being, or becoming, fat. Enclosed you'll find a "Readers Digest Contest", I filled it out and hope that you'll win with it. Just mail it in the enclosed envelope as addressed. Lee told me that you called her from the country. She was very glad that you went for a vacation, and so am I. What do you think of her, Maria? Did she change any since you know her? Let's have your honest of goodness truth. Ok, Maria? Our present plan is for September. I will know more about [it] as soon as I hear from Lee. In New York, marriage is a costly proposition. Just last Sunday I was over to Arthur and family. They are ok. They'll leave for their vacation on the 15th of August to 15th of September. This was a picnic. The Roth's and family were there. They and everyone asked about you and family. Jenny with her boy friend was there. Samuel, too, was there, and inquired about our family. He didn't change. Jenny did not speak much. The only conversation I had was "hello and by." Flora looks good and so did Arthur. They plan to sell the factory after their vacation. Aunt Helen was not there. I saw her a couple of weeks before. She would like to return to Europe. Well, I guess I told you most of the gossip. I'm glad that Hermina and Diana [are] getting along well. I spoke with Eugene via telephone, just after Diana's birthday. How is Linda? Give my best wishes to all. Did you see Herman lately? I hope all is well with him. Let me hear from you when you can, as you can. Till next time, take good care of yourself and regards and love to Hermina, Eugene, Linda, and Diana. To Herman and you too. Love, from Irving

1954/8/10 Marie to Irving (Book 9, 72-74)

8/10/54

[In English]

Dear Irving,

Just a few lines that we are all well and hoping to hear from you the same. I don't know why, but I didn't hear from you for quite some time. I saw Lee last Saturday. She is alright. She told me that she spoke to you on the telephone and also mentioned about the wedding plans. So let's hope for the best. But it is hard when you are so far apart from each other. Oh yes, Irving dear, we were talking with Lee and mentioned about Herman. Maybe it would be a good idea if you would mention to Herman to get a suit for the wedding because I mentioned it to him once and he said he wouldn't get any. I told him then he can't go the way he is. You don't want him to go there like a (shnurer) I know he is almost impossible, but maybe he would listen to you. But if not, I don't know what we will do with him. But don't worry, because we know he is very stubborn, for him everything is good. But we have to make him realize that it isn't so. And he could do that much for his brother. That is all you are asking for. And if he wouldn't listen then he just can't go. You tell him that in a nice way. And how about you, Irving dear. It looks like you will have to get a nice suit - a new blue suit. I wish I could go with you. Please don't get just anything. Lee wants to see you look very nice and me too. It pays to get a good suit, because it lasts longer and always looks nice. And Irving dear, if I can be of any help, please let me know. And take care of yourself and don't worry. And try to get the things before, so you wouldn't have to run [at] the last minute. With best wishes and love, Maria

1954/8/17 Marie to Irving (Book 9, 198-201)

8/17/54

My dear Irving,

[In English] Received your letter and was very happy to hear that you are all right. What is the most important. And also I spoke to Lee last night after she spoke with you and she told me about your position. That you don't know how long you will remain there. That is true, it is hard to get a job, especially with a good pay. But that is not everything. No job is worth it to worry about and get sick. And you should know that it is always for the best. Some cases we make more, [then] we spend more and don't enjoy it. And the idea is you should take care of yourself and not to worry. And let's hope for the best. There must be a good way out. You always will be able to get a job, only thing is it takes time. Or it might not take too long. But don't forget that it would be harder if [you] would wait until you would settle down. First there would be more expenses. And this way if nothing else you can come to N.Y. and try for something else. Or maybe you could look around in Washington, too. So you better take care of yourself. Oh, yes, Lee told me that you are planning to meet in Washington this weekend. I'm sure Lee is more than happy to see you. And it is good for you to see her too and Irving-kem dear, as you are asking about Lee! What I think of her. [In Hungarian] My dear Irving, I know as much that [In English] she is a good girl and she would do anything for me if I would want to. [In Hungarian] She is not selfish nor grabbing everything to herself like some would do. Some girls would be demanding from now on. And I think that you know better than I would because I don't go that often with her. And it is harder for her because she wants to help her mother, too. I think she is probably paying for the cost of the wedding also because as I can see it, her mother wanted a big wedding. She did not have in mind to pay for it, but you don't have to talk about this to her. And now take care of yourself wherever you go and when you travel with the train...and wish you lots of good luck and I hope, that everything will work out the best. About myself, everything is alright. [In English] Hermine and family they are alright. Herman he is alright, too. Everyone sends their love to you. Oh yes, you mentioned about Arthur and family. I know them. That is the reason I wouldn't like to bother with any of them. But don't worry! I got a letter from Dorothy and they send their love to you all. But [the] only thing is Dorothy was operated [on]. An emergency appendix operation. But now it's good [and] she is better. With all my love and best wishes. Love, Maria

1954/8/23 Hermine to Irving (Book 10, 322-324)

New York 8/22 - 54
Dear Irving,
Thank you very much for your lovely gift to Diana. It was nice to see Lee. Maria came over with her. The only thing was that just then we were so busy with both children that we hardly had time to talk to them. Linda is getting better now. She too needs adjustment. She really grew up now because she knows that she is the big sister now. We also received your letter and we wish you mazel tof. The 19th of September is pretty close now. About the job, don't worry. Something just works out in time. The main thing is that you have a nice girl and that's more than you think! Maria told me that you'll meet for the weekend in Washington. Hope everything will work out for you. Herman came over too, but the first week was a very tough one. So we could hardly sit down to talk. Oh! Yes! I'm sorry I couldn't talk to you on the telephone when you called, but you know the reason. Besides, just then I was expecting the doctor to call me and I shouldn't tie up the phone! Let's hear from you. Love from us all. Hermina
Many thanks again from us and Diana

1954/8/26 Irving Intro Letter for Job (Book 16, 58)

1810 Highland Avenue
Portsmouth, Ohio
August 26, 1954

Duquesne Power & Light Co.
Pittsburgh, Pennsylvania

Attention: Personnel Manager

Gentlemen:
Reference is made to your project at Shippingport, Pa. Have had considerable experience as a Buyer and Expediter, and desire to make application for a position with the Shippingport project. Would appreciate receiving an application form from you. Thanking you for this courtesy, I am, Very truly yours, I. Gluck

9/15/54

Dear Irving!

I can't imagine why you became so lazy to write. I am lazy too, but still we need to write a few lines. I should not write now because I wrote to you and you did not respond yet, but I will leave this too. I hope that my lines will find you in the best. I talked to Lee and she said that she talked to you and you probably will come back to New York. As far as your job concerned, it's not worth it to be upset about it because you knew that it will not be permanent before you took it, and you took a chance. So now, take it easy and sooner or later with a few days, it does not matter. Especially if they will fire you, then at least you can get unemployment. That's worth something, too. So, then you can look for another job at ease, even if it is hard to wait, but it's not worth it to rush it. Let's hope for the best! Now where will you go for the holidays? 9/27/54 that is, on Monday night (Rosh Hashanah) starts. Are you going anywhere? [In English] You Irving-kem, better write. And first of all, I want to wish you a very happy holiday and also a very happy New Years. Hoping that the New Year will bring you all the happiness, good health, and good luck. All your dreams should come true. And next year you should come to visit me together with Lee. And take care of yourself. Let me hear from you, too. I'm fine, Hermine and family, Herman too. He is waiting for you, always asking me when you are coming. Now, with all my best wishes for a happy New Year and Love to you. Maria

P.S. Just received your letter and was very happy to hear that you are alright and hoping to hear the best again. Until the next time, take care of yourself, and don't worry. Everything will be alright. How is the weather there? Here it looks like [it's] going to rain. Love, M

9/18/54

Dear Irving,

Just a few words that we are alright and hoping to hear from you the same. First, I saw Herman last night. He is alright and told me that he didn't hear from you for quite some time. Wanted to know when you are planning to be back in N.Y. Otherwise, he is alright and sends his regards and best wishes for a happy New Years. Also gave me this check to make it to you. Take care of yourself and let me hear from you. I didn't hear from Lee as yet, but probably will call later. Hermine and family they are fine except busy, as usual. This is all at present. Until next time, with best wishes and love, Maria

October 5, 1954

Dear Lee and Mr. Gluck:

Well it has been about two weeks since you left the big town of Portsmouth, Ohio. And boy it seems like a month or longer. I haven't anyone to play tennis with now, I sure wish you both were here so we could play a good game, you know how good I am not to mention how good you are. Everyone here that I know that you know is just as always, well maybe a little worse. It rained last night and the weather has sure changed. It is, I would say about 55° or colder. I bet it is cold up in New York also. I guess Alleen and Bob will be moving to Louisville, Ky. in about a month or so. You did know that Bob was working as an electrician now did you not. I sure had a wonderful time in Indiana on my vacation and I hope you like New York as well as I think you do. You and Lee should be married by the time you get this letter and I would like to extend my congratulations to both of you. I hope you got a job like you wanted so some day you can open that store or some little business like you were talking about. By the way you be sure and let know what you are doing, and how well you like it. Have you gotten any mail from Lovell lately, if not he is just as he ever was. The only thing different is that he is going to Roanoke Va in about a month or so. He didn't say exactly when. Boy you know I sure will miss him a lot. I guess you know just how much. He will more than likely write and tell you when he leaves. Well you be sure and write me all the news from the big City, and let me know how everything is with you and your little girl as you always spoke of her. Give your Lee my best wishes. Sincerely, Rosalind Rowsey

Tuesday

Dear Irving:

Received your letter, and as always were so glad to hear from you. My neglect in writing you is due to no special reason, only perhaps lack of time and good intentions that don't seem to materialize. I always say - "tomorrow I must make time to answer letters" and so it goes. Forgive me, please. Maria did write me that you were in New York because of your job. However, I thought it was only a temporary thing. Also, you don't say much about your wedding plans. Is everything all right? I sincerely hope so. With us, there is nothing new. Conditions out this way do not look too favorable, and they haven't been for a while now. I don't mean only with us, but as a general thing. In David's new line of endeavor, it is nothing but work, work, work. I thought we were tied down before, but this exceeds everything. The hours are long and the work is hard. I cannot be there too much, since Freddie goes to school, so the burden falls on David. However, David himself seems to thrive on hard work - he looks fine and has gained weight. We are sure glad Herman is getting along better. Is he able to work yet? That sure was an unfortunate occurrence. Your nephew is getting to be a big boy, and he sure loves school. I only hope he always will. Write again soon and let us know about everything. I promise this time I won't let such a long time elapse before answering. David and Freddie join me in sending our love to you and all there. Dorothy

1954/11/29 Janice Benowitz to Irving (Book 22, 241-242)

Miss Janice Benowitz
2102 Aqueduct Ave.
The Bronx 53, New York

November 29, 1954
New York Times
V609 Times
New York, New York

Dear Sir,

I hope you will accept this letter in the "spirit" in which it is intended. Obviously, I noticed your Ad in the Sunday Times paper. However, this letter is not one offering you a position; instead it is one of a social nature. We are a small group of girls who thought perhaps it would be nice to arrange for an informal gathering some evening. To put it frankly, we would like to meet some nice, intelligent, refined, young men, and I think an informal get-together is a wonderful channel for getting to know people. If you, too, would like to meet some nice, attractive girls, please let me know. My telephone number is: Ludlow-4-7063. I wish to state at this time that I don't know who you are, and of course, the same pertains to you, but please understand that this intent is perfectly honest and legitimate, as well as entirely respectable. Good luck - I certainly hope you landed a nice position! Sincerely, Janice Benowitz

1955/2/17 Rosalind Rowsey to Irving (Book 17, 342-345)

Dear Mr. Gluck,

Well it sure has been a long time since I have heard from you. I was just sitting here thinking about you. I thought I would really like to hear from you and know what you were doing these days and how the world has been doing you. Everyone here is just about the same except they're all just a bit thinner, you know P.K.S. and all the other contractors have been giving a lot of reductions in force. Lee left February 1st and I miss him so much, I would give anything to see him. He received his reduction of force in January the 28th, but he stayed over until the first of February. I have gotten four letters from him and hoping he will write more often. He writes the nicest letters you ever read, I think, and I know you would think so too. You know we usually agreed on everything. I haven't had a single date since Lee's been gone. I wouldn't tell him for the life of me because you just can't tell about these men. Now since I've told you about my lover, you tell me about yours. Are you married? If so, when, where, what time, and all about it. I would love to know. Now listen, you better write me. If you want to know Lee's address well here it is. 2713 North View Dr. S.W. Roanoke, Va. Always, Rosalind
P.S. Write soon

1955/5/26 Rosalind Rowsey to Irving (Book 17, 231-234)

Friday 26, 55

Dear Mr. Gluck,

I received your most welcome letter Wednesday. I intended to write you yesterday, but just couldn't find time. Everything has happen[ed] since I wrote you last time. My Daddy went to Indiana to work for a while. He seems to like it fine. Daddy hasn't been very well lately, but I think he'll be feeling better soon. Anyway I hope so. Guess what? Lee and I are engaged to be married. How do you think Mrs. Rosalind Meadows sounds? I think it will be sometime in July, we're not sure about the date as of yet. I told you he was in Roanoke didn't I. Well he came up the first of March, and the first of April, then I went down the 22nd of April to meet his parents and they are very nice. I took one day off from work, left Huntington at 7:15 Thursday, April 22 and got to Roanoke 9:15. I went by plane by the way, and that was my first trip in the air. Boy I'm telling you there's nothing, no nothing like flying. I'd go on an air plane trip every day if I had the money. Well any way Lee brought me back to Portsmouth Sunday morning April 24th and boy did we have a nice trip. He stayed up here until May 2. And Friday, April 29th he gave me my ring. It sure is a beautiful one. Gluck I'm convinced we're doing the right thing because I love him very much and I'm sure he loves me too, cause Lee just isn't the type that goes around telling girls he's in love with them. I've never been so happy in all my life. Well I guess you're tired of hearing about Lee and I. There is just one fourth of the people here now that were here when you left. Boy they're laying them off by the 100. I tried to get them to lay me off, but they won't do it. That makes me so mad. Well now since I've told you something about the job I'll go back to Lee, you know something, he is the only thing I have on my mind as you can tell. Any way I write him nearly every night and I've not seen him since May second, but he will be up June 11th which is two weeks off. I'm not sure if I can wait that long. He called me Wednesday evening and I guess we talked a good half hour, believe me I could have talked longer. Tuesday May 31 is my birthday and I'll be 19. You'll probably get this letter the same day. Lee got me something, but won't tell me what it is. I never did tell you what he got me for Christmas did I? Well he got me a radio. It's a pretty one, also small. For Valentine's Day he got me a sewing basket and boy did that come in handy cause of the fact I'm doing a lot of sewing. I made Lee a shirt and if I do say so I think it is sure pretty. Also it looks very good on him. You didn't tell me about yourself in your letter so don't forget that the next time OK. I'm going to close for now cause my hand is getting tired so___ Hoping I see you sometime soon. Be careful and be good, your best girl Rosi, will soon be Meadows.

P.S. Write Soon

1955/7/14 Abraham Markhoff (lawyer) to Herman - Injury (Book 21, 309)

July 14, 1955

Mr. Herman Gluck
% Kreitzer
1898 Harrison Avenue
Bronx, N.Y.

Dear Mr. Gluck:

In our last conversation we advised you that the Weisberg Fixture Co. Inc., had communicated with us, and advised us that they did not carry any insurance to cover them for the injuries which you had sustained on December 28, 1953. Their contention was that they had installed the shelves in question exactly in accordance with the instructions of your employer. Furthermore, that their employee had pointed out to your employer that the shelves needed additional support, but that he refused to permit them to do it. We suggested to you that you speak to your employer to ascertain whether these facts are accurate. It is our understanding from the conversation had with you, that your former employer will not cooperate with you in this matter. In view of the foregoing, we do not feel that we would be able to establish a cause of action against the Weisberg Fixture Co. Inc., and due to the fact that theydo not carry insurance, we would not be able to settle this case, but would have to go to trial. It is our considered opinion, therefore, that no further action be taken with reference to the third party claim. We will, however, be pleased to handle the reopening of your compensation case, and would suggest that you call at this office after Labor Day to discuss the matter further. Very truly yours, MARKHOFF, BLOCH & MERLIS by; Abraham Markhoff

---

1955/9/14 Irv to US State Dept -Frozen Funds' Use for Claims is asked (Book 19, 154)

September 14, 1955

State Department
Senate Foreign Relations Committee
Assistant Secretary of Senate
Thruston B. Morton

Dear Sir:

I would like to inquire whether as an American citizen if I am able to file a claim against the Czechoslovakian Government under the Soviet Regime for my property. If so, please advise me what action I should take to enable me to secure an exchange value of funds held by the American Government. I would appreciate any information or assistance for the above. I remain, Very respectfully yours, Irv. Gluck

1955/9/28 US Dept of State to Irv - Frozen Funds' Use for Claims is asked (Book 19, 156-157)

September 28, 1955

In reply refer to
SCS 249.1141 Gluck,
Irving/9-1455

Dear Mr. Gluck:

The receipt is acknowledged of your letter of September 14, 1955 requesting information as to the filing of a claim for property losses against the Czechoslovak Government. With respect to property claims of American citizens arising from the nationalization and other confiscatory measures of Czechoslovakia, you are informed that the United States Government has made and will continue to make every effort to bring an adjustment of this unsettled difference between the two nations. It is of course impossible at this stage to predict the outcome of these efforts. You may expect due public notice to be given to any developments in this regard which may call for action on the part of interested citizens. Sincerely yours, for the Secretary of State:

Francis E. Flaherty
Assistant Director
Office of Special Consular Services

1956/4/24 Dorothy to Irving (Book 12, 307-308) - Irving visited California

April 24, 1956.

Dear Irving:

We were anxiously awaiting your letter since there were so many things that were indefinite until your return home. As far as your job is concerned, I guess you weren't too shocked since you had an idea of their cheapness. I sure hope your dreams of going into some business for yourself will materialize and then you won't have to go through these sort of deals. Good luck with the vending machine business. I'm sorry I can't report a thing about any of the West Coast plants you visited - none of them have contacted me. My thought in this matter is that you would actually have to live here before they seriously would consider your application. I received a letter from home too and of course they told me how happy they were to see you, I had no idea that you would wait so long before phoning them, and they seemed disappointed that the time was so short. At any rate they thought you looked very well, and a short visit was better than none at all. I must tell you that the day after you left the weather took a turn for the worst and we had nothing but cool, dreary, rainy days. Believe it or not, today is the first day the sun has been out in all its glory and it's beautiful once again. I'm glad you had at least one week of nice weather so you can see how it usually is. We felt very badly about your forgetting your coat, since the papers were full of the cold weather in Chicago and New York. I hope you didn't catch cold. You didn't mention about finding an apartment. Did you find one to your liking? I hope so. Before I forget, the family's new address is 7521 South Phillips Ave., Chicago 49, Ill. PINKUS Things with us are just about the same, and business goes on as usual. The Main Stop is still up for sale, and I sure wish someone would come along and buy it so there would be less headaches. I relayed to Freddie your request that he write you about his business, and he said "Oh - Uncle Irving knows I can't write - just read". So I guess you'll have to wait a bit until you receive a personal letter from your

Page 730

nephew. How did you enjoy your train trip home? Anything exciting occur? Which way of travel did you actually enjoy most, the plane or train? Write us soon about everything. In the meantime, our love to all the family and tell the girls I will write them soon. Skippy and Cheeta send their best to you too. Freddie says I should be sure and write you that. Love, Dorothy

1957 Undated Hermine to Elsie (Book 10, 18-19) - draft -Fred is 8 years old

Dear Elsie,

We were very happy to hear from you and as you see I'm answering you already. We are very happy to know that you and the family are well. Jane will have a good time and I'm sure will enjoy her vacation in California. My brother lives there. Maria and Irving visited him and his family, but I have never been there. I would love to meet his wife because in her letters she sounds wonderful. He also has an 8 year old little boy [who] I never met. Irving and Herman were here today and they are well, thank G-d. Irving works very hard. He is also in the vending business. Maria is well thank G. and took a small apartment and she loves it. It's a very nice little place and she is sorry for not fixing up her own apartment years ago. Otherwise, everything is well with us. Mazel tov to the new baby brother. Samuel and his wife were at our house. We are kept busy, but it's worth it. Eugene loves his flowers and is always around them. It sure is a change from the apartment house. Maria and the boys are well. Her address is 1818 Clay Ave. She fixed up her own apartment and she is so happy to have her own. Irv and Herman are using our address for mailing. They are well. Irv works hard, but that's how it is when you work for yourself. Love from us to all of you. Hermine

1958/7/9 Undated Irving to US State Dept - Request for info - Draft (Book 19, 190)

State Department
Washington, D.C.

To whom it may concern:

Gentlemen,

We would be interested to learn about the report of July 9, 1958 in the N.Y. Times with regards to legislation No. S-3557 that may allow U.S. citizens to collect claims against Czechoslovakia because of their taking of American-owned property. We would appreciate any additional information, and/or application for same.

1958/7/22 Undated Dorothy to Marie (Book 12, 258-260) no year

July 22nd

Dear Maria:

Again it's been a long time since I wrote you. Quite a bit has happened during the interim. I was in the hospital for surgery in June, but thank God that is over and I'm beginning to feel myself once more. Also, my stepmother has passed away. This was the end of May, but my family didn't let me know until it was all over. She died very suddenly at home, and it was quite a shock as she apparently was well. In fact she got up that morning, prepared breakfast and didn't complain of not feeling well. The family all left for work and by the time they got home she had died. My poor Dad took it very hard, naturally, and he himself is not at all well. I hope to make a short visit home in early September to see them. And so it goes. My sister has quite a job working and having to take care of the household. David and Freddy are fine. Today Freddy went to the business with David and will be with him. It gives me a chance to just rest. I believe I wrote you before that David has made quite a change in the business, just concentrating on beers and carrying just a few sandwiches and pizza. This has worked out wonderfully well and he is doing better than anything he has attempted before. Enclosed is part of a paragraph which will show you what he has gone into - all foreign beers. No place else has it out here, and if business keeps on as it is going now we shall have no complaints. David just said this morning he wishes Irving and Herman were in it with him. Actually right now we could use a bigger place and more help. Since Irving saw the place it has been remodeled, with a long bar and it looks real nice. I'm keeping my fingers crossed but I really believe David has hit it this time. Please show this page to the boys and Hermina - I'm sure they will find it interesting. Also, here's a picture (not too good) of Freddy, which appeared in a local newspaper. [1958/7/18 Freddy's in Lomita Newspaper Article (Book 7, 302) - Freddy] Enough about us. I hope this finds you, the boys, and Hermina's family well and happy. Give our love to all of them. Write again soon. Love to you, Dorothy

Tuesday

Dear Irving:
I don't have any definite address for you, so will write you in care of Hermina. We received the packages you sent to Freddie, and he sure is enjoying the sets. To tell you the truth, David got as much fun out of building with the Log Stix as did Freddie. Thank you very much for the gift. There is nothing too much new. We are all feeling fine, thank God, and things go on as usual. Maria had asked me to write when the best time would be for you to call David and talk with him. I wrote Maria last week and said David is usually home on Monday and Wednesday evenings. However, this is again changed. David decided to keep the cafe open 24 hours a day, so now he leaves later in the morning and doesn't get home until midnight. He will do this until he breaks in his girl and is able to leave her there alone. So now his hours are worse than ever. I will write you when this changes (soon I hope). I sent Maria some snaps we took of Freddie and enclosed one for you so you can see how big your nephew is getting to be. He is doing very well at school and seems to like it a lot. I sure hope he will always like it. I understand from the girls that you are still not too happy with your job. I'm sure sorry about that, but getting just what you want is never an easy matter. There's always something. David works very, very hard at the cafe, but yet doesn't seem to mind it. Sometimes I wonder how he can do it or how long he can keep going. It makes it hard too that we live so far away from the cafe and traveling back and forth takes so much time. Well, Irving, it's been a long time since we've heard from you with a letter and will be awaiting one soon. Thank you again for Freddie. Love to you and Herman from all of us. Dorothy

January 19, 1959

Mr. Joseph Stein, Ass't General Counsel
Foreign Claims Settlement Commission of the United States
Washington 25, D.C.

Re: Claim No. CZ-1, 321 (I)

Dear Mr. Stein:
Please accept my apologies for the delay in answering your letters of January 12, 1960 and September 11, 1959 requesting evidence in support of my claim. I am enclosing a copy of the letter and information which I received from the Department of State on October 17th, 1950. I have repeatedly requested further information regarding our additional property from the Notary Public (Leleszi Jegyzo) District of Hivatal Kralovsky-Chlumec, Lelesz, Czechoslovak. As of this date, however, I haven't received verification from them. Please advise me if the U.S. Government can be of help in aiding me to establish the additional proof needed. Cordially,

Irving Gluck

Jan 18, 1960
Dear Irving:
Please forgive our not writing you sooner to acknowledge receipt of the check. I don't know whether the New York papers have played up the epidemic of virus flu that has hit California, but all of us were down with it, David, Freddy, and myself. Thank God we are all better now, but it really lays you low for a while. I don't have to tell you how much we appreciate what you did, and Dave says to tell you he will do his best not to let you down in any way. He will write you personally soon, but I thought I'd better get this mailed right away so you will know the reason no one wrote you. It was nice talking to Maria, and wish it could have been with all of you. I'm going to mail this right away so will make this letter short. I don't want another day to go by without letting you know. I hope this finds you and the family well - Again our everlasting thanks! Love from all of us. Dorothy

March 9, 1960

My dear Hermine,

Don't be angry that I'm calling you by your maiden name, however I only know you by that name. I would like to answer your letter completely, however, that which you ask - - the land numbers for your properties cannot be obtained and mailed. Perhaps in 1945 and 1946 through the foreign ministry and through Ignác you have inquired about similar problems. I wrote at that time everything and mailed information about the properties to you. However, I am no longer working in an official capacity because I am retired. Even if I were still working, even then I would not be able to give information about everything because it's impossible to do so today. It's impossible because the district office as it was in 1950 has been dissolved. The documents have been given to the local communes in which the properties belonged to. Therefore Polány - - the properties of that city have been transferred to that city. I have tried to secure these documents from there, but the local adviser would not cooperate. Therefore, with regards to the property, I can only give general information. First, I will begin with the following [advice that] you must not dream about regaining your properties. Every Jew that left the country renounced all of their possessions here. Therefore [ownership of] all your properties has been renounced. Those properties whose owners are in America were confiscated by the state, and they have passed into the state's ownership. The land, forage land, and grazing land, was given by the government to the local land commune of the people of Polány. In all respects, it is now a Communist affair of the community. The whole village uses the property as communal property. All the land and everything else is being used, therefore private land ownership has ceased. The house has also been confiscated and it became government property. The government sold it to Sandor Puskár , who at one time was your tobacco planter [He worked for us as a laborer. He is the one who dug under the building and stole tobacco - Irv]. I'm sure you knew him. The Polány properties are therefore communal agricultural property. Before this took place, Ignác Klein of Lelesz was guardian and rent collector as well. I believe that one of your family authorized him. Ignác does not live in Lelesz now, since he has remarried and left for Nagymihály, that is, Michalovce, to live there with his sister Rozsi. I do not know the nearest address. Regarding your father Jermus' securities, he [your father] withdrew it at the Lelesz security office and paid the debt to the credit union. With this he was lucky, because in 1945 the government confiscated all deposits, including bank deposits. I have lost also, and I'm suffering now. Finally, I am giving information regarding [your grandfather] Samuel Schwartz's house in Lelesz. He sold it to D'Oczy. He was a neighbor, and he attached it to his house. Since then, he [D'Oczy] has also died. Finally, so that you know everything that happened during the time the Jews were taken away, all movable properties were auctioned. Things that were left over were stored. So don't have any reservations about anything. If it happens that the American government would assist the Jews who are still alive, they would compensate them for local compensations. Then you would receive something in return. There must be a law between the two governments. Therefore, follow the local papers and if such a law exists, declare your intentions. That's all I can write about. I have delayed writing because I have been sick almost a month. Now, I'm hardly able to write. Besides being sick, I suffer from high blood pressure. You were very lucky to have gotten in to America before the war and haven't felt the Fascist government in the second world war and the Revolution that followed. I'm wishing that my letter will find you all in the best of health. May you all receive my luckiest wishes and heartiest regards. Respectfully, Pál Lengyel

New York 3/22/60

Polány Land Office, Czechoslovakia

Gentlemen:

I have authorized Lengyel Pál to submit information pertaining to the property from the Land Office. These include all the properties which are listed under Herman, Hermina, Maria, and Ignác as Polány residents, Jeremias Gluck's children. Also Lajos Gluck (brother) Emil and Lenke, his children - - owners. David Gluck, also an American citizen, is legal guardian of Emil and Lenke. Since all are American citizens, we are interested to know the existing legal setting of the properties and the amount of land as recorded as of 1945. Thank you, I. Gluck

1960/5/1 Bertha to Irving (Book 19, 238-239)

Sun May 1 - 1960

Dear Irving,

[In Hungarian] I didn't think it was necessary to explain, Ziga's letters are being sent to you, what do you think about the content? What, if you do, do you want to do? We trust you, I'm sorry I haven't been in New York for 10 years, but I'm really afraid of the trip. [In English] I hope that you don't mind to take care of it for us. Thanks a million in advance. How about spending your vacation with us in Florida and Mariska. We have a room for you both. Regards to Hermina and family, to Herman with love to you and Mariska. Bertha and Mannie

1960/5/2 Bertha to Irving (Book 19, 215)

May 2nd, 1960

Dear Irving:

Enclosed please find all papers pertaining to my claim. I am enclosing a letter September 19, 1948, one of March 20, 1949, and one of April 4, 1960. I know you are more familiar with these papers and know you could explain it to Mr. Stein much better than I could. Hoping this finds you and your sisters enjoying good health. With sincerest thanks for your efforts, Love, Bertha

This is a letter I have sen[t] to Mr. Stein,

Dear Mr. Stein:

I have received your notice about your representative being in New York City on May the 10th, 1960 to interview claimants. At present I am a Florida resident, and if you have no representative coming for similar purposes to this part of the country, I would like to [be] represented by my cousin, Mr. Irving Gluck of 76-20 175th Street, Flushing Long Island #6, New York. Mr. Gluck has a similar claim interview scheduled for 1.00 P.M. on the tenth of May. I will forward Mr. Gluck all my papers. In fact, Mr. Gluck left Europe in 1940 and he is well informed of the location of the properties. Thanking you for your consideration of this matter, I am, very truly yours, Mrs. Bertha Weingarten

1960/5/5 Pál Lengyel to Irving (Book 19, 217-219)

Lelesz. 1960 May 5

Dear Hermine, and all of you,

It has taken time to answer your second letter, due to the fact that I have been hospitalized in order to regulate my blood pressure. I was admitted for three days, and since then I haven't been feeling well. The doctors said I was lucky with this warning. I could have died. Since this doesn't pertain to the problem at hand, I am going to proceed to the present case. It was difficult to secure these papers because the district office in Király Helmec has been closed and all official documents were brought to Terebes [Trebišov], including the Land Registry. From there, I have received the following information: that these documents can only be issued through official channels and officers. Therefore I have to be satisfied with the papers and information that I could obtain locally in Polyán. Regarding this, I have made registration documents of the present existing property, which are enclosed. It's made on two documents, but it contains seven registrars per documented books. I believe everything is in them which incorporates your property. If this is not useful, then there is nothing left to do but to go through the Foreign Ministry, and officially ask for these registered documents. This will be easier now because the numbers are known. The final, official confiscation number is 50-1950.

To be sure, I would not have undertaken similar problems for anyone, since I had to put in a tremendous effort to fulfill your wish. I am doing this for you because your dear father, Mr. Glück, was a very good friend of mine. We have on numerous occasions exchanged loans. For example, in 1938, I loaned him 500 Czechoslovakian korona of which he repaid 40 Hungarian pengős. Therefore figuring 40x7, that amounts to 280 korona, and the rest remains [unpaid]. Of which, it's beyond your own control that he was unable to pay since he was also taken away. Therefore 220 korona are still due me from you, when you inherit it. If you can afford it, mail this amount to me, since my retirement pay is small. Here one dollar is worth seven korona. Therefore, I would request $32 from you. Of course, as you know, legally I cannot ask for this. As for the present documents I have paid for them, however I am not asking for payment on these unless you desire to do so. I would ask this of you, address the payment to my sister, Anna Lengyel Belane Bartko, because my sickness is such that although I'm alive today, I may be dead tomorrow. I've written to Ignác Klein in this matter so that he can help you, since he has used the property after the war. However, he didn't even reply to my letter. I heard that he wanted to hang himself, but they found out and saved him. Who doesn't have problems like this? We are very happy that you are in good health, even though you lost here, you found something greater to compensate for it.

I believe in my previous letter, I have written more, therefore I do not want to duplicate myself since there have been no changes since I greeted you then. I send greetings to you as well as your family, brothers, and sister. I remain with best regards. Pál Lengyel

1960/5/6 Selma Jaeger to Irving

May 6, 1960
Dear Irv,
I know that you're surprised at hearing from me. No, I haven't completely forgotten you. I am presently teaching 6th grade in Maryland. The children are polite, eager to learn, and wonderful. I'm really enjoying working with them. A friend from N.Y. visited me recently. She is a teacher on Long Island. If you are still unmarried, I'd suggest that you telephone her. In my next note, I'll include her name, address and phone number if you wish. Do let me hear how you've been spending your time. How's Bonded Vending Company? Where are you now residing? I hope you are in good health, and that you are happy. As ever, Selma
Sandymount School
25 Ave and School Drive
Marlow Hgts, Md.

1960/5/12 Selma Jaeger to Irving

May 12, 1960
Dear Irv,
Your note was so warm that I can't help responding quickly. The letter gave my spirits a life. Barbara Nagel is my friend's name. Her address is 134-15 231 St, Laurelton, N.Y. [in black ink, Irv's handwriting] LA7-9155 You can probably find her phone number in the phone book. I just finished reading an interesting article in Time Magazine (May 16th edition) about vending machines (page 93) I think you'll find the article enlightening. As the [school] term is rapidly coming to an end, I am engrossed with records, reports, and report cards etc. This is one part of my job that I'd gladly hand over to someone else. Kelcy sends her regards. Each time I see her she asks me if I've heard from you. She's teaching in Plainview. Don't work too hard. Do take time out to have fun. Cordially, Selma
Do let me know how the date turns out.

1960/5/15 Irving to Bertha (Book 19, 236) - draft

May 15, 1960
Dear Bertha and Mannie,
This is my first opportunity to write you since the hearing of May 10, 1960 with regards to the properties. Please be advised that the following are required before the claim is approved:
  1. Verification of ownership;
  2. A claim signed by your brother Fred;
  3. Any additional information of sister's whereabouts;
  4. How has the value been estimated?
  5. What was the productivity of the forest rights?
These letters that [I] have, I'll rewrite them in English, that is, anything that pertains to the properties. To each letter a statement will have to be attached and notarized. If you'll mail me the copy of your claim then I'll make the necessary copy for Fred. Also, you will have to submit a copy of the "Lajstrom" from which you have taken the "Land Numbers as recorded in the European Office." That you have in your possession. I did not mention anything about Ressike from Helmec and any property rights. If you have any statement, please advise.

5/30/60

Dear Selma,

Enclosed herewith please find commission due for services rendered. We are planning to ship shortly a new machine serving double heart candies. Thank you again for the speedy attention in the matter. We remain friends of yours forever.

Bonded Vending and Associate

Irv and Barb.

Miami Beach

Florida June 26 / 1960

Dear Irving!

I hope that you are O.K. and all your loved ones. We are fine except it is quite warm, I hope that you decide to visit real soon with Mariska, yes? Enclosed you [will] find all the letters that I could find. Also my sister's address Moskovitz Zoltan and Rezsi, Boji Street 2855, Kiraly Helmec. Please would you write to Ziga and maybe he could get you all [the] information. I am afraid to correspond with him as I may get in [trouble] with the European government. You can tell him that he shall be taken care of for his trouble. Our best wishes to your sisters Hermina and family, also to Herman and Mariska, with love to you all. Bertha and Mannie

Thursday

Dear Irving:

We received your telegram with the wonderful news, and to say that we are happy for you would be putting it mildly - It goes without saying we wish you the best of everything, and may your newfound happiness continue through a lifetime. You deserve it. Maria called us the other evening and she spoke so highly of Barbara, we were just thrilled. Our heartiest congratulations. Incidentally, we do have an unlisted phone number - so here it is in the event you would want to phone us - Harrison 97884. About David, you undoubtedly know what we have written to Hermina in a recent letter. Since then, the latest tapping showed something in the liquid which did not appear before. What it is they do not as yet know, but another tapping is required to see if it shows up again. David went to a specialist the other morning and he suggested more x-rays and tests be taken so David is going in to the hospital tomorrow for those tests. He may have to be there a day or two (I hope no longer). Just when we will know the results I don't know. It may take a week or so. Let's all hope everything will be all right. It's funny, with all this, David looks wonderful - hasn't lost any weight, and to look at him no one would ever believe he wasn't in excellent health. I will keep you posted, and I hope my next letter to you will contain good news. Again, from all of us to you and Barbara, our congratulations. Is the wedding date set? Write and tell us all about it. David and Freddy join me in sending love. Dorothy

July 17, 1963

Dear Barbara and Irving:

We received your note and were glad to hear from you. No doubt the baby was named after Irving's father. Flora goes to the hospital Sunday for a major operation. May God be willing that she gets well. We will not be able to have visitors for some time. Otherwise, we are O.K. With love to all, as ever, Your cousin, Arthur

P.S. I am having this note typed because since my illness my writing has deteriorated.

Columbus, Ohio

March 29, 1967

Dear Barbara and Irving:-

Such a long time has passed since I have wanted to write - first to tell you how sorry I was to hear of your misfortune and to wish you well in the future. Much has happened since then - We lost Charlotte - Arthur hasn't been well and Aunt Helen spent two weeks in the Hospital - previous to which she was with us - later and now it keeps me busy going back and forth to her house. I am sure Jerritt is making progress every day - he seems to be a mature little boy and very lovable and I am sure you are proud of him Keep well - all of you - give our love and best wishes to the whole family and our love to you. Flora

1967/6/7 Arthur to Irving and Barbara (Book 17, 204-205)

June 6, 1967

Dear Irving and Barbara,

We surely are glad to hear from you and to know that all of you are well. We cannot say the same for ourselves as I am crippled and can barely walk 50 ft. I am in bed about 20 hours a day and must have a nurse to take care of me. It is too much for Flora. Besides she is having several ailments and is losing her eyesight. In addition, she has to take care of Aunt Helen who is in a psychiatric ward and has been failing rapidly. So you can see that we are having all we can do to take care of ourselves. I hope your business is going along nicely and that Jerritt and Irving take care of Barbara efficiently and nicely. With love to all of you from us all, As ever, Arthur Gluck

1968/6/13 Emil Schwartz to Irving, Tape (Book 3, 289-291)

13.6.68

My dearest!

I'm enclosing a few lines to the tape. I thank you very much for working for me [on my behalf]. It's a shame that the tape does not give you the real bell sound of my voice, it's beauty. The tape has recordings on both sides of songs. It was made in a hurry, that is, on a borrowed tape machine, however from this small tape recorded sound can be the judged by those that are interested. They can decide if this is what they want. It is natural that it would sound better if I would sing and they would listen to me in person. (The machine that I taped it on is called Panasonic Radio Recorder.) We thank you for the beautiful package. Lili thanks you separately. She will write to you, however since she is on a job for two months, she has been very busy and didn't have a chance to write to you. We have gotten a letter from Gèza bacsitol and $30 were enclosed and it was noted that it is for the children to buy them something. We thank him, he is a good man, and we are going to write to him also. I want to thank you Irving for thinking of us. Please write Herminkem and Mariska, and you too Irving. With kisses, Lili, Emil and the children.

1972/6/12 Emil and Lili Schwartz - TAXI PERMIT (Book 3, 334-339)

1972 June 12

My dearests!

It has been a long time since I have written to you. Emil took over this assignment. Last week we received a letter from Hermina and from Linda. They wrote that they were in your home and your older son had his birthday. We also congratulate him and wish him happiness for 120 years.

We hope that during the summer someone from your family will come to Israel. It seems like the children are not preparing to come! How is the little boy? I hope that he is developing and we would like to have a picture of you and of them, aren't you going to make some? Please send us some so that we can see you all!!

Thank God that we are well, very happy, and want to share with you that we have gotten the taxi permit. I'm sure you remember that we have been waiting for this for many years. You can imagine that this has given us happiness, that finally it happened, and we have succeeded to receive it. As it's being said, it's not complete happiness because it is quite a problem to secure the automobile. We hope that the almighty will help and that we can get a loan. The biggest problem is that the interest rate is quite high, but unfortunately we can't get it any other way. The main thing is to be healthy. We'll manage it somehow.

Misha doesn't know about this happiness because he's not at home. This is the ninth day that he has not been home. As you know, this is his fifth month that he's a soldier and we can't inform him because we don't know where he is. We hope that God will take care of him!!! Dudi just finished the eighth grade and we have signed him into the high school where Misha finished his studies. We hope that he will study as well as the older boy.

In our family, thank God everybody is well and they ask about you and send their best wishes and kisses. I am going to write to Herminka. Please Barbara, write, because I think Irving doesn't have time. How is your study of Hebrew going for you Barbara? And the older boy? What is with the Israeli friends? Did they leave the country finally?

When I think more about this lady it is laughing matter. You know Irving dear, when they were here in the country, I looked them up and they told us that we should not go to America. We should just stay in Israel. But then they have not returned back, I think?!----- she has a young husband that could purchase a house like my son and my husband, but so it is with that man, he is egotistical, is it true? Please write to us and I promise I'll reply right away.

Sending kisses to Hermine and Mariska and the children. And to you with love and kisses, Lili, Emil, and our children.

My Dearests.

I hope that our letters brought you good news and will find you in good health.

Lili has given you all the information therefore I will write to you only a few lines. Thank God we are well. We are very, very happy for our taxi number. Finally after 20 years of night work I will work in the daytime now and for myself. Now the main problem is to secure the money for the automobile. It will happen somehow, God will help us! Please write us and till then love, kisses to all of you individually. Emil

1972/7/12 Emil Schwartz to Irving (Book 3, 304-305)

Emil Schwartz
H.[enrietta] Sold 13 A
Bat Jam, Israel

[1st of AV תשל'ב = July 12, 1972 - Sherwin's note]

My dearests, until 120

I want to write to you just a few lines. I'm at the airport and I have a half an hour and I would like to thank you for the check. It is natural that you have helped me and that it came in very handy. Really, we thank you a lot. Thank God we are well. I purchased a car and I'm working with it. You can imagine how great our happiness is. Finally after 20 years, I'm working now in the daytime and not at night, and in my own car. That is a great word. Hope that you are also well. Lili will write to you in more detail. Barbara is very good

and explains everything in detail She is an ashes hayil [אשת חיל = a woman of valor], right? Hermina's daughter according to her is not coming. When are you coming to Israel? Please don't be angry that I am writing this in a hurry [grabbing time]. Hencsu Lefkovits' daughter is here on a Kibbutz for two months. There is not much news here. Loads of love and kisses to all of you, again many thanks. Lili, Emil, and the boys.

1973/7/26 Lili Schwartz to Irving (Book 3, 292-296)

Emil Schwartz
Bat Jam, Ramat Josef
Henrietta Sold 13A, Israel

July 25
My dearests!

It is Wednesday afternoon July 25 we have just arrived from the airport. We are going to answer your questions. We waited there one hour and 25 minutes for Dezső's son Freddy. We were told that he had arrived at six o'clock in the morning.

You cannot imagine how we felt. If I wouldn't have been ashamed I would have cried. And we were running from one office to the other so that we can learn where they have gone. The only thing they were able to tell me, regretfully, was that there was a bunch of students and they left.

We also brought Blanka's daughter [Lea] with us so that she would be our interpreter. We arranged everything nicely, we had a plan, we would have taken him from the airport to show [him] places. Unfortunately, it wasn't a success. We hoped that he will call us on the telephone. Emil said that he sent you the telephone number and we hoped that you have given it to him with our address together! My dear Irving, I don't know where we have misunderstood each other. Barbara has written to us that he will arrive on the 21st at the Lod airport in Israel from Rome. We read this letter three of us for an hour and 20 minutes and everyone understood that he would arrive here to the airport and here we were sitting at the telephone and we hoped that he's going to report. The poor child. We don't not even know how old he is, that is, Freddy? Why would he be in Tel Aviv only one day? After that, where is he going? I'm full of questions. It would be very painful if he would travel from here without seeing him. Irving dear, tell Dezső that we are sorry about this matter, but we're not at fault! What's new in your place? Is Hermina's daughter not coming? And you? How are the children? I think they are precious! Our boys thank God are well. Misha is finishing the military requirements. He's a very good boy. A precious one.

Dudi-kam, is working now during his vacation because he needs pocket money and he doesn't want to ask for everything from his father. We are very happy that he thinks that way, that he sees that life is not so simple. He is also a very good boy, like an angel. Thank God we cannot complain. How is Mariska and Herman? Please write about them.

We thank you for both of the two checks that you sent us. I put it in the bank for Dudi for next year's education. It is regretful that it costs a lot of money and they raised it for the next year. If God will help us, next Saturday Jidesz Lefkovits' two daughters from America will be here for the summer. One is here with her husband. We are happy that young people are coming to Israel and happy also that we can accommodate them. I hope that there will be true peace. I would also be grateful to meet you also!!! When?? Please write at once!!! Kisses to you all with lots of love, Lili, Emil and the children

P.S. Our telephone number is 873.194

[from Emil] Kisses with love, Emil.

1973/8/19 Tata Feuereisen (Lili's brother) to David (Book 17, 80-81)

Dear Dezső,

We are sending you regards from my family - the Feuereisen brothers and sisters, Tata, Hajual [Hancsu], Jenő [Ucu], Blanka, Magda, Lili, Aliz, Blanka's husband Geza Zucker. And last, but not least, your cousin Emil, my sister's [Lili] husband and family. Salommal [shalom], Tata

19.8.73

P.S. What do you know about Zseni-ről?

1973/12/16 Emil and Lili Schwartz - Yom Kippur WAR (Book 3, 279-285)

1973 Dec. 16

B"H

Dearests! Until 120

I was preparing to write to you for quite some time, but we are so aggravated and nervous as we live at this time, so that we don't have patience to do anything. I have to tell you what we have gone through and unfortunately what we are going through today with our oldest boy Misha due to them. Thank God he came home just now in good health after three weeks since the war began. He was the first day to be taken from the temple on Yom Kippur at 8 in the morning. From that moment on only God was taking care of him because I cannot write it down what went on. He went through it. He was near where the water flows in Sinai [the Suez Canal]. He worked day and night between the dead and the bullets flying around him, but he didn't care because he was in a hurry to save the lives of as many boys he as could. He's a happy young man because many soldiers will be thankful to him for his medical help to them. The doctors with whom he has been working were very satisfied and they liked him. He received a promotion since his superior wanted to promote him. His heart pains him tremendously for the many soldiers that lost their lives. Perhaps I shouldn't write about this because all of us will get sick from all those losses. At this moment again we are in fear. We live in fear because Misha left two weeks ago and he was sent by his superior to Africa [to the other side] where he continues his work. It's unfortunate that they're firing at them daily from the Egyptian side. What can we do? We hope that the Almighty will continue to help him and take care of him. Therefore, we are praying night and day.

In other words we live in a difficult time. The agricultural life has stopped completely. There aren't any people at home, which can be said officially, the people are mainly in the military, and therefore everything is at a standstill. The tourists have stopped coming [and] the hotels are empty therefore Emil-kem has to work double so that we could earn the minimum that is needed for us. All that is not important, as long as we have dry bread in front of us. The main thing is that Misha and all our soldiers should return home in good health!! Dudi-ka is a very sweet boy and worries a lot about his brother. He studies diligently. He keeps us alive. What's new at your place? How is Hermine's family? They haven't written for quite some time, perhaps they are angry at us? I was thinking perhaps Linda at least would inquire about Misha. It appears that she's not interested in how he is. It's not bad, let it be this way. Not everyone is Barbara!!!---- ---------

We thank you for your beautiful letter and the check. You will be laughing to know what we'll use the money for - Misha lost his watch at the front and I decided that with your money and the amount we had, we'll use it for the watch purchase and therefore we bought him a nice watch.

What is with Dezső's son? I can tell you he is a very sweet, sympathetic, young man. We were happy that we were able to finally meet him. My whole family liked him, We regret that he stayed for such a short time with us. I hope that when peace comes, he will return to us once again. Give my kisses to him, also to Hermina and Mariska.

I hope that the two young men are healthy and you also. It will be Christmas vacation and you will be able to rest yourselves. Please write. It will be very good for us. With lots of love and kisses to all of you and to the boys. My family also sends their kisses. Lili and Emil.
[from Emil] Lots of kisses and love to you, Emil

1974/4/15 Lili Schwartz to Irving (Book 3, 273-278)

1974 April 15
My Dearests!
We received both of your letters and it hurts me that I'm just now replying to you, but I don't have to tell you how difficult are the days we are living here, the business as well as the agricultural situation, I'm sure that you know. We have additional tension because of Misha, the fear, because wherever he goes is very dangerous territory. I can tell you one must be strong to accept this great aggravation. We hope that the good God will help, so that it will be good for us.

We are very happy to get your letters especially now because of the beautiful pictures and also the gift, the check, you included. We cashed both checks and the boys got for Passover shoes and Dudi-ka pants. It is unfortunate that the prices are so high, also we can't even get to it, that is, to anything. Can you imagine that the pants itself cost 100 pounds [font-ba] and not to speak of the shoes which were very costly, prices tripled from what it was before. Thank God, these are big boys who also need pocket money. Misha especially is always on the road. Here you have to drink a lot [I assume water by Irv] and sometimes he gets hungry and there the food costs money. He's watching every penny, should he spend it or not, but even then he needs a lot, but that's not a problem, the main thing is that they should be healthy. He's a beautiful, good child and a serious thoughtful and dependable young man. Also, my little one is the same. I and the children thank you for the check. Misha said that as soon as he has a little time he will write also. They send kisses to you and they do not want to believe that those two little boys have grown up and they were happy to see the pictures.

I hope that Barbara feels well and there isn't any problem. Irving dear, think it over because there isn't such a woman and it is very difficult to find. I believe that she is fantastic and has a great personality, very seldom can you find it and hope that it will remain the same way always, as when you were here, it was great to see you both of you together. How is Freddy? Sending kisses to him. Emil wanted to write but he has been very busy and doesn't have time for anything. Unfortunately, the work is very weak, there aren't any tourists and gasoline is very costly. He has to work for half a day for gas alone. Perhaps it would be good to change the car for diesel, but that would mean 20,000 Pounds extra payment and unfortunately we can't, and we have to forget about that. I'll say it once again, nothing is bad, only if peace would come then everything will be fine. How is Hermina and the family? Mariska and the boys, kisses to them. What is with Linda? We heard that Diana is not living at home. What happened? Is this the way in America, is it natural? I can't imagine it with our boys. Barbara please write to me about this will you?

Thank God that in our family everything is fine. Everyone sends their kisses. Lea was here yesterday and sends her kisses to you also. She became a very fine lady and sweet like a lady. She just finished the military service and during the fall, if God will let us live, she is going to start the university education. She will study Psychology, biology and art. Let the Almighty give her luck she deserves it, she's a wonderful child. And Blanka's children, Nili, she is like a big girl, today it is very seldom to hear about people like that. Aliz's daughter will be getting a doctorate in June together with her husband. They will be going to America to specialize, he as a surgeon and she a gynecologist [woman's doctor]. The time has come for this also, I wish that my Misha would be at that point. We hope that it will be. I would like very much if you would write to us immediately. We want thank you once again for the things that you sent us. Loads of love and kisses, Lili, Emil, and the children.
[from Emil] I also send you everything and kisses with love to all of you, Emil.

1974/10/5 Emil and Lili Schwartz, Happy New Year from Israel (Book 3, 326-329)

Dear Barbara, Yitzhak [Irving] and the children Until 120 years
Wishing you all a good year in peace. Lots of happiness from your children. We wish Barbara individually a [in Hebrew] happy new year [in Hungarian] and only good news from all of you. Thank God we are well. My little son is in the Army and became a lieutenant. The young couple are well. They just began their fourth year. They are studying a lot, and send their kisses. When are you coming back to Israel? It would be good again to see you once more, all of you. We thank you very much for the check. We bought underwear for the children for the holiday. Kisses to you all with love, Lili, Emil, and the children.
[In Hebrew] Happy New Year and g'mar hatima tova.

1975 Emil and Lili Schwartz to Irving (Book 3, 297-298)

My dearests, until 120
We can't imagine why we don't hear anything from you. We sent a telegram to your older son and hoped that you will tell us, so we can account with anything but we haven't heard anything from you. We hope that everything is well and you're well and your whole family. Here with us, thank God, everything is in order only regretfully that we are busy. Due to that we do not have the time to write. My Lili is also working outside and at home all by herself. Unfortunately, she doesn't have any free time either. She is exhausted. Thank God, the children are well. Our Mishale is in the second year at the [Hebrew] University in Jerusalem in the medical faculty, with honors. He is taking the exams. Dudi-ka went into the Army a month ago, naturally with honors because of his education. Let the Almighty maintain quietness so that he doesn't have to play war games. How is the rest of the family? We have no information about them either. We are asking you Barbara, as you do, write to us about everything. How are the boys? How is business? I hope you don't have any problems. We thought perhaps because you plan to come to Israel and that's why you're not writing. We hope that will come in time. Please write to us definitely. With lots of love, Lili, Emil, and the boys

1976/2/3 Lili and Emil Schwartz to Irving (Book 3, 318-325)

1976 February 3
Dearests, until 120
I don't remember the date or time when I've written to you, but you may think badly of me. Emil replied to the last letter from Barbara, and I was at work and I didn't add to the last letter. I don't know whether Emil mentioned that I have been working for more than a year in a shoe factory, in their sales department a half a day. They like me very much. They wanted me to work a full day however, I can't undertake it, is too much for me. I have to tell you that work is waiting for me at home also and I do not have any help. I must do everything by myself. I don't have to tell you that I stand on my feet all day, and I don't have energy and time for anything. This is the reason, explanation, of why I didn't write to you. I'm sure you must be

interested in how Misha is progressing with his learning. Thank God, he is progressing fantastically. He studies day and night and it is very difficult for him, but we hope that he will be able to graduate. As you know he studies in Jerusalem, but on Saturday he comes home, however he lives at the University. He cooks for himself. He takes raw food and prepares it there, therefore, it's much cheaper and the food tastes better. Even this way it costs a lot. Next year the cost will go up to 8 thousand pounds [fontra]. Thank the Almighty that he is at home and that he didn't have to go Italy.

Dudi-ka is also an exceptional student. This year he is studying a lot. He is exceptional in understanding and he selected eastern studies. My opinion is that if God wants him to do that, then after the military he can go into the diplomatic service [political] therefore we can't complain. It is up to the Almighty, they are good dear boys, just let them have good luck in life.

Emil thank God is well but he puts a lot of hours at work. The situation is very difficult in the country and you know it also. The costs are so high and one cannot earn enough to catch up with the cost of living. I don't know where it will lead us. The people are bitter and are afraid of the future, hope that good God will not leave us behind and everything will turn out well! How is your place? Is Barbara as precious a woman as she was before? How are the children progressing? I believe they are smart and good if they reflect the parents, it only can be the best. Please write about them, send pictures of all of you. How is Barbara's dear mother? Is she as always, beautiful and young? Give our regards to them and kisses.

How is it at Herminkem's family? Did her daughters get married? We know nothing about them, only we heard from someone that Diana left home, why? What is with the boys, with Mariska, and with Dezső's son? Kisses to all. Barbara, you are good little girl and you will tell us about everything. You are a good letter writer, not like I. Our families send their kisses. Aliz just came home from Switzerland. She was there at her daughter's place. Both of them are doctors and they are specializing there, both of them are special people. They were back for two weeks to visit.

I ask you, please write and I hope that you are not angry. Kisses to you all, each individually and the children, Lili, Emil, and the children.

[from Emil]
My dearests, until 120
Thank God we are well and hope that you too are well. My Lili has written to you about everything. In the near future I will write more. Kisses to you, Barbara, and the children individually with love. Emil
Thank you for the check that you sent us for the new year. Kisses to Herminket and her family, every member. Emil

1978/2/23 Misha and Adina Schwartz to Irving (Book 3, 286-288)

Michael and Adina Schwartz
Kyriat Yovel
4/A Varburg St.
Jerusalem, Israel

23.2.78
[In English]
Dear Barbara, Irving, Jerritt, and Sherwin,
We want to thank you for your letter and what [was] enclosed in it. I was in the way to my writing desk more than once in order to sit down and answer your letter, but I couldn't find the time to do it because the last 40 days we were loaded with 4 big exams. You asked in your letter if I [am] still studying, so that's a good answer isn't it... And even more than that, my young wife is also a student, she learns General medicine. Both of us now finish the 3rd year and have about 4 years left. How are you Barbara? You wrote about a pelvic problem which was not detected when Sherwin was delivered, and that every movement you do is painful. How do you feel now?
We live in Jerusalem near the Hadassah Hospital in which our school is, in place called 'Kyriat-Hayovel'. We have a small apartment, but a very comfortable one, and we have almost everything we need in it. Both of us learn and work, my wife teaches mathematics in high school two evenings in a week, and I work on the taxi of my father. Send our love to the whole family from the "Old" and "Young" Schwartz families. Our love to you. Michael and Adina

1980/12/15 Emil and Lili Schwartz to Irving (Book 3, 346-347)

My dearests, until 120 B"H

We were very happy to hear about you from Herminkem. We are very sorry that we were together for only a short time. But really, they told you about us also. Dearests, we are asking that you shouldn't be angry at us since we have not written to you for longtime. Hope you will forgive us. We do not have any news. It is a running life. Lili is working and then she runs to the young couple, to (Dudi's family) to help them with whatever is needed. Dudi has completed his military service and began to study at the University. He can't go to work during the first year. His wife is a teacher and works at the same time and studies at the University. They are wonderful children and all of us love her. We thank you very much, on behalf of our children, for the gift that you have sent for the wedding and they have used it very well. Also, we thank you for the money that you have sent with Herminka-val. There are a lot of places that it will be useful because this year Misha has to be helped. And God will help him so that he can receive his doctorate this year. They are studying a lot. Very seldom do they come to us. They do not have time because they are always preparing for the exams. The last year is the most difficult. They are sending their kisses and wishing good health to you and yours, especially to Barbara, with a pure heart that everything for her will turn out for the best. We have seen the pictures of the children, it's unbelievable how beautiful they are and they have developed very well. Let there be a lot of luck in their life. Please write to us even if you can just a few lines. The young couple thanks Mariska-nak for the gift for the wedding. We send you our kisses to her and to the boys. We will write to them. Blanka's whole family is sending kisses to all of you. In conclusion, our thoughts are always with you and hope to see you once again. Many kisses with great love, Lili, Emil, and the children.

1981/11/5 Emil Schwartz to Irving (Book 3, 299-300)

My dearests, until 120

I'm somewhat belated in answering your letters. It was wonderful to hear from you. And we are wishing you a healthy, good year and you should have a lot of happiness from your children. Linda has spoken lots of nice things about you. There is not much news around here only that we became grandmother and grandfather. Our grandchildren, thank God are progressing well, here and there they cry, but eat and sleep and are like gold. My son Dudi, began his second year and he studies nicely to be an attorney. Thank God both he and his wife are well. They live close by and we visit them frequently. My son Misha, thank God, he finished his education and he's now working in Jerusalem. Adina will finish also in two weeks thank God. We give thanks to God that they have arrived to this point. We are well and work a lot. How is Hermina and her family? We were very happy to see Linda. She became a beautiful girl and she should have a lot of luck in her life. We are sending you all our kisses, also to Mariska and the boys.

We thank you for the check that you have mailed to us. With it we purchased small items for our grandchildren. I'm asking you greatly, if you have any time, to write a few lines. We hope to hear from you good news. All of us are sending you our love and kisses. Lili, Emil, and the children

1982/12/12 Emil Schwartz to Irving (Book 3, 301-303)

My dearests, until 120 B"H

We have received your beautiful invitation. We wish we could go to celebrate with you in your happiness in person. We are sorry, but we can't allow an American journey like that for ourselves. So we can only congratulate you in a letter and wish the very best and the nicest to you and Sherwin. [in Hebrew] Good luck in everything the best]. We have received the New Year's greeting and the $30. We thank you very much. What's new at your place? How is the older boy's learning? Hope that all of you are in good health. Thank God we are well. About four weeks ago a little girl was born to Misha, the first little girl. They're very happy with her. At Dudi, his daughter is one and a half years old, but thank God, we are very happy with our dear grandchild. We have gone through a lot of aggravation with the Lebanese War. Here life is sickening until my children come home in good health. How is Hermina and Mariska? What is with Linda, she didn't get married yet? More likely you'll be together with the family during the celebration [in Hebrew] Bar Mitzvah. [In Hungarian] We will be with you in our thoughts. Please give our kisses to all. Please write. With loads of love and kisses to you from Lili, Emil, and the children

1987/9/27 Emil Schwartz to us, New Year's greetings (Book 3, 330-333)

[It's a card with a picture of Tel Aviv wishing us a Happy New Year.]

Dearests, until 120
Wishing all of you good health in the New Year. We hope that all of you are well. Is there any improvement for Barbara? Here the only way you could get any information if you are here, diagnosed in person and the doctors could see you. We met your friends and they gave us the beautiful gift. We thank you very much. It was good to hear from you. We thank God we are well. Kisses to all of you with lots of love. Lili, Emil, and the family, A good year (לשנה טובה)

1990/4/25 Emil and Lili Schwartz to all of us (Book 5, 102-103)

25.4.90
Dearests, until 120
It was good to read your lines [letter]. It is a very sad situation that Barbara cannot be helped. We can imagine how difficult a life you have. We think of you a lot and you are always in our mind. It has been 4 years since Lili was operated on her back. We had no choice, she had to be operated on since she was unable to sit and was lying down for months. Thank God the operation was successful. Today she's well. She can walk nicely. She comes and goes and she became a new person. She had to have another operation for gallstones. They took out 41 pieces. Thank goodness we are over that also and Lili is well. In the past they used to say that (she became very attractive woman). We are well thank God. I have given up the taxi business because I could not do it any longer and I'm looking for some other type of work. It is somewhat difficult at this time to find work since there are many unemployed. I also went through cataract surgery. It was successful. Thank God our children are well and are capable. Our older boy is a dental surgeon and has a private clinic in Jerusalem and as well at the Hadassah Hospital. He has a beautiful family with three beautiful children. Our younger son is a successful attorney and hopes to get his doctorate and also is quite capable at Bar-Ilan University. He too has two beautiful little girls and the third one is on its way. We spoke to Cantor HAS - about your beautiful Torah reading in the temple. We hope to hear beautiful things about your children. Hope that you will have lots of [in Hebrew] 'nahas' [joy]. Lili, Emil, and the children.
Lili and I want to thank you for the check that you mailed me - a little late, hope that you are not angry. How are Hermine and her family? And Maria?

1992/9/12 Emil and Lili to Irving [New Years' card]

Dearests, until 120
Wishing you a healthy, happy new year. We want to thank you for the amount that you sent us with your friends, it came in very handy. As you know, I cannot work, regretfully, and I'm not getting any retirement income. My grandchildren received Sherwin's letter and they were very happy. [In Hebrew] Wishing you a happy new year [In Hungarian] with lots of love. Lili, Emil and the children.

1993/9/22 Emil and Lili Schwartz to Irving and Barbara (Book 18, 18-21)

B'H
My dearests!
I wish all of you [In Hebrew] shana tova and g'mar hatima tova [In Hungarian] good health and peace. We thank you separately for the New Year present! Give my good wishes to everyone in the family. We kiss you with love, Lili + Emil and Misha + Dudi

1994/1/28 Emil and Lili Schwartz to us (Book 3, 344-345)

28.1.94
My dearests, until 120 B"H
We were very happy for your letter and pictures which are very precious for us. Also, thank you for the hundred that you sent me. Thank God we are well and hope that you are also. How is Jerritt with his girlfriend? We wish you a lot of happiness and [In Hebrew] nachos [joy] from the young people. How is Barbara? Is there any improvement by her? Sherwin, your son, writes beautifully in Hebrew. I thank him

that he has time to think of us and that he looks after our heritage. Lili is sending her kisses to all of you with her brothers and sisters. Kisses to you all with love. Lili, Emil, and our boys and grandchildren.

1994/5/7 Emil and Lili Schwartz to Irving (Book 3, 348-349)

Dearests, until 120 B"H

We have been quite affected to see Barbara's lines. It is unbelievable that she has sat down to write to us. I wish that the good God would give a miracle and once again she would be as well as when she was here together with us in Israel. We thank Sherwin that he has translated it into Hebrew. We are very proud of how beautiful he writes and his writing is also beautiful. We hope that your boys are well. Your younger son writes you're very busy fixing the house for your older son. When are they going to be married? We wish the young couple happiness and luck. Your younger son writes to my granddaughter so we know about you. Thank God we are well. The future should never be worse. This year I was better with my dizziness, I hope it will be as good later. Lili is well, thank God, with her problems. She says that -here it pains- and -here it pains - Our children, thank God, are progressing nicely. The family are dear and they love us well. We think of you a lot and hope to hear from you the best. We are preparing what's necessary for the [Yizkor] book. It isn't easy work, but we hope shortly it will be ready, thank God. We thank Barbara and Sherwin for their dear lines. Kisses to all of you, with lots of love. Lili, and Emil, and our family. Emil

2000/9/19 Oyster Bay Jewish Center to Irving Membership (Book 22, 375-376)

September 19, 2000

Mr. Irv Gluck
1 Laurel Lane
Syosset, NY 11791

Dear Irv:

It is my distinct pleasure and honor to advise you that the Board of Trustees, at their monthly meeting held on the 12th of September, unanimously voted to provide you with a fully paid-up Synagogue membership for the year 5761. This membership entitles you to all the benefits and privileges of the Oyster Bay Jewish Center including one ticket for High Holiday services, which is enclosed. This membership is offered to you in [honor] of years of dedicated service to the Oyster Bay Jewish Center and most currently for the services rendered as our Baal Koreh during the past few months when we were without the services of a Rabbi. I add my personal thanks to you and wish you many years of good health and sustenance so that you will be able to continue your good deeds. I wish you and your family a healthy, happy and sweet New Year. Best regards,

Jack Bernstein
President

Epilogue

For the sake of completeness, and to show how the tsunami that was the Holocaust continues to create waves amongst the children of the survivors, I am including the following three vignettes. The first two occurred as my father began to revisit his history, and the third happened to me as I became deeply engrossed in my father's papers.

It happened that my brother-in-law Shmulick Brenner came to the United States to visit us from Israel. While talking to my father in broken English, Shmulick learned that my father's friend Sanyi Klein lived in Israel. When my father had visited Israel in 1968, he had wanted to get in touch with Sanyi, but I suppose the limited time that they stayed there, the language barrier, and the difficulty of finding people without knowing their exact address or their phone number (or not having the internet yet!) made it impossible. Shmulick volunteered to look him up, and my father gave him Sany's last known address. It was just a fragment - Sanyi Klein, Arbel. My wife Hanit's father, a Sabra and a truck driver, recognized the town's name immediately. In no time at all, Shmulick made contact with Sanyi's son, Eli Klein, who still lived in Arbel, which is located on Mount Arbel in the lower Galilee. Shmulick helped arrange an international phone call between my father and Eli, with Hanit as translator. The following are the emails exchanged after that phone call.

2009/3/1 Irving Gluck to Eli Klein

Dear Eli,
It was a pleasure to speak with you today. I will look for more letters from your father and will email them to you as soon as I can. Please email me pictures of him (and you too!) Best regards to you and your family from all of us, Irving (Ignac) Gluck
[Folder attachment with letters from Sanyi]

2009/3/1 Eli Klein to Irving Gluck

[In English]

Dear Mr. Irving (Ignac) Gluck. 1/3/09
It was a very big surprise and a pleasure to speak with you, to hear your voice to listen [to] you reading and translating the letters my father sent you many years ago. I am asking your permission to continue in Hebrew.

I will try to formulate it in Hebrew, and I will ask you to translate it to Mr. Irving.
My father immigrated to Israel on the weapons ship Altalena in 1948 as a World War II refugee after his parents and two sisters were killed and burned at Auschwitz. In any case, this is the information that my father had. Despite this information, he listened for many years, until his last day, to the section for searching for relatives that was broadcast on "Kol Yisrael" all those years.

My father met my Sabra [native Israeli] mother. They married and established their home in Moshav Kerem Maharal on the Carmel coast. It is a moshav that was established at the time on the ruins of the Arab village of Igzim.

My father set up a dairy farm that was considered very big at the time, and was my father's love and pride. In January 1970, my father's tractor, with which he was transporting milk to the dairy, overturned and he died.

I didn't succeed in drawing out information from my father about all the hardships he went through to the extent that would allow me to know and remember facts. When I asked, he answered briefly. I felt that my father did not want to share the hardships of the past. In memory of his parents and sisters, he ordered a klaf [animal parchment] from an artist and engraved their names along with a painting of the crematoria at Auschwitz, the Western Wall, the Tower of David in Jerusalem, and the inscription: Remember what Amalek did to you.

The names: Moshe Frolinger, Shemaiah, Ignat, take me back many years. The letter you read to me awakens within me things forgotten, and maybe with your kind help I will be able to build from the pieces of information so important and exciting, some picture that I so miss and have almost come to terms with [the fact] that I will never be privileged to see.

Tomorrow I will organize pictures of my father (there are few) as well as pictures of the rest of the family and will send them by email.

My wife Dorit and I have three sons, the eldest is 34 years old, the second is 31 and the third is 23. The two eldest sons are married and have two sons. At the time I promised my father that I would never change my last name so that there would be continuity to Klein. Although my father did not live to see his grandchildren, so far there are already six Kleins and the last word has not been said.

My sister Sarah, who is three years younger than I, has four children, three of whom are married. She has four grandchildren. My sister's eldest daughter has lived in the US for a number of years. With your permission, I will give your phone number to my sister so she can contact you.

I write these words as I feel the indescribable excitement of the letters you scanned for me and hope that more will be found. Here they [the letters] are opening new shelves in my life that will allow me to receive missing information that I almost came to terms with losing.

I want to thank you again for everything and feel that this is the opening of a journey into the unknown that is becoming clearer. Thanks, I'll organize the photos soon and send.
Eli Klein Moshav Arbel Farm-23

2/3/09
When I tried to send the email there was a power outage as a result of a lightning storm and the email with the scanned letters plus the introduction sent to me by Mr. Irving was badly damaged. If you [can] send them to me again. Thank you so much Eli Klein.

2009/3/9 Sherwin Gluck to Eli Klein

Hi Eli!
My father is still looking for more letters from your father. In the meantime, he thanks you for your letter and says that you are welcome to give his phone # to your sister. It is 516-921-0819. חג פורים שמח
Sherwin

2009/4/1 Eli Klein to Irving Gluck

Dear Mr. Irving Gluck
I am sending you [a] few pictures of my father & mother with the dates with [the] hope you can recognize my father. Please make me know you get my mail. From the bottom of the heart.
Eli Klein
Moshav Arbel-

2009/4/1 Irving Gluck to Eli Klein

Dear Eli,
I have received the email with the pictures of your father. There is no doubt that he is the same person that I knew so many years ago in Polyan. I want to thank you for sending them to me! You might be interested in this link to a Yizkor book about Kiraly Helmec and its surroundings, including Polany. The link is in English but the Yizkor book can be found in Hebrew at Yad v-Shem. There was also a memorial service

held many years ago in Beit Hatfusot. My son will try to email you a copy of the video tape that was made. I wish you and your family a kosherin pesah.

Ignac - Yitzhak - Irving Gluck

http://www.jewishgen.org/Yizkor/Kralovsky_chlmec/kra006.html

2009/4/26 Sherwin Gluck to Eli Klein

Hi Eli!
My Dad is curious if you received the DVD that we sent? He sends his regards, too...
Sherwin Gluck

2009/4/27 Eli Klein to Sherwin Gluck

Hi Sherwin,
I received the DVD and go deeply in, I try to recognize people, somebody that maybe I saw him in the past or wherever but indeed I could not recognize even one of them. The continuation of the DVD was stories and descriptions about the region, it was very interesting and teach me about the place. Most of the history of my father for me is [a] mystery. My hope is to meet your father and hear more about my father. Thanks [to] you and your father. Eli Klein.

2009/9/14 Irving Gluck to Eli Klein

Hi Eli!
I haven't heard from you in quite some time and hope that you are okay! I want to wish you and your family a "shana tova"! I hope to hear from you… Irv Gluck

2009/12/26 Eli Klein to Irving Gluck

Hi Irv,
Sorry for the very late reply.
We're all doing well here, everything is fine!
We would like to let [you] know that we're planning to visit in the US at the beginning of April.(me and my son). It would be great to meet you face to face and [share] some memories...Generally, our planning is to come for ~ 10 days (visiting new York and Wisconsin). If it sounds good to you just let us know and we'll set a convenient day for you.. Bye
Eli Klein

2010/1/3 Irving Gluck to Eli Klein

Hi Eli!
I am replying for my father.
I too am sorry for not answering your email sooner. I will be very happy to meet you and your son when you come to New York. Please keep me informed as to the dates that you will be here and I will be very glad to meet with you both. As soon as you can let me know exactly which day you want to come to visit me so that I won't make any plans. It is very easy to get to Syosset by train (Long Island Rail Road). I look forward to meeting you and hope that you and your family are well. Sincerely, Irving Gluck

2010/2/2 Eli Klein to Irving Gluck

Hi Irving,
Well, Now it's all set. We have the dates for our visit in the US. We'll be in NY from the 2nd till the 6th on April. (landing on the 2nd evening). If you have a preferred date just say and we will do our best to sync with. Looking forward to see you! Bye
Eli

2010/2/14 Eli Klein to Irving Gluck

Hi Irving,
We're planning to visit you on the 4th on April. Is that ok? Do you have preferred time?
We'll probably come by LIRR from Manhattan. Bye!
Eli

2010/3/8 Irving Gluck to Eli Klein

Hi! 2 PM works best for me. See you soon...
Irving

2010/3/13 Eli Klein to Irving Gluck

Hi Irving,
Can you please send me your home address?
Thanks Eli.

2010/3/14 Sherwin Gluck to Eli Klein

Hi Eli!
My father's address is 1 Laurel Lane in Syosset. However, please call me on my cell phone (516-864-9155) when you know which train you will be on and when it will arrive and I will meet you at the train station. It will be my pleasure to do this and it will not be any trouble at all. Moreover, the taxi drivers here are dishonest and they will take advantage of you. Sincerely,
Sherwin Gluck

2010/3/18 Adi Klein to Sherwin Gluck

Hi Sherwin,
I'm replying [to] you for my father..
Thank you very much for your kindness. Once we know which train we are taking,we will update you.
Thanks!
Adi

2010/4/3 Adi Klein to Sherwin Gluck

Hi Sherwin,
We just landed yesterday evening, everything is going well..
Sorry for the late answer. We will take the train from Penn Station at 12:51 and should be in Syosset station at 1:44. Does that sound ok? Bye and Thanks
Adi & Eli

2010/4/4 Sherwin Gluck to Ade and Eli Klein

Hi Adi and Eli!
It was a pleasure to meet you both! I hope that we will be able to meet again and continue the friendship that had its beginnings 60 years ago!

Here is the link to the English version of the book *A Short History of the Jewish Communities of Kralovsky Chlemc-Kiraly Helmec and the Bodrog District*. When I speak to my father's cousin Emil Schwartz I will ask if there are any more copies in Hebrew available to send to you directly.
http://www.jewishgen.org/YizkorKralovsky_chlmec/Kralovsky_chlmec.html

Here also are the pictures we took today. I will send the video of my father speaking to the High School children separately. Enjoy the rest of your trip and please let us know when you arrive safely back home. We look forward to one day seeing you again. Best regards, Sherwin Gluck

After this visit, we continued to be in touch with Eli. I especially tried to find out information about Ernest Frohlinger, who appeared in the photograph that Eli had emailed, and brought with him.

2010/4/5 Eli Klein to Sherwin Gluck

[in Hebrew]

Hi Sherwin,
First I hope the child [Naomi] who fell off the bike is fine. We received your email with all the data and details. I wanted to say that the meeting was very, very exciting and left us with deep feelings. We of course want to stay in touch and we will be happy at any time to meet you and host you with us in Israel. We were surprised by the vitality and clarity of your father and aunt as a whole. I take advantage of the fact that Hanit is a Sabra and she speaks Hebrew, so if something is not understood, you have a translator nearby. I wanted to thank Hanit too for the warm attitude and lots of patience. We felt with you just like at home. And again thank you for everything. We will be in touch. Eli Klein.

2010/4/5 Sherwin Gluck to Eli Klein

Hi Adi and Eli!
I am glad that I was able to find the information that I sent you yesterday. If my Dad had internet at home I would have done it from there...I hope that you understood that I sent you the phone # for Eugene Frohlinger in New York. He is from Leles! I also sent you the information for his interview with the Shoah Foundation. However, I urge you to try calling him. If they are religious, they might not answer the phone today as it is the end of Hol HaMoed but try anyway, and again tomorrow night after the holiday. If you would prefer that I call on your behalf, let me know. I will try to help in whatever way I can. Thank you for asking about Naomi...she hurt herself but luckily not so badly as to need a doctor. Enjoy your day! Sherwin

2010/4/6 Eli Klein to Sherwin Gluck

We were happy to hear that Naomi was fine and did not need a doctor's treatment. We wanted to say that all the information makes us very happy and we hope that we will eventually be able to obtain data about my late father's family that we are so lacking. We would be very happy if you would try to make contact for us with the Frohlinger family because for us it's a little more complicated mainly because of age and language. We are having a lot of fun in New York. We were at the Natural History Museum most of the day yesterday, and in the afternoon we saw a musical from Mama Mia which we really enjoyed. Thanks again for everything and for the willingness to help. We will keep in touch thanks Adi and Eli Klein.

I easily found a phone number for the Eugene Frohlinger and spoke with his wife. Unfortunately, Eugene had died in 2004.

2010/4/7 Sherwin Gluck to Eli Klein

Hi Eli!
I have just gotten off the phone with Charlotte Frohlinger. Unfortunately, her husband Eugene died in 2004. At first, she did not recognize your father's name. She knew that her husband went to Israel in 1966 or 1967 to visit his brother and his cousin. She said that Eugene and this cousin were together on a death march either from or to Flossenburg Concentration camp (http://www.thirdreichruins.com/flossenburg.htm) and that Eugene carried this cousin on his back. When the opportunity arose they were able to escape because the German guards left out of fear of the approaching Americans. Then she added that this same cousin was killed in a tractor accident. I knew immediately that she had been talking about your father. However, she doesn't know anything further about your father. She will re-watch the interviews that her husband did for Spielberg and for the Fortunoff Archives at Yale University to [see] if Mr. Frohlinger spoke of this incident with your father. She will also ask her cousin to check on the family tree for your father's name. What other names did he have (Tzvi, Sanyi, and ?) Eugene Frohlinger's father was 1 of 10 children. Eugene Frohlinger himself had 2 brothers: Samuel (Shmayu) and Joseph, and two sisters. One sister went into hiding in Budapest but someone recognized her and identified her to the Germans that she was a Jew and she was

killed. The other sister is still alive but old and not well. Mrs. Frohlinger will nonetheless speak to her to see is she remembers anything about your father. Mrs. Frohlinger's email is goldchas@aol.com
She is a native American so her English is perfect. You may email her in English as she says that she knows how to email! I'm glad that I can be of some help to you. Sherwin

2010/4/7 Charlotte Frohlinger to Sherwin Gluck

Dear Sherwin:

I was happy to speak to you on the phone regarding this family matter. I did speak to my sister-in-law but she was unable to remember if she had heard the story of the man who died after being run over by a tractor; however, her daughter Carol said that my husband told her the story about how he and two other men had run away from the march that the Germans were conducting with the survivors of Auschwitz, etc. She said that he never said that he carried anyone or that he was a cousin of his. I might have misunderstood at some point, but I believe that my husband had to help one of the men with whom he was familiar. They ran away in the woods until they came to a farmhouse and hid in the barn until they were able to unite with the advancing American army. I am not sure if my husband actually saw this man when he first went to Israel or if the man already was gone. I might also add that there are several Eugene Frohlingers who are all related. There were frequent mix-ups from people looking for one or the other, but it was my husband who knew the man that had the fatal accident with the tractor. How he knew him, I am not sure. My sister-in-law did not recognize the name of the town that you gave me, but I will still try to find it on a local map that I have from there. Sorry I don't have more information at this time but I will try to find more. Have a good week. Charlotte Frohlinger

2010/4/11 Charlotte Frohlinger to Sherwin Gluck

Dear Sherwin,

This is to inform you that I have been trying to track down your quest for some news about Zvi Klein as he was known in Israel in Beer Sheva. I was in touch with Dr. Stanley Frohlinger in N. Miami, FL, because he has the Frohlinger Family Tree. He told me at once that Sandor Klein was his father's first cousin who survived the Shoah and moved to Israel where he married and had two children, a boy and a girl. He was called by the name of Zvi in Israel. He was cousin to my husband as well. My husband came from the town of Leles, but Stanley's father came from Ludmuc where there were several Klein families. My husband's sister unfortunately could not remember the town of Polyan, but I managed to locate it just above Leles on the map that I have. I am going to give you the email address of Stanley Frohlinger as he asked me to do. He is going to be in touch with his older brother Brian (called Dov in Israel) to see if he is in touch with any of these Klein cousins over there. Stanley's email address is as follows: Bitedoc99@aol.com. You might guess he is a dentist. If he gets any further information, he will email you. I hope that some of what I have written is of some help. I would be interested to hear of any further news from you. Charlotte Frohlinger

2010/4/11 Sherwin Gluck to Charlotte Frohlinger

Hi Charlotte!
Thank you so much for this information! I have already emailed it to Eli Klein (Tvi's son). He is in Wisconsin visiting his sister...I too am interested in how it turns out. I hope to talk to them this week. Be well! Sherwin

2010/4/12 Charlotte Frohlinger to Sherwin Gluck

It's funny, but Stanley's mother was a Klein as well as my husband's uncle's wife. Not all Kleins are related, but in the small towns the Jewish people tended to intermarry with relatives. Stanley's father was Sandor (Alex) Frohlinger with whom we were very close; although, he was a second or third cousin to my husband. All Frohlingers are very clannish and love to find new relatives, but these we are talking about are well-known. You said there was a photograph with my husband's picture on it. Who was with him? My husband's brother Samuel lived in Ashkelon back in the 1960s, and that's who my husband was visiting at that time. Both are now deceased. Stanley would love to add Zvi's children to the family tree, and you seem to know their names and where they are. The plot thickens, and we hope [Eli Klein] gets his answers. Charlotte

2010/4/12 Sherwin Gluck to Charlotte Frohlinger

Hi Charlotte!
Here is the photo taken by your husband (I believe that Eli, Tvi's son, annotated the photo from memory and incorrectly named your husband Ernest and not Eugene.) Sara is Tsvi's daughter. I would love to give you (and Stanley) the details of Tsvi's children and grandchildren but I don't know them. I will ask for them when I hear from Eli and Adi again...According to Stanley's family tree, did Tsvi Klein have sisters? What were their names? Also, I contacted the Yale Library and the Shoah Foundation...I am unable to easily get copies of your husband's testimony. Would it be possible to make a copy of each for me?
Sherwin

2010/4/12 Charlotte Frohlinger to Sherwin Gluck

Sherwin, I believe this photo does show the wife of ERNEST Frohlinger. I have never been to Israel, but Ernest (Alex's brother) actually lived in Israel at one time with his wife Magda. But it was my husband Eugene who together with Zvi Klein ran away from the Nazis into the woods until they came to a farm with a barn where they hid out. Ernest passed away some years ago, and his wife remarried a man by name of --
----Klein! I am now convinced that it was Ernest who took the picture and not Eugene. My husband went to Israel many times, but I never did (yet). How did you get Eugene's name to attach to this picture? I have copies of Eugene's testimony from both Yale and Spielberg. We transferred them to CDs for protection. I will see if I have any copies left to be able to send to you. Thanks for asking. I will send Stanley the names you have supplied me with and he can check to see if they are on the Family Tree. This is really very interesting. Keep well.
Charlotte

2010/4/13 Sherwin Gluck to Charlotte Frohlinger

Hi Charlotte!
I just spoke with Eli Klein (Tsvi's son) and he asked me to thank you for all your help thus far. He asks if Magda is still alive? Is there any way that he could contact her? Where does she live? He also asks if it would be possible to get a copy (by disk or on paper) of the family tree (at least the part that relates to his family)? Thank you again for all your kindness, Sherwin

2010/4/13 Stanley Frohlinger to Sherwin Gluck

Sherwin-
When my cousin Charlotte told me about someone interested in a cousin Zvi Klein in Israel, I was stunned, but well acquainted. Ironically, I learned of another relative by the name of Zvi Klein this past month via a Holocaust Survivor website. Let's just officially call this "Zvi Klein Month". Firstly, I didn't understand the connection between your father and Zvi Klein and my Uncle Ernest. Could you explain that. Secondly, Ernest passed away in 1986. His wife Magda (now remarried to a Klein) lives part time in Boca Raton, Florida/part time in NJ. She is in Florida for a few more days at phone # 561-483-2550. After the 20th, in NJ at 609-860-1266. Where do Eli and Sara live? Married? Children? I have a family tree that needs some updating and I would be glad to share the info. I believe that they are my only second cousins I haven't met. Can you forward this email to Eli or share his email address. with me? Looking forward to hearing from you, Stan Frohlinger
Bitedoc99@aol.com

2010/4/13 Sherwin Gluck to Stanley Frohlinger

Hi Stanley!
Thanks so much for your email. I have already forwarded your email address to Eli (and I spoke with him this morning). He and his son are returning to Israel tomorrow but I am sure they will be in touch with you.

My father, Ignatz (now Irving) Gluck, left Europe in 1940. From mid 1938 to that time the local schools were closed due to the situation, he and Zvi Klein were friends. My understanding is that Zvi and his parents moved to Polyan and lived in a building adjoining the synagogue sometime in 1938. He and my father spent a lot of time talking since they were the same age and there were so few Jews in their small village. After my Dad left Europe in 1940 they exchanged a few letters and then lost contact with each other. At some point in the late 1960's my Dad met with some other people from Polyan-Leles that lived in Brooklyn and they gave him a partial address for Zvi Klein in Israel. However, my father, despite visiting Israel in 1968 was unable to get in touch with him. Flash forward to last year when my brother-in-law visited from Israel. My Dad asked him if, in his spare time, he might locate Zvi Klein or his family from the partial address. Eventually, with a little help from my father in law, we located Zvi's son, Eli, and he and my father spoke by telephone and exchanged several emails. Eli Klein was so moved to find out any information about his long deceased father that he came to visit my father just this past week, bringing with him his son and a stack of old photos! Using the information from the photos, I was able to track down Eugene Frohlinger. From the summary of his testimony on the Shoah Foundation's website, I knew that he was from Leles and that he lived in New York. I found his phone #, left a message, and Charlotte was kind enough to return my call.

One of the pictures that Eli brought with him was taken by Ernest Frohlinger, according to the notation. Not knowing anything about the Frohlinger family except for this notation on the photo, I searched for the name Frohlinger and found Eugene's name. I incorrectly guessed that the notation might have been wrong. Seeing that Eugene was from Leles, I thought we had nothing to lose by trying to contact him for more information. Sure enough, we have found out more than we could have ever hoped for!

Eli lives in Moshav Arbel in Northern Israel while his sister Sara lives in Wisconsin. Eli has three sons, the oldest is named Adi. The others' names I don't know but again, I am sure that Eli will be in touch with you directly when he returns home to Israel and has a chance to digest all the information that I have found for him that he heretofore did not know. Zvi Klein returned from the trauma of the war and did not discuss many things prior to his life in Israel with his son.

The biggest question I have for you right now is: do you have names on your family tree indicating whether or not Zvi Klein had sisters? My father has no memory of them but Eli is sure that his father had sisters.

Thank you for all your help thus far! Sincerely, Sherwin

2010/4/16 Stanley Frohlinger to Sherwin Gluck

Sherwin,
Thanks for the quick response. My apologies about my much slower one. Unbelievable story about reconnecting with the family this past year. Yes. I do have Zvi Klein's two sisters on the family tree, but unfortunately with no names listed. I have two brothers living in Israel and they would also be interested in connecting with Eli. Do you have an email address or phone number? By the way, where are you and your father located? Where in Wisconsin is Sara, Eli's sister?
Incidentally, I showed the picture to Magda Frohlinger. She was delighted to hear the story and would love to hear from Eli too. Thank you for all of your efforts in bringing everyone closer. Stan

2010/4/16 Sherwin Gluck to Stanley Frohlinger

Hi Stan!
I guess the mystery of Zvi Klein's sisters will remain unsolved for now! Eli's email address is elkl23@bezeqint.net and his home address is אלי קליין מושב ארבל משק 23- (Eli Klein, Moshav Arbel, Farm 23) I am forwarding this email to him as well. My father and I both live in Syosset, New York out on Long Island, just a few blocks away from one another. Best wishes and shabbat shalom! Sherwin

2010/9/19 Irving Gluck to Eli Klein

Dear Eli and family!
I want to wish you all a Happy and Healthy New Year! I have been thinking about you and hoping that you are all well. Each time I prepare food and use the olive oil that you brought I think of you. That my friend's son brought it to me. It is unfortunate that he is not here with us. Our best wishes from our families to you, Irving Gluck

2011/1/16 Sherwin Gluck to Eli Klein

Hi Eli!

My father found these additional letters that your father wrote to him. He asked me to send images of them to you as well as the translations. We hope that they find you all in good health. He sends his best regards to you and hopes to hear back from you again soon. All the best, Sherwin Gluck

2011/1/16 Adi Klein to Sherwin Gluck

Hi Sherwin,

Thank you so much for sending & translating these letters. I'm sure my father will be very excited to read these lines as [much as] me...We are ok and hope you all in good health. Thanks
Adi

2011/1/17 Eli Klein to Sherwin Gluck

[in Hebrew]
Hello Sherwin,

I was very happy to receive the email and get more details related to my father. First I wanted to ask how your father and aunt are, and of course your wife and children? I hope everyone is alright. Give everyone warm greetings from me. Regarding the letters I did not understand why the title of the letter says Alex Klein, and at the end of the letter is different Klein. I started to think that maybe the letter that says Alex is something else?? But at the end it is written differently?? That's pretty weird. I was able to contact the Frohlingers in Israel, two brothers, but for some reason I am under the impression that they were not too interested in the relationship. I was very disappointed, but decided I won't obligate anyone to be in touch if it does not interest them. The last pathway I have left to gather information about my father is probably Mrs. Magda Klein who was the wife of Ernest Frohlinger, living alternately in Florida and New York. She visited us with him in about 1968/9, about a year and a half before my father was killed. Possibly from her husband's stories I can know a little more. Unfortunately, on December 31, 2010, about two weeks ago, my mother passed away at the age of 82. I really appreciate the efforts you are making for us and thank you very much. Once again a warm greeting to everyone and be well. With great friendship, Eli Klein.

2011/1/17 Sherwin Gluck to Eli Klein

Hi Eli!

I just translated your email to my father, who is sitting next to me now. Both he and my Aunt are, thank goodness, well. He says that Alex was Shany's father's name (your grandfather's name). My father adds that if he finds anything else as he goes through the remaining letters he will, of course, have me email it to you. Please also accept our deepest condolences on the loss of your mother. Sincerely, Irving Gluck (and Sherwin Gluck)

2011/1/18 Eli Klein to Irving and Sherwin Gluck

[in Hebrew]

Hello Irving and Sherwin,

I'm glad to hear that thank God everyone is in good health, and thank you for sharing in my grief on my mother's death. My grandfather's name (my father's father) was Elimelech and I am named after him, Alex is not a name I am familiar unless it is a second name or another name. Anyway many thanks for the responsiveness and quick responses. With great friendship and appreciation Eli Klein.

This was the last email that we received from Eli Klein. I'm not sure why the correspondence ended, but I think that the information he learned about his father from Charlotte Frohlinger upset him very much. He believed that his father was strong and athletic, a survivor. If he was in fact the man carried by Eugene Frohlinger, his entire foundational story needed to be revised. It was extraordinary that he and his son came to visit my father, and that they shared, even briefly, their reminiscences of a father and of a friend. (Eugene Frohlinger's interview can be seen through the USC Shoah Foundation).

The second incident was also instigated by my father. He asked if I could find out anything on the internet about his friend from Ohio State University, Herbert Baum. What were the odds? Well, I searched and sure enough I found that Herbert Baum had recently become the oldest recipient of a PhD from the University of Chicago. With a few more clicks, I had his phone number and my father made the phone call...and haltingly left Herb a message on his answering machine. Shortly thereafter, Herb Baum returned the call, and they spoke at length. What follows are the emails that they briefly exchanged.

2009/7/15 Sherwin Gluck to Herb Baum

Hi Dr. Baum!
My father asked me to send some pictures to you and here they are! Simply amazing that after 60 years he was able to speak with you. I'm sure that he will be very happy to get a picture from you as well. Since he doesn't have an email account, you can send it to me and I will get it to him. Have a great day! Sincerely, Sherwin Gluck

2009/7/15 Herb Baum to Irving Gluck

Thanks so much for finding me and sending the pictures. I will respond shortly. I have fond memories of our time together at Ohio State and our discussions and lunches together. Time rolls by so quickly and friendships are lost along the way. The internet has been a boon for discovery and engaging. My PhD was based on my book, "Quest for the Perfect Strawberry" an industry I was in for over 40 years. It can be googled as you have for other info on my business and academic life. I have been retired since 1999, served on the local school board and currently substitute teach k-12. I have 3 children, 2 girls and 1 boy, 2 teachers and a lawyer. 6 grandchildren and one great one. One boy in 4th year med school, one girl in 3rd year dental school, one boy at Annapolis and Portland State, and another boy at California state. I am healthy at 82, although have 2 hip implants and a shoulder. All other functions fine. We hike a lot and kayak also. Oregon is a beautiful state and we live on the coast, in Depoe Bay, 900 people and 2 hours from Portland. Will write again and send pictures. Thanks again. Herb Baum, 310 Midden Reach, Depoe Bay Or. 97341

2009/9/14 Irving Gluck to Herb Baum

Hi Herb!
I haven't heard from [you] in quite some time and hope that you are okay! First, I want to wish you and your family a "shana tova"! I hope that you had a chance to watch the DVD that I mailed you. I would like to hear your comments! I am okay. I have mailed to President Obama a copy of a term paper that I wrote back in 1949 regarding the "economics of health." Today's health care is not any different than what it was when I wrote the paper back in 1949. I hope that he will reply with his comments. I wish you the very best and hope to hear from you! With best wishes for a healthy New Year! Irv Gluck

2009/10/30 Herb Baum to Irving Gluck

I am so sorry for not answering your emails and phone calls. I have been sub teaching almost daily and now have a bad cold, no real excuse and I will address your inquires soon. I am certain that any work you do will be exemplary. I will always remember our lunches together as well as our friendship. I promise to study your material very soon. Herb

2010/9/19 Irving Gluck to Herb Baum

Hi Herb!
I hope that you are well. I have been disappointed from not hearing from you. I know you have been busy but I had hoped you would have taken a few minutes to reflect on the past. If you have a chance, at any time, you can drop me a line. Wishing you a happy and healthy year, to you and to your family. As always, I am, Irv Gluck

2010/9/19 Herb Baum to Irving Gluck

I am sorry for neglecting you and your writings. Busy is no excuse, pure and simple neglect is the reason. Also, as you probably are aware, one's memory is not as good as when were learning at OSU. We were in Sedona Az in May and June and I was hospitalized for a few days and weeks of slow recovery with some sort of gastro blockage, which turned out to be nothing except a few very sick days. We have had an exceptionally cool summer and recently had 5 inches of rain. I promise to reply soon. Meanwhile Shana Tova. I too have very fond memories Irv. hb

2010/10/8 Herb Baum to Irving Gluck

Dear friend,
I just completed the viewing and listening of your engrossing and educational video. I was proud to know you, and remember with great joy, the personal and educational experiences we shared at OSU. I remember your "ONE WORLD" dream and agreed that this was a noble goal and hoped that the United Nations would provide a movement in that direction. It has, and as by you noted in your video, progress has been made in Europe and in the world. There has not been another major global conflict and probably will not, thanks to you and many of us who participated in WWII. After academic economics I too was in business my adult life and was CEO of a large Cooperative of mostly Japanese farmers. As you probably know I received my PHD from the University of Chicago in 2006, the oldest to ever receive such. If you do a google search under my name you will see articles about this and my book, "The Quest For The Perfect Strawberry, A case study of the California Strawberry Commission and the Strawberry Industry: A Descriptive Model for Marketing order Evaluation." Incidentally I have 3 children, 6 grandchildren, and 1 great grandson. One lawyer, 2 teachers, 1 doctor, 1 dentist, 1 Annapolis Ensign, and 2 others in school. They should be able to fend for themselves. As you stated, education is the key ingredient to a successful life. I also have a wonderful, second younger wife, whose loving care I really don't deserve. Without these last 20 years with her, my life would have been uneventful and my health not exceptional. I hope that we can meet one day in the future and that she can see my "one friend" at Ohio State, who remembered and reconnected, something I neglected, to my shame and embarrassment. Sincerely, Herb

The third incident involved a wedding photo that was in my Aunt Marie's photo album and a wedding invitation that was amongst the many papers in the cardboard box. The invitation was for the wedding of Irén Mayer to Ernö Riedermann which was to take place on the 6th of November in the well-known city of Satu-Mare, Romania. From the letters, I knew that this invitation had been sent to Dezső in America. I also knew from the letters that Irén survived and eventually was brought to New York by her mother's half sister, our cousin Bertha. I wanted to see what else I could find out about her when I stumbled upon a website called "Szatmári Mementó" that mentioned her name on a Mayer family tree. I reached out to Gyuri Elefant whose email was given as the contact for the website.

2020/11/27 Sherwin Gluck to Gyuri Elefant

Dear Mr. Elefant,
First, please accept my sincerest compliments on your website! You have done an enormous amount of research, and it shows that it is a labor of love. I stumbled upon it serendipitously. As you see below my signature, I have written my father's memoir, and despite it being finished I am always trying to fill in missing puzzle pieces. I was searching to see if I could find anything about Irene Mayer Neuman, and after having almost given up, I found a link to your website. Sure enough, the Irene Henda Maier Riederman Neuman listed on your site, is the very same person I was searching for. Her mother, Sarolta Gluck Maier was my father's first cousin. I have several letters from Sarolta and her daughters, Irene and Jolan, from 1938-1939 as well as a photo of Sarolta. I would be happy to share them with you. Please let me know if you would be interested. Have a shabbat shalom! Sincerely, Mr. Sherwin Gluck

2020/11/28 Gyuri Elefant to Sherwin Gluck

Dear Mr. Gluck
From the beginning I apologize for the fact that my English is through google translation. From your letter I deduce that you have reached my site where I researched the family tree, my mother's ascendants. After researching the family tree, my father's ascendants, I found the lack of interest and lack of collaboration of most relatives, I abandoned the continuation of the genealogical project. I started a bigger project, the reconstruction of the Jews before 1944, from my hometown Satu Mare, the site where you found Henda in

the list of survivors. Sarolta, her daughter and her husband appear on the list of deported martyrs. Gluck Sarolta's husband, Lipot, is my grandmother's cousin. Lipot's brother, Chaim, has a son who lives in Washington DC. I am attaching the descendants of Grunzweig, to be located on Henda. Of course, I am interested in filling in the civil data about them on the site, to display the photo on the page of Sarolta's victims. Jolan's (Penda) letters also interest me as a documentary. Unfortunately, I reached the maximum data that the server accepts, for the volume of the subscription that I can afford. A different fact, my uncle and aunt (Elephant Ammy and Itzhack) played rummy for years in Queens with Henda. I am attaching 3 photos from my cousin Rivka, daughter of Ammy and Itzhack. For Sarolta's photo and his letters, Thank you in advance. Shavua Tov! Gy. Elefant

As soon as I saw the photograph from Mr. Elefant, I knew I had identified the wedding picture. I superimposed the bride's face with the photo of Irén and voilà, it was a match.

2020/11/20 Sherwin Gluck to Gyuri Elefant

Hi Mr. Elefant!
Thank you for the photos! I can confirm that the wedding photo that I sent you is in fact the wedding photo of Irene Mayer Riedermann Neuman (I sent you the wedding invitation earlier). Here I am attaching the facial comparison of the photo you sent and the photo I had…nothing like finding puzzle pieces!

2020/11/29 Sherwin Gluck to Gyuri Elefant

Hi Mr. Elefant!
It was so nice to see your email in my InBox! Your "Google English" is excellent! If Lipot's brother's son has photos, maybe we can compare them with the ones I'm sending you. As the captions show, I am only certain of Sarolta in the photos, not her daughters. I am attaching the photos I have, as well as images of the letters I mentioned, along with their (imperfect) translations into English. The letters are written in Hungarian. They were sent to my father's brother Dezső, who had just arrived to America in January 1938. They mention Bertha. Bertha was Sarolta's half sister. She had been in America for many years by 1938 and was instrumental in bringing Irene out after the war. If you have any questions, please don't hesitate to reach out. Sherwin

2020/11/29 Gyuri Elefant to Sherwin Gluck

Hi Mr. Gluck!
I'm glad I managed to complete the puzzle. I managed to download the photos, but the letters cannot be opened. I propose to send only the letters in Hungarian. Also try at elefantg@gmail.com. Photo 009 is taken in the center of Satu Mare, in the background you can see the fire tower. Sarolta and Jolan's photo will be uploaded in the near future. Gyuri

2020/11/29 Gyuri Elefant to Sherwin Gluck

Dear Sherwin!
I read Jolan's letters, it turns out [s]he tried to get to America desperately. Today we know that [s]he did not succeed, [s]he was a victim of the Holocaust. It is clear from the subtext that the family was a family, modest traditional Jew, like most Jews in Satu Mare, shop owners. They knew about the war, but they could not imagine the fate that awaited them. The desire to emigrate was for economic reasons. Today we know that the whole family was deported, Iren Hinda was the only one who survived. Interestingly, the correspondence was kept only until 1939, it is possible that relations cooled due to the failure of emigration. The mentality in Romania (Satu Mare) is known, people are convinced that American citizens are able to solve all problems. I could not find the reason why Jolan did not marry, it is known that in the Jewish tradition girls are married in the order of birth. Chaim's son from Washington has no data or photos that can contribute to the research. I posted the photos of Sarolta and Jolan on my website. http://egyur.50webs.com/fotok1g.html All the best and success in future puzzle! Gyuri

2020/11/30 Sherwin Gluck to Gyuri Elefant

Hi Gyuri!

Thank you for your email, and all the information that you included! Did you read the letters in Hungarian? If so, I'm envious! My father only taught us to count and a few other words. Although my Dad and Aunt translated many of the letters, of which there are more than 1500, after they died I had to pay someone to translate the remainder, and I'm so glad that I did! It is most likely that my Uncle Dezső became so preoccupied with trying to get his siblings out, and he had such little resources to do even that and had to rely on his Uncle in America, that he passed Jolan's emigration troubles to her Aunt Bertha. She too would have found it difficult to help, and would have turned to the same Uncle. This Uncle, did in fact save my father and his 3 siblings, as well as family from his wife's side. Perhaps he could have done more, but who am I to judge? In hindsight, had they known what was to happen, they may have acted with more haste. In my father's case, he and his siblings were able to leave because they had quota numbers from Czechoslovakia which they had obtained before their region was returned to Hungary. The US allowed them to enter under those quota numbers. Had they tried to leave as Hungarians, it is doubtful that I would be writing this email to you since the US admitted so few. The same was true for Romania. Thank you again for your work on the website which led me to you! Sincerely, Sherwin

Notes about additional letters

The following letters were not included in this volume. The letters from Marie and Hermine were repetitive in nature, and added no new information from the ones that were included. The v-mails from Marie were repetitive. The letters from Herman were extraordinarily difficult to decipher and appeared to be mostly about stock prices and the stock market. The letters from Tonti and Bill Zuhl were primarily about themselves and their lives.

Hermine/Marie

1947/2/4 Marie to Irving (Book 8, 95-97)
1947/2/10 Hermine to Irving (Book 11, 222-227)
1947/3/3 Marie to Irving (Book 8, 99-100)
1947/3/4 Hermine to Irving (Book 11, 236-238)
1947/4/20 Marie and Hermine to Irving (Book 8, 117-121)
1947/7 ? Hermine to Irving (Book 16, 452-457)
1947/7/1 Marie and Hermine to Irving (Book 8, 162-166)
1947/7/27 Hermine to Irving (Book 18, 304-306)
1947/8/2 Hermine to Irving (Book 11, 287-288)
1947/8/18 Marie to Irving (Book 8, 184-186)
1947/8/23 Marie to Irving (Book 8, 188-190)
1947/8/31 Marie to Irving (Book 16, 448-450)
1947/9/7 Marie to Irving (Book 16, 438-440)
1947/11/3 Hermine to Irving (Book 11, 319-321)
1948/1/9 Marie to Irving (Book 8, 198)
1948/1/15 Marie to Irving (Book 8, 200-201)
1948/2/4 Hermine to Irving (Book 10, 90-91)
1948/2/9 Hermine to Irving (Book 16, 183-184)
1948/2/21 Marie to Irving (Book 9, 260-261)
1948/3/11 Marie to Irving (Book 8, 203-204)
1948/4/1 Marie to Irving (Book 8, 212)
1948/4/14 Hermine to Irving (Book 8, 214-215)
1948/4/18 Marie to Irving (Book 8, 217-218)
1948/4/27 Hermine to Irving (Book 8, 220-221)
1948/5/12 Marie to Irving (Book 8, 223-224)
1948/5/18 Hermine to Irving (Book 10, 104-105)
1948/5/26 Marie to Irving (Book 8, 226-227)
1948/6/2 Marie to Irving (Book 8, 229-230)
1948/7/13 Marie to Irving (Book 8, 232-233)
1948/7/20 Marie to Irving (Book 8, 209-210)
1948/9/13 Hermine to Irving (Book 10, 110-112)
1948/10/22 Marie to Irving (Book 15, 209-210)
1948/12/20 Marie to Irving (Book 8, 235-236)
1949/1/18 Marie to Irving (Book 8, 238-239)
1949/2/1 Marie to Irving (Book 2, 42-43)
1949/2/18 Marie and Hermine to Irving (Book 2, 8-13)
1949/4/25 Marie to Irving (Book 8, 244-246)
1949/5/10 Hermine to Irving (Book 10, 155-157)
1949/5/18 Marie to Irving (Book 8, 252-254)
1949/6/3 Hermine to Irving (Book 10, 159-162)
1949/6/7 Marie to Irving (Book 8, 256-257)
1949/8/29 Marie to Irving (Book 8, 258-259)
1949/11/11 Marie to Irving (Book 8, 274-275)
1950/8/15 Marie to Irving (Book 10, 270-271)
1950/9/19 Marie to Irving (Book 9, 256-258)
1954/6/11 Marie to Irving (Book 9, 183-185)
1954/6/14 Marie to Irving (Book 9, 187-189)
Undated 1948 Marie to Irving (Book 6, 31-32) - about insurance transfer - missing page 1

Undated 1950 Fall Hermine to Irving (Book 10, 75-76) - advice to Irving
Undated 1950 or after Marie to Irving (Book 19, 434-435) - missing pages 1-2 of 6 pages - Mayo Clinic
Undated Hermine to Irving (Book 11, 229) winter 1946-47, coal
Undated Hermine to Irving (Book 18, 23-25) - advice for property German girl

v-mail

1944/8/16 Marie to Irving (V-Mail, Slide 224)
1944/9/10 Marie to Irving (V-Mail, Slide 243)
1944/9/19 Marie to Irving (V-Mail, Slide 250)
1944/9/19 Marie to Irving (V-Mail, Slide 251)
1944/9/21 Marie to Irving (V-Mail, Slide 283)
1944/9/24 Marie to Irving (V-Mail, Slide 255)
1944/9/28 Marie to Irving (V-Mail, Slide 260)
1944/9/28 Marie to Irving (V-Mail, Slide 261)
1944/10/2 Marie to Irving (V-Mail, Slide 266)
1944/10/4 Marie to Irving (V-Mail, Slide 267)
1944/10/8 Marie to Irving (V-Mail, Slide 268-269)
1944/10/9 Marie to Irving (V-Mail, Slide 271)
1944/10/12 Marie to Irving (V-Mail, Slide 274)
1944/10/13 Marie to Irving (V-Mail, Slide 275)
1944/10/15 Marie to Irving (V-Mail, Slide 276)
1944/10/15 Marie to Irving (V-Mail, Slide 277)
1944/10/18 Marie to Irving (V-Mail, Slide 279)
1944/10/20 Marie to Irving (V-Mail, Slide 280)
1944/10/20 Marie to Irving (V-Mail, Slide 282)
1944/10/23 Marie to Irving (V-Mail, Slide 284)
1944/10/24 Marie to Irving (V-Mail, Slide 286)
1944/10/28 Marie to Irving (V-Mail, Slide 288)
1944/10/31 Marie to Irving (V-Mail, Slide 289)
1944/11/2 Marie to Irving (V-Mail, Slide 290)
1944/11/5 Marie to Irving (V-Mail, Slide 292)
1944/11/7 Marie to Irving (V-Mail, Slide 293)
1944/11/10 Marie to Irving (V-Mail, Slide 294)
1944/11/10 Marie to Irving #2 (V-Mail, Slide 296)
1944/11/18 Marie to Irving (V-Mail, Slide 295)
1944/11/18 Marie to Irving #2 (V-Mail, Slide 297)
1944/11/20 Marie to Irving #2 (V-Mail, Slide 299)
1944/11/23 Marie to Irving (V-Mail, Slide 300)
1944/11/26 Marie to Irving (V-Mail, 301-302)
1944/11/30 Marie to Irving (V-Mail, Slide 307)
1944/12/1 Marie to Irving (V-Mail, Slide 312)
1944/12/2 Marie to Irving (Vmail, Slide 313)
1944/12/4 Marie to Irving (V-Mail, Slide 315)
1944/12/7 Marie to Irving (V-Mail, Slide 316)
1944/12/14 Marie to Irving (V-Mail, Slide 319)
1944/12/22 Marie to Irving (V-Mail, Slide 323)
1944/12/22 Marie to Irving (V-Mail, Slide 324)
1944/12/27 Marie to Irving (V-Mail, Slide 326)

1944/12/31 Marie to Irving (V-Mail, Slide 327)
1944/12/31 Marie to Irving (V-Mail, Slide 328)
1945/1/4 Marie to Irving (V-Mail, Slide 329)
1945/1/4 Marie to Irving (V-Mail, Slide 330)
1945/1/4 Marie to Irving (V-Mail, Slide 333)
1945/1/8 Marie to Irving (V-Mail, Slide 332)
1945/1/16 Marie to Irving (V-Mail, Slide 336)
1945/1/22 Marie to Irving (V-Mail, Slide 357)
1945/1/24 Marie to Irving (V-Mail, Slide 359)
1945/1/28 Marie to Irving (V-Mail, Slide 361)
1945/1/28 Marie to Irving (V-Mail, Slide 362)
1945/1/30 Marie to Irving (V-Mail, Slide 366)
1945/1/31 Marie to Irving (V-Mail, Slide 390)
1945/2/1 Marie to Irving (V-Mail, Slide 391)
1945/2/22 Marie to Irving (V-Mail, Slide 416)
1945/3/19 Marie to Irving (V-Mail, Slide 423)
1945/3/31 Marie to Irving (V-Mail, Slide 433)
1945/3/31 Marie to Irving (V-Mail, Slide 435)
1945/4/3 Marie to Irving (V-Mail, Slide 437)
1945/4/3 Marie to Irving (V-Mail, Slide 438)
1945/4/8 Marie to Irving (V-Mail, Slide 441)
1945/5/30 Marie to Irving (V-Mail, Slide 458)
1945/5/30 Marie to Irving #2 (V-Mail, Slide 459)
1945/6/2 Marie to Irving (V-Mail, Slide 461)
1945/6/4 Marie to Irving (V-Mail, Slide 462)
1945/6/4 Marie to Irving (V-Mail, Slide 463)
1945/6/7 Marie to Irving (V-Mail, Slide 464)
1945/6/11 Marie to Irving (V-Mail, Slide 465)
1945/7/1 Marie to Irving (V-Mail, Slide 469)
1945/7/1 Marie to Irving #2 (V-Mail, Slide 470)
1945/7/19 Marie to Irving (V-Mail, Slide 477)
1945/7/21 Marie to Irving (V-Mail, Slide 478)
1945/7/25 Marie to Irving (V-Mail, Slide 485)
1945/8/20 Marie to Irving (V-Mail, Slide 493)

Herman

1950/3/27 Herman to Irving, Marie, and Hermine (Book 18, 328-329)
1950/4/3 Herman to Irving, Marie, and Hermine (Book 18, 325-326)
1953/3/9 Herman to Irving (Book 10, 293-294)
1953/9/22 Herman to Irving (Book 16, 45-46)
1953/10/3 Herman to Irving (Book 16, 90-92)
1953/10/14 Herman to Irving (Book 19, 22-23)

1953/10/29 Herman to Irving (Book 19, 25-26)
1953/11/29 Herman to Irving (Book 16, 37-39)
1953/12/14 Herman to Irving (Book 16, 99-102)
1954/1/26 Herman to Irving (Book 14, 249-250)
1954/3/1 Herman to Irving (Book 14, 287-289)
1954//10 Herman to Irving (Book 14, 252-257)
1954/3/29 Herman to Irving (Book 16, 35)
1954/4/7 Herman to Irving (Book 16, 133-134)
1954/6/10 Herman to Irving (Book 14, 245-247)
1954/7/27 Herman to Irving (Book 14, 280-285)
Undated Herman to Irving (Book 14, 259) maybe 1954
Undated Herman to Irving (Book 14, 261-262) maybe 1954

Tonti and Bill Zuhl

1952/11/9 Tonti and Bill Zuhl to Irving (Book 16, 161-164)
1953/10/27 Tonti Zuhl to Irving (Book 17, 51-52)
1954/1/6 Tonti and Bill Zuhl to Irving (Book 17, 62-63)
1954/2/10 Tonti and Bill Zuhl to Irving (Book 17, 58-60)
1954/9/26 Tonti and Bill Zuhl to Irving (Book 17, 65-66)
1954/10/25 Tonti and Bill Zuhl to Irving (Book 16, 68-70) missing pg 3
1954/12/12 Tonti and Bill Zuhl to Irving (Book 17, 54-56)
1956/9/25 Tonti and Bill Zuhl to Irving (Book 16, 172-174)
1957/1/26 Tonti and Bill Zuhl to Irving (Book 16, 167-170) extra page 3
1959/8/8 Tonti and Bill Zuhl to Irving (Book 16, 111-113)
1962/3/19 Tonti and Bill Zuhl to Irving (Book 17, 68-71)
1962/7/3 Tonti and Bill Zuhl to Irving (Book 17, 73-75)
1972/1/7 Tonti Zuhl to Barbara and Irving (Book 19, 437-440)
Undated 6/11 Tonti and Bill Zuhl to Irving (Book 17, 77-78)

INDEX

Using the Index

In order to clarify how to use this index, the following explanations are necessary.

- Semi-colons separate both sub-entries, *sub-sub entries*, and sub-sub-sub entries. while **bold sub-entries** differentiate them to indicate that they have numerous further *sub-sub-entries*, which are italicized. Sub-sub-sub entries are neither bold, nor italicized.

- A single written letter is indicated by ***letter** which puts each letter written by that particular letter writer to the top of the list of sub-entries.

- Sub-entries for the five siblings (David, Hermine, Marie, Herman, Irving) use only their *First Name in English*. All other names are *Last Name, First Name*.

- Entries marked as "**letter from*" act as a Table of Contents for that letter writer and indicate each individual letter that they wrote. The pages numbers for these entries are not hyphenated.

Irving, 344, 424; **Palestine**; *advises Hermine to go to*, 597; **siblings**; *dinner with*, 163, 401, 431, 505, 530, 568; surgery, xix, 184, 198, 200, 202, 206, 212-215, 736; **vacation in**, 695; *Canada*, 357, 365, 600, 637; *Michigan*, 365, 476; *return home from*, 542, 546; visiting with, 693; visits NY, xviii, 710

Gluck, Fred (Feri), xv, xviii, 156, 257, 483, 486, 630

Gluck, Frederick Jerome, xvii, 661, 676, 678, 686, 688, 693, 700, 705, 710, 718, 728, 730, 732, 736, 740, 742; born, 659; flu, 732; in newspaper, 731; record player for, 712; visits Israel, xx, 738; work, goes to with David, 731

Gluck, Gyula (Gyuszi), viii, 161-162, 467; **Agardon, Hungary**; *visiting Gluck, Lajos in*, 51; **America**; *doesn't believe Aunts went to*, 106; barefoot, 137; clothing for, 124; **Hermine**; *crying to write to her*, 129; *won't recognize me*, 136; kisses from, 81, 107, 116, 118, 126-127, 134, 156; **Levente**; *looking for Irving and Herman in*, 122; personality, 108, 124, 129, 131, 137, 148-149, 153; school, is going to, 126, 131; shoes, permission to get for, 145; **Szürte, Hungary**; *thinks Hermine is in*, 119

Gluck, Helen, xxii, xxiii, 22, 38, 40, 63, 84, 90, 125, 148, 215, 331, 371, 440, 443, 461, 479, 505, 533, 661, 667; *letter from, 1, 41, 111, 200, 369, 638; asking about, 64, 155, 266, 563-564, 569, 577, 582, 591, 632, 668, 681, 701, 710; correspondence with, 38, 41-42, 92, 161, 212-213, 289, 325, 539, 602-603, 643, 649, 659, 661, 664, 690; German, writes in, 41, 160; gift from Irving to, 410, 424, 426, 432; **Gluck, Jónász's clothing**; *don't give to strangers*, 158; illness, 578, 737; **Irving**; *her reaction to photograph of*, 404; *package from, to*, 409-410, 424; *she asks about*, 461; megillat Esther, 200; **to David**; *it will be even better to see you again here in the very strange world*, 1; visiting with, 642, 656, 659, 674, 725; visits Weingarten, Bertha in NY, 83

Gluck, Henry, 52, 75

Gluck, Herman, vii-viii, xxii; *letter from, 2, 7, 8, 11, 15, 16, 19, 23, 25, 31, 37, 47, 48, 50, 52, 54, 67, 78, 79, 81, 83, 90, 95, 103, 161, 177, 196, 204, 214, 294, 329, 399, 411, 668, 669, 671, 712; affidavit of support for, 85; **America**; *also wants to go to*, 7; *ok to wait for 2ⁿᵈ ship to*, 104; **army**; *Czechoslovakian*; exam for, 48; inducted into, 34, 81; report to training in, vii, 8; *Hungarian*, vii, 95; discharged from, 60, 86, 89; still at home, 101; *United States*, x, 283; discharge payment, 321; don't join, 180; inducted into, ix, 165-166; smart for not being in, 356; birthdate error on birth certificate of, 105; broken leg, xix, 716-719, 729; **Budapest**; *visa hearing in, without documents for*, viii, 88-89; citizenship, US, 194, 220; correspondence with, 107; **David's**

nickname for; *his majesty*, 274; **Europe**, emigration from; *medical exam before*, 14; *papers not ready*, 33; *pessimistic about leaving*, 48; *Torah will stay until*, 33; **Hermine**; *angry at*, xvi, 666; **Hungarian Levente**; *participates in*, 90; **illness**; *anxious, not eating*, xiii, 550-551; *health unchanged*, 48; *medicine for*, x, 272-273, 275, 278, 283; *nervous stomach*, xvi-xvii, 698; in NY, xviii, 662, 706-707, 710; **jobs**, xviii, 126, 129, 712, 713; *changing*, 407; *gardener*, 119, 120; *works for Arthur*, xv, 519, 588; **Marie**; *won't visit her in new apartment*, xviii, 709; military release from Hungarian army for, vii, 21, 33, 36, 41, 54, 91; moral and district certificate for, 105; **passports**; *Czechoslovakian*, 37; *Hungarian*, 91; military request needed to get, 88; photographs of, 188; **Schwartz, Marton**; *advice from*, 113; share of inherited property listed under, xv, 528, 543, 545, 556, 575, 613, 618, 683-684, 733-734; Slovakian court case, 6; stocks, 710; suit for, 45, 725; **synagogue, goes to**; *for yahrzeit of Gluck, Lena*, 342; *on Passover*, 449; unemployed, xi, xvi, 479, 481, 484-485, 651; upset that Irving returned to Ohio, xviii, 707; visits Chicago, IL, xvii, 676; Zemplen County Orphanage account for, vii, 86

Gluck, Hermine, vi-viii, xxii, 9, 13, 32, 68, 86, 90, 109, 114-115, 117, 121, 129, 131, 151; *letter from, 2, 5, 10, 14, 16, 17, 18, 21, 22, 30, 33, 37, 40, 41, 42, 55, 56, 60, 66, 70, 72, 77, 79, 80, 89, 90, 91, 92, 94, 95, 97, 101, 102, 103, 106, 110, 161, 163, 164, 177, 179, 184, 186, 192, 196, 203, 205, 209, 210, 212, 213, 214, 215, 264, 286, 294, 298, 299, 309, 311, 316, 317, 318, 319, 320, 321, 331, 341, 343, 349, 351, 364, 371, 379, 380, 386, 389, 390, 396, 397, 401, 404, 405, 408, 414, 417, 420, 425, 426, 430, 431, 438, 440, 442, 443, 445, 447, 448, 449, 451, 453, 455, 457, 459, 461, 462, 463, 464, 465, 466, 467, 468, 469, 470, 472, 473, 475, 476, 478, 481, 484, 487, 489, 492, 493, 499, 502, 503, 505, 509, 513, 514, 515, 517, 522, 525, 526, 527, 528, 530, 531, 532, 535, 536, 537, 538, 539, 540, 541, 544, 545, 546, 549, 551, 552, 553, 554, 555, 556, 557, 560, 561, 562, 563, 566, 567, 568, 569, 571, 572, 573, 574, 576, 580, 582, 583, 584, 585, 586, 587, 588, 589, 590, 591, 593, 594, 596, 597, 599, 600, 601, 603, 608, 611, 613, 615, 616, 617, 619, 621, 622, 623, 626, 627, 628, 630, 631, 632, 634, 637, 641, 642, 643, 644, 645, 646, 647, 648, 650, 651, 652, 654, 656, 657, 659, 660, 661, 662, 663, 665, 666, 667, 669, 672, 674, 675, 676, 679, 680, 681, 683, 685, 687, 688, 689, 691, 693, 694, 695, 696, 698, 699, 700, 701, 708, 710, 711, 712, 715, 717, 722, 723, 726, 731; affidavit of support for, 85; **apartment address**; *36-19 167ᵗʰ Street*, 687; birthday, 56, 301; **boyfriends**; *Hungarian*, xiii, 533; *Polish*, xiii, 533, 538-539, 542, 544, 551; **broken**

hope: as long as we are alive, 60
Howard, Warren: *letter from, 663
Humenné, Czechoslovakia / Homonna,
    Hungary, 391, 410, 485, 518, 520, 528
Hunecke, Buddy: army buddies, x, 419
Hunecke, Margaret, x-xi, xxiii, 327, 419-420;
    *letter from; husband killed, same
    handwriting as Irving, 327
Hungarian boyfriend: Hermine, xiii, 533
Hungarian language, 317, 460; formal form,
    189, 193
Hungarian picnic, 530-531, 545-546
Hungary, 356; censorship in, 54; **First Vienna
    Award**, 54, 61; *border changed because of,*
    vii, 53; *business permits after,* 75;
    celebration after, 56-57; car accident during,
    57; *currency changed to pengős after,* 54;
    emigration process after, 56; *hope it will be
    better after,* 61; *Hungarian citizenship after,*
    vii, 54, 57; *Jewish business licenses revoked
    after,* 60, 110; *mail service begins after,* 54;
    military rule imposed after, 59; *transfer
    papers from Czechoslovakia after,* 57, 61;
    war in, 378
hussar, 109
ice-box, 533, 537, 558, 560
Iceland, 271, 290, 298, 310, 314, 326, 341,
    374, 380, 387, 390, 398, 404, 414, 426, 484;
    daylight hours in, 308; Schwartz, Louis
    stationed in, 365, 451
illness: Frye, Jenny, 64; Gluck, Arthur, 44, 146,
    178, 185, 192, 245, 455, 675, 737; Gluck,
    Flora, 199, 427, 576, 578; Gluck, Helen,
    578, 737; Gluck, Jennie, 455; **Herman**;
    anxious, not eating, xiii, 550-551; *health
    unchanged,* 48; *medicine for,* x, 272-273,
    275, 278, 283; *nervous stomach,* xvi, 698;
    Marie, 15; *doesn't feel well,* 146; *operation
    for,* 158; *sickly in America,* 516; Mayer, Irén,
    604; Mayer, Jolan, 39; **Nagel, Barbara**, xx,
    740, 742-744; *struggles to write,* xx, 745;
    Schwartz, Haia, 142; *feeling better from,*
    143; **Weingarten, Bertha**; *angina,* 29;
    asthma, 16; Weingarten, Mannie, 189, 589
Imhoff, Paul, xxiii; *letter from, 490;
    discharged from US army, 490
infantry, ix, 171, 173, 186, 189, 197
infantryman: Irving, 460
inheritance: from Gluck, Jeremias, 528
Irving, Marie's boyfriend in NY, xiv, 567, 571-
    573, 576, 579-580, 583, 586
Israel, xviii, 652-653, 690-691, 696-697, 700,
    702, 713, 737, 738-739, 741-742, 745-746,
    750-754; black market in, 696-697;
    economy; *Arab boycott, impact on,* xx;
    condition of, xviii, 699-700, 742; *Yom
    Kippur War, impact on,* xx, 740; Gluck,
    Frederick Jerome visits, xx, 738; **Mayer,
    Irén**; *arrives to,* 694; *permission to go to,*
    xvi, 656; peace in, 739-741; point system for
    products in, 697; Solomon, Linda visits, xx,
    743
Israeli Defense Forces (IDF), 740-743; reserve
    duty, xviii, 698; **Schwartz, Dudi**, xx, 741;

Eastern Studies in, xx, 742; Schwartz,
    Misha, xx, 737, 739-740
Italia Lines, viii, 102
Italian language, 400
Italy, i, iii, x, xi, 106, 150, 268-73, 277-282,
    284-298, 300-311, 313-315, 317-318, 321-
    325, 328-329, 331-338, 340, 343, 346-352,
    356, 359-366, 368-372, 375-376, 379-380,
    382-383, 386, 388-389, 391-395, 399-400,
    403, 406, 409-411, 413, 415-437, 442, 445,
    458-460, 463, 512, 742; siblings can travel
    to, 94
Ivanyo Family, 545; Ivanyo, Mrs., xiv, xxiii;
    letter from, 128; **Pista**, 495, 499, 544; *died,*
    517; took furniture, 485, 492
Jaeger, Selma, xxiii; *letter from, 735;
    introduces Irving to Nagel, Barbara, 735
Jaffa, Israel, xviii, 696, 698, 700
Japan, 342, 373, 472-473, 488, 580; Goldblatt,
    Louis, stationed in, 474, 502; VJ Day, 476,
    529
Japan China Bank note, 506
Japanese: **Irving**; *would he fight against,* 213
Jenő. *See* Solomon, Eugene
Jerusalem, Israel, xx, 741-744, 747
jewelry: **Szabo, Gyula**; *given to, for
    safekeeping,* xiii, 500; *Klein, Ignácz tried to
    get it back from,* 500
Jewish, 43, 94, 113, 139, 141, 178, 186, 198,
    200, 220, 327, 333, 339, 447, 495, 679, 749,
    751, 757; bible in the army, 172; **businesses**;
    Christian partners in, viii-ix, 123, 141, 146,
    156, 160; *licenses revoked from,* 60, 110;
    must open on Shabbat, 135; *restrictions
    imposed on,* 28; *shut down,* 139; customers,
    want Marie to sew for low price, 263;
    difficult everywhere to be, 62; employment
    office, 662; girl from Oran, Algeria, 343;
    guys in CA are jerks, 413; household to
    place Hermine and Marie in, 9; **identifying
    as**, 89; *in US army,* 176; *life in Europe after
    the war,* 609; marry, 510; newspaper in
    English, 45, 287; notary fired for being, 84;
    population; *in LA,* xvi, 642; *in Lelesz, only
    22 survived,* 485; *in NY,* 608; **religious
    practice**; *maintaining,* 28, 37; **sects**;
    Conservative, 668; *Orthodox,* 668; *Reform,*
    668; store in Ohio, 44; USO group that is,
    194; wedding in army, 183; workers in
    shipyard, 253
Jewish Agency: Gluck, Emil found by, but
    mistaken identity, 515, 517, 523; seeking
    family through, xii, 455, 492, 523; survivors'
    event hosted by, 514
Jewish knights, 447
Jews, xii, 43, 53, 259, 261, 399, 450, 506, 756;
    America; *no Emperor in, to ask for help
    from,* 29; bad news about, 131; baptism of,
    in Lelesz, 149; **Christian neighbors**;
    relations with, 117, 153, 156; *in Lelesz after
    liberation,* 485; *take property for free,* 157;
    Christmas, don't believe in, 645;
    conceptions about; *other people to do their
    work,* 244; *physical strength uncommon in,*

Nancy, France, xi, 458

Naples, Italy, x, 106, 112, 150, 299, 317, 347, 348, 366, 382-383, 389, 402, 410-411, 424, 426, 427; synagogue services in, 369

Nash Automobile, 669

National Bank of Hungary, 107, 115, 117, 119, 148; get dollars from, 94; permit from, to bring Torah, 123

National Council of Jewish Women: *letter from, 524; *Marie's citizenship*, 524

necklace: from Irving to sisters, xi, 425-426, 432; pearl, 305; set, 299

needlepoint, 268

neighbors: Csorosz Family, 495; **Deák Family**; *Anùs*; died, 545; *Mariska*, xxii; died, 545; *Mrs.*, 491; **Gerenyi**; *Ilona*, xxii; *Margit*, xii, 489, 507; goyim, 535, 576; **Ivanyo Family**, 545; *lives in house*, 492; *Mrs.*, xxiii; *Pista*, 495, 499, 544; died, 517; *took furniture*, 485; Kosztyo, Sandor, 489; Lefkovits, Jozsef, xxii, 481; Lefkovits, Malvin, xxiii; packages, asking siblings to send, 545; **Ragány Family**, 545; *Jolán*, xiii, 498; *took furniture*, 485; Simon Family, 495; Szabo, Juliska, xxii; Szmolyák, János, 490; Török, Ilonka, xii, 488, 489; **Toth Family**; *Ilan*, xiii, 512; *Istvan*, xiii; *Istvanne*, 497; *Margit*, xiii, 512; *Pista*, xiii, 512; Walters, Irene, xxiii

Neil House: **Marie**; *cashier in*, xi, 350, 474; *reference from*, 563

Neli. See Gluck, Lenke

nervous stomach: Herman, x, xvii, 698

New Jersey, 170, 647, 704, 707

New York, 20, 35-37, 46, 74, 150, 160, 165, 202, 257, 279, 290, 365, 382, 410, 455, 474, 483, 505, 510, 515, 526, 528-529, 531-535, 540, 542, 547, 549, 557-560, 563-565, 567-568, 572-574, 581, 589, 591-592, 599-602, 606, 609, 616, 618, 622, 626, 629, 630, 632-635, 637-638, 641, 646-647, 650, 654-655, 660, 665, 668, 676, 684, 686-687, 692, 694-695, 708-711, 714, 722-723, 725, 727-728, 730, 732, 734, 748, 750, 753-754, 756; **Bertha**; *housing for sisters in*, 43; *send sisters back to, if necessary*, 49; **David**; *advises Marie to go to*, xiii, 534, 543, 548; *better to live in*, 44; *may go to*, 606-608, 610; Goldblatt, Louis in, xiv, 579; **Hermine**; *visits Weingarten, Bertha in*, xiii, 514-515; **Irving**; *arrived to, after service*, 484; *telephones from, after service*, xi, 484; *visits sisters in*, xiv-xv, 584, 611-612, 614, 631-635; *visits Weingarten, Bertha in, after service*, 486; Marie, thinking about moving to, 547; **siblings**; *arrive to on February 21ˢᵗ, 1940*, viii, 106; *news of arrival to*, 58; *should stay in*, 49; *train from, to Columbus*, 128; World's Fair in, 53, 59

New York Times: legislation S-3557, report about in, 731; want ad in, 728

newspapers, 426, 459, 460; *Already in Parade*, 193; Jews in Hungary, situation of, described in, 354; *New York Times*; *legislation S-3557, report about in*, 731; *want ad in*, 728;

Ohio Jewish Chronicle; *subscription to*, 339; survivors' advertisements in, 495

newsreels: soldier's life, about, 203

Normandy, France, 343

notary, vii, 23, 32-33, 40-41, 88, 147; Fenicky, Bela, 622; fired for being Jewish, vii, 84; Klein, Ignácz goes to, about sister's dowry, 555; Lelesz, 99; Lengyel, Pál, xiii, xiv, 528-529, 532, 543-545, 553, 575, 613, 615, 618, 620-623, 732; none in Ujhely, vii, 66; permission for boys to travel, 73; sale of house arranged with, 69; statement from Gluck, Arthur regarding how many affidavits of support he gave signed by a, 95, 96

Novak, Tony: *letter from, 403

Nuremberg, Germany, 485

Ohio Jewish Chronicle, 237, 293, 302, 334, 339, 355, 409, 433, 436, 560; advertising apartment in, 661; **article about**; *Greenstein, Izy*, 339, 358; *Mendlovetz, Edi hospitalized*, 444; **Irving**; *name appears in*, 373-374; *received first copy of, since leaving Italy*, 458

Ohio State University, ii, xxiii, 171, 178, 537, 545, 653, 692, 755-756; Flo Meizlish, 444; **Irving**; *application to*, 493; *begins classes at*, 493; *classmates from*, 640; *course of study at*, 579, 582, 590, 592, 598-599; *exams in*, 565, 570-571, 581, 589, 596, 598, 603, 618, 632; *graduation from*, 642, 653, 655; *afterwards*, xvi, 646-647, 649, 651, 658; *may go to CA after*, xvi, 641; *play (A man must marry), performs in*, xv, 633; *student at*, xiv, 499, 504-505, 510, 512-516, 519, 527, 530, 534, 538, 541, 543, 547, 549-550, 557, 559, 561, 563-564, 567, 579-581, 586-589, 593, 602, 608, 611, 620, 626-628, 630, 633; *summer school classes at*, 636; Jewish students at, 375; **Legal Aid Clinic**; *letter from*, 685

oil, for fire, 148

oilfields, description of, 171

Oklahoma: Goldblatt, Louis stationed in, xi, 463

Olga, from Lelesz, 15-16, 18, 29-30; regrets going to America, 60

Oran, Algeria: French family, dinner with in, 366; French girl, dates in, x, 331, 357, 359; visits city of, 238, 251, 366

orphanage: clothing from, 507

orphanage accounts, vii, 23, 74, 119; **Gluck, Emil and Lenke's shares held in**, vii, viii, 119, 121, 123; *David must be present to negotiate release of*, 88; Gluck, Herman's shares held in, vii, 86; Gluck, Irving's shares held in, vii, viii, 99; money being held in, 95; share of money deposited to three, vii, 76, 88

Oyster Bay Jewish Center: Irving's membership in, 745

P-38 pistol, Irving brings home captured, 480

packages, 12, 40, 42, 126, 182, 185, 186, 256, 304, 322, 515-516, 519, 525; clothing for children, 118; customs declaration to send, 46; for Gluck, Lenke and Mityu, 69; **from**

www.ingramcontent.com/pod-product-compliance
Lightning Source LLC
Chambersburg PA
CBHW070146120726
47909CB00001B/3